How to use your Connected Casebook

Step 1: Go to **www.CasebookConnect.com** and redeem your access code to get started.

Access Code: SWhCnt853942522

Step 2: Go to your **BOOKSHELF** and select your Connected Casebook to start reading, highlighting, and taking notes in the margins of your e-book.

Step 3: Select the **STUDY** tab in your toolbar to access a variety of practice materials designed to help you master the course material. These materials may include explanations, videos, multiple-choice questions, flashcards, short answer, essays, and issue spotting.

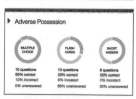

Step 4: Select the **OUTLINE** tab in your toolbar to access chapter outlines that automatically incorporate your highlights and annotations from the e-book. Use the My Notes area for copying, pasting, and editing your book notes or creating new notes.

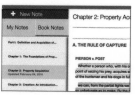

Step 5: If your professor has enrolled your class, you can select the **CLASS INSIGHTS** tab and compare your own study center results against the average of your classmates.

Is this a used casebook? Access code already scratched off?

You can purchase the Digital Version and still access all of the powerful tools listed above. Please visit CasebookConnect.com and select Catalog to learn more.

PIN: 9111149725 WhalCont8

25036

CASES, PROBLEMS, AND MATERIALS
ON
CONTRACTS

ASPEN CASEBOOK SERIES

CASES, PROBLEMS, AND MATERIALS ON CONTRACTS

EIGHTH EDITION

DOUGLAS J. WHALEY
PROFESSOR EMERITUS
MORITZ COLLEGE OF LAW
THE OHIO STATE UNIVERSITY

DAVID HORTON
PROFESSOR OF LAW
UNIVERSITY OF CALIFORNIA, DAVIS

Wolters Kluwer

Published by Wolters Kluwer in New York.

Wolters Kluwer Legal & Regulatory U.S. serves customers worldwide with CCH, Aspen Publishers, and Kluwer Law International products. (www.WKLegaledu.com)

To contact Customer Service, e-mail customer.service@wolterskluwer.com,
call 1-800-234-1660, fax 1-800-901-9075, or mail correspondence to:

Wolters Kluwer
Attn: Order Department
PO Box 990
Frederick, MD 21705

Printed in the United States of America.

1 2 3 4 5 6 7 8 9 0

ISBN 978-1-5438-0249-8

Library of Congress Cataloging-in-Publication Data

Names: Whaley, Douglas J., author. | Horton, David (Law teacher), author.
Title: Cases, problems, and materials on contracts / Douglas J. Whaley,
   Professor Emeritus, Moritz College of Law, The Ohio State University;
   David Horton, Professor of Law, University of California, Davis.
Description: Eighth edition. | New York: Wolters Kluwer, [2019] | Series:
   Aspen casebook series
Identifiers: LCCN 2018030668 | ISBN 9781543802498
Subjects: LCSH: Contracts—United States. | LCGFT: Casebooks (Law)
Classification: LCC KF801.A7 C7 2019 | DDC 346.7302/2—dc23
LC record available at https://lccn.loc.gov/2018030668

About Wolters Kluwer Legal & Regulatory U.S.

Wolters Kluwer Legal & Regulatory U.S. delivers expert content and solutions in the areas of law, corporate compliance, health compliance, reimbursement, and legal education. Its practical solutions help customers successfully navigate the demands of a changing environment to drive their daily activities, enhance decision quality and inspire confident outcomes.

Serving customers worldwide, its legal and regulatory portfolio includes products under the Aspen Publishers, CCH Incorporated, Kluwer Law International, ftwilliam.com and MediRegs names. They are regarded as exceptional and trusted resources for general legal and practice-specific knowledge, compliance and risk management, dynamic workflow solutions, and expert commentary.

This book is dedicated

by Douglas Whaley to
my husband, David Vargo,

and by David Horton to my wife, Annie,
and my kids, Eleanor, Lily, and Claire

SUMMARY OF CONTENTS

CONTENTS

CHAPTER

2

CONSIDERATION   169

CHAPTER

3

REMEDIES   301

CHAPTER

4

THE STATUTE OF FRAUDS

465

CHAPTER

5

THE PAROL EVIDENCE RULE AND
INTERPRETATION OF THE CONTRACT   535

CHAPTER

7

CONDITIONS AND PROMISES: PERFORMANCE AND BREACH   797

CHAPTER

8

ANTICIPATORY REPUDIATION 907

CHAPTER

9

THIRD-PARTY BENEFICIARIES   937

CHAPTER
10
ASSIGNMENT AND DELEGATION   981

ACKNOWLEDGMENTS

We would like to begin by thanking our many students through the years who taught us almost as much law as we taught them. In particular do we thank the students who suffered through this book in earlier forms, pointed out difficulties, and offered suggestions.

Douglas Whaley would like to express his gratitude and admiration for the late Professor Pierre Loiseaux, of the University of California at Davis School of Law, who taught him Contracts all too long ago at the University of Texas. He would also like to thank Jerry Bunge and Barbara Shipek for their help in the preparation of this book. Finally, he would like to acknowledge the research aid of many years' worth of student assistants at Ohio State, most particularly John Walker, class of 1988.

David Horton would like to thank Tom Daughhetee, Darren Kelly, and Sara Nies for their hard work on this book, and Louis Gabriel and Lucas Urgoiti for being outstanding research assistants.

We would also like to thank the following authors and copyright holders for permission to use their materials:

Blinkoff, S., Contracts: Acceptance of an Offer for a Unilateral Contract: Effect of Tender, 14 Cornell L.Q. 81 (1928). Copyright © 1928 by Cornell University. All rights reserved. Reprinted with the permission of Cornell Law Review and Fred B. Rothman & Company.

Childress, Conditions in the Law of Contracts, 45 N.YU. L. Rev. 33 (1970). Reprinted by permission.

Corbin, A., Contracts §§29, 30, 110, 156, 380, 381, 605, 965 (1962). The Yale Law Journal by Yale Law School, Copyright © 1962. Reproduced with permission of Yale Law Journal Company, Inc. via Copyright Clearance Center.

Crandall, T. D., M. J. Herbert, and L. Lawrence, Uniform Commercial Code Law §§3.3, 4.3 (1993). Reprinted by permission.

Fuller and Perdue, The Reliance Interest in Contract Damages, 46 Yale L.J. 52, 53-54, 56, 77 (1936). The Yale Law Journal by Yale Law School. Copyright © 1936. Reproduced with permission of Yale Law Journal Company, Inc. via Copyright Clearance Center.

Palmer, G. E., Law of Restitution, vol. I (1978). Reprinted by permission.

Posner, R., Economic Analysis of the Law (3d ed. 1986). Reprinted by permission.

Restatement of Contracts §§59, 90, 133. Copyright © 1932 by the American Law Institute. Reprinted with permission. All rights reserved.

Restatement (Second) of Contracts §§ 15, 20, 27, 32, 36, 38, 41, 45, 48, 50, 62, 69, 70, 71, 74, 77, 82, 86, 87, 90, 129, 130, 131, 139, 152, 153, 161, 162, 164, 181, 201, 202, 203, 206, 207, 212, 213, 216, 229, 234, 240, 241, 242, 251, 252, 280, 302, 309, 311, 317, 318, 324, 326, 328, 332, 333, 347, 349, 353, 355, 356, 371, 373. Copyright © 1981 by the American Law Institute. Reprinted with permission. All rights reserved.

Uniform Commercial Code §§ 2-201, 2-202 (comment 3), 2-207, 2-209, 2-210, 2-309, 2-313, 2-314, 2-315, 2-316, 2-609, 2-615, 2-703, 2-708, 2-712, 2-713, and 3-311. Uniform Commercial Code (UCC) Article 2 copyright © 2011, Article 3 copyright © 2002 by the American Law Institute and the National Conference of Commissioners on Uniform State Laws. Reproduced with the permission of the Permanent Editorial Board for the UCC. All rights reserved.

Uniform Written Obligations Act, section 1. This excerpt is reprinted through the permission of the National Conference of Commissioners on Uniform State Laws. Copies of the Act may be ordered from NCCUSL at a nominal cost at 676 North St. Clair Street, Suite 1700, Chicago, Illinois, 60611, (312) 915-0195.

Wormser, The True Nature of Unilateral Contracts, 26 Yale L.J. 136-142 (1916). The Yale Law Journal by Yale Law School. Copyright © 1916. Reproduced with permission of Yale Law Journal Company, Inc. via Copyright Clearance Center.

EDITORIAL NOTICE

Most omissions from cases and other quoted materials are indicated either by an ellipsis or by substitution of new material in brackets. Generally, there is no notation of omitted footnotes. All case footnotes that are included retain their original numbering. Author footnotes are indicated with an asterisk.

INTRODUCTION
INTRODUCTION TO THE STUDY OF THE LAW OF CONTRACTS

There is an argument that all of civilization is based on contracts. Consider that no family can exist without many express or implied understandings as to how its members will behave toward one another. As we will see, these agreements may or may not be enforceable in a court, but if they are broken, major disagreements can occur and loved ones may drift apart. Similarly, starting with cautious meetings between tribes of cave dwellers in prehistoric times, human beings have negotiated their progress through contracts — treaties or informal agreements — that have brought us to the complexities of the twenty-first century.

Most of our rules of law are similarly based on contracts. Even the United States Constitution is, at heart, a contract between the adopting states as to how our country will be run. The rules of property law are agreements as to how rights in chattels and realty will be handled, and both tort and criminal law have as their basis the goal of punishing people for outrageous or negligent behavior that violates an established ("agreed-upon") norm for how we will treat one another. Every statute passed by a legislature is contractual in origin, with the language of the law negotiated into being by offer and acceptance, exchange of deals ("consideration"), and other concepts you will study in detail in this course.

The law of contracts derives from many sources. It is necessary for you, the student, to appreciate the relative weight that is given to any one source so that you can gauge its importance in deciding the issue at hand. What follows is a discussion of the hierarchy of sources of law, plus a short explanation of each.

The foundation of law in the United States is the United States Constitution. All other legal rules must be in conformity with it. Immediately under the Constitution in importance are federal statutes and treaties. No state can pass legislation or announce a rule of law in conflict with these federal enactments. For that matter, state law is also subordinate to regulations passed by the various federal agencies. The Supremacy Clause of Article VI of the Constitution states:

1

This Constitution, and the laws of the United States which shall be made in pursuance thereof; and all treaties made, or which shall be made, under the authority of the United States, shall be the supreme law of the land; and the judges in every State shall be bound thereby, anything in the Constitution or laws of any State to the contrary notwithstanding.

Next in line in any given jurisdiction is the state constitution, and under it the laws passed by the state legislature. There will also be regulations passed by state regulatory agencies, and these are the next rung on the legal ladder, followed by the local ordinances passed by municipalities.

That exhausts the legislation that controls our law. Incredible as it may seem, however, that is not the end of it. In spite of all the given structure, there are still many situations unaccounted for that must be subject to rule of law. The development of these rules is left to the courts.

In countries taking their cue from Great Britain (such as the United States), one decision is precedent for subsequent ones, thus building up a body of *common law*, judicially created and followed thereafter by later courts. This concept is called *stare decisis* ("stand by decisions"). As time goes on and society changes, the precedents may lose their weight and be altered or overruled, but this is not done lightly. Our common law system has great respect for the wisdom of the past. Some of the cases you will study are quite old. One, Kingston v. Preston (see Chapter 7), was decided by the great jurist Lord Mansfield in 1773 (and we will refer to others even older). During the

Lord Mansfield

time of the American Revolution, the English court system had Lord Mansfield as its Chief Justice. He believed in pragmatism in his courtroom, and during his tenure the "law merchant" (the law as it was understood in mercantile courts created by merchants themselves) was given much influence in English decisions. Lord Mansfield would call merchants into court to testify as to what mercantile understandings were about the matter before the court, and was not above putting merchants on the jury and then asking them questions as cases proceeded. Mansfield was the father of many of the concepts we will study in this course.

Of course, technically the only decisions that bind a given court are those from the highest court in that particular jurisdiction. Nonetheless, especially where the issue has never arisen in that jurisdiction (or has not arisen in modern times), courts will look to the decisions of other jurisdictions to see how the matter is being handled. When casting about for guidance, the courts will also consult treatises on point as well as the sections of the so-called Restatements (about which more in a moment).

Uniform Laws. In the specialized field of contracts most (but not all) of the law is created at the state level. For many decades each state had rules both legislative and judicial that were similar but not identical. This worked fine as long as merchants stayed within state boundaries to do their trading, but commerce cannot long be so confined. As time went on and the traffic between the states increased, the need for uniform rules became apparent. Various "model" or "uniform" laws were created by different groups and were submitted to the state legislatures with the recommendation of adoption without change. Some of these proposed statutes had greater success than others. Two widely adopted statutes were the Uniform Sales Act (first proposed in 1906, passed by two-thirds of the states) and the Uniform Negotiable Instruments Law (1896, passed by all of the states).

The Uniform Commercial Code. Eventually even these statutes became outdated, and the same body that had created them, the National Conference of Commissioners on Uniform State Laws, along with the American Law Institute, decided in the 1940s to overhaul these and other related statutes and produce a comprehensive code dealing with the issues central to commercial law. The Chief Draftsman of this statute was Professor Karl N. Llewellyn of the Columbia Law School, the leading voice for the "legal realism" school of jurisprudence (very much in Lord Mansfield's tradition). Under his stewardship, committees of drafters produced version after version of a work that was eventually called the Uniform Commercial Code. Starting with Pennsylvania in 1953, the Uniform Commercial Code (abbreviated to UCC, or, simply, the Code) was enacted, with some modifications, in every jurisdiction in the United States (although Louisiana, with its French civil law tradition and very different laws, has enacted only parts of the UCC).

The Code, which repealed prior uniform enactments on point, is divided into distinct parts, called Articles. Article 1 is a general article, containing basic concepts (such as the requirement of good faith, see §1-305)

Karl N. Llewellyn

and definitions (see §1-201).* Article 1 was revised in 2001, and this new version has been adopted in most states. Article 1 citations in this book are to the revised version.

A major focus of this course is Article 2 of the Code. It deals with the *sale of goods. Goods* are defined in §2-105(1) as follows:

> "Goods" means all things (including specially manufactured goods) which are movable at the time of identification to the contract for sale other than the money in which the price is to be paid, investment securities (Article 8) and things in action. "Goods" also includes the unborn young of animals and growing crops and other identified things attached to realty as described in the section of goods to be severed from realty (Section 2-107).

---

* Incidentally, the symbol "§" means "section." Two together ("§§") signify the plural: "sections." The citation "§1-201" refers you to Article 1 of the Uniform Commercial Code with the first digit, and the three numbers after the hyphen refer to the section within that Article that you should consult in your statute book. If the citation contains additional numbers or letters, such as "§2-201(3)(a)," the parenthetical items are references to subsections within the larger section. Look up §2-201(3)(a) to see what is meant by this.

One issue about Article 2 is worth flagging at the outset. Some of its rules only apply if one party is a *merchant* (or both parties are merchants). In general, a merchant is "a person who deals in goods of the kind or otherwise by his occupation holds himself out as having knowledge or skill peculiar to the practices or goods involved in the transaction." UCC §2-104(1). For example, a car dealer is a merchant when he or she enters into a contract involving automobiles. However, a car dealer is *not* a merchant when he or she enters into a contract for boats, computers, books, furniture, or anything else that falls outside his or her area of expertise. In fact, so many doctrines in Article 2 hinge on merchant status that you may lose your moorings and come to believe that the test for whether a transaction falls under Article 2 is whether it involves merchants. That is wrong: Article 2 applies to the sale of *goods*. Believe it or not, this problem is so severe that there is an entire law review article devoted to it. See Scott J. Burnham, Why Do Law Students Insist That Article 2 of the Uniform Commercial Code Applies Only to Merchants and What Can We Do About It?, 63 Brook. L. Rev. 1271 (1997).

As the definition of "goods" in the text above mentions, UCC's Article 2 does not govern *things in action*. Things in action are intangible property, such as insurance policies or intellectual property like patents and trademarks. Thus, the definition of goods refers to *personal* (as opposed to *real*) property, the items that your course in Property calls *chattels*. Article 2 therefore does not apply to transactions involving land or interests in land, to employment agreements, to service contracts (such as contracts with a health spa), to the sale of paper rights (such as stocks or bonds), or to the sale of intangibles (again, insurance). As you study this course, be sensitive to the possible application of UCC Article 2. If a Problem involves a sale of goods, then this statute applies. Application of the common law rules, to the extent they differ from the UCC, will mean that your answer is wrong.

Article 2A of the Uniform Commercial Code deals with the leasing of goods. Its rules are copied from those in Article 2 on the sale of goods, so that anyone who is familiar with the provisions of Article 2 will find Article 2A reassuringly comfortable reading.

The United Nations Convention on Contracts for the International Sale of Goods. Effective January 1, 1988, the United States became bound by a new treaty: the United Nations Convention on Contracts for the International Sale of Goods (hereafter "CISG"). The Convention only covers issues of contract formation and the rights and duties of the parties thereto. It excludes coverage of products liability issues, as well as matters touching on contract validity, such as fraud, illegality, and so on. CISG's rules are divided into different sections called Articles.

Most of the major commercial powers in the world have ratified the CISG. CISG applies if the contracting parties are located in different countries (called "States" by the treaty) and they do not agree that the law of some particular jurisdiction applies. Article 6 clearly allows the parties to avoid the application of CISG by choosing instead to be bound by some other body of law.

Although the law reflected in CISG has some variations from the rules we will study in this book, for the most part its provisions are very similar to those of the common law and the Uniform Commercial Code. This book highlights some of the major changes.

The Restatement. Throughout this book you will also see citations to the Restatement of Contracts. The Restatement, promulgated by the American Law Institute, is one of many similar works created by experts in the various fields of law that attempts to reduce the rules of the common law to set and uniform descriptions. The Restatement of Contracts was first approved by the American Law Institute in 1932; its Chief Reporter was the leading Contracts expert of his day, Professor Samuel Williston of the Harvard Law School. It is important to understand that the Restatement is *not* a statute. It is mere advice to the courts on what the common law *should* be. Thus it is not on the same level as the Uniform Commercial Code, which is a statute and *must* be followed if relevant to the dispute. But even though the Restatement is not binding law, drafted as it was by the then leading commercial authorities, it has been very influential in shaping the development of the common law.

Like the early uniform statutes, the original Restatement became outdated as time passed, so the American Law Institute promulgated a new version in 1979: the Restatement (Second) of Contracts. The late Professor E. Allan Farnsworth of Columbia Law School was the Chief Reporter for the final version.

UNIDROIT Principles of International Commercial Contracts. The International Institute for the Unification of Private Law (UNIDROIT using the French initials) is similar to the Restatement but created by an international body of legal experts who studied all of the world's legal codes and reified them into definite rules (with comments and illustrations). International contracts often adopt its terms, and even where the contracting parties do not do so, courts faced with international contract disputes frequently look to UNIDROIT principles for guidance.

Treatises. Contract law also benefits from a number of well-written treatises on point. Williston wrote one in 1920 and it was very influential. Another important one was written by Professor Arthur L. Corbin of the Yale Law School, published in 1950. These two works are often cited by the courts, and we refer to them (particularly the later work by Corbin) throughout the book (and all Corbin references are to the 1952 version of his treatise). In recent years, other helpful treatises on the law of Contracts have also appeared: J. Murray, *Murray on Contracts* (6th ed. 2015), J. Calamari and J. Perillo, *Perillo's Hornbook on Contracts* (7th ed. 2014), and E. Farnsworth, *Farnsworth on Contracts* (4th ed. 2004). The leading treatise on the UCC is J. White and R. Summers, *Uniform Commercial Code* (6th ed. 2010).

CHAPTER
1
INTENT TO CONTRACT: AGREEMENT

I. INTRODUCTION: THE PRINCIPLE OF MUTUAL ASSENT

This chapter explores the concept of *agreement,* which is at the very heart of contract law. Every contract requires *mutual manifestations of assent.* This is a complex concept, and our next four cases unpack it. In particular, they demonstrate that courts define "agreement" *objectively* (focusing on a party's words and conduct) rather than *subjectively* (trying to determine what a party was actually thinking). Indeed, as we will see, *manifesting* assent (acting *as though* you agreed) is not the same as *assenting* (actually agreeing). In addition, the cases in this subsection introduce the process by which parties reach an agreement. Sometimes, parties manifest assent when an offeror makes a formal *offer* that the offeree may *accept.* In addition, parties can manifest assent through their *conduct.*

LUCY v. ZEHMER
Supreme Court of Virginia, 1954
196 Va. 493, 84 S.E.2d 516

BUCHANAN, Justice.

This suit was instituted by W. O. Lucy and J. C. Lucy, complainants, against A. H. Zehmer and Ida S. Zehmer, his wife, defendants, to have specific performance of a contract by which it was alleged the Zehmers had sold to W. O. Lucy a tract of land owned by A. H. Zehmer in Dinwiddie county containing 471.6 acres, more or less, known as the Ferguson farm, for $50,000. J. C. Lucy, the other complainant, is a brother of W. O. Lucy, to whom W. O. Lucy transferred a half interest in his alleged purchase.

[handwritten margin note: Suit is for "Specific Performance" of a contract]

The instrument sought to be enforced was written by A. H. Zehmer on December 20, 1952, in these words: "We hereby agree to sell to W. O. Lucy the Ferguson Farm complete for $50,000.00, title satisfactory to buyer," and signed by the defendants, A. H. Zehmer and Ida S. Zehmer.

The answer of A. H. Zehmer admitted that at the time mentioned W. O. Lucy offered him $50,000 cash for the farm, but that he, Zehmer, considered that the offer was made in jest; that so thinking, and both he and Lucy having had several drinks, he wrote out "the memorandum" quoted above and induced his wife to sign it; that he did not deliver the memorandum to Lucy, but that Lucy picked it up, read it, put it in his pocket, attempted to offer Zehmer $5 to bind the bargain, which Zehmer refused to accept, and realizing for the first time that Lucy was serious, Zehmer assured him that he had no intention of selling the farm and that the whole matter was a joke. Lucy left the premises insisting that he had purchased the farm. . . .

W. O. Lucy, a lumberman and farmer, thus testified in substance: He had known Zehmer for fifteen or twenty years and had been familiar with the Ferguson farm for ten years. Seven or eight years ago he had offered Zehmer $20,000 for the farm which Zehmer had accepted, but the agreement was verbal and Zehmer backed out. On the night of December 20, 1952, around eight o'clock, he took an employee to McKenney, where Zehmer lived and operated a restaurant, filling station, and motor court. While there he decided to see Zehmer and again try to buy the Ferguson farm. He entered the restaurant and talked to Mrs. Zehmer until Zehmer came in. He asked Zehmer if he had sold the Ferguson farm. Zehmer replied that he had not. Lucy said, "I bet you wouldn't take $50,000.00 for that place." Zehmer replied, "Yes, I would too; you wouldn't give fifty." Lucy said he would and told Zehmer to write up an agreement to that effect. Zehmer took a restaurant check and wrote on the back of it, "I do hereby agree to sell to W. O. Lucy the Ferguson Farm for $50,000 complete." Lucy told him he had better change it to "We" because Mrs. Zehmer would have to sign it too. Zehmer then tore up what he had written, wrote the agreement quoted above and asked Mrs. Zehmer, who was at the other end of the counter ten or twelve feet away, to sign it. Mrs. Zehmer said she would for $50,000 and signed it. Zehmer brought it back and gave it to Lucy, who offered him $5 which Zehmer refused, saying, "You don't need to give me any money, you got the agreement there signed by both of us."

The discussion leading to the signing of the agreement, said Lucy, lasted thirty or forty minutes, during which Zehmer seemed to doubt that Lucy could raise $50,000. Lucy suggested the provision for having the title examined and Zehmer made the suggestion that he would sell it "complete, everything there," and stated that all he had on the farm was three heifers.

Lucy took a partly filled bottle of whiskey into the restaurant with him for the purpose of giving Zehmer a drink if he wanted it. Zehmer did, and he and Lucy had one or two drinks together. Lucy said that while he felt the drinks he took he was not intoxicated, and from the way Zehmer handled the transaction he did not think he was either. . . .

Mr. and Mrs. Zehmer were called by the complainants as adverse witnesses. Zehmer testified in substance as follows:

He bought this farm more than ten years ago for $11,000. He had had twenty-five offers, more or less, to buy it, including several from Lucy, who had never offered any specific sum of money. He had given them all the same answer, that he was not interested in selling it. On this Saturday night before Christmas it looked like everybody and his brother came by there to have a drink. He took a good many drinks during the afternoon and had a pint of his own. When he entered the restaurant around eight-thirty Lucy was there and he could see that he was "pretty high." He said to Lucy, "Boy, you got some good liquor, drinking, ain't you?" Lucy then offered him a drink. "I was already high as a Georgia pine, and didn't have any more better sense than to pour another great big slug out and gulp it down, and he took one too."

After they had talked a while Lucy asked whether he still had the Ferguson farm. He replied that he had not sold it and Lucy said, "I bet you wouldn't take $50,000.00 for it." Zehmer asked him if he would give $50,000 and Lucy said yes. Zehmer replied, "You haven't got $50,000.00 in cash." Lucy said he did and Zehmer replied that he did not believe it. They argued "pro and con for a long time," mainly about "whether he had $50,000 in cash that he could put up right then and buy that farm."

Finally, said Zehmer, Lucy told him if he didn't believe he had $50,000, "you sign that piece of paper here and say you will take $50,000.00 for the farm." He, Zehmer, "just grabbed the back off of a guest check there" and wrote on the back of it. At that point in his testimony Zehmer asked to see what he had written to "see if I recognize my own handwriting." He examined the paper and exclaimed, "Great balls of fire, I got 'Firgerson' for Ferguson. I have got satisfactory spelled wrong. I don't recognize that writing if I would see it, wouldn't know it was mine."

After Zehmer had, as he described it, "scribbled this thing off," Lucy said, "Get your wife to sign it." Zehmer walked over to where she was and she at first refused to sign but did so after he told her that he "was just needling him [Lucy], and didn't mean a thing in the world, that I was not selling the farm." Zehmer then "took it back over there . . . and I was still looking at the dern thing. I had the drink right there by my hand, and I reached over to get a drink, and he said, 'Let me see it.' He reached and picked it up, and when I looked back again he had it in his pocket and he dropped a five dollar bill over there, and he said, 'Here is five dollars payment on it.' . . . I said, 'Hell no, that is beer and liquor talking. I am not going to sell you the farm. I have told you that too many times before.'"

Mrs. Zehmer testified that when Lucy came into the restaurant he looked as if he had had a drink. When Zehmer came in he took a drink out of a bottle that Lucy handed him. She went back to help the waitress who was getting things ready for next day. Lucy and Zehmer were talking but she did not pay too much attention to what they were saying. She heard Lucy ask Zehmer if he had sold the Ferguson farm, and Zehmer replied that he had not and did not want to sell it. Lucy said, "I bet you wouldn't take $50,000.00 cash for that farm," and Zehmer replied, "You haven't got $50,000 cash." Lucy said, "I can get it." Zehmer said he might form a company and get it, "but you haven't got $50,000.00 cash to pay me tonight." Lucy asked him if he would put it in writing that he would sell him this farm. Zehmer then wrote on the back of a pad, "I agree to sell the Ferguson Place to W. O. Lucy for $50,000.00 cash." Lucy said, "All right, get your wife to sign it." Zehmer came back to where she was standing and said, "You want to put your name to this?" She said "No," but he said in an undertone, "It is nothing but a joke," and she signed it.

She said that only one paper was written and it said: "I hereby agree to sell," but the "I" had been changed to "We." However, she said she read what she signed and was then asked, "When you read 'We hereby agree to sell to W. O. Lucy,' what did you interpret that to mean, that particular phrase?" She said she thought that was a cash sale that night; but she also said that when she read that part about "title satisfactory to buyer" she understood that if the title was good Lucy would pay $50,000 but if the title was bad he would have a right to reject it, and that that was her understanding at the time she signed her name.

On examination by her own counsel she said that her husband laid this piece of paper down after it was signed; that Lucy said to let him see it, took it, folded it and put it in his wallet, then said to Zehmer, "Let me give you $5.00," but Zehmer said, "No, this is liquor talking. I don't want to sell the farm, I have told you that I want my son to have it. This is all a joke." Lucy then said at least twice, "Zehmer, you have sold your farm," wheeled around and started for the door. He paused at the door and said, "I will bring you $50,000.00 tomorrow. . . . No, tomorrow is Sunday. I will bring it to you Monday." She said you could tell definitely that he was drinking and she said to her husband, "You should have taken him home," but he said, "Well, I am just about as bad off as he is.". . .

The defendants insist that the evidence was ample to support their contention that the writing sought to be enforced was prepared as a bluff or dare to force Lucy to admit that he did not have $50,000; that the whole matter was a joke; that the writing was not delivered to Lucy and no binding contract was ever made between the parties.

It is an unusual, if not bizarre, defense. When made to the writing admittedly prepared by one of the defendants and signed by both, clear evidence is required to sustain it.

In his testimony Zehmer claimed that he "was high as a Georgia pine," and that the transaction "was just a bunch of two doggoned drunks bluffing to see who could talk the biggest and say the most." That claim is inconsistent with his attempt to testify in great detail as to what was said and what was done. It is contradicted by other evidence as to the condition of both parties, and rendered of no weight by the testimony of his wife that when Lucy left the restaurant she suggested that Zehmer drive him home. The record is convincing that Zehmer was not intoxicated to the extent of being unable to comprehend the nature and consequences of the instrument he executed, and hence that instrument is not to be invalidated on that ground. [Citations omitted.] It was in fact conceded by defendants' counsel in oral argument that under the evidence Zehmer was not too drunk to make a valid contract. . . .

Zehmer Not too Intoxicated whereas the deal is invalid

The appearance of the contract, the fact that it was under discussion for forty minutes or more before it was signed; Lucy's objection to the first draft because it was written in the singular, and he wanted Mrs. Zehmer to sign it also; the rewriting to meet that objection and the signing by Mrs. Zehmer; the discussion of what was to be included in the sale, the provision for the examination of the title, the completeness of the instrument that was executed, the taking possession of it by Lucy with no request or suggestion by either of the defendants that he give it back, are facts which furnish persuasive evidence that the execution of the contract was a serious business transaction rather than a casual, jesting matter as defendants now contend. . . .

Long discussion
multiple drafts
Rewriting
terms/conditions
Completeness
"Serious business transaction"

 Not only did Lucy actually believe, but the evidence shows he was warranted in believing, that the contract represented a serious business transaction and a good faith sale and purchase of the farm.

Lucy was warranted to believe it was a good faith Sale

In the field of contracts, as generally elsewhere, "We must look to the outward expression of a person as manifesting his intention rather than to his secret and unexpressed intention. The law imputes to a person an intention corresponding to the reasonable meaning of his words and acts." First Nat. Exchange Bank of Roanoke v. Roanoke Oil Co., 169 Va. 99, 114, 192 S.E. 764, 770.

The Law
Subjected Intent Irrelevant

At no time prior to the execution of the contract had Zehmer indicated to Lucy by word or act that he was not in earnest about selling the farm. They had argued about it and discussed its terms, as Zehmer admitted, for a long time. Lucy testified that if there was any jesting it was about paying $50,000 that night. The contract and the evidence show that he was not expected to pay the money that night. Zehmer said that after the writing was signed he laid it down on the counter in front of Lucy. Lucy said Zehmer handed it to him. In any event there had been what appeared to be a good faith offer and a good faith acceptance, followed by the execution and apparent delivery of a written contract. Both said that Lucy put the writing in his pocket and then offered Zehmer $5 to seal the bargain. Not until then, even under the defendants' evidence, was anything said or done to indicate that the matter was a joke. Both of the Zehmers testified that when Zehmer asked his wife to sign he whispered that it was a joke so Lucy wouldn't hear and that it was not intended that he should hear.

Zehmer did Not make his Intent known

The mental assent of the parties is not requisite for the formation of a contract. If the words or other acts of one of the parties have but one reasonable meaning, his undisclosed intention is immaterial except when an unreasonable meaning which he attaches to his manifestations is known to the other party. Restatement of the Law of Contracts, Vol. I, §71, p.74. . . .

Mental Assent Defined

Expressed Intentions

The law, therefore, judges of an agreement between two persons exclusively from those expressions of their intentions which are communicated between them. . . . Clark on Contracts, 4 ed., §3, p.4.

Rule Reasonable Person Standard ✱

An agreement or mutual assent is of course essential to a valid contract but the law imputes to a person an intention corresponding to the reasonable meaning of his words and acts. If his words and acts, judged by a reasonable standard, manifest an intention to agree, it is immaterial what may be the real but unexpressed state of his mind. 17 C.J.S., Contracts, §32, p.361; 12 Am. Jur., Contracts, §19, p.515.

So a person cannot set up that he was merely jesting when his conduct and words would warrant a reasonable person in believing that he intended a real agreement. 17 C.J.S., Contracts, §47, p.390; Clark on Contracts, 4 ed., §27, at p.54.

Whether the writing signed by the defendants and now sought to be enforced by the complainants was the result of a serious offer by Lucy and a serious acceptance by the defendants, or was a serious offer by Lucy and an acceptance in secret jest by the defendants, in either event it constituted a binding contract of sale between the parties. . . .

Holding

The complainants are entitled to have specific performance of the contract sued on. The decree appealed from is therefore reversed and the cause is remanded for the entry of a proper decree requiring the defendants to perform the contract in accordance with the prayer of the bill.

Reversed and remanded.

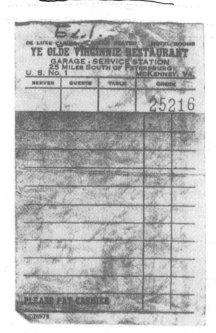

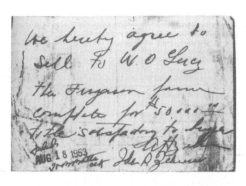

NOTES AND QUESTIONS

1. The front and back of the restaurant check on which Zehmer wrote is reproduced immediately following the opinion. Does it change your opinion of the case?

2. The court mentioned the concession at oral argument that Zehmer was not too drunk to contract. As we shall see in Chapter 6, sometimes the impaired mental state of one of the parties prevents that person from having the legal capacity to enter into a contract.

Problem 1

John Falstaff bought a new car for $25,000, but the first day he drove it to work it broke down on the highway and stranded him. John finally managed to get to his neighborhood bar where he loudly trumpeted his disgust with the car. When the busboy, Francis Feeble, who was known by all to have a very low I.Q., said, "I love your new car," John raised his stein of beer and toasted Francis, replying, "It's yours for $1,500—just go get it." Francis said, "Thanks, Mr. Falstaff, I'll do it now and pay you this evening." Everyone in the tavern laughed as Francis rushed off to rescue the car. Later that day, after Francis had had the car towed to his home, Francis showed up at the bar where John was still consoling himself and put $1,500 on the counter in front of John. When John asked, "What's this?" Francis explained that it was the payment for the car. John refused to take the money, saying that of course he had not been serious earlier in the day. Is Francis entitled to the car in your opinion?

MEYER v. UBER TECHNOLOGIES, INC.
United States Court of Appeals, Second Circuit, 2017
868 F.3d 66

CHIN, Circuit Judge:

In 2014, Spencer Meyer downloaded onto his smartphone a software application offered by Uber Technologies, Inc. ("Uber"), a technology company that operates, among other things, a ride-hailing service. Meyer then registered for an Uber account with his smartphone. After using the application approximately ten times, Meyer brought this action on behalf of himself and other similarly situated Uber accountholders against Uber's co-founder and former Chief Executive Officer, defendant-appellant Travis Kalanick, alleging that the Uber application allows third-party drivers to illegally fix prices. The district court joined Uber as a defendant and denied motions by Kalanick and Uber to compel arbitration. In doing so, the district court concluded that Meyer did not have reasonably conspicuous notice of and did not unambiguously manifest assent to Uber's Terms of Service when he registered. The district court held that Meyer therefore was not bound by the mandatory arbitration provision contained in the Terms of Service.

For the reasons set forth below, we vacate and remand for further proceedings consistent with this opinion.

BACKGROUND

A.   The Facts

The facts are undisputed and are summarized as follows:

Uber offers a software application for smartphones (the "Uber App") that allows riders to request rides from third-party drivers. On October 18, 2014, Meyer registered for an Uber account with the Uber App on a Samsung Galaxy S5 phone running an Android operating system. After registering, Meyer took ten rides with Uber drivers in New York, Connecticut, Washington, D.C., and Paris.

In support of its motion to compel arbitration, Uber submitted a declaration from Senior Software Engineer Vincent Mi, in which Mi represented that Uber maintained records of when and how its users registered for the service and that, from his review of those records, Mi was able to identify the dates and methods by which Meyer registered for a user account. Attached to the declaration were screenshots of the two screens that a user registering in October 2014 with an Android-operated smartphone would have seen during the registration process.

The first screen, at which the user arrives after downloading the application and clicking a button marked "Register," is labeled "Register" and includes fields for the user to enter his or her name, email address, phone number, and a password (the "Registration Screen"). The Registration Screen also offers the user the option to register via a Google+ or Facebook account. According to Uber's records, Meyer did not sign up using either Google or Facebook and would have had to enter manually his personal information.

After completing the information on the Registration Screen and clicking "Next," the user advances to a second screen labeled "Payment" (the "Payment Screen"), on which the user can enter credit card details or elect to make payments using PayPal or Google Wallet, third-party payment services. According to Uber's records, Meyer entered his credit card information to pay for rides. To complete the process, the prospective user must click the button marked "REGISTER" in the middle of the Payment Screen.

Below the input fields and buttons on the Payment Screen is black text advising users that "[b]y creating an Uber account, you agree to the TERMS

OF SERVICE & PRIVACY POLICY." The capitalized phrase, which is bright blue and underlined, was a hyperlink that, when clicked, took the user to a third screen containing a button that, in turn, when clicked, would then display the current version of both Uber's Terms of Service and Privacy Policy. Meyer recalls entering his contact information and credit card details before registering, but does not recall seeing or following the hyperlink to the Terms and Conditions. He declares that he did not read the Terms and Conditions, including the arbitration provision.

When Meyer registered for an account, the Terms of Service contained the following mandatory arbitration clause:

Dispute Resolution

You and Company agree that any dispute, claim or controversy arising out of or relating to this Agreement or the breach, termination, enforcement, interpretation or validity thereof or the use of the Service or Application (collectively, "Disputes") will be settled by binding arbitration, except that each party retains the right to bring an individual action in small claims court and the right to seek injunctive or other equitable relief in a court of competent jurisdiction to prevent the actual or threatened infringement, misappropriation or violation of a party's copyrights, trademarks, trade secrets, patents or other intellectual property rights. You acknowledge and agree that you and Company are each waiving the right to a trial by jury or to participate as a plaintiff or class User in any purported class action or representative proceeding.

DISCUSSION

I. THE ARBITRATION AGREEMENT

A. Applicable Law

1. Procedural Framework

Under the Federal Arbitration Act (the "FAA"), "[a] written provision in . . . a contract . . . to settle by arbitration a controversy thereafter arising out of such contract . . . shall be valid, irrevocable, and enforceable." 9 U.S.C. §2. The FAA reflects "a liberal federal policy favoring arbitration agreements," AT & T Mobility LLC v. Concepcion, 563 U.S. 333, 346, 131 S. Ct. 1740, 179 L. Ed. 2d 742 (2011), and places arbitration agreements on "the same footing as other contracts," Schnabel v. Trilegiant Corp., 697 F.3d 110, 118 (2d Cir. 2012). It thereby follows that parties are not required to arbitrate unless they have agreed to do so. Id.

Thus, before an agreement to arbitrate can be enforced, the district court must first determine whether such agreement exists between the parties. This question is determined by state contract law. Nicosia v.

Amazon.com, Inc., 834 F.3d 220, 229 (2d Cir. 2016). [The court held that California law governed the transaction.]

2. State Contract Law

To form a contract, there must be "[m]utual manifestation of assent, whether by written or spoken word or by conduct." Specht v. Netscape Commc'ns Corp., 306 F.3d 17, 29 (2d Cir. 2002). California law is clear, however, that "an offeree, regardless of apparent manifestation of his consent, is not bound by inconspicuous contractual provisions of which he is unaware, contained in a document whose contractual nature is not obvious." Id. at 30 (quoting Windsor Mills, Inc. v. Collins & Aikman Corp., 101 Cal. Rptr. 347, 351 (1972)). "Thus, California contract law measures assent by an objective standard that takes into account both what the offeree said, wrote, or did and the transactional context in which the offeree verbalized or acted." Id. at 30.

Where there is no evidence that the offeree had actual notice of the terms of the agreement, the offeree will still be bound by the agreement if a reasonably prudent user would be on inquiry notice of the terms. Whether a reasonably prudent user would be on inquiry notice turns on the "[c]larity and conspicuousness of arbitration terms," *Specht*, 306 F.3d at 30; in the context of web-based contracts, as discussed further below, clarity and conspicuousness are a function of the design and content of the relevant interface. See *Nicosia*, 834 F.3d at 233.

Thus, only if the undisputed facts establish that there is "[r]easonably conspicuous notice of the existence of contract terms and unambiguous manifestation of assent to those terms" will we find that a contract has been formed. See *Specht*, 306 F.3d at 35.

3. Web-Based Contracts

"While new commerce on the Internet has exposed courts to many new situations, it has not fundamentally changed the principles of contract." Register.com, Inc. v. Verio, Inc., 356 F.3d 393, 403 (2d Cir. 2004). "Courts around the country have recognized that [an] electronic 'click' can suffice to signify the acceptance of a contract," and that "[t]here is nothing automatically offensive about such agreements, as long as the layout and language of the site give the user reasonable notice that a click will manifest assent to an agreement." Sgouros v. TransUnion Corp., 817 F.3d 1029, 1033-34 (7th Cir. 2016).

With these principles in mind, one way in which we have previously distinguished web-based contracts is the manner in which the user manifests assent—namely, "clickwrap" (or "click-through") agreements, which require users to click an "I agree" box after being presented with a list of terms and conditions of use, or "browsewrap" agreements, which generally post terms and conditions on a website via a hyperlink at the bottom of the screen. Courts routinely uphold clickwrap agreements for the principal reason that the user has affirmatively assented to the terms of agreement by clicking "I agree." Browsewrap agreements, on the other hand, do not require the user to expressly assent. . . . Because no affirmative action is required by the website user to agree to the terms of a contract other than his or her use of the website, the determination of the validity of the browsewrap contract depends on whether the user has actual or constructive knowledge of a website's terms and conditions.

Of course, there are infinite ways to design a website or smartphone application, and not all interfaces fit neatly into the clickwrap or browsewrap categories. Some online agreements require the user to scroll through the terms before the user can indicate his or her assent by clicking "I agree." See Berkson v. Gogo LLC, 97 F. Supp. 3d 359, 386, 398 (E.D.N.Y. 2015) (terming such agreements "scrollwraps"). Other agreements notify the user of the existence of the website's terms of use and, instead of providing an "I agree" button, advise the user that he or she is agreeing to the terms of service when registering or signing up. Id. at 399 (describing such agreements as "sign-in-wraps").

In the interface at issue in this case, a putative user is not required to assent explicitly to the contract terms; instead, the user must click a button marked "Register," underneath which the screen states "By creating an Uber account, you agree to the TERMS OF SERVICE & PRIVACY POLICY," with hyperlinks to the Terms of Service and Privacy Policy.

District courts considering similar agreements have found them valid where the existence of the terms was reasonably communicated to the user. Compare Cullinane v. Uber Techs., Inc., No. 14-14750-DPW, 2016 WL 3751652, at *7 (D. Mass. July 11, 2016) (applying Massachusetts law and granting motion to compel arbitration); Starke v. Gilt Groupe, Inc., No. 13 Civ. 5497(LLS), 2014 WL 1652225, at *3 (S.D.N.Y. Apr. 24, 2014) (applying New York law and granting motion to dismiss); and Fteja, 841 F. Supp. 2d at 839-40 (granting defendant's motion to transfer based on, inter alia, forum selection clause in terms of service); with Applebaum v. Lyft, Inc., No. 16-cv-07062 (JGK), 2017 WL 2774153, at *8-9 (S.D.N.Y. June 26, 2017) (applying New York law and denying motion to compel arbitration where notice of contract terms was insufficient to bind plaintiff).

Classification of web-based contracts alone, however, does not resolve the notice inquiry. Insofar as it turns on the reasonableness of notice, the enforceability of a web-based agreement is clearly a fact-intensive inquiry. See Schnabel, 697 F.3d at 124. Nonetheless, on a motion to compel arbitration, we may determine that an agreement to arbitrate exists where the notice of the arbitration provision was reasonably conspicuous and manifestation of assent unambiguous as a matter of law. See Specht, 306 F.3d at 28.

B. Application

Meyer attests that he was not on actual notice of the hyperlink to the Terms of Service or the arbitration provision itself, and defendants do not point to evidence from which a jury could infer otherwise. Accordingly, we must consider whether Meyer was on inquiry notice of the arbitration provision by virtue of the hyperlink to the Terms of Service on the Payment Screen and, thus, manifested his assent to the agreement by clicking "Register."

1. Reasonably Conspicuous Notice

In considering the question of reasonable conspicuousness, precedent and basic principles of contract law instruct that we consider the perspective of a reasonably prudent smartphone user. "[M]odern cell phones . . . are now such a pervasive and insistent part of daily life that the proverbial visitor from Mars might conclude they were an important feature of human anatomy." Riley v. California, _____ U.S. _____, 134 S. Ct. 2473, 2484, 189 L. Ed. 2d 430 (2014). As of 2015, nearly two-thirds of American adults owned a smartphone, a figure that has almost doubled since 2011. See U.S. Smartphone Use in 2015, Pew Research Center, at 2 (Apr. 2015), http://assets .pewresearch.org/wp-content/uploads/sites/14/2015/03/PI_Smartphones_ 0401151.pdf (last visited Aug. 17, 2017). Consumers use their smartphones for, among other things, following the news, shopping, social networking, online banking, researching health conditions, and taking classes. Id. at 5. In a 2015 study, approximately 89 percent of smartphone users surveyed reported using the internet on their smartphones over the course of the week-long study period. Id. at 33. A purchaser of a new smartphone has his or her choice of features, including operating systems, storage capacity, and screen size.

Smartphone users engage in these activities through mobile applications, or "apps," like the Uber App. To begin using an app, the consumers need to locate and download the app, often from an application store. Many apps then require potential users to sign up for an account to access the app's services. Accordingly, when considering the perspective of a reasonable smartphone user, we need not presume that the user has never before encountered an app or entered into a contract using a smartphone. Moreover, a reasonably prudent smartphone user knows that text that is highlighted in blue and underlined is hyperlinked to another webpage where additional information will be found.

Turning to the interface at issue in this case, we conclude that the design of the screen and language used render the notice provided reasonable as a matter of California law. The Payment Screen is uncluttered, with only fields for the user to enter his or her credit card details, buttons to register for a user account or to connect the user's pre-existing PayPal account or Google Wallet to the Uber account, and the warning that "By creating an Uber account, you agree to the TERMS OF SERVICE & PRIV-ACY POLICY." The text, including the hyperlinks to the Terms and Conditions and Privacy Policy, appears directly below the buttons for registration. The entire screen is visible at once, and the user does not need to scroll beyond what is immediately visible to find notice of the Terms of Service. Although the sentence is in a small font, the dark print contrasts with the bright white background, and the hyperlinks are in blue and underlined.

In addition to being spatially coupled with the mechanism for manifesting assent — i.e., the register button — the notice is temporally coupled. As we observed in Schnabel,

> inasmuch as consumers are regularly and frequently confronted with non-negotiable contract terms, particularly when entering into transactions using the Internet, the presentation of these terms at a place and time that the consumer will associate with the initial purchase or enrollment, or the use of, the goods or services from which the recipient benefits at least indicates to the consumer that he or she is taking such goods or employing such services subject to additional terms and conditions that may one day affect him or her.

Schnabel, 697 F.3d at 127. Here, notice of the Terms of Service is provided simultaneously to enrollment, thereby connecting the contractual terms to the services to which they apply. We think that a reasonably prudent smartphone user would understand that the terms were connected to the creation of a user account.

That the Terms of Service were available only by hyperlink does not preclude a determination of reasonable notice. Moreover, the language "[b]y creating an Uber account, you agree" is a clear prompt directing users to read the Terms and Conditions and signaling that their acceptance of the benefit of registration would be subject to contractual terms. As long as the hyperlinked text was itself reasonably conspicuous — and we conclude that it was — a reasonably prudent smartphone user would have constructive notice of the terms. While it may be the case that many users will not bother reading the additional terms, that is the choice the user makes; the user is still on inquiry notice.

Accordingly, we conclude that the Uber App provided reasonably conspicuous notice of the Terms of Service as a matter of California law and turn to the question of whether Meyer unambiguously manifested his assent to those terms.

2. Manifestation of Assent

Although Meyer's assent to arbitration was not express, we are convinced that it was unambiguous in light of the objectively reasonable notice of the terms, as discussed in detail above. . . . As we described above, there is ample evidence that a reasonable user would be on inquiry notice of the terms, and the spatial and temporal coupling of the terms with the registration button "indicate[d] to the consumer that he or she is . . . employing such services subject to additional terms and conditions that may one day affect him or her." *Schnabel*, 697 F.3d at 127. A reasonable user would know that by clicking the registration button, he was agreeing to the terms and conditions accessible via the hyperlink, whether he clicked on the hyperlink or not.

The fact that clicking the register button had two functions — creation of a user account and assent to the Terms of Service — does not render Meyer's assent ambiguous. The registration process allowed Meyer to review the Terms of Service prior to registration, unlike web platforms that provide notice of contract terms only after the user manifested his or her assent. Furthermore, the text on the Payment Screen not only included a hyperlink to the Terms of Service, but expressly warned the user that by creating an Uber account, the user was agreeing to be bound by the linked terms. Although the warning text used the term "creat[e]" instead of "register," as the button was marked, the physical proximity of the notice to the register button and the placement of the language in the registration flow make clear to the user that the linked terms pertain to the action the user is about to take.

The transactional context of the parties' dealings reinforces our conclusion. Meyer located and downloaded the Uber App, signed up for an account, and entered his credit card information with the intention of entering into a forward-looking relationship with Uber. The registration process clearly contemplated some sort of continuing relationship between the putative user and Uber, one that would require some terms and conditions, and the Payment Screen provided clear notice that there were terms that governed that relationship.

Accordingly, we conclude on the undisputed facts of this case that Meyer unambiguously manifested his assent to Uber's Terms of Service as a matter of California law. . . .

[The Second Circuit also held that the district court should consider the plaintiff's argument that the defendants had waived their right to arbitrate.]

CONCLUSION

For the reasons set forth above, the order of the district court denying defendants' motions to compel arbitration is VACATED, and the case is REMANDED to the district court to consider whether defendants have waived their rights to arbitration and for any further proceedings consistent with this opinion.

NOTES AND QUESTIONS

1. Uber's Payment Screen at the time of this case is reproduced above (at roughly the size it would have appeared on Meyer's smartphone). The tiny print at the bottom says "By creating an Uber account, you agree to the TERMS OF SERVICE & PRIVACY POLICY." Does that change your opinion of the case?

2. As *Meyer* observes, online contracts usually fall into one of two camps. First, there are "browsewrap" terms, which usually appear on websites and say that a user agrees to the terms when he or she accesses the site. Browsewrap terms are usually enforceable if a user has actual or constructive notice of them. Second, there are "clickwrap" terms, which usually involve pop-up boxes that force the user to click "I agree" in order to proceed. Judges usually find that clicking the button manifests assent to the terms. How does the court classify Uber's Terms of Service?

3. Can you explain how the objective theory of contracts (which Lucy v. Zehmer discusses) is connected to the widespread phenomenon of contracts being formed on the Internet or smartphones? If you are the attorney for a company developing an app like Uber's, how would you advise your client to make sure that important legal terms (such as acceptance of arbitration in lieu of a lawsuit, or a disclaimer of warranties) are made part of the resulting deal?

4. The formation of contracts on the Internet has generated a large number of cases. Forcing unread terms on users is often argued to be unfair, and we will address that issue later, as we study doctrines such as unconscionability, fraud, mistake, and various consumer rights.

Problem 2

Bette, who is 85 and lives in a retirement community, is looking for a present for her granddaughter's 16th birthday. She logged on to Amazon. com and found a nice cashmere sweater. She placed it in her "cart" and went to the "Checkout" screen. On that page, there were two buttons — one on the top right and one on the bottom left — entitled "Place your order." Beneath these buttons was small text that read: "By placing your order, you agree to Amazon.com's privacy notice and conditions of use." Bette pushed one of these buttons and ordered the sweater. Has Bette agreed to Amazon's privacy notice and conditions of use?

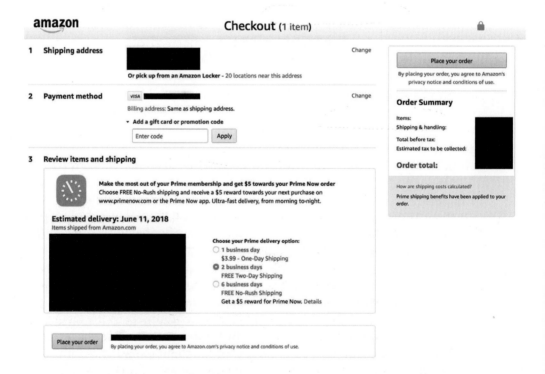

KOLODZIEJ v. MASON
United States Court of Appeals, Eleventh Circuit, 2014
774 F.3d 736

WILSON, Circuit Judge:

This case involves a law student's efforts to form a contract by accepting a "million-dollar challenge" that a lawyer extended on national television while representing a client accused of murder. Since we find that the challenge did not give rise to an enforceable unilateral contract, we hold that the district court properly entered summary judgment for the lawyer and his law firm, Defendants-Appellees James Cheney Mason (Mason) and J. Cheney Mason, P.A., with regard to the breach-of-contract claim brought by the law student, Plaintiff-Appellant Dustin S. Kolodziej.

I

The current dispute—whether Mason formed a unilateral contract with Kolodziej—arose from comments Mason made while representing criminal defendant Nelson Serrano, who stood accused of murdering his former business partner as well as the son, daughter, and son-in-law of a third business partner. During Serrano's highly publicized capital murder trial, Mason participated in an interview with NBC News in which he focused on the seeming implausibility of the prosecution's theory of the case. Indeed, his client ostensibly had an alibi—on the day of the murders, Serrano claimed to be on a business trip in an entirely different state, several hundred miles away from the scene of the crimes in central Florida. Hotel surveillance video confirmed that Serrano was at a La Quinta Inn (La Quinta) in Atlanta, Georgia, several hours before and after the murders occurred in Bartow, Florida.

However, the prosecution maintained that Serrano committed the murders in an approximately ten-hour span between the times that he was seen on the security camera. According to the prosecution, after being recorded by the hotel security camera in the early afternoon, Serrano slipped out of the hotel and, traveling under several aliases, flew from Atlanta to Orlando, where he rented a car, drove to Bartow, Florida, and committed the murders. From there, Serrano allegedly drove to the Tampa International Airport, flew back to Atlanta, and drove from the Atlanta International Airport to the La Quinta, to make an appearance on the hotel's security footage once again that evening.

Mason argued that it was impossible for his client to have committed the murders in accordance with this timeline; for instance, for the last leg of the journey, Serrano would have had to get off a flight in Atlanta's busy airport, travel to the La Quinta several miles away, and arrive in that hotel lobby in only twenty-eight minutes. After extensively describing the delays that would take place to render that twenty-eight-minute timeline even more unlikely,[1] Mason stated, "I challenge anybody to show me, and guess what? Did they bring in any evidence to say that somebody made that route, did so? State's burden of proof. If they can do it, I'll challenge 'em. I'll pay them a million dollars if they can do it."

NBC did not broadcast Mason's original interview during Serrano's trial. At the conclusion of the trial, the jury returned a guilty verdict in Serrano's case. Thereafter, in December 2006, NBC featured an edited version of Mason's interview in a national broadcast of its "Dateline" television program. The edited version removed much of the surrounding commentary, including Mason's references to the State's burden of proof, and Mason's statement aired as, "I challenge anybody to show me — I'll pay them a million dollars if they can do it."

Enter Kolodziej, then a law student at the South Texas College of Law, who had been following the Serrano case. Kolodziej saw the edited version of Mason's interview and understood the statement as a serious challenge, open to anyone, to "make it off the plane and back to the hotel within [twenty-eight] minutes" — that is, in the prosecution's timeline — in return for one million dollars.

Kolodziej subsequently ordered and studied the transcript of the edited interview, interpreting it as an offer to form a unilateral contract — an offer he decided to accept by performing the challenge. In December 2007, Kolodziej recorded himself retracing Serrano's alleged route, traveling from a flight at the Atlanta airport to what he believed was the former location of the now-defunct La Quinta within twenty-eight minutes. Kolodziej then sent Mason a copy of the recording of his journey and a letter stating that Kolodziej had performed the challenge and requested payment. Mason responded with a letter in which he refused payment and denied that he made a serious offer in the interview. Kolodziej again demanded payment, and Mason again refused.

[Kolodziej sued Mason and Mason's law firm, J. Cheney Mason, P.A., for breach of contract. The district court granted summary judgment in favor of the defendants.] . . .

---

1. For example, Mason noted that, "in Atlanta, depending on which concourse you're landing in, you're going to have to wait to get off the airplane. . . . You got people boxed in — the lady with the kids in the carriage. Or people getting down their bags. Or the fat one can't get down the aisle. I mean, whatever the story is, you've got delays in getting off the airplane. . . . Then you have to go from whatever gate you are, . . . to catch the subway train to the terminal. Wait for that. Wait while it stops in the meantime. People getting on and off. Get to that. Go up again, the escalators. Get to where you're in the terminal, out the terminal to ground transportation. And from there to be on the videotape in 28 minutes."

III

The case before us involves the potential creation of an oral, unilateral contract.[3]

Under Florida law, the question of whether a valid contract exists is a threshold question of law that may be properly decided by the court. *See* Acumen Constr., Inc. v. Neher, 616 So. 2d 98, 99 (Fla. Dist. Ct. App. 1993). . . .

"To prove the existence of a contract, a plaintiff must plead: (1) offer; (2) acceptance; (3) consideration; and (4) sufficient specification of the essential terms." Vega v. T-Mobile USA, Inc., 564 F.3d 1256, 1272 (11th Cir. 2009) (citing St. Joe Corp. v. McIver, 875 So. 2d 375, 381 (Fla. 2004)). An oral contract is subject to all basic requirements of contract law, *St. Joe Corp.*, 875 So. 2d at 381, and mutual assent is a prerequisite for the formation of any contract, *see* Gibson v. Courtois, 539 So. 2d 459, 460 (Fla. 1989). . . . A valid contract—premised on the parties' requisite willingness to contract—may be "manifested through written or spoken words, or inferred in whole or in part from the parties' conduct." L & H Constr. Co. v. Circle Redmont, Inc., 55 So. 3d 630, 634 (Fla. Dist. Ct. App. 2011) (internal quotation marks omitted). We use "an objective test . . . to determine whether a contract is enforceable." *See* Robbie v. City of Miami, 469 So. 2d 1384, 1385 (Fla. 1985); *see also Leonard*, 88 F. Supp. 2d at 128 (noting that the determination of whether a party made an offer to enter into a contract requires "the [c]ourt to determine how a reasonable, objective person would have understood" the potential offeror's communication).

IV

We do not find that Mason's statements were such that a reasonable, objective person would have understood them to be an invitation to contract, regardless of whether we look to the unedited interview or the edited television broadcast seen by Kolodziej. Neither the content of Mason's statements, nor the circumstances in which he made them, nor the conduct of the parties reflects the assent necessary to establish an actionable offer—which is, of course, essential to the creation of a contract.

As a threshold matter, the "spoken words" of Mason's purported challenge do not indicate a willingness to enter into a contract. *See L & H Constr. Co.*, 55 So. 3d at 634. Even removed from its surrounding context, the

---

3. While most contracts are bilateral, with promises exchanged between two parties, a unilateral contract is, as the name implies, one-sided—one party promises to do something (for example, pay money) in exchange for performance (an act, forbearance, or conduct producing a certain result). *See* Ballou v. Campbell, 179 So. 2d 228, 229-30 (Fla. Dist. Ct. App. 1965).

edited sentence that Kolodziej claims creates Mason's obligation to pay (that is, "I challenge anybody to show me — I'll pay them a million dollars if they can do it") appears colloquial. The exaggerated amount of "a million dollars" — the common choice of movie villains and schoolyard wagerers alike — indicates that this was hyperbole. As the district court noted, "courts have viewed such indicia of jest or hyperbole as providing a reason for an individual to doubt that an 'offer' was serious." *See* Kolodziej v. Mason, 996 F. Supp. 2d 1237, 1252 (M.D. Fla. 2014) (discussing, in dicta, a laughter-eliciting joke made by Mason's co-counsel during the interview). Thus, the very content of Mason's spoken words "would have given any reasonable person pause, considering all of the attendant circumstances in this case." *See id.*

Those attendant circumstances are further notable when we place Mason's statements in context. As Judge Learned Hand once noted, "the circumstances in which the words are used is always relevant and usually indispensable." N.Y. Trust Co. v. Island Oil & Transp. Corp., 34 F.2d 655, 656 (2d Cir. 1929); *see* Lefkowitz v. Great Minneapolis Surplus Store, Inc., 251 Minn. 188, 86 N.W.2d 689, 691 (1957) (noting that the existence of an offer "depends on the legal intention of the parties and the surrounding circumstances"). Here, Mason made the comments in the course of representing a criminal defendant accused of quadruple homicide and did so during an interview solely related to that representation. Such circumstances would lead a reasonable person to question whether the requisite assent and actionable offer giving rise to contractual liability existed. Certainly, Mason's statements — made as a defense attorney in response to the prosecution's theory against his client — were far more likely to be a descriptive illustration of what that attorney saw as serious holes in the prosecution's theory instead of a serious offer to enter into a contract.

Nor can a valid contract be "inferred in whole or in part from the parties' conduct" in this case. *See* L & H Constr. Co., 55 So. 3d at 634 (internal quotation marks omitted); *see also* Commerce P'ship 8098 LP v. Equity Contracting Co., 695 So. 2d 383, 385 (Fla. Dist. Ct. App. 1997), *as modified on clarification* (June 4, 1997) (noting that contracts that have not been "put into promissory words with sufficient clarity" may still be enforceable, but they "rest upon the assent of the parties" (internal quotation marks omitted)). By way of comparison, consider Lucy v. Zehmer, 196 Va. 493, 84 S.E.2d 516 (1954), the classic case describing and applying what we now know as the objective standard of assent. That court held that statements allegedly made "in jest" *could* result in an offer binding the parties to a contract, since "the law imputes to a person an intention corresponding to the reasonable meaning of his words and acts." *Id.* at 522. Therefore, "a person cannot set up that he was merely jesting when his conduct and words would warrant a reasonable person in believing that he intended a real agreement." *Id.*

In so holding, the *Lucy* court considered that the offeror wrote, prepared, and executed a writing for sale; the parties engaged in extensive, serious discussion prior to preparing the writing; the offeror prepared a second written agreement, having changed the content of the writing in response to the offeree's request; the offeror had his wife separately sign the writing; and the offeror allowed the offeree to leave with the signed writing without ever indicating that it was in jest. *Id.* at 519-22. Given that these "words and acts, judged by a reasonable standard, manifest[ed] an intention to agree," the offeror's "unexpressed state of . . . mind" was immaterial. *Id.* at 522. Under the objective standard of assent, the *Lucy* court found that the parties had formed a contract. *See id.*

Applying the objective standard here leads us to the real million-dollar question: "What did the party say and do?" *See Newman*, 778 F.2d at 464. Here, it is what both parties did not say and did not do that clearly distinguishes this case from those cases where an enforceable contract was formed. Mason did not engage in any discussion regarding his statements to NBC with Kolodziej, and, prior to Kolodziej demanding payment, there was no contact or communication between the parties. Mason neither confirmed that he made an offer nor asserted that the offer was serious.[7] Mason did not have the payment set aside in escrow;[8] nor had he ever declared that he had money set aside in case someone proved him wrong.[9] Mason had not made his career out of the contention that the prosecution's case was implausible;[10] nor did he make the statements in a commercial context for the "obvious purpose of advertising or promoting [his] goods or business." He did not create or promote the video that included his statement,

7. Compare with Barnes v. Treece, where, after seeing news reports that Treece stated he would "put a hundred thousand dollars to anyone to find a crooked board," Barnes telephoned Treece and asked if his earlier statement had been made seriously. 15 Wash. App. 437, 549 P.2d 1152, 1154 (1976). Treece "assured Barnes that the statement had been made seriously [and] advised Barnes that the statement was firm." *Id.* Thus, the trial court found that "Treece's statements before the gambling commission and reiterated to Barnes personally on the telephone constituted a valid offer for a unilateral contract." *Id.* [Further citation omitted.]

8. In the seminal case of Carlill v. Carbolic Smoke Ball Co., which found that an advertisement can constitute an offer to form a unilateral contract, the same advertisement promising the reward included the statement: "1000£ is deposited with the Alliance Bank, Regent Street, shewing our sincerity in the matter." (1892) 2 Q.B. 484, 484-85, *aff'd*, (1893) 1 Q.B. 256 (Eng.); *see also Barnes*, 549 P.2d at 1154 ("[Treece] informed Barnes that the $100,000 was safely being held in escrow.").

9. *Cf.* James v. Turilli, 473 S.W.2d 757, 761 (Mo. Ct. App. 1971). In *James*, Turilli stated before a nationwide television audience that Jesse James didn't die in 1882 and that Turilli "would pay Ten Thousand Dollars ($10,000.00) to anyone . . . who could prove [him] wrong." *Id.* at 759 (internal quotation marks omitted). In finding that this constituted an offer, the court noted that, in addition to other evidence, Turilli had previously said that he had a "certified check of ten thousand dollars" to be collected upon proof that Jesse James had actually died in 1882. *Id.* at 761.

10. In *Newman*, a "self-styled 'tax rebel,'" who "made a career and substantial profits out of his tax protest activities" and "promoted his books by appearing on over five hundred radio and television programs," 778 F.2d at 461-62, made a valid, time-limited offer when, in a live television appearance, he stated, "If anybody calls this show . . . and cites any section of this Code that says an individual is required to file a tax return, I will pay them $100,000," *id.* at 462 (internal quotation marks omitted); *see also James*, 473 S.W.2d at 761 (noting that "[Turilli] had virtually made a career out of his contention Jesse W. James was not killed in 1882").

nor did he increase the amount at issue.[12] He did not, nor did the show include, any information to contact Mason about the challenge.[13] Simply put, Mason's conduct lacks any indicia of assent to contract.

In fact, none of Mason's surrounding commentary — either in the unedited original interview or in the edited television broadcast — gave the slightest indication that his statement was anything other than a figure of speech. In the course of representing his client, Mason merely used a rhetorical expression to raise questions as to the prosecution's case. We could just as easily substitute a comparable idiom such as "I'll eat my hat" or "I'll be a monkey's uncle" into Mason's interview in the place of "I'll pay them a million dollars," and the outcome would be the same. We would not be inclined to make him either consume his headwear or assume a simian relationship were he to be proven wrong; nor will we make him pay one million dollars here.[15]

Additionally, an enforceable contract requires mutual assent as to sufficiently definite essential terms. [Citations omitted.] Here, even the proper starting and ending points for Mason's purported challenge were unspecified and indefinite; Kolodziej had to speculate and decide for himself what constituted the essential terms of the challenge. For instance, in the prosecution's theory of the case, Serrano, using an alias, was seated in the coach section of an aircraft loaded with over one hundred other passengers. Kolodziej, however, purchased a front row aisle seat in first class and started the twenty-eight-minute countdown from that prime location. Comparably, Kolodziej did not finish his performance in the La Quinta lobby; rather, Kolodziej ended the challenge at an EconoLodge, which, based on anecdotal information, he believed was the former location of the La Quinta in which Serrano stayed.

---

12. Compare with Augstein v. Leslie, where, in YouTube videos, news articles, and online postings on social media, Leslie stated he would pay a reward to anyone who returned his stolen laptop, gradually increasing the sum to one million dollars. No. 11 Civ. 7512, 2012 WL 4928914, *2-3 (S.D.N.Y. Oct. 17, 2012). Given the increase in the offer amount, the value of the property lost, and Leslie's postings, the court found that "Leslie's videos and other activities together [were] best characterized as an offer for a reward." *Id.* at *2.

13. *Cf. Newman*, 778 F.2d at 462. During Schiff's live interview on national television program, wherein Schiff made statements constituting an offer, "[t]he words 'Nightwatch Phone-In' and the telephone number [for the show] were flashed on the screen periodically during Schiff's appearance. In addition, [the interviewer] repeated the telephone number and encouraged viewers to call and speak directly with Schiff on the air." *Id.*

15. However, unenforceable is not quite the same as "unlitigable," since some people might still take such a challenge literally. For example, Donald Trump recently sued Bill Maher for breach of contract after Maher stated on national television that he would offer five million dollars to Trump, donatable to the charity of Trump's choice, if Trump proved that he was not the spawn of an orangutan. *See* Compl., Trump v. Maher, No. BC499537 (Cal. Sup. Ct. filed Feb. 4, 2013), *available at* http://pmcdeadline2.files.wordpress.com/2013/02/trump-maher_130205003242.pdf. Trump claimed to accept this offer by providing a copy of his birth certificate as proof of his non-orangutan origin, filing suit when Maher did not respond to his demand for payment. Trump later voluntarily dismissed the suit.

We highlight these differences not to comment as to whether Kolodziej adequately performed the challenge — which the parties dispute for a multitude of additional reasons — but instead to illustrate the lack of definiteness and specificity in any purported offer (and absence of mutual assent thereto). It is challenging to point to anything Mason said or did that evinces a "display of willingness to enter into a contract on specified terms, made in a way that would lead a reasonable person to understand that an acceptance, having been sought, will result in a binding contract." *See Black's Law Dictionary* 1189 (9th ed. 2009) (defining "offer" in contract law); *see also Tiara Condo. Ass'n*, 607 F.3d at 746. Therefore, we conclude that Mason did not manifest the requisite willingness to contract through his words or conduct, and no amount of subsequent effort by Kolodziej could turn Mason's statements into an actionable offer.

In further illustration of the lack of assent to contract in this case, we question whether even Kolodziej's conduct — his "acceptance" — manifested assent to any perceived offer. Under the objective standard of assent, we do not look into the subjective minds of the parties; the law imputes an intention that corresponds with the reasonable meaning of a party's words and acts. *See Lucy*, 84 S.E.2d at 522. We thus find it troublesome that, in all this time — ordering the transcript, studying it, purchasing tickets, recording himself making the trip — Kolodziej never made any effort to contact Mason to confirm the existence of an offer, to ensure any such offer was still valid after Serrano's conviction, or to address the details and terms of the challenge.[16] However, we will not attribute bad intent when inexperience may suffice. Kolodziej may have learned in his contracts class that acceptance by performance results in an immediate, binding contract and that notice may not be necessary, but he apparently did not consider the absolute necessity of first having a specific, definite offer and the basic requirement of mutual assent. We simply are driven to ask, as Mason did in his response letter: "Why did you not just call?" Perhaps a jurist's interpretation of an old aphorism provides the answer: "If, as Alexander Pope wrote, 'a little learning is a dangerous thing,' then a little learning in law is particularly perilous."[17]

. . .

---

16. This is additionally problematic considering the timeline of events. The murders took place in 1997; the interview, trial, conviction, sentencing, and broadcast of the edited interview all occurred in 2006. Yet Kolodziej claims to have accepted Mason's "offer" by attempting the challenge in 2007, a year after the trial had concluded and the sentence had been returned. These factors raise serious doubts as to whether Kolodziej could even accept the purported offer, given that offers must be accepted within a reasonable time and Mason's client had already been convicted. *See* 1 *Williston on Contracts* §5:7 (4th ed.) (observing that, although offers of reward generally do not lapse for a substantial length of time, the reasonable-time analysis requires "taking into account the circumstances surrounding any particular offer"). A reasonable person would have had, at a minimum, hesitations as to whether any actionable offer had lapsed.

17. Chief Judge Gilbert in Ginn v. Farley, 43 Md. App. 229, 403 A.2d 858, 859 (1979) (quoting Alexander Pope, *An Essay on Criticism*, Part II, line 15 (n.p. 1711)).

VI

Just as people are free to contract, they are also free *from* contract, and we find it neither prudent nor permissible to impose contractual liability for offhand remarks or grandstanding. Nor would it be advisable to scrutinize a defense attorney's hyperbolic commentary for a hidden contractual agenda, particularly when that commentary concerns the substantial protections in place for criminal defendants. Having considered the content of Mason's statements, the context in which they were made, and the conduct of the parties, we do not find it reasonable to conclude that Mason assented to enter into a contract with anyone for one million dollars. We affirm the district court's judgment in favor of Mason and J. Cheney Mason, P.A.

AFFIRMED.

NOTES AND QUESTIONS

1. Kolodziej argued that Mason had made an offer to enter into a *unilateral contract*. As we will see later in this chapter, the distinction between unilateral and bilateral contracts is slippery. Very roughly, an offer to enter into a unilateral contract can only be accepted by the offeree *performing an act*. Conversely, an offer to enter into a bilateral contract can be accepted *either* by *performance* or simply by making a return *promise*.

2. Do you think the court thought that Kolodziej truly believed that Mason meant his statement as a serious offer? If not, how does that affect the analysis?

STEPP v. FREEMAN
Court of Appeals of Ohio, 1997
119 Ohio App. 3d 68, 694 N.E.2d 792

FREDERICK N. YOUNG, Presiding Judge.

Donald Freeman, defendant, appeals the trial court's holding in favor of Lionel Stepp, plaintiff, on the issues of equitable estoppel and implied contract.

I

This matter arose out of the events surrounding the purchase of a winning lottery ticket on March 1, 1993. Freeman and Stepp were members of a group of employees at the Chrysler Acustar Plant who jointly purchased lottery tickets. The group had been in existence in excess of five years.

Freeman took over running the group approximately two years prior to the date the group purchased the winning ticket. The group had no written rules, but it had established certain unwritten rules of conduct.

[handwritten margin note: Implied contract between the group]

The group was restricted to only twenty members. Freeman kept a list of the members. The members pooled their money to purchase lottery tickets whenever the jackpot reached $8 million or higher. Each member was expected to contribute $2.20 to the pool. Freeman would keep track of who had paid, whether payment was in advance, and who had not yet paid by noting it in the appropriate column on the list of the members. The group purchased forty tickets and four "kickers" with the pooled money.

To increase their chances of winning, the group would use half of the pooled money to purchase tickets in Cincinnati, Ohio, and the other half to purchase tickets in Beavercreek, Ohio. Freeman purchased the tickets in Beavercreek, Ohio, and Fred Krueger, another member of the group, purchased the tickets in Cincinnati, Ohio. The tickets were purchased either on Monday, for the Wednesday drawing, or on Thursday, for the Saturday drawing. In the weeks that the group played the lottery, Stepp was in charge of making photocopies of the tickets on Tuesday and/or Friday. Sometimes, however, another member of the group, James Saul, would make the copies of the tickets if Stepp was unavailable. Stepp would leave the photocopies on Freeman's desk. Freeman would either leave the copies on his desk for the members to pick up or would sometimes distribute some of the copies to members.

Freeman was recognized as being in charge of receiving the money for the pool. Freeman testified that a few times he had to explicitly inform or remind some members that their money was due. Freeman further stated that he had to remind all of the members of the group at least once or twice during the two years that he ran the group that their shares were due. Freeman also often indirectly reminded members that their shares were due by walking around the plant with the list of members in his hand. When the members saw Freeman with the card in his hand, they knew it was time to contribute, and they would get out their money and pay their shares without Freeman having to expressly ask for their contributions.

Members would sometimes cover other members' shares when they ran into Freeman. Furthermore, Freeman or other members would cover another member's portion of the pool if the member was absent from work. When members knew that they would be on vacation or otherwise unavailable, they would pay their contribution in advance or would inform Freeman that they would pay when they returned. Since the time that Freeman began running the group, none of the members had ever failed to participate, and no fewer than forty tickets, two for each member, had ever been purchased.

Individuals who wanted to join the group had to put their names on a waiting list and could join the group only when one of the existing members decided to leave the group. The members that actually dropped out of the group while Freeman was running it were taken off the list only after Freeman had a conversation with them and the member had conveyed to Freeman that he or she was not going to contribute any longer and that he or she was leaving the group. No member had ever been unilaterally removed from the list by Freeman because the member had not timely paid his or her share. After a member left the group, Freeman would ask the first person on the waiting list if he or she wanted to join the group. If the individual decided to join the group, Freeman would add the individual's name to the list.

In the week prior to the group purchasing the winning lottery ticket, Freeman and Stepp had a serious work-related disagreement. As a result of their disagreement, Freeman called Stepp a derogatory name and, according to Stepp, threatened him. Following their disagreement, Freeman and Stepp did not speak to one another with the exception of a few brief work-related discussions. The lottery jackpot reached $8 million over the weekend following their conflict. On the ensuing Monday, Freeman collected money from the group for the drawing by, in part, walking around with the member list in his hand. Freeman, however, did not ask for Stepp's money, nor did he inform Stepp that the lottery had reached $8 million. Likewise, Stepp, who claims that he was unaware that the lottery had reached $8 million, did not offer his $2.20.

At the end of the day, Freeman gave Krueger the usual $20 to buy tickets in Cincinnati. Freeman put in the extra dollar himself. Freeman did not inform Krueger or Stepp that he did not consider Stepp to be included in the pool, but he did tell some other members that Stepp was out of the group because he had not paid his $2.20. Furthermore, Stepp never conveyed to Freeman that he was dropping out of the pool. Even though Freeman testified that he considered Stepp to be out of the pool, Freeman did not consult anyone on the waiting list to fill Stepp's spot. Freeman did, however, purchase nineteen, rather than twenty, tickets in Beavercreek, Ohio. Conversely, Krueger purchased the usual twenty tickets in Cincinnati. Therefore, the group had one more ticket than the group should have had if the group had purchased only enough tickets for nineteen members.

On Tuesday, Freeman asked James Saul, rather than Stepp, to make copies of the tickets, explaining that "Stepp hasn't come around." On Wednesday, March 3, 1993, the lottery group won the $8 million lottery jackpot. The winning ticket was one of the twenty tickets purchased in Cincinnati by Fred Krueger. When Stepp arrived at work on Thursday, he was informed by some of his coworkers that the group had won the lottery, and that the group considered that he was not entitled to a share of the money because he had failed to contribute his portion to the pool. The group, however, let one of the members, who was on vacation when the money for the lottery was collected, pay his $2.20 on the Friday after the group had won the lottery. The group let that member pay late because he had purportedly made arrangements with Freeman that he would pay when he returned from his vacation.

On September 1, 1993, Stepp commenced an action, claiming that he was denied his rightful share of the lottery winnings. In support of his claim, Stepp asserted three causes of action: breach of express contract, breach of implied contract, and equitable estoppel. The case was referred to a magistrate for a hearing pursuant to Civ. R. 53. The magistrate issued a finding in favor of Stepp on both the equitable estoppel and breach of contract claim, and recommended that the trial court enter judgment for Stepp in the amount of $60,000 for his portion of the accrued winnings in the years 1993-1996 and one-twentieth of each of the future jackpot payouts. Freeman put on objections to the magistrate's findings of fact and conclusions of law. The trial court considered Freeman's objections and independently reviewed the record as well as all of the evidence presented. After the court concluded its review, it rendered a thoughtful opinion in favor of Stepp on both the equitable estoppel and breach of implied contract claims. Freeman now brings this timely appeal of that decision.

Action filed by Stepp

Freeman objected to the findings of fact and the conclusion of law

Court ruled breach of implied contract

Freeman Appeals

II

. . . We determine that we need not consider the assignments of error relating to the equitable estoppel claim because we believe that Stepp proved his cause of action for breach of an implied-in-fact contract, which is sufficient alone to support the court's monetary award. We find both that Stepp proved all of the elements of an implied-in-fact contract and that the court's finding that the contract was breached was not against the manifest weight of the evidence.

Stepp proved all elements of Implied contract (In fact)

It is well established that there are three categories of contracts: express, implied in fact, and implied in law. Legros v. Tarr (1989), 44 Ohio St. 3d 1, 6, 540 N.E.2d 257, 262-263. Express and implied-in-fact contracts differ from contracts implied in law in that contracts implied in law are not true contracts. Sabin v. Graves (1993), 86 Ohio App. 3d 628, 633, 621 N.E.2d 748, 751-752. Implied-in-law contracts are a legal fiction used to effect an equitable result. Id. Because a contract implied in law is a tool of equity, the existence of an implied-in-law contract does not depend on whether the elements of a contract are proven. Id.

Implied-in-law contracts

On the contrary, the existence of express or implied-in-fact contracts does hinge upon proof of all of the elements of a contract. Lucas v. Costantini (1983), 13 Ohio App. 3d 367, 368, 13 OBR 449, 449-451, 469 N.E.2d 927, 928-929. Express contracts diverge from implied-in-fact contracts in the form of proof that is needed to establish each contractual element. Penwell v. Amherst Hosp. (1992), 84 Ohio App. 3d 16, 21, 616 N.E.2d 254, 257-258. In express contracts, assent to the terms of the contract is actually expressed

Difference is the Contractual element

Express Contract

in the form of an offer and an acceptance. *Lucas*, supra. On the other hand, in implied-in-fact contracts the parties' meeting of the minds is shown by the surrounding circumstances, including the conduct and declarations of the parties, that make it inferable that the contract exists as a matter of tacit understanding. Point E. Condominium Owners' Assn. v. Cedar House Assn. (1995), 104 Ohio App. 3d 704, 712, 663 N.E.2d 343, 348-349. To establish a contract implied in fact a plaintiff must demonstrate that the circumstances surrounding the parties' transaction make it reasonably certain that an agreement was intended. *Lucas*, supra.

Stepp proved all of the elements of an implied-in-fact contract. The circumstances surrounding this pool make it inferable that a contract existed as a matter of tacit understanding. The group membership was restricted to twenty. No new members could join until one of the twenty members dropped out of the group. There was a waiting list to join the group. Members joined the group by consulting Freeman and having Freeman place them on the group roster. Placing an individual's name on the roster created an implied agreement that the individual was a member of the group. Furthermore, there was an implied agreement that each member was to contribute $2.20 to the pool whenever the group played the lottery and that the members would share the winnings equally.

The members thought that the group was run very informally and left the details of running the group to Freeman. Many of the members knew very little about how the group was run. Some members did not even know that the group played the lottery only when the jackpot was $8 million or higher. Most members saw their duty as a member of the group as just contributing their share whenever they saw Freeman walking around the plant with the list in his hand or were otherwise informed that their shares were due.

There was an implied agreement among the members that once their names were on the list as members of the group, they would be informed when they owed their share of the pool and how much they owed. The implied agreement was that members would be informed when their money was due either verbally by Freeman, by other members, or by seeing Freeman walking about with the list in his hand. Freeman testified that he had to expressly remind some members that their money was due a few times and that he had to remind every member of the group that their money was due at least once or twice during the period that he ran the group. Freeman also admitted that he indirectly reminded people that their shares were due by frequently walking around the plant with the list in his hand when the group was going to be playing the lottery.

Because the members perceived the group as running informally and because Freeman had reminded the members that their money was due, a member could also count on not being dropped from the group after neglecting to make payment. No members had been unilaterally dropped from the group by Freeman because they had not paid their share in a timely manner. Those who had not paid their shares in a timely manner were dropped from the group only after Freeman had a conversation with them and they conveyed to him that they were not going to pay and that they were leaving the group.

Stepp had belonged to this group for over five years, and he had never failed to contribute to the lottery during those years. Stepp testified that he had always depended upon Freeman, who was in charge of the lottery, to inform him when the jackpot reached $8 million. Stepp testified that Freeman had always told him when his share was due and how much he owed. As consideration for being told that he owed his share, Stepp would contribute his $2.20 or Freeman would cover his $2.20.

Freeman admitted that he would sometimes cover Stepp's share even when Stepp was not absent from work. In particular, Freeman testified that sometimes the group would play the lottery twice a week and that in some instances he would only collect $2.20 from Stepp, and if they ended up playing a second time, he would put in the additional money for Stepp and collect it later. Freeman also admitted to putting in money for Stepp and collecting it later when Stepp was present but did not have enough money to contribute his share. Finally, Freeman sometimes put money in for Stepp and other members of the group when they were absent from work.

In addition to contributing his share to the group, Stepp performed a more formal role in the group than most of the other members in consideration for being informed when the group was playing the lottery. When Stepp was told that the group was playing the lottery, he would make copies of the lottery tickets. Stepp would pick up the tickets from Freeman on either Tuesday morning or Friday morning to make the copies and then return the tickets and copies to Freeman.

We believe from these facts and circumstances that there was an implied contract that Stepp, who had been a member of the group for over five years, who never had failed to contribute his share, who had a formal role in the group, whose share had been previously covered by Freeman under certain circumstances, and who had been reminded that his money was due in the past, would pay his share and perform his role in the group when he was informed that the group was playing the lottery. This contract was breached by Freeman when he failed to inform Stepp that the group was playing the lottery.

Moreover, we are of the opinion that there was an implied agreement that Stepp would not be dropped from the group unless he had expressed his wish to leave the group to Freeman or Freeman had informed him that he was being dropped from the group for the failure to pay his share. We determine that Freeman breached this implied agreement when he unilaterally dropped Stepp from the group. Accordingly, we find that Stepp proved all of the elements of breach of implied contract and that the trial court's decision was not against the manifest weight of the evidence. The assignments of error are overruled.

Affirmed

Based upon the foregoing the judgment of the trial court is affirmed.

NOTE

Distinction Between Express and Implied Contracts

The distinction between an express contract and an implied-in-fact contract relates to whether assent is expressed in words (written or oral) — an express contract — or, as in the case of implied-in-fact contracts, through an interpretation of surrounding circumstances, including declarations of the parties and their conduct. The line is often a fine one, but the <u>issue</u> only has to do with whether there was <u>mutual assent</u> — an issue of formation. The rights and duties of the parties within an enforceable contract do not vary by whether a contract is an express or implied-in-fact contract. (As we shall see in Chapter 3, a contract can also be "implied in law," meaning it is forced on the parties to avoid "unjust enrichment," no matter what they really intended.)

There are a surprising number of cases concerning contracts to share lottery winnings. See Enforceability of Contract to Share Winnings from Legal Lottery Ticket, 90 A.L.R. 4th 784.

Problem 3

Beaumont and Fletcher signed a contract agreeing to each put up $50,000 for a theatrical performance that they were to write themselves. The five-page, single-spaced contract contained this clause: "This contract shall not be enforceable in a court of law." When Beaumont refused to contribute his share of the money or attend any writing sessions, Fletcher sued. Can a court enforce the "contract"? See American Cas. Co. v. Griffith, 107 Ga. App. 224, 129 S.E.2d 549 (1963); Smith v. MacDonald, 37 Cal. App. 503, 174 P. 80 (1918).

II.   THE OFFER

Restatement Definition of offer

In many cases, the first step in analyzing whether the parties have reached an agreement is determining whether one of them has made an *offer*. The <u>Restatement (Second) of Contracts §24</u> defines an "offer" as "the manifestation of willingness to enter into a bargain, so made as to justify another person in understanding that his assent to that bargain is invited and will conclude it."

Problem 4

Should a court find that there is the requisite mutual assent if the response to the following statements is "I accept"?

NO (a) "I'm considering selling my car to you for $1,200."

Yes (b) "I will sell you my car for $1,200."

no (c) "Would it be a good deal if I sold you my car for $1,200?"

NO (d) "You wouldn't consider paying $1,200 for my car, would you?"

A. Preliminary Negotiations

Courts sometimes contrast offers (which become agreements if they are accepted) with "preliminary negotiations" (which are not offers and thus cannot give rise to an agreement even if they are accepted). A preliminary negotiation occurs if the person who hears or reads a communication knows or has reason to know that the person making it does not intend to conclude a bargain until he has made a further manifestation of assent. Restatement (Second) of Contracts §26.

Prelim. Neg. Defined *preliminary negotiation*

PFT ROBERSON, INC. v. VOLVO TRUCKS NORTH AMERICA, INC.

United States Court of Appeals, Seventh Circuit, 2005
420 F.3d 728

The case is about "Preliminary Negotiations"

EASTERBROOK, Circuit Judge.

PFT Roberson operates a fleet of more than 1,200 long-haul trucks and trailers. Freightliner supplies, maintains, and repairs Roberson's vehicles under a fleet agreement. A "fleet agreement" is a comprehensive contract (or series of contracts) specifying the number of trucks, the price of each, how much maintenance costs per mile (a fee that increases as a truck ages and becomes more subject to breakdowns), trade-in and other repurchase details when trucks reach the end of their useful lives, and provisions for winding up the arrangement (the "exit clause"). Exit may be complex, for it can entail early and large-scale replacements, repurchases, or swaps of used trucks, as well as disputes about cause and penalties.

Late in 2001 Freightliner sent Roberson a termination notice, which activated the exit clause. Litigation erupted when the parties could not agree on how it worked; meanwhile Roberson went shopping for another supplier and approached Volvo. The parties discussed a multi-year, $84 million arrangement for the purchase and maintenance of new Volvo trucks plus the trade-in or repair of used Freightliner trucks and trailers that Freightliner did not

Volvo contract agreement terms but nothing was signed

[handwritten margin note: Procedural Hist.]

repurchase. Lengthy drafts were exchanged from November 2001 until late January 2002. Many "Master Agreements" were drafted; none was signed.

[handwritten margin note: Rob. sued Volvo for breach of contract]

In March 2002 Roberson and Freightliner patched up their differences, settled the lawsuit, and extended their fleet agreement. Roberson then sued Volvo for breach of contract and fraud. According to Roberson, an e-mail containing 572 words is the contract that Volvo breached, and the fraud consists in Volvo's efforts to negotiate additional or revised terms after sending the e-mail. Volvo's e-mail, dated December 6, 2001, and captioned "Confirmation of our conversation," recaps the negotiations' status. It identifies items that Roberson and Volvo had "come to agreement on" and others that the parties needed to "review and finalize."

[handwritten margin note: Judge held the email contained Volvo's assent]
[handwritten margin note: At trial]
[handwritten margin note: B-ft Awarded damages to Rob.]
[handwritten margin note: Volvo App]

Although the e-mail states that the contract would be complete only when these other subjects had been resolved and the package approved by senior managers, the district judge held that a jury could find that the e-mail constituted Volvo's assent to the items it mentioned even if a full fleet agreement had not been signed. At the trial, the judge allowed Roberson's managers to testify that they felt they had an agreement with Volvo. (The objection, which the district judge rejected, was that only words exchanged between the parties could create a contract and that private thoughts are irrelevant.) The jury awarded Roberson more than $5 million in damages for breach of contract. Volvo appeals the district court's denial of its motion for judgment as a matter of law under Fed. R. Civ. P. 50 and contends that it is entitled to a new trial if we reject this position. Roberson has filed a cross-appeal in pursuit of damages on its fraud theory, which the district judge did not submit to the jury.

[handwritten margin note: What the parties Allready agree to]

According to the e-mail, the parties "have come to agreement on" the number of new Volvo trucks that Roberson will purchase, the cost per mile of servicing the new trucks and some of the Freightliner trucks, and an outline of an exit clause. They had not agreed on the price per truck, on the cost per mile for all of the older trucks, on the repurchase and trade-in terms for older trucks, or on the details of the exit clause — and recall that the devil was in these details for the arrangement between Roberson and Freightliner. Roberson had not bound itself to buy a single truck; it wants to treat the e-mail as granting it a unilateral option. No reasonable jury could conclude that the items covered in the e-mail were independent bargains to which Volvo had bound itself. The parties were negotiating a comprehensive arrangement, not a series of stand-alone contracts. The e-mail was not something to which Roberson could respond "I accept" and move from the negotiation to the performance stage. Nor did Roberson say "I accept" or any equivalent; the parties negotiated for another two months, and when Volvo submitted its comprehensive proposal (at least 100 times longer than the e-mail), Roberson refused to sign.

[handwritten margin note: Not Independent bargins]
[handwritten margin note: Not a Series of stand alone contracts]

[handwritten margin note: It wasn't an item by item agreement]

True enough, as Roberson stresses, truck purchases can be separated from truck maintenance, and in principle many subjects could be resolved one at a time. If people choose to negotiate and agree item by item, that is their privilege. But that is not what these negotiators were doing, and the e-mail was not an à la carte menu from which Roberson could check off the items it wanted. The e-mail and the other writings these parties exchanged show that the negotiations were global and that Volvo wanted a complete and formal arrangement before being bound. Such caution is to be expected in a multi-million-dollar deal that would last for many years. . . . Here, each item that Roberson and Volvo "have come to agreement on" corresponds to a missing yet required document:

- Termination clause. The e-mail contains some elements of exit arrangements but also states that Volvo must later "provide an exit clause" and that the parties need to "review and finalize" a master agreement "w/exit clause." In later drafts, the parties haggled over whether termination would be allowed at will or only for cause (a question on which the e-mail was silent), and what penalties the party invoking the exit right must pay the other. These particulars were vital in light of the fight between Roberson and Freightliner about precisely such details.
- Truck purchases. According to the e-mail Roberson would purchase at least 811 new Volvo trucks, yet a purchase order or similar recitation would be required to bind Roberson to this provision (Volvo would not allow itself to be bound without a reciprocal commitment), and that was not possible until the parties agreed on the trucks' price, trade-in value, purchase and delivery schedule, and buyer and seller remedies in case of breach, none of which the e-mail covered.
- Maintenance cost per mile. According to the e-mail, Volvo had agreed to maintain Roberson's trucks for a specified cost per mile, but the e-mail added that the parties still needed to reach a "Master CPM [cost-per-mile] agreement" and approve specification sheets to catalog the preexisting damage and condition of each Roberson truck. Drafts of a "Proposed Master CPM agreement" addressed something that the e-mail did not: the cost per mile for trucks older than three years. (Trucks become more expensive to repair over time because of wear and tear, and pennies per mile add up to millions of dollars for a big fleet in which each long-haul truck can average 150,000 miles per year.) At oral argument, Roberson contended that cost per mile could be calculated by plugging data such as manufacturer and length in service into a formula. No such formula appears in either the e-mail or any later communication, however, and "[h]aving neither set a price, nor a mechanism to calculate a price, the draft cannot constitute a contract." Feldman v. Allegheny International, Inc., 850 F.2d 1217, 1223-24 (7th Cir. 1988).
- Trade-in value. A major source of Roberson's supposed damages was the generous (relative to Freightliner) trade-in allowance that Volvo offered for used trucks, yet the e-mail makes the trade-in "subject to trade terms and conditions" derived not from industry practice but

from a document containing "Volvo Trade Terms and conditions" that was never finalized.

Hundreds of pages eventually were needed to furnish these and other details. A telling fact about industry practice and business necessity is that the consummated fleet agreement between Roberson and Freightliner was of length and complexity similar to the final package that Volvo tendered to Roberson in January 2002—and two orders of magnitude longer than the e-mail of December 2001.

Illinois supplies the substantive law: on this, if nothing else, the parties agree. When negotiators say that agreement is subject to a more definitive document, Illinois treats this as demonstrating intent not to be bound until that document has been prepared and signed. See, e.g., Empro Manufacturing Co., Inc. v. Ball-Co Manufacturing, Inc., 870 F.2d 423, 425 (7th Cir. 1989) (Illinois law); Interway, Inc. v. Alagna, 85 Ill. App. 3d 1094, 41 Ill. Dec. 117, 407 N.E.2d 615 (Ill. App. 1 Dist. 1980). Illinois is averse to enforcing tentative agreements that are expressly contingent on the signing of formal or final documents. [Citations omitted.]

And for good reason. Often the parties agree on some items (such as how many trucks the buyer wants) while others (such as the price) require more negotiation. If any sign of agreement on any issue exposed the parties to a risk that a judge would deem the first-resolved items to be stand-alone contracts, the process of negotiation would be more cumbersome (the parties would have to hedge every sentence with cautionary legalese), and these extra negotiating expenses would raise the effective price (for in a competitive market the buyer must cover all of the seller's costs). See Richard Craswell, Passing on the Costs of Legal Rules: Efficiency and Distribution in Buyer-Seller Relationships, 43 Stan. L. Rev. 361, 367-68 (1991).

Illinois permits parties to conserve these costs by reaching agreement in stages without taking the risk that courts will enforce a partial bargain that one side or the other would have rejected as incomplete. We have recognized that contracting parties often approach agreement in stages, not that each fledged stage represents a full agreement. See, e.g., Empro, 870 F.2d at 426. Thus parties may reach agreement on elements A, B, and C, with more negotiation required on D and E. If elements D and E are essential to the mix, Illinois does not bind the parties to A, B, or C alone. Should agreement on essential elements fail, it is a failure of negotiation not performance. And whether extra elements are essential is for the parties themselves to say—as Volvo said they were in the very e-mail that Roberson wanted to sift for favorable terms.

A comprehensive fleet agreement depended on resolving all issues that would affect the long-term dealings. The e-mail lists many documents that contain "more of the required details" and are necessary "for each of us to review and finalize." The e-mail offers a few subjects that the parties agree about but principally is a negotiation tool listing the subjects that the parties agree must be agreed on in the future. . . . Its language demonstrates that no contract has been reached.

Roberson insists that, because the e-mail does not state that agreement is "subject to" these future negotiations and documents, the e-mail binds Volvo on all terms it recites. This magic-words approach is not the law in Illinois; the parties need not recite a formula to demonstrate that a definitive agreement lies in the future. Words expressing contingency or dependence on a subsequent event or agreed-on element will do. . . . Volvo and Roberson failed to agree on the details that the e-mail listed as necessary. So clear is this that there was no need to ask a jury's view.

If Roberson had hit the reply button in the e-mail program and said only "we accept," no contract would have been formed because the e-mail was not a definitive offer; it called for negotiation of the many open details rather than acceptance of any contract limited to a subset of the issues. What Roberson actually did in response to the e-mail was to show enthusiasm ("Let's roll," it wrote), utter some empty phrases ("we look forward" to "this long-term partnership"; see Brian Fugere, Chelsea Hardaway & Jon Warshawsky, Why Business People Speak Like Idiots: A Bullfighter's Guide (2005)), and propose a long list of changes and additions. So even if the December 6 e-mail was an offer, Roberson rejected it—and could not "accept" it months later by filing suit for damages. Roberson never signed anything or tried to accept by performance (as by paying for 811 tractor-trailer sets); it treats the December 6 e-mail as an option. Yet Volvo did not give Roberson a unilateral option, least of all one that could be exercised by suit rather than by payment.

Roberson's position—that as soon as parties agree on any term, it is a jury question whether there is a contract on this term alone—would make negotiations far too risky and is not the law in Illinois or any other jurisdiction of which we are aware. The give-and-take of negotiations will leave parties with bargains on some terms that must be made up for by others that benefit the trading partner. Letting one side accept the favorable terms without the compensatory ones would be like permitting the buyer to say: "We have agreed on quantity but not price; I now accept the quantity term and am entitled to the goods at whatever price a jury thinks reasonable." Firms do not (and Volvo did not) put themselves at the mercy of their counterparts in that way. . . . Volvo protected itself by stating in the e-mail that many "required details" remained to be "finalize[d]"; if the details were "required," there was no agreement without them. See also E. Allan Farnsworth, Precontractual Liability and Preliminary Agreements: Fair Dealing and Failed Negotiations, 87 Colum. L. Rev. 217 (1987).

Suppose we treat the e-mail as an expression of intent to reach agreement. The letter in Interway was even stronger. It stated that "this will confirm our agreement" and that "we have agreed" on certain issues, yet the Illinois judiciary held that it did not create a contract on any term because it showed that negotiations remained open. 85 Ill. App. 3d at 1100-01, 41 Ill.

Dec. 117, 407 N.E.2d at 620-21. [Further citations omitted.] Roberson's arithmetic approach — add accords, subtract discords, the remainder equals a contract — would frustrate negotiations for all but the contemporaneous exchange of commodities (a transaction that requires few preliminaries). Parties may negotiate toward closing a deal without the risk that a jury will think that some intermediate document is a contract, and without the "fear that by reaching a preliminary understanding they have bargained away their privilege to disagree on the specifics." *Empro*, 870 F.2d at 426. . . .

Reversed.

Reversed

B. Statement of Opinion or Intention

Problem 5

You represent John Cabot, an attorney with three years' practice experience. John has been sued by a former client, Martin Frobisher. Frobisher, a boat builder, had come to Cabot and asked if Cabot would bring an antitrust action against a manufacturer of rivets. Frobisher was very distraught. Cabot said that he would bring the action and added: "We'll win, for sure." The case was a loser. Frobisher figures that in addition to Cabot's attorney's fee of $25,000, which was paid in advance, he lost $100,000 in down time, court costs, and the like. Assume the facts show that Cabot was not negligent in any way. What is the best argument you can make for your client? What will be the counterargument?

C. Solicitations

LEFKOWITZ v. GREATER MINNEAPOLIS SURPLUS STORE, INC.

Supreme Court of Minnesota, 1957
251 Minn. 188, 86 N.W.2d 689

Appeal

MURPHY, J.

This is an appeal from an order of the Municipal Court of Minneapolis denying the motion of the defendant for amended findings of fact, or, in the alternative, for a new trial. The order for judgment awarded the plaintiff the sum of $138.50 as damages for breach of contract.

This case grows out of the alleged refusal of the defendant to sell to the plaintiff a certain fur piece which it had offered for sale in a newspaper advertisement. It appears from the record that on April 6, 1956, the defendant published the following advertisement in a Minneapolis newspaper:

[handwritten: Solicitation]

> Saturday 9 A.M. Sharp
> 3 Brand New
> Fur
> Coats
> Worth to $100.00
> First Come
> First Served
> $1
> Each

[handwritten: Not specific details → Not clear and certain terms]

On April 13, the defendant published an advertisement in the same newspaper as follows:

[handwritten: offer]

> Saturday 9 A.M.
> 2 Brand New Pastel
> Mink 3-Skin Scarfs
> Selling for $89.50
> Out they go
> Saturday. Each . . . $1.00
> 1 Black Lapin Stole
> Beautiful,
> Worth $139.50 . . . $1.00
> First Come
> First Served

[handwritten: This is specific — "clear, Definitive and explicit"]

The record supports the findings of the court that on each of the Saturdays following the publication of the above-described ads the plaintiff was the first to present himself at the appropriate counter in the defendant's store and on each occasion demanded the coat and the stole so advertised and indicated his readiness to pay the sale price of $1. On both occasions, the defendant refused to sell the merchandise to the plaintiff, stating on the first occasion that by a "house rule" the offer was intended for women only and sales would not be made to men, and on the second visit that plaintiff knew defendant's house rules.

[handwritten: refused — said House Rule was "women only"]

The trial court properly disallowed plaintiff's claim for the value of the fur coats since the value of these articles was speculative and uncertain. The only evidence of value was the advertisement itself to the effect that the coats were "Worth to $100.00," how much less being speculative especially in view of the price for which they were offered for sale. With reference to the offer of the defendant on April 13, 1956, to sell the "1 Black Lapin Stole . . . worth $139.50 . . ." the trial court held that the value of this article was established and granted judgment in favor of the plaintiff for that amount less the $1 quoted purchase price.

[handwritten: court rejected the claim for the first advertisement]

[handwritten: trial court granted Judgement in favor of the plaintiff]

First Contention

"Unilateral Offer"

Defendant Contention

1. The defendant contends that a newspaper advertisement offering items of merchandise for sale at a named price is a "unilateral offer" which may be withdrawn without notice. He relies upon authorities which hold that, where an advertiser publishes in a newspaper that he has a certain quantity or quality of goods which he wants to dispose of at certain prices and on certain terms, such advertisements are not offers which become contracts as soon as any person to whose notice they may come signifies his acceptance by notifying the other that he will take a certain quantity of them. Such advertisements have been construed as an invitation for an offer of sale on the terms stated, which offer, when received, may be accepted or rejected and which therefore does not become a contract of sale until accepted by the seller; and until a contract has been so made, the seller may modify or revoke such prices or terms. . . .

The defendant relies principally on Craft v. Elder & Johnston Co. supra. In that case, the court discussed the legal effect of an advertisement offering for sale, as a one-day special, an electric sewing machine at a named price. The view was expressed that the advertisement was (38 N.E.2d 417, 34 Ohio L.A. 605) "not an offer made to any specific person but was made to the public generally. Thereby it would be properly designated as a unilateral

Issue

not being supported by any consideration could be withdrawn without notice." It is true that such an offer may be withdrawn ...ptance. Since all offers are by their nature unilateral because they ...e necessarily made by one party or on one side in the negotiation of a contract, the distinction made in that decision between a unilateral offer and a unilateral contract is not clear. On the facts before us we are concerned *Issue* with whether the advertisement constituted an offer, and, if so, whether the plaintiff's conduct constituted an acceptance.

There are numerous authorities which hold that a particular advertisement in a newspaper or circular letter relating to a sale of articles may be construed by the court as constituting an offer, acceptance of which would complete a contract. . . .

The "test" for a binding obligation

The test of whether a binding obligation may originate in advertisements addressed to the general public is "whether the facts show that some performance was promised in positive terms in return for something requested." 1 Williston, Contracts (rev. ed.) §27.

The authorities . . . emphasize that, where the offer is clear, definite, and explicit, and leaves nothing open for negotiation, it constitutes an offer, acceptance of which will complete the contract. The most recent *Most Recent case on the merits* case on the subject is Johnson v. Capital City Ford Co., La. App., 85 So. 2d 75, in which the court pointed out that a newspaper advertisement relating to the purchase and sale of automobiles may constitute an offer, acceptance of which will consummate a contract and create an obligation in the offeror to perform according to the terms of the published offer.

Whether in any individual instance a newspaper advertisement is an offer rather than an invitation to make an offer depends on the legal intention of the parties and the surrounding circumstances. Annotation, 157 A.L.R. 744, 751; 77 C.J.S., Sales, §25b; 17 C.J.S., Contracts, §389. We are of the view on the facts before us that the offer by the defendant of the sale of the Lapin fur was clear, definite, and explicit, and left nothing open for negotiation. The plaintiff having successfully managed to be the first one to appear at the seller's place of business to be served, as requested by the advertisement, and having offered the stated purchase price of the article, he was entitled to performance on the part of the defendant. We think the trial court was correct in holding that there was in the conduct of the parties a sufficient mutuality of obligation to constitute a contract of sale.

2. The defendant contends that the offer was modified by a "house rule" to the effect that only women were qualified to receive the bargains advertised. The advertisement contained no such restriction. This objection may be disposed of briefly by stating that, while an advertiser has the right at any time before acceptance to modify his offer, he does not have the right, after acceptance, to impose new or arbitrary conditions not contained in the published offer.

Affirmed.

NOTE ON DECEPTIVE PRACTICES

A *bait and switch* advertisement is a solicitation for the sale of a product that the seller does not really plan to sell. The purpose of the ad is to get the customer into the store (or the seller into the customer's living room) where the advertised product will be disparaged and a more expensive one promoted. The Federal Trade Commission has the power to prevent "unfair and deceptive acts or practices in or affecting interstate commerce." 15 U.S.C. §45(a)(1). The FTC occasionally issues informal guides to help people avoid such acts or practices.

The following bait advertising guide is an example:

Acts or practices considered in determining if an advertisement is a bona fide offer are:

(a) the refusal to show, demonstrate, or sell the product offered in accordance with the terms of the offer,

(b) the disparagement by acts or words of the advertised product or the disparagement of the guarantee, credit terms, availability of service, repairs or parts, or in any other respect, in connection with it,

(c) the failure to have available to all outlets listed in the advertisement a sufficient quantity of the advertised product to meet reasonably anticipated demands, unless the advertisement clearly and adequately discloses the supply is limited and/or the merchandise is available only at designated outlets,

(d) the refusal to take orders for the advertised merchandise to be delivered within a reasonable period of time,

(e) the showing or demonstrating of a product which is defective, unusable, or impractical for the purpose represented or implied in the advertisement,

(f) use of a sale plan or method of compensation for salesmen or penalizing salesmen, designed to prevent or discourage them from selling the advertised product.

Problem 6

You represent Susan Morel. She owns 160 acres of prime land on the border of Rock City, Wyoming. Susan is not sure she wants to sell the land. Sidney Chanterelle wants the property for investment purposes and has called her a number of times to ask the price and terms Susan thinks acceptable. Other interested parties have called at least once. So far she has told everyone that she is not ready to sell. Now Susan wants to develop a more active negotiating stance and to begin "feeling out" potential buyers. She has decided to write those who have inquired to date and also to place an ad in the newspaper. What can she do to avoid making an offer?

Like ads in newspapers, ads on television are usually not offers. One of the best-known examples is Leonard v. Pepsico, Inc., 88 F. Supp. 2d 116, 122 (S.D.N.Y. 1999), aff'd, 210 F.3d 88 (2d Cir. 2000). Pepsi ran a spot that featured its "Pepsi stuff" promotion, in which customers could redeem "Pepsi points" that they earned by drinking the soda for Pepsi-branded merchandise. One commercial featured a teenage boy wearing a Pepsi T-shirt (which the ad said could be purchased for 75 Pepsi points), leather jacket (which the ad said could be purchased for 1,450 Pepsi points), and sunglasses (which the ad said could be purchased for 175 Pepsi points), who then flew to school in a Harrier jet (which the ad said could be purchased for 7 million Pepsi points). John Leonard, who was 20 years old, saw the commercial. He read the fine print in the Pepsi Stuff catalogue and saw that as long as you earned at least 15 Pepsi points from drinking Pepsi, you could buy any remaining points that you needed to purchase an item for ten cents each. He did the math and determined that the $699,999 it would take to buy 6,999,985 Pepsi Points was much less than the $23 million fair market value of a Harrier. So he found investors, raised the funds, and tried to accept the offer he contended Pepsi had made via the advertisement. Unfortunately for John, the court held that the commercial was not an offer, finding that no reasonable person would have taken it seriously and that it lacked language that limited the universe of potential acceptances, such as "first come, first served." (You can watch the commercial at https://www.youtube.com/watch?v = ZdackF2H7Qc.)

─────────

Problem 7

The advertisement in the newspaper said:

Radial snow tires, major brand, four for $99.00 each, now through July 5 at Tire Warehouse, Inc., 44 E. Main Street.

Is this an offer that a buyer could accept by calling up the seller or going down to the store and saying, "I accept!"?

D.   *Written Contract to Follow*

By now you should no longer be wedded to the notion that an enforceable contract requires a piece of paper entitled "Contract." Even most oral agreements are enforceable, a truth not often appreciated by those untrained in the law.

Nonetheless, a writing or group of writings attempting to express the exact terms of the agreement is frequently of critical importance to the parties. It may provide the best evidence of the actual agreement and gives the parties greater certainty as to the terms to which they are bound. Also, a writing is sometimes required by law—a *statute of frauds* issue to be discussed in Chapter 4 at considerable length. Further, a court may find that, even though no writing is generally required under the law for the particular type of agreement at issue, the parties did not intend to be bound until a writing was executed.

────────────────────

CONTINENTAL LABORATORIES v. SCOTT PAPER CO.
United States District Court, Southern District of Iowa, 1990
759 F. Supp. 538, aff'd, 938 F.2d 184 (8th Cir. 1991)

VIETOR, Chief Judge.

[handwritten margin note: Motion for Summary Judgment]

The court has before it defendant Scott Paper Company's (Scott) motion for summary judgment. Plaintiff Continental Laboratories, Inc. (Continental) has resisted and oral arguments have been heard.

BACKGROUND

A.   FACTS

Entered into negotiations for a potential S—supply and distribution agreement

During early 1987, representatives of Continental and Scott[1] entered into negotiations concerning a potential supply and distribution agreement whereby Continental would supply hotel amenity products[2] to Scott and Scott would distribute the products within designated areas of the United States. In the course of negotiations, the parties also discussed the possibility of a partial or total acquisition of Continental by Scott, but this possibility was not pursued to fruition. Beginning in May, 1987 and continuing throughout the negotiations period, Scott representatives prepared at least five drafts of a written Supply and Distribution Agreement, which they submitted to Continental. Each new draft incorporated changes which had resulted from negotiations about the prior draft and the subsequent revised draft then became the basis for further negotiations.

5 drafts w/ incorporated changes in each one

On July 19, 1987, Scott, through Jim Smith, announced internally that Scott and Continental had reached a supply and distribution agreement in principle. The parties' representatives exchanged phone calls and participated in numerous meetings between July 29 and August 26, 1987. Mr. Krislov's affidavit and deposition testimony show that Continental representatives believed that a binding oral contract was reached by the parties during a telephone conference call on either August 25 or 26, 1987, between Krislov, Hirsch, Smith, and Steve Ford, Scott's legal counsel. Continental, through Krislov, further believed that Scott representatives would reduce the terms of the allegedly binding oral contract to written form in a document entitled "Supply and Distribution Agreement," as a memorial of the contract. Mr. Smith's affidavit, on the other hand, demonstrates that Scott through Smith never intended to be bound by an oral agreement, but only by a written contract executed by both parties.

Binding custom doc What Continental Believed

Scott representatives sent Continental representatives a copy of a written "Supply and Distribution Agreement" which bears the stamp "DRAFT" and the stamp "REC'D SEP 02 1987." It is believed that Continental employees placed the "REC'D" stamp on the document when they received the copy on September 2, 1987, but the origin of the "DRAFT" stamp is not known for certain. The September 2nd document contains a space for the "Commencement Date," which the Scott representatives left blank. Although the September 2nd document contains a signature page showing Scott

Scott Sent Continental a written doc that Said "Draft" only

---

1. The individuals who represented Continental were: 1. Clinton A. Krislov, who has a legal degree and is also chairman of the board for Continental, 2. David Bequeaith, Continental's vice-president of operations, and 3. Austin Hirsch, legal counsel for Continental. Mr. Hirsch became involved in the negotiations in July 1987. James Smith, Scott's Director, New Business Development, was the primary representative for Scott.

2. Hotel amenity products consist of the complimentary, personal sized, health and beauty products that are often provided by hotels to their patrons, i.e.: shampoo, bath gel, hand lotion, bar soap, shower caps, shoe polishing cloths, etc.

vice-president P. N. White's signature, no officer of Continental ever signed the document.

After Continental representatives received the September 2nd document, the parties' representatives conducted meetings on September 9th and 10th to further discuss implementation of the venture. Subsequent to these meetings, Mr. Smith, on behalf of Scott, prepared a revised copy of the "Supply and Distribution Agreement," which he presented to Mr. Krislov at O'Hare Airport in Chicago. On September 16, 1987, the parties' representatives met in Madrid, Iowa. During the September 16th meeting, Mr. Smith informed the Continental representatives that Scott was no longer interested in the venture and he terminated the meeting and any further discussions regarding the proposed venture.

B. PROCEEDINGS

Continental filed suit against Scott in the Iowa District Court for Boone County, alleging that the parties had entered into a final and binding, oral contract during the August telephone conference and that Mr. Smith's actions on September 16, 1987 constituted a breach of that contract by Scott. On April 6, 1988, defendant Scott removed the action to this court on the basis of diversity of citizenship jurisdiction. Defendant Scott has moved for summary judgment on the ground that there was no binding contract. Alternatively, Scott argues that even if there was a binding contract, it contained a condition precedent to Scott's performance, which Continental never fulfilled and Scott properly canceled the contract. . . .

Under Iowa law, a binding oral contract may exist even though the parties intend to memorialize their agreement in a fully executed document. Elkader Coop. Co. v. Matt, 204 N.W.2d 873, 875 (Iowa 1973); Severson v. Elberon Elevator, Inc., 250 N.W.2d 417, 421 (Iowa 1977). On the other hand, the parties can make the execution of a written document a condition precedent to the birth of a binding contract. Elkader, 204 N.W.2d at 875; Emmons v. Ingebretson, 279 F. Supp. 558, 566 (N.D. Iowa 1968). If either party intends not to be bound in the absence of a fully executed document, no amount of negotiation or oral agreement as to specific terms will result in the formation of a binding contract. [Citations omitted.]

It is the parties' intent which will determine the time of the contract formation. Emmons, 279 F. Supp. at 566. Plaintiff contends that the parties, through their representatives, intended to and did enter into a binding oral contract on August 25 or 26, 1987, during a telephone conference call. Defendant, however, argues that it never intended to be bound until the parties had fully executed a written contract. The court must determine the intent of the parties objectively from their words and actions viewed within the context of the situation and surrounding circumstances. Fairway Center Corp. v. U.I.P. Corp., 502 F.2d 1135, 1141 (8th Cir. 1974).

In ascertaining whether the parties intended to be bound prior to execution of a written document, the court should consider the following

Multiple factors test

factors: 1. whether the contract is of a class usually found to be in writing; 2. whether it is of a type needing a formal writing for its full expression; 3. whether it has few or many details; 4. whether the amount is large or small; 5. whether the contract is common or unusual; 6. whether all details have been agreed upon or some remain unresolved; and 7. whether the negotiations show a writing was discussed or contemplated. *Emmons*, 279 F. Supp. at 572, cited in *Severson*, 250 N.W.2d at 421. See Restatement (Second) of Contracts §27 comment c (1981). After considering these factors in the context of this case, I conclude that the summary judgment record lacks sufficient evidence from which it could be found that Scott intended to be bound in the absence of an executed written contract.

Concluded in Fvr of Scott

Factors 1 and 2 support Scott's position. The matter was a large and complex commercial undertaking, which is usually put into written form. The parties, who were both represented by legal counsel, negotiated for over seven months and exchanged numerous drafts of a written proposed agreement. Mr. Smith, Scott's representative, stated in his affidavit that he considered the potential relationship with Continental to be a significant matter and that it was Scott's and his own custom and practice to require all significant business agreements to be in writing. The written Agreement does not mention the August 26th phone conference nor does it contain any language which indicates that it is a written memorial of an oral contract. It does, however, contain a clause which states: "[e]xcept as specifically provided herein, this Agreement and the Exhibits hereto reflect the complete agreement of the parties and there are no other agreements or understandings applicable hereto."

Express?

Similarly, factors 3, 4, and 5 support Scott's contention. First, the 12-page contract contains many details and references numerous exhibits. The Agreement addresses such issues as exclusivity of distributorship, products and services supplied, pricing, purchase commitment, payment terms, advance payments, confidentiality, and termination. Additionally, the Agreement references a related agreement between Continental and Redken. Second, the transaction at issue involves a commitment by Scott to purchase a minimum of $2.25 million worth of products from Continental during the term of the contract. Lastly, although supply and distribution agreements are fairly common in the commercial world, this particular contract was unusual for Scott because it involved Scott's entrance into a new market.

Under factor 6, although Mr. Smith announced internally to Scott officials that the parties had reached an agreement in principle in July, 1987, many details were still unresolved. Even after the August telephone conference and the exchange of the September 2nd written agreement, the parties held several meetings in September, 1987, to finalize all of the details regarding manufacture and distribution of the products. On September 14, Mr. Smith even presented Mr. Krislov with another revised draft of the agreement, which Mr. Krislov accepted grudgingly. This evidence suggests that Scott, through Smith, did not consider that there was a final and binding oral agreement.

Finally, an analysis of the summary judgment record under factor 7 also supports Scott's position that it intended to be bound only by a written and executed contract. During the negotiations, the parties had exchanged drafts of proposed written agreements. Also, Scott representatives had left the space for the Commencement Date of the September 2nd Agreement blank, suggesting that they did not consider August 26th to be that date. In the Agreement itself, the parties required that modifications, amendments, terminations territorial expansions, etc., would all require a writing. See Exhibit *~plaint, pgs. 2, 4, 8, 9, 10, 11, and 12. It would be strange for ~ written modifications without first contemplating a written co.

Reasoning

Conclusion

Based upon the preceding analysis of the relevant factors, ~ ~~~ that Continental has failed to overcome Scott's summary judgment motion. Continental has failed to generate a genuine issue of material fact regarding whether Scott intended to be bound by an oral agreement or only by a written and executed agreement. The summary judgment record shows that, based upon all of the circumstances, Scott communicated its intent to be bound only by a written contract, signed by both parties. No such contract ever existed. Therefore, defendant's motion for summary judgment is granted.

decision

NOTES AND QUESTIONS

1. Restatement (Second) of Contracts §27, comment c, cite. ~ court, lists some factors "which may be helpful" in determining wh ~ contract is concluded even though an anticipated writing is never exe~ ~ted:

> [T]he extent to which express agreement has been reached on all the terms to be included, whether the contract is of a type usually put in writing, whether it needs a formal writing for its full expression, whether it has few or many details, whether it is a common or unusual contract, whether a standard form of contract is widely used in similar transactions, and whether either party takes any action in preparation for performance during the negotiation.

2. Why would this last criterion be important, and was it relevant in this case?

3. What advice do you have for a party who definitely does not want to have an enforceable contract until the agreement is reduced to a final writing? For a party who wants to ensure that there is an enforceable contract whether or not the agreement is reduced to a formal writing?

Problem 8

Arthur Greenbaum agreed to sell his apartment building to David Vargo. They hired Lorri Latek, a lawyer, to put their contract into acceptable legal form, and after she had drawn it up, they met in her office to sign the written agreement. Each man read the copy of the contract she had prepared, and both agreed that the writing correctly reflected their understanding. Each signed the copy in front of the other. They were about to exchange copies and sign the one the other had signed when Vargo casually mentioned that he was going to pay by personal check. This bothered Greenbaum, who insisted on a cashier's check. Vargo proposed that they meet in Latek's office the following day, and he would bring a cashier's check. They left, each man taking with him the copy of the contract that he had signed. That night Vargo changed his mind and decided not to purchase the building. When Greenbaum found this out, he sued. Was there a contract here? See Schwartz v. Greenberg, 304 N.Y. 250, 107 N.E.2d 65 (1952).

III.   ACCEPTANCE

A.   *Effect of Acceptance*

Problem 9

Archie Goodwin signed a purchase order for a new car to be sold by Wolf Motors. The purchase order stated that $800 would be deducted from the price as a trade-in allowance on his old car. When he delivered the old car, Rex Stout, Wolf's sales manager, told him that a mistake had been made and that the car was worth only $600. Stout stated that Wolf Motors would not go through with the deal unless Goodwin agreed to this reduction. Goodwin sued. How should this come out? See Trowbridge v. Jefferson Auto Co., 92 Conn. 569, 103 A. 843 (1918).

The moment of acceptance has an important legal consequence: it fixes the terms of the contract to those agreed upon in the offer. While the parties thereafter are free to modify the contract by mutual agreement, unless the original contract reserves the power to do so one party may not unilaterally alter the contract by changing its terms. Sellers, banks, and insurance companies often forget this and send out notices of additional matters (typically limitations of liability) after the acceptance has taken place. Such "Oh, by the way, we forgot to mention" sorts of changes are not effective unless agreed to by the recipient or unless they are mere clarifications of implied understandings. See, e.g., Tropicana Pools, Inc. v. Boysen, 296 So. 2d 104 (Fla. Dist. Ct. App. 1974) ("Lifetime Guarantee" of swimming pool sent after construction had begun held ineffective to change terms of the existing warranties); Comeaux v. Brown & Williamson Tobacco Co., 915 F.2d 1264, 1271 (9th Cir. 1990) ("A party may not protect itself from liability under a contract by asserting that a heretofore hidden term is somehow part of the agreement"); Dunkelman v. Cincinnati Bengals, Inc., 158 Ohio App. 3d 604, 821 N.E.2d 198 (2004) (arbitration agreement comes too late as an addition in an invoice to sports ticket sale).

B. *Manifesting Assent to an Offer*

RESTATEMENT (SECOND) OF CONTRACTS

§50. ACCEPTANCE OF OFFER DEFINED; ACCEPTANCE BY PERFORMANCE; ACCEPTANCE BY PROMISE

(1) Acceptance of an offer is a manifestation of assent to the terms thereof made by the offeree in a manner invited or required by the offer.

(2) Acceptance by performance requires that at least part of what the offer requests be performed or tendered and includes acceptance by a performance which operates as a return promise.

(3) Acceptance by a promise requires that the offeree complete every act essential to the making of the promise.

The next case addresses the issue of the moment of acceptance (and its effect on attempts to change the "deal") in the sale of computer software.

PROCD, INC. v. ZEIDENBERG
United States Court of Appeals, Seventh Circuit, 1996
86 F.3d 1447

EASTERBROOK, Circuit Judge.

Must buyers of computer software obey the terms of shrinkwrap licenses? The district court held not, for two reasons: first, they are not contracts because the licenses are inside the box rather than printed on the outside; second, federal law forbids enforcement even if the licenses are contracts. 908 F. Supp. 640 (W.D. Wis. 1996). The parties and numerous amici curiae have briefed many other issues, but these are the only two that matter — and we disagree with the district judge's conclusion on each. Shrinkwrap licenses are enforceable unless their terms are objectionable

*Are
Exceptions
to
forcible*

on grounds applicable to contracts in general (for example, if they violate a rule of positive law, or if they are unconscionable). Because no one argues that the terms of the license at issue here are troublesome, we remand with instructions to enter judgment for the plaintiff.

I

*What ProCD
does*

ProCD, the plaintiff, has compiled information from more than 3,000 telephone directories into a computer database. We may assume that this database cannot be copyrighted, although it is more complex, contains more information (nine-digit zip codes and census industrial codes), is organized differently, and therefore is more original than the single alphabetical directory at issue in Feist Publications, Inc. v. Rural Telephone Service Co., 499 U.S. 340 (1991). [Citations omitted.] ProCD sells a version of the database, called SelectPhone^{TM}, on CD-ROM discs. (CD-ROM means "compact disc—read only memory." The "shrinkwrap license" gets its name from the fact that retail software packages are covered in plastic or cellophane "shrinkwrap," and some vendors, though not ProCD, have written licenses that become effective as soon as the customer tears the wrapping from the package. Vendors prefer "end user license," but we use the more common term.) A proprietary method of compressing the data serves as effective encryption too. Customers decrypt and use the data with the aid of an application program that ProCD has written. This program, which is copyrighted, searches the database in response to users' criteria (such as "find all people named Tatum in Tennessee, plus all firms with 'Door Systems' in the corporate name"). The resulting lists (or, as ProCD prefers, "listings") can be read and manipulated by other software, such as word processing programs.

*license otherwise
as soon as you
open it*

The database in SelectPhone^{TM} cost more than $10 million to compile and is expensive to keep current. It is much more valuable to some users than to others. The combination of names, addresses, and zip codes enables manufacturers to compile lists of potential customers. Manufacturers and retailers pay high prices to specialized information intermediaries for such mailing lists; ProCD offers a potentially cheaper alternative. People with nothing to sell could use the database as a substitute for calling long distance information, or as a way to look up old friends who have moved to unknown towns, or just as an electronic substitute for the local phone book. ProCD decided to engage in price discrimination, selling its database to the general public for personal use at a low price (approximately $150 for the set of five discs) while selling information to the trade for a higher price. It has adopted some intermediate strategies too: access to the SelectPhone^{TM} database is available via the America Online service for the price America Online charges to its clients (approximately $3 per hour), but this service has been tailored to be useful only to the general public.

If ProCD had to recover all of its costs and make a profit by charging a single price — that is, if it could not charge more to commercial users than to the general public — it would have to raise the price substantially over $150. The ensuing reduction in sales would harm consumers who value the information at, say, $200. They get consumer surplus of $50 under the current arrangement but would cease to buy if the price rose substantially. If because of high elasticity of demand in the consumer segment of the market the only way to make a profit turned out to be a price attractive to commercial users alone, then all consumers would lose out — and so would the commercial clients, who would have to pay more for the listings because ProCD could not obtain any contribution toward costs from the consumer market.

To make price discrimination work, however, the seller must be able to control arbitrage. An air carrier sells tickets for less to vacationers than to business travelers, using advance purchase and Saturday-night-stay requirements to distinguish the categories. A producer of movies segments the market by time, releasing first to theaters, then to pay-per-view services, next to the videotape and laserdisc market, and finally to cable and commercial TV. Vendors of computer software have a harder task. Anyone can walk into a retail store and buy a box. Customers do not wear tags saying "commercial user" or "consumer user." Anyway, even a commercial-user-detector at the door would not work, because a consumer could buy the software and resell to a commercial user. That arbitrage would break down the price discrimination and drive up the minimum price at which ProCD would sell to anyone.

Instead of tinkering with the product and letting users sort themselves — for example, furnishing current data at a high price that would be attractive only to commercial customers, and two-year-old data at a low price — ProCD turned to the institution of contract. Every box containing its consumer product declares that the software comes with restrictions stated in an enclosed license. This license, which is encoded on the CD-ROM disks as well as printed in the manual, and which appears on a user's screen every time the software runs, limits use of the application program and listings to non-commercial purposes.

Matthew Zeidenberg bought a consumer package of SelectPhone™ in 1994 from a retail outlet in Madison, Wisconsin, but decided to ignore the license. He formed Silken Mountain Web Services, Inc., to resell the information in the SelectPhone™ database. The corporation makes the database available on the Internet to anyone willing to pay its price — which, needless to say, is less than ProCD charges its commercial customers. Zeidenberg has purchased two additional SelectPhone™ packages, each with an updated version of the database, and made the latest information available over the World Wide Web, for a price, through his corporation. ProCD filed this suit seeking an injunction against further dissemination that exceeds the rights specified in the licenses (identical in each of the three packages Zeidenberg purchased). The district court held the licenses ineffectual because their terms do not appear on the outside of the packages. The court added that the second and third licenses stand no different from the first, even though they are identical, because they *might* have been different, and a purchaser does not agree to—and cannot be bound by—terms that were secret at the time of purchase. 908 F. Supp. at 654.

II

Following the district court, we treat the licenses as ordinary contracts accompanying the sale of products, and therefore as governed by the common law of contracts and the Uniform Commercial Code. Whether there are legal differences between "contracts" and "licenses" (which may matter under the copyright doctrine of first sale) is a subject for another day. See Microsoft Corp. v. Harmony Computers & Electronics, Inc., 846 F. Supp. 208 (E.D.N.Y. 1994). Zeidenberg does not argue that Silken Mountain Web Services is free of any restrictions that apply to Zeidenberg himself, because any effort to treat the two parties as distinct would put Silken Mountain behind the eight ball on ProCD's argument that copying the application program onto its hard disk violates the copyright laws. Zeidenberg does argue, and the district court held, that placing the package of software on the shelf is an "offer," which the customer "accepts" by paying the asking price and leaving the store with the goods. Peeters v. State, 154 Wis. 111, 142 N.W. 181 (1913). In Wisconsin, as elsewhere, a contract includes only the terms on which the parties have agreed. One cannot agree to hidden terms, the judge concluded. So far, so good—but one of the terms to which Zeidenberg agreed by purchasing the software is that the transaction was subject to a license. Zeidenberg's position therefore must be that the printed terms on the outside of a box are the parties' contract—except for printed terms that refer to or incorporate other terms. But why would Wisconsin fetter the parties' choice in this way? Vendors can put the entire terms of a contract on the outside of a box only by using microscopic type, removing other information that buyers might find more useful (such as what the software does, and on which computers it works), or both. The "Read Me" file included with most software, describing system requirements and potential incompatibilities, may be equivalent to ten pages of type; warranties and license restrictions take still more space. Notice on the outside, terms on the inside, and a right to return the software for a refund if the terms are unacceptable (a right that the license expressly extends), may be a means of doing business valuable to buyers and sellers alike. See E. Allan Farnsworth, 1 Farnsworth on Contracts §4.26 (1990); Restatement (2d) of Contracts §211 comment a (1981) ("Standardization of agreements serves many of the same functions as standardization of goods and services; both are essential to a system of mass production and distribution. Scarce and costly time and skill can be devoted to a class of transactions rather than the details of individual transactions."). Doubtless a state could forbid the use of standard contracts in the software business, but we do not think that Wisconsin has done so.

Transactions in which the exchange of money precedes the communication of detailed terms are common. Consider the purchase of insurance. The buyer goes to an agent, who explains the essentials (amount of coverage, number of years) and remits the premium to the home office, which sends back a policy. On the district judge's understanding, the terms of the policy are irrelevant because the insured paid before receiving them. Yet the device of payment, often with a "binder" (so that the insurance takes effect immediately even though the home office reserves the right to withdraw coverage later), in advance of the policy, serves buyers' interests by accelerating effectiveness and reducing transactions costs. Or consider the purchase of an airline ticket. The traveler calls the carrier or an agent, is quoted a price, reserves a seat, pays, and gets a ticket, in that order. The ticket contains elaborate terms, which the traveler can reject by canceling the reservation. To use the ticket is to accept the terms, even terms that in retrospect are disadvantageous. See Carnival Cruise Lines, Inc. v. Shute, 499 U.S. 585 (1991). [Further citation omitted.] Just so with a ticket to a concert. The back of the ticket states that the patron promises not to record the concert; to attend is to agree. A theater that detects a violation will confiscate the tape and escort the violator to the exit. One *could* arrange things so that every concertgoer signs this promise before forking over the money, but that cumbersome way of doing things not only would lengthen queues and raise prices but also would scotch the sale of tickets by phone or electronic data service.

Consumer goods work the same way. Someone who wants to buy a radio set visits a store, pays, and walks out with a box. Inside the box is a leaflet containing some terms, the most important of which usually is the warranty, read for the first time in the comfort of home. By Zeidenberg's lights, the warranty in the box is irrelevant; every consumer gets the standard warranty implied by the UCC in the event the contract is silent; yet so far as we are aware no state disregards warranties furnished with consumer products. Drugs come with a list of ingredients on the outside and an elaborate package insert on the inside. The package insert describes drug interactions, contraindications, and other vital information — but, if Zeidenberg is right, the purchaser need not read the package insert, because it is not part of the contract.

Next consider the software industry itself. Only a minority of sales take place over the counter, where there are boxes to peruse. A customer may place an order by phone in response to a line item in a catalog or a review in a magazine. Much software is ordered over the Internet by purchasers who have never seen a box. Increasingly software arrives by wire. There is no box; there is only a stream of electrons, a collection of information that includes data, an application program, instructions, many limitations ("MegaPixel 3.14159 cannot be used with BytePusher 2.718"), and the terms of sale. The user purchases a serial number, which activates the software's features. On Zeidenberg's arguments, these unboxed sales are unfettered by terms — so the seller has made a broad warranty and must pay consequential damages for any shortfalls in performance, two "promises" that if taken seriously would drive prices through the ceiling or return transactions to the horse-and-buggy age.

According to the district court, the UCC does not countenance the sequence of money now, terms later. (Wisconsin's version of the UCC does not differ from the Official Version in any material respect, so we use the regular numbering system. Wis. Stat. §402.201 corresponds to UCC §2-201, and other citations are easy to derive.) One of the court's reasons—that by proposing as part of the draft Article 2B a new UCC §2-2203 that would explicitly validate standard-form user licenses, the American Law Institute and the National Conference of Commissioners on Uniform Laws have conceded the invalidity of shrinkwrap licenses under current law, see 908 F. Supp. at 655-66—depends on a faulty inference. To propose a change in a law's text is not necessarily to propose a change in the law's *effect*. New words may be designed to fortify the current rule with a more precise text that curtails uncertainty. To judge by the flux of law review articles discussing shrinkwrap licenses, uncertainty is much in need of reduction—although businesses seem to feel less uncertainty than do scholars, for only three cases (other than ours) touch on the subject, and none directly addresses it. See Step-Saver Data Systems, Inc. v. Wyse Technology, 939 F.2d 91 (3d Cir. 1991); Vault Corp. v. Quaid Software Ltd., 847 F.2d 255, 268-70 (5th Cir. 1988); Arizona Retail Systems, Inc. v. Software Link, Inc., 831 F. Supp. 759 (D. Ariz. 1993). As their titles suggest, these are not consumer transactions. *Step-Saver* is a battle-of-the-forms case, in which the parties exchange incompatible forms and a court must decide which prevails. See Northrop Corp. v. Litronic Industries, 29 F.3d 1173 (7th Cir. 1994) (Illinois law); Douglas G. Baird & Robert Weisberg, Rules, Standards, and the Battle of the Forms: A Reassessment of §2-207, 68 Va. L. Rev. 1217, 1227-31 (1982). Our case has only one form; UCC §2-207 is irrelevant. *Vault* holds that Louisiana's special shrinkwrap-license statute is preempted by federal law, a question to which we return. And *Arizona Retail Systems* did not reach the question, because the court found that the buyer knew the terms of the license before purchasing the software.

What then does the current version of the UCC have to say? We think that the place to start is §2-204(1): "A contract for sale of goods may be made in any manner sufficient to show agreement, including conduct by both parties which recognizes the existence of such a contract." A vendor, as master of the offer, may invite acceptance by conduct, and may propose limitations on the kind of conduct that constitutes acceptance. A buyer may accept by performing the acts the vendor proposes to treat as acceptance. And that is what happened. ProCD proposed a contract that a buyer would accept by *using* the software after having an opportunity to read the license at leisure. This Zeidenberg did. He had no choice, because the software splashed the license on the screen and would not let him proceed without indicating acceptance. So although the district judge was right to say that a contract can be, and often is, formed simply by paying the price and walking out of the store, the UCC permits contracts to be formed in other ways. ProCD proposed such a different way, and without protest Zeidenberg agreed. Ours is not a case in which a consumer opens a package to find an insert saying "you owe us an extra $10,000" and the seller files suit to collect. Any buyer finding such a demand can prevent formation of the contract by returning the package, as can any consumer who concludes that the terms of the license make the software worth less than the purchase price. Nothing in the UCC requires a seller to maximize the buyer's net gains. . . .

Some portions of the UCC impose additional requirements on the way parties agree on terms. A disclaimer of the implied warranty of merchantability must be "conspicuous." UCC §2-316(2), incorporating UCC §1-201(10). Promises to make firm offers, or to negate oral modifications, must be "separately signed." UCC §§2-205, 2-209(2). These special provisos reinforce the impression that, so far as the UCC is concerned, other terms may be as inconspicuous as the forum-selection clause on the back of the cruise ship ticket in *Carnival Lines.* Zeidenberg has not located any Wisconsin case—for that matter, any case in any state—holding that under the UCC the ordinary terms found in shrinkwrap licenses require any special prominence, or otherwise are to be undercut rather than enforced. In the end, the terms of the license are conceptually identical to the contents of the package. Just as no court would dream of saying that SelectPhone™ must contain 3,100 phone books rather than 3,000, or must have data no more than 30 days old, or must sell for $100 rather than $150—although any of these changes would be welcomed by the customer, if all other things were held constant—so, we believe, Wisconsin would not let the buyer pick and choose among terms. Terms of use are no less a part of "the product" than are the size of the database and the speed with which the software compiles listings. Competition among vendors, not judicial revision of a package's contents, is how consumers are protected in a market economy. Digital Equipment Corp. v. Uniq Digital Technologies, Inc., 73 F.3d 756 (7th Cir. 1996). ProCD has rivals, which may elect to compete by offering superior software, monthly updates, improved terms of use, lower price, or a better compromise among these elements. As we stressed above, adjusting terms in buyers' favor might help Matthew Zeidenberg today (he already has the software) but would lead to a response, such as a higher price, that might make consumers as a whole worse off.

[The court then held that federal copyright law did not forbid ProCD's restriction on the use of the software.]

Reversed and remanded.

NOTES AND QUESTIONS

1. Does the result in this case seem right to you? Fair? If the buyer has purchased the product through a retailer, is there sufficient legal connection ("privity") with the manufacturer to allow the buyer to avoid the sale? Common sense also tells us that buyers are loathe to return goods once they

have taken possession of them. Is this retention necessarily an agreement to all the manufacturer's new terms?

2. There has been a furious debate about *ProCD* and similar cases. See Hillman, Rolling Contracts, 71 Fordham L. Rev. 743 (2002); Knapp, Opting Out or Copping Out?, 40 Loy. L.A. L. Rev. 95 (2006); Posner, ProCD v. Zeidenberg and Cognitive Overload in Contractual Bargaining, 77 U. Chi. L. Rev. 1181 (2010); and Murray, Jr., The Dubious Status of Rolling Contract Formation Theory, 50 Duq. L. Rev. 35 (2012). We will return to the issue when we talk about the battle of the forms later in the chapter.

Problem 10

This photo was taken of a sign posted at the entrance to a fast food restaurant. If you were a judge, would you rule that patrons entering the restaurant have agreed to binding arbitration? Would it matter whether or not the patron saw the sign or understood what arbitration means?

BEARD IMPLEMENT CO. v. KRUSA
Appellate Court of Illinois, 1991
208 Ill. App. 3d 953, 567 N.E.2d 345

[handwritten: Plaintiff] [handwritten: Defendant]

Justice STEIGMANN delivered the opinion of the court:

This action involves an alleged breach of contract between plaintiff seller, Beard Implement Company, Inc., a farm implement dealership, and defendant buyer, Carl Krusa, a farmer, for the purchase of a 1985 Deutz-Allis N-5 combine. The dispositive issue on appeal is whether the trial court in a bench trial erred in finding a contract existed between the parties. Specifically, defendant contends that plaintiff never accepted defendant's offer to purchase the combine. We agree and reverse.

[margin: Was positive issue on Appeal. Defendant contends that Plaintiff never accepted his offer to purchase the combine]

At trial, defendant testified that between December 20 and December 23, 1985, he had several conversations with plaintiff's representatives concerning the purchase of a new combine. Defendant owned a 1980 Deutz-Allis N-5 combine at that time. In fall 1985, both spindles on his combine had broken and defendant spoke with plaintiff's representatives about repairing them.

On December 23, 1985, defendant met with plaintiff's representatives at plaintiff's office in Arenzville, Illinois. Defendant testified that one of plaintiff's representatives, either Jim Beard or Gerry Beard, filled out a purchase order for a new combine for the price of $52,800 cash and the trade-in of the combine defendant then owned. . . . Defendant signed the Allis-Chalmers purchase order, which was dated December 23, 1985. None of plaintiff's representatives signed that order on December 23, 1985, or at any time thereafter. The bottom left corner of this order reads as follows:

[margin: Filled out purchase order. Defendant signed but Plaintiff never did]

> DEALER'S SALESMAN
> This order subject to acceptance by dealer.
> Accepted by: _____
> DEALER

At the same time defendant signed the purchase order, he also signed a counter check drawn on a local bank in the amount of $5,200. Defendant testified that because he did not have his checkbook, plaintiff provided him with the counter check. The check was undated and intended to represent a down payment on the combine. Defendant testified that the check was not dated because he was to call plaintiff later and let plaintiff know if he wanted to proceed with the transaction. At that time, plaintiff would put a date on the check.

[margin: Defendant was to call Plaintiff later and confirm]

Defendant testified that he had misgivings over the Christmas weekend and, after discussing the situation with his wife, telephoned plaintiff's manager, Duane Hess, on December 26, 1985, and told Hess that he did not wish to proceed with the transaction. Defendant explained to Hess that

[margin: Backed out of transaction]

[margin bottom: Hess is Plaintiff's Manager]

defendant and his wife had determined that "the price was too high" and they "did not want to go further into debt to finance the transaction." Defendant testified that Hess told him that if defendant thought the combine was too expensive, Hess would let defendant out of the deal. Hess did not indicate whether he had signed the order.

Earlier on December 26, 1985, defendant had met with a representative of Cox Implement Company. Defendant identified a copy of the order form that one of Cox's salesman had filled out. This order was dated December 26, 1985, but was signed on December 27. Defendant testified that he told Cox's salesman that his price was too high and that defendant could not go through with either that bid or plaintiff's bid. However, after Cox's quoted price was reduced and the figures on the purchase order were scratched out, defendant signed the purchase order with Cox on December 27, 1985. Defendant stated the agreement with Cox was for the same model combine he was negotiating for with plaintiff but at a lower price. He wanted to consummate the transaction by December 31, 1985, in order to take advantage of the investment tax credit.

Defendant wrote a letter to plaintiff that was dated December 26, 1985, but sent on December 27, 1985. That letter read as follows:

Dec. 26, '85

Dear Sirs:

As I told you by phone on Dec. 26, '85, I do not wish to purchase the 1985 N-5 combine we talked about so please send me the uncashed counter check on the Bank of Bluffs for the amount of $5,200. Since my "Purchase Order Sheet" had not yet been signed by the dealer rep, the check wasn't cashed before notification, & the combine wasn't picked up, the [inconvenience] should have been slight.

Feel free to consult my attorney, John D. Coonrod, for details. Again, excuse these changes of events.

Sincerely,

Carl W. Krusa
(FOR "K" FARMS)

Defendant testified that Jim Beard visited defendant at his farm around lunchtime on December 27, 1985. During this visit, Jim told defendant, "There's no problem, Carl, just please send a check to Tony Thomas for his time explaining the differences between models and options." Defendant recalled that their conversation was friendly and that Jim told him something to the effect that, "Carl, we maybe lost a little bit of commission on this, but don't worry about it. I'll make it up on the next sales." Defendant signed the contract with Cox later that afternoon.

Defendant testified that when he spoke with Hess on the evening of December 26, Hess did not indicate that he had signed the order that had been signed earlier by defendant. Defendant testified that in his letter to plaintiff, he enclosed a check for $100 made payable to Thomas for Thomas' time. Defendant believed that once this sum was paid, he was released from any obligation to plaintiff seller.

Jim Beard testified that in fall 1985, he approached defendant several times about purchasing a new combine. Jim testified that he again spoke with defendant about purchasing a new combine at plaintiff's Arenzville office at 3:30 or 4 P.M. on December 23, 1985. Gerry Beard was also present. Jim stated that he did not have the authority to sell the combine at a given price; only Gerry and Hess had that authority. The price quoted by Gerry to defendant was $52,800 and the trade-in of defendant's existing combine. Jim identified the purchase order bearing defendant's signature. Jim filled in all the other information on that order.

Jim testified that defendant did not make any statements that he was going to consider the purchase further after signing the purchase order. Jim also stated that defendant did not make any statements to the effect that the purchase order was not to be considered a completed contract.

Jim identified the counter check payable to plaintiff for $5,200. He stated that he filled out the check and defendant signed it, but that he forgot to fill in the date on the check. Jim did not recall any statement made by defendant that the check should be held. Jim recalled that the purchase order and check were signed at approximately 5:30 P.M. He stated that defendant was not threatened or told that he could not leave the office until he signed the order. Jim stated that he would not have signed the order if defendant had said anything about reserving the right to call back later and cancel the deal.

Jim next spoke with defendant on December 27, 1985. Hess told Jim that defendant did not want to buy the combine and asked Jim to visit defendant. Jim met with defendant that same day and asked defendant why he could not buy the combine. Defendant told him that he could not afford it. Jim stated that defendant did not mention that he had purchased a combine from someone else.

On cross-examination, Jim admitted that he did not sign the purchase order which defendant had signed. He testified that Gerry and Hess are authorized to accept offers on behalf of plaintiff, but that neither one signed the order.

Gerry Beard testified that defendant came to plaintiff's office in the afternoon of December 23. Gerry stated that he attempted to persuade defendant to purchase a new combine. Gerry testified that he offered to sell the new combine to defendant for $52,800 and that defendant replied, "I'll take the deal." Defendant then signed the order and counter check and left plaintiff's offices.

Gerry stated that he is authorized to accept contracts on behalf of plaintiff. He testified that he accepted the contract with defendant. Gerry stated that defendant did not indicate, after signing the counter check and purchase order, that the transaction was not a completed deal.

On appeal, defendant argues that the trial court erred in finding that a contract existed between him and plaintiff for the purchase of a combine. Defendant argues plaintiff never accepted defendant's offer to purchase the combine because the purchase order defendant signed required a signature by a "dealer" on behalf of plaintiff for acceptance and none of plaintiff's representatives ever signed that order. Accordingly, defendant's subsequent refusal to "go through with the deal" constituted a valid revocation of his offer.

Plaintiff argues that a contract existed between the parties even before their agreement was reduced to writing. Essentially, plaintiff contends that after the verbal agreement was reached, the terms of that agreement were memorialized on the purchase order, which was then signed by defendant. Further, plaintiff argues that this verbal agreement was evidenced by a counter check, which was also signed by defendant and which represented a down payment on the combine. Plaintiff asserts that it accepted both the purchase order and the down payment by placing those documents in its office.

In deciding whether the offer in the present case has been accepted, this court must first identify both the offeror and the offer. A treatise on contract law provides some guidance on this issue: "A problem arises when A, through a salesman, has frequently solicited orders from B, the contract to arise when approved by A at A's home office. As we have seen in this situation[,] B is the offeror and A the offeree." J. Calamari & J. Perillo, Contracts §2-18, at 85 (3d ed. 1987). . . .

In the instant case, the purchase order form signed by defendant constitutes an offer made by defendant to plaintiff. Thus, this court needs to determine whether defendant's offer was accepted by plaintiff.

Section 2-206 of the Uniform Commercial Code — Sales (Code) states the following:

> (1) Unless otherwise unambiguously indicated by the language or circumstances
>> (a) an offer to make a contract shall be construed as inviting acceptance in any manner and by any medium reasonable in the circumstances;
>> (b) an order or other offer to buy goods for prompt or current shipment shall be construed as inviting acceptance either by a prompt promise to ship or by the prompt or current shipment of conforming or nonconforming goods, but such a shipment of non-conforming goods does not constitute an acceptance if the seller seasonably notifies the buyer that the shipment is offered only as an accommodation to the buyer.

(2) Where the beginning of a requested performance is a reasonable mode of acceptance an offeror who is not notified of acceptance within a reasonable time may treat the offer as having lapsed before acceptance.

(Ill. Rev. Stat. 1989, ch. 26, par. 2-206.) For the purposes of the present case, the key word in this statute is the term "unambiguously." If defendant's offer contained on the purchase order is unambiguous in inviting acceptance only by the signature of plaintiff's "dealer," no contract exists until the purchase order is signed accordingly. If, however, defendant's offer is ambiguous in inviting plaintiff's acceptance, a contract between plaintiff and defendant could be found to exist.

On appeal, defendant has cited several cases supporting the argument that the purchase order he signed unambiguously invites acceptance only by signature of plaintiff's "dealer." One such case is Brophy v. City of Joliet (1957), 14 Ill. App. 2d 443, 144 N.E.2d 816, which involved the sale of revenue bonds. In that case, the court stated that where an offer requires an acceptance to be made in writing, no other form of acceptance can be made. The offer in *Brophy* read as follows:

> The signed acceptance of this proposal shall constitute a contract between the undersigned and the city. . . .

> Accepted for and on behalf of . . . , which is hereby acknowledged by the duly, qualified officials.

> [ ] _____
>   Mayor
> [ ] _____
>   City Clerk

Brophy, 14 Ill. App. 2d at 448, 144 N.E.2d at 819.

In La Salle National Bank v. Vega (1988), 167 Ill. App. 3d 154, 117 Ill. Dec. 778, 520 N.E.2d 1129, the court dealt with a real estate sales document which was signed by the seller as offeror and clearly stated that a contract would be in full force upon execution by the purchasing trust. The court held that the document did not constitute a valid contract in the absence of acceptance by the written execution of the purchasing trust. The court noted that an offeror has complete control over his offer and its terms of acceptance, and no other mode may be used where a written acceptance is required. *La Salle National Bank*, 167 Ill. App. 3d at 161-62, 117 Ill. Dec. at 782, 520 N.E.2d at 1133.

In Zinni v. Royal Lincoln-Mercury, Inc. (1980), 84 Ill. App. 3d 1093, 40 Ill. Dec. 511, 406 N.E.2d 212, the court wrote the following:

Although the modes of a valid acceptance may be varied, the requirement of an acceptance by the offeror still exists. . . . Where an order form, containing the buyer's offer, requires the acceptance of the seller, no contract will exist until the seller has manifested acceptance of the offer. The record before us contains no manifestation of the defendant's acceptance of the plaintiff's offer. Although the order form contains a space for the defendant's signature, defendant did not sign it. While we believe defendant's acceptance may be manifested in ways other than its signature, plaintiff's complaint fails to allege an alternative manifestation of defendant's acceptance. Absent an acceptance by the defendant, no contract existed between the parties.

Zinni, 84 Ill. App. 3d at 1094-95, 40 Ill. Dec. at 513, 406 N.E.2d at 214. . . .

Plaintiff counters defendant's argument by contending that plaintiff was the one to offer the combine to defendant and defendant accepted plaintiff's offer by signing a counter check and giving that check to plaintiff as a down payment on the combine. We are unpersuaded.

We construe section 2-206 of the Code as giving approval to an ancient and cardinal rule of the law of contracts: the offeror is the master of his offer. An offeror may prescribe as many conditions or terms of the method of acceptance as he may wish, including, but not limited to, the time, place, and manner. (Kroeze v. Chloride Group Ltd. (5th Cir. 1978), 572 F.2d 1099, 1105.) We also note that contracts are generally construed against the party who drafted the document (see Restatement (Second) of Contracts §206, at 105 (1981)) and that plaintiff drafted the purchase order in the present case, and then gave it to defendant to use for his offer to purchase the combine.

Based on the foregoing, we conclude that the purchase order in this case "unambiguously" required the signature by plaintiff's "dealer" in order to be a proper acceptance of defendant's offer. Because plaintiff's "dealer" never signed the purchase order, no contract ever existed.

For the reasons stated, the judgment in favor of plaintiff is reversed. Reversed.

NOTES AND QUESTIONS

1. Exactly who was the offeror and who the offeree in this case?
2. Consider the following statute:

Uniform Commercial Code §2-204. Formation in General

(1) A contract for sale of goods may be made in any manner sufficient to show agreement, including conduct by both parties which recognizes the existence of such a contract.

(2) An agreement sufficient to constitute a contract for sale may be found even though the moment of its making is undetermined.

(3) Even though one or more terms are left open a contract for sale does not fail for indefiniteness if the parties have intended to make a contract and there is a reasonably certain basis for giving an appropriate remedy.

Does subsection (1) dictate a different result in *Beard?*

3. Is it a good idea to postpone effectiveness until the home office or some other official approves? Why would the implement dealer have done this?

4. The Federal Trade Commission has promulgated a rule that generally allows individuals who make purchases of $25 or more for a personal, family, or household purpose a three-day cooling off period (that is, three days to cancel the transaction) when the buyer's "agreement or offer to purchase" is made at a place other than the regular place of business of the seller. 16 C.F.R. §429.1. The purpose of the rule is to give consumers who buy from door-to-door sellers a time within which to reconsider the transaction. The "agreement or offer to purchase" language prevents a door-to-door seller from requiring home office approval and then arguing that the sale is at the regular place of the seller's business.

FUJIMOTO v. RIO GRANDE PICKLE CO.
United States Court of Appeals, Fifth Circuit, 1969
414 F.2d 648

GOLDBERG, Circuit Judge. This appeal involves claims by George Fujimoto and Jose Bravo against the Rio Grande Pickle Company upon written contracts of employment. The questions before us are of contract formation and construction.

Rio Grande Pickle Company, a Colorado corporation engaged in the business of raising and selling cucumbers for the pickling industry, hired Fujimoto in the Spring of 1965 and Bravo in the following Fall. Both of these employees were given important jobs. Fujimoto was employed as the supervisor of the planting and growing operations, while Bravo functioned as the labor recruiter.

In order to encourage them to work with zeal and not to leave the company's employ, Rio Grande offered contracts with profit sharing bonus provisions to both Fujimoto and Bravo. Prior to the offer of the written contracts, the company had responded to the offerees' demands for more compensation by orally agreeing to pay them a salary plus a bonus of ten percent of the company's annual profits. Bravo told the president of Rio Grande that he wanted the agreement in writing, and the president replied "I will prepare one and send you a contract in writing." The contractual documents sent to Fujimoto and Bravo did not specify how the offers could be accepted or how the acceptances should be communicated to the company. Under these circumstances Fujimoto and Bravo signed their respective contracts but did not return them to the company. Believing that they had accepted the company's offers and that they were working under the proffered bonus contracts, the two employees remained in the employ of Rio Grande until November 30, 1966.

The written contracts called for the employees to devote their best efforts to Rio Grande and promised in return that the company would pay each offeree a bonus amounting to ten percent of the company's net profits for each fiscal year. Each employee was to agree to return half of his bonus to the company as an investment in company stock.

Partly as a consequence of projected changes in the nature of the corporation's business, Fujimoto and Bravo quit their jobs with Rio Grande on November 30, 1966. Shortly thereafter the company ceased doing business in Texas. Fujimoto and Bravo then brought this suit, claiming that they had accepted the offered contracts and that they had not received the ten percent bonuses due them. They alleged that they were each entitled to ten percent of the company's net profits for the fiscal year ending September 30, 1966, and ten percent of the profits of the subsequent two months, October and November, 1966.

In answer to special interrogatories the jury found that Fujimoto and Bravo each had entered into a written contract in October, 1965. It was then determined that Fujimoto and Bravo should each recover the sum of $8,964.25 as damages for the company's breach of contract.

On appeal Rio Grande argues that there is insufficient evidence in the record to support the jury's finding that Fujimoto and Bravo had accepted the offered bonus contracts. The company further argues that even if the contracts had been accepted, the district court's judgment still should be reversed because the court erred in charging the jury as to how to compute the net profits of the corporation.

We have concluded that employment contracts were accepted and that they subsisted throughout the fiscal year ending September 30, 1966, and for two months into the following fiscal year. However, we have also concluded that the district court erred in instructing the jury on how to compute Rio Grande's net profits for the truncated period of October and November, 1966. The judgment of the district court is, therefore, affirmed in part and reversed and remanded in part.

I

Rio Grande argues that there were no contracts because Fujimoto and Bravo did not accept the written bonus offers by signing and returning the written instruments to the company. Each contract was signed by the respective employee, but neither was returned. Thus the first issue is whether the

1st Issue

offers, which by their terms did not specify the means by which they could be accepted, could be accepted by a mode other than the return of the signed instruments.

Professor Corbin has summarized the law on this issue as follows:

> In the first place, there is no question that the offeror can require notice of acceptance in any form that he pleases. He can require that it shall be in any language and transmitted in any manner. He may require notice to be given by a nod of the head, by flags, by wig-wag, by a smoke signal on a high hill. He may require that it be by letter, telegraph or radio, and that there shall be no contract unless and until he is himself made conscious of it.
>
> Secondly, the offeror can specify a mode of making an acceptance of his offer, without making that method exclusive of all others. If the mode that he specifies is one that may not bring home to him the knowledge that his offer has been accepted, then such knowledge by him is not a requisite. The offeror can specify a mode of acceptance without any knowledge of the law of contract and without thinking in terms of offer and acceptance at all. This will be considered below.
>
> Thirdly, if the offeror specifies no mode of acceptance, the law requires no more than that the mode adopted shall be in accord with the usage and custom of men in similar cases. If proof of such usage and custom is wanting or is uncertain, the court must consider probable convenience and results and then help by its decision to establish a custom for the future and a rule of law. Corbin on Contracts §67, p.109 [student ed. 1952].

See also Allied Steel & Conveyors, Inc. v. Ford Motor Company, 6 Cir. 1960, 277 F.2d 907, 910-911.

This case falls within the third of Professor Corbin's rules. Neither written offer specified a particular mode of acceptance, and there is no evidence that Rio Grande ever manifested any intent that the offers could be accepted only by the return of the signed instruments. Moreover, there is substantial and convincing evidence to the contrary. The record is replete with evidence that the company conditioned the bonus offers primarily upon the offerees remaining in the company's employment and that the employees understood that they did not have to return the signed contracts in order to have contracts under which they would each get a ten percent bonus.

Never Manifested

Since we have found that the return of the signed documents was not the exclusive means by which the offerees could convey their acceptances, we must now determine whether Fujimoto and Bravo in fact adequately communicated such acceptances to the company. Where, as here, the offer and surrounding circumstances are silent as to permissible modes of acceptance, the law requires only that there be some clear and unmistakable expression of the offeree's intention to accept. In the words of Professor Corbin:

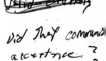

Did they communicate acceptance?

What the law requires

> Whenever the case is such as to require a notice of acceptance, it is not enough for the offeree to express mental assent, or even to do some overt act

that is not known to the offeror and is not one that constitutes a customary method of giving notice. *If the overt act is one that clearly expresses an intention* to accept the specific offer and is in fact known by the offeror, there is an effective acceptance. This is because the offeror has actual knowledge. [Emphasis added.] Corbin on Contracts, supra, §67 at p.111.

As Professor Corbin indicates, the mode of expressing assent is inconsequential so long as it effectively makes known to the offeror that his offer has been accepted. One usually thinks of acceptance in terms of oral or written incantations, but in many situations acts or symbols may be equally effective communicative media. See Restatement of Contracts §21. In the words of Chief Judge Brown in Aetna Casualty & Surety Co. v. Berry, 5 Cir. 1965, 350 F.2d 49, 54:

> "That the communication from the Berry Companies to Aetna was not in words express goes only to the weight and clarity of the message, but it does not mean that no contract came into existence. Of necessity, the law has long recognized the efficacy of nonverbal communications. From the formation of contracts by an offeree's silence, nod, hand signal or 'x' on an order blank to the doctrine of admission by silence, the law has legally realized that to offer guidance and comment meaningfully on the full range of human conduct, cognizance must be taken of communications other than by words. Symbols for words often suffice. Lawyers and Judges live by them, as the citation to this very case may sometime demonstrate." See also McCarty v. Langdeau, Tex. Civ. App. 1960, 337 S.W.2d 407, 412 (writ ref'd n.r.e.).

In the case at bar there is substantial evidence to support the jury's finding that the company knew that the offerees had agreed to the terms of the proffered bonus contracts. Of particular importance is the fact that Fujimoto and Bravo, who had threatened to quit unless their remuneration was substantially increased, continued to work for the company for fourteen months after receiving the offers. Moreover, during this fourteen-month period they did not again express dissatisfaction with their compensation. There is also evidence that Fujimoto and Bravo discussed the bonus contracts with the company president in such circumstances and in such a manner that their assent and acceptance should have been unmistakable to him. In view of these circumstances, Rio Grande could not have been besieged with any Hamlet-like doubts regarding the existence of a contract. Since Rio Grande knew that Fujimoto and Bravo had accepted its offer, there was a valid and binding contract. See Williston on Contracts §90 (1957).

II

[The court then concluded that the district court miscomputed the 10 percent bonus.]

The judgment of the district court is correct in all respects but one. The court properly held that the company's offers were accepted and that the contracts subsisted until the end of November, 1966. Contracts do not evanesce because of the perplexities in their construction, and their consequences cannot be ignored because of vexations in damage ascertainment. We hold, however, that the court should have allowed the jury a backward glance at losses carried over on the company's books from prior years. It is from this fiscal vista that the jury should have been instructed to determine Rio Grande's net profits for the October-November, 1966, period. The judgment of the district court is, therefore, affirmed in part and reversed and remanded in part.

Damages were wrong

Problem 11

Frederick Bean went to Centerboro Grocery and filled up a basket with items. As he got near the checkout counter, a carton of cola in his basket exploded, causing him to lose his footing, fall to the floor, and sustain personal injuries. Bean sued the store for breach of warranty (an action under Article 2 of the UCC; we will discuss such actions in greater detail later). The store defended by arguing that such a warranty action exists only if there is a sale or a contract to sell the cola. The store reasoned that because Bean had not paid for the cola there was no contract. Do you agree? See UCC §§2-204 and 2-206, and Giant Food, Inc. v. Washington Coca-Cola Bottling Co., 273 Md. 592, 332 A.2d 1 (Md. App. 1975).

Problem 12

Hannibal Hamlin ran a business concern that produced cheap cigars. One day he received in the mail the following purchase order:

August 8th

Dear Mr. Hamlin:
I hereby offer to purchase 42 cartons of your West Coast cigars at $200 a carton, shipment to be made F.O.B. truck your plant by September 25th. If acceptable, please write me immediately.

/s/ Thomas R. Marshall

Under UCC §2-206 (which appears in the *Beard* case above), decide which of the following responses create a contract.

(a) Hamlin telephoned Marshall and said, "I accept." Is there an acceptance? If the original letter had not contained the last sentence therein, would your answer be easier?

(b) Marshall sent the letter overnight express. Hamlin responded by regular mail: "I accept." See Defeo v. Amfarms Assoc., 161 A.D.2d 904, 557 N.Y.S.2d 469 (1990) (offer by overnight express; purported acceptance sent by regular mail to agent of offeror who had not been associated with offer).

(c) Hamlin shipped the cigars on September 20 without prior agreement, though he immediately telephoned Marshall's agent notifying him of the shipment (see UCC §2-504). Is this an acceptance according to §2-206(1) (b)? If the cigars are defective (they explode, say, or are infected with a pesticide), can Hamlin escape liability by arguing in this way: The buyer only offered to buy a product that was usable as a cigar, but the cigars I sent did not conform to this offer so no "acceptance" arose and there is no "contract" between us?

(d) You are Hamlin's attorney and he phones you with this dilemma: Marshall's letter asked for "West Coast cigars," but Hamlin is all out of that brand. He has a slightly different brand on hand ("East Coast"), and he would be willing to sell them for the price Marshall quoted, but he cannot get in touch with Marshall to get approval of the change. If he ships the goods, will he be in breach? Is there any language he should add to the invoice or cover letter to protect himself? See UCC §2-206(1)(b) and Official Comment 4 to that section, and Corinthian Pharmaceutical Systems, Inc. v. Lederle Laboratories, 724 F. Supp. 605 (S.D. Ind. 1989).

C.   Silence as Acceptance

RESTATEMENT (SECOND) OF CONTRACTS

§69. Acceptance by Silence or Exercise of Dominion

(1) Where an offeree fails to reply to an offer, his silence and inaction operate as an acceptance in the following cases only:

(a) Where an offeree takes the benefit of offered services with reasonable opportunity to reject them and reason to know that they were offered with the expectation of compensation.

(b) Where the offeror has stated or given the offeree reason to understand that assent may be manifested by silence or inaction and the offeree in remaining silent and inactive intends to accept the offer.

(c) Where because of previous dealings or otherwise, it is reasonable that the offeree should notify the offeror if he does not intend to accept.

(2) An offeree who does any act inconsistent with the offeror's ownership of offered property is bound in accordance with the offered terms

unless they are manifestly unreasonable. But if the act is wrongful as against the offeror it is an acceptance only if ratified by him.

Problem 13

In the beginning of their commerce, the Mikado Manufacturing Company and the Ruddigore Retailer had done business on a formal basis, agreeing among other things that all items were delivered for immediate purchase at the invoice price. Eventually the parties stopped using formal contracts. A five-year period of extensive dealings was followed by a slack period of one year in which they had no dealings. Then, suddenly, Mikado Manufacturing sent Ruddigore a shipment of its latest product line along with a bill for $8,000. If Ruddigore objects immediately, must it pay? What if it says nothing, but one week later sends Mikado Manufacturing a letter objecting to the shipment? Suppose instead that Ruddigore says nothing, but immediately resells the goods to another company. Is this an acceptance? See UCC §1-303. Hobbs v. Massasoit Whip Co., 158 Mass. 194, 33 N.E. 495 (1893).

DAY v. CATON
Supreme Judicial Court of Massachusetts, 1876
119 Mass. 513

Contract to recover the value of one-half of a brick party wall built by the plaintiff upon and between the adjoining estates, 27 and 29 Greenwich Park, Boston.

[handwritten: 29 = Plaintiff / 27 = Defendant]

At the trial in the Superior Court, before Allen, J., it appeared that, in 1871, the plaintiff, having an equitable interest in lot 29, built the wall in question, placing one half of it on the vacant lot 27, in which the defendant then had an equitable interest. The plaintiff testified that there was an

[handwritten: Express Agreement]

express agreement on the defendant's part to pay him one half the value of the wall when the defendant should use it in building upon lot 27. The defendant denied this, and testified that he never had any conversation with the plaintiff about the wall; and there was no other direct testimony on this point.

[handwritten: Plaintiff thinks defendant should pay 1/2 of wall but defendant denies]

The defendant requested the judge to rule that:

(1) The plaintiff can recover in this case only upon an express agreement.
(2) If the jury find there was no express agreement about the wall, but the defendant knew that the plaintiff was building upon land in which the defendant had an equitable interest, the defendant's rights would not be affected by such

knowledge, and his silence and subsequent use of the wall would raise no implied promise to pay anything for the wall.

The judge refused so to rule, but instructed the jury as follows:

A promise would not be implied from the fact that the plaintiff, with the defendant's knowledge, built the wall and the defendant used it, but it might be implied from the conduct of the parties. If the jury find that the plaintiff undertook and completed the building of the wall with the expectation that the defendant would pay him for it, and the defendant had reason to know that the plaintiff was so acting with that expectation, and allowed him so to act without objection, then the jury might infer a promise on the part of the defendant to pay the plaintiff.

The jury found for the plaintiff, and the defendant alleged exceptions.

DEVENS, J. The ruling that a promise to pay for the wall would not be implied from the fact that the plaintiff, with the defendant's knowledge, built the wall, and that the defendant used it, was substantially in accordance with the request of the defendant, and is conceded to have been correct. Chit. Cont. (11th Ed.) 86; Wells v. Banister, 4 Mass. 514; Knowlton v. Plantation No. 4, 14 Me. 20; Davis v. School Dist., 24 Me. 349.

The [defendant], however, contends that the presiding judge incorrectly ruled that such promise might be inferred from the fact that the plaintiff undertook and completed the building of the wall with the expectation that the defendant would pay him for it, the defendant having reason to know that the plaintiff was acting with that expectation, and allowed him thus to act without objection.

The fact that the plaintiff expected to be paid for the work would certainly not be sufficient of itself to establish the existence of a contract, when the question between the parties was whether one was made. Taft v. Dickinson, 6 Allen, 553. It must be shown that in some manner the party sought to be charged assented to it. If a party, however, voluntarily accepts and avails himself of valuable services rendered for his benefit, when he has the option whether to accept or reject them, even if there is no distinct proof that they were rendered by his authority or request, a promise to pay for them may be inferred. His knowledge that they were valuable, and his exercise of the option to avail himself of them, justify this inference. . . . And when one stands by in silence and sees valuable services rendered upon his real estate by the erection of a structure (of which he must necessarily avail himself afterward in his proper use thereof), such silence, accompanied with the knowledge on his part that the party rendering the services expects payment therefore, may fairly be treated as evidence of an acceptance of it, and as tending to show an agreement to pay for it.

The maxim, *Qui tacet consentire videtur*, is to be construed indeed as applying only to those cases where the circumstances are such that a party is fairly called upon either to deny or admit his liability. But if silence may be interpreted as assent where a proposition is made to one which he is bound to deny or admit, so also it may be if he is silent in the face of facts which fairly call upon him to speak. [Citations omitted.]

If a person saw day after day a laborer at work in his field doing services, which must of necessity inure to his benefit, knowing that the laborer expected pay for his work, when it was perfectly easy to notify him if his services were not wanted, even if a request were not expressly proved, such a request, either previous to or contemporaneous with the performance of the services, might fairly be inferred. But if the fact was merely brought to his attention upon a single occasion and casually, if he had little opportunity to notify the other that he did not desire the work and should not pay for it, or could only do so at the expense of much time and trouble, the same inference might not be made. The circumstances of each case would necessarily determine whether silence, with a knowledge that another was doing valuable work for his benefit, and with the expectation of payment, indicated that consent which would give rise to the inference of a contract. The question would be one for the jury, and to them it was properly submitted in the case before us by the presiding judge.

Exceptions overruled.

NOTES AND QUESTIONS

1. As discussed in the beginning of this chapter and in Chapter 3 on Remedies, courts draw a distinction between a contract *implied in fact* and a contract *implied in law*. The former term refers to a contract intentionally created by the parties (typically by their conduct) and is enforced just as any express contract would be. A contract implied in law, on the other hand, is one forced on the parties by the court (regardless of their actual intention) to avoid one party being unjustly enriched at the expense of the other. Was the contract in this case one actually intended by the parties (a contract implied in fact) or one created by the court to reach an equitable result (a contract implied in law)?

2. It is not easy to avoid using a wall erected by a neighbor. If your neighbor builds a wall and you allow ivy to grow up your side, do you now have to pay your fair share, even though nothing was said about this before the wall was built? What is the result if you put up a basketball hoop on your side? Use the wall to keep out prying eyes while you sunbathe?

Problem 14

Reginald Bunthorne was considerably annoyed to receive in the mail a copy of a new magazine *Country Music Today*. He liked only classical music.

Under common law, good argument that he did accepted the offers

The cover letter with the magazine stated that he was being sent a 12-month subscription for only $18, and that if he didn't want this fabulous limited offer he should return the enclosed card ("Please attach postage, the post office will not deliver unstamped letter," he was told by the envelope). Bunthorne threw the magazine away after a hurried reading confirmed his worst fears. He threw 11 more issues away, too, before the bill for $18 arrived. He then threw it away, and eventually the magazine threatened suit. At a cocktail party, Bunthorne asks you for a free bit of legal advice about his contractual liability. Would it help to know about the following federal statute?

Under Statute, good argument he didn't Accept it

The Postal Reorganization Act of 1970, 39 U.S.C.A. §3009. Mailing of Unordered Merchandise

(a) Except for (1) free samples clearly and conspicuously marked as such, and (2) merchandise mailed by a charitable organization soliciting contributions, the mailing of unordered merchandise or of communications prohibited by subsection (c) of this section constitutes an unfair method of competition and an unfair trade practice [under §5 of the Federal Trade Commission Act].

(b) Any merchandise mailed in violation of subsection (a) of this section, or within the exceptions contained therein, may be treated as a gift by the recipient, who shall have the right to retain, use, discard, or dispose of it in any manner he sees fit without any obligation whatsoever to the sender. All such merchandise shall have attached to it a clear and conspicuous statement informing the recipient that he may treat the merchandise as a gift to him and has the right to retain, use, discard, or dispose of it in any manner he sees fit without any obligation whatsoever to the sender.

(c) No mailer of any merchandise mailed in violation of subsection (a) of this section, or within the exceptions contained therein, shall mail to any recipient of such merchandise a bill for such merchandise or any dunning communications.

(d) For the purposes of this section, "unordered merchandise" means merchandise mailed without the prior expressed request or consent of the recipient.

Problem 15

Mr. and Mrs. Smith signed a contract with the Book-of-the-Month Club (BOMC), whereby BOMC monthly sends the Smiths a notice describing the next selection, and if it hears no objection from them it then mails out the book (and bill, of course). Is such a "negative option plan," as it is called, in conflict with the preceding statute? (Negative option plans are regulated by the Federal Trade Commission, 16 C.F.R. §425.)

NORCIA v. SAMSUNG TELECOMMUNICATIONS AMERICA, LLC
United States Court of Appeals, Ninth Circuit, 2017
845 F.3d 1279

IKUTA, Circuit Judge.

Daniel Norcia filed a class action complaint against Samsung Telecommunications America, LLC, and Samsung Electronics America, Inc., (collectively, "Samsung"), alleging that Samsung made misrepresentations as to the performance of the Galaxy S4 phone. Samsung moved to compel arbitration of the dispute on the ground that an arbitration provision, which was contained in a warranty brochure included in the Galaxy S4 box, was binding on Norcia. We affirm the district court's denial of Samsung's motion.

I

On May 23, 2013, Norcia entered a Verizon Wireless store in San Francisco, California, to purchase a Samsung Galaxy S4 phone. Norcia paid for the phone at the register, and a Verizon Wireless employee provided a receipt entitled "Customer Agreement" followed by the name and address of the Verizon Wireless store. The receipt stated the order location, Norcia's mobile number, the product identification number, and the contract end date. Under the heading "Items," the receipt stated "WAR6002 1 YR. MFG. WARRANTY." Under the heading "Agreement," the receipt included three provisions, including a statement (in all capital letters):

> I agree to the current Verizon Wireless Customer Agreement, including the calling plan, (with extended limited warranty/service contract, if applicable), and other terms and conditions for services and selected features I have agreed to purchase as reflected on the receipt, and which have been presented to me by the sales representative and which I had the opportunity to review.

The receipt also stated (in all capital letters): "I understand that I am agreeing to . . . settlement of disputes by arbitration and other means instead of jury trials, and other important terms in the Customer Agreement." The Customer Agreement did not reference Samsung or any other party. Norcia signed the Customer Agreement, and Verizon Wireless emailed him a copy.

After signing the Customer Agreement, Norcia and a Verizon Wireless employee took the Galaxy S4 phone, still in its sealed Samsung box, to a table. The front of the product box stated "Samsung Galaxy S4." The back of the box stated: "Package Contains . . . Product Safety & Warranty Brochure." The Verizon Wireless employee opened the box, unpacked the phone and materials, and helped Norcia transfer his contacts from his old phone to the new phone. Norcia took the phone, the phone charger, and the headphones with him as he left the store, but he declined the offer by the Verizon Wireless employee to take the box and the rest of its contents.

The Samsung Galaxy S4 box contained, among other things, a "Product Safety & Warranty Information" brochure. The 101-page brochure consisted of two sections. Section 1 contained a wide range of health and safety information, while Section 2 contained Samsung's "Standard Limited Warranty" and "End User License Agreement for Software." The Standard Limited Warranty section explained the scope of Samsung's express warranty. In addition to explaining Samsung's obligations, the procedure for obtaining warranty service, and the limits of Samsung's liability, the warranty section included the following (in all capital letters):

Warranty

> All disputes with Samsung arising in any way from this limited warranty or the sale, condition or performance of the products shall be resolved exclusively through final and binding arbitration, and not by a court or jury.

Later in the section, a paragraph explained the procedures for arbitration and stated that purchasers could opt out of the arbitration agreement by providing notice to Samsung within 30 calendar days of purchase, either through email or by calling a toll-free telephone number. It also stated that opting out "will not affect the coverage of the Limited Warranty in any way, and you will continue to enjoy the benefits of the Limited Warranty." Norcia did not take any steps to opt out.

In February 2014, Norcia filed a class action complaint against Samsung, alleging that Samsung misrepresented the Galaxy S4's storage capacity and rigged the phone to operate at a higher speed when it was being tested. The complaint alleged that these deceptive acts constituted common law fraud and violated California's Consumers Legal Remedies Act (Cal. Civ. Code §§1750-1784), California's Unfair Competition Law (Cal. Bus. & Prof. Code §§17200-17210), and California's False Advertising Law (Cal. Bus. & Prof. Code §§17500-17509). The complaint sought certification of the case as a class action for all purchasers of the Galaxy S4 phone in California. Norcia did not bring any claims for breach of warranty.

Instead of filing an answer to the complaint, Samsung moved to compel arbitration by invoking the arbitration provision in the Product Safety & Warranty Information brochure. The district court denied Samsung's motion. It held that even though Norcia should be deemed to have received the Galaxy S4 box, including the Product Safety & Warranty Information brochure, the receipt of the brochure did not form an agreement to arbitrate non-warranty claims. Samsung timely appealed the district court's order. . . .

II

"[A]rbitration is a matter of contract and a party cannot be required to submit to arbitration any dispute which he has not agreed so to submit."

AT&T Techs., Inc. v. Commc'ns Workers of Am., 475 U.S. 643, 648, 106 S. Ct. 1415, 89 L. Ed. 2d 648 (1986). . . . Therefore, to evaluate the district court's denial of Samsung's motion to compel arbitration, we must first determine "whether a valid agreement to arbitrate exists." Chiron Corp. v. Ortho Diagnostic Sys., Inc., 207 F.3d 1126, 1130 (9th Cir. 2000). . . . As the party seeking to compel arbitration, Samsung bears "the burden of proving the existence of an agreement to arbitrate by a preponderance of the evidence." Knutson v. Sirius XM Radio Inc., 771 F.3d 559, 565 (9th Cir. 2014). . . .

Samsung claims that the inclusion of the arbitration provision in the Product Safety & Warranty Information brochure created a valid contract between Samsung and Norcia to arbitrate all claims related to the Galaxy S4 phone. . . .

A

We first evaluate whether the Product Safety & Warranty Information brochure in the Galaxy S4 box created a binding contract between Norcia and Samsung to arbitrate the claims in Norcia's complaint. . . .

We begin with the basic principles of California contract law. Generally, under California law, "the essential elements for a contract are (1) '[p]arties capable of contracting;' (2) '[t]heir consent;' (3) '[a] lawful object;' and (4) '[s]ufficient cause or consideration.'" United States ex rel. Oliver v. Parsons Co., 195 F.3d 457, 462 (9th Cir. 1999) (alterations in original) (quoting Cal. Civ. Code §1550). A party who is bound by a contract is bound by all its terms, whether or not the party was aware of them. "A party cannot avoid the terms of a contract on the ground that he or she failed to read it before signing." Marin Storage & Trucking, Inc. v. Benco Contracting & Eng'g, Inc., 89 Cal. App. 4th 1042, 1049, 107 Cal. Rptr. 2d 645 (2001).

"A contract for sale of goods may be made in any manner sufficient to show agreement, including conduct by both parties which recognizes the existence of such a contract." Cal. Com. Code §2204(1). "Courts must determine whether the outward manifestations of consent would lead a reasonable person to believe the offeree has assented to the agreement." *Knutson,* 771 F.3d at 565. . . .

As a general rule, "silence or inaction does not constitute acceptance of an offer." Golden Eagle Ins. Co. v. Foremost Ins. Co., 20 Cal. App. 4th 1372, 1385, 25 Cal. Rptr. 2d 242 (1993). . . . California courts have long held that "[a]n offer made to another, either orally or in writing, cannot be turned into an agreement because the person to whom it is made or sent makes no reply, even though the offer states that silence will be taken as consent, for the offerer cannot prescribe conditions of rejection so as to turn silence on the part of the offeree into acceptance." Leslie v. Brown Bros. Inc., 208 Cal. 606, 621, 283 P. 936 (1929). . . .

There are exceptions to this rule, however. An offeree's silence may be deemed to be consent to a contract when the offeree has a duty to respond to an offer and fails to act in the face of this duty. *Golden Eagle*, 20 Cal. App. 4th at 1386. . . . For example, in Gentry v. Superior Court, an employee signed an "easily readable, one-page form" acknowledging that he would be required to arbitrate all employment-related legal disputes unless he opted out. 42 Cal. 4th 443, 468. . . . By signing this agreement, the employee "manifested his intent to use his silence, or failure to opt out, as a means of accepting the arbitration agreement." Id. Therefore, the California Supreme Court held that the employee's failure to act constituted acceptance of the agreement. Id.

An offeree's silence may also be treated as consent to a contract when the party retains the benefit offered. See *Golden Eagle*, 20 Cal. App. 4th at 1386, 25 Cal. Rptr. 2d 242; see also Cal. Civ. Code §1589 ("A voluntary acceptance of the benefit of a transaction is equivalent to a consent to all the obligations arising from it, so far as the facts are known, or ought to be known, to the person accepting."). In *Golden Eagle*, a couple received a renewal certificate from their insurance company, and retained the benefit of the renewed insurance policy without paying the premium. 20 Cal. App. 4th at 1386, 25 Cal. Rptr. 2d 242. The court held that in light of the existing relationship between the couple and the insurance company, the couple's retention of the renewal certification was "sufficient evidence of acceptance of the renewal policy" under California law. Id. at 1386-87, 25 Cal. Rptr. 2d 242.

Even if there is an applicable exception to the general rule that silence does not constitute acceptance, courts have rejected the argument that an offeree's silence constitutes consent to a contract when the offeree reasonably did not know that an offer had been made. See Windsor Mills, Inc. v. Collins & Aikman Corp., 25 Cal. App. 3d 987, 993, 101 Cal. Rptr. 347 (1972). In *Windsor Mills*, a buyer ordered yarn from a supplier, and the supplier acknowledged the order on a printed form which stated "in small print" on the reverse side of the form, "15. Arbitration: Any controversy arising out of or relating to this contract shall be settled by arbitration in the City of New York. . . ." Id. at 989-90, 101 Cal. Rptr. 347. The court concluded that the buyer was not bound by this provision because "an offeree, regardless of apparent manifestation of his consent, is not bound by inconspicuous contractual provisions of which he was unaware, contained in a document whose contractual nature is not obvious." Id. at 993, 101 Cal. Rptr. 347; see also Marin Storage, 89 Cal. App. 4th at 1049-50, 107 Cal. Rptr. 2d 645 (noting that a party is not bound by a document that "does not appear to be a contract and the terms are not called to the attention of the recipient").

We now apply these principles of California law to determine whether Norcia engaged in any conduct sufficient to show that he agreed to be bound by the arbitration agreement in the Product Safety & Warranty Information brochure. There is no dispute that Norcia did not expressly assent to any agreement in the brochure. Nor did Norcia sign the brochure or otherwise act in a manner that would show "his intent to use his silence, or failure to opt out, as a means of accepting the arbitration agreement." *Gentry*, 42 Cal. 4th at 468, 64 Cal. Rptr. 3d 773, 165 P.3d 556. Under California law, an offeree's inaction after receipt of an offer is generally insufficient to form a contract. *Leslie*, 208 Cal. at 621, 283 P. 936. Therefore, Samsung's offer to arbitrate all disputes with Norcia "cannot be turned into an agreement because the person to whom it is made or sent makes no reply, even though the offer states that silence will be taken as consent," id. unless an exception to this general rule applies.

Samsung fails to demonstrate the applicability of any exception to the general California rule that an offeree's silence does not constitute consent. Samsung has not pointed to any principle of California law that imposed a duty on Norcia to act in response to receiving the Product Safety & Warranty Information brochure. *Gentry*, 42 Cal. 4th at 468, 64 Cal. Rptr. 3d 773, 165 P.3d 556. Nor was there any previous course of dealing between the parties that might impose a duty on Norcia to act. See *Beatty Safway Scaffold*, 180 Cal. App. 2d at 655, 4 Cal. Rptr. 543. Moreover, Samsung has not alleged that Norcia retained any benefit by failing to act. See Cal. Civ. Code §1589. Indeed, the brochure states that Norcia was entitled to "the benefits of the Limited Warranty" regardless whether Norcia opted out of the arbitration agreement.

In the absence of an applicable exception, California's general rule for contract formation applies. Because Norcia did not give any "outward manifestations of consent [that] would lead a reasonable person to believe the offeree has assented to the agreement," *Knutson*, 771 F.3d at 565, no contract was formed between Norcia and Samsung, and Norcia is not bound by the arbitration provision contained in the brochure. . . .

AFFIRMED.

D.   *Knowledge of Offer*

Problem 16

After detective Philo Vance unraveled the murder mystery and identified the killer, the police took the miscreant away. The next day Vance learned for the first time that there was a $10,000 reward outstanding for anyone who furnished information leading to the solving of the crime. The reward had been issued by the brother of the murder victim, but when Vance applied for the promised money he was told that he was not entitled to it because he had solved the case without knowledge of the reward offer and could not possibly have made an acceptance by his actions (which the reward offeror viewed as gratuitous). Is this the correct legal result? See Gadsden Times v. Doe, 345 So. 2d 1361 (Ala. App. 1977) (agreeing with the argument).

Does the rule that the offeree must know of the offer to accept it follow as a matter of logic? Is it good policy in reward cases? Listen to Judge Nearn, dissenting in Stephens v. City of Memphis, 565 S.W.2d 213, 218 (Tenn. Ct. App. 1977):

> What policy could be more fraught with impediments to justice and with fraud than one that says to the public, "Citizen, if you come forward and do your civic duty promptly as you should, without knowledge or thought of reward, you shall forfeit all claims to any funds which have been offered by other public-minded citizens to induce the citizenry to come forward and do their duty as they should. However, citizen, if you do not do your duty as you should, but on the contrary, wait until the 'pot is right' and you are assured that top dollar will be paid for the information which you ought to have promptly given in the first instance, then you may come forward with your concealed information and you will be amply rewarded for your delay of justice and personal advice." To hold "prior knowledge" necessary for recovery is to make this statement to the people of this state.

And to Judge Frazer in Dawkins v. Sapplington, 26 Ind. 199, 201 (1866):

> If the offer was made in good faith, why should the defendant inquire whether the plaintiff knew that it had been made? Would the benefit to him be diminished by the discovery that the plaintiff, instead of acting from mercenary motive, had been impelled solely by a desire to prevent the larceny from being profitable to the person who had committed it? Is it not well that anyone who has an opportunity to prevent the success of a crime, may know that by doing so he not only performs a virtuous service, but also entitles himself to whatever reward has been offered therefor to the public?

Most jurisdictions will hold that if the reward offer is made by a *governmental entity*, the usual rules of contract do not apply, and any citizen who performs the requested service is entitled to the reward, even if the claimant had no idea that the reward was being offered.

E. Mode of Acceptance

In a contract there is always a *promise* on at least one side and sometimes on both. Where two promises are exchanged for one another ("I promise to buy your car" and "I promise to sell it to you") the contract is said to be *bilateral*. Conversely, in a *unilateral* contract, a promise is exchanged for an act or a forbearance to act ("I promise to give you $20 if you wash my car" or "I promise to pay you $50 if you don't tell Mom what time I got home"). The distinction (albeit much less important than was once the case) occasionally raises a number of legal issues as we shall see in this and the next chapter. In the case that follows, the dichotomy between bilateral and unilateral contracts challenges the California Supreme Court as to the proper mode of acceptance.

DAVIS v. JACOBY
Supreme Court of California, 1934
1 Cal. 2d 370, 34 P.2d 1026

PER CURIAM. Plaintiffs appeal from a judgment refusing to grant specific performance of an alleged contract to make a will. The facts are not in dispute and are as follows:

The plaintiff Caro M. Davis was the niece of Blanche Whitehead, who was married to Rupert Whitehead. Prior to her marriage in 1913 to her coplaintiff Frank M. Davis, Caro lived for a considerable time at the home of the Whiteheads, in Piedmont, Cal. The Whiteheads were childless and extremely fond of Caro. The record is replete with uncontradicted testimony of the close and loving relationship that existed between Caro and her aunt and uncle. During the period that Caro lived with the Whiteheads, she was treated as and often referred to by the Whiteheads as their daughter. In 1913, when Caro was married to Frank Davis, the marriage was arranged at the Whitehead home and a reception held there. After the marriage Mr. and Mrs. Davis went to Mr. Davis' home in Canada, where they have resided ever since. During the period 1913 to 1931 Caro made many visits to the Whiteheads, several of them being of long duration. The Whiteheads visited Mr. and Mrs. Davis in Canada on several occasions. After the marriage and continuing down to 1931 the closest and most friendly relationship at all times existed between these two families. They corresponded frequently, the record being replete with letters showing the loving relationship.

By the year 1930 Mrs. Whitehead had become seriously ill. She had suffered several strokes and her mind was failing. Early in 1931 Mr. Whitehead had her removed to a private hospital. The doctors in attendance had informed him that she might die at any time or she might linger for many months. Mr. Whitehead had suffered severe financial reverses. He had had several sieges of sickness and was in poor health. The record shows that during the early part of 1931 he was desperately in need of assistance with his wife, and in his business affairs, and that he did not trust his friends in Piedmont. On March 18, 1931, he wrote to Mrs. Davis telling her of Mrs. Whitehead's condition and added that Mrs. Whitehead was very wistful.

Today I endeavored to find out what she wanted. I finally asked her if she wanted to see you. She burst out crying and we had great difficulty in getting her to stop. Evidently, that is what is on her mind. It is a very difficult matter to decide. If you come it will mean that you will have to leave again, and then things may be serious. I am going to see the doctor, and get his candid opinion and will then write you again. . . . Since writing the above, I have seen the doctor, and he thinks it will help considerably if you come.

Shortly thereafter, Mr. Whitehead wrote to Caro Davis further explaining the physical condition of Mrs. Whitehead and himself. On March 24, 1931, Mr. Davis, at the request of his wife, telegraphed to Mr. Whitehead as follows:

> Your letter received. Sorry to hear Blanche not so well. Hope you are feeling better yourself. If you wish Caro to go to you can arrange for her to leave in about two weeks. Please wire me if you think it advisable for her to go.

On March 30, 1931, Mr. Whitehead wrote a long letter to Mr. Davis, in which he explained in detail the condition of Mrs. Whitehead's health and also referred to his own health. He pointed out that he had lost a considerable portion of his cash assets but still owned considerable realty, that he needed someone to help him with his wife and some friend he could trust to help him with his business affairs and suggested that perhaps Mr. Davis might come to California. He then pointed out that all his property was community property; that under his will all the property was to go to Mrs. Whitehead; that he believed that under Mrs. Whitehead's will practically everything was to go to Caro. Mr. Whitehead again wrote to Mr. Davis under date of April 9, 1931, pointing out how badly he needed someone he could trust to assist him, and giving it as his belief that if properly handled he could still save about $150,000. He then stated: "Having you [Mr. Davis] here to depend on and to help me regain my mind and courage would be a big thing." Three days later, on April 12, 1931, Mr. Whitehead again wrote, addressing his letter to "Dear Frank and Caro," and in this letter made the definite offer, which offer it is claimed was accepted and is the basis of this action. In this letter he first pointed out that Blanche, his wife, was in a private hospital and that "she cannot last much longer . . . my affairs are not as bad as I supposed at first. Cutting everything down I figure 150,000 can be saved from the wreck." He then enumerated the values placed upon his various properties and then continued:

> My trouble was caused by my friends taking advantage of my illness and my position to skin me.
>
> Now if Frank could come out here and be with me, and look after my affairs, we could easily save the balance I mention, provided I don't get into another panic and do some more foolish things.
>
> The next attack will be my end, I am 65 and my health has been bad for years, so, the Drs. Don't give me much longer to live. So if you can come, Caro will inherit everything and you will make our lives happier and see Blanche is provided for to the end.
>
> My eyesight has gone back on me, I can't read only for a few lines at a time. I am at the house alone with Stanley [the chauffeur] who does everything for me and is a fine fellow. Now, what I want is some one who will take charge of my

affairs and see I don't lose any more. Frank can do it, if he will and cut out the booze.

Will you let me hear from you as soon as possible, I know it will be a sacrifice but times are still bad and likely to be, so by settling down you can help me and Blanche and gain in the end. If I had you here my mind would get better and my courage return, and we could work things out.

This letter was received by Mr. Davis at his office in Windsor, Canada, about 9:30 A.M. April 14, 1931. After reading the letter to Mrs. Davis over the telephone, and after getting her belief that they must go to California, Mr. Davis immediately wrote Mr. Whitehead a letter, which, after reading it to his wife, he sent by air mail. This letter was lost, but there is no doubt that it was sent by Davis and received by Whitehead; in fact, the trial court expressly so found. Mr. Davis testified in substance as to the contents of this letter. After acknowledging receipt of the letter of April 12, 1931, Mr. Davis unequivocally stated that he and Mrs. Davis accepted the proposition of Mr. Whitehead and both would leave Windsor to go to him on April 25. This letter of acceptance also contained the information that the reason they could not leave prior to April 25 was that Mr. Davis had to appear in court on April 22 as one of the executors of his mother's estate. The testimony is uncontradicted and ample to support the trial court's finding that this letter was sent by Davis and received by Whitehead. In fact, under date of April 15, 1931, Mr. Whitehead again wrote to Mr. Davis and stated:

Your letter by air mail received this A.M. Now, I am wondering if I have put you to unnecessary trouble and expense, if you are making any money don't leave it, as things are bad here. . . . You know your business and I don't and I am half crazy in the bargain, but I don't want to hurt you or Caro.

Then on the other hand if I could get some one to trust and keep me straight I can save a good deal, about what I told you in my former letter.

This letter was received by Mr. Davis on April 17, 1931, and the same day Mr. Davis telegraphed to Mr. Whitehead: "Cheer up — we will soon be there, we will wire you from the train."

Between April 14, 1931, the date the letter of acceptance was sent by Mr. Davis, and April 22, Mr. Davis was engaged in closing out his business affairs, and Mrs. Davis in closing up their home and in making other arrangements to leave. On April 22, 1931, Mr. Whitehead committed suicide. Mr. and Mrs. Davis were immediately notified and they at once came to California. From almost the moment of her arrival Mrs. Davis devoted herself to the care and comfort of her aunt, and gave her aunt constant attention and care until Mrs. Whitehead's death on May 30, 1931. On this point the trial court found:

From the time of their arrival in Piedmont, Caro M. Davis administered in every way to the comforts of Blanche Whitehead and saw that she was cared for and provided for down to the time of the death of Blanche Whitehead on May 30, 1931; during said time Caro M. Davis nursed Blanche Whitehead, cared for her and administered to her wants as a natural daughter would have done toward and for her mother.

This finding is supported by uncontradicted evidence and in fact is conceded by respondents to be correct. In fact, the record shows that after their arrival in California Mr. and Mrs. Davis fully performed their side of the agreement.

After the death of Mrs. Whitehead, for the first time it was discovered that the information contained in Mr. Whitehead's letter of March 30, 1931, in reference to the contents of his and Mrs. Whitehead's wills was incorrect. By a duly witnessed will dated February 28, 1931, Mr. Whitehead, after making several specific bequests, had bequeathed all of the balance of his estate to his wife for life, and upon her death to respondents Geoff Doubble and Rupert Ross Whitehead, his nephews. Neither appellant was mentioned in his will. It was also discovered that Mrs. Whitehead by a will dated December 17, 1927, had devised all of her estate to her husband. The evidence is clear and uncontradicted that the relationship existing between Whitehead and his two nephews, respondents herein, was not nearly as close and confidential as that existing between Whitehead and appellants.

After the discovery of the manner in which the property had been devised was made, this action was commenced upon the theory that Rupert Whitehead had assumed a contractual obligation to make a will whereby "Caro Davis would inherit everything"; that he had failed to do so; that plaintiffs had fully performed their part of the contract; that damages being insufficient, quasi specific performance should be granted in order to remedy the alleged wrong, upon the equitable principle that equity regards that done which ought to have been done. The requested relief is that the beneficiaries under the will of Rupert Whitehead, respondents herein, be declared to be involuntary trustees for plaintiffs of Whitehead's estate.

It should also be added that the evidence shows that as a result of Frank Davis leaving his business in Canada he forfeited not only all insurance business he might have written if he had remained, but also forfeited all renewal commissions earned on past business. According to his testimony this loss was over $8,000.

The trial court found that the relationship between Mr. and Mrs. Davis and the Whiteheads was substantially as above recounted and that the other facts above stated were true; that prior to April 12, 1931, Rupert Whitehead had suffered business reverses and was depressed in mind and ill in body; that his wife was very ill; that because of his mental condition he "was unable to properly care for or look after his property or affairs"; that on April 12, 1931, Rupert Whitehead in writing made an offer to plaintiffs that, if within a reasonable time thereafter plaintiffs would leave and abandon their said home in Windsor, and if Frank M. Davis would abandon or dispose of his said business, and if both of the plaintiffs would come to Piedmont in the said county of Alameda where Rupert Whitehead then resided and thereafter reside at said place and be with or near him, and if Frank M. Davis would thereupon and thereafter look after the business and affairs of said Rupert Whitehead until his condition improved to such an extent as to permit him so to do, and if the plaintiffs would look after and administer to the comforts of Blanche Whitehead and see that she was properly cared for until the time of her death, that, in consideration thereof, Caro M. Davis would inherit everything that Rupert Whitehead possessed at the time of his death and that by last will and testament Rupert Whitehead would devise and bequeath to Caro M. Davis all property and estate owned by him at the time of his death, other than the property constituting the community interest of Blanche Whitehead; that shortly prior to April 12, 1931, Rupert Whitehead informed plaintiffs of the supposed terms of his will and the will of Mrs. Whitehead. The court then finds that the offer of April 12 was not accepted. As already stated, the court found that plaintiffs sent a letter to Rupert Whitehead on April 14 purporting to accept the offer of April 12, and also found that this letter was received by the Whiteheads, but finds that in fact such letter was not a legal acceptance. The court also found that the offer of April 12 was

> fair and just and reasonable, and the consideration therefor, namely, the performance by plaintiffs of the terms and conditions thereof, if the same had been performed, would have been an adequate consideration for said offer and for the agreement that would have resulted from such performance; said offer was not, and said agreement would not have been, either harsh or oppressive or unjust to the heirs at law, or devisees, or legatees, of Rupert Whitehead, or to each or any of them, or otherwise.

The court also found that plaintiffs did not know that the statements made by Whitehead in reference to the wills were not correct until after Mrs. Whitehead's death, that after plaintiffs arrived in Piedmont they cared for Mrs. Whitehead until her death and "Blanche Whitehead was greatly comforted by the presence, companionship and association of Caro M. Davis, and by her administering to her wants."

The theory of the trial court and of respondents on this appeal is that the letter of April 12 was an offer to contract, but that such offer could only be accepted by performance and could not be accepted by a promise to perform, and that said offer was revoked by the death of Mr. Whitehead before performance. In other words, it is contended that the offer was an offer to enter into a unilateral contract, and that the purported acceptance of April 14 was of no legal effect.

The distinction between unilateral and bilateral contracts is well settled in the law. It is well stated in section 12 of the American Institute's Restatement of the Law of Contracts as follows: "A unilateral contract is one in which no

promisor receives a promise as consideration for his promise. A bilateral contract is one in which there are mutual promises between two parties to the
contract; each party being both a promisor and a promisee.". . .

In the case of unilateral contracts no notice of acceptance by performance is required. Section 1584 of the Civil Code provides: "Performance of
the conditions of a proposal . . . is an acceptance of the proposal." [Citation
omitted.]

Although the legal distinction between unilateral and bilateral contracts
is thus well settled, the difficulty in any particular case is to determine whether
the particular offer is one to enter into a bilateral or unilateral contract. Some
cases are quite clear cut. Thus an offer to sell which is accepted is clearly a
bilateral contract, while an offer of a reward is a clear-cut offer of a unilateral
contract which cannot be accepted by promise to perform, but only by performance. Berthiaume v. Doe, 22 Cal. App. 78, 133 P. 515. Between these two
extremes is a vague field where the particular contract may be unilateral or
bilateral depending upon the intent of the offer and the facts and circumstances of each case. The offer to contract involved in this case falls within this
category. By the provisions of the Restatement of the Law of Contracts it is
expressly provided that there is a *presumption* that the offer is to enter into
bilateral contract. Section 31 provides: "In case of doubt it is presumed that an
offer invites the formation of a bilateral contract by an acceptance amounting
in effect to a promise by the offeree to perform what the offer requests, rather
than the formation of one or more unilateral contracts by actual performance
on the part of the offeree."

Professor Williston, in his Treatise on Contracts, volume 1, §60, also
takes the position that a presumption in favor of bilateral contracts exists.

In the comment following section 31 of the Restatement the reason for
such presumption is stated as follows: "It is not always easy to determine
whether an offerer requests an act or a promise to do the act. As a bilateral
contract immediately and fully protects both parties, the interpretation is
favored that a bilateral contract is proposed."

While the California cases have never expressly held that a presumption
in favor of bilateral contracts exists, the cases clearly indicate a tendency to
treat offers as offers of bilateral rather than of unilateral contracts. [Citations
omitted.]

Keeping these principles in mind, we are of the opinion that the offer of
April 12 was an offer to enter into a bilateral as distinguished from a unilateral contract. Respondents argue that Mr. Whitehead had the right as offerer
to designate his offer as either unilateral or bilateral. That is undoubtedly the
law. It is then argued that from all the facts and circumstances it must be
implied that what Whitehead wanted was performance and not a mere
promise to perform. We think this is a non sequitur, in fact the surrounding
circumstances lead to just the opposite conclusion. These parties were not
dealing at arm's length. Not only were they related, but a very close and
intimate friendship existed between them. The record indisputably

demonstrates that Mr. Whitehead had confidence in Mr. and Mrs. Davis, in fact that he had lost all confidence in every one else. The record amply shows that by an accumulation of occurrences Mr. Whitehead had become desperate, and that what he wanted was the promise of appellants that he could look to them for assistance. He knew from his past relationship with appellants that if they gave their promise to perform he could rely upon them. The correspondence between them indicates how desperately he desired this assurance. Under these circumstances he wrote his offer of April 12, above quoted, in which he stated, after disclosing his desperate mental and physical condition, and after setting forth the terms of his offer: "*Will you let me hear from you as soon as possible*—I know it will be a sacrifice but times are still bad and likely to be, so by settling down you can help me and Blanche and gain in the end." By thus specifically requesting an immediate reply Whitehead expressly indicated the nature of the acceptance desired by him, namely, appellants' promise that they would come to California and do the things requested by him. This promise was immediately sent by appellants upon receipt of the offer, and was received by Whitehead. It is elementary that when an offer has indicated the mode and means of acceptance, an acceptance in accordance with that mode or means is binding on the offerer. *[margin note: Rule]*

Another factor which indicates that Whitehead must have contemplated a bilateral rather than a unilateral contract, is that the contract required Mr. and Mrs. Davis to perform services until the death of both Mr. and Mrs. Whitehead. It is obvious that if Mr. Whitehead died first some of these services were to be performed after his death, so that he would have to rely on the promise of appellants to perform these services. It is also of some evidentiary force that Whitehead received the letter of acceptance and acquiesced in that means of acceptance. . . .

For the foregoing reasons we are of the opinion that the offer of April 12, 1931, was an offer to enter into a bilateral contract which was accepted by the letter of April 14, 1931. Subsequently appellants fully performed their part of the contract. Under such circumstances it is well settled that damages are insufficient and specific performance will be granted. Wolf v. Donahue, 206 Cal. 213, 273 P. 547. Since the consideration has been fully rendered by appellants the question as to mutuality of remedy becomes of no importance. 6 Cal. Jur. §140. *[margin note: It was an offer to enter into a bilateral contract which the appellants accepted by performance in the future]*

Respondents also contend the complaint definitely binds appellants to the theory of a unilateral contract. This contention is without merit. The complaint expressly alleges the parties entered into a contract. It is true that the complaint also alleged that the contract became effective by performance. However, this is an action in equity. Respondents were not misled. No objection was made to the testimony offered to show the acceptance of April 14. A fair reading of the record clearly indicates the case was tried by the parties on the theory that the sole question was whether there was a contract—unilateral or bilateral. *[margin note: Sole question]*

For the foregoing reasons the judgment appealed from is reversed. *[margin note: Reversed]*

QUESTIONS

1. If Frank and Caro had changed their minds and had never left Canada, would they have been in breach of contract?

2. Does the fact that Mr. Whitehead committed suicide when he knew they were coming help or hurt them in their contractual arguments? Good attorneys marshal the facts to support their arguments. What facts would you highlight as to this issue if you represented the plaintiff? The defendant?

IV.   TERMINATION OF THE POWER OF ACCEPTANCE

RESTATEMENT (SECOND) OF CONTRACTS

§36. METHODS OF TERMINATION OF THE POWER OF THE ACCEPTANCE

(1) An offeree's power of acceptance may be terminated by
   (a) rejection or counter-offer by the offeree, or
   (b) lapse of time, or
   (c) revocation by the offeror, or
   (d) death or incapacity of the offeror or offeree.
(2) In addition, an offeree's power of acceptance is terminated by the non-occurrence of any condition of acceptance under the terms of the offer.

A.   Revocation by Offeror

Offerors are "masters of the offer." In general, this means that they can revoke an offer before it is accepted. In order to revoke an offer, the offeror needs to inform the offeree that the offeror is no longer willing to go through with the exchange. See Restatement (Second) of Contracts §42 ("An offeree's power of acceptance is terminated when the offeree receives from the offeror a manifestation of an intention not to enter into the proposed contract.").

Problem 17

Hoover Motor Express Company sent a written offer to purchase certain real estate from Clements Paper Company. Prior to accepting the offer, the vice president of Clements phoned Mr. Hoover to discuss some details of the transaction. He was very surprised to hear Mr. Hoover say, "Well, I don't know if we are ready. We have not decided; we might not want to go through with it." Clements's VP wrote Hoover Motor Express and accepted the offer as soon as he hung up the phone. Hoover Motor Express responded that the acceptance came after the revocation and was therefore too late. Who prevails? Is it good policy to hold for the offeror here? See Hoover Motor Express Co. v. Clements Paper Co., 193 Tenn. 6, 241 S.W.2d 851 (1951).

℗ DICKINSON v. DODDS *D*
Court of Appeal, Chancery Division, 1876
2 Ch. Div. 463

On Wednesday, the 10th of June, 1874, the Defendant John Dodds signed and delivered to the Plaintiff, George Dickinson, a memorandum, of which the material part was as follows:

> I hereby agree to sell to Mr. George Dickinson the whole of the dwelling-houses, garden ground, stabling, and outbuildings thereto belonging, situate at Croft, belonging to me, for the sum of £800. As witness my hand this tenth day of June, 1874.
>
> £800. (Signed) John Dodds
>
> P.S. — This offer to be left over until Friday, 9 o'clock, A.M. J.D. (the twelfth), 12th June, 1874.
>
> (Signed) J. Dodds

The bill alleged that Dodds understood and intended that the Plaintiff should have until Friday 9 A.M. within which to determine whether he would or would not purchase, and that he should absolutely have until that time the refusal of the property at the price of £800, and that the Plaintiff in fact determined to accept the offer on the morning of Thursday, the 11th of June, but did not at once signify his acceptance to Dodds, believing that he had the power to accept it until 9 A.M. on the Friday.

In the afternoon of the Thursday the Plaintiff was informed by a Mr. Berry that Dodds had been offering or agreeing to sell the property to Thomas Allan, the other Defendant. Thereupon, the Plaintiff, at about half-past seven in the evening, went to the house of Mrs. Burgess, the mother-in-law of Dodds, where he was then staying, and left with her a formal acceptance in writing of the offer to sell the property. According to the evidence of Mrs. Burgess this document never in fact reached Dodds, she having forgotten to give it to him.

On the following (Friday) morning, at about seven o'clock, Berry, who was acting as agent for Dickinson, found Dodds at the Darlington railway station, and handed to him a duplicate of the acceptance by Dickinson, and explained to Dodds its purport. He replied that it was too late, as he had sold the property. A few minutes later Dickinson himself found Dodds entering a railway carriage, and handed him another duplicate of the notice of acceptance, but Dodds declined to receive it, saying, "You are too late. I have sold the property."

It appeared that on the day before, Thursday, the 11th of June, Dodds had signed a formal contract for the sale of the property to the Defendant Allan for £800, and had received from him a deposit of £40.

The bill in this suit prayed that the Defendant Dodds might be decreed specifically to perform the contract of the 10th of June, 1874; that he might be restrained from conveying the property to Allan; that Allan might be restrained from taking any such conveyance; that, if any such conveyance had been or should be made, Allan might be declared a trustee of the property for, and might be directed to convey the property to, the Plaintiff; and for damages.

The cause came on for hearing before Vice-Chancellor Bacon on the 25th of January, 1876 [who awarded the plaintiff specific performance].

JAMES, L.J., after referring to the document of the 10th of June, 1874, continued: The document, though beginning "I hereby agree to sell," was nothing but an offer, and was only intended to be an offer, for the Plaintiff himself tells us that he required time to consider whether he would enter into an agreement or not. Unless both parties had then agreed there was no concluded agreement then made; it was in effect and substance only an offer to sell. The Plaintiff, being minded to complete the bargain at that time, added this memorandum — "This offer to be left over until Friday, 9 o'clock A.M., 12th June, 1874." That shews it was only an offer. There was no consideration given for the undertaking or promise, to whatever extent it may be considered binding, to keep the property unsold until 9 o'clock on Friday morning; but apparently Dickinson was of opinion, and probably Dodds was of the same opinion, that he (Dodds) was bound by that promise, and could not in any way withdraw from it, or retract it, until 9 o'clock on Friday morning, and this probably explains a good deal of what afterwards took place. But it is clear settled law, on one of the clearest principles of law, that this promise, being a mere *nudum pactum*, was not binding, and that at any moment before a complete acceptance by Dickinson of the offer, Dodds was as free as Dickinson himself. Well, that being the state of things, it is said that the only mode in which Dodds could assert that freedom was by actually and distinctly saying to Dickinson, "Now I withdraw my offer." It appears to me that there is neither principle nor authority for the proposition that there must be an express and actual withdrawal of the offer, or what is called a retraction. It must, to constitute a contract, appear that the two minds were at one, at the same moment of time, that is, that there was an offer continuing up to the time of the acceptance. If there was not such a continuing offer, then the acceptance comes to nothing. Of course it may well be that the one man is bound in some way or other to let the other man know that his mind with regard to the offer has been changed; but in this case, beyond all question, the Plaintiff knew that Dodds was no longer minded to sell the property to him as plainly and clearly as if Dodds had told him in so many words, "I withdraw the offer." This is evident from the Plaintiff's own statements in the bill. The Plaintiff says in effect that, having heard and knowing that Dodds was no longer minded to sell to him, and that he was selling or had sold to someone else, thinking that he could not in point of law withdraw his offer, meaning to fix him to it, and endeavouring to bind him, "I went to the house where he was lodging, and saw his mother-in-law, and left with her an acceptance of the offer, knowing all the while that he had entirely changed his mind. I got an agent to watch for him at 7 o'clock the next morning, and I went to the train just before 9 o'clock, in order that I might catch him and give him my notice of acceptance just before 9 o'clock, and when that occurred he told my agent, and he told me, you are too late, and he then threw back the paper." It is to my mind quite clear that before there was any attempt at acceptance by the Plaintiff, he was perfectly well aware that Dodds had changed his mind, and that he had in fact agreed to sell the property to Allan. It is impossible, therefore, to say there was ever that existence of the same mind between the two parties which is essential in point of law to the making of an agreement. I am of opinion, therefore, that the Plaintiff has failed to prove that there was any binding contract between Dodds and himself.

MELLISH, L.J. I am of the same opinion. [T]he law says—and it is a perfectly clear rule of law—that, although it is said that the offer is to be left open until Friday morning at 9 o'clock, that did not bind Dodds. He was not in point of law bound to hold the offer over until 9 o'clock on Friday morning. He was not so bound either in law or in equity. Well, that being so, when on the next day he made an agreement with Allan to sell the property to him, I am not aware of any ground on which it can be said that that contract with Allan was not as good and binding a contract as ever was made. Assuming Allan to have known (there is some dispute about it, and Allan does not admit that he knew of it, but I will assume that he did) that Dodds had made the offer to Dickinson, and had given him till Friday morning at 9 o'clock to accept it, still in point of law that could not prevent Allan from making a more favourable offer than Dickinson, and entering at once into a binding agreement with Dodds.

Then Dickinson is informed by Berry that the property has been sold by Dodds to Allan. Berry does not tell us from whom he heard it, but he says that he did hear it, that he knew it, and that he informed Dickinson of it. Now, stopping there, the question which arises is this—If an offer has been made for the sale of the property, and before that offer is accepted, the person who has made the offer enters into a binding agreement to sell the property to somebody else, and the person to whom the offer was first made receives notice in some way that the property has been sold to another person, can he after that make a binding contract by the acceptance of the offer? I am of opinion that he cannot. The law may be right or wrong in saying that a person who has given to another a certain time within which to accept an offer is not bound by his promise to give that time; but, if he is not bound by that promise, and may still sell the property to someone else, and if it be the law that, in order to make a contract, the two minds must be in agreement at some one time, that is, at the time of the acceptance, how is it possible that when the person to whom the offer has been made knows that the person who has made the offer has sold the property to someone else, and that, in fact, he has not remained in the same mind to sell it to him, he can be at liberty to accept the offer and thereby make a binding contract? It seems to me that would be simply absurd. If a man makes an offer to sell a particular horse in his stable, and says, "I will give you until the day after tomorrow to accept the offer," and the next day goes and sells the horse to somebody else, and receives the purchase-money from him, can the person to whom the offer was originally made then come and say, "I accept," so as to make a binding contract, and so as to be entitled to recover damages for the non-delivery of the horse? If the rule of law is that a mere offer to sell property, which can be withdrawn at any time, and which is made dependent on the acceptance of the person to whom it is made, is a mere *nudum pactum*, how is it possible that the person to whom the offer has been made can by acceptance make a binding contract after he knows that the person who has made the offer has sold the property to someone else? It is admitted law that, if a man who makes an offer dies, the offer cannot be accepted after he is dead, and parting with the property has very much the same effect as the death of the owner, for it makes the performance of the offer impossible. I am clearly of opinion that, just as when a man who has made an offer dies before it is accepted it is impossible that it can then be accepted, so when once the person to whom the offer was made knows that the property has been sold to someone else, it is too late for him to accept the offer, and on that ground I am clearly of opinion that there was no binding contract for the sale of this property by Dodds to Dickinson, and even if there had been, it seems to me that the sale of the property to Allan was first in point of time. However, it is not necessary to consider, if there had been two binding contracts, which of them would be entitled to priority in equity, because there is no binding contract between Dodds and Dickinson.

BAGGALLAY, J.A. I entirely concur in the judgments which have been pronounced.

JAMES, L.J. The bill will be dismissed with costs.

QUESTIONS

1. Do we get the same result if all that Dickinson had learned on that Friday morning was that Dodds had offered to sell the property to Allan but had not yet done so? See Corbin on Contracts, supra, at §40.

2. If Dodds had actually sold the property to Allan would that have automatically revoked the offer to Dickinson?

3. Do we get the same result if Berry were lying and the property had not been sold to anyone? What if Berry were merely wrong?

4. Why isn't Dodds bound by his statement that he would keep the offer open? Are there good reasons for allowing him to change his mind? For the resolution of this issue as a matter of international law, see Article 16 of the United Nations Convention on Contracts for the Sale of Goods.

B. Limits on the Power to Revoke: Option Contracts and Firm Offers

Although the offeror is usually the master of the offer — and thus can revoke before the offeree accepts — parties can change this rule and make an offer irrevocable by forming an *option contract.* Under the common law, an option is an agreement in which the offeror promises not to revoke an offer in return for the offeree providing *consideration.* Although we will study consideration in Chapter 2, for now you should know that consideration, very roughly, means something of *value.*

Suppose A is thinking about buying B's house. To encourage A to take that matter seriously, B might offer (1) to sell her house to A for $500,000 and (2) in exchange for A paying B $100, promise not to revoke this offer for the next seven days. This is an option because B has contracted away her prerogative to revoke during this week.

Options create a kind of force field around an offer. As mentioned, the offeror cannot revoke during the option period. In addition, a *rejection* or *counteroffer* by the offeree does *not* necessarily terminate the offer.

Even though options under the common law require the offeree to provide consideration to the offeror, UCC §2-205 carves out a limited exception for *firm offers.* If the parties fulfil the requirements of §2-205, they can make an offer irrevocable even if the offeree does not provide a valuable right or item in exchange for the offeror's promise not to revoke. Our next case addresses this issue in the context of a lease of goods. Although leases fall under Article 2A of the UCC (rather than Article 2, which governs sales, the primary focus of our study) both Article 2A and Article 2 impose the same preconditions to making a firm offer.

2949 INC. v. McCORKLE
Court of Appeals of Washington, 2005
127 Wash. App. 1039

AGID, J.

Taletha and Terry McCorkle signed a contract to lease a sign from Sign-O-Lite, but revoked their offer before receiving notice that Sign-O-Lite accepted it. Sign-O-Lite sued the McCorkles for breach of contract because the contract contained an irrevocability clause. The trial court agreed and entered summary judgment against the McCorkles. On appeal, the McCorkles argue that the contract's irrevocability clause is unenforceable because there was no consideration for it and in light of RCW 62A.2A-205. We agree. . . .

FACTS

Appellants Taletha and Terry McCorkle own a floral design company. Respondent 2949, Inc., operates a commercial signage company called Sign-O-Lite Signs. On February 21, 2003, the McCorkles signed a pre-printed form contract provided by a Sign-O-Lite sales representative. In the contract, the McCorkles agreed to lease commercial signage that would be designed, manufactured, and installed by Sign-O-Lite. On February 26, 2003, the owner of Sign-O-Lite signed the contract, but did not send it to the McCorkles. On February 28, 2003, the McCorkles notified Sign-O-Lite that they were canceling the contract. Nevertheless, on March 19, 2003, the McCorkles received a letter dated March 11 from Sign-O-Lite notifying them that the company accepted their contract offer.

The McCorkles continued to avoid the contract, and Sign-O-Lite brought this breach of contract action arguing that paragraph 23 of the contract made the McCorkles' offer irrevocable. That paragraph states:

> Acceptance by the Owner [Sign-O-Lite] must be by an executive officer of the Owner. This Agreement shall not be binding upon the Owner after execution by the Advertiser(s) [the McCorkles] and this Agreement shall constitute an irrevocable offer by the Advertiser(s) to the Owner for a period of sixty (60) days from the date of execution by the Advertiser(s). The execution of the Agreement by a sales representative of the Owner is in no way acceptance by the Owner.

In light of this irrevocability clause, a district court judge granted summary judgment in Sign-O-Lite's favor and awarded Sign-O-Lite approximately $11,000 plus interest, attorney fees, and costs.

Discussion

In reviewing a trial court's decision to grant summary judgment, we consider all facts and reasonable inferences in the light most favorable to the nonmoving party. Absent a genuine issue of any material fact, the moving party is entitled to summary judgment as a matter of law. This case raises questions of law, which we review de novo.

I. IS THE IRREVOCABILITY CLAUSE ENFORCEABLE?

A. Consideration

An offer may generally be revoked anytime before it is accepted. . . . [However,] option contracts are valid irrevocable offers. An option contract is a promise which meets the requirements for the formation of a contract and limits the promisor's power to revoke an offer. . . . The option itself is a contract and is sometimes called an "option contract" to distinguish it from the main contract. Option contracts are often necessary because an offeree may need time to decide whether to accept the offer and, during that time, may need to spend money and effort.

The promise not to revoke must be supported by consideration, even if that consideration is nominal. . . . Options typically benefit the one qualified to exercise the option, known as the optionee. If the optionee stands to make a substantial gain by exercising the option and the optionor must stand by idly awaiting the decision, it is appropriate that the optionee pay for the privilege.

Here, paragraph 23 makes the McCorkles' offer irrevocable for a period of time before acceptance, and thus it is an option contract. The district court judge found that the parties' mutual promises constituted adequate consideration to support the option. We disagree. There is no new consideration for the clause. Sign-O-Lite offered nothing to the McCorkles in exchange for their inability to revoke their offer before acceptance. While Sign-O-Lite points out that it promised to do such things as prepare, manufacture, and install commercial signage for the McCorkles, this was the consideration offered for their performance under the contract as a whole. An option contract requires separate consideration, and there is none here. Because insufficient consideration supported the option, the irrevocability clause is unenforceable.

B. RCW 62A.2A-205

The McCorkles also argue that the irrevocability clause is unenforceable because it was not accompanied by a separate signature as required by RCW 62A.2A-205.19. That is Washington's version of the Uniform Commercial Code's (U.C.C.) section 2A-205, and it provides that an irrevocability clause in a contract to lease goods is valid despite a lack of consideration if the clause is separately signed by the offeror:

Firm offers. An offer by a merchant to lease goods to or from another person in a signed writing that by its terms gives assurance it will be held open is not revocable, for lack of consideration, during the time stated or, if no time is stated, for a reasonable time, but in no event may the period of irrevocability exceed three months. Any such term of assurance on a form supplied by the offeree must be separately signed by the offeror.

Under this statute, paragraph 23 of the parties' contract would be valid and enforceable despite its lack of consideration if the McCorkles had separately signed that clause. But because there is no separate signature, the clause is not enforceable. . . .

We reverse and remand for entry of summary judgment in the McCorkles' favor.

NOTES AND QUESTIONS

1. As the opinion illustrates, parties who are considering selling or leasing goods to each other can make offers irrevocable in two ways. First, just as under the common law, they can form option contracts if the offeree gives the offeror consideration. Second, in some circumstances — including when the offeror is a merchant and the offer only needs to remain open for three months or less — they can create firm offers without the offeree providing something of value to the offeror. In the case, why was there no consideration for the McCorkles' promise not to revoke for 60 days?

2. The court holds that Sign-O-Lite and the McCorkles also failed to create a valid firm offer because the McCorkles failed to "separately sign" next to the language that made their offer irrevocable. Why do you think the UCC imposes this "separate signing" requirement?

3. If you were litigating this case and representing the McCorkles, could you see another argument to support your theory that the parties had failed to form a valid firm offer? Here is a hint: Who was the offeror? Does this party regularly enter into contracts for commercial signs?

4. Even when the parties have satisfied all the elements of the firm offer rule, the maximum period of irrevocability is three months. If the offer states that it will remain open for longer, the firm offer is still valid for three months. But once the three-month period has expired, the offer becomes revocable.

Problem 18

Pecos Bill wanted to buy some logging equipment owned by Paul Bunyan, who was in the business of selling such equipment. The parties negotiated for some time before Paul submitted a signed proposal to Bill stating, "I hereby give you the option to purchase this equipment for $12,000, the option to expire on Friday at noon unless exercised." Bill paid nothing for the option. On Friday at 11:00 A.M. he showed up at Paul's office but before he could tender the money, Paul said, "I revoke."

(a) At common law, who prevails? What should Bill have done?

(b) Assume that the UCC applies to this Problem. If Paul Bunyan makes the same written offer to Bill, who again pays nothing for the option, could Paul revoke prior to Friday at noon?

(c) Suppose that Paul Bunyan is a logger but that he does not normally sell logging equipment. Does that affect things? See also §2-104(1) and its Official Comment 2.

(d) If the offer stated that it would be held open for six months, would Paul be bound for that entire period?

Problem 19

Newman-Money Department Store wanted to buy 500 pairs of rain boots for a special sale. Newman-Money's buyer phoned Shoe World, a manufacturer, and asked for a quotation. Shoe World's sales manager said, "We will sell you the 500 pairs for $10,000 and guarantee that we will hold this offer open until next Monday." Shortly after this phone call ended, Shoe World learned it could sell the boots elsewhere at a greater profit. It phones you, its attorney, and asks if it can revoke its offer to Newman-Money. What do you say?

The United Nations Convention on Contracts for the International Sale of Goods (described in the Introduction of this book) expands the firm offer rule by making irrevocable any offer stating a period of time for acceptance (there is no requirement that the statement be in writing or that it be made by a merchant); see Article 16(2)(a). The same article also makes irrevocable any offer so stating, even if no period of time is proposed.

C. Revocation and Acceptance of Offers to Enter into Unilateral Contracts

Under traditional law, the offeror's power to revoke before acceptance generated harsh results in the context of unilateral contracts. As we saw in Kolodziej v. Mason and Davis v. Jacoby, the only way to accept an offer to enter into a unilateral contract is to completely perform the *act* that the offeree requested. But performance can be hard. And even after the offeree had spent time, energy, or money trying to perform, the offeror was free to revoke.

The classic illustration of this dilemma appears in a law review article written by Professor Maurice Wormser:

> Suppose A says to B, "I will give you $100 if you walk across the Brooklyn Bridge," and B walks — is there a contract? It is clear that A is not asking B for B's promise to walk across the Brooklyn Bridge. What A wants from B is the act of walking across the bridge. When B has walked across the bridge there is a contract, and A is then bound to pay to B $100. At that moment there arises a unilateral contract. . . .
>
> Let us suppose that B starts to walk across the Brooklyn Bridge and has gone about one-half of the way across. At that moment A overtakes B and says to him, "I withdraw my offer." Has B then any rights against A? Again let us suppose that after A has said, "I withdraw my offer," B continues to walk across the Brooklyn Bridge and completes the act of crossing. Under these circumstances, has B any rights against A?
>
> In the first of the cases just suggested, A withdrew his offer before B had walked across the bridge. What A wanted from B, what A asked for, was the act of walking across the bridge. Until that was done, B had not given to A what A had requested. The acceptance by B of A's offer could be nothing but the act on B's part of crossing the bridge. It is elementary that an offeror may withdraw his offer until it has been accepted. It follows logically that A is perfectly within his rights in withdrawing his offer before B has accepted it by walking across the bridge — the act contemplated by the offeror and the offeree as the acceptance of the offer. A did not want B to walk half-way across or three-quarters of the way across the bridge. What A wanted from B, and what A asked for from B, was a certain and entire act. B understood this. It was for that act that A was willing to barter his volition with regard to $100. B understood this also. Until this act is done, therefore, A is not bound, since no contract arises until the completion of the act called for. Then, and not before, would A be bound.
>
> The objection is made, however, that it is very "hard" upon B that he should have walked half-way across the Brooklyn Bridge and should get no compensation. This suggestion, invariably advanced, might be dismissed with the remark that hard cases should not make bad law. But going a step further, by way of reply, the pertinent inquiry at once suggests itself, "Was B bound to walk across the Brooklyn Bridge?" The answer to this is obvious. By hypothesis, B was not bound to walk across the Brooklyn Bridge. . . . If B is not bound to continue to cross the bridge, if B is will-free, why should not A also be will-free? Suppose that after B has crossed half the bridge he gets tired and tells A that he refuses to continue crossing. B, concededly, would be perfectly within his rights in so speaking and acting. A would have no cause of action against B for damages.

Wormser, The True Nature of Unilateral Contracts, 26 Yale L.J. 136-140 (1916).

Likewise, our next case, Petterson v. Pattberg, illustrates another way in which offers to enter into a unilateral contract are challenging: determining whether the offeree has done what is necessary to accept.

PETTERSON v. PATTBERG

Court of Appeals of New York, 1928
248 N.Y. 86, 161 N.E. 428

KELLOGG, J. The evidence given upon the trial sanctions the following statement of facts: John Petterson, of whose last will and testament the plaintiff is the executrix, was the owner of a parcel of real estate in Brooklyn, known as 5301 Sixth Avenue. The defendant was the owner of a bond executed by Petterson, which was secured by a third mortgage upon the parcel. On April 4, 1924, there remained unpaid upon the principal the sum of $5,450. This amount was payable in installments of $250 on April 25, 1924, and upon a like monthly date every three months thereafter. Thus the bond and mortgage had more than five years to run before the entire sum became due. Under date of the 4th of April, 1924, the defendant wrote Petterson as follows:

> I hereby agree to accept cash for the mortgage which I hold against premises 5301 6th Ave., Brooklyn, N.Y. It is understood and agreed as a consideration I will allow you $780 providing said mortgage is paid on or before May 31, 1924, and the regular quarterly payment due April 25, 1924, is paid when due.

On April 25, 1924, Petterson paid the defendant the installment of principal due on that date. Subsequently, on a day in the latter part of May, 1924, Petterson presented himself at the defendant's home, and knocked at the door. The defendant demanded the name of his caller. Petterson replied: "It is Mr. Petterson. I have come to pay off the mortgage." The defendant answered that he had sold the mortgage. Petterson stated that he would like to talk with the defendant, so the defendant partly opened the door. Thereupon Petterson exhibited the cash, and said he was ready to pay off the mortgage according to the agreement. The defendant refused to take the money. Prior to this conversation, Petterson had made a contract to sell the land to a third person free and clear of the mortgage to the defendant. Meanwhile, also, the defendant had sold the bond and mortgage to a third party. It therefore became necessary for Petterson to pay to such person the full amount of the bond and mortgage. It is claimed that he thereby sustained a loss of $780, the sum which the defendant agreed to allow upon the bond and mortgage, if payment in full of principal, less that sum, was made on or before May 31, 1924. The plaintiff has had a recovery for the sum thus claimed, with interest.

Clearly the defendant's letter proposed to Petterson the making of a unilateral contract, the gift of a promise in exchange for the performance of an act. The thing conditionally promised by the defendant was the reduction of the mortgage debt. The act requested to be done, in consideration of the offered promise, was payment in full of the reduced principal of the debt prior to the due date thereof. "If an act is requested, that very act, and no other, must be given." Williston on Contracts, §73. "In case of offers for a consideration, the performance of the consideration is always deemed a condition." Langdell's Summary of the Law of Contracts, §4. It is elementary that any offer to enter into a unilateral contract may be withdrawn before the act requested to be done has been performed. Williston on Contracts, §60; Langdell's Summary, §4; Offord v. Davies, 12 O.B. (N.S.) 748. A bidder at a sheriff's sale may revoke his bid at any time before the property is struck down to him. Fisher v. Seltzer, 23 Pa. 308, 62 Am. Dec. 335. The offer of a reward in consideration of an act to be performed is revocable before the very act requested has been done. [Citations omitted.] So, also, an offer to pay a broker commissions, upon a sale of land for the offeror, is revocable at any time before the land is sold, although prior to revocation the broker performs services in an effort to effectuate a sale. [Citations omitted.]

An interesting question arises when, as here, the offeree approaches the offeror with the intention of proffering performance and, before actual tender is made, the offer is withdrawn. Of such a case Williston says:

> The offeror may see the approach of the offeree and know that an acceptance is contemplated. If the offeror can say "I revoke" before the offeree accepts, however brief the interval of time between the two acts, there is no escape from the conclusion that the offer is terminated. Williston on Contracts, §60b.

In this instance Petterson, standing at the door of the defendant's house, stated to the defendant that he had come to pay off the mortgage. Before a tender of the necessary moneys had been made, the defendant informed Petterson that he had sold the mortgage. That was a definite notice to Petterson that the defendant could not perform his offered promise, and that a tender to the defendant, who was no longer the creditor, would be ineffective to satisfy the debt. "An offer to sell property may be withdrawn before acceptance without any formal notice to the person to whom the offer is made. It is sufficient if that person has actual knowledge that the person who made the offer has done some act inconsistent with the continuance of the offer, such as selling the property to a third person." Dickinson v. Dodds, 2 Ch. Div. 463, headnote. To the same effect is Coleman v. Applegarth, 68 Md. 21, 11 A. 284, 6 Am. St. Rep. 417. Thus it clearly appears that the defendant's offer was withdrawn before its acceptance had been tendered. It is unnecessary to determine, therefore, what the legal situation might have been had tender been made before withdrawal. It is the individual view of the writer that the same result would follow. This would be so, for the act requested to be performed was the completed act of payment, a thing incapable of performance, unless assented to by the person to be paid. Williston on Contracts, §60b. Clearly an offering party has the right to name the precise act performance of which would convert his offer into a binding promise. Whatever the act may be until it is performed, the offer must be revocable. However, the supposed case is not before us for decision. We think that in this particular instance the offer of the defendant was withdrawn before it became a binding promise, and therefore that no contract was ever made for the breach of which the plaintiff may claim damages.

[handwritten: The offer was withdrawn before it became binding. No contract]

The judgment of the Appellate Division and that of the Trial Term should be reversed, and the complaint dismissed, with costs in all courts.

[handwritten: Reversed]

LEHMAN, J. (dissenting). The defendant's letter to Petterson constituted a promise on his part to accept payment at a discount of the mortgage he held, provided the mortgage is paid on or before May 31, 1924. Doubtless, by the terms of the promise itself, the defendant made payment of the mortgage by the plaintiff, before the stipulated time, a condition precedent to performance by the defendant of his promise to accept payment at a discount. If the condition precedent has not been performed, it is because the defendant made performance impossible by refusing to accept payment, when the plaintiff came with an offer of immediate performance. "It is a principle of fundamental justice that if a promisor is himself the cause of the failure of performance either of an obligation due him or of a condition upon which his own liability depends, he cannot take advantage of the failure." Williston on Contracts, §677. The question in this case is not whether payment of the mortgage is a condition precedent to the performance of a promise made by the defendant, but, rather, whether, at the time the defendant refused the offer of payment, he had assumed any binding obligation, even though subject to condition.

[handwritten: Promisor being the fundamental cause of failure to perform]

The promise made by the defendant lacked consideration at the time it was made. Nevertheless, the promise was not made as a gift or mere gratuity to the plaintiff. It was made for the purpose of obtaining from the defendant something which the plaintiff desired. It constituted an offer which was to become binding whenever the plaintiff should give, in return for the defendant's promise, exactly the consideration which the defendant requested.

Here the defendant requested no counter promise from the plaintiff. The consideration requested by the defendant for his promise to accept payment was, I agree, some act to be performed by the plaintiff. Until the act requested was performed, the defendant might undoubtedly revoke his offer. Our problem is to determine from the words of the letter, read in the light of surrounding circumstances, what act the defendant requested as consideration for his promise.

The defendant undoubtedly made his offer as an inducement to the plaintiff to "pay" the mortgage before it was due. Therefore, it is said, that "the act requested to be performed was the completed act of payment, a thing incapable of performance, unless assented to by the person to be paid." In unmistakable terms the defendant agreed to accept payment, yet we are told that the defendant intended, and the plaintiff should have understood, that the act requested by the defendant, as consideration for his promise to accept payment, included performance by the defendant himself of the very promise for which the act was to be consideration. The defendant's promise was to become binding only when fully performed; and part of the consideration to be furnished by the plaintiff for the defendant's promise was to be the performance of that promise by the defendant. So construed, the defendant's promise or offer, though intended to induce action by the plaintiff, is but a snare and delusion. The plaintiff could not reasonably suppose that the defendant was asking him to procure the performance by the defendant of the very act which the defendant promised to do, yet we are told that, even after the plaintiff had done all else which the defendant requested, the defendant's promise was still not binding because the defendant chose not to perform.

I cannot believe that a result so extraordinary could have been intended when the defendant wrote the letter. "The thought behind the phrase proclaims itself misread when the outcome of the reading is injustice or absurdity." See opinion of Cardozo, C.J., in Surace v. Danna, 248 N.Y. 18, 161 N.E. 315. If the defendant intended to induce payment by the plaintiff and yet reserve the right to refuse payment when offered he should have used a phrase better calculated to express his meaning than the words: "I agree to accept." A promise to accept payment, by its very terms, must necessarily become binding, if at all, not later than when a present offer to pay is made.

I recognize that in this case only an offer of payment, and not a formal tender of payment, was made before the defendant withdrew his offer to accept payment. Even the plaintiff's part in the act of payment was then not technically complete. Even so, under a fair construction of the words of the letter, I think the plaintiff had done the act which the defendant requested as consideration for his promise. The plaintiff offered to pay, with present intention and ability to make that payment. A formal tender is seldom made in business transactions, except to lay the foundation for subsequent assertion in a court of justice of rights which spring from refusal of the tender. If the defendant acted in good faith in making his offer to accept payment, he could not well have intended to draw a distinction in the act requested of the plaintiff in return, between an offer which, unless refused, would ripen into completed payment, and a formal tender. Certainly the defendant could not have expected or intended that the plaintiff would make a formal tender of payment without first stating that he had come to make payment. We should not read into the language of the defendant's offer a meaning which would prevent enforcement of the defendant's promise after it had been accepted by the plaintiff in the very way which the defendant must have intended it should be accepted, if he acted in good faith.

The judgment should be affirmed.

CARDOZO, C.J., and POUND, CRANE, and O'BRIEN, JJ., concur with KELLOGG, J. LEHMAN, J., dissents in opinion, in which ANDREWS, J., concurs.
Judgments reversed, etc.

NOTES AND QUESTIONS

1. A _tender_ means an offer to perform, but a tender of money, in strict legal terms, means much more than a mere offer to pay. It must be accompanied by the current presentment of the exact amount due in official currency. Checks, even certified or cashier's checks, are not sufficient. (But see §2-511 of the UCC.) Given these rules, at what moment would the contract have come into being in the following series?

    (a) As in the actual case, Petterson, money in hand, states: "It is Mr. Petterson. I have come to pay off the mortgage."

    (b) Pattberg opens the door and sees Petterson.

    (c) Petterson holds out the money and says, "Here."

    (d) Pattberg takes the money.

2. When would dissenting Judge Lehman say that the contract arose in the above sequence?

3. Near the end of the majority opinion, Judge Kellogg expresses "the individual view of the writer" on this same issue. When would Judge Kellogg say that the contract arose in the above sequence?

4. Judge Kellogg's "individual view" was _dictum_ (do you see why?), but it worried the New York legislature enough to lead to this strange statute:

New York General Obligations Law §15-503(1) (McKinney 1978)

Offer of accord followed by tender. An offer in writing, signed by the offeror or by his agent, to accept a performance therein designated in satisfaction or discharge in whole or in part of any claim, cause of action, contract, obligation, or lease, or any mortgage or other security interest in personal or real property, followed by tender of such performance by the offeree or by his agent before revocation of the offer, shall not be denied effect as a defense or as the basis of an action or counter-claim by reason of the fact that such tender was not accepted by the offeror or by his agent.

5. If this famous court seems rather hard on poor Mr. Petterson, consider that the court had more information about the equities than the opinion reflects. According to an often-quoted student piece:

Other facts in the case, not appearing in the opinion, may have influenced the court. The record of the trial (folios 95-97) reveals that the defendant was prevented from testifying as to a letter, sent to the plaintiff's testator, revoking the offer because such testimony was inadmissible under §347 of the Civil Practice Act, which excludes the testimony of one of the interested parties, to a transaction, where the other is dead and so unable to contradict the evidence. The record (folio 59) also seems to suggest that the mortgagor knew of the previous sale of the mortgage, since he brought $4,000 in cash with him and was accompanied by his wife and a notary public as witnesses: anticipation of the defendant's refusal by seeking to get evidence on which to base this action seems to be a plausible explanation. There was no actual proof of knowledge of the defendant's inability to carry out his offer but the situation was suspicious.

Note, 14 Cornell L.Q. 81, 84 n.18 (1928).

NOTE ON THE MODERN APPROACH TO UNILATERAL CONTRACTS

Allowing the offeror to revoke an offer to enter into a unilateral contract after the offeree had begun to perform reflected a nineteenth-century view of contract law. During that period, courts and scholars believed that contracts arose from the "will" of the parties. Thus, to return to Professor Wormser's hypothetical, it made sense that A could offer to pay B to walk across the bridge and then change her mind after B had completed half of the task. As Wormser points out, at that moment B was still "will-free," meaning that B was not *required* to complete the task. Thus, Wormser asks, why shouldn't A "also be will-free" and at liberty to revoke?

But in the twentieth century, the "will" theory fell from favor, and contract law became more concerned with issues such as fairness and protecting reasonable reliance. As a result, the Restatement of Contracts revamped the rules that govern offers to enter into unilateral contracts. Even Professor Wormser retreated, "clad in sackcloth," from his original defense of the orthodox approach to the revocability of offers to enter into unilateral contracts. Wormser, 3 J. Leg. Educ. 145, 146 (1950).

RESTATEMENT (SECOND) OF CONTRACTS

§32. INVITATION OF PROMISE OR PERFORMANCE

In case of doubt an offer is interpreted as inviting the offeree to accept either by promising to perform what the offer requests or by rendering the performance, as the offeree chooses.

RESTATEMENT (SECOND) OF CONTRACTS

§45. OPTION CONTRACT CREATED BY PART PERFORMANCE OR TENDER

(1) Where an offer invites an offeree to accept by rendering a performance and does not invite a promissory acceptance, an option contract is created when the offeree tenders or begins the invited performance or tenders a beginning of it.

(2) The offeror's duty of performance under any option contract so created is conditional on completion or tender of the invited performance in accordance with the terms of the offer.

RESTATEMENT (SECOND) OF CONTRACTS

§62. Effect of Performance by Offeree Where Offer Invites Either Performance or Promise

(1) Where an offer invites an offeree to choose between acceptance by promise and acceptance by performance, the tender or beginning of the invited performance or a tender of a beginning of it is an acceptance by performance.(2) Such an acceptance operates as a promise to render complete performance.

Section 32 instructs courts to assume that an offer can be accepted *either* by promise *or* by performance. We have already seen this presumption in action in Davis v. Jacoby (although the case refers to the Restatement (First) of Contracts, which set forth this principle in what was then §31). Suppose A says to B, "I will give you $100 if you walk across the Brooklyn Bridge." If B replies, "I accept," then A and B have a contract right then and there. A cannot revoke, because B has *already* accepted. But by the same token, B is now *bound* to walk across the bridge. If B decides not to perform, B has breached the contract with A.

However, §32 only applies to "case[s] of doubt" as to whether an offer can be accepted by either promise or performance. Sometimes, the offeror makes it obvious that she only wants *performance*. This scenario is called an offer to enter into a "true" unilateral contract. For example, A might say to B: "I will give you $100 if you walk across the Brooklyn Bridge, and the only way to accept is to perform." Alternatively, something about the offer might suggest that the offeror wouldn't be satisfied with a mere promise in return, because it's not even clear that the offeree *can* perform. If A offers B $100 to find A's lost dog, A doesn't intend to form a contract upon B's promise to find the dog. Instead, A only wants to pay *if* B *actually* finds the dog.

When an offeror makes an offer to enter into a true unilateral contact, §45 kicks in. It changes the normal rule that an offeror can revoke at any time before acceptance. Instead, it specifies that when the offeree starts to try to perform, the offeror *loses the power to revoke*. The offeree enjoys the opportunity to finish the task (in which case she accepts the offer and consummates a binding contract) or to abandon her attempts to perform (in which case there is no contract between the parties).

"Not true unilateral contracts" *§62*

Finally, §62 governs agreements that are *similar to* unilateral contracts, but *aren't* true unilateral contracts. Specifically, it applies when the offer can be accepted either by promise or performance, and instead of promising, the offeree begins to perform. According to §62, the offeree's "tender . . . or beginning of the invited performance" operates as an acceptance, thus forming a contract. Suppose A orders china plates from B. B packs the plates in bubble wrap and places them on a truck. At that point, both A and B are bound. Even though B has never expressly accepted A's offer, B's conduct is the functional equivalent of B saying, "I accept."

Problem 20

Jack works for a real estate company. For two years, the company has been trying to sell a run-down house on a steep hillside. On May 1, Kate, Jack's boss, tells Jack that she'll pay him a $1,000 bonus if he can sell the property by the end of the month.

(a) "I accept," Jack replies to Kate. Have the parties formed a binding contract?

(b) Suppose that instead of saying, "I accept," Jack spends a week organizing and publicizing an open house. At the end of the week, he runs into Kate in the office. "Oh by the way," Kate says, "I revoke my offer to pay you the bonus." Has she revoked?

(c) Same facts as (b) above. What would the parties' rights and duties be if Jack is able to sell the house by the end of May? And what if he can't sell the house by that deadline?

Problem 21

Three Pigs Restaurant hired Wolf Construction Company to put a new roof on the building, agreeing to pay Wolf $4,000 "on completion." Wolf quit the job when it was halfway done, leaving Three Pigs with a mess to clean up (a second contractor charged $5,000 for finishing the job). Three Pigs sued Wolf for its damages. Can Wolf defend by arguing that it had never made an acceptance? What, if any, is the moment of acceptance here? See Los Angeles Traction Co. v. Wilshire, 135 Cal. 654, 67 P. 1086 (1902).

D. Lapse of Time

RESTATEMENT (SECOND) OF CONTRACTS

§41. LAPSE OF TIME

(1) An offeree's power of acceptance is terminated at the time specified in the offer, or, if no time is specified, at the end of a reasonable time.

(2) What is a reasonable time is a question of fact, depending on all the circumstances existing when the offer and attempted acceptance are made.

(3) Unless otherwise indicated by the language or the circumstances, and subject to the rule stated in §49, an offer sent by mail is seasonably accepted if an acceptance is mailed at any time before midnight on the day on which the offer is received.

LORING v. CITY OF BOSTON

Supreme Judicial Court of Massachusetts, 1844
7 Metc. 409, 48 Mass. 409

Assumpsit to recover a reward of $1,000, offered by the defendants for the apprehension and conviction of incendiaries. Writ dated September 30th 1841.

At the trial before Wilde, J., the following facts were proved: On the 26th of May 1837, this advertisement was published in the daily papers in Boston: "$500 reward. The above reward is offered for the apprehension and conviction of any person who shall set fire to any building within the limits of the city. May 26 1837. Samuel A. Eliot, Mayor." On the 27th of May 1837, the following advertisement was published in the same papers: "$1000 reward. The frequent and successful repetition of incendiary attempts renders it necessary that the most vigorous efforts should be made to prevent their recurrence. In addition to the other precautions, the reward heretofore offered is doubled. One thousand dollars will be paid by the city for the conviction of any person engaged in these nefarious practices. May 27 1837. Samuel A. Eliot, Mayor." These advertisements were continued in the papers for about a week; but there was no vote of the city government, or notice by the mayor, revoking the advertisements, or limiting the time during which they should be in force. Similar rewards for the detection of incendiaries had been before offered, and paid on the conviction of the offenders; and at the time of the trial of this case, a similar reward was daily published in the newspapers.

In January 1841, there was an extensive fire on Washington Street, when the Amory House (so called) and several others were burned. The plaintiffs suspected that Samuel Marriott, who then boarded in Boston, was concerned in burning said buildings. Soon after the fire, said Marriott departed for New York. The plaintiffs declared to several persons their intention to pursue him and prosecute him, with the intention of gaining the reward of $1,000 which had been offered as aforesaid. They pursued said Marriott to New York, carried with them a person to identify him, arrested him, and brought him back to Boston. They then complained of him to the county attorney, obtained other witnesses, procured him to be indicted and prosecuted for setting fire to the said Amory House. And at the March term 1841 of the municipal court, on the apprehension and prosecution of said Marriott, and on the evidence given and procured by the plaintiffs, he was convicted of setting fire to said house, and sentenced to ten years' confinement in the state prison.

William Barnicoat, called as a witness by the defendants, testified that he was chief engineer of the fire department in Boston, in 1837, and for several years after; that alarms of fire were frequent before the said advertisement in May 1837; but that from that time till the close of the year 1841, there were but few fires in the city.

As the only question in the case was, whether said offer of reward continued to be in force when the Amory House was burnt, the case was taken from the jury, by consent of the parties, under an agreement that the defendants should be defaulted, or the plaintiffs become nonsuit, as the full court should decide.

SHAW, C.J. There is now no question of the correctness of the legal principle on which this action is founded. The offer of a reward for the detection of an offender, the recovery of property, and the like, is an offer or proposal, on the part of the person making it, to all persons, which anyone, capable of performing the service, may accept at any time before it is revoked, and perform the service; and such offer on one side, and acceptance and performance of the service on the other, is a valid contract made on good consideration, which the law will enforce.

The ground of defence is, that the advertisement, offering the reward of $1,000 for the detection and conviction of persons setting fire to buildings in the city, was issued almost four years before the time at which the plaintiffs arrested Marriott and prosecuted him to conviction; that this reward was so offered, in reference to a special emergency in consequence of several alarming fires; that the advertisement was withdrawn and discontinued; that the recollection of it has passed away; that it was obsolete, and by most persons forgotten; and that it could not be regarded as a perpetually continuing offer on the part of the city.

We are then first to look at the terms of the advertisement, to see what the offer was. It is competent to the party offering such reward to propose his own terms; and no person can entitle himself to the promised reward without a compliance with all its terms. The first advertisement offering the reward demanded in this action was published March 26th 1837, offering a reward of $500; and another on the day following, increasing it to $1,000. No time is inserted, in the notice, within which the service is to be done for which the reward is claimed. It is therefore relied on as an unlimited and continuing offer.

In the first place, it is to be considered that this is not an ordinance of the city government, of standing force and effect; it is an act temporary in its nature, emanating from the executive branch of the city government, done under the exigency of a special occasion indicated by its terms, and continued to be published but a short time. Although not limited in its terms, it is manifest, we think that it could not have been intended to be perpetual, or to last ten or twenty years, or more; and therefore must have been understood to have some limit. It was insisted, in the argument, that it had no limit but the statute of limitations. But it is obvious that the statute of limitations would not operate so as to make six years from the date of the offer a bar. The offer of a reward is a proposal made by one party, and does not become a contract, until acted upon by the performance of the service by the other, which is the acceptance of such offer, and constitutes the agreement of minds essential to a contract. The six years, therefore, would begin to run only from the time of the service performed and the cause of action accrued, which might be ten, twenty, or fifty years from the time of the offer, and would in fact leave the offer itself unlimited by time.

Supposing then that, by fair implication, there must be some limit to this offer, and there being no limit in terms, then by a general rule of law it must be limited to a *reasonable time,* that is, the service must be done within a reasonable time after the offer made.

What is a reasonable time, when all the facts and circumstances are proved on which it depends, is a question of law. To determine it, we are first to consider the objects and purposes for which such reward is offered. The principal object obviously must be, to awaken the attention of the public, to excite the vigilance and stimulate the exertions of police officers, watchmen and citizens generally, to the detection and punishment of offenders. Possibly, too, it may operate to prevent offences, by alarming the fears of those who are under temptation to commit them, by inspiring the belief that the public are awake, that any suspicious movement is watched, and that the crime cannot be committed with impunity. To accomplish either of these objects, such offer of a reward must be notorious, known and kept in mind by the public at large; and, for that purpose, the publication of the offer, if not actually continued in newspapers, and placarded at conspicuous places, must have been recent. After the lapse of years, and after the publication of the offer has been long discontinued, it must be presumed to be forgotten by the public generally, and if known at all, known only to a few individuals who may happen to meet with it in an old newspaper. The expectation of benefit, then, from such a promise of reward, must in a great measure have ceased. Indeed, every consideration arising from the nature of the case confirms the belief that such offer of reward, for a special service of this

Not unlimited

nature, is not unlimited and perpetual in its duration, but must be limited to some reasonable time. The difficulty is in fixing it. One circumstance, perhaps a slight one, is, that the act is done by a board of officers, who themselves are annual officers. But as they act for the city, which is a permanent body, and exercise its authority for the time being, and as such a reward might be offered near the end of the year, we cannot necessarily limit it to the time for which the same board of mayor and aldermen have to serve; though it tends to mark the distinction between a temporary act of one branch and a permanent act of the whole city government.

We have already alluded to the fact of the discontinuance of the advertisement, as one of some weight. It is some notice to the public that the exigency has passed, for which such offer of a reward was particularly intended. And though such discontinuance is not a revocation of the offer, it proves that those who made it no longer hold it forth conspicuously as a continuing offer; and it is not reasonable to regard it as a continuing offer for any considerable term of time afterwards.

But it is not necessary, perhaps not proper, to undertake to fix a precise time, as reasonable time; it must depend on many circumstances.

Court opinion

Under the circumstances of the present case, the court are of the opinion, that three years and eight months is not a reasonable time within which, or rather to the extent of which, the offer in question can be considered as a continuing offer on the part of the city. In that length of time, the exigency under which it was made having passed, it must be presumed to have been forgotten by most of the officers and citizens of the community, and cannot be presumed to have been before the public as an actuating motive to vigilance and exertion on this subject; nor could it justly and reasonably have been so understood by the plaintiffs. We are therefore of opinion, that the

No Contract

offer of the city had ceased before the plaintiffs accepted and acted upon it as such, and that consequently no contract existed upon which this action, founded on an alleged express promise, can be maintained.

QUESTION

If the reward had been for information leading to the arrest of the person setting *one particular fire,* would the statute of limitations for the criminal prosecution have been relevant? See In re Stephen Kelly, 39 Conn. 159 (1872).

Problem 22

Outraged at being robbed, Octopus National Bank put up a poster in its lobby offering a $500 reward to anyone furnishing information leading to the arrest of the individual who had stolen $80,000 at gunpoint in late 2019. The poster (24′ × 24′) stayed up until early 2021, when a bank employee took it down.

(a) If the robber is caught five minutes later in another part of town by someone who had seen the bank's poster, is Octopus National bound in contract?

(b) If the bank had also advertised in the local newspaper, how would the bank revoke the offer on January 1, 2021? Shuey v. United States, 92 U.S. 73 (1875).

(c) Assume a revocation-of-reward poster went up in January 2021. Would the reward offer be revoked by June of that year? December 2021? February 2022? February 2023? See Carr v. Mahaska County Bankers Ass'n, 222 Iowa 411, 269 N.W. 494 (1936).

(d) To avoid this issue (and conserve the $500) what would you, the bank's attorney, advise it to do?

Problem 23

Alphonse and Gaston met on the street one day. Alphonse said, "I have long wanted to buy the painting you have hanging in your dining room. I offer you $800 for it." Gaston replied, "Well, I'm not sure I want to sell it. I'm very fond of that painting." The conversation drifted on to other matters, and eventually they shook hands and parted. The next day Gaston decided that he wasn't as fond of the painting as he was of having $800, so he phoned Alphonse and accepted the offer. The latter retorted that there was no deal and refused to pay the $800. If Gaston sues, who should win here? See Corbin on Contracts, supra, §36; Akers v. J. B. Sedberry, Inc., 39 Tenn. App. 633, 286 S.W.2d 617 (1955). If in the original conversation Alphonse had said, "I'll give you until tomorrow at noon to make up your mind," could Gaston have accepted the next day at 5:00 P.M.? At 1:00 P.M.? Would it make any difference if Alphonse were hard to find the next morning?

PHILLIPS v. MOOR
Supreme Judicial Court of Maine, 1880
71 Me. 78

BARROWS, J. Negotiations by letter, looking to the purchase by the defendant of a quantity of hay in the plaintiff's barn, had resulted in the pressing of the hay by the defendant's men, to be paid for at a certain rate if the terms of sale could not be agreed on; and in written invitations from plaintiff's guardian to defendant, to make an offer for the hay, in one of which he says: "If the price is satisfactory I will write you on receipt of it"; and in the other: "If your offer is satisfactory I shall accept it; if not, I will send you the money for pressing." Friday, June 14th, defendant made an examination of the hay after it had been pressed, and wrote to plaintiff's guardian, same day . . . "Will give $9.50 per ton, for all but three tons, and for that I will give $5.00." Plaintiff's guardian lived in Carmel, 14 miles from Bangor where defendant lived, and there is a daily mail communication each way between the two places. The card containing defendant's offer was mailed at Bangor, June 15, and probably received by plaintiff in regular course, about nine o'clock, A.M., that day. The plaintiff does not deny this, though he says he does not always go to the office, and the mail is sometimes carried by. Receiving no better offer, and being offered less by another dealer, on Thursday, June 20th, he went to Bangor, and there, not meeting the defendant, sent him through the post office a card, in which he says he was in hopes defendant would have paid him $10.00 for the best quality: "But you can take the hay at your offer, and when you get it hauled in, if you can pay the $10.00 I would like to have you do it, if the hay proves good enough for the price." Defendant received this card that night or the next morning, made no reply, and Sunday morning the hay was burnt in the barn. Shortly after, when the parties met, the plaintiff claimed the price of the hay and defendant denied his liability, and asserted a claim for the pressing. Hence this suit.

The guardian's acceptance of the defendant's offer was absolute and unconditional. It is not in any legal sense qualified by the expression of his hopes, as to what the defendant would have done, or what he would like to have him do, if the hay when hauled proved good enough. Aside from all this, the defendant was told that he could take the hay at his own offer. It seems to have been the intention and understanding of both the parties that the property should pass. The defendant does not deny what the guardian testifies he told him at their conference after the hay was burned, — that he had agreed with a man to haul the hay for sixty cents a ton. The guardian does not seem to have claimed any lien for the price, or to have expected payment until the hay should have been hauled by the defendant. But the defendant insists that the guardian's acceptance of his offer was not seasonable; that in the initiatory correspondence the guardian had in substance promised an immediate acceptance or rejection of such offer as he might make, and that the offer was not, in fact, accepted within a reasonable time.

If it be conceded that for want of a more prompt acceptance the defendant had the right to retract his offer, or to refuse to be bound by it when notified of its acceptance, still the defendant did not avail himself of such right. Two days elapsed before the fire after the defendant had actual notice that his offer was accepted, and he permitted the guardian to consider it sold, and made a bargain with a third party to haul it.

It is true that an offer, to be binding upon the party making it, must be accepted within a reasonable time. Peru v. Turner, 10 Maine, 185; but if the party to whom it is made, makes known his acceptance of it to the party making it, within any period which he could fairly have supposed to be reasonable, good faith requires the maker, if he intends to retract on account of the delay, to make known that intention promptly. If he does not, he must be regarded as waiving any objection to the acceptance as being too late.

[margin note: He never made his intentions known]

The question here is, — In whom was the property in the hay at the time of its destruction?

It is true, as remarked by the court, in Thompson v. Gould, 20 Pick. 139, that — "When there is an agreement for the sale and purchase of goods and chattels, and, after the agreement, and before the sale is completed, the property is destroyed by casualty, the loss must be borne by the vender, the property remaining vested in him at the time of its destruction." [Citations omitted.]

[margin note: If the sale was not completed, but the agreement was made — the vendor bears the loss]

But we think, that, under the circumstances here presented, the sale was completed, and the property vested in the vendee. The agreement was completed by the concurrent assent of both parties; Adams v. Lindsell, 1 Barn. & Ald. 681; Mactier v. Frith, 6 Wend. 103.

[margin note: Court thinks sale and agreement was completed]

In Dixon v. Yates, 5 Barn, & Adol. 313, Parke, J., remarks (E.C.L.R. vol. 27, p.92),:

> Where there is a sale of goods, generally no property in them passes till delivery, because until then the very goods sold are not ascertained; but when, by the contract itself the vender appropriates to the vendee a specific chattel, and the latter thereby agrees to take that specific chattel, and to pay the stipulated price, the parties are then in the same situation as they would be after a delivery of goods in pursuance of a general contract. The very appropriation of the chattel is equivalent to delivery by the vender, and the assent of the vendee to take the specific chattel and to pay the price is equivalent to his accepting possession. The effect of the contract, therefore, is to vest the property in the bargainee.

The omission to distinguish between general contracts for the sale of goods of a certain kind and contracts for the sale of specific articles, will account for any seeming confusion in the decisions. Chancellor Kent, 2 Com. 492, states the doctrine thus: "When the terms of sale are agreed on and the bargain is struck, and everything that the seller has to do with the goods is complete, the contract of sale becomes absolute without actual payment or delivery, and the property and risk of accident to the goods vest in the buyer." That doctrine was expressly approved by this court in Wing v. Clarke, 24 Maine, 366, 372, where its origin in the civil law is referred to. And this court went farther in Waldron v. Chase, 37 Maine, 414; and held that when the owner of a quantity of corn in bulk, sold a certain number of bushels therefrom and received his pay, and the vendee had taken away a part only, the property in the whole quantity sold, vested in the buyer, although it had not been measured and separated from the heap, and that it thenceforward remained in charge of the seller at the buyer's risk.

In the case at bar all the hay was sold. The quality had been ascertained by the defendant. The price was agreed on. The defendant had been told that he might take it and had nothing to do but to send the man whom he had engaged to haul it, and appropriate it to himself without any further act on the part of the seller.

NOTE ON THE RISK OF LOSS

At the time Phillips v. Moor was decided, the risk of loss concerning the sale of goods was on the person having *title* ("property") to the goods at the time of their destruction. Under §2-509(3) of the UCC, title is no longer important—see §2-401—and risk of loss is generally determined by other factors such as possession or the parties' agreement.

What point does this case make about late acceptances? According to the Restatement (Second) of Contracts §70, "[a] late or otherwise defective acceptance may be effective as an offer to the original offeror, but his silence operates as an acceptance in such a case only as stated in §69." (Section 69 (dealing with "silence as acceptance") is reprinted above.) Do these sections codify the part of the *Phillips* decision concerning the effect of a late acceptance?

E.   Termination by Death or Incapacity of the Offeror or Offeree

RESTATEMENT (SECOND) OF CONTRACTS

§48. DEATH OR INCAPACITY OF OFFEROR OR OFFEREE

An offeree's power of acceptance is terminated when the offeree or offeror dies or is deprived of legal capacity to enter into the proposed contract.

Problem 24

When Scrooge's nephew Donald opened an animal feed store, he entered into a contract to buy needed inventory on a continuing basis from Fantasia Feeds, agreeing to pay for each shipment within 60 days after receiving it. Before Fantasia Feeds signed the contract with Donald, it insisted he get a guarantor for his payment liabilities, so Donald's Uncle Scrooge signed such a guaranty. It contained a clause providing that Scrooge would guarantee the repayment of all shipments made to Donald until Scrooge sent Fantasia Feeds a notice cancelling this undertaking. Two years later Scrooge suddenly died, but Fantasia Feeds, unaware of his demise, continued to make shipments to his nephew. Is Scrooge's estate still liable on its guaranty for these shipments if Donald fails to make payment? Do we get the same result if Scrooge did not die, but instead underwent a court proceeding declaring him incompetent to conduct his affairs? See Swift & Co. v. Smigel, 115 N.J. Super. 391, 279 A.2d 895, aff'd, 60 N.J. 348, 289 A.2d 793 (N. J. App. 1972).

F.   *Termination by Rejection*

RESTATEMENT (SECOND) OF CONTRACTS

§38. REJECTION

(1) An offeree's power of acceptance is terminated by his rejection of the offer, unless the offeror has manifested a contrary intention.

(2) A manifestation of intention not to accept an offer is a rejection unless the offeree manifests an intention to take it under further advisement.

Problem 25

Zorba wrote Nikos and offered to be his guide for a summer tour of Greece, stating a price for his services and adding that he would leave this offer open until April 30. On April 9, Nikos wrote back that he was "not interested," but the next day his plans changed and he decided to take the tour. He immediately wrote Zorba and accepted the offer. Zorba, however, was outraged by the first letter and refused to act as Nikos's guide. Nikos consults you. Does he have a contract or not?

Would your answer change if Nikos had purchased an option that allowed him to retain Zorba's services at a fixed price until April 30? Ryder v. Wescoat, 535 S.W.2d 269 (Mo. Ct. App. 1976).

Assuming there was no binding option, if Nikos had replied that he would employ Zorba, but at a lower price than Zorba proposed, would this counteroffer also be a rejection and terminate his power of acceptance?

If Nikos responds that he is considering Zorba's offer, but in the mean-time would like to propose that the tour include Turkey as well as Greece, with an appropriate adjustment in the price of Zorba's services, is this counteroffer also a rejection?

G.   The "Mail Box" Rule

MORRISON v. THOELKE
District Court of Appeals of Florida, Second District, 1963
155 So. 2d 889

ALLEN, Acting Chief Judge. Appellants, defendants and counter-plaintiffs in the lower court, appeal a summary final decree for appellees, plaintiffs and counter-defendants below. The plaintiff-appellees, owners of certain realty, sued to quiet title, specifically requesting that defendant-appellants be enjoined from making any claim under a recorded contract for the sale of the subject realty. Defendant-appellants counterclaimed, seeking specific performance of the same contract and conveyance of the subject property to them. The lower court, after hearing, entered a summary decree for plaintiffs.

A number of undisputed facts were established by the pleadings, including the facts that appellees are the owners of the subject property, located in Orange County; that on November 26, 1957, appellants, as purchasers, executed a contract for the sale and purchase of the subject property and mailed the contract to appellees who were in Texas; and that on November 27, 1957, appellees executed the contract and placed it in the mails addressed to appellants' attorney in Florida. It is also undisputed that after mailing said contract, but prior to its receipt in Florida, appellees called appellants' attorney and cancelled and repudiated the execution and contract. Nonetheless, appellants, upon receipt of the contract caused the same to be recorded. . . .

In appealing the summary decree the appellants argue that the lower court erred in determining the contract void. . . . The question is whether a contract is complete and binding when a letter of acceptance is mailed, thus barring repudiation prior to delivery to the offeror, or when the letter of acceptance is received, thus permitting repudiation prior to receipt. Appellants, of course, argue that posting the acceptance creates the contract; appellees contend that only receipt of the acceptance bars repudiation. . . .

The appellant, in arguing that the lower court erred in giving effect to the repudiation of the mailed acceptance, contends that this case is controlled by the general rule that insofar as the mail is an acceptable medium of communication, a contract is complete and binding upon posting of the letter of acceptance. [Citations omitted.] Appellees, on the other hand, argue that the right to recall mail makes the Post Office Department the agent of the sender, and that such right coupled with communication of a renunciation prior to receipt of the acceptance voids the acceptance. In short, appellees argue that acceptance is complete only upon receipt of the mailed acceptance. They rely, inter alia, on Rhode Island Tool Company v. United States, 128 F. Supp. 417, 130 Ct. Cl. 698 (1955) and Dick v. United States, 82 F. Supp. 326, 113 Ct. Cl. 94 (1949).

Appellees Argues only complete upon receipt

Turning first to the general rule relied upon by appellant some insight may be gained by reference to the statement of the rule in leading encyclopedias and treatises. . . .

A . . . statement of the general rule is found in 1 Williston, Contracts §81 (3d ed. 1957):

> Contracts are frequently made between parties at some distance and therefore it is of vital importance to determine at what moment the contract is complete. . . .
>
> It was early decided that the contract was completed upon the mailing of the acceptance. The reason influencing the court was evidently that when the acceptance was mailed, there had been an overt manifestation of assent to the proposal. The court failed to consider that since the proposed contract was bilateral, as is almost invariably any contract made by mail, the so-called acceptance must also have become effective as a promise to the offeror in order to create a contract. The result thus early reached, however, has definitely established the law not only in England but also in the United States, Canada and other common law jurisdictions. It is, therefore, immaterial that the acceptance never reaches its destination.

. . . A second leading treatise on the law of contracts, Corbin, Contracts §§78 and 80 (1950 Supp. 1961), also devotes some discussion to the "rule" urged by appellants. Corbin writes:

> Where the parties are negotiating at a distance from each other, the most common method of making an offer is by sending it by mail; and more often than not the offeror has specified no particular mode of acceptance. In such a case, it is now the prevailing rule that the offeree has power to accept and close the contract by mailing a letter of acceptance, properly stamped and addressed, within a reasonable time. The contract is regarded as made at the time and place that the letter of acceptance is put into the possession of the post office department.

Like the editor of Williston, Corbin negates the effect of the offeree's power to recall his letter:

> The postal regulations have for a long period made it possible for the sender of a letter to intercept it and prevent its delivery to the addressee. This has caused some doubt to be expressed as to whether an acceptance can ever

be operative upon the mere mailing of the letter, since the delivery to the post office has not put it entirely beyond the sender's control.

It is believed that no such doubt should exist. . . . In view of common practices, in view of the difficulties involved in the process of interception of a letter, and in view of the decisions and printed discussions dealing with acceptance by post, it is believed that the fact that a letter can be lawfully intercepted by the sender should not prevent the acceptance from being operative on mailing. If the offer was made under such circumstances that the offeror should know that the offeree might reasonably regard this as a proper method of closing the deal, and the offeree does so regard it, and makes use of it, the contract is consummated even though the letter of acceptance is intercepted and not delivered. . . .

The rule that a contract is complete upon deposit of the acceptance in the mails, hereinbefore referred to as "deposited acceptance rule" and also known as the "rule in Adams v. Lindsell," had its origin, insofar as the common law is concerned, in Adams v. Lindsell, 1 Barn. & Ald. 681, 106 Eng. Rep. 250 (K.B. 1818). In that case, the defendants had sent an offer to plaintiffs on September 2nd, indicating that they expected an answer "in course of post." The offer was misdirected and was not received and accepted until the 5th, the acceptance being mailed that day and received by defendant-offerors on the 9th. However, the defendants, who had expected to receive the acceptance on or before the 7th, sold the goods offered on the 8th of September. It was conceded that the delay had been occasioned by the fault of the defendants in initially misdirecting the offer.

Defendants contended that no contract had been made until receipt of the offer on the 9th. . . .

Examination of the decision in Adams v. Lindsell reveals three distinct factors deserving consideration. The first and most significant is the court's obvious concern with the necessity of drawing a line, with establishing some point at which a contract is deemed complete and their equally obvious concern with the thought that if communication of each party's assent were necessary, the negotiations would be interminable. A second factor, again a practical one, was the court's apparent desire to limit but not over-rule the decision in Cooke v. Oxley, 3 T.R. 653 [1790] that an offer was revocable at any time prior to acceptance. In application to contracts nego-tiated by mail, this latter rule would permit revocation even after unqualified assent unless the assent was deemed effective upon posting. Finally, having chosen a point at which negotiations would terminate and having effectively circumvented the inequities of Cooke v. Oxley, the court, apparently con-strained to offer some theoretical justification for its decision, designated a mailed offer as "continuing" and found a meeting of the minds upon the instant of posting assent. Significantly, the factor of the offeree's loss of control of his acceptance is not mentioned. . . .

The unjustified significance placed on the "loss of control" in the cases relied upon by appellee follows from two errors. The first error is failure to distinguish between relinquishment of control as a factual element of manifest intent, which it is, and as *the* legal predicate for completion of contract, which it is not. The second error lies in confusing the "right" to recall mail with the "power" to recall mail. Under current postal regulations, the sender has the "power" to regain a letter, but this does not necessarily give him the "right" to repudiate acceptance. The existence of the latter right is a matter of contract law and is determinable by reference to factors which include, but are not limited to the existence of the power to recall mail. In short, the power to recall mail is a factor, among many others, which may be significant in determining when an acceptance is effective, but the right to effectively withdraw and repudiate an acceptance must be dependent upon the initial determination of when the acceptance is effective and irrevocable.

From the foregoing it is clear that a change in postal regulations does not, ipso facto, alter or affect the validity of the rule in Adams v. Lindsell. To the extent that the cases relied upon by appellee mistakenly assumed that "loss of control" and "agency" were determinative of the validity of the rule they are not authority for rejecting the rule. Rather, the adoption of the rule in this jurisdiction must turn on an evaluation of its justifications, quite apart from the fallacious theories of agency and control sometimes advanced in its support. . . .

The justification for the "deposited acceptance" rule proceeds from the uncontested premise of Adams v. Lindsell that there must be, both in practical and conceptual terms, a point in time when a contract is complete. In the formation of contracts *inter praesentes* this point is readily reached upon expressions of assent instantaneously communicated. In the formation of contracts *inter absentes* by post, however, delay in communication prevents concurrent knowledge of assents and some point must be chosen as legally significant. The problem raised by the impossibility of concurrent knowledge of manifest assent is discussed and a justification for the traditional rule is offered in Corbin, Contracts §78 (1950).

> A better explanation of the existing rule seems to be that in such cases the mailing of a letter has long been a customary and expected way of accepting the offer. It is ordinary business usage. More than this, however, is needed to explain why the letter is operative on mailing rather than on receipt by the offeror. Even though it is business usage to send an offer by mail, it creates no power of acceptance until it is received. Indeed, most notices sent by mail are not operative unless actually received.
>
> The additional reasons for holding that a different rule applies to an acceptance and that it is operative on mailing may be suggested as follows: When an offer is by mail and the acceptance also is by mail, the contract must date either from the mailing of the acceptance or from its receipt. In either

case, one of the parties will be bound by the contract without being actually aware of that fact. If we hold the offeror bound on the mailing of the acceptance, he may change his position in ignorance of the acceptance; even though he waits a reasonable time before acting, he may still remain unaware that he is bound by contract because the letter of acceptance is delayed, or is actually lost or destroyed, in the mails. Therefore this rule is going to cause loss and inconvenience to the offeror in some cases. But if we adopt the alternative rule that the letter of acceptance is not operative until receipt, it is the offeree who is subjected to the danger of loss and inconvenience. He can not know that his letter has been received and that he is bound by contract until a new communication is received by him. His letter of acceptance may never have been received and so no letter of notification is sent to him; or it may have been received, and the letter of notification may be delayed or entirely lost in the mails. One of the parties must carry the risk of loss and inconvenience. We need a definite and uniform rule as to this. We can choose either rule; but we must choose one. We can put the risk on either party; but we must not leave it in doubt. The party not carrying the risk can then act promptly and with confidence in reliance on the contract; the party carrying the risk can insure against it if he so desires. The business community could no doubt adjust itself to either rule; but the rule throwing the risk on the offeror has the merit of closing the deal more quickly and enabling performance more promptly. It must be remembered that in the vast majority of cases the acceptance is neither lost nor delayed; and promptness of action is of importance in all of them. Also it is the offeror who has invited the acceptance. . . .

Opponents of the rule argue as forcefully that all of the disadvantages of delay or loss in communication which would potentially harm the offeree are equally harmful to the offeror. Why, they ask, should the offeror be bound by an acceptance of which he has no knowledge? Arguing specific cases, opponents of the rule point to the inequity of forbidding the offeror to withdraw his offer after the acceptance was posted but before he had any knowledge that the offer was accepted; they argue that to forbid the offeree to withdraw his acceptance, as in the instant case, scant hours after it was posted but days before the offeror knew of it, is unjust and indefensible. Too, the opponents argue, the offeree can always prevent the revocation of an offer by providing consideration, by buying an option.

In short, both advocates and critics muster persuasive argument. As Corbin indicated, there must be a choice made, and such choice may, by the nature of things, seem unjust in some cases. Weighing the arguments with reference not to specific cases but toward a rule of general application and recognizing the general and traditional acceptance of the rule as well as the modern changes in effective long-distance communication, it would seem that the balance tips, whether heavily or near imperceptively, to continued adherence to the "Rule in Adams v. Lindsell." This rule, although not entirely compatible with ordered, consistent and sometime artificial principles of contract advanced by some theorists, is, in our view, in accord with the practical considerations and essential concepts of contract law. See Llewellyn, Our Case Law of Contracts; Offer and Acceptance II, 48 Yale L.J. 779, 795 (1939). Outmoded precedents may, on occasion, be discarded and the function of justice should not be the perpetuation of error, but, by the same token, traditional rules and concepts should not be abandoned save on compelling ground.

In choosing to align this jurisdiction with those adhering to the deposited acceptance rule, we adopt a view contrary to that of the very able judge below, contrary to the decisions of other respected courts and possibly contrary to the decision which might have been reached had this case been heard in a sister court in this State. However, we are constrained by *hute* factors hereinbefore discussed to hold that an acceptance is effective upon mailing and not upon receipt. Necessarily this decision is limited in any prospective application to circumstances involving the mails and does not purport to determine the rule possibly applicable to cases involving other modern methods of communication. [Citations omitted.]

In the instant case, an unqualified offer was accepted and the acceptance made manifest. Later, the offerees sought to repudiate their initial assent. Had there been a delay in their determination to repudiate permitting the letter to be delivered to appellant, no question as to the invalidity of the repudiation would have been entertained. As it were, the repudiation antedated receipt of the letter. However, adopting the view that the acceptance was effective when the letter of acceptance was deposited in the mails, the repudiation was equally invalid and cannot alone support the summary decree for appellees.

The summary decree is reversed and the cause remanded for further proceedings.

Problem 26

(1) By mail, Phillip offered to buy 300 dwarf apple tree saplings from Mildred, adding that the offer would remain open until midnight of August 21. Mildred wrote a letter of acceptance to Phillip. The letter was properly addressed and mailed, but Phillip never received the letter. Three weeks later, Mildred called Phillip and was told that there was no contract. Was there an acceptance?

(2) If Phillip had hand delivered the original offer to Mildred, would her mailed acceptance have created a contract on dispatch?

(3) What is the result with this sequence:

(a) On August 1, Phillip mailed his offer, but on August 2, he changed his mind and mailed her a revocation of the offer.

(b) On August 4, Mildred received the offer and the next morning she posted a written acceptance. Later that same day, she received his second letter. Does she have a contract?

(4) Consider this variation:

(a) On August 1, Phillip mailed his offer and Mildred received it on August 4.

(b) On August 5, Mildred mailed her acceptance, but later that day changed her mind and phoned Phillip, telling him she was rejecting. She did not mention her en route letter.

(c) Phillip immediately contracted with someone else to purchase the 300 dwarf apple seedlings. The next day he received her letter of acceptance, but threw it away.

(d) Mildred changed her mind again and now wants to sell the seedlings to Phillip. Her attorney points to Morrison v. Thoelke (the last case) and argues that there is a contract. Is Phillip bound?

(5) In (1) above, what is the result if Phillip's offer had stated, "If I do not receive a written reply from you by August 21, I will assume you do not accept"? See Restatement (Second) of Contracts §63(a) and comment b, and American Heritage Life Ins. Co. v. Virginia Koch, 721 S.W.2d 611 (Tex. App. 1986).

(6) What if the acceptance letter Mildred sent had the correct address for Phillip, but had the zip code wrong by one digit? Would her acceptance be effective on mailing? See Phillips Exploration, Inc. v. Tomich, 2013 WL 3983643 (S.D. Ohio 2013).

NOTE ON THE MAIL BOX RULE AND OPTION CONTRACTS

When an offeree tries to accept an offer under an option contract or a firm offer, the mail box rule does *not* apply. The acceptance must be *received* within the option period to be effective. See Restatement (Second) of Contracts §63(b); River Development Corp. v. Slemmer, 781 S.W.2d 525 (Ky. Ct. App. 1989).

NOTE ON OFFERS IN INTERNATIONAL SALES

Under the United Nations Convention on Contracts for the International Sale of Goods, the mail box rule (acceptance effective on dispatch) is altered. In international sales to which the treaty applies, an acceptance is not effective until *received* (Article 18(2)). However, the offeror is not permitted to revoke an offer once the acceptance has been dispatched (Article 16(1)), thus effectively reaching the same result as American law.

H. Termination by Counteroffer and the "Battle of the Forms"

As we mentioned in the Introduction to this book, one of the most important distinctions in contract law is whether the common law or the UCC governs a transaction. This choice is particularly important in the following common situation: One party makes an offer, and the other party responds with a document that claims to accept the offer *but changes its terms.* Under the common law, the analysis is straightforward. Under what is known as the "mirror image rule," an acceptance must *mirror* the offer exactly. Adding or deleting any terms makes a reply to the offer *not* an acceptance, but a *counteroffer.* See Restatement (Second) of Contracts §§36(1)(a), 37. However, UCC §2-207 abandons the mirror image rule and adopts a much more nuanced approach.

1. The Common Law

PRINCESS CRUISE LINES, INC. v. GENERAL ELECTRIC CO.
United States Court of Appeals, Fourth Circuit, 1998
143 F.3d 828

Goodwin, District Judge:

This suit arises out of a contract between General Electric Company (GE) and Princess Cruises, Inc. (Princess) for inspection and repair services relating to Princess's cruise ship, the SS Sky Princess. In January 1997, a jury found GE liable for breach of contract and awarded Princess $4,577,743.00 in damages. On appeal, GE contends that the district court erred in denying its renewed motion for judgment as a matter of law, which requested that the court vacate the jury's award of incidental and consequential damages. Specifically, GE argues that the district court erroneously applied Uniform Commercial Code principles, rather than common-law principles, to a contract primarily for services. We agree and hold that when the predominant purpose of a contract is the rendering of services rather than the furnishing of goods, the U.C.C. is inapplicable, and courts must draw on common-law doctrines when interpreting the contract. Accordingly, we reverse the district court's decision denying GE's renewed motion for judgment as a matter of law and remand for modification of the judgment consistent with this opinion.

I. FACTUAL BACKGROUND

Princess scheduled the SS Sky Princess for routine inspection services and repairs in December 1994 and requested that GE, the original manufacturer of the ship's main turbines, perform services and provide parts incidental to the ship's inspection and repair. Princess issued a Purchase Order in October 1994. The Purchase Order included a proposed contract price of $260,000.00 and contained a brief description of services to be performed by GE. The reverse side of the Purchase Order listed terms and conditions which indicated that Princess intended the Purchase Order to be an offer. These terms and conditions also stated that GE could accept the Purchase Order through acknowledgment or performance; that the terms and conditions could not be changed unilaterally; and that GE would provide a warranty of workmanlike quality and fitness for the use intended.

On the same day that GE received the Purchase Order, GE faxed a Fixed Price Quotation to Princess. The Fixed Price Quotation provided a more detailed work description than Princess's Purchase Order and included a parts and materials list, an offering price of $201,888.00, and GE's own terms and conditions. When GE reviewed Princess's Purchase Order, it discovered that Princess requested work not contemplated by GE in its Fixed Price Quotation. GE notified Princess of GE's error. On October 28, 1994, GE faxed a Final Price Quotation to Princess. In the Final Price Quotation, GE offered to provide all services, labor, and materials for $231,925.00. Attached to both GE Quotations were GE's terms and conditions, which: (1) rejected the terms and conditions set forth in Princess's Purchase Order; (2) rejected liquidated damages; (3) limited GE's liability to repair or replacement of any defective goods or damaged equipment resulting from defective service, exclusive of all written, oral, implied, or statutory warranties; (4) limited GE's liability on any claims to not more than the greater of either $5000.00 or the contract price; and (5) disclaimed any liability for consequential damages, lost profits, or lost revenue. During an October 31, 1994 telephone call, Princess gave GE permission to proceed based on the price set forth in GE's Final Price Quotation.

On November 1, 1994, GE sent a confirmatory letter to Princess acknowledging receipt of Princess's Purchase Order and expressing GE's intent to perform the services. The letter also restated GE's $231,925.00 offering price from its Final Price Quotation and specified that GE's terms and conditions, attached to the letter, were to govern the contract.

When the SS Sky Princess arrived for inspection, GE noted surface rust on the rotor and recommended that it be taken ashore for cleaning and balancing. The parties agree that during the cleaning, good metal was removed from the rotor, rendering the rotor unbalanced. Although GE attempted to correct the imbalance, Princess canceled a ten-day Christmas cruise as a result of delays caused by the repair. At trial, Princess alleged that the continued vibration and high temperatures caused damage to the ship, forcing additional repairs and the cancellation of a ten-day Easter cruise. It was undisputed, however, that Princess paid GE the full amount of the contract: $231,925.00.

On April 22, 1996, Princess filed a four-count complaint against GE, alleging breach of contract, breach of express warranty, breach of implied maritime warranty, and negligence. The district court granted GE's motion for summary judgment as to the negligence claim. Following Princess's presentation of evidence at trial, GE made a motion for judgment as a matter of law, which the district court denied. At the conclusion of the defendant's presentation of evidence, the district court denied GE's second motion for judgment as a matter of law. In instructing the jury, the district court drew on principles set forth in U.C.C. §2-207 and allowed the jury to imply the following terms as part of the contract: (1) the warranty of merchantability; (2) the warranty of fitness for a particular purpose; (3) the warranty of workmanlike performance; (4) Princess's right to recover damages for GE's alleged breach of the contact; and (5) Princess's right to recover incidental and consequential damages, as well as lost profits, proximately caused by GE's alleged breach. On January 24, 1997, the jury returned a $4,577,743.00 verdict in favor of Princess. On February 3, 1997, GE renewed its motion for judgment as a matter of law requesting that the court vacate the jury's award of incidental and consequential damages. The district court heard oral argument on May 6, 1997. Following oral argument, the district court denied GE's renewed motion for judgment as a matter of law and issued an opinion clarifying its ruling.

[The court held that even though the contract fell under maritime law, the same principles that governed land-based contracts would control the choice between the common law and the UCC.]

THE GE-PRINCESS CONTRACT WAS PREDOMINANTLY FOR SERVICES

Although the U.C.C. governs the sale of goods, the U.C.C. also applies to certain mixed contracts for goods and services. Whether a particular transaction is governed by the U.C.C., rather than the common law or other statutory law, hinges on the predominant purpose of the transaction, that is, whether the contract primarily concerns the furnishing of goods or the rendering of services. See *Coakley & Williams*, 706 F.2d at 458 ("Whether the U.C.C. applies turns on a question as to whether the contract . . . involved principally a sale of goods, on the one hand, or a provision of services, on the other."). Thus, before applying the U.C.C., courts generally examine the transaction to determine whether the sale of goods predominates. See *Coakley & Williams*, 706 F.2d at 458. Because the facts in this case are sufficiently developed and undisputed, it is proper for the Court to determine on appeal whether the GE-Princess transaction was a contract for the sale of goods within the scope of the U.C.C.

In determining whether goods or services predominate in a particular transaction, we are guided by the seminal case of Bonebrake v. Cox, 499 F.2d 951 (8th Cir. 1974). In holding the U.C.C. applicable, the Bonebrake court stated:

> The test for inclusion or exclusion is not whether they are mixed but, granting that they are mixed, whether their pre dominant factor, their thrust, their purpose, reasonably stated, is the rendition of service, with goods incidentally involved (e.g., contract with artist for painting) or is a transaction of sale, with labor incidentally involved (e.g., installation of a water heater in a bathroom).

Bonebrake, 499 F.2d at 960. The Fourth Circuit has deemed the following factors significant in determining the nature of the contract: (1) the language of the contract, (2) the nature of the business of the supplier, and (3) the intrinsic worth of the materials. See *Coakley & Williams*, 706 F.2d at 460 (applying Maryland law).

It is plain that the GE-Princess transaction principally concerned the rendering of services, specifically, the routine inspection and repair of the SS Sky Princess, with incidental — albeit expensive — parts supplied by GE. Although Princess's standard fine-print terms and conditions mention the sale of goods, Princess's actual purchase description requests a GE "service engineer" to perform service functions: the opening of valves for survey and the inspection of the ship's port main turbine. GE's Final Price Quotation also contemplates service functions, stating in large print on every page that it is a "Quotation for Services." The Final Price Quotation's first page notes that GE is offering a quotation for "engineering services." GE's Quotation further specifies that the particular type of service offered is "Installation/Repair/Maintenance." The Final Price Quotation then lists the scope of the contemplated work — opening, checking, cleaning, inspecting, disassembling — in short, service functions. Although GE's materials list shows that GE planned to manufacture a small number of parts for Princess, Princess appeared to have had most of the needed materials onboard. Thus, the language of both the Purchase Order and the Final Price Quotation indicates that although GE planned to supply certain parts, the parts were incidental to the contract's predominant purpose, which was inspection, repair, and maintenance services.

As to the second Coakley factor — the nature of the business of the supplier — although GE is known to manufacture goods, GE's correspondence and Quotations came from GE's Installation and Service Engineering Department. Evidence at trial showed that GE's Installation and Service Engineering division is comprised of twenty-seven field engineers who perform service functions, such as overhauls and repairs. Finally, the last Coakley factor — the intrinsic worth of the materials supplied — cannot be determined because neither Princess's Purchase Order nor GE's Final Price Quotation separately itemized the value of the materials. Instead, both the Purchase Order and the Final Price Quotation blend the cost of the materials into the final price of a services contract, thereby confirming that services rather than materials predominated in the transaction. Although not a Coakley factor, it is also telling that, during oral argument, Princess's counsel admitted that the gravamen of Princess's complaint did not arise out of GE's furnishing of deficient parts, but rather out of GE's deficient services. Accordingly, we find as a matter of law that services rather than goods predominated in the GE-Princess contract.

UNDER COMMON LAW, GE'S FINAL PRICE QUOTATION WAS A COUNTEROFFER ACCEPTED BY PRINCESS

Under the common law, an acceptance that varies the terms of the offer is a counteroffer which rejects the original offer. Restatement (Second) of Contracts §59 (1981) ("A reply to an offer which purports to accept it but is conditional on the offeror's assent to terms additional to or different from those offered is not an acceptance but is a counter-offer."). Virginia follows the same rule. See Chang v. First Colonial Savs. Bank, 242 Va. 388, 410 S.E.2d 928, 931 (1991). Here, GE's Final Price Quotation materially altered the terms of Princess's Purchase Order by offering a different price, limiting damages and liability, and excluding warranties. Thus, GE's Final Price Quotation was a counteroffer rejecting Princess's Purchase Order. Although Princess could have rejected GE's counteroffer, Princess accepted the Final Price Quotation by giving GE permission to proceed with the repair and maintenance services, by not objecting to the confirmatory letter sent by GE, and by paying the amount set forth in GE's Final Price Quotation, $231,925.00, rather than the $260,000.00 price term set forth in Princess's Purchase Order. At common law, an offeror who proceeds under a contract after receiving the counteroffer can accept the terms of the counteroffer by performance. Although GE and Princess never discussed the Purchase Order's and the Final Price Quotation's conflicting terms and conditions, both Princess's actions and inaction gave GE every reason to believe that Princess assented to the terms and conditions set forth in GE's Final Price Quotation. See Restatement (Second) of Contracts §19(1) (1981) ("The manifestation of assent may be made wholly or partly by written or spoken words or by other acts or by failure to act."). Accordingly, we find that the terms and conditions of GE's Final Price Quotation control liability and damages in the GE-Princess transaction.

THE VERDICT DEMONSTRATES THAT THE JURY IMPERMISSIBLY RELIED ON A CONTRACT OTHER THAN GE'S FINAL PRICE QUOTATION

For the reasons stated above, the jury could only have considered one contract in awarding damages: GE's Final Price Quotation. The Quotation restricted damages to the contract price, $231,925.00, and eliminated liability for incidental or consequential damages and lost profits or revenue. Moreover, GE's Final Price Quotation controlled the warranties available to its customers. Yet the jury awarded $4,577,743.00 in damages to Princess. This verdict demonstrates that the jury relied on Princess's Purchase Order or some other contract when awarding damages. As a matter of law, the jury could only have awarded damages consistent with the terms and conditions of GE's Final Price Quotation and could not have awarded incidental or consequential damages. By requesting that the Court award Princess the maximum amount available under the Final Price Quotation, GE concedes that it breached its contract with Princess and that damages consistent with its Final Price Quotation are appropriate. Accordingly, we find it unnecessary to remand for a new trial on this issue. We reverse the district court's decision denying GE's motion for judgment as a matter of law and remand for entry of judgment against GE in the amount of $231,925.00, interest to accumulate from the date of the original judgment.

REVERSED AND REMANDED.

Problem 27

Assume that Gandalf, a prestidigitator, offers to perform magic tricks for an extravaganza put on by Frodo, an impresario, for $3,000. Frodo replies, "I accept, but I plan to videotape your performance and show it monthly thereafter at park concerts." Is there a contract? If Gandalf says nothing, but does perform and is videotaped, can he later object to the monthly showings? What if, instead of the above, Frodo had replied, "I agree to pay you $3,000, but you must be sober during the performance." Is this a counteroffer?

2.   The Uniform Commercial Code

The UCC tries to deal with the problem of purported "acceptances" that deviate from the terms of the offer (as well as a few other, similar issues) in §2-207. It is no exaggeration to say that §2-207 is a rite of passage for law students. Read it and you'll see why.

UNIFORM COMMERCIAL CODE

§2-207. ADDITIONAL TERMS IN ACCEPTANCE OR CONFIRMATION

(1) A definite and seasonable expression of acceptance or a written confirmation which is sent within a reasonable time operates as an acceptance even though it states terms additional to or different from those

offered or agreed upon, unless acceptance is expressly made conditional on assent to the additional or different terms.

(2) The additional terms are to be construed as proposals for addition to the contract. Between merchants such terms become part of the contract unless:

(a) the offer expressly limits acceptance to the terms of the offer;

(b) they materially alter it; or

(c) notification of objection to them has already been given or is given within a reasonable time after notice of them is received.

(3) Conduct by both parties which recognizes the existence of a contract is sufficient to establish a contract for sale although the writings of the parties do not otherwise establish a contract. In such case the terms of the particular contract consist of those terms on which the writings of the parties agree, together with any supplementary terms incorporated under any other provisions of this Act.

Section 2-207 governs a situation that is known as the "battle of the forms." Buyers and sellers often have their lawyers create standard sales contracts for all of their transactions. Good attorneys will try to make these documents as favorable as possible to their clients. (Although disputes rarely arise, it's always good to plan for the worst.) Thus, in many deals, Party A sends its self-serving form to Party B, which responds with its own self-serving form. Princess Cruise Lines v. GE reveals how the common law treats this scenario. Under the mirror image rule, Party A's form is an offer, and Party B's form adds new or different terms and thus is a counteroffer. If, as in Princess Cruise Lines v. General Electric, the parties then perform, Party A has accepted Party B's counteroffer by conduct, and the parties have a contract that consists entirely of Party B's form. [*common law rule*]

Section 2-207 changes this result. It provides that a reply to an offer *can* be an acceptance even though its terms deviate from the terms of the offer. Section 2-207(1) helps us determine *whether* a reply to an offer with additional or different terms *is* an acceptance. It declares that such a reply is an acceptance provided that it is (1) seasonable (meaning timely), (2) a definite expression of acceptance (meaning that it doesn't drastically change the offer), and (3) the reply to the offer doesn't say "this acceptance is expressly conditioned on your assent to our additional or different terms." This third element — the "expressly conditioned" language — is known as the "proviso." It permits the party who is replying to the offer to clarify that the party is not willing to accept the offeror's terms. [*2-207 (1)*]

However, if the reply to the offer does qualify as an acceptance, §2-207(2) tells us what to do with "additional terms." (We deal with "different terms" below.) According to §2-207(2), additional terms become [*2-207 (2)*] part of the contract if (1) both parties are merchants, (2) the offer doesn't express limit acceptance to its terms, (3) the additional terms don't "materially alter" the offer,* and (4) the offeror hasn't objected to them or doesn't object to them within a reasonable time.

If the reply to the offer *doesn't* qualify as an acceptance, then it's a counteroffer. Like any counteroffer, it can simply never be accepted, which means that the parties don't have a contract. But if the parties then perform (as in *Princess Cruise Lines*), §2-207 departs from the common law by stating that the contract only "consist[s] of those terms on which the writings of the parties agree." Can you see why the district court in *Princess Cruise Lines*—which applied the UCC, not the common law—held that GE's liability limitations were *not* part of the contract?

[handwritten margin note: Yes. acceptance was Not made conditional on the additional terms. And mate was No Further Discussion between parties~ silence acted as acceptance]

[handwritten margin note: or]

Problem 28

After some preliminary negotiations over the telephone, the purchasing agent of the Galsworthy Oil Company sent off the usual company purchase order to the Forsyte Shipbuilding firm for the purchase of a $100,000 tugboat, the price quoted in the phone conversation. On receiving this, the sales agent of Forsyte Shipbuilding sent off the usual company sales acknowledgment slip, which included the following clause: "Seller does not warrant its goods in any way, and specifically disclaims any warranty of MERCHANTABILITY or of fitness." No further discussion was had by the parties. The seller shipped the tugboat, and the buyer used it for two days before it broke apart and sank due to a manufacturing defect. Is the seller's disclaimer of warranty liability (generally permitted by the UCC if the seller uses the above language) effective here?

[handwritten margin note: It between merchants. Yes, under 2-207(2)(a) The contract is between merchants and the Merchants limits warranty expressly to the terms of the offer]

COMMERCE & INDUSTRY INSURANCE CO. v. BAYER CORP.

Supreme Judicial Court of Massachusetts, 2001
433 Mass. 388, 742 N.E.2d 567

[handwritten margin note: Determining enforceability of an Arbitration provision]

GREANEY, J. We granted the application for direct appellate review of the defendant, Bayer Corporation (Bayer), to determine the enforceability of an arbitration provision appearing in the plaintiff's, Malden Mills Industries, Inc. (Malden Mills), orders purchasing materials from Bayer. In a written

---

*Terms in the acceptance "materially alter" the offer if they are either (1) harsh or (2) surprising (uncommon in the industry). Comment 4 to §2-207 explains that material alterations might include disclaimers of warranties and clauses those that deviate from industry norms. On the flip side, Comment 5 lists terms that normally aren't material alterations, including those that impose reasonable limits on the time for complaints or require the buyer to pay a normal amount of interest on overdue invoices.

decision, a judge in the Superior Court concluded that the provision was not enforceable. An order entered denying Bayer's motion to compel arbitration and to stay further litigation against it. We affirm the order.

The background of the case is as follows. Malden Mills manufactures internationally-known apparel fabrics and other textiles. On December 11, 1995, an explosion and fire destroyed several Malden Mills's buildings at its manufacturing facility. Subsequently, Malden Mills and its property insurers, the plaintiffs Commerce and Industry Insurance Company and Federal Insurance Company, commenced suit in the Superior Court against numerous defendants, including Bayer. In their complaint, the plaintiffs allege, insofar as relevant here, that the cause of the fire was the ignition, by static electrical discharge, of nylon tow (also known as bulk nylon fiber), which was sold by Bayer (but manufactured by a French business entity) to Malden Mills and used by Malden Mills to manufacture "flocked fabric," a fabric used primarily for upholstery application.[3]

Malden Mills initiated purchases of nylon tow from Bayer either by sending its standard form purchase order to Bayer, or by placing a telephone order to Bayer, followed by a standard form purchase order. Each of Malden Mills's purchase orders contained, on the reverse side, as one of its "terms and conditions," an arbitration provision stating:

> Any controversy arising out of or relating to this contract shall be settled by arbitration in the City of New York or Boston as [Malden Mills] shall determine in accordance with the Rules then obtaining of the American Arbitration Association or the General Arbitration Council of the Textile Industry, as [Malden Mills] shall determine.

Another "term and condition" appearing in paragraph one on the reverse side of each purchase order provides:

> This purchase order represents the entire agreement between both parties, not withstanding any Seller's order form, whether sent before or after the sending of this purchase order, and this document cannot be modified except in writing and signed by an authorized representative of the buyer.

In response, Bayer transmitted Malden Mills's purchase orders to the manufacturer with instructions, in most instances, that the nylon tow was to be shipped directly to Malden Mills. Thereafter, Bayer prepared and sent Malden Mills an invoice. Each of the Bayer invoices contained the following language on its face, located at the bottom of the form in capital letters:

> TERMS AND CONDITIONS: NOTWITHSTANDING ANY CONTRARY OR INCONSISTENT CONDITIONS THAT MAY BE EMBODIED IN YOUR

---

3. The plaintiffs' claims against Bayer allege negligence and breach of implied warranties of merchantability and of fitness for a particular purpose.

PURCHASE ORDER, YOUR ORDER IS ACCEPTED SUBJECT TO THE PRICES, TERMS AND CONDITIONS OF THE MUTUALLY EXECUTED CONTRACT BETWEEN US, OR, IF NO SUCH CONTRACT EXISTS, YOUR ORDER IS ACCEPTED SUBJECT TO OUR REGULAR SCHEDULED PRICE AND TERMS IN EFFECT AT TIME OF SHIPMENT AND SUBJECT TO THE TERMS AND CONDITIONS PRINTED ON THE REVERSE SIDE HEREOF.

The following "condition" appears in paragraph fourteen on the reverse side of each invoice:

> This document is not an Expression of Acceptance or a Confirmation document as contemplated in Section 2-207 of the Uniform Commercial Code. The acceptance of any order entered by [Malden Mills] is expressly conditioned on [Malden Mills's] assent to any additional or conflicting terms contained herein.

Malden Mills usually remitted payment to Bayer within thirty days of receiving an invoice.

Based on the arbitration provision in Malden Mills's purchase orders, Bayer demanded that Malden Mills arbitrate its claims against Bayer. After Malden Mills refused, Bayer moved to compel arbitration and to stay the litigation against it. The judge denied Bayer's motion, concluding, under §2-207 of the Massachusetts enactment of the Uniform Commercial Code, that the parties' conduct, as opposed to their writings, established a contract. As to whether the arbitration provision was an enforceable term of the parties' contract, the judge concluded that subsection (3) of §2-207 governed, and, pursuant thereto, the arbitration provision was not enforceable because the parties had not agreed in their writings to arbitrate. Finally, the judge rejected Bayer's argument that the plaintiffs should be equitably estopped from refusing to proceed under the arbitration provision.

1. This case presents a dispute arising from what has been styled a typical "battle of the forms" sale, in which a buyer and a seller each attempt to consummate a commercial transaction through the exchange of self-serving preprinted forms that clash, and contradict each other, on both material and minor terms. See 1 J. J. White & R. S. Summers, Uniform Commercial Code §1-3, at 6-7 (4th ed. 1995) (White & Summers). Here, Malden Mills's form, a purchase order, contains an arbitration provision, and Bayer's form, a seller's invoice, is silent on how the parties will resolve any disputes. Oddly enough, the buyer, Malden Mills, the party proposing the arbitration provision, and its insurers, now seek to avoid an arbitral forum.

Section 2-207 was enacted with the expectation of creating an orderly mechanism to resolve commercial disputes resulting from a "battle of the forms."[6] The section has been characterized as "an amphibious tank that was originally designed to fight in the swamps, but was sent to fight in the desert." White & Summers, supra at §1-3, at 8.[7] Section 2-207 sets forth rules and principles concerning contract formation and the procedures for determining the terms of a contract. Id. at 9. As to contract formation, under §2-207, there are essentially three ways by which a contract may be formed. Id. at 19-20. See also JOM, Inc. v. Adell Plastics, Inc., 193 F.3d 47, 53 (1st Cir. 1999) (*JOM*). "First, if the parties exchange forms with divergent terms, yet the seller's invoice does not state that its acceptance is made 'expressly conditional' on the buyer's assent to any additional or different terms in the invoice, a contract is formed [under subsection (1) of §2-207]." Id. at 53. "Second, if the seller does make its acceptance 'expressly conditional' on the buyer's assent to any additional or divergent terms in the seller's invoice, the invoice is merely a counteroffer, and a contract is formed [under subsection (1) of §2-207] only when the buyer expresses its affirmative acceptance of the seller's counteroffer." Id. Third, "where for any reason the exchange of forms does not result in contract formation (e.g., the buyer 'expressly limits acceptance to the terms of [its offer]' under §2-207(2)(a), or the buyer does not accept the seller's counteroffer under the second clause of §2-207[1]), a contract nonetheless is formed [under subsection (3) of §2-207] if their subsequent conduct—for instance, the seller ships and the buyer accepts the goods—demonstrates that the parties believed that a binding agreement had been formed." Id. at 54.

Bayer correctly concedes that its contract with Malden Mills resulted from the parties' conduct, and, thus, was formed pursuant to subsection (3) of §2-207. A contract never came into being under subsection (1) of §2-207 because (1) paragraph fourteen on the reverse side of Bayer's invoices expressly conditioned acceptance on Malden Mills's assent to

---

6. Section 2-207 was intended to restrict application of the common law "mirror image" rule to defeat the formation of a contract for the sale of goods. See JOM, Inc. v. Adell Plastics, Inc., 193 F.3d 47, 53 (1st Cir. 1999). "Under the common law, the inclusion of an additional term in an acceptance rejected the original offer and constituted a counteroffer which did not become a contract unless it was accepted by the offeror. . . . [Section 2-207] converts what would have been a counteroffer under the common law into an acceptance or confirmation even where the acceptance or confirmation includes additional terms or terms different from those offered or agreed upon." Anderson, supra at §2-207:4, at 560-561. See Moss v. Old Colony Trust Co., 246 Mass. 139, 148, 140 N.E. 803 (1923).

7. The tank metaphor was meant to convey the notion that §2-207 has not worked satisfactorily in practice. Another treatise on the Uniform Commercial Code has been more direct in criticizing §2-207. "Few provisions of the Code (or indeed of any statute) have gained the notoriety of §2-207. Scores of cases have explored its every nuance; dozens of law review articles have analyzed its minutiae. A virtual cottage industry has been created to suggest amendments, and agreement is nearly universal that it is at best a 'murky bit of prose.' Its workmanship is further honored by Grant Gilmore's characterization of the provision as 'a miserable, bungled, patched-up job . . . to which various hands . . . contributed at various points, each acting independently of the others (like the blind men and the elephant).' No similar provision exists elsewhere in the Code." (Footnotes omitted.) 1 T. D. Crandall, M. J. Herbert & L. Lawrence, Uniform Commercial Code §3.2.4, at 3:12 (1996). . . .

"additional or different" terms,[8] and (2) Malden Mills never expressed "affirmative acceptance" of any of Bayer's invoices. See id. at 53. In addition, the exchange of forms between Malden Mills and Bayer did not result in a contract because Malden Mills, by means of language in paragraph one of its purchase orders, expressly limited Bayer's acceptance to the terms of Malden Mills's offers. . . .

Although Bayer acknowledges that its contract with Malden Mills was formed under subsection (3) of §2-207, it nonetheless argues, relying on language in both *JOM*, supra at 55, and official comment 6 to §2-207 of the Code, 1 U.L.A. 378 (Master ed. 1989), that the terms of the contract are determined through an application of the principles in subsection (2) of §2-207. Under this analysis, Bayer asserts that the arbitration provision became part of the parties' contract because it was not a "material alteration," and to include the provision would cause no "surprise or hardship" to the plaintiffs. This analysis is incorrect.

Bayer ignores the significance of the method of contract formation in determining the terms of a contract. See White & Summers, supra at §1-3, at 19-20 (discussing three routes of contract formation under §2-207, and noting "the terms of any resulting contracts will vary, depending on which route to contract formation a court adopts"). Where a contract is formed by the parties' conduct (as opposed to writings), as is the case here, the terms of the contract are determined exclusively by subsection (3) of §2-207. [Citations omitted.] Official comment 7, which Bayer overlooks, expressly directs as much. See 1 U.L.A. §2-207 official comment 7, at 378 (Master ed. 1989) ("In many cases, as where goods are shipped, accepted and paid for before any dispute arises, there is no question whether a contract has been made. In such cases, where the writings of the parties do not establish a contract, it is not necessary to determine which act or document constituted the offer and which the acceptance. . . . The only question is what terms are included in the contract, and subsection [3] furnishes the governing rule"). Under subsection (3) of §2-207, "the terms of the particular contract consist of those terms on which the writings of the parties agree, together with any supplementary terms incorporated under any other provisions of this chapter." G. L. c. 106, §2-207(3). In this respect, one commentator has aptly referred to subsection (3) of §2-207 as the "fall-back" rule. See 1 T. M. Quinn, Uniform Commercial Code Commentary and Law Digest par. 2-207[A][14], at 2-134 (2d ed. 1991). Under this rule, the Code accepts "common terms but rejects

---

8. Bayer's invoices contain terms "additional" and "different" from those in Malden Mills's purchase orders. For example, Bayer's invoices disclaim certain warranties (implied warranties) for which Malden Mills's purchase orders provide. In addition, Bayer's invoices exclude liability for consequential damages for which Malden Mills' purchase orders provide. It cannot be said that these terms are immaterial. See Anderson, supra at §2-207:79, §2-207:88 (Code is not concerned with presence of additional term unless it is material; limitation of warranties provision and clause excluding liability for consequential damages are material new terms).

all the rest." Id. at 2-135. While this approach "serves to leave many matters uncovered," terms may be filled by "recourse to usages of trade or course of dealing under §1-205 or, perhaps, the gap filling provisions of §2-300s." Id. See also Anderson, supra at §2-207:78, at 602 ("'supplementary terms' authorized by UCC §2-207[3] include those that may be established by a course of dealing, course of performance, and usage of the trade").

Contrary to Bayer's contentions, subsection (2) of §2-207 is not applicable for several reasons. First, subsection (2) instructs on how to ascertain the terms of a contract when the contract is formed either by the parties' writings or by a party's written confirmation of an oral contract, situations not present here (the parties' contract was formed by their conduct). See 1 U.L.A. §2-207 official comments 1 and 2, supra at 377. See also Anderson, supra at §2-207:28, at 574-575; §2-207:30, at 576; §2-207:160, at 647. Second, the rules set forth in subsection (2), concerning how the terms of a contract between merchants are determined, apply only when the acceptance or written confirmation contains "additional or different terms," a situation also not present here (Bayer's invoice is silent concerning how to resolve disputes). See 1 U.L.A. §2-207 official comment 3, supra at 377. See also Anderson, supra at §2-207:160, at 647-648. In addition, official comment 6, read in its entirety,[9] does not support Bayer's argument because the comment expressly applies to a situation where there are "conflicting" terms. Id. There are no provisions in Bayer's invoices that "conflict" with Malden Mills's arbitration provision because the invoices do not contain any provision stating how the parties intend to resolve their disputes. See White & Summers, supra at §1-3, at 15 (official comment 6 not applicable when term appears in first form, but not in second; there are no terms that "conflict").

Bayer argues that this case is governed by the language in *JOM*, supra at 54, stating that "[t]he terms of [the parties' contract formed by the parties' conduct] would then be determined under the 'default' test in §2-207(3), *which implicitly incorporates the criteria prescribed in §2-207(2)*" (emphasis supplied). We disagree. As discussed above, the criteria in subsection (2)

---

9. Official comment 6 to §2-207, 1 U.L.A. 378 (Master ed. 1989), provides:

6. If no answer is received within a reasonable time after additional terms are proposed, it is both fair and commercially sound to assume that their inclusion has been assented to. Where clauses on confirming forms sent by both parties conflict each party must be assumed to object to a clause of the other conflicting with one on the confirmation sent by himself. As a result the requirement that there be notice of objection which is found in subsection (2) is satisfied and the conflicting terms do not become a part of the contract. The contract then consists of the terms originally expressly agreed to, terms on which the confirmations agree, and terms supplied by this Act, including subsection (2). The written confirmation is also subject to Section 2-201. Under that section a failure to respond permits enforcement of a prior oral agreement; under this section a failure to respond permits additional terms to become part of the agreement.

determine what "additional or different terms" will or will not be part of a contract that is formed by the exchange of writings. Where the writings do not form a contract, subsection (3) states its own criteria — "those terms on which the writings agree" plus any terms that would be provided by other Code sections. One cannot turn to subsection (2) as another Code section that would supply a term when, by its express provisions, subsection (2) simply does not apply to the transaction.

Holding

Thus, the judge correctly concluded, under subsection (3) of §2-207, that the arbitration provision in Malden Mills's purchase orders did not become a term of the parties' contract. The arbitration provision was not common to both Malden Mills's purchase orders and Bayer's invoices. Bayer properly does not argue that any of the gap-filling provisions of G.L. c. 106, apply. Because Bayer concedes that it never previously arbitrated a dispute with Malden Mills, we reject Bayer's claim that the parties' course of dealing requires us to enforce the arbitration provision. Bayer also cites Pervel Indus., Inc. v. T M Wallcovering, Inc., 871 F.2d 7 (2d Cir. 1989), in arguing that industry custom and usage favors enforcing Malden Mills's arbitration provision. That case, however, is not helpful to Bayer. The court upheld the existence of an enforceable arbitration agreement because the manufacturer had "a well established custom of sending purchase order confirmations containing an arbitration clause," and the buyer, who had "made numerous purchases over a period of time," received "in each instance a standard confirmation form which it either signed and returned or retained without objection." Id. at 8. Although Bayer never objected to the arbitration provision in Malden Mills's purchase orders, as we have previously explained, no agreement to arbitrate ever arose due, in part, to the expressly conditional language appearing in paragraph fourteen of Bayer's invoices, and to the lack of an arbitration provision in its invoices. It is significant also that Bayer did not provide the judge with any evidence of industry custom and usage. We decline to conclude that industry custom and usage favors enforcing Malden Mills's arbitration provision. . . .

3. Bayer may be right that the drafters of the Massachusetts version of the Code did not intend that §2-207 should provide "an avenue for a party to strike the terms of its own purchase documents." Bayer, however, cannot ignore the fact that the use of its own boilerplate invoices contributed to the result that Bayer now finds problematic. The order denying the motion to compel arbitration and to stay litigation is affirmed.

So ordered.

NOTE

It Not used as Part of the accepting form Then goes to §(2)

Commerce & Industry Ins. Co. v. Bayer stands for the idea that the proviso clause acts like a railroad switch. If it is *not* used as part of the accepting form, then the purported acceptance does create a contract, and the parties are directed to subsection (2) to determine its terms. If the proviso is put into the accepting document, the exchange of forms does not create a contract, and the parties are directed to subsection (3) to see what results from their dealings. The point is this: The use or not of the proviso shunts the parties into either subsection (2) or subsection (3), *but never both.*

[handwritten margin note: If IS used as Part of The Accepting form, Then goes to § 3]

So far, we've discussed how to treat "additional" terms in an acceptance under §2-207. An additional term adds some right or duty that the offer doesn't mention. But what happens if a term is "different," in the sense that it alters an issue that *does* appear in the offer? Our next case tackles that conundrum.

NORTHROP CORP. v. LITRONIC INDUSTRIES
United States Court of Appeals, Seventh Circuit, 1994
29 F.3d 1173

POSNER, Chief Judge.

"Battle of the forms" refers to the not uncommon situation in which one business firm makes an offer in the form of a preprinted form contract and the offeree responds with its own form contract. At common law, any discrepancy between the forms would prevent the offeree's response from operating as an acceptance. So there would be no contract in such a case. This was the "mirror image" rule, which Article 2 of the Uniform Commercial Code jettisoned by providing that "a definite and seasonable expression of acceptance or a written confirmation which is sent within a reasonable time operates as an acceptance even though it states terms additional to or different from those offered or agreed upon, unless acceptance is made conditional on assent to the additional or different terms." Mischief lurks in the words "additional to or different from." The next subsection of 2-207 provides that if additional terms in the acceptance are not materially different from those in the offer, then, subject to certain other qualifications they become part of the contract, §2-207(2), while if the additional terms are materially different they operate as proposals and so have no effect unless the offeror agrees to them; if the offeror does not agree to them, therefore, the terms of the contract are those in the offer. A clause providing for interest at normal rates on overdue invoices, or limiting the right to reject goods because of defects falling within customary trade tolerances for acceptance with adjustment, would be the sort of additional term that is not deemed material, and hence it would become a part of the contract even if the offeror never signified acceptance of it.

The Code does not explain, however, what happens if the offeree's response contains different terms (rather than additional ones) within the meaning of section 2-207(1). There is no consensus on that question. We know there is a contract because an acceptance is effective even though it contains different terms; but what are the terms of the contract that is brought into being by the offer and acceptance? One view is that the discrepant terms in both the nonidentical offer and the acceptance drop out, and default terms found elsewhere in the Code fill the resulting gap. Another view is that the offeree's discrepant terms drop out and the offeror's become part of the contract. A third view, possibly the most sensible, equates "different" with "additional" and makes the outcome turn on whether the new terms in the acceptance are materially different from the terms in the offer — in which event they operate as proposals, so that the offeror's terms prevail unless he agrees to the variant terms in the acceptance — or not materially different from the terms in the offer, in which event they become part of the contract. This interpretation equating "different" to "additional," bolstered by drafting history which shows that the omission of "or different" from section 2-207(2) was a drafting error, substitutes a manageable inquiry into materiality for a hair-splitting inquiry into the difference between "different" and "additional." It is hair-splitting ("metaphysical," "casuistic," "semantic," in the pejorative senses of these words) because all different terms are additional and all additional terms are different.

Unfortunately, the Illinois courts — whose understanding of Article 2 of the UCC is binding on us because this is a diversity suit governed, all agree, by Illinois law — have had no occasion to choose among the different positions on the consequences of an acceptance that contains "different" terms from the offer. We shall have to choose.

The battle of the forms in this case takes the form of something very like a badminton game, but we can simplify it a bit without distorting the issues. The players are Northrop, the giant defense firm, and Litronic, which manufactures electronic components, including "printed wire boards" that are incorporated into defense weapon systems. In 1987 Northrop sent several manufacturers, including Litronic, a request to submit offers to sell Northrop a customized printed wire board designated by Northrop as a "1714 Board." The request stated that any purchase would be made by means of a purchase order that would set forth terms and conditions that would override any inconsistent terms in the offer. In response, Litronic mailed an offer to sell Northrop four boards for $19,000 apiece, to be delivered within six weeks. The offer contained a 90-day warranty stated to be in lieu of any other warranties, and provided that the terms of the offer would take precedence over any terms proposed by the buyer. Lynch, a purchasing officer of Northrop, responded to the offer in a phone conversation in which he told Litronic's man, Lair, that he was accepting the offer up to the limit of his authority, which was $24,999, and that a formal purchase order for all four boards would follow. Litronic was familiar with Northrop's purchase order form, having previously done business with Northrop, which had been using the same form for some time. Had Lair referred to any of the previous orders, he would have discovered that Northrop's order form provided for a warranty that contained no time limit.

Lynch followed up the phone conversation a month later with a "turn on" letter, authorizing Litronic to begin production of all four boards (it had done so already) and repeating that a purchase order would follow. The record is unclear when the actual purchase order was mailed; it may have been as much as four months after the phone conversation and three months after the turn-on letter. The purchase order required the seller to send a written acknowledgment to Northrop. Litronic never did so, however, and Northrop did not complain; it does not bother to follow up on its requirement of a signed acknowledgment.

Although Litronic had begun manufacturing the boards immediately after the telephone call from Lynch, for reasons that are unknown but that Northrop does not contend are culpable Litronic did not deliver the first three boards until more than a year later, in July of 1988. Northrop tested the boards for conformity to its specifications. The testing was protracted, either because the boards were highly complex or because Northrop's inspectors were busy, or perhaps for both reasons. At all events it was not until December and January, five or six months after delivery, that Northrop returned the three boards (the fourth had not been delivered), claiming that they were defective. Litronic refused to accept the return of the boards, on the ground that its 90-day warranty had lapsed. Northrop's position of course is that it had an unlimited warranty, as stated in the purchase order.

Litronic's 90-day warranty, if a term of the contract, not only barred Northrop from complaining about defects that showed up more than 90 days after the delivery of the boards but also limited to 90 days the time within which Northrop was permitted to reject the boards because of defects that rendered them nonconforming.

Litronic's appeal concerns the breach of its warranty on the No. 1714 boards. It wins if the warranty really did expire after only 90 days. The parties agree that Litronic's offer to sell the No. 1714 boards to Northrop, the offer made in response to Northrop's request for bids, was — the offer. So far, so good. If Northrop's Mr. Lynch accepted the offer over the phone, the parties had a contract then and there, but the question would still be on what terms. Regarding the first question, whether there was a contract, we may assume to begin with that the acceptance was sufficiently "definite" to satisfy the requirement of definiteness in section 2-207(1); after all, it impelled Litronic to begin production immediately, and there is no suggestion that it acted precipitately in doing so. We do not know whether Lynch in his conversation with Lair made acceptance of the complete contract expressly conditional on approval by Lynch's superiors at Northrop. We know that he had authority to contract only up to $24,999, but we do not know whether he told Lair what the exact limitation on his authority was or whether Litronic knew it without being told. It does not matter. The condition, if it was a condition, was satisfied and so drops out.

We do not think that Northrop's acceptance, via Lynch, of Litronic's offer could be thought conditional on Litronic's yielding to Northrop's demand for an open-ended warranty. For while Lynch's reference to the purchase order might have alerted Litronic to Northrop's desire for a warranty not limited to 90 days, Lynch did not purport to make the more extensive warranty a condition of acceptance. So the condition, if there was one, was not an express condition, as the cases insist it be.

There was a contract, therefore; further, and, as we shall note, decisive, evidence being that the parties acted as if they had a contract — the boards were shipped and paid for. The question is then what the terms of the warranty in the contract were. Lynch's reference in the phone conversation to the forthcoming purchase order shows that Northrop's acceptance contained different terms from the offer, namely the discrepant terms in the purchase order, in particular the warranty — for it is plain that the Northrop warranty was intended to be indefinite in length, so any limitation on the length of the warranty in the offer would be a materially different term. Of course the fact that Northrop preferred a longer warranty than Litronic was offering does not by itself establish that Northrop's acceptance contained different terms. But Lynch did not accept Litronic's offer and leave it at that. He said that he would issue a Northrop purchase order, and both he and Lair knew (or at least should have known) that the Northrop purchase order form contained a different warranty from Litronic's sale order form. And we have already said that Lynch did not, by his oral reference to the purchase order, condition Northrop's purchase on Litronic's agreeing to comply with all the terms in the purchase order form, given the courts' insistence that any such condition be explicit. (Judges are skeptical that even businesspeople read boilerplate, so they are reluctant, rightly or wrongly, to make a contract fail on the basis of a printed condition in a form contract.) But Lynch said enough to make clear to Lair that the acceptance contained different terms from the offer.

The Uniform Commercial Code, as we have said, does not say what the terms of the contract are if the offer and acceptance contain different terms, as distinct from cases in which the acceptance merely contains additional terms to those in the offer. The majority view is that the discrepant terms fall out and are replaced by a suitable UCC gap-filler. The magistrate judge followed this approach and proceeded to section 2-309, which provides that nonconforming goods may be rejected within a "reasonable" time (see also §2-601(1)), and she held that the six months that Northrop took to reject Litronic's boards was a reasonable time because of the complexity of the required testing. The leading minority view is that the discrepant terms in the acceptance are to be ignored, and that would give the palm to Litronic. Our own preferred view — the view that assimilates "different" to "additional," so that the terms in the offer prevail over the different terms in the acceptance only if the latter are materially different, has as yet been adopted by only one state, California. Under that view, as under what we are calling the "leading" minority view, the warranty in Litronic's offer, the 90-day warranty, was the contractual warranty, because the unlimited warranty contained in Northrop's acceptance was materially different.

Because Illinois in other UCC cases has tended to adopt majority rules, and because the interest in the uniform nationwide application of the Code argues for nudging majority views, even if imperfect (but not downright bad), toward unanimity, we start with a presumption that Illinois, whose position we are trying to predict, would adopt the majority view. We do not find the presumption rebutted. The idea behind the majority view is that the presence of different terms in the acceptance suggests that the offeree didn't really accede to the offeror's terms, yet both parties wanted to contract, so why not find a neutral term to govern the dispute that has arisen between them? Of course the offeree may not have had any serious objection to the terms in the offer at the time of contracting; he may have mailed a boilerplated form without giving any thought to its contents or to its suitability for the particular contract in question. But it is just as likely that the discrepant terms in the offer itself were the product of a thoughtless use of a boilerplate form rather than a considered condition of contracting. And if the offeror doesn't want to do business other than on the terms in the offer, he can protect himself by specifying that the offeree must accept all those terms for the parties to have a contract. Now as it happens Litronic did state in its offer that the terms in the offer "take precedence over terms and conditions of the buyer, unless specifically negotiated otherwise." But, for reasons that we do not and need not fathom, Litronic does not argue that this language conditioned the existence of the contract on Northrop's acceding to the 90-day warranty in the offer; any such argument is therefore waived.

It is true that the offeree likewise can protect himself by making his acceptance of the offer conditional on the offeror's acceding to any different terms in the acceptance. But so many acceptances are made over the phone by relatively junior employees, as in this case, that it may be unrealistic to expect offerees to protect themselves in this way. The offeror goes first and therefore has a little more time for careful specification of the terms on which he is willing to make a contract. What we are calling the leading minority view may tempt the offeror to spring a surprise on the offeree, hoping the latter won't read the fine print. Under the majority view, if the offeree tries to spring a surprise (the offeror can't, since his terms won't prevail if the acceptance contains different terms), the parties move to neutral ground; and the offeror can, we have suggested, more easily protect himself against being surprised than the offeree can protect himself against being surprised. The California rule dissolves all these problems, but has too little support to make it a plausible candidate for Illinois, or at least a plausible candidate for our guess as to Illinois's position.

There is a further wrinkle, however. The third subsection of section 2-207 provides that even if no contract is established under either of the first two subsections, it may be established by the "conduct of the parties," and in that event (as subsection (3) expressly provides) the discrepant terms vanish and are replaced by UCC gap fillers. This may seem to make it impossible for the offeror to protect himself from being contractually bound by specifying that the acceptance must mirror his offer. But subsection (3) comes into play only when the parties have by their conduct manifested the existence of a contract, as where the offeror, having specified that the acceptance must mirror the offer yet having received an acceptance that deviates from the offer, nonetheless goes ahead and performs as if there were a contract. That is one way to interpret what happened here but it leads to the same result as applying subsection (2) interpreted as the majority of states do, so we need not consider it separately.

Given the intricacy of the No. 1714 boards, it is unlikely that Northrop would have acceded to a 90-day limitation on its warranty protection. Litronic at argument stressed that it is a much smaller firm, hence presumably unwilling to assume burdensome warranty obligations; but it is a curious suggestion that little fellows are more likely than big ones to get their way in negotiations between firms of disparate size. And Northrop actually got only half its way, though enough for victory here; for by virtue of accepting Litronic's offer without expressly conditioning its acceptance on Litronic's acceding to Northrop's terms, Northrop got not a warranty unlimited in duration, as its purchase order provides, but (pursuant to the majority understanding of UCC §2-207(2)) a warranty of "reasonable" duration, courtesy the court. If special circumstances made a 90-day warranty reasonable, Litronic was free to argue for it in the district court.

On the view we take, the purchase order has no significance beyond showing that Northrop's acceptance contained (albeit by reference) different terms. The fact that Litronic never signed the order, and the fact that Northrop never called this omission to Litronic's attention, also drop out of the case.

AFFIRMED

NOTE

As *Northrop* explains, there are three separate views on what to do with "different" terms under §2-207. The majority approach, known as the "knockout rule," dictates that the different terms cancel each other out. The leading minority view is that because the text of §2-207(2) never says that "different" terms can become part of the contract, the offeror's terms control. Finally, other jurisdictions assume that the omission of the word "different" from §2-207(2) was a drafting error, and treat "different" terms just like "additional terms."

Problem 29

The Galsworthy Oil Company ordered a $100,000 tugboat and specifically demanded that all disputes be subject to binding arbitration. The acknowledgment form from Forsyte Shipbuilding agreed to all of the terms except this one and specifically stated that "the parties agree to settle or litigate any disputes without resorting to arbitration." Neither party read the other's form, so the tugboat was shipped, accepted, and then had major problems remaining afloat. You are the attorney for the buyer. Advise your client on whether arbitration can be demanded here.

Finally, §2-207 also applies when the parties reach an agreement, and then one of them sends a written confirmation of the agreement that contains terms that are additional to or different from the agreement. Section 2-207(1) instructs courts that the additional or different terms only become part of the contract if they satisfy all the elements of §2-207(2).

KLOCEK v. GATEWAY, INC. *offense*
United States District Court, Kansas, 2000
104 F. Supp. 2d 1332, 41 U.C.C. Rep. Serv. 2d 1059

[handwritten: # PPCD was switch]

VRATIL, District Judge.

William S. Klocek brings suit against Gateway, Inc. and Hewlett-Packard, Inc. on claims arising from purchases of a Gateway computer and a Hewlett-Packard scanner. . . . For reasons stated below, the Court overrules Gateway's motion to dismiss, sustains Hewlett-Packard's motion to dismiss, and overrules the motions filed by plaintiff.

A. GATEWAY'S MOTION TO DISMISS

Plaintiff brings individual and class action claims against Gateway, alleging that it induced him and other consumers to purchase computers and special support packages by making false promises of technical support. *Complaint*, ¶¶3 and 4. Individually, plaintiff also claims breach of contract and breach of warranty, in that Gateway breached certain warranties that its computer would be compatible with standard peripherals and standard internet services. *Complaint*, ¶¶2, 5, and 6.

[handwritten: plaintiff Alleged claim]

Gateway asserts that plaintiff must arbitrate his claims under Gateway's Standard Terms and Conditions Agreement ("Standard Terms"). Whenever it sells a computer, Gateway includes a copy of the Standard Terms in the box

[handwritten: Gateway Asserts Arbitration]

which contains the computer battery power cables and instruction manuals. At the top of the first page, the Standard Terms include the following notice:

Note to the Customer: *Condition?*

Privso?   This document contains Gateway 2000's Standard Terms and Conditions. By keeping your Gateway 2000 computer system beyond five (5) days after the date of delivery, you accept these Terms and Conditions.

The notice is in <u>emphasized type</u> and is located inside a printed box which sets it <u>apart</u> from other provisions of the document. The Standard Terms are four <u>pages</u> long and contain 16 numbered paragraphs. Paragraph 10 provides the following arbitration clause:

Arbitration clause   DISPUTE RESOLUTION. Any dispute or controversy arising out of or relating to this Agreement or its interpretation shall be settled exclusively and finally by arbitration. . . . [1]

FAA   Gateway urges the Court to dismiss plaintiff's claims under the Federal Arbitration Act ("FAA"), 9 U.S.C. §1 et seq. <u>The FAA</u> ensures that written arbitration agreements in maritime transactions and transactions involving interstate commerce are "valid, irrevocable, and enforceable." 9 U.S.C. §2. Federal policy favors arbitration agreements and requires that we "rigorously enforce" them. [Citations omitted.] "[A]ny doubts concerning the scope of arbitrable issues should be resolved in favor of arbitration." *Moses*, 460 U.S. at 24-25, 103 S. Ct. 927. . . .

Federal policy favors Arbitration and gives it the benefit of the doubt

Gateway bears an initial summary-judgment-like burden of establishing *Issue* that it is entitled to arbitration. [Citations omitted.] <u>Thus</u>, Gateway must present evidence sufficient to demonstrate the existence of an enforceable agreement to arbitrate. See, e.g., Oppenheimer & Co. v. Neidhardt, 56 F.3d 352, 358 (2d Cir. 1995). If Gateway makes such a showing, the burden shifts to plaintiff to submit evidence demonstrating a genuine issue for trial. Id.; see also Naddy v. Piper Jaffray, Inc., 88 Wash. App. 1033, 1997 WL 749261, *2, Case Nos. 15431-9-III, 15681-8-III (Wash. App. Dec. 4, 1997). <u>In this case, Gateway fails to present evidence establishing the most basic facts regarding the transaction.</u> The gaping holes in the evidentiary record preclude the Court from determining what state law controls the formation of the contract in this case, and, consequently, prevent the Court from agreeing that Gateway's motion is well taken.

If Gateway makes an Initial showing of the Arbitration clause, then Burden falls on the Plaintiff

holes in evidentiary record for Gateway's claim

---

1. Gateway states that after it sold plaintiff's computer, it mailed all existing customers in the United States a copy of its quarterly magazine, which contained notice of a change in the arbitration policy set forth in the Standard Terms. The new arbitration policy afforded customers the option of arbitrating before the International Chamber of Commerce ("ICC"), the American Arbitration Association ("AAA"), or the National Arbitration Forum ("NAF") in Chicago, Illinois, or any other location agreed upon by the parties. Plaintiff denies receiving notice of the amended arbitration policy. Neither party explains why—if the arbitration agreement was an enforceable contract—Gateway was entitled to unilaterally amend it by sending a magazine to computer customers.

Before granting a stay or dismissing a case pending arbitration, the Court must determine that the parties have a written agreement to arbitrate. See 9 U.S.C. §§3 and 4. [Citation omitted.] When deciding whether the parties have agreed to arbitrate, the Court applies ordinary state law principles that govern the formation of contracts. First Options of Chicago, Inc. v. Kaplan, 514 U.S. 938, 944, 115 S. Ct. 1920, 131 L. Ed. 2d 985 (1995). The existence of an arbitration agreement "is simply a matter of contract between the parties; [arbitration] is a way to resolve those disputes — but only those disputes — that the parties have agreed to submit to arbitration." Avedon, 126 F.3d at 1283 (quoting Kaplan, 514 U.S. at 943-945, 115 S. Ct. 1920). If the parties dispute making an arbitration agreement, a jury trial on the existence of an agreement is warranted if the record reveals genuine issues of material fact regarding the parties' agreement. See Avedon, 126 F.3d at 1283. . . .

The Uniform Commercial Code ("UCC") governs the parties' transaction under both Kansas and Missouri law. [Citations omitted.] Regardless whether plaintiff purchased the computer in person or placed an order and received shipment of the computer, the parties agree that plaintiff paid for and received a computer from Gateway. This conduct clearly demonstrates a contract for the sale of a computer. See, e.g., Step-Saver Data Sys., Inc. v. Wyse Techn., 939 F.2d 91, 98 (3d Cir. 1991). Thus the issue is whether the contract of sale includes the Standard Terms as part of the agreement.

State courts in Kansas and Missouri apparently have not decided whether terms received with a product become part of the parties' agreement. Authority from other courts is split. [Citations omitted.] It appears that at least in part, the cases turn on whether the court finds that the parties formed their contract *before* or *after* the vendor communicated its terms to the purchaser. [Citations omitted.]

Gateway urges the Court to follow the Seventh Circuit decision in *Hill [v. Gateway 2000*, 105 F. 3d 1147 (7th Cir. 1997)]. That case involved the shipment of a Gateway computer with terms similar to the Standard Terms in this case, except that Gateway gave the customer 30 days — instead of 5 days — to return the computer. In enforcing the arbitration clause, the Seventh Circuit relied on its decision in *ProCD*, where it enforced a software license which was contained inside a product box. See *Hill*, 105 F.3d at 1148-50. In *ProCD*, the Seventh Circuit noted that the exchange of money frequently precedes the communication of detailed terms in a commercial transaction. See *ProCD*, 86 F.3d at 1451. Citing UCC §2-204, the court reasoned that by including the license with the software, the vendor proposed a contract that the buyer could accept by using the software after having an opportunity to read the license.[8] *ProCD*, 86 F.3d at 1452. Specifically, the court stated:

---

8. Section 2-204 provides: "A contract for sale of goods may be made in any manner sufficient to show agreement, including conduct by both parties which recognizes the existence of such contract." K.S.A. §84-2-204; V.A.M.S. §400.2-204.

> A vendor, as master of the offer, may invite acceptance by conduct, and may propose limitations on the kind of conduct that constitutes acceptance. A buyer may accept by performing the acts the vendor proposes to treat as acceptance.

ProCD, 86 F.3d at 1452. The *Hill* court followed the *ProCD* analysis, noting that "[p]ractical considerations support allowing vendors to enclose the full legal terms with their products." *Hill*, 105 F.3d at 1149.

The Court is not persuaded that Kansas or Missouri courts would follow the Seventh Circuit reasoning in *Hill* and *ProCD*. In each case the Seventh Circuit concluded without support that UCC §2-207 was irrelevant because the cases involved only one written form. See *ProCD*, 86 F.3d at 1452 (citing no authority); *Hill*, 105 F.3d at 1150 (citing *ProCD*). This conclusion is not supported by the statute or by Kansas or Missouri law. Disputes under §2-207 often arise in the context of a "battle of forms," see, e.g., Diatom, Inc. v. Pennwalt Corp., 741 F.2d 1569, 1574 (10th Cir. 1984), but nothing in its language precludes application in a case which involves only one form. The statute provides:

Additional terms in acceptance or confirmation.

(1) A definite and seasonable expression of acceptance or a written confirmation which is sent within a reasonable time operates as an acceptance even though it states terms additional to or different from those offered or agreed upon, unless acceptance is expressly made conditional on assent to the additional or different terms.

(2) The additional terms are to be construed as proposals for addition to the contract [if the contract is not between merchants]. . . .

K.S.A. §84-2-207; V.A.M.S. §400.2-207. By its terms, §2-207 applies to an acceptance or written confirmation. It states nothing which requires another form before the provision becomes effective. In fact, the official comment to the section specifically provides that §2-207(1) and (2) apply "where an agreement has been reached orally . . . and is followed by one or both of the parties sending formal memoranda embodying the terms so far agreed and adding terms not discussed." Official Comment 1 of UCC §2-207. Kansas and Missouri courts have followed this analysis. [Citations omitted.] Thus, the Court concludes that Kansas and Missouri courts would apply §2-207 to the facts in this case. Accord *Avedon*, 126 F.3d at 1283 (parties agree that §2-207 controls whether arbitration clause in sales confirmation is part of contract).

In addition, the Seventh Circuit provided no explanation for its conclusion that "the vendor is the master of the offer." See *ProCD*, 86 F.3d at 1452 (citing nothing in support of proposition); *Hill*, 105 F.3d at 1149 (citing *ProCD*). In typical consumer transactions, the purchaser is the offeror, and the vendor is the offeree. [Citations omitted.] While it is possible for the vendor to be the offeror, . . . Gateway provides no factual evidence which would support such a finding in this case. The Court therefore assumes for purposes of the motion to dismiss that plaintiff offered to purchase the computer (either in person or through catalog order) and that Gateway accepted plaintiff's offer (either by completing the sales transaction in person or by agreeing to ship and/or shipping the computer to plaintiff). . . .

Under §2-207, the Standard Terms constitute either an expression of acceptance or written confirmation. As an expression of acceptance, the Standard Terms would constitute a counter-offer only if Gateway expressly made its acceptance conditional on plaintiff's assent to the additional or different terms. K.S.A. §84-2-207(1); V.A.M.S. §400.2-207(1). "[T]he conditional nature of the acceptance must be clearly expressed in a manner sufficient to notify the offeror that the offeree is unwilling to proceed with the transaction unless the additional or different terms are included in the contract." *Brown Machine [v. Hercules, Inc.*, 770 S.W.2d 416, 420 (Mo. App. 1989)]. Gateway provides no evidence that at the time of the sales transaction, it informed plaintiff that the transaction was conditioned on plaintiff's acceptance of the Standard Terms. Moreover, the mere fact that Gateway shipped the goods with the terms attached did not communicate to plaintiff any unwillingness to proceed without plaintiff's agreement to the Standard Terms. . . .

Because plaintiff is not a merchant, additional or different terms contained in the Standard Terms did not become part of the parties' agreement unless plaintiff expressly agreed to them. [Citations omitted.] Gateway argues that plaintiff demonstrated acceptance of the arbitration provision by keeping the computer more than five days after the date of delivery. Although the Standard Terms purport to work that result, Gateway has not presented evidence that plaintiff expressly agreed to those Standard Terms. Gateway states only that it enclosed the Standard Terms inside the computer box for plaintiff to read afterwards. It provides no evidence that it informed plaintiff of the five-day review-and-return period as a condition of the sales transaction, or that the parties contemplated additional terms to the agreement. . . . [14] The Court finds that the act of keeping the computer past five days was not sufficient to demonstrate that plaintiff expressly agreed to the Standard Terms. Accord *Brown Machine*, 770 S.W.2d at 421 (express assent cannot be presumed by silence or mere failure to object). Thus, because Gateway has not provided evidence sufficient to support a finding under Kansas or Missouri law that plaintiff agreed to the arbitration

14. The Court is mindful of the practical considerations which are involved in commercial transactions, but it is not unreasonable for a vendor to clearly communicate to a buyer—at the time of sale—either the complete terms of the sale or the fact that the vendor will propose additional terms as a condition of sale, if that be the case.

provision contained in Gateway's Standard Terms, the Court overrules Gateway's motion to dismiss. . . .

Problem 30

The purchasing agent of the Galsworthy Oil Company phoned the sales agent of Forsyte Shipbuilding, and the two parties completely negotiated the terms of a contract for the purchase of a $100,000 tugboat, with the phone conversation ending with an agreement that they had reached a deal. The purchasing agent said that a purchase order would be forthcoming and promptly put one in the mail. Forsyte Shipbuilding replied with an acknowledgment form that added a disclaimer of warranty and then used the exact language of the proviso to make it clear that the seller was insisting on its own terms. You are the attorney for the Galsworthy Oil Company, and the company has asked you the following questions. Do the parties have a contract prior to the shipment of the boat? Is the disclaimer of warranty effective? See Air Products & Chemical, Inc. v. Fairbanks Morse, Inc., 58 Wis. 2d 193, 206 N.W.2d 414, 12 U.C.C. Rep. Serv. 794 (1973) (once a contract has been formed by mutual agreement, a written confirmation thereof cannot use the proviso to avoid the existing contract). If you are the attorney for the seller, what can you do in all these situations to make sure that your client's disclaimer of warranties is effective?

V.   INDEFINITENESS

As a general rule, no mutual assent exists and thus no contract is formed unless the agreement of the parties is sufficiently certain. Certain as to what? All terms? What degree of certainty must be shown? Must certainty be established only by the terms of the offer? Are terms in the acceptance relevant? Is evidence other than the language of the offer and acceptance to be considered?

[handwritten margin note: Need to be "Sufficiently Certain"]

CORBIN ON CONTRACTS §29

We must not jump too readily to the conclusion that a contract has not been made from the fact of apparent incompleteness. People do business in a very informal fashion, using abbreviated and elliptical language. A transaction is complete when the parties mean it to be complete. It is a mere matter of interpretation of their expressions to each other, a question of fact. An expression is no less effective than it is found by the method of implication. The parties may not give verbal expression to such vitally important matters as price, place and time of delivery, time of payment, amount of goods, and yet they may actually have agreed upon them. This may be shown by their antecedent expression, their past action and custom, and other circumstances.

———

The UCC requires the courts to look to the following matters as aids for construction of the contract: *usage of trade,* meaning the custom within any given industry; *course of dealing,* meaning the parties' past interactions with each other; and *course of performance,* meaning what the parties do while performing this *one* contract (what the common law called *practical construction*). Read §1-303 of the UCC. The UCC has a number of provisions designed to fill in the blanks left in the contract. Read §§2-305 (Open Price Term), 2-306 (Output, Requirements and Exclusive Dealings), 2-307 (Delivery in Single or Several Lots), 2-308 (Absence of Specified Place for Delivery), and 2-309 (Absence of Specific Time Provisions).

———

WALKER v. KEITH
Court of Appeals of Kentucky, 1964
382 S.W.2d 198

CLAY, Commissioner. . . .

In July 1951 appellants, the lessors, leased a small lot to appellee, the lessee, for a 10-year term at a rent of $100 per month. The lessee was given an option to extend the lease for an additional 10-year term, under the same terms and conditions except as to rental. The renewal option provided:

> rental will be fixed in such amount as shall actually be agreed upon by the lessors and the lessee with the monthly rental fixed on the comparative basis of rental values as of the date of the renewal with rental values at this time reflected by the comparative business conditions of the two periods.

The lessee gave the proper notice to renew but the parties were unable to agree upon the rent. Preliminary court proceedings finally culminated in this lawsuit. Based upon the verdict of an advisory jury, the Chancellor fixed the new rent at $125 per month.

The question before us is whether the quoted provision is so indefinite and uncertain that the parties cannot be held to have agreed upon this essential rental term of the lease. There have been many cases from other jurisdictions passing on somewhat similar lease provisions and the decisions are in hopeless conflict. We have no authoritative Kentucky decision.

At the outset two observations may be made. One is that rental in the ordinary lease is a very uncomplicated item. It involves the number of dollars the lessee will pay. It, or a method of ascertaining it, can be so easily fixed with certainty. From the standpoint of stability in business transactions, it should be so fixed.

Secondly, as an original proposition, uncomplicated by subtle rules of law, the provision we have quoted, on its face, is ambiguous and indefinite. The language used is equivocal. It neither fixes the rent nor furnishes a positive key to its establishment. The terminology is not only confusing but inherently unworkable as a formula.

The above observations should resolve the issue. Unfortunately it is not that simple. Many courts have become intrigued with the possible import of similar language and have interpolated into it a binding obligation. The lease renewal option has been treated as something different from an ordinary contract. The law has become woefully complicated. For this reason we consider it necessary and proper to examine this question in depth.

The following basic principles of law are generally accepted:

It is a necessary requirement in the nature of things that an agreement in order to be binding must be sufficiently definite to enable a court to give it an exact meaning. Williston on Contracts (3d ed.) Vol. 1, section 37 (page 107).

Like other contracts or agreements for a lease, the provision for a renewal must be certain in order to render it binding and enforceable. Indefiniteness, vagueness, and uncertainty in the terms of such a provision will render it void unless the parties, by their subsequent conduct or acts supplement the covenant and thus remove an alleged uncertainty. The certainty that is required is such as will enable a court to determine what has been agreed upon. 32 Am. Jur., Landlord and Tenant, section 958 (page 806).

The terms of an extension or renewal, under an option therefor in a lease, may be left for future determination by a prescribed method, as by future arbitration or appraisal; but merely leaving the terms for future ascertainment, without providing a method for their determination, renders the agreement unenforceable for uncertainty. 51 C.J.S. Landlord and Tenant 56b(2), page 597.

A renewal covenant in a lease which leaves the renewal rental to be fixed by future agreement between the parties has generally been held unenforceable and void for uncertainty and indefiniteness. Also, as a general rule, provisions for renewal rental dependent upon future valuation of premises without indicating when or how such valuation should be made have been held void for uncertainty and indefiniteness. 32 Am. Jur., Landlord and Tenant, section 965 (page 810).

Many decisions supporting these principles may be found in 30 A.L.R. 572; 68 A.L.R. 157; 166 A.L.R. 1237.

The degree of certainty is the controlling consideration. An example of an appropriate method by which a non-fixed rental could be determined appears in Jackson v. Pepper Gasoline Co., 280 Ky. 226, 113 S.W.2d 91, 126 A. L.R. 1370. The lessee, who operated an automobile service station, agreed to pay "an amount equal to one cent per gallon of gasoline delivered to said station." Observing that the parties had created *a definite objective standard* by which the rent could with certainty be *computed*, the court upheld the lease as against the contention that it was lacking in mutuality. (The Chancellor cited this case as authoritative on the issue before us, but we do not believe it is. Appellee apparently agrees because he does not even cite the case in his brief.)

On the face of the rent provision, the parties had not agreed upon a rent figure. They left the amount to future determination. If they had agreed upon a specific method of making the determination, such as by computation, the application of a formula, or the decision of an arbitrator, they could be said to have agreed upon whatever rent figure emerged from utilization of the method. This was not done.

It will be observed the rent provision expresses two ideas. The first is that the parties agree to agree. The second is that the future agreement will be based on a comparative adjustment in the light of "business conditions." We will examine separately these two concepts and then consider them as a whole.

The lease purports to fix the rent at such an amount as shall "actually be agreed upon." It should be obvious that an agreement to agree cannot constitute a binding contract. [Citations omitted.]

Slade v. City of Lexington, 141 Ky. 214, 132 S.W. 404, 32 L.R.A., N.S., 201, has been cited as adopting a contrary view. Certain language in that opinion would seem to justify such contention. However, that case involved very unusual features and some of the broad language used was unnecessary to the decision. The parties (being a legislatively created public service corporation and a municipality) had agreed to renew a contract "upon terms as mutually agreed upon." When the time came for renewal, *both parties agreed upon new terms.* Thus the contract in this respect was *executed.* Since the parties had actually complied with all of its provisions, it was properly held valid and binding as of its inception. No question was raised with respect to the enforceability of the contract as between the parties thereto, which is the issue before us. If this case may be construed to hold that an agreement to agree, standing alone, constitutes a binding contract, we believe it unsound.

As said in Williston on Contracts (3d ed.) Vol. 1, section 45 (page 149):

> Although a promise may be sufficiently definite when it contains an option given to the promisor, yet if an essential element is reserved for the future agreement of both parties, the promise gives rise to no legal obligation until such future agreement. Since either party, by the very terms of the

agreement, may refuse to agree to anything the other party will agree to, it is impossible for the law to fix any obligation to such a promise.

We accept this because it is both sensible and basic to the enforcement of a written contract. We applied it in Johnson v. Lowery, Ky., 270 S.W.2d 943, page 946, wherein we said:

> To be enforceable and valid, a contract to enter into a future covenant must specify all material and essential terms and leave nothing to be agreed upon as a result of future negotiations.

[handwritten margin note: Courts applied it in another case]

This proposition is not universally accepted as it pertains to renewal options in a lease. Hall v. Weatherford, 32 Ariz. 370, 259 P. 282, 56 A.L.R. 903; Rainwater v. Hobeika, 208 S.C. 433, 38 S.E.2d 495, 166 A.L.R. 1228. We have examined the reasons set forth in those opinions and do not find them convincing. The view is taken that the renewal option is for the benefit of the lessee; that the parties intended something; and that the lessee should not be deprived of his right to enforce his contract. This reasoning seems to overlook the fact that a party must have an enforceable contract before he has a right to enforce it. We wonder if these courts would enforce an *original* lease in which the rent was not fixed, but agreed to be agreed upon.

[handwritten margin note: Not universally accepted tho]

Surely there are some limits to what equity can or should undertake to compel parties in their private affairs to do what the court thinks they should have done. See Slayter v. Pasley, Or., 199 Or. 616, 264 P.2d 444, 449; and dissenting opinion of Judge Weygandt in Moss v. Olson, 148 Ohio 625, 76 N.E.2d 875. In any event, we are not persuaded that renewal options in leases are of such an exceptional character as to justify emasculation of one of the basic rules of contract law. An agreement to agree simply does not fix an enforceable obligation.

[handwritten margin note: An agreement to agree is Not an enforceable contract]

As noted, however, the language of the renewal option incorporated a secondary stipulation. Reference was made to "comparative business conditions" which were to play some part in adjusting the new rental. It is contended this provides the necessary certainty, and we will examine a leading case which lends support to the argument.

[handwritten margin note: "Comparative Business Condition"]

In Edwards v. Tobin, 132 Or. 38, 284 P. 562, 68 A.L.R. 152, the court upheld and enforced a lease agreement which provided that the rent should be "determined" at the time of renewal, "said rental to be *a reasonable rental* under the then existing conditions." (Our emphasis.) Significance was attached to the last quoted language, the court reasoning that since the parties had agreed upon a reasonable rent, the court would hold the parties to the agreement by fixing it.

[handwritten margin note: Edwards v. Tobin]

[handwritten margin note: Court held Parties Agreeable]

All rents tend to be reasonable. When parties are trying to reach an agreement, however, their ideas or claims of reasonableness may widely differ. In addition, they have a right to bargain. They cannot be said to be in *agreement* about what is a reasonable rent until they specify a figure or an

[handwritten margin note: current Court Not Persuaded]

exact method of determining it. The term "reasonable rent" is itself indefinite and uncertain. Would an original lease for a "reasonable rent" be enforceable by either party? The very purpose of a rental stipulation is to remove this item from an abstract area.

It is true courts often must *imply* such terms in a contract as "reasonable time" or "reasonable price." This is done when the parties fail to deal with such matters in an otherwise enforceable contract. Here the parties were undertaking to fix the terms rather than leave them to implication. Our problem is not what the law would imply if the contract did not purport to cover the subject matter, but whether the parties, in removing this material term from the field of implication, have fixed their mutual obligations.

We are seeking what the agreement actually was. When dealing with such a specific item as rent, to be payable in dollars, the area of possible agreement is quite limited. If the parties did not agree upon such an unequivocal item or upon a definite method of ascertaining it, then there is a clear case of nonagreement. The court, in fixing an obligation under a nonagreement, is not enforcing the contract but is binding the parties to something they were patently unable to agree to when writing the contract.

The opinion in the *Tobin* case, which purportedly was justifying the enforcement of a contractual obligation between the lessor and the lessee, shows on its face the court was doing something entirely different. This question was posed in the opinion: "What logical reason is there for equity to refuse to act when the parties themselves *fail to agree* on the rental?" (Our emphasis.) The obvious logical answer is that even equity cannot enforce as a contract a nonagreement. No distortion of words can hide the fact that when the court admits the parties "fail to agree," then the contract it enforces is one it makes for the parties.

It has been suggested that rent is not a material term of a lease. It is said in the *Tobin* case: "The method of determining the rent pertains more to form than to substance. It was not the essence of the contract, but was merely incidental and ancillary thereto." This seems rather startling. Nothing could be more vital in a lease than the amount of rent. It is the price the lessee agrees to pay and the lessor agrees to accept for the use of the premises. Would a contract to buy a building at a "reasonable price" be enforceable? Would the method of determining the price be a matter of "form" and "incidental and ancillary" to the transaction? In truth it lies at the heart of it. This seems to us as no more than a grammatical means of sweeping the problem under the rug. It will not do to say that the establishment of the rent agreed upon is not of the essence of a lease contract.

We have examined the *Tobin* case at length because it exemplifies lines of reasoning adopted by some courts to dredge certainty from uncertainty. Other courts balk at the process. The majority of cases, passing upon the question of whether a renewal option providing that the future rent shall be dependent upon or proportionate to *the valuation of the property* at the time of renewal, hold that such provision is not sufficiently certain to constitute an enforceable agreement. See cases cited in 30 A.L.R. 579 and 68 A.L.R. 159. The valuation of property and the ascertainment of "comparative business conditions," which we have under consideration, involve similar uncertainties.

A case construing language closely approximating that in the lease before us is Beal v. Dill, 173 Kan. 879, 252 P.2d 931. The option to extend the lease provided: "said rental shall be subject to reasonable adjustment, up or down, depending upon general business conditions then existing." The Kansas Supreme Court, purporting to follow what it deemed the "majority" rule (and citing numerous authorities), held this language was too indefinite to be enforceable.

The opposite conclusion on similar language was reached in Greene v. Leeper, 193 Tenn. 153, 245 S.W.2d 181. The option provided for: "a rental to be agreed on according to business conditions at that time." The court, declaring that "rental can be determined with reasonable certainty by dis-interested parties," adjudged this was an enforceable provision. The court indicated in the opinion that real estate experts would have no difficulty in fixing the rental agreed upon. The trouble is the parties did not agree to leave the matter to disinterested parties or real estate experts, and it is a false assumption that there will be no differences of opinion.

A similar renewal option was enforced in Fuller v. Michigan National Bank, 342 Mich. 92, 68 N.W.2d 771. In that case the language was "at a rent to be agreed upon, dependent on then existing conditions. . . ." The court treated the problem as one involving an *ambiguity*. Synonyms for the word "ambiguous" are: indeterminate, indefinite, unsettled. This dubiosity is of course what makes it clear the parties had failed to reach an *agreement*.

We do not think our problem can be solved by determining which is the "majority" rule and which is the "minority" rule. We are inclined, however, to adhere to a sound basic principle of contract law unless there are impel-ling reasons to depart from it, particularly so when the practical problems involved in such departure are so manifest. Let us briefly examine those practical problems.

What the law requires is an adequate key to a mutual agreement. If "comparative business conditions" afforded sufficient certainty, we might possibly surmount the obstacle of the unenforceable agreement to agree. This term, however, is very broad indeed. Did the parties have in mind local conditions, national conditions, or conditions affecting the lessee's particular business?

That a controversy, rather than a mutual agreement, exists on this very question is established in this case. One of the substantial issues on appeal is whether the Chancellor properly admitted in evidence the consumer price index of the United States Labor Department. At the trial the lessor was attempting to prove the change in local conditions and the lessee sought to prove changes in national conditions. Their minds to this day have never met on a criterion to determine the rent. It is pure fiction to say the court, in deciding upon some figure, is enforcing something the parties agreed to.

One aspect of this problem seems to have been overlooked by courts which have extended themselves to fix the rent and enforce the contract. This is the Statute of Frauds. The purpose of requiring a writing to evidence an agreement is to assure certainty of the essential terms thereof and to avoid controversy and litigation. See 49 Am. Jur., Statute of Frauds, section 313 (page 629); section 353 (page 663); section 354 (page 664). This very case is living proof of the difficulties encountered when a court undertakes to supply a missing essential term of a contract.

In the first place, when the parties failed to enter into a new agreement as the renewal option provided, their rights were no longer *fixed* by the contract. The determination of what they were was automatically shifted to the courtroom. There the court must determine the scope of relevant evidence to establish that certainty which obviously cannot be culled from the contract. Thereupon extensive proof must be taken concerning business conditions, valuations of property, and reasonable rentals. Serious controversies develop concerning the admissibility of evidence on the issue of whether "business conditions" referred to in the lease are those on the local or national level, or are those particularly affecting the lessee's business. An advisory jury is impanelled to express its opinion as to the proper rental figure. The judge then must decide whether the jury verdict conforms to the proof and to his concept of equity. On appeal the appellate court must examine alleged errors in the trial. Assuming some error in the trial (which appears likely on this record), the case may be reversed and the whole process begun anew. All of this time we are piously clinging to a concept that the contract itself fixed the rent with some degree of certainty.

We realize that litigation is oft times inevitable and courts should not shrink from the solution of difficult problems. On the other hand, courts should not expend their powers to establish contract rights which the parties, with an opportunity to do so, have failed to define. As said in Morrison v. Rossingnol, 5 Cal. 64, quoted in 30 A.L.R. at page 579:

> A court of equity is always chary of its power to decree specific performance, and will withhold the exercise of its jurisdiction in that respect, unless there is such a degree of certainty in the terms of the contract as will enable it at one view to do complete equity.

That cannot be done in this case.

Stipulations such as the one before us have been the source of interminable litigation. Courts are called upon not to enforce an agreement or to determine what the agreement was, but to write their own concept of what would constitute a proper one. Why this paternalistic task should be undertaken is difficult to understand when the parties could so easily provide any number of workable methods by which rents could be adjusted. As a practical matter, courts sometimes must assert their right not to be imposed upon. . . .

Rule ✗

Rent is a material term in v lease

We think the basic principle of contract law that requires substantial certainty as to the material terms upon which the minds of the parties have met is a sound one and should be adhered to. A renewal option stands on the same footing as any other contract right. Rent is a material term of a lease. If the parties do not fix it with reasonable certainty, it is not the business of courts to do so.

Holding

The renewal provision before us was fatally defective in failing to specify either an agreed rental or an agreed method by which it could be fixed with certainty. Because of the lack of agreement, the lessee's option right was illusory. The Chancellor erred in undertaking to enforce it.

Reversed

The judgment is reversed.

NOTES AND QUESTIONS

1. Compare Miller v. Bloomberg, 26 Ill. App. 3d 18, 324 N.E.2d 207 (Ill. App. 1975), in which the court was willing to uphold a contract allowing a tenant to purchase at the "then prevailing price." For an annotation on point, see 2 A.L.R.3d 701.

2. Would the UCC's statutory provisions listed prior to the case have solved the problem here? See UCC §§2-102 and 2-105(1).

---

lessor   **REGO v. DECKER**   *lessee*

Supreme Court of Alaska, 1971
482 P.2d 834

RABINOWITZ, J. Appellant Joseph Rego and his wife leased land with a three bay service station on it to appellee Robert Decker for one year, 1966.

Rent

Agreed to pave road

Option to renew with increased rent

Also an option to Purchase

The rent was to be $65 per month, plus 2 cents per gallon on all gasoline sold in excess of 4,000 gallons per month and "a sum equal to the net profit realized from the sale of diesel fuel." The Regos agreed in part to pave the grounds with asphalt before July 31, 1966. Under the lease Decker was given an option to renew for four years on the same terms except that the minimum rent was to be increased to $125 per month during 1969 and 1970. The lease also included an option to purchase provision which provided:

> The lessors shall grant the lessee the firm option to purchase the leased premises, upon the giving of thirty days written notice of the exercise of the option by certified mail, at any time during the term of this lease or the renewed term thereof. Upon the lessee's exercise of his option to purchase, the terms of the transaction shall be as follows:
>
> A. The purchase price of the premises shall be Eighty-One Thousand ($81,000.00) Dollars.

B. If lessee exercises his option to purchase within the term of this lease, the amount of all rents paid to the lessors shall be deducted from the purchase price. If the lessee exercises his option to purchase within the first two years of the renewed lease term seventy-five (75%) percent of all rents paid to the lessors shall be deducted from the purchase price. If the lessee exercises his option to purchase within the last two years of the renewed lease term, fifty (50%) percent of all rents paid to the lessors shall be deducted from the purchase price. The terms for payment of the remaining balance due on the purchase price in the event the lessee exercises his option to so purchase shall be identical to the terms hereinbefore set forth as rent herein.

C. The lessors shall furnish the lessee with a Warranty Deed to the property. The lessors shall also furnish the lessee with a title insurance policy for the amount of the purchase price subject to no exceptions other than deed restrictions, easements and patent reservations of record.

D. The parties shall have the right to terminate this lease, or any renewal thereof, at any time upon the giving of thirty (30) days written notice by certified mail. Provided, however, any options in existence on the effective date of such termination may be exercised in the manner herein provided for a period of ninety (90) days following said effective termination date.

The Regos never paved the grounds of the service station. Prior to the expiration of the initial one-year period of the lease, Decker renewed the same for a four-year period. In February of 1967, Decker notified the Regos that he was exercising his option to purchase the property, and demanded a warranty deed and title insurance policy within 30 days. The Regos did not comply with Decker's demand, and conveyed the property instead to others, who took with notice of Decker's interest. Decker sued the Regos and their grantees for specific performance by the Regos of their obligations under the option to purchase provisions of the lease, damages flowing from the Regos' failure to pave the premises and other relief. After trial to the superior court without a jury, judgment was entered ordering the Regos to execute and deliver a warranty deed to Decker, declaring that Decker would, in the event the Regos refused to convey to Decker, have title to the property not subject to any interest of the Regos or their grantees, and ordering the Regos to deliver to Decker an $81,000 title insurance policy on the property. The Regos were also ordered to pave the premises with an asphalt covering by July 15, 1969, or Decker was to have judgment for $15,000. From this judgment the Regos appeal. They argue that specific performance should have been denied because the terms of the option provisions of the lease were uncertain and too harsh, or in the alternative, that if granted, the specific performance provisions of the decree should have been conditioned upon various provisions protecting their interests. The Regos also contend that the court erred in providing for a $15,000 money judgment against them if they failed to pave the premises of the service station.

UNCERTAINTY OF THE TERMS OF THE CONTRACT

Regos Contend The
terms were uncertain

In this appeal the Regos argue that specific performance should have
been denied because the terms of the purchase option were uncertain. In
their view the uncertainty of the option is reflected in the provisions pertaining to the amount of monthly payments, the lack of definition concerning
the phrase "net profit" on diesel fuel sales, the omission of any provision for
interest and stipulated time for its payment, and the further omission of any
security for Decker's performance. Decker argues that monthly payments
under the purchase option clearly were to continue at $125 plus 2 cents per
gallon on gasoline sold in excess of 4,000 gallons and net profit on diesel
fuel; "net profits" on diesel fuel need not be certain because no diesel fuel
has been or is likely to be sold; extrinsic evidence indicated that the parties
intended no interest payments or security agreement.

"uncertain"
terms
claimed by
Regos

Decker Argues

To be specifically enforceable, a contract "must be reasonably definite
and certain as to its terms."[2] In Alaska Creamery Products, Inc. v. Wells,[3] a
contract for sale of goods was held too uncertain because the amount of the
down payment and the terms of future payments were left for future determination by the parties. The inadequate contract in *Alaska Creamery* was an
oral attempt to enter into an executory accord. Lewis v. Lockhart[4] reiterates
the *Alaska Creamery* rule,[5] but finds adequate certainty for specific performance of a promise to sell land on the strength of a lessee's option to
purchase on terms to be agreed on at the time of exercise, plus an "earnest
money receipt" acknowledging part payment of the purchase price and
reciting that the balance was to be obtained "from an FHA secured loan."
Lewis said that the earnest money receipt cured the uncertainty of the option
as drafted in the lease because the trial court could reasonably provide for
payment within four months on the basis of the common knowledge that
FHA loans generally were processed within that period.

Regarding the rule requiring reasonable certainty and its application to
particular factual situations, *Alaska Creamery* and *Lewis* demonstrate that:

> The dream of a mechanical justice is recognized for what it is — only a dream
> and not even a rosy or desirable one.[6]

In general it has been said that the primary underlying purpose of the
law of contracts is the attempted "realization of reasonable expectations that
have been induced by the making of a promise."[7] In light of this underlying

2. Alaska Creamery Products, Inc. v. Wells, 373 P.2d 505, 510 (Alaska 1962).
3. Id.
4. 379 P.2d 618 (Alaska 1963).
5. Id. at 622.
6. 5A A. Corbin, Contracts §1136, at 94 (1964).
7. 1 A. Corbin, Contracts §1, at 2 (1963).

purpose, two general considerations become relevant to solution of reasonable certainty-specific performance problems. <u>On the one hand</u>, courts should fill gaps in contracts to ensure fairness where the reasonable expectations of the parties are fairly clear. The parties to a contract often cannot negotiate and draft solutions to all the problems which may arise. Except in transactions involving very large amounts of money or adhesion contracts to be imposed on many parties, contracts tend to be skeletal, because the amount of time and money needed to produce a more complete contract would be disproportionate to the value of the transaction to the parties. Courts would impose too great a burden on the business community if the standards of certainty were set too high. <u>On the other hand</u>, the courts should not impose on a party any performance to which he did not and probably would not have agreed. Where the character of a gap in an agreement manifests failure to reach an agreement rather than a sketchy agreement, or where gaps cannot be filled with confidence that the reasonable expectations of the parties are being fulfilled, then specific enforcement should be denied for lack of reasonable certainty.

Two general considerations

Several other considerations affect the standard of certainty. A greater degree of certainty is required for specific performance than for damages, because of the difficulty of framing a decree specifying the performance required, as compared with the relative facility with which a breach may be perceived for purposes of awarding damages. Less certainty is required where the party seeking specific performance has substantially shifted his position in reliance on the supposed contract, than where the contract is wholly unperformed on both sides. While option contracts for the sale of land such as the one at issue are not technically within the scope of the Uniform Commercial Code, we consider relevant here the recent legislative decision to provide in contracts for sale of goods that

Technically Not within the UCC

> [e]ven though one or more terms are left open, a contract for sale <u>does not fail</u> <u>for indefiniteness</u> if the parties intended to make a contract and there is a reasonably certain basis for giving an appropriate remedy.[13]

We turn now to consideration of the Regos' specific claims of uncertainty. Appellants' first three claims of uncertainty are that the monthly minimum payment after 1970 was not clearly established, that the meaning of "net profit" on diesel fuel sales was unclear, and that the option did not clearly establish whether interest was to be due on the unpaid balance. Appellants further argue that the agreement was fatally uncertain because it failed to say what sort of security, if any, was required while appellee was paying for the gas station. Our disposition on the issue of security obviates the necessity for passing on appellants' first three contentions.

Appellants' Three Contentions of uncertainty

13. [Uniform Commercial Code §2-204(3).]

Normal business practice, appellants contend, would require a real estate contract, deed of trust, or mortgage, but here the purchase option agreement is too uncertain to determine what security provisions should be put into a decree. Appellee Decker argues that the parties intended that there should be no security agreement, so the contract is not uncertain. The trial court did not make a finding of fact on the question of whether security was intended. If the parties intended not to provide for security, then the silence of the contract does not amount to uncertainty. A finding by the trial court that the parties intended to have a security agreement but failed to specify its character would have amounted to uncertainty in the contract in question. Such uncertainty, however, should not result in unconditional denial of specific performance, at least where the vendee has entered into possession in part in reliance on the option to purchase agreement. But as we hold below, in the circumstances of this case, specific performance on the Regos' part should not have been required without conditioning such performance on the giving of security by Decker for his performance. In granting specific performance, the decree can be fashioned to provide that the plaintiff furnish adequate security for his agreed performance. In so doing, the courts are fulfilling their function of achieving justice between the parties without requiring additional or unnecessary litigation. . . .

Thus, although we believe the trial court was correct in granting Decker specific performance of the purchase option agreement, we further hold that the court's decree should have been made conditional upon Decker's either paying the purchase price in full or furnishing adequate security embodying such terms as the court considered appropriate. We therefore affirm the decree insofar as it awards Decker specific performance and the case is remanded for such further proceedings as are deemed necessary to condition the grant of specific performance upon the giving of appropriate security.

QUESTION

The court here is applying the old Latin maxim *ut res magis valeat quam pereat* ("let it be saved rather than destroyed"). Can this case be reconciled with the Kentucky case (Walker v. Keith) immediately preceding it?

Problem 31

Race Manhattan Bank agreed to purchase 100,000 loan forms from Mykos Printing. All terms were set but the price. Because of a recent amendment to New York statutes, Race and Mykos were not certain of the language

[handwritten margin notes: "Trial court didn't make finding on security question"; "Affirm Specific Performance"]

that would ultimately be required in the forms. Therefore, rather than specifying a price for the forms, it was agreed that the parties would later meet and set a price. When that time came, the parties could not agree on a price for the forms. Is there a contract? See UCC §2-305. What if the missing term were the place for delivery? See UCC §2-308.

Problem 32

Ms. Lovett owned a company that sold meat pies. In early May one year she contracted with a Mr. Todd to deliver 1,000 pies to his establishment on December 1. She regularly sold two different types of meat pies: Juicy (costing $2.89 each) and Extra Juicy ($3.89). Todd told her in May that he wasn't yet sure how much he wanted of each type, but he was certain he would want a total of 1,000. He agreed to phone her in November and specify the types desired. November arrived and she became worried when she did not hear from him. He told her that he had converted to vegetarianism and he refused to discuss the matter further. Read UCC §2-311 and decide if she had a contract. If so, advise her how to settle the specificity issue.

CHAPTER 1 ASSESSMENT

Multiple Choice Questions

1. Ronald went to Floors, Inc. and purchased 20 cartons of cork floor panels to install in his home, doing the work himself. While he was performing the installation on the second day of work, he checked his mail box and discovered a letter from Floors, Inc., which stated, "We forgot to give you the warranty that came with the product — it is enclosed." He didn't read the warranty, but put it with his bill of sale in a file on his desk. When the flooring proved defective months later and Floors, Inc. refused to refund his money, he threatened to file suit against the company. At this point Floors, Inc.'s lawyer told him that the warranty paperwork contained a clause that waived the right to sue and required purchasers to submit any disputes to arbitration. For the first time he read the warranty, and it did have such a requirement. He calls you, his cousin and favorite lawyer. Is he required to arbitrate? Choose the best response:

    a. Yes, since his silence on receiving the warranty was an acceptance of its terms even though he did not read the warranty.

    b. No. Ronald hadn't read the warranty terms so his silence meant nothing.

    c. Yes, because the whole deal included all the paperwork, and since he benefitted from the warranty he also agreed to the arbitration.

    d. No. The warranty was delivered after the close of the offer and acceptance had already created a contract, and is too late to modify that contract. He can sue based on the agreement to supply him with adequate flooring and ignore the paper warranty delivered after the deal was already formed.

    e. Yes. The warranty was a proposal to modify the contract and his retention of it without objection was an agreement to the modification, which included the arbitration requirement.

2. When the owner of the Chicago Pups professional baseball team became tired of its losing record after owning the team for many years, he sold it for $25 million to his daughter. The contract for this was 20 pages long and took two weeks to negotiate. After the sale, the Pups did very well and won the World Series two years in a row. At a family holiday party that second December, the father, eggnog in hand, told his daughter he would give her $40 million if she would let him repurchase the club. She was a non-drinker and thought this was a pretty good price, so she asked him if he was serious. He said, "Of course I am," and she said, "Then shake on it." They promptly shook hands, and the rest of the family applauded. Two days later when the father called his daughter to set up a conference to iron out the details, she laughed and told him that she had changed her mind and was not going to sell him the Pups for any price. He sued, and you are the judge in the case. Is there a binding contract here?

    a. No. It was too festive an occasion and the father was drinking, so no intent to contract is present.

    b. Yes. Witnesses will testify that it was a definite deal, and the father, the drinker, still wants to pay the large sum. There's no indication he was too drunk make a contract. It's simply too late for her to change her mind.

    c. No. Agreement on the price is only one part of this complicated sale and the other major details are unresolved, making the contract too indefinite to enforce.

    d. Yes. The prior contract supplies the details, and the major issue, the price (a fair amount) was settled by a handshake.

    e. No. Family gatherings are not a reliable setting for a multimillion dollar transaction to be settled by a handshake.

3. When Carrie visited the museum owned by the Thomas family, she was most impressed by the Picasso collection the family had exhibited in one special room. Her favorite was a stunning painting called "Woman of Smiles," which she had never heard of before. Nancy Thomas, the owner of the collection, told her that it was a new acquisition and that she had paid $2 million for it. Carrie, very rich herself, promptly offered her $4 million for the painting. Awed at the sum, and in need of money, Nancy accepted, and the women shook hands, agreeing that Carrie could come by the next day and pick up the painting in return for a check for the named price. That evening Nancy sent Carrie an email stating, "Thank you for your offer to buy 'Woman of Smiles' for $4 million, payable tomorrow at the museum. The sale is subject to a disclaimer my attorney requires me to make that there is no warranty that the painter is necessarily the one to whom any given painting is routinely attributed, and the risk that the painter is someone else is on the buyer." Carrie received the email, and the next day the exchange of the check for the painting took place at the museum. Nothing was said about the disclaimer in the email. When the painting proved to be a forgery, Carrie demanded her money back. Nancy's lawyer said that the email created a term that became part of the contract and protected Nancy. Carrie's attorney pointed to §2-207 of the Uniform Commercial Code. How does this come out?

a. There is no contract since the parties failed to agree on a key term. Thus the painting still belongs to Nancy and Carrie gets her $4 million back.

b. This is what subsection (1) of §2-207 calls "a written confirmation" and sends us to subsection (2), where the key question (assuming both parties qualify as "merchants") will be whether this is a "material alteration" to the original deal, as, of course, it is. In that case the disclaimer is not part of the contract and Nancy loses. If the parties aren't merchants, then subsection (2) makes this disclaimer a proposal for addition to the contract and the court will have to decide if Carrie's payment without objection was an acceptance of the new term.

c. The disclaimer is invalid because no one would pay $4 million for a forgery of a Picasso painting, so Carrie could not be understood to have agreed to so outrageous a term.

d. This a "rolling" contract, with the parties understanding that until delivery either party could add new terms to the contract and the other party could cancel the deal if unwilling to accept these new terms. Thus Nancy wins since Carrie didn't object.

e. Since the parties have failed to reach agreement on this important term, there is no contract until they perform the exchange. Then subsection (3) of §2-207 creates the contract using the terms agreed upon plus those supplied by the Uniform Commercial Code. Since the Code does not favor disclaimers, Carrie will win.

4. Diego sent an email to Maria offering to sell her his award-winning race car, El Jefe, for $80,000. El Jefe had just beaten Maria's car in a major race and he knew she was interested in buying. She replied that she wanted a week to think about it, that being a steep price for the car. He emailed

back that he had other possible buyers, but would give her a week to think it over if she paid him a non-refundable $100 for the right to make her decision in that period. Maria agreed, and wired him that amount through PayPal. The parties agreed the week would end at midnight on the following Thursday. Two minutes before midnight on that day Maria wired Diego the $80,000, and also sent him an email right before midnight saying she was accepting and the money would be in his account by the next day, and the email arrived in his email account at two minutes after midnight. Diego had changed his mind about selling El Jefe to anyone, and refused to go through with the sale when she phoned him at 5 P.M. the next day to discuss the details. Furious, she sued. What result?

a. He wins. The parties had specified the time period for acceptance, for which she'd paid money. That created an option contract and the law requires receipt of the acceptance within the option period. The "mail box rule" does not apply to option contracts.

b. She wins. She sent the payment before midnight and he received it the next day, so the money was transferred within the required period. And her email was sent just before midnight, so he's in no way deceived about her intentions when he got it shortly thereafter. He'd taken no steps to sell the car to anyone else, so he should be bound by his contract with her.

c. She wins. Even if the argument in B doesn't work for some reason, he had a duty to speak up immediately if he thought she was too late. A late acceptance creates a duty to speak if it will be used as the basis for objection, and he waited too long to do so if he didn't tell her until the next day in the late afternoon.

d. He wins. She had only herself to blame if she failed to act within the period she so carefully negotiated. He told her the next day that she'd missed the deadline, a fact she already knew. She has no reliance interest to protect.

e. She wins. Our rules of law are not so picky or technical that a few minutes destroys an important deal where there's no harm caused by the insignificant delay. The mail box rule makes acceptances effective on *dispatch*, and here she dispatched the acceptance by sending the email before the midnight deadline.

5. Daredevil aerialist Hugo Steady walked tightropes across major landmarks, earning his living by such dangerous stunts. When he was on a late-night TV talk show and the other guest was Donald Hair, a bouncy millionaire and loud talker, Hair publicly challenged him to walk across the top of the Golden Gate bridge, using the existing spans, blindfolded, and said to Steady, "If you can do this and not fall I'll pay you a million dollars and pay for the expenses of the telecast myself, win or lose." Steady replied that he would try the walk next March, and the two men shook hands on the air. Steady gave up other projects and spent

much time preparing for the Golden Gate attempt, scheduled for March 5, a date announced by both Steady and Hair in a joint news conference promoting the stunt. On March 4 Steady changed his mind and announced that he thought the walk would be too dangerous, so he declined to try it. At that point, Hair demanded that Steady pay the considerable expenses Hair had already incurred in buying the air time and promoting the event. When Steady refused, a lawsuit followed. Who prevails?

a. It will depend on whether the fact finder decides this was a bilateral or unilateral contract. Did the parties shake hands while exchanging a promise to pay for the event in return for a promise to attempt the stunt? That would create a bilateral contract and Steady would have to pay for Hair's reliance expenses when he breached by not performing his promise. If there was no exchange, this was simply a promise for a unilateral act (walking the bridge on the spans), and Steady, having made no *promise* to do the walk, was free of liability if he decided not to try.

b. The shaking of hands on the TV show coupled with the later joint appearance made it clear that both parties were committed to the deal, and there was no ability to walk away from the stunt without at least paying the reliance expenses Hair incurred. The law struggles to protect reliance interests, and thus Steady should pay up. Professional daredevils are always risking at least the expenses of their foolish promises, and if they don't want to have that financial risk, they should go into a safer business.

c. Steady should win. No one would *commit* to risking his life for money in so dangerous an endeavor, and the law should not force him to risk his life or pay up. The very reason for entering into a unilateral contract is to preserve the ability to do the act or not without liability until the performance occurs. Hair is not Steady's regular promoter, but a daredevil himself, eager to risk his own money, and here the risk didn't pay off.

Answers

1. D is the best answer. At best the late-arriving warranty is an attempt to modify the existing contract and would take an acceptance by Ronald before it added the arbitration term. Merely receiving the warranty and filing it away without reading it is not likely to be construed as an acceptance, and Floors, Inc. cannot argue it relied in any way on his inactivity.

2. C is the best answer. The sale of a major business is a complicated matter—witness the two weeks of negotiations for the prior sale—and agreeing on the price is just the first step. Until the parties work out the other issues (dates, timing of the payment, form of the payment, what is

included in the sale, etc.) this is just an agreement to agree, which is unenforceable.

3. B is the best answer. When the parties have already created a contract through offer and acceptance, new terms are added only if accepted by the other party. Between merchants non-material terms can be added, but not material ones. Carrie, for all we are told, is not a merchant (though Nancy probably qualifies if she often buys and sells paintings for her museum), but even if she were, a disclaimer of Picasso's status as the painter is obviously a major matter, and therefore would not become part of the contract. Subsection (3) of §2-207 is irrelevant since the parties did have an offer and acceptance, and also because their contract was not created by an exchange of writings, which is the scenario for the application of that subsection.

4. A is the best answer. Fair or not, the law is clear that in option contracts the acceptance must be received within the option period, and mere dispatch within that period won't do. Lawyers must be ever sensitive to this rule if an option contract is involved. Of course, the recipient may not care, or may waive application of the rule by conduct indicating the deal is still on, but that's not what happened here.

5. A is the best answer, though the arguments in the other two answers have their merits. This is really a factual question: What did the parties decide about the ability to cancel the walk? If this were in writing, that would be a question of law, because what a writing means has always been a question of law (dating from the time when jurors could not read), and the judge decides questions of law. But here the agreement was oral and witnessed by millions of people. The jury will have to decide who wins after viewing the TV show, listening to witnesses, and finally hearing lawyers make the arguments in answers B and C.

CONSIDERATION

Civilization itself has arisen in no small part because of the exclusively human trait of swapping things. Much of what we know of early civilization derives from still extant commercial records. Certainly commercial law is very old law. By 3000 B.C. Egypt and what is now Iraq had reached a thriving commerce, and from there we have progressed to a system that is so complicated that no one understands it. Certain fundamentals, though, still obtain. The very essence of such a commerce, then and now, is the necessity of exchange.

Exchange is also important in contract law. In every contract, a promise is exchanged for something else, or, phrased another way, in "consideration" of something else. In the field of contracts, the word "consideration" refers to whatever is exchanged for a promise (money, a cow, another promise, etc.). Very roughly, the consideration doctrine requires that every agreement involve an exchange of things of value—that each party promises to do (or not do) something because of what they are getting in return.

I. THE BASIC CONCEPT

A. *Definition*

ADAM SMITH, THE WEALTH OF NATIONS
(1776)

In almost every other race of animals each individual, when it is grown up to maturity, is entirely independent, and in its natural state has occasion for the assistance of no other living creature. But man has almost constant occasion for the help of his brethren, and it is in vain for him to expect it from their benevolence only. He will be more likely to prevail if he can interest their self-love in his favour, and show them that it is for their own advantage to do for him what he requires of them. Whoever offers to another a bargain of any kind, proposes to do this. Give me that which I want, and you shall have this which you want, is the meaning of every such offer; and it is in this manner that we obtain from one another the far greater part of those good offices which we stand in need of. It is not from the benevolence of the butcher, the brewer, or the baker that we expect our dinner, but from their regard to their own interest.

CORBIN ON CONTRACTS §110

The mere fact that one man promises something to another creates no legal duty and makes no legal remedy available in case of nonperformance. To be enforceable, the promise must be accompanied by some other factor. This seems to be true of all systems of law. The question now to be discussed is what is this other factor. What fact or facts must accompany a promise to make it enforceable at law?

A contract is defined as a promise that the law will enforce. See Corbin §3. This means that a true contract will always contain at least one promise, and in a typical commercial setting that promise will be exchanged for something else, a *quid pro quo*. That "something else" is what the law calls *consideration*.

RESTATEMENT (SECOND) OF CONTRACTS

§71. Requirement of Exchange; Types of Exchange

(1) To constitute consideration, a performance or a return promise must be bargained for.

(2) A performance or return promise is bargained for if it is sought by the promisor in exchange for his promise and is given by the promisee in exchange for that promise.

(3) The performance may consist of
    (a) an act other than a promise, or
    (b) a forbearance, or
    (c) the creation, modification, or destruction of a legal relation.

(4) The performance or return promise may be given to the promisor or to some other person. It may be given by the promisee or by some other person.

Problem 33

Should the following promises, without more, be enforced?

NO (a) I promise to give you $500. *No Act other than a promise*

yes (b) I promise to give you $500 if you go to Chicago. ← *An Act*

yes (c) I promise to give you $500 if you do not go to Chicago next Friday. ← *forbearance*

HAMER v. SIDWAY
Court of Appeals of New York, 1891
124 N.Y. 538, 27 N.E. 256

Appeal from an order of the general term of the supreme court in the fourth judicial department, reversing a judgment entered on the decision of the court at special term in the county clerk's office of Chemung county on the 1st day of October, 1889. The plaintiff presented a claim to the executor of William E. Story, Sr., for $5,000 and interest from the 6th day of February, 1875. She acquired it through several mesne assignments from William E. Story, 2d. The claim being rejected by the executor, this action was brought. *The claim being rejected by the executor* It appears that William E. Story, Sr., was the uncle of William E. Story, 2d; that at the celebration of the golden wedding of Samuel Story and wife, father and mother of William E. Story, Sr., on the 20th day of March, 1869, in the presence of the family and invited guests, he promised his nephew that if he *The promise* would refrain from drinking, using tobacco, swearing, and playing cards or billiards for money until he became 21 years of age, he would pay him the sum of $5,000. The nephew assented thereto, and fully performed the conditions inducing the promise. When the nephew arrived at the age of 21 years, and on the 31st day of January, 1875, he wrote to his uncle, informing *Nephew informing uncle he had performed his part of the agreement* him that he had performed his part of the agreement, and had thereby become entitled to the sum of $5,000. The uncle received the letter, and a few days later, and on the 6th day of February, he wrote and mailed to his nephew the following letter:

> Buffalo, Feb. 6, 1875
> W. E. Story, Jr.

Dear Nephew:

Your letter of the 31st ultimately came to hand all right, saying that you had lived up to the promise made to me several years ago. I have no doubt but you have, for which you shall have five thousand dollars, as I promised you. I had the money in the bank the day you was twenty-one years old that I intend for you, and you shall have the money certain. Now, Willie, I do not intend to interfere with this money in any way till I think you are capable of taking care of it, and the sooner that time comes the better it will please me. I would hate very much to have you start out in some adventure that you thought all right and lose this money in one year. The first five thousand dollars that I got together cost me a heap of hard work. You would hardly believe me when I tell you that to obtain this I shoved a jack-plane many a day, butchered three or four years, then came to this city, and, after three months' perserverance, I obtained a situation in a grocery store. I opened this store early, closed late, slept in the fourth story of the building in a room 30 by 40 feet, and not a human being in the building but myself. All this I done to live as cheap as I could to save something. I don't want you to take up with this kind of fare. I was here in the cholera season of '49 and '52, and the deaths averaged 80 to 125 daily, and plenty of small-pox. I wanted to go home, but Mr. Fisk, the gentleman I was working for, told me, if I left them, after it got healthy he probably would not want me. I stayed. All the money I have saved I know just how I got it. It did not come to me in any mysterious way, and the reason I speak of this is that money got in this way stops longer with a fellow that gets it with hard knocks than it does when he finds it. Willie, you are twenty-one, and you have many a thing to learn yet. This money you have earned much easier than I did, besides acquiring good habits at the same time, and you are quite welcome to the money. Hope you will make good use of it. I was ten long years getting this together after I was your age. Now, hoping this will be satisfactory, I stop. . . .

Willie, I have said much more than I expected to. Hope you can make out what I have written. To-day is the seventeenth day that I have not been out of my room, and have had the doctor as many days. Am a little better today. Think I will get out next week. You need not mention to father, as he always worries about small matters.

Truly yours,
W. E. Story

P.S. You can consider this money on interest.

> The nephew received the letter, and thereafter consented that the money should remain with his uncle in accordance with the terms and conditions of the letter. The uncle died on the 29th day of January, 1887, without having paid over to his nephew any portion of the said $5,000 and interest. . . .

[handwritten margin notes: Nephew Consented to the letter; Uncle Died before paying the nephew]

PARKER, J. (after stating the facts as above). The question which provoked the most discussion by counsel on this appeal, and which lies at the foundation of plaintiff's asserted right of recovery, is whether by virtue of a contract defendant's testator, William E. Story, became indebted to his nephew, William E. Story, 2d, on his twenty-first birthday in the sum of $5,000. The trial court found as a fact that "on the 20th day of March, 1869, . . . William E. Story agreed to and with William E. Story, 2d, that if he would refrain from drinking liquor, using tobacco, swearing, and playing cards or billiards for money until he should become twenty-one years of age, then he, the said William E. Story, would at that time pay him, the said William E. Story, 2d, the sum of $5,000 for such refraining, to which the said William E. Story, 2d, agreed," and that he "in all things fully performed his part of said agreement." The defendant contends that the contract was without consideration to support it, and therefore invalid. He asserts that the promisee, by refraining from the use of liquor and tobacco, was not harmed, but benefited; that that which he did was best for him to do, independently of his uncle's promise, — and insists that it follows that, unless the promisor was benefited, the contract was without consideration, — a contention which, if well founded, would seem to leave open for controversy in many cases whether that which the promisee did or omitted to do was in fact of such benefit to him as to leave no consideration to support the enforcement of the promisor's agreement. Such a rule could not be tolerated, and is without foundation in the law. The exchequer chamber in 1875 defined "consideration" as follows: "A valuable consideration, in the sense of the law, may consist either in some right, interest, profit, or benefit accruing to the one party, or some forbearance, detriment, loss, or responsibility given, suffered, or undertaken by the other." Courts "will not ask whether the thing which forms the consideration does in fact benefit the promisee or a third party, or is of any substantial value to any one. It is enough that something is promised, done, forborne, or suffered by the party to whom the promise is made as consideration for the promise made to him." Anson, Cont. 63. "In general a waiver of any legal right at the request of another party is a sufficient consideration for a promise." Pars. Cont. 444. "Any damage, or suspension, or forbearance of a right will be sufficient to sustain a promise." 2 Kent, Comm. (12th ed.) 465. Pollock in his work on Contracts (page 166), after citing the definition given by the exchequer chamber, already quoted, says: "The second branch of this judicial description is really the most important one. 'Consideration' means not so much that one party is profiting as that the other abandons some legal right in the present, or limits his legal freedom of action in the future, as an inducement for the promise of the first." Now, applying this rule to the facts before us, the promisee used tobacco, occasionally drank liquor, and he had a legal right to do so. That right he abandoned for a period of years upon the strength of the promise of the testator that for such forbearance he would give him $5,000. We need not speculate on the effort which may have been required to give up the use of those stimulants. It is sufficient that he restricted his lawful freedom of action within certain prescribed limits upon the faith of his uncle's agreement, and now, having fully performed the conditions imposed, it is of no moment whether such performance actually proved a benefit to the promisor, and the court will not inquire into it; but, were it a proper subject of inquiry, we see nothing in this record that would permit a determination that the uncle was not benefited in a legal sense. Few cases have been found which may be said to be precisely in point, but such as have been, support the position we have taken. In Shadwell v. Shadwell, 9 C.B. (N.S.) 159, an uncle wrote to his nephew as follows:

My dear Lancey:

I am so glad to hear of your intended marriage with Ellen Nicholl, and, as I promised to assist you at starting, I am happy to tell you that I will pay you 150 pounds yearly during my life and until your annual income derived from your profession of a chancery barrister shall amount to 600 guineas, of which your own admission will be the only evidence that I shall receive or require.

Your affectionate uncle,
Charles Shadwell

It was held that the promise was binding, and made upon good consideration. In Lakota v. Newton, (an unreported case in the superior court of Worcester, Mass.,) the complaint averred defendant's promise that "if you [meaning the plaintiff] will leave off drinking for a year I will give you $100." Plaintiff's assent thereto, performance of the condition by him, and demanded judgment therefor. Defendant demurred, on the ground, among others, that the plaintiff's declaration did not allege a valid and sufficient consideration for the agreement of the defendant. The demurrer was overruled. In Talbott v. Stemmons, 12 S.W. Rep. 297, (a Kentucky case, not yet officially reported,) the step-grandmother of the plaintiff made with him the following agreement: "I do promise and bind myself to give my grandson Albert R. Talbott $500 at my death if he will never take another chew of tobacco or smoke another cigar during my life, from this date up to my death; and if he breaks this pledge he is to refund double the amount to his mother." The executor of Mrs. Stemmons demurred to the complaint on the ground that the agreement was not based on a sufficient consideration. The demurrer was sustained, and an appeal taken therefrom to the court of appeals, where the decision of the court below was reversed. In the opinion of the court it is said that "the right to use and enjoy the use of tobacco was a right that belonged to the plaintiff, and not forbidden by law. The abandonment of its use may have saved him money, or contributed to his health; nevertheless, the surrender of that right caused the promise, and, having the right to contract with reference to the subject matter, the abandonment of the use was a sufficient consideration to uphold the promise. . . ."

The order appealed from should be <u>reversed</u>, and the judgment of the special term affirmed, with costs payable out of the estate. All concur.

QUESTIONS

1. Analyze this case under the Restatement provision that precedes the case. What exactly was the consideration?

2. After quoting the classic definition of "valuable" consideration as being something of benefit to the promisor or of detriment to the promisee, the court states that the latter alone is enough but that if both were required there was benefit to the uncle here. What does the court mean? What benefit did the uncle receive from the nephew's asceticism?

Problem 34

Meriwether, who is wealthy, has a credit account at Barney's (a fancy department store). One cold winter's afternoon, Meriwether is walking down the street near Barney's when he sees Lewis, a homeless man, shivering on a street corner. Meriwether, feeling a rush of sympathy, approaches Lewis. Pointing to Barney's, Meriwether says, "If <u>you walk</u> to that store, you can buy a coat on my credit account." "Thank you! I accept," replies Lewis. Have the parties formed a binding contract?

Performance done by an Act

Lewis has to Actually walk to the store first

B. Sufficiency

Traditionally, the <u>common law</u> rule was that the courts would inquire into the sufficiency of the consideration, but <u>not</u> the adequacy of the consideration. *Sufficiency* means that the offered consideration must be something that has value in the eyes of the law; <u>*adequacy*</u> refers to the quantity of the amounts exchanged. The Restatement (Second) of Contracts no longer refers to the issue of sufficiency, but this does not necessarily mean that the issue has disappeared.

common Law

WILLIAMS v. ORMSBY
Supreme Court of Ohio, 2012
131 Ohio St. 3d 427, 966 N.E.2d 255

LANZINGER, J.

[¶1] We are asked to determine whether merely resuming a romantic relationship by moving into a home with another can serve as consideration for a contract. We hold that it cannot.

I. Factual Background

[¶2] This case arises in the context of a nonmarital relationship between Amber Williams, the appellee, and Frederick Ormsby, the appellant. In May 2004, Frederick moved into Amber's house on Hardwood Hollow in Medina to which she had received title through her divorce settlement. Frederick began making the mortgage payments in August and paid the 2004 property taxes. He eventually paid the remaining mortgage balance of approximately $310,000. In return, Amber gave Frederick title to the property by executing a quitclaim deed dated December 15, 2004, that was recorded the same day.

[¶3] Although the couple had planned to marry, they canceled their plans in January 2005 when Frederick's divorce did not occur. They did, however, continue to live together. After a disagreement in March 2005, Amber left the house, and Frederick obtained a restraining order against her. As a result of this separation, Amber and Frederick signed a document dated March 24, 2005, to immediately sell the Medina house and allocate the proceeds.

[¶4] Two months later, the couple tried to reconcile and attended couples counseling. Amber refused to move back into the house with Frederick unless he granted her an undivided one-half interest in the property. On June 2, 2005, they signed a second document, purportedly making themselves "equal partners" in the Medina house and, among other things, providing for property disposition in the event that their relationship ended. Amber then returned to the house, and the couple resumed their relationship. But by April 2007, they were living in separate areas of the house, and although they tried counseling again, Amber ended the relationship in September 2007. The two continued living in separate areas of the house until Frederick left in April 2008.

[¶5] The next month, Amber and Frederick filed suit against each other in two separate actions, which the trial court consolidated. Amber sought either specific performance of the contract that she alleged was created in June 2005 to give her a half-interest in the property or damages stemming from breach of that contract. In his complaint, Frederick alleged causes of action for quiet title and unjust enrichment or quantum meruit and sought a declaratory judgment that both the March 2005 and June 2005 documents are invalid for lack of consideration. He also alleged causes of action for breach of contract, partition, and contribution if either or both agreements were held valid.

[¶6] Both parties filed motions for summary judgment. On April 16, 2009, the trial court determined that the March 2005 agreement was supported by consideration but that the June 2005 agreement was not. The court granted judgment to Frederick on Amber's complaint and held that title to the property was vested in him exclusively. Amber was granted judgment on Frederick's causes of action for contribution and unjust enrichment. The trial court ruled that the only issue remaining for trial was whether Frederick was entitled to damages for any possible breach of the March 2005 contract.

[¶7] Over the next several months, the parties amended their pleadings and attempted to dismiss various claims. A judgment entry was issued in October 2009 pursuant to Civ. R. 54(B) to declare that the court's summary judgment order was final and appealable and that there was no just reason for delay. Amber appealed.

[¶8] The Ninth District Court of Appeals reversed the trial court's judgment, concluding that under the facts of this case, "moving into a home with another and resuming a relationship can constitute consideration sufficient to support a contract." Williams v. Ormsby, 190 Ohio App. 3d 815, 2010-Ohio-4664, 944 N.E.2d 699, ¶19 (9th Dist.). The court of appeals also held that the June 2005 contract was not conditioned upon marriage, and thus, the consideration had not failed. Id. at ¶22.

[¶9] Frederick appealed, and we accepted jurisdiction on his sole proposition of law: "Moving into a home with another and resuming a romantic relationship cannot serve as legal consideration for a contract; love and affection is [sic] insufficient consideration for a contract."

II. Legal Analysis

[¶10] We must first note that the proposition accepted does not refer broadly to all circumstances of cohabitation. As we have held, "[t]he essential elements of 'cohabitation' are (1) sharing of familial or financial responsibilities and (2) consortium." State v. Williams, 79 Ohio St. 3d 459, 683 N.E.2d 1126 (1997), paragraph two of the syllabus. In the case before us, the issue is only whether the emotional aspect of resuming a relationship by moving in together can serve as consideration for a contract—separate and apart from the sharing of financial resources and obligations.

[¶11] Although the dissenting opinion takes a rather cynical view of the relationship between the parties and seems to liken it to a business transaction allowing Amber to avoid her creditors, we disagree. Speculation and innuendo are not evidence. While it is not surprising that there was no longer any love or affection between the parties at the time of their depositions, both Amber and Frederick agreed that they began a romantic relationship on April 30, 2004, moved in together the next month, became engaged in July 2004, separated in March 2005, and in June 2005, reunited and "plan[ned] to be married." Furthermore, although there was some evidence that Amber had some outstanding financial obligations from her divorce at the time Frederick moved into the house, there is absolutely no evidence that she was unable or unwilling to meet those obligations.

[¶12] Frederick contends that the only consideration offered for the June 2005 agreement was resuming a romantic relationship, which cannot serve as consideration for a contract. He argues that to enforce such a contract is the same as enforcing a contract to make a gift in consideration of love and affection.

[¶13] Amber counters that the March 2005 agreement was novated, i.e., legally substituted, by the June 2005 agreement and that Frederick received a benefit that he bargained for. She maintains that the June 2005 agreement was supported by consideration.

A. GENERAL CONTRACT PRINCIPLES

[¶14] We have stated, "'A contract is generally defined as a promise, or a set of promises, actionable upon breach. Essential elements of a contract include an offer, acceptance, contractual capacity, consideration (the bargained for legal benefit and/or detriment), a manifestation of mutual assent and legality of object and of consideration.'" Kostelnik v. Helper, 96 Ohio St. 3d 1, 2002-Ohio-2985, 770 N.E.2d 58, ¶16, quoting Perlmuter Printing Co. v. Strome, Inc., 436 F. Supp. 409, 414 (N.D. Ohio 1976).

1. The Need for Consideration

[¶15] In this case, we are concerned with the legal enforceability of the June 2005 writing, for a contract is not binding unless supported by consideration. Judy v. Louderman, 48 Ohio St. 562, 29 N.E. 181 (1891), paragraph two of the syllabus.

[¶16] Consideration may consist of either a detriment to the promisee or a benefit to the promisor. Irwin v. Lombard Univ., 56 Ohio St. 9, 19, 46 N. E. 63 (1897). A benefit may consist of some right, interest, or profit accruing to the promisor, while a detriment may consist of some forbearance, loss, or responsibility given, suffered, or undertaken by the promisee. *Id.* at 20, 46 N. E. 63.

[¶17] We also have a long-established precedent that courts may not inquire into the adequacy of consideration, which is left to the parties as "'the sole judges of the benefits or advantages to be derived from their contracts.'" Hotels Statler Co., Inc. v. Safier, 103 Ohio St. 638, 644-645, 134 N.E. 460 (1921), quoting Newhall v. Paige, 10 Gray (76 Mass.) 366, 368 (1858). But whether there is consideration at all is a proper question for a court.

> Gratuitous promises are not enforceable as contracts, because there is no consideration. . . . A written gratuitous promise, even if it evidences an intent by the promisor to be bound, is not a contract. . . . Likewise, conditional gratuitous promises, which require the promisee to do something before the promised act or omission will take place, are not enforceable as contracts. . . . While it is true, therefore, that courts generally do not inquire into the adequacy of consideration once it is found to exist, it must be

determined in a contract case whether any "consideration" was really bargained for. If it was not bargained for, it could not support a contract.

Carlisle v. T & R Excavating, Inc., 123 Ohio App. 3d 277, 283-284, 704 N.E.2d 39 (9th Dist. 1997).

2. Novation

[¶18] Amber argues that the June 2005 agreement is a valid novation of the March 2005 agreement. "A contract of novation is created where a previous valid obligation is extinguished by a new valid contract, accomplished by substitution of parties or of the undertaking, with the consent of all the parties, and based on valid consideration." McGlothin v. Huffman, 94 Ohio App. 3d 240, 244, 640 N.E.2d 598 (12th Dist. 1994). A novation can never be presumed but must be evinced by a clear and definite intent on the part of all the parties to the original contract to completely negate the original contract and enter into the second. King Thompson, Holzer-Wollam, Inc. v. Anderson, 10th Dist. No. 93APE08-1155, 1994 WL 14791, *2 (Jan. 20, 1994).

[¶19] Because a novation is a new contract, it too must meet all the elements of a contract. Therefore, even if the June 2005 document is a novation of the original March 2005 agreement, it must be supported by consideration.

3. Distinction Between Contract and Gift

[¶20] The trial court concluded that the June 2005 agreement was nothing more than a written gratuitous promise because there was no consideration for that agreement. In fact, the requirement for consideration is what distinguishes a contract from a gift. The essential elements of an inter vivos gift are (1) an intention on the part of the donor to transfer the title and right of possession to the donee, (2) delivery by the donor to the donee, (3) relinquishment of ownership, dominion, and control over the gift by the donor, and (4) acceptance by the donee. Bolles v. Toledo Trust Co., 132 Ohio St. 21, 26-27, 4 N.E.2d 917 (1936). Therefore, a gift is a voluntary transfer by the donor to the donee without any consideration or compensation.

[¶21] Even if we were to construe the June 2005 agreement as a promise to make a gift of one-half interest in the property, we must still examine whether there is consideration, because even a written promise to make a gift is not binding on the promisor if the promise lacks consideration. Hendrie v. Hendrie, 94 F.2d 534, 535 (5th Cir. 1938).

B. THE AGREEMENTS

[¶22] To be enforceable between the parties, therefore, the agreements must be supported by consideration. Although the enforceability of the

March agreement is not before us, the terms of both documents signed by the parties will be summarized.

1. The March 2005 Agreement

[¶23] The trial court found that in March 2005, the parties executed a valid, written contract supported by mutual consideration. This agreement provided that the Hardwood Hollow house would be sold, with the first $324,000 of the proceeds to Frederick and the balance to Amber. Both Frederick and Amber specified their separate rights to reside at the subject property until it was sold. Under the March 2005 agreement, Amber assumed responsibility for the real estate taxes if the property was not sold in two months. The two also were to equally share the costs necessary to operate and maintain the house as long as both were living there. This agreement also detailed who was responsible for certain bills and repairs to the residence.

[¶24] The March 2005 agreement also provided an alternative plan whereby Frederick could pay Amber the difference between $324,000 and the fair market value of the property, and Amber would then vacate the residence.

2. The June 2005 Agreement

[¶25] With respect to the second document, signed in June 2005, the trial court found that the writing was not a valid contract, because there was no consideration to support it. The June document, which asserted the March contract to be void, stated that "for valuable consideration," the parties agree that although titled solely in Frederick's name, the house was owned jointly by Frederick and Amber and that they were equal partners. In addition, Amber's name would be placed on the deed at a time she specified, and she could file a lien against the house for her share of the property until it was retitled. This writing required Frederick to pay all expenses on the property, including taxes and insurance. If the house was sold, Amber and Frederick would divide the proceeds from the sale after expenses were paid. Finally, if their relationship ended and they chose not to sell the house, Frederick could elect to keep the house and pay Amber for her share of the property or to leave the house to Amber after being paid for his share.

C.   THE COURT OF APPEALS' OPINION

[The court distinguished three cases relied upon by the court of appeals.]

E. THE JUNE 2005 DOCUMENT—A FAILED CONTRACT AND NOVATION

[¶42] The court of appeals used both *Snyder* and *Roccamonte* to conclude that consideration supported the June 2005 document: "As in *Roccamonte,* by resuming the relationship, [Amber] agreed to undertake a way of life that entailed among other things 'providing companionship, and fulfilling each other's needs, financial, emotional, physical, and social, as best as [she was] able,' as well as foregoing other romantic possibilities." *Williams,* 190 Ohio App. 3d 815, 2010-Ohio-4664, 944 N.E.2d 699, at ¶20, quoting *Roccamonte,* 174 N.J. at 392, 808 A.2d 838. Nevertheless, the record does not show evidence of this statement. The June 2005 document states that Amber has "inhabited" the house since 1997. It states that she and Frederick plan to be married and reside there. Apart from stating that Frederick will pay all the expenses for the property, the document makes no mention of fulfilling each other's needs— financial, emotional, physical, social, or otherwise.

[¶43] Although the June document states that the agreement was made "for valuable consideration," it does not specify what the consideration is. The document does not refer to "fulfilling each other's needs, financial, emotional, physical, and social." The court of appeals supplied those terms on its own. And unlike the March 2005 agreement, which contains mutual obligations and benefits (i.e., both parties had a right to reside at the property and equally shared costs necessary to maintain the house, with Amber being responsible for real estate taxes starting the second half of 2004), the June 2005 document requires Frederick to pay all expenses, taxes, and insurance costs. Nonetheless, the court of appeals relied on Amber's reply to a question of whether she had paid Frederick or given him anything of value in exchange for the June 2005 agreement. She stated, "I didn't pay him anything, no. I thought what was of value was the fact that we were sharing all sorts of things. He had my love. He had—I shared my assets with him, too. We were living together as a couple." But this vague statement falls short of establishing that she shared her assets as consideration for the June 2005 agreement and appears to refer to how she had previously shared her assets before entering into the June agreement.

[¶44] Rather, the evidence demonstrates that the only consideration offered by Amber for the June 2005 agreement was her resumption of a romantic relationship with Frederick. There is no detriment to Amber in the June 2005 document, only benefit. Essentially, this agreement amounts to a gratuitous promise by Frederick to give Amber an interest in property based solely on the consideration of her love and affection. Therefore, the June 2005 document is not an enforceable contract, because it fails for want of consideration.

[¶45] Amber argues, and the dissent agrees, that the voiding of the March agreement in the June document was consideration for the June agreement, and thus Amber contends that the March agreement amounted to a novation. The substitution of one of the original parties to a contract by a third party who assumes the responsibilities and benefits of that original party is a novation. *See* Bacon v. Daniels, 37 Ohio St. 279 (1881), paragraph two of the syllabus ("An agreement between the parties to a contract and a third person, whereby one party is released from the obligations of the contract, and the third person substituted in his stead, is a *novation,* and requires no further consideration than such release and substitution"). In this case, there is no substitution of party but rather an attempt to change the obligations of the parties under an existing contract. But a novation is effective only when a previous valid obligation is extinguished by a *new valid contract.* In order to qualify as a novation, the June agreement must be a valid contract in its own right *before* it can be used to void the March agreement.

[¶46] Amber had been living in the house for more than seven years, having lived there with her husband and having retained the residence as part of the property division in their divorce. Despite having transferred legal ownership to Frederick in December 2004, Amber already had the contractual right to reside in the property by virtue of the March 2005 contract, which had required her to vacate the guest bedroom and bath to accommodate Frederick. She was also to have been granted upon the sale of the residence the net proceeds of the sale after Frederick received $324,000. It was Amber's demand that she be given an equal property interest in the house before she would move back in and resume her romantic relationship with Frederick — there was no consideration.

[¶47] Because there is no consideration for the June agreement, it cannot extinguish the existing obligations established under the March agreement. Therefore, the June document was not an enforceable novation of the March 2005 agreement.

[¶48] We hold that merely moving into a home with another while engaging in a romantic relationship is not consideration for the formation of a contract. To hold otherwise would open the door to palimony claims and invite a number of evidentiary problems.

III. Conclusion

[¶49] We will not contractually bind parties to promises based merely on their resumption of a romantic relationship in residing together. We therefore reverse the judgment of the Ninth District Court of Appeals.

Judgment reversed.

Pfeifer, Judge, concurring in part and dissenting in part.

[¶50] One can hardly disavow the syllabus law in the majority opinion. It is good law, and it should be, though it is irrelevant to this case. I dissent to the balance of the majority opinion aside from its recitation of the facts, upon which I will rely.

[¶51] The majority seems to have chased a red herring ("love and affection") all the way upstream until it reached a dry creek bed. Love and affection were not offered in consideration of the June 2005 contract. Although the contract refers to a contemplated marriage, it never mentions love and affection.

[¶52] The record is replete with shadings and innuendo that there was no love and affection between the parties. The record includes statements that suggest or allege that Williams and Ormsby were searching for a way to continue living well without engaging in full-time work, that Williams was seeking to both delude and elude creditors, that Williams's name may have been fraudulently signed on the quitclaim deed or that the person who notarized her signature did so without being present when Williams signed, that domestic-violence charges had been filed, and that each had promised not to accuse the other of domestic violence. That Williams wouldn't move back into the house until Ormsby signed the agreement, which he wrote, was not offered as consideration and was not consideration. It was a simple fact of life — a fact that is outside the contract and is of no relevance.

[¶53] The resolution of this case should be straightforward. Among the consideration that Williams and Ormsby offered for the second agreement was the voiding of the first agreement, which denied to each of them rights that the first agreement granted. That either or both of them offered additional consideration is beside the point because we consider only the existence of consideration, not its adequacy. Judy v. Louderman, 48 Ohio St. 562, 29 N.E. 181 (1891), paragraph two of the syllabus ("While it is necessary that the consideration of a promise should be of some value, it is sufficient if it be such as *could* be valuable to the party promising; and the law will not enter into an inquiry as to the adequacy of the consideration, but will leave the parties to be the sole judges of the benefits to be derived from their contracts, unless the inadequacy of consideration is so gross as of itself to prove fraud or imposition." (Emphasis added)); Rogers v. Runfola & Assocs., Inc., 57 Ohio St. 3d 5, 6, 565 N.E.2d 540 (1991).

[¶54] Amber Williams and Frederick Ormsby entered into two contracts. The first was entered into in March 2005 "FOR VALUABLE CONSIDERATION that is mutually agreed upon" but unstated. (Capitalization sic.) Williams, Ormsby, their respective attorneys, the trial court, the court of appeals, and this court all agree that the March 2005 agreement is a valid, binding contract. The second contract was entered into in June 2005 "FOR VALUABLE CONSIDERATION that is mutually agreed upon" but unstated. (Capitalization sic.) The exact same consideration language is used in both contracts — yet it is sufficient in one instance but not in the other. The parties are the same, the subject matter is the same, the consideration is stated the same way — but this court concludes that there is no consideration for the second contract.

[¶55] The first clause of the June 2005 contract resolves the issue before us. It states: "FOR VALUABLE CONSIDERATION that is mutually agreed upon, the AGREEMENT deems all other agreements concerning the items stated below to be null and void. . . ." Could it be more clear? The March

2005 contract required that the house be sold and entitled Williams to, among other things, sales proceeds in excess of $324,000 and to live in the house until its sale. In consideration for giving up those rights, Williams entered into the June 2005 contract, which entitled her to different rights. How can it be argued that by voiding a contract that entitled her to specific rights, Williams was not offering consideration for the June 2005 contract, which entitled her to different rights? For instance, under the March agreement, if the property sold for $650,000, Williams would be entitled to $326,000; under the June agreement, she would be entitled to $325,000. If the property sold for $1,000,000, under the March agreement, Williams would get $726,000; under the June agreement, she would get $500,000. In that scenario, the March agreement benefits her considerably. Under the June contract, she also gives up the right to get proceeds from an immediate sale. Ormsby, meanwhile, under the June agreement does not have to vacate the house or pay Williams her equity portion to remain there — obligations of his under the March agreement. Under the June agreement, Ormsby gains more control over the timing of any sale of the house. For these benefits, he forfeits some equity in the house.

[¶56] I am convinced that Williams and Ormsby offered consideration for the second contract. The case is so fact specific and so riven with bizarre, if irrelevant, details, however, that it provides no meaningful guidance to the bench and bar. Accordingly, I believe that this case should be dismissed as having been improvidently accepted. . . .

QUESTION

If you represent a client in the position of Amber Williams, how will you draft the agreement to create sufficient consideration to support the other contractual promises?

Problem 35

Should the following promises be enforced?

(a) When Claudius adopted his nephew Hamlet, he was disturbed by the lack of affection the boy showed toward him. He tried everything to get the boy to like him, but nothing seemed to work. Finally, he signed an agreement with Hamlet, promising to pay his nephew $5,000 a year if his nephew would agree to like him. If Hamlet develops a genuine affection for his uncle, but Claudius refuses to pay the money, does Hamlet have a contract claim? That is, is the consideration that he promised *sufficient* in the eyes of the law? No, Not Sufficient Consideration

↳ law at Contracts doesnt recongnize love and affection

(b) On his deathbed, John Roberts tried everything to keep alive. Finally, a local fortune teller, Mrs. McGruder, did some "conjuring" over him in return for his promissory note for $250. Her conjuring and incantations did not work, and he died, but she sued his estate on the note anyway. Has she given consideration for his $250 promise? See Cooper v. Livingston, 19 Fla. 684 (1883).

[handwritten margin note: She did something. She was Not legally obligated to do, but she did it anyway]

(c) Jack Point contacted the Yeoman Corporation and offered to sell it a marketing idea that would increase the corporation's profits from the sale of its product. If they adopted the idea, Jack wanted one-half of the increased profits. Figuring that it couldn't lose from this deal, the corporation signed such an agreement. Jack then disclosed his idea: raise the wholesale price slightly. Shortly thereafter the Yeoman Corporation did so, and increased profits resulted. Must Jack be paid half of these profits? See Soule v. Bon Ami, 201 A.D. 794, 195 N.Y.S. 574 (1922), aff'd without opinion, 235 N.Y. 609, 139 N.E. 754, modified, 236 N.Y. 555, 142 N.E. 281 (1923).

(d) Mr. Meyer mailed an advertising scheme to the makers of Chesterfield cigarettes suggesting billboards showing two well-dressed men in conversation, one extending to the other a package of cigarettes saying, "Have one of these," and the other replying, "No thanks; I smoke Chesterfields." The company did not reply, but two years later adopted an advertising campaign showing two men and a caddy with golf clubs, one man having an open cigarette case and the other a package of Chesterfields, and the slogan "I'll stick to Chesterfields." Should the company have to pay for this? See Liggett & Myers Tobacco Co. v. Meyer, 101 Ind. App. 420, 194 N.E. 206 (1935) ("a property right subject to sale . . . must be something novel and new; in other words, one cannot claim any right in the multiplication table").

(e) Girard had never had any education, but nonetheless had managed to make a lot of money. Late in life he decided to remedy his ignorance, and hired Descartes to teach him the multiplication table. Has Descartes furnished consideration for Girard's promise of payment?

C. Adequacy of Consideration

BATSAKIS v. DEMOTSIS
Court of Civil Appeals of Texas, El Paso, 1949
226 S.W.2d 673

McGILL, J. This is an appeal from a judgment of the 57th judicial District Court of Bexar County. Appellant was plaintiff and appellee was defendant in the trial court. The parties will be so designated.

Plaintiff sued defendant to recover $2,000 with interest at the rate of 8 percent per annum from April 2, 1942, alleged to be due on the following instrument, being a translation from the original, which is written in the Greek language:

Peiraeus
April 2, 1942

Mr. George Batsakis:
Konstantinou Diadohou #7
Peiraeus
Mr. Batsakis:

I state by my present (letter) that I received today from you the amount of two thousand dollars ($2,000.00) of United States of America money, which I borrowed from you for the support of my family during these difficult days and because it is impossible for me to transfer dollars of my own from America.

The above amount I accept with the expressed promise that I will return to you again in American dollars either at the end of the present war or even before in the event that you might be able to find a way to collect them (dollars) from my representative in America to whom I shall write and give him an order relative to this. You understand until the final execution (payment) to the above amount an eight percent interest will be added and paid together with the principal.

I thank you and I remain yours with respects.

(Signed) *Eugenia The. Demotsis*

<u>Trial</u> to the court without the intervention of a jury resulted in a judgment in favor of plaintiff for $750.00 principal, and interest at the rate of 8 percent per annum from April 2, 1942 to the date of judgment, totaling $1,163.83, with interest thereon at the rate of 8 percent per annum until paid. Plaintiff has perfected his appeal.

The court sustained certain special exceptions of plaintiff to defendant's first amended original answer on which the case was tried, and struck therefrom paragraphs II, III and V. Defendant excepted to such action of the court, but has not crossassigned error here. The answer, stripped of such paragraphs, consisted of a general denial contained in paragraph I thereof, and of paragraph IV, which is as follows:

IV. That under the circumstances alleged in Paragraph II of this answer, the consideration upon which said written instrument sued upon by plaintiff herein is founded, is wanting and has failed to the extent of $1,975.00, and defendant pleads specially under the verification hereinafter made the want and failure of consideration stated, and now tenders, as defendant has heretofore tendered to plaintiff, $25.00 as the value of the loan of money received by defendant from plaintiff, together with interest thereon.

Further, in connection with this plea of want and failure of consideration defendant alleges that she at no time received from plaintiff himself or from anyone for plaintiff any money or thing of value other than, as hereinbefore alleged, the original loan of 500,000 drachmae. That at the time of the loan by plaintiff to defendant of said 500,000 drachmae the value of 500,000 drachmae in the Kingdom of Greece in dollars of money of the United States of America, was $25.00, and also at said time the value of 500,000 drachmae of Greek money in the United States of America in dollars was $25.00 of money of the United States of America. The plea of want and failure of consideration is verified by defendant as follows.

The allegations in paragraph II which were stricken, referred to in paragraph IV, were that the instrument sued on was signed and delivered in the Kingdom of Greece on or about April 2, 1942, at which time both plaintiff and defendant were residents of and residing in the Kingdom of Greece, and

Plaintiff . . . avers that on or about April 2, 1942 she owned money and property and had credit in the United States of America, but was then and there in the Kingdom of Greece in straitened financial circumstances due to the conditions produced by World War II and could not make use of her money and property and credit existing in the United States of America. That in the circumstances the plaintiff agreed to and did lend to defendant the sum of 500,000 drachmae, which at that time, on or about April 2, 1942, had the value of $25.00 in money of the United States of America. That the said plaintiff, knowing defendant's financial distress and desire to return to the United States of America, exacted of her the written instrument plaintiff sues upon, which was a promise by her to pay to him the sum of $2,000.00 of United States of America money.

Plaintiff specially excepted to paragraph IV because the allegations thereof were insufficient to allege either want of consideration or failure of consideration, in that it affirmatively appears therefrom that defendant received what was agreed to be delivered to her, and that plaintiff breached no agreement. The court overruled this exception, and such action is ~Court Error~ assigned as error. Error is also assigned because of the court's failure to enter judgment for the whole unpaid balance of the principal of the instrument with interest as therein provided.

Defendant testified that she did receive 500,000 drachmas from plaintiff. It is not clear whether she received all the 500,000 drachmas or only a portion of them before she signed the instrument in question. Her testimony clearly shows that the understanding of the parties was that plaintiff would give her the 500,000 drachmas if she would sign the instrument.

She testified:

Q.   . . . who suggested the figure of $2,000.00?
A.   That was how he asked me from the beginning. He said he will give me five hundred thousand drachmas provided

I signed that I would pay him $2,000.00 American money.

The transaction amounted to a sale by plaintiff of the 500,000 drachmas in consideration of the execution of the instrument sued on, by defendant. It is not contended that the drachmas had no value. Indeed, the judgment indicates that the trial court placed a value of $750.00 on them or on the other consideration which plaintiff gave defendant for the instrument if he believed plaintiff's testimony. Therefore the plea of want of consideration was unavailing. A plea of want of consideration amounts to a contention that the instrument never became a valid obligation in the first place. National Bank of Commerce v. Williams, 125 Tex. 619, 84 S.W.2d 691.

Mere inadequacy of consideration will not void a contract.

Nor was the plea of failure of consideration availing. Defendant got exactly what she contracted for according to her own testimony. The court should have rendered judgment in favor of plaintiff against defendant for the principal sum of $2,000.00 evidenced by the instrument sued on, with interest as therein provided. We construe the provision relating to interest as providing for interest at the rate of 8 percent per annum. The judgment is reformed so as to award appellant a recovery against appellee of $2,000.00 with interest thereon at the rate of 8 percent per annum from April 2, 1942. Such judgment will bear interest at the rate of 8 percent per annum until paid on $2,000.00 thereof and on the balance interest at the rate of 6 percent per annum. As so reformed, the judgment is affirmed.

Reformed and affirmed.

QUESTIONS

1. Does this case seem right to you? What policy is behind the idea that the law will not inquire into the adequacy of the consideration? Go back to the last Problem. In the situations described there, were we looking at the *adequacy* of the consideration?

2. In 1942, Greece was occupied by the Nazis. Food was scarce, and inflation was rampant. Do these facts make it *more* or *less* likely that there was consideration for the defendant's promise to pay $2,000 with interest in return for a loan of much less money (perhaps $750, or perhaps as little as $25)?

SCHNELL v. NELL
Supreme Court of Indiana, 1861
17 Ind. 29

PERKINS, J. Action by J. B. Nell against Zacharias Schnell, upon the following instrument:

This agreement, entered into this 13th day of February, 1856, between Zach. Schnell, of Indianapolis, Marion county, State of Indiana, as party of the first part, and J. B. Nell, of the same place, Wendelin Lorenz, of Stilesville, Hendricks county, State of Indiana, and Donata Lorenz, of Frickinger, Grand Duchy of Baden, Germany, as parties of the second part, witnesseth: The said Zacharias Schnell agrees as follows: whereas his wife, Theresa Schnell, now deceased, has made a last will and testament, in which, among other provisions, it was ordained that every one of the above named second parties, should receive the sum of $200; and whereas the said provisions of the will must remain a nullity, for the reason that no property, real or personal, was in the possession of the said Theresa Schnell, deceased, in her own name, at the time of her death, and all property held by Zacharias and Theresa Schnell jointly, therefore reverts to her husband; and whereas the said Theresa Schnell has also been a dutiful and loving wife to the said Zach. Schnell, and has materially aided him in the acquisition of all property, real and personal, now possessed by him; for, and in consideration of all this, and the love and respect he bears to his wife; and, furthermore, in consideration of one cent, received by him of the second parties, he the said Zach. Schnell, agrees to pay the above named sums of money to the parties of the second part, to wit: $200 to the said J. B. Nell; $200 to the said Wendelin Lorenz; and $200 to the said Donata Lorenz, in the following installment, viz., $200 in one year from the date of these presents; $200 in two years, and $200 in three years; to be divided between the parties in equal portions $66 2/3 each year, or as they may agree, till each one has received his full sum of $200.

And the said parties of the second part, for, and in consideration of this, agree to pay the above named sum of money [one cent], and to deliver up to said Schnell, and abstain from collecting any real or supposed claims upon him or his estate, arising from the said last will and testament of the said Theresa Schnell, deceased.

In witness whereof, the said parties on this 13th day of February, 1856, set hereunto their hands and seals.

Zacharias Schnell, [SEAL.]

J. B. Nell, [SEAL.]

Wen. Lorenz, [SEAL.]

The complaint contained no averment of a consideration for the instrument, outside of those expressed in it; and did not aver that the one cent agreed to be paid, had been paid or tendered.

A demurrer to the complaint was overruled.

The defendant answered, that the instrument sued on was given for no consideration whatever.

He further answered, that it was given for no consideration, because his said wife, Theresa, at the time she made the will mentioned, and at the time of her death, owned, neither separately, nor jointly with her husband, or any one else (except so far as the law gave her an interest in her husband's property), any property, real or personal, etc.

The will is copied into the record, but need not be into this opinion.

The Court sustained a demurrer to these answers, evidently on the ground that they were regarded as contradicting the instrument sued on, which particularly set out the considerations upon which it was executed. But the instrument is latently ambiguous on this point. See Ind. Dig., p. 110.

The case turned below, and must turn here, upon the question whether the instrument sued on does express a consideration sufficient to give it legal obligation, as against Zacharias Schnell. It specifies three distinct considerations for his promise to pay $600:

(1) A promise, on the part of the plaintiffs, to pay him one cent.
(2) The love and affection he bore his deceased wife, and the fact that she had done her part, as his wife, in the acquisition of property.
(3) The fact that she had expressed her desire, in the form of an inoperative will, that the persons named therein should have the sums of money specified.

The consideration of one cent will not support the promise of Schnell. It is true, that as a general proposition, inadequacy of consideration will not vitiate an agreement. Baker v. Roberts, 14 Ind. 552. But this doctrine does not apply to a mere exchange of sums of money, of coin, whose value is exactly fixed, but to the exchange of something of, in itself, indeterminate value, for money, or, perhaps, for some other thing of indeterminate value. In this case, had the one cent mentioned, been some particular one cent, a family piece, or ancient, remarkable coin, possessing an indeterminate value, extrinsic from its simple money value, a different view might be taken. As it is, the mere promise to pay six hundred dollars for one cent, even had the portion of that cent due from the plaintiff been tendered, is an unconscionable contract, void, at first blush, upon its face, if it be regarded as an earnest one. Hardesty v. Smith, 3 Ind. 39. The consideration of one cent is, plainly, in this case, merely nominal, and intended to be so. As the will and testament of Schnell's wife imposed no legal obligation upon him to discharge her bequests out of his property, and as she had none of her own, his promise to discharge them was not legally binding upon him, on that ground. A moral consideration, only, will not support a promise. Ind. Dig., p. 13. And for the same reason, a valid consideration for his promise cannot be found in the fact of a compromise of a disputed claim; for where such claim is legally groundless, a promise upon a compromise of it, or of a suit upon it, is not legally binding. Spahr v. Hollingshead, 8 Blackf. 415. There was no mistake of law or fact in this case, as the agreement admits the will inoperative and void. The promise was simply one to make a gift. The past services of his wife, and the love and affection he had borne her, are objectionable as legal considerations for Schnell's promise, on two grounds: 1. They are past considerations. Ind. Dig., p. 13. 2. The fact that Schnell loved his wife, and that she had been industrious, constituted no consideration for his promise to pay J. B. Nell, and the Lorenzes, a sum of money. Whether, if his wife, in her lifetime, had made a bargain with Schnell, that, in consideration of his promising to pay, after her death, to the persons named, a sum of money, she would be industrious, and worthy of his affection, such a promise would have been valid and consistent with public policy, we need not decide. Nor is the fact that Schnell now venerates the memory of his deceased wife, a legal consideration for a promise to pay any third person money.

The instrument sued on, interpreted in the light of the facts alleged in the second paragraph of the answer, will not support an action. The demurrer to the answer should have been overruled. See Stevenson v. Druley, 4 Ind. 519.

PER CURIAM. The judgment is reversed, with costs. Cause remanded, etc.

QUESTION

Does *Schnell* conflict with *Batsakis?*

Problem 36

Is there consideration in the following hypotheticals if the promise or act requested is given?

(a) I promise to deliver 800 bushels of wheat to you in return for your promise to deliver 500 bushels of wheat to me. No

(b) I promise to give you $10,000 in return for your promise to sell me the silver dollar that George Washington threw across the Potomac. Yes

(c) I promise to give you one dollar if you will give me two quarters so that I can operate this vending machine. Yes -> Need it Now

(d) I promise to sell you Blackacre in return for your promise to pay $1.00. (Blackacre is worth around $500,000.) No, Nominal (gift offer)

(e) Would your answer to (d) change if the $1.00 were in fact paid?

(f) The contract recited that "In return for $1.00, in hand received, I hereby give you an option to buy Blackacre for the sum of $500,000; this option must be exercised prior to December 1, 2020." Is the dollar adequate consideration here? Does it matter that the recital is a sham because the dollar was never paid? Compare the Restatement section quoted next with Hermes v. Wm. F. Meyer Co., 65 Ill. App. 3d 745, 382 N.E.2d 841 (1978), and Board of Control v. Burgess, 45 Mich. App. 183, 206 N.W.2d 256 (1973).

RESTATEMENT (SECOND) OF CONTRACTS

§87. OPTION CONTRACT

(1) An offer is binding as an option contract if it

(a) is in writing and signed by the offeror, recites a purported consideration for the making of the offer, and proposes an exchange on fair terms within a reasonable time; or

(b) is made irrevocable by statute.

(2) An offer which the offeror should reasonably expect to induce action or forbearance of a substantial character on the part of the offeree before acceptance and which does induce such action or forbearance is binding as an option contract to the extent necessary to avoid injustice.

1464-EIGHT, LTD. v. JOPPICH
Supreme Court of Texas, 2004
154 S.W.3d 101

STEVEN WAYNE SMITH, Justice.

The question presented is whether section 87(1)(a) of the Restatement (Second) of Contracts should be incorporated into the common law of Texas. See 3 Williston & Lord, A Treatise on the Law of Contracts §7:23 (4th ed. 1992) ("As far as option contracts are concerned, the Restatement (Second) has taken the position, adopted by some common law courts, that a false recital of nominal consideration is sufficient to support the irrevocability of an offer so long as the underlying exchange is fair and the offer is to be accepted within a reasonable time.").

The petitioners, citing section 87(1)(a) of the Restatement (Second) of Contracts, assert that the respondent's offer to sell real property should be binding as an option contract because the offer was in writing and signed by the respondent, acknowledged the receipt of a nominal consideration of ten dollars, and proposed an exchange on fair terms within a reasonable time. The respondent, contending that the parties' written option agreement is unenforceable, asserts that the agreement lacks consideration because the recited nominal consideration was never actually paid, and that the offer was revoked before it was properly accepted.

In this case of first impression, we agree with the petitioners that the nonpayment of the recited nominal consideration does not preclude enforcement of the parties' written option agreement. Therefore, we will reverse and remand.

I

In July 1997, Gail Ann Joppich entered into an earnest money contract with 1464-Eight, Ltd. and Millis Management Corporation (collectively "Millis") under which Joppich agreed to buy, and Millis agreed to convey, an undeveloped residential lot located in a subdivision being developed by Millis. The purchase price was $65,000. An addendum attached to the earnest money contract provided:

> All Lots being sold in Shiloh Lake Estates Subdivision are being sold pursuant to an Option Agreement to be executed by Buyer and Seller at closing that shall survive closing and provide Seller with an option to purchase the Property from the Buyer at a price equal to 90% of the sale price herein if Buyer fails to commence construction of a private residence on the Property within 18 months from the date of closing.

At the closing later the same month, Millis executed a special warranty deed conveying the lot to Joppich. In addition, the parties executed a separate four-page document entitled "Option Agreement." The notarized document, which was signed by both Joppich and Millis, provided:

> 1. *Grant of Option.* In consideration of the sum of Ten and No/100 ($10.00) Dollars ("Option Fee") paid in cash by Developer, the receipt and sufficiency of which is hereby acknowledged and confessed, Purchaser hereby grants to Developer the exclusive right and option to purchase [the Property]. This Option may be exercised at any time from and after January 21, 1999.
> 2. *Purchase Price.* The total purchase price for the Property shall be [$58,500] and shall be due and payable at closing.
> 3. *Expiration Date.* This Option shall automatically expire at 5:00 o'clock p. m. on the date which is five (5) years after the date of execution and recording in the Office of the County Clerk of Fort Bend County, Texas unless prior to the expiration date this Option is exercised by Developer.
> 4. *Termination.* This Option shall automatically terminate on the date that Purchaser, or Purchaser's assigns, commence construction of a primary residence which has been approved by [the appropriate committee].

In October 1999, Joppich filed suit against Millis, seeking a declaratory judgment that the Option Agreement was unenforceable. In her original petition, Joppich asserted that "[a]lthough the Option Agreement states that a sum of Ten and No/100 dollars was given to Plaintiff in consideration for granting the option, this sum was not then nor has it ever been tendered to nor paid to Plaintiff," and she requested that "the Court declare that the Agreement granting the exclusive right and option to purchase [the Property] to the Developer is void and unenforceable for lack of consideration or alternatively, failure of consideration." Millis answered with a general denial.

In September 2000, Millis filed a counterclaim seeking specific performance, damages, and attorney's fees, asserting:

> Counter Defendant failed to begin construction of a primary residence on the property, therefore, Counter Plaintiffs sent notice of their exercising of the option to Counter Defendant on September 4, 1999. . . . Counter Defendant refused and continues to refuse to convey the property pursuant to the terms of the option.

In January 2001, Joppich moved for final summary judgment "based on failure and/or lack of consideration." Joppich asserted that "[s]ince no consideration flowed from Defendants to Plaintiff and she revoked the Option Agreement before consideration had in fact passed, the Option Agreement is void and unenforceable." In her affidavit, which was attached to the motion, Joppich stated: "The Option Agreement states that a sum of Ten and No/100 dollars was given to me in consideration for granting Defendants the right to repurchase the property under certain conditions. This sum was not then nor has it ever been tendered to or paid to me."

In February 2001, the trial court denied Joppich's motion for final summary judgment and granted Millis's motion for partial summary judgment. In May 2001, the trial court rendered a final judgment declaring that the Option Agreement was enforceable, requiring Joppich to sell the property in compliance with the terms of the Option Agreement, and awarding attorney's fees to Millis.

In December 2002, the court of appeals reversed and remanded, concluding that "summary judgment for [Millis] was improper." 96 S.W.3d 614, 617. . . .

II

"[A] promise to give an option is valid if supported by an independent consideration. For example, if a sum of money be paid for the option, the promisee may, at his election, enforce the contract." Nat'l Oil & Pipe Line Co. v. Teel, 95 Tex. 586, 68 S.W. 979, 980 (1902); see also Restatement (Second) of Contracts §25 (1981) ("An option contract is a promise which meets the requirements for the formation of a contract and limits the promisor's power to revoke an offer.") . . .

Section 87(1) of the Restatement (Second) of Contracts provides:

> (1) An offer is binding as an option contract if it
>   (a) is in writing and signed by the offeror, recites a purported consideration for the making of the offer, and proposes an exchange on fair terms within a reasonable time; or
>   (b) is made irrevocable by statute.

Restatement (Second) of Contracts §87(1) (1981).

The official comment to section 87 states:

> b. Nominal consideration. Offers made in consideration of one dollar paid or promised are often irrevocable under Subsection (1)(a). . . .
>
> [A] nominal consideration is regularly held sufficient to support a short-time option proposing an exchange on fair terms. The fact that the option is an appropriate preliminary step in the conclusion of a socially useful transaction provides a sufficient substantive basis for enforcement, and a signed writing taking a form appropriate to a bargain satisfies the desiderata of form. . . .

Id. §87 cmts. b-c (illustrations omitted).

The illustration following comment c states:

> 3. A executes and delivers to B a written agreement "in consideration of one dollar in hand paid" giving B an option to buy described land belonging to A for $15,000, the option to expire at noon six days later. The fact that the dollar is not in fact paid does not prevent the offer from being irrevocable.

Id. §87 cmt. c, illus. 3.

The authors of the national treatises on contracts have generally endorsed section 87(1)(a) of the Restatement (Second) of Contracts. For example, Corbin on Contracts states:

> . . . Consideration is designed primarily to protect promisors from their own donative promises. Options, however, are one commercial step in a commercial deal. A number of cases have followed the forthright approach taken by the Restatement (Second). Indeed, it may be urged that the Restatement fails to lead the way to more progressive reform. Having recognized the value of the enforceability of options as commercial devices, it still insists on the fictional recital of a purported consideration. Such fictional charades should not be a part of a mature legal system. Commercial promises such as options . . . should be enforceable without consideration.

2 Perillo & Bender, Corbin on Contracts §5.17 (rev. ed. 1995) (footnotes omitted). . . .

III

The position taken by section 87(1)(a) of the Restatement (Second) of Contracts is admittedly the minority position among the limited number of state supreme courts that have addressed the question. [Citations omitted.]

Nevertheless, we are persuaded that the position of the Restatement (Second) of Contracts, which is supported by a well-articulated and sound rationale, represents the better approach. . . . Gordon, Consideration and the Commercial-Gift Dichotomy, 44 Vand. L. Rev. 283, 293-94 (1991)

("Option contracts are related to economic exchanges — transactions based on self-interest, not altruism. Moreover, people expect that option contracts are serious and binding commitments.") (footnote omitted).

Based on the foregoing analysis, we reverse the court of appeals's judgment and remand the case to the court of appeals for further proceedings.

Chief Justice JEFFERSON, joined by Justice BRISTER, concurring.

Today the Court adopts section 87(1)(a) of the Restatement (Second) of Contracts to hold that an option contract in which consideration is recited, but not paid, is enforceable. But if the Court enforces option contracts containing fictional recitals of consideration, why mandate such recitals at all? Why recognize and require parties to recite "a lie, a sham"? James D. Gordon III, Consideration and the Commercial-Gift Dichotomy, 44 Vand. L. Rev. 283, 294 (1991) (commenting on section 87 of the Restatement (Second) of Contracts); see also John P. Dawson, Gifts and Promises 4 (1980) (criticizing consideration requirement as a "needless hindrance to the processes by which agreement is reached and, being artificial as well as needless, was soon made to look silly, so that a dollar, a hairpin, or a false recital would do").

Instead, I agree with the authors of a leading treatise that while the Restatement approach is a step in the right direction, it "fails to lead the way to more progressive reform. Having recognized the value of the enforceability of options as commercial devices, it still insists on the fictional recital of a purported consideration. Such fictional charades should not be part of a mature legal system. Commercial promises such as options and credit guaranties should be enforceable without consideration." 2 Joseph M. Perillo & Helen Hadjiyannakis Bender, Corbin on Contracts §5.17 (rev. ed. 1995) (footnote omitted); see also id. §5.17 n.19 (noting that "undue deference is being paid to fictional recitals and the appropriate solution is that options should not require consideration").[1] Although I am not prepared to advocate elimination of the consideration requirement in all commercial contracts, I believe it is time to acknowledge that the doctrine serves no justifiable purpose in option agreements.

Typically, courts require consideration to separate binding agreements from unenforceable donative promises. See id. §5.17 (rev. ed.1995). But option contracts rarely involve gifts. . . .

Moreover, enforcing option agreements even without consideration comports with the parties' expectations. "[P]eople expect that option contracts are serious and binding commitments." Gordon, 44 Vand. L. Rev. at

---

1. Yet another problem with the Restatement approach is that, in addition to mandating a recital of consideration, the Restatement requires that an option be "on fair terms" and that the exchange occur "within a reasonable time." Restatement (Second) of Contracts §87(1)(a) (1981). This approach unduly complicates enforcement of option contracts, requiring a factual inquiry regarding fairness of terms and reasonableness of time in each case.

294. We can safely presume that was the case here. Millis and Joppich entered into a detailed, four-page option agreement, which was signed and notarized. It expressed the parties' intent to be bound. It was incident to Joppich's purchase of the lot for $65,000. Joppich agreed to begin construction within eighteen months. The option included the familiar refrain, "[i]n consideration of the sum of Ten and No/100 ($10.00) Dollars ("Option Fee") paid in cash by Developer, the receipt and sufficiency of which is hereby acknowledged and confessed," something the parties likely paid little attention to, until Joppich sought a means to avoid her promise. I agree with the Court that the option should be enforced even though Millis did not actually pay the recited ten dollars. But we should go further and dispense with that recital requirement in option contracts.

For these reasons, I concur in the Court's judgment but not in its reasoning.

NOTE AND QUESTION

1. As the majority opinion concedes, most courts have not adopted Restatement §87's approach to option contracts. As a result, they hold that the offeree must actually provide consideration (even in the form of small payment, such as $10) in return for the offeror's promise not to revoke the offer for a period of time.

2. Recall our discussion of firm offers under UCC §2-205 from Chapter 1. How would you analyze *1464-Eight, Ltd.* under the following circumstances: (1) both Joppich and Millis sold vintage pinball machines and (2) the contract between them was for the sale of a broken but rare pinball machine, and it gave Millis the right to repurchase the machine at 90 percent of the sales price if Joppich was not able to get the machine working within two months? Would it matter whether the governing jurisdiction adopted Restatement §87?

II. FORBEARANCE AS CONSIDERATION

▷ FIEGE v. BOEHM ◁

Court of Appeals of Maryland, 1956
210 Md. 352, 123 A.2d 316

DELAPLAINE, J. This suit was brought in the Superior Court of Baltimore City by Hilda Louise Boehm against Louis Gail Fiege to recover for breach of a contract to pay the expenses incident to the birth of his bastard child and to provide for its support upon condition that she would refrain from prosecuting him for bastardy.

Plaintiff alleged in her declaration substantially as follows: (1) that early in 1951 defendant had sexual intercourse with her although she was unmarried, and as a result thereof she became pregnant, and defendant acknowledged that he was responsible for her pregnancy; (2) that on September 29, 1951, she gave birth to a female child; that defendant is the father of the child; and that he acknowledged on many occasions that he is the father; (3) that before the child was born, defendant agreed to pay all her medical and miscellaneous expenses and to compensate her for the loss of her salary caused by the child's birth, and also to pay her ten dollars per week for its support until it reached the age of 21, upon condition that she would not institute bastardy proceedings against him as long as he made the payments in accordance with the agreement; (4) that she placed the child for adoption on July 13, 1954, and she claimed the following sums: Union Memorial Hospital, $110; Florence Crittenton Home, $100; Dr. George Merrill, her physician, $50; medicines $70.35; miscellaneous expenses, $20.45; loss of earnings for 26 weeks, $1,105; support of the child $1,440; total, $2,895.80; and (5) that defendant paid her only $480, and she demanded that he pay her the further sum of $2,415.80, the balance due under the agreement, but he failed and refused to pay the same.

Defendant demurred to the declaration on the ground that it failed to allege that in September, 1953, plaintiff instituted bastardy proceedings against him in the Criminal Court of Baltimore, but since it had been found from blood tests that he could not have been the father of the child, he was acquitted of bastardy. The Court sustained the demurrer with leave to amend.

Plaintiff then filed an amended declaration, which contained the additional allegation that, after the breach of the agreement by defendant, she filed a charge with the State's Attorney that defendant was the father of her bastard child; and that on October 8, 1953, the Criminal Court found defendant not guilty solely on a physician's testimony that "on the basis of certain blood tests made, the defendant can be excluded as the father of the said child, which testimony is not conclusive upon a jury in a trial court."

Defendant also demurred to the amended declaration, but the Court overruled that demurrer.

Plaintiff, a typist, now over 35 years old, who has been employed by the Government in Washington and Baltimore for over thirteen years, testified in the Court below that she had never been married, but that at about midnight on January 21, 1951, defendant, after taking her to a moving picture theater on York Road and then to a restaurant, had sexual intercourse with her in his automobile. She further testified that he agreed to pay all her medical and hospital expenses, to compensate her for loss of salary caused by the pregnancy and birth, and to pay her ten dollars per week for the support of the child upon condition that she would refrain from instituting bastardy proceedings against him. She further testified that between September 17, 1951, and May, 1953, defendant paid her a total of $480.

Defendant admitted that he had taken plaintiff to restaurants, had danced with her several times, had taken her to Washington, and had brought her home in the country; but he asserted that he had never had sexual intercourse with her. He also claimed that he did not enter into any agreement with her. He admitted, however, that he had paid her a total of $480. His father also testified that he stated "that he did not want his mother to know, and if it were just kept quiet, kept principally away from his mother and the public and the courts, that he would take care of it."

Defendant further testified that in May, 1953, he went to see plaintiff's physician to make inquiry about blood tests to show the paternity of the child; and that those tests were made and they indicated that it was not possible that he could have been the child's father. He then stopped making payments. Plaintiff thereupon filed a charge of bastardy with the State's Attorney.

The testimony which was given in the Criminal Court by Dr. Milton Sachs, hematologist at the University Hospital, was read to the jury in the Superior Court. In recent years the blood-grouping test has been employed in criminology, in the selection of donors for blood transfusions, and as evidence in paternity cases. The Landsteiner blood-grouping test is based on the medical theory that the red corpuscles in human blood contain two affirmative agglutinating substances, and that every individual's blood falls into one of the four classes and remains the same throughout life. According to Mendel's law of inheritance, this blood individuality is an hereditary characteristic which passes from parent to child, and no agglutinating substance can appear in the blood of a child which is not present in the blood of one of its parents. The four Landsteiner blood groups, designated as AB, A, B, and O, into which human blood is divided on the basis of the compatibility of the corpuscles and serum with the corpuscles and serum of other persons, are characterized by different combinations of two agglutinogens in the red blood cells and two agglutinins in the serum. Dr. Sachs reported that Fiege's blood group was Type O, Miss Boehm's was Type B, and the infant's was Type A. He further testified that on the basis of these tests, Fiege could not have been the father of the child, as it is impossible for a mating of Type O and Type B to result in a child of Type A.

Although defendant was acquitted by the Criminal Court, the Superior Court overruled his motion for a directed verdict. In the charge to the jury the Court instructed them that defendant's acquittal in the Criminal Court was not binding upon them. The jury found a verdict in favor of plaintiff for $2,415.80, the full amount of her claim.

Defendant filed a motion for judgment n.o.v. or a new trial. The Court overruled that motion also, and entered judgment on the verdict of the jury. Defendant appealed from that judgment.

Defendant contends that, even if he did enter into the contract as alleged, it was not enforceable, because plaintiff's forbearance to prosecute was not based on a valid claim, and hence the contract was without consideration. He, therefore, asserts that the Court erred in overruling (1) his demurrer to the amended declaration, (2) his motion for a directed verdict, and (3) his motion for judgment n.o.v. or a new trial.

It was originally held at common law that a child born out of wedlock is *filius nullius,* and a putative father is not under any legal liability to contribute to the support of his illegitimate child, and his promise to do so is unenforceable because it is based on purely a moral obligation. Some of the courts in this country have held that, in the absence of any statutory obligation on the father to aid in the support of his bastard child, his promise to the child's mother to pay her for its maintenance, resting solely on his natural affection for it and his moral obligation to provide for it, is a promise which the law cannot enforce because of lack of sufficient consideration. [Citations omitted.] On the contrary, a few courts have stated that the natural affection of a father for his child and the moral obligation upon him to support it and to aid the woman he has wronged furnish sufficient consideration for his promise to the mother to pay for the support of the child to make the agreement enforceable at law. [Citations omitted.]

However, where statutes are in force to compel the father of a bastard to contribute to its support, the courts have invariably held that a contract by the putative father with the mother of his bastard child to provide for the support of the child upon the agreement of the mother to refrain from invoking the bastardy statute against the father, or to abandon proceedings already commenced, is supported by sufficient consideration. [Citations omitted.]

In Maryland it is now provided by statute that whenever a person is found guilty of bastardy, the court shall issue an order directing such person (1) to pay for the maintenance and support of the child until it reaches the age of eighteen years, such sum as may be agreed upon, if consent proceedings be had, or in the absence of agreement, such sum as the court may fix, with due regard to the circumstances of the accused person; and (2) to give bond to the State of Maryland in such penalty as the court may fix, with good and sufficient securities, conditioned on making the payments required by the court's order, or any amendments thereof. Failure to give such bond shall be punished by commitment to the jail or the House of Correction until bond is given but not exceeding two years. Code Supp. 1955, art. 12, §8.

Prosecutions for bastardy are treated in Maryland as criminal proceedings, but they are actually civil in purpose. [Citations omitted.] While the prime object of the Maryland Bastardy Act is to protect the public from the burden of maintaining illegitimate children, it is so distinctly in the interest of the mother that she becomes the beneficiary of it. Accordingly a contract by the putative father of an illegitimate child to provide for its support upon condition that bastardy proceedings will not be instituted is a compromise of civil injuries resulting from a criminal act, and not a contract to compound a criminal prosecution, and if it is fair and reasonable, it is in accord with the Bastardy Act and the public policy of the State.

Of course, a contract of a putative father to provide for the support of his illegitimate child must be based, like any other contract, upon sufficient consideration. The early English law made no distinction in regard to the sufficiency of a claim which the claimant promised to forbear to prosecute, as the consideration of a promise, other than the broad distinction between good claims and bad claims. No promise to forbear to prosecute an unfounded claim was sufficient consideration. In the early part of the Nineteenth Century, an advance was made from the criterion of the early authorities when it was held that forbearance to prosecute a suit which had already been instituted was sufficient consideration, without inquiring whether the suit would have been successful or not. Longridge v. Dorville, 5 B. & Ald. 117.

In 1867 the Maryland Court of Appeals, in the opinion delivered by Judge Bartol in Hartle v. Stahl, 27 Md. 157, 172, held: (1) that forbearance to assert a claim before institution of suit, if not in fact a legal claim, is not of itself sufficient consideration to support a promise; but (2) that a compromise of a doubtful claim or a relinquishment of a pending suit is good consideration for a promise; and (3) that in order to support a compromise, it is sufficient that the parties entering into it thought at the time that there was a bona fide question between them, although it may eventually be found that there was in fact no such question.

We have thus adopted the rule that the surrender of, or forbearance to assert, an invalid claim by one who has not an honest and reasonable belief in its possible validity is not sufficient consideration for a contract. 1 Restatement, Contracts, sec. 76(b). We combine the subjective requisite that the claim be bona fide with the objective requisite that it must have a reasonable basis of support. Accordingly a promise not to prosecute a claim which is not founded in good faith does not of itself give a right of action on an agreement to pay for refraining from so acting, because a release from mere annoyance and unfounded litigation does not furnish valuable consideration.

Professor Williston was not entirely certain whether the test of reasonableness is based upon the intelligence of the claimant himself, who may be an ignorant person with no knowledge of law and little sense as to facts; but he seemed inclined to favor the view that "the claim forborne must be neither absurd in fact from the standpoint of a reasonable man in the position of the claimant, nor, obviously unfounded in law to one who has an elementary knowledge of legal principles." 1 Williston on Contracts, rev. ed., sec. 135. We agree that while stress is placed upon the honesty and good faith of the claimant, forbearance to prosecute a claim is insufficient consideration if the claim forborne is so lacking in foundation as to make its assertion incompatible with honesty and a reasonable degree of intelligence. Thus, if the mother of a bastard knows that there is no foundation, either in law or fact, for a charge against a certain man that he is the father of the child, but that man promises to pay her in order to prevent bastardy proceedings against him, the forbearance to institute proceedings is not sufficient consideration.

On the other hand, forbearance to sue for a lawful claim or demand is sufficient consideration for a promise to pay for the forbearance if the party forbearing had an honest intention to prosecute litigation which is not frivolous, vexatious, or unlawful, and which he believed to be well founded. [Citations omitted.] Thus the promise of a woman who is expecting an illegitimate child that she will not institute bastardy proceedings against a certain man is sufficient consideration for his promise to pay for the child's support, even though it may not be certain whether the man is the father or whether the prosecution would be successful, if she makes the charge in good faith. The fact that a man accused of bastardy is forced to enter into a contract to pay for the support of his bastard child from fear of exposure and the shame that might be cast upon him as a result, as well as a sense of justice to render some compensation for the injury he inflicted upon the mother, does not lessen the merit of the contract, but greatly increases it. [Citations omitted.]

In the case at bar there was no proof of fraud or unfairness. Assuming that the hematologists were accurate in their laboratory tests and findings, nevertheless plaintiff gave testimony which indicated that she made the charge of bastardy against defendant in good faith. For these reasons the Court acted properly in overruling the demurrer to the amended declaration and the motion for a directed verdict. . . .

As we have found no reversible error in the rulings and instructions of the trial Court, we will affirm the judgment entered on the verdict of the jury.

Judgment affirmed, with costs.

Problem 37

Ebenezer Scrooge hired Robert Cratchit, an expert in energy resources, to do advisory work for Scrooge's company, which was looking into new possibilities for the fracking of rock and coal to produce natural gas. The employment contract expressly stated that it was "at will," meaning that either party was free to terminate the contract at any time without liability. Cratchit's efforts were quite successful, and Scrooge's company profited tremendously by his advice. After one year, Scrooge proposed a change to the contract by which Cratchit agreed that on the termination of their agreement he would not be employed by any of Scrooge's competitors for a three-year period. Cratchit did sign this amendment to the at-will employment contract. Six months later Cratchit quit and immediately took a job giving similar advice to Scrooge's largest competitor. When Scrooge sued both Cratchit and the competitor for breach of the non-competition clause, the defense was that there was no consideration for this change in the contract since Scrooge still could have terminated Cratchit's employment at time. How should this come out? See Lucht's Concrete Pumping, Inc Horner, 255 P.3d 1058 (Colo. 2011).

RESTATEMENT (SECOND) OF CONTRACTS

§74. SETTLEMENT OF CLAIMS

(1) Forbearance to assert or the surrender of a claim or defense which proves to be invalid is not consideration unless
    (a) the claim or defense is in fact doubtful because of uncertainty as to the facts or the law, or
    (b) the forbearing or surrendering party believes that the claim or defense may be fairly determined to be valid. (Intend Faith)
    (2) The execution of a written instrument surrendering a claim or defense by one who is under no duty to execute it is consideration if the execution of the written instrument is bargained for even though he is not asserting the claim or defense and believes that no valid claim or defense exists.

Problem 38

Mark Queensberry was the current holder of a promissory note signed by Sebastian Melmouth. When the note matured, Queensberry came to Melmouth's house to collect. Mrs. Melmouth met him at the door and handed him a promissory note she had signed for the same amount; it was payable exactly one year later. She said to Queensberry that if he would promise her to forbear collecting on her husband's note for one year, at the end of that period she would pay her note if her husband was unable to pay his. Queensberry just grunted and walked away with her note. He did forbear collection activities for one year. Now Queensberry is trying to collect from Mrs. Melmouth. She is arguing that she had asked for a promise and did not get it, and that there is, therefore, no consideration. Is she correct? See Strong v. Sheffield, 144 N.Y. 392, 39 N.E. 330 (1895); Restatement (Second) of Contracts, §74, comment d.

Problem 39

Romeo Montague married Juliet and they lived happily for a year until he was struck by a car. The doctors told Juliet that it was unlikely he would recover and that he would probably live for a few days at best. That night, worried, Juliet searched through their family papers and discovered that her father-in-law, Vern Montague, was still named as beneficiary in Romeo's will. The next morning she obtained a change-of-beneficiary form from the insurance agent and took it to the hospital, hoping to catch Romeo in a lucid moment and have him sign it. Outside of Romeo's hospital room, Juliet ran into Vern Montague, and she told him about her plan. He was horrified, saying that bothering Romeo about death benefits at this moment would certainly hasten his end. Vern added that if she would forget changing the beneficiary, he would pay the insurance money over to her when he received it. Relieved, she agreed. Ten minutes later, Romeo died. When Vern received the insurance money, he told Juliet that he had never liked her and that he was particularly upset that she would extort a promise out of him by using the ugly threat of killing his son. He refused to give her the money and she sued. How should this come out? See Orr v. Orr, 181 Ill. App. 148 (1913).

Problem 40

When she took the course in Property and learned about title searches, Portia Moot, first-year law student, decided to search the title of the home she had owned for five years. She was disturbed to learn that the house was on land once owned by a Native American tribe. More research convinced her that the tribe had been duped into signing the original treaty deeding the land to the government. When she asked her Property professor about this, she was told not to worry because the statute of limitations had long since run out on this sort of claim. Still concerned, Portia tracked down the remnants of the tribe involved and offered to pay the tribe $1,000 if its governing council would sign a contract promising to forbear to press its possible claim against her property; she also asked the tribe to sign a quit-claim deed. The council initially refused, saying that the tribe's lawyer had advised that the tribe definitely had no possible claim; the tribe said it didn't want to take her money for nothing. She persisted, and the tribe finally signed the documents. When her check bounced, Portia suddenly realized that she needed the money for other matters and told the tribe to forget the whole thing. The tribe, thoroughly annoyed by this time, sued. Portia argued that the tribe had given no consideration. How should this come out? See Restatement §74(2), and Mullen v. Hawkins, 141 Ind. 363, 40 N.E. 797 (1895).

III.   THE ILLUSORY PROMISE

As we have seen, the consideration doctrine requires each party to surrender his or her free will in some meaningful way by either (1) doing (or not doing) something or (2) promising to do (or not do) something. But suppose a party makes such a promise and also reserves the right to change his or her mind? When A says to B, "I'll sell you my Contracts casebook for $100 if I feel like it," and B accepts, is there a contract? This section examines the problem of the so-called illusory promise.

RESTATEMENT (SECOND) OF CONTRACTS

§77. ILLUSORY AND ALTERNATIVE PROMISES

A promise or apparent promise is not consideration if by its terms the promisor or purported promisor reserves a choice of alternative performances unless

(a) each of the alternative performances would have been consideration if it alone had been bargained for; or *(Implied)*
(b) one of the alternative performances would have been consideration and there is or appears to the parties to be a substantial possibility that before the promisor exercises his choice events may eliminate the alternative which would not have been consideration.

Problem 41

Illusory Promise

After two years of negotiations over the sale of her ancestral home, Tara, Scarlett finally sent Rhett, the proposed buyer, a letter stating, "I hereby offer to sell you Tara for $3,000,000, provided I don't change my mind again." Rhett immediately tendered the money, but Scarlett refused to take it. She made him a counteroffer to sell for $3,500,000. He refused and sued on the basis of the offer in her letter. If you were the judge, would you hold her liable?

She did Not bind herself - No Consideration here - She didn't bind herself

Problem 42

Archibald Craven made the following proposal to Mary Lennox: "I promise to sell you my car for $499 if you want to buy it, but I reserve the right to cancel this deal by giving you notice before midnight Friday." To this Mary replied, "That's fine with me." Does this conversation create a contract?

WOOD v. LUCY, LADY DUFF-GORDON
Court of Appeals of New York, 1917
222 N.Y. 88, 118 N.E. 214

CARDOZO, J. The defendant styles herself "a creator of fashions." Her favor helps a sale. Manufacturers of dresses, millinery, and like articles are glad to pay for a certificate of her approval. The things which she designs, fabrics, parasols, and what not, have a new value in the public mind when issued in her name. She employed the plaintiff to help her to turn this vogue into money. He was to have the exclusive right, subject always to her approval, to place her indorsements on the designs of others. He was also to have the exclusive right to place her own designs on sale, or to license others to market them. In return she was to have one-half of "all profits and revenues" derived from any contracts he might make. The exclusive right was to last at least one year from April 1, 1915, and thereafter from year to year unless terminated by notice of 90 days. The plaintiff says that he kept the contract on his part, and that the defendant broke it. She placed her indorsement on fabrics, dresses, and millinery without his knowledge, and withheld the profits. He sues her for the damages, and the case comes here on demurrer.

The agreement of employment is signed by both parties. It has a wealth of recitals. The defendant insists, however, that it lacks the elements of a contract. She says that the plaintiff does not bind himself to anything. It is true that he does not promise in so many words that he will use reasonable efforts to place the defendant's indorsements and market her designs. We think, however, that such a promise is fairly to be implied. The law has outgrown its primitive stage of formalism when the precise word was the sovereign talisman, and every slip was fatal. It takes a broader view today. A promise may be lacking, and yet the whole writing may be "instinct with an obligation," imperfectly expressed (Scott, J., in McCall Co. v. Wright, 133 App. Div. 62, 117 N.Y. Supp. 775; Moran v. Standard Oil Co., 211 N.Y. 187, 198, 105 N.E. 217). If that is so, there is a contract.

The implication of a promise here finds support in many circumstances. The defendant gave an exclusive privilege. She was to have no right for at least a year to place her own indorsements or market her own designs except through the agency of the plaintiff. The acceptance of the exclusive agency was an assumption of its duties. [Citations omitted.] We are not to suppose that one party was to be placed at the mercy of the other. . . . Many other terms of the agreement point the same way. We are told at the outset by way of recital that: "The said Otis F. Wood possesses a business organization adapted to the placing of such indorsements as the said Lucy, Lady Duff-Gordon, has approved."

The implication is that the plaintiff's business organization will be used for the purpose for which it is adapted. But the terms of the defendant's compensation are even more significant. Her sole compensation for the grant of an exclusive agency is to be one-half of all the profits resulting from the plaintiff's efforts. Unless he gave his efforts, she could never get anything. Without an implied promise, the transaction cannot have such business "efficacy, as both parties must have intended that at all events it should have." Bowen, L.J., in the Moorcock, 14 P.D. 64, 68. But the contract does not stop there. The plaintiff goes on to promise that he will account monthly for all moneys received by him, and that he will take out all such patents and copyrights and trade-marks as may in his judgment be necessary to protect the rights and articles affected by the agreement. It is true, of course, as the Appellate Division has said, that if he was under no duty to try to market designs or to place certificates of indorsement, his promise to account for profits or take out copyrights would be valueless. But in determining the intention of the parties the promise has a value. It helps to enforce the conclusion that the plaintiff had some duties. His promise to pay the defendant one-half of the profits and revenues resulting from the exclusive agency and to render accounts monthly was a promise to use reasonable efforts to bring profits and revenues into existence. For this conclusion the authorities are ample. . . .

The judgment of the Appellate Division should be reversed, and the order of the Special Term affirmed, with costs in the Appellate Division and in this court.

CUDDEBACK, MCLAUGHLIN, and ANDREWS, JJ., concur. HISCOCK, C.J., and CHASE and CRANER, JJ., dissent.

Order reversed, etc.

NOTES

1. Lady Duff-Gordon was a famous woman in her day. She was one of the survivors of the *Titanic* disaster and went on to make (and subsequently lose) her fortune as a designer. She invented the word "chic" and introduced slits in skirts, pockets in women's clothing, and the practice of using mannequins to display new fashions. See Charles Pellegrino, *Ghosts of the Titanic* 257 (2000).

2. Had Cardozo decided the other way, the great legal realist Karl Llewellyn once suggested that the facts might have been stated very differently. Llewellyn, A Lecture on Appellate Advocacy, 29 U. Chi. L. Rev. 627, 637-638 (1962):

The plaintiff in this action rests his case upon his own carefully prepared form agreement, which has as its first essence his own omission of any expression whatsoever of any obligation of any kind on the part of this same plaintiff. We thus have the familiar situation of a venture in which one party, here the defendant, has an asset, with what is, in advance, of purely speculative value. The other party, the present plaintiff, who drew the agreement, is a marketer eager for profit, but chary of risk. The legal question presented is whether the plaintiff, while carefully avoiding all risk in the event of failure, can nevertheless claim full profit in the event that the market may prove favorable in its response. The law of consideration joins with the principles of business decency in giving the answer. And the answer is no.

SYLVAN CREST SAND & GRAVEL CO. v. UNITED STATES
United States Court of Appeals, Second Circuit, 1945
150 F.2d 642

SWAN, Circuit Judge. This is an action for damages for breach of four alleged contracts under each of which the plaintiff was to deliver trap rock to an airport project "as required" and in accordance with delivery instructions to be given by the defendant. The breach alleged was the defendant's refusal to request or accept delivery within a reasonable time after the date of the contracts, thereby depriving the plaintiff of profits it would have made in the amount of $10,000. The action was commenced in the District Court, federal jurisdiction resting on 28 U.S.C.A. §41(20). Upon the pleadings, consisting of complaint, answer and reply, the defendant moved to dismiss the action for failure of the complaint to state a claim or, in the alternative, to grant summary judgment for the defendant on the ground that no genuine issue exists as to any material fact. The contracts in suit were introduced as exhibits at the hearing on the motion. Summary judgment for the defendant was granted on the theory that the defendant's reservation of an unrestricted power of cancellation caused the alleged contracts to be wholly illusory as binding obligations. The plaintiff has appealed.

The plaintiff owned and operated a trap rock quarry in Trumbull, Conn. Through the Treasury Department, acting by its State Procurement Office in Connecticut, the United States invited bids on trap rock needed for the Mollison Airport, Bridgeport, Conn. The plaintiff submitted four bids for different sized screenings of trap rock and each bid was accepted by the Assistant State Procurement Officer on June 29, 1937. The four documents are substantially alike and it will suffice to describe one of them. It is a printed government form, with the blank spaces filled in in typewriting, consisting of a single sheet bearing the heading:

Invitation, Bid, and Acceptance
(Short Form Contract)

Below the heading, under the subheadings, follow in order the "Invitation," the "Bid," and the "Acceptance by the Government." The Invitation, signed by a State Procurement Officer, states that "Sealed bids in triplicate, subject to the conditions on the reverse hereof, will be received at this office . . . for furnishing supplies . . . for delivery at WP 2752 — Mollison Airport, Bridgeport, Ct." Then come typed provisions which, so far as material, are as follows:

> Item No. 1. 1/2[inch] Trap Rock to pass the following screening test . . . approx. 4,000 tons, unit price $2.00 amount $8,000. To be delivered to project as required. Delivery to start immediately. Communicate with W. J. Scott, Supt. W.P.A. Branch Office, 147 Canon Street, Bridgeport, Ct., for definite delivery instructions. Cancellation by the Procurement Division may be effected at any time.

[handwritten margin note: unrestricted power to cancel]

The Bid, signed by the plaintiff, provides that

> In compliance with the above invitation for bids, and subject to all of the conditions thereof, the undersigned offers, and agrees, if this bid be accepted . . . to furnish any or all of the items upon which prices are quoted, at the prices set opposite each item, delivered at the point(s) as specified. . . .

The Acceptance, besides its date and the signature of an Assistant State Procurement Officer, contains only the words "Accepted as to items numbered 1." The printing on the reverse side of the sheet under the heading "Conditions" and "Instructions to Contracting Officers" clearly indicates that the parties supposed they were entering into an enforceable contract. For example, Condition 3 states that "in case of default of the contractor" the government may procure the articles from other sources and hold the contractor liable for any excess in cost; and Condition 4 provides that "if the contractor refuses or fails to make deliveries . . . within the time specified . . . the Government may by written notice terminate the right of the contractor to proceed with deliveries. . . ." The Instructions to Contracting Officers also presupposes the making of a valid contract; No. 2 reads:

> Although this form meets the requirements of a formal contract (R.S. 3744), if the execution of a formal contract with bond is contemplated, U.S. Standard Forms 31 and 32 should be used.

No one can read the document as a whole without concluding that the parties intended a contract to result from the Bid and the Government's Acceptance. If the United States did not so intend, it certainly set a skillful trap for unwary bidders. No such purpose should be attributed to the government. See United States v. Purcell Envelope Co., 249 U.S. 313, 318. In construing the document the presumption should be indulged that both parties were acting in good faith.

Although the Acceptance contains no promissory words, it is conceded that a promise by the defendant to pay the stated price for rock delivered is to be implied. Since no precise time for delivery was specified, the implication is that delivery within a reasonable time was contemplated. [Citations omitted.] This is corroborated by the express provision that the rock was "to be delivered to the project as required. Delivery to start immediately." There is also to be implied a promise to give delivery instructions; nothing in the language of the contracts indicates that performance by the plaintiff was to be conditional upon the exercise of the defendant's discretion in giving such instructions. A more reasonable interpretation is that the defendant was placed under an obligation to give instructions for delivery from time to time when trap rock was required at the project. Such were the duties of the defendant, unless the cancellation clause precludes such a construction of the document.

Beyond question the plaintiff made a promise to deliver rock at a stated price; and if the United States were suing for its breach the question would be whether the "acceptance" by the United States operated as a sufficient consideration to make the plaintiff's promise binding. Since the United States is the defendant the question is whether it made any promise that has been broken. Its "acceptance" should be interpreted as a reasonable business man would have understood it. Surely it would not have been understood thus: "We accept your offer and bind you to your promise to deliver, but we do not promise either to take the rock or pay the price." The reservation of a power to effect cancellation at any time meant something different from this. We believe that the reasonable interpretation of the document is as follows: "We accept your offer to deliver within a reasonable time, and we promise to take the rock and pay the price unless we give you notice of cancellation within a reasonable time." Only on such an interpretation is the United States justified in expecting the plaintiff to prepare for performance and to remain ready and willing to deliver. Even so, the bidder is taking a great risk and the United States has an advantage. It is not "good faith" for the United States to insist upon more than this. It is certain that the United States intended to bind the bidder to a "contract," and that the bidder thought that the "acceptance" of his bid made a "contract." A reasonable interpretation of the language used gives effect to their mutual intention. Consequently we cannot accept the contention that the defendant's power of cancellation was unrestricted and could be exercised merely by failure to give delivery orders. The words "cancellation may be effected at any time" imply affirmative action, namely, the giving of notice of intent to cancel. The defendant itself so construed the clause by giving notice of cancellation on July 11, 1939, as alleged in its answer. While the phrase "at any time" should be liberally construed, it means much less than "forever." If taken literally, it would mean that after the defendant had given instructions for delivery and the plaintiff had tendered delivery in accordance therewith, or even after delivery had actually been made, the defendant could refuse to accept and when sued for the price give notice of cancellation of the contract. Such an interpretation would be not only unjust and unreasonable, but would make nugatory the entire contract, contrary to the intention of the parties, if it be assumed that the United States was acting in good faith in accepting the plaintiff's bid. The words should be so construed as to support the contract and not render illusory the promises of both parties. This can be accomplished by interpolating the word "reasonable," as is often done with respect to indefinite time clauses. See Starkweather v. Gleason, 221 Mass. 552, 109 N.E. 635. Hence the agreement obligated the defendant to give delivery instructions or notice of cancellation within a reasonable time after the date of its "acceptance." This constituted consideration for the plaintiff's promise to deliver in accordance with delivery instructions, and made the agreement a valid contract.

It must be conceded that the cases dealing with agreements in which one party has reserved to himself an option to cancel are not entirely harmonious. Where the option is completely unrestricted some courts say that the party having the option has promised nothing and the contract is void for lack of mutuality. [Citations omitted.] These cases have been criticized by competent text writers and the latter case cited by this court "with distinct lack of warmth," as Judge Clark noted in Bushwick-Decatur Motors v. Ford Motor Co., 2 Cir., 116 F.2d 675, 678. But where, as in the case at bar, the option to cancel "does not wholly defeat consideration," the agreement is not *nudum pactum.* Corbin, The Effect of Options on Consideration, 34 Yale L.J. 571, 585; see Hunt v. Stimson, 6 Cir., 23 F.2d 447; Gurfein v. Werbelovsky, 97 Conn. 703, 118 A. 32. A promise is not made illusory by the fact that the promissor has an option between two alternatives, if each alternative would be sufficient consideration if it alone were bargained for. ALI Contracts, §79. As we have construed the agreement the United States promised by implication to take and pay for the trap rock or give notice of cancellation within a reasonable time. The alternative of giving notice was not difficult of performance, but it was a sufficient consideration to support the contract.

The judgment is reversed and the cause remanded for trial.

UNIFORM COMMERCIAL CODE

§2-309. Absence of Specific Time Provisions; Notice of Termination.

. . .

(2) Where the contract provides for successive performances but is indefinite in duration it is valid for a reasonable time but unless otherwise agreed may be terminated at any time by either party.

(3) Termination of a contract by one party except on the happening of an agreed event requires that reasonable notification be received by the other party and an agreement dispensing with notification is invalid if its operation would be unconscionable.

NOTES AND QUESTIONS

1. *Sylvian Crest* was decided before the UCC was enacted. Is §2-309(3) consistent with the court's holding?

2. Parties often enter into dealer-distributor relationships (which are sometimes called "franchise" contracts). Stores selling well-known brands (for example, Goodyear tires) and fast food restaurants (from Pizza Hut to McDonald's) are usually owned by local businesspeople who have purchased the right to use the products and intellectual property of a parent corporation. The contracts often have no end date, which means that the parent company can end the relationship if it satisfies §2-309(3). Given this background, what does §2-309(3) mean when it requires one party to give "reasonable notification" to the other before terminating the agreement? If you owned a local Goodyear tire store, what would you need to do once Goodyear notified you that you could no longer operate the business?

3. Section 2-309 also states that one party may terminate an ongoing contract "on the happening of an agreed event" without providing reasonable notice. What kind of "event[s]" do you think might trigger the end of the contract? Why would it be fair to allow a party to terminate the relationship when these events occur?

McMICHAEL v. PRICE
Supreme Court of Oklahoma, 1936
177 Okla. 186, 58 P.2d 549

OSBORN, Vice Chief Justice. This action was instituted in the district court of Tulsa county by Harley T. Price, doing business as Sooner Sand Company, hereinafter referred to as plaintiff, against W. M. McMichael, hereinafter referred to as defendant, as an action to recover damages for the breach of a contract. The cause was tried to a jury and a verdict returned in favor of plaintiff for $7,512.51. The trial court ordered a remittitur of $2,500, which was duly filed. Thereafter the trial court rendered judgment upon the verdict for $5,012.51, from which judgment defendant has appealed.

The pertinent provisions of the contract, which is the basis of this action, are as follows:

> This Contract and Agreement entered into on this 25th day of February, 1929, by and between Harley T. Price, doing business as the Sooner Sand Company, party of the first part, and W. M. McMichael, party of the second part, Witnesseth:
>
> Whereas, the party of the first part is engaged in the business of selling and shipping sand from Tulsa, Oklahoma, to various points in the United States; and,

Whereas, the party of the second part is the owner of a plot of ground hereinafter described as follows, to-wit:

Lot 11, Section 11, Township 19 North,

Range 12 East, Tulsa County, and,

Whereas, the party of the second part has agreed to build a switch connecting with the Frisco Railway and having its terminal in or at said plot of ground above described; and,

Whereas, the party of the first part is desirous of buying and the party of the second part is desirous of selling various grades and qualities of sand as hereinafter set forth;

Now, therefore, in consideration of the mutual promises herein contained, the said second party agrees to furnish all of the sand of various grades and qualities which the first party can sell for shipment to various and sundry points outside of the City of Tulsa, Oklahoma, and to load all of said sand in suitable railway cars on said aforesaid switch for delivery to said Frisco Railway Company as initial carrier. Said second party agrees to furnish the quantity and quality of sand at all and various times as the first party may designate by written or oral order, and agrees to furnish and load same within a reasonable time after said verbal or written order is received.

In consideration of the mutual promises herein contained, first party agrees to purchase and accept from second party all of the sand of various grades and quality which the said first party can sell, for shipment to various and sundry points outside of the City of Tulsa, Oklahoma, provided that the sand so agreed to be furnished and loaded by the said second party shall at least be equal to in quality and comparable with the sand of various grades sold by other sand companies in the City of Tulsa, Oklahoma, or vicinity. First party agrees to pay and the second party agrees to accept as payment and compensation for said sand so furnished and loaded, a sum per ton which represents sixty percent (60 percent) of the current market price per ton of concrete sand at the place of destination of said shipment. It is agreed that statements are to be rendered by second party to first party every thirty days; the account is payable monthly by first party with a discount to be allowed by second party of four cents per ton for payment within ten days after shipment of any quantity of sand. . . .

This contract and agreement shall cover a period of ten years from the date hereof, and shall be binding and effective during said period, and shall extend to the heirs, executors, administrators and assigns of both parties hereto.

Dated this 25th day of February, 1929.

Sooner Sand Company,
By *Harley T. Price,*
Party of the first part
W. M. McMichael,
By *J. O. McMichael,*
Party of the second part

Plaintiff alleged the execution of the above contract, and further alleged that defendant at various and sundry times, beginning about five months after the execution of the contract, failed, neglected, and refused to furnish all of the sand which plaintiff had sold for shipment to various points outside of the city of Tulsa; that on or about November 15, 1929, defendant expressly repudiated and renounced the contract and stated to plaintiff that he would no longer consider himself bound thereby and would not further comply therewith. Plaintiff alleged various items of damages in the nature of loss of profits arising by reason of the alleged repudiation and breach of the contract by defendant. It will not be necessary to set out the various items of damage claimed.

Defendant admitted the execution of the contract and alleged his full performance thereof from March, 1929, to November, 1929, and further alleged that plaintiff breached the terms of the contract by failing and refusing to pay for the sand shipped each month as required by the contract; that he advised plaintiff that he would cease making further shipments unless plaintiff paid the accounts monthly as provided in the agreement; that in November, 1929, at a time when the sum of $2,143.32 was due and owing by plaintiff to defendant, defendant refused to make further shipments of sand until said account was paid; that plaintiff has been in default on the contract since April, 1929. For counterclaim against plaintiff, defendant alleged the indebtedness of $2,143.32, and prayed for judgment against plaintiff in said amount.

By way of reply to defendant's answer and counterclaim, plaintiff denied the correctness of the accounts sued on in the counterclaim and alleged that defendant only furnished to plaintiff one statement which was on the date of November 10, 1929, which statement was incorrect, false, and fraudulent. In this connection plaintiff claims that in order to make settlements with defendant he was forced to go to the office of defendant and examine the books; that at no time did the books of defendant reflect the correct balance due and owing; that plaintiff from time to time made payments on the account and was assured by defendant from time to time that the books would be adjusted and they would determine the exact amount due and owing to defendant. Plaintiff insists that he was able and willing at all times to make full and complete settlement with defendant whenever the exact amount of the indebtedness could be determined.

Defendant contends that the contract between the parties was a mere revocable offer and is not a valid and binding contract of purchase and sale for want of mutuality. The general rule is that in construing a contract where the consideration on the one side is an offer or an agreement to sell, and on the other side an offer or agreement to buy, the obligation of the parties to sell and buy must be mutual, to render the contract binding on either party, or, as it is sometimes stated, if one of the parties, not having suffered any previous detriment, can escape future liability under the contract, that party may be said to have a "free way out" and the contract lacks mutuality.

Consolidated Pipe Line Co. v. British American Oil Co., 163 Okl. 171, 21 P.2d 762. Attention is directed to the specific language used in the contract binding the defendant to "furnish all of the sand of various grades and qualities which the first party can sell" and whereby plaintiff is bound "to purchase and accept from second party all of the sand of various grades and qualities which the said first party (plaintiff) can sell." It is urged that plaintiff had no established business and was not bound to sell any sand whatever and might escape all liability under the terms of the contract by a mere failure or refusal to sell sand. In this connection it is to be noted that the contract recites that plaintiff is "engaged in the business of selling and shipping sand from Tulsa, Oklahoma, to various points." The parties based their contract on this agreed predicate.

A number of the applicable authorities were discussed by this court in the case of Baker v. Murray Tool & Supply Co., 137 Okl. 288, 279 P. 340, 344, where the court was called upon to determine the force and effect of a contract somewhat similar to the contract involved herein. We quote from the body of the opinion:

In the case of Minnesota Lumber Co. v. Whitebreast Coal Co., 160 Ill. 85, 43 N.E. 774, 31 L.R.A. 529, the court, in sustaining the validity of a contract of sale by mining company to a dealer in coal of his requirements, said: *"Season Requirement"*

1. A contract wherein defendant agreed to buy of plaintiff all its "requirements" of coal for the season at a specified price is not void for uncertainty, in that the actual amount of the requirement was not stated, it being, manifestly, the amount of coal defendant needed and used in its business during the season.

2. Where defendant agreed to buy its "requirements" of coal of plaintiff, the contract is mutual, as such provision required defendant to buy all its coal from plaintiff, and was one on which plaintiff could maintain an action for breach, should defendant purchase coal elsewhere.

If the word "requirements," as here used, is so interpreted as to mean that appellee was only to furnish such coal as appellant should require it to furnish, then it might be said that appellant was not bound to require any coal unless he chose, and that therefore there was a want of mutuality in the contract. But the rule is that, where the terms of a contract are susceptible of two significations, that will be adopted which gives some operation to the contract, rather than that which renders it inoperative. . . . A contract should be construed in such a way as to make the obligation imposed by its terms mutually binding upon the parties, unless such construction is wholly negatived by the language used. . . . It cannot be said that appellant was not bound by the contract. It had no right to purchase coal elsewhere for use in its business, unless, in case of a decline in the price, appellee should conclude to release it from further liability. . . .

It is said in the syllabus of Texas Co. v. Pensacola Maritime Corporation (C.C.A.) 279 F. 19, 24 A.L.R. 1336:

A contract for the sale of plaintiff's requirements of oil for resale to ships does not lack mutuality, even though the plaintiff had as yet no established business for the sale of fuel oil for ships, and especially where plaintiff did have an established business in the sale of coal as a fuel for ships, since plaintiff's agreement to buy its oil only from defendant was a <u>detriment</u> to it sufficient to support the contract. . . .

Crane v. C. Crane & Co., 105 F. 869, 45 C.C.A. 96, cited by the appellee in support of the position of the District Court, involved material points of difference from the case made by the complaint under examination. The contract examined in that case left the plaintiff at liberty to buy the lumber he desired elsewhere if the prices of such lumber were more favorable to him, and it did not appear from the complaint that the vendor had knowledge of the purchaser's requirements. These points of distinction are well brought out in Grand Prairie Gravel Co. v. Wills Co. (Tex. Civ. App.) 188 S.W. 689.

At the time the contract involved herein was executed, plaintiff was not the owner of an established sand business. The evidence shows, however, that he was an experienced salesman of sand, which fact was well known to defendant, and that it was anticipated by both parties that on account of the experience, acquaintances, and connections of plaintiff, he would be able to sell a substantial amount of sand to the mutual profit of the contracting parties. The record discloses that for the nine months immediately following the execution of the contract plaintiff's average net profit per month was $516.88.

 By the terms of the contract the price to be paid for sand was definitely fixed. Plaintiff was bound by a solemn covenant of the contract to purchase all the sand he was able to sell from defendant and for a breach of such covenant could have been made to respond in damages. The argument of defendant that the plaintiff could escape liability under the contract by going out of the sand business is without force in view of our determination, in line with the authorities hereinabove cited, that it was the intent of the parties to enter into a contract which would be mutually binding. . . .

<u>Defendant contends</u> that even though the contract is valid and enforceable, plaintiff failed to make out a case under his own theory. Under the specification defendant argues that the evidence shows that plaintiff, and not defendant, breached the contract by failure to make monthly payments as provided by the contract and by his failure to keep his accounts with defendant settled in full. In this connection the court gave a special instruction to the jury upon the issue of waiver and instructed the jury in detail upon the issues of fact involved by the pleadings and evidence regarding plaintiff's claim that defendant did not keep a correct account of the indebtedness and did not furnish correct statements of the accounts so that plaintiff at no time was able to determine from said books the correct status of his account. The evidence on this point is conflicting, but the finding of the jury under said special instruction is supported by ample competent evidence and will not be disturbed. . . .

The judgment is affirmed.

UNIFORM COMMERCIAL CODE

§2-306. Output, Requirements and Exclusive Dealings.

(1) A term which measures the quantity by the output of the seller or the requirements of the buyer means such actual output or requirements as may occur in good faith, except that no quantity unreasonably disproportionate to any stated estimate or in the absence of a stated estimate to any normal or otherwise comparable prior output or requirements may be tendered or demanded.

(2) A lawful agreement by either the seller or the buyer for exclusive dealing in the kind of goods concerned imposes unless otherwise agreed an obligation by the seller to use best efforts to supply the goods and by the buyer to use best efforts to promote their sale.

CORBIN ON CONTRACTS §156

A promise to buy of another person or company all of some commodity or service that the promisor may thereafter need or require in his business is not an illusory promise; and such a promise is a sufficient consideration for a return promise. It is true that the amount to be delivered or paid for cannot be determined at the time the contract is made; but the terms of the promise give a sufficiently definite objective standard to enable a court to determine the amount when the time comes for enforcement. It is not a promise to buy all that the buyer wishes or may thereafter choose to order; the amount is not left to the will of the promisor himself.

The word "require" is not here used in the sense of request or order; instead, it is the equivalent of need or use. The promisor's duty is conditional upon the existence of an objective need for the commodity or service, and the promisor may have a high degree of control over the happening of this condition; but this does not render the promise illusory and empty of content. It states a limitation upon the promisor's future liberty of action; he no longer has an unlimited option.

It makes no difference how great or small this limitation is — at least, until it approaches near to the vanishing point.

Corbin's basic test here — whether the promise states a limitation upon the promisor's future liberty of action — is useful in determining whether any promise is illusory. Use it and the other ideas just quoted to resolve the following matters.

Problem 43

Under UCC §2-306, is there a valid contract in the following situations?

(a) Portia agreed to buy and the Antonio Casket Company agreed to sell her all the caskets that the company produced the next year. *Yes*

(b) Portia agreed with the Antonio Casket Company to buy from it all the caskets that she would need the next year, and they agreed to sell her that amount. *Yes*

(c) Portia agreed to buy and the Antonio Casket Company agreed to sell her all the caskets <u>she wished</u> to order during the coming year. If she does place an order, is there a contract? *No, under 2-309 (3)*

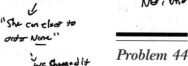

Illusional

"She can elect to order None"

"we changed it"

Problem 44

(a) Ralph Rackstraw was contemplating purchasing a yacht named *Pinafore* and hiring it out to others for pleasure cruises. He signed a contract with Josephine Corcoran in which he promised to charter the yacht to her *if* he decided to purchase it. Is there a contract *prior* to his purchase? This Problem is based on Scott v. Moragues Lumber Co., 202 Ala. 312, 80 So. 394 (1918).

(b) Wanting to make a binding gift and being aware of the doctrine of consideration, Uncle Scrooge signed an agreement promising to give his nephew Donald $10,000 a year for ten years in return for which Donald promised never to become a professor of law. Donald has no legal training, has no interest in law, and is in fact a sand dealer. Is this a valid contract?

IV.   PAST CONSIDERATION

As we have seen, the consideration doctrine is satisfied when each party commits itself to doing something in the future. Yet what if one party makes such a promise in return for something that the other party has *already* done?

HAYES v. PLANTATIONS STEEL CO.
Supreme Court of Rhode Island, 1982
438 A.2d 1091

SHEA, J. The defendant employer, Plantations Steel Company (Plantations), appeals from a Superior Court judgment for the plaintiff employee, Edward J. Hayes (Hayes). The trial justice, sitting without a jury, found that

IV. Past Consideration

Plantations was obligated to Hayes on the basis of an implied-in-fact contract to pay him a yearly pension of $5,000. The award covered three years in which payment had not been made. . . . The trial justice, however, found in part for Plantations in ruling that the payments to Hayes were not governed by the Employee Retirement Income Security Act, 29 U.S.C.A. §§1001-1461 (West 1975), and consequently he was not entitled to attorney's fees under §1132(g) of that act. Both parties have appealed.

We reverse the findings of the trial justice regarding Plantations's contractual obligation to pay Hayes a pension. Consequently we need not deal with the cross-appeal concerning the award of attorney's fees under the federal statute.

Plantations is a closely held Rhode Island corporation engaged in the manufacture of steel reinforcing rods for use in concrete construction. The company was founded by Hugo R. Mainelli, Sr., and Alexander A. DiMartino. A dispute between their two families in 1976 and 1977 left the DiMartinos in full control of the corporation. Hayes was an employee of the corporation from 1947 until his retirement in 1972 at the age of sixty-five. He began with Plantations as an "estimator and draftsman" and ended his career as general manager, a position of considerable responsibility. Starting in January 1973 and continuing until January 1976, Hayes received the annual sum of $5,000 from Plantations. Hayes instituted this action in December 1977, after the then company management refused to make any further payments.

Hayes testified that in January 1972 he announced his intention to retire the following July, after twenty-five years of continuous service. He decided to retire because he had worked continuously for fifty-one years. He stated, however, that he would not have retired had he not expected to receive a pension. After he stopped working for Plantations, he sought no other employment.

Approximately one week before his actual retirement Hayes spoke with Hugo R. Mainelli, Jr., who was then an officer and a stockholder of Plantations. This conversation was the first and only one concerning payments of a pension to Hayes during retirement. Mainelli said that the company "would take care" of him. There was no mention of a sum of money or a percentage of salary that Hayes would receive. There was no formal authorization for payments by Plantations's shareholders and/or board of directors. Indeed, there was never any formal provision for a pension plan for any employee other than for unionized employees, who benefit from an arrangement through their union. The plaintiff was not a union member.

Mr. Mainelli, Jr., testified that his father, Hugo R. Mainelli, Sr., had authorized the first payment "as a token of appreciation for the many years of [Hayes's] service." Furthermore, "it was implied that that check would continue on an annual basis." Mainelli also testified that it was his "personal intention" that the payments would continue for "as long as I was around."

Mainelli testified that after Hayes's retirement, he would visit the premises each year to say hello and renew old acquaintances. During the course of his visits, Hayes would thank Mainelli for the previous check and ask how long it would continue so that he could plan an orderly retirement. The payments were discontinued after 1976. At that time a succession of several poor business years plus the stockholders' dispute, resulting in the takeover by the DiMartino family, contributed to the decision to stop the payments.

Trial

The trial justice ruled that Plantations owed Hayes his annual sum of $5,000 for the years 1977 through 1979. The ruling implied that barring bankruptcy or the cessation of business for any other reason, Hayes had a right to expect continued annual payments.

Promise

Consideration

Implied Contract

The trial justice found that Hugo Mainelli, Jr.'s statement that Hayes would be taken care of after his retirement was a promise. Although no sum of money was mentioned in 1972, the four annual payments of $5,000 established that otherwise unspecified term of the contract. The trial justice also found that Hayes supplied consideration for the promise by voluntarily retiring, because he was under no obligation to do so. From the words and conduct of the parties and from the surrounding circumstances, the trial justice concluded that there existed an implied contract obligating the company to pay a pension to Hayes for life. . . .

The findings of fact of a trial justice sitting without a jury are entitled to great weight when reviewed by this court. His findings will not be disturbed unless it can be shown that they are clearly wrong or that the trial justice misconceived or overlooked material evidence. Lisi v. Marra, R.I., 424 A.2d 1052 (1981); Raheb v. Lemenski, 115 R.I. 576, 350 A.2d 397 (1976). After careful review of the record, however, we conclude that the trial justice's findings and conclusions must be reversed.

Reversed

Assuming for the purpose of this discussion that Plantations in legal effect made a promise to Hayes, we must ask whether Hayes did supply the required consideration that would make the promise binding? And, if Hayes did not supply consideration, was his alleged reliance sufficiently induced by the promise to estop defendant from denying its obligation to him? We answer both questions in the negative.

Problem of Consideration

We turn first to the problem of consideration. The facts at bar do not present the case of an express contract. As the trial justice stated, the existence of a contract in this case must be determined from all the circumstances of the parties' conduct and words. Although words were expressed initially in the remark that Hayes "would be taken care of," any contract in this case would be more in the nature of an implied contract. Certainly the statement of Hugo Mainelli, Jr., standing alone is not an expression of a direct and definite promise to pay Hayes a pension. Though we are analyzing an implied contract, nevertheless we must address the question of consideration.

Need Consideration for Implied Contracts

Contracts implied in fact require the element of consideration to support them as is required in express contracts. The only difference between the two is the manner in which the parties manifest their assent. [Citations omitted.] In this jurisdiction, consideration consists either in some right, interest, or benefit accruing to one party or some forbearance, detriment, or responsibility given, suffered, or undertaken by the other. [Citations omitted.] Valid consideration furthermore must be bargained for. It must induce the return act or promise. To be valid, therefore, the purported consideration must not have been delivered before a promise is executed, that is, given without reference to the promise. Plowman v. Indian Refining Co., 20 F. Supp. 1 (E.D. Ill. 1937). Consideration is therefore a test of the enforceability of executory promises, Angel v. Murray, 113 R.I. 482, 322 A.2d 630 (1974), and has no legal effect when rendered in the past and apart from an alleged exchange in the present. Zanturjian v. Boornazian, 25 R.I. 151, 55 A. 199 (1903).

In the case before us, Plantations's promise to pay Hayes a pension is quite clearly not supported by any consideration supplied by Hayes. Hayes had announced his intent to retire well in advance of any promise, and therefore the intention to retire was arrived at without regard to any promise by Plantations. Although Hayes may have had in mind the receipt of a pension when he first informed Plantations, his expectation was not based on any statement made to him or on any conduct of the company officer relative to him in January 1972. In deciding to retire, Hayes acted on his own initiative. Hayes's long years of dedicated service also is legally insufficient because his service too was rendered without being induced by Plantations's promise. See Plowman v. Indian Refining Co., supra.

Clearly then this is not a case in which Plantations's promise was meant to induce Hayes to refrain from retiring when he could have chosen to do so in return for further service. 1 Williston on Contracts, §130B (3d ed., Jaeger 1957). Nor was the promise made to encourage long service from the start of his employment. Weesner v. Electric Power Board of Chattanooga, 48 Tenn. App. 178, 344 S.W.2d 766 (1961). Instead, the testimony establishes that Plantations's promise was intended "as a token of appreciation for [Hayes's] many years of service." As such it was in the nature of a gratuity paid to Hayes for as long as the company chose. In Spickelmier Industries, Inc. v. Passander, 172 Ind. App. 49, 359 N.E.2d 563 (1977), an employer's promise to an employee to pay him a year-end bonus was unenforceable because it was made after the employee had performed his contractual responsibilities for that year.

The plaintiff's most relevant citations are still inapposite to the present case. Bredemann v. Vaughan Mfg. Co., 40 Ill. App. 2d 232, 188 N.E.2d 746 (1963), presents similar yet distinguishable facts. There, the appellate court reversed a summary judgment granted to the defendant employer, stating that a genuine issue of material fact existed regarding whether the plaintiff's retirement was in consideration of her employer's promise to pay her a lifetime pension. As in the present case, the employer made the promise one week prior to the employee's retirement, and in almost the same words.

However, *Bredemann* is distinguishable because the court characterized that promise as a concrete offer to pay *if she would retire immediately.* In fact, the defendant wanted her to retire. *Id.* 188 N.E.2d at 749. On the contrary, Plantations in this case did not actively seek Hayes's retirement. DiMartino, one of Plantations's founders, testified that he did not want Hayes to retire. Unlike *Bredemann*, here Hayes announced his unsolicited intent to retire.

Hayes also argues that the work he performed during the week between the promise and the date of his retirement constituted sufficient consideration to support the promise. He relies on Ulmann v. Sunset-McKee Co., 221 F.2d 128 (9th Cir. 1955), in which the court ruled that work performed during the one-week period of the employee's notice of impending retirement constituted consideration for the employer's offer of a pension that the employee had solicited some months previously. But there the court stated that its prime reason for upholding the agreement was that sufficient consideration existed in the employee's consent not to compete with his employer. These circumstances do not appear in our case. Hayes left his employment because he no longer desired to work. He was not contemplating other job offers or considering going into competition with Plantations. Although Plantations did not want Hayes to leave, it did not try to deter him, nor did it seek to prevent Hayes from engaging in other activity.

[The court also rejected Hayes's promissory estoppel claim. We discuss promissory estoppel later in this chapter — EDS.].

For the foregoing reasons, the defendant's appeal is sustained and the judgment of the Superior Court is reversed. The papers of the case are remanded to the Superior Court.

NOTE

Some pensions are enforceable under statutes such as Employee Retirement Income Security Act of 1974 (ERISA), Pub. L. No. 93-406, 88 Stat. 829 (codified in various sections of 26, 29 U.S.C.).

MILLS v. WYMAN

Supreme Judicial Court of Massachusetts, 1825
3 Pick. 207

This was an action of assumpsit brought to recover a compensation for the board, nursing, etc. of Levi Wyman, son of the defendant, from the 5th to the 20th of February 1821. The plaintiff then lived at Hartford, in Connecticut; the defendant, at Shrewsbury, in this county. Levi Wyman, at the time when the services were rendered, was about 25 years of age, and had long ceased to be a member of his father's family. He was on his return from a voyage at sea, and being suddenly taken sick at Hartford, and being poor and in distress, was relieved by the plaintiff in the manner and to the extent above stated. On the 24th of February, after all the expenses had been incurred, the defendant wrote a letter to the plaintiff, promising to pay him such expenses. There was no consideration for this promise, except what grew out of the relation which subsisted between Levi Wyman and the defendant, and Howe J., before whom the cause was tried in the Court of Common Pleas, thinking this not sufficient to support the action, directed a nonsuit. To this direction the plaintiff filed exceptions.

PARKER C.J. General rules of law established for the protection and security of honest and fair-minded men, who may inconsiderately make promises without any equivalent, will sometimes screen men of a different character from engagements which they are bound in *foro conscientiae* to perform. This is a defect inherent in all human systems of legislation. The rule that a mere verbal promise, without any consideration, cannot be enforced by action, is universal in its application, and cannot be departed from to suit particular cases in which a refusal to perform such a promise may be disgraceful.

The promise declared on in this case appears to have been made without any legal consideration. The kindness and services towards the sick son of the defendant were not bestowed at his request. The son was in no respect under the care of the defendant. He was twenty-five years old, and had long left his father's family. On his return from a foreign country, he fell sick among strangers, and the plaintiff acted the part of the good Samaritan, giving him shelter and comfort until he died. The defendant, his father, on being informed of this event, influenced by transient feeling of gratitude, promises in writing to pay the plaintiff for the expenses he had incurred. But he has determined to break this promise, and is willing to have his case appear on record as a strong example of particular injustice sometimes necessarily resulting from the operation of general rules.

It is said a moral obligation is a sufficient consideration to support an express promise; and some authorities lay down the rule thus broadly; but upon examination of the cases we are satisfied that the universality of the rule cannot be supported, and that there must have been some pre-existing obligation, which has become inoperative by positive law, to form a basis for an effective promise. The cases of debts barred by the statute of limitations, of debts incurred by infants, of debts of bankrupts, are generally put for illustration of the rule. Express promises founded on such pre-existing equitable obligations may be enforced; there is a good consideration for them; they merely remove an impediment created by law to the recovery of debts honestly due, but which public policy protects the debtors from being compelled to pay. In all these cases there was originally a quid pro quo; and according to the principles of natural justice the party receiving ought to pay; but the legislature has said he shall not be coerced; then comes the promise to pay the debt that is barred, the promise of the man to pay the debt

[Margin annotations:] No legal consideration

Son was Not under the care of the defendant

Father of son who died promises to pay the plaintiff for expenses, but then decided to break his promise

Must have been some pre-existing obligation to form a basis for an effective promise of the infant, of the discharged bankrupt to restore to his creditor what by the law he had lost. In all these cases there is a moral obligation founded upon an antecedent valuable consideration. These promises therefore have a sound legal basis. They are not promises to pay something for nothing; not naked pacts; but the voluntary revival or creation of obligation which before existed in natural law, but which had been dispensed with, not for the benefit of the party obliged solely, but principally for the public convenience. If moral obligation, in its fullest sense, is a good substratum for an express promise, it is not easy to perceive why it is not equally good to support an implied promise. What a man ought to do, generally he ought to be made to do, whether he promise or refuse. But the law of society has left most of such obligations to the interior forum, as the tribunal of conscience has been aptly called. Is there not a moral obligation upon every son who has become affluent by means of the education and advantages bestowed upon him by his father, to relieve that father from pecuniary embarrassment, to promote his comfort and happiness, and even to share with him his riches, if thereby he will be made happy? And yet such a son may, with impunity, leave such a father in any degree of penury above that which will expose the community in which he dwells, to the danger of being obliged to preserve him from absolute want. Is not a wealthy father under strong moral obligation to advance the interest of an obedient, well disposed son, to furnish him with the means of acquiring and maintaining a becoming rank in life, to rescue him from the horrors of debt incurred by misfortune? Yet the law will uphold him in any degree of parsimony, short of that which would reduce his son to the necessity of seeking public charity.

Without doubt there are great interests of society which justify withholding the coercive arm of the law from these duties of imperfect obligation, as they are called; imperfect, not because they are less binding upon the conscience than those which are called perfect, but because the wisdom of the social law does not impose sanctions upon them.

A deliberate promise, in writing, made freely and without any mistake, one which may lead the party to whom it is made into contracts and expenses, cannot be broken without a violation of moral duty. But if there was nothing paid or promised for it, the law, perhaps wisely, leaves the execution of it to the conscience of him who makes it. It is only when the party making the promise gains something, or he to whom it is made loses something, that the law gives the promise validity. And in the case of the promise of the adult to pay the debt of the infant, of the debtor discharged by the statute of limitations or bankruptcy, the principle is preserved by looking back to the origin of the transaction, where an equivalent is to be found. An exact equivalent is not required by the law; for there being a consideration, the parties are left to estimate its value: though here the courts of equity will step in to relieve from gross inadequacy between the consideration and the promise.

These principles are deduced from the general current of decided cases upon the subject, as well as from the known maxims of the common law. The general position, that moral obligation is a sufficient consideration for an express promise, is to be limited in its application to cases where at some time or other a good or valuable consideration has existed.

A legal obligation is always a sufficient consideration to support either an express or an implied promise; such as an infant's debt for necessaries, or a father's promise to pay for the support and education of his minor children. But when the child shall have attained to manhood, and shall have become his own agent in the world's business, the debts he incurs, whatever may be their nature, create no obligation; and it seems to follow, that a promise founded upon such a debt has no legally binding force. . . .

For the foregoing reasons we are all of opinion that the nonsuit directed by the Court of Common Pleas was right, and that judgment be entered thereon for costs for the defendant.

NOTES

1. For an article arguing that this case is wrong on both the facts (the son apparently lived for a number of years, for example) and the law, see Watson, In the Tribunal of Conscience: *Mills v. Wyman* Reconsidered, 71 Tul. L. Rev. 1749 (1997).

2. The Utah Supreme Court in Manwill v. Oyler, 11 Utah 2d 433, 361 P.2d 177, 178 (1961), had this to say about the doctrine of moral consideration:

> The difficulty we see with the doctrine is that if a mere moral, as distinguished from a legal, obligation were recognized as valid consideration for a contract, that would practically erode to the vanishing point the necessity for finding a consideration. This is so, first because in nearly all circumstances where a promise is made there is some moral aspect of the situation which provides the motivation for making the promise even if it is to make an outright gift. And second, if we are dealing with the moral concepts, the making of a promise itself creates a moral obligation to perform it. It seems obvious that if a contract to be legally enforceable need be anything other than a naked promise, something more than mere moral consideration is necessary. The principle that in order for a contract to be valid and binding, each party must be bound to give some legal consideration to the other by conferring a benefit upon him or suffering a legal detriment at his request is firmly implanted in the roots of our law.

Note, however, that *Mills* states a number of exceptions to the general rule against the use of the moral obligation doctrine as a substitute for traditional consideration. These exceptions are still generally applicable. For example, if a defaulting obligor promises not to plead the statute of limitations or undertakes to pay a debt voidable because of the statute, the promise is enforceable. For that matter the mere acknowledgment of the debt or the part payment of principal or interest may be found to be an enforceable implied promise to pay the obligation. See Restatement (Second) of Contracts §82 (reprinted later). All but a few states provide by statute that such a promise or acknowledgment must be in writing to be enforceable.

3. *Mills* also recognizes the historical exception for promises to pay debts discharged in bankruptcy. Such a reaffirmation promise is now regulated by federal law. The Bankruptcy Code, at 11 U.S.C. §524(c) and (d), allows a bankrupt 60 days to rescind a promise to pay a discharged debt and, unless the debt is secured by real property, authorizes the bankruptcy court to disallow any consumer agreements not in the best interests of the promisor. Typically, bankruptcy serves to discharge the bankrupt's obligations. However, the bankrupt cannot receive such a discharge again for eight years. When would it ever be in the consumer's best interest to agree to pay a debt dischargeable in bankruptcy?

4. *Mills* also mentions the still generally accepted special treatment of promises to pay an obligation otherwise voidable because of infancy. Upon reaching majority, if a person voluntarily and with knowledge of the facts promises to pay an obligation that was voidable because that person was a minor when the contract was made, the new promise is enforceable. It is generally assumed that this special treatment applies to promises to perform all or part of any antecedent contract previously voidable because of such defects as fraud, mistake, duress, or undue influence. See Restatement (Second) of Contracts §85. Another rationale that is often used for enforcing such promises is that the obligor has "affirmed" the original promise made during infancy.

_____

Problem 45

Alexander Selkirk was shipwrecked for a ten-year period on a deserted island. When he returned to civilization, one of his creditors, Daniel Defoe, to whom he owed $5,000, hunted him up and asked him for payment. The statute of limitations had recently run out on the debt.

(a) If Selkirk makes no promise to pay the time-barred debt, must he do so? What policies are at work here?

(b) If he makes a written promise to pay the debt, what consideration does Defoe give for the new promise?

(c) If Selkirk makes a written promise to pay Defoe, but states that he will only pay $1,000, does he owe any amount?

(d) When Defoe made his payment demand, Selkirk said nothing, but the next day he sent a check to Defoe for $100. Must he now pay the remaining debt?

RESTATEMENT (SECOND) OF CONTRACTS

§82. PROMISE TO PAY INDEBTEDNESS; EFFECT ON THE STATUTE OF LIMITATIONS

(1) A promise to pay all or part of an antecedent contractual or quasi-contractual indebtedness owed by the promisor is binding if the indebtedness is still enforceable or would be except for the effect of a statute of limitations.

(2) The following facts operate as such a promise unless other facts indicate a different intention:

(a) A voluntary acknowledgment to the obligee, admitting the present existence of the antecedent indebtedness; or

(b) A voluntary transfer of money, a negotiable instrument, or other thing by the obligor to the obligee, made as interest on or part payment of or collateral security for the antecedent indebtedness; or

(c) A statement to the obligee that the statute of limitations will not be pleaded as a defense.

Problem 46

When his car broke down the night before he had to drive 40 miles to the big game, Coach Pigskin of Football University was frantic. He phoned his next-door neighbor, Al Garage, who owned a repair shop and who always performed the coach's repair work, and asked Al if he could do an emergency repair, "for a friend in need who must get to the football game." Al agreed to try to help, and after working on the car for four hours, he put it in running condition. Coach Pigskin's team won the game, and when he returned home he told Al that he would pay him $200 for his work the night before. The two friends had never discussed payment at the time of the repair, though Al had always charged the coach for previous repair work. Al agreed to the $200 figure, and they shook hands on the deal. Later Coach Pigskin decided the work was worth only $100, and he refused to pay more. If Al sues, what amount, if any, can he recover?

Appellant WEBB v. McGOWIN _Appellee_
Court of Appeals of Alabama, 1935
27 Ala. App. 82, 168 So. 196

BRICKEN, Presiding Judge. This action is in assumpsit. The complaint as originally filed was amended. The demurrers to the complaint as amended were sustained, and because of this adverse ruling by the court the plaintiff took a nonsuit, and the assignment of errors on this appeal are predicated upon said action or ruling of the court.

A fair statement of the case presenting the questions for decision is set out in appellant's brief, which we adopt.

On the 3d day of August, 1925, appellant while in the employ of the W. T. Smith Lumber Company, a corporation, and acting within the scope of his employment, was engaged in clearing the upper floor of mill No. 2 of the company. While so engaged he was in the act of dropping a pine block from the upper floor of the mill to the ground below; this being the usual and ordinary way of clearing the floor, and it being the duty of the plaintiff in the course of his employment to so drop it. The block weighed about 75 pounds.

As appellant was in the act of dropping the block to the ground below, he was on the edge of the upper floor of the mill. As he started to turn the block loose so that it would drop to the ground, he saw J. Greeley McGowin, testator of the defendants, on the ground below and directly under where the block would have fallen had appellant turned it loose. Had he turned it loose it would have struck McGowin with such force as to have caused him serious bodily harm or death. Appellant could have remained safely on the upper floor of the mill by turning the block loose and allowing it to drop, but had he done this the block would have fallen on McGowin and caused him serious injuries or death. The only safe and reasonable way to prevent this was for appellant to hold to the block and divert its direction in falling from the place where McGowin was standing and the only safe way to divert it so as to prevent its coming into contact with McGowin was for appellant to fall with it to the ground below. Appellant did this, and by holding to the block and falling with it to the ground below, he diverted the course of its fall in such way that McGowin was not injured. In thus preventing the injuries to McGowin appellant himself received serious bodily injuries, resulting in his right leg being broken, the heel of his right foot torn off and his right arm broken. He was badly crippled for life and rendered unable to do physical or mental labor.

On September 1, 1925, in consideration of appellant having prevented him from sustaining death or serious bodily harm and in consideration of the injuries appellant had received, McGowin agreed with him to care for and maintain him for the remainder of appellant's life at the rate of $15 every two weeks from the time he sustained his injuries to and during the remainder of appellant's life; it being agreed that McGowin would pay this sum to appellant for his maintenance. Under the agreement McGowin paid or caused to be paid to appellant the sum so agreed on up until McGowin's death on January 1, 1934. After his death the payments were continued to and including January 27, 1934, at which time they were discontinued. Thereupon plaintiff brought suit to recover the unpaid installments accruing up to the time of the bringing of the suit.

The material averments of the different counts of the original complaint and the amended complaint are predicated upon the foregoing statement of facts.

In other words, the complaint as amended averred in substance: (1) That on August 3, 1925, appellant saved J. Greeley McGowin, appellee's testator, from death or grievous bodily harm; (2) that in doing so appellant sustained bodily injury crippling him for life; (3) that in consideration of the services rendered and the injuries received by appellant, McGowin agreed to care for him the remainder of appellant's life, the amount to be paid being $15 every two weeks; (4) that McGowin complied with this agreement until he died on January 1, 1934, and the payments were kept up to January 27, 1934, after which they were discontinued.

The action was for the unpaid installments accruing after January 27, 1934, to the time of the suit.

The principal grounds of demurrer to the original and amended complaint are: (1) It states no cause of action; (2) its averments show the contract was without consideration; (3) it fails to allege that McGowin had, at or before the services were rendered, agreed to pay appellant for them; (4) the contract declared on is void under the Statute of Frauds.

<u>1</u>. The averments of the complaint show that appellant saved McGowin from death or grievous bodily harm. This was a material benefit to him of infinitely more value than any financial aid he could have received. Receiving this benefit, McGowin became morally bound to compensate appellant for the services rendered. Recognizing his moral obligation, he expressly agreed to pay appellant as alleged in the complaint and complied with this agreement up to the time of his death; a period of more than eight years.

Had McGowin been accidentally poisoned and a physician, without his knowledge or request, had administered an antidote, thus saving his life, a subsequent promise by McGowin to pay the physician would have been valid. Likewise, McGowin's agreement as disclosed by the complaint to compensate appellant for saving him from death or grievous bodily injury is valid and enforceable.

Where the promisee cares for, improves, and preserves the property of the promisor, though done without his request, it is sufficient consideration for the promisor's subsequent agreement to pay for the service, because of the material benefit received. [Citations omitted.]

In Boothe v. Fitzpatrick, 36 Vt. 681, the court held that a promise by defendant to pay for the past keeping of a bull which had escaped from defendant's premises and been cared for by plaintiff was valid, although there was no previous request, because the subsequent promise obviated that objection; it being equivalent to a previous request. On the same principle, had the promisee saved the promisor's life or his body from grievous harm, his subsequent promise to pay for the services rendered would have been valid. Such service would have been far more material than caring for his bull. Any holding that saving a man from death or grievous bodily harm is not a material benefit sufficient to uphold a subsequent promise to pay for the service, necessarily rests on the assumption that saving life and preservation of the body from harm have only a sentimental value. The converse of this is true. Life and preservation of the body have material, pecuniary values, measurable in dollars and cents. Because of this, physicians practice their profession charging for services rendered in saving life and curing the body of its ills, and surgeons perform operations. The same is true as to the law of negligence, authorizing the assessment of damages in personal injury cases based upon the extent of the injuries, earnings, and life expectancies of those injured.

In the business of life insurance, the value of a man's life is measured in dollars and cents according to his expectancy, the soundness of his body, and his ability to pay premiums. The same is true as to health and accident insurance.

It follows that if, as alleged in the complaint, appellant saved J. Greeley McGowin from death or grievous bodily harm, and McGowin subsequently agreed to pay him for the service rendered, it became a valid and enforceable contract.

2. It is well settled that a moral obligation is a sufficient consideration to support a subsequent promise to pay where the promisor has received a material benefit, although there was no original duty or liability resting on the promisor. . . . In the case of State ex rel. Bayer v. Funk, supra, the court held that a moral obligation is a sufficient consideration to support an executory promise where the promisor has received an actual pecuniary or material benefit for which he subsequently expressly promised to pay.

The case at bar is clearly distinguishable from that class of cases where the consideration is a mere moral obligation or conscientious duty unconnected with receipt by promisor of benefits of a material or pecuniary nature. Park Falls State Bank v. Fordyce, supra. Here the promisor received a material benefit constituting a valid consideration for his promise.

3. Some authorities hold that, for a moral obligation to support a subsequent promise to pay, there must have existed a prior legal or equitable obligation, which for some reason had become unenforceable, but for which the promisor was still morally bound. This rule, however, is subject to qualification in those cases where the promisor, having received a material benefit from the promisee, is morally bound to compensate him for the services rendered and in consideration of this obligation promises to pay. In such cases the subsequent promise to pay is an affirmance or ratification of the services rendered carrying with it the presumption that a previous request for the service was made. [Citations omitted.]

Under the decisions above cited, McGowin's express promise to pay appellant for the services rendered was an affirmance or ratification of what appellant had done raising the presumption that the services had been rendered at McGowin's request.

4. The averments of the complaint show that in saving McGowin from death or grievous bodily harm, appellant was crippled for life. This was part of the consideration of the contract declared on. McGowin was benefited. Appellant was injured. Benefit to the promisor or injury to the promisee is a

sufficient legal consideration for the promisor's agreement to pay. Fisher v. Bartlett, 8 Greenl. (Me.) 122, 22 Am. Dec. 225; State ex rel. Bayer v. Funk, supra.

5. Under the averments of the complaint the services rendered by appellant were not gratuitous. The agreement of McGowin to pay and the acceptance of payment by appellant conclusively shows the contrary. . . .

From what has been said, we are of the opinion that the court below erred in the ruling complained of; that is to say, in sustaining the demurrer, and for this error the case is reversed and remanded.

Reversed and remanded. *Reversed*

SAMFORD, J. (concurring). The questions involved in this case are not free from doubt, and perhaps the strict letter of the rule, as stated by judges, though not always in accord, would bar a recovery by plaintiff, but following the principle announced by Chief Justice Marshall in Hoffman v. Porter, Fed. Cas. No. 6,577, 2 Brock. 156, 159, where he says, "I do not think that law ought to be separated from justice, where it is at most doubtful," I concur in the conclusions reached by the court.

[The Supreme Court of Alabama denied certiorari in this case, writing a short opinion in which it expressly approved the decision of the lower appellate court, 232 Ala. 374, 168 So. 199 (1936).]

case was Appealed again, but it was Denied

NOTES AND QUESTIONS

1. Is this case distinguishable from Mills v. Wyman?
2. Would the case have been decided differently if McGowin had made no promise at all and had never made any payments?

Courts have frequently enforced promises on the simple ground that the promisor was only promising to do what he ought to have done anyway. These cases have either been condemned as wanton departures from legal principle, or reluctantly accepted as involving the kind of compromise logic must inevitably make at times with sentiment. I believe that these decisions are capable of rational defense. When we say the defendant was morally obligated to do the thing he promised, we in effect assert the existence of a substantive ground for enforcing the promise. . . . The court's conviction that the promisor ought to do the thing, plus the promisor's own admission of his obligation, may tilt the scales in favor of enforcement where neither standing alone would be sufficient. If it be argued that moral consideration threatens certainty, the solution would seem to lie, not in rejecting the doctrine, but in taming it by continuing the process of judicial exclusion and inclusion already begun in the cases involving infants' contracts, barred debts, and discharged bankrupts.

Fuller, Consideration and Form, 41 Colum. L. Rev. 799, 821-822 (1941).

Problem 47

When his parents died, Oliver, age 9, was taken into the home of his aunt, Mrs. Corney, who cared for him until he reached the age of majority. Twenty years later, Mrs. Corney appealed to him for financial aid, and he signed a contract obligating himself to pay her $50 a week for the rest of her life "in return for her many acts of kindness to me." By a twist of fate, the next day he met the love of his life and ran off with her. Two years later Mrs. Corney died, and her executor brought suit against him for all of the missed weekly payments. Must he pay?

RESTATEMENT (SECOND) OF CONTRACTS

§86. PROMISE FOR BENEFIT RECEIVED

(1) A promise made in recognition of a benefit previously received by the promisor from the promisee is binding to the extent necessary to prevent injustice.

(2) A promise is not binding under Subsection (1)

(a) if the promisee conferred the benefit as a gift or for other reasons the promisor has not been unjustly enriched; or

(b) to the extent that its value is disproportionate to the benefit.

Problem 48

Decide *Hayes, Mills,* and *Webb* as if the preceding Restatement provision expressed the law of the jurisdiction.

V.   THE PREEXISTING DUTY RULE

A.   *The Basic Concept*

HARRIS v. WATSON
King's Bench, 1791
Peake 72, 170 Eng. Rep. 94

In this case the declaration stated, that the Plaintiff being a seaman on board the ship *Alexander*, of which the Defendant was master and commander, and which was bound on a voyage to Lisbon: whilst the ship was on her voyage, the Defendant, in consideration that the plaintiff would perform some extra work, in navigating the ship, promised to pay him five guineas over and above his common wages. There were other counts for work and labour, etc.

Defendant told Plaintiff he would pay him more to do extra work

The Plaintiff proved that the ship being in danger, the Defendant, to induce the seamen to exert themselves, made the promise stated in the first count.

Lord KENYON. If this action was to be supported, it would materially affect the navigation of this kingdom. It has been long since determined, that when the freight is lost, the wages are also lost. This rule was founded on a principle of policy, for if sailors were in all events to have their wages, and in time of danger entitled to insist on an extra charge on such a promise as this, they would in many cases suffer a ship to sink, unless the captain would pay any extravagant demand they might think proper to make.

Principle of Policy

The plaintiff was nonsuited.

STILK v. MYRICK
Court of Common Pleas, 1809
6 Esp. 129, 170 Eng. Rep. 1168

This was an action for seaman's wages, on a voyage from London to the Baltic and back.

By the ship's articles, executed before the commencement of the voyage, the plaintiff was to be paid at the rate of 5 pounds a month; and the principal question in the cause was, whether he was entitled to a higher rate of wages. In the course of the voyage two of the seamen deserted, and the captain, having in vain attempted to supply their places at Cronstadt, there entered into an agreement with the rest of the crew, that they should have the wages of the two who had deserted equally divided among them if he could not procure two other hands at Gottenburgh. This was found impossible, and the ship was worked back to London by the plaintiff and eight more of the original crew, with whom the agreement had been made at Cronstadt.

Principle Question

Two men deserted ship so the crew had to take on more work

Lord ELLENBOROUGH. I think Harris v. Watson (Peake, 72) was rightly decided; but I doubt whether the ground of public policy, upon which Lord Kenyon is stated to have proceeded, be the true principle on which the decision is to be supported. Here, I say, the agreement is void for want of consideration. There was no consideration for the ulterior pay promised to the mariners who remained with the ship. Before they sailed from London they had undertaken to do all they could under all the emergencies of the

Void for want of consideration

voyage. They had sold all their services till the voyage should be completed. If they had been at liberty to quit the vessel at Cronstadt, the case would have been quite different; or if the captain had capriciously discharged the two men who were wanting, the others might not have been compelled to take the whole duty upon themselves, and their agreeing to do so might have been a sufficient consideration for the promise of an advance of wages. But the desertion of a part of the crew is to be considered an emergency of the voyage as much as their death, and those who remain are bound by the terms of their original contract to exert themselves to the utmost to bring the ship in safety to her destined port. Therefore, without looking to the policy of this agreement, I think it is void for want of consideration, and that the plaintiff can only recover at the rate of 5 pounds a month.

Verdict accordingly.

LINGENFELDER v. WAINWRIGHT BREWERY CO.
Supreme Court of Missouri, 1891
103 Mo. 578, 15 S.W. 844

[Plaintiff was the executor of the estate of Edmund Jungenfeld, who was employed by the defendant brewery as an architect. During the performance of a contract to design new brewery buildings, Jungenfeld discovered that defendant had awarded a separate contract for a refrigeration plant to one of his competitors. Angry, Jungenfeld threatened to quit, but agreed to continue when defendant promised him an extra payment of 5 percent of the refrigeration plant's cost. When Jungenfeld finished the brewery building, defendant refused to pay anything more than the original contract amount. The trial court, refusing to adopt the portion of a report on this point prepared by a referee to whom the case was assigned, held for the plaintiff on the issue presented here.]

GANTT, P.J. (after stating the facts). . . . Was there any consideration for the promise of Wainwright to pay Jungenfeld the 5 percent on the refrigerator plant? If there was not, plaintiffs cannot recover the $3,449.75, the amount of that commission. The report of the referee and the evidence upon which it is based alike show that Jungenfeld's claim to this extra compensation is based upon Wainwright's promise to pay him this sum to induce him, Jungenfeld, to complete his original contract under its original terms. It is urged upon us by respondents that this was a new contract. New in what? Jungenfeld was bound by his contract to design and supervise this building. Under the new promise he was not to do any more or anything different. What benefit was to accrue to Wainwright? He was to receive the same service from Jungenfeld under the new, that Jungenfeld was bound to render under the original, contract. What loss, trouble, or inconvenience could result to

Jungenfeld that he had not already assumed? No amount of metaphysical reasoning can change the plain fact that Jungenfeld took advantage of Wainwright's necessities, and extorted the promise of 5 percent of the refrigeration plant as the condition of his complying with his contract already entered into. Nor was there even the flimsy pretext that Wainwright had violated any of the conditions of the contract on his part. Jungenfeld himself put it upon the simple proposition that "if he, as an architect, put up the brewery, and another company put up the refrigerating machinery, it would be a detriment to the Empire Refrigerating Company," of which Jungenfeld was president. To permit plaintiff to recover under such circumstances would be to offer a premium upon bad faith, and invite men to violate their most sacred contracts that they may profit by their own wrong. "That a promise to pay a man for doing that which he is already under contract to do is without consideration" is conceded by respondents. The rule has been so long imbedded in the common law and decisions of the highest courts of the various states that nothing but the most cogent reasons ought to shake it. . . . But "it is carrying coals to New Castle" to add authorities on a proposition so universally accepted, and so inherently just and right in itself.

The learned counsel for respondents do not controvert the general proposition. Their contention is, and the circuit court agreed with them, that when Jungenfeld declined to go further on his contract, that defendant then had the right to sue for damages, and, not having elected to sue Jungenfeld, but having acceded to his demand for the additional compensation, defendant cannot now be heard to say his promise is without consideration. While it is true Jungenfeld became liable in damages for the obvious breach of his contract we do not think it follows that defendant is estopped from showing its promise was made without consideration. It is true that as eminent a jurist as Judge Cooley, in Goebel v. Linn, 47 Mich. 489, 11 N.W. Rep. 284, held that an ice company which had agreed to furnish a brewery with all the ice they might need for their business from November 8, 1879, until January 1, 1881, at $1.75 per ton, and afterwards, in May, 1880, declined to deliver any more ice unless the brewery would give it $3 per ton, could recover on a promissory note given for the increased price. Profound as is our respect for the distinguished judge who delivered that opinion, we are still of the opinion that his decision is not in accord with the almost universally accepted doctrine, and is not convincing, and certainly so much of the opinion as held that the payment by a debtor of a part of his debt then due would constitute a defense to a suit for the remainder is not the law of this state, nor, do we think, of any other where the common law prevails. The case of Bishop v. Busse, 69 Ill. 403, is readily distinguishable from the case at bar. The price of brick increased very considerably, and the owner changed the plan of the building, so as to require nearly double the number. Owing to the increased price and change in the plans the contractor notified the party for whom he was building that he could not complete the house at the original prices, and thereupon a new arrangement was made and it is expressly upheld by the court on the ground that the change in the buildings was such a modification as necessitated a new contract. Nothing we have said is intended as denying parties the right to modify their contracts, or make new contracts, upon new or different considerations, and binding themselves thereby. What we hold is that, when a party merely does what he has already obligated himself to do, he cannot demand an additional compensation therefor, and although by taking advantage of the necessities of his adversary he obtains a promise for more, the law will regard it as *nudum pactum*, and will not lend its process to aid in the wrong. So holding, we reverse the judgment of the circuit court of St. Louis to the extent that it allows the plaintiffs below (respondents here) the sum $3,449.75, the amount of commission at 5 per cent on the refrigerator plant. . . .

[handwritten margin note: Holding]

[handwritten margin note: Reversed The trial Courts Decision]

Problem 49

When Tony was murdered, Maria offered a $5,000 reward for the arrest of his killer. Officer Krupke of the New York police force tracked down the killer while Krupke was taking a day off from work. Maria refused to pay Krupke the reward. Is the preexisting duty rule involved in this? What policy considerations affect the result? See N.Y. Penal Law §§200.30 and 200.35, making it a crime to offer or accept a gratuity for the performance of a public servant's official duties. There is a similar federal statute: 18 U.S.C.A. §201(f) and (g).

[handwritten: Yes. It was already his job - had preexisting Duty]

[handwritten: - Bad Policy => only catching criminals on weekends]

Problem 50

The Gilberts School of Law hired Professor Chalk to teach Contracts for an agreed salary of $80,000 for the first year. The day after Chalk agreed to this new employment, he received an offer to join the faculty of the Nutshell Law School at a yearly salary of $85,000. He phoned the dean of the Gilberts School of Law and said, "Will you advise me as a friendly matter what to do?" The dean, worried, replied, "I don't want to lose you. Let's agree to forget the first contract, and I'll see that you are paid $85,000 for next year." Chalk did join the Gilberts faculty, but the school paid him only $80,000. Is he entitled to the extra $5,000? See Schwartzreich v. Bauman-Basch, Inc., 231 N.Y. 196, 131 N.E. 887 (1921); Corbin §186. Is it possible to characterize the extra amount as a *gift*? See Watkins & Sons, Inc. v. Carrig, 91 N.H. 459, 21 A.2d 591 (1941).

[handwritten: Yes - New contract, First Contract was rescinded and a New Contract was formed.]

UNIFORM COMMERCIAL CODE

§2-209. MODIFICATION, RESCISSION AND WAIVER.

(1) An agreement modifying a contract within this Article needs no consideration to be binding. . . .

[handwritten margin note: No Consideration Needed under the UCC]

OFFICIAL COMMENT

1. This section seeks to protect and make effective all necessary and desirable modifications of sales contracts without regard to the technicalities which at present hamper such adjustments.

2. Subsection (1) provides that an agreement modifying a sales contract needs no consideration to be binding.

However, modifications made thereunder must meet the test of good faith imposed by this Act. The effective use of bad faith to escape performance on the original contract terms is barred, and the extortion of a "modification" without legitimate commercial reason is ineffective as a violation of the duty of good faith.

[handwritten margin note: Needs to be in "good faith"]

Problem 51

Abby Brewster had wanted to have a cellar under her house for a long time. She hired the Teddy Construction Company to do the excavation for $1,500. Shortly after the work began, it was discovered that the house was built over swampland, and the cellar could be dug only with almost super-human effort and great expense. Teddy wanted to quit, but Abby insisted on the cellar, promising to pay any additional cost. Teddy finally did complete the cellar, but Abby refused to pay anything more than $1,500. Must she? If it is clear from the usage of trade that in this situation the contractor bears the risk of soil problems, how is this result squared with the preexisting duty rule? See Corbin §§183 and 184. If this were a sale of goods instead of a construction agreement, is the answer easier? See above for UCC §2-209(1) and its Official Comment 2. *[handwritten: Yes, unforeseen supervening circumstance]*

Problem 52

The U.S. Army contracted with Treads, Inc., to supply a special type of tread for a new tank the Army was developing. When the tanks were in production and it was too late for the Army to procure the treading else-where, Treads suddenly announced that it was doubling the price — take it or leave it. The Army complained but finally gave in "under protest." After Treads had completely performed, must the Army pay the doubled amount? Compare Austin Instrument, Inc. v. Loral Corp., 29 N.Y.2d 124, 324 N.Y.S.2d 22, 272 N.E.2d 533 (1971), and United States v. Bethlehem Steel Corp., 315 U.S. 289 (1942), with Ruble Forest Products, Inc. v. Lancer Mobile Homes, Inc., 269 Or. 315, 524 P.2d 1204 (1974). The seminal article on point is Dawson, Economic Duress: An Essay in Perspective, 45 Mich. L. Rev. 253 (1947).

Problem 53

The owner of the sailboat *Indefatigable* hired Horatio Hornblower to sail her in the America's Cup Race and agreed to pay Hornblower $50,000 if he won. The *Indefatigable* had been built by the Forester Marine Works, which stood to gain a great deal of business if the boat won the race, so the president of Forester contracted to pay Hornblower an extra $10,000 if he won. The *Indefatigable* did prove to be the victor, and Hornblower collected his $50,000 from her owner. Must Forester Marine Works pay up, or is the preexisting duty rule a bar? Compare McDivitt v. Stokes, 174 Ky. 515, 192 S.W. 681 (1917), with Corbin §§176-179.

B.   Past Due Monetary Debts

Problem 54

Thomas Pettifog, an attorney, did a lot of debt collection work for clients. On behalf of a client, Pettifog phoned a debtor, I. M. Pecunious, and asked her what she was going to do about the past due amount of $1,000 that she owed Pettifog's client. She replied that she was short of funds. When Pettifog threatened suit, she asked him if he would accept an immediate payment of $750 and forget the rest. He agreed to do so. When her check for that amount arrived, he cashed it and then, secure in his knowledge of the preexisting duty rule, he filed suit against her for the extra $250. Will the suit succeed?

In Pinnel's Case, 5 Coke's Rep. 117a, 77 Eng. Rep. 237 (Com. Pl. 1602), Lord Coke said in dictum that "payment of a less sum on the day [due] in satisfaction of a greater, cannot be satisfaction of the whole," but he added that "the gift of a horse, hawk, or robe, etc., in satisfaction is good." In 1884 in the famous case of Foakes v. Beer, L.R. 9 A.C. 605, the House of Lords (Great Britain's highest court) cited to Pinnel's Case when holding that there was no consideration for a modification agreement in which a creditor agrees to accept as satisfaction a lesser amount than that admittedly due. Does the "Rule of Foakes v. Beer" follow logically from the preexisting duty rule? Is it good policy?

In Pinnel's Case, Lord Coke himself had provided the way out of the partial payment puzzle — simply substitute a nonfungible item (for example, a hawk) for the amount due and, since the law will not inquire into the adequacy of the consideration, a valid modification agreement arises. In a modern context an additional promise to do something new in substitution for the original undertaking, such as paying a debt earlier than due, would be sufficient consideration. It is a favorite legal maxim that "the law favors a compromise." Further, note again that the decision in *Foakes* only serves to keep a new agreement unenforceable if the obligation is admittedly due. That is, if there is either a good faith dispute about whether there is any debt owed or the amount of debt owed, an agreement to pay less than requested by the creditor is supported by consideration.

An *accord* is the agreement to accept a substituted or different performance, and a *satisfaction* is the execution of the new agreement.

Problem 55

In the last Problem, would your answer change if I. M. Pecunious (a) truly believed that she only owed $750 or (b) she did not believe she owed any money to Pettifog's client because Pettifog's client was rude to I. M. Pecunious when she purchased goods on credit from him?

Problem 56

Attorney Pettifog phoned the debtor, I. M. Pecunious, and demanded that she pay his client the $1,000 she owed. She replied that she had decided to file for bankruptcy and Pettifog's client should submit his claim to the bankruptcy court. Knowing that the chance of getting any payment out of a bankruptcy court is slim, Pettifog said, "Look, why don't you forget about filing a bankruptcy petition and send me $750 as a full satisfaction of the debt?" She agreed to do so. Is this a valid accord and satisfaction or may Pettifog still collect the extra $250? See Citibank v. Perez, 191 Ohio App. 3d 575, 947 N.E.2d 191 (2010). If Pecunious violates this agreement and files her bankruptcy petition anyway, may Pettifog's client file a claim for $1,000 or only $750?

CLARK v. ELZA

Court of Appeals of Maryland, 1979
286 Md. 208, 406 A.2d 922

ELDRIDGE, J. This case presents the question of whether an executory oral agreement to settle a pending law suit may be raised as a defense to prevent a plaintiff from pursuing his original cause of action. It also presents the threshold issue of whether a trial court's refusal to enforce such a settlement agreement, where enforcement was sought in the underlying legal action, may be immediately appealed. We answer these questions in the affirmative.

As a result of injuries sustained in an automobile accident, the plaintiffs, Floyd L. Elza and his wife Myrtle E. Elza, filed suit in the Circuit Court for Baltimore County. They alleged that the defendants, Swannie B. Clark and Linda Sue Woodward, were legally responsible for their injuries. After the case was scheduled for trial, settlement negotiations ensued between the parties. A figure of $9,500.00 was verbally agreed upon; the trial judge was notified; and the case was removed from the trial calendar. The defendants forwarded a release and an order of satisfaction to the plaintiff's attorney, and later sent a settlement draft to the plaintiffs' attorney. Thereafter, these papers were returned unexecuted with the statement that the $9,500.00 settlement was no longer adequate. The reason given for this change of mind was that on the day after the oral agreement, Mr. Elza had visited a new physician who informed him that his injuries were more extensive than he originally believed.

The plaintiffs then advised the court that they were no longer willing to go through with the settlement. In response, the defendants filed in the tort action a "Motion to Enforce Settlement." At a hearing on the motion the plaintiffs argued that the settlement agreement was not binding on them because it was merely an executory accord, and could only be enforced upon satisfaction. The court observed that if the agreement were a substituted contract, as opposed to an executory accord, then it would be binding. Finding that the intention of the parties was to create an executory accord, the trial judge denied the motion of the defendants to enforce the settlement. The effect of this ruling was that trial upon the original tort action could proceed, notwithstanding the supposed settlement.

The defendants then took an appeal to the Court of Special Appeals, and the plaintiffs moved to dismiss the appeal. The Court of Special Appeals, in an unreported opinion, dismissed the appeal as premature because the trial court had not yet rendered a final judgment in the tort case. The court reasoned:

> Here, the order . . . denying appellants' motion to enforce settlement did not deny appellees the means of further prosecuting their claims nor did it deny appellants the right to defend against those claims. In short, it did not settle

and conclude the rights of the parties involved in the action and, thus, constituted an interlocutory order which is not appealable at this time.

The defendants petitioned this Court for a writ of certiorari, challenging the ruling that the case was not appealable and arguing that the purported settlement was effective. We granted the petition with respect to both issues.

[The court first concluded that the case was appealable.]

As previously mentioned, the trial court refused to enforce the settlement agreement on the ground that it was an "executory accord" and not a "substitute contract." An executory accord is defined in 6 Corbin on Contracts §1268, p.71 (1962) as follows:

> The term "accord executory" is and always has been used to mean an agreement for the future discharge of an existing claim by a substituted performance. In order for an agreement to fall within this definition, it is the promised performance that is to discharge the existing claim, and not the promise to render such performance. Conversely, all agreements for a future discharge by a substituted performance are accords executory. It makes no difference whether or not the existing claim is liquidated or unliquidated, undisputed or disputed, except as these facts bear upon the sufficiency of the consideration for some promise in the new agreement. It makes no difference whether or not a suit has already been brought to enforce the original claim; or whether that claim arised out of an alleged tort or contract or quasi-contract.

See also J. Calamari and J. Perillo, The Law of Contracts §21-4 (2d ed. 1977); II Restatement of Contracts §417 (1932). See generally Gold, Executory Accords, 21 Boston U. L. Rev. 465 (1941); Comment, Executory Accord, Accord and Satisfaction, and Novation—The Distinctions, 26 Baylor L. Rev. 185 (1974). On the other hand, where the parties intend the new agreement itself to constitute a substitute for the prior claim, then this substituted contract immediately discharges the original claim. Under this latter type of arrangement, since the original claim is fully extinguished at the time the agreement is made, recovery may only be had upon the substituted contract. 6 Corbin, supra, pp. 74-75; Calamari and Perillo, supra, §21-5.

It is often extremely difficult to determine the factual question of whether the parties to a compromise agreement intended to create an executory accord or a substitute contract. However, unless the evidence demonstrates that the new agreement was designed to be a substitute for the original cause of action, it is presumed that the parties each intended to surrender their old rights and liabilities only upon performance of the new agreement. In other words, unless there is clear evidence to the contrary, an agreement to discharge a pre-existing claim will be regarded as an executory accord. [Citations omitted.]

In light of the above-discussed principles, we agree with the trial court that the settlement agreement in this case was an executory accord and not a substitute contract. This conclusion is supported by the fact that a "release" was to be executed upon performance of the settlement contract. If a substitute contract were intended, the underlying tort cause of action would have been released when the agreement was made, notwithstanding the fact that performance had not yet been rendered. Holding in abeyance the release of the tort claim until the settlement agreement was performed would be inconsistent with the principle that a substitute contract serves to replace the initial claim. See Warner v. Rossignol, 513 F.2d 678, 682 (1st Cir. 1975). Furthermore, to the extent that there is any doubt, under this Court's decision in Porter v. Berwyn Fuel & Feed, supra, 244 Md. at 639, 224 A.2d 662, such doubt is resolved in favor of finding an executory accord.

Issue 2

After concluding that the oral settlement agreement was an executory accord, the circuit court permitted the plaintiffs to proceed to trial on their original cause of action. In so ruling, we believe that the circuit court erred as to the effect of an unexecuted accord.

It is true that several cases set forth the principle, adopted by the court below, that an executory accord is unenforceable and is no defense against a suit on the prior claim. See the discussion in 6 Corbin on Contracts §§1271-1275 (1962). See also Addison v. Sommers, 404 F. Supp. 715 (D. Md. 1975). Nevertheless the modern view, and in our judgment the better view, is summarized by 6 Corbin, supra, §1274, p. 104, as follows:

> An accord executory does not in itself operate as a discharge of the previous claim, for the reason that it is not so intended or agreed. In nearly every case, however, the parties intend that the duty created by the previous transaction shall be suspended during the period fixed for performance of the accord. As long as the debtor has committed no breach of the accord, therefore, the creditor should be allowed to maintain no action for the enforcement of the prior claim. His right of action should be held to be suspended as the parties intended.

This is also the position adopted by the Restatement of Contracts, Vol. II, §417 (1932):

§417. An Accord; Its Effect When Performed and When Broken

Except as stated in §§142, 143 with reference to contracts for the benefit of third persons and as stated in §418, the following rules are applicable to a contract to accept in the future a stated performance in satisfaction of an existing contractual duty, or a duty to make compensation:

(a) Such a contract does not discharge the duty, but suspends the right to enforce it as long as there has been neither a breach of the contract nor a justification for the creditor in changing his position because of its prospective non-performance.

(b) If such a contract is performed, the previously existing duty is discharged.

(c) If the debtor breaks such a contract the creditor has alternative rights. He can enforce either the original duty or the subsequent contract.

(d) If the creditor breaks such a contract, the debtor's original duty is not discharged. The debtor acquires a right of action for damages for the breach, and if specific enforcement of that contract is practicable, he acquires an alternative right to the specific enforcement thereof. If the contract is enforced specifically, his original duty is discharged.

Comment . . .

b. The rules governing the validity and effect of accord and satisfaction are applicable as well where the pre-existing duty arises from a tort as where it is based on contract.

Thus, an executory accord does not discharge the underlying claim until it is performed. Until there is a breach of the accord or a justifiable change of position based upon prospective nonperformance, the original cause of action is suspended. As long as the "debtor" (i.e., the defendant in a tort case) neither breaches the accord nor provides a reasonable basis for concluding that he will not perform, the "creditor" (i.e., the plaintiff) has no right to enforce the underlying cause of action. . . .

Although the precise question here presented does not appear to have been discussed by this Court in any prior opinion, nevertheless our decisions seem to reflect the position of the above-cited cases, the Restatement, and Corbin. See, e.g., Chicora Fer. Co. v. Dunan, 91 Md. 144, 46 A. 347 (1900). Moreover, it is logical to hold that executory accords are enforceable. An executory accord is simply a type of bilateral contract. As long as the basic requirements to form a contract are present, there is no reason to treat such a settlement agreement differently than other contracts which are binding. This is consistent with the public policy dictating that courts should "look with favor upon the compromise or settlement of law suits in the interest of efficient and economical administration of justice and the lessening of friction and acrimony." Chertkof v. Harry C. Weiskittel Co., 251 Md. 544, 550, 248 A.2d 373, 377 (1968), cert. denied, 394 U.S. 974, 89 S. Ct. 1467, 22 L. Ed. 2d 754 (1969).

In sum, the circuit court should not have permitted the plaintiffs to proceed with the underlying tort action in violation of their settlement agreement.

Judgment of the court of special appeals reversed and case remanded to that court with directions to reverse the judgment of the circuit court for Baltimore County and remand the case for further proceedings not inconsistent with this opinion. Respondents to pay costs.

Problem 57

When attorney Pettifog finally contacted I. M. Pecunious, a debtor, he asked her when she was going to pay the $1,000 she owed his client; she replied that she did not owe that amount. She insisted that all she owed was $750. She mailed Pettifog a check for $750 and marked both on the check and on the accompanying letter that the check was tendered as "payment in full" of the debt owed to Pettifog's client. What results in the following circumstances?

(a) Pettifog's client cashes the check. Compare Hudson v. Yonkers Fruit Co., 258 N.Y. 168, 179 N.E. 373 (1932), with Kellogg v. Iowa State Traveling Men's Ass'n, 239 Iowa 196, 29 N.W.2d 559 (1947).

(b) Pettifog's client holds onto the check, not cashing it or replying in any way. See Hoffman v. Ralston Purina Co., 86 Wis. 2d 445, 273 N.W.2d 214 (1979).

(c) Pecunious is lying. She owes $1,000 and knows it all too well. Pettifog's client cashes the check and sues her for the other $250. See Hayden v. Coddington, 169 Pa. Super. 174, 82 A.2d 285 (1951).

The 1990 revision of Article 3 of the UCC addressed this problem of the "payment-in-full" check for the first time (the courts had reached varying results). One of your authors has written a blog post discussing such checks at length; see http://douglaswhaley.blogspot.com/2011/04/payment-in-full-check-powerful-legal.html.

UNIFORM COMMERCIAL CODE

§3-311. Accord and Satisfaction by Use of Instrument

(a) If a person against whom a claim is asserted proves that (i) that person in good faith tendered an instrument to the claimant as full satisfaction of the claim, (ii) the amount of the claim was unliquidated or subject to a bona fide dispute, and (iii) the claimant obtained payment of the instrument, the following subsections apply.

(b) Unless subsection (c) applies, the claim is discharged if the person against whom the claim is asserted proves that the instrument or an accompanying written communication contained a conspicuous statement to the effect that the instrument was tendered as full satisfaction of the claim.

(c) Subject to subsection (d), a claim is not discharged under subsection (b) if either of the following applies:

(1) The claimant, if an organization, proves that (i) within a reasonable time before the tender, the claimant sent a conspicuous statement to the person against whom the claim is asserted that communications concerning disputed debts, including an instrument tendered as full

satisfaction of a debt, are to be sent to a designated person, office, or place, and (ii) the instrument or accompanying communication was not received by that designated person, office, or place.

(2) The claimant, whether or not an organization, proves that within 90 days after payment of the instrument, the claimant tendered repayment of the amount of the instrument to the person against whom the claim is asserted. This paragraph does not apply if the claimant is an organization that sent a statement complying with paragraph (1)(i).

(d) A claim is discharged if the person against whom the claim is asserted proves that within a reasonable time before collection of the instrument was initiated, the claimant, or an agent of the claimant having direct responsibility with respect to the disputed obligation, knew that the instrument was tendered in full satisfaction of the claim.

Problem 58

Robert Startup picked out a beautiful Persian rug for his living room when he visited the carpet department of Merchandise World, agreeing to pay $5,500 for it. He charged it on his Merchandise World credit card. When the rug was delivered, he was annoyed to discover that it was badly wrinkled, apparently because it had been rolled up and stored in the delivery truck under much heavier items. He immediately complained to Merchandise World, but got no satisfactory resolution of the problem, so he had the rug professionally cleaned, which cost him $150. When he received his credit card bill from Merchandise World, he sent back a check for $5,350, along with a cover letter explaining what had happened, stating in the letter that the check was tendered as "payment in full" for the rug. The check was routinely cashed by the credit card department.

(a) The next month Merchandise World sent him a bill for $150. Must he pay it? See UCC §3-311(b). What should Merchandise World have done when it received the check?

(b) Is it too late for Merchandise World to do anything to avoid the accord and satisfaction? See UCC §3-311(c)(2).

(c) You are the attorney for Merchandise World. Alice Mayberry, the head of the credit card department, wants a realistic chance to avoid the accidental settlement of these disputes. She asks: Is there any way for checks like these to be sent to her office for her personal consideration? See UCC §3-311(c)(1).

(d) Alice also asks if, when she gets such checks, she can just scratch off the "payment in full" language on the check, write "cashed under protest, all rights reserved," and avoid settling the dispute. See UCC §1-308; Wolfe v. Eagle Ridge Holding Co., LLC, 869 N.E.2d 521 (Ind. App. 2007).

VI.   PROMISSORY ESTOPPEL

The consideration doctrine can generate harsh results. Suppose Party A promises to do something for Party B. Unless Party B makes a return promise, there is no enforceable contract. Party A can simply decide to change his or her mind. But until Party A does so, Party B might change position in reliance on the promise being fulfilled.

In the early twentieth century, some courts and commentators began experimenting with a remedy for this unjust-seeming situation. They drew on an idea that appears throughout the law: *estoppel.* Think of estoppel as the legal equivalent of a gag stuck in someone's mouth. Thus the doctrine of judicial estoppel bars a litigant from making one argument and then later making a completely inconsistent argument. For instance, judicial estoppel prevents a party from arguing that a traffic light was red at the beginning of a case and then turning around and arguing that the traffic light was green. In addition, equitable estoppel prevents a person or entity from lulling another into a false belief by first making a representation of fact and then denying it is true. For instance, if a party reassures another that he or she has no intention to sue about a particular issue, he or she may be equitably estopped from later filing litigation about that issue.

Most importantly for our purposes, §90 of the first and second Restatements of Contract established a principle called "promissory estoppel." In theory, the concept is simple: If someone makes a promise on which there is foreseeable reliance, that person is forbidden ("estopped") from bringing up many traditional defenses to the enforcement of the promise (no consideration, no acceptance, no written agreement). This section focuses on the historical development and modern application of promissory estoppel.

A.   *Historical Development*

ALLEGHENY COLLEGE v. NATIONAL CHAUTAUQUA COUNTY BANK
New York Court of Appeals, 1927
246 N.Y. 369, 159 N.E. 173

CARDOZO, C.J. The plaintiff, Allegheny College, is an institution of liberal learning at Meadville, Pa. In June, 1921, a "drive" was in progress to secure for it an additional endowment of $1,250,000. An appeal to contribute to this fund was made to Mary Yates Johnston, of Jamestown, New York. In response thereto, she signed and delivered on June 15, 1921, the following writing:

Estate Pledge, Allegheny College Second
Century Endowment.
Jamestown, N.Y., June 15, 1921

In consideration of my interest in Christian education, and in consideration of others subscribing, I hereby subscribe and will pay to the
order of the treasurer of Allegheny College, Meadville, Pennsylvania,
the sum of five thousand dollars; $5,000.

 This obligation shall become due thirty days after my death, and I
hereby instruct my executor, or administrator, to pay the same out of
my estate. This pledge shall bear interest at the rate of _____ percent
per annum, payable annually, from _____ till paid. The proceeds of
this obligation shall be added to the Endowment of said Institution, or
expended in accordance with instructions on reverse side of this
pledge.

Name: *Mary Yates Johnston,*
Address: 306 East 6th Street, Jamestown, N.Y.
Dayton E. McClain, Witness,
T. R. Courtis, Witness,
To authentic signature

 On the reverse side of the writing is the following indorsement:

In loving memory this gift shall be known as the Mary Yates Johnston
memorial fund, the proceeds from which shall be used to educate
students preparing for the ministry, either in the United States or in
the Foreign Field.

 This pledge shall be valid only on the condition that the provisions
of my will, now extant, shall be first met.

Mary Yates Johnston

 The subscription was not payable by its terms until 30 days after the
death of the promisor. The sum of $1,000 was paid, however, upon account
in December, 1923, while the promisor was alive. The college set the money
aside to be held as a scholarship fund for the benefit of students preparing
for the ministry. Later, in July, 1924, the promisor gave notice to the college
that she repudiated the promise. Upon the expiration of 30 days following
her death, this action was brought against the executor of her will to recover
the unpaid balance.

 The law of charitable subscriptions has been a prolific source of controversy in this state and elsewhere. We have held that a promise of that order
is unenforceable like any other if made without consideration. . . . On the
other hand, though professing to apply to such subscriptions the general law

of contract, we have found consideration present where the general law of contract, at least as then declared, would have said that it was absent. . . .

A classic form of statement identifies consideration with detriment to the promisee sustained by virtue of the promise. [Citations omitted.] So compendious a formula is little more than a half truth. There is need of many a supplementary gloss before the outline can be so filled in as to depict the classic doctrine. "The promise and the consideration must purport to be the motive each for the other, in whole or at least in part. It is not enough that the promise induces the detriment or that the detriment induces the promise if the other half is wanting." . . .

The half truths of one generation tend at times to perpetuate themselves in the law as the whole truth of another, when constant repetition brings it about that qualifications, taken once for granted, are disregarded or forgotten. The doctrine of consideration has not escaped the common lot. As far back as 1881, Judge Holmes in his lectures on the Common Law (page 292), separated the detriment, which is merely a consequence of the promise from the detriment, which is in truth the motive or inducement, and yet added that the courts "have gone far in obliterating this distinction." The tendency toward effacement has not lessened with the years. On the contrary, there has grown up of recent days a doctrine that a substitute for consideration or an exception to its ordinary requirements can be found in what is styled "a promissory estoppel." Williston, Contracts, §§139, 116. Whether the exception has made its way in this state to such an extent as to permit us to say that the general law of consideration has been modified accordingly, we do not now attempt to say. Cases such as Siegel v. Spear & Co., 234 N.Y. 479, 138 N.E. 414, 26 A.L.R. 1205, and De Cicco v. Schweizer, 221 N.Y. 431, 117 N.E. 807, L.R.A. 1918E, 1004, Ann. Cas. 1918C, 816, may be signposts on the road. Certain, at least, it is that we have adopted the doctrine of promissory estoppel as the equivalent of consideration in connection with our law of charitable subscriptions. So long as those decisions stand, the question is not merely whether the enforcement of a charitable subscription can be squared with the doctrine of consideration in all its ancient rigor. The question may also be whether it can be squared with the doctrine of consideration as qualified by the doctrine of promissory estoppel.

We have said that the cases in this state have recognized this exception, if exception it is thought to be. Thus, in Barnes v. Perine, 12 N.Y. 18, the subscription was made without request, express or implied, that the church do anything on the faith of it. Later, the church did incur expense to the knowledge of the promisor, and in the reasonable belief that the promise would be kept. We held the promise binding, though consideration there was none except upon the theory of a promissory estoppel. In Presbyterian Society v. Beach, 74 N.Y. 72, a situation substantially the same became the basis for a like ruling. So in Roberts v. Cobb, 103 N.Y. 600, 9 N.E. 500, and Keuka College v. Ray, 167 N.Y. 96, 60 N.E. 325, the moulds of consideration

as fixed by the old doctrine were subjected to a like expansion. Very likely, *Public Policy*
conceptions of public policy have shaped, more or less subconsciously, the
rulings thus made. Judges have been affected by the thought that "defenses
of that character" are "breaches of faith towards the public, and especially
towards those engaged in the same enterprise, and an unwarrantable disappointment of the reasonable expectations of those interested." . . . The
result speaks for itself irrespective of the motive. Decisions which have stood
so long, and which are supported by so many considerations of public policy
and reason, will not be overruled to save the symmetry of a concept which
itself came into our law, not so much from any reasoned conviction of its
justice, as from historical accidents of practice and procedure. 8 Holdsworth,
History of English Law, 7 et seq. The concept survives as one of the distinctive
features of our legal system. We have no thought to suggest that it is obsolete
or on the way to be abandoned. As in the case of other concepts, however,
the pressure of exceptions has led to irregularities of form.

It is in this background of precedent that we are to view the problem
now before us. The background helps to an understanding of the implications inherent in subscription and acceptance. This is so though we may find
in the end that without recourse to the innovation of promissory estoppel
the transaction can be fitted within the mould of consideration as established by tradition.

The promisor wished to have a memorial to perpetuate her name. She
imposed a condition that the "gift" should "be known as the Mary Yates
Johnston Memorial Fund." The moment that the college accepted $1,000 as
a payment on account, there was an assumption of a duty to do whatever acts
were customary or reasonably necessary to maintain the memorial fairly and
justly in the spirit of its creation. The college could not accept the money and
hold itself free thereafter from personal responsibility to give effect to the
condition. . . . The purpose of the founder would be unfairly thwarted or at
least inadequately served if the college failed to communicate to the world,
or in any event to applicants for the scholarship, the title of the memorial. By
implication it undertook, when it accepted a portion of the "gift," that in its
circulars of information and in other customary ways when making
announcement of this scholarship, it would couple with the announcement
the name of the donor. The donor was not at liberty to gain the benefit of
such an undertaking upon the payment of a part and disappoint the expectation that there would be payment of the residue. If the college had stated
after receiving $1,000 upon account of the subscription, that it would apply
the money to the prescribed use, but that in its circulars of information and
when responding to prospective applicants it would deal with the fund as an
anonymous donation, there is little doubt that the subscriber would have
been at liberty to treat this statement as the repudiation of a duty impliedly
assumed, a repudiation justifying a refusal to make payments in the future.
Obligation in such circumstances is correlative and mutual. A case much in
point is New Jersey Hospital v. Wright, 95 N.J. Law, 462, 464, 113 A. 144,

where a subscription for the maintenance of a bed in a hospital was held to be enforceable by virtue of an implied promise by the hospital that the bed should be maintained in the name of the subscriber. Cf. Board of Foreign Missions v. Smith, 209 Pa. 361, 58 A. 689. A parallel situation might arise upon the endowment of a chair or a fellowship in a university by the aid of annual payments with the condition that it should commemorate the name of the founder or that of a member of his family. The university would fail to live up to the fair meaning of its promise if it were to publish in its circulars of information and elsewhere the existence of a chair or a fellowship in the prescribed subject, and omit the benefactor's name. A duty to act in ways beneficial to the promisor and beyond the application of the fund to the mere uses of the trust would be cast upon the promisee by the acceptance of the money. We do not need to measure the extent either of benefit to the promisor or of detriment to the promisee implicit in this duty. "If a person chooses to make an extravagant promise for an inadequate consideration, it is his own affair." 8 Holdsworth, History of English Law, p. 17. It was long ago said that "when a thing is to be done by the plaintiff, be it never so small, this is a sufficient consideration to ground an action." Sturlyn v. Albany, 1587, Cro. Eliz. 67, quoted by Holdsworth, supra; cf. Walton Water Co. v. Village of Walton, 238 N.Y. 46, 51, 143 N.E. 786. The longing for posthumous remembrance is an emotion not so weak as to justify us in saying that its gratification is a negligible good.

We think the duty assumed by the plaintiff to perpetuate the name of the founder of the memorial is sufficient in itself to give validity to the subscription within the rules that define consideration for a promise of that order. When the promisee subjected itself to such a duty at the implied request of the promisor, the result was the creation of a bilateral agreement. Williston, Contracts, §§60a, 68, 90, 370; Brown v. Knapp, supra; Grossman v. Schenker, supra; Williams College v. Danforth, 12 Pick. (Mass.) 541, 544; Ladies Collegiate Institute v. French, 16 Gray (Mass.) 196, 200. There was a promise on the one side and on the other a return promise, made, it is true, by implication, but expressing an obligation that had been exacted as a condition of the payment. A bilateral agreement may exist though one of the mutual promises be a promise "implied in fact," an inference from conduct as opposed to an inference from words. Williston, Contracts, §§90, 22a; Pettibone v. Moore, 75 Hun. 461, 27 N.Y.S. 455. We think the fair inference to be drawn from the acceptance of a payment on account of the subscription is a promise by the college to do what may be necessary on its part to make the scholarship effective. The plan conceived by the subscriber will be mutilated and distorted unless the sum to be accepted is adequate to the end in view. Moreover, the time to affix her name to the memorial will not arrive until the entire fund has been collected. The college may thus thwart the purpose of the payment on account if at liberty to reject a tender of the residue. It is no answer to say that a duty would then arise to make restitution of the money. If such a duty may be imposed, the only reason for its existence must be that there is then a failure of "consideration." To say that there is a failure of consideration is to concede that a consideration has been promised, since otherwise it could not fail. No doubt there are times and situations in which limitations laid upon a promisee in connection with the use of what is paid by a subscriber lack the quality of a consideration, and are to be classed merely as conditions. Williston, Contracts, §112; Page, Contracts, §523. "It is often difficult to determine whether words of condition in a promise indicate a request for consideration or state a mere condition in a gratuitous promise. An aid, though not a conclusive test in determining which construction of the promise is more reasonable is an inquiry whether the happening of the condition will be a benefit to the promisor. If so, it is a fair inference that the happening was requested as a consideration." Williston, supra, §112. Such must be the meaning of this transaction unless we are prepared to hold that the college may keep the payment on account, and thereafter nullify the scholarship which is to preserve the memory of the subscriber. The fair implication to be gathered from the whole transaction is assent to the condition and the assumption of a duty to go forward with performance. . . .

The subscriber does not say: I hand you $1,000, and you may make up your mind later, after my death, whether you will undertake to commemorate my name. What she says in effect is this: I hand you $1,000, and if you are unwilling to commemorate me, the time to speak is now.

The conclusion thus reached makes it needless to consider whether, aside from the feature of a memorial, a promissory estoppel may result from the assumption of a duty to apply the fund, so far as already paid, to special purposes not mandatory under the provisions of the college charter (the support and education of students preparing for the ministry) — an assumption induced by the belief that other payments sufficient in amount to make the scholarship effective would be added to the fund thereafter upon the death of the subscriber. Ladies Collegiate Institute v. French, 16 Gray (Mass.) 196; Barnes v. Perine, 12 N.Y. 18, and cases there cited.

The judgment of the Appellate Division and that of the Trial Term should be reversed, and judgment ordered for the plaintiff as prayed for in the complaint, with costs in all courts.

Kellogg, J. (dissenting). The Chief Judge finds in the expression, "In loving memory this gift shall be known as the Mary Yates Johnston Memorial Fund," an offer on the part of Mary Yates Johnston to contract with Allegheny College. The expression makes no such appeal to me. Allegheny College was not requested to perform any act through which the sum offered might bear the title by which the offeror states that it shall be known. The sum offered was termed a "gift" by the offeror. Consequently, I can see no reason why we should strain ourselves to make it, not a gift, but a trade. Moreover, since the donor specified that the gift was made, "In consideration of my interest in Christian education, and in consideration of others subscribing," considerations not adequate in law, I can see no excuse for asserting that it was otherwise made in consideration of an act or promise on the part of the donee, constituting a sufficient quid pro quo to convert the gift into a contract obligation. To me the words used merely expressed an expectation or wish on the part of the donor and failed to exact the return of an adequate consideration. But if an offer indeed was present, then clearly it was an offer to enter into a unilateral contract. The offeror was to be bound provided the offeree performed such acts as might be necessary to make the gift offered become known under the proposed name. This is evidently the thought of the Chief Judge, for he says: "She imposed a condition that the 'gift' should be known as the Mary Yates Johnston Memorial Fund." In other words, she proposed to exchange her offer of a donation in return for acts to be performed. Even so, there was never any acceptance of the offer, and therefore no contract, for the acts requested have never been performed. The gift has never been made known as demanded. Indeed, the requested acts, under the very terms of the assumed offer, could never have been performed at a time to convert the offer into a promise. This is so for the reason that the donation was not to take effect until after the death of the donor, and by her death her offer was withdrawn. Williston on Contracts, §62. Clearly, although a promise of the college to make the gift known, as requested, may be implied, that promise was not the acceptance of an offer which gave rise to a contract. The donor stipulated for acts, not promises.

> In order to make a bargain it is necessary that the acceptor shall give in return for the offer or the promise exactly the consideration which the offeror requests. If an act is requested, that very act and no other must be given. If a promise is requested, that promise must be made absolutely and unqualifiedly. Williston on Contracts, §73.
>
> It does not follow that an offer becomes a promise because it is accepted; it may be, and frequently is, conditional, and then it does not become a promise until the conditions are satisfied; and in case of offers for a consideration, the performance of the consideration is always deemed a condition. Langdell, Summary of the Law of Contracts, §4.

It seems clear to me that there was here no offer, no acceptance of an offer, and no contract. Neither do I agree with the Chief Judge that this court "found consideration present where the general law of contract, at least as then declared, would have said that it was absent" in the cases of Barnes v. Perine, 12 N.Y. 18, Presbyterian Society v. Beach, 74 N.Y. 72, and Keuka College v. Ray, 167 N.Y. 96, 60 N.E. 325. In the *Keuka College* case an offer to contract, in consideration of the performance of certain acts by the offeree, was converted into a promise by the actual performance of those acts. This form of contract has been known to the law from time immemorial (Langdell, §46), and for at least a century longer than the other type, a bilateral contract (Williston, §13). It may be that the basis of the decisions in Barnes v. Perine and Presbyterian Society v. Beach, supra, was the same as in the *Keuka College* Case. See Presbyterian Church of Albany v. Cooper, 112 N.Y. 517, 20 N.E. 352, 3 L.R.A. 468, 8 Am. St. Rep. 767. However, even if the basis of the decisions be a so-called "promissory estoppel," nevertheless they initiated no new doctrine. A so-called "promissory estoppel," although not so termed, was held sufficient by Lord Mansfield and his fellow judges as far back as the year 1765. Pillans v. Van Mierop, 3 Burr. 1663. Such a doctrine may be an anomaly; it is not a novelty. Therefore I can see no ground for the suggestion that the ancient rule which makes consideration necessary to the formation of every contract is in danger of effacement through any decisions of this court. To me that is a cause for gratulation rather than regret. However, the discussion may be beside the mark, for I do not understand that the holding about to be made in this case is other than a holding that consideration was given to convert the offer into a promise. With that result I cannot agree and, accordingly, must dissent.

POUND, CRANE, LEHMAN, and O'BRIEN, JJ., concur with CARDOZO, C.J.

KELLOGG, J., dissents in opinion, in which ANDREWS, J., concurs. Judgment accordingly.

QUESTIONS

1. Was Justice Cardozo's discussion of estoppel necessary to his decision?

2. If the case had been decided solely on promissory estoppel grounds, how would it have come out?

3. For a line-by-line analysis of this case, see Konefsky, How to Read, Or at Least Not Misread, Cardozo in the *Allegheny College* Case, 36 Buff. L. Rev. 645 (1987). For a general treatment of the doctrine's complicated changing uses through the years, see Teeven, A History of Promissory Estoppel: Growth in the Face of Doctrinal Resistance, 72 Tenn. L. Rev. 1111 (2005).

B.   *Basic Applications*

RESTATEMENT OF CONTRACTS

§90. PROMISE REASONABLY INDUCING DEFINITE AND SUBSTANTIAL RELIANCE

A promise which the promisor should reasonably expect to induce action or forbearance of a definite and substantial character on the part of the promisee and which does induce such action or forbearance is binding if injustice can be avoided only by enforcement of the promise.

RESTATEMENT (SECOND) OF CONTRACTS

§90 Promise Reasonably Inducing Action or Forbearance

(1) A promise which the promisor should reasonably expect to induce action or forbearance on the part of the promisee or a third person and which does induce such action or forbearance is binding if injustice can be avoided only by enforcement of the promise. The remedy granted for breach may be limited as justice requires.

(2) A charitable subscription or a marriage settlement is binding under Subsection (1) without proof that the promise induced action or forbearance.

(without element 2)

There are minor variances in these two sections, and we will discuss those later. First, note their similarity. There is little substantive difference in their scope. There is no language in either section that limits coverage to donative promises, although nearly all pre-Restatement cases were so limited. In fact, most cases concerning §90 have not involved donative promises but promises in a bargaining context. The three major limitations on the scope of the section under the Restatement (Second) are the same under the original Restatement: (1) The promisor must reasonably expect that his or her promise will induce action or forbearance; (2) the promise must in fact induce such action or forbearance; and (3) injustice can be avoided only by the enforcement of the promise.

Note the language of subsection (2) of §90 of the Restatement (Second) of Contracts. Why do you suppose there is this difference for promissory estoppel in charitable subscription cases? Does *Allegheny* give you any hint? The courts have been slow to adopt the idea that charitable subscriptions are so freely enforceable. See In re Bashas' Inc., 468 B.R. 381 (D. Ariz. 2012).

Problem 59

When Earnest was about to turn 40, he became very depressed. To cheer him up, his rich Aunt Augusta told him that she was going to give him $1,000 for each year of his life as a birthday gift. Overjoyed, Earnest lived it up in the month before his birthday. He spent his savings on a new car, a wild day at the races, and a hot air balloon. When his Aunt Augusta learned this, she became disgusted at his profligacy and for his birthday she sent him a simple birthday card. He calls your office for advice. Does he have an action against her?

Problem 60

Valentine and Proteus, two friends, pooled their money and decided to buy a $75,000 yacht. On the day it was delivered, they painted the name *Silvia* on the bow, and Valentine promised Proteus that he would procure insurance for the craft on the next day. One week later a hurricane destroyed the yacht, and Valentine felt sick when he revealed to Proteus that he had forgotten to apply for the insurance. "It's okay," Proteus replied, "just replace the boat." When Valentine declined to do so, Proteus sued. Is promissory estoppel applicable here? Is there traditional consideration for Valentine's promise? Compare Rayden Engr. Corp. v. Church, 337 Mass. 652, 151 N.E.2d 57 (1958) (promise by insurance agent); Graddon v. Knight, 138 Cal. App. 2d 577, 292 P.2d 632 (1956) (promise by mortgagee-bank); Spiegel v. Metropolitan Life Ins. Co., 6 N.Y.2d 91, 160 N.E.2d 40 (1959) (promise by insurance agent); with Northern Commercial Co. v. United Airmotive, 101 F. Supp. 169 (D. Alaska 1951); Nichols v. Acers Co., 415 S.W.2d 683 (Tex. Civ. App. 1967); Dillow v. Phalen, 106 Ohio App. 106, 153 N.E.2d 687 (1957). Comment (e) to Restatement (Second) §90 urges caution in applying the doctrine in such cases.

Problem 61

Aunt Augusta promised her nephew Earnest the sum of $5,000 if he studied hard in law school and made the law review. Earnest had always been an indifferent student who made modestly impressive grades by force of talent rather than application to his lessons. Taking her at her word, Earnest concentrated on his courses, finished his first year at the top of his class, and eventually became the editor in chief of the law review. By this time Aunt Augusta was repulsed by the snob he had become, and she refused to make the $5,000 payment, saying it was clearly a gift promise on which she had changed her mind. The day he was sworn into the bar, Earnest filed suit against her pro se. How does this come out? Does it differ from Hamer v. Sidway, supra section IA, at all?

UNIVERSAL COMPUTER SYSTEMS v. MEDICAL SERVICES ASSOCIATION OF PENNSYLVANIA
United States Court of Appeals, Third Circuit, 1980
628 F.2d 820

ROSENN, Circuit Judge. This is a diversity action in which we are asked to consider questions of agency and promissory estoppel under Pennsylvania law. Specifically, we are asked to consider whether a principal is bound under a theory of promissory estoppel when an employee promised to pick up a bid from a potential bidder. We hold that the employee possessed apparent authority to make a binding promise on which the promisee relied to its detriment and accordingly reinstate the verdict of the jury awarding damages for the breach of that promise.

I

In July of 1975, Medical Services Association of Pennsylvania (Blue Shield) located in Camp Hill, Pennsylvania, solicited bids for the lease of a computer. Pursuant to the bid solicitation, Universal Computer Systems, Inc. (Universal) of Westport, Connecticut, prepared a bid proposal. In order to be considered, the terms of the solicitation required that it be received by Blue Shield at Harrisburg, Pennsylvania, no later than 12:00 Noon on August 18, 1975.

Joel Gebert, an employee of Blue Shield, served as liaison between Blue Shield and prospective bidders on this contract. Shortly before the date of the bidding deadline, most probably on Friday, August 15, Warren Roy Wilson, President of Universal, telephoned Gebert and informed him that Universal could furnish a computer which would meet the required specifications. Being reluctant to entrust the bid to a conventional courier source, Wilson informed Gebert that he expected to transmit the bid via Allegheny Airlines to Harrisburg, Pennsylvania, and asked Gebert if he could arrange to have someone pick up the proposal at the Harrisburg airport on Monday morning. Gebert assured Wilson that the proposal would be picked up at the airport and delivered to Blue Shield in time to meet the bidding deadline.

On the appointed day, Wilson dispatched the bid proposal from La Guardia Airport in New York by Allegheny Airlines PDQ Service on August 18, 1975, at approximately 8:30 A.M. Wilson called Gebert again to give him the necessary information so that the bid could be picked up at Harrisburg as Gebert had agreed and timely delivered to Blue Shield. Gebert, however, informed Wilson that he had changed his mind and could not pick up the proposal. Wilson then unsuccessfully attempted to make other arrangements with Allegheny to have the proposal picked up by courier or other agents and timely delivered to Blue Shield.

Allegheny originally refused to allow anyone to pick up the proposal other than a direct employee of either plaintiff or Blue Shield. Wilson was finally able to contact the supervisors of the airline manager who instructed the manager to release the package to a courier. The bid proposal, however, was released too late to meet the noon deadline. Consequently, Blue Shield rejected the bid as untimely and returned it unopened.

Thereafter, Universal filed a complaint in the United States District Court for the Middle District of Pennsylvania seeking damages for the alleged breach of Blue Shield's promise. The case was tried before a jury which returned a verdict in the amount of $13,000 against Blue Shield. Thereafter Blue Shield filed a motion for judgment non obstante veredicto (n.o.v.) and a motion for a new trial. The district court granted the motion for judgment n.o.v. but denied the motion for a new trial. Universal appealed from the court's entry of judgment n.o.v. and Blue Shield cross-appeals from the denial of its motion for a new trial.

II

In this diversity action brought in a Pennsylvania forum, Pennsylvania law applies as the place where the promise was made and where it was to be performed. See Craftmark Homes, Inc. v. Nanticoke Construction Co., 526 F.2d 790, 792 n.2 (3d Cir. 1975). The district court's order entering judgment n.o.v. rests on two findings. The first is that Gebert, whom Universal alleged made the promise to pick up the bid proposal, lacked actual and apparent authority to make that promise and thereby bind Blue Shield. The second is whether Wilson's reliance upon Gebert's promise was justified.

It is undisputed that Gebert lacked *actual* authority to make the promise. The issue, however, is whether he possessed *apparent* authority under Pennsylvania law to make such a promise. Under the decisional law of Pennsylvania, "apparent authority" is the power to bind a principal in the absence of actual authorization from the principal, but under circumstances in which the principal leads persons with whom his agent deals to believe that the agent has authority. Revere Press, Inc. v. Blumberg, 431 Pa. 370, 375, 246 A.2d 407, 410 (1968). The test for determining whether an agent possesses apparent authority is whether "a man of ordinary prudence, diligence and discretion would have a right to believe and would actually believe that the agent possessed the authority he purported to exercise." Apex Financial Corp. v. Decker, 245 Pa. Super. 439, 369 A.2d 483, 485-486 (1976). Nevertheless, a principal is not bound by the unauthorized act of his agent if the third person had notice of the agent's lack of authority. Schenker v. Indemnity Insurance Co., 340 Pa. 81, 87, 16 A.2d 304, 306 (1940).

The district court stated that Gebert "received all calls from prospective bidders and was the sole contact pursuant to the request for bids." Nevertheless, the court found that Universal should have been aware that Gebert lacked the authority to promise to pick up the bid at the airport and, therefore, Blue Shield was not bound by Gebert's promise. The court based its holding on three findings. First, it found that the bidding process was covered by the federal procurement regulations. Second, the court found that those regulations prohibited Blue Shield from showing a preference for any bidder by receiving a bid at a time or place other than that specified in the Invitation for Bids. Finally, the court found that Universal should have known that the procurement regulations applied to the bidding process and that those regulations prohibited the act which Gebert allegedly promised to perform. Accordingly, our discussion of the agency issue focuses upon the district court's conclusions about the relevance of the federal regulations.

The first two points do not require extended discussion because we believe that the district court erred in holding, as a matter of law, that Universal should have known the federal regulations were applicable. The invitation for bids apparently contained only two indications that federal procurement regulations might be applicable. There was, however, apparently no mention of the regulation at issue here, 41 C.F.R. §1-2.301(a), which the district court construed as forbidding the accommodation Gebert allegedly promised. The first mention of federal regulations occurs at page 2 of the Invitation for Bids and states: "specifications are presented in a 'Brand Name or Equal' modes for optional equipment, as described in Federal Procurement Regulations, Section 1-1.307-4 and 1-1.307-5 through 1-1.307-9." The second reference to federal regulations evidently appears at page 10 of the Invitation for Bids. Both parties apparently agree that the invitation did not mention the federal regulation at issue here, nor did it give any notice that federal procurement regulations were generally applicable.

In addition, Blue Shield argues that the Invitation for Bids contained a notice that the successful bidder had to be approved by the Secretary of the United States Department of Health, Education, and Welfare (HEW). Even so, that would nonetheless be insufficient to support the holding of the district court. By its ruling, the court concluded that as a matter of law a reasonable man should have been aware that the bidding procedure was governed by the federal procurement regulations. We disagree.

The references to the federal procurement regulations in the Invitation for Bids are not to the relevant regulation involving the issue before us, 41 C.F.R. §1-2.301(a) (1979), supra, and the references give no notice whatever that the bid procedures are covered by the federal procurement regulations. In addition, there is no indication that the Invitation for Bids contained a copy of the relevant federal regulations. Finally, although the invitation contained a notice that the successful bidder had to be approved by HEW, we do not believe that requirement provided a sufficient basis to conclude as a matter of law that a reasonable person should have been aware that the bidding procedures were governed by the Federal procurement regulations. Thus, the district court erred in concluding that Gebert lacked apparent authority to make the promise. Therefore, the jury could conclude, as it appears to have done, that Wilson reasonably was unaware of the applicability of the federal regulations and that they possibly interdicted Gebert's promised action.

For essentially the same reasons, we believe that the district court erred in ruling that Gebert's promise should not be enforced on principles of promissory estoppel. To create liability on the basis of promissory estoppel, a promise must be of such a nature and made under such circumstances that the promisor should reasonably anticipate that it will induce action or forbearance of a definite and substantial character on the part of the promisee. Further, the promise must actually induce such action or forbearance and the circumstances must be such that injustice can only be avoided by enforcement of the promise. Restatement of Contracts §90 (1932). The remedy may be limited as justice requires. Restatement of Contracts §201 (Tent. Draft No. 2, April 30, 1965).

In the case before us, the district court found that, assuming that there had been authority to make a promise, the jury reasonably could have found that there was a promise upon which Universal had relied to its detriment. The court, however, concluded that Universal's reliance was unjustified. As we have already alluded, the court reasoned that Universal should have been aware of the federal procurement regulations and of their prohibition against the kind of service Gebert had agreed to perform for Universal. Thus, the court found Universal's reliance unjustified and declined to enforce the promise on principles of promissory estoppel. For the reasons we have stated above, however, we believe the court erred in concluding that Universal should have been aware of the applicability of federal procurement regulations to Gebert's promise to pick up their bid at the airport.

Nor do we believe that our holding is contrary to Stelmack v. Glen Alden Coal Co., 339 Pa. 410, 14 A.2d 127 (1940), and TMA Fund, Inc. v. Biever, 380 F. Supp. 1248 (E.D. Pa. 1974), as urged by Blue Shield.

In *Stelmack* the defendant coal company requested permission to enter upon the plaintiffs' land and erect supports about their building so as to protect it against damage from defendant's impending subsurface mining operations. Plaintiffs granted permission and the supports were erected. As the mining operations continued, the defendant made repairs to the building from time to time but later refused to restore it to its previous condition. The plaintiffs later brought an action, seeking to recover on various theories of contract and promissory estoppel. In rejecting the promissory estoppel theory, the court stated:

> The doctrine of promissory estoppel . . . may be invoked only in those cases where all the elements of a true estoppel are present, for if it is loosely applied any promise, regardless of the complete absence of consideration, would be enforceable.

339 Pa. at 416, 14 A.2d at 129. The court, however, proceeded to analyze the case under section 90 of the Restatement of Contracts. The court stated:

> Here no action was taken by plaintiffs in reliance upon the defendant's promise which resulted in disadvantage to them. They did not alter their position adversely or substantially. They have suffered no injustice in being deprived of a gratuitous benefit to which they have no legal or equitable right.

Id., 14 A.2d at 130.

The instant case is different, however. Here it is clear that plaintiff incurred a <u>substantial detriment</u> as a result of relying upon defendant's promise. Plaintiff has <u>suffered an injustice</u> in being deprived of the service promised by Blue Shield's employee, Gebert.

TMA Fund is also distinguishable. There, defendants were induced to sign a promissory note to support a failing business on the false representation that other financing had also been arranged. On an action against defendants to enforce the terms of the note, the court held the note unenforceable for lack of consideration. The court noted that TMA Fund "did not agree to do anything when the agreement and notes were executed in return for the payment on the notes. TMA Fund is to this day not required to do anything or to refrain from doing any act which it had a right to do under the terms of the purported agreement." 380 F. Supp. at 1254. In the instant case, however, Blue Shield promised to pick up the bid and Universal relied upon that promise to its detriment.

Accordingly, <u>we believe that</u>, under Pennsylvania law, the jury could reasonably have found that Gebert possessed apparent authority to make a promise binding upon Blue Shield, that Universal relied upon that promise to its detriment, and that that promise should be enforced on the basis of promissory estoppel.

III

We now turn to an examination of the damages issue raised by Blue Shield in its cross-appeal. The jury returned a verdict of $13,000 against Blue Shield. This was apparently based upon the jury's conclusion that, had Gebert's promise been carried out, Universal's bid would have been timely submitted and Universal would have been awarded the computer lease contract. The figure $13,000 seems to represent the jury's calculation of the amount of profits lost by Universal because of Blue Shield's failure to perform its promise. The district court held that the damages were proven with reasonable certainty and that the amount awarded was within the jury's discretion. Accordingly, the court denied Blue Shield's motion for judgment n.o.v. and the motion for a new trial on this basis. On its cross-appeal, Blue Shield argues that the jury's finding that Universal suffered damages by virtue of Blue Shield's failure to carry out its promise could only have been based on conjecture and speculation. Blue Shield argues that even if Universal's bid would have been the lowest, there is <u>no guarantee</u> Universal would have been awarded the contract because the final contract still had to be approved by the Federal Bureau of Health Insurance. Blue Shield points particularly to the low bid that was actually opened as not in fact having been selected for the contract which was awarded.

From our examination of the record, however, we believe that the jury could reasonably have concluded that, had Blue Shield carried out its promise, Universal's bid would have been timely submitted and it would have been awarded the contract. There is evidence, first, that had Universal's bid been timely received, it would have been the low bid. The record indicates that Universal's bid was approximately $450 per month lower than the bid submitted by the company that was awarded the contract. Second, Gebert testified that had there been a lower bid received at a point earlier in time, all other things being equal, he would have recommended that negotiations be conducted with the lowest bidder. Ray Eichelberger, Administrative Assistant to the Controller, indicated in his deposition that, all other factors being equal, "the lowest bid price would be [the] sole determining factor as to acceptability." Finally, there is no evidence in the record of other factors which would have prevented an award of the contract to Universal. Eichelberger also stated in his deposition that if Universal's bid had been submitted in a timely fashion, it is likely that a contract would have been approved if the bid was the lowest on a cost basis. We therefore believe the jury could reasonably have concluded that had Gebert performed as promised and picked up Universal's bid at the airport, Universal would have been awarded the contract. Accordingly, we affirm the district court's judgment denying Blue Shield's motions for judgment n.o.v. and for a new trial on the issue of damages.

[handwritten margin note: The court thinks They would have]

IV

The order of the district court denying Blue Shield's motions for judgment n.o.v. and for a new trial (No. 79-2401) will be affirmed. The court's order entering judgment n.o.v. for Blue Shield on the issue of liability (No. 79-2400) will be reversed and the case remanded to the district court with directions to reinstate the jury's verdict. Costs taxed against Blue Shield in both appeals.

NOTES

1. It has been argued that the first requirement for the application of the promissory estoppel doctrine is really part of the second because a promisor should expect every promise to induce the promisee's reasonable action or forbearance. "The real issue is not whether the promisor should have expected the promisee to rely, but whether the extent of the promisee's reliance was reasonable." 1A Corbin, Contracts §13 (1963). See also Eisenberg, Principles of Consideration, 67 Cornell L. Rev. 640, 659 (1982).

2. The reliance interest is the plaintiff's interest in being reimbursed for loss caused by reliance on the contract — the plaintiff's out-of-pocket loss. In

a famous reliance case, <u>Goodman v. Dicker</u>, 169 F.2d 684 (D.C. Cir. 1948), retailer A applied to distributor B for a franchise to sell radios. Such franchises were revocable at will. B erroneously informed A that the application was accepted and A would soon receive the franchise. A expended $1,150 in preparing to do business, but did not receive the franchise. The court awarded the $1,150 to A but no lost profits. Corbin has argued that reliance damages should be the preferred measure of damages for detrimental reliance because the "injustice" that should be avoided is the loss or minus quantity to the relying party. Corbin §205. Some commentators would award the expectancy in commercial contracts where it is possible to measure it. In protecting the restitution interest the court attempts to restore to the plaintiff any benefit the plaintiff has conferred on the other party. Illustration 12 to Restatement (Second) §90 gives the following example of the award of such damages in the estoppel case.

> A promises to make a gift of a tract of land to B, his son-in-law. B takes possession and lives on the land for 17 years, making valuable improvements. A then dispossesses B, and specific performance is denied because the proof of the terms of the promise is not sufficiently clear and definite. B is entitled to a lien on the land for the value of the improvements, not exceeding their cost.

3. There are specific sections of the Restatement (Second) that allow the use of the reliance doctrine to enforce an otherwise unenforceable promise. Section 87(2) of the Restatement (Second), relevant to the two cases that follow, expresses the drafters' impression of the law concerning the irrevocability of certain subcontractors' bids and similar offers when the offeree has detrimentally reasonably relied on the continued viability of the offer. Section 88 at times preserves the obligation of a surety without consideration where there has been reasonable reliance on the promise to be a surety. Section 89 upholds the modification of an executory contract even without consideration where the modification was fair and equitable and justice requires its enforcement in view of a material change of position in reliance on the new contract. Modifications will be discussed in some detail later.

JAMES BAIRD CO. v. GIMBEL BROS.
United States Court of Appeals, Second Circuit, 1933
64 F.2d 344

L. Hand, Circuit Judge. The <u>plaintiff sued</u> the defendant for breach of a contract to deliver linoleum under a contract of sale; the defendant denied the making of the contract; the parties tried the case to the judge under a written stipulation and he directed judgment for the defendant. The facts as found, bearing on the making of the contract, the only issue necessary to

Defendant Denied making a Contract

Judgment for Defendant

discuss, were as follows: The defendant, a New York merchant, knew that the Department of Highways in Pennsylvania had asked for bids for the construction of a public building. It sent an employee to the office of a contractor in Philadelphia, who had possession of the specifications, and the employee there computed the amount of the linoleum which would be required on the job, underestimating the total yardage by about one-half the proper amount. In ignorance of this mistake, on December twenty-fourth the defendant sent to some twenty or thirty contractors, likely to bid on the job, an offer to supply all the linoleum required by the specifications at two different lump sums, depending upon the quality used. These offers concluded as follows: "If successful in being awarded this contract, it will be absolutely guaranteed, . . . and . . . we are offering these prices for reasonable" [sic], "prompt acceptance after the general contract has been awarded." The plaintiff, a contractor in Washington, got one of these on the twenty-eighth, and on the same day the defendant learned its mistake and telegraphed all the contractors to whom it had sent the offer, that it withdrew it and would substitute a new one at about double the amount of the old. This withdrawal reached the plaintiff at Washington on the afternoon of the same day, but not until after it had put in a bid at Harrisburg at a lump sum, based as to linoleum upon the prices quoted by the defendant. The public authorities accepted the plaintiff's bid on December thirtieth, the defendant having meanwhile written a letter of confirmation of its withdrawal, received on the thirty-first. The plaintiff formally accepted the offer on January second, and, as the defendant persisted in declining to recognize the existence of a contract, sued it for damages on a breach.

Unless there are circumstances to take it out of the ordinary doctrine, since the offer was withdrawn before it was accepted, the acceptance was too late. Restatement of Contracts, §35. To meet this the plaintiff argues as follows: It was a reasonable implication from the defendant's offer that it should be irrevocable in case the plaintiff acted upon it, that is to say, used the prices quoted in making its bid, thus putting itself in a position from which it could not withdraw without great loss. While it might have withdrawn its bid after receiving the revocation, the time had passed to submit another, and as the item of linoleum was a very trifling part of the cost of the whole building, it would have been an unreasonable hardship to expect it to lose the contract on that account, and probably forfeit its deposit. While it is true that the plaintiff might in advance have secured a contract conditional upon the success of its bid, this was not what the defendant suggested. It understood that the contractors would use its offer in their bids, and would thus in fact commit themselves to supplying the linoleum at the proposed prices. The inevitable implication from all this was that when the contractors acted upon it, they accepted the offer and promised to pay for the linoleum, in case their bid were accepted.

It was of course possible for the parties to make such a contract, and the question is merely as to what they meant; that is, what is to be imputed to the words they used. Whatever plausibility there is in the argument, is in the fact that the defendant must have known the predicament in which the contractors would be put if it withdrew its offer after the bids went in. However, it seems entirely clear that the contractors did not suppose that they accepted the offer merely by putting in their bids. If, for example, the successful one had repudiated the contract with the public authorities after it had been awarded to him, certainly the defendant could not have sued him for a breach. If he had become bankrupt, the defendant could not prove against his estate. It seems plain therefore that there was no contract between them. And if there be any doubt as to this, the language of the offer sets it at rest. The phrase, "if successful in being awarded this contract," is scarcely met by the mere use of the prices in the bids. Surely such a use was not an "award" of the contract to the defendant. Again, the phrase, "we are offering these prices for . . . prompt acceptance after the general contract has been awarded," looks to the usual communication of an acceptance, and precludes the idea that the use of the offer in the bidding shall be the equivalent. It may indeed be argued that this last language contemplated no more than an early notice that the offer had been accepted, the actual acceptance being the bid, but that would wrench its natural meaning too far, especially in the light of the preceding phrase. The contractors had a ready escape from their difficulty by insisting upon a contract before they used the figures; and in commercial transactions it does not in the end promote justice to seek strained interpretations in aid of those who do not protect themselves.

But the plaintiff says that even though no bilateral contract was made, the defendant should be held under the doctrine of "promissory estoppel." This is to be chiefly found in those cases where persons subscribe to a venture, usually charitable, and are held to their promises after it has been completed. It has been applied much more broadly, however, and has now been generalized in section 90, of the Restatement of Contracts. We may arguendo accept it as it there reads, for it does not apply to the case at bar. Offers are ordinarily made in exchange for a consideration, either a counter-promise or some other act which the promisor wishes to secure. In such cases they propose bargains; they presuppose that each promise or performance is an inducement to the other. Wisconsin, etc., Ry. v. Powers, 191 U.S. 379, 386, 387; Banning Co. v. California, 240 U.S. 142, 152, 153. But a man may make a promise without expecting an equivalent; a donative promise, conditional or absolute. The common law provided for such by sealed instruments, and it is unfortunate that these are no longer generally available. The doctrine of "promissory estoppel" is to avoid the harsh results of allowing the promisor in such a case to repudiate, when the promisee has acted in reliance upon the promise. Siegel v. Spear & Co., 234 N.Y. 479, 138 N.E. 414, 26 A.L.R. 1205. Cf. Allegheny College v. National Bank, 246 N.Y. 369, 159 N.E. 173, 57 L.R.A. 980. But an offer for an exchange is not meant to become a promise until a consideration has been received, either a counter-

promise or whatever else is stipulated. To extend it would be to hold the
offeror regardless of the stipulated condition of his offer. In the case at bar
the defendant offered to deliver the linoleum in exchange for the plaintiff's
acceptance, not for its bid, which was a matter of indifference to it. That offer
could become a promise to deliver only when the equivalent was received;
that is, when the plaintiff promised to take and pay for it. There is no room in
such a situation for the doctrine of "promissory estoppel."

Nor can the offer be regarded as of an option, giving the plaintiff the
right seasonably to accept the linoleum at the quoted prices if its bid was
accepted, but not binding it to take and pay, if it could get a better bargain
elsewhere. There is not the least reason to suppose that the defendant meant
to subject itself to such a one-sided obligation. True, if so construed, the
doctrine of "promissory estoppel" might apply, the plaintiff having acted in
reliance upon it, though, so far as we have found, the decisions are otherwise.
Ganss v. Guffey Petroleum Co., 125 App. Div. 760, 110 N.Y.S. 176;
Comstock v. North, 88 Miss. 754, 41 So. 374. As to that, however, we need
not declare ourselves.

Judgment affirmed.

BRANCO ENTERPRISES, INC. v. DELTA ROOFING, INC.

Missouri Court of Appeals, 1994
886 S.W.2d 157

PARRISH, Judge.

Branco Enterprises, Inc. (Branco), brought an action against Delta
Roofing, Inc. (Delta), to recover damages for Delta's refusal to install a
roof on a Consumers Market building renovated by Branco. The trial
court determined (a) the parties had a contract that required Delta to install
the required roof at a price of $21,545, and (b) Branco was entitled to and
did rely on Delta's bid of $21,545 to its detriment. Judgment was entered for
Branco in the amount of $18,695.

Delta appeals contending the determination that the parties had a contract was erroneous and there was insufficient evidence for the trial court to
have found that Branco was entitled to rely on Delta's bid of $21,545 as the
cost for installing the required roof. Appellate review is undertaken in accordance with Rule 73.01(c). The judgment is affirmed.

Branco desired to bid on a proposed renovation of a Consumers Market
building in Neosho, Missouri. It undertook to subcontract part of the job.
Branco requested bids from subcontractors for installation of a new roof on
the Neosho store. The architectural specifications for the job required the
new roof to be a modified bitumen roof using Derbigum, a product of
Owens-Corning Fiberglass Corporation (Owens-Corning), or an approved
substitute of equal quality. Any substitute was required to be approved by the

architect. In order to obtain a manufacturer's warranty on a Derbigum roof, the roof had to be installed by a roofer who was certified by Owens-Corning to install the product.

Delta submitted a bid to Branco of $21,545 for installation, plus $1,200 for warranty of the roof. Delta's bid was significantly lower than other bids Branco received.

Branco's president, John Branham, called Delta to confirm its bid. He spoke to Cliff Cook, an estimator for Delta. Mr. Cook told Branham that Delta was seeking approval of alternative roofing from the architect; that if Delta could not get approval for its alternative roofing, Delta could get Owens-Corning certification.

Mr. Branham told Mr. Cook that Branco was relying on Delta's bid in placing its bid as general contractor for the project. Cook answered, "That's fine." Branco's bid was accepted. The contract was signed April 9, 1990.

On April 12, 1990, Branco sent three copies of a written subcontract agreement to Delta, together with a transmittal letter requesting Delta to execute and return all copies of the contract and to provide Branco certificates of insurance evidencing certain insurance coverage. Delta did not execute and return the contracts. It did send Branco a certificate of insurance. James Spears, president of Delta, explained why Delta sent the certificate of insurance to Branco. He testified, "We had intentions of doing the job."

On June 4, 1990, after the work on the project had begun, Mr. Branham had a telephone conversation with Mr. Cook. Cook told Branham, "We're not going to do the job." Cook explained that Delta had not gotten certified by Owens-Corning to apply Derbigum.

Branco then contracted with another roofing company for the work Delta was to have performed. The contract price with the new company was $40,240 — $18,565 more than Delta's bid.

The trial court's conclusions of law included:

1. That [Delta's] bids to [Branco] on March 6, 1990 were offers to perform.

2. That [Branco] conditionally accepted [Delta's] $21,545.00 bid on March 6, 1990, said acceptance being contingent only on the award of the prime contract for renovation of the Consumer's [sic] Market in Neosho, Missouri to [Branco]. . . .

4. That on March 19, 1990, the oral agreement between [Branco] and [Delta] became final when [Branco] signed said prime contract, creating a contractual obligation in [Delta].

5. That [Delta] breached its oral agreement with [Branco] by refusing to perform.

6. That in Missouri, detrimental reliance on an oral bid can be enforced under the doctrine of promissory estoppel. . . .

7. That [Branco] relied on [Delta's] March 6, 1990 bid to its detriment.

8. That [Delta] knew or should have known that [Branco] was relying on its bid.

9. That [Branco] had the right to rely on [Delta's] represDeltations [sic].

10. [Branco's] reliance on [Delta's] bid and [Delta's] breach of agreement resulted in damage to [Branco] in the amount of $18,695.00 and it should have judgment on its petition and against [Delta] in that amount.

Delta presents two points on appeal. Both go to the question of whether there was an offer and acceptance between the parties that was sufficiently specific as to terms of a contract to manifest a common assent by them. If there was, a contract exists. If not, there was no contract. Bare v. Kansas City Federation of Musicians Local 34-627, 755 S.W.2d 442, 444 (Mo. App. 1988).

[handwritten: Delta contends that there was no offer and Acceptance]

Point I contends the trial court erred in finding that there was a contract because there was "no unequivocal acceptance of Delta's bid by Branco." Point II claims the trial court erred in applying the doctrine of promissory estoppel because "no unequivocal promise had been made by [Delta] in making its bid to [Branco] sufficient to permit [Branco] to unquestionably expect performance and to reasonably rely thereon." The facts relevant to each point are the same. The points will be discussed together.

Clifford Cook, the estimator for Delta who bid the roofing subcontract, testified by deposition. He testified that he had seen the plans or specifications for the job before he submitted Delta's bid. Based on the job requirements, he submitted an initial bid on behalf of Delta and, on the day Branco was compiling its bid, a revised bid. The representative of Branco with whom Mr. Cook talked told Cook that Branco was relying on Delta's bid in formulating its bid for the general contract with the owner.

In Delmo, Inc. v. Maxima Elec. Sales, Inc., 878 S.W.2d 499 (Mo. App. 1994), this court held that a contract may be effected between a general contractor and a subcontractor based on the general contractor's reliance on the subcontractor's bid for a component of the project being bid. The decision in Delmo was based on application of the doctrine Missouri courts refer to as promissory estoppel.[2] Id. at 504. The necessary elements for promissory estoppel are "(1) a promise, (2) foreseeable reliance, (3) reliance, and (4) injustice absent enforcement." Id.

[handwritten: Delmo based holding on promissory estoppel]

[handwritten: Elements of promissory estoppel]

Delmo is consistent with Drennan v. Star Paving Co., 51 Cal. 2d 409, 333 P.2d 757 (1958), a case with facts similar to those in this appeal. Drennan was a general contractor. He sought bids from subcontractors and relied on them in computing his own bid. On the day bids had to be submitted, he received the bid from Star Paving Co. For paving work Drennan planned to

[handwritten: Drennan]

---

2. It has been suggested that the term "promissory estoppel" almost defies definition. See Corbin, Corbin on Contracts §204 (one vol. ed. 1952). Corbin suggests, "The use of this phrase made some headway, because it satisfied the need of the courts for a justification of their enforcement of certain promises in the absence of any bargain or agreed exchange." Id. at p. 293 (footnote omitted). He suggests, "The American Law Institute was well advised in not adopting this phrase and in stating its rule in terms of action or forbearance in reliance on the promise." Id. at 293-94. See Restatement (Second) of Law of Contracts §90 (1979).

subcontract. Star Paving Co.'s bid was the lowest bid for the paving. Drennan used it in his calculation of his bid on the general contract. Drennan was awarded the contract.

Star Paving Co. refused to perform the work it had bid. The California court, following the reasoning in Northwestern Engineering Co. v. Ellerman, 69 S.D. 397, 408, 10 N.W.2d 879, 884 (1943), held that Star Paving Co.'s bid became binding upon Drennan being awarded the general contract. The court explained:

> When [Drennan] used [Star Paving Co.'s] offer in computing his own bid, he bound himself to perform in reliance on [Star Paving Co.'s] terms. Though [Star Paving Co.] did not bargain for this use of its bid neither did [Star Paving Co.] make it idly, indifferent to whether it would be used or not. On the contrary it is reasonable to suppose that [Star Paving Co.] submitted its bid to obtain the subcontract. It was bound to realize the substantial possibility that its bid would be the lowest, and that it would be included by [Drennan] in his bid. It was to its own interest that the contractor be awarded the general contract; the lower the subcontract bid, the lower the general contractor's bid was likely to be and the greater its chance of acceptance and hence the greater [Star Paving Co.'s] chance of getting the paving subcontract. [Star Paving Co.] had reason not only to expect [Drennan] to rely on its bid but to want him to. Clearly [Star Paving Co.] had a stake in [Drennan's] reliance on its bid. Given this interest and the fact that [Drennan] is bound by his own bid, it is only fair that [Drennan] should have at least an opportunity to accept [Star Paving Co.'s] bid after the general contract has been awarded to him.

333 P.2d at 760.

Clifford Cook, Delta's representative, had seen the specifications for the required work. He knew that the specifications for the roof required use of the Owens-Corning product Derbigum with complete warranty that was available only when the material was installed by a roofer who was certified by Owens-Corning. A variance based on installation of other roofing material of equal quality could be granted only by the architect for the project.

The trial court heard testimony that Cook, knowing these things, told Mr. Branham, Branco's president, that if Delta could not get an alternative product approved, Delta could be certified by Owens-Corning. Branham testified he told Mr. Cook that Branco was relying on Delta's bid in seeking award of the general contract. There was testimony that Mr. Cook agreed on behalf of Delta. Deferring to the trial court's opportunity to judge the credibility of the witnesses, Rule 73.01(c)(2), this court holds the trial court's finding that an oral agreement was made on March 6, 1990, that became final when Branco signed the general contract is not erroneous.

Delta's contention, in Point I, that there was no "unequivocal acceptance of Delta's bid by Branco" fails. The fact that a written subcontract was not tendered to Delta by Branco until after the general contract was signed is

[Handwritten margin notes: "oral Agreement became binding after Branco signature several correct" and "Point I fails"]

of no significance under the facts of this case. As explained by Mr. Branham, "The [written] contract [was] just a confirmation." He further explained, "I had already committed to Delta that I was using them. I committed to them at 2:48 on the day of the bid letting. I specifically said, 'We are using your bid. If we get it, you will get the job.'"

Point 2 — Fails

Delta's contention in Point II also fails. Delta argues that Delta's bid did not make an unequivocal promise to Branco "sufficient to permit [Branco] to unquestionably expect performance and to reasonably rely thereon."

There was testimony that Mr. Branham was told that Delta would obtain a variance to permit it to substitute another product for Derbigum or would obtain Owens-Corning certification to permit Delta to apply Derbigum and provide a full warranty; that Delta would perform the roofing task for the amount of its bid. A promise was made by Delta to Branco.

Mr. Branham told Delta that Branco was relying on Delta's bid. Mr. Cook acknowledged that the reliance was acceptable to Delta. It was foreseeable that Branco would rely on Delta's promise to perform at the bid price.

Branco submitted its bid to the owner and included in its calculation Delta's bid for roofing. Branco relied on Delta's promise.

Delta refused to perform in accordance with its promise. Branco was required to expend a greater sum to get the work done than the amount to which Delta had agreed. Absent Branco obtaining reimbursement from Delta, an injustice would occur.

Missouri's doctrine of promissory estoppel applies. This court holds that the trial court's judgment is supported by substantial evidence and is not against the weight of the evidence; that it neither erroneously declares or applies the law. See Thurmond v. Moxley, 879 S.W.2d 709, 710 (Mo. App. 1994). Judgment affirmed. *Affirmed*

PE Applies

NOTES AND QUESTIONS

1. *James Baird Co.* and *Branco* conflict, don't they? Which represents the best solution to the issue?

2. In resolving this problem, you should know something about the customary practices of the construction industry.

When the owner of property desires to improve it, the owner typically employs an architect to draw up plans and supervise the project. The construction is usually accomplished by inviting *general contractors* to bid on the project, which they do by submitting a bid that is a composite of the bids they in turn have received from the *subcontractors* ("subs" are specialists in such matters as electrical work, plumbing and heating, sheet metal and roofing, painting and decorating, and the like). General contractors may do some of the construction work themselves, or they may do none of it at all, being merely an office for organizing the concerted efforts of the subs. In some projects there is no general contractor; the owner in effect acts as the general and contracts directly with the subs. In such a case the subs are each called *prime contractors.*

3. As the preceding case shows, general contractors run the risk that reliance on the sub's bid by including it in the overall bid may be a mistake. The sub may try to back out after the general receives the bid but before the general has made a formal acceptance of the sub's offer. Absent legal adoption of the doctrine of promissory estoppel in this circumstance, the sub would appear to have the legal right to do so. Why don't the generals insist that the subs sign contracts for the amount quoted (with the contract contingent on the general being awarded the overall job)? When asked, the generals give a number of reasons. First, the subs' bids often come in at the last moment and the general simply has no time to set up formal contracts before the general must submit the overall bid. Second, the subs' bids are frequently complicated, proposing alternatives that must in turn be submitted to the architect and approved. Third, the construction industry relies in large part on a system of mutual trust, and the parties involved rarely resort to law. Reputation is very important, and subs who do not honor their bids are blacklisted thereafter.

Subcontractors would add a fourth reason. They maintain that it is not at all uncommon for the general contractor who has received the award to turn around and engage in a process known as "bid shopping," whereby the general shows the sub's low bid to other subs and asks them to try and beat it. If this is true (and of course it does go on), is it fair to use promissory estoppel to bind the sub to the price quoted?

4. In very large projects more attention is paid to legal relations, and a host of devices — contracts, "firm offers," bid bonds, and escalation clauses — are employed to fix the various responsibilities. Even in these big money transactions, however, an enormous number of the deals are informal and are based largely on trust and reputation.

5. Subcontractors bitterly complain that they do not have the bargaining position to protect their own interests, and that many of the generals do not play fair. They point to the substantial costs they incur in preparing their bids and maintain that this expense is often wasted. In a famous article on which these notes were in part based, Shultz, The Firm Offer Puzzle: A Study of Business Practice in the Construction Industry, 19 U. Chi. L. Rev. 237 (1952), the author concluded that general contractors do not need the protection of a legal doctrine that would bind the sub to the original quotation (absent a formal contract doing so), and that the application of promissory estoppel in this situation was most often unfair to subcontractors.

6. In a jurisdiction not permitting the general contractors to use promissory estoppel as a way to bind the subcontractor, what can the general do to make sure that the sub will not back off from the original estimate?

C.   *The Limits of the Doctrine*

ᵖ HOFFMAN v. RED OWL STORES ᵒ
Supreme Court of Wisconsin, 1965
26 Wis. 2d 683, 133 N.W.2d 267

Action by Joseph Hoffman (hereinafter "Hoffman") and wife, plaintiffs, against defendants Red Owl Stores, Inc. (hereinafter "Red Owl") and Edward Lukowitz.

The complaint alleged that Lukowitz, as agent for Red Owl, represented to and agreed with plaintiffs that Red Owl would build a store building in Chilton and stock it with merchandise for Hoffman to operate in return for which plaintiffs were to put up and invest a total sum of $18,000; that in reliance upon the above mentioned agreement and representations plaintiffs sold their bakery building and business and their grocery store and business; also in reliance on the agreement and representations Hoffman purchased the building site in Chilton and rented a residence for himself and his family in Chilton; plaintiffs' action in reliance on the representations and agreement disrupted their personal and business life; plaintiffs lost substantial amounts of income and expended large sums of money as expenses. Plaintiffs demanded recovery of damages for the breach of defendants' representations and agreements.

The action was tried to a court and jury. The facts hereafter stated are taken from the evidence adduced at the trial. Where there was a conflict in the evidence the version favorable to plaintiffs has been accepted since the verdict rendered was in favor of plaintiffs.

Hoffman assisted by his wife operated a bakery at Wautoma from 1956 until sale of the building late in 1961. The building was owned in joint tenancy by him and his wife. Red Owl is a Minnesota corporation having its home office at Hopkins, Minnesota. It owns and operates a number of grocery supermarket stores and also extends franchises to agency stores which are owned by individuals, partnerships and corporations. Lukowitz resides at Green Bay and since September, 1960, has been divisional manager for Red Owl in a territory comprising Upper Michigan and most of Wisconsin in charge of 84 stores. Prior to September, 1960, he was district manager having charge of approximately 20 stores.

In November, 1959, Hoffman was desirous of expanding his operations by establishing a grocery store and contacted a Red Owl representative by the name of Jansen, now deceased. Numerous conversations were had in 1960 with the idea of establishing a Red Owl franchise store in Wautoma. In September, 1960, Lukowitz succeeded Jansen as Red Owl's representative in the negotiations. Hoffman mentioned that $18,000 was all the capital he had available to invest and he was repeatedly assured that this would be sufficient to set him up in business as a Red Owl store. About Christmastime, 1960, Hoffman thought it would be a good idea if he bought a small grocery store in Wautoma and operated it in order that he gain experience in the grocery business prior to operating a Red Owl store in some larger community. On February 6, 1961, on the advice of Lukowitz and Sykes, who had succeeded Lukowitz as Red Owl's district manager, Hoffman bought the inventory and fixtures of a small grocery store in Wautoma and leased the building in which it was operated.

After three months of operating this Wautoma store, the Red Owl representatives came in and took inventory and checked the operations and found the store was operating at a profit. Lukowitz advised Hoffman to sell the store to his manager, and assured him that Red Owl would find a larger store for him elsewhere. Acting on this advice and assurance, Hoffman sold the fixtures and inventory to his manager on June 6, 1961. Hoffman was reluctant to sell at that time because it meant losing the summer tourist business, but he sold on the assurance that he would be operating in a new location by fall and that he must sell this store if he wanted a bigger one. Before selling, Hoffman told the Red Owl representatives that he had $18,000 for "getting set up in business" and they assured him that there would be no problems in establishing him in a bigger operation. The makeup of the $18,000 was not discussed; it was understood plaintiff's father-in-law would furnish part of it. By June, 1961, the towns for the new grocery store had been narrowed down to two, Kewaunee and Chilton. In Kewaunee, Red Owl had an option on a building site. In Chilton, Red Owl had nothing under option, but it did select a site to which plaintiff obtained an option at Red Owl's suggestion. The option stipulated a purchase price of $6,000 with $1,000 to be paid on election to purchase and the balance to be paid within 30 days. On Lukowitz's assurance that everything was all set plaintiff paid $1,000 down on the lot on September 15th.

On September 27, 1961, plaintiff met at Chilton with Lukowitz and Mr. Reymund and Mr. Carlson from the home office who prepared a projected financial statement. Part of the funds plaintiffs were to supply as their investment in the venture were to be obtained by sale of their Wautoma bakery building.

On the basis of this meeting Lukowitz assured Hoffman: ". . . [E]verything is ready to go. Get your money together and we are set." Shortly after this meeting Lukowitz told plaintiffs that they would have to sell their bakery business and bakery building, and that their retaining this property was the only "hitch" in the entire plan. On November 6, 1961, plaintiffs sold their bakery building for $10,000. Hoffman was to retain the bakery equipment as he contemplated using it to operate a bakery in connection with his Red Owl store. After sale of the bakery Hoffman obtained employment on the night shift at an Appleton bakery.

The record contains different exhibits which were prepared in September and October, some of which were projections of the fiscal operation of the business and others were proposed building and floor plans. Red Owl was to procure some third party to buy the Chilton lot from Hoffman, construct the building, and then lease it to Hoffman. No final plans were ever made, nor were bids let or a construction contract entered. Some time prior to November 20, 1961, certain of the terms of the lease under which the building was to be rented by Hoffman were understood between him and Lukowitz. The lease was to be for 10 years with a rental approximating $550 a month calculated on the basis of 1 percent per month on the building cost, plus 6 percent of the land cost divided on a monthly basis. At the end of the 10-year term he was to have an option to renew the lease for an additional 10-year period or to buy the property at cost on an installment basis. There was no discussion as to what the installments would be or with respect to repairs and maintenance.

On November 22nd or 23rd, Lukowitz and plaintiffs met in Minneapolis with Red Owl's credit manager to confer on Hoffman's financial standing and on financing the agency. Another projected financial statement was there drawn up entitled, "Proposed Financing For An Agency Store." This showed Hoffman contributing $24,100 of cash capital of which only $4,600 was to be cash possessed by plaintiffs. Eight thousand was to be procured as a loan from a Chilton bank secured by a mortgage on the bakery fixtures, $7,500 was to be obtained on a 5 percent loan from the father-in-law, and $4,000 was to be obtained by sale of the lot to the lessor at a profit.

A week or two after the Minneapolis meeting Lukowitz showed Hoffman a telegram from the home office to the effect that if plaintiff could get another $2,000 for promotional purposes the deal could go through for $26,000. Hoffman stated he would have to find out if he could get another $2,000. He met with his father-in-law, who agreed to put $13,000 into the business provided he could come into the business as a partner. Lukowitz told Hoffman the partnership arrangement "sounds fine" and that Hoffman should not go into the partnership arrangement with the "front office." On January 16, 1962, the Red Owl credit manager teletyped Lukowitz that the father-in-law would have to sign an agreement that the $13,000 was either a gift or a loan subordinate to all general creditors and that he would prepare the agreement. On January 31, 1962, Lukowitz teletyped the home office that the father-in-law would sign one or other of the agreements. However, Hoffman testified that it was not until the final meeting some time between January 26th and February 2nd, 1962, that he was told that his father-in-law expected to sign an agreement that the $13,000 he was advancing was to be an outright gift. No mention was then made by the Red Owl representatives of the alternative of the father-in-law signing a subordination agreement. At this meeting the Red Owl agents presented Hoffman with the following projected financial statement:

Capital required in operation:

Cash	$ 5,000.00
Merchandise	20,000.00
Bakery	18,000.00
Fixtures	17,500.00
Promotional Funds	1,500.00
TOTAL:	$62,000.00

Source of funds:

Red Owl 7-day terms	$ 5,000.00	
Red Owl Fixture contract (Term 5 years)	14,000.00	
Bank loans (Term 9 years Union State Bank of Chilton) (Secured by Bakery Equipment)	8,000.00	
Other loans (Term No-pay) No interest		
Father-in-law (Secured by None)	13,000.00	
(Secured by Mortgage on Wautoma Bakery Bldg.)	2,000.00	
Resale of land	6,000.00	
Equity Capital:	$5,000.00	Cash
Amount owner has to invest	17,500.00	Bakery Equip.
	22,500.00	
TOTAL:	$70,500.00	

Hoffman interpreted the above statement to require of plaintiffs a total of $34,000 cash made up of $13,000 gift from his father-in-law, $2,000 on mortgage, $8,000 on Chilton bank loan, $5,000 in cash from plaintiff, and $6,000 on the resale of the Chilton lot. Red Owl claims $18,000 is the total of the unborrowed or unencumbered cash, that is, $13,000 from the father-in-law and $5,000 cash from Hoffman himself. Hoffman informed Red Owl he could not go along with this proposal, and particularly objected to the requirement that his father-in-law sign an agreement that his $13,000 advancement was an absolute gift. This terminated the negotiations between the parties.

The case was submitted to the jury on a special verdict with the first two questions answered by the court.

This verdict, as returned by the jury, was as follows:

Question No. 1:   Did the Red Owl Stores, Inc. and Joseph Hoffman on or about mid-May of 1961 initiate negotiations looking to the establishment of Joseph Hoffman as a franchise operator of a Red Owl Store in Chilton?

Answer: Yes. (Answered by the Court.)

Question No. 2: Did the parties mutually agree on all of the details of the proposal so as to reach a final agreement thereon?

Answer No. (Answered by the Court.)

Question No. 3: Did the Red Owl Stores, Inc., in the course of said negotiations, make representations to Joseph Hoffman that if he fulfilled certain conditions that they would establish him as a franchise operator of a Red Owl Store in Chilton?

Answer: Yes.

Question No. 4: If you have answered Question No. 3 "Yes," then answer this question: Did Joseph Hoffman rely on said representations and was he induced to act thereon?

Answer: Yes.

Question No. 5: If you have answered Question No. 4 "Yes," then answer this question: Ought Joseph Hoffman, in the exercise of ordinary care, to have relied on said representations?

Answer: Yes.

Question No. 6: If you have answered Question No. 3 "Yes," then answer this question: Did Joseph Hoffman fulfill all the conditions he was required to fulfill by the terms of the negotiations between the parties up to January 26, 1962?

Answer: Yes.

Question No. 7: What sum of money will reasonably compensate the plaintiffs for such damages as they sustained by reason of:

(a) The sale of the Wautoma store fixtures and inventory?

Answer: $16,735.00.

(b) The sale of the bakery building?

Answer: $2,000.00.

(c) Taking up the option on the Chilton lot?

Answer: $1,000.00.

(d) Expenses of moving his family to Neenah?

Answer: $140.00.

(e) House rental in Chilton?

Answer: $125.00.

Plaintiffs moved for judgment on the verdict while defendants moved to change the answers to Questions 3, 4, 5, and 6 from "Yes" to "No," and in the alternative for relief from the answers to the subdivisions of Question 7 or a new trial. On March 31, 1964, the circuit court entered the following order:

IT IS ORDERED in accordance with said decision on motions after verdict hereby incorporated herein by reference:

1. That the answer of the jury to Question No. 7(a) be and the same is hereby vacated and set aside and that a new trial be had on the sole issue of the damages for loss, if any, on the sale of the Wautoma store, fixtures and inventory.

2. That all other portions of the verdict of the jury be and hereby are approved and confirmed and all after-verdict motions of the parties inconsistent with this order are hereby denied.

Defendants have appealed from this order and plaintiffs have cross-appealed from paragraph 1 thereof.

CURRIE, C.J. The instant appeal and cross-appeal present these questions:

(1)   Whether this court should recognize causes of action grounded on promissory estoppel as exemplified by sec. 90 of Restatement, 1 Contracts?
(2)   Do the facts in this case make out a cause of action for promissory estoppel?
(3)   Are the jury's findings with respect to damages sustained by the evidence?

RECOGNITION OF A CAUSE OF ACTION GROUNDED ON PROMISSORY ESTOPPEL

Sec. 90 of Restatement, 1 Contracts, provides (at p. 110):

A promise which the promisor should reasonably expect to induce action or forbearance of a definite and substantial character on the part of the promisee and which does induce such action or forbearance is binding if injustice can be avoided only by enforcement of the promise.

The Wisconsin Annotations to Restatement, Contracts, prepared under the direction of the late Professor William H. Page and issued in 1933, stated (at p. 53, sec. 90):

The Wisconsin cases do not seem to be in accord with this section of the Restatement. It is certain that no such proposition has ever been announced by the Wisconsin court and it is at least doubtful if it would be approved by the court.

Since 1933, the closest approach this court has made to adopting the rule of the Restatement occurred in the recent case of Lazarus v. American Motors Corp. (1963), 21 Wis. 2d 76, 85, 123 N.W.2d 548, 553, wherein the court stated:

We recognize that upon different facts it would be possible for a seller of steel to have altered his position so as to effectuate the equitable considerations inherent in sec. 90 of the Restatement.

While it is not necessary to the disposition of the *Lazarus* Case to adopt the promissory estoppel rule of the Restatement, we are squarely faced in the instant case with that issue. Not only did the trial court frame the special verdict on the theory of sec. 90 of Restatement, 1 Contracts, but no other possible theory has been presented to or discovered by this court which would permit plaintiffs to recover. Of other remedies considered that of an action for fraud and deceit seemed to be the most comparable. An action at law for fraud, however, cannot be predicated on unfulfilled promises unless the promisor possessed the present intent not to perform. Suskey v. Davidoff (1958), 2 Wis. 2d 503, 507, 87 N.W.2d 306, and cases cited. Here, there is no evidence that would support a finding that Lukowitz made any of the promises, upon which plaintiffs' complaint is predicated, in bad faith with any present intent that they would not be fulfilled by Red Owl.

Many courts of other jurisdictions have seen fit over the years to adopt the principle of promissory estoppel, and the tendency in that direction continues. As Mr. Justice McFaddin, speaking in behalf of the Arkansas court, well stated, that the development of the law of promissory estoppel "is an attempt by the courts to keep remedies abreast of increased moral consciousness of honesty and fair representations in all business dealings." . . .

Because we deem the doctrine of promissory estoppel, as stated in sec. 90 of Restatement, 1 Contracts, is one which supplies a needed tool which courts may employ in a proper case to prevent injustice, we endorse and adopt it.

APPLICABILITY OF DOCTRINE TO FACTS OF THIS CASE

The record here discloses a number of promises and assurances given to Hoffman by Lukowitz in behalf of Red Owl upon which plaintiffs relied and acted upon to their detriment.

Foremost were the promises that for the sum of $18,000 Red Owl would establish Hoffman in a store. After Hoffman had sold his grocery store and paid the $1,000 on the Chilton lot, the $18,000 figure was changed to $24,100. Then in November, 1961, Hoffman was assured that if the $24,100 figure were increased by $2,000 the deal would go through. Hoffman was induced to sell his grocery store fixtures and inventory in June, 1961, on the promise that he would be in his new store by fall. In November, plaintiffs sold their bakery building on the urging of defendants and on the assurance that this was the last step necessary to have the deal with Red Owl go through.

We determine that there was ample evidence to sustain the answers of the jury to the questions of the verdict with respect to the promissory representations made by Red Owl, Hoffman's reliance thereon in the exercise of ordinary care, and his fulfillment of the conditions required of him by the terms of the negotiations had with Red Owl.

There remains for consideration the question of law raised by defendants that agreement was never reached on essential factors necessary to establish a contract between Hoffman and Red Owl. Among these were the size, cost, design, and layout of the store building; and the terms of the lease with respect to rent, maintenance, renewal, and purchase options. This poses the question of whether the promise necessary to sustain a cause of action for promissory estoppel must embrace all essential details of a proposed transaction between promisor and promisee so as to be equivalent of an offer that would result in a binding contract between the parties if the promisee were to accept the same.

Originally the doctrine of promissory estoppel was invoked as a substitute for consideration rendering a gratuitous promise enforceable as a contract. See Williston, Contracts (1st ed.), p. 307, sec. 139. In other words, the acts of reliance by the promisee to his detriment provided a substitute for consideration. If promissory estoppel were to be limited to only those situations where the promise giving rise to the cause of action must be so definite with respect to all details that a contract would result were the promise supported by consideration, then the defendants' instant promises to Hoffman would not meet this test. However, sec. 90 of Restatement, 1 Contracts, does not impose the requirement that the promise giving rise to the cause of action must be so comprehensive in scope as to meet the requirements of an offer that would ripen into a contract if accepted by the promisee. Rather the conditions imposed are:

(1) Was the promise one which the promisor should reasonably expect to induce action or forbearance of a definite and substantial character on the part of the promisee?
(2) Did the promise induce such action or forbearance?
(3) Can injustice be avoided only by enforcement of the promise?

We deem it would be a mistake to regard an action grounded on promissory estoppel as the equivalent of a breach of contract action. As Dean Boyer points out, it is desirable that fluidity in the application of the concept be maintained. 98 U. of Pa. L. Rev. (1950), 459, at page 497. While the first two of the above listed three requirements of promissory estoppel present issues of fact which ordinarily will be resolved by a jury, the third requirement, that the remedy can only be invoked where necessary to avoid injustice, is one that involves a policy decision by the court. Such a policy decision necessarily embraces an element of discretion.

We conclude that injustice would result here if plaintiffs were not granted some relief because of the failure of defendants to keep their promises which induced plaintiffs to act to their detriment.

DAMAGES

Defendants attack all the items of damages awarded by the jury.

The bakery building at Wautoma was sold at defendants' instigation in order that Hoffman might have the net proceeds available as part of the cash capital he was to invest in the Chilton store venture. The evidence clearly establishes that it was sold at a loss of $2,000. Defendants contend that half of this loss was sustained by Mrs. Hoffman because title stood in joint tenancy. They point out that no dealings took place between her and defendants as all negotiations were had with her husband. Ordinarily only the promisee and not third persons are entitled to enforce the remedy of promissory estoppel against the promisor. However, if the promisor actually foresees, or has reason to foresee, action by a third person in reliance on the promise, it may be quite unjust to refuse to perform the promise. 1A Corbin, Contracts, p. 220, sec. 200. Here not only did defendants foresee that it would be necessary for Mrs. Hoffman to sell her joint interest in the bakery building, but defendants actually requested that this be done. We approve the jury's award of $2,000 damages for the loss incurred by both plaintiffs in this sale.

Defendants attack on two grounds the $1,000 award because of Hoffman's payment of that amount on the purchase price of the Chilton lot. The first is that this $1,000 had already been lost at the time the final negotiations with Red Owl fell through in January, 1962, because the remaining $5,000 of purchase price had been due on October 15, 1961. The record does not disclose that the lot owner had foreclosed Hoffman's interest in the lot for failure to pay this $5,000. The $1,000 was not paid for the option, but had been paid as part of the purchase price at the time Hoffman elected to exercise the option. This gave him an equity in the lot which could not be legally foreclosed without affording Hoffman an opportunity to pay the balance. The second ground of attack is that the lot may have had a fair market value of $6,000, and Hoffman should have paid the remaining $5,000 of purchase price. We determine that it would be unreasonable to require Hoffman to have invested an additional $5,000 in order to protect the $1,000 he had paid. Therefore, we find no merit to defendants' attack upon this item of damages.

We also determine it was reasonable for Hoffman to have paid $125 for one month's rent of a home in Chilton after defendants assured him everything would be set when plaintiff sold the bakery building. This was a proper item of damage.

Plaintiffs never moved to Chilton because defendants suggested that Hoffman get some experience by working in a Red Owl store in the Fox River Valley. Plaintiffs, therefore, moved to Neenah instead of Chilton. After moving, Hoffman worked at night in an Appleton bakery but held himself available for work in a Red Owl store. The $140 moving expense would not have been incurred if plaintiffs had not sold their bakery building in

Wautoma in reliance upon defendants' promises. We consider the $140 moving expense to be a proper item of damage.

We turn now to the damage item with respect to which the trial court granted a new trial, i.e., that arising from the sale of the Wautoma grocery store fixtures and inventory for which the jury awarded $16,735. The trial court ruled that Hoffman could not recover for any loss of future profits for the summer months following the sale on June 6, 1961, but that damages would be limited to the difference between the sales price received and the fair market value of the assets sold, giving consideration to any goodwill attaching thereto by reason of the transfer of a going business. There was no direct evidence presented as to what this fair market value was on June 6, 1961. The evidence did disclose that Hoffman paid $9,000 for the inventory, added $1,500 to it and sold it for $10,000 or a loss of $500. His 1961 federal income tax return showed that the grocery equipment had been purchased for $7,000 and sold for $7,955.96. Plaintiffs introduced evidence of the buyer that during the first eleven weeks of operation of the grocery store his gross sales were $44,000 and his profit was $6,000 or roughly 15 percent. On cross-examination he admitted that this was gross and not net profit. Plaintiffs contend that in a breach of contract action damages may include loss of profits. However, this is not a breach of contract action.

The only relevancy of evidence relating to profits would be with respect to proving the element of goodwill in establishing the fair market value of the grocery inventory and fixtures sold. Therefore, evidence of profits would be admissible to afford a foundation for expert opinion as to fair market value.

Where damages are awarded in promissory estoppel instead of specifically enforcing the promisor's promise, they should be only such as in the opinion of the court are necessary to prevent injustice. Mechanical or rule of thumb approaches to the damage problem should be avoided. In discussing remedies to be applied by courts in promissory estoppel we quote the following views of writers on the subject:

> Enforcement of a promise does not necessarily mean Specific Performance. It does not necessarily mean Damages for breach. Moreover the amount allowed as Damages may be determined by the plaintiff's expenditures or change of position in reliance as well as by the value to him of the promised performance. Restitution is also an "enforcing" remedy, although it is often said to be based upon some kind of a rescission. In determining what justice requires, the court must remember all of its powers, derived from equity, law merchant, and other sources, as well as the common law. Its decree should be molded accordingly. 1A Corbin, Contracts, p. 221, sec. 200.
>
> The wrong is not primarily in depriving the plaintiff of the promised reward but in causing the plaintiff to change position to his detriment. It would follow that the damages should not exceed the loss caused by the change of position, which would never be more in amount, but might be

less, than the promised reward. Seavey, Reliance on Gratuitous Promises or Other Conduct, 64 Harv. L. Rev. (1951), 913, 926.

There likewise seems to be no positive legal requirement, and certainly no legal policy, which dictates the allowance of contract damages in every case where the defendant's duty is consensual. Shattuck, Gratuitous Promises — A New Writ?, 35 Mich. L. Rev. (1936), 908, 912.[3]

At the time Hoffman bought the equipment and inventory of the small grocery store at Wautoma he did so in order to gain experience in the grocery store business. At that time discussion had already been had with Red Owl representatives that Wautoma might be too small for a Red Owl operation and that a larger city might be more desirable. Thus Hoffman made this purchase more or less as a temporary experiment. Justice does not require that the damages awarded him, because of selling these assets at the behest of defendants, should exceed any actual loss sustained measured by the difference between the sales price and the fair market value.

Since the evidence does not sustain the large award of damages arising from the sale of the Wautoma grocery business, the trial court properly ordered a new trial on this issue.

Order affirmed. Because of the cross-appeal, plaintiffs shall be limited to taxing but two-thirds of their costs.

QUESTIONS

1. This case caused a stir when it was first handed down. Can you see why? How does the use of promissory estoppel here differ from its use in prior cases?

2. One sentence in particular struck the commentators as extraordinary. Can you identify it?

3. Promissory estoppel, as applied here, puts severe limitations on the bargaining process. Is this a good idea?

4. Would the reasoning of this case reverse the result in Petterson v. Pattberg (see Chapter 1)?

Protecting as it does the reliance interest, which is at the very heart of contract law, promissory estoppel appears to be a theory that an attorney would want to use as often as possible. As the cases suggest, this assumption is wrong. There are significant reasons for avoiding pressing a promissory estoppel claim if it is possible to make a case for a traditional contracts action. First, promissory estoppel theory is not available if an enforceable contract exists. Second, the use of promissory estoppel may indicate to the judge that

---

3. For expression of the opposite view, that courts in promissory estoppel cases should treat them as ordinary breach of contract cases and allow the full amount of damages recoverable in the later, see Note, 13 Vand. L. Rev. (1960), 705.

the very attorney who may have failed to help create an enforceable contract is now trying to use promissory estoppel to pervert the usual rules so as to snatch chestnuts from a fire of the attorney's own making.

NOTES

Negotiating in good faith

1. The Colorado Supreme Court in Vigoda v. Denver Urban Renewal Auth., 646 P.2d 900 (Colo. 1982), cited *Hoffman* with approval. The plaintiff's complaint alleged that the defendant had promised to negotiate with her in good faith for the purchase of her property; that the defendant knew that the plaintiff would devote time and make expenditures in reliance on that promise; and that the promise of the defendant was relied on by the plaintiff, inducing her to expend time and money in furtherance of the anticipated negotiations. The court felt that these allegations were sufficient to support a claim based on the doctrine of promissory estoppel. The court stated:

> We believe that the doctrine as set forth in the Restatement should be applied to prevent injustice where there has not been mutual agreement by the parties on all essential terms of a contract, but a promise was made which the promisor should reasonably have expected would induce action or forbearance, and the promise in fact induced such action or forbearance.

The case was remanded in part for a determination of whether there was sufficient proof to support the allegations by the plaintiff.

On the issue of the parties' duties to negotiate in good faith, see generally Summers, "Good Faith" in General Contract Law and the Sales Provisions of the Uniform Commercial Code, 54 Va. L. Rev. 195 (1968).

2. Compare with *Hoffman*, the lead case, and *Vigoda*, cited in the last note, the case of Wheeler v. White, 398 S.W.2d 93 (Tex. 1965). Wheeler was to build a shopping center on White's land. White agreed to furnish Wheeler with construction financing. Because of White's assurances that the financing would be provided, Wheeler demolished existing buildings and generally prepared the site. The loan was not made, and Wheeler sued White for breach of contract. The court held the contract was too indefinite to enforce because the terms of repayment of the loan were not specified. However, the court held that the complaint stated a cause of action for promissory estoppel and reversed and remanded for a finding pursuant to that ruling. The court, like many courts (including the Wisconsin Supreme Court in *Hoffman*) would not award lost profits in a promissory estoppel action. The Texas Supreme Court justified this result by saying that the promisee is partially at fault in not getting a traditional contract, so traditional damages are not recoverable, and the promisee is restricted to out-of-pocket losses only. To the same effect is First Natl. Bank v. Logan Mfg. Co., 577

N.E.2d 949 (Ind. 1991). Because several courts have held that oral commitments to loan money are actionable, many states have enacted statutes that provide that loan commitments must be in writing to be enforceable.

3. There were predictions in the last 30 years that the doctrine of promissory estoppel would prove so appealing to the courts that it would come to dominate contracts cases, but time has proven otherwise. Employment cases have proven to be the least futile for the doctrine. Most states are "at will" jurisdictions — an employee may be fired at any time with no reason as long as it is not on a prohibited basis such as race. When employers make what appears to be a promise of employment with limits on the employer's right to fire at will, employees have often argued that promissory estoppel can be used to prevent a firing not in accord with employer's promise, an argument that rarely succeeds. See, e.g., Martens v. Minnesota Min. & Mfg. Co., 616 N.W.2d 732 (Minn. 2000). See also Conner, A Study of the Interplay Between Promissory Estoppel and At-Will Employment in Texas, 53 SMU L. Rev. 579 (2000).

DIXON v. WELLS FARGO BANK
United States District Court, Massachusetts, 2011
798 F. Supp. 2d 336

YOUNG, District Judge.

I. INTRODUCTIONS

Frank and Deana Dixon (collectively "the Dixons") bring this cause of action against Wells Fargo Bank, N.A. ("Wells Fargo"), seeking (1) an injunction prohibiting Wells Fargo from foreclosing on their home; (2) specific performance of an oral agreement to enter into a loan modification; and (3) damages. Wells Fargo, having removed the action from state court, now moves for dismissal of the Dixons' complaint under Fed. R. Civ. P. 12(b)(6), arguing that the allegations are insufficient to invoke the doctrine of promissory estoppel and that, to the extent the Dixons have stated a state-law claim, it is preempted by the Home Owners' Loan Act ("HOLA"), 12 U.S.C. §§1461-1700, and its implementing regulations, 12 C.F.R. §§500-99. . . .

B. FACTS ALLEGED

The Dixons reside at their home in Scituate, Plymouth County, Massachusetts. Compl. ¶2. Wells Fargo is a corporation doing business in the Commonwealth of Massachusetts. *Id.* ¶3. Wells Fargo alleges that it is the holder of a mortgage on the Dixons' home. *Id.* ¶6.

On or about June 8, 2009, the Dixons orally agreed with Wells Fargo to take the steps necessary to enter into a mortgage loan modification. *Id.* ¶7. As part of this agreement, Wells Fargo instructed the Dixons to stop making payments on their loan. *Id.* It was contemplated that the unpaid payments would be added to the note as modified. *Id.* In addition, Wells Fargo requested certain financial information, which the Dixons promptly supplied. *Id.*

Notwithstanding the Dixons' diligent efforts and reliance on Wells Fargo's promise, Wells Fargo has failed, and effectively refused, to abide by the oral agreement to modify the existing mortgage loan. *Id.* ¶8.

On or about December 8, 2010, the Dixons received notice from the Massachusetts Land Court that Wells Fargo was proceeding with a foreclosure on their home. *Id.* ¶9. The return date on the order of notice in the Land Court was January 10, 2011, and so the Dixons sought a temporary restraining order in the Superior Court to prevent the loss of their home. *See* Procedural History, *supra.*

The Dixons state that, on information and belief, the fair market value of their home is in excess of the mortgage loan balance and any arrearage. Compl. ¶10.

II. ANALYSIS

. . .

B. PROMISSORY ESTOPPEL

The gravamen of the Dixons' complaint is that Wells Fargo promised to engage in negotiations to modify their loan, provided that they took certain "steps necessary to enter into a mortgage modification." Compl. ¶7. On the basis of Wells Fargo's representation, the Dixons stopped making payments on their loan and submitted the requested financial information — only to learn subsequently that the bank had initiated foreclosure proceedings against them. They contend that Wells Fargo ought to have anticipated their compliance with the terms of its promise to consider them for a loan modification. Not only was it reasonable that they would rely on the promise, but also their reliance left them considerably worse off, for by entering into default they became vulnerable to foreclosure.

The question whether these allegations are sufficient to state a claim for promissory estoppel requires a close look at the doctrine's evolution in the law of Massachusetts. In Loranger Const. Corp. v. E.F. Hauserman Co., 376 Mass. 757, 384 N.E.2d 176 (1978), the Supreme Judicial Court recognized the enforceability of a promise on the basis of detrimental reliance, but declined to "use the expression 'promissory estoppel,' since it tends to confusion rather than clarity." *Id.* at 760-61, 384 N.E.2d 176. The court reasoned that "[w]hen a promise is enforceable in whole or in part by virtue of reliance, it is a 'contract,' and it is enforceable pursuant to a 'traditional contract theory' antedating the modern doctrine of consideration." *Id.* at 761, 384 N.E.2d 176. Since *Loranger,* the court has adhered to its view that "an action based on reliance is equivalent to a contract action, and the party bringing such an action must prove all the necessary elements of a contract other than consideration." Rhode Island Hosp. Trust Nat'l Bank v. Varadian, 419 Mass. 841, 850, 647 N.E.2d 1174 (1995).

"An essential element in the pleading and proof of a contract claim is, of course, the 'promise' sought to be enforced." Kiely v. Raytheon Co., 914 F. Supp. 708, 712 (D. Mass. 1996) (O'Toole, J.). Thus, even where detrimental reliance acts as a substitute for consideration, the promise on which a claim for promissory estoppel is based must be interchangeable with an offer "in the sense of 'commitment.'" Cataldo Ambulance Serv., Inc. v. City of Chelsea, 426 Mass. 383, 386 n.6, 688 N.E.2d 959 (1998). The promise must demonstrate "an intention to act or refrain from acting in a specified way, so as to justify a promisee in understanding that a *commitment* has been made." *Varadian,* 419 Mass. at 849-50, 647 N.E.2d 1174 (quoting Restatement (Second) of Contracts §2 (1981)). That the representation is of future, rather than present, intention will not preclude recovery, so long as the promisor's expectation to be legally bound is clear. [Citations omitted.]

In addition to demonstrating a firm commitment, the putative promise, like any offer, must be sufficiently "definite and certain in its terms" to be enforceable. Moore v. La-Z-Boy, Inc., 639 F. Supp. 2d 136, 142 (D. Mass. 2009) (Stearns, J.) (quoting *Kiely,* 914 F. Supp. at 712). "[I]f an essential element is reserved for the future agreement of both parties, as a general rule, the promise can give rise to no legal obligation until such future agreement." 1 Richard A. Lord, Williston on Contracts §4:29 (4th ed. 1990); *see* Lucey v. Hero Int'l Corp., 361 Mass. 569, 574-75, 281 N.E.2d 266 (1972). Under well-settled Massachusetts law, "an agreement to enter into a contract which leaves the terms of that contract for future negotiation is too indefinite to be enforced." Caggiano v. Marchegiano, 327 Mass. 574, 580, 99 N.E.2d 861 (1951); . . . Restatement (Second) of Contracts §33, comment (c) ("The more terms the parties leave open, the less likely it is that they have intended to conclude a binding agreement.").

The longstanding reluctance of courts to enforce open-ended "agreements to agree" reflects a belief that, unless a "fall-back standard" exists to supply the missing terms, there is no way to know what ultimate agreement, if any, would have resulted. E. Allan Farnsworth, *Precontractual Liability and Preliminary Agreements: Fair Dealing and Failed Negotiations,* 87 Colum. L. Rev. 217, 255-56 (1987). It is the vague and indefinite nature of that potential final agreement—not the preliminary agreement to agree—that troubles courts. *See* Armstrong v. Rohm & Haas Co., Inc., 349 F. Supp. 2d 71, 78 (D. Mass. 2004) (Saylor, J.) (holding that an agreement must be sufficiently definite to enable courts to give it an exact meaning). Judges are justifiably unwilling to endorse one party's aspirational view of the terms of an unrea-lized agreement. *See* Farnsworth, *supra* at 259. Just as "[i]t is no appropriate part of judicial business to rewrite contracts freely entered into," RCI North-east Servs. Div. v. Boston Edison Co., 822 F.2d 199, 205 (1st Cir. 1987), courts must not force parties into contracts into which they have not entered freely, *Armstrong*, 349 F. Supp. 2d at 80 (holding a promise unenforceable where the court could not "supply the missing terms without 'writing a contract for the parties which they themselves did not make'" (quoting Held v. Zamparelli, 13 Mass. App. Ct. 957, 958, 431 N.E.2d 961 (1982))).

Moreover, parties ought to be allowed to step away unscathed if they are unable to reach a deal. *Cf.* R.W. Int'l Corp. v. Welch Food, Inc., 13 F.3d 478, 484-85 (1st Cir. 1994). To impose rights and duties at "the stage of 'imperfect negotiation,'" *Lafayette Place Assocs.*, 427 Mass. at 517, 694 N.E.2d 820, would be to interfere with the liberty to contract—or not to contract. Thus, the concern is that if a court were to order specific performance of an agreement to agree, where the material terms of the final agreement were left open by the parties, not only would there be "little, if anything, to enforce," Lambert v. Fleet Nat'l Bank, 449 Mass. 119, 123, 865 N.E.2d 1091 (2007), but also future negotiations would be chilled. [Citation omitted.]

Wells Fargo would have this Court end its inquiry here. The complaint plainly alleges that the parties had an "agreement to enter into a loan mod-ification agreement," but as matter of law "[a]n agreement to reach an agreement is a contradiction in terms and imposes no obligations on the parties thereto." *Rosenfield*, 290 Mass. at 217, 195 N.E. 323. As such, the complaint would appear to fail to state a claim.

During the course of opposing Wells Fargo's motion to dismiss, however, the Dixons have made clear that they do not seek specific perfor-mance of a promised loan modification. *See* Pls.' Supplemental Mem. Opp'n 1-2. They admit that there was no guarantee of a modification by Wells Fargo, only a verbal commitment to determine their eligibility for a modification if they followed the bank's prescribed steps. Thus, the Dixons' request that Wells Fargo be held to its promise to consider them for a loan modification is not a covert attempt to bind the bank to a final agreement it had not con-templated. There is no risk that this Court, were it to uphold the promissory estoppel claim, would be "trapping" Wells Fargo into a vague, indefinite, and unintended loan modification masquerading as an agreement to agree. Teachers Ins. & Annuity Ass'n of Am. v. Tribune Co., 670 F. Supp. 491, 497 (S.D.N.Y. 1987).

Furthermore, because the parties had not yet begun to negotiate the terms of a modification, the Court questions whether Wells Fargo's promise ought to even be characterized as a preliminary agreement to agree. Instead, it more closely resembles an "agreement to negotiate." *See* Farnsworth, *supra* at 263-69; *cf.* Aceves v. U.S. Bank, N.A., 192 Cal. App. 4th 218, 120 Cal. Rptr. 3d 507, 514 (2011) ("[T]he question here is simply whether U.S. Bank made and kept a promise to *negotiate* with Aceves, not whether . . . the bank promised to make a loan or, more precisely, to modify a loan.").

To be sure, Massachusetts courts have tended to treat agreements to negotiate as variants of open-ended agreements to agree. The view that "[a]n agreement to negotiate does not create a binding contract," *Sax,* 639 F. Supp. 2d at 171, again reflects a concern that a promise of further negotiations is too indefinite, too undefined in scope, to be enforceable. *See Bell,* 359 Mass. at 763, 270 N.E.2d 926 (finding an agreement to negotiate "for as long as the parties agreed" to be "void for vagueness"). This is particularly true where the parties have not specified the terms on which they will continue negotiating. *See* Farnsworth, *supra* at 264. Conventional wisdom holds that courts ought not "strain[ ] to find an agreement to negotiate in the absence of a clear indication of assent" by the parties to a governing standard of conduct, e.g., "good faith" or "best efforts," *Id.* at 266-67, because "there is no meaningful content in a general duty to negotiate, standing alone," Steven J. Burton & Eric G. Anderson, Contractual Good Faith §8.4.2, at 361 (1995). *See* Pinnacle Books, Inc. v. Harlequin Enters. Ltd., 519 F. Supp. 118, 122 (S.D.N.Y. 1981). As with open-ended agreements to agree, judicial enforcement of vague agreements to negotiate would risk imposing on parties contractual obligations they had not taken on themselves.

In this case, Wells Fargo and the Dixons had not yet contemplated the terms of a loan modification, but they had contemplated negotiations. Their failure to elaborate on the boundaries of that duty to negotiate, however, would seem to militate against enforcement of it. Yet, Wells Fargo made a specific promise to consider the Dixons' eligibility for a loan modification if they defaulted on their payments and submitted certain financial information. [Citations omitted.] Importantly, it was not a promise made in exchange for a bargained-for legal detriment, as there was no bargain between the parties; rather, the legal detriment that the Dixons claim to have suffered was a direct consequence of their reliance on Wells Fargo's promise. Joseph Perillo, Calamari & Perillo on Contracts §6.1, at 218 (6th ed. 2009). Under the theory of promissory estoppel, "[a] negotiating party may not with impunity break a promise made during negotiations if the other party has relied on it." Farnsworth, *supra* at 236.

Promissory estoppel has developed into "an attempt by the courts to keep remedies abreast of increased moral consciousness of honesty and fair representations in all business dealings." Peoples Nat'l Bank of Little Rock v. Linebarger Constr. Co., 219 Ark. 11, 240 S.W.2d 12, 16 (1951). While it began as "a substitute for (or the equivalent of) consideration" in the context of an otherwise binding contract, Perillo, *supra* §6.1, at 218, "promissory estoppel has come to be a doctrine employed to rescue failing contracts where the cause of the failure is not related to consideration," *Id.* §6.3, at 229. It now "provides a remedy for many promises or agreements that fail the test of enforceability under many traditional contract doctrines," *Id.* §6.1, at

218, but whose enforcement is "necessary to avoid injustice," Restatement (Second) of Contracts §90, comment (b).

Admittedly, the courts of Massachusetts have yet to formally embrace promissory estoppel as more than a consideration substitute. *See, e.g., Varadian*, 419 Mass. at 850, 647 N.E.2d 1174. Nonetheless, without equivocation, they have adopted section 90 of the Restatement (Second) of Contracts, which reads, "A promise which the promisor should reasonably expect to induce action or forbearance on the part of the promisee or a third person and which does induce such action or forbearance is binding if injustice can be avoided only by enforcement of the promise." . . . Nowhere in the comments to section 90 nor in section 2 of the Restatement, which defines the word "promise," is there an explicit "requirement that the promise giving rise to the cause of action must be so comprehensive in scope as to meet the requirements of an offer that would ripen into a contract if accepted by the promisee." Hoffman v. Red Owl Stores, Inc., 26 Wis. 2d 683, 133 N.W.2d 267, 275 (1965). In fact, the Restatement "has expressly approved" promissory estoppel's use to protect reliance on indefinite promises. *See* Michael B. Metzger & Michael J. Phillips, *Promissory Estoppel and Reliance on Illusory Promises,* 44 Sw. L.J. 841, 842 (1990). [Citation omitted.]

Massachusetts's continued insistence that a promise be definite — at least to a degree likely not met in the present case — is arguably in tension with its adoption of the Restatement's more relaxed standard. This tension is not irreconcilable, however. Tracing the development of promissory estoppel through the case law reveals a willingness on courts' part to enforce even an indefinite promise made during preliminary negotiations where the facts suggest that the promisor's words or conduct were designed to take advantage of the promisee. The promisor need not have acted fraudulently, deceitfully, or in bad faith. McLearn v. Hill, 276 Mass. 519, 524-25, 177 N.E. 617 (1931). Rather, "[f]acts falling short of these elements may constitute conduct contrary to general principles of fair dealing and to the good conscience which ought to actuate individuals and which it is the design of courts to enforce." *Id.* at 524, 177 N.E. 617. As the Supreme Judicial Court remarked in an early promissory estoppel case:

> [I]t is not essential that the representations or conduct giving rise to [the doctrine's] application should be fraudulent in the strictly legal significance of that term, or with intent to mislead or deceive; the test appears to be whether in all the circumstances of the case conscience and duty of honest dealing should deny one the right to repudiate the consequence of his representations or conduct; whether the author of a proximate cause may justly repudiate its natural and reasonably anticipated effect; fraud, in the sense of a court of equity, properly including all acts, omissions, and concealments which involve a breach of legal or equitable duty, trust, or confidence, justly reposed, and are injurious to another or by which an undue and unconscientious advantage is taken of another.

Id. at 525, 177 N.E. 617 (quoting Howard v. West Jersey & Seashore R.R., 102 N.J. Eq. 517, 141 A. 755, 757 (N.J. Ch. 1928), *aff'd,* 104 N.J. Eq. 201, 144 A. 919 (N.J. 1929)).

Typically, where the Massachusetts courts have applied the doctrine of promissory estoppel to enforce an otherwise unenforceable promise, "there has been a pattern of conduct by one side which has dangled the other side on a string." [citing cases]. In *Greenstein,* where a landlord submitted a lease to a prospective tenant and then strung him along for more than four months before repudiating the lease he had submitted, the Massachusetts Appeals Court concluded that the conduct of the landlord "was calculated to misrepresent the true situation to the [tenant], keep him on a string, and make the [tenant] conclude — reasonably — that the deal had been made and that only a bureaucratic formality remained." 19 Mass. App. Ct. at 356, 474 N.E.2d 1130. Because this conduct "was misleading, it fit[ ] comfortably 'within at least the penumbra of some common-law, statutory, or other established concept of unfairness.'" *Id.* (quoting PMP Assocs., Inc. v. Globe Newspaper Co., 366 Mass. 593, 596, 321 N.E.2d 915 (1975)). [Citation omitted.] While *Greenstein* presented a situation ripe for a straightforward application of promissory estoppel, the court noted that "[i]t is not even necessary that the conduct complained of fit into a precise tort or contract niche" for relief to be appropriate. 19 Mass. App. Ct. at 356, 474 N.E.2d 1130 (citing Slaney v. Westwood Auto, Inc., 366 Mass. 688, 693, 322 N.E.2d 768 (1975)).

The circumstances of the *McLearn* case, quoted from above, are also instructive. *See* 276 Mass. 519, 177 N.E. 617. There, after the plaintiff timely filed his tort claim in a municipal court, the defendant convinced him to dismiss it and refile in the Superior Court, where a number of other lawsuits arising from the same motor vehicle accident were pending a consolidated trial. *Id.* at 521, 177 N.E. 617. But, in so doing, the plaintiff's second action was filed after the one-year statute of limitations had run, and the defendant promptly asserted this as a defense. *Id.* at 521-22, 177 N.E. 617. The defendant had not expressly promised not to plead the statute of limitations, but the court deemed it "a necessary implication," as "the arrangement suggested by the defendant could be carried out only by not pleading the statute." *Id.* at 527, 177 N.E. 617. The court observed that "the plaintiff ha[d] suffered direct harm brought about by conduct of the defendant when he discontinued an action seasonably brought to enforce his claim; and the defendant ha[d] acquired the direct advantage of being enabled to interpose a defence resting on that conduct alone." *Id.* at 526, 177 N.E. 617. Having acted in a manner "not consonant with fairness and designed to induce action by the plaintiff to his harm," the defendant was estopped from raising the statute as a defense. *Id.* at 527, 177 N.E. 617.

One final case, the core allegations of which mirror those presented in the Dixons' complaint, merits mention. In Cohoon v. Citizens Bank, No. 002774, 2000 WL 33170737 (Mass. Super. Nov. 11, 2000) (Agnes, J.), the parties orally agreed to a discounted payoff in full satisfaction of the plaintiff's original mortgage obligation. *Id.* at *1. The defendant encouraged the plaintiff to default on a mortgage payment to ensure approval of the discounted payoff. *Id.* at *4. Until that time, the plaintiff had made timely payments. *Id.* Once in default, however, the defendant sold the note to a buyer who promptly commenced foreclosure. *Id.* The court upheld the plaintiff's claim for promissory estoppel because, "[t]aking the facts in the light most favorable to the plaintiff, it could be found that [the defendant] encouraged [the plaintiff] to delay mortgage payment and, as a result of that reliance, the eventual buyer . . . took advantage of [the plaintiff's] vulnerable state by initiating foreclosure on [the plaintiff's] property interest." *Id.* While the court indicated that, to prevail at trial, the plaintiff would need to establish that he "was misled or induced to believe that by defaulting he would achieve the discounted purchase of the note that he was seeking," *Id.* at *6, he was at least entitled to "th[is] opportunity to prove facts in support of his claim of detrimental reliance," *Id.* at *4.

In the present case, Wells Fargo convinced the Dixons that to be eligible for a loan modification they had to default on their payments, and it was only because they relied on this representation and stopped making their payments that Wells Fargo was able to initiate foreclosure proceedings. While there is no allegation that its promise was dishonest, Wells Fargo distinctly gained the upper hand by inducing the Dixons to open themselves up to a foreclosure action. In specifically telling the Dixons that stopping their payments and submitting financial information were the "steps necessary to enter into a mortgage modification," Wells Fargo not only should have known that the Dixons would take these steps believing their fulfillment would lead to a loan modification, but also must have intended that the Dixons do so. The bank's promise to consider them for a loan modification if they took those steps necessarily "involved as matter of fair dealing an undertaking on [its] part not to [foreclose] based upon facts coming into existence solely from" the making of its promise. *McLearn*, 276 Mass. at 523-24, 177 N.E. 617; *see Aceves*, 120 Cal. Rptr. 3d at 514 ("U.S. Bank agreed to 'work with [Aceves] on a mortgage reinstatement and loan modification' if she no longer pursued relief in the bankruptcy court. . . . [This promise] indicates that U.S. Bank would not foreclose on Aceves's home without first engaging in negotiations with her to reinstate and modify the loan on mutually agreeable terms."); *cf.* Vigoda v. Denver Urban Renewal Auth., 646 P.2d 900, 905 (Colo. 1982) (ruling that the plaintiff's allegation that she incurred losses in reasonable reliance on the defendant's promise to negotiate in good faith was sufficient to state a claim for relief). Wells Fargo's decision to foreclose without warning was unseemly conduct at best. In the opinion of this Court, such conduct presents "an identifiable occasion for applying the principle of promissory estoppel." *Greenstein*, 19 Mass. App. Ct. at 356-57, 474 N.E.2d 1130.

As the cases reveal, where, like here, the promisor opportunistically has strung along the promisee, the imposition of liability despite the preliminary stage of the negotiations produces the most equitable result. This balancing of the harms "is explicitly made an element of recovery under the doctrine of promissory estoppel by the last words of [section 90 of the Restatement], which make the promise binding only if injustice can be avoided by its enforcement." Metzger & Phillips, *supra* at 849. Binding the promisor to a promise made to take advantage of the promisee is also the most efficient result. *Cf.* Richard Craswell, *Offer, Acceptance, and Efficient Reliance,* 48 Stan. L. Rev. 481, 538 (1996). In cases of opportunism, "[the] willingness to impose a liability rule can be justified as efficient since such intervention may be the most cost-effective means of controlling opportunistic behavior, which both parties would seek to control ex ante as a means of maximizing joint gains. Because private control arrangements may be costly, the law-supplied rule may be the most effective means of controlling opportunism and maximizing joint gain." Juliet P. Kostritsky, *The Rise and Fall of Promissory Estoppel or Is Promissory Estoppel Really as Unsuccessful as Scholars Say It Is: A New Look at the Data,* 37 Wake Forest L. Rev. 531, 574 (2002). [Citations omitted.]

There remains the concern that, by imposing precontractual liability for specific promises made to induce reliance during preliminary negotiations, courts will restrict parties' freedom to negotiate by reading in a duty to bargain in good faith not recognized at common law. While this concern does not fall on deaf ears, it can be effectively minimized by limiting the promisee's recovery to his or her reliance expenditures. [Citations omitted.]

Moreover, because the promisee's reliance must be not only reasonable and foreseeable but also detrimental, such that injustice would result if the promise were not binding, "the doctrine renders the motive of the promisor a secondary consideration in deciding whether to award relief." Metzger & Phillips, *supra* at 888. Although some sense that the promisor has acted to take unfair advantage of the promisee is typically what prompts courts to enforce promises made during preliminary negotiations, the foreseeability and injustice requirements of section 90 render inquiry into whether the promisor acted in bad faith unnecessary, which, in turn, obviates any need to impose a precontractual duty to negotiate in good faith. . . . [1]

---

1. While the law does not recognize a duty to negotiate in good faith, at least one scholar has argued that, where the parties to an agreement take it upon themselves to negotiate a modification of that agreement, "they are bound by a duty of fair dealing imposed by their existing agreement and do not enjoy the freedom of the regime of negotiation." Farnsworth, *supra* at 244; *see also* Restatement (Second) of Contracts §205, comment (c). *But see* Burton & Andersen, *supra* §8.5.4, at 384 (stating that most courts have "decline[d] to impose obligations concerning revision or renewal merely because the parties already have a contract between them"). Furthermore, Massachusetts law imposes on mortgage holders seeking to foreclose an obligation to "act in good faith and . . . use reasonable diligence to protect the interests of the mortgagor." U.S. Bank Nat'l Ass'n v. Ibanez, 458 Mass. 637, 647 n.16, 941 N.

Finally, contrary to the conventional wisdom that precontractual liability unduly restricts the freedom to negotiate, a default rule allowing recovery but limiting it to reliance expenditures may in fact promote more efficient bargaining. [Citations omitted.] It is only under the current regime of either no liability or strict liability that negotiating parties are discouraged from making early and "exploratory investments that are a necessary precondition to the later writing of efficient final contracts." *Id.* at 690. . . . In contrast, a scheme of reliance-only precontractual liability makes negotiations more desirable by inducing optimal-level commitment from each party. [Citation omitted.] Certainly, enforcement of specific promises made to induce reliance during preliminary negotiations "might sometimes work an injustice on promisors." Metzger & Phillips, *supra* at 851; *see* Katz, *supra* at 1273. But reliance-based recovery in such instances offers the most equitable and efficient result without "distort[ing] the incentives to enter negotiations" in the first place. [Citation omitted.]

This Court, therefore, holds that the complaint states a claim for promissory estoppel: Wells Fargo promised to engage in negotiating a loan modification if the Dixons defaulted on their payments and provided certain financial information, and they did so in reasonable reliance on that promise, only to learn that the bank had taken advantage of their default status by initiating foreclosure proceedings. Assuming they can prove these allegations by a preponderance of the evidence, their damages appropriately will be confined to the value of their expenditures in reliance on Wells Fargo's promise.

Without question, this is an uncertain result. But the "type of life-situation" out of which the Dixons' case arises—a devastating and nationwide foreclosure crisis that is crippling entire communities—cannot be ignored. Karl N. Llewellyn, Jurisprudence Realism in Theory and Practice 219-20 (1962). Distressed homeowners are turning to the courts in droves, hoping for relief for what they perceive as misconduct by their mortgage lenders. Many of these cases are factually similar, if not identical to, the Dixons' case. Yet, with the notable exception of three Massachusetts federal district court cases, virtually no other court has upheld a claim for promissory estoppel premised on such facts.

To the extent that today's result is an anomaly, this Court has sought to explain its decision "openly and with respect for precedent, not by sleight of hand." David L. Shapiro, *Mr. Justice Rehnquist: A Preliminary View*, 90 Harv. L.

E.2d 40 (2011) (quoting Williams v. Resolution GGF OY, 417 Mass. 377, 382-83, 630 N.E.2d 581 (1994)).

The Dixons have not alleged that a duty of good faith governed their negotiations with Wells Fargo over a loan modification, and thus this Court need not address the issue. The fact that the parties already were bound to the special contractual relationship of mortgagor-mortgagee, however, lends support to today's conclusion that Wells Fargo's conduct, at a minimum, was "shabby and doubtless would not be followed by conscientious mortgagees." *Williams*, 417 Mass. at 385, 630 N.E.2d 581.

Rev. 293, 355 (1976). [Citation omitted.] It is the view of this Court that "[f]oreclosure is a powerful act with significant consequences," *Ibanez*, 458 Mass. at 655, 941 N.E.2d 40 (Cordy, J., concurring), and where a bank has obtained the opportunity to foreclose by representing an intention to do the exact opposite — i.e., to negotiate a loan modification that would give the homeowner the right to stay in his or her home — the doctrine of promissory estoppel is properly invoked under Massachusetts law to provide at least reliance-based recovery.

[The court also held that federal law did not preempt the promissory estoppel claim.]

Accordingly, this case is ordered placed on the September running trial list, and the parties shall be ready for trial on Tuesday, September 6, 2011.

SO ORDERED.

VII.   THE NEED FOR CONSIDERATION

What function does the doctrine of consideration serve? If a bill were introduced in the state legislature that stated: "Promises, seriously meant, shall be enforceable even if no consideration is given for them," would you, as a legislator, vote in favor?

In a series of cases decided in England around the time of the American Revolution, Lord Mansfield, often called the "father of commercial law," tried to eliminate the requirement of consideration. In Pillans v. Van Mierop, 3 Burr. 1663, 97 Eng. Rep. 1035 (K.B. 1765), Lord Mansfield declared, "In commercial cases amongst merchants, the want of consideration is not an objection." This iconoclastic idea, however, did not prevail. In the next decade, the case of Rann v. Hughes, 7 T.R. 350n, 101 Eng. Rep. 1014n (1778), reinstated consideration as a viable issue in contract disputes.

In the 1930s, the Commissioners of Uniform State Laws proposed the following simple statute, which only Pennsylvania adopted. What is its effect?

Uniform Written Obligations Act

Section 1. A written release or promise hereafter made and signed by the person releasing or promising shall not be invalid or unenforceable for lack of consideration, if the writing also contains an additional express statement, in any form of language, that the signer intends to be legally bound.

Two final things: The United Nations Convention on Contracts for the International Sale of Goods says not a word about the need for consideration, and the Uniform Commercial Code (UCC) does not make much of the doctrine. You should review the inroads that the UCC has made on the necessity for consideration. Read UCC §§1-107, 2-205, and 2-209(1).

CHAPTER 2 ASSESSMENT

Multiple Choice Questions

1. Wonder Mouse Theme Park was opening a new version of its park on Berker Island, and had announced its grand opening for the first of November of the following year. Berker Island was connected to the mainland by a bridge and the state signed a contract to have a new bridge built from the mainland to the island, replacing the old bridge. The state promised to pay the contractor $4 million if the bridge would be completed by September of the coming year, and a clause to this effect was in the contract. However, the contractor proved to be slower than expected, and Wonder Mouse's executives became worried that the bridge would not be finished in time for the grand opening. Wonder Mouse then signed a contract promising the contractor an extra $1 million if the bridge was complete by the original September date. Spurred on by the money, the contractor sped up its efforts and did the work as agreed with the state on time. When Wonder Mouse refused to pay the extra $1 million, the contractor sued it. How should this come out?
   a. Wonder Mouse should win. The contractor only performed the work it was already bound to perform under the preexisting duty it had to the state to finish the job by September 1st, so it has given no consideration to Wonder Mouse that it wasn't already entitled to receive as a beneficiary of the contract between the state and the contractor.
   b. Wonder Mouse should lose. It has a stake in the completion of the contract on time and paid to make sure that would happen, and the assurance it received from the contractor's promise to avoid breaching the contract with the state is sufficient consideration to support the second contract.
   c. Wonder Mouse should win. The last argument is wrong because the contractor had no right to breach the contract with the state, so there is no new consideration given by the contractor to Wonder Mouse other than a duty to complete a contract to which it was already bound.
   d. Wonder Mouse should lose. The contractor had the ability to go to the state, explain why the project was behind schedule, and negotiate a later completion date. The contract with Wonder Mouse is valid because the contractor forbore its right to propose such a modification to the state, and that forbearance is sufficient consideration for the contract signed with Wonder Mouse.

2. Carrie and Mark have decided to live together but never marry (they think that marriage is a bad institution). They do plan to have children. They have signed a contract stating: "In return for love, affection, mutual respect, and a promise to care for each other and their children, the parties will live together, do the chores of the household, have hot sex regularly, share equally any monies earned by either of them from outside employment, and in the event of parting divide up their property by giving half to each party." You are their best friend, a lawyer. They ask you if this contract is enforceable.

   a. Yes it is, though it's probably a good idea to remove the reference to "hot sex," which isn't enforceable in a court of law ("meretricious" consideration is invalid). There's enough there to indicate the parties intend to be bound and are exchanging valid promises to share and even deciding how to divorce themselves from this agreement if things don't work out.

   b. No. It's all too vague and unrealistic. Either make it a lot more specific, including how to deal with the children in the event of a breakup, or, better yet, get married and have the benefit of laws that will protect them both.

   c. Maybe, but a lawyer could do a much better job of writing it and it would be worth the money for a lawyer to do so.

   d. No. There is not sufficient consideration for these so-called promises, since nothing is specific enough. How do you divide a house, should they purchase one? Who will care for the children if they break up? Is there even an intent to contract here?

3. Arnold Pound was the head coach at Football College, and his teams had won three national championships. When he was touring the country recruiting potential players for future teams at FC, he was very impressed by Milo Stells, a high school quarterback with much talent. Milo very much wanted to attend FC and said he'd do anything for the chance to make the team. Coach Pound told him that he wasn't quite ready, but if he attended Quarterback Summer Camp in the coming summer, he would give Arnold a chance to make the team if he did well there. The coach mentioned that he was a part owner of the camp and could vouch for the value of its training program because he'd helped create it. The camp cost Arnold and his parents $5,000, but he did attend and graduated at the top of the summer class. But when he called Coach Pound with the news, the coach told him that "my quarterbacks are all picked for this year, but I will give you a good recommendation for any school where you want to apply." Instead Milo hired a lawyer and sued Coach Pound and FC for breach of contract. Who wins?

   a. The coach and the college win. There are two problems: The coach's "promise" is too vague, and Milo gave them back nothing in return.

Instead he got valuable training for his money and now can pursue his dream elsewhere with the coach's help.

b. Milo wins. There is sufficient consideration in the money the coach got as part owner of the camp.

c. Milo wins. Promissory estoppel applies here. The coach made him a promise on which he foreseeably relied to his detriment, and injustice can be avoided only by enforcing the promise to give him a chance to be on the college's team.

d. It's a toss-up. A court might say that a promise to "give him a chance" is too vague for any reliance on it to be reasonable, so that promissory estoppel won't work, but the equities lean toward Milo, particularly where the coach profited by Milo's payment to the camp the coach created. The court will be hard pressed to come up with a remedy should it decide there is an enforceable contract here, but that's a matter for the chapter on remedies, coming up next.

4. Patrick had an eccentric aunt named Mame, but he liked her and always agreed with whatever she wanted. Mame had a lot of money and when Patrick was choosing his career in college she offered to give him $10,000 a year for five years after he graduated if he would not become a teacher. Mame had hated all her teachers when she was a schoolgirl, and she didn't want her favorite relative to become a teacher. Patrick told her that he too wasn't fond of teachers and had no intention of ever becoming one. "I want you to have the money anyway," she replied, "so just sign the agreement and that will make it all legal." "I hate to pretend to give you something that isn't there," he said. She asked, "Would you take it if were a gift?" He shrugged and said, "Sure." "Then let's do it my way," she said and pointed to the written contract. He shrugged again and signed it. After college he became a paralegal, but the money stopped two years later when Patrick married a teacher. He asked Mame why, and she replied that she didn't like his wife's occupation and she wasn't going to pay any more. He promptly sued Mame for breach of contract. How should this come out?

a. He should win. He has not violated his promise. While Patrick's wife is a teacher, he is not.

b. Mame should win. Bilateral contracts must have valid promises on each side, and here both parties knew that Patrick's promise was a mere pretense of an obligation to match her promise to pay the money. But a fake promise is not sufficient consideration, so there was no exchange and hence no contractual obligation. A promise to make a gift is not legally enforceable.

c. Patrick should win. While he didn't believe he would ever want to be a teacher, Mame wanted to foreclose even that remote possibility, which was important to her. She is allowed to bargain for a will-o-the-wisp if she truly desires it, as happened here. Thus, his promise, dearly wanted by her, was given and foreclosed any consideration of a teaching career. That's a valid exchange, deliberately negotiated, even if he only went along with it with the pretense that it would be thought of as a gift in his mind. He has not violated the contract, so she should keep making the payments.

   d. Mame should win. She told Patrick she didn't want a teacher in the family, and then he married one, which violates the clear intent of their agreement.

   e. Patrick should win. He relied on her promise in planning his financial life, and particularly by entering into his recent marriage, and his detrimental reliance on her promise was foreseeable, so promissory estoppel keeps her from stopping the payments she had promised.

5. Damon and Pythius were close friends who went into business together and did very well. Damon, however, had a lavish lifestyle and frequently went into debt. In these situations, Pythius would always lend him money, but the parties would sign a promissory note that included interest, thus making the nature of the transactions clear. When kidnappers stole Damon's prize show dog, Syracuse, and demanded that $2,000 be immediately wired to an offshore account, Damon, frantic, phoned Pythius and told him all this, adding, "I'm broke, but please, as my best friend, help me save my dog!" Pythius immediately sent off the money, but the thieves killed Syracuse anyway, and the money was not recovered. When five days later Pythius asked Damon for repayment, using the usual interest rate, Damon, distraught over the loss of his pet, nodded, but later repudiated the promise. When Pythius sued, Damon's lawyer said there was no consideration for Damon's promise since Pythius had made the loan days before and nothing was later exchanged for Damon promising repayment when he finally made it. Who wins?

   a. Pythius should win. He relied on Damon's implied promise to repay the money when he sent off the money to the thieves, so promissory estoppel is the theory that allows him to prevail. Justice can only be avoided by making Damon pay for the foreseeable reliance Pythius incurred after Damon's implied promise was made.

   b. Damon should win. Sure, the equities are with Pythius, but if someone makes a gift that person cannot later repent and now claim it was a contract. When true loans had been made between the two in the past, contracts were properly signed. No such actions occurred here, and from Damon's point of view his friend was being generous in a time of great need. That's admirable, but it doesn't lead to legal liability on Damon's part.

   c. Damon should win. When he made his promise to pay Pythius there was nothing exchanged for it. Yes, Pythius had parted with money sent to someone else to help Damon out, but that happened days before any promise occurred. Either Pythius's payment to the thieves was done gratuitously, or, even if not, it was *past consideration*, which is not sufficient consideration for a later promise to repay the amount.

d. Pythius should win. At no point did the parties discuss repayment because there was no time for formalities. Nonetheless, this was otherwise a familiar situation: a loan to help out a distressed friend, with the implied understanding that the details would be settled later, as they were when Damon finally made his promise of repayment. The exchange going on at that moment was the settlement of an unsettled debt, one that that still due and floating around in the minds of both parties. That settlement is a valid current exchange (an agreement on how much was due) and not merely past consideration of a gratuitous act exchanged for a later gift promise of repayment.

Answers

1. D is the best answer. Since parties to a contract are always free by mutual agreement to alter its terms, the contractor has given consideration to Wonder Mouse by not proposing such a modification to the state in the contract it had with the state. Wonder Mouse benefitted greatly by this forbearance and by the subsequent completion of the bridge on time.

2. C is the best answer. Something as important as a contract for a relationship should be very specific as to things that matter, and vague generalities will only lead to a lawsuit. This couple needs to convince the courts that their "contract" involves a real exchange of substantive promises. They wouldn't perform major medical procedures on each other, so they shouldn't do their own legal work on something as important as planning a future that the courts will help enforce and that either party can point to in the event of disputes. They're happy now, but a long-term relationship will inevitably have stormy periods.

3. D is the best answer. Promissory estoppel cases are frequently messy, involving, as here, statements that are vague and "reliance" where the wisdom of counting on the promise being fulfilled is doubtful. Leaving aside the remedy problem, Milo should argue the chance to be a quarterback at the college was clearly made as a promise by the coach, and the coach made it to induce the very reliance that occurred, thus requiring justice to step in and give some sort of relief. If it could be shown that the coach never intended to give Milo serious consideration (say a witness will testify the coach laughed about Milo's abilities and bragged he'd talked the kid into parting with $5,000), then there might be a remedy in fraud (which includes punitive damages), an issue to be considered in Chapter 6.

4. C is the best answer. This is similar to Problem 40 in which Portia Moot persuaded a Native American tribe to sign a contract giving up property

rights the tribe didn't believe it had. Even if one party thinks the deal is unnecessary, if the other bargains for the promise there is a real exchange going on. Here Mame gets her wish that he won't become a teacher and he signs in order to give her the peace of mind that his promise brings. But he never promised not to marry a teacher, and if she wanted that to be part of the deal she should have put it into the contract. He has not breached the contract as written, and Mame owes him the money. Promissory estoppel to enforce a gift promise rarely succeeds, even for charities.

5. D is the best answer. Our law struggles to avoid one party being unjustly enriched at the expense of another (something to be discussed in detail in the next chapter). If the law didn't enforce Damon's promise of repayment, Pythius would have parted with his money rightly expecting to be repaid and Damon would have gotten the benefit of trying to save his dog from the thieves (fruitless though that endeavor proved to be). If the parties both understood there was an unsettled debt, then the promise and acceptance of the settlement amount is a current exchange, and a valid contract is formed at that moment. This is similar to Problem 46 in which the garage owner helped the football coach with a car emergency, and it comes out the same way.

CHAPTER
3
REMEDIES

When a contract is breached, the injured party has the burden of proving that a particular remedy is appropriate. This involves both the rules of evidence (which we largely leave for your Evidence class) and contract law (which is the primary focus of this chapter). In particular, the plaintiff must convince the court that the relief requested is proper. In some situations, the plaintiff doesn't want money damages, but instead will ask the court to order the other side to perform the contract or, at the very least, issue an order forbidding the defendant from taking actions that would harm the plaintiff further. We will get to those extraordinary requests (and some others) later in this chapter. We begin with the interesting question of how monetary damages are assessed.

I. DAMAGES

A. Introduction

A little civil procedure. At the end of the complaint, the plaintiff must specify the relief requested. This part of the complaint is called, fittingly enough, the "prayer." In an action founded on a contract, the prayer may request extraordinary relief, such as an injunction (a court order forbidding certain conduct) or specific performance (a court decree commanding the other party to perform the contract as agreed), or simply a declaratory judgment (a ruling interpreting the contract or clarifying the parties' rights). Typically, however, the complaint will ask for money damages because such extraordinary relief is generally not available, for reasons we will explore later. In a tort suit, the injured party usually asks for enough damages to return to the pre-injury position, the status quo prior to the commission of

the tort. In contracts cases the goal is different. Section 1-305(a) of the
Uniform Commercial Code of Article 1 puts it this way:

> (1) The remedies provided by this Act shall be liberally administered to
> the end that the aggrieved party may be put in as good a position as if the other
> party had fully performed.

Thus, contract law gives the injured person the benefit of the broken
bargain. A famous law review article, Fuller and Perdue, The Reliance Interest
in Contract Damages, 46 Yale L. Rev. 52, 53-54 (1936-1937), elaborates:

> It is convenient to distinguish three principal purposes which may be
> pursued in awarding contract damages. These purposes, and the situations
> in which they become appropriate, may be stated briefly as follows:
>
> *First*, the plaintiff has in reliance on the promise of the defendant con-
> ferred some value on the defendant. The defendant fails to perform his
> promise. The court may force the defendant to disgorge the value he received
> from the plaintiff. The object here may be termed the prevention of gain by
> the defaulting promisor at the expense of the promisee; more briefly, the
> prevention of unjust enrichment. The interest protected may be called the
> *restitution interest.* For our present purposes it is quite immaterial how the suit
> in such a case be classified, whether as contractual or quasi-contractual,
> whether as a suit to enforce the contract or as a suit based upon a rescission
> of the contract. These questions relate to the superstructure of the law, not to
> the basic policies with which we are concerned.
>
> *Secondly*, the plaintiff has in reliance on the promise of the defendant
> changed his position. For example, the buyer under a contract for the sale
> of land has incurred expense in the investigation of the seller's title, or has
> neglected the opportunity to enter other contracts. We may award damages to
> the plaintiff for the purpose of undoing the harm which his reliance of the
> defendant's promise has caused him. Our object is to put him in as good a
> position as he was in before the promise was made. The interest protected in
> this case may be called the *reliance interest.*
>
> *Thirdly*, without insisting on reliance by the promisee or enrichment of
> the promisor, we may seek to give the promisee the value of the expectancy
> which the promise created. We may in suit for specific performance actually
> compel the defendant to render the promised performance to the plaintiff, or,
> in suit for damages, we may make the defendant pay the money value of this
> performance. Here our object is to put the plaintiff in as good a position as he
> would have occupied had the defendant performed his promise. The interest
> protected in this case we may call the *expectation interest.*

You should also see that these remedial possibilities fit inside each other
like Russian nesting dolls. If the expectation interest is to land the plaintiff in
the position performance would have achieved, it will typically recompense
both the restitution and reliance elements, while reliance damages are often

treated as including restitution of the consideration given to the other side as an obvious "reliance" expenditure to be recovered.

The expectation interest therefore is the general goal of an award of damages in a contracts case. The Restatement (Second) of Contracts provides:

§347. Measure of Damages in General

Subject to the limitations stated in §§350-353, the injured party has a right to damages based on his <u>expectation interest</u> as measured by

(a) the loss in the value to him of the other party's performance caused by its failure or deficiency, plus

(b) any other loss, including incidental or consequential loss, caused by the breach, less

(c) any cost or other loss that he has avoided by not having to perform.

Consequential damages are one step removed from the core lost value to the nonbreaching party, but nevertheless were caused by the breach. Without the breach they never would have occurred. Suppose a breach of a warranty in the sale of an automobile causes personal injury and the buyer ends up in the hospital. The core lost value to the buyer is the difference between the value of the car he or she received and a car that had no defects. Awarding her this difference in value protects her expectancy. In addition, the buyer's medical costs would be consequential damages. These damages must be tacked on to the expectancy to put the buyer in the position he or she would have occupied but for the breach. Thus, the buyer should be awarded both expectancy damages (the value of a car that had no defects) and consequential damages (hospital bills, pain and suffering, lost wages, etc.).

Even with the expectancy goal in mind, courts often struggle in arriving at a dollar figure that meets the typical expectations of the plaintiff and does not go beyond or below that figure. The next subsection considers the issues involved in calculating an expectation measure of money damages, after which we will return to the issue of consequential damages.

B. Measuring Expectation Damages

We begin with one of the most famous cases in all of law.

HAWKINS v. McGEE
Supreme Court of New Hampshire, 1929
84 N.H. 114, 146 A. 641

Assumpsit against a surgeon for breach of an alleged warranty of the success of an operation. Trial by jury. <u>Verdict for the plaintiff.</u> The writ also

Breach of Alleged Warranty

contained a count in negligence upon which a nonsuit was ordered, without exception.

Defendant's motions for a nonsuit and for a directed verdict on the count in assumpsit were denied, and the defendant excepted. During the argument of plaintiff's counsel to the jury, the defendant claimed certain exceptions, and also excepted to the denial of his requests for instructions and to the charge of the court upon the question of damages, as more fully appears in the opinion. The defendant seasonably moved to set aside the verdict upon the grounds that it was (1) contrary to the evidence; (2) against the weight of the evidence; (3) against the weight of the law and evidence; and (4) because the damages awarded by the jury were excessive. The court denied the motion upon the first three grounds, but found that the damages were excessive, and made an order that the verdict be set aside, unless the plaintiff elected to remit all in excess of $500. The plaintiff having refused to remit, the verdict was set aside "as excessive and against the weight of the evidence," and the plaintiff excepted. . . .

BRANCH, J.

1. The operation in question consisted in the removal of a considerable quantity of scar tissue from the palm of the plaintiff's right hand and the grafting of skin taken from the plaintiff's chest in place thereof. The scar tissue was the result of a severe burn caused by contact with an electric wire, which the plaintiff received about nine years before the time of the transactions here involved. There was evidence to the effect that before the operation was performed the plaintiff and his father went to the defendant's office, and that the defendant, in answer to the question, "How long will the boy be in the hospital?" replied, "Three or four days, not over four; then the boy can go home and it will be just a few days when he will go back to work with a good hand." Clearly this and other testimony to the same effect would not justify a finding that the doctor contracted to complete the hospital treatment in three or four days or that the plaintiff would be able to go back to work within a few days thereafter. The above statements could only be construed as expressions of opinion or predictions as to the probable duration of the treatment and plaintiff's resulting disability, and the fact that these estimates were exceeded would impose no contractual liability upon the defendant. The only substantial basis for the plaintiff's claim is the testimony that the defendant also said before the operation was decided upon, "I will guarantee to make the hand a hundred percent perfect hand or a hundred percent good hand." The plaintiff was present when these words were alleged to have been spoken, and, if they are to be taken at their face value, it seems obvious that proof of their utterance would establish the giving of a warranty in accordance with his contention.

The defendant argues, however, that, even if these words were uttered by him, no reasonable man would understand that they were used with the intention of entering "into any contractual relation whatever," and that they could reasonably be understood only "as his expression in strong language that he believed and expected that as a result of the operation he would give the plaintiff a very good hand." It may be conceded, as the defendant contends, that, before the question of the making of a contract should be submitted to a jury, there is a preliminary question of law for the trial court to pass upon, i.e. "whether the words could possibly have the meaning imputed to them by the party who founds his case upon a certain interpretation," but it cannot be held that the trial court decided this question erroneously in the present case. It is unnecessary to determine at this time whether the argument of the defendant, based upon "common knowledge of the uncertainty which attends all surgical operations," and the improbability that a surgeon would ever contract to make a damaged part of the human body "one hundred percent perfect," would, in the absence of countervailing considerations, be regarded as conclusive, for there were other factors in the present case which tended to support the contention of the plaintiff. There was evidence that the defendant repeatedly solicited from the plaintiff's father the opportunity to perform this operation, and the theory was advanced by plaintiff's counsel in cross-examination of defendant that he sought an opportunity to "experiment on skin grafting," in which he had had little previous experience. If the jury accepted this part of plaintiff's contention, there would be a reasonable basis for the further conclusion that if defendant spoke the words attributed to him, he did so with the intention that they should be accepted at their face value, as an inducement for the granting of consent to the operation by the plaintiff and his father, and there was ample evidence that they were so accepted by them. The question of the making of the alleged contract was properly submitted to the jury.

2. The substance of the charge to the jury on the question of damages appears in the following quotation: "If you find the plaintiff entitled to anything, he is entitled to recover for what pain and suffering he has been made to endure and for what injury he has sustained over and above what injury he had before." To this instruction the defendant seasonably excepted. By it, the jury was permitted to consider two elements of damage: (1) Pain and suffering due to the operation; and (2) positive ill effects of the operation upon the plaintiff's hand. Authority for any specific rule of damages in cases of this kind seems to be lacking, but, when tested by general principle and by analogy, it appears that the foregoing instruction was erroneous.

"By 'damages,' as that term is used in the law of contracts, is intended compensation for a breach, measured in the terms of the contract." Davis v. New England Cotton Yarn Co., 77 N.H. 403, 404, 92 A. 732, 733. The purpose of the law is "to put the plaintiff in as good a position as he would have been in had the defendant kept his contract." 3 Williston Cont. §1338;

Hardie-Tynes Mfg. Co. v. Easton Cotton Oil Co., 150 N.C. 150, 63 S.E. 676, 134 Am. St. Rep. 899. The measure of recovery "is based upon what the defendant should have given the plaintiff, not what the plaintiff has given the defendant or otherwise expended." 3 Williston Cont. §1341. "The only losses that can be said fairly to come within the terms of a contract are such as the parties must have had in mind when the contract was made, or such as they either knew or ought to have known would probably result from a failure to comply with its terms." Davis v. New England Cotton Yarn Co., 77 N.H. 403, 404, 92 A. 732, 733, Hurd v. Dunsmore, 63 N.H. 171.

The present case is closely analogous to one in which a machine is built for a certain purpose and warranted to do certain work. In such cases, the usual rule of damages for breach of warranty in the sale of chattels is applied, and it is held that the measure of damages is the difference between the value of the machine, if it had corresponded with the warranty and its actual value, together with such incidental losses as the parties knew, or ought to have known, would probably result from a failure to comply with its terms. . . .

The rule thus applied is well settled in this state. "As a general rule, the measure of the vendee's damages is the difference between the value of the goods as they would have been if the warranty as to quality had been true, and the actual value at the time of the sale, including gains prevented and losses sustained, and such other damages as could be reasonably anticipated by the parties as likely to be caused by the vendor's failure to keep his agreement, and could not by reasonable care on the part of the vendee have been avoided." Union Bank v. Blanchard, 65 N.H. 21, 23, 18 A. 90, 91; Hurd v. Dunsmore, supra; Noyes v. Blodgett, 58 N.H. 502; P.L. ch. 166, §69, subd. 7. We therefore conclude that the true measure of the plaintiff's damage in the present case is the difference between the value to him of a perfect hand or a good hand, such as the jury found the defendant promised him, and the value of his hand in its present condition, including any incidental consequences fairly within the contemplation of the parties when they made their contract. 1 Sutherland, Damages (4th ed.) §92. Damages not thus limited, although naturally resulting, are not to be given.

The extent of the plaintiff's suffering does not measure this difference in value. The pain necessarily incident to a serious surgical operation was a part of the contribution which the plaintiff was willing to make to his joint undertaking with the defendant to produce a good hand. It was a legal detriment suffered by him which constituted a part of the consideration given by him for the contract. It represented a part of the price which he was willing to pay for a good hand, but it furnished no test of the value of a good hand or the difference between the value of the hand which the defendant promised and the one which resulted from the operation.

It was also erroneous and misleading to submit to the jury as a separate element of damage any change for the worse in the condition of the plaintiff's hand resulting from the operation, although this error was probably more prejudicial to the plaintiff than to the defendant. Any such ill effect of the operation would be included under the true rule of damages set forth above, but damages might properly be assessed for the defendant's failure to improve the condition of the hand, even if there were no evidence that its condition was made worse as a result of the operation. . . .

New trial.

QUESTIONS AND NOTES

1. What exactly did the trial court judge do wrong here? How should the plaintiff's damages have been measured?

2. If the goal of contract law is to put the injured person in the same position that performance would have done (thus giving the "expectancy"), consider which of the following items should be relevant on retrial, and how each is to be classified (restitution, reliance, consequential damages):

(a) The cost of the operation
(b) The pain plaintiff suffered in the original operation
(c) The pain plaintiff suffered that would not have been suffered if the hand had been as promised
(d) The embarrassment plaintiff suffered as a result of the operation
(e) The difference between a hand with hair and scars and a hand without these defects
(f) The difference between plaintiff's hand before and after the operation

What would be Hawkins's *restitution* element in this fact pattern? Which of all these possible recoveries would be most important to the plaintiff in the actual case?

3. Tort damages strive to return the plaintiff to the pre-tort position, but a contractual recovery goes much further — putting the plaintiff in the position that would have resulted from full performance. Why is this right? Wouldn't a return to the precontract position be a better goal (it would certainly be simpler to calculate)?

4. This famous decision is often referred to as the "hairy hand" case because Dr. McGee grafted skin from Hawkins's chest onto his hand, and, since it came from his chest, it grew hair, causing him extreme embarrassment. For an account of what actually happened after the decision in this case, see the investigative follow-up done by students in the Harvard Law Record, Vol. 66, March 17, 1978. It reveals that the original jury verdict was for $3,000 and that the case was finally settled for $1,400 and attorney's fees.

SANTORINI CAB CORP. v. BANCO POPULAR NORTH AMERICA

Appellate Court of Illinois, 2013
999 N.E.2d 46

Justice LAMPKIN delivered the judgment of the court, with opinion.

OPINION

¶1 Plaintiff Santorini Cab Corp. (Santorini) sued defendant Banco Popular North America (Banco) for breach of contract concerning the sale of two taxicab medallions.* Following a bench trial, the trial court found that Banco had breached the contracts and awarded Santorini $37,550 in damages.

¶2 Santorini appeals, contending the trial court made erroneous partial summary judgment rulings in Banco's favor prior to the bench trial. Specifically, Santorini argues the trial court erred by . . . failing to calculate Santorini's damages by using the market price of the medallions at the time the case went to trial. For the reasons that follow, we affirm the judgment of the [trial] court.

¶3 I. BACKGROUND

¶4 Santorini and Banco entered into two contracts for the sale of taxicab medallions. The May 2006 contract was for the sale of medallion number 2408 from Banco to Santorini for $48,000. The July 2006 contract was for the sale of medallion number 2361 from Banco to Santorini for $48,000. Both contracts contained substantially the same terms, including paragraph 6, which provided that if the parties were unable to obtain final approval from the department of consumer services of the City of Chicago (DCS) for the transfer of the medallions within 90 days of the date of the parties' contract, or if during the 90-day period the DCS indicated that it would not approve Santorini as a qualified purchaser of the medallions, then in either event, Banco's sole liability would be to refund Santorini's deposit, and upon such refund, neither party would have any further rights, obligations, or claims against the other, and the contract would be deemed void and of no further force or effect. The contracts also contained provisions that any notice or other communication was to be delivered by hand, sent by

---

* [A taxicab medallion is a permit from a city issued to the operator of a cab authorizing the picking up of passengers. — EDS.]

overnight courier or mailed by registered or certified mail. Both contracts also contained clauses stating that time was of the essence.

¶5 Plaintiff paid the required earnest money under each contract and at all relevant times was financially and otherwise able to purchase the two medallions.

¶6 After the 90-day period had expired under each of the contracts, the parties still continued to work together to close the sale. The last written communication between the parties was a letter from Banco's counsel to Santorini's counsel, dated December 15, 2006, which stated that an issue arose concerning whether Banco's borrower had received the requisite notice in the underlying foreclosure proceedings on the medallions. Until that issue was resolved, Banco was not in a position to move forward with the sale to Santorini. Furthermore, although the DCS had received the documents concerning the medallion transfer, the DCS had not given its final approval to allow the transfer. Accordingly, Banco's counsel stated:

> No further steps should be taken to consummate the transaction until the issue of the borrower's notice has been resolved. I will continue to work on this matter and try and bring it to an amicable resolution. Until that time, the transaction is being stayed.

However, at the December 2011 bench trial in this case, Banco's counsel testified that he had telephone calls with Santorini's counsel in January and February 2007 and told him that the deals concerning both contracts were "dead."

¶7 In September 2007, Santorini filed this breach of contract lawsuit against Banco. Santorini alleged that its damages included the appreciation in the value of the medallions and the lost profits it would have derived from ownership of the medallions. . . .

¶9 In September 2009, Banco attempted to return to Santorini the earnest money Banco had been holding in escrow, but Santorini did not cash the check due to the pending litigation. . . .

¶11 Banco . . . moved for partial summary judgment on the issue of the damage calculation. Specifically, Banco argued that damages should be based on the difference between the contract price of the medallions and the value of the medallions at the time of the breach of contract. In response, Santorini argued that damages should be based on the difference between the contract price of the medallions and the value of the medallions at the time of trial. In January 2011, the trial court granted Banco's motion and held that "damages for breach of contract will be determined as the difference of the contract at the time of breach and the time of contract; no damages based on the price of medallions at trial are allowed." . . .

¶13 After a bench trial, the trial court found that Banco had breached the two contracts because it failed to either transfer the medallions or cancel the contracts in writing. The court also found that Banco waived all the provisions of paragraph 6, including the limitation of liability clause, by continuing to work with Santorini to close the sales after the relevant 90-day time periods had lapsed. The trial court also ruled that the proper measure of damages was the difference between the market price at the time Santorini learned of the breach and the contract price, plus any consequential damages less expenses saved as a result of the breach. Although Santorini could have been entitled to lost profits under this measurement, the trial court had previously barred Santorini from seeking those profits as a result of Santorini's repeated failure to comply with discovery requests and the court's orders on the issue of lost profits. The trial court found that Santorini knew of the breach of contract by February 2007. According to the evidence, there were 6,999 medallions in the City of Chicago, and over 2,550 medallions were bought and sold during the 3 1/2-year time period from December 4, 2006, through June 15, 2010. In addition, Santorini's medallion broker had testified that medallions had always been available for buying in the years 2006, 2007, 2008 and 2009. The trial court determined that the average sale price of taxi medallions in Chicago during February 2007 was $66,775. The difference between $66,775 and the $48,000 contract price was $18,775. Accordingly, for the two contracts, Santorini's total damages were $37,550.

¶14 Santorini timely appealed.

¶15 II. Analysis

¶16 On appeal, Santorini challenges the trial court's summary judgment rulings concerning the . . . measurement of Santorini's damages. Summary judgment is appropriate when the pleadings, affidavits, depositions, and admissions on file, when viewed in a light most favorable to the non-movant, present no genuine issue as to any material fact and show that the moving party is entitled to a judgment as a matter of law. . . .

¶24 B. Damage Calculation

¶25 Santorini argues the trial court's damage calculation was erroneous as a matter of law. Santorini contends the trial court made an erroneous legal determination that damages should be measured as the difference between the contract price of medallions and the price of the medallions at the time Banco breached the contract, which was February 2007. Santorini complains that the trial court's award denied Santorini the full benefit of its bargain with Banco and deprived Santorini of the increased value of the medallions at the time of trial in December 2011. According to Santorini, when the trial court set February 2007 as the date to use for the damage calculation, the court failed to consider the fundamental purpose of contract damage awards and failed to place Santorini into the position it would have been in if Banco had not breached the contracts. We disagree.

¶26 The measure of damages for breach of contract is the amount that will compensate the aggrieved party for the loss "which either fulfillment of the contract would have prevented or which the breach of it has entailed." LeFevour v. Howorka, 224 Ill. App. 3d 428, 430-31, 166 Ill. Dec. 698, 586 N. E.2d 656 (1991). "The purpose of damages is to put the nonbreaching party into the position he or she would have been in had the contract been performed, but not in a better position." Walker v. Ridgeview Construction Co., 316 Ill. App. 3d 592, 596, 249 Ill. Dec. 746, 736 N.E.2d 1184 (2000). "In determining which measure of damages to use, the trial court must examine the exact interest harmed." Gvillo v. Stutz, 306 Ill. App. 3d 766, 770, 239 Ill. Dec. 840, 715 N.E.2d 285 (1999). "Compensation awarded in a breach of contract action should not provide plaintiff with a windfall." Walker, 316 Ill. App. 3d at 596, 249 Ill. Dec. 746, 736 N.E.2d 1184.

¶27 "It has long been the law in Illinois that the measure of damages in a breach of contract for the sale of personal property where the article is one obtainable in the market, is the difference between the contract price and the market price at the time of the breach." Quad County Distributing Co. v. Burroughs Corp., 68 Ill. App. 3d 163, 165, 24 Ill. Dec. 818, 385 N.E.2d 1108 (1979) (citing Loescher v. Deisterberg, 26 Ill. App. 520, 523 (1887)). When a breach has occurred, the buyer has the right to treat the contract as rescinded and to go into the market and purchase the article at its merchantable value, and then he has the right to recover the difference in the price which he was thus compelled to pay, with interest on the difference which he has paid. Slueter v. Wallbaum, 45 Ill. 43, 45-46 (1867).

¶28 ... Nevertheless, in order to recover, it is not essential that the buyer must purchase the article after the breach occurs, and, if he does not, then the true measure of damages is the difference between the contract and the market price at the time of the breach. Slueter, 45 Ill. at 46–47. ... This rule, however, is not applicable if the buyer cannot obtain the article purchased in the market and resort must be had to other elements of value. Loescher, 26 Ill. App. at 523. If the article cannot be obtained in the market or elsewhere, the measure of damages is the actual loss the buyer has sustained. ...

¶30 Santorini claims it is entitled to damages calculated as the difference between the medallions' contract price of $48,000 each and the increased market price of the medallions at the time of the December 2011 bench trial. ... [However], the trial court concluded, based on the telephone conversations between counsel for the parties, that the contract was breached in February 2007. In order to establish the price of medallions in February 2007, the trial court referred to the evidence concerning the City of Chicago's medallion transfer history for the month of February 2007, which recorded many medallion sales for that month. The trial court discarded three sales that were abnormally low and then averaged the remaining sales for an average market price of $66,775 per medallion. The difference between that average price and the $48,000 contract price was $18,775, which was multiplied by two for the two contracts for total damages of $37,550. We find no error in the trial court's measure of damages for this breach of contract involving the sale of personal property that was available for purchase in the market. . . .

¶36 III. Conclusion

¶37 For the foregoing reasons, the judgment of the [trial] court is affirmed.

QUESTIONS AND NOTES

1. What would Santorini Cab Corp.'s damages have been if it made reasonable efforts to find substitute medallions and ended up buying two medallions from a different seller in February 2007 for $60,000 each?

2. As the opinion mentions, the transaction was supposed to terminate if the department of consumer services of the City of Chicago did not approve of the sale within 90 days. This is an example of an *express condition*, an issue we will study in Chapter 7. As we will see, a party can *waive* its right to invoke an express condition, which is exactly what Banco did by continuing to treat the agreement as effective after the 90-day windows had closed.

3. Santorini Cab Corp. was upset with the trial court's damage award because the value of the taxi medallions had increased between the breach in February 2007 and the trial four years later. Today, the pendulum has swung in the opposite direction: because of ride-sharing services like Uber and Lyft, the value of medallions has plummeted. See, e.g., Winnie Hu, Taxi Medallions, Once a Safe Investment, Now Drag Owners into Debt, N.Y. Times, Sept. 10, 2017, at https://www.nytimes.com/2017/09/10/nyregion/new-york-taxi-medallions-uber.html.

─────

Problem 62

Roderick Murgatroyd had always thought his family house was worth little because it was so old, and therefore he was surprised when Rose Maybud offered to buy it from him for $280,000. He signed the contract with her immediately. As he finished signing, he asked her why she was willing to pay so much for the property, and she replied, "Because it's worth twice the amount you have just sold it for, and I plan to enjoy the profit I'll make when I resell." Astounded, Roderick tore up the contract and told her that he was not going to sell her the property. When she sues, what damages should she ask for, considering that she never paid him a cent (although the property is worth $560,000)? Does the fact that she has paid nothing and has in no way made any expenditures in reliance on this contract furnish him with a defense?

As we saw in *Santorini Cab Corp.*, expectation damages seek to put the plaintiff in the financial position he or she would have occupied if the defendant had fully performed. Sometimes, however, there is more than one plausible way to achieve this objective. Suppose a builder breaches a construction contract. How can we give the plaintiff the benefit of the defendant's performance? One way might be to compensate the plaintiff for the amount that his or her property declined in value because of the breach. But another equally logical approach would be to award the plaintiff the cost of remedying the defect. Our next, quite famous, case tackles this problem.

PEEVYHOUSE v. GARLAND COAL & MINING CO.
Supreme Court of Oklahoma, 1962
382 P.2d 109

JACKSON, J. In the trial court, plaintiffs Willie and Lucille Peevyhouse sued the defendant, Garland Coal and Mining Company, for damages for breach of contract. Judgment was for plaintiffs in an amount considerably less than was sued for. Plaintiffs appeal and defendant cross-appeals.

In the briefs on appeal, the parties present their argument and contentions under several propositions; however, they all stem from the basic question of whether the trial court properly instructed the jury on the measure of damages.

Briefly stated, the facts are as follows: plaintiffs owned a farm containing coal deposits, and in November, 1954, leased the premises to defendant for a period of five years for coal mining purposes. A "strip-mining" operation was contemplated in which the coal would be taken from pits on the surface of the ground, instead of from underground mine shafts. In addition to the usual covenants found in a coal mining lease, defendant specifically agreed to perform certain restorative and remedial work at the end of the lease period. It is unnecessary to set out the details of the work to be done, other than to say that it would involve the moving of many thousands of cubic yards of dirt, at a cost estimated by expert witnesses at about $29,000.00. However, plaintiffs sued for only $25,000.00.

During the trial, it was stipulated that all covenants and agreements in the lease contract had been fully carried out by both parties, except the remedial work mentioned above; defendant conceded that this work had not been done.

Plaintiffs introduced expert testimony as to the amount and nature of the work to be done, and its estimated cost. Over plaintiffs' objections, defendant thereafter introduced expert testimony as to the "diminution in value" of plaintiffs' farm resulting from the failure of defendant to render performance as agreed in the contract — that is, the difference between the present value of the farm, and what its value would have been if defendant had done what it agreed to do.

At the conclusion of the trial, the court instructed the jury that it must return a verdict for plaintiffs, and left the amount of damages for jury determination. On the measure of damages, the court instructed the jury that it might consider the cost of performance of the work defendant agreed to do, "together with all of the evidence offered on behalf of either party."

It thus appears that the jury was at liberty to consider the "diminution in value" of plaintiffs' farm as well as the cost of "repair work" in determining the amount of damages. It returned a verdict for plaintiffs for $5000.00 — only a fraction of the "cost of performance," *but more than the total value of the farm even after the remedial work is done.*

On appeal, the issue is sharply drawn. Plaintiffs contend that the true measure of damages in this case is what it will cost plaintiffs to obtain performance of the work that was not done because of defendant's default. Defendant argues that the measure of damages is the cost of performance "limited, however, to the total difference in the market value before and after the work was performed."

It appears that this precise question has not heretofore been presented to this court. In Ardizonne v. Archer, 72 Okl. 70, 178 P. 263, this court held that the measure of damages for breach of a contract to drill an oil well was the reasonable cost of drilling the well, but here a slightly different factual situation exists. The drilling of an oil well will yield valuable geological information, even if no oil or gas is found, and of course if the well is a producer, the value of the premises increases. In the case before us, it is argued by defendant with some force that the performance of the remedial work defendant agreed to do will add at the most only a few hundred dollars to the value of plaintiffs' farm, and that the damages should be limited to that amount because that is all plaintiffs have lost.

Plaintiffs rely on Groves v. John Wunder Co., 205 Minn. 163, 286 N.W. 235, 123 A.L.R. 502. In that case, the Minnesota court, in a substantially similar situation, adopted the "cost of performance" rule as opposed to the "value" rule. The result was to authorize a jury to give plaintiff damages in the amount of $60,000, where the real estate concerned would have been worth only $12,160, even if the work contracted for had been done.

It may be observed that Groves v. John Wunder Co., supra, is the only case which has come to our attention in which the cost of performance rule has been followed under circumstances where the cost of performance greatly exceeded the diminution in value resulting from the breach of contract. . . .

The explanation may be found in the fact that the situations presented are artificial ones. It is highly unlikely that the ordinary property owner would agree to pay $29,000 (or its equivalent) for the construction of "improvements" upon his property that would increase its value only about ($300) three hundred dollars. The result is that we are called upon to apply principles of law theoretically based upon reason and reality to a situation which is basically unreasonable and unrealistic.

In Groves v. John Wunder Co., supra, in arriving at its conclusions, the Minnesota court apparently considered the contract involved to be analogous to a building and construction contract, and cited authority for the proposition that the cost of performance or completion of the building as contracted is ordinarily the measure of damages in actions for damages for the breach of such a contract.

In an annotation following the Minnesota case beginning at 123 A.L.R. 515, the annotator places the three cases relied on by defendant (*Sandy Valley, Bigham* and *Sweeney*) under the classification of cases involving "grading and excavation contracts."

We do not think either analogy is strictly applicable to the case now before us. The primary purpose of the lease contract between plaintiffs and defendant was neither "building and construction" nor "grading and excavation." It was merely to accomplish the economical recovery and marketing of coal from the premises, to the profit of all parties. The special provisions of the lease contract pertaining to remedial work were incidental to the main object involved.

Even in the case of contracts that are unquestionably building and construction contracts, the authorities are not in agreement as to the factors to be considered in determining whether the cost of performance rule or the value rule should be applied. The American Law Institute's Restatement of the Law, Contracts, Volume 1, Sections 346(1)(a)(i) and (ii) submits the proposition that the cost of performance is the proper measure of damages "if this is possible and does not involve *unreasonable economic waste*"; and that the diminution in value caused by the breach is the proper measure "if construction and completion in accordance with the contract would involve *unreasonable economic waste*." (Emphasis supplied.) In an explanatory comment immediately following the text, the Restatement makes it clear that the "economic waste" referred to consists of the destruction of a substantially completed building or other structure. Of course no such destruction is involved in the case now before us.

On the other hand, in McCormick, Damages, Section 168, it is said with regard to building and construction contracts that ". . . in cases where the defect is one that can be repaired or cured without *undue expense*" the cost of performance is the proper measure of damages, but where ". . . the defect in material or construction is one that cannot be remedied without *an expenditure for reconstruction disproportionate to the end to be attained*" (emphasis supplied) the value rule should be followed. The same idea was expressed in

Jacob & Youngs, Inc. v. Kent, 230 N.Y. 239, 129 N.E. 889, 23 A.L.R. 1429, as follows:

> The owner is entitled to the money which will permit him to complete, unless the cost of completion is grossly and unfairly out of proportion to the good to be attained. When that is true, the measure is the difference in value.

It thus appears that the prime consideration in the Restatement was "economic waste"; and that the prime consideration in McCormick, Damages, and in Jacob & Youngs, Inc. v. Kent, supra, was the relationship between the expense involved and the "end to be attained"—in other words, the "relative economic benefit."

In view of the unrealistic fact situation in the instant case, and certain Oklahoma statutes to be hereinafter noted, we are of the opinion that the "relative economic benefit" is a proper consideration here. This is in accord with the recent case of Mann v. Clowser, 190 Va. 887, 59 S.E.2d 78, where, in applying the cost rule, the Virginia court specifically noted that "... the defects are remediable from a practical standpoint and the costs *are not grossly disproportionate to the results to be obtained*" (emphasis supplied).

23 O.S. 1961 §§96 and 97 provide as follows:

> §96. ... Notwithstanding the provisions of this chapter, no person can recover a greater amount in damages for the breach of an obligation, than he would have gained by the full performance thereof on both sides. ...
>
> §97. ... Damages must, in all cases, be reasonable, and where an obligation of any kind appears to create a right to unconscionable and grossly oppressive damages, contrary to substantial justice no more than reasonable damages can be recovered.

Although it is true that the above sections of the statute are applied most often in tort cases, they are by their own terms, and the decisions of this court, also applicable in actions for damages for breach of contract. It would seem that they are peculiarly applicable here where, under the "cost of performance" rule, plaintiffs might recover an amount about nine times the total value of their farm. Such would seem to be "unconscionable and grossly oppressive damages, contrary to substantial justice" within the meaning of the statute. Also, it can hardly be denied that if plaintiffs here are permitted to recover under the "cost of performance" rule, they will receive a greater benefit from the breach than could be gained from full performance, contrary to the provisions of Sec. 96. ...

We therefore hold that where, in a coal mining lease, lessee agrees to perform certain remedial work on the premises concerned at the end of the lease period, and thereafter the contract is fully performed by both parties except that the remedial work is not done, the measure of damages in an action by lessor against lessee for damages for breach of contract is ordinarily the reasonable cost of performance of the work; however, where the contract ✗ *Incidental provision* provision breached was merely incidental to the main purpose in view, and where the economic benefit which would result to lessor by full performance of the work is grossly disproportionate to the cost of performance, the damages which lessor may recover are limited to the diminution in value resulting to the premises because of the nonperformance.

. . . It should be noted that the rule as stated does not interfere with the property owner's right to "do what he will with his own" (Chamberlain v. Parker, 45 N.Y. 569), or his right, if he chooses, to contract for "improvements" which will actually have the effect of reducing his property's value. Where such result is in fact contemplated by the parties, and is a main or principal purpose of those contracting, it would seem that the measure of damages for breach would ordinarily be the cost of performance. . . .

Under the most liberal view of the evidence herein, the diminution in value resulting to the premises because of nonperformance of the remedial work was $300.00. After a careful search of the record, we have found no evidence of a higher figure, and plaintiffs do not argue in their briefs that a greater diminution in value was sustained. It thus appears that the judgment was clearly excessive, and that the amount for which judgment should have been rendered is definitely and satisfactorily shown by the record. . . .

We are of the opinion that the judgment of the trial court for plaintiffs should be, and it is hereby, modified and reduced to the sum of $300.00, and as so modified it is affirmed.

WELCH, DAVISON, HALLEY, and JOHNSON, JJ., concur.

WILLIAMS, C.J., BLACKBIRD, V.C.J., and IRWIN and BERRY, JJ., dissent.

IRWIN, J. (dissenting). By the specific provisions in the coal mining lease under consideration, the defendant agreed as follows:

> 7b. Lessee agrees to make fills in the pits dug on said premises on the property line in such manner that fences can be placed thereon and access had to opposite sides of the pits.
> 7c. Lessee agrees to smooth off the top of the soil banks on the above premises.
> 7d. Lessee agrees to leave the creek crossing the above premises in such a condition that it will not interfere with the crossings to be made in pits as set out in 7b. . . .
> 7f. Lessee further agrees to leave no shale or dirt on the high wall of said pits.

Following the expiration of the lease, plaintiffs made demand upon defendant that it carry out the provisions of the contract and to perform those covenants contained therein.

Defendant admits that it failed to perform its obligations that it agreed and contracted to perform under the lease contract and there is nothing in the record which indicates that defendant could not perform its obligations. Therefore, in my opinion defendant's breach of the contract was wilful and not in good faith.

Although the contract speaks for itself, there were several negotiations between the plaintiffs and defendant before the contract was executed. Defendant admitted in the trial of the action, that plaintiffs insisted that the above provisions be included in the contract and that they would not agree to the coal mining lease unless the above provisions were included.

In consideration for the lease contract, plaintiffs were to receive a certain amount as royalty for the coal produced and marketed and in addition thereto their land was to be restored as provided in the contract.

Defendant received as consideration for the contract, its proportionate share of the coal produced and marketed and in addition thereto, the *right to use* plaintiffs' land in the furtherance of its mining operations.

The cost for performing the contract in question could have been reasonably approximated when the contract was negotiated and executed and there are no conditions now existing which could not have been reasonably anticipated by the parties. Therefore, defendant had knowledge, when it prevailed upon the plaintiffs to execute the lease, that the cost of performance might be disproportionate to the value or benefits received by plaintiff for the performance.

Defendant has received its benefits under the contract and now urges, in substance, that plaintiffs' measure of damages for its failure to perform should be the economic value of performance to the plaintiffs and not the cost of performance.

If a peculiar set of facts should exist where the above rule should be applied as the proper measure of damages, (and in my judgment those facts do not exist in the instant case) before such rule should be applied, consideration should be given to the benefits received or contracted for by the party who asserts the application of the rule.

Defendant did not have the right to mine plaintiffs' coal or to use plaintiffs' property for its mining operations without the consent of plaintiffs. Defendant had knowledge of the benefits that it would receive under the contract and the approximate cost of performing the contract. With this knowledge, it must be presumed that defendant thought that it would be to its economic advantage to enter into the contract with plaintiffs and that it would reap benefits from the contract, or it would have not entered into the contract.

Therefore, if the value of the performance of a contract should be considered in determining the measure of damages for breach of a contract, the value of the benefits received under the contract by a party who breaches a contract should also be considered. However, in my judgment, to give consideration to either in the instant action, completely rescinds and holds for naught the solemnity of the contract before us and makes an entirely new contract for the parties. . . .

In Great Western Oil & Gas Company v. Mitchell, Okl., 326 P.2d 794, we held:

> The law will not make a better contract for parties than they themselves have seen fit to enter into, or alter it for the benefit of one party and to the detriment of the others; the judicial function of a court of law is to enforce a contract as it is written.

I am mindful of Title 23 O.S. 1961 §96, which provides that no person can recover a greater amount in damages for the breach of an obligation than he could have gained by the full performance thereof on both sides, except in cases not applicable herein. However, in my judgment, the above statutory provision is not applicable here.

In my judgment, we should follow the case of Groves v. John Wunder Company, 205 Minn. 163, 286 N.W. 235, 123 A.L.R. 502, which defendant agrees "that the fact situation is apparently similar to the one in the case at bar," and where the Supreme Court of Minnesota held:

> The owner's or employer's damages for such a breach (i.e. breach hypothesized in 2d syllabus) are to be measured, not in respect to the value of the land to be improved, but by the reasonable cost of doing that which the contractor promised to do and which he left undone.

The hypothesized breach referred to states that where the contractor's breach of a contract is wilful, that is, in bad faith, he is not entitled to any benefit of the equitable doctrine of substantial performance.

In the instant action defendant has made no attempt to even substantially perform. The contract in question is not immoral, is not tainted with fraud, and was not entered into through mistake or accident and is not contrary to public policy. It is clear and unambiguous and the parties understood the terms thereof, and the approximate cost of fulfilling the obligations could have been approximately ascertained. There are no conditions existing now which could not have been reasonably anticipated when the contract was negotiated and executed. The defendant could have performed the contract if it desired. It has accepted and reaped the benefits of its contract and now urges that plaintiffs' benefits under the contract be denied. If plaintiffs' benefits are denied, such benefits would inure to the direct benefit of the defendant. . . .

I therefore respectfully dissent to the opinion promulgated by a majority of my associates.

QUESTIONS

1. How do we measure the value of land? Is market value all that land is worth to a farmer? To you?

2. Is the decision wise as a matter of policy? If *Peevyhouse* were decided today, is it possible that increased public awareness of environmental concerns would affect the court's decision? See Rock Island Improvement Co. v. Helmerick & Payne, 698 F.2d 1075 (10th Cir. 1983) (prediction that Oklahoma would no longer follow *Peevyhouse*). Where the defendant is guilty of a willful breach, some courts opt for the cost of repair even where this arguably results in economic waste, in effect imposing a form of punitive damages on the bad faith party; see American Standard, Inc. v. Schectman, 439 N.Y.S.2d 529 (N.Y. App. Div. 1981).

3. Should a court attempt to determine whether the plaintiff in a case like *Peevyhouse* has particular environmental or aesthetic values before determining whether to award damages under the cost of performance rule or the diminution in value rule? What other factors should control the court's adoption of either rule?

4. The burden is on the breaching party to show that the cost of repairs is unreasonable when compared to the diminution of value due to the breach. See Andrulis v. Levin Construction Corp., 331 Md. 354, 628 A.2d 197 (Md. App. 1993); Greene v. Bearden Enterprises, 598 S.W.2d 649 (Tex. Civ. App. 1980).

5. Suppose that after this case was decided you are the attorney for the Smiths, who have the farm next door to the Peevyhouses. Garland is proposing to strip mine on their land. What do you advise be put into the contract to make sure the land will be returned to its original condition when the mining is done?

6. For a fascinating study of this case that includes pictures of the farm and the strip mine and an investigation as to whether members of the court were bribed, see Maute, Peevyhouse v. Garland Coal Co. Revisited: The Ballad of Willie and Lucille, 89 Nw. U. L. Rev. 1341 (1995).

Problem 63

Helen's Contracting agreed to build a huge horse for the town of Troy's annual pioneer parade. Helen agreed to build the horse for $24,000. It was going to cost Helen $20,000 to build the horse. After three months' work and the expenditure of $15,000, the horse was three-fourths completed. On that date, the town of Troy told Helen to stop construction on the horse. Troy had already paid Helen $5,000 but refused to pay any more. Helen can sell the horse for $2,000 salvage value. What is the loss in expectation value to Helen?

C.   The Reliance Interest

Instead of expectation damages, courts sometimes award *reliance* damages. In general, courts do so because the plaintiff did not suffer or cannot prove expectation damages (although, as we will see, judges occasionally also choose the reliance measure as a matter of public policy). Unlike expectation damages, which give the injured party the benefit of the bargain, reliance damages restore the injured party to the position the plaintiff would have been in if the contract had never been made. The Restatement (Second) of Contracts provides:

§349. Damages Based on Reliance Interest

As an alternative to the measure of damages stated in §347, the injured party has a right to damages based on reliance interest, including expenditures made in preparation for performance or in performance, less any loss that the party in breach can prove with reasonable certainty the injured party would have suffered had the contract been performed.

SULLIVAN v. O'CONNOR
Supreme Judicial Court of Massachusetts, 1973
363 Mass. 579, 296 N.E.2d 183

KAPLAN, J. The plaintiff patient secured a jury verdict of $13,500 against the defendant surgeon for breach of contract in respect to an operation upon the plaintiff's nose. The substituted consolidated bill of exceptions presents questions about the correctness of the judge's instructions on the issue of damages.

The declaration was in two counts. In the first count, the plaintiff alleged that she, as patient, entered into a contract with the defendant, a surgeon, wherein the defendant promised to perform plastic surgery on her nose and thereby to enhance her beauty and improve her appearance; that he performed the surgery but failed to achieve the promised result; rather the result of the surgery was to disfigure and deform her nose, to cause her pain in body and mind, and to subject her to other damage and expense. The second count, based on the same transaction, was in the conventional form for malpractice, charging that the defendant had been guilty of negligence in performing the surgery. Answering, the defendant entered a general denial.

On the plaintiff's demand, the case was tried by jury. At the close of the evidence, the judge put to the jury, as special questions, the issues of liability under the two counts, and instructed them accordingly. The jury returned a verdict for the plaintiff on the contract count, and for the defendant on the negligence count. The judge then instructed the jury on the issue of damages.

As background to the instructions and the parties' exceptions, we mention certain facts as the jury could find them. The plaintiff was a professional entertainer, and this was known to the defendant. The agreement was as alleged in the declaration. More particularly, judging from exhibits, the plaintiff's nose had been straight, but long and prominent; the defendant undertook by two operations to reduce its prominence and somewhat to shorten it, thus making it more pleasing in relation to the plaintiff's other features. Actually the plaintiff was obliged to undergo three operations, and her appearance was worsened. Her nose now had a concave line to about the midpoint, at which it became bulbous; viewed frontally, the nose from bridge to midpoint was flattened and broadened, and the two sides of the tip had lost symmetry. This configuration evidently could not be improved by further surgery. The plaintiff did not demonstrate, however, that her change of appearance had resulted in loss of employment. Payments by the plaintiff covering the defendant's fee and hospital expenses were stipulated at $622.65.

The judge instructed the jury, first, that the plaintiff was entitled to recover her out-of-pocket expenses incident to the operations. Second, she could recover the damages flowing directly, naturally, proximately, and foreseeably from the defendant's breach of promise. These would comprehend damages for any disfigurement of the plaintiff's nose — that is, any change of appearance for the worse — including the effects of the consciousness of such disfigurement on the plaintiff's mind, and in this connection the jury should consider the nature of the plaintiff's profession. Also consequent upon the defendant's breach, and compensable, were the pain and suffering involved in the third operation, but not in the first two. As there was no proof that any loss of earnings by the plaintiff resulted from the breach, that element should not enter into the calculation of damages.

By his exceptions the defendant contends that the judge erred in allowing the jury to take into account anything but the plaintiff's out-of-pocket expenses (presumably at the stipulated amount). The defendant excepted to the judge's refusal of his request for a general charge to that effect, and, more specifically, to the judge's refusal of a charge that the plaintiff could not recover for pain and suffering connected with the third operation or for impairment of the plaintiff's appearance and associated mental distress.

The plaintiff on her part excepted to the judge's refusal of a request to charge that the plaintiff could recover the difference in value between the nose as promised and the nose as it appeared after the operations. However, the plaintiff in her brief expressly waives this exception and others made by her in case this court overrules the defendant's exceptions; thus she would be content to hold the jury's verdict in her favor.

We conclude that the defendant's exceptions should be overruled.

It has been suggested on occasion that agreements between patients and physicians by which the physician undertakes to effect a cure or to bring about a given result should be declared unenforceable on grounds of public policy. See Guilmet v. Campbell, 385 Mich. 57, 76, 188 N.W.2d 601 (dissenting opinion). But there are many decisions recognizing and enforcing such contracts, see annotation, 43 A.L.R.3d 1221, 1225, 1229-1233, and the law of

Massachusetts has treated them as valid, although we have had no decision meeting head on the contention that they should be denied legal sanction. [Citations omitted.] These causes of action are, however, considered a little suspect, and thus we find courts straining sometimes to read the pleadings as sounding only in tort for negligence, and not in contract for breach of promise, despite sedulous efforts by the pleaders to pursue the latter theory. [Citations omitted.]

It is not hard to see why the courts should be unenthusiastic or skeptical about the contract theory. Considering the uncertainties of medical science and the variations in the physical and psychological conditions of individual patients, doctors can seldom in good faith promise specific results. Therefore it is unlikely that physicians of even average integrity will in fact make such promises. Statements of opinion by the physician with some optimistic coloring are a different thing, and may indeed have therapeutic value. But patients may transform such statements into firm promises in their own minds, especially when they have been disappointed in the event, and testify in that sense to sympathetic juries.[2] If actions for breach of promise can be readily maintained, doctors, so it is said, will be frightened into practicing "defensive medicine." On the other hand, if these actions were outlawed, leaving only the possibility of suits for malpractice, there is fear that the public might be exposed to the enticements of charlatans, and confidence in the profession might ultimately be shaken. See Miller, The Contractual Liability of Physicians and Surgeons, 1953 Wash. L.Q. 413, 416-423. The law has taken the middle of the road position of allowing actions based on alleged contract, but insisting on clear proof. Instructions to the jury may well stress this requirement and point to tests of truth, such as the complexity or difficulty of an operation as bearing on the probability that a given result was promised. See annotation, 43 A.L.R.3d 1225, 1225-1227.

If an action on the basis of contract is allowed, we have next the question of the measure of damages to be applied where liability is found. Some cases have taken the simple view that the promise by the physician is to be treated like an ordinary commercial promise, and accordingly that the successful plaintiff is entitled to a standard measure of recovery for breach of contract — "compensatory" ("expectancy") damages, an amount intended to put the plaintiff in the position he would be in if the contract had been performed, or, presumably, at the plaintiff's election, "restitution" damages, an amount corresponding to any benefit conferred by the plaintiff upon the defendant in the performance of the contract disrupted by the defendant's breach. See Restatement: Contracts §329 and comment a, §§347, 384(1).

---

2. Judicial skepticism about whether a promise was in fact made derives also from the possibility that the truth has been tortured to give the plaintiff the advantage of the longer period of limitations sometimes available for actions on contract as distinguished from those in tort or for malpractice. See Lillich, The Malpractice Statute of Limitations in New York and Other Jurisdictions, 47 Cornell L.Q. 339; annotation, 80 A.L.R.2d 368.

Thus in Hawkins v. McGee, 84 N.H. 114, 146 A. 641, the defendant doctor was taken to have promised the plaintiff to convert his damaged hand by means of an operation into a good or perfect hand, but the doctor so operated as to damage the hand still further. The court, following the usual expectancy formula, would have asked the jury to estimate and award to the plaintiff the difference between the value of a good or perfect hand, as promised, and the value of the hand after the operation. (The same formula would apply, although the dollar result would be less, if the operation had neither worsened nor improved the condition of the hand.) If the plaintiff had not yet paid the doctor his fee, that amount would be deducted from the recovery. There could be no recovery for the pain and suffering of the operation, since that detriment would have been incurred even if the operation had been successful; one can say that this detriment was not "caused" by the breach. But where the plaintiff by reason of the operation was put to more pain than he would have had to endure, had the doctor performed as promised, he should be compensated for that difference as a proper part of his expectancy recovery. It may be noted that on an alternative count for malpractice the plaintiff in the *Hawkins* case had been nonsuited; but on ordinary principles this could not affect the contract claim, for it is hardly a defense to a breach of contract that the promisor acted innocently and without negligence. The New Hampshire court further refined the *Hawkins* analysis in McQuaid v. Michou, 85 N.H. 299, 157 A. 881, all in the direction of treating the patient-physician cases on the ordinary footing of expectancy. [Citations omitted.]

Other cases, including a number in New York, without distinctly repudiating the *Hawkins* type of analysis, have indicated that a different and generally more lenient measure of damages is to be applied in patient-physician actions based on breach of alleged special agreements to effect a cure, attain a stated result, or employ a given medical method. This measure is expressed in somewhat variant ways, but the substance is that the plaintiff is to recover any expenditures made by him and for other detriment (usually not specifically described in the opinions) following proximately and foreseeably upon the defendant's failure to carry out his promise. [Citations omitted.] Cf. Carpenter v. Moore, 51 Wash. 2d 795, 322 P.2d 125. This, be it noted, is not a "restitution" measure, for it is not limited to restoration of the benefit conferred on the defendant (the fee paid) but includes other expenditures, for example, amounts paid for medicine and nurses; so also it would seem according to its logic to take in damages for any worsening of the plaintiff's condition due to the breach. Nor is it an "expectancy" measure, for it does not appear to contemplate recovery of the whole difference in value between the condition as promised and the condition actually resulting from the treatment. Rather the tendency of the formulation is to put the plaintiff back in the position he occupied just before the parties entered upon the agreement, to compensate him for the detriments he suffered in reliance upon the agreement. This kind of intermediate pattern of recovery for breach of contract is discussed in the suggestive article by Fuller and Perdue, The Reliance Interest in Contract Damages, 46 Yale L.J. 52, 373, where the authors show that, although not attaining the currency of the standard measures, a "reliance" measure has for special reasons been applied by the courts in a variety of settings, including noncommercial settings. See 46 Yale L.J. at 396-401.[4]

For breach of the patient-physician agreements under consideration, a recovery limited to restitution seems plainly too meager, if the agreements are to be enforced at all. On the other hand, an expectancy recovery may well be excessive. The factors, already mentioned, which have made the cause of action somewhat suspect, also suggest moderation as to the breadth of the recovery that should be permitted. Where, as in the case at bar and in a number of the reported cases, the doctor has been absolved of negligence by the trier, an expectancy measure may be thought harsh. We should recall here that the fee paid by the patient to the doctor for the alleged promise would usually be quite disproportionate to the putative expectancy recovery. To attempt, moreover, to put a value on the condition that would or might have resulted, had the treatment succeeded as promised, may sometimes put an exceptional strain on the imagination of the fact finder. As a general consideration, Fuller and Perdue argue that the reasons for granting damages for broken promises to the extent of the expectancy are at their strongest when the promises are made in a business context, when they have to do with the production or distribution of goods or the allocation of functions in the market place; they become weaker as the context shifts from a commercial to a noncommercial field. 46 Yale L.J. at 60-63.

There is much to be said, then, for applying a reliance measure to the present facts, and we have only to add that our cases are not unreceptive to the use of that formula in special situations. We have, however, had no previous occasion to apply it to patient-physician cases.

The question of recovery on a reliance basis for pain and suffering or mental distress requires further attention. We find expressions in the decisions that pain and suffering (or the like) are simply not compensable in actions for breach of contract. The defendant seemingly espouses this proposition in the present case. True, if the buyer under a contract for the purchase of a lot of merchandise, in suing for the seller's breach, should claim damages for mental anguish caused by his disappointment in the transaction, he would not succeed; he would be told, perhaps, that the asserted psychological injury was not fairly foreseeable by the defendant as a probable consequence of the breach of such a business contract. See Restatement: Contracts, §341, and comment a. But there is no general rule

4. Some of the exceptional situations mentioned where reliance may be preferred to expectancy are those in which the latter measure would be hard to apply or would impose too great a burden; performance was interfered with by external circumstances; the contract was indefinite. See 46 Yale L.J. at 373-386, 394-396.

barring such items of damage in actions for breach of contract. It is all a question of the subject matter and background of the contract, and when the contract calls for an operation on the person of the plaintiff, psychological as well as physical injury may be expected to figure somewhere in the recovery, depending on the particular circumstances. The point is explained in Stewart v. Rudner, 349 Mich. 459, 469, 84 N.W.2d 816. Cf. Frewen v. Page, 238 Mass. 499, 131 N.E. 475; McClean v. University Club, 327 Mass. 68, 97 N. E.2d 174. Again, it is said in a few of the New York cases, concerned with the classification of actions for statute of limitations purposes, that the absence of allegations demanding recovery for pain and suffering is characteristic of a contract claim by a patient against a physician, that such allegations rather belong in a claim for malpractice. See Robins v. Finestone, 308 N.Y. 543, 547, 127 N.E.2d 330; Budoff v. Kessler, 2 A.D.2d 760, 153 N.Y.S.2d 654. These remarks seem unduly sweeping. Suffering or distress resulting from the breach going beyond that which was envisaged by the treatment as agreed, should be compensable on the same ground as the worsening of the patient's condition because of the breach. Indeed it can be argued that the very suffering or distress "contracted for" — that which would have been incurred if the treatment achieved the promised result — should also be compensable on the theory underlying the New York cases. For that suffering is "wasted" if the treatment fails. Otherwise stated, compensation for this waste is arguably required in order to complete the restoration of the status quo ante.

In the light of the foregoing discussion, all the defendant's exceptions fail: the plaintiff was not confined to the recovery of her out-of-pocket expenditures; she was entitled to recover also for the worsening of her condition, and for the pain and suffering and mental distress involved in the third operation. These items were compensable on either an expectancy or a reliance view. We might have been required to elect between the two views if the pain and suffering connected with the first two operations contemplated by the agreement, or the whole difference in value between the present and the promised conditions, were being claimed as elements of damage. But the plaintiff waives her possible claim to the former element, and to so much of the latter as represents the difference in value between the promised condition and the condition before the operations.

Plaintiff's exceptions waived.

Defendant's exceptions overruled.

ANGLIA TELEVISION LTD. v. REED
Court of Appeals, Civil Division, 1971
3 All Eng. Rep. 690

Lord DENNING. Anglia Television Ltd. were minded in 1968 to make a film of a play for television entitled "The Man in the Wood." It portrayed an

American married to an English woman. The American has an adventure in an English wood. The film was to last for 90 minutes. Anglia Television made many arrangements in advance. They arranged for a place where the play was to be filmed. They employed a director, a designer and a stage manager, and so forth. They involved themselves in much expense. All this was done before they got the leading man. They required a strong actor capable of holding the play together. He was to be on the scene the whole time. Anglia Television eventually found the man. He was Mr. Robert Reed, an American who has a very high reputation as an actor. He was very suitable for this part. By telephone conversation on 30th August 1968 it was agreed by Mr. Reed through his agent that he would come to England and be available between 9th September and 11th October 1968 to rehearse and play in this film. He was to get a performance fee of £1,050, living expenses of £100 a week, his first class fares to and from the United States, and so forth. It was all subject to the permit of the Ministry of Labour for him to come here. That was duly given on 2nd September 1968. So the contract was concluded. But unfortunately there was some muddle with the bookings. It appears that Mr. Reed's agent had already booked him in America for some other play. So on 3rd September 1968 the agent said that Mr. Reed would not come to England to perform in this play. He repudiated his contract. Anglia Television tried hard to find a substitute but could not do so. So on 11th September they accepted his repudiation. They abandoned the proposed film. They gave notice to the people whom they had engaged and so forth.

Anglia Television then sued Mr. Reed for damages. He did not dispute his liability, but a question arose as to the damages. Anglia Television do not claim their profit. They cannot say what their profit would have been on this contract if Mr. Reed had come here and performed it. So, instead of claim for loss or profits, they claim for the wasted expenditure. They had incurred the director's fees, the designer's fees, the stage manager's and assistant manager's fees, and so on. It comes in all to £2,750. Anglia Television say [sic] that all that money was wasted because Mr. Reed did not perform his contract.

Mr. Reed's advisers take a point of law. They submit that Anglia Television cannot recover for expenditure incurred *before* the contract was concluded with Mr. Reed. They can only recover the expenditure *after* the contract was concluded. They say that the expenditure *after* the contract was only £854.65, and that is all that Anglia Television can recover. The master rejected that contention; he held that Anglia Television could recover the whole £2,750; and now Mr. Reed appeals to this court.

Counsel for Mr. Reed has referred us to the recent unreported case of Perestrello & Compania Limitada v. United Paint Co. Ltd. (No. 2),[1] in which

---

1. (1969) 113 Sol. Jo. 324.

Thesiger J. quoted the words of Lord Tindal C.J. in 1835 in Hodges v. Earl of Litchfield:[2]

> The expenses preliminary to the contract ought not to be allowed. The party enters into them for his own benefit at a time when it is uncertain whether there will be any contract or not.

Thesiger J. applied those words, saying: "In my judgment pre-contract expenditure, though thrown away, is not recoverable. . . ."

I cannot accept the proposition as stated. It seems to me that a plaintiff in such a case as this had an election: he can either claim for his loss of profits; or for his wasted expenditure. But he must elect between them. He cannot claim both. If he has not suffered any loss of profits — or if he cannot prove what his profits would have been — he can claim in the alternative the expenditure which has been thrown away, that is, wasted, by reason of the breach. That is shown by Cullinane v. British "Rema" Manufacturing Co. Ltd.[3]

If the plaintiff claims the wasted expenditure, he is not limited to the expenditure incurred *after* the contract was concluded. He can claim also the expenditure incurred *before* the contract, provided that it was such as would reasonably be in the contemplation of the parties as likely to be wasted if the contract was broken. Applying that principle here, it is plain that, when Mr. Reed entered into this contract, he must have known perfectly well that much expenditure had already been incurred on director's fees and the like. He must have contemplated — or, at any rate, it is reasonably to be imputed to him — that if he broke his contract, all that expenditure would be wasted, whether or not it was incurred before or after the contract. He must pay damages for all the expenditure so wasted and thrown away. This view is supported by the recent decision of Brightman J. in Lloyd v. Stanbury.[4] There was a contract for the sale of land. In anticipation of the contract — and before it was concluded — the purchaser went to much expense in moving a caravan to the site and in getting his furniture there. The seller afterwards entered into a contract to sell the land to the purchaser, but afterwards broke his contract. The land had not increased in value, so the purchaser could not claim for any loss of profit. But Brightman J. held that he could recover the cost of moving the caravan and furniture, because it was[5] "within the contemplation of the parties when the contract was signed." That decision is in accord with correct principle, namely, that wasted expenditure can be recovered when it is wasted by reason of the defendant's breach of contract. It is true that, if the defendant had never entered into the contract, he would not be liable, and the expenditure would have been

2. (1835) 1 Bing. N.C. 492 at 498, [1835-42] All E.R. Rep. 551 at 552, 553.
3. [1953] 2 All E.R. 1257 at 1261, 1264, 1265, [1954] 1 Q.B. 292 at 303, 308.
4. [1971] 2 All E.R. 267, [1971] 1 W.L.R. 535.
5. [1971] 2 All E.R. at 276, [1971] 1 W.L.R. at 547.

incurred by the plaintiff without redress; but, the defendant having made his contract and broken it, it does not lie in his mouth to say he is not liable, when it was because of his breach that the expenditure has been wasted.

I think the master was quite right and this appeal should be dismissed.

PHILLIMORE L.J. I agree.

MEGAW L.J. I also agree.   *Affirmed for Plaintiff*

Appeal dismissed.

QUESTIONS AND NOTES

1. If the expectation measure is the "normal" remedy for the plaintiff, why did the court in *Sullivan* choose the reliance measure as the appropriate measure for the plaintiff? Why did the plaintiff opt for the reliance measure over the expectancy measure in *Anglia*?

2. In *Anglia* what would be the award if it appeared that the plaintiff was going to lose money on the film? Whose obligation is it to show that a loss is likely to occur?

3. Would it affect the result in *Anglia* if the amount of the reliance interest had been $22 million?

4. For more on the issue of whether preparation costs are recoverable in reliance actions, see Bebchuk and Ben-Shahar, Precontractual Reliance, 30 J. Legal Stud. 423 (2001); Crespi, Recovering Pre-Contractual Expenditures as an Element of Reliance Damages, 49 SMU L. Rev. 43 (1995).

NOTE ON THE PRESUMPTION OF BREAKING EVEN

If the expectancy is too difficult to prove, the plaintiff is entitled to recover out-of-pocket expenses unless the defendant can prove that the contract was a losing one and that the plaintiff would not have made enough from the contract to make up these expenditures. Thus, the courts in effect are indulging in a presumption that the plaintiff will "break even"; that the expectancy would have been at least the amount of the expenditures. See J. Calamari and J. Perillo, *Perillo's Hornbook on Contracts* §14-9 (7th ed. 2014). Reasonable reliance and restitution expenses are awarded on "the assumption that the value of the contract would at least have covered the outlay," C. McCormick, *Damages* 586 (1935). If the defendant can carry the burden of showing that the contract was really a losing one, the court will deduct the loss from the plaintiff's outlay.

Assumption is the plaintiff will break even

Problem 64

Rogette began drafting the fourteenth edition of her tour guide pursuant to an agreement with White Publishing. After Rogette was one-quarter done, White repudiated the agreement. Rogette sued White for the amount of money she had expended touring the world to gather updated information for the book. She also sued White for the "expectancy" — that is, the total amount she expected she would have earned as royalties on the book. White admits liability but alleges the damages should be measured either by the expectancy or the amount spent but should not include both. Rogette argues that she had suffered the loss of both elements of damages and should receive both. Who is right?

What would the plaintiff have recovered in Problem 63 if the suit there sought recovery for only the reliance interest?

NOTE ON DAMAGES FOR PROMISSORY ESTOPPEL CLAIMS

Courts disagree over which remedies are available under a promissory estoppel claim. The majority rule is that "court[s] may award [either] expectation, reliance, or restitutionary damages for promissory estoppel claims." Dynalectric Co. of Nevada v. Clark & Sullivan Constructors, Inc., 255 P.3d 286, 289 (Nev. 2011); accord Daigle Commercial Grp., Inc. v. St. Laurent, 734 A.2d 667, 674-675 (Me. 1999); Tour Costa Rica v. Country Walkers, Inc., 758 A.2d 795, 802 (Vt. 2000). In some states, however, "[a] successful promissory[]estoppel claimant's recovery . . . is limited to reliance damages, that is, the party may recover only the amount necessary to restore it to the position it would have occupied if it had not relied on the adverse party's promise." Range v. Calvary Christian Fellowship, 530 S.W.3d 818, 831 (Tex. App. 2017); see also Hi-Pac, Ltd. v. Avoset Corp., 26 F. Supp. 2d 1230, 1237 n.5 (D. Haw. 1997). In other jurisdictions, there is authority for both propositions. See, e.g., Cosgrove v. Bartolotta, 150 F.3d 729, 734 (7th Cir. 1998) (noting contradictory authority under Wisconsin law).

D.   Limitations on the Recovery

Along with the type of expectancy damages discussed earlier — damages representing a "loss in value" to the plaintiff because of the breach (general damages) — *incidental* and *consequential* damages (special damages) may also be included in the final award. As we briefly mentioned earlier, consequential damages are expenses or other losses beyond general damages that the plaintiff would never have incurred but for the breach. For example, if the breach involves a faulty furnace that blows up and injures a family, the consequential damages would include pain and suffering and medical expenses. In a commercial context, consequential damages frequently consist of lost profits for a nonbreaching buyer. If the builder of a motel fails to build a structure as promised, loss in value damages for the owner will consist of the cost of substitute performance or the diminution in value occasioned by the defective performance. In addition, the owner may be entitled to consequential damages such as the profit lost on another contract between the motel owner and a convention group that cancels because the motel is not ready. *Incidental* Incidental damages are consequential damages incurred in trying to prevent or limit the impact of the breach. See UCC §2-715. An example would be *UCC 2-715* storage costs incurred by a nonbreaching seller who holds goods for a buyer for a reasonable time after the buyer fails to pick up the goods as promised.

Both the loss of value and the consequential portions of a damage award are subject to various limitations. Of primary importance are the doctrines of certainty, foreseeability, and avoidability. Read the cases with two purposes in mind: (1) to understand how the limitations work and (2) to get a feel for the losses that may be reimbursed as consequential damages, meaning that they fall into this category.

1. Certainty

Courts deny plaintiffs any relief that is too speculative. Requested relief can be too speculative because there is too much uncertainty as to either (1) the fact that the breach caused the type of injury that plaintiff alleges (a "causation" limitation); (2) the extent to which the plaintiff suffered from the breach (the dollar amount of the damage caused); or (3) both the causation and amount. Most cases on certainty concern requests by the plaintiff for consequential damages. Claims for general damages must also have the requisite degree of certainty, although through the years formulas have been developed for measuring general damages in such a way as to satisfy this requirement as to at least the causation issue (number 1 above) without the trouble caused by the same issue when applied to consequential losses. For example, it is generally presumed that the general damage as measured by the cost of substitute performance is caused by a breach by the contractor. The diversity of potential claims for consequential damages (for want of a horse a kingdom was lost, etc.) makes for some hard questions as to causation as well as amount. For example, the breach by the contractor does not necessarily cause the owner who hired the contractor to suffer lost profits on third-party contracts, nor tort damages because the owner fell through a defective floor.

MERRY GENTLEMAN, LLC. v. GEORGE AND LEONA PRODUCTIONS, INC.
United States Court of Appeals for the Seventh Circuit, 2015
799 F.3d 827

Hamilton, Circuit Judge.
Plaintiff Merry Gentleman, LLC produced the motion picture *The Merry Gentleman*, which was released in 2009. Despite some critical acclaim, the film

was a commercial flop. Merry Gentleman blames defendant Michael Keaton, the film's lead actor and director, for the bust. It brought this breach of contract action against Keaton and defendant George and Leona Productions, Inc., Keaton's "loan-out company" that he uses for professional contracting, alleging that Keaton violated his directing contract by (1) failing to prepare the first cut of the film in a timely fashion, (2) submitting a first cut that was incomplete, (3) submitting a revised cut that was not ready for the producers to watch, (4) communicating directly with officials at the Sundance Film Festival and threatening to boycott the festival if they did not accept his director's cut instead of the producers' preferred cut, (5) failing to cooperate with the producers during the post-production process, and (6) failing to promote the film adequately.

If the case were to go to trial, one might expect Keaton to dispute that any of these alleged breaches actually violated the directing contract. After all, Keaton completed the movie. It was accepted at the prestigious Sundance Film Festival. It received critical praise — Roger Ebert, for example, gave it 3.5 stars out of 4 and called it "original, absorbing and curiously moving." And the film's executive producer, Paul Duggan, admitted during his deposition that he was unaware of any director who did more publicity than Keaton did for a movie with a comparable budget.

Keaton moved for summary judgment, however, on the narrow ground that Merry Gentleman had failed to produce sufficient evidence that his alleged breaches of the directing contract caused it damages. For purposes of deciding this appeal, we must therefore assume as the district court did that Keaton in fact breached the contract.

Illinois law governs the directing contract. Under Illinois law, a "party injured by another's breach or repudiation of a contract usually seeks recovery in the form of damages based on his 'expectation interest,' which involves obtaining the 'benefit of the bargain,' or his 'reliance interest,' which involves reimbursement for loss caused by reliance on a contract." MC Baldwin Financial Co. v. DiMaggio, Rosario & Veraja, LLC, 364 Ill. App. 3d 6, 300 Ill. Dec. 601, 845 N.E.2d 22, 30 (2006), quoting Restatement (Second) of Contracts §344 (1981). The district court granted Keaton's motion for summary judgment, concluding that Merry Gentleman had failed to present a genuine issue of material fact on either damages theory.

First, the district court held that Merry Gentleman forfeited the expectation damages theory by not addressing it sufficiently in its response to summary judgment. Merry Gentleman, LLC v. George & Leona Productions, Inc., 76 F. Supp. 3d 756, 761 (N.D. Ill. 2014). Merry Gentleman does not dispute this conclusion on appeal, so expectation damages are out.

Second, the district court held that Merry Gentleman failed to produce evidence from which a reasonable trier of fact could find that Keaton's alleged breaches caused the damages Merry Gentleman seeks: all $5.5 million it spent producing the movie. Id. at 761-66. This holding is the focus of Merry Gentleman's appeal.

We review the grant of summary judgment de novo, reviewing the record in the light most favorable to Merry Gentleman, as the non-moving party, and drawing all reasonable inferences in its favor. E.g., Bentrud v. Bowman, Heintz, Boscia & Vician, P.C., 794 F.3d 871, 873-74, 2015 WL 4509935, at *2 (7th Cir. 2015). Summary judgment is appropriate only where there are no genuine issues of material fact and the moving party is entitled to judgment as a matter of law. Fed. R. Civ. P. 56(a).

Illinois follows the approach of §349 of the Restatement (Second) of Contracts (1981), which provides that as an alternative to expectation damages, "the injured party has a right to damages based on his reliance interest, including expenditures made in preparation for performance or in performance, less any loss that the party in breach can prove with reasonable certainty the injured party would have suffered had the contract been performed." See, e.g., Herbert W. Jaeger & Associates v. Slovak American Charitable Ass'n, 156 Ill. App. 3d 106, 107 Ill. Dec. 710, 507 N.E.2d 863, 868 (1987) (discussing §349). Reliance damages are designed to put the injured party "in as good a position as [the injured party] would have been in had the contract not been made." Restatement (Second) of Contracts §344; *MC Baldwin Financial*, 300 Ill. Dec. 601, 845 N.E.2d at 30 (discussing §344). . . .

Merry Gentleman argues that the district court required too much when it held that Merry Gentleman failed to establish a causal connection between its expenditures on the film and Keaton's alleged breaches. The causation standard is minimal when the injured party seeks reliance damages under §349, Merry Gentleman contends, and it cleared this low hurdle when it submitted an affidavit from Duggan stating that the production company spent over $5 million in reliance on the directing contract. Once it produced that evidence, Merry Gentleman continues, the burden shifted to Keaton to prove that the production company would have suffered the alleged losses even if Keaton had fully performed. And because Keaton did not submit evidence with his motion for summary judgment showing beyond reasonable dispute that these losses were inevitable, summary judgment against Merry Gentleman was improper. Or so goes the argument.

We agree with Merry Gentleman that a party seeking reliance damages under §349 has a relatively low bar to clear to establish causation and that once it makes this showing, the burden shifts to the breaching party to prove any reduction in those damages. This causation threshold is low because the injured party is forced to prove a counterfactual: what would have happened if the contract had not been signed in the first place. See Autotrol Corp. v. Continental Water Systems Corp., 918 F.2d 689, 695 (7th Cir. 1990). Proving this kind of counterfactual is difficult because the value of performance can be so difficult to establish. That is especially true in cases where the injured party is seeking reliance damages. If damages were easy to calculate, the injured party likely would have sought expectation damages to begin with on a benefit-of-the-bargain theory under §347. Reliance damages are appropriate precisely because the injured party is at an evidentiary disadvantage.

Cf. Restatement (Second) of Contracts §349, cmt. a (1981) (reliance damages are appropriate where the injured party "cannot prove his profit with reasonable certainty"). That is why courts use the burden-shifting framework of §349. As Judge Hand explained long ago:

> It is often very hard to learn what the value of the performance would have been; and it is a common expedient, and a just one, in such situations to put the peril of the answer upon that party who by his wrong has made the issue relevant to the rights of the other. On principle therefore the proper solution would seem to be that the promisee may recover his outlay in preparation for the performance, subject to the privilege of the promisor to reduce it by as much as he can show that the promisee would have lost, if the contract had been performed.

L. Albert & Son v. Armstrong Rubber Co., 178 F.2d 182, 189 (2d Cir. 1949) (footnote omitted).

The burden does not shift to the breaching party until the injured party first satisfies this threshold showing of causation, however. And just because the causation threshold under §349 is low does not mean it is not there, as Merry Gentleman seems to suggest. To oppose summary judgment on this point, the injured party must still produce evidence sufficient to permit a reasonable trier of fact to find that the losses claimed were caused by the breach. . . .

In the typical case where reliance damages are sought, the defendant has simply repudiated the contract and walked away from the deal. This causal link will be straightforward in those cases. As the district court explained, in such cases the non-breaching plaintiff is left "holding the bag after having made its expenditures." *Merry Gentleman*, 76 F. Supp. 3d at 763. In those cases, it is appropriate for the injured party to claim as damages all expenditures it made in preparation for performance because the other side failed to perform at all. In such cases, the complete loss of investment will often be the proximate result of the breach.

But in cases like this one, where the breaching party has substantially performed and the alleged breaches have to do with the quality of the final product, the causal link between reliance damages and the breach is not so direct. An injured party cannot reasonably claim that all of its expenditures were caused by the other party's breach without some reason to think the breach destroyed the entire value of the breaching party's performance. In this context, the breach does not cause the complete loss of investment.

Take this case, for example. Who can say why a critically praised movie did not make money? Merry Gentleman claims as damages all $5.5 million it spent to produce the movie. If Keaton had somehow prevented completion of the movie, Merry Gentleman might well have been entitled to all expenditures made in preparation for his performance (subject, of course, to the "losing contract" limitation in §349). But here, Keaton actually made the movie. Merry Gentleman complains that Keaton slowed down the production process and failed to publicize the movie adequately after it was finished. No doubt, these services have economic value and, on a proper showing, Merry Gentleman might have been entitled to recover damages for these shortcomings. (Imagine, for instance, if Keaton's tardiness in submitting the first cut forced Merry Gentleman to pay the film editors for a longer period. Or, to take a more extreme example, imagine if Keaton had publicly criticized the film released to theaters so harshly that no one bought tickets to see it.) But no reasonable trier of fact could find that Merry Gentleman lost its entire investment of $5.5 million because Keaton failed to submit his first cut on time or failed to publicize the movie better. Merry Gentleman entered the directing contract to have Keaton deliver a finished movie, and he delivered one that showed well at Sundance and won some critical praise. The breaches by Keaton that Merry Gentleman alleges cannot reasonably be said to have rendered the investment completely worthless. . . .

We agree with the district court that Merry Gentleman, in seeking $5.5 million in reliance damages, "effectively wants to shift the entire cost — and risk — of producing The Merry Gentleman to Keaton for his alleged breaches, giving it a windfall and placing it in a better position than it would have been in had the contract never been signed." *Merry Gentleman*, 76 F. Supp. 3d at 766. Reliance damages are not insurance. . . .

As noted, we must assume here that Keaton breached the $100,000 contract as alleged, but these alleged breaches did not render his performance completely worthless. He directed the movie, it was accepted by Sundance, and it was released to the public. Reimbursing Merry Gentleman for all $5.5 million it spent, even though it received from Keaton a finished film praised by critics, would put it in a better position than if the contract had not been made. Perhaps Merry Gentleman might have been able to present a genuine issue for trial on a more modest damages theory, but it decided to shoot for the moon and missed. A reasonable trier of fact could not find that Keaton's alleged breaches caused Merry Gentleman to sustain $5.5 million in damages.

The district court's judgment is AFFIRMED.

FREUND v. WASHINGTON SQUARE PRESS
Court of Appeals of New York, 1974
34 N.Y.2d 379, 357 N.Y.S.2d 857, 314 N.E.2d 419

RABIN, J. In this action for breach of a publishing contract, we must decide what damages are recoverable for defendant's failure to publish plaintiff's manuscript. In 1965, plaintiff, an author and a college teacher, and defendant, Washington Square Press, Inc., entered into a written agreement which, in relevant part, provided as follows. Plaintiff ("author")

[handwritten margin note: Plaintiff and Defendant entered into a written Agreement]

granted defendant ("publisher") exclusive rights to publish and sell in book form plaintiff's work on modern drama. Upon plaintiff's delivery of the manuscript, defendant agreed to complete payment of a nonreturnable $2,000 advance. Thereafter, if defendant deemed the manuscript not "suitable for publication," it had the right to terminate the agreement by written notice within 60 days of delivery. Unless so terminated, defendant agreed to publish the work in hard-bound edition within 18 months and afterwards in paperbound edition. The contract further provided that defendant would pay royalties to plaintiff, based upon specified percentages of sales. (For example, plaintiff was to receive 10 percent of the retail price of the first 10,000 copies sold in the continental United States.) If defendant failed to publish within 18 months, the contract provided that "this agreement shall terminate and the rights herein granted to the Publisher shall revert to the Author. In such event all payments theretofore made to the Author shall belong to the Author without prejudice to any other remedies which the Author may have." The contract also provided that controversies were to be determined pursuant to the New York simplified procedure for court determination of disputes (CPLR 3031-3037, Consol. Laws, c.8).

Plaintiff performed by delivering his manuscript to defendant and was paid his $2,000 advance. Defendant thereafter merged with another publisher and ceased publishing in hardbound. Although defendant did not exercise its 60-day right to terminate, it has refused to publish the manuscript in any form.

Plaintiff commenced the instant action pursuant to the simplified procedure practice and initially sought specific performance of the contract. The Trial Term Justice denied specific performance but, finding a valid contract and a breach by defendant, set the matter down for trial on the issue of monetary damages, if any, sustained by the plaintiff. At trial, plaintiff sought to prove: (1) delay of his academic promotion; (2) loss of royalties which would have been earned; and (3) the cost of publication if plaintiff had made his own arrangements to publish. The trial court found that plaintiff had been promoted despite defendant's failure to publish, and that there was no evidence that the breach had caused any delay. Recovery of lost royalties was denied without discussion. The court found, however, that the cost of hardcover publication to plaintiff was the natural and probable consequence of the breach and, based upon expert testimony, awarded $10,000 to cover this cost. It denied recovery of the expenses of paperbound publication on the ground that plaintiff's proof was conjectural.

The Appellate Division (3 to 2) affirmed, finding that the cost of publication was the proper measure of damages. In support of its conclusion, the majority analogized to the construction contract situation where the cost of completion may be the proper measure of damages for a builder's failure to complete a house or for use of wrong materials. The dissent concluded that the cost of publication is not an appropriate measure of damages and consequently, that plaintiff may recover nominal damages only. We agree with the dissent. In so concluding, we look to the basic purpose of damage recovery and the nature and effect of the parties' contract.

It is axiomatic that, except where punitive damages are allowable, the law awards damages for breach of contract to compensate for injury caused by the breach—injury which was foreseeable, i.e., reasonably within the contemplation of the parties, at the time the contract was entered into. (Swain v. Schieffelin, 134 N.Y. 471, 473, 31 N.E. 1025, 1026.) Money damages are substitutional relief designed in theory "to put the injured party in as good a position as he would have been put by full performance of the contract, at the least cost to the defendant and without charging him with harms that he had no sufficient reason to foresee when he made the contract." (5 Corbin, Contracts, §1002, pp. 31-32; 11 Williston, Contracts [3d ed.], §1338, p. 198.) In other words, so far as possible, the law attempts to secure to the injured party the benefit of his bargain, subject to the limitations that the injury—whether it be losses suffered or gains prevented—was foreseeable, and that the amount of damages claimed be measurable with a reasonable degree of certainty and, of course, adequately proven. (See, generally, Dobbs, Law of Remedies, p. 148; see, also, Farnsworth, Legal Remedies for Breach of Contract, 70 Col. L. Rev. 1145, 1159.) But it is equally fundamental that the injured party should not recover more from the breach than he would have gained had the contract been fully performed. . . .

Measurement of damages in this case according to the cost of publication to the plaintiff would confer greater advantage than performance of the contract would have entailed to plaintiff and would place him in a far better position than he would have occupied had the defendant fully performed. Such measurement bears no relation to compensation for plaintiff's actual loss or anticipated profit. Far beyond compensating plaintiff for the interests he had in the defendant's performance of the contract—whether restitution, reliance or expectation (see Fuller & Perdue, Reliance Interest in Contract Damages, 46 Yale L.J. 52, 53-56) an award of the cost of publication would enrich plaintiff at defendant's expense.

Pursuant to the contract, plaintiff delivered his manuscript to the defendant. In doing so, he conferred a value on the defendant which, upon defendant's breach, was required to be restored to him. Special Term, in addition to ordering a trial on the issue of damages, ordered defendant to return the manuscript to plaintiff and plaintiff's restitution interest in the contract was thereby protected. . . .

At the trial on the issue of damages, plaintiff alleged no reliance losses suffered in performing the contract or in making necessary preparations to perform. Had such losses, if foreseeable and ascertainable, been incurred, plaintiff would have been entitled to compensation for them.

As for plaintiff's expectation interest in the contract, it was basically twofold—the "advance" and the royalties. (To be sure, plaintiff may have expected to enjoy whatever notoriety, prestige or other benefits that might have attended publication, but even if these expectations were compensable, plaintiff did not attempt at trial to place a monetary value on them.) There is no dispute that plaintiff's expectancy in the "advance" was fulfilled — he has received his $2,000. His expectancy interest in the royalties — the profit he stood to gain from sale of the published book — while theoretically compensable, was speculative. Although this work is not plaintiff's first, at trial he provided no stable foundation for a reasonable estimate of royalties he would have earned had defendant not breached its promise to publish. In these circumstances, his claim for royalties fails for uncertainty. . . .

Since the damages which would have compensated plaintiff for anticipated royalties were not proved with the required certainty, we agree with the dissent in the Appellate Division that nominal damages alone are recoverable. . . .

. . . Though these are damages in name only and not at all compensatory, they are nevertheless awarded as a formal vindication of plaintiff's legal right to compensation which has not been given a sufficiently certain monetary valuation. . . .

In our view, the analogy by the majority in the Appellate Division to the construction contract situation was inapposite. In the typical construction contract, the owner agrees to pay money or other consideration to a builder and expects, under the contract, to receive a completed building in return. The value of the promised performance to the owner is the properly constructed building. In this case, unlike the typical construction contract, the value to plaintiff of the promised performance — publication — was a percentage of sales of the books published and not the books themselves. Had the plaintiff contracted for the printing, binding and delivery of a number of hardbound copies of his manuscript, to be sold or disposed of as he wished, then perhaps the construction analogy, and measurement of damages by the cost of replacement or completion, would have some application.

Here, however, the specific value to plaintiff of the promised publication was the royalties he stood to receive from defendant's sales of the published book. Essentially, publication represented what it would have cost the defendant to confer that value upon the plaintiff, and, by its breach, defendant saved that cost. The error by the courts below was in measuring damages not by the value to plaintiff of the promised performance but by the cost of that performance to defendant. Damages are not measured, however, by what the defaulting party saved by the breach, but by the natural and probable consequences of the breach *to the plaintiff.* In this case, the consequence to plaintiff of defendant's failure to publish is that he is prevented from realizing the gains promised by the contract — the royalties. But, as we have stated, the amount of royalties plaintiff would have realized was not ascertained with adequate certainty and, as a consequence, plaintiff may recover nominal damages only.

Accordingly, the order of the Appellate Division should be modified to the extent of reducing the damage award of $10,000 for the cost of publication to six cents, but with costs and disbursements to the plaintiff.

NOTE ON NOMINAL DAMAGES

Six cents doesn't go far these days. It would be safe to say that it is a "nominal" amount. Nominal damages are awarded for breach of contract when the plaintiff has a valid cause of action against the defendant but actual damages have not been proven and cannot be presumed (in some types of torts, damages are presumed to have been incurred, for example, when the tort of defamation of a commercial entity has occurred). An award of nominal damages may be better than an outright dismissal of the plaintiff's action. In awarding nominal damages, the court is necessarily finding that the plaintiff's position concerning breach is correct. This may influence other parties' behavior in dealing with the plaintiff. Finally, nominal damages can also be the basis for an award of punitive damages (which we discuss later in this chapter).

Problem 65

Suzie Temple entered her dog in the "Perfect Pet" contest at the Savabit store. The grand prize was $25,000. Suzie's dog and three other dogs made it to the finals. Two hours before the final judging among Suzie's dog and the other finalists, the company running the contest, Big Winner, Inc., withdrew. Suzie sues, requesting the money. Big Winner defends, alleging insufficient certainty. Who wins? Cf. Wachtel v. National Alfalfa Journal, 190 Iowa 1293, 176 N.W. 801 (1920). *- Not reasonably certain she would win (expected damages) (reliance) - bought tickets -> (restitution)*

HUMETRIX, INC. v. GEMPLUS S.C.A.
United States Court of Appeals, Ninth Circuit, 2001
268 F.3d 910

RICHARD C. TALLMAN, Circuit Judge:

Happy contractual relationships are all alike; but every unhappy contractual relationship is unhappy in its own way.[1]

In this case, a United States health care consulting company, Humetrix, Inc. ("Humetrix"), contracted with the world's leading manufacturer of Smart Card technology, Gemplus S.C.A. ("Gemplus"), to provide portable patient data storage solutions to the United States health care market.[2] By all

---

1. See Leo Tolstoy, *Anna Karenina* 1 (C. Garnett trans. 1933).

2. A Smart Card is a credit card-sized microprocessor that stores data files. With the proper hardware, the data files can be downloaded, viewed, updated, and restored. Smart Cards also contain security protocols that protect the confidentiality of the data stored on them. The initial health care application envisioned by Humetrix and Gemplus permitted a

indications, Gemplus and Humetrix were poised on the threshold of a promising business opportunity. Humetrix labored industriously to capitalize on this opportunity, raising finances, increasing its sales staff, and developing a client base in the United States.

Unbeknownst to Humetrix, however, two events occurred within Gemplus that threatened the vitality of their partnership. First, Guy Guistini, a Gemplus senior manager and the progenitor of the French health care Smart Card program, learned that Humetrix had registered the trademark "Vaccicard" in the United States. Guistini was a 45% shareholder in Inovaction S.A.R.L. ("Inovaction"), a French company that held the French trademarks "Vaccicarte" and "Vaccicard." Second, Gemplus acquired a new U.S. subsidiary that could perform many of the functions that Humetrix was to have performed as Gemplus's American partner.

As a result of these events, Gemplus's cooperative efforts with Humetrix came to a grinding halt. For more than a month, Gemplus ignored Humetrix's increasingly urgent entreaties to honor the parties' agreements. Finally, Gemplus explained that, contrary to its prior representations, it viewed Humetrix not as its partner, but merely as a reseller. Humetrix had already invested significant time and resources in market research, client development, and product development, and had closed contracts with two California counties.

Humetrix sued Gemplus for breach of contract and breach of its fiduciary duty as Humetrix's partner. Humetrix also sued Guistini for intentional interference with contractual relations and Inovaction seeking a declaration that Humetrix was entitled to use the "Vaccicard" trademark in the United States. The jury awarded Humetrix $15 million in damages for breach of contract and breach of fiduciary duty. The jury also declared that Humetrix was entitled to use the trademark "Vaccicard" in the U.S. market.

Gemplus argues on appeal that the district court erred by: (1) allowing the jury to consider evidence of two oral agreements between the parties; (2) allowing the jury to consider evidence of lost profit damages despite Humetrix's use of equitable estoppel to overcome the statute of frauds; (3) allowing the jury to consider the testimony of Humetrix's experts regarding lost profits; (4) excluding evidence of Humetrix's attempts to contract with a replacement supplier of Smart Cards; and (5) entering judgment on a jury verdict that resulted from passion, confusion, or wild speculation.

Inovaction argues on appeal that the district court erred by: (1) holding that Humetrix's trademark application comported with the Lanham Act; and (2) entering judgment based on the jury's determination that Humetrix's trademark application was valid and prior to Inovaction's when there was insufficient evidence to support that determination.

We have jurisdiction under 28 U.S.C. §1291, and we affirm.

---

cardholder to maintain his or her current immunization records in this computerized credit card storage medium.

I

In 1994, Gemplus's Health Applications Sales Manager, Dr. Bruno Lassus, spoke at a medical conference about health care applications of Smart Card technology. Humetrix's founder, president, and sole shareholder, Dr. Bettina Experton, was among those in attendance. She approached Dr. Lassus after his presentation, and the two struck up a conversation about opportunities in the United States for Smart Card technology. Gemplus had no presence to speak of in the United States, and Dr. Lassus was impressed and enticed by Dr. Experton's suggestions. Humetrix and Gemplus began negotiations that spanned much of the next year. Dr. Experton visited Gemplus's headquarters in France on three occasions. Drs. Experton and Lassus initially envisioned Humetrix only as a U.S. reseller of Gemplus's Smart Card products because Gemplus already had a U.S. subsidiary, Gemplus Card International Corp. ("Gemplus USA"). At Dr. Lassus's request, Humetrix negotiated an Agency Agreement with Gemplus USA.

Dr. Lassus became increasingly impressed, however, with the opportunities available in the United States and with Humetrix's ingenuity and resourcefulness in exploiting those opportunities. As Humetrix earned a more prominent role in Gemplus's efforts to penetrate the U.S. health care market, Drs. Lassus and Experton discussed a new role for Humetrix, a role as Gemplus's partner. The negotiations proceeded, in the words of Dr. Lassus, "discreetly so as not to hurt Gemplus [USA]."

In April 1995, Dr. Lassus visited Gemplus USA and was disappointed to discover that Gemplus USA had not organized any meetings with U.S. health care companies. By contrast, Dr. Lassus reported that during a subsequent visit with Humetrix, Dr. Experton secured meetings with a number of important decision-makers in the U.S. health care industry. Dr. Lassus concluded that Humetrix was uniquely qualified to engineer Gemplus's successful entrance into the U.S. market. He observed, by contrast, that "neither Gemplus [USA] nor our competitors know how to tackle the U.S. health care market." Dr. Lassus continued to feel that "[t]he U.S. represents an extraordinary market for our technology in the health care and social services area."

By May, Gemplus and Humetrix were engaged in what Dr. Lassus described as a "pure partnership/collaboration." As Dr. Experton wrote shortly thereafter to a potential investor, Humetrix had "already generated firm orders and more interest than [Humetrix's] development and sales forces [we]re able to handle." Dr. Lassus directed Dr. Experton to draft an agreement between Humetrix and Gemplus reflecting their "partnership" and a new compensation scheme pursuant to which, in addition to the commission provided by the Agency Agreement with Gemplus USA, Humetrix was to keep the full margin of each unit sold in the United States. Humetrix drafted such an agreement, entitled the Representative Agreement, and sent it to Gemplus to be signed.

Dr. Lassus also encouraged Dr. Experton to develop a name for the vaccination Smart Card they intended to offer on the U.S. market and to obtain legal protection for that name. After researching market reaction to several names, Dr. Experton settled on "Vaccicard." Humetrix applied to register the trademark "Vaccicard" on June 14, 1995.

In July and August 1995, even as Humetrix closed contracts with two California counties and expanded its sales and development resources to meet the burgeoning supply of U.S. health care clients, its partnership with Gemplus suffered two setbacks.

First, Guy Guistini learned that Humetrix had registered the trademark "Vaccicard" for use in the United States. Guistini was the progenitor of the French Smart Card application that stored vaccination records. In addition to being the "personal adviser" to Gemplus's president, he held 45% of the shares of Inovaction, the French company that registered the trademarks "Vaccicarte" and "Vaccicard" in France. Guistini insisted that Inovaction hold the American trademark as well. He ordered Dr. Experton to withdraw Humetrix's trademark application and to stop using the Vaccicard trademark. When Dr. Experton did not accede to his demands, Guistini resorted to threats and intimidation. Inovaction filed its own American trademark application on July 19, 1995, more than a month after Humetrix's application.

Second, Gemplus acquired a new U.S. subsidiary. At Dr. Lassus's direction, Gemplus USA refrained from mentioning the acquisition to Dr. Experton.

As August drew to a close, Dr. Experton again visited France. Dr. Lassus and Gemplus's president assured her that Gemplus would execute the Representative Agreement at a meeting during her visit. Gemplus first rescheduled, then canceled, the meeting, however, and Dr. Experton returned to the United States without an executed Representative Agreement in hand.

After Dr. Experton returned to the United States, Gemplus's communication and cooperation stopped abruptly. In the ensuing six weeks, Humetrix tried in vain to communicate with Gemplus. As the deadline for performance of Humetrix's contracts with its U.S. purchasers neared, Gemplus ignored Humetrix's entreaties to cooperate or, at the very least, communicate. Humetrix sent increasingly desperate memoranda to Gemplus portending increasingly dire consequences if Gemplus and Humetrix did not re-establish contact and deliver a product to their customers in the United States. In late September, Dr. Experton sent Dr. Lassus a four-page letter, imploring Gemplus to cooperate with Humetrix in meeting customer demands.

Finally, by telephoning Gemplus's office and pretending to be someone else, Dr. Experton succeeded in reaching Dr. Lassus on October 3. Their conversation, as chronicled by Dr. Experton's letter of the following day, was a frustrating procession of dissembling explanations and hollow reassurances. On October 16, Gemplus's president wrote Dr. Experton that the Agency Agreement between Humetrix and Gemplus USA was the only agreement between them, that Humetrix was "not entitled to hold the trademark Vaccicard in the USA since Gemplus already holds a worldwide license to this product," and that Humetrix bore no ownership interest in the Vaccicard software to be marketed in the United States. The letter closed with the rebuke: "It does not seem to me appropriate to maintain hostility with my personal adviser Guy Guistini who originated the Vaccicarte project and who has all of my confidence in this sphere as in other spheres within his competence." A draft of the letter produced during discovery revealed that Guistini himself had dictated the letter for the president's signature. Without Gemplus's cooperation, Humetrix was forced to cancel its contracts with customers in the United States.

In February 1996, Humetrix sued Gemplus, Inovaction, and Guistini. Because Gemplus never executed the Representative Agreement, Humetrix made no claims for breach of its terms. Instead, Humetrix alleged that the discussions between Humetrix and Gemplus culminated in the formation of two oral contracts, the Sales Agreement and the Partnership Agreement, and that Gemplus breached them both. Humetrix attributed Gemplus's breach, in part, to the interference of Guistini, for which Humetrix sought compensatory and punitive damages. Finally, Humetrix sought a declaration that it had properly registered the trademark "Vaccicard" in the United States.

Gemplus countered that the Agency Agreement constituted the sole agreement between Humetrix and Gemplus or its subsidiaries and moved to compel arbitration in accordance with the Agency Agreement's mandatory arbitration clause. The district court denied Gemplus's motion. On interlocutory appeal, we affirmed on the grounds that "Gemplus was not a party to the Agency Agreement that contained the arbitration provision," only Gemplus USA and Humetrix were parties to the Agency Agreement, and that "Humetrix enjoyed a distinct and separate contractual relationship with parent company Gemplus." Humetrix, Inc. v. Gemplus, S.C.A., No. 97-55080, 1997 WL 683301, at *1, *3 (9th Cir. Oct. 23, 1997) (unpublished disposition; see 9th Cir. R. 36-3).

Humetrix's claims against Gemplus, Guistini and Inovaction were tried before a jury. The jury found that Humetrix and Gemplus entered into the Sales Agreement and the Partnership Agreement. The jury further found that:

(1) Gemplus breached the Sales Agreement, damaging Humetrix in the amount of $5 million;

(2) Gemplus breached the Partnership Agreement, damaging Humetrix in the amount of $10 million;

(3) Guistini intentionally interfered with Humetrix's contractual relations, damaging Humetrix in the amount of $1.2 million;

(4) Guistini's conduct warranted an award of punitive damages to Humetrix in the amount of $1.3 million; and,

(5) Humetrix was the proper legal owner of the Vaccicard trademark in the United States. Gemplus and Inovaction appeal.[3]

II

. . . Under California law, a plaintiff that prevails on a breach of contract claim "should receive as nearly as possible the equivalent of the benefits of performance," meaning the plaintiff should be put "in as good a position as he would have been had performance been rendered as promised." Brandon & Tibbs v. George Kevorkian Accountancy Corp., 226 Cal. App. 3d 442, 277 Cal. Rptr. 40, 47 (Ct. App. 1990). This may include lost profits if the plaintiff can prove that the defendant's failure to perform caused the plaintiff to lose profits. See id. at 48-49.

c

Gemplus contends that the district court erred by admitting Humetrix's damages experts' testimony regarding lost profits. Gemplus claims that the testimony was speculative and was unsupported by the evidence. District courts, in their capacity as evidentiary gatekeepers, have broad discretion in deciding what evidence is relevant, reliable, and helpful to the trier of fact. Desrosiers v. Flight Int'l of Florida Inc., 156 F.3d 952, 961 (9th Cir. 1998); Shore v. Mohave, Arizona, 644 F.2d 1320, 1322 (9th Cir. 1981). . . .

Both we and California state courts have recognized that lost profits are "necessarily an estimate," Portland 76 Auto/Truck Plaza, Inc. v. Union Oil Co., 153 F.3d 938, 947 (9th Cir. 1998), cert. denied, 526 U.S. 1064, 119 S. Ct. 1454, 143 L. Ed. 2d 541 (1999), and that their "amount cannot be shown with mathematical precision." Berge v. Int'l Harvester Co., 142 Cal. App. 3d 152, 190 Cal. Rptr. 815, 822 (Ct. App. 1983). We uphold awards of lost profit damages so long as they are supported by substantial evidence. [Citations omitted.]

Humetrix's request for lost profit damages is supported by the testimony of two experts. The experts based their testimony on contracts Humetrix had closed, pilot projects for which Humetrix had received commitments, and contracts in negotiation at the time of breach; Humetrix's partnership with Gemplus, the world's leading manufacturer of Smart Cards; Gemplus's success in foreign markets; Dr. Experton's contacts with government health care officials; and market forecasts, including Gemplus's own. Their testimony is borne out by Gemplus's own contemporaneous

---

3. The district court vacated the punitive damages award against Guistini, and Humetrix and Guistini subsequently settled.

observations that "the real market boom is still ahead of us," and that "the U. S. represents an extraordinary market for our technology in the health care and social services area." Humetrix's request for lost profits was supported by substantial evidence.

To the extent Gemplus sought to challenge the correctness of Humetrix's experts' testimony, its recourse is not exclusion of the testimony, but, rather, refutation of it by cross-examination and by the testimony of its own expert witnesses. Gemplus availed itself of both of these opportunities. Gemplus cross-examined Humetrix's experts and presented its own expert.

Authority to determine the victor in such a "battle of expert witnesses" is properly reposed in the jury. Wyler Summit P'ship v. Turner Broad. Sys., Inc., 235 F.3d 1184, 1192 (9th Cir. 2000) ("Weighing the credibility of conflicting expert witness testimony is the province of the jury."). As one California court of appeal observed:

> As to the reasonableness of the assumptions underlying the experts' lost profit analysis, criticisms of an expert's method of calculation [are] a matter for the jury's consideration in weighing that evidence. It is for the trier of fact to accept or reject this evidence, and this evidence not being inherently improbable provides a substantial basis for the trial court's award of lost profits.

Arntz Contracting Co. v. St. Paul Fire & Marine Ins. Co., 47 Cal. App. 4th 464, 54 Cal. Rptr. 2d 888, 903 (Ct. App. 1996) (internal quotations and citations omitted). . . . Humetrix's experts based their testimony on substantial evidence. The district court did not abuse its discretion by allowing the jury to weigh the conflicting testimony of the parties' experts regarding lost profit damages.

Gemplus also argues that lost profit damages are inappropriate for a "new business" because, without a record of past performance as a standard, future profits are necessarily speculative. In light of the "new business rule," Gemplus argues, the district court abused its discretion by allowing the jury even to consider Humetrix's future profits in determining its damages.

The new business rule is more empirical than normative, however. As an empirical matter, new businesses often cannot offer reliable proof of prospective profits. As a normative matter, if a business can offer reliable proof of profits, there is no reason to deprive it of the profits it would have garnered had the contract been performed merely because it is "new." As one California court put it: "[T]he [new business] rule is not a hard and fast one and loss of prospective profits may nevertheless be recovered if the evidence shows with reasonable certainty both their occurrence and the extent thereof." Gerwin v. Southeastern California Ass'n of Seventh Day Adventists, 14 Cal. App. 3d 209, 92 Cal. Rptr. 111, 119 (Cal. Ct. App. 1971).

Moreover, Humetrix was not exactly a new business. When it contracted with Gemplus it had been offering health care consulting and information systems services to the California and national markets for ten years. See

Maggio, Inc. v. United Farm Workers, 227 Cal. App. 3d 847, 278 Cal. Rptr. 250, 264 (Ct. App. 1991) ("Cases applying the 'new business rule' generally involve businesses which have been in operation only a very short period of time."). Indeed, the experience, the contacts, and the dynamism of its principal, Dr. Experton, led Dr. Lassus to observe that Humetrix was uniquely capable of successfully marketing Smart Card technology in the United States.

Humetrix's experts were also able to draw on Gemplus's own experience introducing Smart Card technology into previously untapped markets. Humetrix's profits were, in a sense, dependent on and derivative of Gemplus's profits so that if one could be determined reliably, the other followed as a matter of course. Under these circumstances, the profits Humetrix could expect to garner from its contracts with Gemplus were not so speculative that the district court abused its discretion by allowing the jury to hear evidence regarding profits. . . .

E

Gemplus argues, finally, that the district erred by entering the jury's $15 million award of damages, an award Gemplus claims could only be the result of passion, confusion, or wild speculation by the jury. Our role in reviewing a jury award entered under California law is limited:

> [A]s a reviewing court, we view the evidence through a different lens than does the trier of fact. The judgment comes to us cloaked with the presumption that it is correct. In assessing a claim that the jury's award of damages is excessive, we do not reassess the credibility of witnesses or reweigh the evidence. To the contrary, we consider the evidence in the light most favorable to the judgment, accepting every reasonable inference and resolving all conflicts in its favor. We may interfere with an award of damage only when it is so large that it shocks the conscience and suggests passion, prejudice or corruption on the part of the jury.

Westphal v. Wal-Mart Stores, Inc., 68 Cal. App. 4th 1071, 81 Cal. Rptr. 2d 46, 48 (Ct. App. 1998).

Humetrix and Gemplus were poised at the inception of a promising business opportunity — to provide a technological breakthrough in personal health care documentation to government and private health care entities around the country. Gemplus's similar foreign endeavors had been very profitable. Gemplus was confident that its campaign in the United States would be equally profitable. Under these circumstances, the jury's determination that Humetrix could have earned $15 million in net profits over the ensuing five years does not shock the conscience or suggest passion, prejudice, or corruption. The district court did not abuse its discretion by entering the jury's verdict on damages as the proper judgment. . . .

For the foregoing reasons, the judgment of the district court is affirmed.

2. Foreseeability

HADLEY v. BAXENDALE
Court of the Exchequer, 1854
9 Exch. 341, 156 Eng. Rep. 145

At the trial before Crompton, J., at the last Gloucester Assizes, it appeared that the plaintiffs carried on an extensive business as millers at Gloucester; and that, on the 11th of May, their mill was stopped by a breakage of the crank shaft by which the mill was worked. The steam-engine was manufactured by Messrs. Joyce & Co., the engineers, at Greenwich, and it became necessary to send the shaft as a pattern for a new one to Greenwich. The fracture was discovered on the 12th, and on the 13th the plaintiffs sent one of their servants to the office of the defendants, who are the well-known carriers trading under the name of Pickford & Co., for the purpose of having the shaft carried to Greenwich. The plaintiffs' servant told the clerk that the mill was stopped, and that the shaft must be sent immediately; and in answer to the inquiry when the shaft would be taken, the answer was, that if it was sent up by twelve o'clock any day, it would be delivered at Greenwich on the following day. On the following day the shaft was taken by the defendants, before noon, for the purpose of being conveyed to Greenwich, and the sum of 2l. 4s. was paid for its carriage for the whole distance; at the same time the defendants' clerk was told that a special entry, if required, should be made to hasten its delivery. The delivery of the shaft at Greenwich was delayed by some neglect; and the consequence was, that the plaintiffs did not receive the new shaft for several days after they would otherwise have done, and the working of their mill was thereby delayed, and they thereby lost the profits they would otherwise have received.

On the part of the defendants, it was objected that these damages were too remote, and that the defendants were not liable with respect to them. The learned Judge left the case generally to the jury, who found a verdict with 25l. damages beyond the amount paid into Court.

Whateley, in last Michaelmas Term, obtained a rule nisi for a new trial, on the ground of misdirection. . . .

ALDERSON, B. We think that there ought to be a new trial in this case; but, in so doing, we deem it to be expedient and necessary to state explicitly the rule which the Judge, at the next trial, ought, in our opinion, to direct the jury to be governed by when they estimate the damages.

It is, indeed, of the last importance that we should do this; for, if the jury are left without any definite rule to guide them, it will, in such cases as these, manifestly lead to the greatest injustice. The Courts have done this on several occasions; and, in Blake v. Midland Railway Company (18 Q.B. 93), the Court granted a new trial on this very ground, that the rule had not been definitely laid down to the jury by the learned Judge at Nisi Prius.

"There are certain established rules," this Court says, in Alder v. Keighley (15 M.&W. 117), "according to which the jury ought to find." And the Court, in that case, adds: "and here there is a clear rule, that the amount which would have been received if the contract had been kept, is the measure of damages if the contract is broken."

Now we think the proper rule in such a case as the present is this: Where two parties have made a contract which one of them has broken, the damages which the other party ought to receive in respect of such breach of contract should be such as may fairly and reasonably be considered either arising naturally, i.e., according to the usual course of things, from such breach of contract itself, or such as may reasonably be supposed to have been in the contemplation of both parties, at the time they made the contract, as the probable result of the breach of it. Now, if the special circumstances under which the contract was actually made were communicated by the plaintiffs to the defendants, and thus known to both parties, the damages resulting from the breach of such a contract, which they would reasonably contemplate, would be the amount of injury which would ordinarily follow from a breach of contract under these special circumstances so known and communicated. But, on the other hand, if these special circumstances were wholly unknown to the party breaking the contract, he, at the most, could only be supposed to have had in his contemplation the amount of injury which would arise generally, and in the great multitude of cases not affected by any special circumstances, from such a breach of contract. For, had the special circumstances been known, the parties might have specially provided for the breach of contract by special terms as to the damages in that case; and of this advantage it would be very unjust to deprive them. Now the above principles are those by which we think the jury ought to be guided in estimating the damages arising out of any breach of contract. It is said, that other cases such as breaches of contract in the non-payment of money, or in the not making a good title to land, are to be treated as exceptions from this, and as governed by a conventional rule. But, as in such cases, both parties must be supposed to be cognisant of that well-known rule, these cases may, we think, be more properly classed under the rule above enunciated as to cases under known special circumstances, because there both parties may reasonably be presumed to contemplate the estimation of the amount of damages according to the conventional rule. Now, in the present case, if we are to apply the principles above laid down, we find that the only circumstances here communicated by the plaintiffs to the defendants at the time the contract was made, were that the article to be carried was the broken shaft of a mill, and that the plaintiffs were the millers of that mill. But how do these circumstances show reasonably that the profits of the mill must be stopped by an unreasonable delay in the delivery of the broken shaft by the carrier to the third person? Suppose the plaintiffs had another shaft in their possession put up or putting up at the time, and that they only wished to send back the broken shaft to the engineer who made it; it is clear that this would be quite consistent with the above circumstances, and yet the unreasonable delay in the delivery would have no effect upon the intermediate profits of the mill. Or, again, suppose that, at the time of the delivery to the carrier, the machinery of the mill had been in other respects defective, then, also, the same results would follow. Here it is true that the shaft was actually sent back to serve as a model for a new one, and that the want of a new one was the only cause of the stoppage of the mill, and that the loss of profits really arose from not sending down the new shaft in proper time, and that this arose from the delay in delivering the broken one to serve as a model. But it is obvious that, in the great multitude of cases of millers sending off broken shafts to third persons by a carrier under ordinary circumstances, such consequences would not, in all probability, have occurred; and these special circumstances were here never communicated by the plaintiffs to the defendants. It follows, therefore, that the loss of profits here cannot reasonably be considered such a consequence of the breach of contract as could have been fairly and reasonably contemplated by both the parties when they made this contract. For such loss would neither have flowed naturally from the breach of this contract in the great multitude of such cases occurring under ordinary circumstances, nor were the special circumstances, which, perhaps, would have made it a reasonable and natural consequence of such breach of contract, communicated to or known by the defendants. The Judge ought, therefore, to have told the jury, that, upon the facts then before them, they ought not to take the loss of profits into consideration at all in estimating the damages. There must therefore be a new trial in this case.

Rule absolute.

NOTES AND QUESTIONS

1. Baron Alderson refers to "other cases" in which the usual consequential damages are measured by different standards. These are, first, the non-payment of money, in which the typical consequential loss is limited to unpaid interest, and, second, the failure of a seller of realty to deliver good title, where most courts will allow the seller who makes this mistake in good faith to repay the buyer's expenses but not give the buyer the loss of bargain damages.

2. UCC §2-715(2)(b) entitles plaintiffs in breach of warranty cases to recover consequential damages for "injury to person or property proximately resulting from any breach of warranty." The UCC thus takes the position that a breach of warranty plaintiff need *not* prove that these types of harm are foreseeable. Why would the drafters have done this?

(handwritten top margin: UCC – 2-715 → reflects tacit agreement)

(handwritten left margin: Services)

Problem 66

Bill Gilbert was offered $50,000 for his new play *Engaged* if he could get it to the producer, Dick Carte, by October 12. He finished writing the play on October 10, and called up a private courier, Overnight Delivery, Inc., telling the woman he talked to on the phone all of the above details. He ended the conversation by saying, "I'll lose $50,000 if this package does not arrive by October 12." She told him not to worry. The Overnight Delivery courier picked up the package on October 11 and put it on board its airplane for delivery the next day. That night the plane crashed, and the package was never delivered. Gilbert's play was not produced, and he sued Overnight Delivery, Inc. for $50,000. Are either of the following defenses valid?

(handwritten left margin: Consequential Damages)

(handwritten left margin: – No defense A) There was a tacit agreement when she told him not to worry – It was implied or endorsed)

(a) Mere *knowledge* of the possible damages flowing from the breach is not the same thing as an *agreement* to accept the liability for such damages. Before the liability attaches, there must be at least a tacit agreement under which the defendant assumes the risk of the consequential loss.

(b) The plane crash was totally unforeseeable, so that Overnight Delivery is not liable for the consequential damages.

(handwritten: b) No → harm was foreseeable ...)

AM/PM FRANCHISE ASS'N v. ATLANTIC RICHFIELD CO.
Pennsylvania Supreme Court, 1990
526 Pa. 110, 584 A.2d 915

(handwritten: D)

(handwritten left margin: P–A)

CAPPY, J. Before us is an appeal by members of a franchisee association from an order of the Superior Court of Pennsylvania at No. 01958 Philadelphia 1987, issued April 14, 1988, affirming the order of the Court of Common Pleas at No. 157 November Term 1986, dated June 16, 1987, sustaining defendant's preliminary objections in the nature of a demurrer and dismissing the action.

(handwritten left margin: Plaintiff claim they suffered Econic harm)

We granted allocatur to determine whether the named appellants ("plaintiffs") have alleged sufficient facts to sustain a cause of action when they aver that the gasoline they purchased from the appellee ("ARCO") was not in conformance with the warranties made and resulted in their suffering economic harm. In making such a determination, we address the question of whether such damages constitute a "loss of good will," and whether good will damages are too speculative as a matter of law to permit recovery. For the reasons set forth herein, we find that the plaintiffs have alleged sufficient facts to entitle them to proceed with their claim and that the damages claimed are not good will nor so speculative as to deny them an attempt at recovery. We reverse the decision of the Superior Court in part and affirm in part.

(handwritten left margin: Issue "loss of good will" ↓ too speculative?)

(handwritten left margin: Reversed in part Affirmed in part)

PROCEDURAL HISTORY

ARCO filed preliminary objections in the nature of a demurrer to appellants' complaint, claiming that the damages sought by appellants stemmed from a loss of good will, which are speculative and not recoverable as a matter of law. Additionally, the defendants claim that the plaintiffs should not be entitled to recover under a tort theory.

[margin note: loss of goodwill are too speculative and nonrecoverable as a matter of law]

[margin note: Tort claim too]

The trial court sustained ARCO's preliminary objections and dismissed appellants' complaint.

[margin note: Tral court for Defendt]

The Superior Court affirmed the ruling of the trial court, holding that under current Pennsylvania law, damages sought for the breach of warranty claims due to a loss of good will are not recoverable as they have traditionally been considered to be too speculative. Additionally, the Superior Court held that the plaintiff was not entitled to recover in tort, finding that the duty of the parties to act in good faith arises under contract and not tort principles.

[margin note: Affirmed b Superior court]

[margin note: Dismiss tort claim]

[margin note: Dissent] In the dissent to the opinion of the Superior Court, Judge Brosky remarked that the majority characterizes the claim as one for loss of good will, while he "view[s] appellants' claim as a request for lost profits occasioned by appellee's delivery of an unmerchantable product." 373 Pa. Super. 572, 580, 542 A.2d 90, 94 (1988). Additionally, Judge Brosky disagreed with the characterization of the loss as speculative, stating "[a]lthough calculating damages may have been a problem in the past, and in certain cases, may still be a problem, I cannot see that it presents a problem here. . . . Further, a comparison of the business profits before and after the delivery of the unmerchantable gasoline should prove to be enlightening." Id. at 581, 542 A.2d at 94-95.

[margin note: Dissent → viewed it as lost profits]

[margin note: Calculating damages Not a problem in this case]

FACTUAL HISTORY

The Plaintiffs claim to represent a class of over 150 franchisees of ARCO that operated AM/PM Mini Markets in Pennsylvania and New York during a three and one-half year period.

ARCO entered into franchise agreements with the plaintiffs which were comprised of a premises lease, a lessee dealer gasoline agreement, and an AM/PM mini-market agreement. The products agreement mandated that the franchisees sell only ARCO petroleum products.

The complaint sets forth the following facts: ARCO began experimenting with its formula for unleaded gasoline and provided its franchisees with an unleaded gasoline blended with oxinol, consisting of 4.5% methanol and 4.5% gasoline grade tertiary butyl alcohol (hereinafter "the oxinol blend") from early 1982 through September 30, 1985.

[margin note: ARCO started experimenting with a new gas formula]

During this three and a half year period, the franchisees were required to sell the oxinol blend to their clients who desired unleaded gasoline. The franchisees were given no opportunity to buy regular unleaded gasoline from ARCO during that period.

*New formula
created problems*

Plaintiffs claim that numerous purchasers of the oxinol blend gasoline experienced poor engine performance and physical damage to fuel system components. Specifically, plaintiffs claim that the oxinol gasoline permitted an excess accumulation of alcohol and/or water which interfered with the efficiency of gasoline engines and, in certain vehicles, caused swelling of plastic or rubber components in the fuel delivery system and resulted in

loss of sales due to poor quality of gas

engine damage. The plaintiffs claim that the gasoline did not conform to ARCO's warranties about the product.

As the problems with the oxinol blend became known, the plaintiffs claim to have suffered a precipitous drop in the volume of their business and an attendant loss of profits. Specifically, plaintiffs point to the rise in sales from 1973 until 1982, when sales began to fall dramatically; allegedly due to defective oxinol blend gasoline.

requested Damages for lost profits, consequential, and Incidental

In their complaint, plaintiffs allege three counts of breach of warranty, breach of implied duty, misrepresentation, and exemplary damages. They request damages for "lost profits, consequential and incidental damages."

DISCUSSION

The point at which we start our inquiry is the Uniform Commercial Code ("the U.C.C."), codified at 13 Pa C.S. §1101 et seq. Section 2-714, entitled "Damages of buyer for breach in regard to accepted goods" is one of the governing provisions in the case before us, and provides, in pertinent part:

UCC 2-714

(2) Measure of damages for breach of warranty. The measure of damages for breach of warranty is the difference at the time and place of acceptance between the value of the goods accepted and the value they would have had if they had been as warranted, unless special circumstances show proximate damages of a different amount.

(3) Incidental and consequential damages. In a proper case any incidental and consequential damages under section 2-715 (relating to incidental and consequential damages of buyer) may also be recovered.

Section 2-715 is entitled "Incidental and Consequential Damages of Buyer" and provides, in pertinent part:

UCC 2-715

(1) Incidental damages. Incidental damages resulting from the breach of the seller include: . . .

(c) any other reasonable expenses incident to the delay or other breach.

(2) Consequential damages. Consequential damages resulting from the breach of the seller include:

(a) any loss resulting from general or particular requirements and needs of which the seller at the time of contracting had reason to know and which could not reasonably be prevented by cover or otherwise.

Pursuant to the provisions of the U.C.C., plaintiffs are entitled to seek "general" damages, so-called, under §2-714(2), and consequential damages as provided by §2-714(3).

There has been substantial confusion in the courts and among litigants about what consequential damages actually are and what types of consequential damages are available in a breach of warranty case. Where a buyer in the business of reselling goods can prove that a breach by the seller has caused him to lose profitable resales, the buyer's lost profits constitute a form of consequential damages. We now hold that in addition to general damages, there are three types of lost profit recoverable as consequential damages that may flow from a breach of warranty: (1) loss of primary profits; (2) loss of secondary profits; and (3) a loss of good will damages (or prospective damages, as they are sometimes termed).

In order to alleviate the confusion that has developed concerning the various damages, we use an example to help illustrate the different types.

General damages in the case of accepted goods (such as occurred here) are the actual difference in value between the goods as promised and the goods as received. Thus, suppose a buyer bought five hundred tires from a wholesaler that were to be delivered in good condition, and in that condition would be worth $2,500. The tires were delivered with holes in them which rendered them worthless. The buyer would be entitled to $2,500 from the seller — the difference between the value of the tires as warranted and the value of the tires as received; those would be the general damages.

Consequential damages are generally understood to be other damages which naturally and proximately flow from the breach and include three types of lost profit damages: (1) lost primary profits; (2) lost secondary profits; and (3) loss of prospective profits, also commonly referred to as good will damages.

Lost primary profits are the difference between what the buyer would have earned from reselling the goods in question had there been no breach and what was earned after the breach occurred. Thus, if the buyer of the tires proved that he would have resold the tires for $5,000, he would be able to claim an additional $2,500 for loss of tire profits; the difference between what he would have earned from the sale of the tires and what he actually did earn from the sale (or lack of sales) from the tires.

If the buyer of the tires also sold, for example, hubcaps with every set of tires, he would also suffer a loss of hubcap profits. These types of damages are what we term "loss of secondary profits."

If the buyer's regular customers were so disgruntled about the defective tires that they no longer frequented the buyer's business and began to patronize a competitor's business, the buyer would have suffered a "loss of good will" beyond the direct loss of profits from the nonconforming goods; his future business would be adversely affected as a result of the defective tires. Thus, good will damages refer to profits lost on future sales rather than on sales of the defective goods themselves.

While this example provides a simple framework to understand the different types of possible damages in a breach of warranty case, it does not encompass the myriad of circumstances in which a claim for damages can arise, nor does it specify which of these different damages have been allowed in Pennsylvania.

In addition to recognizing general damages under §2-714 of the Code, Pennsylvania allows consequential damages in the form of lost profits to be recovered.

Pennsylvania has, however, disallowed good will damages; finding them to be too speculative to permit recovery. In the cases disallowing good will damages, part of the reason we found them too speculative is that the damages were not contemplated by the parties at the time the contract was made. . . .

Turning to the case at hand, we must determine whether the plaintiffs have alleged sufficient facts to permit them to proceed with a claim for consequential damages. . . .

Loss of Profits for Gasoline Sales

The first claim the plaintiff makes for damages is for the profits lost from the sales of gasoline. The plaintiffs claim that the breach of warranty by the defendant concerning the gasoline caused the plaintiffs to lose sales during a three and one half year period while they received nonconforming gasoline from ARCO. In the case of Kassab v. Central Soya, 432 Pa. 217, 246 A.2d 848 (1968), we permitted lost profits for cattle sales when the plaintiff showed that the defective feed caused harm to their cattle, causing the public to stop buying their cattle. The allegation here is similar. When the gasoline buying public discovered that the gasoline was defective, many stopped purchasing ARCO gasoline.

Employing the reasoning of _Kassab_ and taking it one step further, we believe that the plaintiffs here are entitled to show that the gasoline buying community did not buy their gasoline from 1982 through 1985 because of the reasonable belief that the gasoline was defective and would harm their engines. The lost gasoline sales are comparable to the lost cattle sales in _Kassab_. The distinction between the two cases is that the Kassabs had bought the feed all at one time and thus all their livestock was affected. The instant plaintiffs bought their gasoline in regular intervals and could only earn a profit on what they could sell per month. The defendant's argument — that the plaintiffs sold all the gasoline they bought — misses the point. While they may have sold every gallon, they sold significantly fewer gallons during the period that ARCO allegedly delivered nonconforming gasoline. Thus, during this period, the plaintiffs' lost sales were just as directly attributable to the defective gasoline as the lost profits were attributable to the defective tires in the example we used previously.

Thus, if prior to the manufacture of defective gasoline the plaintiffs sold 100,000 gallons per month every month and then as a result of the defective gasoline, they sold only 60,000 gallons per month every month until ARCO discontinued that gasoline, then the plaintiffs have lost the profits they would have received on 40,000 gallons per month for the three year claimed period. Lost profits are, in fact, the difference between what the plaintiff actually earned and what they would have earned had the defendant not committed the breach. Because the gasoline was allegedly not in conformance with the warranties, the plaintiffs may be entitled to lost profits for the gasoline on a breach of warranty theory. The lost gasoline sales are what we have termed "loss of primary profits," and they are recoverable pursuant to §2-715 of the U.C.C. upon proper proof. . . .

Furthermore, we note that §1-106 of the U.C.C. provides:

[t]he remedies provided by this title shall be *liberally administered to the end that the aggrieved party may be put in as good a position as if the other party had fully performed* but neither consequential or special nor penal damages may be had except as specifically provided in this title or by other rule of law. (Emphasis supplied.)

The Code itself compels us to be liberal in our interpretation of the types of damages we permit. We would therefore allow the plaintiffs to proceed with their claims for lost gasoline profits during the period ARCO supplied allegedly nonconforming gasoline.

LOSS OF PROFITS FOR ITEMS OTHER THAN GASOLINE SALES

The plaintiffs allege that in addition to a loss of profits for sales of gasoline, they had a concomitant loss of sales for other items that they sold in their mini-marts during the period of time that ARCO supplied nonconforming gasoline. Their rationale is that when the number of customers buying gasoline decreased, so did the number of customers buying items at the mini-mart. In other words, related facets of their business suffered as a result of the defective gasoline. This type of injury is what we characterize as "loss of secondary profits"; meaning that the sales of other products suffered as a result of the breach of warranty. This court has not had an opportunity to address whether these types of damages are recoverable.

In the case before us, the essence of plaintiffs' allegations is that customers frequent the mini-marts because it is convenient to do so at the time they purchase gasoline. Customers of the mini-mart are foremost gasoline buying patrons; gasoline is their primary purchase and sundries are their incidental purchases. Here, the plaintiffs claim that the *primary product* sales so affected the incidental sales as to create a loss in other aspects of their business. It is reasonable to assume that if the gasoline sales dropped

[Handwritten margin notes, top left: "Foreseeability"]

[Handwritten margin notes, left: "When loss of primary profits, its foreseeable to have loss of secondary profits"]

dramatically, there was a ripple effect on the mini-mart sales. Additionally, when a primary product does not conform to the warranty, we believe that it is foreseeable that there will be a loss of secondary profits. Thus, permitting these damages would correspond with the requirement of foreseeability as set forth in *Lampus*, supra, and the Code. It is much less foreseeable to assume there will be a loss of secondary profits when the nonconforming products are not the primary ones. We believe that unless it is a primary product that does not conform to the warranty, the causal relationship between the breach and the loss is too attenuated to permit damages for the loss of secondary profits.[12]

We also find that the fact situation before us presents a further problem in that the plaintiffs were not able to mitigate the harm in any way by buying substitute goods or "cover." Thus, the plaintiffs' primary product was defective and they were unable to remedy the situation by buying gasoline from another supplier.

[Handwritten margin note, left: "Rule"]

We find that the present case presents compelling reasons for permitting damages for loss of secondary profits. Henceforth, in a breach of warranty case, when a primary product of the plaintiff is alleged to be nonconforming and the plaintiff is unable to cover by purchasing substitute goods, we hold that upon proper proof, the plaintiff should be entitled to sue for loss of secondary profits.[13]

LOSS OF GOOD WILL

Historically, Pennsylvania has disallowed recovery for loss of good will damages or prospective profits in breach of warranty cases. The cases generally relied upon for this proposition are Michelin Tire Co. v. Schultz, 295 Pa. 140, 145 A. 67 (1929); Harry Rubin & Sons, Inc. v. Consolidated Pipe Co. of America, 396 Pa. 506, 153 A.2d 472 (1959); and Kassab v. Central Soya, 432 Pa. 217, 246 A.2d 848 (1968)....

As one commentator aptly noted, "[l]oss of good will is a mercurial concept and, as such, is difficult to define. In a broad sense, it refers to a

---

12. As with all cases involving breach of warranty, the plaintiff is charged with the burden of proving that the defendant's breach is the proximate cause of the harm suffered. Thus, in order to proceed with their case, the plaintiffs here must prove that the alleged nonconformance of the gasoline caused both their loss of gasoline sales as well as their loss of mini-mart sales. This requirement is an arduous one and we render no opinion as to whether the plaintiffs can meet this burden. However, we note that this is for the trial court, in its wisdom, to decide whether the plaintiffs have met the threshold of proof to submit the case to the factfinder.

13. What constitutes a "primary product" will be dependent on the facts of each case. However, we would define a "primary product" as an item upon which the aggrieved party relies for a substantial amount of its revenue. The plaintiff must show that without that product, his business would be severely incapacitated.

loss of future profits."[14] Other jurisdictions have considered loss of good will to be a loss of profits and reputation among customers.[15] Generally, good will refers to the reputation that businesses have built over the course of time that is reflected by the return of customers to purchase goods and the attendant profits that accompanies such sales. Thus the phrase "good will damages" is coextensive with prospective profits and loss of business reputation.

Secondly, we must decide when good will damages arise in a breach of warranty situation. Essentially, damage to good will in a case in which the seller supplies a quantity dictated by the buyer's requirements arises only *after* the seller has ceased providing nonconforming goods — or the buyer has purchased substitute goods. Damage to good will in this case would refer to the loss of business sales that occurred after the buyer was able to provide acceptable goods to his customers; it does not refer to the period of time during which he is forced to sell the nonconforming goods.

Thirdly, we must address whether good will damages are too speculative to permit recovery, as we held in *Michelin, Rubin & Sons*, supra, and *Kassab*, supra. Although we disallowed good will damages in those cases, they are not recent. They were written in a time when business was conducted on a more simple basis, where market studies and economic forecasting were unexplored sciences.

We are now in an era in which computers, economic forecasting, sophisticated marketing studies and demographic studies are widely used and accepted. As such, we believe that the rationale for precluding prospective profits under the rubric of "too speculative" ignores the realities of the marketplace and the science of modern economics. We believe that claims for prospective profits should not be barred ab initio. Rather, plaintiffs should be given an opportunity to set forth and attempt to prove their damages.

Twenty years ago, the Third Circuit Court of Appeals noted in a case disallowing claims for prospective profits that damages once considered speculative may not be in the future:

> This is not to say we approve the Pennsylvania view or believe it will be the Pennsylvania position in the future [prohibiting good will damages]. Considering the advances made in techniques of market analysis and the use of highly sophisticated computers it may be that lost profits of this nature are no more speculative than lost profits from the destruction of a factory or hotel, and perhaps Pennsylvania will reconsider the reason for its rule in a future case.

Neville Chemical Co. v. Union Carbide Corp., 422 F.2d 1205, 1227 (1970).

We believe the time has come to reconsider that rule. In doing so, we find our position on recovery for good will damages (or prospective profits)

14. Anderson, Incidental and Consequential Damages, 7 J. L. & Com. 327, 420 (1987).
15. Texsun Feed Yards, Inc. v. Ralston Purina Co., 447 F.2d 660 (5th Cir. 1971).

to be out of step with modern day business practices and techniques, as well as the law of other jurisdictions. As noted by Professor Anderson in his well-crafted article on incidental and consequential damages,

> [t]o date, only the Pennsylvania courts have categorically denied recovery for loss of goodwill under any circumstances, an issue which has been oft-litigated in Pennsylvania. If one removes the Pennsylvania cases from the count, a significant majority of the cases have allowed for the recovery of lost goodwill in proper circumstances.[17]

Furthermore, our rule has been repeatedly criticized by other courts and commentators. In reviewing our case law on the issue of prospective profits, we have not had a significant case come before us since *Kassab* was decided in 1968. Since that time, astronauts have walked on the moon, engineers have developed computers capable of amazing feats and biomedical engineers and physicians have made enormous strides in organ transplantation and replacement. It is evident that the world of 1990 is not the same world as it was in 1929 when the *Michelin* case was decided, nor even the same world as it was in 1968 when *Kassab* was decided. While these rapid technological developments have not been without their concomitant problems, they have made possible many things that were not possible before; including the calculation of prospective profits. For these reasons, we overrule *Michelin*, supra, *Rubin & Sons, Inc.*, supra, and *Kassab*, supra, to the extent they prohibit a plaintiff from alleging a claim for damage to good will as a matter of law.

Inextricably entwined with the issue of speculation is the difficulty in proving the damages are causally related to the breach. As we stated earlier, difficulty in proving causation should not operate as a bar to permitting plaintiffs to claim the damages. Furthermore, we note that pursuant to our case law and the Uniform Commercial Code, damages need not be proved with mathematical certainty. As long as the plaintiffs can provide a reasonable basis from which the jury can calculate damages, they will be permitted to pursue their case.

Thus, we now hold that plaintiffs should be entitled to try to prove good will damages; provided they are able to introduce sufficient evidence (1) to establish that such profits were causally related to a breach of warranty and (2) to provide the trier of fact with a reasonable basis from which to calculate damages.

Turning to the facts of this case, we note that the plaintiffs have made no claim for good will damages, since none was incurred; ARCO having cured the breach by stopping the supply of the nonconforming gasoline. The damages claimed are only for the period of time that the plaintiffs were forced to purchase the gasoline with oxinol. Thus, we reverse the decision of the lower courts in holding that the plaintiffs' claim was for good will damages.

---

17. Anderson, Incidental and Consequential Damages, 7 J.L. & Com. 327, 421 (1987).

CONCLUSION

We now hold that there are three types of lost profits recoverable as consequential damages available under §2-714 and §2-715 of the Uniform Commercial Code: (1) loss of primary profits; (2) loss of secondary profits; and (3) good will damages, defined as a loss of prospective profits or business reputation. While this categorization of damages represents a new direction for the court, we believe it is the better direction. . . .

It is so ordered. . . .

Problem 67

When their young daughter died in a tragic accident, the parents contracted with a funeral home to prepare her body for burial. When they went to the funeral home to view the body, the mortician was apologetic. He had misplaced the body, and "I think she's in Ohio" was all that he could say. Both parents suffered extreme mental anguish because of this mishap. Can they recover consequential damages for their suffering? The actual case is Renihan v. Wright, 125 Ind. 536, 25 N.E. 823 (1890); Annot., 54 A.L.R. 4th 901; see Douglas Whaley, Paying for the Agony: The Recovery of Emotional Distress Damages in Contract Actions, 26 Suffolk U. L. Rev. 935 (1992).

Note the following excerpt from the Restatement (Second) of Contracts:

§353. Loss Due to Emotional Disturbance

Recovery for emotional disturbance will be excluded unless the breach also causes bodily harm or the contract or the breach is of such a kind that serious emotional disturbance was a particularly likely result.

Problem 68

On graduating from law school, Andrew Advocate received a gift of $25,000 from his wealthy parents and used it to buy a sports car that he had long desired. The car proved to be a lemon; four times it stalled and stranded Andrew in dangerous traffic situations. He took time off from his new job 18 times to take the car to and from the dealer's repair shop. Finally, when it stalled for the fifth time and made him miss a court appearance, he parked the car at the dealership and gave notice that he was revoking his acceptance (UCC §2-608) and wanted his money back (UCC §§2-711 and 2-715). When the dealer ignored him, he sued, asking for a return of his purchase money plus consequential damages of $5,000 for "mental anguish." Is this last element of damages recoverable? Compare Volkswagen of Am., Inc. v. Dillard, 579 So. 2d 1301, 14 U.C.C. Rep. Serv. 2d 475 (Ala. 1991) (yes), with Kwan v. Mercedes-Benz of N. Am., Inc., 28 Cal. Rptr. 371, 23 Cal. App. 4th 174 (1994) (no, distinguishing *Volkswagen* in part because of nonuniform language in Alabama's UCC).

━━━━━━━

In Bogner v. General Motors Corp., 117 Misc. 2d 929, 459 N.Y.S.2d 679 (N. Y. Civ. Ct. 1982), the plaintiff alleged damages for emotional harm for being stranded in a remote area of Nova Scotia for three days of her vacation while waiting for a part needed to repair her auto. The car was under warranty, but the manufacturer had excluded liability for: "loss of the use of the car during warranty repairs. This includes lodging bills, car rentals, other travel costs, or loss of pay." The court held that this disclaimer was not broad enough to disclaim damages for emotional distress. Further, the court held that although general principles of contract law normally dictate no damages for emotional injury because of a breach of contract, exceptions relating to public policy exist. The court then cited a couple of cases concerning defective caskets and the like. The court added: "This court feels that similar considerations apply when the rendering of automobile warranty service is unreasonably delayed, such that the customer has to languish in the boondocks for several days."

What if a Vermont resident were stranded in New York City? A member of Gamblers Anonymous in front of Caesar's Palace? Do not most individual plaintiffs suffer great inconvenience and mental turmoil because of breaches of contract?

Attorney's fees would also seem to be an obvious consequential expense, meeting all the relevant tests for recovery (foreseeability, causation, etc.). Nonetheless, it is the American rule that attorney's fees are not recoverable in contract actions unless awarded by a special statute (for example, in some consumer cases they are an element of the recovery) or contracted for in the agreement itself.

3. Avoidability

━━━━━━━

◊ ROCKINGHAM COUNTY v. LUTEN BRIDGE CO. ρ
United States Circuit Court of Appeals, Fourth Circuit, 1929
35 F.2d 301

PARKER, Circuit Judge. This was an action at law instituted in the court below by the Luten Bridge Company, as plaintiff, to recover of Rockingham county, North Carolina, an amount alleged to be due under a contract for the construction of a bridge. The county admits the execution and breach of the contract, but contends that notice of cancellation was given the bridge company before the erection of the bridge was commenced, and that it is liable only for the damages which the company would have sustained, if it had abandoned construction at that time. The judge below refused to strike out an answer filed by certain members of the board of commissioners of the county, admitting liability in accordance with the prayer of the complaint, allowed this pleading to be introduced in evidence as the answer of the county, excluded evidence offered by the county in support of its contentions as to notice of cancellation and damages, and instructed a verdict for plaintiff for the full amount of its claim. From judgment on this verdict the county has appealed.

The facts out of which the case arises, as shown by the affidavits and offers of proof appearing in the record, are as follows: On January 7, 1924, the board of commissioners of Rockingham county voted to award to plaintiff a contract for the construction of the bridge in controversy. Three of the five commissioners favored the awarding of the contract and two opposed it. Much feeling was engendered over the matter, with the result that on February 11, 1924, W. K. Pruitt, one of the commissioners who had voted in the affirmative, sent his resignation to the clerk of the superior court of the county. The clerk received this resignation on the same day, and immediately accepted same and noted his acceptance thereon. Later in the day, Pruitt called him over the telephone and stated that he wished to withdraw the resignation, and later sent him written notice to the same effect. The clerk, however, paid no attention to the attempted withdrawal, and proceeded on the next day to appoint one W. W. Hampton as a member of the board to succeed him.

After his resignation, Pruitt attended no further meetings of the board, and did nothing further as a commissioner of the county. Likewise Pratt and McCollum, the other two members of the board who had voted with him in favor of the contract, attended no further meetings. Hampton, on the other hand, took the oath of office immediately upon his appointment and entered upon the discharge of the duties of a commissioner. He met regularly with the two remaining members of the board, Martin and Barber, in the courthouse at the county seat, and with them attended to all of the business of the county. Between the 12th of February and the first Monday in December following, these three attended, in all, 25 meetings of the board.

At one of these meetings, a regularly advertised called meeting held on February 21st, a resolution was unanimously adopted declaring that the contract for the building of the bridge was not legal and valid, and directing the clerk of the board to notify plaintiff that it refused to recognize same as a valid contract, and that plaintiff should proceed no further thereunder. This resolution also rescinded action of the board theretofore taken looking to the construction of a hard-surfaced road, in which the bridge was to be a mere connecting link. The clerk duly sent a certified copy of this resolution to plaintiff.

At the regular monthly meeting of the board on March 3d, a resolution was passed directing that plaintiff be notified that any work done on the bridge would be done by it at its own risk and hazard, that the board was of the opinion that the contract for the construction of the bridge was not valid and legal, and that, even if the board were mistaken as to this, it did not desire to construct the bridge, and would contest payment for same if constructed. A copy of this resolution was also sent to plaintiff. At the regular monthly meeting on April 7th, a resolution was passed, reciting that the board had been informed that one of its members was privately insisting that the bridge be constructed. It repudiated this action on the part of the member and gave notice that it would not be recognized. At the September meeting, a resolution was passed to the effect that the board would pay no bills presented by plaintiff or any one connected with the bridge. At the time of the passage of the first resolution, very little work toward the construction of the bridge had been done, it being estimated that the total cost of labor done and material on the ground was around $1,900; but, notwithstanding the repudiation of the contract by the county, the bridge company continued with the work of construction.

On November 24, 1924, plaintiff instituted this action against Rockingham county, and against Pruitt, Pratt, McCollum, Martin, and Barber, as constituting its board of commissioners. Complaint was filed, setting forth the execution of the contract and the doing of work by plaintiff thereunder, and alleging that for work done up until November 3, 1924, the county was indebted in the sum of $18,301.07. On November 27th, three days after the filing of the complaint, and only three days before the expiration of the term of office of the members of the old board of commissioners, Pruitt, Pratt, and McCollum met with an attorney at the county seat, and, without notice to or consultation with the other members of the board, so far as appears, had the attorney prepare for them an answer admitting the allegations of the complaint. This answer, which was filed in the cause on the following day, did not purport to be an answer of the county, or of its board of commissioners, but of the three commissioners named.

On December 1, 1924, the newly elected board of commissioners held its first meeting and employed attorneys to defend the action which had been instituted by plaintiff against the county. . . .

At the trial, plaintiff, over the objection of the county, was allowed to introduce in evidence the answer filed by Pruitt, Pratt, and McCollum, the contract was introduced, and proof was made of the value under the terms of the contract of the work done up to November 3, 1924. The county elicited on cross-examination proof as to the state of the work at the time of the passage of the resolutions to which we have referred. It then offered these resolutions in evidence, together with evidence as to the resignation of

Pruitt, the acceptance of his resignation, and the appointment of Hampton; but all of this evidence was excluded, and the jury was instructed to return a verdict for plaintiff for the full amount of its claim. The county preserved exceptions to the rulings which were adverse to it, and contends that there was error on the part of the judge below in denying the motion to strike out the answer filed by Pruitt, Pratt, and McCollum; in allowing same to be introduced in evidence; in excluding the evidence offered of the resignation of Pruitt, the acceptance of his resignation, and the appointment of Hampton, and of the resolutions attempting to cancel the contract and the notices sent plaintiff pursuant thereto; and in directing a verdict for plaintiff in accordance with its claim.

As the county now admits the execution and validity of the contract, and the breach on its part, the ultimate question in the case is one as to the measure of plaintiff's recovery, and the exceptions must be considered with this in mind. Upon these exceptions, three principal questions arise for our consideration, viz.: (1) Whether the answer filed by Pruitt, Pratt, and McCollum was the answer of the county. If it was, the lower court properly refused to strike it out, and properly admitted it in evidence. (2) Whether, in the light of the evidence offered and excluded, the resolutions to which we have referred, and the notices sent pursuant thereto, are to be deemed action on the part of the county. If they are not, the county has nothing upon which to base its position as to minimizing damages, and the evidence offered was properly excluded. And (3) whether plaintiff, if the notices are to be deemed action by the county, can recover under the contract for work done after they were received, or is limited to the recovery of damages for breach of contract as of that date.

[The court decided the first issue in the negative and the second affirmatively.]

Coming, then, to the third question—i.e., as to the measure of plaintiff's recovery—we do not think that, after the county had given notice, while the contract was still executory, that it did not desire the bridge built and would not pay for it, plaintiff could proceed to build it and recover the contract price. It is true that the county had no right to rescind the contract, and the notice given plaintiff amounted to a breach on its part; but, after plaintiff had received notice of the breach, it was its duty to do nothing to increase the damages flowing therefrom. If A enters into a binding contract to build a house for B, B, of course, has no right to rescind the contract without A's consent. But if, before the house is built, he decides that he does not want it, and notifies A to that effect, A has no right to proceed with the building and thus pile up damages. His remedy is to treat the contract as broken when he receives the notice, and sue for the recovery of such damages as he may have sustained from the breach, including any profit which he would have realized upon performance, as well as any other losses which may have resulted to him. In the case at bar, the county decided not to build the road of which the bridge was to be a part, and did not build it. The bridge, built in the midst of the forest, is of no value to the county because of this change of circumstances. When, therefore, the county gave notice to the plaintiff that it would not proceed with the project, plaintiff should have desisted from further work. It had no right thus to pile up damages by proceeding with the erection of a useless bridge.

The contrary view was expressed by Lord Cockburn in Frost v. Knight, L. R. 7 Ex. 111, but, as pointed out by Prof. Williston (Williston on Contracts, vol. 3, p. 2347), it is not in harmony with the decisions in this country. The American rule and the reasons supporting it are well stated by Prof. Williston as follows:

> There is a line of cases running back to 1845 which holds that, after an absolute repudiation or refusal to perform by one party to a contract, the other party cannot continue to perform and recover damages based on full performance. This rule is only a particular application of the general rule of damages that a plaintiff cannot hold a defendant liable for damages which need not have been incurred; or, as it is often stated, the plaintiff must, so far as he can without loss to himself, mitigate the damages caused by the defendant's wrongful act. The application of this rule to the matter in question is obvious. If a man engages to have work done, and afterwards repudiates his contract before the work has been begun or when it has been only partially done, it is inflicting damage on the defendant without benefit to the plaintiff to allow the latter to insist on proceeding with the contract. The work may be useless to the defendant, and yet he would be forced to pay the full contract price. On the other hand, the plaintiff is interested only in the profit he will make out of the contract. If he receives this it is equally advantageous for him to use his time otherwise.

The leading case on the subject in this country is the New York case of Clark v. Marsiglia, 1 Denio (N.Y.) 317, 43 Am. Dec. 670. In that case defendant had employed plaintiff to paint certain pictures for him, but countermanded the order before the work was finished. Plaintiff, however, went on and completed the work and sued for the contract price. In reversing a judgment for plaintiff, the court said:

> The plaintiff was allowed to recover as though there had been no countermand of the order; and in this the court erred. The defendant, by requiring the plaintiff to stop work upon the paintings, violated his contract, and thereby incurred a liability to pay such damages as the plaintiff should sustain. Such damages would include a recompense for the labor done and materials used, and such further sum in damages as might, upon legal principles, be assessed for the breach of the contract; but the plaintiff had no right, by obstinately persisting in the work, to make the penalty upon the defendant greater than it would otherwise have been.

And the rule as established by the great weight of authority in America is summed up in the following statement in 6 R.C.L. 1029, which is quoted with approval by the Supreme Court of North Carolina in the recent case of Novelty Advertising Co. v. Farmers' Mut. Tobacco Warehouse Co., 186 N. C. 197, 119 S.E. 196, 198:

> While a contract is executory a party has the power to stop performance on the other side by an explicit direction to that effect, subjecting himself to such damages as will compensate the other party for being stopped in the performance on his part at that stage in the execution of the contract. The party thus forbidden cannot afterwards go on, and thereby increase the damages, and then recover such damages from the other party. The legal right of either party to violate, abandon, or renounce his contract, on the usual terms of compensation to the other for the damages which the law recognizes and allows, subject to the jurisdiction of equity to decree specific performance in proper cases, is universally recognized and acted upon.

This is in accord with the earlier North Carolina decision of Heiser v. Mears, 120 N.C. 443, 27 S.E. 117, in which it was held that, where a buyer countermands his order for goods to be manufactured for him under an executory contract, before the work is completed, it is notice to the seller that he elects to rescind his contract and submit to the legal measure of damages, and that in such case the seller cannot complete the goods and recover the contract price.

We have carefully considered the cases upon which plaintiff relies; but we do not think that they are at all in point. . . . It follows that there was error in directing a verdict for plaintiff for the full amount of its claim. The measure of plaintiff's damage, upon its appearing that notice was duly given not to build the bridge, is an amount sufficient to compensate plaintiff for labor and materials expended and expense incurred in the part performance of the contract, prior to its repudiation, plus the profit which would have been realized if it had been carried out in accordance with its terms.

Our conclusion, on the whole case, is that there was error in failing to strike out the answer of Pruitt, Pratt, and McCollum, and in admitting same as evidence against the county, in excluding the testimony offered by the county to which we have referred, and in directing a verdict for plaintiff. The judgment below will accordingly be reversed, and the case remanded for a new trial.

Reversed.

QUESTION

Assume the facts of this last case are that the contract price was $10,000, the amount spent prior to repudiation was $3,000, and the amount spent after repudiation was $4,000. What recovery would the court permit?

Problem 69

The Garland Coal Company signed a contract with Willie and Lucille Peevyhouse by which they agreed to let the company strip mine their farm at an agreed price. Garland also agreed to restore the land to its former appearance at the conclusion of the mining. When it failed to do so, offering instead to pay the Peevyhouses $300 (this being the market value lost by the failure to replace the strip mines), the Peevyhouses immediately hired another company to cover up the strip mines. This work cost $29,000. The Peevyhouses then brought suit against the Garland Coal Company for that amount. Should they recover it?

Problem 70

For the Cleveland World's Fair, Balloons of America had contracted with the government of Cuba to build a giant balloon in the shape of a cigar. It was halfway finished when Cuba decided to abandon the project. Balloons of America phones you, its attorney, and wants to know whether it should complete the cigar-shaped balloon (contract price: $13,000) or stop now (when it has expended only $8,000) and sell the partially completed balloon for its scrap value ($120). The cost of completion is $2,500 and the salvage value after completion is $1,000. Read UCC §§2-704 and 2-709 and advise your client.

ℙ   PARKER v. TWENTIETH CENTURY-FOX FILM CORP. 𝒟
Supreme Court of California, 1970
3 Cal. 3d 176, 89 Cal. Rptr. 737, 474 P.2d 689

BURKE, J. Defendant Twentieth Century-Fox Film Corporation appeals from a summary judgment granting to plaintiff the recovery of agreed compensation under a written contract for her services as an actress in a motion picture. As will appear, we have concluded that the trial court correctly ruled in plaintiff's favor and that the judgment should be affirmed.

Plaintiff is well known as an actress, and in the contract between plaintiff and defendant is sometimes referred to as the "Artist." Under the contract, dated August 6, 1965, plaintiff was to play the female lead in defendant's contemplated production of a motion picture entitled "Bloomer Girl." The contract provided that defendant would pay plaintiff a minimum "guaranteed compensation" of $53,571.42 per week for 14 weeks commencing May 23, 1966, for a total of $750,000. Prior to May 1966 defendant decided not to produce the picture and by a letter dated April 4, 1966, it notified plaintiff of that decision and that it would not "comply with our obligations to you under" the written contract.

By the same letter and with the professed purpose "to avoid any damage to you," defendant instead offered to employ plaintiff as the leading actress in another film tentatively entitled "Big Country, Big Man" (hereinafter, "Big Country"). The compensation offered was identical, as were 31 of the 34 numbered provisions or articles of the original contract. Unlike "Bloomer Girl," however, which was to have been a musical production, "Big Country" was a dramatic "western type" movie. "Bloomer Girl" was to have been filmed in California; "Big Country" was to be produced in Australia. Also, certain terms in the proffered contract varied from those of the original.[2]

Plaintiff was given one week within which to accept; she did not and the offer lapsed. Plaintiff then commenced this action seeking recovery of the agreed guaranteed compensation.

The complaint sets forth two causes of action. The first is for money due under the contract; the second, based upon the same allegations as the first, is for damages resulting from defendant's breach of contract. Defendant in its answer admits the existence and validity of the contract, that plaintiff complied with all the conditions, covenants and promises and stood ready to complete the performance, and that defendant breached and "anticipatorily repudiated" the contract. It denies, however, that any money is due to

---

2. Article 29 of the original contract specified that plaintiff approved the director already chosen for "Bloomer Girl" and that in case he failed to act as director plaintiff was to have approval rights of any substitute director. Article 31 provided that plaintiff was to have the right of approval of the "Bloomer Girl" dance director, and Article 32 gave her the right of approval of the screenplay.

Defendant's letter of April 4 to plaintiff, which contained both defendant's notice of breach of the "Bloomer Girl" contract and offer of the lead in "Big Country," eliminated or impaired each of those rights. It read in part as follows:

> The terms and conditions of our offer of employment are identical to those set forth in the "Bloomer Girl" Agreement, Articles 1 through 34 and Exhibit A to the Agreement, except as follows:
>
> 1. Article 31 of said Agreement will not be included in any contract of employment regarding "Big Country, Big Man" as it is not a musical and it thus will not need a dance director.
>
> 2. In the "Bloomer Girl" agreement, in Articles 29 and 32, you were given certain director and screenplay approvals and you had preapproved certain matters. Since there simply is insufficient time to negotiate with you regarding your choice of director and regarding the screenplay and since you already expressed an interest in performing the role in "Big Country, Big Man," we must exclude from our offer of employment in "Big Country, Big Man" any approval rights as are contained in said Articles 29 and 32; however, we shall consult with you respecting the director to be selected to direct the photoplay and will further consult with you with respect to the screenplay and any revisions or changes therein, provided, however, that if we fail to agree . . . the decision of [defendant] with respect to the selection of a director and to revisions and changes in the said screenplay shall be binding upon the parties to said agreement.

[margin note: Defendant claims No Damages because The plaintiff Failed to mitigate damages by not accepting the other role]

plaintiff either under the contract or as a result of its breach, and pleads as an affirmative defense to both causes of action plaintiff's allegedly deliberate failure to mitigate damages, asserting that she unreasonably refused to accept its offer of the leading role in "Big Country."

Plaintiff moved for summary judgment under Code of Civil Procedure section 437c, the motion was granted, and summary judgment for $750,000 plus interest was entered in plaintiff's favor. This appeal by defendant followed.

The familiar rules are that the matter to be determined by the trial court on a motion for summary judgment is whether facts have been presented which give rise to a triable factual issue. The court may not pass upon the issue itself. Summary judgment is proper only if the affidavits *or* declarations in support of the moving party would be sufficient to sustain a judgment in his favor and his opponent does not by affidavit show facts sufficient to present a triable issue of fact. The affidavits of the moving party are strictly construed, and doubts as to the propriety of summary judgment should be resolved against granting the motion. Such summary procedure is drastic and should be used with caution so that it does not become a substitute for the open trial method of determining facts. . . .

[margin note: Defendants Sole Defense]

As stated, defendant's sole defense to this action which resulted from its deliberate breach of contract is that in rejecting defendant's substitute offer of employment plaintiff unreasonably refused to mitigate damages.

[margin note: General Rule]

The general rule is that the measure of recovery by a wrongfully discharged employee is the amount of salary agreed upon for the period of service, less the amount which the employer affirmatively proves the employee has earned or with reasonable effort might have earned from other employment. However, before projected earnings from other employment opportunities not sought or accepted by the discharged employee can be applied in mitigation, the employer must show that the other employment was comparable, or substantially similar, to that of which the employee has been deprived; the employee's rejection of or failure to seek other available employment of a different or inferior kind may not be resorted to in order to mitigate damages.

[margin note: Rule — employment must be substantially similar]

[margin note: Issue]

In the present case defendant has raised no issue of *reasonableness of efforts* by plaintiff to obtain other employment; the sole issue is whether plaintiff's refusal of defendant's substitute offer of "Big Country" may be used in mitigation. Nor, if the "Big Country" offer was of employment different or inferior when compared with the original "Bloomer Girl" employment, is there an issue as to whether or not plaintiff acted reasonably in refusing the substitute offer. Despite defendant's arguments to the contrary, no case cited or which our research has discovered holds or suggests that reasonableness is an element of a wrongfully discharged employee's option to reject, or fail to seek, different or inferior employment lest the possible earnings therefrom be charged against him in mitigation of damages.

Applying the foregoing rules to the record in the present case, with all intendments in favor of the party opposing the summary judgment motion—here, defendant—it is clear that the trial court correctly ruled that plaintiff's failure to accept defendant's tendered substitute employment could not be applied in mitigation of damages because the offer of the "Big Country" lead was of employment both different and inferior, and that no factual dispute was presented on that issue. The mere circumstance that "Bloomer Girl" was to be a musical review calling upon plaintiff's talents as a dancer as well as an actress, and was to be produced in the City of Los Angeles, whereas "Big Country" was a straight dramatic role in a "Western Type" story taking place in an opal mine in Australia, demonstrates the difference in kind between the two employments; the female lead as a dramatic actress in a western style motion picture can by no stretch of imagination be considered the equivalent of or substantially similar to the lead in a song-and-dance production.

Additionally, the substitute "Big Country" offer proposed to eliminate or impair the director and screenplay approvals accorded to plaintiff under the original "Bloomer Girl" contract (see fn. 2, ante), and thus constituted an offer of inferior employment. No expertise or judicial notice is required in order to hold that the deprivation or infringement of an employee's rights held under an original employment contract converts the available "other employment" relied upon by the employer to mitigate damages, into inferior employment which the employee need not seek or accept. . . .

In view of the determination that defendant failed to present any facts showing the existence of a factual issue with respect to its sole defense—plaintiff's rejection of its substitute employment offer in mitigation of damages—we need not consider plaintiff's contention that for various reasons, including the provisions of the original contract set forth in footnote 1, ante, plaintiff was excused from attempting to mitigate damages.

The judgment is affirmed.

McComb, Peters, and Tobriner, JJ., and Kaus, J. pro tem., and Roth, J. pro tem., concur.

Sullivan, Acting Chief Justice (dissenting). The basic question in this case is whether or not plaintiff acted reasonably in rejecting defendant's offer of alternate employment. The answer depends upon whether that offer (starring in "Big Country, Big Man") was an offer of work that was substantially similar to her former employment (starring in "Bloomer Girl") or of work that was of a different or inferior kind. To my mind this is a factual issue which the trial court should not have determined on a motion for summary judgment. The majority have not only repeated this error but have compounded it by applying the rules governing mitigation of damages in the employer-employee context in a misleading fashion. Accordingly, I respectfully dissent.

The familiar rule requiring a plaintiff in a tort or contract action to mitigate damages embodies notions of fairness and socially responsible behavior which are fundamental to our jurisprudence. Most broadly stated, it precludes the recovery of damages which, through the exercise of due diligence, could have been avoided. Thus, in essence, it is a rule requiring reasonable conduct in commercial affairs. This general principle governs the obligations of an employee after his employer has wrongfully repudiated or terminated the employment contract. Rather than permitting the employee simply to remain idle during the balance of the contract period, the law requires him to make a reasonable effort to secure other employment. He is not obliged, however, to seek or accept any and all types of work which may be available. Only work which is in the same field and which is of the same quality need be accepted.[2]

Over the years the courts have employed various phrases to define the type of employment which the employee, upon his wrongful discharge, is under an obligation to accept. Thus in California alone it has been held that he must accept employment which is "substantially similar." . . .

For reasons which are unexplained, the majority cite several of these cases yet select from among the various judicial formulations which contain one particular phrase, "Not of a different or inferior kind," with which to analyze this case. I have discovered no historical or theoretical reason to adopt this phrase, which is simply a negative restatement of the affirmative standards set out in the above cases, as the exclusive standard. Indeed, its emergence is an example of the dubious phenomenon of the law responding not to rational judicial choice or changing social conditions, but to unrecognized changes in the language of opinions or legal treatises. However, the phrase is a serviceable one and my concern is not with its use as the standard but rather with what I consider its distortion.

. . . It has never been the law that the mere existence of *differences between two jobs in the same field* is sufficient, as a matter of law, to excuse an employee wrongfully discharged from one from accepting the other in order to mitigate damages. Such an approach would effectively eliminate any obligation of an employee to attempt to minimize damage arising from a wrongful discharge. The only alternative job offer an employee would be required to accept would be an offer of his former job by his former employer.

Although the majority appear to hold that there was a difference "in kind" between the employment offered plaintiff in "Bloomer Girl" and that offered in "Big Country," an examination of the opinion makes crystal clear that the majority merely point out differences between the two *films* (an

2. This qualification of the rule seems to reflect the simple and humane attitude that it is too severe to demand of a person that he attempt to find and perform work for which he has no training or experience. Many of the older cases hold that one need not accept work in an inferior rank or position nor work which is more menial or arduous. This suggests that the rule may have had its origin in the bourgeois fear of resubmergence in lower economic classes.

obvious circumstance) and then apodically assert that these constitute a difference in the *kind* of *employment*. The entire rationale of the majority boils down to this: that the "*mere circumstances*" that "Bloomer Girl" was to be a musical review while "Big Country" was a straight drama "demonstrates the difference in kind" since a female lead in a western is not "the equivalent of or substantially similar to" a lead in a musical. This is merely attempting to prove the proposition by repeating it. It shows that the vehicles for the display of the star's talents are different but it does not prove that her employment as a star in such vehicles is of necessity different *in kind* and either inferior or superior.

I believe that the approach taken by the majority (a superficial listing of differences with no attempt to assess their significance) may subvert a valuable legal doctrine.[5] The inquiry in cases such as this should not be whether differences between the two jobs exist (there will always be differences) but whether the differences which are present are substantial enough to constitute differences in the *kind* of employment or, alternatively, whether they render the substitute work employment of an *inferior kind.*

It seems to me that *this* inquiry involves, in the instant case at least, factual determinations which are improper on a motion for summary judgment. Resolving whether or not one job is substantially similar to another or whether, on the other hand, it is of a different or inferior kind, will often (as here) require a critical appraisal of the similarities and differences between them in light of the importance of these differences to the employee. This necessitates a weighing of the evidence, and it is precisely this undertaking which is forbidden on summary judgment.

This is not to say that summary judgment would never be available in an action by an employee in which the employer raises the defense of failure to mitigate damages. No case has come to my attention, however, in which summary judgment has been granted on the issue of whether an employee was obliged to accept available alternate employment. Nevertheless, there may well be cases in which the substitute employment is so manifestly of a dissimilar or inferior sort, the declarations of the plaintiff so complete and those of the defendant so conclusionary and inadequate that no factual issues exist for which a trial is required. This, however, is not such a case.

It is not intuitively obvious, to me at least, that the leading female role in a dramatic motion picture is a radically different endeavor from the leading female role in a musical comedy film. Nor is it plain to me that the rather qualified rights of director and screenplay approval contained in the first contract are highly significant matters either in the entertainment industry

5. The values of the doctrine of mitigation of damages in this context are that it minimizes the unnecessary personal and social (e.g., nonproductive use of labor, litigation) costs of contractual failure. If a wrongfully discharged employee can, through his own action and without suffering financial or psychological loss in the process, reduce the damages accruing from the breach of contract, the most sensible policy is to require him to do so. I fear the majority opinion will encourage precisely opposite conduct.

in general or to this plaintiff in particular. Certainly, none of the declarations introduced by plaintiff in support of her motion shed any light on these issues. Nor do they attempt to explain why she declined the offer of starring in "Big Country, Big Man." Nevertheless, the trial court granted the motion, declaring that these approval rights were "critical" and that their elimination altered "the essential nature of the employment."

The plaintiff's declarations were of no assistance to the trial court in its effort to justify reaching this conclusion on summary judgment. Instead, it was forced to rely on judicial notice of the definitions of "motion picture," "screenplay" and "director" (Evid. Code, §451, subd. (e)) and then on judicial notice of practices in the film industry which were purportedly of "common knowledge." (Evid. Code, §451, subd. (f) or §452, subd. (g).) This use of judicial notice was error. Evidence Code section 451, subdivision (e) was never intended to authorize resort to the dictionary to solve essentially factual questions which do not turn upon conventional linguistic usage. More important, however, the trial court's notice of "facts commonly known" violated Evidence Code section 455, subdivision (a). Before this section was enacted there were no procedural safeguards affording litigants an opportunity to be heard as to the propriety of taking judicial notice of a matter or as to the tenor of the matter to be noticed. Section 455 makes such an opportunity (which may be an element of due process, see Evid. Code, §455, Law Revision Com. Comment (a)) mandatory and its provisions should be scrupulously adhered to. "Judicial notice can be a valuable tool in the adversary system for the lawyer as well as the court" (Kongsgaard, Judicial Notice (1966), 18 Hastings L.J. 117, 140) and its use is appropriate on motions for summary judgment. Its use in this case, however, to determine on summary judgment issues fundamental to the litigation without complying with statutory requirements of notice and hearing is a highly improper effort to "cut the Gordion knot of involved litigation." . . .

The majority do not confront the trial court's misuse of judicial notice. They avoid this issue through the expedient of declaring that neither judicial notice nor expert opinion (such as that contained in the declarations in opposition to the motion) is necessary to reach the trial court's conclusion. *Something*, however, clearly *is* needed to support this conclusion. Nevertheless, the majority make no effort to justify the judgment through an examination of the plaintiff's declarations. Ignoring the obvious insufficiency of these declarations, the majority announce that "the deprivation or infringement of an employee's rights held under an original employment contract" changes the alternate employment offered or available into employment of an inferior kind.

I cannot accept the proposition that an offer which eliminates *any* contract right, regardless of its significance, is, as a matter of law, an offer of employment of an inferior kind. Such an absolute rule seems no more sensible than the majority's earlier suggestion that the mere existence of differences between two jobs is sufficient to render them employment of different kinds. Application of such per se rules will severely undermine the principle of mitigation of damages in the employer-employee context.

I remain convinced that the relevant question in such cases is whether or not a particular contract provision is so significant that its omission creates employment of an inferior kind. This question is, of course, intimately bound up in what I consider the ultimate issue: whether or not the employee acted reasonably. This will generally involve a factual inquiry to ascertain the importance of the particular contract term and a process of weighing the absence of that term against the countervailing advantages of the alternate employment. In the typical case, this will mean that summary judgment must be withheld.

In the instant case, there was nothing properly before the trial court by which the importance of the approval rights could be ascertained, much less evaluated. Thus, in order to grant the motion for summary judgment, the trial court misused judicial notice. In upholding the summary judgment, the majority here rely upon per se rules which distort the process of determining whether or not an employee is obliged to accept particular employment in mitigation of damages.

Court misused Judicial Notice

I believe that the judgment should be reversed so that the issue of whether or not the offer of the lead role in "Big Country, Big Man" was of employment comparable to that of the lead role in "Bloomer Girl" may be determined at trial.

NOTES AND QUESTIONS

1. In his dissent Judge Sullivan objects to the majority's use of *judicial notice.* Judicial notice means the ability of the court to apply its own knowledge (without the need of evidence being introduced) of things within the common knowledge of all humankind. For example, the court can take judicial notice that the litigants are on the planet Earth, or that people breathe oxygen. What is Judge Sullivan's complaint with the majority's application of judicial notice in this case? Is he right? Would the Supreme Court of North Dakota have had as easy a time with the issue as the Supreme Court of California did?

Judicial Notice

2. The "well-known actress" in this case is Shirley MacLaine (whose married name is "Parker"). The musical *Bloomer Girl* (with music by Harold Arlen and lyrics by E. Y. Harburg, the same duo that wrote the songs for *The Wizard of Oz*) was a Broadway hit in 1944, running 654 performances. It tells the story of the American feminist reformer Amelia Jenks ("Dolly") Bloomer (1818-1894). Ms. Bloomer was the founder and editor of a monthly journal, the *Lilly*, the first American magazine published by and for women. Among the many issues raised by the magazine were temperance, unjust marriage laws, inadequate education for women, and woman's suffrage. Ms. Bloomer became most famous for her advocacy of a reform in woman's clothing,

appearing in public in a short dress with trousers gathered at the ankle (called "bloomers"), intended to reduce the weight and discomfort of the usual female dresses of the period.

3. Would the court have reached the same result if instead of a western, the studio had offered Ms. MacLaine the part of Scarlett O'Hara in a remake of *Gone With the Wind* (the famous movie in which a Southern woman struggles with the trials of the Civil War)? What if the substituted picture were *My Fair Lady* and Ms. MacLaine was given the chance to play Eliza Doolittle (an early 1900s London flower girl who is given voice lessons to turn her into a lady)?

4. Contractual provisions in which a party agrees that the other has no duty to mitigate may be unenforceable as a matter of public policy. Durman Realty Co. Ltd. Partnership v. Jindo Corp., 865 F. Supp. 1093 (S.D.N.Y. 1994) (interpreting New Jersey law).

5. If the plaintiff elects to take a new job that is inferior to the one promised in the original contract are the earnings from it a mitigation of her damages?

Problem 71

Basketball star Michael Jordan entered into a contract with WorldCom, Inc., in which he received an annual sum of $2 million to do endorsements for its telecommunications products during the next ten years. After two years of such endorsements, WorldCom filed a bankruptcy petition, and Jordan filed a claim in the bankruptcy court for the amounts still due under his contract. The objection to this claim was that Jordan had not mitigated his damages by seeking other endorsement contracts, to which he responded he had cut back on the number of endorsements he'd been doing for fear of diluting his reputation and also because he was investigating becoming the owner of a NBA team. How should this come out? See In re WorldCom, Inc., 361 B.R. 675 (Bankr. S.D.N.Y. 2007).

Problem 72

Hearing a report that Alice Chalk, a popular high school teacher, was a drug dealer on the side, the school's principal marched down to her classroom and fired Alice on the spot. Her horrified students' jaws dropped open when the principal accused her of selling drugs and ordered her from the building. Later that day, the principal learned that the report was false, and he phoned Alice at home, apologized, and offered her job back. She declined and took a job as an evening waitress in an all-night diner. She also sued the school for wrongful termination. Is it a defense that she refused to return to her job? Is the salary she receives as a waitress a mitigating factor? See John Call Engineering v. Manti City Corp., 795 P.2d 678 (Utah Ct. App. 1990). What if she had accepted unemployment compensation? See Corl v. Huron Castings, Inc., 450 Mich. 620, 544 N.W.2d 278 (1996).

4. Damages by Agreement

RESTATEMENT (SECOND) OF CONTRACTS

§356(1). LIQUIDATED DAMAGES AND PENALTIES

Damages for breach by either party may be liquidated in the agreement but only at an amount that is reasonable in the light of the anticipated or actual loss caused by the breach and the difficulties of proof of loss. A term fixing unreasonably large liquidated damages is unenforceable on grounds of public policy as a penalty.

LAKE RIVER CORP. v. CARBORUNDUM CO.
United States Court of Appeals, Seventh Circuit, 1985
769 F.2d 1284

POSNER, Circuit Judge. This diversity suit between Lake River Corporation and Carborundum Company requires us to consider questions of Illinois commercial law, and in particular to explore the fuzzy line between penalty clauses and liquidated-damages clauses.

Carborundum manufactures "Ferro Carbo," an abrasive powder used in making steel. To serve its midwestern customers better, Carborundum made a contract with Lake River by which the latter agreed to provide distribution services in its warehouse in Illinois. Lake River would receive Ferro Carbo in bulk from Carborundum, "bag" it, and ship the bagged product to Carborundum's customers. The Ferro Carbo would remain Carborundum's property until delivered to the customers.

Carborundum insisted that Lake River install a new bagging system to handle the contract. In order to be sure of being able to recover the cost of the new system ($89,000) and make a profit of 20 percent of the contract price, Lake River insisted on the following minimum-quantity guarantee:

> In consideration of the special equipment [i.e., the new bagging system] to be acquired and furnished by Lake-River for handling the product, Carborundum shall, during the initial three-year term of this Agreement, ship to Lake-

River for bagging a minimum quantity of [22,500 tons]. If, at the end of the three-year term, this minimum quantity shall not have been shipped, Lake-River shall invoice Carborundum at the then prevailing rates for the difference between the quantity bagged and the minimum guaranteed.

If Carborundum had shipped the full minimum quantity that it guaranteed, it would have owed Lake River roughly $533,000 under the contract.

After the contract was signed in 1979, the demand for domestic steel, and with it the demand for Ferro Carbo, plummeted, and Carborundum failed to ship the guaranteed amount. When the contract expired late in 1982, Carborundum had shipped only 12,000 of the 22,500 tons it had guaranteed. Lake River had bagged the 12,000 tons and had billed Carborundum for this bagging, and Carborundum had paid, but by virtue of the formula in the minimum-guarantee clause Carborundum still owed Lake River $241,000 — the contract price of $533,000 if the full amount of Ferro Carbo had been shipped, minus what Carborundum had paid for the bagging of the quantity it had shipped.

When Lake River demanded payment of this amount, Carborundum refused, on the ground that the formula imposed a penalty. At the time, Lake River had in its warehouse 500 tons of bagged Ferro Carbo, having a market value of $269,000, which it refused to release unless Carborundum paid the $241,000 due under the formula. Lake River did offer to sell the bagged product and place the proceeds in escrow until its dispute with Carborundum over the enforceability of the formula was resolved, but Carborundum rejected the offer and trucked in bagged Ferro Carbo from the East to serve its customers in Illinois, at an additional cost of $31,000.

Lake River brought this suit for $241,000, which it claims as liquidated damages. Carborundum counterclaimed for the value of the bagged Ferro Carbo when Lake River impounded it and the additional cost of serving the customers affected by the impounding. The theory of the counterclaim is that the impounding was a conversion, and not as Lake River contends the assertion of a lien. The district judge, after a bench trial, gave judgment for both parties. Carborundum ended up roughly $42,000 to the good: $269,000 + $31,000 − $241,000 − $17,000, the last figure representing prejudgment interest on Lake River's damages. (We have rounded off all dollar figures to the nearest thousand.) Both parties have appealed.

[The court first decided that Lake River did not have a valid lien on the bagged powder.]

The hardest issue in the case is whether the formula in the minimum-guarantee clause imposes a penalty for breach of contract or is merely an effort to liquidate damages. Deep as the hostility to penalty clauses runs in the common law, see Loyd, Penalties and Forfeitures, 29 Harv. L. Rev. 117 (1915), we still might be inclined to question, if we thought ourselves free to do so, whether a modern court should refuse to enforce a penalty clause where the signator is a substantial corporation, well able to avoid improvident commitments. Penalty clauses provide an earnest of performance. The clause here enhanced Carborundum's credibility in promising to ship the minimum amount guaranteed by showing that it was willing to pay the full contract price even if it failed to ship anything. On the other side it can be pointed out that by raising the cost of a breach of contract to the contract breaker, a penalty clause increases the risk to his other creditors; increases (what is the same thing and more, because bankruptcy imposes "deadweight" social costs) the risk of bankruptcy; and could amplify the business cycle by increasing the number of bankruptcies in bad times, which is when contracts are most likely to be broken. But since little effort is made to prevent businessmen from assuming risks, these reasons are no better than makeweights.

A better argument is that a penalty clause may discourage efficient as well as inefficient breaches of contract. Suppose a breach would cost the promisee $12,000 in actual damages but would yield the promisor $20,000 in additional profits. Then there would be a net social gain from breach. After being fully compensated for his loss the promisee would be no worse off than if the contract had been performed, while the promisor would be better off by $8,000. But now suppose the contract contains a penalty clause under which the promisor if he breaks his promise must pay the promisee $25,000. The promisor will be discouraged from breaking the contract, since $25,000, the penalty, is greater than $20,000, the profits of the breach; and a transaction that would have increased value will be forgone.

On this view, since compensatory damages should be sufficient to deter inefficient breaches (that is, breaches that cost the victim more than the gain to the contract breaker), penal damages could have no effect other than to deter some efficient breaches. But this overlooks the earlier point that the willingness to agree to a penalty clause is a way of making the promisor and his promise credible and may therefore be essential to inducing some value-maximizing contracts to be made. It also overlooks the more important point that the parties (always assuming they are fully competent) will, in deciding whether to include a penalty clause in their contract, weigh the gains against the costs — costs that include the possibility of discouraging an efficient breach somewhere down the road — and will include the clause only if the benefits exceed those costs as well as all other costs.

On this view the refusal to enforce penalty clauses is (at best) paternalistic — and it seems odd that courts should display parental solicitude for large corporations. But however this may be, we must be on guard to avoid importing our own ideas of sound public policy into an area where our proper judicial role is more than usually deferential. The responsibility for making innovations in the common law of Illinois rests with the courts of Illinois, and not with the federal courts in Illinois. And like every other state, Illinois, untroubled by academic skepticism of the wisdom of refusing to enforce penalty clauses against sophisticated promisors, see, e.g., Goetz & Scott, Liquidated Damages, Penalties and the Just Compensation Principle,

77 Colum. L. Rev. 554 (1977), continues steadfastly to insist on the distinction between penalties and liquidated damages. To be valid under Illinois law a liquidation of damages must be a reasonable estimate at the time of contracting of the likely damages from breach, and the need for estimation at that time must be shown by reference to the likely difficulty of measuring the actual damages from a breach of contract after the breach occurs. If damages would be easy to determine then, or if the estimate greatly exceeds a reasonable upper estimate of what the damages are likely to be, it is a penalty. [Citation omitted.]

The distinction between a penalty and liquidated damages is not an easy one to draw in practice but we are required to draw it and can give only limited weight to the district court's determination. Whether a provision for damages is a penalty clause or a liquidated-damages clause is a question of law rather than fact, [citations omitted], and unlike some courts of appeals we do not treat a determination by a federal district judge of an issue of state law as if it were a finding of fact, and reverse only if persuaded that clear error has occurred, though we give his determination respectful consideration.

Mindful that Illinois courts resolve doubtful cases in favor of classification as a penalty, we conclude that the damage formula in this case is a penalty and not a liquidation of damages, because it is designed always to assure Lake River more than its actual damages. The formula — full contract price minus the amount already invoiced to Carborundum — is invariant to the gravity of the breach. When a contract specifies a single sum in damages for any and all breaches even though it is apparent that all are not of the same gravity, the specification is not a reasonable effort to estimate damages; and when in addition the fixed sum greatly exceeds the actual damages likely to be inflicted by a minor breach, its character as a penalty becomes unmistakable. This case is within the gravitational field of these principles even though the minimum-guarantee clause does not fix a single sum as damages.

Suppose to begin with that the breach occurs the day after Lake River buys its new bagging system for $89,000 and before Carborundum ships any Ferro Carbo. Carborundum would owe Lake River $533,000. Since Lake River would have incurred at that point a total cost of only $89,000, its net gain from the breach would be $444,000. This is more than four times the profit of $107,000 (20 percent of the contract price of $533,000) that Lake River expected to make from the contract if it had been performed: a huge windfall.

Next suppose (as actually happened here) that breach occurs when 55 percent of the Ferro Carbo has been shipped. Lake River would already have received $293,000 from Carborundum. To see what its costs then would have been (as estimated at the time of contracting), first subtract Lake River's anticipated profit on the contract of $107,000 from the total contract price of $533,000. The difference — Lake River's total cost of performance — is $426,000. Of this, $89,000 is the cost of the new bagging system, a fixed cost. The rest ($426,000 − $89,000 = $337,000) presumably consists of variable costs that are roughly proportional to the amount of Ferro Carbo bagged; there is no indication of any other fixed costs. Assume, therefore, that if Lake River bagged 55 percent of the contractually agreed quantity, it incurred in doing so 55 percent of its variable costs, or $185,000. When this is added to the cost of the new bagging system, assumed for the moment to be worthless except in connection with the contract, the total cost of performance to Lake River is $274,000. Hence a breach that occurred after 55 percent of contractual performance was complete would be expected to yield Lake River a modest profit of $19,000 ($293,000 − $274,000). But now add the "liquidated damages" of $241,000 that Lake River claims, and the result is a total gain from the breach of $260,000, which is almost two and a half times the profit that Lake River expected to gain if there was no breach. And this ignores any use value or salvage value of the new bagging system, which is the property of Lake River—though admittedly it also ignores the time value of money; Lake River paid $89,000 for that system before receiving any revenue from the contract.

To complete the picture, assume that the breach had not occurred till performance was 90 percent complete. Then the "liquidated damages" clause would not be so one-sided, but it would be one-sided. Carborundum would have paid $480,000 for bagging. Against this, Lake River would have incurred its fixed cost of $89,000 plus 90 percent of its variable costs of $337,000, or $303,000. Its total costs would thus be $392,000, and its net profit $88,000. But on top of this it would be entitled to "liquidated damages" of $53,000, for a total profit of $141,000—more than 30 percent more than its expected profit of $107,000 if there was no breach.

The reason for these results is that most of the costs to Lake River of performing the contract are saved if the contract is broken, and this saving is not reflected in the damage formula. As a result, at whatever point in the life of the contract a breach occurs, the damage formula gives Lake River more than its lost profits from the breach—dramatically more if the breach occurs at the beginning of the contract; tapering off at the end, it is true. Still, over the interval between the beginning of Lake River's performance and nearly the end, the clause could be expected to generate profits ranging from 400 percent of the expected contract profits to 130 percent of those profits. And this is on the assumption that the bagging system has no value apart from the contract. If it were worth only $20,000 to Lake River, the range would be 434 percent to 150 percent.

Lake River argues that it would never get as much as the formula suggests, because it would be required to mitigate its damages. This is a dubious argument on several grounds. First, mitigation of damages is a doctrine of the law of court-assessed damages, while the point of a liquidated-damages clause is to substitute party assessment; and that point is blunted, and the certainty that liquidated-damages clauses are designed to give the process of assessing damages impaired, if a defendant can force the plaintiff to take less than the damages specified in the clause, on the ground that the plaintiff could have avoided some of them. It would seem therefore that the clause in this case should be read to eliminate any duty of mitigation, that what Lake River is doing is attempting to rewrite the clause to make it more reasonable, and that since actually the clause is designed to give Lake River the full damages it would incur from breach (and more) even if it made no effort to find a substitute use for the equipment that it bought to perform the contract, this is just one more piece of evidence that it is a penalty clause rather than a liquidated-damages clause. [Citation omitted.]

But in any event mitigation would not mitigate the penal character of this clause. If Carborundum did not ship the guaranteed minimum quantity, the reason was likely to be — the reason was — that the steel industry had fallen on hard times and the demand for Ferro Carbo was therefore down. In these circumstances Lake River would have little prospect of finding a substitute contract that would yield it significant profits to set off against the full contract price, which is the method by which it proposes to take account of mitigation. At argument Lake River suggested that it might at least have been able to sell the new bagging equipment to someone for something, and the figure $40,000 was proposed. If the breach occurred on the first day when performance under the contract was due and Lake River promptly sold the bagging equipment for $40,000, its liquidated damages would fall to $493,000. But by the same token its costs would fall to $49,000. Its profit would still be $444,000, which as we said was more than 400 percent of its expected profit on the contract. The penal component would be unaffected.

With the penalty clause in this case compare the liquidated-damages clause in Arduini v. Board of Education [93 Ill. App. 3d 925, 49 Ill. Dec. 460, 418 N.E.2d 104 (1981)], which is representative of such clauses upheld in Illinois. The plaintiff was a public school teacher whose contract provided that if he resigned before the end of the school year he would be docked 4 percent of his salary. This was a modest fraction of the contract price. And the cost to the school of an untimely resignation would be difficult to measure. Since that cost would be greater the more senior and experienced the teacher was, the fact that the liquidated damages would be greater the higher the teacher's salary did not make the clause arbitrary. Even the fact that the liquidated damages were the same whether the teacher resigned at the beginning, the middle, or the end of the school year was not arbitrary, for it was unclear how the amount of actual damages would vary with the time of resignation. Although one might think that the earlier the teacher resigned the greater the damage to the school would be, the school might find it easier to hire a replacement for the whole year or a great part of it than to bring in a replacement at the last minute to grade the exams left behind by the resigning teacher. Here, in contrast, it is apparent from the face of the contract that the damages provided for by the "liquidated damages" clause are grossly disproportionate to any probable loss and penalize some breaches much more heavily than others regardless of relative cost.

Lake River's Damages Would be grossly Disproportionate

We do not mean by this discussion to cast a cloud of doubt over the "take or pay" clauses that are a common feature of contracts between natural gas pipeline companies and their customers. Such clauses require the customer, in consideration of the pipeline's extending its line to his premises, to take a certain amount of gas at a specified price — and if he fails to take it to pay the full price anyway. The resemblance to the minimum-guarantee clause in the present case is obvious, but perhaps quite superficial. Neither party has mentioned take-or-pay clauses, and we can find no case where such a clause was even challenged as a penalty clause — though in one case it was argued that such a clause made the damages unreasonably *low*. See National Fuel Gas Distribution Corp. v. Pennsylvania Public Utility Commn., 76 Pa. Commw. 102, 126-127 n.8, 464 A.2d 546, 558 n.8 (1983). If, as appears not to be the case here but would often be the case in supplying natural gas, a supplier's fixed costs were a very large fraction of his total costs, a take-or-pay clause might well be a reasonable liquidation of damages. In the limit, if *all* the supplier's costs were incurred before he began supplying the customer, the contract revenues would be an excellent measure of the damages from breach. But in this case, the supplier (Lake River, viewed as a supplier of bagging services to Carborundum) incurred only a fraction of its costs before performance began, and the interruption of performance generated a considerable cost saving that is not reflected in the damage formula.

The fact that the damage formula is invalid does not deprive Lake River of a remedy. The parties did not contract explicitly with reference to the measure of damages if the agreed-on damage formula was invalidated, but all this means is that the victim of the breach is entitled to his common law damages. See, e.g., Restatement, Second, Contracts §356, comment a (1981). In this case that would be the unpaid contract price of $241,000 minus the costs that Lake River saved by not having to complete the contract (the variable costs on the other 45 percent of the Ferro Carbo that it never had to bag). The case must be remanded to the district judge to fix these damages. . . .

NOTES

1. For another excellent case setting out the history and policy behind liquidated damages clauses, see Wasserman's Inc. v. Township of Middletown, 137 N.J. 238, 645 A.2d 100 (1994). There the court concludes, after citing several commentators, that the real issue is one of reasonableness and that the categorization of the parties of a clause as one for "liquidated damages" versus "penalty" is of no import and adds little to the overall analysis. Of course a provision that is labeled a "penalty" clause gives a broad hint of the impermissible intent of the parties as to this matter, and shows that the drafter paid little attention to the liquidated damages segment of the Contracts course.

2. The court distinguishes "take and pay" contracts, which historically have not been held to be unenforceable. For an excellent case on the distinction between take-and-pay contracts and contracts with an unenforceable penalty, see Superfos Investments Ltd. v. Firstmiss Fertilizer, Inc., 821 F. Supp. 432 (S.D. Miss. 1993) (liquidated damages clause really a penalty and not like take-and-pay contract because contract at issue (1) specifically relieved seller of risk of its producer's failure to supply product and (2) buyer was not given the right to purchase additional product in future to make up any quantity of product not purchased by the buyer in previous years).

Problem 73

Dr. Watson signed a contract to purchase land in Florida, agreeing to pay a set amount each month to the sellers. A liquidated damages clause provided that if he missed a payment the sellers could foreclose their purchase money mortgage and reclaim the land, plus keep all payments made to date as liquidated damages. Is the clause valid? See Hutchinson v. Tompkins, 259 So. 2d 129 (Fla. 1972). What about a clause that provides for liquidated damages of 15 percent of the contract price? Should the result be affected by the fact that before trial the seller sold the land for a price greater than the original sale price? Compare Leeber v. Deltona Corp., 546 A.2d 452 (Me. 1988) (a "fortuitous resale" should not affect the result), with Lind Bldg. Corp. v. Pacific Bellevue Dev., 55 Wash. App. 70, 776 P.2d 977 (1989) (no liquidated damages should be allowed where the seller in fact suffered no damages).

Problem 74

The construction contract contained a liquidated damages clause stating that the contractor must complete the bridge by August 10 or pay $500 a day for each day thereafter that the bridge remained uncompleted. On August 10 the bridge was still uncompleted, but the road on the other side of the river to which it was to be connected was not completed by other contractors until September 8, by which time the bridge was done. Must the bridge contractor pay the liquidated amount? What was the purpose of the clause at the time it was drafted? Compare Massman Construction Co. v. City Council, 147 F.2d 925 (5th Cir. 1945), with Southwest Engineer Co. v. United States, 341 F.2d 998 (8th Cir.), cert. denied, 382 U.S. 819 (1965). For a more modern view on the issue see Boone v. Coleman Constr., Inc. v. Piketon, 145 Ohio St. 3d 450, 50 N.E.3d 502 (2016).

Problem 75

When student Portia Moot tried to rent an apartment near the law school, she was required to sign a lease and put down a deposit of $600. The lease provided that this amount would be kept by the lessor as liquidated damages if Portia did any of the following things: damage the apartment in any way, cause a disturbance, bother the other tenants, keep a pet, put holes in the wall, move out without giving 30 days' notice, or fail to pay the usual $600 rent each month. The clause also provided that Portia would have to pay such other actual damages as the lessor might be able to prove. Is this clause valid? See Perillo, Contracts §14-32.

What about the validity of a clause that provides that if the tenant does not fulfill the entire term of the one-year lease that there is a penalty equal to all of the remaining rent? Two months' rent? See Paragon Group, Inc. v. Ampleman, 878 S.W.2d 878 (Mo. Ct. App. 1994).

Problem 76

Portia Moot next decided to sign up with a health spa to improve her physical fitness, which was suffering from the law school regimen. The spa manager talked her into a three-year contract under which she obligated herself for a total of $3,500 in lessons and training. She went once and then the strain of her studies forced her to discontinue the program. The spa sued her for $3,450 (she had put down a $50 deposit). Is it entitled to this amount? See Cellphone Termination Cases, 193 Cal. App. 4th 298, 122 Cal. Rptr. 3d 726 (2011); Vogue Models, Inc. v. Reina, 6 Ill. App. 3d 211, 285 N.E.2d 256 (1972); Westmount Country Club v. Kameny, 82 N.J. Super. 200, 197 A.2d 379 (1964); Nu Dimensions Figure Salon v. Becerra, 73 Misc. 2d 917, 340 N. Y.S.2d 268 (Civ. Ct. 1973).

NOTE

In reading the following case, depending on the order in which your instructor assigns these materials, you may get your first introduction to warranties for the quality of goods. A breach of warranty under UCC Article 2's §§2-313, 2-314, or 2-315 may give rise to the right of damages under §§2-714 and 2-715. At this point, do not concern yourself with either how warranties arise (a topic we address in Chapter 5) or the typical measure of damages for a breach of warranty. Instead concentrate on what the court has to say about agreements limiting damages and their effectiveness under §2-719.

SCHURTZ v. BMW OF NORTH AMERICA
Utah Supreme Court, 1991
814 P.2d 1108

ZIMMERMAN, J. . . .

In February 1982, Hugh Schurtz purchased a 1982 BMW 320i from BMW of Murray. The car carried a written warranty limiting BMW's responsibility to the repair or replacement of defective parts within three years or 38,000 miles. The limited warranty specified that the decision to repair or replace was within the sole discretion of BMW. Of central concern for the purposes of the appeal were additional warranty provisions stating that "BMW of North America, Inc., makes no other express warranty on this product" and the "BMW of North America, Inc., hereby excludes incidental and consequential damages . . . for any breach of any express or implied warranty."

After allegedly encountering numerous problems with the car, Schurtz filed the present action. He claimed that immediately after purchase, he experienced difficulties with the car. He further asserted that BMW breached the limited warranty because it was either unable or unwilling to repair or replace the car. Schurtz claimed (i) breach of written and implied warranties in contravention of the Magnuson Moss Act, 15 U.S.C. §§2301(6) and 2310(d)(1) (1974); (ii) negligent misrepresentation; (iii) breach of the Utah Consumer Sales Practices Act, Utah Code Ann. §§13-11-1 to -23 (1990); and (iv) breach of express and implied warranties made actionable by code §§70A-2-715 and -719 (1990). Schurtz sought damages including the purchase price of the automobile, incidental and consequential damages, attorney fees, costs, and punitive damages.

BMW filed a motion for summary judgment, seeking dismissal of all Schurtz's warranty claims. Pertinent to this appeal is the alternative motion for partial summary judgment in which BMW sought to have Schurtz's claims for incidental and consequential damages dismissed, arguing that these claims were barred by the express provisions of the limited warranty.

In response to this alternative motion, Schurtz argued that the limited warranty's provision excluding incidental and consequential damages and limiting the remedy for breach to repair or replacement was invalid under §2-719(2) of the Utah U.C.C. He reasoned that a provision excluding incidental and consequential damages is invalid under §2-719(2) if the warranty to repair or replace "fails of its essential purpose" and that the limited BMW warranty failed of its essential purpose because BMW was either unable or unwilling to repair his car.

BMW responded to this argument by contending that under the U.C.C. the limited warranty provision excluding incidental and consequential damages remains valid even if the warranty of repair or replacement fails of its essential purpose. BMW argued that §2-719(3) governs incidental and consequential damage provisions and specifically allows a provision to exclude incidental and consequential damages unless it is "unconsciona- ble." BMW argued that "unconscionability" under subpart (2) does not arise merely because a limited warranty to repair or replace fails of its "essential purpose."

The issue thus joined is the critical issue of this appeal. Specifically, are subparts (2) and (3) of §2-719 of the Utah U.C.C. to be read dependently, as Schurtz argues, or independently, as BMW claims and the trial court found? A dependent reading would mean that any limitation on incidental and consequential damages under subpart (3) would be ineffective in the event that the contingency in subpart (2), a failure of the essential purpose of the limited warranty, occurred. An independent reading would mean that the occurrence of the condition specified in subpart (2) would not mean the automatic invalidity of a limitation on incidental and consequential damages. Because the disposition of this issue turns on §2-719 of the Utah U.C.C., we set it forth here:

> (1) Subject to the provisions of subsections (2) and (3) of this section and of the preceding section on liquidation and limitation of damages,
> (a) the agreement may provide for remedies in addition to or in substitution for those provided in this chapter and may limit or alter the measure of damages recoverable under this chapter, as by limiting the buyer's remedies to return of the goods and repayment of the price or to repair and replacement of non-conforming goods or parts; and
> (b) resort to a remedy as provided is optional unless the remedy is expressly agreed to be exclusive, in which case it is the sole remedy.
> (2) Where circumstances cause an exclusive remedy or limited remedy to fail of its essential purpose, remedy may be had as provided in this act.
> (3) Consequential damages may be limited or excluded unless the limitation or exclusion is unconscionable. Limitation of consequential damages for injury to the person in the case of consumer goods is prima facie unconscionable but limitation of damages where the loss is commercial is not.

The motion for partial summary judgment was heard on July 22, 1988, and taken under advisement by the court. The matter came for trial on August 1, 1988. On the first day of trial, a jury was impaneled, counsel made their opening statements, and Schurtz was called as the first witness. On the second day of trial, before any further evidence was taken, the court ruled on the summary judgment motion filed previously by BMW. The court denied BMW's motion to dismiss all Schurtz's warranty claims, but it granted BMW's motion with respect to Schurtz's claim for incidental and consequen- tial damages. The court agreed with BMW and concluded that subparts 2-719(2) and (3) operate independently. When a warranty limits the reme- dies available to the buyer to repair or replacement and also provides that the buyer may not recover incidental and consequential damages, if the repair or replacement provision fails of its essential purpose, the incidental and consequential damages limitation in the warranty remains valid.

Following this decision, an agreement was reached between the parties under which BMW, although not conceding the issues of breach of warranty and breach of contract, would refund the car's purchase price of $14,500 to Schurtz upon return of the car, minus a credit to BMW for actual use by Schurtz in the amount of 16 cents per mile for 22,516 miles, for a total credit of $3,602.56. It was further agreed that Schurtz would be deemed the prevailing party for the purpose of obtaining attorney fees as provided for by the Magnuson-Moss Act, 15 U.S.C. §2310(d)(2). Under that provision, the prevailing party is entitled to such fees as the court determines were "reasonably incurred" in prosecuting the action.

Following entry of the parties' agreement, the court held a hearing to determine the reasonable attorney fees due Schurtz. Schurtz requested fees of $44,069.15, the amount which he claimed he had incurred in prosecuting the claim. BMW contended that he was not entitled to any attorney fees or, in the alternative, entitled only to an award sufficient to compensate him to the point where he filed his complaint and received an offer for settlement based on rescission on the theory that the lawsuit was unnecessary and the fees were unreasonable. The court awarded Schurtz only $10,000 on the ground that the matter "could have been and probably should have been settled very early in the proceedings, for an amount roughly equal to the ultimate outcome." The court, in awarding a discounted sum of fees to Schurtz, operated on the assumption that Schurtz should have known that he was not entitled to incidental and consequential damages and therefore spent more money prosecuting the action than was justified. Schurtz appeals from the grant of summary judgment and from the award of fees. . . .

The fundamental question before us is whether the trial court correctly held that the failure of essential purpose of a repair or replace provision in a limited warranty does not affect the validity of a companion provision in the warranty precluding incidental and consequential damages or, in other words, that subparts (2) and (3) should operate independently. To determine the answer, we must determine the proper interpretation of subparts 2-719(2) and (3) of the Utah U.C.C. In so doing, we review the language of the statute, the legislative history, and the relevant policy considerations. . . .

Section 2-719 states the contractual limitations or modifications that may be made in the remedies provided for in the earlier sections of part 7. Subpart (1) of §2-719 states that, consistent with subparts (2) and (3) of that section, the parties may limit the remedies provided in chapter two of the agreement between the buyer and seller to, for example, "repair and replacement of non-conforming goods or parts." Subpart 2-719(2) then provides that a limitation of remedies may become ineffective: "[W]here circumstances cause an exclusive remedy or limited remedy to fail of its essential purpose, [then] remedy may be had as provided in this act." As we recognized in Devore v. Bostrom, 632 P.2d 832, 835 (Utah 1981), where a limited remedy fails of its essential purpose, the buyer may pursue all remedies provided in that part of the U.C.C., including the recovery of incidental and consequential damages under §2-715.

Subpart 2-719(3) deals separately with provisions expressly limiting damages otherwise available under §2-715. That section provides, "[C]onsequential damages may be limited or excluded unless the limitation or exclusion is unconscionable."

From the statute's language, it appears that subparts (2) and (3) are to operate independently. A scheme is established under which express agreements disclaiming incidental and consequential damages are to be governed by subpart (3), and the validity of these exclusions is tested by "unconscionability," while agreements disclaiming all the other contractual remedies provided in chapter two are governed by subparts (1) and (2) and their validity is tested by "failure of essential purpose as well as the general unconscionability requirements of the Code."

This independent reading of the two provisions also conforms to the general rule that we should construe statutory provisions so as to give full effect to all their terms, where possible. Madsen v. Borthick, 769 P.2d 245, 252 n.11 (Utah 1988). If we were to read subparts (2) and (3) as dependent, we would effectively read out the unconscionability test of subpart (3) for determining the validity of a provision limiting incidental and consequential damages and substitute "failure of essential purpose" from subpart (2) as the operative text. Such a reading seems to fly in the face of the plain language of the statute.

The statute's terms lead us to conclude that subparts (2) and (3) should be read independently. We recognize that courts across the country are split on the question, suggesting that a number of courts find the statute's language less than clear. Our position is in accord with the Third Circuit's statement in [Chatlos Systems v. National Cash Register Corp., 635 F.2d 1081 (3d Cir. 1980)]:

> It appears to us that the better reasoned approach is to treat the consequential damages disclaimer as an independent provision, valid unless unconscionable [subpart (3)]. . . . The limited remedy of repair [subpart (2)] and a consequential damages exclusion are two discrete ways of attempting to limit recovery for breach of warranty. . . . The code, moreover, treats each by a different standard. The former survives unless it fails of its essential purpose, while the latter is valid unless it is unconscionable. We therefore see no reason to hold, as a general proposition, that the failure of the limited remedy provided in the contract, without more, invalidates a wholly distinct term in the agreement excluding consequential damages. The two are not mutually exclusive.

Chatlos Systems, 635 F.2d at 1086 (bracketed material added).

Our independent reading of the two subparts is consistent with the only thing that could be described as legislative history on the issue, the comments of the drafters of the Uniform Commercial Code. The comment to §2-719 does not expressly state whether the remedies provided for by §2-719(2) should include incidental and consequential damages when a limited warranty specifically excludes them. See U.C.C. §2-719 comment (1990). However, the general terms of the comment, when viewed in light of the other provisions of part 7, are furthered by an independent reading of §2-719(2) and §2-719(3). The comment explains that §2-719 permits contractual limitations on remedies to be overthrown in certain circumstances, and consequently, parties who conclude a contract for sale, even one with limitations of remedies, "must accept the legal consequence that there be at least a fair quantum of remedy for breach of the obligations or duties outlined in the contract." Such a "fair quantum of remedy for breach" is available when subparts (2) and (3) are given an independent reading.

Our independent reading of subparts (2) and (3) is also supported by sound policy considerations. And with some careful tuning, our independent reading of the two subparts can accommodate the values that appear to have driven a number of courts to read these two provisions as dependent.

As noted above, there is a split among the courts across the country, with some courts reading (2) and (3) independently and others reading them dependently. These positions may appear irreconcilable. However, when the facts of the cases are taken into account, the policy considerations that seem to underlie the decisions holding the two subparts dependent appear reconcilable with the considerations underlying those holding them independent, and the split of authority on the question of a dependent or independent construction seems largely a result of the context in which the question was presented to the courts.

In cases where the buyer is a consumer, there is a disparity in bargaining power, and the contractual limitations on remedies, including incidental and consequential damages, are contained in a preprinted document rather than one that has been negotiated between the parties, the courts have held uniformly that if the limited warranty fails of its essential purpose, the consumer should be permitted to seek incidental and consequential damages. The courts usually reach this result by reading the two subparts dependently. See, e.g., Clark v. International Harvester, 99 Idaho 326, 581 P.2d 784 (1978). On the other hand, in cases where the parties are operating in a commercial setting, there is no disparity in bargaining power, and the contract and its limitations on remedies are negotiated, most courts have concluded that if a limited warranty fails of its essential purpose, any contractual limitation on incidental and consequential damages is not automatically void. The subparts are read independently and the surviving limitation on incidentals and consequentials remains valid absent a showing of unconscionability. E.g., V-M Corp. v. Bernard Distrib. Co., 447 F.2d 864, 869 (7th Cir. 1971); *American Elec. Power Co.*, 418 F. Supp. at 457-59.

In our view, both the consumer and the nonconsumer situation can be dealt with in a manner that reconciles the apparent split of authority in the cases by giving an independent reading to subparts (2) and (3). When trial courts are addressing the subpart (3) issue of unconscionability in any specific case, they should take an approach that frankly recognizes the differences that inhere in consumer, as opposed to commercial, settings and affect the determination of unconscionability. This distinction is recognized in other areas of the U.C.C. See, e.g., J. White & R. Summers, U.C.C. §§4-2 to 4-9 (difference in unconscionability determination in consumer and commercial setting); 12-1 to 12-5 (difference in warranties to consumers and merchants); 14-8 to 14-9 (consumer/merchant distinction in rights of holders in due course) (2d ed. 1980). We think the results in the cases we have canvassed amount to a recognition of this distinction in §2-719 cases. Under such an approach, the trial court confronted with an issue of unconscionability takes into account any disparities in bargaining power between the parties, the negotiation process, if any, and the type of contract entered into by the parties, specifically addressing whether the contract was one of adhesion. As noted above, in practice after these factors are examined and weighed, a trial court will generally find that provisions limiting incidental and consequential damages are unconscionable in consumer settings and conscionable in commercial settings. We acknowledge that the outcome in any particular case may diverge from this pattern because of the facts; but that is only a recognition of the difficulty of neatly categorizing transactions as commercial or consumer.

An analysis that takes a case-by-case approach to the question of unconscionability accommodates the results in virtually all the cases dealing with the relationship between subparts (2) and (3). It also provides the courts with a flexible tool for determining the validity of limitations on incidental and consequential damages that serves well the different policies appropriate to consumer and commercial settings. For example, where such a limitation is freely negotiated between sophisticated parties, which will most likely occur in a commercial setting, it seems unlikely that a court will find a provision limiting incidental and consequential damages unconscionable and free the buyer from that provision simply because some other limited warranty provision has failed of its essential purpose. On the other hand, where a limitation of incidentals and consequentials is nonnegotiable and preprinted on a standard form limited warranty that is sealed in a package with consumer goods or stuffed in a glovebox, where it will never be seen until after the goods are sold, as may often occur in consumer transactions, then it seems more likely that a court will find that the freedom to contract for limitations on remedies described in subparts 2-719(1) and (3) has not really been meaningfully exercised by both parties and the limitation will be held unconscionable. [Citations omitted.]

In light of the foregoing, we conclude that the trial court erred in ruling on the motion for partial summary judgment that, as a matter of law, Schurtz was not entitled to incidental and consequential damages. Although the trial court correctly held that subparts (2) and (3) of §2-719 are to be read independently, it erred by not then determining whether the facts of this case warrant a finding that the limitation of incidental and consequential damages is unconscionable under subpart 2-719(3). And if it had so found, it should have made findings of fact to support the result. We vacate the summary judgment and remand for further proceedings on the warranty question in accordance with this opinion.

Schurtz also claims that it was an error for the court to award a discounted sum of attorney fees because it was based on the legal assumption that Schurtz could not recover incidental and consequential damages and should have known that fact. Because that assumption was incorrect, the trial court must readdress the attorney fees question after deciding the warranty issues.

HALL, C.J., and DURHAM, J., concur.

HOWE, Associate C.J. (concurring and dissenting). [Omitted.]

STEWART, J. (concurring and dissenting). I agree with the majority opinion that Utah's U.C.C. §2-719(2) does not mandate that consequential damages be allowed every time a limited warranty fails of its essential purpose. However, there may be circumstances in which the failure of a limited warranty will also result in the failure of a clause limiting consequential damages. The question is primarily one of contract interpretation, in my view, rather than one of statutory construction, as both the majority and Justice Howe in his opinion seem to suggest.

Section §2-719(1) authorizes a limited or exclusive remedy. Section 2-719(2) provides that if "circumstances cause an exclusive or limited remedy to fail of its essential purpose, remedy may be had as provided in this act." The phrase "as provided in this act" does not invalidate an otherwise valid contractual provision. The true question is whether, based on an interpretation of the contract, the failure of an exclusive or limited remedy also causes the failure of a consequential damages limitation. The answer to this question depends on the contract rather than the U.C.C. In other words, if the contract is interpreted in such a way that the consequential damages limitation must fail with the limited remedy, then incidental and consequential damages may be recovered as provided in the U.C.C. On the other hand, if the failure of the limited remedy does not cause the failure of the consequential damages limitation, then that limitation must be evaluated under the unconscionability standard of §2-719(3).

Sustaining an otherwise valid consequential damages limitation, even though a limited remedy has failed of its essential purpose, is entirely consistent with the terms and framework of the U.C.C. Under the U.C.C., a seller may limit consequential damages without otherwise limiting a buyer's remedies. See, e.g., Adams Laboratories, Inc. v. Jacobs Eng'g Co., 486 F. Supp. 383, 388 (N.D. Ill. 1980). There is no reason to hold that a seller and a buyer may not enter into a contract which provides for the limitation of consequential damages, so long as it is not unconscionable, in the event that a limited remedy fails of its essential purpose. The U.C.C. certainly does not mandate such a conclusion. Although generally the failure of the essential purpose of a limited remedy will also invalidate a consequential damages limitation, there are cases when it will not. . . .

Case law from other jurisdictions, including that cited in the majority opinion, if not expressly following this reasoning, at least does so implicitly. Those cases allowing consequential damages in spite of an express limitation have done so either because the seller repudiated the warranty and therefore could not rely on the warranty's limitation of consequential damages or because the two limitations were so interrelated that the failure of one necessarily caused the failure of the other. See, e.g., Jones & McKnight Corp. v. Birdsboro Corp., 320 F. Supp. 39, 43 (N.D. Ill. 1970) (court "would be in an untenable position if it allowed the defendant to shelter itself behind one segment of the warranty when it has allegedly repudiated and ignored its very limited obligations under another segment of the same warranty"); Clark v. International Harvester Co., 99 Idaho 326, 343, 581 P.2d 784, 801 (1978) (both limitations were "integral parts of the provision, reciprocal to one another, and together they represented the agreed allocation of risk between the parties"); Adams v. J.I. Case Co., 125 Ill. App. 2d 388, 402, 261 N.E.2d 1, 7 (1970) ("[L]imitations of remedy and of liability are not separable from the obligations of the warranty. Repudiation of the obligations of the warranty destroy its benefits."); Kelynack v. Yamaha Motor Corp., USA, 152 Mich. App. 105, 115, 394 N.W.2d 17, 21 (1986) ("repair and replace remedy and the exclusion of consequential damages are integral and interdependent parts of the warranty"; seller cannot "repudiate its limited obligation under the warranty while shielding itself behind another provision of the very warranty it has repudiated"); Ehlers v. Chrysler Motor Corp., 88 S.D. 612, 620, 226 N.W.2d 157, 161 (1975) (seller cannot "repudiate its obligation under the warranty" and at the same time attempt "to shield itself behind the beneficial limitation clause" of the same warranty).

On the other hand, many courts are willing to enforce a completely separate and otherwise valid consequential damages limitation provision. See, e.g., Chatlos Sys., Inc. v. National Cash Register Corp., 635 F.2d 1081, 1086 (3d Cir. 1980) ("limited remedy of repair and a consequential damages exclusion are two discrete ways of attempting to limit recovery"; the consequential damages limitation is "valid unless it is unconscionable"); AES Technology Sys., Inc. v. Coherent Radiation, 583 F.2d 933, 941 (7th Cir. 1978) (court rejected "the contention that failure of the essential purpose of the limited remedy automatically means that a damage award will include consequential damages"; "purpose of the courts in contractual disputes is not to rewrite contracts by ignoring parties' intent; rather it is to interpret the existing contract as fairly as possible when all events did not occur as planned"); V-M Corp. v. Bernard Distrib. Co., 447 F.2d 864, 869 (7th Cir. 1971) (court "not persuaded that Section 2-719(2) . . . requires the negation of the specific limitations of the contract"); American Elec. Power Co. v. Westinghouse Elec. Corp., 418 F. Supp. 435, 458 (S.D.N.Y. 1976) ("totally separate provision" limiting consequential damages does not fail with limited remedy; limited remedy which "fails of its essential purpose . . . may be ignored, and other clauses in the contract which limit remedies for breach may be left to stand or fall independently of the stricken clause. Section 2-719 was intended to encourage and facilitate consensual allocations of risks"); Stutts v. Green Ford, Inc., 47 N.C. App. 503, 516, 267 S.E.2d 919, 926 (1980) (failure of limited remedy does not invalidate a "contractual limitation on the recovery of consequential damages").

Although, as a practical matter, the various courts deciding these cases might not agree on how to interpret a particular set of facts, the principle derived from the cases is well-reasoned. In sum, if a consequential damages limitation is not so integrally related to a limited remedy that the failure of the essential purpose of that remedy, or its repudiation by the seller, necessarily invalidates the damages limitation, the consequential damages limitation should be upheld if not unconscionable. . . .

NOTES AND QUESTIONS

1. Unconscionability, a doctrine we will discuss in some detail in Chapter 6, means that the contractual provision is so unfair that the court will not enforce it. See Uniform Commercial Code §2-302.

2. What does "failure of its essential purpose" mean? When would a remedy limitation do this? Official Comment 1 to §2-719 states:

> [I]t is of the very essence of a sales contract that at least minimum adequate remedies be available. If the parties intend to conclude a contract for sale within this Article they must accept the legal consequence that there be at least a fair quantum of remedy for breach of the obligations or duties outlined in the contract. . . . [W]here an apparently fair and reasonable clause because of circumstances fails in its purpose or operates to deprive either party of the substantial value of the bargain, it must give way to the general remedy provisions of this Article.

3. Where the seller limited the buyer's remedy to repair and also disclaimed any consequential damages (such as loss of the use of the car while it was in the shop), the parties probably understood that the repair would be done in an efficient manner, and during this period buyer would have to bear the consequential damages himself. But where the seller is not able to repair the goods after numerous attempts, is it still fair to uphold the denial of consequential damages?

4. When this case is returned to the lower court for retrial, what will the parties now argue concerning §2-719?

5. Note that a consequential damages limitation for personal injury in the sale of consumer goods is prima facie unconscionable under §2-719(3)'s last sentence. Thus in Collins v. Uniroyal, 64 N.J. 260, 315 A.2d 16, 14 U.C.C. Rep. Serv. 294 (1974), where a family was killed when the tire on their automobile blew out, the New Jersey Supreme Court tossed out a limitation in the warranty attempting to avoid liability for damages due to wrongful death.

5. Punitive Damages

See the following excerpt from the Restatement (Second) of Contracts:

§355. Punitive Damages

Punitive damages are not recoverable for a breach of contract unless the conduct constituting the breach is also a tort for which punitive damages are recoverable.

HIBSCHMAN PONTIAC, INC. v. BATCHELOR
Supreme Court of Indiana, 1977
266 Ind. 310, 362 N.E.2d 845

Givan, C.J. Batchelor brought an action for breach of contract and oppressive conduct by Hibschman Pontiac, Inc. and General Motors Corporation. A trial before a jury resulted in a verdict for Batchelor and against Hibschman Pontiac and General Motors Corporation in the amount of $1,500.00. Further, the jury assessed punitive damages against Hibschman Pontiac, Inc. in the amount of $15,000.00.

Plaintiff got 15,000 in punitive damages

The Court of Appeals, Third District, reversed the grant of punitive damages. See 340 N.E.2d 377. Batchelor now petitions for transfer.

Reversed on Appeals

The record reveals the following evidence: Prior to buying the Pontiac GTO automobile involved in this case, Batchelor inquired of the salesman, the service manager and the vice president as to the quality of Hibschman Pontiac's service department, as it was important that any deficiencies in the car be corrected. The salesman and the service manager responded that the service department at Hibschman Pontiac was above average. Jim Hibschman, the vice president, assured him that he would personally see that any difficulties would be corrected. Batchelor stated that he relied on the statements of the three men and ordered a 1969 GTO Pontiac automobile.

When Batchelor picked up his new car he discovered several problems with it. As requested by the service manager of Hibschman Pontiac,

Batchelor made a list of his complaints and brought the car in for repair a few days later. The service manager attached the list to a work order but did not list the deficiencies on the work order. Later the manager called Batchelor and said that the car was ready. When he picked up the car Batchelor noticed that several items on the list had not been touched. Batchelor testified that there were many occasions when he took the car to Hibschman Pontiac for repairs and the service manager told him that the defects had been fixed when in fact they were not fixed. Batchelor testified that the service manager knew the defects were not corrected, but represented to him that the defects were corrected. Batchelor stated that he relied on the service manager's statements and took the car on several trips, only to have it break down. Some of the deficiencies resulted in abnormal wear of the car and break-downs after the warranty period had expired.

Batchelor testified that he had taken the car in for repairs five times before he had owned it a month but that the defects had not been corrected. Batchelor had taken the car in 12 times during the warranty period for overnight repair and at least 20 times in all during the period. During the warranty period Batchelor lost use of the car approximately 45 days while it was at Hibschman Pontiac.

Batchelor had appealed to Jim Hibschman on several occasions to take care of his car. Hibschman replied that he realized the repairs were not effected properly but that Hibschman Pontiac would "do everything to get you happy." On another occasion Jim Hibschman responded they had done all they could with the car but that Batchelor was just a particular, habitual complainer whom they could not satisfy and "I would rather you would just leave and not come back. We are going to have to write you off as a bad customer."

On several occasions Batchelor attempted to see Dan Shaules, an area service representative from Pontiac Division, about the car but was kept waiting so long that he had to leave without seeing him. Batchelor did see Shaules in Buchanan, Michigan, when he took the car to an authorized Pontiac dealer there after the warranty had expired. Shaules inspected the car and told Batchelor to return the car to Hibschman Pontiac for repairs.

Hugh Haverstock, the owner of the garage where several of the deficiencies were corrected after the expiration of the warranty, testified that Batchelor was a good customer and paid his bills. He stated that an average transmission man could have corrected the problem with the transmission and that a problem with the timing chain was discovered and corrected when a tune up lasted only 800 miles. Haverstock stated that the difference in value of the car without defects and with the defects it had was approximately $1,500.00. Haverstock testified that when a person complains about problems with cars that have not been fixed by dealerships, word gets out and others do not want to work on the cars.

Arnold Miexel, the service manager for Hibschman Pontiac during the time in question, testified that his representation to Batchelor regarding Hibschman Pontiac service department was based on the fact that the mechanics were factory trained and that he had received no complaints regarding their work. He further stated that he could not check the work of the mechanics. Miexel testified that if their work was unsatisfactory it was done over but no work order was written for it. He stated that it was possible Batchelor made complaints about the car, but the defects were not corrected. The warranty expired and, as a consequence, later work was not considered under warranty.

Dan Shaules testified that Miexel was an average service manager. He testified that not all of the deficiencies in the car were corrected properly. He further stated that if any defects in the car were brought to their attention within the warranty period, items would be corrected if necessary after the warranty had expired.

Appellant first argues that there was insufficient evidence to permit the issue of punitive damages to go to the jury and that the court should have rendered a directed verdict on the issue of punitive damages on behalf of Hibschman Pontiac. This Court has recently dealt with the question of punitive damages in a contract action. In Vernon Fire & Casualty Ins. Co. v. Sharp (1976), Ind., 349 N.E.2d 173, the majority restated the general provision that punitive damages are not recoverable in contract actions and went on to state exceptions to this rule. Where the conduct of a party, in breaching his contract, independently establishes the elements of a common law tort, punitive damages may be awarded for the tort.

Punitive damages may be awarded in addition to compensatory damages "whenever the elements of fraud, malice, gross negligence or oppression *mingle* in the controversy." (Emphasis supplied.) Vernon Fire & Casualty Ins. Co. v. Sharp, supra, Ind., 349 N.E.2d 178, 180, quoting Taber v. Hutson (1854), 5 Ind. 322.

Further, where a separate tort accompanies the breach or the elements of tort mingle with the breach, it must appear that the public interest will be served by the deterrent effect of the punitive damages. Vernon Fire & Casualty Ins. Co. v. Sharp, supra.

Appellant urges that the evidence presented does not indicate tortious conduct of any sort on its part. While a reasonable inference could be made from the evidence that appellant merely attempted to fulfill its contract and to do no more than that contract required, it is also reasonable to infer that Hibschman Pontiac acted tortiously and in willful disregard of the right of Batchelor. This Court has often stated the maxim that it will not reweigh the evidence nor determine the credibility of witnesses, but will sustain a verdict if there is any evidence of probative value to support it. Moore v. Waitt (1973), Ind. App., 298 N.E.2d 456; Smart and Perry Ford Sales, Inc. v. Weaver (1971), 149 Ind. App. 693, 274 N.E.2d 718.

A corporation can act only through its agents, and their acts, when done within the scope of their authority, are attributable to the corporation. Soft Water Utilities, Inc. v. Lefevre (1974), Ind. App., 308 N.E.2d 395.

Here, the jury could reasonably have found elements of fraud, malice, gross negligence or oppression mingled into the breach of warranty. The evidence showed that requested repairs were not satisfactorily completed although covered by the warranty and capable of correction. Some of these defects were clearly breaches of warranty. Paint was bubbled, the radio never worked properly, the hood and bumper were twisted and misaligned, the universal joints failed, the transmission linkage was improperly adjusted, the timing chain was defective causing improper tune-ups and the carburetor was defective, among other things. Batchelor took the car to the defendant with a list of defects on numerous occasions and picked up the car when told it was "all ready to go." It was reasonable to infer that the defendant's service manager represented repairs to have been made when he knew that the work had not been done and that in reliance on his representations, Batchelor drove the car on trips and had breakdowns. Before purchasing the car Batchelor was given special representations on the excellence of Hibschman's service department, and the jury could find that Batchelor relied on these in buying the car from the defendant. After having brought the car in on numerous occasions, Batchelor was told by Jim Hibschman, "I would rather you would just leave and not come back. We are going to have to write you off as a bad customer." And he was told by one of Hibschman's mechanics that, "If you don't get on them and get this fixed, they will screw you around and you will never get it done." From these statements the jury could infer that the defendant was attempting to avoid making certain repairs by concealing them during the period of the warranty. Batchelor gave the defendant numerous opportunities to repair the car and the defendant did not do so; instead he tried to convince Batchelor that the problems were not with the car, but rather with Batchelor. We are of the opinion that in this case the jury could have found there was cogent proof to establish malice, fraud, gross negligence and oppressive conduct.

Although fraudulent conduct was not alleged in the complaint, evidence on the subject was admitted. Any inconsistency between the pleadings and proof will be resolved in favor of the proof at trial. Ayr-Way Stores, Inc. v. Chitwood (1973), 261 Ind. 86, 300 N.E.2d 335; Vernon Fire & Casualty Ins. Co. v. Sharp, supra. Thus there was probative evidence supporting the claim for punitive damages. The trial court did not err in denying a directed verdict as to that issue. See Jordanich v. Gerstbauer (1972), 153 Ind. App. 416, 287 N.E.2d 784.

Appellant next presents a collective argument for three issues: whether there was sufficient evidence to support an award for punitive damages in the amount of $15,000; whether the award of $15,000 punitive damages bears a reasonable relationship to the actual damages; and whether punitive damages of $15,000 is excessive in this case.

Appellant here urges that there was no evidence presented concerning its worth or ability to pay. In Physicians Mutual Ins. Co. v. Savage (1973), 156 Ind. App. 283, 296 N.E.2d 165, the Court of Appeals held that the assessment of punitive damages in the amount of $50,000 "was not excessive when considered in relation to the evidence available to the trial court." The opinion noted that included in the evidence was a statement of net worth of the defendant. In Manning v. Lynn Immke Buick, Inc. (1971), 28 Ohio App. 2d 203, 276 N.E.2d 253, the court held that where punitive damages are to be assessed, the wealth of the defendant may be shown so that the jury will assess damages that will punish him. Such a rule is based on the theory that it will take a greater amount of penalty to dissuade a rich person than a poor person from oppressive conduct. However there appears to be no requirement that evidence of worth be submitted in cases of punitive damages.

Indiana has followed a rule that punitive damages in a proper case may be assessed by the jury within their sound discretion guided by proper instructions given by the court. Murphy Auto Sales v. Coomer (1953), 123 Ind. App. 709, 112 N.E.2d 589. There is no rule that the amount of punitive damages must be within a certain ratio to compensatory damages, although in the case of Bangert v. Hubbard (1955), 127 Ind. App. 579, 126 N.E.2d 778, a malicious prosecution suit, the court held that punitive damages of $10,500, being 105 times the compensatory damages, was so excessive as to indicate that the verdict was given under the influence of passion and prejudice. In Lou Leventhal Auto Co. v. Munns (1975), Ind. App., 328 N. E.2d 734, the Court of Appeals held that punitive damages in the amount of $1,500 was not excessive, although it was 50 times greater than the compensatory damages proven. That case involved an action to replevin an automobile wrongfully repossessed by a dealer. As noted by Judge Lowdermilk, the high ratio of punitive damages to compensatory damages "alone is not conclusive of an improper award. The amount here awarded is not so large as to appear the result of passion or prejudice, and is therefore not excessive." 328 N.E.2d at 742.

In the case at bar, although it was within the province of the jury to assess punitive damages, the amount in this case is so high as to violate the "first blush" rule as set out in City of Indianapolis v. Stokes (1914), 182 Ind. 31, 105 N.E. 477:

> Damages are not [to be] considered excessive unless at first blush they appear to be outrageous and excessive or it is apparent that some improper element was taken into account by the jury in determining the amount.

For the above reasons transfer is granted and the cause is remanded to the trial court with instruction to order remittitur of $7,500 of the punitive damages. In the event the remittitur is not made, the trial court shall order a new trial. The trial court is in all other matters affirmed.

DeBruler, J., concurring in result. I agree that the punitive damage award of $15,000.00 was excessive, and that remittitur of $7,500.00 is reasonable. However, I doubt the efficacy of the standard enunciated by the majority for the review of punitive damages awards, the "first blush" rule. This rule is vague and contains no objective standards for the evaluation of such awards in view of their purpose, the deterrence of tortious conduct, and the danger to be guarded against, awards motivated by vindictiveness and prejudice. I believe that we should undertake to define a standard of review of punitive damages which imposes objective limitations upon such damages.

NOTES AND QUESTIONS

1. How does the Indiana rule vary from that expressed in the Restatement provision preceding the case?

2. In Travelers Indemnity Co. v. Armstrong, 442 N.E.2d 349 (Ind. 1982), the Indiana Supreme Court adopted a "clear and convincing" standard; that is, that any element of fraud, malice, gross negligence, or oppression that provides the basis for a claim for punitive damages must be established by clear and convincing evidence. The court added:

> [P]unitive damages should not be allowable upon evidence that is merely consistent with the hypothesis of malice, fraud, gross negligence or oppressiveness. Rather some evidence should be required that is inconsistent with the hypothesis that the tortious conduct was the result of a mistake of law or fact, honest error of judgment, over-zealousness, mere negligence or other such iniquitous human failing.

3. Under the Indiana standard should punitive damages be awarded if the defendant purposefully breaches a contract because it can get a better deal from a third party despite the cost of compensatory damages? Judge Posner of the Seventh Circuit Court of Appeals says no because society would suffer a net social gain. Can you explain what he means? Judge Posner would hold the breaching party liable for punitives under the Indiana rule when the breach is

> opportunistic; the promisor wants the benefit of the bargain without bearing the agreed-upon cost, and exploits the inadequacies of purely compensatory remedies (the major inadequacies being that pre- and postjudgment interest rates are frequently below market levels when the risk of nonpayment is taken into account and that the winning party cannot recover his attorney's fees). This seems the common element in most of the Indiana cases that have allowed punitive damages to be awarded in breach of contract cases.

Patton v. Mid-Continent Systems, 841 F.2d 742, 751 (7th Cir. 1988).

4. In *Hibschman*, other than failing to repair the car, what, if anything, did the defendant do to deserve punishment?

5. Factors that may affect the amount of punitive damages include the plaintiff's costs of litigation, the financial condition of the defendant, and the grossness of the conduct of the defendant.

[handwritten margin note: Factors considered when awarding punitive damages]

6. When punitive damages are sought, courts have often allowed as part of discovery an investigation of the financial records of the defendant to determine what amount is necessary to make the award truly pinch. Annot., 54 A.L.R. 4th 998. Of course, defendants don't want their financial records examined, and this gives added menace to a claim for punitive damages.

7. The United States Supreme Court has held that punitive damages greatly exceeding the compensatory damages are unconstitutional as violating the Due Process Clause of the Fourteenth Amendment; see State Farm Mut. Auto. Ins. Co. v. Campbell, 538 U.S. 408 (2003) (punitive damages of $145 million excessive where actual damages were $1 million); BMW of North America, Inc. v. Gore, 517 U.S. 559 (1996) (punitive damages of $2 million excessive where actual damages were $4,000); Phillip Morris USA v. Williams, 549 U.S. 346 (2007) (punitive damages used to punish injury to nonparties violates Due Process Clause). State courts have also struggled with this issue; see Parrot v. Carr Chevrolet, Inc., 331 Or. 537, 17 P.3d 473 (2001) (jury award of $1 million punitive damages upheld in lemon used car sale where the actual damages were $11,496).

E. Damages Under the Uniform Commercial Code

1. Buyer's Damages

If the seller fails to tender delivery in the manner promised or the quantity or the quality of the goods does not conform to the contract, the buyer generally has the right to *reject* the goods. UCC §2-601. (There are some limitations to this right; for example, the seller may have the right to cure the defect under UCC §2-508.) The right to reject is an important remedy because on rejection the seller is in control of the goods and ultimately responsible for any decline in value that may occur after rejection. If the buyer holds on to nonconforming goods for too long or uses them without regard to the seller's rights, the right to reject the goods disappears — *acceptance* has occurred. UCC §2-606. Even after acceptance, the buyer may still be entitled to *revoke* acceptance of the goods depending on the nature of the defect and exactly when the buyer attempts to revoke acceptance. UCC §2-608. We discuss the issues involved in rejection/acceptance/revocation in depth in Chapter 7. At this stage it is important to know that the proper exercise of the right of rejection or revocation will affect the measure of damages for breach.

If the buyer has rightfully rejected or revoked acceptance or the seller never delivered the goods at all, the buyer's actual damages are determined by either UCC §2-712 or 2-713. If the buyer "covers" by acting reasonably and trying to find substitute goods from a different seller, §2-712 entitles the buyer to the difference between the cover price and the contract price. Conversely, if the buyer does not cover or covers in an unreasonable fashion (not shopping around hard enough or buying vastly superior substitute goods), §2-712 limits the buyer to the difference between the market price and the contract price. In either situation, the buyer may also be entitled to incidental and consequential damages under §2-715. (However, the amount of damages may be limited by provisions in the sales contract that set a maximum amount for damages. §§2-718, 2-719.)

UNIFORM COMMERCIAL CODE

§2-712. "Cover"; Buyer's Procurement of Substitute Goods

(1) After a breach within the preceding section the buyer may "cover" by making in good faith and without unreasonable delay any reasonable purchase of or contract to purchase goods in substitution for those due from the seller.

(2) The buyer may recover from the seller as damages the difference between the cost of cover and the contract price together with any incidental or consequential damages as hereinafter defined (Section 2-715), but less expenses saved in consequence of the seller's breach.

(3) Failure of the buyer to effect cover within this Section does not bar him from any other remedy.

OFFICIAL COMMENT

1. This section provides the buyer with a remedy aimed at enabling him to obtain the goods he needs thus meeting his essential need. This remedy is the buyer's equivalent of the seller's right to resell.

2. The definition of "cover" under subsection (1) envisages a series of contracts or sales, as well as a single contract or sale; goods not identical with those involved but commercially usable as reasonable substitutes under the circumstances of the particular case; and contracts on credit or delivery terms differing from the contract in breach, but again reasonable under the circumstances. The test of proper cover is whether at the time and place the buyer acted in good faith and in a reasonable manner, and it is immaterial that hindsight may later prove that the method of cover used was not the cheapest or most effective. . . .

The test of Proper cover

3. Subsection (3) expresses the policy that cover is not a mandatory remedy for the buyer. The buyer is always free to choose between cover and damages for non-delivery under the next section.

However, this subsection must be read in conjunction with the section which limits the recovery of consequential damages to such as could not have been obviated by cover. Moreover, the operation of the section on specific performance of contracts for "unique" goods must be considered in this connection for availability of the goods to the particular buyer for his particular needs is the test for that remedy and inability to cover is made an express condition to the right of the buyer to replevy the goods. . . .

UNIFORM COMMERCIAL CODE

§2-713. Buyer's Damages for Non-Delivery or Repudiation

(1) . . . [T]he measure of damages for non-delivery or repudiation by the seller is the difference between the market price at the time when the buyer learned of the breach and the contract price together with any incidental and consequential damages provided in this Article (Section 2-715), but less expenses saved in consequence of the seller's breach.

(2) Market price is to be determined as of the place for tender or, in cases of rejection after arrival or revocation of acceptance, as of the place of arrival.

OFFICIAL COMMENT

1. The general baseline adopted in this section uses as a yardstick the market in which the buyer would have obtained cover had he sought that relief. So the place for measuring damages is the place of tender (or the place of arrival if the goods are rejected or their acceptance is revoked after reaching their destination) and the crucial time is the time at which the buyer learns of the breach. . . .

3. When the current market price under this section is difficult to prove the section on determination and proof of market price is available to permit a showing of a comparable market price or, where no market price is available, evidence of spot sale prices is proper. Where the unavailability of a market price is caused by a scarcity of goods of the type involved, a good case is normally made for specific performance under this Article. Such scarcity conditions, moreover, indicate that the price has risen and under the section providing for liberal administration of remedies, opinion evidence as to the value of the goods would be admissible in the absence of a market price and a liberal construction of allowable consequential damages should also result. . . .

5. The present section provides a remedy which is completely alternative to cover under the preceding section and applies only when and to the extent that the buyer has not covered.

Problem 77

Roget agreed to purchase 40 new computer workstations with state-of-the-art speakers from Sleazic Computers located in Quartz, California. The workstations were to be delivered by the seller to Roget's place of business in Lewiston, Indiana, on March 1, 2020. The cost of each was $3,000.

When the workstations were delivered, Roget discovered that the built-in speakers were barely audible and totally worthless. Roget properly revoked acceptance of the products on March 25, 2020, pursuant to UCC §2-608. On April 1, Roget purchased another brand at the cost of $4,000 each. The new workstations had excellent speakers and were essentially identical to those purchased from Sleazic except that the substitute workstations had a keyboard with a built-in mouse, a feature worth $200. This feature was of no importance to Roget, who had purchased the substitute workstations because they were readily available (a must).

What are Roget's damages under §2-712 if you presume that Roget suffered no consequential or incidental damages?

Problem 78

Assume the same facts as in the last Problem, except also assume that the market price of processors like that purchased by Roget was $5,000 in Lewiston and $3,000 in Quartz. Roget has sued Sleazic for damages under UCC §2-713. If you assume Roget is entitled to sue under that section, what would be the amount of damages assuming no incidental or consequential damages? Is Roget entitled to sue under that section or should Roget be limited to damages as measured by §2-712? See Official Comment 3 to §2-712, and Official Comment 5 to §2-713. If Roget had consequential damages that could have been avoided by cover, are those damages recoverable in an action under §2-713? See UCC §2-715(2)(a) and Official Comment 3 to §2-712.

If a buyer accepts the goods, the buyer's damages are determined by §§2-714 and 2-715. The basic remedy of §2-714 is the difference between the value of the goods in the condition as sold and the value of the goods as promised. Section 2-715 allows the additional recovery of consequential and incidental damages within various limitations.

2. Seller's Damages

If the buyer breaches before acceptance or wrongfully revokes the acceptance, the seller's right to damages is determined by UCC §§2-706, 2-708(1), or 2-708(2). The seller's right to damages under §2-706 is similar to the buyer's right to cover damages. Under §2-706, the seller is entitled to resell the goods under the procedure set out in that section. The measure of damages under the section is then the difference between the resale price and the contract price. The seller may add any incidental damages under §2-710 but must deduct any expenses saved.

UNIFORM COMMERCIAL CODE

§2-703. Seller's Damages for Non-Delivery or Repudiation

(1). . . . [T]he seller may resell the goods concerned or the undelivered balance thereof. Where the resale is made in good faith and in a commercially reasonable manner the seller may recover the difference between the resale price and the contract price together with any incidental damages allowed under the provisions of this Article (Section 2-710), but less expenses saved in consequence of the buyer's breach. . . .

UNIFORM COMMERCIAL CODE

§2-708. Seller's Damages for Non-Acceptance or Repudiation

(1) Subject to subsection (2) . . . , the measure of damages for non-acceptance or repudiation by the buyer is the difference between the market price at the time and place for tender and the unpaid contract price together with any incidental damages provided in this Article (Section 2-710), but less expenses saved in consequence of the buyer's breach.

(2) If the measure of damages provided in subsection (1) is inadequate to put the seller in as good a position as performance would have done then the measure of damages is the profit (including reasonable overhead) which the seller would have made from full performance by the buyer, together with any incidental damages provided in this Article (Section 2-710), due allowance for costs reasonably incurred and due credit for payments or proceeds of resale.

Problem 79

H. Majesty sold 3,000 plates to Corner Surprises in the City of Devane. Majesty was to deliver at Corner's back door on May 3. The plates celebrated the 100th anniversary of the Order of the Weasel, which was holding its 100th anniversary in Devane, and were sold to Corner for $20 each. The plates were delivered when promised. Both the manner of delivery and the plates' quality were also as promised. No matter, Corner sent the plates back, a clear breach of their agreement. Following this, Majesty resold the plates to another dealer at $18 each. No notice was given to Corner. The plates had a market value in Devane of $14 on May 3. H. Majesty has sued Corner for breach and asked for damages as measured by §2-708(1). Corner argues that damages must be measured by §2-706 because a resale occurred. Majesty rebuts that the section is not applicable because it failed to follow its limitations.

(a) Did Majesty follow the procedures of §2-706?

(b) If Majesty did fail to follow the restrictions of the section, can Majesty nonetheless opt for recovery under §2-708(1)? See Official Comment 2 to §2-708(1); §1-106; Official Comment 1 to §2-703; White and Summers, *Uniform Commercial Code* §7-7 (6th ed. 2010).

P TERADYNE, INC. v. TELEDYNE INDUSTRIES D

Seller **United States Court of Appeals, First Circuit, 1982** Buyer
676 F.2d 865

Wyzanski, Senior District Judge. In this diversity action, Teradyne, Inc. sued Teledyne Industries, Inc. and its subsidiary for damages pursuant to §2-708(2) of the UCC, Mass. Gen. Laws c.106 §2-708(2) (hereafter "§2-708(2)"). Teledyne does not dispute the facts that it is bound as a buyer under a sales contract with Teradyne, that it broke the contract, and that Teradyne's right to damages is governed by §2-708(2). The principal dispute concerns the calculation of damages.

The district court referred the case to a master whose report the district court approved and made the basis of the judgment here on appeal.

The following facts, derived from the master's report, are undisputed.

Quantity Purchase Contract

On July 30, 1976 Teradyne, Inc. ("the seller"), a Massachusetts corporation, entered into a Quantity Purchase Contract ("the contract") which, though made with a subsidiary, binds Teledyne Industries, Inc., a California corporation ("the buyer"). That contract governed an earlier contract resulting from the seller's acceptance of the buyer's July 23, 1976 purchase order to buy at the list price of $98,400 (which was also its fair market value) a T-347A transistor test system ("the T-347A"). One consequence of such governance was that the buyer was entitled to a $984 discount from the $98,400 price.

The buyer canceled its order for the T-347A when it was packed ready for shipment scheduled to occur two days later. The seller refused to accept the cancellation.

The buyer offered to purchase instead of the T-347A a $65,000 Field Effects Transistor System ("the FET") which would also have been governed by "the contract." The seller refused the offer.

After dismantling, testing, and reassembling at an estimated cost of $614 the T-347A, the seller, pursuant to an order that was on hand prior to the cancellation, sold it for $98,400 to another purchaser (hereafter "resale purchaser").

Teradyne would have made the sale to the resale purchaser even if Teradyne had not broken its contract. Thus if there had been no breach, Teradyne would have made two sales and earned two profits rather than one.

The seller was a volume seller of the equipment covered by the July 23, 1976 purchase order. The equipment represented standard products of the seller and the seller had the means and capacity to duplicate the equipment for a second sale had the buyer honored its purchase order.

Teradyne being of the view that the measure of damages under §2-708(2) was the contract price less ascertainable costs saved as a result of the breach — see Jericho Sash and Door Company, Inc. v. Building Erectors, Inc., 362 Mass. 871, 872, 286 N.E.2d 343, (1972) (hereafter "*Jericho*") — offered as evidence of its cost prices its Inventory Standards Catalog ("the Catalog") — a document which was prepared for tax purposes not claimed to have been illegitimate, but which admittedly disclosed "low inventory valuations." Relying on that Catalog, Teradyne's Controller, McCabe, testified that the *only* costs which the seller saved as a result of the breach were:

direct labor costs associated with production	$3,301
material charges	17,045
sales commission on one T-347A	492
Expense	1,800
TOTAL	$22,638

McCabe admitted that he had not included as costs saved the labor costs of employees associated with testing, shipping, installing, servicing, or fulfilling 10-year warranties on the T-347A (although he acknowledged that in forms of accounting for purposes other than damage suits the costs of those employees would not be regarded as "overhead"). His reason was that those costs would not have been affected by the production of one machine more or less. McCabe also admitted that he had not included fringe benefits which amounted to 12% in the case of both included and excluded labor costs.

During McCabe's direct examination, he referred to the 10-K report which Teradyne had filed with the SEC. On cross-examination McCabe admitted that the 10-K form showed that on average the seller's revenues were distributed as follows:

profit	9%
"selling and administrative" expense	26%
interest	1%
"cost of sales and engineering" (including substantial research and developmental costs incidental to a high technology business)	64%

He also admitted that the average figures applied to the T-347A.

Teledyne contended that the 10-K report was a better index of lost profits than was the Catalog. The master disagreed and concluded that the more appropriate formula for calculating Teradyne's damages under §2-708(2) was the one approved in *Jericho*, supra — "'gross profit' including fixed costs but not costs saved as a result of the breach." He then stated:

> In accordance with the statutory mandate that the remedy "be liberally administered to the end that the aggrieved party may be put in as good a position as if the other party had fully performed," M.G.L. c.106 §1-106(1), I find that the plaintiff has met its burden of proof of damages, and has established the accuracy of its direct costs and the ascertainability of its variable costs with reasonable certainty and "whatever definiteness and accuracy the facts permit." Comment 1 to §1-106(1) of the UCC.

In effect, this was a finding that Teradyne had saved only $22,638 as a result of the breach. Subtracting that amount and also the $984 quantity discount from the original contract price of $98,400, the master found that the lost "profit (including reasonable overhead)" was $74,778. To that amount the master added $614 for "incidental damages" which Teradyne incurred in preparing the T-347A for its new customer. Thus he found that Teradyne's total §2-708(2) damages amounted to $75,392.

The master declined to make a deduction from the $75,392 on account of the refusal of the seller to accept the buyer's offer to purchase an FET tester in partial substitution for the repudiated T-347A.

At the time of the reference to the master, the court, without securing the agreement of the parties, had ordered that the master's costs should be paid by them in equal parts.

Teradyne filed a motion praying that the district court (1) should adopt the master's report allowing it to recover $75,392, and (2) should require Teledyne to pay all the master's costs. The district court, without opinion, entered a judgment which grants the first prayer and denies the second. Teledyne appealed from the first part of the judgment; Teradyne appealed from the second part.

1. The parties are agreed that §2-708(2) applies to the case at bar. Inasmuch as this conclusion is not plain from the text, we explain the reasons why we concur in that agreement.

Section 2-708(2) applies only if the damages provided by §2-708(1) are inadequate to put the seller in as good a position as performance would have done. Under §2-708(1) the measure of damages is the difference between unpaid contract price and market price. Here the unpaid contract price was $97,416 and the market price was $98,400. Hence no damages would be recoverable under §2-708(1). On the other hand, if the buyer had performed, the seller (1) would have had the proceeds of two contracts, one with the buyer Teledyne and the other with the "resale purchaser" and (2) *it seems* would have had in 1976-7 one more T-347A sale.

A literal reading of the last sentence of §2-708(2) — providing for "due credit for payments or proceeds of resale" — would indicate that Teradyne recovers nothing because the proceeds of the resale exceeded the price set in the Teledyne-Teradyne contract. However, in light of the statutory history of the subsection, it is universally agreed that in a case where after the buyer's default a seller resells the goods, the proceeds of the resale are not to be credited to the buyer if the seller is a lost volume seller[2] — that is, one who had there been no breach by the buyer, could and would have had the benefit of both the original contract and the resale contract.

Thus, despite the resale of the T-347A, Teradyne is entitled to recover from Teledyne what §2-708(2) calls its expected "profit (including reasonable overhead)" on the broken Teledyne contract.

2. Teledyne not only "does not dispute that damages are to be calculated pursuant to §2-708(2)" but concedes that the formula used in Jericho Sash & Door Co. v. Building Erectors Inc., 362 Mass. 871, 286 N.E.2d 343 (1972), for determining lost profit including overhead — that is, the formula under which direct costs of producing and selling manufactured goods are deducted from the contract price in order to arrive at "profit (including reasonable overhead)" as that term is used in §2-708(2) — "is permissible provided any variable expenses are identified."

What Teledyne contends is that all variable costs were not identified because the cost figures came from a catalog, prepared for tax purposes, which did not fully reflect all direct costs. The master found that the statement of costs based on the catalog was reliable and that Teledyne's method of calculating costs based on the 10-K statements was not more accurate. Those findings are not clearly erroneous and therefore we may not reverse the judgment on the ground that allegedly the items of cost which were deducted are unreliable. . . .

2. The term "lost volume seller" was apparently coined by Professor Robert J. Harris in his article A Radical Restatement of the Law of Seller's Damages: Sales Act and Commercial Code Results Compared, 18 Stan. L. Rev. 66 (1965). The terminology has been widely adopted. See Famous Knitwear Corp. v. Drug Fair Inc., 493 F.2d 251, 254 n.5 (4th Cir. 1974); Snyder v. Herbert Greenbaum & Assoc. Inc., 38 Md. App. 144, 157, 380 A.2d 618, 624 (1977); Publicker Industries, Inc. v. Roman Ceramics Corp., 652 F.2d 340, 346 (3d Cir. 1981). See Restatement (Second) Contracts §347 Comment f; J. White and R. Summers, Uniform Commercial Code, 2d ed. (1980) (hereafter "White and Summers") §7-9, particularly p. 276 first full paragraph.

Teledyne's more significant objection to Teradyne's and the master's application of the *Jericho* formula in the case at bar is that neither of them made deductions on account of the wages paid to testers, shippers, installers, and other Teradyne employees who directly handled the T-347A, or on account of the fringe benefits amounting in the case of those and other employees to 12 percent of wages. Teradyne gave as the reason for the omission of the wages of the testers, etc. that those wages would not have been affected if each of the testers, etc. handled one product more or less. However, the work of those employees entered as directly into production and supplying the T-347A as did the work of a fabricator of a T-347A. Surely no one would regard as "reasonable overhead" within §2-708(2) the wages of a fabricator of a T-347A even if his wages were the same whether he made one product more or less. We conclude that the wages of the testers, etc. likewise are not part of overhead and as a "direct cost" should have been deducted from the contract price. A fortiori fringe benefits amounting to 12 percent of wages should also have been deducted as direct costs. Taken together we cannot view these omitted items as what *Jericho* called "relatively insignificant items." We, therefore, must vacate the district court's judgment. In accordance with the procedure followed in Publicker Industries, Inc. v. Roman Ceramics Corp., 603 F.2d 1065, 1072-1073 (3d Cir. 1979) and Famous Knitwear Corp. v. Drug Fair, Inc., 493 F.2d 251, 255-256 (4th Cir. 1974), we remand this case so that with respect to the omitted direct labor costs specified above the parties may offer further evidence and the court may make findings "with whatever definiteness and accuracy the facts permit, but no more." *Jericho*, p. 872, 286 N.E.2d 343.

There are two other matters which may properly be dealt with before the case is remanded to the district court.

3. Teledyne contends that Teradyne was required to mitigate damages by acceptance of Teledyne's offer to purchase instead of the T-347A the FET system.

That point is without merit.

The meaning of Teledyne's offer was that if Teradyne would forego its profit-loss claim arising out of Teledyne's breach of the T-347A contract, Teledyne would purchase another type of machine which it was under no obligation to buy. The seller's failure to accept such an offer does not preclude it from recovering the full damages to which it would otherwise be entitled. As Restatement (Second) Contracts, §350 Comment c indicates, there is no right to so-called mitigation of damages where the offer of a substitute contract "is conditioned on surrender by the injured party of his claim for breach." "One is not required to mitigate his losses by accepting an arrangement with the repudiator if that is made conditional on his surrender of his rights under the repudiated contract." 5 Corbin, Contracts 2nd (1964) §1043 at 274. . . .

The district court's judgment is vacated and the case is remanded to the district court to proceed in accordance with this opinion.

QUESTIONS AND NOTE

1. Are all sellers of goods "lost volume sellers"? If you agree to sell your car to your neighbor and he later changes his mind, are you entitled to lost volume profits?

"Lost volume sellers" may be found outside of the coverage of the UCC, and a recovery similar to that under §2-708(2) is typically available in such cases. For an interesting case applying the term to a volume lessor of rental laundry equipment, see Jetz Service Co., Inc. v. Salina Properties, 19 Kan. App. 2d 144, 865 P.2d 1051 (1993). The court allowed the plaintiff to recover the lost profit without accounting for any amounts received on other leases under the common law equivalent of §2-708(2): comment f of Restatement (Second) of Contracts §347. The plaintiff there had sufficient customers and rental equipment so that leasing the equipment defendant leased to another lessee did not make the plaintiff whole.

2. Why does the court draw a distinction between overhead costs and variable expenses (which the court calls "direct costs")? Which was which here?

3. If the buyer of goods does not reject them and tries to recover their price, but instead accepts them in spite of their nonconformities, the buyer may wish to sue for breach of warranty damages. Under the UCC such damages are measured the same way that the common law measured them (see Hawkins v. McGee at the beginning of this chapter): the difference between the value of the goods as warranted and the value of the goods delivered, plus incidental and consequential damages. See UCC §§2-714(2) and (3) and 2-715. Where the goods are in disrepair, that amount will typically equal the cost of repair. As we shall see in Chapter 7, the buyer also may be able to reject the goods or revoke acceptance of the goods in an appropriate case.

4. Return the facts of the Michael Jordan case discussed in Problem 71. Can Jordan escape from a duty to mitigate on the theory that he is in a position similar to a "lost volume seller" in that he has a virtually limitless capacity to endorse products so the existence of "cover" is irrelevant to his damages?

II. RESTITUTION

A true contract is based on the intention of the parties, and this intention is found in the express or implied terms of the agreement. Most contracts need not comply with any particular formalities (although some must be reflected by a writing; see Chapter 4). Where the past dealings of the parties so indicate, a contract can be said to be *implied in fact*, meaning that a contract is intended by the parties even though none of its terms are expressly agreed on. If, for example, the parties originally sign a sales agreement but through the years deviate from its terms as the circumstances change, their agreement becomes a contract implied in fact; see UCC §1-303 (Course of Performance), though, again, its meaning depends on the intention of the parties, which is gathered from their conduct.

With this sort of true contract, contrast a contract *implied in law*, sometimes called a *quasi-contract*. Such a contract is imposed upon the parties irrespective of their actual intent. This arises in the situation where one party has the benefit of money, property, or services of another, and it would be unjust to allow that party to keep the benefit without paying for it. Where this unjust enrichment would occur, the law conclusively presumes a promise of restitution. For this reason, such an action is also known as an action in *restitution*. The concept includes a number of actions that have as a common goal the prevention of the defendant's unjust enrichment. Examples of such actions include the constructive trust and equitable accounting utilized when a fiduciary relationship has been violated by an agent or trustee. We do not have the space to develop the subject of restitution completely in these materials. However, we will explore the doctrine to the extent it is recognized by the drafters of the Restatement (Second) of Contracts as particularly relevant in the contractual setting.* There the concept of restitution is often used:

(1) as an independent theory of recovery when there is no enforceable contract because of lack of mutual assent or some other formation defect — "quasi-contract" actions;

(2) as an alternative method to measure damages, or as an independent remedy, for a party not in breach of an enforceable contract;

(3) as an independent remedy for a party who has breached an enforceable contract;

(4) as an independent theory of recovery when a contract is unenforceable because of some defect such as a lack of a requisite writing (a statute of frauds problem), impossibility, mistake, or incapacity.

The following materials consider the use of restitution in the first three instances. The fourth use of restitution will be discussed as the statute of frauds, impossibility, and other bars to enforceability are explored in later chapters.

---

* There is also a Restatement of Restitution.

A.   *Restitution When There Is No Contract: Quasi-Contract*

Quasi-contract actions developed from the common law action of general assumpsit, which was used to provide relief for *both* contracts implied in fact (based on the intention of the parties) and contracts implied in law (imposed regardless of the parties' intent). The latter are also called quasi-contracts because a true contract is primarily based on the intention of the parties to be bound.

The writ of general assumpsit was divided into different parts called the <u>*common counts,*</u> three of which are still in widespread use today. These theories of action are:

(1)   <u>*Quantum meruit:*</u> the value of services rendered to another.
(2)   *Quantum valebant:* the value of property delivered to another.
(3)   *Money had and received:* money held by one person but belonging to another.

In a quasi-contractual action one person will have received services, property, or money under circumstances where that person would be unjustly enriched if allowed to keep same, so the law allows an action in restitution to recover the benefits conferred.

KAFKA v. HESS

United States District Court for the District of Maryland, 2017
NO. JKB-16-1757, 2017 WL 2439142

MEMORANDUM

James K. Bredar, United States District Judge

I. Background

This case began as a one-count complaint filed on May 31, 2016, by Plaintiff George J. Kafka, Jr., for declaratory judgment against his aunt, Defendant Gladys C. Hess. (ECF No. 1.) Nearly two months later, Hess filed suit for both declaratory relief and damages against Kafka in Maryland state court, and that case was removed to this Court. (16-2789, ECF Nos. 1, 2.) . . . Pending before the Court in this consolidated case [is] a motion for summary judgment filed by Kafka (16-1757, ECF No. 10). . . . Kafka's motion for summary judgment will be granted. . . .

III. Evidence Pertaining to the Motion for Summary Judgment

In his affidavit, Kafka avers he is retired and living in North Carolina. (Mot. Summ. J. Ex. 1, Kafka Aff. ¶ 2 (undated; filed Nov. 26, 2016), ECF No. 10-1.) Kafka is the only son of Dorothy J. Smith ("Smith"), who passed away March 31, 2015. (Id. ¶ 3.) Smith executed a durable power of attorney on September 17, 1999, appointing Kafka as her agent. (Id. ¶ 4.) Over a period of many years, Kafka knew that Smith and her husband, Emory H. Smith, Jr., who was Kafka's stepfather, planned for Kafka to become sole owner of all their property upon their deaths. (Id. ¶¶ 4, 5.)...

Emory Smith, Kafka's stepfather, passed away on June 2, 2009, making Dorothy Smith the sole owner of their residential property at 7313 Geis Avenue, Baltimore, Maryland (the "Property"). (Id. ¶¶ 3, 5.) During the preceding two-month period in which the stepfather's health was failing, Kafka traveled back and forth between North Carolina and Maryland. (Id. ¶ 5.) Kafka attended the funeral. (Id.) On June 9, 2009, Smith executed a deed, which had been drafted by her attorney, Raymond Rudacille, granting herself a life estate in the Property with the remainder to Kafka. (Id. ¶ 6; Ex. 2, Deed June 9, 2009, ECF No. 10-2.) That deed was recorded by the attorney on April 30, 2010. (Kafka Aff. ¶ 7; Deed June 9, 2009.)

Hess notified Kafka of Smith's death and indicated there was no need for Kafka to come to the funeral, but Kafka did come, driving all night to get there. (Id. ¶ 11.) While in Maryland, he saw that most of the valuable personal property in Smith's home was missing. (Id.) In addition, after Smith's funeral, Kafka and his wife went to Smith's home, but Hess demanded they leave. (Id.) Kafka states, "I was unsure of my rights and, given the circumstances, I elected to stay away from Maryland and Gladys Hess." (Id. ¶ 12.)

In early 2016, Kafka learned Hess was trying to sell the Property. (Id. ¶ 13.) Hess contacted Kafka and indicated a title search revealed the 2009 deed in Kafka's favor. (Id. ¶ 14.) Kafka contacted the same prospective buyers in an effort to sell the Property to them, but a 2011 deed for the Property made title underwriters unwilling to insure the title, leaving Kafka unable to sell it. (Id. ¶¶ 15, 16; Ex. 3, Deed Aug. 4, 2011, ECF No. 10-3.) The 2011 deed by Smith purported to convey a life estate to Smith and the remainder to Hess, contingent upon Smith's not having exercised her reserved power of disposition during her lifetime. (Deed Aug. 4, 2011.) Attorney Tara K. Frame authored a letter dated May 19, 2016, on Hess's behalf to Kafka; Frame wrote,

> [P]rior to Ms. Hess learning of the previously executed deed, she had spent a substantial sum of money getting the property ready for sale. . . . [Hess] has had to deal with maintaining the property and expending monies to repair and renovate the property for sale out of her own funds. She has had to deal with hiring and working with the real estate agent to list the property.

In light of the time and effort that Ms. Hess has invested in this property, she believes she should receive 50% of the net proceeds from the sale of the property, in addition to reimbursement for the monies she has spent on the property since Ms. Smith's death in March of 2015.

(Ex. 4, Frame Letter, ECF No. 10-4.) Attached to the letter was a list of each expenditure Hess had made, totaling $71,336.30. (Id.) Frame requested Kafka contact her to discuss the matter. (Id.)

[Hess conceded that Kafka was the rightful owner of the Property because the 2009 Deed had been filed in the land records first, but sought restitution for] the money she spent "maintaining the Property, as well as getting the Property ready to be placed on the market for sale." (Id. Ex. 1, Hess Aff. ¶¶ 5, 8, Dec. 12, 2016, ECF No. 16-1.)

IV. Analysis of Motion for Summary Judgment

. . . After reviewing the evidence, the Court concludes Kafka was not unjustly enriched by Hess's making repairs and improvements to the Property. The three elements of an unjust-enrichment claim are as stated in Hill v. Cross Country Settlements, LLC, 936 A.2d 343, 351 (Md. 2007):

> 1. A benefit conferred upon the defendant by the plaintiff;
> 2. An appreciation or knowledge by the defendant of the benefit; and
> 3. The acceptance or retention by the defendant of the benefit under such circumstances as to make it inequitable for the defendant to retain the benefit without the payment of its value.

"A defendant, however, 'is not unjustly enriched, and therefore not required to make restitution where the benefit was conferred by a volunteer or intermeddler.'" Id. at 352 (citing Daniel B. Dobbs, Handbook on the Law of Remedies §4.9 (1973)). This qualifying principle to the doctrine of unjust enrichment "is based on the notion that 'one who confers a benefit upon another without affording that other the opportunity to reject the benefit, has no equitable claim for relief against the recipient of the benefit in the absence of some special policy. . . . '" Id. (citing Dobbs, §4.9). A distinction is drawn between voluntary payment by a plaintiff of a defendant's debt, which ordinarily may be readily rejected or accepted by the defendant, and the voluntary rendering of services or the addition of value to the defendant. Id. at 352, 354-55. An "apt example" of the latter is given in Hill:

> While the homeowner is away, a house painter paints the entire house, without the owner's consent, thereby adding value to the homeowner's property. The added value of the home cannot be separated easily and returned to the house painter. Therefore, a court should not permit the house painter to

> recover. Dobbs notes that, although the homeowner is enriched, this result "is preferable to payment of the intermeddler, who should not thus be encouraged to invade another's freedom of choice about his own affairs." Dobbs, supra, §4.9. If, however, the benefit is something that can be easily returned, such as money or personal property, "the fact that it is retained and used is a choice. When this choice is available, the choice principle is satisfied and restitution . . . ought to be required." Dobbs, supra, §4.9.

Id. at 355 n.12.

The present case is one step removed from Dobbs's hypothetical about the house painter. Here, it is not the house painter, or other type of contractor, who is seeking payment for services rendered. According to Hess, the contractors who made repairs or improvements to the Property have all been paid by her, and it is Hess who is seeking reimbursement from Kafka. Even so, assuming arguendo that the contractors' actions added some value to the Property, Kafka has no option to decline it. As is true with Dobbs's example of the house painter, Hess has not presented any evidence that the repairs and improvements can be separated easily and returned to the contractors. Kafka has been given no opportunity to decline whatever benefit to the Property was derived from the contractors' services. As noted earlier, the Frame Letter clearly indicates that Kafka first learned about the various repairs and improvements to the Property after they had been completed. No evidence indicates he was aware of them beforehand, that he requested the services be undertaken, or that he stood by and silently suffered their rendition. As the *Hill* opinion indicated, the ability of the defendant to decline the benefit is the essence of the second element of an unjust-enrichment claim. Id. at 354. Hess has failed to establish the second element.

Hess's endeavor to be reimbursed exposes another frailty in her claim that Kafka has been unjustly enriched. The measure of recovery in this cause of action "is the gain to the defendant, not the loss by the plaintiff." Mass Transit v. Granite Construction, 471 A.2d 1121, 1126 (Md. Ct. Spec. App. 1984), quoted in Alternatives Unlimited, Inc. v. New Baltimore City Bd. of Sch. Comm'rs, 843 A.2d 252, 293 (Md. Ct. Spec. App. 2004). Hess has only posited that Kafka benefited by the same amount she paid various contractors. But even if she could provide credible evidence of some increase in value to the Property, she still has not provided evidence that Kafka has been given a realistic choice to decline that increased value.

In cases where improvements to another's property have resulted in restitution to the one making improvements, the courts have required proof of three elements: (1) the plaintiff must have held possession of the property under color of title, (2) the plaintiff's possession must have been adverse to the title of the true owner, and (3) the plaintiff must have acted in good faith. Bryan v. Councilman, 67 A. 279, 282 (Md. 1907). "By good faith is meant an honest belief on the part of the occupant that he has secured a good title to the property in question and is the rightful owner thereof. And for this belief there must be some reasonable grounds such as would lead a man of ordinary prudence to entertain it." Id. See also Welsh v. Welsh, 255 A.2d 368, 373 (Md. Ct. Spec. App. 1969) ("a person to be a bona fide possessor must not only believe that he has title to the property but it must appear also that he has had no notice of an adverse claim of title by another person or of facts which would require an investigation that would lead to a discovery of the adverse claim").

"'In all these cases, however, the element of good faith and innocent mistake is essential for if a person lays out money on another's property with knowledge or notice of the true state of the title—e.g., a purchaser with notice of another's claim—he has no claim to be reimbursed, and of course no lien.'" Goldberg v. Ford, 53 A.2d 665, 668 (Md. 1947) (quoting Pomeroy, Equity Jurisprudence, 5th ed., §§1241, 1242). Kafka's title to the Property was on record and, by law, that recorded title was notice to Hess. Frazee v. Frazee, 28 A. 1105, 1106 (Md. 1894). She has not shown that her failure to learn the true state of affairs with regard to Kafka's title was within the realm of ordinary prudence. See *Bryan*, 67 A. at 282. As a result, Hess cannot show she acted in good faith when she paid for repairs and improvements to the Property; this is especially so given her order to Kafka to leave the Property immediately after Smith's funeral and Hess's subsequent intentional exclusion of him from the Property. Consequently, Hess is not entitled to reimbursement for her expenditures on the Property.

NOTE

As *Kafka* illustrates, a restitution plaintiff must usually show that the defendant either requested the benefit, accepted the benefit, or at least acquiesced to the benefit. However, this rule is subject to an exception for emergencies. Under the Restatement of Restitution §116, "[a] person who has supplied things or services to another, *although acting without the other's knowledge or consent*, is entitled to restitution if . . . the things or services were necessary to prevent the other from suffering serious bodily harm or pain [and] . . . it was impossible for the other to give consent." If the recipient would have refused the benefit if conscious, the plaintiff can still recover unless the plaintiff knew or should have known this fact.

Problem 80

When Elsie Maynard passed out in the department store, she was rushed to Tower Hospital for emergency medical care. After two weeks in a coma, she died. May the hospital recover its expenses from her estate? Was its behavior "officious"? See In re Crisan Estate, 362 Mich. 569, 107 N.W.2d

907 (1961). Would it make a difference if she had tried to commit suicide? If she were a well-known Christian Scientist?

Problem 81

All the neighbors on the block, except Ruth McCarty, signed contracts with Quick Construction, Inc., to have curbing installed. Ruth decided that the price was too high and she told Quick's manager that she did not want the curbing. Deciding that the block would look odd if her lot were left uncurbed, Quick put curbing along McCarty's property at the same time it installed the rest. Quick then sent her a bill for her share of the project. The curbing is beautiful, is worth $500 (and the bill is only for $350), and has improved the value of her house by $1,000. What must she pay? See Enterprises v. Galloway, 192 Ohio App. 3d, 948 N.E.2d 473 (2011).

MAGLICA v. MAGLICA
California Court of Appeal, 1998
66 Cal. App. 4th 442, 78 Cal. Rptr. 2d 101

SILLS, P.J.

I.   INTRODUCTION

Quantum Meruit

This case forces us to confront the legal doctrine known as "quantum meruit" in the context of a case about an unmarried couple who lived together and worked in a business solely owned by one of them. Quantum meruit is a Latin phrase, meaning "as much as he deserves,"[1] and is based on the idea that someone should get paid for beneficial goods or services which he or she bestows on another.

Jury Instructions

The trial judge instructed the jury that the reasonable value of the plaintiff's services was either the value of what it would have cost the defendant to obtain those services from someone else or the "value by which" he had "benefitted as a result" of those services. The instruction allowed the jury to reach a whopping number in favor of the plaintiff — $84 million — because of the tremendous growth in the *value* of the business over the years.

As we explain later, the finding that the couple had no contract in the first place is itself somewhat suspect because certain jury instructions did not

---

1. See Black's Law Dictionary (5th ed. 1979) page 1119, column 1.

accurately convey the law concerning implied-in-fact contracts. However, assuming that there was indeed no contract, the quantum meruit award cannot stand. The legal test for recovery in quantum meruit is not the value of the benefit, but value of the services (assuming, of course, that the services were beneficial to the recipient in the first place). In this case the failure to appreciate that fine distinction meant a big difference. People who work for businesses for a period of years and then walk away with $84 million do so because they have acquired some *equity* in the business, not because $84 million is the going rate for the services of even the most workaholic manager. In substance, the court was allowing the jury to value the plaintiff's services as if she had made a sweetheart stock option deal—yet such a deal was precisely what the jury found she did not make. So the $84 million judgment cannot stand.

[margin note: Test is the Value of Services]

On the other hand, plaintiff was hindered in her ability to prove the existence of an implied-in-fact contract by a series of jury instructions which may have misled the jury about certain of the factors which bear on such contracts. The instructions were insufficiently qualified. They told the jury flat out that such facts as a couple's living together or holding themselves out as husband and wife or sharing a common surname did not mean that they had any agreement to share assets. That is not *exactly* correct. Such factors can, indeed, when taken together with other facts and in context, show the existence of an implied-in-fact contract. At most the jury instructions should have said that such factors do not *by themselves necessarily* show an implied-in-fact contract. Accordingly, when the case is retried, the plaintiff will have another chance to prove that she indeed had a deal for a share of equity in the defendant's business.

II. Facts

The important facts in this case may be briefly stated. Anthony Maglica, a Croatian immigrant, founded his own machine shop business, Mag Instrument, in 1955. He got divorced in 1971 and kept the business. That year he met Claire Halasz, an interior designer. They got on famously, and lived together, holding themselves out as man and wife—hence Claire began using the name Claire Maglica—but never actually got married. And, while they worked side by side building the business, Anthony never agreed—or at least the jury found Anthony never agreed—to give Claire a share of the business. When the business was incorporated in 1974 all shares went into Anthony's name. Anthony was the president and Claire was the secretary. They were paid equal salaries from the business after incorporation. In 1978 the business began manufacturing flashlights, and, thanks in part to some great ideas and hard work on Claire's part (e.g., coming out with a purse-sized flashlight in colors), the business boomed. Mag Instrument, Inc., is now worth hundreds of millions of dollars.

[margin note: Just Found that Claire Never owned a share of the business]

[margin note: Claire had ideas that led to the success of the business]

In 1992 Claire discovered that Anthony was trying to transfer stock to his children but not her, and the couple split up in October. In June 1993 Claire sued Anthony for, among other things, breach of contract, breach of partnership agreement, fraud, breach of fiduciary duty and quantum meruit. The case came to trial in the spring of 1994. The jury awarded $84 million for the breach of fiduciary duty and quantum meruit causes of action, finding that $84 million was the reasonable value of Claire's services.

III.   Discussion

[The court first found that there were no fiduciary duties between the parties.]

B.   Quantum Meruit Allows Recovery for the Value of Beneficial Services, Not the Value by Which Someone Benefits from Those Services

The absence of a contract between Claire and Anthony, however, would not preclude her recovery in quantum meruit: As every first year law student knows or should know, recovery in quantum meruit does not require a contract. (See 1 Witkin, Summary of Cal. Law (9th ed. 1987) Contracts, §112, p. 137; see, e.g., B.C. Richter Contracting Co. v. Continental Cas. Co. (1964) 230 Cal. App. 2d 491, 499-500 [41 Cal. Rptr. 98].)[4]

The classic formulation concerning the measure of recovery in quantum meruit is found in Palmer v. Gregg, supra, 65 Cal. 2d 657. Justice Mosk, writing for the court, said: "The measure of recovery in *quantum meruit* is the reasonable value of the services rendered *provided* they were of direct benefit to the defendant." (Id. at p. 660, italics added; see also Producers Cotton Oil Co. v. Amstar Corp. (1988) 197 Cal. App. 3d 638, 659 [242 Cal. Rptr. 914].)

The underlying idea behind quantum meruit is the law's distaste for unjust enrichment. If one has received a benefit which one may not justly retain, one should "restore the aggrieved party to his [or her] former position by return of the *thing* or its *equivalent* in money." (1 Witkin, Summary of Cal. Law, supra, Contracts, §91, p. 122.)

The idea that one must be *benefited* by the goods and services bestowed is thus integral to recovery in quantum meruit; hence courts have always required that the plaintiff have bestowed some benefit on the defendant as a prerequisite to recovery. (See Earhart v. William Low Co., supra, 25 Cal. 3d 503, 510 [explaining origins of quantum meruit recovery in actions

---

4. The doctrine can become trickier when an actual contract is involved. (See Hedging Concepts, Inc. v. First Alliance Mortgage Co., supra, 41 Cal. App. 4th 1410, 1419-1420 [quantum meruit recovery cannot conflict with terms of actual contract between parties, lest the court in effect impose its own ideas of a fair deal on the parties].)

for recovery of money tortiously retained; law implied an obligation to restore "'benefit,' unfairly retained by the defendant"].)

But the threshold requirement that there be a benefit from the services can lead to confusion, as it did in the case before us. It is one thing to require that the defendant be benefited by services, it is quite another to *measure* the reasonable value of those *services* by the value by which the defendant was "benefited" as a *result* of them. Contract price and the reasonable value of services rendered are two separate things; sometimes the reasonable value of services exceeds a contract price. (See B. C. Richter Contracting Co. v. Continental Cas. Co., supra, 230 Cal. App. 2d at p. 500.) And sometimes it does not. *[margin note: ThB causes Confusion]*

At root, allowing quantum meruit recovery based on "resulting benefit" of services rather than the reasonable value of beneficial services affords the plaintiff the best of both contractual and quasi-contractual recovery. Resulting benefit is an open-ended standard, which, as we have mentioned earlier, can result in the plaintiff obtaining recovery amounting to de facto ownership in a business all out of reasonable relation to the value of services rendered. After all, a particular service timely rendered can have, as Androcles was once pleasantly surprised to discover in the case of a particular lion, disproportionate value to what it would cost on the open market. *[margin note: XX "Resulting-Benefit"]*

The facts in this court's decision in Passante v. McWilliam (1997) 53 Cal. App. 4th 1240 [62 Cal. Rptr. 2d 298] illustrate the point nicely. In *Passante*, the attorney for a fledgling baseball card company gratuitously arranged a needed loan for $100,000 at a crucial point in the company's history; because the loan was made the company survived and a grateful board promised the attorney a 3 percent equity interest in the company. The company eventually became worth more than a quarter of a billion dollars, resulting in the attorney claiming *$33 million* for his efforts in arranging but a single loan. This court would later conclude, because of the attorney's duty to the company as an attorney, that the promise was unenforceable. (See id. at pp. 1247-1248.) Interestingly enough, however, the one cause of action the plaintiff in *Passante* did not sue on was quantum meruit; while this court opined that the attorney should certainly get paid "something" for his efforts, a *$33 million* recovery in quantum meruit would have been too much. Had the services been bargained for, the going price would likely have been simply a reasonable finder's fee. (See id. at p. 1248.) *[margin note: Passante]*

The jury instruction given here allows the value of services to depend on their *impact* on a defendant's business rather than their reasonable value. True, the services must be of benefit if there is to be any recovery at all; even so, the benefit is not necessarily related to the reasonable value of a particular set of services. Sometimes luck, sometimes the impact of others makes the difference. Some enterprises are successful; others less so. Allowing recovery based on resulting benefit would mean the law imposes an exchange of equity for services, and that can result in a windfall—as in the present case—or a serious shortfall in others. Equity-for-service *[margin note: k]*

compensation packages are extraordinary in the labor market, and always
the result of specific bargaining. To impose such a measure of recovery
would make a deal for the parties that they did not make themselves. If courts
cannot use quantum meruit to change the terms of a contract which the
parties did make (see Hedging Concepts, Inc. v. First Alliance Mortgage Co.,
supra, 41 Cal. App. 4th at p. 1420), it follows that neither can they use
quantum meruit to impose a highly generous and extraordinary contract
that the parties did not make. . . .

Telling the jury that it could measure the value of Claire's services by
"[t]he value by which Defendant has benefited as a result of [her] services"
was error. It allowed the jury to value Claire's services as having bought her a
de facto ownership interest in a business whose owner never agreed to give
her an interest. On remand, that part of the jury instruction must be
dropped. . . .

**D.   CERTAIN JURY INSTRUCTIONS MAY HAVE MISLED THE JURY INTO
FINDING THERE WAS NO IMPLIED CONTRACT WHEN IN FACT THERE WAS ONE**

As we have shown, the quantum meruit damage award cannot stand in
the wake of the jury's finding that Claire and Anthony had no agreement to
share the equity in Anthony's business. But the validity of that very finding
itself is challenged in Claire's protective cross-appeal, where she attacks a
series of five jury instructions, specially drafted and proferred by Anthony.
These instructions are set out in the margin.[11] We agree with Claire that it
was error for the trial court to give three of these five instructions. The three
instructions are so infelicitously worded that they might have misled the jury

11. Here are the five:

1. No Contract Results From Parties Holding Themselves out as Husband and
Wife. You cannot find an agreement to share property or form a partnership from
the fact that the parties held themselves out as husband and wife. The fact that
unmarried persons live together as husband and wife and share a surname does not
mean that they have any agreement to share earnings or assets.

2. No Implied Contract From Living Together. You cannot find an implied contract to share property or form a partnership simply from the fact that the parties lived
together[.]

3. Creation of an Implied Contract. . . . The fact the parties are living together
does not change any of the requirements for finding an express or implied contract
between the parties.

4. Companionship Does Not Constitute Consideration. Providing services such as a
constant companion and confidant does not constitute the consideration required by
law to support a contract to share property, does not support any right of recovery and
such services are not otherwise compensable.

5. Obligations Imposed by Legal Marriage. In California, there are various obligations imposed upon parties who become legally and formally married. These obligations do not arise under the law merely by living together without a formal and legal
marriage.

into concluding that evidence which can indeed support a finding of an implied contract could not.

The problem with the three instructions is this: They isolate three uncontested facts about the case: (1) living together, (2) holding themselves out to others as husband and wife, (3) providing services "such as" being a constant companion and confidant — and, seriatim, tell the jury that these facts definitely do not mean there was an implied contract. True, none of these facts *by themselves and alone* necessarily *compels* the conclusion that there was an implied contract. But that does not mean that these facts cannot, in conjunction with all the facts and circumstances of the case, establish an implied contract. In point of fact, they can. Unlike the "quasi-contractual" quantum meruit theory which operates *without* an actual agreement of the parties, an implied-in-fact contract entails an actual contract, but one manifested in conduct rather than expressed in words. (See Silva v. Providence Hospital of Oakland (1939) 14 Cal. 2d 762, 773 [97 P.2d 798] ["The true implied contract, then, consists of obligations arising from a mutual agreement and intent to promise where the agreement and promise have not been expressed in words."]; McGough v. University of San Francisco (1989) 214 Cal. App. 3d 1577, 1584 [263 Cal. Rptr. 404] ["An implied-in-fact contract is one whose existence and terms are manifested by conduct."]; 1 Witkin, Summary of Cal. Law, supra, Contracts, §11, p. 46 ["The distinction between *express* and *implied in fact* contracts relates only to the *manifestation of assent*; both types are based upon the expressed or apparent intention of the parties."].)[14]

In Alderson v. Alderson (1986) 180 Cal. App. 3d 450, 461 [225 Cal. Rptr. 610], the court observed that a number of factors, *including*

- direct testimony of an agreement;
- holding themselves out socially as husband and wife;
- the woman and her children's taking the man's surname;
- pooling of finances to purchase a number of joint rental properties;
- joint decisionmaking in rental property purchases;
- rendering bookkeeping services for, paying the bills on, and collecting the rents of, those joint rental properties; and
- the nature of title taken in those rental properties

14. Because an implied-in-fact contract can be found where there is no expression of agreement in *words*, the line between an implied-in-fact contract and recovery in quantum meruit — where there may be no actual agreement at all — is fuzzy indeed. We will not attempt, in dicta, to clear up that fuzziness here. Suffice to say that because quantum meruit is a theory which implies a promise to pay for services as a *matter of law for reasons of justice* (Hedging Concepts, Inc. v. First Alliance Mortgage Co., supra, 41 Cal. App. 4th at p. 1419), while implied-in-fact contracts are predicated on actual agreements, albeit not ones expressed in words. . . .

could all support a finding there was an implied agreement to share the
rental property acquisitions equally.

We certainly do not say that living together, holding themselves out as
husband and wife, and being companions and confidants, even taken
together, are *sufficient in and of themselves* to show an implied agreement to
divide the equity in a business owned by one of the couple. However, *Alderson*
clearly shows that such facts, together with others bearing more directly on
the business and the way the parties treated the equity and proceeds of the
business, *can* be part of a series of facts which do show such an agreement.
The vice of the three instructions here is that they affirmatively suggested
that living together, holding themselves out, and companionship could not,
as a matter of law, even be *part* of the support for a finding of an implied
agreement. That meant the jury could have completely omitted these facts
when considering the other factors which might also have borne on whether
there was an implied contract.

On remand, the three instructions should not be given. The jury should
be told, rather, that while the facts that a couple live together, hold themselves out as married, and act as companions and confidants toward each
other do not, by themselves, show an implied agreement to share property,
those facts, when taken together and in conjunction with other facts bearing
more directly on the alleged arrangement to share property, can show an
implied agreement to share property.

DISPOSITION

The judgment is reversed. The case is remanded for a new trial. At the
new trial the jury instructions identified in this opinion as erroneous shall
not be given. In the interest of justice both sides will bear their own costs on
appeal.

FEINGOLD v. PUCELLO
Pennsylvania Superior Court, 1995
439 Pa. Super. 509, 654 A.2d 1093

OLSZEWSKI, Judge:
On February 2, 1979, Barry Pucello was involved in a motor vehicle
accident. One of Pucello's co-workers knew Allen Feingold, a personal injury
attorney, and asked if he could give Feingold Pucello's name. Pucello
agreed.

Feingold called Pucello that very evening. Pucello explained that he
wasn't feeling well, having just been in an accident, and would call back
tomorrow. Feingold recommended a doctor he knew, and set up an

appointment for Pucello. The next day, the two discussed the possibility of Feingold's representing Pucello. Pucello gave Feingold some basic information, but did not discuss fee arrangements.

Feingold then went to work on the case. He inspected the accident site, took pictures, obtained the police report, and secured an admission of liability from the other driver. He had still never met with Pucello in person. Towards the end of February, Feingold mailed a formal contingency fee agreement to Pucello, which called for a 50/50 split of the recovery, after costs. Pucello balked at the high fee, and found other counsel. Pucello told Feingold he could keep any pictures, reports, and admissions; Feingold never forwarded the file.

About a year later, Feingold sued Pucello in quantum meruit. A board of arbitrators unanimously found for Pucello. Feingold appealed to the Philadelphia Court of Common Pleas. After much procedural delay, the parties had a de novo bench trial. The trial court found that while Feingold might have had a quantum meruit claim if Pucello retained him and then fired him midway through the case, here the parties never even entered into an attorney-client relationship. The trial court thus found for Pucello, and Feingold appeals.

Feingold argues that Pucello orally agreed to have Feingold represent him, so he is entitled to be paid for the work he did even though Pucello never signed a written fee agreement. The trial court found that by working on the case without the agreement, Feingold proceeded at his own risk. Since there was never a meeting of the minds regarding representation, there was no contract and no obligation to reimburse for his work on the case. Feingold acknowledges the absence of an express contract, but argues that the circumstances imply a contract to support quantum meruit recovery. He contends that Pucello enjoyed the benefits of his efforts despite rejecting his work product: Feingold got Pucello a doctor's appointment, and once the tortfeasor admitted liability, he was unlikely to deny it later.

Quantum meruit is an equitable remedy. Dept. of Environmental Resources v. Winn, 142 Pa. Cmwlth. 375, 597 A.2d 281, 284 n. 3 (1991), alloc. denied 529 Pa. 654, 602 A.2d 863 (1992). We therefore begin our analysis by noting that Feingold comes to this court with hands smudged by the ink which should have been used to sign his fee agreement. Pa. R.C.P. 202, now rescinded, was in effect in the late 1970's. This rule required attorneys to put contingency fee agreements in writing. Pa. R.C.P. 202, 42 Pa. C.S. A. The rule was rescinded because it duplicated Rule 1.5(b) of the Rules of Professional Conduct, which requires attorneys to state their contingency fee in writing "before, or within a reasonable time after commencing representation." As the trial court aptly noted, the whole point of these rules is to avoid precisely the sort of situation Feingold brings to the court. Opinion 3/29/94 at 8.

Secondly, Feingold's proposed contingency fee of 50% of the recovery, after costs, is breathtakingly high. It struck the trial court as unethical. N.T.

7/13/88 at 21. By pricing his services at the top end of the spectrum, Feingold should expect some prospective clients to balk. This makes stating the fee agreement up front all the more important. Contingency fee practice used to be badly abused by practitioners who would assure their injured clients not to worry — the case was in good hands. When the relationship had passed the point of no return and the client's reliance was entrenched, then the attorney mentioned what his hefty percentage of the take would be. The only way to counter this abuse was to require that attorneys state contingency fees up front and in writing. This is also why the requirement evolved from a procedural rule into an ethical rule. We think Feingold's abject failure to comply with this rule precludes any equitable recovery.

Even without these equitable considerations, Feingold's claim still fails on its merits. In rejecting the proposed fee agreement, Pucello told Feingold to keep his work-product. Thus Feingold did not confer any tangible benefit on Pucello. Feingold argues that having admitted liability to Feingold, the tortfeasor was constrained from altering his story, which facilitated settlement. If so, then Feingold's claim would more properly lie against Pucello's attorney, who testified that he still could have won the case without Feingold's preliminary work. Id. at 32. Thus, Pucello would have gotten his recovery either way; it is only Pucello's attorney whose job might have been facilitated by Feingold's services. See Johnson v. Stein, 254 Pa. Super. 41, 385 A.2d 514 (1978).

Feingold likens himself to the surgeon who may render emergency medical treatment first, and then ask for payment later. Appellant's reply brief at 1. Pucello's claim had a two-year statute of limitation, and was for the sole purpose of obtaining money, not saving his life. Feingold could have held off working on the case long enough to properly commence the relationship by stating his contingency fee up front, and should have under our procedural and ethical rules.[3] When Pucello learned of Feingold's exorbitant rates, he understandably balked and told Feingold to keep his file. Feingold's unclean hands and Pucello's rejection of his services clearly preclude any quantum meruit recovery.

Order affirmed.

DEL SOLE, J., concurs in the result.

BECK, J., files a concurring opinion.

BECK, Judge, concurring.

I concur in the result reached by my colleague. I do so, however, on the narrow basis that appellant has failed to make out a claim in quasi-contract that would entitle him to restitution from appellees.

---

2. Pucello's attorney also offered to reimburse Feingold for his out-of-pocket expenses, though not for his time. Id.

3. In fact, both old Pa. R.C.P. 202 and ethics rule 1.5(b) are mandatory, not aspirational.

Appellant has conceded that the facts in this case do not support a finding that a contract for legal services was reached between him and appellee Pucello. His only claim on appeal is that the trial court erred in denying his quantum meruit claim on the basis that there had been no meeting of the minds between the parties. In this appellant is correct, for "[u]nlike true contracts, quasi-contracts are not based on the apparent intention of the parties to undertake the performances in question, nor are they promises. They are obligations created by law for reasons of justice." Schott v. Westinghouse Electric Corporation, 436 Pa. 279, 290, 259 A.2d 443, 449 (1969), quoting Restatement (Second) of Contracts, §5, comment b. at 24. "Quasi contracts may be found in the absence of any expression of assent by the party to be charged and may indeed be found in spite of the party's contrary intention." Schott v. Westinghouse Electric Corporation, supra at 290-91, 259 A.2d at 449. Martin v. Little, Brown and Co., 304 Pa. Super. 424, 430-431, 450 A.2d 984, 988 (1981). However, this error by the trial court does not warrant reversal of its judgment because it is clear that the facts of this case cannot, as a matter of law, support a quantum meruit recovery by appellant.

A cause of action in quasi-contract for quantum meruit, a form of restitution, is made out where one person has been unjustly enriched at the expense of another. Martin v. Little, Brown and Co., supra (citing DeGasperi v. Valicenti, 198 Pa. Super. 455, 457, 181 A.2d 862, 864 (1962)). The elements of unjust enrichment are "benefits conferred on defendant by plaintiff, appreciation of such benefits by defendant, and acceptance and retention of such benefits under such circumstances that it would be inequitable for defendant to retain the benefit without payment of value." Wolf v. Wolf, 527 Pa. 218, 590 A.2d 4 (1991). . . . The most significant element of the doctrine is whether the enrichment of the defendant is unjust. Id. Thus to sustain a claim of unjust enrichment, it must be shown "that a person wrongly secured or passively received a benefit that it would be unconscionable to retain" without making payment. Martin v. Little, Brown and Co., supra (citing Brereton's Estate, 388 Pa. 206, 212, 130 A.2d 453, 457 (1957). . . .

The facts of this case simply cannot support a finding that Pucello was unjustly enriched by appellant Feingold's services. By refusing to accept Feingold's files containing his work product, Pucello affirmatively rejected any direct benefit from Feingold's services. Thus it is clear that acceptance and retention of the benefits of Feingold's services, a necessary element of the claim of unjust enrichment, has not been established.

Appellant argues that despite Pucello's refusal to accept his work product, Pucello nevertheless passively received benefits from Feingold's services. He points to two specific benefits which he contends were received by Pucello. First, he asserts that Pucello's ability to obtain an appointment with a conveniently located physician on short notice was a result of Feingold's established relationships with the physician. Second, Feingold asserts that settlement of Pucello's case was facilitated because Feingold obtained a written admission of liability from the driver of the car which struck Pucello, and the driver was constrained from denying liability when he was later interviewed by Pucello's counsel. I cannot agree that either of these alleged "benefits," even if received by Pucello, was sufficient to establish that Pucello was unjustly enriched.

Feingold's assistance in arranging an appointment with a physician is not the type of service for which one would normally expect to pay, nor is it a professional legal service which has a value because of the professional expertise required to render it. Accordingly, these services did not confer upon Pucello a benefit which it would be unconscionable to retain without making restitution. Similarly, Feingold's claim that settlement of Pucello's case was facilitated by the admissions made by the alleged tortfeasor to Feingold is entirely speculative. Because Feingold introduced no competent evidence to support his assertion that his work on the case had the effect he alleges, the record cannot support his claim that his services conferred a benefit upon Pucello.

Appellant's claim for quantum meruit cannot be sustained in the absence of a finding of unjust enrichment which, in equity, requires restitution. Because the record in this matter will not support such a finding, his quantum meruit claim was properly denied. I would therefore affirm the trial court's order.

B.   Restitution for Breach of Contract

UNITED STATES v. ALGERNON BLAIR, INC.
United States Court of Appeals, Fourth Circuit, 1973
479 F.2d 638

CRAVEN, Circuit Judge. May a subcontractor, who justifiably ceases work under a contract because of the prime contractor's breach, recover in quantum meruit the value of labor and equipment already furnished pursuant to the contract irrespective of whether he would have been entitled to recover in a suit on the contract? We think so, and, for reasons to be stated, the decision of the district court will be reversed.

The subcontractor, Coastal Steel Erectors, Inc., brought this action under the provisions of the Miller Act, 40 U.S.C.A. §270a et seq., in the name of the United States against Algernon Blair, Inc., and its surety, United States Fidelity and Guaranty Company. Blair had entered a contract with the United States for the construction of a naval hospital in Charleston County, South Carolina. Blair had then contracted with Coastal to perform certain steel erection and supply certain equipment in conjunction with Blair's contract with the United States. Coastal commenced performance of its obligations, supplying its own cranes for handling and placing steel. Blair refused to pay for crane rental, maintaining that it was not obligated to do so under the subcontract. Because of Blair's failure to make payments for crane rental, and after completion of approximately 28 percent of the subcontract, Coastal terminated its performance. Blair then proceeded to complete the job with a new subcontractor. Coastal brought this action to recover for labor and equipment furnished.

Blair refused to pay for crane rental, so Coastal terminated the contract

The district court found that the subcontract required Blair to pay for crane use and that Blair's refusal to do so was such a material breach as to justify Coastal's terminating performance. This finding is not questioned on appeal. The court then found that under the contract the amount due Coastal, less what had already been paid, totaled approximately $37,000. Additionally, the court found Coastal would have lost more than $37,000 if it had completed performance. Holding that any amount due Coastal must be reduced by any loss it would have incurred by complete performance of the contract, the court denied recovery to Coastal. While the district court correctly stated the "'normal' rule of contract damages,"[1] we think Coastal is entitled to recover in quantum meruit.

This issue was not questioned on appeal

In United States for Use of Susi Contracting Co. v. Zara Contracting Co., 146 F.2d 606 (2d Cir. 1944), a Miller Act action, the court was faced with a situation similar to that involved here—the prime contractor had unjustifiably breached a subcontract after partial performance by the subcontractor. The court stated:

Miller Act

> For it is an accepted principle of contract law, often applied in the case of construction contracts, that the promisee upon breach has the option to forego any suit on the contract and claim only the reasonable value of his performance.

146 F.2d at 610. The Tenth Circuit has also stated that the right to seek recovery under quantum meruit in a Miller Act case is clear. Quantum meruit recovery is not limited to an action against the prime contractor but may also be brought against the Miller Act surety, as in this case. Further, that the complaint is not clear in regard to the theory of a plaintiff's recovery does not preclude recovery under quantum meruit. Narragansett Improvement Co. v. United States, 290 F.2d 577 (1st Cir. 1961). A plaintiff may join a claim for quantum meruit with a claim for damages from breach of contract.

Rule

In the present case, Coastal has, at its own expense, provided Blair with labor and the use of equipment. Blair, who breached the subcontract, has retained these benefits without having fully paid for them. On these facts, Coastal is entitled to restitution in quantum meruit.

Blair retained the benefits without paying for them

---

1. Fuller and Perdue, The Reliance Interest in Contract Damages, 46 Yale L.J. 52 (1936); Restatement of Contracts §333 (1932).

The "restitution interest," involving a combination of unjust impoverishment with unjust gain, presents the strongest case for relief. If, following Aristotle, we regard the purpose of justice as the maintenance of an equilibrium of goods among members of society, the restitution interest presents twice as strong a claim to judicial intervention as the reliance interest, since if A not only causes B to lose one unit but appropriates that unit to himself, the resulting discrepancy between A and B is not one unit but two.

Fuller & Perdue, The Reliance Interest in Contract Damages, 46 Yale L.J. 52, 56 (1936).

The impact of quantum meruit is to allow a promisee to recover the value of services he gave to the defendant irrespective of whether he would have lost money on the contract and been unable to recover in a suit on the contract. Scaduto v. Orlando, 381 F.2d 587, 595 (2d Cir. 1967). The measure of recovery for quantum meruit is the reasonable value of the performance, Restatement of Contracts §347 (1932); and recovery is undiminished by any loss which would have been incurred by complete performance. 12 Williston on Contracts §1485, at 312 (3d ed. 1970). While the contract price may be evidence of reasonable value of the services, it does not measure the value of the performance or limit recovery. Rather, the standard for measuring the reasonable value of the services rendered is the amount for which such services could have been purchased from one in the plaintiff's position at the time and place the services were rendered.

Since the district court has not yet accurately determined the reasonable value of the labor and equipment use furnished by Coastal to Blair, the case must be remanded for those findings. When the amount has been determined, judgment will be entered in favor of Coastal, less payments already made under the contract. Accordingly, for the reasons stated above, the decision of the district court is reversed and remanded with instructions.

NOTES AND QUESTIONS

1. The Miller Act is a federal statute permitting certain parties to a construction project to recover from the contractor's surety if they remain unpaid.

2. The measure of damages in restitution is the benefit the plaintiff conferred on the defendant. Reliance damages are generally greater than this recovery because all reliance expenditures are reimbursed whether or not they benefit the defendant. (But, as we shall see, if the benefit to the defendant is greater than the cost to produce it, restitution damages could be more.) If expectancy damages are generally greater than reliance damages and reliance damages greater than restitution damages, why were expectancy or reliance damages not sought in *Algernon*?

3. How exactly is the court to determine the value of the benefit to the defendant when awarding restitution damages? What exactly was the measure of restitution according to the court in *Algernon*? Compare Restatement (Second) of Contracts:

§371. Measure of Restitution Interest

If a sum of money is awarded to protect a party's restitution interest, it may as justice requires be measured by either

(a) the reasonable value to the other party of what he received in terms of what it would have cost him to obtain it from a person in the claimant's position, or
(b) the extent to which the other party's property has been increased in value or his other interests advanced.

It should be noted, however, that in suits for restitution there are many cases permitting the plaintiff to recover the value of benefits conferred on the defendant, even though this value exceeds that of the return performance promised by the defendant. In these cases it is no doubt felt that the defendant's breach should work a forfeiture of his right to retain the benefits of an advantageous bargain.

Fuller and Perdue, The Reliance Interest in Contract Damages, 46 Yale L. Rev. 52, 77 (1936-1937).

4. Some courts refuse to limit restitution damages to the contract price, an approach apparently accepted by the court in *Algernon*. See also Southern Painting Co. v. United States, 222 F.2d 431 (10th Cir. 1955); 1 G. Palmer, *Law of Restitution* §4.4 (1978). Authority contra includes Lewis Electric Co. v. Miller, 791 N.W.2d 691 (Iowa 2010); Childress and Garamella, The Law of Restitution and the Reliance Interest in Contract, 64 Nw. U. L. Rev. 433, 439-441 (1969).

The Restatement did not take sides on this issue. It does provide that if the plaintiff has completed performance and the defendant's breach is simply the failure to pay the agreed price, restitution is not a proper measure. Restatement (Second) of Contracts §373(2). The reason given by the Restatement drafters for this limitation is as follows:

> To give him that right would impose on the court the burden of measuring the benefit in terms of money in spite of the fact that this has already been done by the parties themselves when they made their contract.

Is this a convincing reason? What if all performance had been rendered except the attachment of the plastic plates on the electrical outlets? Would the plaintiff be able to seek restitution in an amount exceeding the contract price?

Finally, the Restatement (Third) of Restitution §38 adopts the minority position, and contrary to the case reprinted above, mandates that the contract price is always a cap on the amount the plaintiff can recover in a restitution action. The Reporter's Notes to this section explain that most commentators think the majority rule is wrong because it violates a basic goal of the law of damages: strive to put the parties in the position that performance would have done.

Problem 82

Weekend Construction Company agreed to build a parking garage for Municipal Airport, but it proved to be a foolish contract because the construction would cost Weekend Construction $100,000, although the Airport would pay no more than $80,000, as per the contract. When the construction was halfway completed, Municipal Airport filed for a bankruptcy and repudiated this contract. Weekend Construction has incurred $50,000 in expenses so far, with the same amount yet to go. What is the amount of the claim it should file in the bankruptcy proceeding? *$50h → For the services already rendered*

ROSENBERG v. LEVIN
Supreme Court of Florida, 1982
409 So. 2d 1016

OVERTON, J. This is a petition to review a decision of the Third District Court of Appeal, reported as Levin v. Rosenberg, 372 So. 2d 956 (Fla. 3d D.C.A. 1979). The issue to be decided concerns the proper basis for compensating an attorney discharged without cause by his client after he has performed substantial legal services under a valid contract of employment. We find conflict with our decision in Goodkind v. Wolkowsky, 132 Fla. 63, 180 So. 538 (1938).

We hold that a lawyer discharged without cause is entitled to the reasonable value of his services on the basis of quantum meruit, but recovery is limited to the maximum fee set in the contract entered into for those services. We have concluded that without this limitation, the client would be penalized for the discharge and the lawyer would receive more than he bargained for in his initial contract. In the instant case, we reject the contention of the respondent lawyer that he is entitled to $55,000 as the reasonable value of his services when his contract fee was $10,000. We affirm the decision of the district court and recede from our prior decision in *Goodkind*.

The facts of this case reflect the following. Levin hired Rosenberg and Pomerantz to perform legal services pursuant to a letter agreement which provided for a $10,000 fixed fee, plus a contingent fee equal to fifty percent of all amounts recovered in excess of $600,000. Levin later discharged

Rosenberg and Pomerantz without cause before the legal controversy was resolved and subsequently settled the matter for a net recovery of $500,000. Rosenberg and Pomerantz sued for fees based on a "quantum meruit" eval- *Trial* uation of their services. After lengthy testimony, the trial judge concluded that quantum meruit was indeed the appropriate basis for compensation and awarded Rosenberg and Pomerantz $55,000. The district court also agreed that quantum meruit was the appropriate basis for recovery but low- ered the amount awarded to $10,000, stating that recovery could in no event exceed the amount which the attorneys would have received under their contract if not prematurely discharged. 372 So. 2d at 958.

The issue submitted to us for resolution is whether the terms of an attorney employment contract limit the attorney's quantum meruit recovery to the fee set out in the contract. This issue requires, however, that we answer the broader underlying question of whether in Florida quantum meruit is an appropriate basis for compensation of attorneys discharged by their clients without cause where there is a specific employment contract. The Florida cases which have previously addressed this issue have resulted in confusion and conflicting views.

In Goodkind v. Wolkowsky, this Court held that an attorney who was employed for a specific purpose and for a definite fee, but who was dis- charged without cause after substantial performance, was entitled to recover the fee agreed upon as damages for breach of contract. The attorney in *Goodkind* was employed to represent several clients in a tax case for a fixed fee of $4,000 and was discharged without cause prior to his completion of the matter. He sought damages for breach of contract. The trial court sustained clients' demurrer to the complaint "on the ground that plaintiff's right to recover must be restricted to a reasonable compensation for the value of the services performed prior to the discharge." 180 So. at 540. The attorney appealed and this Court, after an extensive survey of the authorities, reversed the attorney's quantum meruit recovery and found instead that he was enti- tled to recover under the contract. The *Goodkind* court, while following the traditional contract rule, did recognize the right of the client to discharge his attorney at any time with or without cause. The Third District Court of Appeal later applied this contract rule to a contingent fee contract situation in Osius v. Hastings, 97 So. 2d 623 (Fla. 3d D.C.A. 1957), rev'd on other grounds, 104 So. 2d 21 (Fla. 1958).

In Milton Kelner, P.A. v. 610 Lincoln Road, Inc., 328 So. 2d 193 (Fla. 1976), we approved the enforcement of a specific attorney-client contract, but left open the issue of whether quantum meruit was the proper rule in a contingency fee case. The attorney in *Kelner* represented a client on an insurance claim under a contingency fee contract calling for "40 percent of all sums recovered." The insurer agreed to pay the face amount of the policy before trial, but the client rejected the settlement offer and dis- charged the attorney without cause. In effect, the maximum recovery from the insurance company had been obtained at the time of the discharge.

The attorney then sought recovery under the contract in the trial court and was successful, with the jury resolving the dispute relating to fee calculation in favor of the attorney. On appeal, the district court reversed and limited the attorney's recovery to quantum meruit rather than the percentage of the insurance proceeds recovery provided by the contingency contract. The district court emphasized that recovery under the original contract might have a chilling effect on a client's exercise of the right to discharge. The district court then certified to this Court the question it had decided, whether quantum meruit should be the exclusive remedy in contingent fee cases. We chose to decide the *Kelner* case on its unique facts and <u>held</u>:

> Under the peculiar circumstances of this case, where the proceeds of the insurance policy were fully recovered and the real issue of how the contingency fee was to be computed was settled by a jury, we will not disturb the verdict and restrict the computation of the attorney's fee to quantum meruit. We do agree with the District Court that Goodkind v. Wolkowsky applies to a fixed fee contract and does not establish the precedent for contingent fee contracts.

We continued by stating:

> Quantum meruit may well be the proper standard when the discharge under a contingent fee contract occurs *prior* to the obtaining of the full settlement contracted for under the attorney-client agreement, with the cause of action accruing only upon the happening of the contingency to the benefit of the former client. That issue, however, is not factually before us and we do not make that determination in this cause.

328 So. 2d at 196 (citation omitted).

The First District Court of Appeal, in <u>Sohn v. Brockington</u>, 371 So. 2d 1089 (Fla. 1st D.C.A. 1979), cert. denied, 383 So. 2d 1202 (Fla. 1980), subsequently determined that, based on the above-quoted language in *Kelner*, quantum meruit was the appropriate remedy when discharge occurred before the happening of the contingency. In *Sohn*, the attorney was employed under a forty percent contingent fee contract and was discharged without cause before filing the complaint. The client subsequently retained new counsel who secured a settlement of $75,000. The district court affirmed the trial court which had limited the attorney to a quantum meruit recovery and awarded him $950 as the reasonable value of his services. In so holding, the district court concluded that "the [modern] rule . . . is the more logical and should be adopted in this state." 371 So. 2d at 1092. That court also held that the attorney's cause of action accrued immediately upon discharge in accordance with the view expressed in Martin v. Camp, 219 N.Y 170, 177, 114 N.E. 46, 49 (1916).

The existing case law in this state reflects that this Court is on record as favoring the traditional contract means of recovery. We have, however, inferred in dicta in *Kelner* that quantum meruit may be the proper basis for recovery in a contingent fee contract situation. The First District Court of Appeal in *Sohn* expressly held that quantum meruit is proper in a contingency contract. In the instant case, the Third District Court of Appeal held that quantum meruit is proper where the contingency does not control and limited such quantum meruit recovery to the maximum amount of the contract fee.

There are two conflicting interests involved in the determination of the issue presented in this type of attorney-client dispute. The first is the need of the client to have confidence in the integrity and ability of his attorney and, therefore, the need for the client to have the ability to discharge his attorney when he loses that necessary confidence in the attorney. The second is the attorney's right to adequate compensation for work performed. To address these conflicting interests, we must consider three distinct rules.

[margin note: Two conflicting Interests]

CONTRACT RULE

The traditional contract rule adopted by a number of jurisdictions holds that an attorney discharged without cause may recover damages for breach of contract under traditional contract principles. The measure of damages is usually the full contract price, although some courts deduct a fair allowance for services and expenses not expended by the discharged attorney in performing the balance of the contract. . . . Some jurisdictions following the contract rule also permit an alternative recovery based on quantum meruit so that an attorney can elect between recovery based on the contract or the reasonable value of the performed services. . . .

Support for the traditional contract theory is based on: (1) the full contract price is arguably the most rational measure of damages since it reflects the value that the parties placed on the services; (2) charging the full fee prevents the client from profiting from his own breach of contract; and (3) the contract rule is said to avoid the difficult problem of setting a value on an attorney's partially completed legal work.

[margin note: ✗ Agreed to Fee]

QUANTUM MERUIT RULE

To avoid restricting a client's freedom to discharge his attorney, a number of jurisdictions in recent years have held that an attorney discharged without cause can recover only the reasonable value of services rendered prior to discharge. . . . This rule was first announced in Martin v. Camp, 219 N.Y. 170, 114 N.E. 46 (1916), where the New York Court of Appeals held that a discharged attorney could not sue his client for damages for breach of contract unless the attorney had completed performance of the contract. The New York court established quantum meruit recovery for the attorney

[margin note: NY]

on the theory that the client does not breach the contract by discharging the attorney. Rather, the court reasoned, there is an implied condition in every attorney-client contract that the client may discharge the attorney at any time with or without cause. With this right as part of the contract, traditional contract principles are applied to allow quantum meruit recovery on the basis of services performed to date. Under the New York rule, the attorney's cause of action accrues immediately upon his discharge by the client, under the reasoning that it is unfair to make the attorney's right to compensation dependent on the performance of a successor over whom he has no control. See Tillman v. Komar, 259 N.Y. 133, 135-136, 181 N.E. 75, 76 (1932).

The California Supreme Court, in Fracasse v. Brent, 6 Cal. 3d 784, 494 P.2d 9, 100 Cal. Rptr. 385 (1972), also adopted a quantum meruit rule. That court carefully analyzed those factors which distinguish the attorney-client relationship from other employment situations and concluded that a discharged attorney should be limited to a quantum meruit recovery in order to strike a proper balance between the client's right to discharge his attorney without undue restriction and the attorney's right to fair compensation for work performed. The Fracasse court sought both to provide clients greater freedom in substituting counsel and to promote confidence in the legal profession while protecting society's interest in the attorney-client relationship.

Contrary to the New York rule, however, the California court also held that an attorney's cause of action for quantum meruit does not accrue until the happening of the contingency, that is, the client's recovery. If no recovery is forthcoming, the attorney is denied compensation. The California court offered two reasons in support of its position. First, the result obtained and the amount involved, two important factors in determining the reasonableness of a fee, cannot be ascertained until the occurrence of the contingency. Second, the client may be of limited means and it would be unduly burdensome to force him to pay a fee if there was no recovery. The court stated that: "[S]ince the attorney agreed initially to take his chances on recovering any fee whatever, we believe that the fact that the success of the litigation is no longer under his control is insufficient to justify imposing a new and more onerous burden on the client." Id. at 792, 494 P.2d at 14, 100 Cal. Rptr. at 390.

QUANTUM MERUIT RULE LIMITED BY THE CONTRACT PRICE

The third rule is an extension of the second that limits quantum meruit recovery to the maximum fee set in the contract. This limitation is believed necessary to provide client freedom to substitute attorneys without economic penalty. Without such a limitation, a client's right to discharge an attorney may be illusory and the client may in effect be penalized for exercising a right.

The Tennessee Court of Appeals, in Chambliss, Bahner & Crawford v. *[TN handwritten]* Luther, 531 S.W.2d 108 (Tenn. Ct. App. 1975), expressed the need for limitation on quantum meruit recovery, stating: "It would seem to us that the better rule is that because a client has the unqualified right to discharge his attorney, fees in such cases should be limited to the value of the services rendered or the contract price, whichever is less." 531 S.W.2d at 113. In rejecting the argument that quantum meruit should be the basis for the recovery even though it exceeds the contract fee, that court said:

> To adopt the rule advanced by Plaintiff would, in our view, encourage attorneys less keenly aware of their professional responsibilities than Attorney Chambliss, . . . to induce clients to lose confidence in them in cases where the reasonable value of their services has exceeded the original fee and thereby, upon being discharged, reap a greater benefit than that for which they had bargained.

531 S.W.2d at 113. Other authorities also support this position.[1]

CONCLUSION

We have carefully considered all the matters presented, both on the original argument on the merits and on rehearing. It is our opinion that it is in the best interest of clients and the legal profession as a whole that we adopt the modified quantum meruit rule which limits recovery to the maximum amount of the contract fee in all premature discharge cases involving both fixed and contingency employment contracts. The attorney-client relationship is one of special trust and confidence. The client must rely entirely on the good faith efforts of the attorney in representing his interests. This reliance requires that the client have complete confidence in the integrity and ability of the attorney and that absolute fairness and candor characterize all dealings between them. These considerations dictate that clients be given greater freedom to change legal representatives than might be tolerated in other employment relationships. We approve the philosophy that there is an overriding need to allow clients freedom to substitute attorneys without economic penalty as a means of accomplishing the broad objective of fostering public confidence in the legal profession. Failure to limit quantum meruit recovery defeats the policy against penalizing the client for exercising his right to discharge. However, attorneys should not be penalized either and should have the opportunity to recover for services performed.

[handwritten margin notes: "Adopt the Modified Quantum Meruit rule → limits recovery to max amount of the contract fee"; "Rationale"; "Policy"]

---

1. For example, Corbin on Contracts, in the chapter dealing with restitution, cites the quantum meruit rule with this limitation with approval. Contracts §1102 (1980 Supp.) at 207-208. . . .

Holding

Accordingly, we hold that an attorney employed under a valid contract who is discharged without cause before the contingency has occurred or before the client's matters have concluded can recover only the reasonable value of his services rendered prior to discharge, limited by the maximum contract fee. We reject both the traditional contract rule and the quantum meruit rule that allow recovery in excess of the maximum contract price because both have a chilling effect on the client's power to discharge an attorney. Under the contract rule in a contingent fee situation, both the discharged attorney and the second attorney may receive a substantial percentage of the client's final recovery. Under the unlimited quantum meruit rule, it is possible, as the instant case illustrates, for the attorney to receive a fee greater than he bargained for under the terms of his contract. Both these results are unacceptable to us.

Court rejected the traditional contract rule and the traditional quantum meruit rule

We further follow the California view that in contingency fee cases, the cause of action for quantum meruit arises only upon the successful occurrence of the contingency. If the client fails in his recovery, the discharged attorney will similarly fail and recover nothing. We recognize that deferring the commencement of a cause of action until the occurrence of the contingency is a view not uniformly accepted. Deferral, however, supports our goal to preserve the client's freedom to discharge, and any resulting harm to the attorney is minimal because the attorney would not have benefited earlier until the contingency's occurrence. There should, of course, be a presumption of regularity and competence in the performance of the services by a successor attorney.

Computing Value

In computing the reasonable value of the discharged attorney's services, the trial court can consider the totality of the circumstances surrounding the professional relationship between the attorney and client. Factors such as time, the recovery sought, the skill demanded, the results obtained, and the attorney-client contract itself will necessarily be relevant considerations.

factors

We conclude that this approach creates the best balance between the desirable right of the client to discharge his attorney and the right of an attorney to reasonable compensation for his services. With this decision, we necessarily recede from our prior decision in Goodkind v. Wolkowsky. This decision has no effect on our *Kelner* decision concerning completed contracts, whether contingent, fixed fee, or mixed. We find the district court of appeal was correct in limiting the quantum meruit award to the contract price, and its decision is approved.

Goodkind was overruled

Affirmed

━━━━━━━━

Problem 83

Attorney Amos Factory was world famous for his legal abilities in the area of antitrust law. He was employed by a client for the agreed fee of $50,000 to handle a complex negotiation leading to a merger. When he was half done with the task, the client discharged him without cause. He proves to the court's satisfaction that his efforts prior to the discharge were already worth $50,000. May he recover that amount?

C. The Breaching Plaintiff

BRITTON v. TURNER
Supreme Court of New Hampshire, 1834
6 N.H. 481

PARKER, J. delivered the opinion of the court.

It may be assumed, that the labor performed by the plaintiff, and for which he seeks to recover a compensation in this action, was commenced under a special contract to labor for the defendant the term of one year, for the sum of one hundred and twenty dollars, and that the plaintiff has labored but a portion of that time, and has voluntarily failed to complete the entire contract.

It is clear, then, that he is not entitled to recover upon the contract itself, because the service, which was to entitle him to the sum agreed upon, has never been performed.

But the question arises, can the plaintiff, under these circumstances, recover a reasonable sum for the service he has actually performed, under the count in *quantum meruit*.

Upon this, and questions of a similar nature, the decisions to be found in the books are not easily reconciled.

It has been held, upon contracts of this kind for labor to be performed at a specified price, that the party who voluntarily fails to fulfil the contract by performing the whole labor contracted for, is not entitled to recover any thing for the labor actually performed, however much he may have done towards the performance, and this has been considered the settled rule of law upon this subject. [Citations omitted.]

That such rule in its operation may be very unequal, not to say unjust, is apparent.

A party who contracts to perform certain specified labor, and who breaks his contract in the first instance, without any attempt to perform it, can only be made liable to pay the damages which the other party has sustained by reason of such non performance, which in many instances may be trifling — whereas a party who in good faith has entered upon the performance of his contract, and nearly completed it, and then abandoned the further performance — although the other party has had the full benefit of all that has been done, and has perhaps sustained no actual damage — is in fact subjected to a loss of all which has been performed, in the nature of damages for the non fulfilment of the remainder, upon the technical rule,

[handwritten margin notes:] plaintiff voluntarily breached contract

Not entitled to recover under the contract because he didn't fully perform

Can he recover for services already performed under QM?

that the contract must be fully performed in order to [allow] a recovery of any part of the compensation.

By the operation of this rule, then, the party who attempts performance may be placed in a much worse situation than he who wholly disregards his contract, and the other party may receive much more, by the breach of the contract, than the injury which he has sustained by such breach, and more than he could be entitled to were he seeking to recover damages by an action.

The case before us presents an illustration. Had the plaintiff in this case never entered upon the performance of his contract, the damage could not probably have been greater than some small expense and trouble incurred in procuring another to do the labor which he had contracted to perform. But having entered upon the performance, and labored nine and a half months, the value of which labor to the defendant as found by the jury is $95, if the defendant can succeed in this defence, he in fact receives nearly five sixths of the value of a whole year's labor, by reason of the breach of contract by the plaintiff a sum not only utterly disproportionate to any probable, not to say possible damage which could have resulted from the neglect of the plaintiff to continue the remaining two and a half months, but altogether beyond any damage which could have been recovered by the defendant, had the plaintiff done nothing towards the fulfilment of his contract.

Another illustration is furnished in Lantry v. Parks, 8 Cowen, 83. There the defendant hired the plaintiff for a year, at ten dollars per month. The plaintiff worked ten and a half months, and then left saying he would work no more for him. This was on Saturday — on Monday the plaintiff returned, and offered to resume his work, but the defendant said he would employ him no longer. The court held that the refusal of the defendant on Saturday was a violation of his contract, and that he could recover nothing for the labor performed.

There are other cases, however, in which principles have been adopted leading to a different result.

It is said, that where a party contracts to perform certain work, and to furnish materials, as, for instance, to build a house, and the work is done, but with some variations from the mode prescribed by the contract, yet if the other party has the benefit of the labor and materials he should be bound to pay so much as they are reasonably worth. [Citations omitted.] . . .

The party who contracts for labor merely, for a certain period, does so with full knowledge that he must, from the nature of the case, be accepting part performance from day to day, if the other party commences the performance, and with knowledge also that the other may eventually fail of completing the entire term.

If under such circumstances he actually receives a benefit from the labor performed, over and above the damage occasioned by the failure to complete, there is as much reason why he should pay the reasonable worth of what has thus been done for his benefit, as there is when he enters and occupies the house which has been built for him, but not according to the stipulations of the contract, and which he perhaps enters, not because he is satisfied with what has been done, but because circumstances compel him to accept it such as it is, that he should pay for the value of the house. . . .

We hold then, that where a party undertakes to pay upon a special contract for the performance of labor, or the furnishing of materials, he is not to be charged upon such special agreement until the money is earned according to the terms of it, and where the parties have made an express contract the law will not imply and raise a contract different from that which the parties have entered into, except upon some farther transaction between the parties. . . .

But if, where a contract is made of such a character, a party actually receives labor, or materials, and thereby derives a benefit and advantage, over and above the damage which has resulted from the breach of the contract by the other party, the labor actually done, and the value received, furnish a new consideration, and the law thereupon raises a promise to pay to the extent of the reasonable worth of such excess. This may be considered as making a new case, one not within the original agreement, and the party is entitled to "recover on his new case, for the work done, not as agreed, but yet accepted by the defendant." 1 Dane's Abr. 224.

If on such failure to perform the whole, the nature of the contract be such that the employer can reject what has been done, and refuse to receive any benefit from the part performance, he is entitled so to do, and in such case is not liable to be charged, unless he has before assented to and accepted of what has been done, however much the other party may have done towards the performance. He has in such case received nothing, and having contracted to receive nothing but the entire matter contracted for, he is not bound to pay, because his express promise was only to pay on receiving the whole, and having actually received nothing the law cannot and ought not to raise an implied promise to pay. But where the party receives value — takes and uses the materials, or has advantage from the labor, he is liable to pay the reasonable worth of what he has received. 1 Camp. 38, Farnsworth v. Garrard. And the rule is the same whether it was received and accepted by the assent of the party prior to the breach, under a contract by which, from its nature, he was to receive labor, from time to time until the completion of the whole contract; or whether it was received and accepted by an assent subsequent to the performance of all which was in fact done. If he received it under such circumstances as precluded him from rejecting it afterwards, that does not alter the case — it has still been received by his assent. . . .

The amount, however, for which the employer ought to be charged, where the laborer abandons his contract, is only the reasonable worth, or the amount of advantage he receives upon the whole transaction, (6 N.H. 15, Wadleigh v. Sutton) and, in estimating the value of the labor, the contract price for the service cannot be exceeded. 7 Green. 78; 4 Wendell, 285,

Dubois v. Delaware & Hudson Canal Company; 7 Wend. 121, Koon v. Greenman. . . .

If in such case it be found that the damages are equal to, or greater than the amount of the labor performed, so that the employer, having a right to the full performance of the contract, has not upon the whole case received a beneficial service, the plaintiff cannot recover.

Awk ✗

This rule, by binding the employer to pay the value of the service he actually receives, and the laborer to answer in damages where he does not complete the entire contract, will leave no temptation to the former to drive the laborer from his service, near the close of his term, by ill treatment, in order to escape from payment; nor to the latter to desert his service before the stipulated time, without a sufficient reason; and it will in most instances settle the whole controversy in one action, and prevent a multiplicity of suits and cross actions. . . .

Applying the principles thus laid down, to this case, the plaintiff is entitled to judgment on the verdict.

plaintiff is entitled to recover

The defendant sets up a mere breach of the contract in defense of the action, but this cannot avail him. He does not appear to have offered evidence to show that he was damnified by such breach, or to have asked that a deduction should be made upon that account. The direction to the jury was therefore correct, that the plaintiff was entitled to recover as much as the labor performed was reasonably worth, and the jury appear to have allowed a *pro rata* compensation, for the time which the plaintiff labored in the defendant's service. . . .

Judgment on the verdict.

Problem 84

Famous movie star Howard Teeth agreed to accept a $50,000 fee to appear in a low-budget remake of Aristophanes's *The Birds*. As part of his contract, he promised to undertake a publicity tour to promote the film. After the film was over, he flatly refused to go on the tour. The movie was nonetheless a surprise hit and made millions for its producers. Teeth, not having been paid anything, sued for $1 million, the reasonable value of his services. What amount should he recover? Would your answer change if he had been involved in an accident and was not feeling well?

Problem 85

Montgomery sold King several marine charts for $2,000. King sent a $750 down payment. Shortly thereafter, King relinquished his merchant marine commission and told Montgomery that he was not going to buy the charts and wanted his $750 back. Montgomery's actual damages are only $250. Is King entitled to any recovery? If so, how much? See UCC §2-718(2).

III.   EQUITABLE REMEDIES

A.   *The Meaning of "Equity"*

The word *equity* is used by lawyers to mean different things, depending on the context. The most obvious use is as a synonym for *fairness* ("Your Honor, simple equity requires a judgment in favor of my client"). The other uses of the word have a historical background.

As it developed through the centuries, common law pleading in England became a game of technicalities. The law courts only recognized certain specific theories (causes of action) that could be pleaded, and if an injured party's complaint could not be adapted to an approved theory, the courts would not hear it. Moreover, the courts felt that remedial relief was available only in the form of money damages. If the plaintiff wanted other relief (for example, an order from the court telling the defendant to do or not do something), the courts were useless.

Enter the king. Litigants shut out of the law courts sought relief by appealing to the monarch, who, of course, could grant whatever relief was thought necessary. Phrased another way, the king could grant "equitable relief" unbounded by the rules hampering the courts of law. Litigants seeking this extraordinary intervention made their appeals to the monarch through the king's chancellor, and the chancery courts were called courts of "equity."

This end run around the existing legal system caused much friction between the courts of "law" and the courts of "equity" (and had the further result of encouraging the courts of law to loosen up and liberalize some of the constraints on common law pleading). Eventually, rules were established to protect the jurisdiction of each. For our purposes, the most important of these is that the courts of equity limited the relief they would grant to cases in which money damages would not make the parties whole (the usual incantation is that "the remedy at law is inadequate"), as where the plaintiff requested something more than the payment of money from the defendant. Thus by a writ of *mandamus* a public official is ordered to perform his or her job, by a writ of *injunction* a party is forbidden to do something, and by a writ of *specific performance* a party is ordered to perform the contract. Defiance of the court's order would be contempt of court (an altogether nasty business involving an angry judge with almost unlimited powers, including the right to jail the offender).

Modern courts are not typically divided into courts of law and courts of equity (although vestiges of the practice do still exist here and there), but the courts still keep close track of whether the plaintiff is seeking money damages (an action "at law") or extraordinary relief (an action "in equity"). In the materials that follow we will explore the constraints on a judge "sitting in equity."

PHH MORTGAGE CORP. v. BARKER
Court of Appeals of Ohio, 2010
190 Ohio App. 3d 71, 940 N.E.2d 662

SHAW, Judge.

(1) Plaintiff-appellants, PHH Mortgage Corp. (PHH), appeals the December 7, 2009 judgment of the Van Wert County Court of Common Pleas reinstating the mortgage between PHH and defendants-appellees, Denise and Robert Barker, on the Barkers' home.

(2) On December 22, 2005, the Barkers executed a note and a mortgage in the sum of $34,200 with First Financial Bank, N.A ("First Financial"). The note required the Barkers to pay First Financial 360 monthly payments of $227.53. On May 1, 2007, the Barkers failed to make the required monthly payment. Denise Barker testified that she suffered from an illness during this time that prevented her from contacting First Financial about the missed payments until July 2007, when her health improved. Denise attempted to contact a representative at the local First Financial branch in Van Wert. Denise testified that she left several voicemail messages about the missed payments with different First Financial representatives but none of her calls were returned.

(3) Eventually, Denise drove to a First Financial branch in Paulding, located in a neighboring county, where the person who originally worked on the mortgage was now employed.

The Paulding representative gave Denise the name of another representative in a different office to contact about "loss mitigation" — an assistance program that helps the homeowner cure the default and bring the mortgage current. Denise contacted this person, who walked her through the loss-mitigation-assistance process and informed her that she would be receiving a loss-mitigation packet in the mail.

(4) On July 31, 2007, First Financial sent a letter to the Barkers notifying them that as of May 1, 2007, payment on their mortgage remained due and owing. In the letter, First Financial also offered assistance to the Barkers if they were experiencing difficulties maintaining their monthly payments.

(5) In early August 2007, the Barkers received a loss-mitigation packet from an entity called "Mortgage Service Center," which was affiliated with First Financial. The materials in the packet requested the Barkers to provide specific information so that the Mortgage Service Center could review the

Barkers' financial situation. Based on the information provided by the Barkers, the Mortgage Service Center would determine whether they qualified for a "Workout Option to Avoid Foreclosure." The Barkers completed the materials in the loss-mitigation packet and mailed the packet to the Mortgage Service Center on August 17, 2007.

(6) On August 20, 2007, First Financial sent a letter to the Barkers notifying them that their mortgage was in default. The letter further demanded that the Barkers pay $1,288.64 in 30 days to avoid the initiation of foreclosure proceedings. On August 29, 2007, a second notice of default was sent to the Barkers.

(7) Shortly thereafter, the Barkers received a "coupon book" in the mail that listed a new monthly payment on the mortgage in the amount of $312.06 if paid by the first of the month or a payment of $322.16 if made by the 16th of the month. The first payment coupon was dated for October 1, 2007. Denise testified that the coupon book arrived by itself with no other correspondence to provide further explanation. Denise stated that when she received this coupon book, she believed that the mortgage had been reset as a result of the previously mentioned loss-mitigation questionnaire sent to the Mortgage Service Center because the first payment coupon listed a new due date and the monthly payment amount had been increased.

(8) Denise testified that she made a payment of $400 at the end of August 2007 and another payment in the same amount in September. On October 1, 2007, Denise used the new coupon book to tender a payment of $400 to a local First Financial branch office in Van Wert. Denise testified that every time she made a payment, she did so in person at the local branch and that she always either paid in cash or had the teller deduct the payment amount from her paycheck. The teller would accept the payment and give Denise a receipt for the transaction. Denise kept the receipts in the coupon book.

(9) On October 22, 2007, First Financial sent a letter from its corporate office in New Jersey to the Barkers with a check enclosed in the amount of $322.16. The letter informed the Barkers that the money was being returned because their mortgage remained in default and was pending review by the foreclosure department. On October 29, 2007, First Financial sent a second letter with a check for $477.84 enclosed informing the Barkers that the money was returned because the mortgage remained in default and foreclosure proceedings were still pending. However, the Barkers testified that they never received either the letters or the checks. Moreover, no evidence was presented at trial that these checks were ever cashed.

(10) On October 29, 2007, Denise made another payment in the amount of $800 to First Financial's local branch in Van Wert, using the coupon book. Again, the teller processed the payment and gave Denise a receipt for the transaction.

(11) On November 7, 2007, PHH, the appellant in this case, filed a complaint in foreclosure against the Barkers based on their default on the

mortgage with First Financial. During this time, Denise testified, she continued to have communications with the loss-mitigation department, who sent her another packet of paperwork to complete and return. Denise testified that on November 10, 2007, she mailed the second set of loss-mitigation materials to First Financial.

(12) On November 14, 2007, PHH sent a letter to the Barkers with a check refunding a payment of $800. This letter was the first time PHH formally communicated with the Barkers. Unlike the previous two letters sent by First Financial, this letter indicated that the account had "been referred to an attorney to handle the foreclosure process." The letter further directed the Barkers to call the loss-mitigation department to learn about assistance programs to help bring the mortgage current. However, the Barkers testified that they did not receive this letter at this time. Denise testified that she received this refund check nearly five months later, in late February or early March of 2008.

(13) In December 2007 and January 2008, Denise continued to make payments on the mortgage to First Financial's local branch using the coupon book. Just as before, the First Financial teller processed the payment and gave Denise a receipt for the transaction. Denise made two additional payments in this manner each in the amount of $400 on December 11, 2007, and January 3, 2008. There was no attempt by First Financial/PHH to return either of these payments.

(14) On February 4, 2008, when Denise attempted to tender a payment of $400 to First Financial, the teller at the local First Financial branch refused to accept the payment, at the direction of PHH. The teller gave Denise a Cleveland telephone number to call for further information on the matter. Denise testified that she had called the number expecting a representative of the bank to answer and offer her some assistance. However, the number given to Denise belonged to an attorney who informed her that the account was in the process of foreclosure. Shortly thereafter the Barkers retained counsel.

(15) On March 14, 2008, PHH filed a motion for summary judgment claiming that the Barkers were in default on their mortgage, giving PHH the absolute right to accelerate the mortgage and institute foreclosure proceedings on the property. On March 20, 2008, the Barkers filed a response to PHH's motion for summary judgment alleging that genuine issues of material fact remained. Specifically, the Barkers alleged that the coupon book was issued after their communications with First Financial, and therefore, the parties understood that the mortgage was reinstated. Based on this belief, the Barkers began making payments pursuant to the newly issued coupon book, and those payments were accepted by First Financial until February 2008. The Barkers attached the affidavit of Robert Barker in support of their memorandum in opposition to summary judgment. On April 2, 2008, PHH filed a reply to the Barkers' response to its motion for

summary judgment. PHH objected to the use of Robert Barker's affidavit as the only evidence to establish a dispute of fact.

(16) Before the trial court made its ruling on PHH's motion for summary judgment, the Barkers filed a Chapter 7 bankruptcy petition and the matter was stayed pending the disposition of the bankruptcy proceedings. Notably, during the pendency of the court proceedings, the loss-mitigation department continued to send Denise paperwork, which she dutifully completed and returned.

(17) On July, 28, 2008, the trial court overruled and "dismissed" PHH's motion for summary judgment, finding the existence of a genuine issue of material fact in dispute.

(18) Over a year later, on October 20, 2009, the trial court conducted a bench trial. . . .

On December 7, 2009, the trial court entered the following ruling in this case via its judgment entry:

> The court having considered the evidence and the equity of the situation finds that the [Barkers] entered into a reasonable interpretation of their communication with First Financial Bank and attempted to follow through on that interpretation until prevented from doing so by [PHH].
>
> The court, therefore, finds it is equitable and in the best interests of justice, and hereby orders that the mortgage and the note be reinstated at the amount owed by the [Barkers] to [PHH] as of October 1, 2007.

(21) PHH now appeals from this judgment, asserting three assignments of error.

Assignment of Error No. I
The trial court erred in overruling and "dismissing" appellant's motion for summary judgment where the appellant properly demonstrated the nonexistence of any genuine issue of material fact concerning appellee's default.

Assignment of Error No. II
The trial court erred in overruling and "dismissing" appellant's motion for summary [sic] by construing the evidence to find the existence of an agreement to modify the subject mortgage loan agreement in the absence of any admissible evidence demonstrating modification of a contract according to law.

Assignment of Error No. III
The trial court erred in entering judgment against the appellant and ordering "reinstatement" of the subject mortgage loan agreement to a date clearly in default, thereby improperly reforming the parties' agreement.

[The court ruled against PHH on the first two Assignments of Error.]

The Third Assignment of Error

(34) In its third assignment of error, PHH asserts that the trial court erred in ordering the reinstatement of the Barkers' mortgage. Specifically, PHH contends that the trial court committed improper judicial "making of a contract" when it found an agreement between the parties to modify and reinstated the mortgage.

(35) Under applicable Ohio law, a foreclosure involves a two-step process. Once it has been determined as a matter of law that a default on the obligation secured by the mortgage has occurred, the court must then consider the equities to determine if foreclosure is the appropriate remedy. See First Knox Natl. Bank v. Peterson, 5th Dist. No. 08CA28, 2009-Ohio-5096, 2009 WL 3086583, 18, citing Rosselot v. Heimbrock (1988), 54 Ohio App. 3d 103, 105-106, 561 N.E.2d 555. Moreover, because foreclosure is equitable relief, "the simple assertion of the elements of foreclosure does not require, as a matter of law, the remedy of foreclosure." See First Natl. Bank of Am. v. Pendergrass, 6th Dist. No. E-08-048, 2009-Ohio-3208, 2009 WL 1865127, 22. Therefore, as an equitable action, a foreclosure action should be reviewed for abuse of discretion. See Buckeye Retirement Co., L.L.C. v. Walling, 2d Dist. No. 05 MA 119, 2006-Ohio-7059, 2006 WL 3849863, 16. "Abuse of discretion" connotes more than an error of law or judgment; rather, it implies an unreasonable, arbitrary, or unconscionable attitude. Id.

(36) In the instant action, the trial court specifically addressed the equities involved in this action and highlighted the extremely unique circumstances presented by the facts of this case. The court made the following observation at the conclusion of the trial:

> [The Barkers] made every effort to try to get this loan back unlike the other ninety-nine percent of the foreclosure cases that I have. These people have tried to get back on track and get the thing reinstated and made what appears to me to be a good faith effort to do that.

(37) The trial court further addressed its evaluation of the equities in determining whether foreclosure was the appropriate remedy under these specific facts in its judgment entry:

> A foreclosure requires a two step process. Once the [c]ourt has determined a default on an obligation secured by a mortgage they [sic] must then consider the equity of the situation in order to decide if foreclosure is appropriate. It is not enough the contract was breached and the bank can enforce the contract. The [c]ourt has to look at whether it is equitable to take the house of the Defendants under the circumstances.
>
> The [Barkers] testified about the efforts they made to pay this mortgage, the efforts they made to enter into a modification of the mortgage, and the efforts they went to after receiving a mortgage coupon book to maintain

payments on their mortgage. Believing that they had reach[ed] [an] understanding they made payments pursuant to the coupon book they had received from First Financial Bank prior to October 1, 2007, and the First Financial Bank at first accepted the payments. It was at the direction of [PHH] that First Financial Bank eventually refused to accept [the Barkers'] payments on and after February 4, 2008.

(38) The evidence at trial revealed that the Barkers were receiving conflicting communications from First Financial/PHH concerning their mortgage, which obfuscated the situation. On the one hand, First Financial sent the Barkers letters informing them that their loan was in default. Most of these letters were received by the Barkers at the same time they were communicating with the loss-mitigation department about curing the default. It was shortly after receiving the second notice of default that the Barkers received the coupon book purporting to reset the mortgage payments for a new amount beginning October 1, 2007. The evidence showed that it was the Barkers' communication with the loss-mitigation department that resulted in the issuing of a new coupon book.

(39) Using this coupon book, the Barkers made four payments totaling $2,000 — more than the $1,288.64 needed to cure the default — over a period of five months, and the payments were unconditionally accepted by First Financial. Despite PHH's evidence showing that letters containing refunded payments were sent to the Barkers, there was no evidence that the Barkers actually received them. Indeed, the Barkers testified under oath that they never received two of the three letters with the returned payments. The Barkers admitted to receiving the third letter from PHH but not until late February of 2008, when this action was already before the court.

(40) Denise Barker testified that she was dumbfounded when she received a complaint in foreclosure in November of 2007 from PHH. However, at that time, she did not know who PHH was or what its relation was to First Financial because she had never received any notice of the assignment of her mortgage. Thus, believing that her mortgage with First Financial was still in place, she continued to make payments on the mortgage. Notably, even after the Barkers became actively involved in the lawsuit, First Financial's loss-mitigation department continued to send the Barkers paperwork throughout the foreclosure proceedings with PHH.

(41) Based on the record before us, we conclude that there was ample evidence to support the trial court's decision that the equitable principles implicated in this case warranted a reinstatement of the Barkers' mortgage. Further, we find no error in the trial court's order to reinstate the mortgage as of October 1, 2007, because this is the last communication from First Financial/PHH containing the terms of the revised payment schedule on the mortgage. Accordingly, PHH's third assignment of error is overruled.

(42) For all these reasons, the judgment of the Van Wert County Court of Common Pleas is affirmed.

B. Specific Performance

As we have seen, in the usual contracts suit the prevailing plaintiff recovers money damages measured under the rules studied thus far. However, considering that it is the primary remedial goal of contracts law to put injured persons in the position that performance would have done, why is it not more appropriate simply to order specific performance? In a contract in which the defendant is to pay an amount of money, such as in a loan contract, the award of money damages equals that which the plaintiff would have received by performance. But if the plaintiff had bargained for a house to be built, an award of money damages is not the same as the performance sought by the defendant. At first thought, specific performance appears more direct, easier to measure, and fairer to the plaintiff. Is it therefore the preferred solution?

POSNER, ECONOMIC ANALYSIS OF LAW
117-120 (4th ed. 1992)

§4.8. FUNDAMENTAL PRINCIPLES OF CONTRACT DAMAGES

When a breach of contract is established, the issue becomes one of the proper remedy. . . .

It makes a difference in deciding which remedy to grant whether the breach was opportunistic. If a promisor breaks his promise merely to take advantage of the vulnerability of the promisee in a setting (the normal contract setting) where performance is sequential rather than simultaneous, we might as well throw the book at the promisor. An example would be where A pays B in advance for goods and instead of delivering them B uses the money in another venture. Such conduct has no economic justification and ought simply to be deterred. An attractive remedy in such a case is restitution. The promisor broke his promise in order to make money — there can be no other reason in the case of such a breach. We can deter this kind of behavior by making it worthless to the promisor, which we do by making him hand over all his profits from the breach to the promisee; no lighter sanction would deter.

Most breaches of contract, however, are not opportunistic. Many are involuntary; performance is impossible at a reasonable cost. Others are voluntary but (as we are about to see) efficient — which from an economic standpoint is the same case as that of an involuntary breach. These observations both explain the centrality of remedies to the law of contracts (can you see why?) and give point to Holmes's dictum that it is not the policy of the law to compel adherence to contracts but only to require each party to choose between performing in accordance with the contract and compensating the other party for any injury resulting from a failure to perform.[1] This dictum, though overbroad, contains an important economic insight. In many cases it is uneconomical to induce completion of performance of a contract after it has been broken. I agree to purchase 100,000 widgets custom-ground for use as components in a machine that I manufacture. After I have taken delivery of 10,000, the market for my machine collapses. I promptly notify my supplier that I am terminating the contract, and admit that my termination is a breach. When notified of the termination he has not yet begun the custom grinding of the other 90,000 widgets, but he informs me that he intends to complete his performance under the contract and bill me accordingly. The custom-ground widgets have no operating use other than in my machine, and a negligible scrap value. To give the supplier a remedy that induced him to complete the contract after the breach would waste resources. The law is alert to this danger and, under the doctrine of mitigation of damages, would not give the supplier damages for any costs he incurred in continuing production after notice of termination. . . .

Now suppose the contract is broken by the seller rather than the buyer. I really need those 100,000 custom-ground widgets for my machine but the supplier, after producing 50,000, is forced to suspend production because of a mechanical failure. Other suppliers are in a position to supply the remaining widgets that I need but I insist that the original supplier complete his performance of the contract. If the law compels completion (specific performance), the supplier will have to make arrangements with other producers to complete his contract with me. Probably it will be more costly for him to procure an alternative supplier than for me to do so directly (after all, I know my own needs best); otherwise he would have done it voluntarily, to minimize his liability for the breach. To compel completion of the contract (or costly negotiations to discharge the promisor) would again result in a waste of resources, and again the law does not compel completion but confines the victim to simple damages. . . .

NOTES AND QUESTIONS

1. See also Birmingham, Breach of Contract, Damage Measures, and Economic Efficiency, 24 Rutgers L. Rev. 273, 284-292 (1970). Attorney's fees and out-of-pocket costs of litigation (except official court costs) are not normally awarded to a litigant in American courts. What effect do you suppose this has on a plaintiff's willingness to file suit and proceed to trial? Is an

---

1. Oliver Wendell Holmes, The Path of the Law, 10 Harv. L. Rev. 457, 462 (1897) ("The duty to keep a contract at common law means a prediction that you must pay damages if you do not keep it—and nothing else"). [For the argument that Posner misunderstands what Holmes meant by this statement, see J. Perillo, Misreading Oliver Wendell Holmes on Efficient Breach and Tortious Interference, 68 Fordham L. Rev. 1085 (2000).]

award of damages that excludes these costs ever truly in substitution for performance? Some have disagreed that economic theory dictates an award of damages should be the usual remedy for breach of contract. They have argued that specific performance is generally more economically efficient. See Linzer, On the Amorality of Contract Remedies: Efficiency, Equity, and the Second Restatement, 81 Colum. L. Rev. 111 (1981); Schwartz, The Case for Specific Performance, 89 Yale L.J. 271 (1979).

2. The United Nations Convention on Contracts for the International Sale of Goods (described in the Introduction to this book) is divided into different sections called *articles*. The Convention has a presumption in favor of the ability of the parties to get specific performance. See Articles 46, 62. Note, however, that Article 28 does not permit specific performance if the court asked to grant it would not do so were its own law applied. For example, because in the United States specific performance is rarely appropriate if it would require undue court supervision, a United States court might use this ground to duck an order of specific performance.

3. What part does morality play in this discussion? Is breach of contract immoral, and, if so, does the moral obligation to fulfill one's promises tend to support money damages or specific performance?

4. Should such considerations as relative bargaining power affect the amount of an award if the court does opt for the generally accepted expectation measure of damages? See Eisenberg, The Bargain Principle and Its Limits, 95 Harv. L. Rev. 741 (1982).

ℙ CENTEX HOMES CORP. v. BOAG ᵇ
Superior Court of New Jersey, 1974
128 N.J. Super. 385, 320 A.2d 194

GELMAN, J.S.C. Plaintiff Centex Homes Corporation (Centex) is engaged in the development and construction of a luxury high-rise condominium project in the Boroughs of Cliffside Park and Fort Lee. The project when completed will consist of six 31-story buildings containing in excess of 3,600 condominium apartment units, together with recreational buildings and facilities, parking garages and other common elements associated with this form of residential development. As sponsor of the project Centex offers the condominium apartment units for sale to the public and has filed an offering plan covering such sales with the appropriate regulatory agencies of the States of New Jersey and New York.

On September 13, 1972 defendants Mr. & Mrs. Eugene Boag executed a contract for the purchase of apartment unit No. 2019 in the building under construction and known as "Winston Towers 200." The contract purchase price was $73,700, and prior to signing the contract defendants had given

Centex a deposit in the amount of $525. At or shortly after signing the contract defendants delivered to Centex a check in the amount of $6,870 which, together with the deposit, represented approximately 10 percent of the total purchase price of the apartment unit. Shortly thereafter Boag was notified by his employer that he was to be transferred to the Chicago, Illinois, area. Under date of September 27, 1972 he advised Centex that he "would be unable to complete the purchase" agreement and stopped payment on the $6,870 check. Centex deposited the check for collection approximately two weeks after receiving notice from defendant, but the check was not honored by defendants' bank. On August 8, 1973 Centex instituted this action in Chancery Division for specific performance of the purchase agreement or, in the alternative, for liquidated damages in the amount of $6,870. The matter is presently before this court on the motion of Centex for summary judgment.

[handwritten margin notes: "Defendant paid 10% of price"; "Found out he was being transferred for work"; "Plaintiff Centex sued for specific performance or/and liquidated damages"]

Both parties acknowledge, and our research has confirmed, that no court in this State or in the United States has determined in any reported decision whether the equitable remedy of specific performance will lie for the enforcement of a contract for the sale of a condominium apartment. . . .

[U]nder a condominium housing scheme each condominium apartment unit constitutes a separate parcel of real property which may be dealt with in the same manner as any real estate. Upon closing of title the apartment unit owner receives a recordable deed which confers upon him the same rights and subjects him to the same obligations as in the case of traditional forms of real estate ownership, the only difference being that the condominium owner receives in addition an undivided interest in the common elements associated with the building and assigned to each unit. . . .

Centex urges that since the subject matter of the contract is the transfer of a fee interest in real estate, the remedy of specific performance is available to enforce the agreement under principles of equity which are well-settled in this state. . . .

The principle underlying the specific performance remedy is equity's jurisdiction to grant relief where the damage remedy at law is inadequate. The text writers generally agree that at the time this branch of equity jurisdiction was evolving in England, the presumed uniqueness of land as well as its importance to the social order of that era led to the conclusion that damages at law could never be adequate to compensate for the breach of a contract to transfer an interest in land. Hence specific performance became a fixed remedy in this class of transactions. See 11 Williston on Contracts (3d ed. 1968) §1418A; 5A Corbin on Contracts §1143 (1964). The judicial attitude has remained substantially unchanged and is expressed in *Pomeroy* as follows:

> in applying this doctrine the courts of equity have established the further rule that in general the legal remedy of damages is inadequate in all agreements for

the sale or letting of land, or of any estate therein; and therefore in such class of contracts the jurisdiction is always exercised, and a specific performance granted, unless prevented by other and independent equitable considerations which directly affect the remedial right of the complaining party. . . . [1 Pomeroy, Equity Jurisprudence (5th ed. 1941), §221(b).]

While the inadequacy of the damage remedy suffices to explain the origin of the vendee's right to obtain specific performance in equity, it does not provide a *rationale* for the availability of the remedy at the instance of the vendor of real estate. Except upon a showing of unusual circumstances or a change in the vendor's position, such as where the vendee has entered into possession, the vendor's damages are usually measurable, his remedy at law is adequate and there is no jurisdictional basis for equitable relief.

[The] English precedents suggest that the reliability of the remedy in a suit by a vendor was an outgrowth of the equitable concept of mutuality, i.e., that equity would not specifically enforce an agreement unless the remedy was available to both parties. . . .

So far as can be determined from our decisional law, the mutuality of remedy concept has been the prop which has supported equitable jurisdiction to grant specific performance in actions by vendors of real estate. The earliest reported decision in this State granting specific performance in favor of a vendor is Rodman v. Zilley, 1 N.J. Eq. 320 (Ch. 1831), in which the vendee (who was also the judgment creditor) was the highest bidder at an execution sale. In his opinion Chancellor Vroom did not address himself to the question whether the vendor had an adequate remedy at law. The first reported discussion of the question occurs in Hopper v. Hopper, 16 N.J. Eq. 147 (Ch. 1863), which was an action by a vendor to compel specific performance of a contract for the sale of land. In answer to the contention that equity lacked jurisdiction because the vendor had an adequate legal remedy, Chancellor Green said (at p. 148):

> It constitutes no objection to the relief prayed for, that the application is made by the vendor to enforce the payment of the purchase money, and not by the vendee to compel a delivery of the title. The vendor has not a complete remedy at law. Pecuniary damages for the breach of the contract is not what the complainant asks, or is entitled to receive at the hands of a court of equity. He asks to receive the price stipulated to be paid in lieu of the land. The doctrine is well established that the remedy is mutual, and that the vendor may maintain his bill in all cases where the purchaser could sue for a specific performance of the agreement.

No other *rationale* has been offered by our decisions subsequent to *Hopper*, and specific performance has been routinely granted to vendors without further discussion of the underlying jurisdictional issue. . . .

Our present Supreme Court has squarely held, however, that mutuality of remedy is not an appropriate basis for granting or denying specific performance. Fleischer v. James Drug Store, 1 N.J. 138, 62 A.2d 383 (1948); see also, Restatement, Contracts §372; 11 Williston, Contracts (3d ed. 1968), §1433. The test is whether the obligations of the contract are mutual and not whether each is entitled to precisely the same remedy in the event of a breach. In *Fleischer* plaintiff sought specific performance against a cooperative buying and selling association although his membership contract was terminable by him on 60 days' notice. Justice Heher said:

The test ✕

> And the requisite mutuality is not wanting. The contention contra rests upon the premise that, although the corporation "can terminate the contract only in certain restricted and unusual circumstances, any 'member' may withdraw at any time by merely giving notice."
>
> Clearly, there is mutuality of obligation, for until his withdrawal complainant is under a continuing obligation of performance in the event of performance by the corporation. It is not essential that the remedy of specific performance be mutual. . . . The fact that the remedy of specific enforcement is available to one party to a contract is not in itself a sufficient reason for making the remedy available to the other; but it may be decisive when the adequacy of damages is difficult to determine and there is no other reason for refusing specific enforcement. Restatement, Contracts (1932), sections 372, 373. It is not necessary, to serve the ends of equal justice, that the parties shall have identical remedies in case of breach. [At 149, 62 A.2d at 388.]

✕

No more Mutuality

The disappearance of the mutuality of remedy doctrine from our law dictates the conclusion that specific performance relief should no longer be automatically available to a vendor of real estate, but should be confined to those special instances where a vendor will otherwise suffer an economic injury for which his damage remedy at law will not be adequate, or where other equitable considerations require that the relief be granted. . . .

Rule ✕

As Chancellor Vroom noted in King v. Morford, 1 N.J. Eq. 274, 281-282 (Ch. Div. 1831), whether a contract should be specifically enforced is always a matter resting in the sound discretion of the court and

> considerable caution should be used in decreeing the specific performance of agreements, and . . . the court is bound to see that it really does the complete justice which it aims at, and which is the ground of its jurisdiction.

Here the subject matter of the real estate transaction — a condominium apartment unit — has no unique quality but is one of hundreds of virtually identical units being offered by a developer for sale to the public. The units are sold by means of sample, in this case model apartments, in much the same manner as items of personal property are sold in the market place. The sales prices for the units are fixed in accordance with schedule filed by

subject matter is Not unique quality

price is fixed

Centex as part of its offering plan, and the only variance as between apartments having the same floor plan (of which six plans are available) is the floor level or the building location within the project. In actuality, the condominium apartment units, regardless of their realty label, share the same characteristics as personal property.

From the foregoing one must conclude that the damages sustained by a condominium sponsor resulting from the breach of the sales agreement are readily measurable and the damage remedy at law is wholly adequate. No compelling reasons have been shown by Centex for the granting of specific performance relief and its complaint is therefore dismissed as to the first count.

Centex also seeks money damages pursuant to a liquidated damage clause in its contract with the defendants. It is sufficient to note only that under the language of that clause (which was authored by Centex) liquidated damages are limited to such moneys as were paid by defendant at the time the default occurred. Since the default here consisted of the defendant's stopping payment of his check for the balance of the down payment, Centex's liquidated damages are limited to the retention of the "moneys paid" prior to that date, or the initial $525 deposit. Accordingly, the second count of the complaint for damage relief will also be dismissed.

NOTES AND QUESTIONS

1. Is the reason for the court's denial that (a) condominium units are alike and therefore not unique; (b) given the vendor's position in the principal case, it is easy to determine the amount of damages (there is an equitable maxim that "[e]quity withholds its hand if there is an adequate remedy at law"); or (c) specific performance does not lie in favor of the seller?

2. Section 2-506 of the Uniform Land Transactions Act provides that the seller of land is not entitled to specific performance unless the property cannot be resold by him at a reasonable price with reasonable effort.

3. Courts have been even quicker to give vendees of land the right to specific performance. Should it make a difference whether the vendee is buying the land for purposes of speculation rather than for a residence or for recreational use? That the buyer has already arranged a resale at the time of the principal contract? See, e.g., Watkins v. Paul, 95 Idaho 499, 511 P.2d 781 (1973).

4. Occasionally, specific performance will be denied if the court finds that specific performance would be unjust because of fraud, undue influence, or the like, even though the suspect activity does not give rise to an action at law for damages. See, e.g., Hilton v. Nelson, 283 N.W.2d 877 (Minn. 1979).

ᴾ LACLEDE GAS CO. v. AMOCO OIL CO. ᴰ
United States Court of Appeals, Eighth Circuit, 1975
522 F.2d 33

Ross, Circuit Judge. The Laclede Gas Company (Laclede), a Missouri corporation, brought this diversity action alleging breach of contract against the Amoco Oil Company (Amoco), a Delaware corporation. It sought relief in the form of a mandatory injunction prohibiting the continuing breach or, in the alternative, damages. The district court held a bench trial on the issues of whether there was a valid, binding contract between the parties and whether, if there was such a contract, Amoco should be enjoined from breaching it. It then ruled that the "contract is invalid due to lack of mutuality" and denied the prayer for injunctive relief. The court made no decision regarding the requested damages. Laclede Gas Co. v. Amoco Oil Co., 385 F. Supp. 1332, 1336 (E.D. Mo. 1974). This appeal followed, and we reverse the district court's judgment.

On September 21, 1970, Midwest Missouri Gas Company (now Laclede), and American Oil Company (now Amoco), the predecessors of the parties to this litigation, entered into a written agreement which was designed to provide central propane gas distribution systems to various residential developments in Jefferson County, Missouri, until such time as natural gas mains were extended into these areas. The agreement contemplated that as individual developments were planned the owners or developers would apply to Laclede for central propane gas systems. If Laclede determined that such a system was appropriate in any given development, it could request Amoco to supply the propane to that specific development. . . .

[O]n April 3, 1973, Amoco notified Laclede that its Wood River Area Posted Price of propane had been increased by three cents per gallon. Laclede objected to this increase also and demanded a full explanation. None was forthcoming. Instead Amoco merely sent a letter dated May 14, 1973, informing Laclede that it was "terminating" the September 21, 1970, agreement effective May 31, 1973. It claimed it had the right to do this because "the Agreement lacks 'mutuality.'"

The district court felt that the entire controversy turned on whether or not Laclede's right to "arbitrarily cancel the Agreement" without Amoco having a similar right rendered the contract void "for lack of mutuality" and it resolved this question in the affirmative. We disagree with this conclusion and hold that settled principles of contract law require a reversal.

I

A bilateral contract is not rendered invalid and unenforceable merely because one party has the right to cancellation while the other does not.

There is no necessity "that for each stipulation in a contract binding the one party there must be a corresponding stipulation binding the other." ...

We conclude that there is mutuality of consideration within the terms of the agreement and hold that there is a valid, binding contract between the parties as to each of the developments for which supplemental letter agreements have been signed.

II

Since he found that there was no binding contract, the district judge did not have to deal with the question of whether or not to grant the injunction prayed for by Laclede. He simply denied this relief because there was no contract. Laclede Gas Co. v. Amoco Oil Co., supra, 385 F. Supp. at 1336.

Generally the determination of whether or not to order specific performance of a contract lies within the sound discretion of the trial court. ... However, this discretion is, in fact, quite limited; and it is said that when certain equitable rules have been met and the contract is fair and plain "specific performance goes as a matter of right." ...

With this in mind we have carefully reviewed the very complete record on appeal and conclude that the trial court should grant the injunctive relief prayed. We are satisfied that this case falls within that category in which specific performance should be ordered as a matter of right. See Miller v. Coffeen, supra, 280 S.W.2d at 102.

Amoco contends that four of the requirements for specific performance have not been met. Its claims are: (1) there is no mutuality of remedy in the contract; (2) the remedy of specific performance would be difficult for the court to administer without constant and long-continued supervision; (3) the contract is indefinite and uncertain; and (4) the remedy at law available to Laclede is adequate. The first three contentions have little or no merit and do not detain us for long.

There is simply no requirement in the law that both parties be mutually entitled to the remedy of specific performance in order that one of them be given that remedy by the court. ...

While a court may refuse to grant specific performance where such a decree would require constant and long-continued court supervision, this is merely a discretionary rule of decision which is frequently ignored when the public interest is involved. ...

Here the public interest in providing propane to the retail customers is manifest, while any supervision required will be far from onerous.

Section 370 of the Restatement of Contracts (1932) provides:

> Specific enforcement will not be decreed unless the terms of the contract are so expressed that the court can determine with reasonable certainty what is the duty of each party and the conditions under which performance is due.

We believe these criteria have been satisfied here. As discussed in part I of this opinion, as to all developments for which a supplemental agreement has been signed, Amoco is to supply all the propane which is reasonably foreseeably required, while Laclede is to purchase the required propane from Amoco and pay the contract price therefor. The parties have disagreed over what is meant by "Wood River Area Posted Price" in the agreement, but the district court can and should determine with reasonable certainty what the parties intended by this term and should mold its decree, if necessary accordingly. Likewise, the fact that the agreement does not have a definite time of duration is not fatal since the evidence established that the last subdivision should be converted to natural gas in 10 to 15 years. This sets a reasonable time limit on performance and the district court can and should mold the final decree to reflect this testimony.

It is axiomatic that specific performance will not be ordered when the party claiming breach of contract has an adequate remedy at law. . . . This is especially true when the contract involves personal property as distinguished from real estate.

However, in Missouri, as elsewhere, specific performance may be ordered even though personalty is involved in the "proper circumstances." Mo. Rev. Stat. §400.2-716(1); Restatement of Contracts, supra, §361. And a remedy at law adequate to defeat the grant of specific performance "must be as certain, prompt, complete, and efficient to attain the ends of justice as a decree of specific performance." . . .

One of the leading Missouri cases allowing specific performance of a contract relating to personalty because the remedy at law was inadequate is Boeving v. Vandover, 240 Mo. App. 117, 218 S.W.2d 175, 178 (1949). In that case the plaintiff sought specific performance of a contract in which the defendant had promised to sell him an automobile. At that time (near the end of and shortly after World War II) new cars were hard to come by, and the court held that specific performance was a proper remedy since a new car "could not be obtained elsewhere except at considerable expense, trouble or loss, which cannot be estimated in advance."

We are satisfied that Laclede has brought itself within this practical approach taken by the Missouri courts. As Amoco points out, Laclede has propane immediately available to it under other contracts with other suppliers. And the evidence indicates that at the present time propane is readily available on the open market. However, this analysis ignores the fact that the contract involved in this lawsuit is for a long-term supply of propane to these subdivisions. The other two contracts under which Laclede obtains the gas will remain in force only until March 31, 1977, and April 1, 1981, respectively; and there is no assurance that Laclede will be able to receive any propane under them after that time. Also it is unclear as to whether or not Laclede can use the propane obtained under these contracts to supply the Jefferson County subdivisions, since they were originally entered into to provide Laclede with propane with which to "shave" its natural gas supply during peak demand periods. Additionally, there was uncontradicted expert testimony that Laclede probably could not find another supplier of propane willing to enter into a long-term contract such as the Amoco agreement, given the uncertain future of worldwide energy supplies. And, even if Laclede could obtain supplies of propane for the affected developments through its present contracts or newly negotiated ones, it would still face considerable expense and trouble which cannot be estimated in advance in making arrangements for its distribution to the subdivisions.

Specific performance is the proper remedy in this situation, and it should be granted by the district court.

CONCLUSION

For the foregoing reasons the judgment of the district court is reversed and the cause is remanded for the fashioning of appropriate injunctive relief in the form of a decree of specific performance as to those developments for which a supplemental agreement form has been signed by the parties.

NOTES AND QUESTIONS

1. In Sedmak v. Charlie's Chevrolet, Inc., 622 S.W.2d 694 (Mo. App. 1981), the court granted specific performance under UCC §2-716 for a new limited production "Indy 500" Corvette that was in very short supply. In Scholl v. Hartzell, 20 Pa. D.&C. 3d 304, 33 UCC Rep. Serv. 951 (Pa. Ct. Common Pleas 1981), the court refused to allow specific performance for a 1962 Corvette. Is the lesson of these two cases that (a) newer specialty cars are unique and older specialty cars are not, (b) the judge in Pennsylvania does not think Corvettes are so special, or (c) the judge in Missouri is a race fan?

2. The Uniform Commercial Code does not per se allow the *seller* specific performance in a sale of goods. However, §2-709 of the UCC permits the seller of goods to recover, as damages, the price of goods if the buyer has breached the contract after final acceptance of the goods, the goods have been destroyed after the risk of loss of the goods has passed to the buyer, or for "goods identified to the contract if the seller is unable after reasonable effort to resell them at a reasonable price or the circumstances reasonably indicate that such effort will be unavailing."

Problem 86

Home run king Sammy Stocks has played for the same California professional baseball team for his entire career. Recently, he has announced that (in violation of his contract) he will switch teams and play for an east coast ball club. His current team is outraged and has applied to you, a California federal judge, for an order of specific performance, requiring him to continue playing in California as per his contract (which has three years remaining). If you grant such a request, what would you have to do to enforce it? Would you have any difficulties with the Thirteenth Amendment to the United States Constitution, which prohibits involuntary servitude? See Oman, Specific Performance and the Thirteenth Amendment, 93 Minn. L. Rev. 2020 (2009). Is there any other relief that might be adequate?

ᴾ LUMLEY v. WAGNER ᴰ
Lord Chancellor's Court, 1852
1 De C.M.&G. 604, 42 Eng. Rep. 687

Lord T. LEONARDS, L.C. The question which I have to decide in the present case arises out of a very simple contract, the effect of which is, that the defendant Johanna Wagner should sing at Her Majesty's Theatre for a certain number of nights, and that she should not sing elsewhere (for that is the true construction) during that period. As I understand the points taken by the defendants' counsel in support of this appeal they in effect come to this, namely, that a court of equity ought not to grant an injunction except in cases connected with specific performance, or where the injunction, being to compel a party to forbear from committing an act (and not to perform an act), that injunction will complete the whole of the agreement remaining unexecuted. . . .

The present is a mixed case, consisting not of two correlative acts to be done, one by the plaintiff and the other by the defendants, which state of facts may have and in some cases has introduced a very important difference, but of an act to be done by Johanna Wagner alone, to which is superadded a negative stipulation on her part to abstain from the commission of any act which will break in upon her affirmative covenant — the one being ancillary to, and concurrent and operating together with the other. The agreement to sing for the plaintiff during three months at his theatre, and during that time *It's one contract* not to sing for anybody else, is not a correlative contract. It is, in effect, one contract, and though beyond all doubt this court could not interfere to enforce the specific performance of the whole of this contract, yet in all sound construction and according to the true spirit of the agreement, the engagement to perform for three months at one theatre must necessarily exclude the right to perform at the same time at another theatre. It was clearly intended that Johanna Wagner was to exert her vocal abilities to the utmost to aid the theatre to which she agreed to attach herself. I am of opinion that if she had attempted, even in the absence of any negative stipulation, to perform at another theatre, she would have broken the spirit and true meaning of the contract as much as she would now do with reference to the contract into which she has actually entered. Wherever this court has not proper jurisdiction to enforce specific performance, it operates to bind men's consciences, as far as they can be bound, to a true and literal performance of their agreements, and it will not suffer them to depart from their contracts at their pleasure, leaving the party with whom they have contracted to the mere chance of any damages which a jury may give. The exercise of this jurisdiction has, I believe, had a wholesome tendency towards the maintenance of that good faith which exists in this country to a much greater degree perhaps than in any other, and although the jurisdiction is not to be extended, yet a judge would desert his duty who did not act up to what his predecessors have handed down as the rule for his guidance in the administration of such an equity.

It was objected that the operation of the injunction in the present case was mischievous, excluding the defendant Johanna Wagner from performing at any other theatre while this court had no power to compel her to perform at Her Majesty's Theatre. It is true that I have not the means of compelling her to sing, but she has no cause of complaint if I compel her to abstain from the commission of an act which she has bound herself not to do, and thus possibly cause her to fulfil her engagement. The jurisdiction which I now exercise is wholly within the power of the court, and being of opinion that it is a proper case for interfering, I shall leave nothing unsatisfied by the judgment I pronounce. The effect, too, of the injunction, in restraining Johanna Wagner from singing elsewhere may, in the event of an action being brought against her by the plaintiff, prevent any such amount of vindictive damages being given against her as a jury might probably be inclined to give if she had carried her talents and exercised them at the rival theatre. The injunction may also, as I have said, tend to the fulfilment of her engagement, though, in continuing the injunction, I disclaim doing indirectly what I cannot do directly. . . .

For a musical treatment of this famous case, go to YouTube and listen to Professor Richard Craswell's operative duet at https://www.youtube.com/playlist?list=PL36131D32992573A4.

Problem 87

Hammer & Son was a contractor. Hammer made plans to build a large shopping center. One of the stores was to be leased to Jane's Fashions. Jane's store was to be built according to general specifications applicable to all stores in the center. However, no two stores were to be identical, and Jane and Hammer had never particularized the design for Jane's store. Hammer refused to build Jane's store and lease it to her as promised. Jane sued for breach and asked for specific performance — an order requiring Hammer & Son to build Jane's store and lease it to her. The court finds a contract and a breach. Should the court grant Jane's request for specific performance? See City Stores Co. v. Ammerman, 266 F. Supp. 766 (D.D.C.), aff'd per curiam, 394 F.2d 950 (D.C. Cir. 1967).

CHAPTER 3 ASSESSMENT

Multiple Choice Questions

1. TexasBeef contracted to buy 40 steers from Open Range Farms for the price of $50,000, with TexasBeef agreeing to pick up the steers on August 1 and pay the amount immediately, which it did by wire transfer to Open Range Farms's bank. TexasBeef contracted with B&B Railroad to divert seven cattle cars to the farm to pick up the cattle on August 1 and deliver them to the TexasBeef plant 100 miles away for the sum of $7,000. It also contracted with a buyer to purchase the beef to be made from the cattle for a net profit to TexasBeef of $12,000 on the whole transaction. When the cattle cars arrived at Open Range Farms on August 1, there were no cattle to be loaded since ORF had shut down its business. TexasBeef sues for breach of contract. What amount will the law likely award it?
   a. $12,000. That is the profit TexasBeef planned to make, so an award of that amount puts it in the place performance would have.
   b. $50,000. That is the amount that TexasBeef paid ORF, and is the appropriate amount to make TexasBeef whole.
   c. $57,000. That amount gives TexasBeef both its restitution and reliance expense.
   d. All of these amounts added together: $69,000.

2. The contract provided: "In the event of breach the breaching party promises to pay $75,000 in liquidated damages to the injured party. The parties agree that this is not a penalty amount but an honest attempt to pre-estimate damages, which in the event will be hard to estimate, but certain to occur." In the actual event the damages appeared small or, more likely, nonexistent. Will this clause be upheld?
   a. Yes. Actual damages are irrelevant as long as the parties contemplated the possibility of such damages and made a good faith attempt to estimate them.
   b. No. If there are no actual damages or very little, the clause fails of its essential purpose and would have a punitive effect. The law does not

allow the parties to contract for punitive damages even if they do so in the form of an agreement to a so-called liquidated damages clause.

c. Yes. The law doesn't second guess the parties when they have made a good faith estimate of what harm will befall a failure to comply with the contract. Both parties planned their conduct with this clause in mind and it would upset the apple cart not to enforce it.

d. No. Our law is not so rigid as to ignore what really happened and blindly award $75,000 to a party who did not suffer any damages (or at most only a fraction of that amount). We have a strong policy in favor of awarding actual damages and not punitive ones (except where bad behavior, such as fraud, demands the infliction of a penalty).

3. CoolUp is a company that makes and sells air conditioning units for businesses. It contracted with World Wide Widgets to furnish the company with 32 Mega-Units, its most powerful and expensive product, for a total price of $120,000, with a delivery date set for September 25. CoolUp built the units at its factory, at a cost of $80,000, and was ready to ship when a week before the delivery date WWW sent a fax cancelling the purchase. You are the attorney for CoolUp and the sales manager asks you what damages it can sue for. She is sure that the 32 units will sell for the same price, even though it may take a couple of months before another buyer comes along willing to spend that much money. What is your answer?

a. All CoolUp is really out so far is the $80,000 it has spent in building the air conditioning units, so it should sue for that amount. But if the units do sell before the suit is settled, that would cancel out all damages because CoolUp would have successfully mitigated.

b. For the same reason as in A you should advise CoolUp not to sue at all. Its damages can be avoided by the second sale.

c. CoolUp should sue for the $120,000 it lost on the WWW contract. Any resale of the units it made is not a mitigating event because CoolUp is a lost volume seller. It can sell as many units as it finds buyers for, and these units will sell in the ordinary course of its business, as the sales manager has just told you. If the resale were viewed as a mitigating event, that would cut down the profits CoolUp makes for the year because it would have made both sales of these units if WWW had not cancelled.

d. Same argument as C except that the only amount CoolUp can sue for is $40,000. It didn't have to expend the $80,000 in building costs twice, so it saved that amount. All it is really out is the lost profit on the WWW contract.

4. Jane Witherspoon was an elderly rich landowner with a lovely home. The property had an elaborate garden that she had created through the decades with the help of her gardener, David Vargo, whom she paid sporadically when the garden needed tending. However, every April 1st she

had always hired David to thoroughly landscape the garden by cleaning out the debris from the winter and putting the garden in shape for the spring planting that the two of them would then do together, always paying him $500 for this preliminary job. In this particular year during the last week of March Jane fell down her front stairs and was knocked unconscious. She was taken by ambulance to the hospital and was still in a coma on April 1. Certain that she would want him to do the usual landscaping, David did the work, and was dismayed when she died two days after he finished the job. Jane's executor has refused to pay him the $500 he requested, saying (a) there was no contract for him to perform the work, (b) similar work would have only cost $300, and (c) he didn't do a job that was worth even $300 according to other gardening services that were contacted. David comes to you, his attorney cousin, and asks what he should do. He is certain Jane would have paid him the $500 as she has for the last ten years. What do you advise, counselor?

a. He should sue and recover the $500. The parties had created an implied contract for this amount, and that contract was annual. If she wasn't going to have him do the work she would have told him before the last week of March, so the contract was on and he should recover the contracted-for amount. He can produce plenty of witnesses as to how happy she had always been both with him and his work, and how she often bragged that she had the best gardener in the city.

b. There is no implied contract here, as much as David might wish it. Jane may or may not have wanted to do anything with the garden this year, or she might have decided it was time to have a professional company do the work. Probably he's right that she would have hired him for this year's landscaping, but we'll never know since she died before that could be ascertained.

c. David should sue for the value of his services using quasi-contract. This is an action in restitution, asking for quantum meruit (the value of his service conferred) and quantum valebant (the value of any goods he put into the job, such as mulch). He and Jane had always valued his work in this identical task at $500, and while a professional service might have charged less it wouldn't have known exactly what she wanted, while David was an expert at all the details that Jane expected in a finished job. If she had used strangers to do the work, she would have expended huge amounts of time teaching them what to do and supervising their work. The $500 amount was paid in large part because he didn't need any supervision and could be trusted to produce a garden that would please her.

d. There is no contract here. David was nice to do the work without an agreement, but it was at his risk that she wouldn't recover and authorize it. His landscaping was gratuitously conferred ("officious") and does not give rise to an action in restitution/quasi-contract/quantum valebant/quantum meruit.

  e. The quasi-contract action is likely to succeed, but only for the market
      value of David's services and not $500. He will have the burden of
      proving how much his efforts were worth.

Answers

1. D is the best answer. The goal of the law is to put the injured party in the
    position performance would have. Thus the $50,000 restitution amount
    paid must be added to the reliance expense paid to the railroad of $7,000,
    and, finally, the consequential loss of the $12,000 profit TexasBeef would
    have made must also be added in before we have reached the stated goal.
    Of course, TexasBeef must prove these amounts, and ORF may argue the
    lost profit should have been mitigated or was not foreseeable.

2. Take your pick. Any of these could be the result. But these are the argu-
    ments you, future attorney, will make. Be eloquent, sound forceful, and
    good luck.

3. D is the correct answer. If CoolUp really is a lost volume seller (it can sell
    as many units as it has customers to buy them), then it is entitled to the
    contract amount of the cancelled contract ($120,000) minus any
    expenses saved (here $80,000) by not having to build more units for
    the second sale to the later buyer. If WWW had actually bought the
    first units, CoolUp would have had to expend another $80,000 to build
    the units for the second sale, but that reliance expense was saved when
    WWW cancelled and the first units were then used to fulfill the second
    contract.

4. The implied contract argument is interesting, and you should probably
    try it, but the quasi-contract theory should also be a count in the com-
    plaint you file. No outcome is certain, and he might lose completely on
    the theory his work was officiously conferred on the estate. But the equi-
    ties are strong in his favor, and there is a good case for either the $500 (for
    the reasons mentioned in D) or, as a fallback position, the market value of
    his services viewed objectively (E).

CHAPTER
4
THE STATUTE OF FRAUDS

Many people who are not lawyers are under the mistaken impression that *all* contracts have to be in writing before they are legally enforceable. Strangely, our law has the opposite presumption: Only certain kinds of contracts have to be in writing and if a contract isn't on the list, then oral agreements, though often messy to prove, are legally fine. An agreement to pay someone $100,000 to perform a certain task (say, doing makeup for an upcoming movie over the course of the next month) becomes effective at the close of the offer and acceptance process even if done over the phone.

But, as explained immediately below, since 1677 English law (and subsequently American law) has contained statutes requiring certain kinds of contracts to be in writing. The idea behind these statutes is to prevent fraud and perjury by the false assertion of an oral agreement, so the original English statute was commonly called the "statute of frauds," and the term has stuck as a shorthand reference to any statute that requires a contract to be in writing.

I. HISTORY AND PURPOSE

In 1671, in Old Marston, Oxfordshire, England, defendant Egbert was sued by plaintiff John over an alleged oral promise by Egbert to sell to John a fighting cock named Fiste. John's friend, Harold, claimed he overheard the "deal" and by that dubious means John won, though in fact there apparently was no deal. In 1671 courts did not allow parties to a lawsuit to testify so Egbert could not testify to rebut Harold's story. Compounding the problem was the fact that courts then could not throw out jury verdicts manifestly contrary to the evidence. So, in response to the plight of the Egberts of the world and to the recurring mischief of the Johns, as well as to combat possible "Fraude and perjurie" by the Harolds, Parliament passed in 1677 a "Statute of Frauds" which required that certain contracts for the sale of goods be in writing to be enforceable.

Thomson Printing Machinery Co. v. B. F. Goodrich Co., 714 F.2d 744, 746 (7th Cir. 1983).

Given present rules concerning the competency of witnesses, the admissibility of testimony, and the greater confidence in courts and juries, is there still a reason for the statute of frauds? Why not enforce all contracts if they can be proven with sufficient evidence? Professor Corbin states:

> It can hardly be doubted that the statute renders some service by operating *in terrorem* to cause important contracts to be put into writing. Indeed, many laymen have the erroneous notion that an agreement is never binding until it is written and signed.
>
> Reduction to writing undoubtedly tends to prevent not only fraud and perjury but also the disputes and litigation that arise by reason of treacherous memory and the absence of witnesses. . . .
>
> Such good as the statute renders in preventing the making of perjured claims and in causing important agreements to be reduced to writing is attained at a very great cost of two different sorts: First, it denies enforcement to many honest plaintiffs; secondly, it has introduced an immense complexity into the law and has been in part the cause of an immense amount of litigation as to whether a promise is within the statute or can by any remote possibility be taken out of it.

Corbin §275. The United Nations Convention on Contracts for the International Sale of Goods has no requirement that its contracts be in writing; see Article 11.

II.   TYPES OF CONTRACTS TYPICALLY COVERED UNDER STATUTES OF FRAUDS

The English statute of frauds—entitled "An Act for Prevention of Frauds and Perjuries"—had 25 sections and covered transactions other than contracts for the sale of goods. But for our purposes, the important segment of the act (§4) provided:

> And be it further enacted . . . that . . . no action shall be brought
>
> (1) whereby to charge any executor or administrator upon any special promise to answer for damages out of his own estate; or
>
> (2) whereby to charge the defendant upon any special promise to answer for the debt, default or miscarriages of another person; or
>
> (3) to charge any person upon any agreement made upon consideration of marriage; or

(4) upon any contract or sale of lands, tenements or hereditaments, or any interest in or concerning them; or

(5) upon any agreement that is not to be performed within the space of one year from the making thereof; unless the agreement upon which such action shall be brought, or some memorandum or note thereof, shall be in writing, and signed by the party to be charged therewith, or some other person thereunto by him lawfully authorized.

In addition, §17 of the statute required a writing for the sale of any goods having a price of "ten pounds of sterling or upwards."

In 1954, the English Parliament removed the writing requirement for all contracts other than those listed in (2) (suretyship) and (4) (sale of realty).

In the United States, nearly every state has adopted, and retained, a statute of frauds. (Louisiana, Maryland, and New Mexico are the exceptions, but they have similar requirements as the result of judicial decisions.) Typically, these laws require a writing for the same types of contracts as those listed in (1) through (5) above. See Restatement (Second) of Contracts §110.

The writing requirement for certain sales of goods is now found in §2-201 of the Uniform Commercial Code. The official version, adopted by most states, is applicable only when the goods have a price of over $500. Other provisions of the UCC, such as §9-203, which mandates that security agreements be in a "record" (defined in §9-102(a)(69) broadly to encompass any sort of preservable version of the contract), also require signed writings in some other commercial transactions. Article 2A of the UCC, dealing with the leasing of goods, has a statute of frauds requirement in §2A-201 for leases of $1,000 or more. This section is modeled on Article 2's §2-201, discussed in detail later in this chapter.

In any particular state, other statutes may require certain kinds of contracts to be in writing. Typical examples are agreements authorizing brokers to buy or sell real estate, contracts to make a bequest in a will, or warranties by physicians to effect a certain result. Less common writing requirements abound in the statute books. Florida demands that newspaper subscriptions be in writing (Fla. Stat. Ann. §725.03); South Dakota does the same for prearranged burial services and, curiously enough for a landlocked state, ships (S.D. Laws Ann. §§55-11-3 and 43-35-2); Indiana wants all contracts with teachers to be in writing (Ind. Code Ann. §20-6.1-4-3); North Carolina requires contracts with non-English-speaking Cherokee Indians to be in writing (N.C. Gen. Stat. §22-3); North Dakota mandates a writing for contracts involving seeds (N.D. Cent. Code §4-25-02); Arkansas does so for contracts concerning political campaigns (Ark. Stat. Ann. §3-1101); and Minnesota requires a writing for nonmarital cohabitation agreements between a man and a woman who are contemplating sexual relations

(Minn. Stat. Ann. §513.175). Before practicing law in any given jurisdiction you should pore through your state statutes for variations like these.

In the twenty-first century many communications are not consummated by signing a piece of paper, but instead reside in emails, website "click here if you agree" instructions, fax transmissions, and so on. Both state law (the Uniform Electronic Transactions Act, or UETA) and federal law (Electronic Signatures in Global and National Commerce Act, 15 U.S.C. §7001, commonly called "E-Sign") allow electronic records to satisfy most legal requirements mandating a "signed writing." More specifically, courts have found that an email can be a "writing" under the statute of frauds. See Buckles Management, LLC v. InvestorDigs, LLC, 728 F. Supp. 2d 1145 (D. Colo. 2010). More will be said about electronic signatures and the statutes governing them later in this chapter.

A.   Executor/Administrator Contracts

Contracts by an executor or administrator to answer for the debts of a decedent and payable out of the executor/administrator's own personal assets generally must be in writing. For example, assume D died leaving a debt of $5,000 to C. A, the administrator of D's estate, promises C that he will pay D's debt out of his own pocket. Unless A's promise is in writing, the promise is unenforceable. This writing requirement has generated little litigation. Note the similarity of this requirement with the writing requirement for suretyship contracts discussed later. In both types of contracts, one person is agreeing to answer for the debts of another.

B.   Suretyship Contracts

A "surety" is someone who agrees to be liable for paying someone else's debt. People often agree to become sureties with very little thought about the consequences, thus becoming the so-called fool with a pen (the Bible has a similar thought: "A man void of understanding . . . becometh surety in the presence of his friend" — Proverbs 17:18). In the desire to help out a friend or relative who is temporarily financially embarrassed (and who often assures the prospective surety "I guarantee you that you really won't have to pay"), the surety cosigns and, like it or not, understand it or not, takes on liability for the debt. Because becoming a surety is filled with many poorly understood consequences, the statute of frauds provides that a promise to answer for "debt, default or miscarriage of another" (i.e., the promise to become a surety) must be in writing before it is enforceable. Like most doctrines there are exceptions, and the next case explores the primary one.

FILO v. LIBERATO
Court of Appeals of Ohio, 2013
987 N.E.2d 707

WAITE, J.

[¶1] Appellant, Anthony Filo, was a subcontractor on a commercial construction project owned by Appellee, Michael Liberato. Appellant approached Appellee during August of 2006 because the general contractor was behind in making payments to Appellant. According to Appellant, Appellee promised him that he would be fully paid. Appellant subsequently received $7,000.00 of the alleged $33,600.00 owed. Appellee also released payment in full to another subcontractor. Appellant was never paid the remainder of the amount owed.

[¶2] In March of 2010, Appellant filed suit against Appellee for payment. The trial court granted a Civ. R. 12(B)(6) motion and dismissed all of Appellant's claims. The judgment of the trial court dismissing Appellant's conversion claim is affirmed. The trial court's dismissal of Appellant's promissory estoppel, unjust enrichment and fraud claims is reversed, as these claims are supported by the pleadings.

FACTUAL AND PROCEDURAL HISTORY

[¶3] Appellant, Anthony Filo, provided materials and services to build curbing, sidewalks, footers, floors and a trash enclosure as well as other excavation and concrete work on a commercial construction project at 789 Wick Avenue. Appellant performed the work under contract to D & R Construction and Maintenance, the general contractor in charge of the Belleria Pizza commercial building project. Appellee, Michael Liberato, is the owner of the property at 789 Wick Ave., where Appellant worked as a subcontractor pursuant to the contract with D & R Construction. According to Appellant, at some point during August of 2006 he was owed $33,600.00. Appellant was not receiving payment from D & R Construction and approached Appellee directly about the amount due. According to Appellant, Appellee promised him full payment. Appellant later received $7,000.00, but never received the balance. Appellant alleges that Appellee controlled the draws on the financial institution financing the project and Appellee released payment to at least one other subcontractor, who performed work after Appellant, without paying Appellant as promised. As a result, on March 31, 2010, Appellant filed a complaint against Appellee, alleging promissory estoppel, unjust enrichment, conversion and fraud. . . .

On January 7, 2011, the trial court dismissed the amended complaint. The matter is now before us on Appellant's timely appeal.

[¶8] The statute of frauds, R.C. 1335.05, was last amended in 1976 and provides:

> **Certain agreements to be in writing.** No action shall be brought whereby to charge the defendant, upon a special promise, to answer for the debt, default, or miscarriage of another person; . . . or upon a contract or sale of lands, tenements, or hereditaments, or interest in or concerning them . . . unless the agreement upon which such action is brought, or some memorandum or note thereof, is in writing and signed by the party to be charged therewith or some other person thereunto by him or her lawfully authorized. . . .

[¶9] The thrust of Appellant's argument in his first assignment of error is that he is entitled to compensation for the work benefitting and retained by Appellee that was completed in reliance on Appellee's oral promise that he would be paid. Appellant contends that the doctrine of promissory estoppel should be applied in this instance to prevent Appellee from retaining the benefit of Appellant's work without compensating Appellant. The trial court held that because promises to pay the debt of another are subject to the statute of frauds and Appellant failed to allege that a written promise existed, his claim for promissory estoppel "cannot be proven and must be dismissed." (1/7/11 J.E., p. 4.) The trial court was mistaken in this conclusion.

[The court found that promissory estoppel could be used as a cause of action for damages where a contract was not in writing and therefore could not be enforced because of the statute of frauds. This did not mean that the contract was enforced, however, merely that some damages could be recovered. The court then moved on to whether the statute of frauds itself was satisfied by the facts of this case.]

[¶17] In Appellant's first assignment he mentions the "leading object" rule, but does not rely on this theory for the body of his argument. In this assignment, however, Appellant argues that a writing is also not required to enforce the oral promise in this instance because the promise was made to protect Appellee's own pecuniary interest in the completion of the project. In addition to the general rules of pleading, when alleging fraud, "the circumstances constituting fraud or mistake shall be stated with particularity. Malice, intent, knowledge, and other condition of mind of a person may be averred generally." Civ. R. 9(B). Appellant specifically alleges in the amended complaint: "The leading object of Defendant's [Appellee's] promise to Plaintiff [Appellant] was to serve Defendant's own pecuniary or business purpose, i.e. detering [sic] Plaintiff from filing a mechanic's lien against the Property and having Plaintiff complete the Project." (8/6/11 Amend. Compl., ¶11.) Unlike the doctrine of promissory estoppel, which creates a remedy for parties who could not otherwise recover because they acted to their detriment on an unenforceable oral promise, the "leading object" rule excuses the writing requirement of the statute of frauds and, in effect, makes an oral promise into an enforceable contract. The driving principle of the leading object rule is to prevent the use of the writing requirement to "effectuate a wrong" "which the statute's enactment was to prevent." Wilson Floors v. Sciota Park, Ltd., 54 Ohio St. 2d 451, 460, 377 N.E.2d 514 (1978).

[¶18] The use of the "leading object" rule is a matter of first impression in this district. Appellant's complaint contains several allegations. The first, that he relied on Appellee's promise to pay for the benefit conferred by the work Appellant performed for Appellee, falls under a classic promissory estoppel claim and so is not barred by the statute of frauds, as already discussed. The second, however, is that Appellee promised to pay because Appellant would have stopped work and/or taken other legal action that would slow or end construction. At first blush, this promise by Appellee looks to be a promise to pay the debt owed by the general contractor. Ordinarily, this promise to pay the debt of another is required to be in writing, undoubtedly because it would ordinarily not be apparent why one would undertake to pay a debt one does not owe. However, where it is readily apparent that it is the promisor who will benefit from this seemingly altruistic act, the statute of frauds and its protections need not be invoked. The Ohio Supreme Court explains: "When the leading object of the promisor is not to answer for another's debt but to subserve some pecuniary or business purpose of his own involving a benefit to himself, his promise is not within the statute of frauds, although the original debtor may remain liable." *Wilson Floors, supra,* syllabus. In Ohio, when the rule began to emerge as a defense or excuse to the requirements of the statute of frauds, one test for the application of the rule was whether the promisor had become primarily or solely liable for the debt by making the promise. The Supreme Court dispensed with the primary liability requirement in *Wilson Floors,* and clarified two separate tests for the leading object rule, the second of which appears applicable to the facts as alleged by Appellant:

> Under the second test, it is of no consequence that when such promise is made, the original obligor remains primarily liable or that the third party continues to look to the original obligor for payment. So long as the promisor undertakes to pay the subcontractor whatever his services are worth irrespective of what he may owe the general contractor, and so long as the main purpose of the promisor is to further his own business or pecuniary interest, the promise is enforceable.

Wilson Floors at 459, 377 N.E.2d 514, referencing *Williston on Contracts* (3 Ed. 1960). This formulation of the leading object rule has been infrequently, but consistently, applied by state and federal courts throughout Ohio. . . .

[¶20] The leading object rule generally appears in situations similar to the matter at bar: a subcontractor or material supplier has gone unpaid by the general contractor and is promised by the owner, the investor, or the funding source that the debt will be paid in full. The promise is not put into writing and payment is not forthcoming. Under these circumstances the Ohio Supreme Court, the Eighth District Court of Appeals, the Tenth District Court of Appeals, and the United States District Court for the Northern District of Ohio have all found that this oral promise to pay the debt of another is not required to be in writing when the promisor has a pecuniary interest in the outcome that will result from the promise to pay the subcontractor; that is, completion of the subcontractor's work.

[¶21] In *Wilson Floors,* an oral promise was made by a bank officer of the bank financing the project. The bank promised the subcontractor "that payments would be forthcoming upon a resumption of work." The Court held this was an enforceable oral contract to pay the debts of another because "the bank made its guarantee to Wilson to subserve its own business interest of reducing the costs to complete the project." *Id.* at 454 and 460, 377 N.E.2d 514. In F & D Siding Services v. Commarato, 8th Dist. No. 78038, 2001 WL 455829 (April 26, 2001), the owner's oral promise to personally repay the debts of his various businesses to the subcontractor and supplier who provided siding materials and services to multiple construction projects was held valid and enforceable due to the promisor's pecuniary interest in these continued services. The subcontractor's reliance on the promise in this instance was reasonable in the context of a history of oral agreements between the parties and partial payment on demand by means of personal checks. "Since there was evidence that the defendant's 'leading object' or main purpose in making the promise was to promote his own business interest, the trial court's finding that the statute of frauds did not apply is not against the manifest weight of the evidence." *Id.* *4. . . .

Appellant's third assignment of error is sustained. . . .

Problem 88

Mame Dennis took her nephew Patrick to the grocery store near St. Boniface Academy and told the proprietor to let him charge anything he wanted and send the bill to her. The proprietor agreed, and over the course of the semester Patrick charged quite a large amount. On getting the bill, Mame was flabbergasted. She phoned the proprietor and bawled him out for letting the tab get so high, saying that she refused to pay anything. When the grocery store sued, she defended, using the suretyship portion of the statute of frauds. Will this defense succeed? What exactly was Patrick's obligation here?

Problem 89

When Henry Pulling needed a loan, he asked his Aunt Augusta if she would become his surety. When she demurred initially, he promised her that in return for her undertaking this obligation, he would give to her an urn once belonging to his now deceased mother. She agreed to cosign for him in an amount of $10,000. He delivered the urn to her, but she then changed her mind and decided not to cosign the promissory note that the bank had Henry sign. He sued her. May she defend on the basis of the statute of frauds?

NO, promise to be a surity Needs to be in writing [handwritten]

C. Made in Consideration of Marriage

This part of the statute of frauds, contracts "made upon consideration of marriage," is almost never litigated. One case holding an oral promise unenforceable under this requirement involved a promise by A to support B's child if B would marry A; Byers v. Byers, 618 P.2d 930 (Okla. 1980). Another oral promise unenforceable because of this requirement was a promise by X to leave all property to Y upon X's death if Y would promise to marry X; Tatum v. Tatum, 606 S.W.2d 31 (Tex. Civ. App. 1980). Note, however, that the statute of frauds only applies when one person promises to marry and the other person promises *to do something else,* that is, the statute does *not* govern "an agreement which consists only of mutual promises of two persons to marry each other." Restatement (Second) of Contracts §124.

only governs when Not Mutual agreement to Marry [handwritten]

Problem 90

Over supper one evening Edwin proposed to Angelina that he would adopt her child from a previous relationship, Ida, if Angelina married him. She accepted. Edwin and Angelina married, but Edwin now refuses to adopt Ida. Angelina sues him for breach of contract. Edwin defends by pointing to the lack of a writing. Who wins?

Edwin wins, see Byer v. Byer above [handwritten]

D. Land Transactions

There are two main issues with contracts for the sale of realty: What types of "transfers" are covered and what exactly is "realty"? Clearly, agreements to buy or sell land are within the types of transfers contemplated. Generally, assumptions, extensions, or modifications of real estate mortgages are also covered. See, e.g., Marine Midland Bank v. Northeast Kawasaki, Inc., 92 A.D.2d 952, 460 N.Y.S.2d 666 (1983). An agreement affecting the boundary line of adjoining landowners has been held not to require a writing. Norberg v. Fitzgerald, 122 N.H. 1080, 453 A.2d 1301 (1982); but see Restatement (Second) of Contracts §128. A promise to devise land is within the statute; Illustration 5 to Restatement (Second) of Contracts §125. The original statute of frauds covered all leases, but today in most states leases

of a short duration (one to three years, typically) are statutorily exempt from
the writing requirement.

WADDLE v. ELROD
Supreme Court of Tennessee, 2012
367 S.W.3d 217

CORNELIA A. CLARK, C.J.

[handwritten: Two Issues]

[handwritten: 1] In this appeal we must determine whether the Statute of Frauds, Tenn.
Code Ann. §29-2-101(a)(4) (Supp. 2011), applies to a settlement agreement
requiring the transfer of an interest in real property; and, if so, whether
emails exchanged by the parties' attorneys satisfy the Statute of Frauds *[handwritten: 2]*
under the Uniform Electronic Transactions Act ("UETA"), Tenn. Code
Ann. §§47-10-101 to -123 (2001 & Supp. 2011). We hold that the Statute
of Frauds applies to settlement agreements requiring the transfer of an
interest in real property and that the emails, along with a legal description
of the property contained in the cross-claim, satisfy the Statute of Frauds.

Accordingly, we affirm the judgment of the Court of Appeals enforcing
the settlement agreement.

FACTS AND PROCEDURAL HISTORY

On January 29, 2007, Regent Investments 1, LLC ("Regent") sued octo-
genarian Earline Waddle, and her niece, Lorene Elrod. According to the
allegations of the complaint, Regent contracted to purchase from
Ms. Waddle approximately four acres of real property located at 2268
Prim Lane, in Rutherford County, Tennessee ("the Prim Lane property"),
for $230,000. Regent paid Ms. Waddle $10,000 earnest money when the
contract was signed. However, in preparing to close the deal, Regent learned
of a quitclaim deed by which Ms. Waddle had conveyed one-half of her
interest in the Prim Lane property to Ms. Elrod. Regent sued Ms. Waddle,
alleging breach of contract, fraud, and intentional and negligent misrepresentation. Regent requested specific performance, $1,000,000 in damages,
attorney's fees, costs, and pre-judgment interest. Regent also asked the trial
court to set aside the quitclaim deed, arguing that Ms. Elrod had wrongfully
obtained her one-half interest by exercising undue influence over
Ms. Waddle.

[handwritten: Regent sued Waddle]

On May 14, 2007, Ms. Waddle filed a cross-claim against Ms. Elrod, also
alleging that Ms. Elrod had acquired her one-half interest in the Prim
Lane property through undue influence. The cross-claim included a legal
description of the Prim Lane property. According to the allegations of the

[handwritten: Waddle filed cross-claim against Elrod for undue influence]

cross-claim, after Ms. Waddle's husband of more than fifty years died on February 12, 2001, Ms. Elrod began frequently visiting Ms. Waddle. In early March 2001, Ms. Elrod arranged for her own attorney, whom Ms. Waddle did not know, to draft both the quitclaim deed conveying a one-half interest in the Prim Lane property to Ms. Elrod and a durable power of attorney naming Ms. Elrod as Ms. Waddle's attorney-in-fact. On March 15, 2001, Ms. Elrod drove Ms. Waddle to the attorney's office and persuaded her to sign both documents. Ms. Waddle alleged that she did not have the benefit of independent legal counsel prior to signing the documents, that Ms. Elrod provided no money or consideration for the interest she acquired in the Prim Lane property, that she did not willingly or knowingly intend to convey any interest in the Prim Lane property to Ms. Elrod, and that the power of attorney executed contemporaneously with the quitclaim deed created a confidential relationship giving rise to a presumption of undue influence with respect to the quitclaim deed. Ms. Waddle asked the trial court to set aside the quitclaim deed and to award her "any and all damages" caused by Ms. Elrod's undue influence, including, and in particular, the damages resulting from Ms. Waddle's inability to convey Regent marketable title to the Prim Lane property.

On July 10, 2007, Ms. Elrod filed an answer to the cross-claim, denying all allegations of undue influence and wrongdoing and arguing that the assistance she had provided Ms. Waddle served as consideration for the quitclaim deed.

On April 28, 2009, Regent agreed to dismiss with prejudice its claims against Ms. Waddle and Ms. Elrod. In exchange, Ms. Waddle agreed to return Regent's $10,000 earnest money, and both Ms. Waddle and Ms. Elrod agreed that Regent would not be responsible for any portion of the court costs. Ms. Waddle's cross-claim against Ms. Elrod remained pending, however, with a jury trial scheduled for June 2 to June 4, 2009.

The day before trial, Ms. Elrod's attorney, Mr. Gregory Reed, advised Ms. Hagan, counsel for Ms. Waddle, that Ms. Elrod was willing to return her one-half interest in the Prim Lane property to avoid going to trial if Ms. Waddle would settle the case and release all other claims against her. Through her attorney, Ms. Waddle agreed to settle the case on the condition that she would not be responsible for any of the court costs. Around 4:00 P.M., Mr. Reed advised Ms. Hagan that Ms. Elrod had agreed to settle the case with Ms. Waddle's condition. At 4:34 P.M., Ms. Hagan sent the following email to Mr. Reed:

Greg,
This confirms that we have settled this case on the following terms:
Elrod deeds property interest back to Waddle, Both [sic] parties sign full release, Waddle bears no court costs.
Let me know if I have correctly stated our agreement.

Thanks,
Mary Beth

At 5:02 P.M., Mr. Reed responded:

That is the agreement. I understand that you will draft the deed and take a shot at the court's order. No admission of guilt is to be included.

Greg Reed

The attorneys thereafter advised the trial court of the terms of the agreement. Believing that a settlement had been reached and that a written order memorializing the settlement would be entered later, the trial court cancelled the jury trial and excused prospective jurors. Counsel for Ms. Waddle prepared and forwarded the settlement documents to counsel for Ms. Elrod. Ms. Waddle, understanding that the settlement had returned sole ownership of the Prim Lane property to her, paid all outstanding property taxes. Approximately three weeks later, however, Ms. Elrod advised her attorney that she had changed her mind and no longer wanted to settle the case. When Ms. Elrod refused to sign the settlement documents, Mr. Reed moved to withdraw from further representation, and the trial court granted Mr. Reed's motion.

On July 13, 2009, Ms. Waddle filed a motion asking the trial court to enforce the settlement agreement. On September 2, 2009, Ms. Elrod filed a response, arguing that the discussions on June 1, 2009, resulted merely in an agreement to agree, with many important material terms unresolved. Alternatively, Ms. Elrod argued that the Statute of Frauds, Tenn. Code Ann. §29-2-101 (Supp. 2011), bars enforcement of the settlement agreement because it required the transfer of an interest in real property and was not evidenced by a writing signed by Ms. Elrod or her attorney describing with specificity the terms of the agreement and the property at issue. Relying on the Uniform Electronic Transactions Act ("UETA"), *see* Tenn. Code Ann. §§47-10-101 to -123 (2001 & Supp. 2011), Ms. Waddle argued in response that the email from Ms. Elrod's attorney, which confirmed the terms of the settlement and included Mr. Reed's typewritten name, constituted a writing signed by an agent of the party to be charged and satisfied the Statute of Frauds.

Following a hearing, the trial court entered an order on September 15, 2009, enforcing the settlement agreement. The trial court found that Ms. Elrod had agreed through her attorney and authorized agent to settle the case on the terms set out in the June 1, 2009 email. As a result, the trial court divested Ms. Elrod of any right, title, or interest in the Prim Lane property and vested ownership of the property in Ms. Waddle. The trial court also dismissed with prejudice Ms. Waddle's remaining claims against Ms. Elrod, ordered each party to bear her own attorney's fees and discretionary costs, and taxed court costs to Ms. Waddle. The trial court's order did not expressly address either Ms. Elrod's argument that the Statute of Frauds precluded enforcement of the settlement or Ms. Waddle's argument that the emails constituted writings signed by the party to be charged under the UETA and satisfied the Statute of Frauds.

Ms. Elrod appealed, but she did not challenge the trial court's factual finding that the parties had reached an agreement to settle the case. Rather, she argued that the Statute of Frauds precludes enforcement of the settlement agreement. The Court of Appeals rejected this argument and affirmed the trial court's judgment enforcing the settlement agreement, reasoning that the Statute of Frauds applies only to "any contract for the *sale* of lands," Tenn. Code Ann. §29-2-101(a)(4) (emphasis added), and does not apply to a settlement agreement requiring the transfer of an interest in real property. [Citation omitted.]

Appealed

Court of Appeals reasoning ↳ Issue 1

We granted Ms. Elrod's application for permission to appeal. . . .

Appealed to SC

As the Court of Appeals recognized, Ms. Elrod does not dispute that the parties reached an agreement; rather, she argues that the Statute of Frauds applies and precludes enforcement of the settlement agreement because it required the transfer of an interest in real property. In contrast, Ms. Waddle argues that the Court of Appeals' judgment should be affirmed because the relevant portion of the Statute of Frauds applies only to contracts for the sale of land. Alternatively, Ms. Waddle maintains that the emails counsel exchanged and the legal description of the Prim Lane property in Ms. Waddle's cross-claim satisfy the Statute of Frauds.

A settlement agreement made during the course of litigation is a contract between the parties, and as such, contract law governs disputes concerning the formation, construction, and enforceability of the settlement agreement. . . . Like other contracts, a settlement agreement may be subject to the Statute of Frauds. The Statute of Frauds precludes actions to enforce certain types of parol contracts unless the action is supported by written evidence of the parties' agreement. . . .

Settlement agreement is a contract

The settlement agreement in the present case requires a conveyance of real property. With respect to real property, Tennessee's Statute of Frauds provides:

> No action shall be brought . . . [u]pon any contract for the sale of lands, tenements, or hereditaments, . . . unless the promise or agreement, upon which such action shall be brought, or some memorandum or note thereof, shall be in writing, and signed by the party to be charged therewith, or some other person lawfully authorized by such party. In a contract for the sale of lands, tenements, or hereditaments, the party to be charged is the party against whom enforcement of the contract is sought.

TN SoF

Tenn. Code Ann. §29-2-101(a)(4) (Supp. 2011).

The primary purpose of the Statute of Frauds is to reduce the risk of fraud and perjury associated with oral testimony. [Citations omitted.] The Statute of Frauds also fosters certainty in transactions by ensuring that

Purpose of SoF

contract formation is not "based upon loose statements or innuendoes long after witnesses have become unavailable or when memories of the precise agreement have been dimmed by the passage of time." *Price,* 682 S.W.2d at 932 (citing Boutwell v. Lewis Bros. Lumber Co., 27 Tenn. App. 460, 182 S. W.2d 1, 3 (1944)). Another purpose of the Statute of Frauds is to protect property owners against "hasty or inconsiderate agreements concerning a valuable species of property" and "misunderstandings as to the nature and extent of such agreements." Brandel v. Moore Mortg. & Inv. Co., 774 S.W.2d 600, 604 (Tenn. Ct. App. 1989).

While this Court has long emphasized that the Statute of Frauds should be strictly adhered to and construed to accomplish its intended purposes, Newman v. Carroll, 11 Tenn. (3 Yer.) 18, 26 (1832), the Statute of Frauds is an affirmative defense. See Tenn. R. Civ. P. 8.03. In other words, parol agreements within the Statute of Frauds are not void ab initio, and enforcement of such agreements may be barred only if a party pleads the Statute of Frauds. *See, e.g., Cobble,* 230 S.W.2d at 196; Bailey v. Henry, 125 Tenn. 390, 143 S.W. 1124, 1127 (1912); Brakefield v. Anderson, 87 Tenn. 206, 10 S.W. 360, 361 (1889). Parties may choose to abide by parol contracts for the sale of land. *Bailey,* 143 S.W. at 1127 ("[I]f the parties themselves choose to execute the contract, third parties cannot object."); *Brakefield,* 10 S.W. at 361 ("Such a contract may be enforced by the consent and upon the application of both parties."). Indeed, the Statute of Frauds "was not enacted for the purpose of permitting a person to avoid a contract. Its object was not to grant a privilege to a person to refuse to perform what he has agreed to do. It was not enacted as a shield to the dishonest. . . ." *Cobble,* 230 S.W.2d at 196.

The word "sale," used in the statutory phrase "contract for the sale of lands, tenements, or hereditaments," has long been broadly interpreted to mean any alienation of real property, including even a donation of realty. *Bailey,* 143 S.W. at 1127. This Court has previously explained that such a broad construction is consistent both with the purposes of the Statute of Frauds and with the common law understanding of the term:

> The word "sale" in our statute of frauds (section 3142, Shannon's Code) means alienation, and an action on a parol contract made by the owner binding him to give or donate land to another, would, we think, fall within the terms of that statute. A contrary holding would open a wide door to perjury and fraud, and defeat, as we think, one of the purposes of the statute. . . .

[The court then determined that a settlement agreement requiring a transfer of an interest in real property was enough of a "sale" to trigger the application of the statute of frauds.]

We next consider whether the Statute of Frauds bars enforcement of the settlement agreement at issue in this appeal. As already explained, parol contracts are enforceable if "some memorandum or note thereof, shall be in writing and signed by the party to be charged therewith, or some other person lawfully authorized by such party." Tenn. Code Ann. §29-2-101(a)(4). The Statute of Frauds does not require a written contract, only a written memorandum or note evidencing the parties' agreement. *Huffine*, 257 S.W. at 89. Additionally, while the writing required by the Statute of Frauds must contain the essential terms of the contract, it need not be in a single document. *See* Lambert v. Home Fed. Sav. & Loan Ass'n, 481 S.W.2d 770, 773 (Tenn. 1972). As this Court explained in *Lambert*:

> The general rule is that the memorandum, in order to satisfy the statute, must contain the essential terms of the contract, expressed with such certainty that they may be understood from the memorandum itself or some other writing to which it refers or with which it is connected, without resorting to parol evidence. A memorandum disclosing merely that a contract had been made, without showing what the contract is, is not sufficient to satisfy the requirement of the Statute of Frauds that there be a memorandum in writing of the contract.

Id. (quoting 49 Am. Jur. *Statute of Frauds* §353, 363-64). [Citations omitted.]

Of course, even if one or more memoranda are produced sufficiently describing the terms of a parol agreement, the Statute of Frauds also requires that one of the writings be signed by the party to be charged or by some other person authorized to act on that party's behalf. Tenn. Code Ann. §29-2-101(a)(4). The authority of the agent or the evidence of his agency need not be in writing, however. [Citations omitted.] While the Statute of Frauds does not define "signed," many years ago the Court of Appeals considered whether a party's printed name on a bill of sale satisfied the signature requirement. *See* Gessler v. Winton, 24 Tenn. App. 411, 145 S. W.2d 789 (1940). In holding that the printed name was sufficient, the Court of Appeals stated:

> The [S]tatute [of Frauds] does not specify any particular form of signing. It merely requires that the party to be charged shall have signed the memorandum. It has been held that a cross mark is a good signature; also initials; even numerals, when used with the intention of constituting a signature; and a typewritten name or imprint made by a rubber stamp has the same effect; and this is equally true, though the typewriting or stamp impression be made by another, if the person to be charged has directed it. . . . This has been the law in England for more than a century, and has been followed quite generally in this country.

Id. at 794 (citations and internal quotation marks omitted).

While *Gessler* predates email, its holding appears broad enough to encompass typed names appearing in emails. However, we need not rely upon *Gessler* to determine whether the email that includes the name of Ms. Elrod's attorney satisfies the Statute of Frauds requirement of a writing signed by the party to be charged. In 2001 the General Assembly enacted the

UETA

UETA. Ms. Waddle relied upon the UETA in the trial court when arguing that the email constituted a writing for purposes of the Statute of Frauds and that Mr. Reed's name on the email constituted the signature of an agent of Ms. Elrod, the party to be charged. She has continued to advance these arguments on appeal.

The UETA "applies to electronic records and electronic signatures relating to a transaction." Tenn. Code Ann. §47-10-103(a). The General Assembly has declared that the UETA:

must be construed and applied to:

(1) Facilitate electronic transactions consistent with other applicable law;
(2) Be consistent with reasonable practices concerning electronic transactions and with the continued expansion of those practices; and
(3) Effectuate its general purpose to make uniform the law with respect to the subject of [the UETA] among states enacting it.

Determined by Conduct and the Surrounding circumstances

Tenn. Code Ann. §47-10-106. The UETA does not require parties to conduct transactions by electronic means. Tenn. Code Ann. §47-10-105(a). Rather, the UETA governs "transactions between parties each of which has agreed to conduct transactions by electronic means. Whether the parties agree to conduct a transaction by electronic means is determined from the context and surrounding circumstances, including the parties' conduct." Tenn. Code Ann. §47-10-105(a)-(b). "Transaction means an action or set of actions occurring between two (2) or more persons relating to the conduct of business, commercial, or governmental affairs." Tenn. Code Ann. §47-10-102(16). Under the UETA:

(a) A record or signature may not be denied legal effect or enforceability solely because it is in electronic form.
(b) A contract may not be denied legal effect or enforceability solely because an electronic record was used in its formation.
(c) If a law requires a record to be in writing, an electronic record satisfies the law.
(d) If a law requires a signature, an electronic signature satisfies the law.

"Electronic Signature"

Tenn. Code Ann. §47-10-107(a)-(d). "Electronic signature" includes "an electronic sound, symbol, or process attached to or logically associated with a record and executed or adopted by a person with the intent to sign the record." Tenn. Code Ann. §47-10-102(8); *see also id.* cmt. 7 ("[T]he mere inclusion of one's name as part of an email message" qualifies as an electronic signature "so long as in each case the signer executed or adopted the symbol with the intent to sign.").

Holding of Issue

Applying the foregoing principles, we conclude that the Statute of Frauds does not bar enforcement of the settlement agreement at issue in this appeal. The parties, through their attorneys, evidenced an intent to finalize the settlement by electronic means; thus, the UETA applies. *See, e.g.,* Crestwood Shops, L.L.C. v. Hilkene, 197 S.W.3d 641, 651-53 (Mo. Ct. App. 2006) (holding that the UETA applied because the parties manifested their intent to conduct business by email). Pursuant to section 47-10-107(c), the emails counsel exchanged constitute a signed memorandum, note, or writing for purposes of the Statute of Frauds.

Parties showed Intent

Additionally, under the principles discussed in *Lambert,* the emails, considered along with the legal description of the Prim Lane property in the cross-claim, described the terms of the parol agreement with sufficient specificity to satisfy the Statute of Frauds. In particular, the emails described the following four material terms of the settlement: (1) Ms. Elrod would convey her interest "in the property" back to Ms. Waddle; (2) each party would sign a release giving up any claims she may have had against the other party; (3) Ms. Waddle would not be responsible for court costs; and (4) Ms. Elrod would not admit guilt. Ms. Elrod's attorney confirmed the settlement, responding electronically "[t]hat is our agreement." While the emails referred only to "the property," the Prim Lane property was the only realty at issue in the litigation, and Ms. Waddle's cross-claim included a full legal description of the Prim Lane property. As stated in *Lambert,* a writing is sufficient if the terms of the agreement may be understood either from the writing itself or from some other writing connected with it. The emails and cross-claim satisfy this standard.

All material Elements were Satisfied

Furthermore, although Ms. Elrod did not sign the email, there is no dispute that Mr. Reed was acting as her agent when he negotiated the settlement. Had he written his signature on a printed version of the email, rather than typed his name at the end of the email, his signature would undoubtedly have been sufficient to satisfy the Statute of Frauds. The UETA, recognizing that all sorts of transactions are now routinely conducted by electronic means on a daily basis, obviates the need for a handwritten signature. Mr. Reed's typed name at the end of the email constitutes an "electronic signature." Tenn. Code Ann. §47-10-107(d). As the agent of Ms. Elrod, Mr. Reed's electronic signature on the email confirming the terms of the settlement agreement satisfies the signature requirement of the Statute of Frauds. [Citations omitted.]

Elrod's Agent signed the email

CONCLUSION

The Statute of Frauds applies to settlement agreements requiring the transfer of an interest in real property. However, the Statute of Frauds does not bar enforcement of the settlement agreement at issue in this appeal. The emails counsel for the parties exchanged, along with the legal description of the Prim Lane property included in the cross-claim, constitute a sufficiently definite writing, note, or memorandum, and the email confirming the terms of the settlement agreement included the electronic signature of the attorney and authorized agent of Ms. Elrod, the party to be charged. Thus, on these alternate grounds we affirm the Court of Appeals' judgment enforcing the settlement agreement, including the taxing of court costs to Ms. Elrod. Costs of this appeal also are taxed to Ms. Elrod, for which execution may issue if necessary.

———

Electronic signatures. At both the federal and state level statutes have been enacted to facilitate electronic commerce as civilization moves from the world of paper into cyberspace. The states acted first, with many of them adopting the Uniform Electronic Transactions Act (UETA) (used in the case above), and the federal government followed with the similar Electronic Signatures in Global and National Commerce Act, 15 U.S.C. §7001, commonly known as "E-Sign." The latter statute applies only in jurisdictions not adopting UETA. As of 2012, Illinois, New York, and Washington were the only states not to have enacted UETA. Both statutes should be in your statute book. White and Summers have a clear discussion of the statutes. See White and Summers, §§1-3 and 3-9.

The basic thrust of these statutes is to allow electronic records in most commercial transactions even if other statutes, such as the statute of frauds, require a writing or a written signature. With certain exceptions (utility cut-off notices, notices of default, repossession, foreclosure and eviction, insurance cancellations, etc.), almost all legal communications by the parties to a transaction can now be accomplished electronically. The statutes provide only that electronic communications may meet the requirements for a writing or signature. They do not provide substantive rules, such as how contracts are formed or what terms will be included in the contract. See Alliance Laundry Systems, LLC v. Thyssenkrupp Materials, NA, 570 F. Supp. 2d 1061, 66 UCC Rep. Serv. 2d 427 (E.D. Wis. 2008).

There are a number of unsettled issues as to electronic signatures. Both of the statutes mentioned require that if a consumer is involved, he or she must have *agreed* to electronic disclosures, but it is unclear exactly what this means. The federal statute is broader, requiring that there be *electronic agreement or confirmation of agreement,* and this agreement must be "affirmative"; 15 U.S.C. §7001(c)(1)(C)(ii). This means that the consumer must have agreed electronically to receive electronic records or have confirmed this consent electronically. UETA is less clear about this, though Comment 4 to §5 indicates that the consumer's agreement to receive electronic communications must be actual and not imposed unconscionably as part of the fine print in a written contract.

There is also no consensus on what electronic communication means. Is it sufficient for the required information to be posted on a website (the so-called come and get it notice) that the consumer must periodically access (which, of course, most won't do) to keep informed? In the 1990s, AOL posted rate changes only on its website, making customers agree that this was sufficient notice of any hike in the rate, only to back down when 19 Attorneys General objected that the practice was unfair and deceptive. What about email notification? Must it be highlighted in such a way that the consumer will recognize its importance and not delete it as "spam"? If the consumer has switched email addresses, then what? Must the sender do something with bounced-back messages? These matters and others will have to await judicial determination. For a summary of the consumer issues and suggested resolutions, see Braucher, Rent-Seeking and Risk-Fixing in the New Statutory Law of Electronic Commerce: Difficulties in Moving Consumer Protection Online, 2001 Wis. L. Rev. 527.

E.   The One-Year Provision

One of the most challenging aspects of the statute of frauds is its "one-year" provision. This aspect of the statute applies to agreements that cannot be fully performed within a year of their making. See Restatement (Second) of Contracts §130. This principle may sound straightforward, but it is slippery in practice.

PROFESSIONAL BULL RIDERS, INC. v. AUTOZONE, INC.
Supreme Court of Colorado, 2005
113 P.3d 757

COATS, Justice.
Pursuant to 10th Cir. R. 27.1, The United States Court of Appeals for the Tenth Circuit certified to this court the following question:

> Under Col. Rev. Stat. §38-10-112(1)(a), is an oral agreement void when: (1) the agreement contemplates performance for a definite period of more than one year but (2) allows the party to be charged an option to terminate the agreement by a certain date less than a year from the making of the agreement and when (3) the party to be charged has not exercised that option to terminate the agreement?

Issues

Pursuant to C.A.R. 21.1, we agreed to answer the question and do so now (in the context provided us) in the negative.

I

The certifying court provided the following statement of factual and procedural circumstances, giving context to the question.

In the years leading up to this dispute, the defendant AutoZone sponsored events conducted by the plaintiff Professional Bull Riders (PBR). For the years 2001 and 2002, PBR prepared a written agreement to provide for AutoZone's sponsorship. Section I of that agreement states:

> The term of this agreement shall commence as of December 29, 2000 and end on December 31, 2002, unless terminated earlier in accordance with the provisions of this Agreement. Notwithstanding the preceding sentence, AutoZone may, at its option, elect to terminate this Agreement and its sponsorship of PBR and the Series effective as of the end of the Finals in 2001, by giving PBR written notice of termination by no later than August 15, 2001.

AutoZone never signed this agreement. However, PBR alleges that by its actions, AutoZone tacitly accepted its terms set forth in the proposed written agreement and that, as a result, the parties entered into an oral agreement mirroring the terms set forth in writing.

There appears to be a factual dispute as to the communications between the parties during 2001. However, it appears undisputed that in January 2002, AutoZone notified PBR that AutoZone would not be sponsoring PBR events in 2002. However, despite this notice, AutoZone alleges, "PBR continued to use AutoZone's protected trade name and service mark for an indeterminate period of time in its programs."

PBR then sued AutoZone for breach of the oral sponsorship agreement. Speedbar, a wholly-owned subsidiary of AutoZone and the owner of the trade name and service mark, "AutoZone," intervened. AutoZone and Speedbar filed a counterclaim alleging service and trademark infringement, unfair competition, and service mark dilution.

As to PBR's breach of contract claim, the district court granted summary judgment to AutoZone. The court reasoned that the oral contract could not be performed within one year and was therefore unenforceable under the Colorado statute of frauds, Col. Rev. Stat. §38-10-112, which provides, in part:

> (1) Except for contracts for the sale of goods . . . and lease contracts . . . , in the following cases every agreement shall be void, unless such agreement or some note or memorandum thereof is in writing and subscribed by the party charged therewith:
>
>   (a) Every agreement that by the terms is not to be performed within one year after the making thereof.

The district court explained:

> Although no Colorado court has ruled on the question of whether the statute of frauds governs an oral contract which, by its express terms, is to last for more than one year but which contains a provision allowing one party to terminate the contract before the end of the first year, case law from other jurisdictions indicates that the statute of frauds will bar an action on verbal agreements that

the parties intend to put into writing. For example, in Klinke v. Famous Recipe Fried Chicken, Inc. [24 Wash. App. 202], 600 P.2d 1034 (Wash. Ct. App. 1979), after noting the general rule that "a verbal agreement to put in writing a contract which will require more than a year to be performed is within the statute of frauds and thus unenforceable," 600 P.2d at 1037, the court held that "the fact that either party has an option to put an end to the contract within a year does not take it out of the operation of the statute if, independent of the exercise of such power, the agreement cannot be performed within a year." Id. at 1038.

The district court reasoned that the purported oral contract provided for a term of two years and was thus unenforceable.

II

The origin of the statute of frauds traces to the English parliament of 1677, which adopted "An Act for Prevention of Frauds and Perjuries," commonly known as the Statute of Frauds. See Kiely v. St. Germain, 670 P.2d 764, 768 (Colo. 1983); 2 E. Allan Farnsworth, Farnsworth on Contracts §6.4, at 130 (3d ed. 2004). The overriding purpose of the Statute of Frauds was to prevent the perpetration of fraud by the device of perjury. Kiely, 670 P.2d at 768. While the English statute of frauds has since been repealed, almost every state has enacted (and currently has in force) a statute containing language substantially similar to portions of the original act. Id.

Few indicators of the precise intent of the framers of the original English provisions exist. Commentators have noted that the purpose of the one-year provision is especially puzzling.[3] Due to this provision's questionable effectiveness in carrying out the general purposes of the statute, under virtually any rationale, courts have tended to construe it narrowly, to void the fewest number of oral contracts. The provision is therefore universally understood to apply only to agreements that, by their terms, are incapable of being performed within one year.

Nevertheless, courts and commentators have disagreed sharply about the effect of various contingencies that may result in termination of an agreement in less than a year. Debate persists about whether particular kinds of termination amount to performance or merely a defeasance short of breach, such as annulment, frustration of the purposes of the contract, or excuse for nonperformance. Disagreement among authorities is particularly prevalent concerning options for one or both parties to terminate merely by giving notice. See 2 Farnsworth, §6.4, at 129-130 (stating that while some courts have held that a contract is within the statute even though

---

3. See Farnsworth, §6.4, at 130 ("[O]f all the provisions of the statute, it is the most difficult to rationalize."); [further citations omitted].

it provides that one or both parties have the power to terminate the contract within one year of its making, there is a strong contrary view, with a growing number of courts coming to regard a contract as not within the statute if one party can terminate within a year); [further citations omitted].

While there is little agreement whether an option to terminate should itself be considered an alternative way of performing, compare Hopper v. Lennen & Mitchell, Inc., 146 F.2d 364 (9th Cir. 1944) (holding that "the contract would be fulfilled in a sense originally contemplated by the parties," either by performing without exercising option to terminate or by performing until exercising option), and Johnston v. Bowersock, 62 Kan. 148, 61 P. 740, 744 (1900) (holding that if termination is authorized then it is not a breach and "if not a breach, it must be performance"), with French v. Sabey Corp., 134 Wash. 2d 547, 951 P.2d 260 (1998) (holding that option to end contract within a year does not take it out of the statute if, independent of option, the agreement cannot be performed within a year), there is, at the same time, little question that a promise of two or more performances, in the alternative, does not fall within the one-year provision if any one of the alternatives could be fully performed within one year. [Citations omitted.]

Whether a contract actually contemplates alternate performance obligations or merely provides an excuse for nonperformance, however, necessarily depends on the purposes of the parties, as expressed in the terms of the contract. Restatement (Second) of Contracts §130 cmt. b (2004) ("This distinction between performance and excuse for nonperformance is sometimes tenuous; it depends on the terms and the circumstances, particularly on whether the essential purposes of the parties will be attained."). It does not matter which party has the right to name the alternative, 4 Corbin, §19.11; Calamari, §302, at 475 n. 7, as long as the agreement contemplates that the election will establish the performance obligations of the parties rather than merely relieving the electing party of its obligations under the agreement. In keeping with the accepted narrow construction of the one-year provision of the statute of frauds, no contract that may be "fairly and reasonably interpreted such that it may be performed within one year," Cron v. Hargro Fabrics, Inc., 91 N.Y.2d 362, 670 N.Y.S.2d 973, 694 N.E.2d 56 (1998), will be voided by it.

III

Colorado enacted the one-year provision of the statute of frauds in 1861, drawing heavily from the English statute, and the language of that provision has never been amended. See Sec. 12, 1861 Colo. Sess. Laws 241 (currently §38-10-112(1)(a), C.R.S. (2004)). Although we have not before expressly addressed an option like the one presented by the certification, we have long construed the one-year provision narrowly, to bring within the statute only those agreements that exclude, by their very terms, the possibility of

Rule

performance within one year. See Clark v. Perdue, 70 Colo. 589, 203 P. 655 (1922). If the agreement "could have been performed" within one year, the statute is inapplicable. Kuhlmann v. McCormack, 116 Colo. 300, 302, 180 P.2d 863, 864 (1947). That an agreement was not actually performed within one year of its making is, by this construction, clearly of no consequence in determining the applicability of the statute of frauds.

As described by the Tenth Circuit, the agreement that is the subject of its certification required AutoZone to sponsor "PBR and the Series." With regard to the length of AutoZone's required sponsorship, however, the agreement provided an election. By its own terms, the sponsorship agreement was to run for two seasons, unless sooner terminated as contemplated by the agreement itself. The agreement then expressly left to AutoZone the choice to terminate not only the Agreement, but also its obligation of sponsorship, effective upon the conclusion of only one season.

While the agreement was couched in terms of an agreement to sponsor for two seasons, with an option to terminate after sponsoring for only one season, it cannot be reasonably understood as other than an agreement of sponsorship for either one or two seasons, at AutoZone's choice. The agreement did not purport to grant AutoZone an option to terminate the agreement at will or upon the occurrence of some particular event; rather it provided AutoZone with two alternative ways of satisfying its obligations as contemplated by the agreement. Although the agreement contemplated performance for two seasons (a definite period of more than one year), if AutoZone chose that option, it also contemplated that AutoZone could completely perform its obligation by sponsoring PBR for one full season. Whether or not AutoZone effectively elected its option to limit its sponsorship obligation to only one season, the agreement expressly provided, by its own terms, an alternative performance that could be completed in less than one year.

Under the circumstances of this case, it is unnecessary for us to decide whether an option to terminate a contract must always be construed as an alternative and sufficient means of performance. Cf. Bowersock, 61 P. 740. Where the terms of an agreement can fairly and reasonably be interpreted to define alternate obligations, one or more of which can be performed within one year, the agreement in question may be fairly and reasonably interpreted such that it may be performed within one year. The one-year provision therefore does not bring such an agreement within the statute of frauds. And at least where, as here, the word "terminate" not only applies to the agreement itself but expressly limits the electing party's performance obligation to a specific task — sponsorship for one season — an interpretation of the election as defining alternate obligations is not only fair and reasonable, it is clear. . . . We therefore answer the certified question in the negative.

As to this portion of the statute of frauds, the Restatement comments:

> The design was said to be not to trust to the memory of witnesses for a longer time than one year, but the statutory language was not appropriate to carry out

that purpose. The result has been a tendency to construction narrowing the application of the statute. Under the prevailing interpretation, the enforceability of a contract under the one-year provision does not turn on the actual course of subsequent events, nor on the expectations of the parties as to the probabilities. Contracts of uncertain duration are simply excluded; the provision covers only those contracts whose performance cannot possibly be completed within a year. . . .

The period of a year begins when agreement is complete, ordinarily when the offer is accepted. . . . But a subsequent restatement of the terms starts the period again if the manifestation of mutual assent is such that it would be sufficient in the absence of prior agreement. The one-year period ends at midnight of the anniversary of the day on which the contract is made, on the theory that fractions of a day are disregarded in the way most favorable to the enforceability of the contract.

Restatement (Second) of Contracts §130, Comments a and c.

NOTE

The general rule is that a contract that does not specifically state a time that is more than one year is not within the statute even if the time for completion of the contract is very likely to be more than one year. For example, a contract to build a commercial building that does not state a time for completion greater than one year is not within the statute even if it is likely that the contract will not be completed within one year. See, e.g., Linscott v. Shasteen, 288 Neb. 276, 847 N.W.2d 283 (2014). There are some jurisdictions where the law is to the contrary, for example, Texas. See Hall v. Hall, 158 Tex. 95, 308 S.W.2d 12 (1957) (holding that the court must make a determination as to what is a reasonable time to complete performance of the contract by looking at circumstances surrounding the adoption of the agreement, the situation of the parties, and the subject matter of the contract, but not facts arising after formation of the contract).

Problem 91

Are the following contracts within the scope of the one-year portion of the statute of frauds?

 (a) On November 30, Levy Pants offers Ignatius J. Reilly a one-year job as office manager. The job is to begin on December 1, the next day. If Ignatius accepts, can Levy Pants change its mind and avoid liability on the theory that the contract cannot be performed within one year?

(b) Levy Pants orally contracted with Ignatius J. Reilly for a one-year position as its office manager. The contract was entered into on November 30, 2021, and was to begin on the first day of 2022. On the first working day of the year, Ignatius showed up and began his duties. He proved so obnoxious that Levy Pants discharged him the next day. When he sued, the company defended only on the ground of the lack of a writing. Is this a good defense? Could they have refused to recognize the contract in January, when he first reported for duty?

(c) Levy Pants hired Ignatius J. Reilly for a five-year term as its office manager; the contract was oral. Can Ignatius avoid the necessity of a writing by pointing out that he might die within the first year? Would it matter if he were in bad health?

(d) Knowing of his bad health, Levy Pants orally offered to employ Ignatius J. Reilly as its office manager for a five-year period "if you live so long." Is this contract required to be in writing?

(e) Levy Pants contracts for Reilly to work for five years, but the contract provides that either party may terminate the contract at any time. Must this contract be in writing? The majority rule is that it does not. Can you see why? California adopts the minority approach. See White Lighting Co. v. Woldson, 66 Cal. Rptr. 697, 438 P.2d 345 (Cal. 1968), as does Texas, Sullivan v. Leor Energy, LLC, 600 F.3d 542 (5th Cir. 2010) (holding that only events where *performance* is possible within a year are events that abrogate the need for a writing).

(f) Levy contracts for Reilly to work "for life." Most courts would hold that this contract need not be in writing. Do you agree? See also the controversial case of McInerney v. Charter Golf, Inc. 680 N.E.2d 1347 (Ill. 1997), noting the strong dissent. The majority's opinion has also been criticized elsewhere. Note, *McInerney v. Charter Gold, Inc.*: The Court Swings and Misses, 29 Loy. U. Chi. L.J. 907 (1998).

F.   Modification of Contracts

If the parties to an existing contract modify it, the modification must also be in writing if the original contract needed to meet the statute. Also if the contract as modified falls within the statute, the contract with modification must comply with the writing requirement. See, e.g., UCC §2-209(3).

Problem 92

When Dr. Maugham went into partnership with Drs. Doyle and Lewis, they signed an agreement providing that if one of the partners left the partnership, he would not practice medicine anywhere in the city for a five-year period thereafter. When Dr. Maugham decided to leave the partnership, he initially moved to another city. Two months later he phoned his former associates and proposed a modification of the contract whereby he would pay the partnership $40,000 and then be allowed to open up his

[handwritten margin notes: Yes, modification now falls within the SoF requires writing if more than a year]

practice in the old city. The parties all agreed to this, but then Dr. Maugham changed his mind once again and decided not to return. By this time his former partners were less concerned about the possible competition he might provide than the loss of the $40,000, so they sued for the money. Can he successfully defend on the basis that the oral modification needs a writing to be enforceable? Compare Zusy v. International Medical Group, Inc., 500 F. Supp. 2d 1087 (S.D. Ind. 2007), with Modisett v. Jolly, 153 Ind. App. 173, 286 N.E.2d 675 (1972).

The doctrines of waiver and estoppel may serve to permit the enforcement of a modification otherwise unenforceable under the statute of frauds. We discuss these doctrines and their effect on the statute at the end of this chapter.

G.   Sale of Goods

The original statute of frauds required a writing for contracts for the sale of goods for ten pounds or more. It has been replaced in this country by §2-201 of the UCC.

Uniform Commercial Code §2-201. Formal Requirements; Statute of Frauds

(1) Except as otherwise provided in this section a contract for the sale of goods for the price of $500 or more is not enforceable by way of action or defense unless there is some writing sufficient to indicate that a contract for sale has been made between the parties and signed by the party against whom enforcement is sought or by his authorized agent or broker. A writing is not insufficient because it omits or incorrectly states a term agreed upon but the contract is not enforceable under this paragraph beyond the quantity of goods shown in such writing. . . .

EASTERN DENTAL CORP. v. ISAAC MASEL CO.
United States District Court, Eastern District of Pennsylvania, 1980
502 F. Supp. 1354

LUONGO, District Judge. Plaintiff, Eastern Dental Corporation (EDC), is a distributor and manufacturer of products used exclusively in the practice of orthodontics. Defendant, Isaac Masel Co., Inc. (Masel), is a manufacturer and distributor of dental products and instruments. From the time of EDC's incorporation, Masel supplied it with certain of the products Masel manufactured. On August 10, 1978, Masel informed EDC that it would no longer supply its products to EDC. . . .

EDC asserts additional claims [EDC's first claim involved a violation of the antitrust laws]: (1) that the termination of the business relationship between the parties was in breach of a requirements contract and (2) that defendant had supplied defective merchandise in breach of a warranty of merchantability. On all three counts plaintiff claims damages to its business, including a claim for loss of goodwill. . . .

Before me is defendant's motion for partial summary judgment on the antitrust claims, the breach of contract claim and on the issue of whether or not damages for loss of goodwill are recoverable if plaintiff is successful on any one of the three counts of the complaint.

I. Background

EDC was incorporated in December of 1973 for the purpose of distributing products used exclusively in the practice of orthodontics, in particular, disposable orthodontic products, "the braces and the wires and the auxiliary items that go around the fixed appliances." Masel is a manufacturer and distributor of dental products and instruments including those considered to be disposable orthodontic products and instruments. Masel markets its products wholesale through sales to distributors, and retail through direct sales to dentists and orthodontists. Around the time of EDC's incorporation, its President, Vincent Santulli, and its Vice-President and Secretary-Treasurer, H. Neil Miller, began a series of discussions with Jacob J. Masel, the President of defendant, Isaac Masel Co., Inc., concerning the sale of Masel's disposable orthodontic products and instruments to EDC for resale to retail purchasers. As a result of these discussions Masel began to sell a product known as facebows to EDC. Eventually, Masel added what are known as elastics, lingual buttons, cleats, and metal bases to the line of products that it sold to EDC. Pursuant to their negotiations, Masel manufactured and sold to EDC at a wholesale price (the price which Masel charged distributors) products which were resold under EDC's label. In addition, since EDC was a new company, Masel granted it advantageous credit terms. During the course of the four year relationship, the parties operated without a written agreement, doing business solely through invoices and statements.

[handwritten margin note: No written Agreement]

Beginning in late 1976, EDC began to receive many customer complaints concerning breakage of the facebows manufactured by Masel. These complaints of defective facebows are the basis for EDC's breach of warranty count in which EDC seeks to be compensated for loss of customers and goodwill.

[handwritten margin note: Basis for Claims]

In July of 1977, EDC began to manufacture elastics, a product it had theretofore purchased from Masel. Later, in September of 1977, Miller informed Masel that a firm known as Star Dental Company had expressed an interest in acquiring EDC. A meeting took place between Jacob Masel, his son Robert, and Miller and Santulli, concerning the possibility of Masel acquiring EDC. Although Jacob Masel made a proposal to Miller and Santulli, no written offer was ever made. In any event, the possibility of a Masel takeover never left the preliminary negotiation stages as the EDC shareholders rejected the entire concept of the Masel proposal.

Terminated Business Between Them

In March of 1978 EDC submitted a purchase order which was not filled. Eventually, on August 10, 1978, Masel sent a letter to EDC advising that Masel was too busy to handle accounts like EDC's profitably, and that it was therefore terminating their relationship. When it was cut off, EDC attempted to find alternative sources of supply for Masel products. It was unable to find a source for either facebows or metal bases at wholesale prices. While it did find an alternative source of buttons and cleats, it made the business decision not to purchase those items because the price was prohibitive. As of the date of the filing of the complaint, EDC was no longer selling metal bases, cleats, or buttons. It did, however, sell facebows, a product which it has been manufacturing itself since January, 1979.

II.   THE ANTITRUST CLAIMS . . .

III.   THE BREACH OF CONTRACT CLAIM . . .

Masel contends The Agreement Doesn't Satisfy The SoF

Masel contends that it is entitled to summary judgment on the breach of contract claim on the grounds . . . that the contract is not evidenced by a writing sufficient to satisfy the statute of frauds. . . . The statute of frauds' requirement of a writing is applicable to all contracts for the sale of goods for $500 or more, including requirements contracts. . . .

A writing satisfies the statute if it is (1) signed by the party to be charged, (2) evidences a contract for the sale of goods, and (3) specifies a quantity term. . . . In output and requirement contracts the quantity of goods to be delivered under the contract is determined by the good faith output or requirements of the parties. This does not mean, however, that the statute of frauds' requirement of a quantity term is obviated since the inclusion of a quantity term is a mandatory requirement under the Code. . . . While the quantity term in requirements contracts need not be numerically stated, there must be some writing which indicates that the quantity to be delivered under the contract is a party's requirements or output. . . .

Input/requirement Contracts

Rule

EDC asserts that the termination letter dated August 10, 1978, the invoices of the individual transactions between the parties and a letter dated November 18, 1974, satisfy the requisite quantity term. While the above documents may indicate that the parties had an ongoing business relationship, they do not, expressly or by implication, reflect that the contract between the parties was for the supply of EDC's requirements of Masel's products.

First, the invoices of the individual sales transactions do not indicate that a requirements contract was entered into. They reflect only the quantity of goods shipped in each transaction. (Plaintiff's Exhibit III, 25(a).) Invoices which solely reflect the terms of individual transactions do not indicate that quantity is to be measured by requirements and, accordingly, do not satisfy the quantity term requirement of the statute of frauds. . . .

Similarly the letter signed by EDC on Masel's letterhead dated November 18, 1974, fails to satisfy the statute of frauds. It provides:

> Isaac Masel Company is importing a line of dental instruments which they will supply to Eastern Dental Corporation at a very small markup. Isaac Masel Company is advancing a large sum of money for these products, and would like assurance from Eastern Dental Corporation that
>
>   A. Eastern Dental Corporation will not contact Masel's supplier or purchase from Masel's supplier for a period of five years.
>
>   B. Eastern Dental Corporation will not purchase similar instruments from any other source unless Masel cannot supply them or until Masel's stock is exhausted, so that Masel will not get stuck with this merchandise.
>
>   I agree to the above terms.
>
>   Eastern Dental Corporation
> /s/ *Vincent Santulli*
> Vincent Santulli — Pres.
> /s/ *Neil Miller*
> Neil Miller — Vice-Pres.
> Date 11/18/74

Although this letter arguably indicates that EDC would purchase its requirements of a certain line of dental instruments from Masel, the record clearly establishes that it is a memorandum of an agreement unrelated to the contract which EDC is attempting to prove in this case. The subject matter of this letter was dental pliers, a product which neither party had dealt with previously. It is evident from Miller's deposition that the parties viewed their arrangement concerning these pliers as being distinct from any other arrangement they may have had. Miller pointed out that the letter was not a true memorandum of the intent of the parties. He stated that the parties, in fact, had entered into an exclusive dealing arrangement whereby Masel was obligated to market these pliers through EDC. At no point in the course of these proceedings has EDC asserted that the purported requirements contract was also an exclusive dealing contract. Indeed, the record would not support such an assertion.

It is clear that EDC was just one of Masel's many customers for the items which are the subject matter of the purported requirements contract. In fact, both EDC and Masel sold these products on the retail level in competition with each other. Thus, whatever may have been the contractual arrangement between the parties concerning facebows, elastics, lingual buttons and cleats, it is clear that Masel was not obligated to market these products solely through EDC. The November 18, 1974 agreement, therefore, is distinct from the contract which plaintiff is attempting to prove in the instant case. Accordingly, the presence of a quantity term, if it is such, in that agreement cannot serve to satisfy the statute of frauds for the purported contract which is before me.

Quantity term Does Not Satisfy the SoF

Finally, plaintiff's contention that the quantity term is supplied by the termination letter is not supported by the record. The termination letter provides:

> Gentlemen:
>
> We are enclosing our check No. 7290 in the sum of $599.05. At the present time, we are too busy to handle your orders, and we make the least amount of profit manufacturing for other manufacturers. As something had to give, we decided to eliminate this type of account.
>
> If we pick up enough additional, capable, new help making it possible for us to handle your account again, we will contact you.
>
> Please understand our position.
>
> > Very truly yours,
> > ISAAC MASEL CO., INC.
> > *J. J. Masel*

All that this letter indicates is that the parties had an ongoing business relationship. There is nothing in it suggesting that the "type of account" was a requirements account, or that Masel was to supply all that EDC needed. This letter, therefore, also fails to state a quantity term sufficient to satisfy the statute of frauds. The remaining documents submitted by the parties also fail to state the requisite quantity term. There are documents concerning credit terms and future shipments of merchandise, but there is no document expressly or impliedly providing that Masel was to supply all of EDC's requirements. I must, therefore, grant defendant's motion for summary judgment on count III of the complaint because the contract fails to satisfy the statute of frauds.

Holding

Summary Motion granted

Problem 93

Natasha agreed to sell Dan 100 cartons of cigarettes (she had just quit smoking). Dan felt the agreement should be in writing so Natasha typed on a blank piece of her letterhead: "I promise to sell Dan 100 cartons of cigarettes at $7.50 per carton." Natasha did not sign her name at the end. When Natasha backs out of the deal, Dan sues for breach of contract, and Natasha defends, alleging there is no requisite writing because she has signed nothing. Is she correct? UCC §1-201(b)(37); Restatement (Second) of Contracts §134.

[handwritten margin note: letterhead is the signature]

III. SATISFACTION OF THE STATUTE

RESTATEMENT (SECOND) OF CONTRACTS

§131. GENERAL REQUISITES OF A MEMORANDUM

Unless additional requirements are prescribed by the particular statute, a contract within the Statute of Frauds is enforceable if it is evidenced by any writing, signed by or on behalf of the party to be charged, which

(a) reasonably identifies the subject matter of the contract,
(b) is sufficient to indicate that a contract with respect thereto has been made between the parties or offered by the signer to the other party, and
(c) states with reasonable certainty the essential terms of the unperformed promises.

Comment g to this section provides: "What is essential depends on the agreement and its context and also on the subsequent conduct of the parties, including the dispute which arises and the remedy sought."

[handwritten margin note: "ESSential"]

CRABTREE v. ELIZABETH ARDEN SALES CORP.
New York Court of Appeals, 1953
305 N.Y. 48, 110 N.E.2d 551

FULD, J. In September of 1947, Nate Crabtree entered into preliminary negotiations with Elizabeth Arden Sales Corporation, manufacturers and sellers of cosmetics, looking toward his employment as sales manager. Interviewed on September 26th, by Robert P. Johns, executive vice-president and general manager of the corporation, who had apprised him of the possible opening, Crabtree requested a three-year contract at $25,000 a year. Explaining that he would be giving up a secure well-paying job to take a position in

an entirely new field of endeavor — which he believed would take him some
years to master — he insisted upon an agreement for a definite term. And he
repeated his desire for a contract for three years to Miss Elizabeth Arden, the
corporation's president. When Miss Arden finally indicated that she was
offered contract by employer prepared to offer a two-year contract, based on an annual salary of
$20,000 for the first six months, $25,000 for the second six months and
$30,000 for the second year, plus expenses of $5,000 a year for each of
those years, Crabtree replied that that offer was "interesting." Miss Arden
thereupon had her personal secretary make this memorandum on a
telephone order blank that happened to be at hand:

Memo

EMPLOYMENT AGREEMENT WITH

NATE CRABTREE	DATE SEPT. 26 1947
At 681 5th Ave.	6 P.M.

Begin	20000.
6 months	25000.
6 months	30000.

5000 — per year, Expense money
[2 years to make good]

Arrangement with Mr. Crabtree, By Miss
Arden, Present Miss [A]rden, Mr. Johns, Mr. Crabtree, Miss O'Leary

A few days later, Crabtree phoned Mr. Johns and telegraphed Miss
Arden; he accepted the "invitation to join the Arden organization," and
Miss Arden wired back her "welcome." When he reported for work, a "payroll change" card was made up and initialed by Mr. Johns, and then forwarded to the payroll department. Reciting that it was prepared on
September 30, 1947, and was to be effective as of October 22d, it specified
the names of the parties, Crabtree's "Job Classification" and, in addition,
contained the notation that "This employee is to be paid as follows:

First six months of employment	$20,000 Per annum
Next six months of employment	25,000 " "
After one year of employment	30,000 " "

Approved by RPJ [initialed] *Signed*

New 50 Increase to $30k After six months of employment, Crabtree received the scheduled
increase from $20,000 to $25,000, but the further specified increase at the
end of the year was not paid. Both Mr. Johns and the comptroller of the
corporation, Mr. Carstens, told Crabtree that they would attempt to
straighten out the matter with Miss Arden, and, with that in mind, the comptroller prepared another "pay-roll change" card, to which his signature is
appended, noting that there was to be a "Salary increase" from $25,000 to

$30,000 a year, "per contractual arrangements with Miss Arden." The latter, however, refused to approve the increase and, after further fruitless discussion, plaintiff left defendant's employ and commenced this action for breach of contract.

At the ensuing trial, defendant denied the existence of any agreement to employ plaintiff for two years, and further contended that, even if one had been made, the statute of frauds barred its enforcement. The trial court found against defendant on both issues and awarded plaintiff damages of about $14,000, and the Appellate Division, two justices dissenting, affirmed. Since the contract relied upon was not to be performed within a year, the primary question for decision is whether there was a memorandum of its terms, subscribed by defendant, to satisfy the statute of frauds, Personal Property Law, §31.

Each of the two payroll cards — the one initialed by defendant's general manager, the other signed by its comptroller — unquestionably constitutes a memorandum under the statute. That they were not prepared or signed with the intention of evidencing the contract, or that they came into existence subsequent to its execution, is of no consequence, [citations omitted], it is enough, to meet the statute's demands, that they were signed with intent to authenticate the information contained therein and that such information does evidence the terms of the contract. [Citations omitted.] Those two writings contain all of the essential terms of the contract — the parties to it, the position that plaintiff was to assume, the salary that he was to receive — except that relating to the duration of plaintiff's employment. Accordingly, we must consider whether that item, the length of the contract, may be supplied by reference to the earlier unsigned office memorandum, and, if so, whether its notation, "2 years to make good," sufficiently designates a period of employment. The statute of frauds does not require the "memorandum . . . to be in one document. It may be pieced together out of separate writings, connected with one another either expressly or by the internal evidence of subject-matter and occasion." . . . Where each of the separate writings has been subscribed by the party to be charged, little if any difficulty is encountered. . . . Where, however, some writings have been signed, and others have not — as in the case before us — there is basic disagreement as to what constitutes a sufficient connection permitting the unsigned papers to be considered as part of the statutory memorandum. The courts of some jurisdictions insist that there be a reference, of varying degrees of specificity, in the signed writing to that unsigned, and, if there is no such reference, they refuse to permit consideration of the latter in determining whether the memorandum satisfies the statute. . . . That conclusion is based upon a construction of the statute which requires that the connection between the writings and defendant's acknowledgment of the one not subscribed, appear from examination of the papers alone, without the aid of parol evidence. The other position — which has gained increasing support over the years — is that a sufficient connection between the papers is established simply by a reference in them to the same subject matter or transaction. . . . The statute is not pressed "to the extreme of a literal and rigid logic," Marks v. Cowdin, supra, 226 N.Y. 138, 144, 123 N.E. 139, 141, and oral testimony is admitted to show the connection between the documents and to establish the acquiescence, of the party to be charged, to the contents of the one unsigned. . . .

The view last expressed impresses us as the more sound, and, indeed — although several of our cases appear to have gone the other way, . . . — this court has on a number of occasions approved the rule, and we now definitively adopt it, permitting the signed and unsigned writings to be read together, provided that they clearly refer to the same subject matter or transaction. . . .

The language of the statute — "Every agreement . . . is void, unless . . . some note or memorandum thereof to be in writing, and subscribed by the party to be charged," Personal Property Law, §31 — does not impose the requirement that the signed acknowledgment of the contract must appear from the writings alone, unaided by oral testimony. The danger of fraud and perjury, generally attendant upon the admission of parol evidence, is at a minimum in a case such as this. None of the terms of the contract are supplied by parol. All of them must be set out in the various writings presented to the court, and at least one writing, the one establishing a contractual relationship between the parties, must bear the signature of the party to be charged, while the unsigned document must on its face refer to the same transaction as that set forth in the one that was signed. Parol evidence — to portray the circumstances surrounding the making of the memorandum — serves only to connect the separate documents and to show that there was assent, by the party to be charged, to the contents of the one unsigned. If that testimony does not convincingly connect the papers, or does not show assent to the unsigned paper, it is within the province of the judge to conclude, as a matter of law, that the statute has not been satisfied. True, the possibility still remains that, by fraud or perjury, an agreement never in fact made may occasionally be enforced under the subject matter or transaction test. It is better to run that risk, though, than to deny enforcement to all agreements, merely because the signed document made no specific mention of the unsigned writing. . . .

Turning to the writings in the case before us — the unsigned office memo, the payroll change form initialed by the general manager Johns, and the paper signed by the comptroller Carstens — it is apparent, and most patently, that all three refer on their face to the same transaction. The parties, the position to be filled by plaintiff, the salary to be paid him, are all identically set forth; it is hardly possible that such detailed information could refer to another or a different agreement. Even more, the card signed by Carstens notes that it was prepared for the purpose of a "Salary increase per contractual arrangements with Miss Arden." That certainly constitutes a reference of sorts to a more comprehensive "arrangement," and parol is permissible to furnish the explanation.

The corroborative evidence of defendant's assent to the contents of the unsigned office memorandum is also convincing. Prepared by defendant's agent, Miss Arden's personal secretary, there is little likelihood that that paper was fraudulently manufactured or that defendant had not assented to its contents. Furthermore, the evidence as to the conduct of the parties at the time it was prepared persuasively demonstrates defendant's assent to its terms. Under such circumstances, the courts below were fully justified in finding that the three papers constituted the "memorandum" of their agreement within the meaning of the statute.

Nor can there be any doubt that the memorandum contains all of the essential terms of the contract. . . . Only one term, the length of the employment, is in dispute. The September 26th office memorandum contains the notation, "2 years to make good." What purpose, other than to denote the length of the contract term, such a notation could have, is hard to imagine. Without it, the employment would be at will, see Martin v. New York Life Ins. Co., 148 N.Y. 117, 121, 42 N.E. 416, 417, and its inclusion may not be treated as meaningless or purposeless. Quite obviously, as the courts below decided, the phrase signifies that the parties agreed to a term, a certain and definite term, of two years, after which, if plaintiff did not "make good," he would be subject to discharge. And examination of other parts of the memorandum supports that construction. Throughout the writings, a scale of wages, increasing plaintiff's salary periodically, is set out; that type of arrangement is hardly consistent with the hypothesis that the employment was meant to be at will. The most that may be argued from defendant's standpoint is that "2 years to make good," is a cryptic and ambiguous statement. But, in such a case, parol evidence is admissible to explain its meaning. . . . Having in mind the relations of the parties, the course of the negotiations and plaintiff's insistence upon security of employment, the purpose of the phrase — or so the trier of the facts was warranted in finding — was to grant plaintiff the tenure he desired.

The judgment should be affirmed, with costs.

NOTES AND QUESTIONS

1. There were three separate writings in *Crabtree*: the memo on the telephone order blank and the two payroll change cards. Why were each of these, standing alone, insufficient to satisfy the statute of frauds?

2. Suppose Crabtree had worked for Arden for one year and then tried to jump ship to a competitor. Arden sues, arguing that Crabtree is contractually obligated to work for her for two years, and Crabtree defends by citing the statute of frauds. What result?

3. The court held in Heinrichs v. Marshall & Stevens, Inc., 921 F.2d 418 (2d Cir. 1990), that provisions in an employee's manual concerning employment were insufficient to satisfy the statute of frauds where the manual contained no promise or undertaking that employment would be for any definite term.

4. In the last section of these materials, we learned that the general view is that UCC §2-201 requires a quantity to be stated in the writing. In a distributorship contract, would the writing suffice if it did not specifically state the quantity to be distributed? Consider Wood v. Lucy, Lady Duff-Gordon at page 212. Does the implication of good faith in §2-306 help? See Lorenz Supply Co. v. American Standard, Inc., 419 Mich. 610, 358 N.W.2d 845 (1984) (the dissent makes a very strong argument that the good faith requirement and general language about the distributorship implies that the seller will meet the requirements of the distributor in good faith and this, therefore, satisfies the quantity requirement). To the same effect is Advent Systems v. Unisys Corp., 925 F.2d 670 (1991).

5. The Restatement comment quoted before *Crabtree* indicates that the degree of specificity depends on the type of remedy sought. What type of remedy would demand more specificity?

6. Even though a once sufficient writing is later lost, that writing may be used to overcome the statute of frauds. See, e.g., Matter of Serodio, 101 A.3d 1069, 1074 (N.H. 2014).

7. The signature requirement occasionally frustrates a party trying to enforce a contract required to be in writing. Review the definition of "signed" in the UCC at §1-201(b)(37). Would an initial placed on notes taken during a negotiation for a contract prove satisfactory?

Problem 94

After Levy Pants orally agreed to hire Ignatius J. Reilly as its office manager for a five-year period, the president of the company wrote a letter to Ignatius's long-suffering mother. In part the letter stated: "Knowing of your distress at his idleness, we have agreed with him to employ him as our office manager, paying him $30,000 a year for a five-year period, starting at the first of this year." When the company fired Ignatius shortly thereafter, he sued. When the company pointed to the lack of a writing, Ignatius produced the letter sent by the company to his mother. To this the company replied that it was *not* the contract itself, and that the president of the company had no contractual intent when he signed the letter to a third person (i.e., the mother). Does the letter satisfy the statute, or is it defective because it is not the contract itself?

Problem 95

Elizabeth Bennett signed a contract with Jim Darcy to buy his house in Derbyshire and was astounded when he told her that he had changed his mind and no longer was of a mind to sell. She promptly filed suit against him.

Darcy's lawyer asked him to review the negotiations and see if Darcy couldn't remember some detail actually agreed to by the parties but inadvertently left out of the agreement. Darcy then remembered a conversation with Bennett in which he had agreed that if she would purchase the house at the agreed-upon price, he would improve the view by tearing down an ugly ice house on a nearby property he also owned. At the trial, in spite of the parol evidence rule (see the next chapter) and the objections of Bennett's lawyer, Darcy was permitted to testify as to the ice-house agreement, and, when called to the stand, Bennett confirmed his testimony. His attorney immediately moved to have the suit dismissed based on the statute of frauds. Should the judge grant the request?

[handwritten margin notes: Not essential — Term is Not Stated in the writing]

[handwritten note below text: Toring 12 house down is part of the Agreement, and toring it down is Part of performance. The contract is uncertain with duration, and this excluded from the SOF. / NO.]

[handwritten note right: ~ contract over for site of land]

IV.   MITIGATING DOCTRINES AND EXCEPTIONS

A.   Restitution

Problem 96

Bea Potter was hired by MacGregor Agricultural Enterprises as a book-keeper for a two-year period; her salary was to be $34,000 a year. The contract was oral. After she had worked for a two-month period, she was wrongfully accused of stealing and was fired on the spot. When Potter brought suit, MacGregor defended on the basis of the lack of a writing. If this defense is successful, may she nonetheless recover for the two months she worked? Under what theory? How would her damages be measured?

[handwritten note: - recover under quantum merit]

B.   Part Performance

[handwritten notes: - Its whats contemplated in contract which was 2 yrs, so had to be in writing — No wrongful termination cuz No contract]

RESTATEMENT (SECOND) OF CONTRACTS

§129. Action in Reliance; Specific Performance

A contract for the transfer of an interest in land may be specifically enforced notwithstanding failure to comply with the Statute of Frauds if it is established that the party seeking enforcement, in reasonable reliance on the contract and on the continuing assent of the party against whom enforcement is sought, has so changed his position that injustice can be avoided only by specific enforcement.

[Comment d to the section states in part:]

The promisee must act in reasonable reliance on the promise, before the promisor has repudiated it, and the action must be such that the remedy of restitution is inadequate. If these requirements are met, neither taking of possession nor payment of money nor the making of improvements is essential.

Uniform Commercial Code §2-201

. . . (3) A contract which does not satisfy the requirements of [the UCC statute of frauds] but which is valid in other respects is enforceable . . . (c) with respect to goods for which payment has been made and accepted or which have been received and accepted.

WAGERS v. ASSOCIATED MORTGAGE INVESTORS
Washington Court of Appeals, 1978
19 Wash. App. 758, 577 P.2d 622

Dore, J. Plaintiff Ronald L. Wagers sought specific performance of an alleged agreement to purchase real estate lots in Kent, Washington or, in the alternative, for damages for breach of the agreement. Defendant Associated Mortgage Investors (hereinafter called AMI) moved to dismiss the plaintiff's first cause of action for specific performance which the court treated as a motion for summary judgment. The trial court entered partial summary judgment as a final judgment dismissing plaintiff's first cause of action for specific performance. . . .

Plaintiff Wagers was a building contractor with offices in Federal Way, Washington. In the spring of 1975 Wagers commenced negotiations with Tom Benkert, a representative of AMI in Coral Gables, Florida, for the purchase of 104 building lots near Kent, Washington. Negotiations for the sale took place over a period ranging from the spring of 1975 through April of 1976. Benkert indicated that his principal (AMI) owned and controlled the property and had the power to sell to anyone it chose. There was some mention of other persons having an interest in the property but plaintiff was assured that AMI had the authority to make the sale as long as agreeable terms were reached. That on February 9, 1976 Wagers submitted an earnest money agreement to AMI to purchase the lots for $250,000 cash.

After Wagers mailed the executed earnest money agreement to AMI he continued to inquire as to when approval would be forthcoming. On March 29, 1976 Benkert telephonically advised plaintiff that the Board of Trustees of AMI had approved the earnest money agreement for an amended total

cash sales price of $270,000. He further stated the signed earnest money
agreement would be immediately returned to plaintiff through AMI's attorney in Seattle. In this conversation plaintiff was informed that there was only
"one slight problem" with an individual who was "hedging a bit for more
money on settlement of AMI from the sale proceeds; it was a matter of
internal handling, however, and would not delay the close of the sale."

In a letter dated March 30, 1976, AMI's Seattle attorney wrote to plaintiff's attorney as follows:

Dear Mr. Stevenson:

Associated Mortgage Investors has indicated to us that the proposed sale to Mr. Wagers for $270,000 — $10,000 as forfeitable earnest
money with the balance to be paid in cash within 90 days if the necessary
financing can be arranged — is acceptable to AMI *subject to prior approval
by its trustees and subject to its ability to arrange* for delivery of clear title.
AMI is governed by its Board of Trustees and must have approval of the
Board before it can sell the property. However, AMI's officers are confident that the trustees will approve the sale.

Concerning the problems of clearing title, we attempted to explain
to you during our recent phone conversation some of the complexities
of the case. These complexities result in delay, but we do not anticipate
any particular problem. On March 17, 1976, we wrote to the various
parties having an interest in the property outlining the terms of the
proposed sale and suggesting a division of the proceeds. We requested a
response by Monday, March 29, 1976. All except one of the parties have
now responded by indicating that the proposal is acceptable. The one
remaining party has indicated that he is undertaking certain steps to
determine whether the sale price is reasonable and has promised to
respond by Monday, April 5, 1976.

Thus, although we cannot promise that the proposed transaction
will be closed, we are undertaking our best efforts to obtain the
necessary approvals, and it is AMI's intent to sell the property to
Mr. Wagers on the terms indicated if it can successfully arrange to
clear title on terms acceptable to AMI.

/s/ *John H. Strasburger*

(Emphasis added.)

A few days later on April 6, 1976 the attorney for the plaintiff acknowledged Strasburger's letter of March 30 and wrote:

Dear Mr. Strasburger:

Thank you for your letter of March 30, 1976 concerning the *sale* of
the above realty by your client, Associated Mortgage Investors (AMI), to
Ron Wagers, my client.

Your letter confirms Wagers' understanding with Mr. Tom Benkirk [sic], agent for AMI in Coral Gables, Florida, that the above described realty is *sold* to Wagers for $270,000.00, all cash on closing with $10,000.00 down, pending clearance by you of fee title. The *sale* is to be closed at Pioneer National Title Insurance Company here in Seattle under appropriate escrow instructions and within 90 days of AMI furnishing the preliminary title report.

You are proceeding to clear the title and will advise me when this has been accomplished — hopefully within the next week.

Relying on the above, *Wagers is proceeding to obtain the necessary funds for payment and preparing plans and schedules for completion of the tract.*

Tom Benkirk [sic] advised Wagers in a phone conversation on March 29, 1976 that the *trustees of AMI had approved the terms of the above described sale. Therefore, please have the earnest money now in the hands of AMI executed and forwarded to me for my file and for Pioneer National Title Insurance Company. Also, forward to me AMI's appraisal on the property and engineer's report as promised by Tom Benkirk* [sic].

Wagers advises that there may be a problem of the ownership of Lots 1 through 7 by AMI. He discussed this with Tom Benkirk [sic] who has agreed, if there is no ownership, to reduce the total sales price of $270,000.00 by $18,173.05 for the loss of the seven lots. This amount was arrived at by dividing $270,000.00 by 104 lots which gives a price of $2,596.15 for each lot or a total of $18,173.05.

Please advise me when this sale can be moved into closing.

/s/ *Robert H. Stevenson*

(Emphasis added.)

AMI's Seattle counsel, upon receiving the above letter and obviously disagreeing, responded the following day April 7, 1976, as follows:

Dear Mr. Stevenson:

We have received your letter of April 6, 1976. As we stated in our prior letter, *it is not my understanding that the trustees have approved the sale since an agreement has not yet been received from all of the parties who have an interest in the property* concerning the sale and the proposed sale cannot be approved by the trustees until formal agreement has been received. We have contacted four different individuals connected with the property. Three have indicated that the sale appears to be acceptable. The fourth is still questioning the reasonableness of the sale price, but it appears that they will also consent. However, when we informed them of the sale, we stated that the sale price was $270,000. Your letter indicates that the sale price has been reduced. If this is the case, it will be necessary to recontact each of the individual parties.

We are concerned that your letter may be designed to render AMI liable for any financing and other costs incurred by Mr. Wagers if the property is not sold to Mr. Wagers. Therefore, we wish to clarify that although AMI is interested in Mr. Wagers' offer, he is proceeding at his own risk and AMI will not be responsible for any expenses he may incur. *Specifically, your letter indicates that you are confirming Mr. Wagers' understanding that the property has been* "sold to Wagers." *If this is Mr. Wagers' understanding, it is incorrect.* As previously indicated, any sale to Mr. Wagers is contingent upon approval of the Board of Trustees of AMI and approval of each of the individuals who have an interest in the property. We are continuing to exert our best efforts to obtain the necessary approvals on terms acceptable to AMI. *Until these necessary approvals on terms acceptable to AMI's trustees have been obtained, there is no binding and enforceable agreement.*

As we have previously indicated, AMI's officers are acting in good faith, but we felt it necessary to write this letter since your letter implied that the negotiations had now resulted in a binding agreement which is not yet the case.

/s/ *John H. Strasburger*

(Emphasis added.)

ISSUES

1. Whether plaintiff's unilaterally executed earnest money agreement, together with the letters exchanged between the parties' respective attorneys, constitute a sufficient writing of a sale of land to satisfy the statute of frauds?

2. Whether plaintiff's arrangement of financing for development of the subject of the sale constituted sufficient part performance to make the sale an exception to the statute of frauds?

DECISION

ISSUE 1

Sales of land to be enforceable must ordinarily be in writing signed by the party to be charged. However, a writing is not always essential to the validity of the contract. An oral agreement can be equally effective and binding as a written one when the terms are reasonably established in writing by a series of documents and/or written memorandum which would establish the subject matter, consideration, identity of the parties and the terms of the agreement.

Plaintiff argues that the statute of frauds may be satisfied by various kinds of written memorandum. It may consist of one writing or several writings. It may also be pieced together out of separate writings since all that the statute requires is written evidence on which the whole agreement can be made out. Restatement of Contracts §208 (1932); Western Timber Co. v. Kalama River Lbr. Co., 42 Wash. 620, 85 P. 338 (1906); Alexander v. Lewes, 104 Wash. 32, 175 P. 572 (1918). Plaintiff contends that the earnest money agreement signed by Wagers and the letter of defendant's attorney under date of March 30, 1976, together with plaintiff's attorney's answering letter of April 6, 1976, supplies the necessary written information to satisfy the statute of frauds.

Plaintiff and his attorney at all times were advised that the purchaser's earnest money agreement was subject to approval of the board of trustees as well as its ability to arrange for delivery of clear title.

Strasburger's letter of March 30 was written 1 day after plaintiff's earnest money agreement had expired without being accepted, signed and returned. His letter is replete with statements that the subject earnest money agreement was contingent upon the approval of the board of trustees and that there was a number of indications that there was pending trouble with clearing title. At this juncture plaintiff's attorney was obviously disturbed and tried to turn a unilaterally executed earnest money agreement into a consummated sale by answering Strasburger's letter referring to "the sale of the above realty by your client Associated Mortgage Investors to Ronald Wagers, my client." It is clear to the court that on April 6, 1976 plaintiff's attorney was still unsure as to the subject matter of the sale and was trying to establish a formula for reduction of the amount of the total purchase price in the event that title to seven lots might not be cleared. It may well be that the seven deleted lots were far more valuable than the remaining lots and there is no indication that the lots were of the value of $2,596.15 each, as provided for in plaintiff's letter.

Apparently the next day when defendant's attorney received plaintiff's attorney's letter of April 6, he immediately responded in his letter of April 7, 1976 wherein he stated in no uncertain terms that the sale had not been approved and again stating that one of the tenants in common was questioning the reasonableness of the sale price. He further stated that in the event the sale price of $270,000 was to be reduced, it would again require approval from all of the owners. In the same letter he also cautioned plaintiff's attorney not to incur any expenses on the basis that the sale had been consummated.

We hold that the buyer's unilaterally executed earnest money agreement, together with the letters exchanged between the buyer's and seller's attorneys, fail to establish an agreement between the parties on essential contract terms and, therefore, did not constitute a sufficient writing to satisfy the statute of frauds.

[handwritten margin note: SOF Not Satisfied]

ISSUE 2

Part performance is a recognized exception of the requirement of the statute of frauds. One of the requirements of the doctrine of part performance is that the acts relied upon as constituting part performance must unmistakably point to the existence of the claimed agreement. If they may be accounted for by some other hypothesis they are not sufficient. Granquist v. McKean, 29 Wash. 2d 440, 187 P.2d 623 (1947).

The statute of frauds is a positive enactment to the effect that contracts of this nature to be valid and enforceable must be in writing. Courts of equity have no right any more than courts of law to disregard the statute except where it is necessary to do so in order to prevent a gross fraud from being practiced. Granquist v. McKean, supra.

In Richardson v. Taylor Land & Livestock Co., 25 Wash. 2d 518, 171 P.2d 703 (1976), the principal elements involved in determining part performance are elucidated at page 528, 171 P.2d at page 709:

> The principal elements or circumstances involved in determining whether there has been sufficient part performance by a purchaser of real estate under an oral contract otherwise within the statute of frauds, are (1) delivery and assumption of actual and exclusive possession of the land; (2) payment or tender of the consideration, whether in money, other property, or services; and (3) the making of permanent, substantial, and valuable improvements, referable to the contract.

[handwritten margin note: Elements of Part Performance by a purchaser of real estate]

> There is a wide diversity of opinion, as shown by the adjudicated cases regarding the relative importance of these three elements. Where all three of them are united in a given instance, the strongest kind of case is thereby generally presented (Bendon v. Parfit, 74 Wash. 645, 134 P. 185), and, conversely, where none is shown, there is little to warrant a court of equity in decreeing specific performance. There is also a contrariety of opinion, as exemplified in the many cases on the subject, as to whether any single one of these elements is either an indispensable or an all-sufficient ingredient of part performance. As a matter of fact, in most of the cases where the doctrine of part performance has been successfully invoked, it will be found that at least two of the enumerated elements are present. . . .

[handwritten margin note: Don't Need all 3 elements]

[handwritten margin note: Usually at least 2 elements]

. . .

The only act of "part performance" alleged by appellant is contained in Mr. Wagers's affidavit in which he states:

> Affiant told Mr. Beukert [sic] that he was arranging for the financing of the sale and wanted to start breaking ground as soon as possible. . . . In reliance on these conversations, affiant made arrangements for financing this sale with Citizens Federal Savings and Loan in Seattle.

No elements Satisfied

We have none of the three principal elements or circumstances in this case to constitute part performance. At best we have arrangement for financing which presumably had been arranged or provided for before the earnest money agreement was signed. In any event the arrangement for financing was equally consistent with the earnest money agreement or with the decision to make an offer to increase the purchase price rather than a sale. We hold there was no part performance by the plaintiff to con-

Holding

stitute an exception to the statute of frauds.

The doctrine of equitable estoppel is not applicable in this case.

Judgment affirmed.   *Affirmed for Defendant*

NOTES AND QUESTIONS

1. Would the plaintiff in *Wagers* have fared better under Restatement (Second) of Contracts §129 (before the case)? Losh Family, LLC v. Kurtsman, 155 Wash. App. 458, 228 P.2d 793 (Wash. App. Ct. 2010), noted that the third requirement listed in *Wagers* may be met by other types of part performance such as continuing to rent long term (under a five-year oral lease) and paying increased rent because of the length of the lease.

2. Although as indicated by the present case, taking possession is one event often decided as part performance, *retention* of possession by one already in possession claimed under a different right or title is not part performance. See Bank of Alton v. Tanaka, 274 Kan. 443, 799 P.2d 1029 (1990).

3. Typically, payment does not serve as part performance for purposes of circumventing the statute of frauds unless the payment is in full. See, e.g., Marathon Oil Co. v. Collins, 744 N.E.2d 474 (Ind. App. 2001).

4. Part performance is not preparation to perform. See, for example, Mann v. White Marsh Properties, 321 Md. 111, 581 A.2d 819 (Md. 1990), holding that activities in having title to property searched, having plans prepared and reviewed for zoning compliance, and making arrangements for percolation test of soil were insufficient because such actions although consistent with a contract were also consistent with the absence of contract — steps that may have been taken preliminary to a contract.

5. The part performance exception does not allow for enforcement of an oral contract when the contract is for a performance that will take over one year or one in consideration of marriage. Comment d to §130 and comment d to §124. Nor do the courts typically use part performance to escape from the suretyship portion of the statute; see, e.g., Brown & Shinitzky Chartered v. Dentinger, 118 Ill. App. 3d 517, 455 N.E.2d 128 (1983). However, in the one year situation, *full* performance by a person of a promise to render services for over one year does serve to make an oral promise to pay enforceable.

BUFFALOE v. HART
North Carolina Court of Appeals, 1995
441 S.E.2d 172

GREENE, Judge.

Patricia Hart and Lowell Thomas Hart (defendants) appeal from the trial court's denial of their motions for directed verdict and judgment notwithstanding the verdict in this action brought by Homer Buffaloe (plaintiff) for breach of contract.

Plaintiff filed a complaint for breach of contract and damages in Franklin County Superior Court on 13 November 1989. Defendants, in their answers, denied the existence of the contract and contended the alleged contract was unenforceable because it violated the statute of frauds. The case was tried with a jury during the 28 September 1992 term of Franklin County Superior Court. Plaintiff presented evidence that tended to show that he is a tobacco farmer in Franklin County, North Carolina, has known defendants for about ten years and rented tobacco from them in 1988 and 1989. Plaintiff rented from defendants, pursuant to an oral agreement, five "roanoke box [tobacco] barns" (the barns) located on their farm for use in his tobacco farming operations during the 1988 farming year. The agreement with defendants for rental of the tobacco and the barns was not reduced to writing and was based on a "handshake, oral" agreement. Plaintiff stated, "I had bought some equipment prior to then, and we always done it on a handshake agreement, cash basis. That's the way it was." Defendants agreed to provide insurance coverage for the barns in 1988. On 20 October 1988, plaintiff paid the $2,000.00 rent owed for the barns and the $992.64 owed to Patricia Hart (Mrs. Hart) for the tobacco rent.

Plaintiff began negotiating with defendants several days later about purchasing the barns. Plaintiff offered to pay $20,000.00 for the five barns in annual installments of $5,000.00 over a four year period, but did not offer any interest payments. The offer was made in Mrs. Hart's front yard with only defendants and plaintiff present. Defendants accepted the offer, and both parties shook hands. Plaintiff already had possession of the barns under the rental agreement. Plaintiff did not remove the barns from defendants' land because he agreed to farm their land in 1989 with tobacco he rented from defendants.

On 3 January 1989, plaintiff applied for a loan with Production Credit Association in order to pay for the barns. He informed Lowell Thomas Hart (Mr. Hart) that he would pay for all the barns if the loan came through. Mr. Hart responded that it "would be fine with us." On the financial statement portion of the application, he listed the barns, but his loan was denied. Plaintiff and Mr. Hart then reconfirmed that plaintiff was to pay four yearly installments of $5,000.00 for the barns. Because he was unsuccessful in obtaining insurance coverage for the barns, defendants agreed to provide insurance for the five barns for 1989 if plaintiff would reimburse them for the cost. On 20 October 1989, plaintiff promptly reimbursed defendants in full for the insurance coverage. Plaintiff testified that "[a]fter I bought the barns was the only time I agreed to pay insurance" and when he rented the barns in 1988, Mrs. Hart "was supposed to pay" the insurance.

During the 1989 tobacco farming season, plaintiff decided to sell the barns and placed a "for sale" ad which expired 23 October 1989 under farm equipment saying "five roanoke box barns, gas, [plaintiff's] phone number" in The News and Observer. The ad ran two lines for four days and resulted in several calls, including contact with Ashley P. Mohorn (Mr. Mohorn), Ronald E. Stainback (Mr. Stainback), and Lawrence Elliot (Mr. Elliot). Plaintiff received a $500.00 check dated 22 October 1989 as a down payment from Mr. Mohorn for two of the barns after quoting a price of $8,000.00 each. Mr. Stainback met with plaintiff, informed him that he would take two barns, and Mr. Elliot would take one. Mr. Stainback wrote plaintiff a check for $1,000.00 dated 25 October 1989, representing a deposit on the three barns.

Mrs. Hart called plaintiff in the fall of 1989 and asked if he could "straighten up with her," and he "told her it would be in the next two or three days" and that he was going to sell the barns. She responded that would "be fine with her." On the morning of 22 or 23 October 1989, plaintiff delivered a check in person to her for the first $5,000.00 due defendants. The payment was in the form of plaintiff's personal check number 1468, dated 23 October 1989, payable to Patricia Hart, signed by plaintiff, and with written words on the "for" line indicating the check was for payment for the five barns. When plaintiff gave her the check, she asked him if he wanted a receipt, but he said "no, the check would be the receipt." The next night after plaintiff delivered the check, she called him and told him "she didn't want to sell [him] the barns; she'd already sold them" to somebody else. Plaintiff received a letter, postmarked 26 October 1989, with the check in it. "She had torn ... [the check] so bad you couldn't hardly put it back together," and "had tore off [plaintiff's] name-tore off her name, the 'for' line, and the date." Plaintiff was able to piece the check back together to see his signature and the five thousand dollars. He later discovered that defendants sold the five barns to "the same guys" plaintiff had agreed to sell them to.

Randy Baker (Baker) testified that plaintiff told him he had bought the barns and had him repair boxes on the barns. Plaintiff paid Baker for this work. J.R. Fowler, Jr. testified that plaintiff told him he had bought the five barns in 1989, was going to pay five thousand dollars a year until they were paid for, was going to sell them, and had run an ad in the paper. Jack Stone (Stone), an auctioneer for the State of North Carolina, testified that "[plaintiff] approached me and said that he had some bulk barns," "said that he had purchased the barns," and "asked if [Stone] could sell them." Stone received a $41,000.00 check for the five barns and held it in escrow until he could inform plaintiff; however, plaintiff told Stone "he thought he already had them sold." After Stone informed plaintiff to let him know if he had already sold the barns, "[plaintiff] calls back and said that the lady had backed out on him and he couldn't sell the barns to nobody 'til he got this straight." At the close of plaintiff's evidence, defendants moved for a directed verdict which was denied.

Defendants presented evidence tending to show that "[plaintiff] agreed to pay [Mr. Hart] twenty thousand dollars for the five barns, and he agreed to pay it over a four year period of time"; however, plaintiff later called Mr. Hart and wished to make a new arrangement in that plaintiff would secure a loan and pay for the barns all at one time. When the loan was not approved, plaintiff contacted Mr. Hart and "wanted to know if he could continue the rental agreement that he had had the previous year." When Mr. Hart's wife told him that plaintiff "had come over and brought the rent check, and left the five thousand dollars as an enticement to buy the barns, [he] told her that it just wasn't sufficient considering the fact that there had been a tremendous acreage increase in the tobacco poundage." He instructed Mrs. Hart to call plaintiff and "tell him we weren't interested." His wife tore up the check, put it in an envelope, and mailed it to plaintiff. At the close of all the evidence, defendants moved for a directed verdict which was denied.

[The jury found that there was a contract between the parties, that Buffaloe had accepted the tobacco barns, and that the Harts had accepted payment for the barns. Also, the jury found that Buffaloe had not agreed merely to rent the barns from the Harts.]

The jury awarded plaintiff damages of $21,000.00. Defendants filed a motion for judgment notwithstanding the verdict which was denied.

The issues presented are whether (I) a personal check signed by plaintiff, describing the property involved and containing an amount representing partial payment is sufficient to constitute a writing under the statute of frauds; and (II) there is substantial relevant evidence that plaintiff "accepted" the barns and defendants "accepted" plaintiff's check, taking the contract out of the statute of frauds.

Because the barns, the subject of this dispute, are "goods" within the meaning of the Uniform Commercial Code, N.C.G.S. §25-2-105 (1986), and because the price for the barns is at least $500.00, the provisions of N.C. Gen. Stat. §25-2-201 apply. . . .

I

Defendants argue in their brief that the check delivered by plaintiff to Mrs. Hart fails to meet the requirements of N.C. Gen. Stat. §25-2-201(1), commonly referred to as a statute of frauds, because the check "was not negotiated or endorsed by the Defendants and therefore the signature of the Defendants did not appear on the check." A check may constitute a writing sufficient to satisfy the requirements of Section 25-2-201(1) provided it (1) contains a writing sufficient to indicate a contract of sale between the parties; (2) is signed by the party or his authorized agent against whom enforcement is sought; and (3) states a quantity. . . .

The only writing in this case is a personal check which, although specifying the quantity of "five barns" on the "for" line, addressed to Patricia Hart, signed by plaintiff, and containing an amount of $5,000.00, is not sufficient to satisfy Section 25-2-201. Defendants, the parties "against whom enforcement is sought," did not endorse the check, and therefore, their handwriting does not appear anywhere on the check. In fact, the name of defendant, Mr. Hart, is totally absent from the check. Therefore, because the requirement of Section 25-2-201(1) that the writing be "signed by the party against whom enforcement is sought or by his authorized agent or broker" is absent from the check, the alleged oral contract between plaintiff and defendants is unenforceable under that section.

II

Defendants further argue that the part performance exception in Section 25-2-201(3)(c) does not apply because "there was no overt action by the plaintiff, purported buyer, in fact no change from the rental period and therefore no basis for a finding of part performance," "[t]here is no overt action of the Defendants in giving up possession of the tobacco barns," and "the delivery of the check by the Plaintiff to the Defendant, Patricia Hart, did not constitute partial payment of the contract because the check was never accepted legally by the Defendants." We disagree.

To qualify under Section 25-2-201(3)(c), the seller must deliver the goods and have them accepted by the buyer. "Acceptance must be voluntary and unconditional" and may "be inferred from the buyer's conduct in taking physical possession of the goods or some part of them." Howse v. Crumb, 143 Colo. 90, 352 P.2d 285, 288 (Colo.1960). . . .

In this case, the evidence, in the light most favorable to plaintiff, establishes that plaintiff told several people about purchasing the barns, reimbursed defendants for insurance on the barns, paid for improvements, took possession, enlisted the aid of an auctioneer and the paper to sell the barns, and received deposits from three buyers on the barns. The evidence, in the light most favorable to plaintiff, also establishes that plaintiff delivered a check for $5,000.00 on 22 October 1989 to defendants, and the check was not returned to plaintiff until 26 October 1989. . . . [T]his evidence represents substantial relevant evidence that a reasonable mind might accept as adequate to support the conclusions reached by the jury that there was a "contract between the plaintiff, Homer Buffaloe, and the defendants," plaintiff "accept[ed] the tobacco barns under the terms and conditions of the contract," and defendants "accept[ed] a payment for the tobacco barns under the terms and conditions of the contract." [Citations omitted.] Therefore, the trial court did not err in denying defendants' motions for directed verdict or motion for judgment notwithstanding the verdict.

No error.

NOTES AND QUESTIONS

1. It might surprise you to learn that Roanoke tobacco barns are "goods" under the UCC. (Barns hardly sound *moveable*, one of the criteria for a transaction to involve "goods.") However, if one Googles "Roanoke tobacco barns," and selects the "Images" tab, one can find a series of pictures of small, shed-like structures that look as though they can be transported.

2. What would the result have been in *Buffaloe* if the parties were reversed: if Buffaloe had changed his mind and tried to back out, and the Harts had sued to enforce the oral contract? Would the court even need to rely on the part performance exception? Or suppose (as in the actual case) Buffaloe had wanted to enforce the agreement, but the Harts had endorsed the back of the check before they returned it in shreds?

Problem 97

Mary's Used Cars orally agreed to sell Harry a 1978 Special Corvette Pace Car for $4,000. Harry made a $300 down payment. When Harry went to pick up the car, he was told there was no contract because of the lack of a writing. When Harry pointed to UCC §2-201(3)(c), Mary's manager just laughed and offered to give him a bumper worth $300. Who wins? If he had paid by a check, would the check itself have satisfied the writing requirement (Mary's Used Cars would have endorsed it when it was cashed)?

C. Admissions

In many jurisdictions, there is no "judicial admission" exception to the statute of frauds under the common law. Thus, the statute applies even "if the party against whom enforcement . . . is sought has admitted that a contract was made." Orthomet, Inc. v. A.B. Med., Inc., 990 F.2d 387, 391 (8th Cir. 1993). However, as noted below, the UCC takes a contrary view.

Uniform Commercial Code §2-201.

. . . (3) A contract which does not satisfy the requirements of [the UCC statute of frauds] but which is valid in other respects is enforceable . . . (b) if the party against whom enforcement is sought admits in his pleading, testimony or otherwise in court that a contract for sale was made, but the contract is not enforceable under this provision beyond the quantity of goods admitted.

Problem 98

Scarlett decided to sell Tara, her ancestral home, to Rhett, and they entered into an oral contract that specified all of the details. At the closing she decided at the last moment that she just couldn't bear to go through with the deal, so she refused to sign the contract that he had had prepared. When he sued, she defended on the basis of the statute of frauds, although she took the witness stand and when shown the copy of the contract that she had refused to sign she readily admitted that it correctly reflected all of the terms of their oral agreement. As the judge, how would you rule on the statute of frauds issue? Was it unethical to plead the statute in such a case? See Triangle Marketing, Inc. v. Action Indus., Inc., 630 F. Supp. 1578 (N.D. Ill. 1986) ("[T]o allow those who admit to a contract to use the statute of frauds as an insulator not only yields the 'wrong' result on the facts — which can always happen in litigation — but it also allows the litigant to thumb his or her nose at the court"); Corbin §320; Stevens, Ethics and the Statute of Frauds, 37 Cornell L.Q. 355 (1952).

NOTES AND QUESTIONS

1. What would the result be if the contract involved the sale of Tara, Scarlett's racehorse, rather than Tara, Scarlett's home? In Nebraska Builders Products Co. v. Industrial Erectors, Inc., 239 Neb. 744, 478 N.W.2d 257 (1992), the court held that a statement by the manager of the defendant supplier referring to "the contract" was a sufficient admission under the UCC.

2. A more difficult issue concerns implicit admissions arising from the nature of the pleadings. Certain responses to complaints, a demurrer, for example, does not contest the accuracy of the facts pleaded in the complaint. If the plaintiff pleads the existence of a contract, and the defendant files a demurrer, is that an admission of a contract that forbids the use of the statute of frauds defense? The majority and the dissent in the last-cited case differed on the effect that should be given to "technical admissions." Try to formulate their basis for disagreement given the major reason behind the statute of frauds: the prevention of fraud.

Problem 99

[handwritten margin notes: - one year provison; - sale of goods; → CL; → UCC; → UCC trumps the CL when it applies]

Artist Basil Hallward orally agreed to sell his five finest paintings at the rate of one a year for the next five years to Henry Wotton. The price was to be $10,000 for each painting. When the time came for delivery of the first painting, Basil couldn't bring himself to part with it. When Henry sued, Basil admitted the contract from the witness stand. Henry's attorney argued that this admission destroyed Basil's statute of frauds defense, but the other side pointed out that the contract could not be performed within one year and therefore the common law statute of frauds required a writing even if the UCC did not. How should this come out? See *Rajala v. Allied Corp.*, 66 Bankr. Rptr. 582 (D. Kan. 1986).

D. Merchant Confirmations

Uniform Commercial Code §2-201.

. . . (2) Between merchants if within a reasonable time a writing in confirmation of the contract and sufficient against the sender is received and the party receiving it has reason to know its contents, it satisfies the requirements of [the UCC statute of frauds] against such party unless written notice of objection to its contents is given within 10 days after it is received.

THOMSON PRINTING MACHINERY CO. v. B. F. GOODRICH CO.
United States Court of Appeals, Seventh Circuit, 1983
714 F.2d 744

CUDAHY, Circuit Judge. Appellant Thomson Printing Company ("Thomson Printing") won a jury verdict in its suit for breach of contract against appellee B. F. Goodrich Company ("Goodrich"). The district court concluded, however, that as a matter of law the contract could not be enforced against Goodrich because it was an oral contract, the Statute of Frauds applied and the Statute was not satisfied. Because we conclude that the contract was enforceable on the basis of the "merchants" exception to the Statute of Frauds, we reverse.

INTRODUCTION

Thomson Printing buys and sells used printing machinery. On Tuesday, April 10, 1979, the president of Thomson Printing, James Thomson, went to

Goodrich's surplus machinery department in Akron, Ohio to look at some used printing machinery which was for sale. James Thomson discussed the sale terms, including a price of $9,000, with Goodrich's surplus equipment manager, Ingram Meyers. Four days later, on Saturday, April 14, 1979, James Thomson sent to Goodrich in Akron a purchase order for the equipment and a check for $1,000 in part payment.

Procedural History

Thomson Printing sued Goodrich when Goodrich refused to perform. Goodrich asserted by way of defense that no contract had been formed and that in any event the alleged oral contract was unenforceable due to the Statute of Frauds. Thomson Printing argued that a contract had been made and that the "merchants" and "partial performance" exceptions to the Statute of Frauds were applicable and satisfied. The jury found for Thomson Printing, but the district court entered judgment for Goodrich on the grounds that the Statute of Frauds barred enforcement of the contract in Thomson's favor. . . .

THE "MERCHANTS" EXCEPTION

A modern exception to the usual writing requirement is the "merchants" exception of the Uniform Commercial Code, Ohio Rev. Code Ann. §1302.04(B) (Page 1979) (UCC §2-201(2)), which provides:

> Between merchants if within a reasonable time a writing in confirmation of the contract and sufficient against the sender is received and the party receiving it has reason to know its contents, it satisfies the [writing requirement] against such party unless written notice of objection to its contents is given within 10 days after it is received.

We must emphasize that the only effect of this exception is to take away from a merchant who receives a writing in confirmation of a contract the Statute of Frauds defense if the merchant does not object. The sender must still persuade the trier of fact that a contract was in fact made orally, to which the written confirmation applies.

In the instant case, James Thomson sent a "writing in confirmation" to Goodrich four days after his meeting with Ingram Meyers, a Goodrich employee and agent. The purchase order contained Thomson Printing's name, address, telephone number and certain information about the machinery purchase. The check James Thomson sent to Goodrich with the purchase order also had on it Thomson Printing's name and address, and the check carried notations that connected the check with the purchase order.

Goodrich Argues

Goodrich argues, however, that Thomson's writing in confirmation cannot qualify for the 2-201(2) exception because it was not received by anyone at Goodrich who had reason to know its contents.[5] Goodrich claims that Thomson erred in not specifically designating on the envelope, check or purchase order that the items were intended for Ingram Meyers or the surplus equipment department. Consequently, Goodrich contends, it was unable to "find a home" for the check and purchase order despite attempts to do so, in accordance with its regular procedures, by sending copies of the documents to several of its various divisions. Ingram Meyers testified that he never learned of the purchase order until weeks later when James Thomson called to arrange for removal of the machines. By then, however, the machines had long been sold to someone else.

[margin note: wrthng confomion couldnt "find a home"]

We think Goodrich misreads the requirements of 2-201(2). First, the literal requirements of 2-201(2), as they apply here, are that a writing "is received" and that Goodrich "has reason to know its contents." There is no dispute that the purchase order and check were received by Goodrich, and there is at least no specific or express requirement that the "receipt" referred to in 2-201(2) be by any Goodrich agent in particular.

[margin note: Courts explanation of 2-201(2)]

> These issues are not resolved by [2-201(2)], but it is probably a reasonable projection that a delivery at either the recipient's principal place of business, a place of business from which negotiations were conducted, or to which the sender may have transmitted previous communications, will be an adequate receipt.

[margin note: whos constitutes a reasonable place to delivery the receipt ("received")]

3 R. Duesenberg & L. King, Bender's UCC Service §2-204[2] at 2-70 (1982). As for the "reason to know its contents" requirement, this element "is best understood to mean that the confirmation was an instrument which should have been anticipated and therefore should have received the attention of appropriate parties." Perdue Farms, Inc. v. Motts, Inc., 459 F. Supp. 7, 20 (N.D. Miss. 1978) (quoting from Bender's UCC Service, supra, §2-204[2] at 2-69). "The receipt of a spurious document would not burden the recipient with a risk of losing the [Statute of Frauds] defense. . . ." Id. In the case before us there is no doubt that the confirmatory writings were based on actual negotiations (although the legal effect of the negotiations was disputed), and therefore the documents were not "spurious" but could have been anticipated and appropriately handled.

Even if we go beyond the literal requirements of 2-201(2) and read into the "receipt" requirement the "receipt of notice" rule of 1-201(27), we still think Thomson Printing satisfied the "merchants" exception. Section 1-201, the definitional section of the UCC, provides that notice received by an organization

[margin note: UCC 1-201(27) "receipt of Notice"]

---

5. The district court found that both parties were merchants for the purpose of 2-201(2). We agree. "For purposes of [2-201(2)] almost every person in business would, therefore, be deemed to be a 'merchant' . . . since the practices involved in the transaction are nonspecialized business practices such as answering mail." UCC §2-104, Comment 2.

UCC 1-201

is effective for a particular transaction . . . from the time when it would have been brought to [the attention of the individual conducting that transaction] if the organization had executed *due diligence.*

UCC §1-201(27) (emphasis supplied). The Official Comment states:

"Should have been"

[R]eason to know, knowledge, or a notification, although "received" for instance by a clerk in Department A of an organization, is effective for a transaction conducted in Department B only from the time when it was *or should have been* communicated to the individual conducting that transaction.

UCC §1-201(27), Official Comment (emphasis supplied).

Thus, the question comes down to whether Goodrich's mailroom, given the information it had, should have notified the surplus equipment manager, Ingram Meyers, of Thomson's confirmatory writing. At whatever point Meyers should have been so notified, then at that point Thomson's writing was effective even though Meyers did not see it. See 2 A. Squillante & J. Fonseca, Williston on Sales §14-8 at 284 (4th ed. 1974) ("the time of receipt will be measured as if the organization involved had used due diligence in getting the document to the appropriate person").

The definitional section of the UCC also sets the general standard for what mailrooms "should do":

Standard for mailrooms

An organization exercises due diligence if it maintains reasonable routines for communicating significant information to the person conducting the transaction and there is reasonable compliance with the routines.

Court Analysis

UCC §1-201(27). One cannot say that Goodrich's mailroom procedures were reasonable as a matter of law: if Goodrich had exercised due diligence in handling Thomson Printing's purchase order and check, these items would have reasonably promptly come to Ingram Meyers' attention. First, the purchase order on its face should have alerted the mailroom that the documents referred to a purchase of used printing equipment. Since Goodrich had only one surplus machinery department, the documents' "home" should not have been difficult to find. Second, even if the mailroom would have had difficulty in immediately identifying the kind of transaction involved, the purchase order had Thomson Printing's phone number printed on it and we think a "reasonable routine" in these particular circumstances would have involved at some point in the process a simple phone call to Thomson Printing. Thus, we think Goodrich's mailroom mishandled the confirmatory writings. This failure should not permit Goodrich to escape liability by pleading non-receipt. See Williston on Sales, supra, §14-8 at 284-85.

We note that the jury verdict for Thomson Printing indicates that the jury found as a fact that the contract had in fact been made and that the Statute of Frauds had been satisfied. Also, Goodrich acknowledges those facts about the handling of the purchase order which we regard as determinative of the "merchants" exception question. We think that there is *Holding* ample evidence to support the jury findings both of the existence of the contract and of the satisfaction of the Statute.

The district court, in holding as a matter of law that the circumstances failed to satisfy the Statute of Frauds, was impressed by James Thomson's dereliction in failing to specifically direct the purchase order and check to the attention of Ingram Meyers or the surplus equipment department. We agree that Thomson erred in this respect, but, for the reasons we have suggested, Goodrich was at least equally derelict in failing to find a "home" for the well-identified documents. Goodrich argues that in the "vast majority" of cases it can identify checks within a week without contacting an outside party; in the instant case, therefore, if Goodrich correctly states its experience under its procedures, it should presumably have checked with Thomson Printing promptly after the time it normally identified checks by other means — in this case, by its own calculation, a week at most. Under the particular circumstances of this case, we therefore think it inappropriate to set aside a jury verdict on Statute of Frauds grounds.

The district court's order granting judgment for Goodrich is reversed and the cause is remanded for further proceedings consistent with this opinion.

Reversed and remanded. *Reversed*

NOTES AND QUESTIONS

1. The UCC's merchant confirmation exception to the statute of frauds *Elements for merchant Exception* applies when (1) two merchants reach an agreement, (2) one merchant sends the other merchant a writing that mentions the deal, and (3) the recipient fails to object within ten days. What is the logic behind barring the recipient from invoking the statute of frauds in this situation?

2. More specifically, the written confirmation must be "sufficient against the sender": It must satisfy the requirements of the UCC's statute of frauds (evidencing a contract, mentioning a quantity, and being subscribed) *if the statute were invoked against the sender.* For example, in *Thompson Printing,* James Thompson's written confirmation contained details about the parties' agreement and apparently was subscribed by Thompson by virtue of the letterhead and perhaps the signature on the enclosed check. Because the confirmation was "sufficient against the sender" (Thompson), the clock started ticking once Goodrich received it.

3. Recall the facts of Buffaloe v. Hart, which we discussed above. Homer Buffaloe sent a signed check for the purchase of five tobacco barns to the Harts. Homer had signed the check, and it bore the label "for five barns." The Harts kept it for two or three days and then returned it in shreds. The court held that the statute of frauds did not apply because of the part performance exception. Could the court have also applied the merchant confirmation exception?

Problem 100

Despard Murgatroyd, knowing the reputation that the Oakapple Farms had for slow responses, sent a letter to the Farms stating the terms of a mythical phone conversation between the two parties in which Oakapple Farms had supposedly agreed to sell all of its 2021 crop to Despard. The letter was received by Oakapple Farms on the first of December 2022, and on February 8, 2023, the sales manager sent back a letter to Despard informing him that no such deal existed. Despard filed suit, pointing to UCC §2-201(2). What result? See §1-203.* If there really had been an oral deal, but the letter did not correctly reflect its terms, could that still be an issue in the resulting lawsuit? See Columbus Trade Exch., Inc. v. Amca Intl. Corp., 763 F. Supp. 946 (S.D. Ohio 1991).

E.   Estoppel, Waiver, and Special Manufacture

The statute of frauds, being a matter of avoidance, is an affirmative defense. Therefore, if the party claiming the protection of the statute wants to preserve the defense, it must be raised in that party's pleadings. Failing to do so means that the party forfeits the argument.

It has been long settled in most jurisdictions that a party may be estopped to assert the defense of the statute of frauds when the elements of an *equitable estoppel* exist. For an equitable estoppel to arise, there must be some misrepresentation giving rise to the detrimental reliance. In a case where the statute of frauds is at issue, the misrepresentation may be shown by evidence that the party relying on the statute had misrepresented that a writing was needed, that a writing would be executed, or that a writing had already been executed.

Problem 101

When Charles Baskerville decided to sell his house, the buyer was lawyer John Watson. The parties orally agreed to the terms but never signed a writing. If Watson backs out of the deal, is the need for a writing excused where

(a) Watson told Baskerville that no writing was required for the validity of this sale? Would your answer change if Watson were not a lawyer?

(b) Baskerville signed the writing and mailed it to Watson, who phoned Baskerville and told him he had signed it? In fact, Watson never got around to actually putting pen to paper.

* Section 1-404 in the revised version of Article 1.

(c) Watson told Baskerville that they ought to sign a writing but added, *No*
"Never mind about these legal technicalities. I promise never to raise this
issue"?

—————————

In contrast to equitable estoppel, courts traditionally would *not* allow a *Promissory Estoppel*
mere *promissory estoppel* to override the statute of frauds (that is, if there was no
misrepresentation but merely reliance on an oral promise). Nevertheless, the
use of promissory estoppel to trump the statute of frauds gained acceptance in *Now Accepted*
yet another trend-setting case by California Justice Roger Traynor, Monarco v.
Lo Greco, 35 Cal. 2d 621, 220 P.2d 737 (1950). This case and its progeny gave
rise to Restatement (Second) of Contracts §139, reprinted next. See Childres
and Garamella, The Law of Restitution and the Reliance Interest in Contract,
64 Nw. U. L. Rev. 433 (1969); Annotation, 64 A.L.R.3d 1191 (1975).

—————————

RESTATEMENT (SECOND) OF CONTRACTS

§139. Enforcement by Virtue of Action in Reliance

Promissory Estoppel

(1) A promise which the promisor should reasonably expect to induce
action or forbearance on the part of the promisee or a third person and
which does induce the action or forbearance is enforceable notwithstanding
the Statute of Frauds if injustice can be avoided only by enforcement of the
promise. The remedy granted for breach is to be limited as justice requires.

(2) In determining whether injustice can be avoided only by enforcement of the promise, the following circumstances are significant:

(a) the availability and adequacy of other remedies, particularly cancellation and restitution;

(b) the definite and substantial character of the action or forbearance in
relation to the remedy sought;

(c) the extent to which the action or forbearance corroborates evidence
of the making and terms of the promise, or the making and terms are
otherwise established by clear and convincing evidence;

(d) the reasonableness of the action or forbearance;

(e) the extent to which the action or forbearance was foreseeable by the
promisor.

NOTES AND QUESTIONS

1. Section 139 is broader than the part performance doctrine of §129
[reprinted earlier in this chapter]. Part performance, as envisioned under

§129, is typically more difficult to show than the reliance necessary to meet §139. In Ragosta v. Wilder, 156 Vt. 390, 592 A.2d 367 (Vt. 1991), unsuccessful purchasers were unable to show the applicability of the part performance exception because their actions—incurring costs to obtain financing—were merely "preparation to perform" and not part performance. The court remanded for a determination of whether the promissory estoppel doctrine would serve as an exception. In spite of the Restatement most courts have been loath to allow promissory estoppel to trump the writing required by the statute of frauds; see, e.g., Van Hook v. Quinn, 2014 WL 293857 (Ill. App. 2014).

2. Although the UCC does not expressly recognize a promissory estoppel exception to the statute of frauds, "[a] majority of jurisdictions have adopted the rule that promissory estoppel may remove an oral contract [for the sale of goods] from the . . . statute." S & P Brake Supply, Inc. v. STEMCO LP, 385 P.3d 567, 574 (Mont. 2016) (collecting cases). In addition, UCC §2-201(3)(a) establishes a similar doctrine known as the *special manufacture* exception. It states that the statute of frauds does not apply to an order for unique goods "that are not suitable for sale to others in the ordinary course of the seller's business [if] the seller . . . has made either a substantial beginning of their manufacture or commitments for their procurement."

McINTOSH v. MURPHY

Supreme Court of Hawaii, 1970
52 Haw. 29, 469 P.2d 177

LEVINSON, J. This case involves an oral employment contract which allegedly violates the provision of the Statute of Frauds requiring "any agreement that is not to be performed within one year from the making thereof" to be in writing in order to be enforceable, HRS §656-1(5). In this action the plaintiff-employee Dick McIntosh seeks to recover damages from his employer, George Murphy and Murphy Motors, Ltd., for the breach of an alleged one-year oral employment contract.

While the facts are in sharp conflict, it appears that defendant George Murphy was in southern California during March, 1964 interviewing prospective management personnel for his Chevrolet-Oldsmobile dealerships in Hawaii. He interviewed the plaintiff twice during that time. The position of sales manager for one of the dealerships was fully discussed but no contract was entered into. In April, 1964 the plaintiff received a call from the general manager of Murphy Motors informing him of possible employment within thirty days if he was still available. The plaintiff indicated his continued interest and informed the manager that he would be available. Later in April, the plaintiff sent Murphy a telegram to the effect that he would arrive in Honolulu on Sunday, April 26, 1964. Murphy then telephoned McIntosh on Saturday, April 25, 1964 to notify him that the job of assistant sales manager was open and work would begin on the following Monday, April 27, 1964. At that time McIntosh expressed surprise at the change in job title from sales manager to assistant sales manager but reconfirmed the fact that he was arriving in Honolulu the next day, Sunday. McIntosh arrived on Sunday, April 26, 1964 and began work on the following day, Monday, April 27, 1964.

As a consequence of his decision to work for Murphy, McIntosh moved some of his belongings from the mainland to Hawaii, sold other possessions, leased an apartment in Honolulu and obviously forwent any other employment opportunities. In short, the plaintiff did all those things which were incidental to changing one's residence permanently from Los Angeles to Honolulu, a distance of approximately 2200 miles. McIntosh continued working for Murphy until July 16, 1964, approximately two and one-half months, at which time he was discharged on the grounds that he was unable to close deals with prospective customers and could not train the salesmen.

At the conclusion of the trial, the defense moved for a directed verdict arguing that the oral employment agreement was in violation of the Statute of Frauds, there being no written memorandum or note thereof. The trial court ruled that as a matter of law the contract did not come within the Statute, reasoning that Murphy bargained for acceptance by the actual commencement of performance by McIntosh, so that McIntosh was not bound by a contract until he came to work on Monday, April 27, 1964. Therefore, assuming that the contract was for a year's employment, it was performable within a year exactly to the day and no writing was required for it to be enforceable. Alternatively, the court ruled that if the agreement was made final by the telephone call between the parties on Saturday, April 25, 1964, then that part of the weekend which remained would not be counted in calculating the year, thus taking the contract out of the Statute of Frauds. With commendable candor the trial judge gave as the motivating force for the decision his desire to avoid a mechanical and unjust application of the Statute.[1]

The case went to the jury on the following questions: (1) whether the contract was for a year's duration or was performable on a trial basis, thus making it terminable at the will of either party; (2) whether the plaintiff was discharged for just cause; and (3) if he was not discharged for just cause, what damages were due the plaintiff. The jury returned a verdict for the plaintiff in

---

1. The Court:

   You make the law look ridiculous, because one day is Sunday and the man does not work on Sunday; the other day is Saturday; he is up in Fresno. He can't work down there. And he is down here Sunday night and shows up for work on Monday. To me that is a contract within a year. I don't want to make the law look ridiculous, Mr. Clause, because it is one day later, one day too much, and that one day is a Sunday, and a non-working day.

the sum of $12,103.40. The defendants appeal to this court on four principal grounds, three of which we find to be without merit. The remaining ground of appeal is whether the plaintiff can maintain an action on the alleged oral employment contract in light of the prohibition of the Statute of Frauds making unenforceable an oral contract that is not to be performed within one year.

I. Time of Acceptance of the Employment Agreement

The defendants contend that the trial court erred in refusing to give an instruction to the jury that if the employment agreement was made more than one day before the plaintiff began performance, there could be no recovery by the plaintiff. The reason given was that a contract not to be performed within one year from its making is unenforceable if not in writing.

The defendants are correct in their argument that the time of acceptance of an offer is a question of fact for the jury to decide. But the trial court alternatively decided that even if the offer was accepted on the Saturday prior to the commencement of performance, the intervening Sunday and part of Saturday would not be counted in computing the year for the purposes of the Statute of Frauds. The judge stated that Sunday was a nonworking day and only a fraction of Saturday was left which he would not count. In any event, there is no need to discuss the relative merits of either ruling since we base our decision in this case on the doctrine of equitable estoppel which was properly briefed and argued by both parties before this court, although not presented to the trial court.

II. Enforcement by Virtue of Action in Reliance on the Oral Contract

In determining whether a rule of law can be fashioned and applied to a situation where an oral contract admittedly violates a strict interpretation of the Statute of Frauds, it is necessary to review the Statute itself together with its historical and modern functions. The Statute of Frauds, which requires that certain contracts be in writing in order to be legally enforceable, had its inception in the days of Charles II of England. Hawaii's version of the Statute is found in HRS §656-1 and is substantially the same as the original English Statute of Frauds.

The first English Statute was enacted almost 300 years ago to prevent "many fraudulent practices, which are commonly endeavored to be upheld by perjury and subornation of perjury." 29 Car. 2, c.3 (1677). Certainly, there were compelling reasons in those days for such a law. At the time of enactment in England, the jury system was quite unreliable, rules of evidence were few, and the complaining party was disqualified as a witness so he could neither testify on direct-examination nor, more importantly, be cross-examined. Summers, The Doctrine of Estoppel and the Statute of Frauds, 79

U. Pa. L. Rev. 440, 441 (1931). The aforementioned structural and evidentiary limitations on our system of justice no longer exist.

Retention of the Statute today has nevertheless been justified on at least three grounds: (1) the Statute still serves an evidentiary function, thereby lessening the danger of perjured testimony (the original rationale); (2) the requirement of a writing has a cautionary effect which causes reflection by the parties on the importance of the agreement; and (3) the writing is an easy way to distinguish enforceable contracts from those which are not, thus channelling certain transactions into written form.

In spite of whatever utility the Statute of Frauds may still have, its applicability has been drastically limited by judicial construction over the years in order to mitigate the harshness of a mechanical application. Furthermore, learned writers continue to disparage the Statute regarding it as "a statute for promoting fraud" and a "legal anachronism."[4]

Another method of judicial circumvention of the Statute of Frauds has grown out of the exercise of the equity powers of the courts. Such judicially imposed limitations or exceptions involved the traditional dispensing power of the equity courts to mitigate the "harsh" rule of law. When courts have enforced an oral contract in spite of the Statute, they have utilized the legal labels of "part performance" or "equitable estoppel" in granting relief. Both doctrines are said to be based on the concept of estoppel, which operates to avoid unconscionable injury. [Citations omitted.]

Part performance has long been recognized in Hawaii as an equitable doctrine justifying the enforcement of an oral agreement for the conveyance of an interest in land where there has been substantial reliance by the party seeking to enforce the contract. [Citations omitted.] Other courts have enforced oral contracts (including employment contracts) which failed to satisfy the section of the Statute making unenforceable an agreement not to be performed within a year of its making. This has occurred where the conduct of the parties gave rise to an estoppel to assert the Statute. [Citations omitted.]

It is appropriate for modern courts to cast aside the raiments of conceptualism which cloak the true policies underlying the reasoning behind the many decisions enforcing contracts that violate the Statute of Frauds. There is certainly no need to resort to legal rubrics or meticulous legal formulas when better explanations are available. The policy behind enforcing an oral agreement which violated the Statute of Frauds, as a policy of avoiding unconscionable injury, was well set out by the California Supreme Court. In Monarco v. Lo Greco, 35 Cal. 2d 621, 623, 220 P.2d 737, 739 (1950), a case which involved an action to enforce an oral contract for the conveyance of land on the grounds of 20 years performance by the promisee, the court said:

---

4. Burdick, A Statute for Promoting Fraud, 16 Colum. L. Rev, 273 (1916); Willis, The Statute of Frauds—A Legal Anachronism, 3 Ind. L.J. 427, 528 (1928).

The doctrine of estoppel to assert the statute of frauds has been consistently applied by the courts of this state to prevent fraud that would result from refusal to enforce oral contracts in certain circumstances. Such fraud may inhere in the unconscionable injury that would result from denying enforcement of the contract after one party has been induced by the other seriously to change his position in reliance on the contract.

See also Seymour v. Oelrichs, 156 Cal. 782, 106 P. 88 (1909) (an employment contract enforced).

In seeking to frame a workable test which is flexible enough to cover diverse factual situations and also provide some reviewable standards, we find very persuasive section 217A of the Second Restatement of Contracts.[5] That section specifically covers those situations where there has been reliance on an oral contract which falls within the Statute of Frauds.

Section 217A states:

(1) A promise which the promisor should reasonably expect to induce action or forbearance on the part of the promisee or a third person and which does induce the action or forbearance is enforceable notwithstanding the Statute of Frauds if injustice can be avoided only by enforcement of the promise. The remedy granted for breach is to be limited as justice requires.

(2) In determining whether injustice can be avoided only by enforcement of the promise, the following circumstances are significant: (a) the availability and adequacy of other remedies, particularly cancellation and restitution; (b) the definite and substantial character of the action or forbearance in relation to the remedy sought; (c) the extent to which the action or forbearance corroborates evidence of the making and terms of the promise, or the making and terms are otherwise established by clear and convincing evidence; (d) the reasonableness of the action or forbearance; (e) the extent to which the action or forbearance was forseeable by the promisor.

We think that the approach taken in the Restatement is the proper method of giving the trial court the necessary latitude to relieve a party of the hardships of the Statute of Frauds. Other courts have used similar approaches in dealing with oral employment contracts upon which an employee had seriously relied. [Citations omitted.] This is to be preferred over having the trial court bend over backwards to take the contract out of the Statute of Frauds. In the present case the trial court admitted just this inclination and forthrightly followed it.

There is no dispute that the action of the plaintiff in moving 2,200 miles from Los Angeles to Hawaii was foreseeable by the defendant. In fact, it was required to perform his duties. Injustice can only be avoided by the enforcement of the contract and the granting of money damages. No other remedy is adequate. The plaintiff found himself residing in Hawaii without a job.

5. Restatement (Second) of Contracts §217A (Supp. Tentative Draft No. 4, 1969).

It is also clear that a contract of some kind did exist. The plaintiff performed the contract for two and one-half months receiving $3,484.60 for his services. The exact length of the contract, whether terminable at will as urged by the defendant, or for a year from the time when the plaintiff started working, was up to the jury to decide.

In sum, the trial court might have found that enforcement of the contract was warranted by virtue of the plaintiff's reliance on the defendant's promise. Naturally, each case turns on its own facts. Certainly there is considerable discretion for a court to implement the true policy behind the Statute of Frauds, which is to prevent fraud or any other type of unconscionable injury. We therefore affirm the judgment of the trial court on the ground that the plaintiff's reliance was such that injustice could only be avoided by enforcement of the contract.

Affirmed.

ABE, J. (dissenting). The majority of the court has affirmed the judgment of the trial court; however, I respectfully dissent.

Whether alleged contract of employment came within the Statute of Frauds:

As acknowledged by this court, the trial judge erred when as a matter of law he ruled that the alleged employment contract did not come within the Statute of Frauds; however, I cannot agree that this error was not prejudicial as this court intimates.

On this issue, the date that the alleged contract was entered into was all important and the date of acceptance of an offer by the plaintiff was a question of fact for the jury to decide. In other words, it was for the jury to determine when the alleged one-year employment contract was entered into and if the jury had found that the plaintiff had accepted the offer[1] more than one day before plaintiff was to report to work, the contract would have come within the Statute of Frauds and would have been unenforceable. [Citations omitted.]

II

This court holds that though the alleged one-year employment contract came within the Statute of Frauds, nevertheless the judgment of the trial court is affirmed "on the ground that the plaintiff's reliance was such that injustice could only be avoided by enforcement of the contract."

I believe this court is begging the issue by its holding because to reach that conclusion, this court is ruling that the defendant agreed to hire the plaintiff under a one-year employment contract. The defendant has denied

---

1. Plaintiff testified that he accepted the offer in California over the telephone.

that the plaintiff was hired for a period of one year and has introduced into evidence testimony of witnesses that all hiring by the defendant in the past has been on a trial basis. The defendant also testified that he had hired the plaintiff on a trial basis.

Here on one hand the plaintiff claimed that he had a one-year employment contract; on the other hand, the defendant claimed that the plaintiff had not been hired for one year but on a trial basis for so long as his services were satisfactory. I believe the Statute of Frauds was enacted to avoid the consequences this court is forcing upon the defendant. In my opinion, the legislature enacted the Statute of Frauds to negate claims such as has been made by the plaintiff in this case. But this court holds that because the plaintiff in reliance of the one-year employment contract (alleged to have been entered into by the plaintiff, but denied by the defendant) has changed his position, "injustice could only be avoided by enforcement of the contract." Where is the sense of justice?

Now assuming that the defendant had agreed to hire the plaintiff under a one-year employment contract and the contract came within the Statute of Frauds, I cannot agree, as intimated by this court, that we should circumvent the Statute of Frauds by the exercise of the equity powers of courts. As to statutory law, the sole function of the judiciary is to interpret the statute and the judiciary should not usurp legislative power and enter into the legislative field. A. C. Chock, Ltd. v. Kaneshiro, 51 Haw. 87, 93, 451 P.2d 809 (1969); Miller v. Miller, 41 Ohio Op. 233, 83 N.E.2d 254 (Ct. C.P. 1948). Thus, if the Statute of Frauds is too harsh as intimated by this court, and it brings about undue hardship, it is for the legislature to amend or repeal the statute and not for this court to legislate.

KOBAYASHI, J., joins in this dissent.

NOTES

1. The Alaska Supreme Court has cited *McIntosh* with approval in a very similar situation. Alaska Democratic Party v. Rice, 934 P.2d 1313 (Alaska 1997) (promise to employ Rice as executive director was enforced where worker resigned from her job and moved to Alaska in reliance on promise to employ her). However, the prevailing view is to deny the use of the promissory estoppel to overcome the statute of frauds in this fashion. Sterns v. Emery-Waterhouse Co., 596 A.2d 72 (Me. 1991) (oral promise to employ plaintiff until age 55 not enforceable); McInerney v. Charter Golf, Inc., 680 N.E.2d 1347 (Ill. 1997) (must show fraud and not mere promise); and Classic Cheesecake Co. v. JP Morgan Chase Bank, N.A., 546 F.3d 839 (7th Cir. 2008) (reliance on general statement that a sought-after loan was "a go" unreasonable).

In employment-at-will cases estoppel rarely works because of the strong reluctance by courts to undermine the "at will" limitation. This doctrine is relatively straightforward: Subject to few exceptions, without a specific contract to the contrary an employee can be terminated for *any reason at any time.* Exceptions include, for example, prohibitions against discrimination on a prohibited basis such as race, gender, or age. By strictly enforcing the statute of frauds requirement—not allowing promissory estoppel to be used to enforce an oral contract contra to the at-will contract—the at-will doctrine is strengthened. For a review of the at-will doctrine, its history in one state, and the use of promissory estoppel in light of the at-will doctrine, see Connor, A Study of the Interplay Between Promissory Estoppel and At Will Employment in Texas, 53 SMU L. Rev. 579 (2000).

Exceptions

2. Waiver is generally defined as the intentional relinquishment of a known right. The law concerning the use of the doctrine of waiver as it relates to a statute of frauds is somewhat confusing because of conflicting policies: preserving the statute of frauds requirement of a writing, versus the potential of denying recovery when the person using the statute of frauds willfully entered into an oral contract or an oral modification of a written contract on which the other side had reasonably relied.

Waiver

Courts rarely give any serious time to a claim that a party waived a statute of frauds writing requirement for the parties' *initial* contract, such as the one required for the sale of real estate. However, courts have been quite inventive in finding a waiver of a writing requirement for a *modification* of a written contract, and this in spite of the usual rule that a modification of a contract required to be in writing must itself be in writing under statutes of fraud. In fact, the parties may reinforce this by a term in their contract requiring that any change be in writing. Nevertheless, a minority of courts have found waivers of the writing requirement where there has been separate consideration for the modification or significant reliance on the oral modification. For one inventive approach, see Johnson v. Sellers, 798 N.W.2d 690 (S.D. 2011), in which the court found that a change in time for payment was not a modification of a written contract but merely a waiver of the right to enforce a provision requiring payment on the date specified in the original contract.

Cannot really waive the initial contract for sale of land

modifications

CHAPTER 4 ASSESSMENT

Multiple Choice Questions

1. Sarah had a contentious relationship with her mother Alice during much of her life, but things got better as Alice aged. When Alice was 72 her health began to fail and, terrified of living alone, she begged to Sarah to return to the family home and live with her. Sarah was reluctant to do this, so Alice told her that if she did come back, live with her mother for a three-year period, care for Alice as age caused her difficulties, and take over Alice's financial affairs, Alice would pay all of their joint bills, pay

Sarah a thousand dollars a month, and at the end of the three-year period deed the house over to her daughter. Sarah dutifully did all of these things, and the contract was performed on both sides for three years. At the end of the three-year period, Alice told Sarah that she would soon have her lawyer draw up the necessary deed to transfer the house to Sarah, but the next day Alice fainted, was taken to the hospital, and died that night. Sarah comes to your law office and asks if she has any right to the house. Apparently, Alice's will leaves all of her possessions, including the house, to a cat rescue society. What do you tell her?

   a. Sarah is entitled to the house. Even though there is no writing for the sale of the interest in real property as is required by the statute of frauds, there has been sufficient part performance of the contract that a court will award the home to Sarah.

   b. Sarah gets nothing. The part performance was an ongoing exchange from which both parties benefited, but the law requires that a promise to transfer an interest in realty be in writing and here that prevents Sarah from getting the house.

   c. Promissory estoppel should save Sarah. All of the elements are in place, and, indeed, justice demands that a fully performed oral contract be excused from compliance with the strict letter of the law, particularly where, as here, both parties obeyed the contract at all moments and never repudiated it. Application of the statute of frauds would serve no purpose other than to punish innocent people who didn't understand the technicalities of the law. It would work a fraud instead of preventing one.

   d. Sarah should at least get her reliance and restitution expenses, even if the court does not give her the house. These would be computed as the value of Sarah's services over and above what she was paid both as a salary and from being able to live in the home for three years without paying rent.

2. Julio opened an email from his sister Juanita telling him that her daughter Anna was applying for a loan from Octopus National Bank to finance the purchase of a car. Neither the loan amount nor the type of car was mentioned. She asked Julio if he would be willing to be the cosigner on Anna's loan. Julio wasn't much worried about this. Anna had a good job as a veterinarian and was a reliable person, so his email reply was one word: "Sure." Anna called her uncle the next day and told him she had signed a contract to purchase a $65,000 Jaguar at Swank Motors and informed the dealership Julio would be down the next day to cosign the loan. Hearing the amount, Julio was astounded at how expensive this car would be. He told Anna that that was too much for him, and she promptly sued him when the car deal fell through because of his withdrawal. How should this come out?

    a. He has a statute of frauds defense that should protect him because this is a promise to answer for the debt of another and he never signed the contract at the dealership in which he would have made the written promise.

    b. He loses. His email agreement was a sufficient writing to satisfy the statute of frauds.

    c. He wins. His email agreement was a promise to negotiate at best, and the deal was lacking too many details to be enforceable just on the basis of the email, so no contract came into existence, and thus the statute of frauds was never triggered.

    d. The statute of frauds does not require a promise to the borrower (or the borrower's mother, as here) to cosign to be in writing; only a promise to the *creditor* to become the surety is required to be in writing. Thus the email, even if it contemplates a sufficient contract, has no statute of frauds problem. The only issue remaining is whether there was sufficient agreement via the email to create a contract for him to become a surety. This could go either way, with him arguing that too much was left unspecified, and his relatives arguing that if he wanted more details before committing himself, he should have brought that up before he answered, "Sure."

3. The shipping agent at Seller Corporation received a phone call from the sales clerk at Buyer Corporation asking if Seller could immediately send Buyer 1,000 drums of the premium motor oil that Seller Corporation produced, naming a price and a delivery date in the following month. The shipping agent at Seller replied that this was such a large order that she would have to check and see if her company had to capacity to fulfill this request. The sales clerk at Buyer Corporation immediately sent a fax to Seller Corporation stating, "This is to confirm that you have agreed to sell us 1,000 drums of your premium motor oil" and then specified the price and the delivery date above the buyer's signature. Seller Corporation received the fax but it was lost in some paperwork and not found for two weeks. At that point the shipping agent phoned Buyer Corporation and denied that there was any such contract as stated in the fax. Buyer sued Seller for its damages caused by the shipment not being made, and pointed to the fax as establishing the contract per the rule of §2-201(2) that a writing sent between merchants establishes the contract unless objected to in writing within ten days of receipt. The contract was for more than $500, thus triggering that section. How does this come out?

    a. The buyer is right. The cited section does create the contract under this provision, sometimes called the rule that "merchants must read their mail." A fax is a writing and the seller had plenty of time to avoid the contract by making an objection within the ten-day period.

    b. The seller wins. Section 2-201(2) gets rid of the statute of frauds problem all right, but it does not establish that there was a contract.

An actual offer and acceptance must still be proven, and here there were only preliminary negotiations. A contract was never agreed upon.

   c. Buyer wins. The offer was made on the phone and the written fax established a duty of the seller to speak. Since the seller was silent, a contract came into existence and the fax satisfied the statute of frauds per the rule in §2-201(2).

   d. Seller wins. There was no duty to speak here since seller, having lost the fax, never knew about the written offer. The oral offer over the phone was clearly not accepted, and §2-201(2) does not create a contractual duty to speak up, it only deprives the merchant who receives such a writing of the statute of frauds defense that would otherwise be available.

4. Kathy Hyland applied for her dream job with Listening World and was delighted when she was told in a phone call that the position of running the drama program for deaf children was hers. The job would be for a three-year period and pay her $50,000 each year. The caller warned her, however, that it was possible the federal government would not renew its grant of financial assistance to Listening World when the grant came up for renewal this coming summer and if that happened she would immediately be let go. But, the caller added, she shouldn't worry about that because the chances were excellent that the government would keep its financing going. Kathy started work immediately and was very pleased three months later when the government did continue the financing. However, she was very upset when Listening World discharged her at Christmas time, citing financial difficulties that caused it to terminate the entire drama program. When Kathy sued the response was that this contact fell under the one-year rule of the statute of frauds and that the lack of a writing doomed her lawsuit. How does this come out?

   a. Kathy wins. This contract was not required to be in writing because it might have been performed in under a year if the government financing had not come through. If a contract can be performed in less than a year, even if that was not likely to happen and indeed did not happen, nonetheless no writing is required. The oral agreement is enforceable because it might have ended according to its own terms within a year's period.

   b. Listening World wins. The statute of frauds defense defeats her. The contract was for three years and the possibility that it might have been terminated earlier was not "performance" within the year but the occurrence of a destructive event neither party bargained for. You can always think of things that might happen that would keep a contract from being performed (Kathy's death, for example), but the mere possibility of early termination due to a problem does not shorten the announced term of the contract.

Answers

1. All of these are possible solutions, but with equities strongly in Sarah's favor the courts will likely give her the home under either the part performance or promissory estoppel theories. Even if that doesn't happen, she would be entitled to quasi-contractual relief calculated as in D.

2. D is the best answer. There is no statute of frauds issue when the promise to be a surety is only made to the borrower; the statute is triggered when the suretyship promise is made to the creditor (here the auto dealership). That said, there is still the issue of whether there was a definite enough promise to enforce based on the sketchy details agreed upon in the email. Julio has some hope of winning that argument since the car is so pricey and arguably well beyond what he expected.

3. B and D are the best answers. Section 2-201(2) only deals with getting rid of the need of a writing when the parties have truly agreed upon the details of the contract through oral negotiations. Here there was no such agreement and the buyer, who has the burden of proof, will have a hard time convincing a court that seller ever agreed to the terms of the sale.

4. A is the best answer. If the parties have an agreement containing a possible scenario in which the contract might end according to its own terms within a year's period, no writing is required even if that event never occurred. That said, if the event is not specified in the contract, the fact that it's possible to think of things that would unnaturally terminate the contract (say, Kathy's death) would not avoid the necessity of having a writing for a contract clearly lasting more than one year.

5

THE PAROL EVIDENCE RULE AND INTERPRETATION OF THE CONTRACT

Few things are darker than this, or fuller of subtle difficulties.
— Thayer, A Preliminary Treatise on Evidence
at Common Law 390 (1898)

This chapter focuses on defining the parties' rights and obligations. This inquiry involves two basic steps. One requires setting the boundaries of the agreement: a step the parties may have begun by putting their agreement in writing. If the parties have memorialized some or all of their understandings in a writing, to what extent may evidence of prior agreements or negotiations be introduced to add to or vary the text? The resolution of that question requires exploration of the *parol evidence rule.*

The other step requires clarifying the "meaning" of the parties' "agreement." What the parties wrote in the contract is the starting point for that inquiry. But writings (as we know from our own and you may know from yours) are not always a model of clarity. Thus a word or phrase or paragraph or more may be ambiguous (susceptible to more than one meaning). Which meaning should the court apply: what the court presumes to be the intent of the parties after reading the writing, what one of the parties to the contract argues the words mean, or how an outside party or parties may interpret such words? Should the court take into consideration the surrounding circumstances, such as who drafted the contract and the nature of the parties' relationship? Determining the legal significance of the contractual language is the process of *interpretation.*

The parol evidence rule and the process of interpretation are closely related and may be discussed together in any given court decision with no clear indication of which doctrine is truly relevant. We therefore divide the discussion of the two doctrines (with some trepidation) with the hope that the meaning of all this will become clearer.

I.   THE PAROL EVIDENCE RULE

A.   *Introduction*

The parol evidence rule bars a party from using certain forms of proof—called *parol evidence*—for particular purposes in court. "Parol" is a French word meaning "informal" (in other words, not under seal). Thus, "parol evidence" is oral or written negotiations or understandings that are made prior to (or at the same as) the final written contract. The logic of the parol evidence rule is simple: If the parties have taken the trouble to reduce their agreement to a formal, detailed writing, that writing must mention every term to which they *actually* agreed. Accordingly, the parol evidence rule precludes parties from trying to establish that a clause was mysteriously omitted or that the words of a writing do not mean what they seem to mean.

More specifically, the parol evidence rule has two prongs. First, it prevents litigants from using parol evidence to *supplement* a *fully integrated* contract. "Supplementing" is adding additional, consistent terms. As we will see below, a contract is "fully integrated" if it is long, formal, and detailed, revealing that the parties intended it to be a comprehensive account of their rights and obligations. Second, the parol evidence rule bars parties from using parol evidence to *contradict* a written contact (even if it is only "partially" integrated). The cases in this section flesh out these concepts.

RESTATEMENT (SECOND) OF CONTRACTS

§213. Effect of Integrated Agreement on Prior Agreements (Parol Evidence Rule)

(1) A binding integrated agreement discharges prior agreements to the extent that it is inconsistent with them.

(2) A binding completely integrated agreement discharges prior agreements to the extent that they are within its scope. . . .

UNIFORM COMMERCIAL CODE

§2-202. Final Written Expression: Parol or Extrinsic Evidence

Terms with respect to which the confirmatory memoranda of the parties agree or which are otherwise set forth in a writing intended by the parties as a final expression of their agreement with respect to such terms as are included therein may not be contradicted by evidence of any prior agreement or of a contemporaneous oral agreement but may be explained or supplemented:

(a) by course of dealing or usage of trade (Section 1-205) or by course of performance (Section 2-208); and

(b) by evidence of consistent additional terms unless the court finds the writing to have been intended also as a complete and exclusive statement of the terms of the agreement.

Problem 102

For two years World Wide Widgets (WWW) negotiated for the construction and purchase of a new computer system from MegaHard Computers, with teams of lawyers bargaining heatedly over the contract terms. A long, detailed contract was finally signed by the two parties, and the new system was designed and installed. Two days later the president of WWW canceled the purchase, saying that the system was unsatisfactory and that, in addition to all the terms of the written contract, the parties had an oral understanding that WWW could get out of the deal at any time if it didn't like the way the computer system was functioning.

You are the trial judge hearing the lawsuit that arose out of this. Will you allow in evidence of this oral understanding?

[handwritten margin notes: Ascertain the mutual / Whose / Parties / Intended]

[handwritten margin notes: Judicial efficiency]

[handwritten note: Con lead to a miscarriage of justice]

[handwritten note: Be more careful in drafting contracts]

Problem 103

Jane Bean and Hiram Walkup agreed that Jane would build a dock for Hiram on a lake near Big Rock Candy Mountain. They entered into a formal written contract utilizing a construction contract form supplied by Jane's attorney. Construction began. One day while sitting near Lemonade Springs, Jane commented that it was becoming difficult to purchase copper-clad nails as specified in the contract. Hiram said, "Oh, Jane, you can use galvanized nails if you like." And Jane did. Now Hiram has sued Jane for breach of contract because Jane used galvanized nails. Jane has offered evidence of the oral agreement. Hiram objects because of the parol evidence rule. Is it applicable here?

[handwritten note: No, only bars prior or contemporaneous / → this was a subsequent promise]

B. Integration Level

As noted, the parol evidence rule precludes parties from using parol evidence to supplement a fully integrated contract. Thus, the first step in the analysis is to determine whether a writing is either (1) fully integrated (intended to be final and complete), (2) partially integrated (intended to be final and complete with respect to some issues but not others), or (3) unintegrated (oral and therefore not subject to the parol evidence rule). Confusingly, some courts refer to fully integrated writings either as "completely integrated" or simply as "integrated." Likewise, the UCC §2-202 does not use the term "integrated" at all. Nevertheless, no matter the terminology, all approaches to the parol evidence rule start with the same question: Is the writing a complete or only a partial representation of the parties' final agreement?

THOMPSON v. LIBBEY
Supreme Court of Minnesota, 1885
26 N.W. 1

The plaintiff being the owner of a quantity of logs marked "H. C. A.," cut in the winters of 1882 and 1883, and lying in the Mississippi river, or on its banks, above Minneapolis, defendant and the plaintiff, through his agent, D. S. Mooers, having fully agreed on the terms of a sale and purchase of the logs referred to, executed the following written agreement:

> "AGREEMENT.
> "HASTINGS, MINN., June 1, 1883.
> "I have this day sold to R. C. Libbey, of Hastings, Minn., all my logs marked 'H. C. A.,' cut in the winters of 1882 and 1883, for ten dollars a thousand feet, boom scale at Minneapolis, Minnesota. Payment, cash, as fast as scale bills are produced.
> [Signed]
> "J. H. THOMPSON,
> "Per D. S. MOOERS.
> "R. C. LIBBEY."

This action having been brought for the purchase money, and defendant having pleaded a warranty of the quality of the logs, alleged to have been made at the time of the sale, and a breach of it, offered on the trial oral testimony to prove the warranty, which was admitted, over the objection of plaintiff that it was incompetent to prove a verbal warranty, the contract of sale being in writing. This raises the only point in the case. . . .

No rule is more familiar than that parol contemporaneous evidence is inadmissible to contradict or vary the terms of a valid written instrument, and yet none has given rise to more misapprehension as to its application. It is a rule founded on the obvious inconvenience and injustice that would result if matters in writing, made with consideration and deliberation, and intended to embody the entire agreement of the parties, were liable to be controlled by what Lord COKE expressively calls "the uncertain testimony of slippery memory." Hence, where the parties have deliberately put their engagements into writing in such terms as to import a legal obligation, without any uncertainty as to the object or extent of such engagement, it is conclusively presumed that the whole engagement of the parties, and the manner and extent of their undertaking, was reduced to writing. Of course, the rule presupposed that the parties intended to have the terms of their complete agreement embraced in the writing, and hence it does not apply where the writing is incomplete on its face and does not purport to contain the whole agreement; as in the case of mere bills of parcels, and the like.

But in what manner shall it be ascertained whether the parties intended to express the whole of their agreement in the writing? It is sometimes loosely stated that where the whole contract be not reduced to writing, parol evidence may be admitted to prove the part omitted. But to allow a party to lay the foundation for such parol evidence by oral testimony that only part of the agreement was reduced to writing, and then prove by parol the part omitted, would be to work in a circle, and to permit the very evil which the rule was designed to prevent. The only criterion of the completeness of the written contract as a full expression of the agreement of the parties is the writing itself. If it imports on its face to be a complete expression of the whole agreement, — that is, contains such language as imports a complete legal obligation, — it is to be presumed that the parties here introduced into it every material item and term; and parol evidence cannot be admitted to add another term to the agreement, although the writing contains nothing on the particular one to which the parol evidence is directed. The rule forbids to add by parol when the writing is silent, as well as to vary where it speaks. . . . The written agreement in the case at bar, as it appears on its face, in connection with the law controlling its construction and operation, purports to be a complete expression of the whole agreement of the parties as to the sale and purchase of these logs, solemnly executed by both parties. There is nothing on its face (and this is a question of law for the court) to indicate that it is a mere informal and incomplete memorandum. Parol evidence of extrinsic facts and circumstances would, if necessary, be admissible, as it always is, to apply the contract to its subject-matter, or in order to a more perfect understanding of its language. But in that case such evidence is used, not to contradict or vary the written instrument, but to aid, uphold, and enforce it as it stands. The language of this contract "imports a legal obligation, without any uncertainty as to its object or the extent of the engagement," and therefore "it must be conclusively presumed that the whole engagement of the parties, and the manner and extent of the undertaking, was reduced to writing." No new term, forming a mere incident to or part of the contract of sale, can be added by parol. That in case of a sale of personal property a warranty of its quality is an item and term of the contract of sale, and not a separate and independent collateral contract, and therefore cannot be added to the written agreement by oral testimony, has been distinctly held by this court, in accordance, not only with the great weight of authority, but also, as we believe, with the soundest principles. Jones v. Alley, 17 Minn. 292 (Gil. 269.) . . .

We have carefully examined all the cases cited in the quite exhaustive brief of counsel for defendant, and find but very few that are at all in conflict with the views already expressed, and these few do not commend themselves to our judgment. Our conclusion therefore is that the court erred in admitting parol evidence of a warranty, and therefore the order refusing a new trial must be reversed.

NOTES AND QUESTIONS

1. The buyer in *Thompson* argued that the seller had made an oral warranty about the logs: a factual statement such as "these logs are A-1 quality," or "these logs are pine, not fir." However, the parties' written contract said nothing about the topic. Thus, the buyer was trying to supplement the writing by adding consistent — or at least *not inconsistent* terms — to it. As the court observes, the parol evidence rule precludes evidence of this allegedly missing term if the writing is fully integrated. Thus, the outcome of the dispute hinges on the integration level of the contract: full or partial?

2. The court notes that the parol evidence rule is "founded on the obvious inconvenience and injustice that would result" if parol evidence were allowed to add to or alter "matters in writing, made with consideration and deliberation." What does the court mean? What policy purposes does the rule serve by barring parol evidence?

3. Because the parol evidence rule only prohibits the use of parol evidence for particular purposes, it is imperative to ask *why* a party wants to introduce such evidence. For example, in *Thompson*, if the buyer was trying to use parol evidence to *contradict* the writing — perhaps by testifying that the parties had actually agreed to payment on credit, rather than "cash" (as the writing states) — integration level would not matter. Parol evidence cannot override a writing's express text, no matter whether the writing is fully or partially integrated. On the flip side, as we will see later in this chapter, parol evidence *is* admissible to *explain* an ambiguous writing. Thus, if the parties disagreed about whether the contract's reference to logs "cut in the winter[] of 1882" included logs cut in November 1882, each side might be able to bolster their respective readings of this language with parol evidence.

4. *Thompson* finds that the contract is fully integrated based on the face of the writing alone. As the court puts it, "[t]he only criterion of the completeness of the written contract as a full expression of the agreement is the writing itself." Thus, it asks whether the document is long, formal, and detailed (and thus likely to be the complete expression of the parties' rights and duties) or sketchy and casual (in which case it might only cover a fragment of a larger deal). This view, which was championed by Professor

Samuel Williston, is known as the *four-corners test* for determining integration level. It still applies in several jurisdictions. See, e.g., Mellon Bank Corp. v. First Union Real Estate Equity & Mortgage Investments, 750 F. Supp. 711 (W.D. Pa. 1990), aff'd, 951 F.2d 1399 (3d Cir. 1991).

5. Other courts (including the Minnesota Supreme Court, which decided *Thompson*) have abandoned the stringent four-corners test. Following the lead of Professor Arthur Corbin, they categorize a writing as either fully or partially integrated by examining circumstances such as "the situation of the parties, the subject matter[,] and purposes of the transaction." Bussard v. College of St. Thomas, Inc., 294 Minn. 215, 200 N.W.2d 155 (1972); Restatement (Second) of Contracts §214. (Corbin was no fan of the parol evidence rule, believing that it merely restated the obvious: Later agreements cancel prior ones if so intended by the parties; see Corbin §574.) For example, these courts have reasoned that parties who are old friends or longtime business partners may not reduce their entire agreement to writing because they trust each other to honor handshake deals. Our next case exemplifies this approach.

LOPEZ v. REYNOSO
Court of Appeals of Washington, 2005
118 P.3d 398

SCHULTHEIS, J.

¶1 Parol evidence is generally admissible to construe a written contract and to determine the intent of the parties. Berg v. Hudesman, 115 Wash.2d 657, 669, 801 P.2d 222 (1990). However, parol evidence cannot add to, modify, or contradict the terms of a fully integrated contract. Id. at 670, 801 P.2d 222.

¶2 Stephany Lopez bought a used car from Ramon Reynoso (doing business as Triple R Auto Sales) pursuant to an installment sales contract. When Ms. Lopez did not make all the payments listed in her amortization schedule, Mr. Reynoso repossessed the car. Ms. Lopez sued for replevin and additional recovery. She moved to exclude parol evidence offered by Mr. Reynoso to show that a $2,000 payment by Ms. Lopez on the day of the sale or one day later [had already been] deducted from the sale price listed on the contract. She contends the $2,000 was actually an additional payment that reduced her obligation under the contract. The trial court allowed the parol evidence and entered judgment for Mr. Reynoso.

¶3 On appeal, Ms. Lopez contends the trial court erred in admitting parol evidence that contradicted terms in the integrated contract. . . . We conclude that the trial court was justified in examining extrinsic evidence to determine whether the contract was the final expression of the parties' agreement. [Thus], we affirm.

FACTS

¶4 Mr. Reynoso began selling used cars as Triple R Auto Sales in May 2000. His family had known Ms. Lopez for several years. In late May 2000, Ms. Lopez visited Triple R and asked the price of a 1994 Ford Explorer. Mr. Reynoso was out of town, but an employee called him and learned that the asking price was $8,500. Ms. Lopez tried to negotiate a lower price with the employee, but he asked her to return when Mr. Reynoso could talk with her.

¶5 Two days later, on June 2, Ms. Lopez purchased the Explorer from Mr. Reynoso. According to her, the parties agreed to a sale price of $6,500 with $500 down and interest at three percent. She claims she gave Mr. Reynoso $500 down in cash but never received a receipt for the payment. Mr. Reynoso claims he agreed to lower the sale price to $8,000 if Ms. Lopez agreed to pay $2,000 down. He asserts Ms. Lopez's boyfriend, Fernando Ortega, gave him $1,800 on June 2, when the agreement was executed, and Ms. Lopez brought in the additional $200 the next day. . . .

¶6 Mr. Reynoso insists Ms. Lopez did not want the sales contract to show that the couple had paid $2,000 down. He was not sure why Ms. Lopez wanted the contract to state the sale price was $6,500 with a down payment of $500, but because the payments would be the same, he agreed to write it the way he says Ms. Lopez wanted it. At trial, Mr. Reynoso's daughter, a childhood friend of Ms. Lopez, testified that she witnessed the execution of the contract and that Ms. Lopez had the idea to write the contract with a price reduced by $2,000 because she did not want Mr. Ortega's name to be on the title to the car.

¶7 The terms of the contract, as drafted by the Triple R accountant on June 2, state that the price of the vehicle is $6,500, the tax and license fee are over $500, and the down payment is $500, for a total price of $6,533. Language at the bottom of the purchase order form states: "This order cancels and supercedes any prior agreement and as of the date herein comprises the complete and exclusive statement of the terms of this agreement." Clerk's Papers (CP) at 58. After Ms. Lopez signed the agreement, the accountant compiled an amortization schedule for $250 monthly payments and gave a copy to Ms. Lopez. This schedule indicates that Ms. Lopez's last payment was due in September 2002.

¶8 According to Mr. Reynoso, Ms. Lopez was often late with payments and did not make her December 2001 payment. When she appeared at his office in January 2002 with a $250 payment, he refused it, claiming she owed him for two months. Ms. Lopez contends she asserted at that time that her $2,000 payment was made after the sale agreement and lowered her obligation by another $2,000, which would be paid in full by the December 2001 payment. Mr. Reynoso says Ms. Lopez did not claim she had paid the full amount with the December payment. Ms. Lopez again offered to pay $250 in February 2002 and Mr. Reynoso again rejected the payment. He repossessed the Explorer in March 2002. Later that month, Ms. Lopez hired Molly Earhart to prepare an amortization schedule based on a purchase price of $7,033 (the sale price plus tax and license), a down payment of $500, and a post-sale payment of $2,000. According to this new amortization schedule, Ms. Lopez's final payment should have been only $145 in January 2002.

¶9 Ms. Lopez filed a complaint against Mr. Reynoso, his wife, Triple R, and the bonding company on April 11, 2002. She requested return of the Explorer, treble damages, and attorney fees for breach of the contract and violations of chapter 46.70 RCW (proscribing unfair motor vehicle business practices) and chapter 19.86 RCW (Washington's Consumer Protection Act). In September 2002 she moved for an order in limine to exclude parol evidence and for judgment on the pleadings. The motions were denied after a hearing. After a bench trial in September 2003, the court entered judgment for the defendants. Ms. Lopez's motion for reconsideration was denied and the trial court's findings, conclusions, and judgment were entered on November 14, 2003. The notice of appeal was timely filed.

Parol Evidence

¶10 Ms. Lopez first challenges the trial court's consideration of evidence extrinsic to the written contract. She contends the trial court used this evidence to contradict or vary the express, unambiguous terms of the integrated contract. We review the trial court's findings of fact regarding the admissibility of parol evidence for substantial evidence. [Citations omitted.] The evidence is viewed in the light most favorable to the prevailing party, and we defer to the trier of fact on issues of witness credibility. *Weyerhaeuser*, 123 Wash. App. at 65, 96 P.3d 460.

¶11 In Washington, "[t]he touchstone of contract interpretation is the parties' intent." Tanner Elec. Coop. v. Puget Sound Power & Light, 128 Wash. 2d 656, 674, 911 P.2d 1301 (1996). This intent may be discerned from the language of the agreement as well as from viewing the objective of the contract, the circumstances around its making, the subsequent conduct of the parties, and the reasonableness of their respective interpretations. Under the parol evidence rule, "prior or contemporaneous negotiations and agreements are said to merge into the final, written contract," Emrich v. Connell, 105 Wash. 2d 551, 556, 716 P.2d 863 (1986), and evidence is not admissible to add to, modify, or contradict the terms of the integrated agreement. But the parol evidence rule is only applied to writings intended as the final expression of the terms of the agreement. Extrinsic evidence may be used to ascertain the intent of the parties, to properly construe the writing, and to determine whether the writing is actually intended to be the final expression of the agreement.

¶12 Generally people have the right to make their agreements entirely oral, entirely in writing, or partly oral and partly in writing. With a written contract, "it is the court's duty to ascertain from all relevant, extrinsic evidence, either oral or written, whether the entire agreement has been incorporated in the writing or not. That is a question of fact." *Barber*, 52 Wash. 2d at 698, 328 P.2d 711. If the writing is a complete integration, any terms and agreements that are not contained in it are disregarded. If it is not intended to be the complete expression of the parties' intent — in other words, if it is only partially integrated — the writing may be supplemented or replaced by consistent terms or agreements shown by a preponderance of the evidence.

¶13 The Lopez-Reynoso written agreement executed on June 2, 2000 stated that the cash price of the vehicle was $6,500, the down payment was $500, and Ms. Lopez would make 26 payments of $250 and a final payment of $264.87. The sales contract included an integration clause that stated that the writing comprised the complete and exclusive statement of the terms. When Mr. Reynoso responded that the writing was an incomplete expression of the entire negotiations and agreements of the parties, the trial court was obligated to consider any extrinsic evidence to determine whether the agreement was fully integrated, and if not, what other terms consistent with the written agreement were operative.

¶14 After considering the parties' inconsistent recitations of the events leading up to the sale, the testimony of witnesses, and evidence of customary retail business practices, the trial court found Mr. Reynoso's explanation more credible and reasonable and implicitly concluded that the written agreement was only partially integrated. These findings are supported by substantial evidence. For instance, Mr. Reynoso testified that he invested almost $6,000 in the Explorer, suggesting that a sale price of $6,500 was not believable. The trial court also found it unrealistic that a used car dealer financing a sale himself would accept a down payment of less than 10 percent. We defer to the trial court's firsthand determination of the witnesses' credibility.

¶15 Assuming that the written sale agreement was only partially integrated and that the parties had orally agreed to additional terms, we address the remaining question: whether the purported oral agreement contradicts any valid terms of the written contract. Evidence that the parties agreed to reduce the sale price by the $2,000 down payment is not inconsistent with the actual terms of repayment included in the contract and the amortization schedule. The reduced price of $6,000 does contradict the written terms of a $6,500 sale price and a $500 down payment, but the result is the same: a contract price of $6,000 for a vehicle originally priced at $8,500. Ultimately, the extrinsic evidence of prior negotiations reveals terms that do not contradict the written terms of the vehicle's price and the number of payments Ms. Lopez owed.

¶16 Ms. Lopez notes that the integration clause at the bottom of Mr. Reynoso's "vehicle purchase order" explicitly provides that the written agreement is fully integrated. CP at 58. The relevant statements on this standard form are as follows:

> Purchaser agrees that (1) this order includes all the terms and conditions on both the face and the reverse side of, together with any attachments herein referred to. (2) This order cancels and supercedes any prior agreement and as of the date herein comprises the complete and exclusive statement of the terms of this agreement relating to the subject matters covered hereby.

CP at 58. Although an integration clause is a strong indication that the parties intended complete integration of a written agreement, a boilerplate clause will not be given effect if it appears that the provision is factually false. Parol evidence is admissible to show whether language denying the existence of any other agreement is controlling. When material extrinsic evidence shows that outside agreements were relied upon, those parol agreements should be given effect rather than allowing boilerplate "to vitiate the manifest understanding of the parties." *Lyall,* 42 Wash. App. at 258, 711 P.2d 356.

¶17 The integration language here is in a boilerplate clause attached to the vehicle purchase order form. The trial court's decision to ignore the integration clause is supported by substantial evidence that the parties based the sales contract on an outside agreement to lower the sale price by the $2,000 down payment. . . .

Affirmed.

I CONCUR: Brown, J.

Sweeney, A.C.J. (dissenting) — I respectfully dissent.

¶23 Parol evidence tending to contradict the terms of a written contract should not, in the face of oral testimony corresponding with the unambiguous language in the contract, be allowed to nullify the language of the instrument. If the parol evidence rule does not apply to these facts, it is meaningless.

¶24 The parties do not dispute the facts. Stephany Lopez bought a car from Ramon Reynoso pursuant to a[] . . . written contract. The contract states the price as $6,500. Ms. Lopez began missing payments, and Mr. Reynoso repossessed the car. In response to Ms. Lopez's action for replevin, Mr. Reynoso repudiated the plain terms of the written contract and successfully enforced an alleged oral agreement that the price was really $2,000 higher than the written contract price.

¶25 The trial court erred in admitting parol evidence directly contradicting the terms of the written contract.

¶26 The contract Mr. Reynoso now repudiates was his contract. He drafted it. He was responsible for it. Mr. Reynoso included in his contract an ironclad integration clause:

> Purchaser agrees that (1) this order includes all the terms and conditions on both the face and the reverse side of, together with any attachments herein

referred to. (2) This order cancels and supercedes any prior agreement and as of the date herein comprises the complete and exclusive statement of the terms of this agreement relating to the subject matters covered hereby.

Clerk's Papers at 58. This language may be "boilerplate." But, again, it is Mr. Reynoso's boilerplate. Ms. Lopez did not change the language or add anything to this contract as a result of her discussions with the seller. And while the absence of such a clause suggests that the agreement or purchase order was not the complete agreement of the parties, the inclusion of an integration clause suggests just the opposite.

¶27. . . . A central element of any contract is the price. Here, the price is stated as $6,500. The price Mr. Reynoso claims, $8,000, certainly contradicts or varies the terms of this written agreement.

¶28 I would, then, enforce the contract as written. If parties to an integrated written contract have a secret handshake agreement to contrary terms, it is the written agreement the courts will enforce.

NOTES AND QUESTIONS

1. Ms. Lopez argues that she bought the Explorer for about $6,500 and then made an immediate $2,000 payment, lowering the amount she owed to $4,500. Conversely, Mr. Reynoso claims that Ms. Lopez purchased the car for $8,000 and then made a $2,000 down payment, lowering the amount she owned to $6,000. The trial court believed Mr. Reynoso. Do you?

2. As the dissent notes, the existence of an "integration" (or "merger") clause — which addresses the integration issue head on by declaring that the parties intend a writing to be complete — usually tips the scales sharply toward full integration. Why does the majority discount the presence of this provision?

3. Suppose the majority is correct that the contract was only partially integrated. Even then, parol evidence can only *supplement* — not *contradict* — the writing. How would you classify the purpose for which Mr. Reynoso seeks to use the parol evidence?

C. *Exceptions*

Although the parol evidence rule serves important objectives, it can cause injustice. On the plus side, it encourages the parties to be careful when they draft and read contracts. But it also fails to account for the messiness of real world interactions. Few contracts are formed between parties who can afford the luxury of reducing every facet of their agreement to writing. Often, one party dictates terms to the other, offers oral assurances that other matters will be honored, and then adds a merger clause to bar this evidence. Accordingly, the parol evidence rule is riddled with caveats and exceptions.

1. Collateral Agreements

Perhaps the most important limit on the parol evidence rule is that it does not apply to *collateral agreements*: prior or contemporaneous understandings that are distinct from a subsequent written contract (even if that contract is fully integrated). Suppose that Bob orally agrees to work for Stacy's law firm as an associate for $1,000 a week. Later, Bob and Stacy sign a detailed written contract in which Bob agrees to buy Stacy's house for $100,000. Even if the real estate contract is fully integrated, the employment agreement is collateral: Its subject matter is so different that the parties would not necessarily address it when they enshrined the real estate transaction in writing. Thus, the parol evidence rule would *not* prohibit either party from testifying (or offering other proof) that they had reached an oral agreement for employment.

As you will see in the cases that follow, some courts merge the collateral agreement exception with the threshold issue of whether a writing is fully integrated. This is a slightly different way of reaching the same result. Courts that use this terminology conclude that writings can be fully integrated with respect to some topics *but not to others*. In the Bob and Stacy example above, some judges would conclude that the written real estate contract is fully integrated on all matters relating to the house sale, but *not* fully integrated when it comes to issues relating to employment. Whether a court conceptualizes the problem that way or exempts collateral agreements from the parol evidence rule, the outcome is the same: The parol evidence rule does *not* apply to omitted provisions that one would *not* necessarily expect to see in the writing.

RESTATEMENT (SECOND) OF CONTRACTS

§216. CONSISTENT ADDITIONAL TERMS

(1) Evidence of a consistent additional term is admissible to supplement an integrated agreement unless the court finds that the agreement was completely integrated.

(2) An agreement is not completely integrated if the writing omits a consistent additional agreed term which is

    (a) agreed to for separate consideration, or

    (b) such a term as in the circumstances might naturally be omitted from the writing.

UNIFORM COMMERCIAL CODE

§2-202. Final Written Expression: Parol or Extrinsic Evidence, cmt. 3

If the additional terms are such that, if agreed upon, they would certainly have been included in the document in the view of the court, then evidence of their alleged making must be kept from the trier of fact.

MITCHILL v. LATH
Court of Appeals of New York, 1928
247 N.Y. 377, 160 N.E. 646

Andrews, J. In the fall of 1923 the Laths owned a farm. This they wished to sell. Across the road, on land belonging to Lieutenant-Governor Lunn, they had an ice house which they might remove. Mrs. Mitchill looked over the land with a view to its purchase. She found the ice house objectionable. Thereupon "the defendants orally promised and agreed, for and in consideration of the purchase of their farm by the plaintiff, to remove the said ice house in the spring of 1924." Relying upon this promise, she made a written contract to buy the property for $8,400, for cash and a mortgage and containing various provisions usual in such papers. Later receiving a deed, she entered into possession and has spent considerable sums in improving the property for use as a summer residence. The defendants have not fulfilled their promise as to the ice house and do not intend to do so. We are not dealing, however, with their moral delinquencies. The question before us is whether their oral agreement may be enforced in a court of equity.

This requires a discussion of the parol evidence rule—a rule of law which defines the limits of the contract to be construed. Glackin v. Bennett, 226 Mass. 316, 115 N.E. 490. It is more than a rule of evidence and oral testimony even if admitted will not control the written contract, O'Malley v. Grady, 222 Mass. 202, 109 N.E. 829, unless admitted without objection. Brady v. Nally, 151 N.Y. 258, 45 N.E. 547. It applies, however, to attempts to modify such a contract by parol. It does not affect a parol collateral contract distinct from and independent of the written agreement. It is, at times, troublesome to draw the line. Williston, in his work on Contracts (sec. 637) points out the difficulty. "Two entirely distinct contracts," he says, "each for a separate consideration may be made at the same time and will be distinct legally. Where, however, one agreement is entered into wholly or partly in consideration of the simultaneous agreement to enter into another, the transactions are necessarily bound together. . . . Then if one of the agreements is oral and the other is written, the problem arises whether the bond is sufficiently close to prevent proof of the oral agreement." That is the situation here. It is claimed that the defendants are called on to do more than is required by their written contract in connection with the sale as to which it deals.

The principle may be clear, but it can be given effect by no mechanical rule. As so often happens, it is a matter of degree, for as Professor Williston also says where a contract contains several promises on each side it is not difficult to put any one of them in the form of a collateral agreement. If this were enough, written contracts might always be modified by parol. Not form, but substance is the test.

In applying this test the policy of our courts is to be considered. We have believed that the purpose behind the rule was a wise one not easily to be abandoned. Notwithstanding injustice here and there, on the whole it works for good. Old precedents and principles are not to be lightly cast aside unless it is certain that they are an obstruction under present conditions. New York has been less open to arguments that would modify this particular rule, than some jurisdictions elsewhere. . . .

Under our decisions before such an oral agreement as the present is received to vary the written contract at least three conditions must exist, (1) the agreement must be in form a collateral one; (2) it must not contradict express or implied provisions of the written contract; and (3) it must be one that parties would not ordinarily be expected to embody in the writing; or put in another way, an inspection of the written contract, read in the light of surrounding circumstances must not indicate that the writing appears "to contain the engagement of the parties, and to define the object and measure the extent of such engagement." Or again, it must not be so clearly connected with the principal transaction as to be part and parcel of it.

Rule

The respondent does not satisfy the third of these requirements. It may be, not the second. We have a written contract for the purchase and sale of land. The buyer is to pay $8,400 in the way described. She is also to pay her portion of any rents, interest on mortgages, insurance premiums and water meter charges. She may have a survey made of the premises. On their part the sellers are to give a full covenant deed of the premises as described, or as they may be described by the surveyor if the survey is had, executed, and acknowledged at their own expense; they sell the personal property on the farm and represent they own it; they agree that all amounts paid them on the contract and the expense of examining the title shall be a lien on the property; they assume the risk of loss or damage by fire until the deed is delivered; and they agree to pay the broker his commissions. Are they to do more? Or is such a claim inconsistent with these precise provisions? It could not be shown that the plaintiff was to pay $500 additional. Is it also implied that the defendants are not to do anything unexpressed in the writing?

didn't satisfy element 3, or 2

No consideration for removing Ice house

That we need not decide. At least, however, an inspection of this contract shows a full and complete agreement, setting forth in detail the obligations of each party. On reading it one would conclude that the reciprocal obligations of the parties were fully detailed. Nor would his opinion alter if he knew the surrounding circumstances. The presence of the ice house, even the knowledge that Mrs. Mitchill thought it objectionable would not lead to the belief that a separate agreement existed with regard to it. Were such an agreement made it would seem most natural that the inquirer should find it in the contract. Collateral in form it is found to be, but it is closely related to the subject dealt with in the written agreement — so closely that we hold it may not be proved.

Where the line between the competent and the incompetent is narrow the citation of authorities is of slight use. Each represents the judgment of the court on the precise facts before it. How closely bound to the contract is the supposed collateral agreement is the decisive factor in each case. . . .

It is argued that what we have said is not applicable to the case as presented. The collateral agreement was made with the plaintiff. The contract of sale was with her husband and no assignment of it from him appears. Yet the deed was given to her. It is evident that here was a transaction in which she was the principal from beginning to end. We must treat the contract as if in form, as it was in fact, made by her.

Our conclusion is that the judgment of the Appellate Division and that of the Special Term should be reversed and the complaint dismissed, with costs in all courts.

LEHMAN, J. (dissenting). I accept the general rule as formulated by Judge Andrews. I differ with him only as to its application to the facts shown in the record. The plaintiff contracted to purchase land from the defendants for an agreed price. A formal written agreement was made between the sellers and the plaintiff's husband. It is on its face a complete contract for the conveyance of the land. It describes the property to be conveyed. It sets forth the purchase price to be paid. All the conditions and terms of the conveyance to be made are clearly stated. I concede at the outset that parol evidence to show additional conditions and terms of the conveyance would be inadmissible. There is a conclusive presumption that the parties intended to integrate in that written contract every agreement relating to the nature or extent of the property to be conveyed, the contents of the deed to be delivered, the consideration to be paid as a condition precedent to the delivery of the deeds, and indeed all the rights of the parties in connection with the land. The conveyance of that land was the subject-matter of the written contract and the contract completely covers that subject.

The parol agreement which the court below found the parties had made was collateral to, yet connected with, the agreement of purchase and sale. It has been found that the defendants induced the plaintiff to agree to purchase the land by a promise to remove an ice house from land not covered by the agreement of purchase and sale. No independent consideration passed to the defendants for the parol promise. To that extent the written contract and the alleged oral contract are bound together. The same bond usually exists wherever attempt is made to prove a parol agreement which is collateral to a written agreement. Hence "the problem arises whether the bond is sufficiently close to prevent proof of the oral agreement." See Judge Andrews' citation from Williston on Contracts, section 637.

Judge Andrews has formulated a standard to measure the closeness of the bond. Three conditions, at least, must exist before an oral agreement may be proven to increase the obligation imposed by the written agreement. I think we agree that the first condition that the agreement "must in form be a collateral one" is met by the evidence. I concede that this condition is met in most cases where the courts have nevertheless excluded evidence of the collateral oral agreement. The difficulty here, as in most cases, arises in connection with the two other conditions.

The second condition is that the "parol agreement must not contradict express or implied provisions of the written contract." Judge Andrews voices doubt whether this condition is satisfied. The written contract has been carried out. The purchase price has been paid; conveyance has been made, title has passed in accordance with the terms of the written contract. The mutual obligations expressed in the written contract are left unchanged by the alleged oral contract. When performance was required of the written contract, the obligations of the parties were measured solely by its terms. By the oral agreement the plaintiff seeks to hold the defendants to other obligations to be performed by them thereafter upon land which was not conveyed to the plaintiff. The assertion of such further obligation is not inconsistent with the written contract unless the written contract contains a provision, express or implied, that the defendants are not to do anything not expressed in the writing. Concededly there is no such express provision in the contract, and such a provision may be implied, if at all, only if the asserted additional obligation is "so clearly connected with the principal transactions as to be part and parcel of it," and is not "one that the parties would not ordinarily be expected to embody in the writing." The hypothesis so formulated for a conclusion that the asserted additional obligation is inconsistent with an implied term of the contract is that the alleged oral agreement does not comply with the third condition as formulated by Judge Andrews. In this case, therefore, the problem reduces itself to the one question whether or not the oral agreement meets the third condition.

I have conceded that upon inspection the contract is complete. "It appears to contain the engagements of the parties, and to define the object and measure the extent of such engagement"; it constitutes the contract between them and is presumed to contain the whole of that contract. (Eighmie v. Taylor, 98 N.Y. 288.) That engagement was on the one side to convey land; on the other to pay the price. The plaintiff asserts further agreement based on the same consideration to be performed by the defendants after the conveyance was complete, and directly affecting only other land. It is true, as Judge Andrews points out, that "the presence of the ice house, even the knowledge that Mrs. Mitchill thought it objectionable, would not lead to the belief that a separate agreement existed with regard to it"; but the question we must decide is whether or not, *assuming* an agreement was made for the removal of an unsightly ice house from one parcel of land as an inducement for the purchase of another parcel, the parties would ordinarily or naturally be expected to embody the agreement for the removal of the ice house from one parcel in the written agreement to convey the other parcel. Exclusion of proof of the oral agreement on the ground that it varies the contract embodied in the writing may be based only upon a finding or presumption that the written contract was intended to cover the oral negotiations for the removal of the ice house which lead up to the contract of purchase and sale. To determine what the writing was intended to cover "the document alone will not suffice. What it was intended to cover cannot be known till we know what there was to cover. The question being whether certain subjects of negotiation were intended to be covered, we must compare the writing and the negotiations before we can determine whether they were in fact covered." (Wigmore on Evidence (2d ed.), section 2430.)

The subject matter of the written contract was the conveyance of land. The contract was so complete on its face that the conclusion is inevitable that the parties intended to embody in the writing all the negotiations covering at least the conveyance. The promise by the defendants to remove the ice house from other land was not connected with their obligation to convey, except that one agreement would not have been made unless the other was also made. The plaintiff's assertion of a parol agreement by the defendants to remove the ice house was completely established by the great weight of evidence. It must prevail unless that agreement was part of the agreement to convey and the entire agreement was embodied in the writing.

The fact that in this case the parol agreement is established by the overwhelming weight of evidence is, of course, not a factor which may be considered in determining the competency or legal effect of the evidence. Hardship in the particular case would not justify the court in disregarding or emasculating the general rule. It merely accentuates the outlines of our problem. The assumption that the parol agreement was made is no longer obscured by any doubts. The problem then is clearly whether the parties are presumed to have intended to render that parol agreement legally ineffective and non-existent by failure to embody it in the writing. Though we are driven to say that nothing in the written contract which fixed the terms and conditions of the stipulated conveyance suggests the existence of any further parol agreement, an inspection of the contract, though it is complete on its face in regard to the subject of the conveyance, does not, I think, show that it was intended to embody negotiations or agreements, if any, in regard to a matter so loosely bound to the conveyance as the removal of an ice house from land not conveyed. . . .

CARDOZO, C.J., POUND, KELLOGG, and O'BRIEN, JJ., concur with ANDREWS, J.; LEHMAN, J., dissents in opinion in which CRANE, J., concurs.

QUESTIONS

1. If Mrs. Mitchill really did contract for the removal of the ice house, why, as a practical matter, didn't she insist on this agreement being included in the writing?

2. Under Restatement (Second) §216, an omitted term or agreement is collateral if it either boasts its own consideration (apart from the written contract) or "might naturally be omitted from the writing." How would each element apply to *Mitchill*?

BETACO, INC. v. CESSNA AIRCRAFT CO.
United States Court of Appeals, Seventh Circuit, 1994
32 F.3d 1126

ROVNER, Circuit Judge. Betaco, Inc. ("Betaco") agreed in 1990 to purchase a six-passenger CitationJet from the Cessna Aircraft Company ("Cessna"). Betaco's decision was based in part on Cessna's representation in a cover letter accompanying the purchase agreement that the new jet was "much faster, more efficient and has more range than the popular Citation I," a model with which Betaco was familiar. After advancing $150,000 toward the purchase of the new plane, Betaco became convinced that the Citation-Jet would not have a greater range than the Citation I with a full passenger load and decided to cancel the purchase. When Cessna refused to return Betaco's deposit, Betaco filed suit in diversity claiming, inter alia, that Cessna had breached an express warranty that the CitationJet had a greater range than the Citation I. The district court rejected Cessna's contention that the purchase agreement signed by the parties was a fully integrated document that precluded Betaco's attempt to rely on this warranty. A jury concluded that the cover letter's representation as to the range of the plane did amount to an express warranty and that Cessna had breached this warranty, and Betaco was awarded damages of $150,000 with interest. We reverse the district court's entry of partial summary judgment in favor of Betaco on the threshold integration issue, concluding that a question of fact exists as to the parties' intent that can be resolved only after a factual hearing before the district court.

I. BACKGROUND

A. FACTS

Betaco is a Delaware corporation headquartered in Indiana; it is a holding company that acquires aircraft for sale or lease to other companies and also for the personal use of J. George Mikelsons, the company owner. Betaco leases aircraft to Execujet and also to American Transair, an airline that Mikelsons founded in 1973 and of which he is the chairman and chief executive. Both companies interlock with Betaco. Mikelsons is himself an experienced pilot.

In late 1989, Betaco became interested in a new aircraft known as the CitationJet to be manufactured by Cessna, a Kansas corporation. Mikelsons contacted Cessna and asked for information about the forthcoming plane. On January 25, 1990, Cessna forwarded to Mikelsons a packet of materials accompanied by a cover letter which read as follows:

Dear Mr. Mikelsons:

We are extremely pleased to provide the material you requested about the phenomenal new CitationJet.

Although a completely new design, the CitationJet has inherited all the quality, reliability, safety and economy of the more than 1600 Citations before it. At 437 miles per hour, the CitationJet is much faster, more efficient, and has more range than the popular Citation I. And its luxurious first-class cabin reflects a level of comfort and quality found only in much larger jets.

And you get all this for less than an ordinary turboprop!

If you have questions or need additional information about the CitationJet, please give me a call. I look forward to discussing this exciting new airplane with you.

Sincerely,
Robert T. Hubbard
Regional Manager

App. 97. Enclosed with Hubbard's letter was a twenty-three page brochure providing general information about the CitationJet, including estimates of the jet's anticipated range and performance at various fuel and payload weights. A purchase agreement was also enclosed. The preliminary specifications attached and incorporated into that agreement as "Exhibit A" indicated that the CitationJet would have a full fuel range of 1,500 nautical miles, plus or minus four percent, under specified conditions. App. 108.

Mikelsons signed the purchase agreement on January 29, 1990 and returned it to Cessna, whose administrative director, Ursula Jarvis, added her signature on February 8, 1990. The agreement occupied both sides of a single sheet of paper. As completed by the parties, the front side reflected a purchase price of $2.495 million and a preliminary delivery date of March, 1994, with Betaco reserving the right to opt for an earlier delivery in the event one were possible. The payment terms required Betaco to make an initial deposit of $50,000 upon execution of the contract, a second deposit of

$100,000 when Cessna gave notice that the first prototype had been flown, and a third deposit of $125,000 at least six months in advance of delivery. The balance was to be paid when the plane was delivered. The agreement expressly incorporated the attached preliminary specifications, although Cessna reserved the right to revise them "whenever occasioned by product improvements or other good cause as long as such revisions do not result in a reduction in performance standards." Item number 9 on the front page stated:

> The signatories to this Agreement verify that they have read the complete Agreement, understand its contents and have full authority to bind and hereby do bind their respective parties.

Following this provision, in a final paragraph located just above the signature lines (written in capital lettering that distinguished this provision from the preceding provisions), the agreement stated:

PURCHASER AND SELLER ACKNOWLEDGE AND AGREE BY EXECUTION OF THIS AGREEMENT THAT THE TERMS AND CONDITIONS ON REVERSE SIDE HEREOF ARE EXPRESSLY MADE PART OF THIS AGREEMENT. EXCEPT FOR THE EXPRESS TERMS OF SELLER's WRITTEN LIMITED WARRANTIES PERTAINING TO THE AIRCRAFT, WHICH ARE SET FORTH IN THE SPECIFICATION (EXHIBIT A), SELLER MAKES NO REPRESENTATIONS OR WARRANTIES EXPRESS OR IMPLIED, OF MERCHANTABILITY, FITNESS FOR ANY PARTICULAR PURPOSE, OR OTHERWISE WHICH EXTEND BEYOND THE FACE HEREOF OR THEREOF. THE WRITTEN LIMITED WARRANTIES OF SELLER ACCOMPANYING ITS PRODUCT ARE IN LIEU OF ANY OTHER OBLIGATION OR LIABILITY WHATSOEVER BY REASON OF THE MANUFACTURE, SALE, LEASE OR USE OF THE WARRANTED PRODUCTS AND NO PERSON OR ENTITY IS AUTHORIZED TO MAKE ANY REPRESENTATIONS OR WARRANTIES OR TO ASSUME ANY OBLIGATIONS ON BEHALF OF SELLER. THE REMEDIES OF REPAIR OR REPLACEMENT SET FORTH IN SELLER's WRITTEN LIMITED WARRANTIES ARE THE ONLY REMEDIES UNDER SUCH WARRANTIES OR THIS AGREEMENT. IN NO EVENT SHALL SELLER BE LIABLE FOR ANY INCIDENTAL OR CONSEQUENTIAL DAMAGES, INCLUDING, WITHOUT LIMITATION, LOSS OF PROFITS OR GOODWILL, LOSS OF USE, LOSS OF TIME, INCONVENIENCE, OR COMMERCIAL LOSS. THE ENGINES AND ENGINE ACCESSORIES ARE SEPARATELY WARRANTED BY THEIR MANUFACTURER AND ARE EXPRESSLY EXCLUDED FROM THE LIMITED WARRANTIES OF SELLER. THE LAWS OF SOME STATES DO NOT PERMIT CERTAIN LIMITATIONS ON WARRANTIES OR REMEDIES. IN THE EVENT THAT SUCH A LAW APPLIES, THE FOREGOING EXCLUSIONS AND LIMITATIONS ARE AMENDED INSOFAR AND ONLY INSOFAR, AS REQUIRED BY SAID LAW.

App. 99 ¶9 (emphasis in original). On the reverse side, the agreement included the following integration clause among its "General Terms:"

> This agreement is the only agreement controlling this purchase and sale, express or implied, either verbal or in writing, and is binding on Purchaser and Seller, their heirs, executors, administrators, successors or assigns. This Agreement, including the rights of Purchaser hereunder, may not be assigned by Purchaser except to a wholly-owned subsidiary or successor in interest by name change or otherwise and then only upon the prior written consent of Seller. Purchaser acknowledges receipt of a written copy of this Agreement which may not be modified in any way except by written agreement executed by both parties.

App. 100, Section IV ¶7.

In early 1992, Paul Ruley and another Betaco employee visited Cessna's facilities in order to select the radio and navigational equipment to be installed in the plane. In the course of his work as an administrator for Execujet and American Transair, Ruley assesses the suitability of aircraft for particular charter flights based on the distance, passenger load, fuel, aircraft weight, and runway requirements. After his visit to Cessna, Ruley completed some calculations concerning the CitationJet and showed them to Mikelsons. By Ruley's estimate, the new jet would have a greater range than its predecessor, the Citation I, when carrying three to five passengers; but with a full passenger load of six (plus two crew members), the CitationJet would have a range no greater than or slightly less than that of the Citation I. Ruley also believed that the new plane would not meet the full fuel range of 1,500 nautical miles set forth in the preliminary specifications.

After seeing Ruley's numbers, Mikelsons contacted Cessna in March or April 1992. The testimony at trial was in conflict as to exactly what Cessna personnel told Mikelsons about the range of the new plane. In any case, Mikelsons was not satisfied that the CitationJet would live up to his expectations and decided to cancel the purchase. On April 16, 1992, Mick Hoveskeland of Cessna wrote to Mikelsons accepting the cancellation and offering to apply Betaco's deposit toward the purchase of another aircraft. Cessna subsequently refused Betaco's demand for a return of the deposit, however, invoking the contract's proviso that "all cash deposits shall be retained by [Cessna] not as a forfeiture but as liquidated damages for default if this Agreement is canceled or terminated by [Betaco] for any cause whatsoever. . . ." Betaco proceeded to file this suit.

B. PROCEEDINGS BELOW

[Of relevance here is the district court's decision concerning the admissibility of the express warranty made in Hubbard's letter of January 25, 1990.] . . .

The district court granted partial summary judgment in favor of Betaco [on the issue of whether the parol evidence rule of §2-202 excluded evidence of the express warranty]. The court found that Hubbard's January 25, 1990 cover letter to Mikelsons did, in fact, contain an express warranty to the effect that the range of the CitationJet would exceed the range of the Citation I. The court then considered whether the purchase agreement was a fully integrated document that would rule out extrinsic evidence concerning such an independent express warranty. Although the court acknowledged that the terms of the agreement declared it to be fully integrated and disclaimed any express warranties beyond its four corners, the court nonetheless concluded that the parties did not intend the contract to be the sole and exclusive reflection of their agreement. The court reasoned that Hubbard's representation as to the range of the CitationJet vis-à-vis the Citation I was not the type of term that would necessarily have been included in the contract itself; it was not, for example, so central to the agreement that Betaco would have insisted that it be written into the pre-printed purchase agreement. At the same time, the fact that the representation had been made in the cover letter accompanying the purchase agreement (which Mikelsons signed shortly after he received it) suggested to the court that the parties considered that representation to be the basis of their bargain. Finally, the court noted that the purchase agreement had not been the subject of extensive negotiation, and that Mikelsons had simply signed it without first seeking the counsel of an attorney. "Not only does this tend to excuse Betaco for failing to have the representations [as to the relative range of the jet] included in the Purchase Agreement, but it minimizes the impact of the warranty limitation and contract integration clauses in the Purchase Agreement." Mem. Op. at 8. . . .

II. ANALYSIS

The sole issue before us is whether the district court erred in concluding that the contract signed by Betaco and Cessna was not a fully integrated contract containing a complete and exclusive statement of the parties' agreement. . . . Both parties agree that we should look to Kansas law in resolving this issue [that is, UCC §2-202]. . . .

The parties agree that they intended the signed purchase contract as a final expression of the terms set forth within its four corners. Betaco, however, has relied on Hubbard's cover letter as evidence of a "consistent additional term" of the agreement. Section 2-202(b) bars that evidence (and thus Betaco's claim for breach of the warranty in Hubbard's letter) if the parties intended the signed contract to be the "complete and exclusive" statement of their agreement.

An initial question arises as to the appropriate standard of review. Cessna urges us to review the district court's decision de novo, whereas Betaco contends that the court's ruling was a factual determination that we may review for clear error only.

Although the rule set forth in §2-202 is superficially a rule of evidence, Kansas does not treat it as such: "'The parol evidence rule is not a rule of evidence, but of substantive law. Its applicability is for the court to determine, and, when the result is reached it is a conclusion of substantive law.'" In re Estate of Goff, 379 P.2d 225, 234 (Kan. 1963) (quoting Phipps v. Union Stock Yards Nat'l Bank, 34 P.2d 561, 563 (Kan. 1934)); [further citation omitted]. We have likewise treated the rule as a substantive one, and have accordingly considered the determination of whether or not an agreement was completely integrated to be a legal determination subject to de novo review. [Citations omitted.]

Betaco correctly points out, however, that insofar as this determination turns on the intent of the contracting parties, it poses a factual question. See Willner, 848 F.2d at 1022 n.3; Transamerica Oil Corp. v. Lynes, Inc., 723 F.2d 758, 763 (10th Cir. 1983). Thus, in cases where the integration assessment amounts to "a predominantly factual inquiry, revolving around the unwritten intentions of the parties instead of interpretation of a formal integration clause," courts have treated the district court's determination as a finding of fact subject to review only for clear error. [Citations omitted.]

Yet, in this case, the district court decided the question on summary judgment. Essentially, the court determined that the evidence before it could only be construed in one way, and that Betaco was entitled to judgment as a matter of law on the integration issue. Thus, the precise question before us is not who should prevail ultimately on the integration issue, but whether it was appropriate to enter partial summary judgment in favor of Betaco and against Cessna on the matter. Our review of that particular determination is of course, de novo, as it would be in any other appeal from the grant of summary judgment. . . .

The familiar rule of contractual interpretation is that absent an ambiguity, the intent of the parties is to be determined from the face of the contract, without resort to extrinsic evidence. [Citations omitted.] Yet, the drafters of §2-202 rejected any presumption that a written contract sets forth the parties' entire agreement. [Citations omitted.] Instead, in ascertaining whether the parties intended their contract to be completely integrated, a court looks beyond the four corners of the document to the circumstances surrounding the transaction, "including the words and actions of the parties." Burge v. Frey, 545 F. Supp. 1160, 1170 (D. Kan. 1982). *Mid Continent Cabinetry* identifies the relevant considerations:

> The focus is on the intent of the parties. Sierra Diesel Injection Service v. Burroughs Corp., 890 F.2d 108, 112 (9th Cir. 1989). Section 2-202 does not offer any tests for determining if the parties intended their written agreement

to be integrated. Comment three to §2-202 offers one measure of when a statement is complete and exclusive: "If the additional terms are such that, if agreed upon, they would certainly have been included in the document in the view of the court, then evidence of their alleged making must be kept from the trier of fact." The courts have looked to several factors, not just the writing, in deciding if the writing is integrated. These factors include merger or integration clauses, [citations omitted]; disclaimer clauses, [citations omitted]; the nature and scope of prior negotiations and any alleged extrinsic terms, [citations omitted]; and the sophistication of the parties [citations omitted].

favors the court. Consider of course is honored

1991 WL 151074, at *8. . . .

We look first to the warranty limitation and integration clauses of the purchase agreement, as these speak directly to the completeness and exclusivity of the contract. The warranty limitation clause states that "[e]xcept for the express terms of seller's written limited warranties pertaining to the aircraft, which are set forth in the specification (Exhibit A), [Cessna] makes no representations or warranties express or implied, of merchantability, fitness for any particular purpose, or otherwise *which extend beyond the face hereof or thereof.*" (Emphasis supplied.) The clause goes on to admonish the buyer that no individual is authorized to make representations or warranties on behalf of Cessna. On its face, this clause might be construed to disavow the types of representations found in Hubbard's letter to Mikelsons. However, as a general rule, express warranties, once made, cannot be so easily disclaimed. Section 2-316(1) of the Kansas U.C.C. provides that "subject to the provisions of this article on parol or extrinsic evidence (K.S.A. §84-2-202), negation or limitation [of an express warranty] is inoperative to the extent such construction is unreasonable." Kan. Stat. Ann. §84-2-316(1) [further citations omitted]. The commentary explains that the purpose of this provision is to "protect a buyer from unexpected and unbargained language of disclaimer." Kan. Stat. Ann. §84-2-316(1), Official U.C.C. Comment (1); [further citations omitted]. On the other hand, the disclaimer rule is, by its express terms, subject to the provisions of §2-202 (see Kan. Stat. Ann. §84-2-316(1) & Kansas Comment 1983); thus, if the signed contract is deemed fully integrated, the plaintiff is precluded from attempting to establish any express warranty outside the signed contract. [Citations omitted.]

We thus turn to the integration clause of the contract. Although not dispositive, "the presence of a merger clause is strong evidence that the parties intended the writing to be the complete and exclusive agreement between them. . . ." *L. S. Heath & Co.,* 9 F.3d at 569 (citing *Sierra Diesel,* 890 F.2d at 112; [further citations omitted]). Here the clause states that "[t]his agreement is the only agreement controlling this purchase and sale, express or implied, either verbal or in writing, and is binding on Purchaser and Seller" and that the agreement "may not be modified in any way except by written agreement executed by both parties." (Emphasis supplied.)[2]

The language is simple and straightforward; and Betaco does not suggest that a reasonable buyer would find it difficult to comprehend. On the other hand, Betaco does note, as the district court did (Mem. Op. at 8), that this was, like most other provisions in the contract, a preprinted clause that was not the subject of negotiation by the parties. Yet, that fact alone does not render the provision unenforceable. See Northwestern Nat'l Ins. Co. v. Donovan, 916 F.2d 372, 377 (7th Cir. 1990). The clause was not buried in fine print, nor was it written so as to be opaque. See id. It was relegated to the back of the contract rather than the front, but the front page admonished the signatories in bold, capitalized lettering that the terms on the back were part of the agreement, and although the reverse side contained a number of provisions, they were neither so many nor so complicated that the reader would have given up before he or she reached the integration clause. Mikelsons signed the contract, and there is no dispute that he had the opportunity to review it in as much detail as he wished before signing it. Under these circumstances, the integration provision should have come as no surprise to Betaco. Compare *Transamerica Oil*, 723 F.2d at 763 (where plaintiff's order was taken over telephone, document that plaintiff received and signed upon delivery did not constitute fully integrated agreement); *Hemmert*, 663 F. Supp. at 1553 (same). In our view, therefore, the clause is strong evidence that the parties intended and agreed for the signed contract to be the complete embodiment of their agreement.

The district court focused on another circumstance that courts frequently consider in assessing the degree to which a contract is integrated: is the term contained in a purported warranty outside the contract one that the parties would have included in the contract itself had they intended it to be part of the agreement? U.C.C. §2-202, Official Comment (3); *Mid-Continent Cabinetry*, 1991 WL 151074, at *8. The court thought that Hubbard's representation as to the relative range of the CitationJet was not such a term, although neither the court nor Betaco has cited any evidence in the record to support that proposition. The court did note that "[t]he representation made by Mr. Hubbard was not so formally presented nor central to the purchase that Mr. Mikelsons of Betaco would most likely have insisted it be included, especially where the Purchase Agreement was a standard form. The representation did not include the word 'warranty,' a

---

2. Betaco points out that the integration clause purports only to disavow other agreements, not other warranties. We do not find the distinction persuasive, however. The essence of the integration inquiry, after all, is whether the parties intended their written contract to embody the entirety of their agreement; if so, extrinsic evidence of an additional warranty that Cessna purportedly made cannot be admitted. Thus, although the integration clause speaks in terms of agreements rather than warranties, if it is given effect and the signed purchase contract is deemed to be a fully integrated agreement, it effectively operates so as to preclude the plaintiff from relying on purported warranties beyond the four corners of that agreement.

red flag that might have clued a non-attorney into the necessity of including it in the Purchase Agreement." Mem. Op. at 7. Our analysis is somewhat different on this score, however.

We are not persuaded that the range of the aircraft was not something that certainly would be included in the agreement. On the contrary, the specifications made part of the contract do contain an express representation as to the range of the CitationJet, and, in fact, it was that warranty that formed the basis for Count I of Betaco's complaint. In that sense, an extraneous reference to the range of the aircraft arguably is less like a supplemental term on a subject as to which the contract is otherwise silent, and more like a potentially conflicting term that section 2-202 would explicitly exclude from admission into evidence. See generally Souder v. Tri-County Refrigeration Co., 373 P.2d 155, 159-60 (Kan. 1962) (noting the distinction between using extrinsic evidence to explain or supplement the contract and using it to vary the terms of the agreement).

The context of the representation does not alter our analysis in this regard. It may well be, as the district court emphasized, that because the statement as to the relative range of the CitationJet was contained in the cover letter accompanying the purchase agreement, Mr. Mikelsons may have given it more weight than he would a more isolated statement. Mem. Op. at 7. At the same time, as the court pointed out, the reference was informal, without language that might alert the reader that the contract should include a comparable provision. Id. But in our view, one might just as readily infer from this that the contents of the letter were not meant to supplement the purchase agreement. Recall the wording of the passage on which Betaco relies: "At 437 miles per hour, the CitationJet is much faster, more efficient, and has more range than the popular Citation I." Like the balance of the letter, this statement is long on adjectives and short on details — how much faster? how much more efficient? how much more range? Consider, in contrast, the following excerpt from the specifications incorporated into the purchase agreement:

ESTIMATED PERFORMANCE (Preliminary) Conditions:
   All estimated performance data are based on a standard aircraft and International Standard Atmosphere. Takeoff and landing field lengths are based on level, hard surface, dry runways with zero wind.

Range +/−4%	At 10,000 lbs. (4536 kg)
(Includes Takeoff, Climb,	TOGW 1500 nautical miles
Cruise at 41,000 Feet,	(2779 km) with full fuel
Descent, and 45-Minute Reserve)	
Stall Speed 81 knots	(150 km/hr) (93 MPH)
	CAS at 9500 lbs
(Landing Configuration)	(4309 kg)
Maximum Altitude	41,000 ft (12,497 m)

Single Engine Climb Rate (Sea Level, ISA, 10,000 lbs)	1070 feet per minute
Takeoff Runway Length (Sea Level, ISA, Balanced Field Length per FAR 25)	2960 ft (902 m) at 10,000 lbs (4536 kg)
Landing Runway Length (Sea Level, ISA, per FAR 25)	2800 ft (854 m) at 9500 lbs (4309 kg)
Cruising Speed +/−3% (Maximum Cruise Thrust, ISA Conditions at 35,000 Feet)	380 kts (704 km/hr) (437 mph) TAS at 8500 lbs (3856 kg) cruise weight

App. 108. This summary of the aircraft's performance capabilities is, in stark contrast to the letter, quite precise and quite explicit about the assumptions underlying each of the estimates. Given the marked difference in style and detail between these specifications and the indeterminate braggadocio in the cover letter, we find it somewhat implausible that the parties might have considered the "more range" reference to be part of their agreement yet failed to include it in the purchase contract with the level of specificity characteristic of that document.

Finally, we do not find it particularly significant that Mikelsons did not consult a lawyer before signing the purchase agreement. Again, the contract was neither lengthy nor obtuse. Nor was this a contract of adhesion. These were two seemingly sophisticated parties entering into a commercial agreement, and Mikelsons's significant experience as a pilot, as an airline executive, and as a purchaser of an earlier model of the Citation aircraft surely went a long way toward balancing whatever advantage Cessna may have enjoyed as the drafter of the agreement. [Citations omitted.] Furthermore, there is no evidence that the contract was tainted by fraud, mutual mistake, or any other circumstance that would call into question the binding nature of the agreement. See generally *Prophet*, 462 P.2d at 126. That Betaco chose not to have the contract reviewed by an attorney before Mikelsons signed it does not, standing alone, permit Betaco to escape the operation of the terms it signed on to, including the integration clause. As the Kansas Supreme Court has stated:

> This court follows the general rule that a contracting party is under a duty to learn the contents of a written contract before signing it. Sutherland v. Sutherland, 187 Kan. 599, 610, 358 P.2d 776 (1961). We have interpreted this duty to include the duty to obtain a reading and explanation of the contract, and we have held that the negligent failure to do so will estop the contracting party from avoiding the contract on the ground of ignorance of its contents. Maltby v. Sumner, 169 Kan. 417, Syl. ¶5, 219 P.2d 395 (1950). As a result of this duty, a person who signs a written contract is bound by its terms regardless of his or her failure to read and understand its terms.

Rosenbaum v. Texas Energies, Inc., 736 P.2d 888, 891-92 (Kan. 1987). [Citations omitted.] That we would make this assumption should come as no surprise to Betaco, for in signing the contract, Mikelsons also assented to its provision that "[t]he signatories to this Agreement verify that they have read the complete Agreement, understand its contents and have full authority to bind and hereby do bind their respective parties."

The circumstances identified by the district court do not, in sum, establish as a matter of law that the purchase agreement was not fully integrated and that extrinsic evidence of additional, consistent terms was therefore admissible. Nor has Betaco identified anything more in the record that would support partial summary judgment in its favor on this question. The district court's decision to grant partial summary judgment in favor of Betaco and against Cessna therefore must be reversed, and the jury's verdict (which was based upon the extrinsic evidence admitted pursuant to the district court's summary judgment ruling) must be vacated. . . .

Holding

However...

[At this point the Seventh Circuit seemed prepared to award summary judgment in Cessna's favor. However, the court found, without the help of either party's briefs, statements in a supporting affidavit of Mikelsons (president of Betaco) that the court felt had bearing on the issue of the admissibility of the parol evidence. This evidence was in the form of statements about conversations Mikelsons had had concerning the performance of the aircraft. This evidence prompted the court in part to add:]

If, in fact, there were substantial discussions preceding Betaco's commitment to the purchase of the CitationJet focusing specifically on the range of the new jet vis-à-vis the Citation I, one might infer that the signed agreement did not, ultimately, embody the complete agreement between the parties. In that respect, the case could be viewed as being more like *Transamerica Oil*, for example, where the court concluded that the parties' agreement extended beyond the signed "Sales and Service Invoice" to include the representations that the plaintiff had seen in trade journals and the assurances that the seller had given it over the telephone prior to the purchase. 723 F.2d at 761, 763. We do not mean to suggest that the evidence ought to be viewed in that way, of course. Although Mikelsons' affidavit appears to characterize Hubbard's letter as the culmination of prior discussions about the range of the new plane, the wording of the letter is far more consistent with that of a standard promotional letter than a confirmation of prior discussions concerning what Betaco contends was an essential contract term. Moreover, as we have noted, Mikelsons was an apparently sophisticated businessman who had the opportunity to review the contract at length before deciding to purchase, very much in contrast to the situation in *Transamerica Oil.* Still, as we consider the merits of Cessna's cross-motion for summary judgment, we must take care to give Betaco the benefit of every reasonable inference that may be drawn from the record. Construed favorably to Betaco, we believe that Mikelsons' affidavit raises a question of fact as to whether the parties considered the purchase contract to be the complete and exclusive statement of their agreement.

Both parties seem to have forgotten that where competing inferences may be drawn from facts that are otherwise undisputed, summary judgment is improper. [Citations omitted.] Just as we believe that plausible inferences from the record rendered partial summary judgment in Betaco's favor on the integration issue improper, so we believe that contrary inferences preclude summary judgment in favor of Cessna. We therefore remand the case for a hearing in which the district judge will sit as a finder of fact and decide, based on whatever evidence the parties choose to submit, whether the parties intended the purchase agreement to be the complete embodiment of their understanding or not. In the event the court answers this question in the affirmative, of course, the rule set forth in §2-202 would bar Betaco's warranty claim and compel the entry of final judgment in Cessna's favor on Count II of the complaint. We express no opinion as to the appropriate outcome of this hearing; that is a matter for the district court to decide based on the totality of the circumstances and the resolution of the competing inferences that the evidence permits.

III. Conclusion

Because we find that the record before the court on summary judgment was reasonably subject to contrary assessments of whether the parties intended their signed contract to be the complete embodiment of their agreement, we reverse the entry of partial summary judgment against Cessna on this question and vacate the final judgment subsequently entered in favor of Betaco on Count II of the complaint. The case is remanded for a factual hearing before the bench on the integration issue and for appropriate disposition based on the outcome of that hearing. . . .

NOTES AND QUESTIONS

1. On remand, the district court held that the contract was not integrated and that, therefore, the express warranty was admissible. The Seventh Circuit promptly reversed again, holding that the decision of the district court was "clearly erroneous" and directing a judgment in the favor of Cessna; 103 F.3d 1281 (7th Cir. 1996).

2. Courts often state that the parol evidence rule is a rule of substantive law and not a rule of evidence. This can be important for a number of reasons, most of them having to do with civil procedure or conflict of laws issues. For example, a federal court considering a case governed by state law will apply its own rules of evidence but import the state's substantive rules (including that state's parol evidence rule). Similarly, one state that is applying another state's substantive laws (because the contract requires this) will

also use that state's parol evidence rule, while otherwise observing its own rules of evidence.

3. As we have already seen, judges disagree about how much weight to give a merger clause. As the court in *Betaco* indicates, a merger clause in a form contract foisted off on hapless consumers is very suspect. Indeed, the Restatement (Second) drafters have stated that a merger clause should generally not be conclusive in most contexts; see comment e to §216. However, the failure to include a merger clause does not necessarily mean that the parties did not intend an integrated agreement. Intershoe, Inc. v. Bankers Trust Co., 571 N.E.2d 641 (N.Y. App. Div. 1991).

LEE v. JOSEPH E. SEAGRAM & SONS
United States Court of Appeals, Second Circuit, 1977
552 F.2d 447

GURFEIN, Circuit Judge. This is an appeal by defendant Joseph E. Seagram & Sons, Inc. ("Seagram") from a judgment entered by the District Court, Hon. Charles H. Tenney, upon the verdict of a jury in the amount of $407,850 in favor of the plaintiffs on a claim asserting common law breach of an oral contract. The court also denied Seagram's motion under Rule 50(b), Fed. R. Civ. P., for judgment notwithstanding the verdict. Harold S. Lee, et al. v. Joseph E. Seagram and Sons, 413 F. Supp. 693 (S.D.N.Y. 1976). It had earlier denied Seagram's motion for summary judgment. The plaintiffs are Harold S. Lee (now deceased) and his two sons, Lester and Eric ("the Lees"). Jurisdiction is based on diversity of citizenship. We affirm.

The jury could have found the following. The Lees owned a 50 percent interest in Capitol City Liquor Company, Inc. ("Capitol City"), a wholesale liquor distributorship located in Washington, D.C. The other 50 percent was owned by Harold's brother, Henry D. Lee, and his nephew, Arthur Lee. Seagram is a distiller of alcoholic beverages. Capitol City carried numerous Seagram brands and a large portion of its sales were generated by Seagram lines.

The Lees and the other owners of Capitol City wanted to sell their respective interests in the business and, in May 1970, Harold Lee, the father, discussed the possible sale of Capitol City with Jack Yogman ("Yogman"), then Executive Vice President of Seagram (and now President), whom he had known for many years. Lee offered to sell Capitol City to Seagram but conditioned the offer on Seagram's agreement to relocate Harold and his sons, the 50 percent owners of Capitol City, in a new distributorship of their own in a different city.

About a month later, another officer of Seagram, John Barth, an assistant to Yogman, visited the Lees and their co-owners in Washington and began negotiations for the purchase of the assets of Capitol City by Seagram on behalf of a new distributor, one Carter, who would take it over after the purchase. The purchase of the assets of Capitol City was consummated on September 30, 1970 pursuant to a written agreement. The promise to relocate the father and sons thereafter was not reduced to writing.

Harold Lee had served the Seagram organization for thirty-six years in positions of responsibility before he acquired the half interest in the Capitol City distributorship. From 1958 to 1962, he was chief executive officer of Calvert Distillers Company, a wholly-owned subsidiary. During this long period he enjoyed the friendship and confidence of the principals of Seagram.

In 1958, Harold Lee had purchased from Seagram its holdings of Capitol City stock in order to introduce his sons into the liquor distribution business, and also to satisfy Seagram's desire to have a strong and friendly distributor for Seagram products in Washington, D.C. Harold Lee and Yogman had known each other for 13 years.

The plaintiffs claimed a breach of the oral agreement to relocate Harold Lee's sons, alleging that Seagram had had opportunities to procure another distributorship for the Lees but had refused to do so. The Lees brought this action on January 18, 1972, fifteen months after the sale of the Capitol City distributorship to Seagram. They contended that they had performed their obligation by agreeing to the sale by Capitol City of its assets to Seagram, but that Seagram had failed to perform its obligation under the separate oral contract between the Lees and Seagram. The agreement which the trial court permitted the jury to find was "an oral agreement with defendant which provided that if they agreed to sell their interest in Capitol City, defendant in return, within a reasonable time, would provide the plaintiffs a Seagram distributorship whose price would require roughly an amount equal to the capital obtained by the plaintiffs for the sale of their interest in Capitol City, and which distributorship would be in a location acceptable to plaintiffs." No specific exception was taken to this portion of the charge. By its verdict for the plaintiffs, we must assume — as Seagram notes in its brief — that this is the agreement which the jury found was made before the sale of Capitol City was agreed upon.[2] Appellant urges several grounds for reversal. It contends that, as a matter of law, (1) plaintiffs' proof of the alleged oral agreement is barred by the parol evidence rule; and (2) the oral agreement is too vague and indefinite to be enforceable. Appellant also contends that plaintiffs' proof of damages is speculative and incompetent.

2. The complaint alleged that Seagram agreed to "obtain" or "secure" or "provide" a "similar" distributorship within a reasonable time, and plaintiffs introduced some testimony to that effect. Although other testimony suggested that Seagram agreed merely to provide an opportunity for the Lees to negotiate with third parties, and Judge Tenney indicated in his denial of judgment n.o.v. that Seagram merely agreed "to notify plaintiffs as they learned of distributors who were considering the sale of their businesses," 413 F. Supp. at 698-699, the jury was permitted to find that the agreement was in the nature of a commitment to provide a distributorship. There was evidence to support such a finding, and the jury so found.

I

Judge Tenney, in a careful analysis of the application of the parol evidence rule, decided that the rule did not bar proof of the oral agreement. We agree.

The District Court, in its denial of the defendant's motion for summary judgment, treated the issue as whether the written agreement for the sale of assets was an "integrated" agreement not only of all the mutual agreements concerning the sale of Capitol City assets, but also of *all* the mutual agreements of the parties. Finding the language of the sales agreement "somewhat ambiguous," the court decided that the determination of whether the parol evidence rule applies must await the taking of evidence on the issue of whether the sales agreement was intended to be a complete and accurate integration of all of the mutual promises of the parties.

Seagram did not avail itself of this invitation. It failed to call as witnesses any of the three persons who negotiated the sales agreement on behalf of Seagram regarding the intention of the parties to integrate all mutual promises or regarding the failure of the written agreement to contain an integration clause.

Appellant contends that, as a matter of law, the oral agreement was "part and parcel" of the subject-matter of the sales contract and that failure to include it in the written contract barred proof of its existence. Mitchill v. Lath, 247 N.Y. 377, 380, 160 N.E. 646 (1928). The position of appellant, fairly stated, is that the oral agreement was either an inducing cause for the sale or was a part of the consideration for the sale, and in either case, should have been contained in the written contract. In either case, it argues that the parol evidence rule bars its admission.

Appellees maintain, on the other hand, that the oral agreement was a collateral agreement and that, since it is not contradictory of any of the terms of the sales agreement, proof of it is not barred by the parol evidence rule. Because the case comes to us after a jury verdict we must assume that there actually was an oral contract, such as the court instructed the jury it could find. The question is whether the strong policy for avoiding fraudulent claims through application of the parol evidence rule nevertheless mandates reversal on the ground that the jury should not have been permitted to hear the evidence. See Fogelson v. Rackfay Constr. Co., 300 N.Y. 334 at 337-338, 90 N.E.2d 881 (1950).

The District Court stated the cardinal issue to be whether the parties "intended" the written agreement for the sale of assets to be the complete and accurate integration of all the mutual promises of the parties. If the written contract was not a complete integration, the court held, then the parol evidence rule has no application. We assume that the District Court determined intention by objective standards. See 3 Corbin on Contracts §§573-574. The parol evidence rule is a rule of substantive law. [Citations omitted.]

The law of New York is not rigid or categorical, but is in harmony with this approach. As Judge Fuld said in *Fogelson:*

> Decision in each case must, of course, turn upon the type of transaction involved, the scope of the written contract and the content of the oral agreement asserted.

300 N.Y. at 338, 90 N.E.2d at 883. And the Court of Appeals wrote in Ball v. Grady, 267 N.Y. 470, 472, 196 N.E. 402, 403 (1935):

> In the end, the court must find the limits of the integration as best it may by reading the writing in the light of surrounding circumstances.

Accord, *Fogelson*, supra, 300 N.Y. at 338, 90 N.E.2d 881. Thus, certain oral collateral agreements, even though made contemporaneously, are not within the prohibition of the parol evidence rule "because [if] they are separate, independent, and complete contracts, although relating to the same subject . . . [t]hey are allowed to be proved by parol, because they were made by parol, and no part thereof committed to writing." Thomas v. Scutt, 127 N.Y. 133, 140-141, 27 N.E. 961, 963 (1891).

Although there is New York authority which in general terms supports defendant's thesis that an oral contract inducing a written one or varying the consideration may be barred, see, e.g., Fogelson v. Rackfay Constr. Co., supra, 300 N.Y. at 340, 90 N.E.2d 881, the overarching question is whether, in the context of the particular setting, the oral agreement was one which the parties would ordinarily be expected to embody in the writing. Ball v. Grady, supra, 267 N.Y. at 470, 196 N.E. 402; accord, Fogelson v. Rackfay Constr. Co., supra, 300 N.Y. at 338, 90 N.E.2d 881. See Restatement on Contracts §240. For example, integration is most easily inferred in the case of real estate contracts for the sale of land, e.g., Mitchill v. Lath, supra, 247 N.Y. 377, 160 N.E. 646, or leases, *Fogelson,* supra; Plum Tree, Inc. v. N.K. Winston Corp., 351 F. Supp. 80, 83 (S.D.N.Y. 1972). In more complex situations, in which customary business practice may be more varied, an oral agreement can be treated as separate and independent of the written agreement even though the written contract contains a strong integration clause. See Gem Corrugated Box Corp. v. National Kraft Container Corp., 427 F.2d 499, 503 (2d Cir. 1970).

Thus, as we see it, the issue is whether the oral promise to the plaintiffs, as individuals, would be an expectable term of the contract for the sale of assets by a corporation in which plaintiffs have only a 50 percent interest, considering as well the history of their relationship to Seagram.

Here, there are several reasons why it would *not* be expected that the oral agreement to give Harold Lee's sons another distributorship would be integrated into the sales contract. In the usual case, there is an identity of parties in both the claimed integrated instrument and in the oral agreement asserted. Here, although it would have been physically possible to insert a provision dealing with only the shareholders of a 50 percent interest, the transaction itself was a *corporate* sale of assets. Collateral agreements which survive the closing of a corporate deal, such as employment agreements for particular shareholders of the seller or consulting agreements, are often set forth in separate agreements. See Gem Corrugated Box Corp. v. National Kraft Container Corp., supra, 427 F.2d at 503 ("it is . . . plain that the parties ordinarily would not embody the stock purchase agreement in a writing concerned only with box materials purchase terms"). It was expectable that such an agreement as one to obtain a new distributorship for certain persons, some of whom were not even parties to the contract, would not necessarily be integrated into an instrument for the sale of *corporate* assets. As with an oral condition precedent to the legal effectiveness of an otherwise integrated written contract, which is not barred by the parol evidence rule if it is not directly contradictory of its terms, Hicks v. Bush, 10 N.Y.2d 488, 225 N.Y.S.2d 34, 180 N.E.2d 425 (1962); cf. 3 Corbin on Contracts §589, "it is certainly not improbable that parties contracting in these circumstances would make the asserted oral agreement. . . ." 10 N.Y.2d at 493, 225 N.Y. S.2d at 39, 180 N.E.2d at 428.

Similarly, it is significant that there was a close relationship of confidence and friendship over many years between two old men, Harold Lee and Yogman, whose authority to bind Seagram has not been questioned. It would not be surprising that a handshake for the benefit of Harold's sons would have been thought sufficient. In point, as well, is the circumstance that the negotiations concerning the provisions of the sales agreement were not conducted by Yogman but by three other Seagram representatives, headed by John Barth. The two transactions may not have been integrated in their minds when the contract was drafted.

Finally, the written agreement does not contain the customary integration clause, even though a good part of it (relating to warranties and negative covenants) is boilerplate. The omission may, of course, have been caused by mutual trust and confidence, but in any event, there is no such strong presumption of exclusion because of the existence of a detailed integration clause, as was relied upon by the Court of Appeals in *Fogelson*, supra, 300 N.Y. at 340, 90 N.E. 881.

Nor do we see any contradiction of the terms of the sales agreement. Mitchill v. Lath, supra, 247 N.Y. at 381, 160 N.E. 646; 3 Corbin on Contracts §573, at 357. The written agreement dealt with the sale of corporate assets, the oral agreement with the relocation of the Lees. Thus, the oral agreement does not vary or contradict the money consideration recited in the contract as flowing to the selling corporation. That is the only consideration recited, and it is still the only consideration to the corporation.[5] We affirm Judge

---

5. Cf. Mitchill v. Lath, 247 N.Y. 377, 380-381, 160 N.E. 646, 647 (1928) (to escape the parol evidence rule, the oral agreement "must not contradict express or implied provisions of the written contract"). The parties do not contend, and we would be unwilling to hold, that the oral agreement was not "in form a collateral one." Id.

Tenney's reception in evidence of the oral agreement and his denial of the motion under Rule 50(b) with respect to the parol evidence rule.

[The court also found that the contract was not too indefinite for enforcement and that the trial court's award of damages was reasonable.]

Affirmed.

NOTES AND QUESTIONS

1. As *Lee* demonstrates, the collateral agreement exception can be another way of addressing the partial versus complete integration issue. If the court finds that there is an independent collateral agreement, this is tantamount to finding that there was never a complete integration. "While there is some distinction between these two doctrines, there is nevertheless a considerable similarity between them, both in their general application and also in the limitations governing them." Buyken v. Ertner, 205 P.2d 628 (Wash. 1949). *Lee* and *Betaco* (which uses the UCC's "would certainly have been included" test) uses an omitted term's relationship to the written contract to decide whether a writing is fully or partially integrated (not whether there is a collateral agreement exception to fully integrated writings).

2. Is there any difference between the Restatement (Second)'s "naturally be omitted" test and the UCC's "certainly would have been included" test? Most courts have indicated that they do not see much distinction between the two. See, e.g., Singh v. Southland Stone, 186 Cal. App. 4th 338, 112 Cal. Rptr. 3d 455 (2010).

Problem 104

Your client is Howard Damon, an eccentric entrepreneur, who is having his dream house built by his best friend, architect James Pythias (they have known each other since the first grade). They have been planning the house for decades and have finally decided to have a lawyer draft up the formal agreement. Should you put in a merger clause or not?

2.   Avoidance

In the next chapter we will discuss some doctrines that allow a party to avoid the contract entirely (for reasons such as fraud or duress). Where this is the case, the parol evidence rule has no relevance and the reason for the avoidance is admissible in spite of a signed writing with an iron-clad merger clause. See, e.g., Star Insurance Co. v. United Commercial Insurance Agency, Inc., 392 F. Supp. 2d 927 (E.D. Mich. 2005) (fraud in failing to include negotiated terms); Riverisland Cold Storage, Inc. v. Fresno-Madera

Production Credit Ass'n, 55 Cal. 4th 1169, 151 Cal. Rptr. 3d 93, 291 P.3d 315 (2013) (fraudulent misrepresentation of the terms of the contract presented at the closing); but see Sherrodd, Inc. v. Morrison-Knudsen Co., 249 Mont. 282, 815 P.2d 1135 (1991) (allegation of fraud barred by parol evidence rule where it would contradict a definite statement in the written contract).

3.   Oral Conditions Precedent

Finally, the parol evidence rule does not preclude a party from using parol evidence to show the *failure of an oral condition precedent.* Suppose the parties orally agree to be bound by a fully integrated written contract only if something happens, such as the price of oil stays above $60 per barrel or the zoning board approves an application to build a factory on a vacant lot. The parol evidence rule does not preclude a party from demonstrating that this event has not occurred and no written contract has come into existence.

PYM v. CAMPBELL
Queen's Bench, 1856
6 Ellis & Blackburn 370

First count. That defendants agreed to purchase of the plaintiff, for 800£., the eighth parts of the benefits to accrue from an invention of plaintiff's. General averments of readiness to convey, and tender of a conveyance of the three eighths. Breach: that defendants refused to accept them. Counts for shares in inventions bargained and sold, and on accounts stated. Pleas. 1st, to first count: That defendants did not agree. 9th, to the other counts: Never indebted. It is not necessary to notice the other seven pleas.

On the trial, before Lord Campbell C.J., at the Sittings at Guildhall after last Hilary term, the plaintiff was called as a witness. He produced and gave in evidence a paper of which the following is a copy.

500£. for a quarter share. 300£. for one eighth, and 50£. to be paid to Mr. Sadler. No other shares to be sold without mutual consent for three months. London, 17th January 1854.

One eighth.	R. J. R. Campbell.
	John Pym.
One eighth.	J. T. Mackenzie.
One eighth.	R. P. Pritchard.

With reference to the above agreement and in consideration of the sum of five pounds paid me I engage, within two days from this date, to execute the legal documents, to the satisfaction of your solicitors, to complete your title to the respective interests against your names in my Crushing, Washing and Amalgamating Machine.

London. 17 January 1854.

John Pym

He gave evidence that he was inventor of a machine which he wished to sell through the instrumentality of one Sadler, who had introduced the defendants to him; that, after some negotiations, the defendant Campbell drew out the above paper, which both plaintiff and defendants then signed, and which plaintiff took away.

The defendants gave evidence that, in the course of the negotiations with the plaintiff, they had got so far as to agree on the price at which the invention should be purchased if bought at all, and had appointed a meeting at which the plaintiff was to explain his invention to two engineers appointed by the defendants, when, if they approved, the machine should be bought. At the appointed time the defendants and two engineers of the names of Fergusson and Abernethie attended; but the plaintiff did not come; and the engineers went away. Shortly after they were gone the plaintiff arrived. Fergusson was found, and expressed a favourable opinion; but Abernethie could not then be found. It was then proposed that, as the parties were all present, and might find it troublesome to meet again, an agreement should be then drawn up and signed, which, if Abernethie approved of the invention, should be the agreement, but, if Abernethie did not approve, should not be one. Abernethie did not approve of the invention when he saw it; and the defendants contended that there was no bargain.

The Lord Chief Justice told the jury that, if they were satisfied that, before the paper was signed, it was agreed amongst them all that it should not operate as an agreement until Abernethie approved of the invention, they should find for the defendant on the pleas denying the agreement. Verdict for the defendants.

Thomas Serjt., in the ensuing term, obtained a rule nisi for a new trial on the ground of misdirection.

Watson and Manisty now shewed cause. The direction was correct. When parties have signed an instrument in writing as the record of their contract, it is not competent to them to shew by evidence that the contract really was something different from that contained in the writing; and therefore in this case, if the defendants had signed this as an agreement, they could not have shewn that the agreement was subject to condition. But they may shew that the writing was signed on the terms that it should be merely void till a condition was fulfilled; for that shews there never was a contract; Davies v. Jones (17 Com. B. 625). So, where the holder of a bill writes his name on it and hands it over, that is no indorsement if it was done on the terms that it should not operate as an indorsement till a condition is fulfilled;

Bell v. Lord Ingestre (12 Q.B. 317), Marston v. Allen. It is true that a deed cannot be delivered as an escrow to the party (Co. Litt. 36, a): but that is for purely technical reasons, inapplicable to parol contracts.

Thomas SERJT and J. H. HODGSON, contra. The very object of reducing a contract to writing and signing it is to prevent all disputes as to the terms of the contract. Here the attempt is to shew by parol that the agreement to take this invention was subject to a condition that Abernethie approved; while the writing is silent as to that. Davies v. Jones (17 Com. B. 625) proceeded on the ground that the instrument was imperfect; the cases as to bills of exchange proceed upon the necessity that there should be a delivery to make an indorsement.

ERLE J. I think that this rule ought to be discharged. The point made is that this is a written agreement, absolute on the face of it, and that evidence was admitted to shew it was conditional: and if that had been so it would have been wrong. But I am of opinion that the evidence shewed that in fact there was never any agreement at all. The production of a paper purporting to be an agreement by a party, with his signature attached, affords a strong presumption that it is his written agreement; and, if in fact he did sign the paper animo contrahendi, the terms contained in it are conclusive, and cannot be varied by parol evidence: but in the present case the defence begins one step earlier: the parties met and expressly stated to each other that, though for convenience they would then sign the memorandum of the terms, yet they were not to sign it as an agreement until Abernethie was consulted. I grant the risk that such a defence may be set up without ground; and I agree that a jury should therefore always look on such a defence with suspicion: but, if it be proved that in fact the paper was signed with the express intention that it should not be an agreement, the other party cannot fix it as an agreement upon those so signing. The distinction in point of law is that evidence to vary the terms of an agreement in writing is not admissible, but evidence to shew that there is not an agreement at all is admissible.

CROMPTON J. I also think that the point in this case was properly left to the jury. If the parties had come to an agreement, though subject to a condition not shewn in the agreement, they could not shew the condition, because the agreement on the face of the writing would have been absolute, and could not be varied: but the finding of the jury is that this paper was signed on the terms that it was to be an agreement if Abernethie approved of the invention, not otherwise. I know of no rule of law to estop parties from shewing that a paper, purporting to be a signed agreement, was in fact signed by mistake, or that it was signed on the terms that it should not be an agreement till money was paid, or something else done. When the instrument is under seal it cannot be a deed until there is a delivery; and when there is a delivery that estops the parties to the deed; that is a technical reason why a deed cannot be delivered as an escrow to the other party. But parol contracts, whether by word of mouth or in writing, do not estop. There is no distinction between them, except that where there is a writing it is the record of the contract. The decision in Davis v. Jones (17 Com. B. 625) is, I think, sound law, and proceeds on a just distinction: the parties may not vary a written agreement; but they may shew that they never came to an agreement at all, and that the signed paper was never intended to be the record of the terms of the agreement; for they never had agreeing minds. Evidence to shew that does not vary an agreement, and is admissible.

Lord CAMPBELL C. J. I agree. No addition to or variation from the terms of a written contract can be made by parol: but in this case the defence was that there never was any agreement entered into. Evidence to that effect was admissible; and the evidence given in this case was overwhelming. It was proved in the most satisfactory manner that before the paper was signed it was explained to the plaintiff that the defendants did not intend the paper to be an agreement till Abernethie had been consulted, and found to approve of the invention; and that the paper was signed before he was seen only because it was not convenient to the defendants to remain. The plaintiff assented to this, and received the writing on those terms. That being proved, there was no agreement.

(WIGHTMAN J., not having heard the whole argument, gave no opinion.)
Rule discharged.

II.   INTERPRETATION

Thus far, we have been considering the extent to which parol evidence can be introduced to *add to* a fully integrated agreement. Often, however, disputes hinge on the meaning of words that *already appear* within the contract. This involves the process of *interpretation.*

A.   *Interpretation and the Parol Evidence Rule*

The parol evidence rule throws a long shadow over the field of interpretation. Recall that although parties cannot use parol evidence to *contradict* a written contract (by showing that "black" means "white"), they *can* use parol evidence to explain an *ambiguous* written contract (by showing that the word "widgets" means widgets of a certain size, color, or quality). Because parol evidence can be powerful proof of what the parties intended, the first skirmish in battles over contract interpretation usually revolves around whether a writing is ambiguous (and thus can be explained by parol evidence).

ANGUS CHEMICAL CO. v. GLENDORA PLANTATION, INC.
United States Court of Appeals, Fifth Circuit, 2015
782 F.3d 175

FORTUNATO P. BENAVIDES, Circuit Judge:

This contract dispute involves a Right-of-Way Easement Option ("Agreement") involving Plaintiff-Appellee Angus Chemical Company ("Angus") and Defendant-Appellant Glendora Plantation, Inc. ("Glendora"). This appeal arises from the district court's grant of Angus's motion for partial summary judgment[and] denial of Glendora's motion for partial summary judgment. . . . The specific issues brought on appeal are . . . whether Angus had authority under the Agreement to abandon the original 12″ pipeline in place when it constructed a new 16″ pipeline. . . .

Issue

I. FACTUAL AND PROCEDURAL HISTORY

Angus owns a facility in Sterlington, Louisiana, that produces nitroparaffin products, a byproduct of which is wastewater containing formaldehyde and acetone. The wastewater is removed through an underground pipeline that goes through land owned by others to a wastewater treatment plant three and one-half miles away. In 1978, IMC Chemical Group, Inc. ("IMC"), Angus's predecessor-in-interest, obtained rights of way or servitudes from the other landowners to construct and operate a wastewater pipeline. At issue here is the "Right of Way Easement Option" granted by George and Mary Tilford Smelser on March 28, 1978, to IMC and its successors and assigns. The Agreement provides in relevant part:

> GEORGE P. SMELSER and MARY TILFORD SMELSER[ ] . . . does hereby grant, bargain, sell and convey unto IMC CHEMICAL GROUP, INC., . . . its successors and assigns, . . . an option to acquire a right of way and easement with the right to construct, maintain, inspect, operate, protect, alter, repair, replace and change the size of a pipeline for the transportation of liquids, gases, solids in either singular or mixed form or any other substances which can be transported through pipelines, together with all incidental equipment and appurtenances, either above or below ground, including but not limited to filtering devices, valves, meters, drips and other necessary and convenient installations, on, over, under, across and through the following described property, along a route to be selected by the Grantee[.]

IMC exercised the option on August 31, 1978, after which the option "automatically [became] an indefeasible right of way agreement without further actions being necessary, and all of the rights, title and privileges herein granted . . . thereafter [became] vested in [IMC], its successors or assigns."

In 1979, IMC constructed a 12″ pipeline from its Sterlington plant, across the Smelser property, and to its wastewater treatment facility. Angus subsequently purchased the rights from IMC, and Glendora purchased the Smelser property. Leaks from the pipeline occurred in 2007, 2010, and 2011, after which Angus decided to replace the pipeline. In 2010, Angus began to design a 16″ pipeline to replace the 12″ pipeline.[1]

Angus sought permission to abandon the 12″ pipeline from the affected landowners, and all but Glendora agreed. On January 26, 2012, Angus proposed a "Supplemental Agreement" that provided in relevant part:

> It is further understood and agreed that, after the sixteen inch (16″) pipeline is installed and in service, then the existing twelve inch (12″) pipeline currently in service across [Glendora's] property will be flushed and cleaned and [Angus] will be allowed by [Glendora] to abandon in place, and [Angus] shall have no future responsibility or obligations for the twelve inch (12″) pipeline abandoned on [Glendora's] property.

On January 27, 2012, Angus proposed a "Pipeline Servitude Ratification and Acknowledgement" that, inter alia, sought to "acknowledge[ ] and confirm [ ]" that the right of way included the right to "abandon[ ] in place" one 12″ pipeline, and offered to pay Glendora for authorization. Glendora did not agree to either of these proposals.

p Filed Complaint

On June 14, 2012, Angus filed a complaint seeking a declaratory judgment that (1) Angus has a valid servitude; (2) per the servitude, Angus may abandon the 12″ pipeline after a new pipeline is in service; (3) Angus may lay a 16″ pipeline, fiber optic cables, and a tracer wire; (4) the servitude will be 50′ wide during construction of the 16″ pipeline and 30′ wide thereafter; and (5) Angus will have right of ingress and egress during construction.

D Filed Counterclaim

Glendora filed an answer and counterclaim on August 13, 2012, and an amended answer and counterclaims on October 25, 2012.

After the suit was filed, Angus began construction of the 16″ pipeline. Angus also installed two fiber optic cables parallel to the 16″ pipeline, and a tracer wire on top of the pipeline. The 16″ pipeline was completed and placed into service on October 3, 2012. The 12″ pipeline was taken out of service that same day. By the end of November of 2012, Angus flushed, cleared, plugged, and abandoned the 12″ pipeline in place. . . .

District court granted P's SJ and Denied D's SJ

On November 20, 2013, the district court granted Angus's motion for partial summary judgment and denied Glendora's motion for partial summary judgment and motion to compel discovery. The court found:

> [(1)] that Angus has a valid and enforceable servitude through the property of Glendora; [(2)] that the Right–of–Way Agreement created a personal

---

1. Internal Angus emails from March 2011 suggest that Angus initially planned to remove the 12″ pipeline after the 16″ pipeline was put into service.

servitude of rights of use; [and] (3) that Angus had the authority under the Right-of-Way Agreement to construct the 16″ pipe and abandon the original 12″ pipeline in place. . . .

III. Applicable Law

Louisiana law governs this dispute. . . . Under the Louisiana Civil Code, "[i]nterpretation of a contract is the determination of the common intent of the parties." LA. CIV. CODE ANN. art. 2045. "The language of the policy is the starting point for determining that common intent." Six Flags, Inc. v. Westchester Surplus Lines Ins. Co., 565 F.3d 948, 954 (5th Cir. 2009). "The words of a contract must be given their generally prevailing meaning." LA. CIV. CODE ANN. art. 2047. "Words susceptible of different meanings must be interpreted as having the meaning that best conforms to the object of the contract." Id. art. 2048.

> The determination of whether a contract is clear or ambiguous is a question of law. Moreover, when a contract can be construed from the four corners of the instrument without looking to extrinsic evidence, the question of contractual interpretation is answered as a matter of law and summary judgment is appropriate.

Sims v. Mulhearn Funeral Home, Inc., 956 So.2d 583, 590 (La. 2007) (internal citations omitted). "When the words of a contract are clear and explicit and lead to no absurd consequences, no further interpretation may be made in search of the parties' intent." LA. CIV. CODE ANN. art. 2046. "[O]nly when there is a choice of reasonable interpretations of the contract is there a material fact issue concerning the parties' intent that would preclude summary judgment." Amoco Prod. Co. v. Tex. Meridian Res. Exploration Inc., 180 F.3d 664, 669 (5th Cir. 1999).

IV. Discussion

A. Whether Angus had authority under the agreement to abandon the original 12″ pipeline in place after constructing the 16″ pipeline

. . .

i. Whether the Agreement Required Removal of the 12″ Pipeline

1. Interpretation of "Replace"

The crux of the dispute as to the meaning of "replace" in the Agreement is that Glendora contends that one cannot "replace" something without removing the original while Angus claims that "replace" does not impart an obligation to remove the substitute's predecessor.

[margin: language permitted P to replace the pipe]

The district court found that "[t]he clear and unambiguous language of the Right-of-Way Agreement permit[ted] Angus to 'replace' the 12″ pipeline." To give the term "replace" its generally prevailing meaning, as required by Louisiana Civil Code article 2047, the court considered various dictionary definitions of "replace" proffered by both parties. The following are relevant definitions of "replace":

> Merriam-Webster:
> 2: to take the place of especially as a substitute or successor
> 3: to put something new in the place of (replace a worn carpet).[5]
> American Heritage Dictionary:
> 2. To take the place of: Jets have largely replaced propeller planes. Nurse practitioners are replacing doctors in some clinics.
> 3. To fill the place of; provide a substitute for: replaced the team's coach; replaced the wall-to-wall carpeting with hardwood floors.[6]

[margin: replace = substitute]

After reviewing these definitions, the court concluded that "[a]lthough the term 'replace' could, in some cases, imply a corresponding duty to remove, the Court agrees with Angus that the appropriate definition in this case is to 'substitute.'" However, "substitute" was not actually a full definition that was proffered to the court. Angus's argument, which the court refers to, was that in common usage, the term "replace" is more akin to "substitute." This does not actually define the term "replace." None of the dictionary definitions of "to replace" is simply "to substitute." Furthermore, the closest dictionary definitions involving "substitute" — "to take the place of especially as a substitute or successor" and "to fill the place of; provide a substitute for" — still lead to ambiguity as to whether the taking or filling the place of a previous item necessitates the previous item's removal. One could reasonably interpret that one can "replace" something in operation without physically removing the item that has been replaced (the interpretation taken by the district court and Angus), and one could also reasonably interpret that one can "replace" something by switching one item out for another (the interpretation taken by Glendora). . . .

[margin: Multiple Interpretations]

It is too much of a stretch to say that the Agreement is clear and unambiguous in its language when there are multiple reasonable interpretations of the implications of the word "replace." We find that there is a material fact issue as to whether the Agreement requires the removal of the 12″ pipeline, and on that basis, we conclude that awarding partial summary judgment to Angus was improper. . . .

5. *Replace Definition*, MERRIAM-WEBSTER ONLINE DICTIONARY, http://www.merriam-webster.com/dictionary/replace (last visited Mar. 2, 2015).
6. Replace Definition, THE AMERICAN HERITAGE DICTIONARY OF THE ENGLISH LANGUAGE (5th ed. 2014), https://www.ahdictionary.com/word/search. html?q=replace&submit.x=0&submit.y=0 (last visited Mar. 2, 2015).

2. Consideration of Extrinsic Evidence

. . .

The record includes extrinsic evidence that supports the idea that the Agreement did not include the right to abandon the older pipeline. Glendora argues that the court should have considered another servitude between Angus and Glendora, which explicitly included the right to abandon. Viewing this most favorably to Glendora, . . . the inclusion of the right to abandon in a subsequent agreement indicates an acknowledgement that the terms of the Agreement at issue here either did not include that same right to abandon, or at least was ambiguous as to whether the right to abandon existed. Glendora also points to Angus's internal documents that give the impression that Angus believed it did not have the right to abandon the pipeline, such as an "Assumption & Clarification" from a 2010 capital cost estimate prepared by Mustang Engineering that "[d]ue to the existence of the single line right, which will continue to be utilized, Angus/Dow will be required to obtain new servitudes for the installation of the 16 inch pipeline." . . .

Considering this matter in the light most favorable to the non-movant, we conclude that there is ambiguity in the Agreement as to whether the right to "replace" a pipeline includes an obligation to remove the older pipeline that is being replaced. Recognizing that a genuine dispute of material facts exists, we VACATE the district court's grant of partial summary judgment to Angus as to this issue.

NOTES AND QUESTIONS

1. The term *extrinsic evidence* is broader than *parol evidence*. Typically, the latter term is limited to describing evidence of oral or written negotiations or agreements that predate or are contemporaneous with a final agreement. Extrinsic evidence includes such parol evidence but also encompasses statements by a contracting party, whenever made, concerning the party's intended meaning for a contractual term. The term is also broad enough to include evidence of the "circumstances" surrounding the making of a contract—"the entire situation, as it appeared to the parties." See Restatement (Second) of Contracts §202. Further, the term *extrinsic evidence* includes evidence of usage of trade, course of dealing, or a course of performance. See UCC §§1-205 and 2-208 [§1-303 in the revised version of Article 1].

2. Just as there are two approaches to determining whether a writing is fully or partially integrated under the parol evidence rule—the orthodox four-corners approach and the more flexible modern approach—there are dueling views on how to decide whether a contract is ambiguous. *Angus Chemical Company* applies the traditional perspective, which focuses exclusively on the text of the agreement. The court considers the words and dictionary definitions—but not extrinsic evidence—before deciding that the term "replace" is reasonably susceptible to more than one meaning.

Only *after* the court finds an ambiguity does it consider extrinsic evidence such as the language of similar agreements and Angus's internal documents.

3. Professor Samuel Williston was a leading proponent of the four-corners approach to determining whether a contract was ambiguous. Williston felt that interpretation should be accomplished by determining the meaning that would be attached "by a reasonably intelligent person acquainted with all operative usages and knowing all the circumstances prior to and contemporaneous with the making of the integration, other than oral statements by the parties of what they intended it to mean." 4 Williston §607 (3d ed. 1961). Thus, when a contract was clear on its face, Williston would exclude any parol evidence and any other statements of intended meaning, including any attempt to show that the parties shared a "private understanding." See Murray §109 at 242. However, Williston would have permitted extrinsic evidence of surrounding circumstances under which the writing was executed. Not all proponents of the plain meaning rule would be this liberal; see, for example, Carey Canada, Inc. v. Columbia Casualty Co., 940 F.2d 1548 (D.C. Cir. 1991) (evidence of surrounding circumstances not admissible unless the writing is ambiguous after looking at only the four corners of the instrument; not admissible for initially determining ambiguity).

4. Professors Samuel Williston and Arthur Corbin could not have been further apart on the desirability of the effect of parol evidence on the issue of interpretation. Williston thought the rule of obvious benefit because it promoted certainty. It did not bother him that occasionally a strict application of the rule would mean that the contract would be interpreted in a manner neither party intended. Williston §95 (1st ed.). Corbin was outraged at the suggestion. Corbin §574. To his mind fulfilling the intention of the parties was the only goal of this or any other interpretive rule. When questions of ambiguity arise, Corbin would urge the judge to send the jury from the room, hear the evidence, and ask this question: If the proffered evidence were true, is it inconsistent with the contract as written? If the contract might reasonably be read to mean what the parol evidence demonstrated, the jury was then permitted to hear the evidence and decide its veracity. Williston would never have permitted parol evidence to *create* an ambiguity in an otherwise apparently unambiguous writing. Justice Traynor, the author of the next case, was certainly a proponent of the Corbin approach.

PACIFIC GAS & ELECTRIC CO. v. G. W. THOMAS DRAYAGE & RIGGING CO.
Supreme Court of California, 1968
442 P.2d 641

TRAYNOR, C.J. Defendant appeals from a judgment for plaintiff in an action for damages for injury to property under an indemnity clause of a contract.

In 1960 defendant entered into a contract with plaintiff to furnish the labor and equipment necessary to remove and replace the upper metal cover of plaintiff's steam turbine. Defendant agreed to perform the work "at [its] own risk and expense" and to "indemnify" plaintiff "against all loss, damage, expense and liability resulting from . . . injury to property, arising out of or in any way connected with the performance of this contract." Defendant also agreed to procure not less than $50,000 insurance to cover liability for injury to property. Plaintiff was to be an additional named insured, but the policy was to contain a cross-liability clause extending the coverage to plaintiff's property.

[margin note: Indemnity clause]

During the work the cover fell and injured the exposed rotor of the turbine. Plaintiff brought this action to recover $25,144.51, the amount it subsequently spent on repairs. During the trial it dismissed a count based on negligence and thereafter secured judgment on the theory that the indemnity provision covered injury to all property regardless of ownership.

[margin note: P wanted to recover $25k]
[margin note: Trial]

Defendant offered to prove by admissions of plaintiff's agents, by defendant's conduct under similar contracts entered into with plaintiff, and by other proof that in the indemnity clause the parties meant to cover injury to property of third parties only and not to plaintiff's property. Although the trial court observed that the language used was "the classic language for a third party indemnity provision" and that "one could very easily conclude that . . . its whole intendment is to indemnify third parties," it nevertheless held that the "plain language" of the agreement also required defendant to indemnify plaintiff for injuries to plaintiff's property. Having determined that the contract had a plain meaning, the court refused to admit any extrinsic evidence that would contradict its interpretation.

[margin note: D offered other extrinsic evidence]
[margin note: Trial court only considered the language of K, and not any extrinsic evidence]

When a court interprets a contract on this basis, it determines the meaning of the instrument in accordance with the ". . . extrinsic evidence of the judge's own linguistic education and experience." (3 Corbin on Contracts (1960 ed.) [1964 Supp. §579, p. 225, fn. 56].) The exclusion of testimony that might contradict the linguistic background of the judge reflects a judicial belief in the possibility of perfect verbal expression. (9 Wigmore on Evidence (3d ed. 1940) §2461, p. 187.) This belief is a remnant of a primitive faith in the inherent potency[2] and inherent meaning of words.[3]

---

2. E.g., "The elaborate system of taboo and verbal prohibitions in primitive groups; the ancient Egyptian myth of Khern, the apotheosis of the word, and of Thoth, the Scribe of Truth, the Giver of Words and Script, the Master of Incantations; the avoidance of the name of God in Brahmanism, Judaism and Islam; totemistic and protective names in mediaeval Turkish and Finno-Ugrian languages; the misplaced verbal scruples of the 'Précieuses'; the Swedish peasant custom of curing sick cattle smitten by witchcraft, by making them swallow a page torn out of the psalter and put in dough." [F]rom Ullman, The Principles of Semantics (1963 ed.) 43. (See also Ogden and Richards, The Meaning of Meaning (rev. ed. 1956) pp. 24-47.)

3. "'Rerum enim vocabula immutabilia sunt, homines mutabilia,'" (Words are unchangeable, men changeable) from Dig. XXXIII, 10, 7, §2, de sup. leg. as quoted in 9 Wigmore on Evidence, op. cit. supra, §2461, p.187.

The test of admissibility of extrinsic evidence to explain the meaning of a written instrument is not whether it appears to the court to be plain and unambiguous on its face, but whether the offered evidence is relevant to prove a meaning to which the language of the instrument is reasonably susceptible. . . .

A rule that would limit the determination of the meaning of a written instrument to its four-corners merely because it seems to the court to be clear and unambiguous, would either deny the relevance of the intention of the parties or presuppose a degree of verbal precision and stability our language has not attained.

Some courts have expressed the opinion that contractual obligations are created by the mere use of certain words, whether or not there was any intention to incur such obligations.[4] Under this view, contractual obligations flow, not from the intention of the parties but from the fact that they used certain magic words. Evidence of the parties' intention therefore becomes irrelevant.

In this state, however, the intention of the parties as expressed in the contract is the source of contractual rights and duties. A court must ascertain and give effect to this intention by determining what the parties meant by the words they used. Accordingly, the exclusion of relevant, extrinsic evidence to explain the meaning of a written instrument could be justified only if it were feasible to determine the meaning the parties gave to the words from the instrument alone.

If words had absolute and constant referents, it might be possible to discover contractual intention in the words themselves and in the manner in which they were arranged. Words, however, do not have absolute and constant referents. "A word is a symbol of thought but has no arbitrary and fixed meaning like a symbol of algebra or chemistry." (Pearson v. State Social Welfare Board (1960) 54 Cal. 2d 184, 195, 5 Cal. Rptr. 553, 559, 353 P.2d 33, 39.) The meaning of particular words or groups of words varies with the ". . . verbal context and surrounding circumstances and purposes in view of the linguistic education and experience of their users and their hearers or readers (not excluding judges). . . . A word has no meaning apart from these factors; much less does it have an objective meaning, one true meaning." (Corbin, The Interpretation of Words and the Parol Evidence Rule (1965) 50 Cornell L.Q. 161, 187.) Accordingly, the meaning of a writing ". . . can only be found by interpretation in the light of all the circumstances that reveal the sense in which the writer used the words. The exclusion of parol evidence regarding such circumstances merely

---

4. "A contract has, strictly speaking, nothing to do with the personal, or individual, intent of the parties. A contract is an obligation attached by the mere force of law to certain acts of the parties, usually words, which ordinarily accompany and represent a known intent." (Hotchkiss v. National City Bank of New York (S.D.N.Y. 1911) 200 F. 287, 293 [further citations omitted].

because the words do not appear ambiguous to the reader can easily lead to the attribution to a written instrument of a meaning that was never intended." . . .

Although extrinsic evidence is not admissible to add to, detract from, or vary the terms of a written contract, these terms must first be determined before it can be decided whether or not extrinsic evidence is being offered for a prohibited purpose. The fact that the terms of an instrument appear clear to a judge does not preclude the possibility that the parties chose the language of the instrument to express different terms. That possibility is not limited to contracts whose terms have acquired a particular meaning by trade usage,[6] but exists whenever the parties' understanding of the words used may have differed from the judge's understanding.

Accordingly, rational interpretation requires at least a preliminary consideration of all credible evidence offered to prove the intention of the parties.[7] (Civ. Code, §1647; Code Civ. Proc. §1860; see also 9 Wigmore on Evidence, op. cit. supra, §2470, fn. 11, p. 227.) Such evidence includes testimony as to the "circumstances surrounding the making of the agreement . . . including the object, nature and subject matter of the writing . . ." so that the court can "place itself in the same situation in which the parties found themselves at the time of contracting." (Universal Sales Corp. v. Cal. Press Mfg. Co., supra, 20 Cal. 2d 751, 761, 128 P.2d 665, 671; Lemm v. Stillwater Land & Cattle Co., supra, 217 Cal. 474, 480-481, 19 P.2d 785.) If the court decides, after considering this evidence, that the language of a contract, in the light of all the circumstances, is "fairly susceptible of either one of the two interpretations contended for, . . ." extrinsic evidence relevant to prove either of such meanings is admissible.[8]

6. Extrinsic evidence of trade usage or custom has been admitted to show that the term "United Kingdom" in a motion picture distribution contract included Ireland (Ermolieff v. R.K.O. Radio Pictures (1942) 19 Cal. 2d 543, 549-552, 122 P.2d 2); that the word "ton" in a lease meant a long ton or 2,240 pounds and not the statutory ton of 2,000 pounds (Higgins v. Ca. Petroleum, etc. Co. (1898) 120 Cal. 629, 630-632, 52 P. 1080); that the word "stubble" in a lease included not only stumps left in the ground but everything "left on the ground after the harvest time" (Callahan v. Stanley (1881) 57 Cal. 476, 477-479); that the term "north" in a contract dividing mining claims indicated a boundary line running along the "magnetic and not the true meridian" (Jenny Lind Co. v. Bower & Co. (1858) 11 Cal. 194, 197-199) and that a form contract for purchase and sale was actually an agency contract (Body-Steffner Co. v. Flotill Products (1944) 63 Cal. App. 2d 555, 558-562, 147 P.2d 84). See also Code Civ. Proc. §1861; Annot., 89 A.L.R. 1228; Note (1942) 30 Cal. L. Rev. 679.

7. When objection is made to any particular item of evidence offered to prove the intention of the parties, the trial court may not yet be in a position to determine whether in the light of all the offered evidence, the item objected to will turn out to be admissible as tending to prove a meaning of which the language of the instrument is reasonable susceptible or inadmissible as tending to prove a meaning of which the language is not reasonably susceptible. In such case the court may admit the evidence conditionally by either reserving its ruling on the objection or by admitting the evidence subject to a motion to strike. (See Evid. Code, §403.)

8. Extrinsic evidence has often been admitted in such cases on the stated ground that the contract was ambiguous (e.g., Universal Sales Corp. v. Cal. Press Mfg. Co., supra, 20 Cal. 2d

Present case

In the present case the court erroneously refused to consider extrinsic evidence offered to show that the indemnity clause in the contract was not intended to cover injuries to plaintiff's property. Although that evidence was not necessary to show that the indemnity clause was reasonably susceptible of the meaning contended for by defendant, it was nevertheless relevant and admissible on that issue. Moreover, since that clause was reasonably susceptible of that meaning, the offered evidence was also admissible to prove that the clause had that meaning and did not cover injuries to plaintiff's property.[9] Accordingly, the judgment must be reversed.

Reversed

NOTES AND QUESTIONS

1. In a jurisdiction like California that will hear evidence to create the ambiguity, what procedure should the court follow when such evidence is first proffered? See footnote 7 of the opinion. Note the limitation: If the extrinsic evidence advances an interpretation to which the language of the contract is not "reasonably susceptible," the evidence is not admissible. See, e.g., A. Kemp Fisheries, Inc. v. Castle & Cooke, Inc., Bumble Bee Seafoods Div., 852 F.2d 493 (9th Cir. 1988) (extrinsic evidence as to warranty of seaworthiness not admissible where clause in charter agreement for vessel clearly and unequivocally communicated that risk of unseaworthiness would fall on charterer once it accepted vessel because contract not reasonably susceptible of meaning advanced by company chartering vessel).

2. Professor Corbin has argued that a party who is advancing a counterintuitive interpretation of the language of a contact must carry a heavy burden:

> The more bizarre and unusual an asserted interpretation is, the more convincing must be the testimony that supports it. At what point the court should cease listening to testimony that white is black and that a dollar is fifty cents is a matter for sound judicial discretion and common sense.

Corbin, The Parol Evidence Rule, 53 Yale L.J. 603, 623 (1944). What language in *Pacific Gas* indicates the court's recognition of Corbin's limitation on extrinsic evidence?

751, 761, 128 P.2d 665). This statement of the rule is harmless if it is kept in mind that the ambiguity may be exposed by extrinsic evidence that reveals more than one possible meaning.

9. The court's exclusion of extrinsic evidence in this case would be error even under a rule that excluded such evidence when the instrument appeared to the court to be clear and unambiguous on its face. The controversy centers on the meaning of the word "indemnify" and the phrase "all loss, damage, expense and liability." The trial court's recognition of the language as typical of a third party indemnity clause and the double sense in which the word "indemnify" is used in statutes and defined in dictionaries demonstrate the existence of an ambiguity . . . .

3. There are strong proponents of the approach taken by Justice Traynor — see Berg v. Hudesman, 115 Wash. 2d 657, 801 P.2d 222 (1990); Watkins v. Ford, 239 P.3d 526 (Utah App. 2010) — but others feel Justice Traynor was way off the mark. Consider the dissent of Justice Mosk in Delta Dynamics, Inc. v. Arioto, 69 Cal. 2d 525, 72 Cal. Rptr. 785, 446 P.2d 785 (1968):

> It can be contended that there may be no evil per se in considering testimony about every discussion and conversation prior to and contemporaneous with the signing of a written instrument and that social utility may result in some circumstances. The problem, however, is that which devolves upon members of the bar who are commissioned by clients to prepare a written instrument able to withstand future assaults. Given two experienced businessmen dealing at arm's length, both represented by competent counsel, it has become virtually impossible under recently evolving rules of evidence to draft a written contract that will produce predictable results in court. The written word, heretofore deemed immutable, is now at all times subject to alteration by self-serving recitals based upon fading memories of antecedent events. This, I submit, is a serious impediment to the certainty required in commercial transactions.

Further criticism is found in Trident Center v. Connecticut General Life Ins., 847 F.2d 564 (9th Cir. 1988), and Bank v. Truck Ins. Exchange, 51 F.2d 736 (7th Cir. 1995). For the California Supreme Court's most recent pronouncements on point, see Dore v. Arnold Worldwide, Inc., 39 Cal. 4th 384, 139 P.3d 56 (Cal. 2006) (particularly the criticism in the concurring opinion).

NOTE ON COURSE OF DEALING, USAGE OF TRADE, AND COURSE OF PERFORMANCE

Under the common law, the general rule is that "a document must first be found to be incomplete or ambiguous before said document may be explained, but not contradicted, by extrinsic evidence." J. O. Hooker & Sons, Inc. v. Roberts Cabinet Co., 683 So. 2d 396, 400 (Miss. 1996). However, the UCC adopts a different approach to certain kinds of extrinsic evidence. A written contract for the sale of goods "may be explained or supplemented by *course of dealing* or *usage of trade* or by *course of performance.*" Wayman v. Amoco Oil Co., 923 F. Supp. 1322, 1339-1340 (D. Kan. 1996), aff'd, 145 F.3d 1347 (10th Cir. 1998) (emphasis added). *Course of dealing* is the parties' previous conduct that "establish[es] a common basis of understanding for interpreting their expressions and other conduct." U.C.C. §1-205(1). *Usage of trade* "is any practice or method of dealing having such regularity of observance in a place, vocation or trade as to justify an expectation that it will be observed with respect to the transaction in question." UCC §1-205(2). *Course of performance* is evidence that one party repeatedly performed in a particular way, and "[t]he other party, with knowledge of the nature of the performance and opportunity for objection to it, accept[ed] the performance . . . without objection." RBC Nice Bearings, Inc. v. SKF USA, Inc., 123 A.3d 417, 425 n.6 (Conn. 2015). Critically, these important forms of extrinsic evidence may be admissible *even if a contract does not seem ambiguous.* See, e.g., O'Neill v. United States, 50 F.3d 677, 684 (9th Cir. 1995).

The best-known illustration of the UCC's liberal policy in this regard is Nanakuli Paving & Rock Co. v. Shell Oil Co., 664 F.2d 772 (9th Cir. 1981). The plaintiff was a paving constructor in Hawaii and bought all of the asphalt it needed from the defendant between 1963 and 1974. The contract stated that the price for the asphalt would be the price the defendant posted at the time of delivery. However, paving contractors in Hawaii received price protection from their suppliers. In fact, in 1970 and 1971, the defendant raised its prices, but offered price protection to the plaintiff. Then, in 1974, the defendant raised its prices again and did not offer to shield the plaintiff from its increased cost. Despite the express contractual term giving the defendant the right to set the price, the Ninth Circuit held that the plaintiff could use (1) trade usage to prove that the parties' agreement incorporated the common practice in the asphalt industry of extending price protection to buyers and (2) course of performance to demonstrate that the plaintiff reasonably expected price protection based on the defendant's previous policy of offering price protection.

However, not every judge is so willing to admit evidence of course of dealing, trade usage, or course of performance. See, e.g., H & W Industries v. Occidental, Titone, Hancock & Bellacosa, 911 F.2d 1118 (5th Cir. 1990) (court refused evidence of trade usage where the term of other contracts and the market for products was different); Aero Consulting Corp. v. Cessna Aircraft Co., 867 F. Supp. 1480 (D. Kan. 1994) (finding that buyer could not introduce evidence that the seller had promised to reduce the price of the aircraft when that would contradict a contractual term that required the buyer to pay the entire sales price at the time of delivery).

B.   General Rules of Interpretation

As we have seen, the parol evidence rule acts as a gatekeeper in contract interpretation cases. Usually, each party offers a reading of the relevant language and tries to bolster that reading with extrinsic evidence. The parol evidence rule then weeds out any proposed interpretation that is unreasonable.

However, there is more to contract interpretation than the parol evidence rule. For example, if both litigants' legal theories are plausible, a court must choose between them. Likewise, if the parties have reached an oral agreement, the parol evidence rule is irrelevant. This subsection examines the tools that judges use to finalize the meaning of the contract.

RESTATEMENT (SECOND) OF CONTRACTS

§201. Whose Meaning Prevails

(1) Where the parties have attached the same meaning to a promise or agreement or a term thereof, it is interpreted in accordance with that meaning.

(2) Where the parties have attached different meanings to a promise or agreement or a term thereof, it is interpreted in accordance with the meaning attached by one of them if at the time the agreement was made

(a) that party did not know of any different meaning attached by the other, and the other knew the meaning attached by the first party; or

(b) that party had no reason to know of any different meaning attached by the other, and the other had reason to know the meaning attached by the first party.

(3) Except as stated in this Section, neither party is bound by the meaning attached by the other, even though the result may be a failure of mutual assent.

Restatement §201(1) governs contexts where the parties *agree* about what a term means. It acknowledges the primacy of the parties' intent by allowing them to adopt idiosyncratic definitions of particular words or phrases:

[P]arties, like Humpty Dumpty, may use words as they please. If they wish the symbols "one Caterpillar D9G tractor" to mean "500 railroad cars full of watermelons," that's fine — provided parties share this weird meaning. A meaning held by one party only may not be invoked to change the ordinary denotation of a word, however. Intent must be mutual to be effective; unilateral intent does not count.

TKO Equip. Co. v. C & G Coal Co., 863 F.2d 541, 545 (7th Cir. 1988). Thus, "[i]n rare instances . . . where parties share a common meaning, [the] prevailing view is that their subjective understanding controls" — even if a hypothetical third party would not understand the language the same way. In re Old Carco LLC, 551 B.R. 124, 129 (Bankr. S.D.N.Y. 2016) (quotation omitted).

Sometimes parties create unusual meanings by *expressly* defining a term or phrase in a way that deviates from common usage. See, e.g., NeuroGrafix v. United States, 111 Fed. Cl. 501, 506 (2013) (contract's recital that "[t]hird [p]arty" meant "any individual, corporation, partnership or other business entity" excluded the U.S. government and was "more narrow [] than the ordinary meaning"). However, if a litigant tries to use *extrinsic evidence* to prove that the parties agreed to give words an unusual meaning, the parol evidence rule will rear its head. Indeed, in states that follow the four-corners approach to determining ambiguity, a court cannot consider evidence other than the text itself, and such a claim will fail.

Restatement §201(2) deals with the common situation in which the parties understood language *differently*. It instructs the court to ask whether each party knew or should have known of the other's interpretation. If Party A was aware of should have been aware of Party B's meaning, but Party B did not know and had no reason to know of Party A's meaning, Party B wins. As such, the Restatement "codifies a rule based on concerns of fairness that prevents a party who knows that the other party has attached a different meaning to a term from taking advantage of the misunderstanding." Farmington Police Officers Ass'n Commc'n Workers of Am. Local 7911 v. City of Farmington, 137 P.3d 1204, 1211 (N.M. 2006).

Finally, as the Restatement provisions below reveal, courts can rely on several canons of interpretation. None of these canons are absolutes; they are mere guidelines for the courts. For the most part they should strike you as restatements of the obvious.

RESTATEMENT (SECOND) OF CONTRACTS

§202. RULES IN AID OF INTERPRETATION

(1) Words and other conduct are interpreted in the light of all the circumstances, and if the principal purpose of the parties is ascertainable it is given great weight.

(2) A writing is interpreted as a whole, and all writings that are part of the same transaction are interpreted together.

(3) Unless a different intention is manifested,

(a) here language has a generally prevailing meaning, it is interpreted in accordance with that meaning;

(b) technical terms and words of art are given their technical meaning when used in a transaction within their technical field.

(4) Where an agreement involves repeated occasions for performance by either party with knowledge of the nature of the performance and opportunity for objection to it by the other, any course of performance accepted or acquiesced in without objection is given great weight in the interpretation of the agreement.

(5) Wherever reasonable, the manifestations of intention of the parties to a promise or agreement are interpreted as consistent with each other and with any relevant course of performance, course of dealing, or usage of trade.

§203. STANDARDS OF PREFERENCE IN INTERPRETATION

In the interpretation of a promise or agreement or a term thereof, the following standards of preference are generally applicable: (a) an interpretation which gives a reasonable, lawful, and effective meaning to all the terms is preferred to an interpretation which leaves a part unreasonable, unlawful, or of no effect; (b) express terms are given greater weight than course of performance, course of dealing, and usage of trade, course of performance is given greater weight than course of dealing or usage of trade, and course of dealing is given greater weight than usage of trade; (c) specific terms and exact terms are given greater weight than general language; (d) separately negotiated or added terms are given greater weight than standardized terms or other terms not separately negotiated.

§206. INTERPRETATION AGAINST THE DRAFTSMAN

In choosing among the reasonable meanings of a promise or agreement or a term thereof, that meaning is generally preferred which operates against the party who supplies the words or from whom a writing otherwise proceeds.

§207. INTERPRETATION FAVORING THE PUBLIC

In choosing among the reasonable meanings of a promise or agreement or a term thereof, a meaning that serves the public interest is generally preferred.

RUSSELL v. CITIGROUP, INC.
United States Court of Appeals, Sixth Circuit, 2014
748 F.3d 677

SUTTON, Circuit Judge.

When Keith Russell accepted a job with Citicorp Credit Services, he agreed to arbitrate "all employment-related disputes" with the company. Does that mean he must arbitrate a case already pending in court when he signed the agreement? We think not.

I

From 2004 to 2009, Russell worked at Citicorp's call center in Florence, Kentucky. As a condition of employment, he signed a standard contract to arbitrate his disputes with the company. The agreement covered individual claims but not class actions.

In January 2012, Russell filed a class action against the company. He claimed that the company did not pay its employees for time spent logging into and out of their computers at the beginning and end of each workday. Because the arbitration agreement with Russell did not reach class claims, the company did not seek arbitration.

At this point, a confluence of improbable circumstances complicated this once-simple case. In late 2012, with the lawsuit still in progress, Russell applied to work once more at Citicorp's call center in Florence. The call center agreed to rehire him. By this time, Citicorp had updated its standard arbitration contract to cover class claims as well as individual ones. Russell signed the new contract, and in January 2013 he began work in the call center.

Russell did not consult with his lawyers before signing the new contract. And the lawyers directly representing Citicorp in this case, an outside law firm, did not know that Russell had applied to work at the call center. About a month after Russell began his new job, they found out. Relying on the new contract, Citicorp sought to compel Russell to arbitrate the class action, which by then had begun discovery. The district court concluded that the new arbitration agreement did not cover lawsuits commenced before the agreement was signed. Citicorp appealed this interlocutory decision, as it may under 9 U.S.C. §16(a). See Grain v. Trinity Health, Mercy Health Servs., 551 F.3d 374, 377 (6th Cir. 2008).

II

A section of the arbitration agreement, captioned "Scope of Policy," provides:

> This Policy applies to both you and to Citi, and makes arbitration the required and exclusive forum for the resolution of all employment-related disputes (other than disputes which by statute are not subject to arbitration) which are based on legally protected rights (i.e., statutory, regulatory, contractual, or common-law rights) and arise between you and Citi, its predecessors, successors and assigns, its current and former parents, subsidiaries, and affiliates, and its and their current and former officers, directors, employees, and agents. . . .

R. 52-7 at 2. The question is whether this language applies to the pending class action.

The text suggests that the agreement does not evict pending lawsuits from court. It covers only disputes that "arise between [Russell] and Citi." Id. The use of the present-tense "arise," rather than the past-tense "arose" or present-perfect "have arisen," suggests that the contract governs only disputes that begin — that arise — in the present or future. The present tense usually does not refer to the past.

The preamble of the agreement — labeled "Statement of Intent" — adds force to what the conjugation of this verb suggests. It explains, "Citi values each of its employees and looks forward to good relations with, and among, all of its employees. Occasionally, however, disagreements may arise between an individual employee and Citi . . . Citi believes that the resolution of such disagreements will be best accomplished . . . by external arbitration." R. 52-7 at 2. This language exudes prospectivity. It says that the company "looks forward" to a good relationship with Russell, not that it looks back on their earlier relationship with fond memories. It then acknowledges that disagreements "may arise," not that disagreements "might have arisen." As used here, the auxiliary verb "may" signals a hazard that is yet to come rather than an incident that has come to pass. See "may, v.1," Oxford English Dictionary (3d ed. 2012). Bringing the point home, the agreement explains that the resolution of these disputes "will be best accomplished" by arbitration. So far as the text of the agreement and its preamble show, the parties signed this agreement to head off future lawsuits, not to cut off existing ones.

The common expectations of the parties reinforce the point. [Citation omitted.] Russell for one says that he expected the contract to apply only to future lawsuits. Citicorp does not question his state of mind, and in any event the circumstances corroborate it. Russell's behavior — signing the contract without consulting counsel and carrying on with the lawsuit as before — would make little sense if Russell understood the contract to cover the case at hand.

As for Citicorp, it seems doubly improbable that the company expected the contract to govern pending lawsuits. In the first place, the company entered into this contract — binding itself to arbitrate its disputes with Russell — without first consulting its lawyers in this case. Would a sophisticated company allow a supervisor at a local call center to sign away rights in a pending case without first speaking to the lawyers representing it in that case? Not likely.

In the second place, the company sent the contract to Russell rather than to his lawyer. One party's lawyer may not communicate about a pending case with an opposing litigant he knows has legal representation. Ky. Sup. Ct. R. 3.130; see also Model Rules of Professional Conduct R. 4.2 (1983). If Citicorp's in-house counsel prepared a contract, expecting it to be given to a represented litigant but also expecting it to govern existing cases, they might find themselves near the edge of this rule. It makes no difference who handed Russell the arbitration agreement, whether a member of the legal department or a supervisor at the call center. The canons preclude a lawyer not only from communicating with a represented adversary but also (for the most part) from helping his client do so. See Restatement (Third) of the Law Governing Lawyers §99, cmt. k (2000). And it makes no difference who prompted the dialogue, whether Russell or Citicorp. The lawyer's obligations remain in place either way. See Ky. Sup. Ct. R. 3.130, cmt. (3).

To be sure, we do not mean to suggest that Citicorp's in-house counsel violated the rules of ethics. Perhaps they did not participate in the drafting of this contract. Or perhaps they did not know that the company planned to give the contract to represented employees. But we do mean to ask: Did Citicorp expect the contract to bear a meaning that would even raise these questions? Again, not likely.

Against all of this, Citicorp offers no evidence that it did expect the contract to govern pending lawsuits. In the final analysis, that leaves a situation in which one party (Russell) certainly and the other party (Citicorp) likely expected the contract to govern only lawsuits still to come. This common understanding fixes the meaning of the contract. See Restatement (Second) of Contracts §201(1) (1981).

No matter, Citicorp claims: The provision before us — "This Policy [covers] all employment-related disputes . . . which . . . arise between [Russell] and Citi" — still proclaims with a clear throat that the arbitrator will decide pending and impending cases alike. But milieu limits the reach of general words like "all." See United States v. Palmer, 3 Wheat. 610, 631-32, 4 L. Ed. 471 (1818) (Marshall, C.J.). If the poissonier tells the chef, "I have marinated all the salmon," we know from context that he means all the salmon on the kitchen counter, not all the salmon in the universe. So too here. We know from context — from the use of "arise," from the preamble and from the parties' probable expectations — that the contract refers to all future lawsuits, not all lawsuits from the beginning of time to the end.

Citicorp persists that our interpretation nullifies language extending the contract to disputes between Russell and the company's "predecessors, successors and assigns, its current and former parents, subsidiaries, and affiliates, and its and their current and former officers, directors, employees, and agents." R. 527 at 2 (emphasis added). Not so. Imagine that yesterday a supervisor suspended Russell because of his sex, today the company fires the supervisor for her misconduct, and tomorrow Russell sues the company and the supervisor for discrimination. The phrase "former officers, directors, employees, and agents" brings this hypothetical dispute within the agreement's grasp, even though the supervisor no longer works for the company. The references to past employees and past affiliates do not establish that the agreement governs past cases.

[The court also rejected Citicorp's argument that the Federal Arbitration Act's pro-arbitration policy mandated a different result, reasoning that the statute does not override the parties' intent to exclude a claim from arbitration.]

. . .

For these reasons, we affirm.

NOTE AND QUESTIONS

Even though the parol evidence rule requires courts to decide as a threshold matter whether a contract is ambiguous, courts often breeze past this step on their way to ruling in favor of one party. *Russell* exemplifies this tendency. Would you characterize the court as holding that (1) the agreement was only reasonable susceptible to Russell's interpretation or (2) the agreement is ambiguous but Russell had the better reading? Ultimately, does it matter?

Problem 105

In 1939, when Orson Welles wrote, directed, and starred in the famous movie *Citizen Kane*, he signed a contract with movie distributor RKO for a two-picture deal that stated that RKO shall own the negative and positive prints of each of the Pictures and all rights of every kind and nature in and to each Picture, and all parts thereof and all material, tangible and intangible, used therein, as soon as such rights come into existence, including, but not being limited to, the exclusive rights of distribution, exploitation, manufacture, recordation, broadcasting, televising (other than in connection with the advertising or exploitation of a commercial product or service), and reproduction by any art or method, and the literary, dramatic, musical and other works included in such Picture.

The contract went on to add:

> In case of any original story written by [Welles] or any of its employees and used as the basis of either Picture, however, [RKO] shall acquire the motion picture and television rights in such story for such Picture only. [RKO] shall not remake any such Picture unless [Welles] produces or directs the same or unless [RKO] buys the remake rights from [Welles] at a price satisfactory to both parties. [Welles] shall own the publication, radio, dramatic and other rights in any such story but shall not use the same in any way to compete with or injure the distribution of the Picture based on such story.

The original movie lost money, no second picture was made, and in late 1944 the parties signed an "exit agreement" with this language in it:

> It is now the mutual desire of the parties to terminate and cancel each and all of the existing agreements between [RKO] and . . . Welles, and to mutually release and discharge each party to each of said agreements from all rights, duties, liabilities and obligations thereunder and from all claims, demands and causes of action of every kind and nature of each party as against the other party.

In subsequent decades the movie gained in stature and is now arguably the finest movie ever made. When RKO's successor refused to share any of the DVD profits, Welles's daughter Beatrice sued. You are on the bench. Would you allow the Welles estate any claim to royalties from the use of the movie in media not in existence in 1939? See Welles v. Turner Entertainment Co., 503 F.3d 728 (9th Cir. 2007).

NOTE ON THE LAW OF WARRANTY IN THE SALE OF GOODS

A final issue that can breathe meaning into the parties' agreement is *warranties*. Warranties are of two basic types: warranties of title and warranties of quality.

The warranty of title is basically what it sounds like, a guarantee that the seller will convey good title to the buyer at the time of sale. See UCC §2-312. Fortunately, this warranty is rarely at issue.

Quality warranties are also divisible into two categories: express and implied warranties. Under UCC §2-313, a seller creates an express warranty by making an affirmation of fact ("this is a new car"), describing the item ("when it arrives, it will be painted yellow"), making a promise relating to the goods ("if it doesn't work, I'll fix it"), or displaying a sample or model ("this is what it will look like"). The statement need not be in writing or even intended by the seller to be a warranty, but it must go to the "basis of the bargain." This phrase means that it must contain enough substance to it that it *might* have played some part in the buyer's decision to purchase. If so, the statement is *presumed* to be part of the basis of the bargain unless the seller can prove that the buyer did not rely on the statement.

Implied warranties are created by the legislature (and thus are often said to be "children of the law") to fulfill the buyer's typical expectations concerning the item purchased. The implied warranty of merchantability (UCC §2-315) is basically a warranty that the goods will fulfill their usual functions. The implied warranty of fitness for a particular purpose (UCC §2-315) arises when the seller has reason to know of some *special* use the buyer has for the goods ("I need some boots for climbing Mt. Everest") and this creates a warranty that the goods will fulfill that particular purpose.

However, sellers have several weapons against warranties. First, express warranties can fall prey to the parol evidence rule. As we have seen earlier in this chapter, a buyer cannot supplement a fully integrated contract with proof of what a seller said before the parties entered into the contract. Second, under UCC §2-316, sellers can *disclaim* (in other words, eliminate) implied warranties and buyers can forfeit implied warranty claims by failing to discover obvious defects.

UNIFORM COMMERCIAL CODE

§2-313. Express Warranties by Affirmation, Promise, Description, Sample

(1) Express warranties by the seller are created as follows:

(a) Any affirmation of fact or promise made by the seller to the buyer which relates to the goods and becomes part of the basis of the bargain creates an express warranty that the goods shall conform to the affirmation or promise.

(b) Any description of the goods which is made part of the basis of the bargain creates an express warranty that the goods shall conform to the description.

(c) Any sample or model which is made part of the basis of the bargain creates an express warranty that the whole of the goods shall conform to the sample or model.

UNIFORM COMMERCIAL CODE

§2-314. Implied Warranty: Merchantability. . . .

(1) . . . [A] warranty that the goods shall be merchantable is implied in a contract for their sale if the seller is a merchant with respect to goods of that kind. Under this section the serving for value of food or drink to be consumed either on the premises or elsewhere is a sale.

(2) Goods to be merchantable must be at least such as

(a) pass without objection in the trade under the contract description; and

(b) in the case of fungible goods, are of fair average quality within the description; and . . .

(d) run, within the variations permitted by the agreement, of even kind, quality and quantity within each unit and among all units involved; and

(e) are adequately contained, packaged, and labeled as the agreement may require; and

(f) conform to the promises or affirmations of fact made on the container or label if any.

UNIFORM COMMERCIAL CODE

§2-315. IMPLIED WARRANTY: FITNESS FOR PARTICULAR PURPOSE

Where the seller at the time of contracting has reason to know any particular purpose for which the goods are required and that the buyer is relying on the seller's skill or judgment to select or furnish suitable goods, there is . . . an implied warranty that the goods shall be fit for such purpose.

UNIFORM COMMERCIAL CODE

§2-316. EXCLUSION OR MODIFICATION OF WARRANTIES

(1) Words or conduct relevant to the creation of an express warranty and words or conduct tending to negate or limit warranty shall be construed wherever reasonable as consistent with each other; but subject to the provisions of this Article on parol or extrinsic evidence (Section 2-202) negation or limitation is inoperative to the extent that such construction is unreasonable.

(2) Subject to subsection (3), to exclude or modify the implied warranty of merchantability or any part of it the language must mention merchantability and in case of a writing must be conspicuous, and to exclude or modify any implied warranty of fitness the exclusion must be by a writing and conspicuous. Language to exclude all implied warranties of fitness is sufficient if it states, for example, that "There are no warranties which extend beyond the description on the face hereof."

(3) Notwithstanding subsection (2)

(a) unless the circumstances indicate otherwise, all implied warranties are excluded by expressions like "as is", "with all faults" or other language which in common understanding calls the buyer's attention to the exclusion of warranties and makes plain that there is no implied warranty; and

(b) when the buyer before entering into the contract has examined the goods or the sample or model as fully as he desired or has refused to examine the goods there is no implied warranty with regard to defects which an examination ought in the circumstances to have revealed to him. . . .

Problem 106

Honest John told Mr. and Mrs. Consumer that the used car he was selling them was in "great condition and was never mistreated by its prior owner, a nun." In fact, unknown to Honest John, the nun had been a bad driver and repeatedly wrecked and repaired the vehicle. The Consumers signed a contract of sale that conspicuously stated there were "no express or implied warranties, particularly not the implied warranty of MERCHANT-ABILITY," involved in the sale. Two days later the car fell to pieces because of its many prior accidents, and the Consumers were injured. May they sue for breach of express warranty? Does it help Honest John that he did not know nor have reason to know of the car's defects? Did Honest John disclaim any implied warranties?

Problem 107

The restaurant menu had beautiful photographs of the food. When Portia Moot and her friend Ralph Res were ready to order, Portia pointed at the picture of the plate of spaghetti and told the waitress, "I'll take that." Ralph ordered fish chowder.

(a) When the food arrived, Portia was annoyed to note that there were only two meatballs (the picture showed three). May she refuse the food for this reason? See UCC §2-313. Is the service of food a sufficient sale to trigger the UCC? See UCC §2-314(1).

(b) If Ralph chokes on a bone in the fish chowder, what commercial theory will offer possible relief to him or his heirs? See UCC §2-314(2)(c); Webster v. Blue Ship Tea Room, Inc., 347 Mass. 421, 198 N.E.2d 309 (1964). Is the question easier if the offending object in the fish chowder is a piece of gravel?

(c) If the water glass that Portia is holding proves to be defective and suddenly shatters, lacerating her hand, does any part of UCC §2-314 apply? See Shaffer v. Victoria Station, Inc., 91 Wash. 2d 295, 588 P.2d 233 (1978).

(d) Assume that Portia told the waitress that she was allergic to milk and asked her to make sure that the dishes she was served contained none. The waitress made no express promise (indeed, she said nothing when Portia gave her this information), but the food Portia was served made her very sick because it was laced with milk. May she sue in warranty? See UCC §2-315.

The warranties created by the UCC are supplemented by special statutes, both federal and state, that change the usual rules in certain situations, typically involving consumer buyers. On the federal level, the chief statute is the Magnuson-Moss Warranty Act, 15 U.S.C. §§2301-2312 (passed in 1975), which regulates written warranties given in the sale of consumer goods. Among other things, the act forbids the disclaimer of implied warranties when a written warranty is furnished and provides for an award of attorney's fees to the consumer who prevails in litigation.

III.   CONCLUSION

The parol evidence rule is all too often a trap for the unwary or the careless. It presumes a greater validity to a writing than most people give writings. Should the rule be abolished? Watered down?*

ZELL v. AMERICAN SEATING CO.
United States Court of Appeals, Second Circuit, 1943
138 F.2d 641

FRANK, Circuit Judge. On defendant's motion for summary judgment, the trial court, after considering the pleadings and affidavits, entered judgment dismissing the action. From that judgment, plaintiff appeals. . . .

Plaintiff, by a letter addressed to defendant company dated October 17, 1941, offered to make efforts to procure for defendant contracts for manufacturing products for national defense or war purposes, in consideration of defendant's agreement to pay him $1,000 per month for a three months' period if he were unsuccessful in his efforts, but, if he were successful, to pay him a further sum in an amount not to be less than 3 percent nor more than 8 percent of the "purchase price of said contracts." On October 31, 1941, at a meeting in Grand Rapids, Michigan, between plaintiff and defendant's President, the latter, on behalf of his company, orally made an agreement with plaintiff substantially on the terms set forth in plaintiff's letter, one of the terms being that mentioned in plaintiff's letter as to commissions; it was orally agreed that the exact amount within the two percentages was to be later determined by the parties.

After this agreement was made, the parties executed, in Grand Rapids, a written instrument dated October 31, 1941, appearing on its face to embody a complete agreement between them; but that writing omitted the provision of their agreement that plaintiff, if successful, was to receive a bonus varying from three to eight percent; instead, there was inserted in the writing a clause that the $1,000 per month "will be full compensation, but the company may, if it desires, pay you something in the nature of a bonus." However, at the time when they executed this writing, the parties orally

---

*The United Nations Convention on Contracts for the International Sale of Goods (CISG) has no parol evidence rule. Article 8(3) provides:

> (3) In determining the intent of a party or the understanding a reasonable person would have had, due consideration is to be given to all relevant circumstances of the case including the negotiations, any practices which the parties have established between themselves, usages and any subsequent conduct of the parties.

The courts have disallowed the use of the parol evidence rule in CISG cases; see MCC-Marble Ceramic Center, Inc. v. Ceramica Nuova D'Agostino, S.P.A., 144 F.3d 1384 (11th Cir. 1998).

agreed that the previous oral agreement was still their actual contract, that the writing was deliberately erroneous with respect to plaintiff's commissions, and that the misstatement in that writing was made solely in order to "avoid any possible stigma which might result" from putting such a provision "in writing," the defendant's President stating that "his fears were based upon the criticism of contingent fee contracts." Nothing in the record discloses whose criticism the defendant feared; but plaintiff, in his brief, says that defendant was apprehensive because adverse comments had been made in Congress of such contingent-fee arrangements in connection with war contracts. The parties subsequently executed further writings extending, for two three-month periods, their "agreement under date of October 31, 1941." Through plaintiff's efforts and expenditures of large sums for traveling expenses, defendant, within this extended period, procured contracts between it and companies supplying aircraft to the government for war purposes, the aggregate purchase price named in said contracts being $5,950,000. The defendant has refused to pay the plaintiff commissions thereon in the agreed amount (i.e., not less than three percent) but has paid him merely $8,950 (at the rate of $1,000 a month) and has offered him, by way of settlement, an additional sum of $9,000 which he has refused to accept as full payment.

Defendant argues that the summary judgment was proper on the ground that, under the parol evidence rule, the court could not properly consider as relevant anything except the writing of October 31, 1941, which appears on its face to set forth a complete and unambiguous agreement between the parties. If defendant on this point is in error, then, if the plaintiff at a trial proves the facts as alleged by him, and no other defenses are successfully interposed, he will be entitled to a sum equal to 3 percent of $5,950,000. . . .

It is not surprising that confusion results from a rule called "the parol evidence rule" which is not a rule of evidence, which relates to extrinsic proof whether written or parol,[7] and which has been said to be virtually no rule at all.[8] As Thayer said of it, "Few things are darker than this, or fuller of subtle difficulties."[9] The rule is often loosely and confusingly stated as if, once the evidence establishes that the parties executed a writing containing what appears to be a complete and unambiguous agreement, then no evidence may be received of previous or contemporaneous oral understandings which contradict or vary its terms. But, under the parol evidence rule correctly stated, such a writing does not acquire that dominating position if it has been proved by extrinsic evidence that the parties did not intend it to be

---

7. Restatement of Contracts, §237, comment a. Indeed the agreement, protected by the rule from competition with extrinsic proof, may itself be wholly oral. See Wigmore, Evidence, 3d ed., §2425.

8. Cf. Corbin, Delivery of Written Contracts, 36 Yale L.J. (1927) 443.

9. Thayer, A Preliminary Treatise on Evidence (1898) 390.

an exclusive authoritative memorial of their agreement. If they did intend it to occupy that position, their secret mutual intentions as to the terms of the contract or its meaning are usually irrelevant, so that parties who exchange promises may be bound, at least "at law" as distinguished from "equity," in a way which neither intended, since their so-called "objective" intent governs. When, however, they have previously agreed that their written promises are not to bind them, that agreement controls and no legal obligations flow from the writing. It has been held virtually everywhere, when the question has arisen that (certainly in the absence of any fraudulent or illegal purpose) a purported written agreement, which the parties designed as a mere sham, lacks legal efficacy, and that extrinsic parol or other extrinsic evidence will always be received on that issue. . . .

We need not here consider cases where third persons have relied on the delusive agreement to their detriment or cases in other jurisdictions (we find none in Michigan) where the mutual purpose of the deception was fraudulent or illegal. For the instant case involves no such elements. As noted above, the pleadings and affidavits are silent as to the matter of whom the parties here intended to mislead, and we cannot infer a fraudulent or illegal purpose. Even the explanation contained in plaintiff's brief discloses no fraud or illegality: No law existed rendering illegal the commission provision of the oral agreement which the parties here omitted from the sham writing; while it may be undesirable that citizens should prepare documents so contrived as to spoil the scent of legislators bent on proposing new legislation, yet such conduct is surely not unlawful and does not deserve judicial castigation as immoral or fraudulent; the courts should not erect standards of morality so far above the customary. . . .

Candor compels the admission that, were we enthusiastic devotees of that rule, we might so construe the record as to bring this case within the rule's scope; we could dwell on the fact that plaintiff, in his complaint, states that the acceptance of his offer "was partly oral and partly contained" in the October 31 writing, and could then hold that, as that writing unambiguously covers the item of commissions, the plaintiff is trying to use extrinsic evidence to "contradict" the writing. But the plaintiff's affidavit, if accepted as true and liberally construed, makes it plain that the parties deliberately intended the October 31 writing to be a misleading, untrue, statement of their real agreement.

We thus construe the record because we do not share defendant's belief that the rule is so beneficent, so promotive of the administration of justice, and so necessary to business stability, that it should be given the widest possible application. The truth is that the rule does but little to achieve the ends it supposedly serves. Although seldom mentioned in modern decisions, the most important motive for perpetuation of the rule is distrust of juries, fear that they cannot adequately cope with, or will be unfairly prejudiced by, conflicting "parol" testimony.

If the rule were frankly recognized as primarily a device to control juries, its shortcomings would become obvious, since it is not true that the execution by the parties of an unambiguous writing, "facially complete," bars extrinsic proof. The courts admit such "parol" testimony (other than the parties' statements of what they meant by the writing) for a variety of purposes: to show "all the operative usages" and "all the surrounding circumstances prior to and contemporaneous with the making" of a writing; to show an agreed oral condition, nowhere referred to in the writing, that the writing was not to be binding until some third person approved; to show that a deed, absolute on its face, is but a mortgage. These and numerous other exceptions have removed most of that insulation of the jury from "oral" testimony which the rule is said to provide.

The rule, then, does relatively little to deserve its much advertised virtue of reducing the dangers of successful fraudulent recoveries and defenses brought about through perjury. The rule is too small a hook to catch such a leviathan. Moreover, if at times it does prevent a person from winning, by lying witnesses, a lawsuit which he should lose, it also, at times, by shutting out the true facts, unjustly aids other persons to win lawsuits they should and would lose, were the suppressed evidence known to the courts. Exclusionary rules, which frequently result in injustice, have always been defended — as was the rule, now fortunately extinct, excluding testimony of the parties to an action — with the danger-of-perjury argument.

Perjury, of course, is pernicious and doubtless much of it is used in our courts daily with unfortunate success. The problem of avoiding its efficacious use should be met head on. Were it consistently met in an indirect manner — in accordance with the viewpoint of the adulators of the parol evidence rule — by wiping out substantive rights provable only through oral testimony, we would have wholesale destruction of familiar causes of action such as, for instance, suits for personal injury and for enforcement of wholly oral agreements.

The parol evidence rule is lauded as an important aid in the judicial quest for "objectivity," a quest which aims to avoid that problem the solution of which was judicially said in the latter part of the fifteenth century to be beyond even the powers of Satan — the discovery of the inner thoughts of man. The policy of stern refusal to consider subjective intention, prevalent in the centralized common law courts of that period, later gave way; in the latter part of the eighteenth and the early part of the nineteenth century, the recession from that policy went far, and there was much talk of the "meeting of the minds" in the formation of contracts, of giving effect to the actual "will" of the contracting parties. The obstacles to learning that actual intention have, more recently, induced a partial reversion to the older view. Today a court generally restricts its attention to the outward behavior of the parties: the meaning of their acts is not what either party or both parties intended but the meaning which a "reasonable man" puts on those acts; the expression of mutual assent, not the assent itself, is usually the essential element.

Externality

We now speak of "externality," insisting on judicial consideration of only those manifestations of intention which are public ("open to the scrutiny and knowledge of the community") and not private ("secreted in the heart" of a person). This objective approach is of great value, for a legal system can be more effectively administered if legal rights and obligations ordinarily attach only to overt conduct. Moreover, to call the standard "objective" and candidly to confess that the actual intention is not the guiding factor serves desirably to highlight the fact that much of the "law of contracts" has nothing whatever to do with what the parties contemplated but consists of rules—founded on considerations of public policy—by which the courts impose on the contracting parties obligations of which the parties were often unaware; this "objective" perspective discloses that the voluntary act of entering into a contract creates a jural "relation" or "status" much in the same way as does being married or holding public office.

But we should not demand too much of this concept of "objectivity"; like all useful concepts it becomes a thought-muddler if its limitations are disregarded. We can largely rid ourselves of concern with the subjective reactions of the parties; when, however, we test their public behavior by inquiring how it appears to the "reasonable man," we must recognize, unless we wish to fool ourselves, that although one area of subjectivity has been conquered, another remains unsubdued. For instance, under the parol

Standard

evidence rule, the standard of interpretation of a written contract is usually "the meaning that would be attached to" it "by a *reasonably intelligent person* acquainted with all operative usages and knowing all the circumstances prior to, and contemporaneous with, the making" of the contract, "other than oral statements by the parties of what they intended it to mean." We say that "the objective viewpoint of a third person is used." But where do we find that "objective" third person? We ask judges or juries to discover that "objective viewpoint" through their own subjective processes. Being but human, their beliefs cannot be objectified, in the sense of being standardized. . . . Early in the history of our legal institutions, litigants strongly objected to a determination of the facts by mere fallible human beings. A man, they felt, ought to be allowed to demonstrate the facts "by supernatural means, by some such process as the ordeal or the judicial combat; God may be for him, though his neighbors be against him."[25] We have accepted the "rational" method of trial based on evidence but the longing persists for some means of counteracting the fallibility of the triers of the facts. Mechanical devices, like the parol evidence rule, are symptoms of that longing,[26] a longing particularly strong when juries participate in trials. But a mechanical device like the parol

25. Maitland, The Constitutional History of England (1908) 130.
26. Thayer delightfully described the fatuous notion of a "lawyer's Paradise, where all words have a fixed, precisely ascertained meaning; where men may express their purposes, not only with accuracy, but with fulness; and where, if the writer has been careful, a lawyer, having a document referred to him, may sit in his chair, inspect the text, and answer all questions without raising his eyes." Thayer, loc. cit., 428, 429.

evidence rule cannot satisfy that longing, especially because the injustice of applying the rule rigidly has led to its being riddled with exceptions.

Those exceptions have, too, played havoc with the contention that business stability depends upon that rule, that, as one court put it "the tremendous but closely adjusted machinery of modern business cannot function at all without" the assurance afforded by the rule and that, "if such assurance were removed today from our law, general disaster would result. . . ."[28] We are asked to believe that the rule enables businessmen, advised by their lawyers, to rely with indispensable confidence on written contracts unimpeachable by oral testimony. In fact, seldom can a conscientious lawyer advise his client, about to sign an agreement, that, should the client become involved in litigation relating to that agreement, one of the many exceptions to the rule will not permit the introduction of uncertainty-producing oral testimony. As Corbin says, "That rule has so many exceptions that only with difficulty can it be correctly stated in the form of a rule."[29] One need but thumb the pages of Wigmore, Williston, or the Restatement of Contracts to see how illusory is the certainty that the rule supplies. "Collateral parol agreements contradicting a writing are inadmissible," runs the rule as ordinarily stated; but in the application of that standard there exists, as Williston notes, "no final test which can be applied with unvarying regularity."[30] Wigmore more bluntly says that only vague generalizations are possible, since the application of the rule, "resting as it does on the parties' intent, can properly be made only after a comparison of the kind of transaction, the terms of the document, and the circumstances of the parties. . . . Such is the complexity of circumstances and the variety of documentary phraseology, and so minute the indicia of intent, that one ruling can seldom be controlling authority or even of utility for a subsequent one."[31] The recognized exceptions to the rule demonstrate strikingly that business can endure even when oral testimony competes with written instruments. If business stability has not been ruined by the deed-mortgage exception, or because juries may hear witnesses narrate oral understandings that written contracts were not to be operative except on the performance of extrinsic conditions, it is unlikely that commercial disaster would follow even if legislatures abolished the rule in its entirety.

In sum, a rule so leaky cannot fairly be described as a stout container of legal certainty. John Chipman Gray, a seasoned practical lawyer, expressed grave doubts concerning the reliance of businessmen on legal precedents

---

28. Cargill Commission Co. v. Swartwood, 159 Minn. 1, 198 N.W. 536, 538.

29. Corbin, Delivery of Written Contracts, 36 Yale L.J. (1927) 443.

30. 3 Williston, Contracts, rev. ed., §1837. Proof of "collateral" agreements seems generally to be more freely permitted when the writing is a negotiable instrument, a lease or a deed—precisely the types of instrument on which one would suppose that business stability would peculiarly depend.

31. Wigmore, loc. cit., §2442.

generally.[33] If they rely on the parol evidence rule in particular, they will often be duped. It has been seriously questioned whether in fact they do so to any considerable extent. We see no good reason why we should strain to interpret the record facts here to bring them within such a rule.

Reversed and remanded.

Reversed in favor of Plaintiff

NOTE

Judge Frank's triumph over the parol evidence rule was short lived. The United States Supreme Court reversed, 322 U.S. 709 (1944):

Scotus reversed and Affirmed the District Courts holding in favor of Defendant

> PER CURIAM. In this case two members of the Court think that the judgment of the Circuit Court of Appeals should be affirmed. Seven are of the opinion that the judgment should be reversed and the judgment of the District Court affirmed — four because proof of the contract alleged in respondent's affidavits on the motion for summary judgment is precluded by the applicable state parol evidence rule, and three because the contract is contrary to public policy and void.

CHAPTER 5 ASSESSMENT

Multiple Choice Questions

1. When Alice Kim was trying to sell her house one of the prospective buyers was Howard Lee. When she showed him around he was most impressed when they reached the huge garden in the back, which featured a large seven-foot high statue of Jumong, a Korean god, shooting an arrow into the sky. He asked if it came with the property, and Alice replied that it did not. They eventually agreed on a price for the property, and the resulting contract contained a statement that the sale of the realty did not include the Jumong statue. Both parties signed the contract. As he was leaving Alice's lawyer's office where the signing took place, Howard said to Alice, "I will add another $5,000 to the price if you'll leave the Jumong statue right where it is when you go." "Wow!" she replied, "that's a lot of money." Then she added, "All right," and they shook hands. At the closing a week later, however, she told him she had changed his mind and refused to add the Jumong statue to the deal. He sued and both

---

33. See Gray, The Nature and Sources of Law (1921) §225; cf. Austin, Jurisprudence, 4th ed., 674; concurring opinion in Aero Spark Plug Co. v. B.G. Corp., 2 Cir., 130 F.2d 290, 292, 297, 298; Wigmore, The Judicial Function, in the Science of Legal Method (1917) Editorial Introduction, xxxvi-xxxix.

parties testified to all of the above on the witness stand. How does this come out?

a. The contract about the statue is a collateral matter and would not normally be included in a contract for the sale of the real property, so the parol evidence rule does not bar evidence of this oral agreement. Howard wins.

b. The sale of the realty included the garden and the statue was a large part of that garden. Thus the sale of the statue is not "collateral" at all, but very much at issue when considering what was being sold and what was not. Alice had made it obvious she was not selling the statue when she first agreed to sell the main property, and made it very clear this was not part of the deal. Thus any agreement about the statue that is oral violates the parol evidence rule because it is the sort of thing that would naturally be included in the sale of the property. Alice wins.

c. Howard loses for another reason: The sale of realty has to be in writing, according to the statute of frauds. Since the statue is part of the realty an oral agreement as to it is unenforceable. Even if the statue is considered personal property, UCC §2-201(1) requires a writing for the sale of goods costing more than $500.

d. Howard wins. The parol evidence rule is no bar to agreements that occur after the signing of the writing, as here. The statute of frauds for the sale of realty also doesn't apply to a statue easily removable from the property, and the UCC statute of frauds for the sale of personal property over $500 is satisfied by Alice's admission on the witness stand to the terms of the oral deal; UCC §2-201(3)(b).

2. Mrs. Mitchell wanted to purchase a farm from Mr. and Mrs. Lath, but didn't like the ugly ice house across the road from the farm. The Laths told her that, as it happened, they also owned the ice house and had been thinking about tearing it down, so they promised if she would purchase the farm for the amount they had all agreed would be fair, the Laths would, in addition, tear down the ice house before Mrs. Mitchell moved in five months from the date of the closing. Mrs. Mitchell looked over the contract at that closing and noticed the ice house wasn't mentioned. She pointed this out and the Laths assured her that it was just a drafting error. They said they would draw up an amendment to the contract immediately and send it to her, but she should sign the contract now so that they could begin moving out and taking down the ice house immediately. Mrs. Mitchell did so and paid for the house by check, but weeks later was distressed to realize that the ice house hadn't been touched. When the Laths denied there was an agreement to remove it, Mrs. Mitchell sued. How should this come out?

a. The same way it did in the actual case with which this chapter began: The parol evidence rule bars the admission of the ice house agreement because the writing appears to integrate into it all the major terms of the contract, including the consideration to be given by each side. The ice house removal, supposedly part of the Laths' consideration, is not mentioned in the writing, so it's not part of the agreement. The Laths win.

b. Mrs. Mitchell should sue for her money back, ignoring the contract, and asking for quasi-contractual relief: money had and received. The Laths, evil people, would be unjustly enriched if they could keep her money without fulfilling an agreement that was so very important to her.

c. Mrs. Mitchell should win. The Laths made the oral promise just to trick her, with no intent to follow through. That is fraud, it voids the contract, and matters of avoidance, like fraud, are exceptions to the parol evidence rule. Fraud not only gets her money back, but also might lead to the award of punitive damages (see the next chapter).

d. The Laths lose. The ice house agreement is a collateral matter, just incidental to the sale and therefore is the sort of thing that might easily have been left out of the more formal contract of deed.

3. Racehorse American Sphinx had won the first two races of the Triple Crown and was a favorite to win the Belmont Stakes, which would make the horse the first Triple Crown winner in a decade. Nelson Cash, a rich man, wanted to buy American Sphinx if the horse did win the Belmont Stakes, so he approached the horse's owner, Melvin Sanders, and made him an offer of $2 million, making it clear that the offer was contingent on American Sphinx winning the Triple Crown. Sanders liked the offer and they agreed to all the terms. Cash wanted to register the horse in his name minutes after it won the Belmont Stakes, so the Cash and Sanders signed a simple piece of paper stating that Cash had bought the horse from Sanders for $2 million. The writing said nothing about American Sphinx winning the final race. When the race was held American Sphinx came in second, and Cash was very disappointed. But Sanders still demanded the $2 million. When Cash protested that the sale was contingent on that final victory, Sanders pointed to the writing and asserted that the parol evidence rule would keep out the evidence of the oral agreement that added a condition to the contract. A lawsuit followed. Who should prevail?

a. Sanders should win. The requirement that the horse win the final race is not a collateral matter — it is central to the deal. The parol evidence rule clearly bars the introduction of such an important term that was mysteriously left out of the writing. If something this big could change the terms of the writing, then the parol evidence rule would have no meaning at all.

b. Cash should win. This evidence does not contradict the writing, but is evidence of a condition precedent to the effectiveness of the writing. The parties clearly meant for the written contract to have no legal effect until American Sphinx won the final race, and the parol evidence rule allows oral conditions precedent to effectiveness to be an exception to the necessity of the writing.

    c. Sanders should win. This isn't just a condition on some small matter, it goes to the very heart of the deal, and the parol evidence rule demands that all the important terms be in the writing and forbids oral terms from changing the clear meaning of the written ones.

    d. Cash should win. It would be fraud to have an oral agreement stopping the enforcement of the contract if American Sphinx lost the final race and then try to use the parol evidence rule to wipe out the oral agreement, enforce the writing, and steal $2 million. The parol evidence rule does not operate to bar evidence of fraud.

4. Weekend Construction Company (WCC) was involved in a massive project to build a skyscraper in the middle of a large city and needed monthly deliveries of a certain quantity of steel each month, so it signed a contract with Steel Sales of Mexico (SSM) agreeing to pay a named amount for each delivery made on the first of the month for the next two years. The contract provided that if a delivery was made late, the seller would suffer a 5 percent deduction from the original amount due. SSM made the first three deliveries on time, but missed the fourth by being one day late. SSM explained that a train derailment had caused the delay and was assured by a phone call from WCC's purchasing agent that a one-day delay was no problem and no deduction would be made. In the subsequent six deliveries SSM was early one month, on time twice, and delivered one day late the other three. When SSM finally submitted its bill, WCC made deductions for these three late deliveries, and SSM was annoyed. You are SSM's lawyer. Can it prevail in a suit to recover the full amounts with no deductions?

    a. Yes. The express term of the contract requiring delivery on time has been changed by the "course of performance" of the contract, which allowed some fluctuation in compliance with the literal language of the agreement. Here WCC had said that a one-day late delivery was fine and would not trigger the penalty, and that changed the express term of the contract to permit this variation. Section 1-303(f) of the Uniform Commercial Code allows course of performance to show a waiver or modification of the express terms of the contract, which is what happened here.

    b. SSM should win. Parties cannot contract for a penalty, but only actual damages. Thus SSM should get the full amount due each month except to the extent that WCC can show damages from the minor delays.

    c. WCC should win. The parties did not contract for a penalty but merely a price adjustment (in effect a liquidated damages clause) for the harm obviously caused by late deliveries. WCC was nice about not enforcing this the first time, but thereafter SSM's sloppy deliveries should trigger the contracted-for deductions from the amount due.

d. Section 1-303(e)(1) clearly provides that "express terms prevail over course of performance." Application of that rule means at SSM must suffer the deductions for the three late deliveries; WCC had not made an express waiver of the relevant contract term for these three (as it had the first time it occurred).

Answers

1. D is the best answer. The parol evidence rule only bars testimony of oral agreements happening *before* the signing of the writing, so it's no issue here. Assuming the court finds that the statue is not a fixture (personal property that becomes so attached to the realty that it becomes part of it and is not easily removable), no writing would be required here under the "sale of real property" part of the statute of frauds. The UCC statute of frauds is satisfied by the admission on the witness stand.

2. The court might choose A, but C is the more likely answer to prevail. Fraud vitiates all contracts, as we shall see, and the parol evidence rule is not designed to let villains take advantage of such a technicality in the law as a shield for protecting their villainy. A court might also say that a promise to amend the writing leads to an estoppel to raise the parol evidence rule, though that is trickier to sell to most courts; if promissory estoppel were enough to get around the parol evidence rule, it could be used to cancel out its efficacy in most cases.

3. B is the best answer. This is similar to Pym v. Campbell in this chapter. There the parties agreed that the writing would not go into effect until it was approved by a third party, which never happened, and the court held that the parol evidence rule does not bar the admission of evidence of a condition precedent to the effectiveness of a written agreement. The same thing happened here. The parties never meant for there to be a sale unless the oral condition occurred, which did not happen, so the writing never had any legal effect. Sure, it would have been smarter to write the condition into the contract, but nonetheless the law does not require formation conditions to be in the writing itself.

4. A is the best answer. It's true that §1-303(e)(1) says express terms prevail over course of performance, but §1-303(f) trumps that by providing that course of performance (here accepting late deliveries without protest, as it had done in the past) means that WCC had waived this express term. The law struggles to protect reliance that is reasonable, and WCC had made it clear that a one-day delay did not violate the express term so SSM rightly came to feel that a one-day delay was still in compliance with the terms of the contract.

6

AVOIDANCE OF THE CONTRACT

Pacta Sunt Servanda (Agreements are to be observed)

Yes, agreements are to be observed, a motto worth quoting to the court when your opponent is arguing that the contract should be changed or completely cancelled. Nonetheless, there are so-called contracts that must not or cannot be observed (ones created at gunpoint, or entered into by eight-year-olds, or where one or both of the parties are talking about very different things, etc.). This chapter explores the extraordinary situations where the court may be asked to either nullify the contract or reform it. Attorneys must be aware of these possibilities before assuring their clients that the contract is fixed and unassailable, lest ugly words like "malpractice" come up in the aftermath of some judge ruling otherwise.

I. INTRODUCTION

Even though the parties have engaged in a valid agreement, exchanged sufficient consideration, and complied with formalities such as the requirement of a writing, events occurring prior or subsequent to the contract's formation may permit one or more of the parties to escape from the bargain. In some cases the contract is completely rescinded, and in others it is reformed by the court in a manner that solves the difficulty.

II. MISTAKE

A. Misunderstanding

The issue of misunderstanding is sometimes taught as part of the doctrine of mistake, sometimes taught as part of law of offer and acceptance (because it deals with confusion in the bargaining process), and sometimes taught as part of the law of interpretation (because it revolves around parties who assign different meanings to the same provision). The leading case on misunderstanding as a doctrine of avoidance — the story of the good ship(s) *Peerless*—follows.

RAFFLES v. WICHELHAUS
Court of the Exchequer, 1864
2 Hurl. & C. 906, 159 Eng. Rep. 375

Declaration. For that it was agreed between the plaintiff and the defendants, to wit, at Liverpool, that the plaintiff should sell to the defendants, and the defendants buy of the plaintiff, certain goods, to wit, 125 bales of Surat cotton, guaranteed middling fair merchant's Dhollorah, to arrive ex "Peerless" from Bombay; and that the cotton should be taken from the quay, and that the defendants would pay the plaintiff for the same at a certain rate, to wit, at the rate of $17\frac{1}{4}$ per pound, within a certain time then agreed upon after the arrival of the said goods in England. Averments: that the said goods did arrive by the said ship from Bombay in England, to wit, at Liverpool, and the plaintiff was then and there ready, and willing and offered to deliver the said goods to the defendants, etc. Breach: that the defendants refused to accept the said goods or pay the plaintiff for them.

Plea. That the said ship mentioned in the said agreement was meant and intended by the defendants to be the ship called the "Peerless," which sailed from Bombay, to wit, in October; and that the plaintiff was not ready and willing and did not offer to deliver to the defendants any bales of cotton which arrived by the last mentioned ship, but instead thereof was only ready and willing and offered to deliver to the defendants 125 bales of Surat cotton which arrived by another and different ship, which was also called the "Peerless," and which sailed from Bombay, to wit, in December.

Demurrer, and joinder therein.

MILWARD, in support of the demurrer. The contract was for the sale of a number of bales of cotton of a particular description, which the plaintiff was ready to deliver. It is immaterial by what ship the cotton was to arrive, so that it was a ship called the "Peerless." The words "to arrive ex 'Peerless,'" only mean that if the vessel is lost on the voyage, the contract is to be at an end. [POLLOCK, C.B. It would be a question for the jury whether both parties meant the same ship called the "Peerless."] That would be so if the contract was for the sale of a ship called the "Peerless"; but it is for the sale of cotton on board a ship of that name. [POLLOCK, C.B. The defendant only bought that cotton which was to arrive by a particular ship. It may as well be said, that if there is a contract for the purchase of certain goods in warehouse A., that is satisfied by the delivery of goods of the same description in warehouse B.] In that case there would be goods in both warehouses; here it does not appear that the plaintiff had any goods on board the other "Peerless." [MARTIN, B. It is imposing on the defendant a contract different from that which he entered into. POLLOCK, C.B. It is like a contract for the purchase of wine coming from a particular estate in France or Spain, where there are two estates of that name.] The defendant has no right to contradict by parol evidence a written contract good upon the face of it. He does not impute misrepresentation or fraud, but only says that he fancied the ship was a different one. Intention is of no avail, unless stated at the time of the contract. [POLLOCK, C.B. One vessel sailed in October and the other in December.] The time of sailing is no part of the contract.

MELLISH (COHEN with him), in support of the plea. There is nothing on the face of the contract to shew that any particular ship called the "Peerless" was meant; but the moment it appears that two ships called the "Peerless" were about to sail from Bombay there is a latent ambiguity, and parol evidence may be given for the purpose of shewing that the defendant meant one "Peerless," and the plaintiff another. That being so, there was no consensus ad idem, and therefore no binding contract. He was then stopped by the Court.

No contract due to mutual Misunderstanding

PER CURIAM. There must be judgment for the defendants.

Judgment for the defendants.

NOTES AND QUESTIONS

1. What does "ex Peerless" mean? See UCC §2-322.

2. Would it matter which of the parties (the seller or the buyer) wanted to rescind the deal?

3. If the parties discovered the mistake, could they elect to live with it and take the late-arriving cotton? That is, does the mistake make the contract *void* or merely *voidable*?

4. Professor Grant Gilmore, The Death of Contract 39 (1974):

None of the judges thought of asking Mellish what would seem to be obvious questions. Would a reasonably well-informed cotton merchant in

Liverpool have known that there were two ships called *Peerless*? Ought this buyer to have known? If in fact the October *Peerless* had arrived in Liverpool first, had the buyer protested the seller's failure to tender the cotton? The failure of the judges, who had given Milward such a hard time, to put any questions to Mellish suggests that they were entirely content to let the case go off on the purely subjective failure of the minds to meet at the time the contract was entered into.

5. For a complete description of the historical background of this famous case, see Simpson, Contracts for Cotton to Arrive: The Case of the Two Ships *Peerless*, 11 Cardozo L. Rev. 287 (1989). The cotton famine of this period put 500,000 people out of work in Great Britain as the textile mills shut down. Trivia question: What event was the likely cause of this cotton shortage?

RESTATEMENT (SECOND) OF CONTRACTS

§20. EFFECT OF MISUNDERSTANDING

(1) There is no manifestation of mutual assent to an exchange if the parties attach materially different meanings to their manifestations and

      (a) neither party knows or has reason to know the meaning attached by the other; or

      (b) each party knows or each party has reason to know the meaning attached by the other.

(2) The manifestations of the parties are operative in accordance with the meaning attached to them by one of the parties if

      (a) that party does not know of any different meaning attached by the other, and the other knows the meaning attached by the first party; or

      (b) that party has no reason to know of any different meaning attached by the other, and the other has reason to know the meaning attached by the first party.*

The Reporter's Note to this section explains: "A contract should be held nonexistent under this Section only when the misunderstanding goes to

---

*As you might remember from Chapter 5, Restatement (Second) of Contracts §201 contains the same rule when the parties assign different meanings to language in a contract.

conflicting and irreconcilable meanings of a material term that could have either but not both meanings."

Problem 108

(a) Seller offered to sell Buyer goods to be shipped from Bombay ex steamer *Peerless*. Buyer accepted. There are two steamers with the name *Peerless*, each sailing from Bombay but at materially different times. Is *No* there a contract if both of the parties have reason to know there are two ships named *Peerless*, but they mean different ships? What if both parties intend the same ship? *No*

(b) Is there a contract if Seller knows that Buyer means the later sailing *Peerless* and Buyer does not know that there are two ships named *Peerless*? *Yes §20(2)(a)*

Problem 109

For a week Andrew Carnes had been negotiating with Will Parker over *Materially Different* the sale of a cow from Will to Andrew. Finally, in the presence of witnesses, Will said, "All right. I'll sell you my horse for $499." Andrew knew that Will loved his only horse and would never sell it, so that the word *horse* was a slip of the tongue. Nonetheless, he quickly accepted, planning to buy the horse. Both the cow and the horse are worth about $499. Is there a contract here? If so, is it for the sale of a cow or a horse?

B. Mutual Mistake

Because a contract is founded upon the agreement of the parties, if they are unaware of critical facts existing at the contract's inception, a mistake has occurred and the courts may feel compelled to straighten out the resulting confusion.

RESTATEMENT (SECOND) OF CONTRACTS

§152. WHEN MISTAKE OF BOTH PARTIES MAKES A CONTRACT VOIDABLE

Where a mistake of both parties at the time a contract was made as to a basic assumption on which the contract was made has a material effect on the agreed exchange of performances, the contract is voidable by the adversely

affected party unless he bears the risk of the mistake under the rule stated
in §154. . . .

§154. When a Party Bears the Risk of a Mistake

A party bears the risk of a mistake when—

(a) the risk is allocated to him by agreement of the parties, or
(b) he is aware, at the time the contract is made, that he has only limited
     knowledge with respect to the facts to which the mistake relates but
     treats his limited knowledge as sufficient, or
(c) the risk is allocated to him by the court on the ground that it is
     reasonable in the circumstances to do so.

The typical remedy for mutual mistake is to permit either party to elect
rescission, an equitable decree by which the contract is simply cancelled, at
which point the court typically orders restitution of the considerations
already exchanged. Other losses, such as reliance expenses and consequential damages, fall where they may. Restatement (Second) of Contracts §158
would permit "relief on such terms as justice requires including protection
of the parties' reliance interests."

SHERWOOD v. WALKER
Supreme Court of Michigan, 1887
66 Mich. 568, 33 N.W. 919

Morse, J. Replevin for a cow. Suit commenced in justice's court; judgment for plaintiff; appealed to circuit court of Wayne county, and verdict and
judgment for plaintiff in that court. The defendants bring error, and set out
25 assignments of the same.

The main controversy depends upon the construction of a contract for
the sale of the cow. The plaintiff claims that the title passed, and bases his
action upon such claim. The defendants contend that the contract was executory, and by its terms no title to the animal was acquired by plaintiff. The
defendants reside at Detroit, but are in business at Walkerville, Ontario, and
have a farm at Greenfield, in Wayne county, upon which were some blooded
cattle supposed to be barren as breeders. The Walkers are importers and
breeders of polled Angus cattle. The plaintiff is a banker living at Plymouth,

in Wayne county. He called upon the defendants at Walkerville for the purchase of some of their stock, but found none there that suited him. Meeting one of the defendants afterwards, he was informed that they had a few head upon their Greenfield farm. He was asked to go out and look at them, with the statement at the time that they were probably barren, and would not breed. May 5, 1886, plaintiff went out to Greenfield, and saw the cattle. A few days thereafter, he called upon one of the defendants with the view of purchasing a cow, known as "Rose 2d of Aberlone." After considerable talk, it was agreed that defendants would telephone Sherwood at his home in Plymouth in reference to the price. The second morning after this talk he was called up by telephone, and the terms of the sale were finally agreed upon. He was to pay five and one-half cents per pound, live weight, fifty pounds shrinkage. He was asked how he intended to take the cow home, and replied that he might ship her from King's cattle-yard. He requested defendants to confirm the sale in writing, which they did by sending him the following letter:

[handwritten margin notes: Didnt Think cow cowd breed / P wanted to purchase cow / D Agreed to sell / confirmed in writing]

Walkerville, May 15, 1886.

T. C. Sherwood, President, etc. — Dear Sir:

We confirm sale to you of the cow Rose 2d of Aberlone, lot 56 of our catalogue, at five and a half cents per pound, less fifty pounds shrink. We inclose herewith order on Mr. Graham for the cow. You might leave check with him, or mail to us here, as you prefer.

Yours, truly,
Hiram Walker & Sons.

The order upon Graham inclosed in the letter read as follows:

Walkerville, May 15, 1886.

George Graham:

You will please deliver at King's cattle-yard to Mr. T. C. Sherwood, Plymouth, the cow Rose 2d of Aberlone, lot 56 of our catalogue. Send halter with the cow, and have her weighed.

Yours, truly,
Hiram Walker & Sons.

On the twenty-first of the same month the plaintiff went to defendants' farm at Greenfield, and presented the order and letter to Graham, who informed him that the defendants had instructed him not to deliver the

refused to Deliver cow

cow. Soon after, the plaintiff tendered to Hiram Walker, one of the defendants, $80, and demanded the cow. Walker refused to take the money or deliver the cow. The plaintiff then instituted this suit. After he has secured possession of the cow under the writ of replevin, the plaintiff caused her to be weighed by the constable who served the writ, at a place other than King's cattle-yard. She weighed 1,420 pounds.

Trial

When the plaintiff, upon the trial in the circuit court, had submitted his proofs showing the above transaction, defendants moved to strike out and exclude the testimony from the case, for the reason that it was irrelevant and did not tend to show that the title to the cow passed, and that it showed that the contract of sale was merely executory. The court refused the motion, and an exception was taken. The defendants then introduced evidence tending to show that at the time of the alleged sale it was believed by both the plaintiff and themselves that the cow was barren and would not breed; that she cost $850, and if not barren would be worth from $750 to $1,000; that after the date of the letter, and the order to Graham, the defendants were informed by said Graham that in his judgment the cow was with calf, and therefore they instructed him not to deliver her to plaintiff, and on the twentieth of May, 1886, telegraphed plaintiff what Graham thought about the cow being with calf, and that consequently they could not sell her. The cow had a calf in the month of October following. On the nineteenth of May, the plaintiff wrote Graham as follows:

Mr. George Graham, Greenfield—Dear Sir:

I have bought Rose or Lucy from Mr. Walker, and will be there for her Friday morning, nine or ten o'clock. Do not water her in the morning.

Yours, etc.,
T. C. Sherwood.

Plaintiff explained the mention of the two cows in this letter by testifying that, when he wrote this letter, the order and letter of defendants was at his home, and writing in a hurry, and being uncertain as to the name of the cow, and not wishing his cow watered, he thought it would do no harm to name them both, as his bill of sale would show which one he had purchased. Plaintiff also testified that he asked defendants to give him a price on the balance of their herd at Greenfield, as a friend thought of buying some, and received a letter dated May 17, 1886, in which they named the price of five cattle, including Lucy, at $90, and Rose 2d at $80. When he received the letter he called defendants up by telephone, and asked them why they put Rose 2d in the list, as he had already purchased her. They replied that they knew he had, but thought it would make no difference if plaintiff and his friend concluded to take the whole herd.

The foregoing is the substance of all the testimony in the case. The circuit judge instructed the jury that if they believed the defendants, when they sent the order and letter to plaintiff, meant to pass the title to the cow, and that the cow was intended to be delivered to plaintiff, it did not matter whether the cow was weighed at any particular place, or by any particular person; and if the cow was weighed afterwards, as Sherwood testified, such weighing would be a sufficient compliance with the order. If they believed that defendants intended to pass the title by writing, it did not matter whether the cow was weighed before or after suit [was] brought, and the plaintiff would be entitled to recover. The defendants submitted a number of requests which were refused. The substance of them was that the cow was never delivered to plaintiff, and the title to her did not pass by the letter and order; and that under the contract, as evidenced by these writings, the title did not pass until the cow was weighed and her price thereby determined; and that, if the defendants only agreed to sell a cow that would not breed, then the barrenness of the cow was a condition precedent to passing title, and plaintiff cannot recover. The court also charged the jury that it was immaterial whether the cow was with calf or not. It will therefore be seen that the defendants claim that, as a matter of law, the title of this cow did not pass, and that the circuit judge erred in submitting the case to the jury, to be determined by them, upon the intent of the parties as to whether or not the title passed with the sending of the letter and order by the defendants to the plaintiff.

This question as to the passing of title is fraught with difficulties, and not always easy of solution. An examination of the multitude of cases bearing upon this subject, with their infinite variety of facts, and at least apparent conflict of law, oft times tends to confuse rather than to enlighten the mind of the inquirer. It is best, therefore, to consider always, in cases of this kind, the general principles of the law, and then apply them as best we may to the facts of the case in hand. [The location of title was an issue in this case because only a plaintiff having title could bring an action in replevin. The court concluded that the buyer had sufficient title to maintain his action — EDS.] It appears from the record that both parties supposed this cow was barren and would not breed, and she was sold by the pound for an insignificant sum as compared with her real value if a breeder. She was evidently sold and purchased on the relation of her value for beef, unless the plaintiff had learned of her true condition, and concealed such knowledge from the defendants. Before the plaintiff secured the possession of the animal, the defendants learned that she was with calf, and therefore of great value, and undertook to rescind the sale by refusing to deliver her. The question arises whether they had a right to do so. The circuit judge rules that this fact did not avoid the sale and it made no difference whether she was barren or not. I am of the opinion that the court erred in this holding. I know that this is a close question, and the dividing line between the adjudicated cases is not easily discerned. But it must be considered as well settled that a party who has given

Rule

an apparent consent to a contract of sale may refuse to execute it, or he may avoid it after it has been completed, if the assent was founded, or the contract made, upon the mistake of a material fact, — such as the subject-matter of the sale, the price, or some collateral fact materially inducing the agreement; and this can be done when the mistake is mutual. [Citations omitted.]

Mistake was mutual

If there is a difference or misapprehension as to the substance of the thing bargained for; if the thing actually delivered or received is different in substance from the thing bargained for, and intended to be sold, — then there is no contract; but if it be only a difference in some quality or accident, even though the mistake may have been the actuating motive to the purchaser or seller, or both of them, yet the contract remains binding. "The difficulty in every case is to determine whether the mistake or misapprehension is as to the substance of the whole contract, going, as it were, to the root of the matter, or only to some point, even though a material point, an error as to which does not affect the substance of the whole consideration." Kennedy v. Panama, etc., Mail Co., L.R. 2 Q.B. 580, 587. It has been held, in accordance with the principles above stated, that where a horse is bought under the belief that he is sound, and both vendor and vendee honestly believe him to be sound, the purchaser must stand by his bargain, and pay the full price, unless there was a warranty.

Exception

Need to figure out if mistake is as to the substance of the whole contract

Court Analysis

It seems to me, however, in the case made by this record, that the mistake or misapprehension of the parties went to the whole substance of the agreement. If the cow was a breeder, she was worth at least $750; if barren, she was worth not over $80. The parties would not have made the contract of sale except upon the understanding and belief that she was incapable of breeding, and of no use as a cow. It is true she is now the identical animal that they thought her to be when the contract was made; there is no mistake as to the identity of the creature. Yet the mistake was not of the mere quality of the animal, but went to the very nature of the thing. A barren cow is substantially a different creature than a breeding one. There is as much difference between them for all purposes of use as there is between an ox and a cow that is capable of breeding and giving milk. If the mutual mistake had simply related to the fact whether she was with calf or not for one season, then it might have been a good sale, but the mistake affected the character of the animal for all time, and for its present and ultimate use. She was not in fact the animal, or the kind of animal, the defendants intended to sell or the plaintiff to buy. She was not a barren cow, and, if this fact had been known, there would have been no contract. The mistake affected the substance of the whole consideration, and it must be considered that there was no contract to sell or sale of the cow as she actually was. The thing sold and bought had in fact no existence. She was sold as a beef creature would be sold; she is in fact a breeding cow, and a valuable one. The court should have instructed the jury that if they found that the cow was sold, or contracted to be sold, upon the understanding of both parties that she was barren, and useless for the purpose of breeding, and that in fact she

Substantially Different

How The Jury Should have been Instructed

was not barren, but capable of breeding, then the defendants had a right to rescind, and to refuse to deliver, and the verdict should be in their favor.

The judgment of the court below must be reversed, and a new trial *Reversed* granted, with costs of this court to defendants.

CAMPBELL, C.J., and CHAMPLIN, J., concurred.

SHERWOOD, J., (dissenting.) I do not concur in the opinion given by my brethren in this case. I think the judgments before the justice and at the circuit were right. I agree with my Brother Morse that the contract made was not within the statute of frauds, and the payment for the property was not a condition precedent to the passing of the title from the defendants to the plaintiff. And I further agree with him that the plaintiff was entitled to a delivery of the property to him when the suit was brought, unless there was a mistake made which would invalidate the contract, and I can find no such mistake. There is no pretense there was any fraud or concealment in the case, and an intimation or insinuation that such a thing might have existed on the part of either of the parties would undoubtedly be a greater surprise to them than anything else that has occurred in their dealings or in the case.

As has already been stated by my brethren, the record shows that the plaintiff is a banker and farmer as well, carrying on a farm, and raising the best breeds of stock, and lived in Plymouth, in the county of Wayne, 23 miles from Detroit; that the defendants lived in Detroit, and were also dealers in stock of the higher grades; that they had a farm at Walkerville, in Canada, and also one in Greenfield in said county of Wayne, and upon these farms the defendants kept their stock. The Greenfield farm was about 15 miles from the plaintiff's. In the spring of 1886 the plaintiff, learning that the defendants had some "polled Angus cattle" for sale, was desirous of purchasing some of that breed, and meeting the defendants, or some of them, at Walkerville, inquired about them, and was informed that they had none at Walkerville, "but had a few head left on their farm in Greenfield, and asked the plaintiff to go and see them, stating that in all probability they were sterile and would not breed." In accordance with said request, the plaintiff, on the fifth day of May, went out and looked at the defendants' cattle at Greenfield, and found one called "Rose, Second," which he wished to purchase, and the terms were finally agreed upon at five and a half cents per pound, live weight, 50 pounds to be deducted for shrinkage. The sale was in writing, and the defendants gave an order to the plaintiff directing the man in charge of the Greenfield farm to deliver the cow to plaintiff. This was done on the fifteenth of May. On the twenty-first of May plaintiff went to get his cow, and the defendants refused to let him have her; claiming at the time that the man in charge at the farm thought the cow was with calf, and, if such was the case, they would not sell her for the price agreed upon. The record further shows that the defendants, when they sold the cow, believed the cow was not with calf, and barren; that from what the plaintiff had been told by defendants (for it does not appear he had any other knowledge or facts from which he could form an opinion) he believed the cow was farrow, but still thought she could be made to breed. The foregoing shows the entire interview and treaty between the parties as to the sterility and qualities of the cow sold to the plaintiff. The cow had a calf in the month of October.

There is no question but that the defendants sold the cow representing her of the breed and quality they believed the cow to be, and that the purchaser so understood it. And the buyer purchased her believing her to be of the breed represented by the sellers, and possessing all the qualities stated, and even more. He believed she would breed. There is no pretense that the plaintiff bought the cow for beef, and there is nothing in the record indicating that he would have bought her at all only that he thought she might be made to breed. Under the foregoing facts, — and these are all that are contained in the record material to the contract, — it is held that because it turned out that the plaintiff was more correct in his judgment as to one quality of the cow than the defendants, and a quality, too, which could not by any possibility be positively known at the time by either party to exist, the contract may be annulled by the defendants at their pleasure. I know of no law, and have not been referred to any, which will justify any such holding, and I think the circuit judge was right in his construction of the contract between the parties.

It is claimed that a mutual mistake of a material fact was made by the parties when the contract of sale was made. There was no warranty in the case of the quality of the animal. When a mistaken fact is relied upon as ground for rescinding, such fact must not only exist at the time the contract is made, but must have been known to one or both of the parties. Where there is no warranty, there can be no mistake of fact when no such fact exists, or, if in existence, neither party knew of it, or could know of it; and that is precisely this case. If the owner of a Hambletonian horse had speeded him, and was only able to make him go a mile in three minutes, and should sell him to another, believing that was his greatest speed, for $300, when the purchaser believed he could go much faster, and made the purchase for that sum, and a few days thereafter, under more favorable circumstances, the horse was driven a mile in 2 min. 16 sec., and was found to be worth $20,000, I hardly think it would be held, either at law or in equity, by any one, that the seller in such case could rescind the contract. The same legal principles apply in each case. . . .

In this case, if either party had superior knowledge as to the qualities of this animal to the other, certainly the defendants had such advantage. I understand the law to be well settled that "there is no breach of any implied confidence that one party will not profit by his superior knowledge as to facts and circumstances" actually within the knowledge of both, because neither party reposes in any such confidence unless it be specially tendered or required, and that a general sale does not imply warranty of any quality, or the absence of any; and if the seller represents to the purchaser what he himself believes as to the qualities of an animal, and the purchaser buys relying upon his own judgment as to such qualities, there is no warranty in the case, and neither has a cause of action against the other if he finds himself to have been mistaken in judgment.

The only pretense for avoiding this contract by the defendants is that they erred in judgment as to the qualities and value of the animal. I think the principles adopted by Chief Justice Campbell in Williams v. Spurr completely cover this case, and should have been allowed to control in its decision. See 24 Mich. 335. See, also, Story, Sales, §§174, 175, 382, and Benj. Sales, §430. The judgment should be affirmed.

QUESTIONS AND NOTE

1. Do the majority and the dissenter disagree on the law of mistake?

2. Sherwood v. Walker was decided before the Restatement (Second) of Contracts refined the black letter test for mistake in §§152 and 154. How would the Michigan Supreme Court have decided the opinion under the Restatement rules? Do we have enough information about the facts of the case?

3. If, unknown to Walker, Sherwood had conducted a fertility test on Rose and determined she was with calf and then decided to offer $80 for her, would the court still allow rescission?

4. For Professor Brainerd Currie's famous poem on point, see Currie, Rose of Aberlone, Harvard Law School Record (Thursday, March 4, 1954), or Student Lawyer Journal 4 (April 1965). It can also be found at http://www.inspirationalstories.com/poems/rose-of-aberlone-brainerd-currie-poems/. For a history of the case, see Stockmeyer, To Err Is Human, to Moo Bovine: The Rose of Aberlone Story, 24 T.M. Cooley L. Rev. 491 (2007).

WOOD v. BOYNTON
Wisconsin Supreme Court, 1885
64 Wis. 265, 25 N.W. 42

TAYLOR, J. This action was brought in the circuit court for Milwaukee county to recover the possession of an uncut diamond of the alleged value of $1,000. The case was tried in the circuit court, and after hearing all the evidence in the case, the learned circuit judge directed the jury to find a verdict for the defendants. The plaintiff excepted to such instruction, and, after a verdict was rendered for the defendants, moved for a new trial upon the minutes of the judge. The motion was denied, and the plaintiff duly excepted, and after judgment was entered in favor of the defendants, appealed to this court. The defendants are partners in the jewelry business. On the trial it appeared that on and before the twenty-eighth of December,

1883, the plaintiff was the owner of and in the possession of a small stone of the nature and value of which she was ignorant; that on that day she sold it to one of the defendants for the sum of one dollar. Afterwards it was ascertained that the stone was a rough diamond, and of the value of about $700. After hearing this fact the plaintiff tendered the defendants the one dollar, and ten cents as interest, and demanded a return of the stone to her. The defendants refused to deliver it, and therefore she commenced this action.

The plaintiff testified to the circumstances attending the sale of the stone to Mr. Samuel B. Boynton, as follows:

> The first time Boynton saw that stone he was talking about buying the topaz, or whatever it is, in September or October. I went into the store to get a little pin mended, and I had it in a small box, — the pin, — a small earring; . . . this stone, and a broken sleeve-button were in the box. Mr. Boynton turned to give me a check for my pin. I thought I would ask him what the stone was, and I took it out of the box and asked him to please tell me what that was. He took it in his hand and seemed some time looking at it. I told him I had been told it was a topaz, and he said it might be. He says, "I would buy this; would you sell it?" I told him I did not know but what I would. What would it be worth? And he said he did not know; he would give me a dollar and keep it as a specimen, and I told him I would not sell it; and it was certainly pretty to look at. He asked me where I found it, and I told him in Eagle. He asked about how far out, and I said right in the village, and I went out. Afterwards, and about the twenty-eighth of December, I needed money pretty badly, and thought every dollar would help, and I took it back to Mr. Boynton and told him I had brought back the topaz, and he says, "Well, yes; what did I offer you for it?" and I says, "One dollar," and he stepped to the change drawer and gave me the dollar, and I went out.

In another part of her testimony she says: "Before I sold the stone I had no knowledge whatever that it was a diamond. I told him that I had been advised that it was probably a topaz, and he said probably it was. The stone was about the size of a canary bird's egg, nearly the shape of an egg, — worn pointed at one end; it was nearly straw color, — a little darker." She also testified that before this action was commenced she tendered the defendants $1.10, and demanded the return of the stone, which they refused. This is substantially all the evidence of what took place at and before the sale to the defendants, as testified to by the plaintiff herself. She produced no other witness on that point.

The evidence on the part of the defendant is not very different from the version given by the plaintiff, and certainly is not more favorable to the plaintiff. Mr. Samuel B. Boynton, the defendant to whom the stone was sold, testified that at the time he bought this stone, he had never seen an uncut diamond; had seen cut diamonds, but they are quite different from the uncut ones; "he had no idea this was a diamond, and it never entered his brain at the time." Considerable evidence was given as to what took place after the sale and purchase, but that evidence has very little if any bearing, upon the main point in the case.

This evidence clearly shows that the plaintiff sold the stone in question to the defendants, and delivered it to them in December, 1883, for a consideration of one dollar. By such sale the title to the stone passed by the sale and delivery to the defendants. How has that title been divested and again vested in the plaintiff? The contention of the learned counsel for the appellant is that the title became vested in the plaintiff by the tender to the Boyntons of the purchase money with interest, and a demand of a return of the stone to her. Unless such tender and demand revested the title in the appellant, she cannot maintain her action. The only question in the case is whether there was anything in the sale which entitled the vendor (the appellant) to rescind the sale and so revest the title in her. The only reasons we know of for rescinding a sale and revesting the title in the vendor so that he may maintain an action at law for the recovery of the possession against his vendee are (1) that the vendee was guilty of some fraud in procuring a sale to be made to him; (2) that there was a mistake made by the vendor in delivering an article which was not the article sold,—a mistake in fact as to the identity of the thing sold with the thing delivered upon the sale. This last is not in reality a rescission of the sale made, as the thing delivered was not the thing sold, and no title ever passed to the vendee by such delivery.

In this case, upon the plaintiff's own evidence, there can be no just ground for alleging that she was induced to make the sale she did by any fraud or unfair dealings on the part of Mr. Boynton. Both were entirely ignorant at the time of the character of the stone and of its intrinsic value. Mr. Boynton was not an expert in uncut diamonds, and had made no examination of the stone, except to take it in his hand and look at it before he made the offer of one dollar, which was refused at the time, and afterwards accepted without any comment or further examination made by Mr. Boynton. The appellant had the stone in her possession for a long time, and it appears from her own statement that she had made some inquiry as to its nature and qualities. If she chose to sell it without further investigation as to its intrinsic value to a person who was guilty of no fraud or unfairness which induced her to sell it for a small sum, she cannot repudiate the sale because it is afterwards ascertained that she made a bad bargain. Kennedy v. Panama, etc., Mail Co., L.R. 2 Q.B. 580. There is no pretense of any mistake as to the identity of the thing sold. It was produced by the plaintiff and exhibited to the vendee before the sale was made, and the thing sold was delivered to the vendee when the purchase price was paid. [Citations omitted.] Suppose the appellant had produced the stone, and said she had been told it was a diamond, and she believed it was, but had no knowledge herself as to its character or value, and Mr. Boynton had given her $500 for it, could he have rescinded the sale if it had turned out to be a topaz or any other stone of very small value? Could Mr. Boynton have rescinded the sale on the ground of mistake? Clearly not, nor could he rescind it on the ground that there had been a breach of warranty, because there was no warranty, nor could he rescind it on the ground of fraud, unless he could show that she falsely declared that she had been told it was a diamond, or, if she had been so told, still she knew it was not a diamond. See Street v. Blay, supra.

It is urged, with a good deal of earnestness, on the part of the counsel for the appellant that, because it has turned out that the stone was immensely more valuable than the parties at the time of the sale supposed it was, such fact alone is a ground for the rescission of the sale, and that fact was evidence of fraud on the part of the vendee. Whether inadequacy of price is to be received as evidence of fraud, even in a suit in equity to avoid a sale, depends upon the facts known to the parties at the time the sale is made. When this sale was made the value of the thing sold was open to the investigation of both parties, neither knowing its intrinsic value, and, so far as the evidence in this case shows, both supposed that the price paid was adequate. How can fraud be predicated upon such a sale, even though after-investigation showed that the intrinsic value of the thing sold was hundreds of times greater than the price paid? It certainly shows no such fraud as would authorize the vendor to rescind the contract and bring an action at law to recover the possession of the thing sold. Whether that fact would have any influence in an action in equity to avoid the sale we need not consider. See Stettheimer v. Killip, 75 N.Y. 287; Etting v. Bank of U.S., 11 Wheat. 59.

We can find nothing in the evidence from which it could be justly inferred that Mr. Boynton, at the time he offered the plaintiff one dollar for the stone, had any knowledge of the real value of the stone, or that he entertained even a belief that the stone was a diamond. It cannot, therefore, be said that there was a suppression of knowledge on the part of the defendant as to the value of the stone which a court of equity might seize upon to avoid the sale. The following cases show that, in the absence of fraud or warranty, the value of the property sold, as compared with the price paid, is no ground for a rescission of a sale. [Citations omitted.] However unfortunate the plaintiff may have been in selling this valuable stone for a mere nominal sum, she has failed entirely to make out a case either of fraud or mistake in the sale such as will entitle her to a rescission of such sale so as to recover the property sold in an action at law.

The judgment of the circuit court is affirmed.

QUESTION

Does this case conflict with Sherwood v. Walker (the barren cow case), or can you find some way to reconcile the two?

CORBIN ON CONTRACTS §605

In making this contract of exchange, either party may be mistaken as to the appetite of others for the commodity. He finds that he cannot sell for as much as he paid. Practically never is this such a mistake as will justify rescission. The parties are conscious of the uncertainty of value. Value is one of the principal subjects of agreement. Each party is consciously assuming the risk of error of judgment. As to this, by business custom, by prevailing mores, by social policy, and by existing law, the rule is caveat emptor. It is also, and in equal degree, caveat vendor.

Value

Problem 110

At an auction of an estate, one item to be auctioned off was a safe. When the auctioneer came to this item, he described the safe's features and casually mentioned that the safe contained an inner door that was locked and would have to be opened by a professional locksmith. The safe was then sold to a buyer for $50. When the locksmith hired by the buyer opened the safe's inner door, $32,307 was found. The estate demanded its return, claiming the money to be an asset of the estate. The buyer naturally refused. Who gets the money? See UCC §§2-403(1) and 1-103; City of Everett v. Estate of Sumstad, 95 Wash. 2d 853, 631 P.2d 366 (1981).

Problem 111

Mistakenly believing that he was the father of her illegitimate child, John promised Mary to pay for the child's support. Mary also believed that John was the father of the child. When blood tests showed that he could not possibly be the father, John quit paying and she sued. Does the law of mistake provide him with a defense?

WILLIAMS v. GLASH
Supreme Court of Texas, 1990
789 S.W.2d 261

DOGGETT, Justice. The question presented is whether execution of the *Issue* release for personal injuries in this cause bars a subsequent suit for an injury unknown at the time of signing. The trial court granted summary judgment against Petitioners Margaret and David Williams based on execution of a release. The court of appeals affirmed. 769 S.W.2d 684. We reverse the judgment of the court of appeals and remand this case to the trial court for further proceedings.

Margaret Williams ("Williams") was a passenger in her family car when it was struck from behind by a car driven by the respondent Stephen Glash. While damage to the Petitioners' car was apparent at the time of the accident, there were no observable injuries. Williams immediately contacted State Farm Mutual Automobile Insurance Company, Glash's insurer, who advised Williams to bring the car to its local office for an appraisal of the property damage claims. State Farm estimated the cost of repairs at $889.46 and provided Williams a check payable for that precise amount.

At the State Farm office, Williams was asked to complete a claim form containing a question as to whether anyone had been injured by the accident. She checked "No" in response. There was no negotiating or bargaining for release of a personal injury claim; only property damage to the car was discussed. Nonetheless, the back of the check contained language purporting to release personal injury claims, providing that:

> The undersigned payee accepts the amount of this payment in full settlement of all claims for damages to property and for bodily injury whether known or unknown which payee claims against any insured under the policy shown on the face hereof, or their respective successors in interest, arising out of an accident which occurred on or about the date shown. This release reserves all rights of the parties released to pursue their legal remedies, if any, against such payee.

This release language was never explained to nor discussed with Williams or her husband. The face of the check contained a State Farm code, "200-1," denoting the settlement of a property claim, rather than a separate code used by the insurer for personal injury claims. Petitioners subsequently endorsed the check over to the garage that repaired their car.

Williams was later diagnosed as having temporomandibular joint syndrome ("TMJ"), causing head and neck pain, as a result of the accident. Both the trial court and the court of appeals found that suit for this injury was barred by execution of the release.

Petitioners seek to avoid the effect of the release, imploring this court to follow the "modern trend" of setting aside releases when the injury later sued for was unknown at the time of signing. See generally, Annot., 13 A.L.R. 4th 686 (1982 and Supp. 1989). It is true that a majority of our sister states would, under a variety of theories, permit invalidation of the release under the circumstances presented in this case. Id.[1] The most common basis for

---

1. See, e.g., Witt v. Watkins, 579 P.2d 1065 (Alaska 1978); Dansby v. Buck, 92 Ariz. 1, 373 P.2d 1 (1962); Casey v. Proctor, 59 Cal. 2d 97, 28 Cal. Rptr. 307, 378 P.2d 579 (1963) (applying California statute); Gleason v. Guzman, 623 P.2d 378 (Colo. 1981); McGuirk v. Ross, 53 Del. 141, 166 A.2d 429 (1960); Wells v. Rau, 129 App. D.C. 253, 393 F.2d 362 (1968); Boole v.

invalidation is the doctrine of mutual mistake, which mandates that a contract be avoided "[w]here a mistake of both parties at the time the contract was made as to a basic assumption on which the contract was made has a material effect on the agreed exchange of performances." Restatement (Second) of Contracts §152 (1981). Following the modern trend, the Restatement expressly recognizes avoidance of personal injury releases when, in view of the parties' knowledge and negotiations, the release language "flies in the face of what would otherwise be regarded as a basic assumption of the parties." Id. comment f.

Under Texas law, a release is a contract and is subject to avoidance, on grounds such as fraud or mistake, just like any other contract. Cf. Loy v. Kuykendall, 347 S.W.2d 726, 728 (Tex. Civ. App. — San Antonio 1961, writ ref'd n.r.e.) (treating release as a contract subject to rules governing construction thereof). Pursuant to the doctrine of mutual mistake, when parties to an agreement have contracted under a misconception or ignorance of a material fact, the agreement will be avoided. See, e.g., ALG Enterprises v. Huffman, 660 S.W.2d 603, 606 (Tex. App. — Corpus Christi 1983), aff'd as reformed per curiam, 672 S.W.2d 230 (Tex. 1984). The parol evidence rule does not bar extrinsic proof of mutual mistake. Santos v. Mid-Continent Refrigerator Co., 471 S.W.2d 568, 569 (Tex. 1971) (per curiam). The law of mutual mistake does not, of course, preclude a person from intentionally assuming the risk of unknown injuries in a valid release.

However, whether the parties to a release intended to cover an unknown injury cannot always be determined exclusively by reference to the language of the release itself. It may require consideration of the conduct of the parties and the information available to them at the time of signing. In a subsequent suit for an unknown injury, once the affirmative defense of release has been pleaded and proved, the burden of proof is on the party seeking to avoid the release to establish mutual mistake. The question of mutual mistake is determined not by self-serving subjective statements of the parties' intent, which would necessitate trial to a jury in all such cases, but rather solely by objective circumstances surrounding execution of

---

Florida Power & Light Co., 147 Fla. 589, 3 So. 2d 335 (1941); Ranta v. Rake, 91 Idaho 376, 421 P.2d 747 (1966); Ruggles v. Selby, 25 Ill. App. 2d 1, 165 N.E.2d 733 (Ill. App. Ct. 1960, cert. denied); Reed v. Harvey, 253 Iowa 10, 110 N.W.2d 442 (1961); Dorman v. Kansas City Terminal Ry. Co., 231 Kan. 128, 642 P.2d 976 (1982) (FELA case not distinguishable from state law); Hall v. Strom Constr. Co., 368 Mich. 253, 118 N.W.2d 281 (1962); Doud v. Minneapolis S.R. Co., 259 Minn. 341, 107 N.W.2d 521 (1961); Frahm v. Carlson, 214 Neb. 532, 334 N.W.2d 795 (1983); Poti v. New England Road Co., 83 N.H. 232, 140 A. 587 (1928); Mangini v. McClurg, 24 N.Y.2d 556, 301 N.Y.S.2d 508, 249 N.E.2d 386 (1969); Caudill v. Chatham Mfg. Co., 258 N.C. 99, 128 S.E.2d 128 (1962); Mitzel v. Schatz, 175 N.W.2d 659 (N.D. 1970); Sloan v. Standard Oil Co., 177 Ohio St. 149, 203 N.E.2d 237 (1964); K.C. Motor Co. v. Miller, 185 Okl. 84, 90 P.2d 433 (1939); Herndon v. Wright, 257 S.C. 98, 184 S.E.2d 444 (1971); Bowman v. Johnson, 83 S.D. 265, 158 N.W.2d 528 (1968) (applying state statute); Warren v. Crockett, 211 Tenn. 173, 364 S.W.2d 352 (1962); Reynolds v. Merrill, 23 Utah 2d 155, 460 P.2d 323 (1969); Seaboard Ice Co. v. Lee, 199 Va. 243, 99 S.E.2d 721 (1957); Finch v. Carlton, 84 Wash. 2d 140, 524 P.2d 898 (1974); Krezinski v. Hay, 77 Wis. 2d 569, 253 N.W.2d 522 (1977).

Considerations ✱

Factors

the release, such as the knowledge of the parties at the time of signing concerning the injury, the amount of consideration paid, the extent of negotiations and discussions as to personal injuries, and the haste or lack thereof in obtaining the release. See Restatement (Second) of Torts §152 comment f (1981).

We then turn to an application of the mutual mistake factors in this case. As this is a summary judgment case, the issue on appeal is whether State Farm met its burden of establishing that there exists no genuine issue of material fact, thereby entitling it to judgment as a matter of law. City of Houston v. Clear Creek Basin Authority, 589 S.W.2d 671, 678 (Tex. 1979). All doubts as to the existence of a genuine issue of material fact are resolved against the movant, and we must view the evidence in the light most favorable to the Petitioners. Great American Reserve Insurance Co. v. San Antonio Plumbing Supply Co., 391 S.W.2d 41, 47 (Tex. 1965). Summary judgment evidence manifesting Williams' objective intent shows that she had no knowledge of the TMJ injury at the time of signing the release. She neither discussed nor bargained for settlement of a personal injury claim, and the amount of consideration received was the exact amount of the property damage to her car. State Farm similarly had no knowledge of the TMJ injury and, in fact, used a code on the check indicating the settlement of property damage claims only. The only evidence that these parties intended to release a claim for unknown personal injuries is the language of the release itself. This summary judgment evidence is sufficient to establish the existence of a genuine issue of fact as to whether the parties intended the release to cover the injury for which suit was later brought.

Application of the Factors

Issue of Fact

The one case cited by State Farm as controlling precedent misapplies the Texas law of mutual mistake and is, therefore, unpersuasive. McClellan v. Boehmer, 700 S.W.2d 687 (Tex. App. — Corpus Christi 1985, no writ). In *McClellan* and in Houston & T.C.R. Co. v. McCarty, 94 Tex. 298, 60 S.W. 429 (1901), the courts were willing to look to the intent of the parties for the purpose of interpreting and applying the release but not to alter the unambiguous language of the contract. *McClellan*, 700 S.W.2d at 692; *McCarty*, 94 Tex. at 303, 60 S.W. at 432. When mutual mistake is alleged, the task of the court is not to interpret the language contained in the release, but to determine whether or not the release itself is valid. We overrule *McCarty* and disapprove *McClellan* to the extent that they give controlling weight to the language of the release to defeat a claim of mutual mistake.[2]

We do not today, as the dissent claims, release an injured tort victim from an unfair bargain. Rather, we hold only that the law of mutual mistake

2. Although Berry v. Guyer, 482 S.W.2d 719 (Tex. Civ. App.—Houston [14th Dist.] 1972, writ ref'd n.r.e.), Champlin v. Pruitt, 539 S.W.2d 356 (Tex. Civ. App. — Fort Worth 1976, writ ref'd n.r.e.), and Lawson v. Ulschmid, 578 S.W.2d 434 (Tex. Civ. App. — Waco 1979, writ ref'd n.r.e), are not cited by State Farm and are factually distinguishable, to the extent any language of those opinions conflicts with our decision today, they are disapproved.

applies to personal injury releases the same as to other contracts. If it can be
established that a release sets out a *bargain that was never made*, it will be
invalidated. If the objective manifestation of the parties' intent—i.e.,
their conduct—indicates that no release of unknown personal injuries
was contemplated, the courts cannot provide intent for them. The dissent
is willing to hold the parties to a written agreement that is contrary to their
intent and understanding and to ignore the law of mutual mistake, granting
as a result a windfall to the insurer by releasing it from claims that it is
contractually obligated to pay. A majority of our sister states have refused
to follow such a harsh rule; and today we join them.[3]

The doctrine of mutual mistake must not routinely be available to avoid
the results of an unhappy bargain. Parties should be able to rely on the
finality of freely bargained agreements. However, in narrow circumstances
a party may raise a fact issue for the trier of fact to set aside a release under
the doctrine of mutual mistake. Because there is some evidence of such
circumstances here, we reverse the judgment of the court of appeals and
remand this cause to the trial court for further proceedings consistent with
this opinion.

SPEARS, J., joined by COOK and HECHT, JJ., dissent.

SPEARS, Justice, dissenting. What the court has really decided today is
that an injured tort victim should not be held to his bargain if the bargain
later appears unfair. In order to reach this result, the court relies on the
doctrine of mutual mistake and a long string citation. Yet, the reality is that
the cases from other jurisdictions present a jumbled mish-mash of reason-
ings and results. The "mutual mistake" rationale does not adequately
explain their holdings. See Casey v. Proctor, 59 Cal. 2d 97, 28 Cal. Rptr.
307, 378 P.2d 579, 587 (1963). Therefore, rather than trying to resolve
this case by simple string citation, the court ought to engage in a straightforward analysis of the issue. Cf. Holmes, The Path of the Law, 10 Harv. L.
Rev. 457, 466-67 (1897) (encouraging the candid articulation of judicial
reasoning).

Two competing interests are involved. On the one hand, the law favors
the peaceful settlement of disputes and the orderly resolution of claims. On
the other hand, the law favors the just compensation of accident victims. Our
dilemma is to resolve these competing interests, and we ought to do so
openly rather than hiding behind the facade of mutual mistake.

---

3. While condemning the use in this opinion of a string-cite of cases from other states,
the dissent nonetheless relies on a string-cite of its own to support deviation from the majority
rule avoiding releases for unknown injuries. While in each of these cases the release scruti-
nized was upheld, it is far from clear that those courts would uphold the release before the
court today. See, e.g., Maltais v. National Grange Ins. Co., 118 N.H. 318, 386 A.2d 1264, 1269
(1978) (release upheld because no evidence that "accident caused an injury more severe than
originally thought or aggravated a preexisting condition of which the parties were originally
unaware").

Because I believe the law, in general, is better served by encouraging settlements, I would uphold the release and affirm the summary judgment in favor of Glash. In its effort to afford equitable relief, the court renders useless most releases. How is one to buy peace and settle a claim? If the release here can be avoided, then no release buys peace until the statute of limitations has run. "Consideration of the conduct of the parties and the information available to them at the time" will present a fact question so as to require a trial in every instance. Bad facts make bad law and that is what has happened here.

Insurers are now faced with a Hobson's choice. If they settle claims promptly, they are not protected from the later assertion of unknown claims. If they refuse to settle until all injuries are known, then they face potential liability under a bad faith claim. See Aranda v. Insurance Co. of North America, 748 S.W.2d 210 (Tex. 1988). Their only alternative is to settle known damages only and this defeats their reason for settling. What the insurer wants is to buy peace and put an end to any further claims; this is the very essence of its position. Any mistake as to the nature of injuries is strictly unilateral, not mutual.

Unilaterally, Not mutual

Courts cannot legitimately cast themselves in the role of saving people from bad bargains. This sort of benevolent paternalism oversteps the boundaries of our proper role in society. In the short run, it may make life easier for one injured party, but in the long run it distorts the law and creates more problems than it solves. The Maryland court expressed a similar view when it stated:

> We are convinced that our society will be best served by adherence to the traditional methodology for interpreting contracts. . . . In our view, the bastardization of the well-founded principles concerning mutual mistake of fact is entirely too high a price to pay for the obtention of an unprincipled, if temporarily desirable, result.

Bernstein v. Kapneck, 290 Md. 452, 430 A.2d 602, 606-608 (1981). And numerous other sister states have also refused to go along with the so-called "modern trend."[1] Boles v. Blackstock, 484 So. 2d 1077 (Ala. 1986); Kennedy v. Bateman, 217 Ga. 458, 123 S.E.2d 656 (1961); Castro v. Chicago, R.I. & P.R. Co., 83 Ill. 2d 358, 47 Ill. Dec. 360, 415 N.E.2d 365 (Ill. 1980), cert. denied, 452 U.S. 941 (1981); Hybarger v. American States Ins. Co., 498 N. E.2d 1015 (Ind. Ct. App. — 1st Dist. 1986); Reynard v. Bradshaw, 196 Kan. 97, 409 P.2d 1011 (1966); Johns v. Kubaugh, 450 S.W.2d 259 (Ky. 1970); Tewksbury v. Fellsway Laundry, Inc., 319 Mass. 386, 65 N.E.2d 918 (1946); Pearson v. Weaver, 252 Miss. 724, 173 So. 2d 666, 669 (1965); Sanger v. Yellow Cab Co., 486 S.W.2d 477 (Mo. 1972); Sibson v. Farmers Ins. Group, 88 Nev.

---

1. I dislike the use of string-cites, but it was the majority's choice to rely on this mode of analysis. I would be happy to delete *all* citation to other states and rely solely on Texas authority for this decision.

417, 498 P.2d 1331 (1972); Maltais v. National Grange Mut. Ins. Co., 118 N.H. 318, 386 A.2d 1264 (1978);[2] Raroha v. Earle Finance Corp., 47 N.J. 229, 220 A.2d 107 (1966); Wheeler v. White Rock Bottling Co., 229 Or. 360, 366 P.2d 527 (1961); Emery v. Mackiewicz, 429 Pa. 322, 240 A.2d 68 (1968); Boccarossa v. Watkins, 112 R.I. 551, 313 A.2d 135 (1973).

Moreover, in some of the cases that have allowed releases to be avoided, the courts have at least moderated their decisions by imposing a higher burden of proof on the plaintiff. They have required clear and convincing proof that a mutual mistake was made or that the release was not fairly and knowingly made. E.g., Witt v. Watkins, 579 P.2d 1065 (Alaska 1978); Ranta v. Rake, 91 Idaho 376, 421 P.2d 747 (1966); Birch v. Keen, 449 P.2d 700 (Okla. 1969); Seaboard Ice Co. v. Lee, 199 Va. 243, 99 S.E.2d 721 (1957). By refusing to impose any higher burden, this court steps beyond even these more moderate decisions in other jurisdictions.

Finally, almost as an afterthought, the court looks to Texas precedent. In order to allow for the invalidation of this release, the court must overrule Houston & T.C.R. Co. v. McCarty, 94 Tex. 298, 60 S.W. 429 (1901), and must disapprove Lawson v. Ulschmid, 578 S.W.2d 434 (Tex. Civ. App.—Waco 1979, writ ref'd n.r.e.); Champlin Petroleum Co. v. Pruitt, 539 S.W.2d 356 (Tex. Civ. App.—Fort Worth 1976, writ ref'd n.r.e.); Berry v. Guyer, 482 S.W.2d 719 (Tex. Civ. App.—Houston [14th Dist.] 1972, writ ref'd n.r.e.); and McClellan v. Boehmer, 700 S.W.2d 687 (Tex. App.—Corpus Christi 1985, no writ). In all of these cases, Texas courts upheld the validity of personal injury releases, and the *Ulschmid* case even involved the same "200-1" notation as exists in this case. This is a lot of Texas precedent for the court to address it in such a summary fashion.

I can understand the desire to do equity,[3] but the court's decision today is too one-sided to fall under the rubric of equity. If the court is determined to reach this result, it ought to at least be candid about its reasons. I respectfully dissent. I would affirm the judgment of the court of appeals.

COOK and HECHT, JJ., join in this dissent.

---

2. The majority attacks *Maltais* as an example of how, for each case that upheld a release, "it is far from clear that those courts would uphold the release before the court today." However, the same can be said of the cases cited by the majority. In cases that have invalidated releases, it is far from clear that those courts would invalidate the release before this court today. See, e.g., Dorman v. Kansas City Terminal Ry. Co., 231 Kan. 128, 642 P.2d 976, 978 (1982) (In an FELA suit for back injuries, the court recognized a fact question on mistake since the release specifically described the plaintiff's injuries as being "to my left thigh and a laceration to my forehead.").

3. I would prefer that Texas address this problem by legislation rather than by judicial fiat. For example, in Idaho, a personal injury release executed within fifteen days after the occurrence may be disavowed at anytime within one year after the occurrence. Idaho Code §29-113 (1961). For other similar statutes, see also Md. Ann. Code art. 79, §11 (1957); Utah Code Ann. §78-27-3 (1953); N.D. Cent. Code §9-08-08 (1987); Cal. Civ. Code §1542 (West 1982); Me. Rev. Stat. Ann. tit. 17, §3964 (1964); Conn. Gen. Stat. §52-572a (1958).

QUESTION AND NOTE

1. If you were a member of the Texas Supreme Court when this case was argued, how would you have voted?

2. Where both parties are aware generally of the type of injury and the injury later appears more severe, a general release is typically found to be effective. In Cordovez v. High-Rise Installation, Inc. 46 So. 3d 1120 (Fla. App. 2010), the employer hit the employee on the head with a radio. Yes, that is what happened. Employee complained of head pain but signed a general release. An early decision by the health care provider was that there was no serious problem. Later that assessment was proved wrong, but the employee was denied recovery beyond that given in the release.

BAILEY v. EWING

Court of Appeals of Idaho, 1983
105 Idaho 636, 671 P.2d 1099

SWANSTROM, J. This case involves a boundary dispute between the purchasers of adjoining lots which had been sold by a decedent's personal representative. The dispute is over a strip of land lying between the conflicting boundary lines claimed by the purchasers. One purchaser, Fred Bailey, brought this suit to eject the other purchaser, Guy Ewing, from the disputed strip and to quiet title to the land in himself. Ewing filed a counterclaim against Bailey and a third party complaint against the personal representative, Gary Erhardt, to reform the deeds so that Ewing would own the disputed strip. The trial court found for Bailey and Erhardt. Ewing appealed.

Appellant Ewing raises several issues in this appeal. However, because we decide that one issue requires a reversal of the judgment entered in the trial court, we discuss only that issue: Did the trial court err in ruling that any mistake concerning the location of the boundary line was a unilateral mistake by Ewing?

Issue

The pertinent facts as shown by the record are as follows. On October 1, 1977, Erhardt, as the personal representative of decedent Mary Ellen Erhardt, conducted an auction sale of decedent's real and personal property. The real property consisted of two city lots, numbered "five" and "six," plus an additional twenty-foot strip of land adjoining the east side of lot six. This real property had been owned by decedent for many years, as a single parcel, improved by a house, a shop and other outbuildings. Sometime shortly before the sale the personal representative and the auctioneer decided that the real estate would likely sell for more money if it were divided into two parcels, to be sold separately. It was decided that lot five would be sold as one parcel; lot six, to the east, and the twenty-foot strip would be sold

Subdivided land

as the second parcel. When the bidding was conducted Ewing purchased lot five, but because no satisfactory bid was received for the second parcel, it was not sold on the day of the auction.

On the day of the sale, Erhardt conducted a tour of lot five and the house situated on that lot. During that tour, he indicated to Ewing and other prospective purchasers that he thought the east boundary line of lot five was at or near some lilac bushes about thirteen feet east of the house. He stated several times that he was not sure of the actual location of the boundary line. In addition, the auctioneer mentioned, before bidding began, that nobody knew exactly where the property lines were. Two later surveys showed, in fact, that the boundary line between lots five and six was less than one foot east of the base of the house on lot five. The vertical plane of the true line passed through the eaves of the house. Domestic water and sewer lines serving the house were located alongside the house beneath the surface of lot six.

[handwritten margin note: Clearly stated he didn't know exactly where the property line was]

A week after the auction, the personal representative sold the remaining parcel to Bailey, who had attended the auction. The personal representative later deeded lot five to Ewing, and lot six and the adjoining strip to Bailey. During his occupancy of the house on lot five, Ewing mowed the grass, trimmed the lilac bushes and otherwise acted as owner of the property between the house and the lilacs. In June of 1978, Ewing erected a fence just to the east of the lilac bushes. Bailey then caused a survey to be conducted and learned where the "true" line was. He asserted his claim to the strip of property between the bushes and the line, demanding that the fence be removed. After Ewing failed to remove the fence and relinquish the property, Bailey brought this quiet title action. Ewing counterclaimed and filed a third-party complaint, seeking reformation of his deed and of the deed to Bailey. He alleged mutual mistake, as well as fraud or misrepresentation on the part of the personal representative. The trial court found no fraud or misrepresentation had occurred. We do not question this finding and it is not material to our decision. The trial court also held that Ewing had made a unilateral mistake as to the location of the boundary line between lots five and six and was therefore not entitled to relief. We focus on this conclusion.

[handwritten margin note: P Surveyed land to determine the true property line]

[handwritten margin note: D alleges]

[handwritten margin note: Issues]

A mistake is an unintentional act or omission arising from ignorance, surprise, or misplaced confidence. See 13 Williston on Contracts §1535 (3d ed. 1970). The mistake must be material or, in other words, so substantial and fundamental as to defeat the object of the parties. Woodahl v. Matthews, 639 P.2d 1165 (Mont. 1982). A unilateral mistake is not normally grounds for relief for the mistaken party, whereas a mutual mistake is. . . . A mutual mistake occurs when both parties, at the time of contracting, share a misconception about a basic assumption or vital fact upon which they based their bargain. . . . Some courts require the parties to have the *same* misconception about the *same* basic assumption or vital fact. . . . However, mutual mistake also has been defined to include situations in which the parties labor under *differing* misconceptions as to the *same* basic assumption or vital fact.

[handwritten margin note: Mistake]

Restatement (Second) Contracts §152, comment h (1981) (hereafter cited as Restatement). We believe the Restatement presents the better view. The assumption or fact must be the same; otherwise two unilateral mistakes, instead of one mutual mistake, would result.

It is undisputed that Erhardt intended to sell the house with lot five and that he assumed the boundary line was located so as to allow him to sell the *whole* house. Erhardt believed the boundary line was somewhere east of its subsequently determined "true" location. Ewing shared this belief. Thus, both Ewing and Erhardt mistakenly believed that the boundary line was further east than it turned out to be. As a result of their ignorance concerning the true location, an act that neither of them intended occurred. Neither intended that the property sold as lot five would fail to include the whole house. Thus, there was an "unintentional act . . . arising from ignorance." We hold, therefore, that Ewing and Erhardt made a mutual mistake regarding the location of the boundary line between lots five and six.

The mere presence of a mutual mistake does not always afford relief to the party adversely affected by the mistake. A party is said to bear the risk of a mistake when "he is aware, at the time the contract is made, that he has limited knowledge with respect to the facts to which the mistake relates but treats his limited knowledge as sufficient." Restatement §154. It is sometimes said in such a situation that, in a sense, there was not mistake but "conscious ignorance." Id. §154 comment c, at 404.

In this case it is clear that — at the time of the auction — neither Erhardt nor Ewing knew where the boundary line was. It is also clearly implied in the findings made by the trial judge and from the trial testimony, that Erhardt thought the boundary line was in the vicinity of the lilacs. The findings go only so far as to say Erhardt "did not represent to [Ewing] specifically that the lilac trees were the East side line of said Lot 5, Block 8." Nevertheless, the record clearly shows that before the sale Erhardt indicated that the line of lilacs was a possible location of the lot boundary. There was no misrepresentation. Erhardt and the auctioneer made it clear that they did not know the actual location of the line. Erhardt sold and Ewing bought lot five with awareness that the true location of the boundary was not known.

We believe that both parties assumed a risk of uncertainty as to the line. However, the extent to which the doctrine of "conscious ignorance" applies depends upon the scope of the risk assumed. Clearly Ewing assumed the risk that the lilac bushes might not be within lot five. Ewing had no right to rely upon the uncertain belief of Erhardt that the lilac bushes represented the line. Nevertheless, it is equally clear that neither party consciously assumed a risk that the line would run beneath the eaves of the house. Nothing in the record indicates that either party intended, or reasonably should have anticipated, such a result. The mutual mistake which occurred was beyond the scope of the assumed risk. Therefore, the doctrine of "conscious ignorance" is not a bar to relief for Ewing in this case.

Because we have said that a mutual mistake was made, we need to offer some guidance to the trial judge, so that on remand he may determine whether reformation of the deeds is available to Ewing as a remedy. Given the proper circumstances a court may reform the instrument for an aggrieved party. . . . A court acts properly "in reforming an instrument when it appears from the evidence . . . that the instrument does not reflect the intentions of the parties" because of mutual mistake. . . . The court reforms the instrument to reflect the intention of the parties, i.e., the agreement the parties would have made but for the mistake. . . . What the parties actually intended is a question for the trier of fact. Pollard Oil Co. v. Christensen, 103 Idaho 110, 645 P.2d 344 (1982). Normally the intent of the parties must be derived from the language of the instrument itself if that instrument is unambiguous. Gardner v. Fliegel, 92 Idaho 767, 450 P.2d 990 (1969). In the present case the deed is clearly unambiguous as to the land conveyed. The deed conveys to Ewing: "Lot 5 of Block 8, Galloways addition to the City of Weiser, Idaho, as same appears on the official plat thereof on file in the office of the County Recorder of Washington County, Idaho." From the language of the instrument, Erhardt intended to convey lot five. This was, in fact, conveyed and therefore the instrument normally could not be reformed.

However, the intent as expressed in the written instrument is incompatible with a finding of mutual mistake. To restrict evidence on the true intent of the parties to the four-corners of the instrument would be to nullify the finding of mutual mistake. In *Collins*, our Supreme Court held that parol evidence may be admitted to show a modification of the instrument when mutual mistake is proved. "The parol evidence rule applies only to integrated writings, and if the mistake is mutual the writing is not integrated. Therefore parol evidence is admissible in this instance." . . . In Bilbao v. Krettinger, supra, parol evidence was held admissible to prove that by reason of mutual mistake the parties' true intent was not expressed by the written instrument. Parol evidence may also be used to show what that true intent was.

[margin note: If AppLied TC "4 corners" rule, 9hen mutual Mistake would be irrelevant]

[margin note: If mutual Mistake, Then contract isn't integrated, and Parol evidence is allowed]

Before reformation of the deeds is granted, however, other questions must be answered. It is undeniable that if the personal representative had not sold lot six, but merely sold lot five to Ewing, the deed to Ewing could be reformed. Only the rights of the estate and Ewing would be affected. However, Erhardt sold lot six to Bailey, thereby involving a third party. Any reformation of Ewing's deed adding land to lot five must result necessarily in reformation of Bailey's deed subtracting land from lot six. Under what circumstances, then, may the deed to a subsequent purchaser of a lot be reformed when the prior deed for an adjoining lot is reformed because of mutual mistake?

[margin note: reforming a deed Due to mutual Mistake]

The general rule is that reformation will not be granted if it appears such relief will prejudice the rights of bona fide and innocent purchasers. See cases collected in 44 A.L.R. 78 (1926), supplemented by 79 A.L.R.2d 1180 (1961). A purchaser must lack notice both of the mistake and of the true intent of the parties, in order to prevent reformation. . . . Actual notice

[margin note: Rule]

however is not required. . . . If there are circumstances which ought to put a party on inquiry as to ownership of property, that party is not considered a purchaser without notice and so cannot avoid reformation of the instrument. . . .

Another example of this rule is presented by Deubel v. Dearwester, 36 Ohio App. 60, 172 N.E. 640 (1930). There the plaintiffs sued to eject the defendant and the defendant counterclaimed to reform the deeds. The original grantor had built improvements on one lot, which improvements encroached upon the adjoining lot. The Ohio Court of Appeals in affirming the trial court's reformation of *both* deeds said:

> We think that the physical presence of the house and improvements upon the property conveyed by the original grantor indicated beyond question that the grantor intended to convey all the premises occupied by said improvement to [defendant's] predecessors in title, and, such deed having been made while the original grantor . . . still owned both lots, the subsequent grantees of the adjacent lot, now owned by the plaintiffs, took title to such adjacent lot impressed with that intention manifest by the physical occupation of the premises.

Whether a party is aware of circumstances sufficient to put him on inquiry is a question of fact. . . . The question becomes whether Bailey was a bona fide purchaser without notice. On remand the trial court will need to determine whether Bailey was a bona fide purchaser without notice. He bears the burden of proof on this point. . . . If Bailey was not a bona fide purchaser, then Ewing may obtain relief by having both deeds reformed in accordance with the parties' intentions. However, if Bailey is found to be a bona fide purchaser then reformation can be decreed only if some way is found for Bailey to be satisfactorily and fully compensated. We leave it to the trial court to properly exercise its fact-finding powers and its equitable jurisdiction to fashion a fair and proper solution to the dispute.

Judgment reversed. Cause remanded for proceedings consistent with this opinion. Costs to appellant.

QUESTION

Would this court have reached a different result in Wood v. Boynton, the uncut diamond case?

C. Unilateral Mistake

As we have seen, courts sometimes grant relief for mutual mistake (where both parties are wrong about a basic assumption on which the contract is made). However, where the mistake is *unilateral*—meaning that just one party has blundered—courts are less sympathetic. With the exceptions we shall explore in the materials that follow, courts typically deny relief to the erroneous party, encouraging that party to be more careful in the future.

RESTATEMENT (SECOND) OF CONTRACTS

§153. WHEN MISTAKE OF ONE PARTY MAKES A CONTRACT VOIDABLE

Where a mistake of one party at the time a contract was made as to a basic assumption on which he made the contract has a material effect on the agreed exchange of performances that is adverse to him, the contract is voidable by him if he does not bear the risk of the mistake under the rule stated in §154, and

(a) the effect of the mistake is such that enforcement of the contract would be unconscionable, or

(b) the other party had reason to know of the mistake or his fault caused the mistake.

ZIPPYSACK LLC v. ONTEL PRODUCTS CORP.

United States District Court for the Northern District of Illinois, 2016
182 F. Supp. 3d 867

HARRY D. LEINENWEBER, Judge

Plaintiffs ZippySack LLC and its licensee, LF Centennial Limited (hereinafter, collectively "ZippySack"), brought this suit against Defendant Ontel Products Corporation ("Ontel") for breach of contract. . . . The dispute arose after Ontel allegedly breached a prior settlement agreement between the parties. The Motion now before the Court is to enforce that settlement. For the reasons stated herein, the Court grants the Motion and dismisses this case.

I. BACKGROUND

A predecessor lawsuit to the current action was filed in August 2015. At that time, ZippySack alleged that Ontel infringed its patents covering a specialty bed sheet. The sheet, marketed for children, is designed to be zipped up rather than folded and tucked, obviating the everyday drudgery of making the bed. ZippySack's product is appropriately named "ZippySack," while Ontel's allegedly infringing product is known as "ZipIt Friends." The parties settled the 2015 matter and stipulated to a dismissal with prejudice. . . .

As part of the settlement, Ontel agreed to cease producing ZipIt Friends, and ZippySack in turn relinquished all relevant legal claims against Ontel. Ontel also agreed that it would sell no more than its existing inventory of ZipIt Friends, which at the time it believed numbered at 80,000. The agreement required Ontel to report monthly on the status of its effort to sell off the remaining inventory.

That number — 80,000 — is at the heart of the current dispute. Shortly after the Court dismissed the predecessor litigation, in November 2015, Ontel sent a letter to ZippySack stating:

> Ontel has discovered a discrepancy that existed with the prior inventory numbers. . . . Specifically, the prior inventory number . . . included only retail inventory. Ontel tracks mail order inventory separately and there was a miscommunication between the business and finance groups when this information was gathered in connection with our discussions, which caused it to unintentionally understate its inventory number. As such, in accordance with [the settlement], Ontel reports that it has 119,432 ZipIt Friends units remaining in inventory. Ontel will continue to dispose of its inventory in accordance with the terms of the [settlement] with respect to the channels of distribution and timing.

(Compl. Ex. C.)

ZippySack, concerned about the larger inventory of ZipIt Friends, sent a letter requesting clarification:

> First, does the number 119,432 mean the number of ZipIt Friends products that Ontel had on hand as of the date of the [settlement], or the number on hand now? Either way, ZippySack and LF Centennial do not agree to allowing more than 80,000 ZipIt Friends products to be sold by Ontel after the [settlement] date. Ontel represented . . . that it had 80,000 units at the time of the [settlement], and that representation was a key and material term that led to the settlement. We also do not accept as reasonable that Ontel could be 150% off from its representation — or even more if the 119,432 is a current number and not a past number. . . .

(Compl. Ex. D.). . . .

In response to the back-and-forth, ZippySack filed the present lawsuit. . . .

III. THE SETTLEMENT AGREEMENT

. . . The settlement is fairly straightforward. The parties relinquished all relevant legal claims, subject to compliance with the other terms of the agreement. This included Ontel's promise that it would not challenge the validity of the underlying ZippySack patent. The key clause regarding inventory reads:

> Ontel represents that is has no more than approximately 80,000 current units of the ZipIt Friends product in existing on-hand inventory or goods to be delivered from its manufacturer(s) (the "Inventory"), and the Parties agree that Ontel may sell off that Inventory and shall not thereafter sell any further ZipIt Friends product after that Inventory is exhausted.

(Compl. Ex. B.) The clause is unambiguous. It clearly defines "Inventory" to mean "no more than approximately 80,000" units. Thus, Ontel cannot sell more than that number, and the word "approximately" cannot be read reasonably to include thousands of additional units. . . .

Ontel's only discernable defense against enforcement is unilateral mistake of fact. It thought it had only 80,000 remaining ZipIt Friends, and then later learned it had neglected its mail-order inventory; now the number is significantly higher. The defense of unilateral mistake is available under Illinois law where the aggrieved party "shows by clear and convincing evidence that (1) the mistake is of a material nature; (2) the mistake is of such consequence that enforcement is unconscionable; (3) the mistake occurred notwithstanding the exercise of due care by the party seeking rescission; and (4) rescission can place the other party in status quo." Blue Cross Blue Shield v. BCS Ins., 517 F. Supp. 2d 1050, 1061 (N.D. Ill. 2007). [Quotation and citation omitted.]

[handwritten margin note: Elements for unilateral mistake]

Ontel's mistake does not invalidate this contract, because enforcement on these terms is not unconscionable. Under Illinois law, "[a] contract is unconscionable when, viewed as a whole, it is improvident, oppressive, or totally one-sided." Id. [Quotation and citation omitted.] The parties had full and fair opportunity to negotiate the preliminary terms of settlement. If Ontel believed that it had a strong case for the invalidity of the ZippySack patent, it could have continued litigating in 2015. Instead, it relinquished its rights to produce ZipIt Friends going forward, and at the time, it thought the right to offload 80,000 existing units was an acceptable tradeoff to ending the suit. Its mistake was not clerical; by all accounts, Ontel believed that 80,000 was the correct number at the time. If the term was acceptable to Ontel then, it is not unconscionable now. It is also unclear how Ontel could have exercised due care when its estimate was so far off the mark. . . .

[handwritten margin note: unconscionable Defined]

In sum, the Court holds that the settlement is valid and enforceable against both parties. . . .

NOTES

1. For a similar case, see Murphey v. Mid-Century Ins. Co., No. 13-2598-JAR-JPO, 2014 WL 2619073, at *1 (D. Kan. June 12, 2014). An insurance

adjuster and a plaintiff's lawyer were discussing the amount for which a personal injury plaintiff would settle her claim. The adjuster meant to offer $121,000, but accidentally typed "$221,000" in an email to the attorney. The court refused to invoke the doctrine of unilateral mistake, reasoning that because the plaintiff's lawyer had originally offered $310,000 to settle the case, he reasonably could have believed that the offer of $221,000 was authentic.

2. Conversely, unilateral mistake claims are most likely to succeed in what are known as "snapping up" cases: where one party tries to take advantage of the other party's obvious error. In addition, outside of the "snapping up" context, courts sometimes grant relief to contractors or subcontractors that submit a bid to work on a project, but make a serious clerical error:

Two examples were unilateral mistake usually works [handwritten note]

> In response to B's invitation for bids on the construction of a building according to stated specifications, A submits an offer to do the work for $150,000. A believes that this is the total of a column of figures, but he has made an error by inadvertently omitting a $50,000 item, and in fact the total is $200,000. B, having no reason to know of A's mistake, accepts A's bid. If A performs for $150,000, he will sustain a loss of $20,000 instead of making an expected profit of $30,000. If the court determines that enforcement of the contract would be unconscionable, it is voidable by A.

Restatement (Second) of Contracts §153 ill. 1; First Baptist Church of Moultrie v. Barber Contracting Co., 377 S.E.2d 717, 719 (Ga. 1989) (applying the doctrine of unilateral mistake when contractor accidentally submitted a bid that was too low by $143,120).

Problem 112

When computing its bid on the new schoolhouse, Careless Construction Company turned two pages of its estimate book at once and thereby accidentally omitted a huge portion of the true amount of its bid. Other bidders bid amounts ranging from $2,500,000 to $3,000,000. Careless's bid was $1,250,000, and the school board snapped it up by an immediate acceptance. Performing at this low rate will put Careless into bankruptcy. Is there relief in the law of mistake? Will it help Careless if the school board unduly rushed it, while giving the other bidders greater time in which to compute their bids?

Yes, "snapping up" applies here. obvious mistake, also, would be unconscionable cuz they would go into bankruptcy [handwritten note]

— rescind would hurt the other party [handwritten note]

Problem 113

How would your answer change, if at all, if Careless had made a bid of $1,250,000, not because of missing pages in the estimate, but because

Careless believed that the work could be completed in five months rather than the six months that were actually required?

(handwritten margin notes: - Negligence - Conscious Ignorance • Assumed risk willfully)

Problem 114

When Careless Construction Company discovered that it had made a mistake that lowered its bid by $4,000, it nonetheless decided to go through with the project and accept the loss. The second lowest bidder was the Prudent Construction Company; its bid was $2,000 higher than that of Careless. Arguing that it would have been awarded the contract if Careless's mistake were taken into account, Prudent demanded that Careless's contract be voided for mistake and that Prudent be awarded the job. Is this argument valid?

(handwritten margin note: NO)

Problem 115

In October of 2014, in an expensive restaurant, the host of a party of ten asked Joe Lentini, one of his guests, if he would choose a bottle of wine from the wine list. Mr. Lentini, who was an infrequent wine drinker, told the waitress he knew little about wine and asked her to suggest a bottle. She pointed to one on the list. Telling her he didn't have his glasses, Lentini asked her the price. "Thirty-seven fifty," she replied. Lentini and the others around him agreed to this price, so the wine was served. When the bill came it showed that the bottle cost $3,750.00! Must the host of the party pay this amount? For a news report on the actual incident, see http://www.nj.com/business/index.ssf/2014/11/bamboozled_what_happens_when_a_3750_bottle_of_wine_really_costs_3750.html.

(handwritten margin notes: No, unilateral mistake b) unconscionable, used due care but meaning witness on NO gloss, and do-sw have knowledge)

D. Reformation

Reformation is an equitable action whereby the court is asked to rewrite the contract so that it represents the "true" agreement of the parties. Reformation is most often used to correct a "scrivener's error": The writing was written down wrong and therefore incorrectly reflects the parties' agreement, and can even be used to correct a unilateral mistake if the other side knew of the mistake and remained silent in order to benefit from it; see Scion Breckenridge Managing Member, LLC v. ASB Allegiance Real Estate Fund, 68 A.3d 665 (Del. 2013). It is occasionally used to correct contracts where there is fraud, duress, undue influence, and unconscionability. Because the primary allegation in a reformation action is that the contract is incorrectly reflected by the writing, the parol evidence rule is inapplicable in

(handwritten margin note: Can bring in Parol evidence)

such a suit. See Palmer, Reformation and the Parol Evidence Rule, 65 Mich. L. Rev. 833 (1967).

Problem 116

Green Acres Country Club held a golf tournament that included a $25,000 prize for any golfer hitting a hole-in-one during the event on certain selected holes. Green Acres purchased an insurance policy from Great Coverage Insurance Company that charged it a premium for guaranteeing the prize should a hole-in-one be made. The insurance company offered premiums of various amounts depending on how far the golfer had to hit the ball in order to claim the big prize, and the parties settled on 150 yards minimum (though they could have chosen a bigger premium for a shorter distance). When the tournament was held a mistake was made and one of the holes on which the prize could be won was only 125 yards from tee to the hole, and (as these things happen) it was the hole on which a golfer made the required shot and claimed the prize. The insurance company refused payment because the yardage was smaller due to the error. If you were the trial court judge would you reform the insurance contract to up the premium and then allow the country club to claim the $25,000 so it could pay the winner? See Servo Pacific Ins. v. Axis Ins, 129 F. Supp. 3d 1143 (W.D. Wash. 2015).

III. FRAUD

The doctrine of fraud takes two basic forms. The first is *misrepresentation*: a false assertion of fact. The second is *nondisclosure*: misleading the other party by failing to speak up.

A. Misrepresentation

RESTATEMENT (SECOND) OF CONTRACTS

§162. When a Misrepresentation Is Fraudulent or Material

(1) A misrepresentation is fraudulent if the maker intends his assertion to induce a party to manifest his assent and the maker

(a) knows or believes that the assertion is not in accord with the facts, or

(b) does not have the confidence that he states or implies in the truth of the assertion, or

(c) knows that he does not have the basis that he states or implies for the assertion.

(2) A misrepresentation is material if it would be likely to induce a reasonable person to manifest his assent, or if the maker knows that it would be likely to induce the recipient to do so.

§164. When a Misrepresentation Makes a Contract Voidable

If a party's manifestation of assent is induced by either a fraudulent or a material misrepresentation by the other party upon which the recipient is justified in relying, the contract is voidable by the recipient. . . .

VOKES v. ARTHUR MURRAY, INC.
District Court of Appeals of Florida, 1968
212 So. 2d 906

Pierce, J. This is an appeal by Audrey E. Vokes, plaintiff below, from a final order dismissing with prejudice, for failure to state a cause of action, her fourth amended complaint, hereinafter referred to as plaintiff's complaint.

Defendant Arthur Murray, Inc., a corporation, authorizes the operation throughout the nation of dancing schools under the name of "Arthur Murray School of Dancing" through local franchised operators, one of whom was defendant J. P. Davenport whose dancing establishment was in Clearwater. Plaintiff Mrs. Audrey E. Vokes, a widow of 51 years and without family, had a yen to be "an accomplished dancer" with the hopes of finding "new interest in life." So, on February 10, 1961, a dubious fate, with the assist of a motivated acquaintance, procured her to attend a "dance party" at Davenport's "School of Dancing" where she whiled away the pleasant hours, sometimes in a private room, absorbing his accomplished sales technique, during which her grace and poise were elaborated upon and her rosy future as "an excellent dancer" was painted for her in vivid and glowing colors. As an incident to this interlude, he sold her eight 1/2-hour dance lessons to be utilized within one calendar month therefrom, for the sum of $14.50 cash in hand paid, obviously a baited "come-on." Thus she embarked upon an almost endless pursuit of the terpsichorean art during which, over a period of less than sixteen months, she was sold fourteen "dance courses" totalling in the aggregate 2,302 hours of dancing lessons for a total cash outlay of $31,090.45, all at Davenport's dance emporium. All of these fourteen courses were evidenced by execution of a written "Enrollment Agreement — Arthur Murray's School of Dancing" with the addendum in heavy black print, "No one will be informed that you are taking dancing lessons. Your relations with us are held in strict confidence," setting forth the number of "dancing lessons" and the "lessons in rhythm sessions" currently sold to her from time to time, and always of course accompanied by payment of cash of the realm.

These dance lesson contracts and the monetary consideration therefor of over $31,000 were procured from her by means and methods of Davenport and his associates which went beyond the unsavory, yet legally permissible, perimeter of "sales puffing" and intruded well into the forbidden area of undue influence, the suggestion of falsehood, the suppression of truth, and the free exercise of rational judgment, if what plaintiff alleged in her complaint was true. From the time of her first contact with the dancing school in February, 1961, she was influenced unwittingly by a constant and continuous barrage of flattery, false praise, excessive compliments, and panegyric encomiums, to such extent that it would be not only inequitable, but unconscionable, for a Court exercising inherent chancery power to allow such contracts to stand.

She was incessantly subjected to over-reaching blandishment and cajolery. She was assured she had "grace and poise"; that she was "rapidly improving and developing in her dancing skill"; that the additional lessons would "make her a beautiful dancer, capable of dancing with the most accomplished dancers"; that she was "rapidly progressing in the development of her dancing skill and gracefulness," etc., etc. She was given "dance aptitude tests" for the ostensible purpose of "determining" the number of remaining hours of instructions needed by her from time to time. At one point she was sold 545 additional hours of dancing lessons to be entitled to award of the "Bronze Medal" signifying that she had reached "the Bronze Standard," a supposed designation of dance achievement by students of Arthur Murray, Inc.

At one point, while she still had to her credit about 900 unused hours of instructions, she was induced to purchase an additional 24 hours of lessons to participate in a trip to Miami at her own expense, where she would be "given the opportunity to dance with members of the Miami Studio." She was induced at another point to purchase an additional 126 hours of lessons in order to be not only eligible for the Miami trip but also to become "a life member of the Arthur Murray Studio," carrying with it certain dubious emoluments, at a further cost of $1,752.30.

At another point, while she still had over 1,000 unused hours of instruction she was induced to buy 151 additional hours at a cost of $2,049.00 to be eligible for a "Student Trip to Trinidad," at her own expense as she later learned.

Also, when she still had 1,100 unused hours to her credit, she was prevailed upon to purchase an additional 347 hours at a cost of $4,235.74, to qualify her to receive a "Gold Medal" for achievement, indicating she had advanced to "the Gold Standard." On another occasion, while she still had over 1,200 unused hours, she was induced to buy an additional 175 hours of instruction at a cost of $2,472.75 to be eligible "to take a trip to Mexico." Finally, sandwiched in between other lesser sales promotions, she was influenced to buy an additional 481 hours of instruction at a cost of $6,523.81 in order to "be classified as a Gold Bar Member, the ultimate achievement of the dancing studio." All the foregoing sales promotions, illustrative of the entire fourteen separate contracts, were procured by defendant Davenport and Arthur Murray, Inc., by false representations to her that she was improving in her dancing ability, that she had excellent potential, that she was responding to instructions in dancing grace, and that they were developing her into a beautiful dancer, whereas in truth and in fact she did not develop in her dancing ability, she had no "dance aptitude," and in fact had difficulty in "hearing the musical beat." The complaint alleged that such representations to her "were in fact false and known by the defendant to be false and contrary to the plaintiff's true ability, the truth of plaintiff's ability being fully known to the defendants, but withheld from the plaintiff for the sole and specific intent to deceive and defraud the plaintiff and to induce her in the purchasing of additional hours of dance lessons." It was averred that the lessons were sold to her "in total disregard to the true physical rhythm, and mental ability of the plaintiff." In other words, while she first exulted that she was entering the "spring of her life," she finally was awakened to the fact there was "spring" neither in her life nor in her feet.

The complaint prayed that the Court decree the dance contracts to be null and void and to be cancelled, that an accounting be had, and judgment entered against the defendants "for that portion of the $31,090.45 not charged against specific hours of instruction given to the plaintiff." The Court held the complaint not to state a cause of action and dismissed it with prejudice. We disagree and reverse.

The material allegations of the complaint must, of course, be accepted as true for the purpose of testing its legal sufficiency. Defendants contend that contracts can only be rescinded for fraud or misrepresentation when the alleged misrepresentation is as to a material fact, rather than an opinion, prediction or expectation, and that the statements and representations set forth at length in the complaint were in the category of "trade puffing," within its legal orbit.

It is true that "generally a misrepresentation, to be actionable, must be one of fact rather than of opinion." Tonkovich v. South Florida Citrus Industries, Inc., Fla. App. 1966, 185 So. 2d 710; Kutner v. Kalish, Fla. App. 1965, 173 So. 2d 763. But this rule has significant qualifications, applicable here. It does not apply where there is a fiduciary relationship between the parties, or where there has been some artifice or trick employed by the representor, or where the parties do not in general deal at "arm's length" as we understand the phrase, or where the representee does not have equal opportunity to become apprised of the truth or falsity of the fact represented. 14 Fla. Jur. Fraud and Deceit, §28; Kitchen v. Long, 1914, 67 Fla. 72, 64 So. 429. As stated by Judge Allen of this Court in Ramel v. Chasebrook Construction Company, Fla. App. 1961, 135 So. 2d 876:

> A statement of a party having . . . superior knowledge may be regarded as a statement of fact although it would be considered as opinion if the parties were dealing on equal terms.

It could be reasonably supposed here that defendants had "superior knowledge" as to whether plaintiff had "dance potential" and as to whether she was noticeably improving in the art of terpsichore. And it would be a reasonable inference from the undenied averments of the complaint that the flowery eulogiums heaped upon her by defendants as a prelude to her contracting for 1,944 additional hours of instruction in order to attain the rank of the Bronze Standard, thence to the bracket of the Silver Standard, thence to the class of the Gold Bar Standard, and finally to the crowning plateau of a Life Member of the Studio, proceeded as much or more from the urge to "ring the cash register" as from any honest or realistic appraisal of her dancing prowess or a factual representation of her progress.

Even in contractual situations where a party to a transaction owes no duty to disclose facts within his knowledge or to answer inquiries respecting such facts, the law is if he undertakes to do so he must disclose the *whole truth*. Ramel v. Chasebrook Construction Company, supra; Beagle v. Bagwell, Fla. App. 1964, 169 So. 2d 43. From the face of the complaint, it should have been reasonably apparent to defendants that her vast outlay of cash for the many hundreds of additional hours of instruction was not justified by her slow and awkward progress, which she would have been made well aware of if they had spoken the "whole truth." In Hirschman v. Hodges, etc., 1910, 59 Fla. 517, 51 So. 550, it was said that "what is plainly injurious to good faith ought to be considered as a fraud sufficient to impeach a contract," and that an improvident agreement may be avoided "because of surprise, or mistake, *want of freedom, undue influence, the suggestion of falsehood, or the suppression of truth.*" (Emphasis supplied.) We repeat that where parties are dealing on a contractual basis at arm's length with no inequities or inherently unfair practices employed, the Courts will in general "leave the parties where they find themselves." But in the case sub judice, from the allegations of the unanswered complaint, we cannot say that enough of the accompanying ingredients, as mentioned in the foregoing authorities, were not present which otherwise would have barred the equitable arm of the Court to her. In our view, from the showing made in her complaint, plaintiff is entitled to her day in Court.

It accordingly follows that the order dismissing plaintiff's last amended complaint with prejudice should be and is reversed.

Reversed.

NOTES AND QUESTIONS

1. *"Reasonable" reliance.* Was her reliance reasonable? Should the reasonableness of the plaintiff's conduct be an issue in a fraud suit? As a judge would you allow the defendant this defense: "It's true I told the plaintiff an outrageous lie, but only an idiot would have believed me"?

In the leading case of Chamberlin v. Fuller, 59 Vt. 247, 9 A. 832 (1887), the court made this point: "No rogue should enjoy his ill-gotten plunder for the simple reason that his victim is by chance a fool."

While courts will sometimes carelessly say that reliance must be reasonable, when pressed they change the standard to "justifiable." However, where the victim signed up for a foolish venture having full knowledge of the facts, which include *no misrepresentations,* an action in fraud will not lie. See Stahl v. Balsara, 60 Haw. 144, 587 P.2d 1210 (1978) ("utterly unreasonable" to rely on astrologer's future predictions); Ellis v. Newbrough, 6 N.M. 181, 27 P. 490 (1891) (no relief for believer who gave all his property to a "land of Shalam" commune in the desert). As stated in In re Vann, 67 F.3d 277, 283 (11th Cir. 1995) (citing Prosser and Keeton on Torts and Restatement (Second) of Torts §545A comment b (1977), "[I]t is only, where, under the circumstances, the facts should be apparent to one of the plaintiff's knowledge and intelligence from a cursory glance, or he has discovered something which should serve as warning that he is being deceived, that he is required to make an investigation of his own."

[margin note: "justifiable" reliance]

2. *Actions as misrepresentations.* Fraud does not necessarily consist of verbal or written statements. Conduct by itself can be fraudulent. Where the defendant takes *affirmative steps* to conceal a problem, a "misrepresentation" occurs, Lindberg Cadillac Co. v. Aron, 371 S.W.2d 651 (Mo. Ct. App. 1963) (used car's engine spray-painted black to look shiny), as it does where the defendant knows that under no circumstances would plaintiff have gone through with the transaction had the truth been known, Jewish Center v. Whale, 86 N.J. 619, 432 A.2d 521 (1981) (rabbi failed to mention his past criminal record and disbarment as an attorney when hired by synagogue).

[margin note: "Affirmative steps"]

3. *Merger clauses and fraud.* Nothing can hide fraud—at least in theory. The common law maxim is "*fraus omnia corrumpit*" ("fraud vitiates everything it touches"). Thus most courts will not allow either a merger clause or the parol evidence rule to bar evidence of fraud in the creation of the contract. Texas has an ugly history with this issue, and most recently has held (in a 4-3 decision) that the usual merger clause won't bar evidence of fraud unless it specifically states that there was no "reliance" on any statements made prior to signing of the writing; see Italian Cowboy Partners, Ltd. v. Prudential Ins. Co. of America, 341 S.W.3d 323 (Tex. 2011). The problem with this squirrelly result is that adding such boilerplate language to the contract would insulate those who lied from any penalty for their bad actions, and "non-reliance" clauses are likely to become standard in Texas contracts. The Texas Supreme Court quoted the above Latin phrase even as it reached a result that violates

it. As noted in the last chapter, California has had similar battles with fraud and the parol evidence rule; see Riverisland Cold Storage, Inc. v. Fresno-Madera Production Credit Ass'n, 55 Cal. 4th 1169, 151 Cal. Rptr. 3d 93, 291 P.3d 315 (2013).

4. *Superior knowledge.* Where the misrepresentor has superior knowledge of the situation, the courts have deemed *opinions* as fraudulent. For instance, while ordinarily a misrepresentation of the rules of law is not fraudulent, it is actionable where the statement is made by an attorney, Ward v. Arnold, 52 Wash. 2d 581, 328 P.2d 164 (1958). This rule frequently traps insurance companies making predictions about the benefits of its policies; see Anderson v. Knox, 297 F.2d 702 (9th Cir. 1961), cert. denied, 370 U.S. 915 (1962).

Problem 117

Randy Long and Ralph Rice were farmers, and Long heard through a friend that Rice had an old tractor for sale. The two men met, away from Rice's farm. Long said he needed a tractor that would be "ready to go in the field" and that the hydraulics had to work, to which Rice replied that his tractor was "field ready." The men shook hands when Long traded in his current fully operational tractor and paid Rice $2,000 as the sales price of the latter's tractor, which Long did not inspect (nor even see) prior to the sale. Rice's tractor never worked properly; it was smoking and needed a new fuel pump immediately, but even that did not make the tractor work adequately. Long sued in fraud, and Rice defended by saying that Long's reliance was not justifiable because he should have inspected and test driven the tractor before agreeing to buy it. How should this come out? See Long v. Rice, 992 N.W.2d 1220 (Ohio App. 2013).

Problem 118

When Portia Moot bought a used car from Honest John Motors, Honest John told her that he believed that it would be "maintenance free" for the first six months and that if anything went wrong in that period he would repair it. The car blew up a week after she bought it. When she asked Honest John to repair it, he told her she had bought a piece of junk "as is," that he never warranted his vehicles, and that he never did repair work. She sued him in fraud, producing a witness who had offered to buy the same car from Honest John a week before she did; this witness testified that John had told him that the car was worthless and "wouldn't run a month without major trouble." Honest John responded to the suit by claiming that fraud consists of the knowing misrepresentation of an *existing* fact, and that his statement of *opinion* and promises of repair in the future were not misrepresentations of existing matters. Who wins? See Vulcan Metals Co. v. Simmons Manufacturing Co., 248 F. 853 (2d Cir. 1918) (misrepresentation by someone with superior knowledge is a misrepresentation of fact). In a famous English case, Lord Bowen addressed this issue in oft-quoted language:

> There must be a misstatement of an existing fact; but the state of a man's mind is as much a fact as the state of his digestion. It is true that it is very difficult to prove what the state of a man's mind at a particular time is but if it can be ascertained it is as much a fact as anything else.

Edginton v. Fitzmaurice, 29 Chan. 459 (1882).

The Great Recession of 2008 and the mortgage mess. The 1980s were a grand time for unscrupulous lenders. Just as banks and other lending institutions pulled out of minority and poor areas, the federal government greatly slackened its enforcement of fair housing laws, and the tax code was changed so as to encourage second mortgage lending by making the interest payments tax deductible. Deregulation also played a part, allowing unscrupulous entities to enter the lending business and go after those who had equity in their homes but who otherwise could not attract the attention of legitimate lenders (particularly the uneducated and the elderly). "Subprime" lending of this stripe was a $140 billion industry by 2000 (and currently constitutes 13 percent of all home loans), leading to predatory loans made at outrageously high interest rates or to "packing" the deal with unwanted extras (such as very high credit insurance) and extra-high closing costs known in the trade as "garbage fees" or "junk charges." Often, dilapidated homes are purchased at a low price and then resold at exorbitant rates to unsophisticated buyers, a process called "flipping."

Many of these loans were called "No Doc" deals because the lenders didn't even require verification of the borrowers' incomes. Much of the paperwork contained out-and-out fraud: fictional numbers pulled from the air, past financial troubles ignored, absurd misstatements about the terms of the loan, and so much more that "subprime loans" morphed into "liar loans" in the vernacular of the times.

When the housing market collapsed in 2008 and the financial situation became dire for both institutions and individuals, people trapped in mortgages they could not afford often found some relief in the law of fraud and/or various consumer protection statutes, both federal and state. For an egregious fact pattern and relief awarding attorney's fees and litigation costs in the total amount of $596,199.89, and punitive damages in the amount of $2,168,868.75, see Quicken Loans, Inc. v. Brown, 230 W. Va. 306, 737 S.E.2d 640 (2012). A similar case follows. Note that this plaintiff was proceeding *pro se* (for herself, probably because she was too poor to afford an attorney — think how daunting that would be).

WEST v. JPMORGAN CHASE BANK, N.A.
California Court of Appeal, 2013
214 Cal. App. 4th 780, 154 Cal. Rptr. 3d 285

Genevieve West, pro se, for Plaintiff and Appellant.

Alvarado Smith, John M. Sorich, S. Christopher Yoo, Santa Ana, Yunnie Youn Ahn, Fountain Valley, and Jenny L. Merris, Santa Ana, for Defendant and Respondent.

OPINION

FYBEL, J.

INTRODUCTION

As authorized by Congress, the United States Department of the Treasury implemented the Home Affordable Mortgage Program (HAMP) to help homeowners avoid foreclosure during the housing market crisis of 2008. "The goal of HAMP is to provide relief to borrowers who have defaulted on their mortgage payments or who are likely to default by reducing mortgage payments to sustainable levels, without discharging any of the underlying debt." (Bosque v. Wells Fargo Bank, N.A. (D. Mass. 2011) 762 F. Supp. 2d 342, 347.)

After her home loan went into default, plaintiff Genevieve West agreed to a trial period plan (TPP), a form of temporary loan payment reduction under HAMP, from defendant JPMorgan Chase Bank, N.A. (Chase Bank), which had acquired her loan from the original lender. West complied with the terms of the TPP, and timely made every reduced monthly payment on her loan during the trial period and afterwards. Nonetheless, Chase Bank denied West a permanent loan modification, and West's home was sold at a trustee's sale just two days after Chase Bank told her, so West alleged, that no foreclosure sale was scheduled.

West brought this lawsuit alleging fraud, breach of written contract, promissory estoppel, and other causes of action, against Chase Bank. The trial court sustained without leave to amend Chase Bank's demurrer to the third amended complaint, and West appealed from the subsequent judgment. We hold that West stated causes of action for fraud, negligent misrepresentation, breach of written contract, promissory estoppel, and unfair competition, and therefore reverse the judgment on those causes of action. We affirm only on the causes of action for conversion, to set aside or vacate void trustee sale, for slander of title, and to quiet title.

In holding that West stated a cause of action for breach of written contract, we agree with the analysis and interpretation of HAMP presented in the recent opinion of the United States Court of Appeals for the Seventh Circuit in Wigod v. Wells Fargo Bank, N.A. (7th Cir. 2012) 673 F.3d 547, 556-557 (*Wigod*). Core to our decision is the court's conclusion in *Wigod, supra*, 673 F.3d at page 557, that when a borrower complies with all the terms of a TPP, and the borrower's representations remain true and correct, the loan servicer must offer the borrower a permanent loan modification. As a party to a TPP, a borrower may sue the lender or loan servicer for its breach. (*Id.* at p. 559, fn. 4.) Because West complied with all the terms of the TPP, Chase Bank had to offer her a permanent loan modification.

HAMP

[The court summarized the HAMP program. During the financial crisis in 2008, Congress created the Troubled Asset Relief Program, which authorized the Secretary of the Treasury to create incentives for home loan servicers to offer loan modifications to struggling homeowners. HAMP required lenders to offer temporary loan modifications to borrowers who met certain criteria. This led to a Trial Period Plan (TPP): a kind of probationary period in which the homeowner tried to make regular payments under the new loan terms. If the homeowner did not miss a payment, HAMP mandated that lenders offer a permanent modification.]

ALLEGATIONS

West's third amended complaint alleged the following facts.

West obtained an adjustable rate home loan in the sum of $645,000, secured by a deed of trust on her home. The deed of trust, which was recorded in September 2006, named Washington Mutual Bank, F.A. (Washington Mutual), as the lender and beneficiary, California Reconveyance Company as the trustee, and West as the borrower. In 2008, Chase Bank acquired Washington Mutual and purchased certain of its assets, including West's loan.

West failed to make payments on the home loan. As a consequence, a notice of default and election to sell under the deed of trust was recorded in March 2009. According to the notice of default, West was $17,795.91 in arrears as of March 17, 2009.

In April 2009, a substitution of trustee was recorded. It named Quality Loan Service Corporation (QLSC) as trustee in place of California Reconveyance Company.

In July 2009, Washington Mutual informed West she had been approved for a TPP, which Washington Mutual called a "Trial Plan Agreement." The approval letter stated: "Since you have told us you're committed to pursuing a stay-in-home option, you have been approved for a Trial Plan Agreement. If you comply with all the terms of this Agreement, we'll consider a permanent workout solution for your loan once the Trial Plan has been completed." In August 2009, West entered into the Trial Plan Agreement with Washington Mutual. The Trial Plan Agreement required West to make an initial payment of $1,931.86 by August 1, 2009, and additional payments in that amount on September 1 and October 1. The Trial Plan Agreement stated: "If you do not make your payments on time, or if any of your payments are returned for nonsufficient funds, this Agreement will be in breach and collection and/or foreclosure activity will resume."

West made all three payments under the Trial Plan Agreement and continued thereafter to make monthly payments in the required amount. In January 2010 and again in March 2010, Chase Bank confirmed receipt of documents that West had submitted in support of her request for a permanent loan modification under HAMP. In the letters confirming receipt of those documents, Chase Bank advised West to "continue to make your trial period payments on time."

By letter dated April 5, 2010, Chase Bank notified West that "we have determined that you do not qualify for a modification through the Making Home Affordable ('MHA') modification program or through other modification programs offered by Chase at this time." Chase Bank's determination was based on a calculation of West's "Net Present Value" (NPV) under a formula developed by the Department of the Treasury. The letter stated: "If we receive a request from you within thirty (30) calendar days from the date of this letter, we will provide you with the date the NPV calculation was completed and the input values noted below. If, within thirty (30) calendar days of receiving this information you provide us with evidence that any of these input values are inaccurate, and those inaccuracies are material, for example a significant difference in your gross monthly income or an inaccurate zip code, we will conduct a new NPV evaluation. While there is no guarantee that a new NPV evaluation will result in the owner of your Loan approving a modification, we want to ensure that the NPV evaluation is based on accurate information."

On April 8, 2010, West "and or" her representative contacted Chase Bank, informed the bank it had used outdated financial information, and requested a "re-evaluation" (boldface & underscoring omitted) using updated financial information. Chase Bank did not send West the NPV data and input values that she had requested.

On May 24, 2010, West again informed Chase Bank that it had used outdated financial information and that she would submit "updated financial information, and any other information necessary to make the input data accurate." West alleged: "On or about May 24, 2010, [West] and or her representative conducted a conference call with the loan modification department of CHASE BANK, who [sic] agreed and promised [West] that

[she] could resubmit her updated financial data for re-evaluation for HAMP modification solutions, and that there was no foreclosure sale date or sale scheduled." (Boldface & underscoring omitted.)

Also on May 24, West made her 10th reduced payment of $1,931.86, which Chase Bank rejected and returned to her.

Although Chase Bank had told West no foreclosure sale had been scheduled, her home was sold at a trustee's sale conducted on May 26, 2010. "In violation of its promises and said letter, and HAMP rules (and Supplemental Directives), two (2) days later, CHASE BANK secretly, sold [West]'s home, on May 26, 2010 during the re-evaluation period. CHASE BANK issued letters dated May 20, 2010, received May 24, 2010, rejecting [West]'s 10th payment . . . , made pursuant to the continuing forbearance agreement."

A trustee's deed upon sale was recorded on June 10, 2010. The deed identified Green Island Holdings, LP, as the grantee, and recited, "[s]aid property was sold by said Trustee at public auction on 5/26/2010 at the place named in the Notice of Sale. . . ."

PROCEDURAL HISTORY

West filed the initial complaint in November 2010. A series of demurrers and amendments resulted in the third amended complaint, which asserted these causes of action: fraud[,] negligent misrepresentation[,] and breach of written contract. . . .

Chase Bank demurred to the third amended complaint on the ground none of the causes [of] action stated facts sufficient to state a cause of action. . . .

The trial court sustained Chase Bank's demurrer in its entirety without leave to amend . . . .

DISCUSSION

I. FRAUD AND NEGLIGENT MISREPRESENTATION CAUSES OF ACTION

West asserted fraud in the first cause of action and negligent misrepresentation in the second cause of action. In the fraud cause of action, West alleged that starting on August 6, 2009, Chase Bank made false representations in the Trial Plan Agreement and "verbally" that she was granted "a continuing Making Home Affordable (HAMP) Trial Modification, and or forbearance agreement, during the re-evaluation of the HAMP Modification." She alleged that Chase Bank concealed from her "the fact that there was a foreclosure sale date pending against the subject Property, and that it did intend to [foreclose] during the re-evaluation period."

The elements of fraud are (1) the defendant made a false representation as to a past or existing material fact; (2) the defendant knew the representation was false at the time it was made; (3) in making the representation, the defendant intended to deceive the plaintiff; (4) the plaintiff justifiably relied on the representation; and (5) the plaintiff suffered resulting damages. (Lazar v. Superior Court (1996) 12 Cal. 4th 631, 638, 49 Cal. Rptr. 2d 377, 909 P.2d 981.) The elements of negligent misrepresentation are the same except for the second element, which for negligent misrepresentation is the defendant made the representation without reasonable ground for believing it to be true. [Citations omitted.]

Chase Bank argues the trial court was correct to sustain the demurrer to those causes of action without leave to amend because West did not allege (1) fraud with the required particularity, (2) justifiable reliance, and (3) causation.

A. Specificity

Fraud must be pleaded with specificity rather than with "'general and conclusory allegations.'" (Small v. Fritz Companies, Inc. (2003) 30 Cal. 4th 167, 184, 132 Cal. Rptr. 2d 490, 65 P.3d 1255.) The specificity requirement means a plaintiff must allege facts showing how, when, where, to whom, and by what means the representations were made, and, in the case of a corporate defendant, the plaintiff must allege the names of the persons who made the representations, their authority to speak on behalf of the corporation, to whom they spoke, what they said or wrote, and when the representation was made. (Lazar v. Superior Court, *supra*, 12 Cal. 4th at p. 645, 49 Cal. Rptr. 2d 377, 909 P.2d 981.)

We enforce the specificity requirement in consideration of its two purposes. The first purpose is to give notice to the defendant with sufficiently definite charges that the defendant can meet them. (Committee on Children's Television, Inc. v. General Foods Corp. (1983) 35 Cal. 3d 197, 216, 197 Cal. Rptr. 783, 673 P.2d 660.) The second is to permit a court to weed out meritless fraud claims on the basis of the pleadings; thus, "the pleading should be sufficient "'to enable the court to determine whether, on the facts pleaded, there is any foundation, prima facie at least, for the charge of fraud.'"'" (*Id.* at pp. 216-217, 197 Cal. Rptr. 783, 673 P.2d 660.)

West met that specificity requirement. She alleged quite specifically that Chase Bank made misrepresentations in the Trial Plan Agreement, in the April 5, 2010 letter, and in telephone conferences on April 8 and May 24, 2010. Both the Trial Plan Agreement and the April 5 letter were attached to the third amended complaint. The Trial Plan Agreement was sent to West on July 24, 2009 by a Washington Mutual loan workout specialist identified as Russell Buelna.

West alleged that, in the April 5, 2010 letter, Chase Bank falsely represented that it would reevaluate her case and send her the NPV input data if she so requested within 30 days. The April 5 letter is from the Chase Fulfillment Center and, though the letter does not identify the preparer, West did not have to plead that information because it was uniquely within Chase Bank's knowledge. [Citations omitted.]

West alleged that on April 8, 2010, she spoke with a supervisor in the loan modification department of Chase Bank, and, on May 24, 2010, spoke with someone in that department. She specifically described the misrepresentations allegedly made during those conferences and alleged the misrepresentations were communicated by telephone. She alleged that, in a telephone call on May 24, 2010, a Chase Bank representative told her she "could resubmit her updated financial data for re-evaluation for HAMP modification solutions, and that there was no foreclosure sale date or sale scheduled." (Boldface & underscoring omitted.) Her allegation of the persons who made the alleged misrepresentations was sufficient to give notice to Chase Bank of the charges. The identification of the Chase Bank employees who spoke with West on those dates is or should be within Chase Bank's knowledge.

B. Justifiable Reliance

"'Besides actual reliance, [a] plaintiff must also show "justifiable" reliance, i.e., circumstances were such to make it *reasonable* for [the] plaintiff to accept [the] defendant's statements without an independent inquiry or investigation.' [Citation omitted.] The reasonableness of the plaintiff's reliance is judged by reference to the plaintiff's knowledge and experience. [Citation omitted.] '"Except in the rare case where the undisputed facts leave no room for a reasonable difference of opinion, the question of whether a plaintiff's reliance is reasonable is a question of fact." [Citations omitted.]' [Citation omitted.]" (OCM Principal Opportunities Fund, L.P. v. CIBC World Markets Corp. (2007) 157 Cal. App. 4th 835, 864-865, 68 Cal. Rptr. 3d 828.) "Reliance can be proved in a fraudulent omission case by establishing that 'had the omitted information been disclosed, [the plaintiff] would have been aware of it and behaved differently.'" (Boschma v. Home Loan Center, Inc., *supra*, 198 Cal. App. 4th at pp. 250-251, 129 Cal. Rptr. 3d 874.)

West alleged in the third amended complaint that she "justifiably relied [on] the representations made by CHASE BANK, on the phone, and in its letters" and, "[a]t all related times, Defendants knew or should have known that Plaintiff would justifiably rely on its representations made in writing, and on the phone."

Chase Bank argues those allegations did not satisfy the justifiable reliance requirement because (1) the Trial Plan Agreement makes no promise of a permanent loan modification agreement and (2) the April 5, 2010 letter informed West that Chase Bank had determined she did not qualify for a permanent loan modification.

The Trial Plan Agreement represented only that Chase Bank would reevaluate West's application for a permanent loan modification if West made all payments as scheduled. But the April 5, 2010 letter stated that Chase Bank would provide West with the NPV input values if she requested them within 30 days and that Chase Bank would conduct a new evaluation if West provided evidence that any of those input values were inaccurate. West could justifiably rely on those representations, and she alleged she asked for those input values on April 8 and on May 24, 2010. Chase Bank never sent them to her before foreclosing.

West also alleged that from the time of the Trial Plan Agreement, Chase Bank concealed the fact it was pursuing foreclosure and that on May 24, a Chase Bank representative told West that no trustee's sale was scheduled. West could have justifiably relied on that representation too, particularly considering she was requesting a reevaluation of Chase Bank's decision to deny her a permanent loan modification.

C. Causation

Chase Bank argues West has not pleaded, and cannot plead, her reliance on the alleged misrepresentations caused her to suffer damages; that is, she did not "'establish a complete causal relationship' between the alleged misrepresentations and the harm claimed to have resulted therefrom." (See Mirkin v. Wasserman (1993) 5 Cal. 4th 1082, 1092, 23 Cal. Rptr. 2d 101, 858 P.2d 568.)

West alleged that in reliance on the representations and Chase Bank's alleged concealment of the foreclosure sale, she suffered damages "including loss of mortgage payments made under false pretenses, attorney fees, legal costs, personal injuries, pain and suffering, anxiety, humiliation, fear, extreme emotional distress, and physical injuries." As Chase Bank argues, West already owed the mortgage payments and was obligated to make them notwithstanding the alleged misrepresentations. West also alleged, however, that Chase Bank "lull[ed]" her into "a false sense of security, so she would not hire an attorney to protect her rights," and then pursued the foreclosure sale despite telling her, on May 24, 2010, that no foreclosure sale had been scheduled.

The third amended complaint, read as a whole, may be reasonably construed to allege that West's reliance on Chase Bank's alleged misrepresentations caused West to forego taking legal action to stop the foreclosure sale. Under the allegations of the third amended complaint, West likely would have been successful in taking legal action to stop the sale. In the April 5, 2010 letter denying a loan modification, Chase Bank offered to conduct a new NPV evaluation if West made a timely request for input values and provided evidence those values were inaccurate. West alleged she timely requested the input values, but Chase Bank never provided her the information. In January 2010 and again in March 2010, Chase Bank advised West to "continue to make your trial period payments on time." She made all of her payments.

II. BREACH OF WRITTEN CONTRACT CAUSE OF ACTION

In the seventh cause of action for breach of written contract, West alleged the Trial Plan Agreement constituted a written contract, which Chase Bank breached by denying her a permanent loan modification after "secretly" selling her home. We conclude the third amended complaint stated a cause of action for breach of written contract.

Chase Bank does not dispute the Trial Plan Agreement constituted a written contract. Many federal courts have concluded a trial loan modification under HAMP constitutes a valid, enforceable contract under state law, at least at the pleading stage of litigation. [Citations omitted.] Chase Bank does not argue lack of offer and acceptance, consideration, certain terms, or any element necessary to create an enforceable contract.

Instead, Chase Bank argues it did not as a matter of law breach the terms of the Trial Plan Agreement because the exhibits to the third amended complaint establish that Chase Bank did reevaluate West's application for a permanent loan modification. Chase Bank relies on the term of the Trial Plan Agreement stating, "[i]f all payments are made as scheduled, we will reevaluate your application for assistance and determine if we are able to offer you a permanent workout solution to bring your loan current." Attached to the third amended complaint was Chase Bank's letter, dated April 5, 2010, notifying West that Chase Bank had determined she did not qualify for a loan modification based on a calculation of her NPV under a formula developed by the Department of the Treasury.

This argument ignores Chase Bank's obligations under HAMP and the express and implied obligations under the Trial Plan Agreement. When Chase Bank received public tax dollars under the Troubled Asset Relief Program, it agreed to offer TPP's and loan modifications under HAMP according to guidelines, procedures, instructions, and directives issued by the Department of the Treasury. (*Wigod, supra,* 673 F.3d at p. 556.) Under the United States Department of the Treasury, HAMP Supplemental Directive 09-01 (Apr. 6, 2009) (Directive 09-01), if the lender approves a TPP, and the borrower complies with all the terms of the TPP and all of the borrower's representations remain true and correct, the lender *must offer* a permanent loan modification. (*Wigod, supra,* at p. 557.) Directive 09-01, *supra,* at page 18, states: "If the borrower complies with the terms and conditions of the [TPP], the loan modification will become effective on the first day of the month following the trial period. . . ."

. . .

Unlike the TPP in *Wigod*, the Trial Plan Agreement signed by West, and prepared by Chase Bank, did not expressly include the proviso that Chase Bank would offer a permanent loan modification if she complied with that agreement's terms. But such a proviso is imposed by the United States Department of the Treasury through Directive 09-01, *supra,* page 18 (see *Wigod, supra,* 673 F.3d at p. 557), and a contract must be interpreted in a way to make it lawful (Civ. Code, §1643). To make the Trial Plan Agreement lawful, it must be interpreted to include the proviso imposed by Directive 09-01. In addition, HAMP guidelines "informed the reasonable expectations of the parties to [the Trial Plan Agreement]." (*Wigod, supra,* at p. 565.)

Thus, in light of Directive 09-01 and HAMP guidelines, the reasonable interpretation of the Trial Plan Agreement — and the one necessary to make it lawful and in compliance with HAMP — is that Chase Bank's reevaluation upon completion of the trial period would be limited to determining whether West complied with the terms of the Trial Plan Agreement and whether West's original representations remained true and correct. Applying *Wigod* to this case, "[a]lthough [Chase Bank] may have had some limited discretion to set the precise terms of an offered permanent modification, it was certainly required to offer *some* sort of good-faith permanent modification to [West] consistent with HAMP guidelines. It has offered none." (*Wigod, supra,* 673 F.3d at p. 565.)

In addition, Chase Bank stated in its April 5, 2010 letter that, upon timely request from West, it would provide her with the input values used to calculate her NPV and, if within 30 days of receiving that information, West provided Chase Bank with evidence that any of the input values were inaccurate, and those inaccuracies were material, Chase Bank would conduct a new NPV evaluation. As a matter of contract law, the import of this letter is twofold. First, under Chase Bank's interpretation of the Trial Plan Agreement, the April 5, 2010 letter constituted a modification of that agreement. A modification of a contract is a change in the obligations of a party by a subsequent mutual agreement of the parties. (1 Witkin, Summary of Cal. Law (10th ed. 2005) Contracts, §964, p. 1055.) A contract in writing may be modified by a contract in writing. (Civ. Code, §1698, subd. (a).) Though not signed by anyone at Chase Bank, the April 5, 2010 letter bears the Chase Bank letterhead, which suffices as a signature. (Rest. 2d Contracts, §134.)

Second, to the extent the Trial Plan Agreement is ambiguous, the April 5, 2010 letter is relevant under the practical construction doctrine in determining Chase Bank's intent. "'[W]hen a contract is ambiguous, a construction given to it by the acts and conduct of the parties with knowledge of its terms, before any controversy has arisen as to its meaning, is entitled to great weight, and will, when reasonable, be adopted and enforced by the court. [Citation omitted.] The reason underlying the rule is that it is the duty of the court to give effect to the intention of the parties where it is not wholly at variance with the correct legal interpretation of the terms of the contract, and a practical construction placed by the parties upon the instrument is the best evidence of their intention.'" (Employers Reinsurance Co. v. Superior Court (2008) 161 Cal. App. 4th 906, 921, 74 Cal. Rptr. 3d 733.) The April 5, 2010 letter, which was drafted before a controversy arose over the Trial Plan Agreement, shows that Chase Bank intended, at the very least, to give West the option and ability — before any foreclosure sale — to challenge the decision to deny her a permanent loan modification.

Thus, as alleged in the third amended complaint, the Trial Plan Agreement required Chase Bank to offer West a permanent loan modification because she had complied with the terms of that agreement. In addition, West alleged she was entitled to challenge Chase Bank's decision to deny her a permanent loan modification by providing information to support a different NPV calculation. She is correct. The third amended complaint alleged Chase Bank breached the Trial Plan Agreement in these two ways, and therefore stated a cause of action for breach of written contract. . . .

DISPOSITION

[The court reversed and remanded on the fraud, negligent misrepresentation, and breach of contract theories. The court also awarded West, the plaintiff representing herself, her costs on appeal.]

What happens if one party to the contract makes a false statement to the other when negotiating the terms but does not know that it is false? Is this fraud? Mistake? The next case deals with this difficulty.

COUSINEAU v. WALKER
Supreme Court of Alaska, 1980
613 P.2d 608

BOOCHEVER, J. The question in this case is whether the appellants are entitled to rescission of a land sale contract because of false statements made by the sellers. The superior court concluded that the buyers did not rely on any misrepresentations made by the sellers, that the misrepresentations were not material to the transaction, and that reliance by the buyers was not justified. Restitution of money paid under the contract was denied. We reverse and remand the case to the superior court to determine the amount of damages owed the appellants. *[Procedural History]*

In 1975, Devon Walker and his wife purchased 9.1 acres of land in Eagle River, Alaska, known as Lot 1, Cross Estates. They paid $140,000.00 for it. A little over a year later, in October, 1976, they signed a multiple listing agreement with Pat Davis, an Anchorage realtor. The listing stated that the property had 580 feet of highway frontage on the Old Glenn Highway and that "Engineer Report Says Over 1 Million in Gravel on Prop." The asking price was $245,000.00.

When the multiple listing expired, Walker signed a new agreement to retain Davis as an exclusive agent. In the broker's contract, the property was again described as having 580 feet of highway frontage, but the gravel content was listed as "minimum 80,000 cubic yds of gravel." The agreement also stated that 2.6 acres on the front of the parcel had been proposed for B-3 zoning (a commercial use), and the asking price was raised to $470,000.00.

An appraisal was prepared to determine the property's value as of December 31, 1976. Walker specifically instructed the appraiser not to include the value of gravel in the appraisal. A rough draft of the appraisal and the appraiser's notes were introduced at trial. Under the heading, "Assumptions and Limiting Conditions," the report stated the appraisal "does not take into account any gravel. . . ." But later in the report the ground was described as "all good gravel base . . . covered with birch and spruce trees." The report did not mention the highway footage of the lot.

Wayne Cousineau, a contractor who was also in the gravel extraction business, became aware of the property when he saw the multiple listing. He consulted Camille Davis, another Anchorage realtor, to see if the property was available. In January, Cousineau and Camille Davis visited the property and discussed gravel extraction with Walker, although according to Walker's testimony commercial extraction was not considered. About this time Cousineau offered Walker $360,000.00 for the property. Cousineau tendered a proposed sales agreement which stated that all gravel rights would be granted to the purchaser at closing.

Sometime after his first offer, Cousineau attempted to determine the lot's road frontage. The property was covered with snow, and he found only one boundary marker. At trial the appraiser testified he could not find any markers. Cousineau testified that he went to the borough office to determine if any regulations prevented gravel extraction. . . .

In February, 1977, the parties agreed on a purchase price of $385,000.00 and signed an earnest money agreement. The sale was contingent upon approval of the zoning change of the front portion of the lot to commercial use. The amount of highway frontage was not included in the agreement. Paragraph 4(e) of the agreement conditionally granted gravel rights to Cousineau. According to the agreement, Cousineau would be entitled to remove only so much gravel as was necessary to establish a construction grade on the commercial portion of the property. To remove additional gravel, Cousineau would be required to pay releases on those portions of ground where gravel was removed. This language was used to prevent Walker's security interest in the property from being impaired before he was fully paid.

Soon after the earnest money agreement was signed, the front portion of the property was rezoned and a month later the parties closed the sale.

There is no reference to the amount of highway frontage in the final purchase agreement. An addendum to a third deed of trust incorporates essentially the same language as the earnest money agreement with regard to the release of gravel rights.

After closing, Cousineau and his partners began developing the commercial portion of the property. They bought a gravel scale for

$12,000.00 and used two of Cousineau's trucks and a loader. The partners contracted with South Construction to remove the gravel. According to Cousineau's testimony, he first learned of discrepancies in the real estate listing which described the lot when a neighbor threatened to sue Cousineau because he was removing gravel from the neighbor's adjacent lot. A recent survey shows that there is 415 feet of highway frontage on the property — not 580 feet, as advertised.

At the same time Cousineau discovered the shortage in highway frontage, South Construction ran out of gravel. They had removed 6,000 cubic yards. To determine if there was any more gravel on the property, a South Construction employee bulldozed a trench about fifty feet long and twenty feet deep. There was no gravel. A soils report prepared in 1978 confirmed that there were no gravel deposits on the property.

After December, 1977, Cousineau and his partners stopped making monthly payments. At that time they had paid a total of $99,000.00 for the property, including a down payment and monthly installments. In March, 1978, they informed Walker of their intention to rescind the contract. A deed of trust foreclosure sale was held in the fall of 1978, and Walker reacquired the property. At a bench trial in December, Cousineau and his partners were denied rescission and restitution.

Among his written findings of fact, the trial judge found:

> At some point in time, between October 24, 1976, and January 11, 1977, there existed a multiple listing advertisement which included information relating to gravel as well as road frontage, said information subsequently determined to be incorrect.

He further found:

> The plaintiffs did not rely on any misinformation or misrepresentations of defendants. The claimed misinformation about gravel on the property and the road frontage was not a material element of the parties' negotiations, and these pieces of information did not appear in the February 16, 1977 purchase agreement document prepared by attorney Harland Davis, attorney for the plaintiffs and signed by the parties. . . .

I. Rescission of the Contract

Numerous cases hold and the Restatement provides that an innocent misrepresentation may be the basis for rescinding a contract.[3] There is no

---

3. We decline to consider whether Walker's statements amounted to fraudulent or negligent misrepresentations. The trial judge made no findings on the question and our resolution makes it unnecessary to consider it. It is apparent, however, that Walker had little basis for making statements regarding gravel content. For example, the basis for the statement in the first listing, "over 1 million in gravel," was Walker's neighbor, Riley Curtis, not the

question, as the trial judge's findings of fact state, that the statements made by Walker and his real estate agent in the multiple listing were false. Three questions must be resolved, however, to determine whether Cousineau is entitled to rescission and restitution of the amount paid for the property on the basis of the misrepresentations. First, it must be determined whether Cousineau in fact relied on the statements. Second, it must be determined whether the statements were material to the transaction — that is, objectively, whether a reasonable person would have considered the statements important in deciding whether to purchase the property. Finally, assuming that Cousineau relied on the statements and that they were material, it must be determined whether his reliance was justified.[5]

A.   RELIANCE ON THE FALSE STATEMENTS

. . . In our opinion, the trial judge's finding that Cousineau and his partners did not rely on the statements made by Walker is clearly erroneous.

Regardless of the credibility of some witnesses, the uncontroverted facts are that Wayne Cousineau was in the gravel extraction business. He first became aware of the property through a multiple listing that said "1 Million in Gravel." The subsequent listing stated that there were 80,000 cubic yards of gravel. Even if Walker might have taken the position that the sale was based on the appraisal, rather than the listings, the appraisal does not disclaim the earlier statements regarding the amount of highway frontage and the existence of gravel. In fact, the appraisal might well reaffirm a buyer's belief that gravel existed, since it stated there was a good gravel base. All the documents prepared regarding the sale from the first offer through the final deed of trust make provisions for the transfer of gravel rights. Cousineau's first act upon acquiring the property was to contract with South Construction for gravel removal, and to purchase gravel scales for $12,000.00. We

---

"Engineer Report." Walker claimed that Curtis told him an engineering firm had dug core samples on the property and had prepared a report which estimated the amount of gravel. At trial, Curtis denied telling Walker that there was gravel on the property. He testified that he told Walker there was over one million in *material*, not gravel. As discussed in the text, Walker never actually saw the report. Moreover, Pat Davis, Walker's real estate agent, was aware of these facts, but included the statement on the listing anyway.

5. Restatement (Second) of Contracts §306, comment (a) (Tent. Draft no. 11, 1976) states:

> A misrepresentation may make a contract voidable under the rule stated in this Section, even though it does not prevent the formulation of a contract under the rule stated in the previous section. Three requirements must be met in addition to the requirement that there must have been a misrepresentation. First, the misrepresentation must have been either fraudulent or material. . . . Second, the misrepresentation must have induced the recipient to make the contract. . . . Third, the recipient must have been justified in relying on the misrepresentation.

conclude that the court erred in finding that Cousineau did not rely on Walker's statement that there was gravel on the property.

We are also convinced that the trial court's finding that Cousineau did not rely on Walker's statement regarding the amount of highway frontage was clearly erroneous. The Cousineaus were experienced and knowledgeable in real estate matters. In determining whether to purchase the property, they would certainly have considered the amount of highway frontage to be of importance. Despite Walker's insistence that Cousineau knew the location of the boundary markers, neither Cousineau nor the appraiser ever found them. It is improbable that Cousineau would have started removing gravel from a neighbor's property had he known the correct location of his boundary line.

B. MATERIALITY OF THE STATEMENTS

Materiality is a mixed question of law and fact. A material fact is one "to which a reasonable man might be expected to attach importance in making his choice of action." W. Prosser, Law of Torts §108, at 719 (4th ed. 1971). It is a fact which could reasonably be expected to influence someone's judgment or conduct concerning a transaction. . . . Under §306 of the tentative draft of the Restatement (Second) of Contracts, a misrepresentation may be grounds for voiding a contract if it is either fraudulent or material. Restatement (Second) of Contracts §306 (Tent. Draft no. 11, 1976). The reason behind the rule requiring proof of materiality is to encourage stability in contractual relations. The rule prevents parties who later become disappointed at the outcome of their bargain from capitalizing on any insignificant discrepancy to void the contract.

We conclude as a matter of law that the statements regarding highway frontage and gravel content were material. A reasonable person would be likely to consider the existence of gravel deposits an important consideration in developing a piece of property. Even if not valuable for commercial extraction, a gravel base would save the cost of obtaining suitable fill from other sources. Walker's real estate agent testified that the statements regarding gravel were placed in the listings because gravel would be among the property's "best points" and a "selling point." It seems obvious that the sellers themselves thought a buyer would consider gravel content important.

The buyers received less than three-fourths of the highway frontage described in the listings. Certainly the amount of highway frontage on a commercial tract would be considered important. Numerous cases from other jurisdictions have held discrepancies to be material which were similar in magnitude to those here.

C. JUSTIFIABLE RELIANCE

The trial judge concluded as a matter of law that the plaintiffs "were not entitled to rely on the alleged misrepresentation." The bulk of the appellee's brief is devoted to the argument that Cousineau's unquestioning reliance on Walker and his real estate agent was imprudent and unreasonable. Cousineau failed to obtain and review the engineer's report. He failed to obtain a survey or examine the plat available at the recorder's office. He failed to make calculations that would have revealed the true frontage of the lot. Although the property was covered with snow, the plaintiffs, according to Walker, had ample time to inspect it. The plaintiffs were experienced businessmen who frequently bought and sold real estate. Discrepancies existed in the various property descriptions which should have alerted Cousineau and his partners to potential problems. In short, the appellees urge that the doctrine of caveat emptor precludes recovery.

. . .

There is a split of authority regarding a buyer's duty to investigate a vendor's fraudulent statements, but the prevailing trend is toward placing a minimal duty on a buyer. . . .

[A]s noted in Williston on Contracts,

> [t]he growing trend and tendency of the courts will continue to move toward the doctrine that negligence in trusting in a misrepresentation will not excuse positive willful fraud or deprive the defrauded person of his remedy.

W. Jaeger, Williston on Contracts §1515B at 487 (3d ed. 1970).

There is also authority for not applying the doctrine of caveat emptor even though the misrepresentation is innocent. The Restatements, case law, and a ready analogy to express warranties in the sale of goods support this view.

The recent draft of the Restatement of Contracts allows rescission for an innocent material misrepresentation unless a buyer's fault was so negligent as to amount to "a failure to act in good faith and in accordance with reasonable standards of fair dealing."[13] Restatement (Second) of Contracts §314, Comment b (Tent. Draft. no. 11, 1976).

In Van Meter v. Bent Construction Co., 46 Cal. 2d 588, 297 P.2d 644 (1956), the city of San Diego failed to properly mark the area of a reservoir

---

13. As an illustration of "fair dealing," the proposed Restatement suggests the following example:

> A, seeking to induce B to make a contract to buy land, tells B that the land is free from encumbrances. Unknown to either A or B, C holds a recorded and unsatisfied mortgage on the land. B could easily learn this by walking across the street to the register of deeds in the courthouse but does not do so. B is induced by A's statement to make the contract. B's reliance is justified since his fault does not amount to a failure to act in good faith and in accordance with reasonable standards of fair dealing, and the contract is voidable by B.

Restatement (Second) of Contracts §314, Comment b, Illustration 2 (Tent. Draft no. 11, 1976).

that needed to be cleared of brush. A lower court concluded that the city's failure to mark the area properly was an innocent mistake, and that a bidder's actions in failing to discover the true area to be cleared was negligent. Recovery was denied because the city's misrepresentation was not willful. The California Supreme Court reversed, first noting that a party's negligence does not bar rescission for mutual mistake, and then concluding:

> There is even more reason for not barring a plaintiff from equitable relief where his negligence is due in part to his reliance in good faith upon the false representations of a defendant, although the statements were not made with intent to deceive. A defendant who misrepresents the facts and induces the plaintiff to rely on his statements should not be heard in an equitable action to assert that the reliance was negligent unless plaintiff's conduct, in the light of his intelligence and information, is preposterous or irrational.

Id. 297 P.2d at 648 (citations omitted). The Massachusetts Supreme Judicial Court has expressed a similar view in Yorke v. Taylor, 332 Mass. 368, 124 N.E.2d 912, 916 (1955).[14]

. . .

We conclude that a purchaser of land may rely on material representations made by the seller and is not obligated to ascertain whether such representations are truthful.

---

14. See also Sorenson v. Adams, 98 Idaho 708, 571 P.2d 769, 776 (1977), in which the tillable acreage sold was misrepresented by reference to an erroneous form prepared by the Department of Agriculture. The buyers sought damages for the shortage, and the Supreme Court of Idaho reversed a judgment of nonsuit, stating:

> In short, the general rule is that "a vendor may be liable in tort for misrepresentations as to the area of land conveyed, notwithstanding such misrepresentations were made without actual knowledge of their falsity." The reason, of course, is that the parties to a real estate transaction do not deal on equal terms. An owner is presumed to know the boundaries of his own land, the quantity of his acreage, and the amount of water available. If he does not know the correct information, he must find out or refrain from making representations to unsuspecting strangers. "Even honesty in making a mistake is no defense as it is incumbent upon the vendor to know the facts."

Id. 571 P.2d at 776 (citations omitted). In addition, the sellers argued that the buyers had no right to rely on the A.S.C. figures, since they could have checked the figures themselves or conducted their own survey. In rejecting this argument, the court stated:

> False statements found . . . to have been made and relied on cannot be avoided by the appellants by the contention that the respondents could have, by independent investigation, ascertained the truth.

The appellants having stated what was untrue cannot now complain because respondents believed what they were told. Lack of caution on the part of respondents because they so believed, and the contention that the respondents could have made an independent investigation and determined the true facts, is no defense to the action. Weitzel v. Jukich, 73 Idaho 301, 305, 251 P.2d 542, 544 (1953). And see, Lanning v. Sprague, [71 Idaho 138, 227 P.2d 347,] supra.

Rule

A buyer of land, relying on an innocent misrepresentation, is barred from recovery only if the buyer's acts in failing to discover defects were wholly irrational, preposterous, or in bad faith.

Holding

Although Cousineau's actions may well have exhibited poor judgment for an experienced businessman, they were not so unreasonable or preposterous in view of Walker's description of the property that recovery should be denied. Consequently, we reverse the judgment of the superior court.

Reversed

II. RESTITUTION

Walker received a total of $99,000.00 from Cousineau and his partners, but the appellants are not entitled to restitution of this amount. Cousineau apparently caused extensive damage to one building on the property, and he removed 6,000 cubic yards of gravel. Walker should be allowed some recoupment for these items, plus an amount for the fair rental value of the property less reasonable costs of rental.

Remanded for damages

It is necessary to remand this case to the trial court to determine the correct amount of damages.

Reversed and remanded.

Problem 119

When John Smith went into the Navy Recruitment Center, he told the recruiter on duty that he wanted to learn how to fly. He was told that his lack of 20/20 vision would prevent this, but that he could become a member of a flight crew if he went to a naval school to qualify as an air technician. He filled out the recruitment papers with this goal in mind, after being assured that he would be able to attend the air technician school. After he completed boot camp, John was denied entry to the school because he had indicated on his medical form that he suffered from hay fever. Instead the Navy sent him orders telling him to report for duty aboard a ship in the Mediterranean, where he would be a simple deck-hand. John Smith hired a lawyer who filed a petition for a writ of habeas corpus. Is he going to be able to get out of the Navy? See Brown v. Dunleavy, 722 F. Supp. 1343 (E.D. Va. 1989).

Election of remedies. If the complaint in a fraud action asks for rescission, most courts hold that all the plaintiff can then recover is out-of-pocket expenses, and that by electing the remedy of rescission, the plaintiff has forfeited any claim for lost expectancy. Thus the lawyer drawing the complaint and wanting benefit-of-the-bargain damages has to be careful not to request rescission. Some jurisdictions ignore this election of remedies doctrine and permit the recovery of benefit-of-the-bargain damages no matter how the complaint is phrased. See Annot., 13 A.L.R.3d 875. The UCC adopts this latter position; read §2-721.

Punitive damages. From the plaintiff's point of view, one attractive feature of a fraud suit is the possibility of substantial punitive damages, which in many jurisdictions also include an award of attorney's fees; see Annot., 44 A.L.R.4th 776. Such damages are most appropriate where there is *intentional* conduct of the defendant which is "malicious, oppressive, or gross," Winn-Dixie Montgomery, Inc. v. Henderson, 395 So. 2d 475 (Ala. 1981), or "willful and wanton," Jeffers v. Nysse, 98 Wis. 2d 543, 297 N.W.2d 495 (1980). Where the plaintiff is a consumer or the defendant has a fiduciary relationship with the plaintiff, simple intentional fraud may be enough to allow for punitive damages, F. D. Borkholder Co. v. Sandock, 274 Ind. 612, 413 N.E.2d 567 (1980); Ford v. Guarantee Abstract & Title Co., 220 Kan. 244, 553 P.2d 254 (1976).

NOTE ON THE FEDERAL TRADE COMMISSION ACT AND STATE UNFAIR AND DECEPTIVE TRADE PRACTICE ACTS

Although a number of federal agencies have authority to protect consumers from a variety of wrongdoing, the agency considered to be the primary consumer protector is the Federal Trade Commission. The commission was formed in 1914 with the passage of the Federal Trade Commission Act. ch. 311, 38 Stat. 717 (1914). Although the FTC has been given authority through the years to enforce a wide variety of trade statutes, the commission's authority to enforce the FTC Act remains its major source of consumer protection power. Under the Act, it has the power to prohibit "unfair and deceptive trade practices." One method by which the FTC may do so is through its "cease and desist" procedure. Once a complaint is filed with the FTC alleging a violation of the FTC Act, an investigation is conducted. If the commission staff concludes that a violation has occurred, the violator may be asked to enter into a "consent" to a "cease and desist order." Such a consent order applies only to prospective behavior and generally provides that the "consent" is not an admission of wrongdoing. If there is a refusal to enter into a consent order or the FTC decides the consent order is not in the public interest, the FTC may file a formal complaint and hold a public hearing before an administrative law judge of the FTC. After hearing testimony, the administrative judge may issue a cease and desist order. Any party to the initial decision of the administrative judge may appeal to the full commission. Further appeal must be to the U.S. Court of Appeals within any circuit where the method of competition or the act or practice in question was used or where such person resides or carries on its business. Final appeal is to the Supreme Court upon certiorari.

The FTC also has the authority to issue "trade regulation rules." To do so, the commission must (1) publish notice of proposed rulemaking stating with particularity the reason for the proposed rule; (2) allow interested persons to submit written data, views, and arguments, and make all such submissions publicly available; (3) provide for an informal hearing; and (4) promulgate, if appropriate, a final rule based on the rulemaking record together with a statement of basis and purpose. Judicial review of rules may be requested by interested persons including consumers or consumer organizations not later than 60 days after the promulgation of a rule. Appeal must be to the U.S. Court of Appeals for the District of Columbia Circuit or for the circuit in which such person resides or has his principal place of business. Final appeal is to the Supreme Court.

The 1975 FTC Improvement Act amendments specifically provide that the FTC has no power to issue rules that regulate banks. Within 60 days after the FTC promulgates a trade regulation rule, the Federal Reserve Board must issue "substantially similar" regulations prohibiting acts or practices of banks that are "substantially similar" to those prohibited by the FTC rules. However, the FRB is not required to issue such rules if it finds that the acts or practices of banks are not unfair or deceptive or that the implementation of similar regulations with respect to banks would seriously conflict with essential monetary and payment systems policies of the FRB. 15 U.S.C. §57a(f)(1). It is generally accepted that there is no private right of action for the violation of the FTC Act. See, e.g., Alfred Dunhill Ltd. v. Interstate Cigar Co., 499 F.2d 232 (2d Cir. 1974); Carlson v. Coca-Cola Co., 483 F.2d 279 (9th Cir. 1973). Contra, Guernsey v. Rich Plan of the Midwest, 408 F. Supp. 582, 586-589 (N.D. Ind. 1976).

Upon violation of commission orders and trade regulation rules, the FTC may seek a variety of statutory remedies and penalties. The FTC may obtain preliminary injunctions against unfair or deceptive acts or practices that are unfair or deceptive to consumers. The commission may bring an action for a civil penalty of up to $10,000 for each violation against any person who is the subject of a cease and desist order. The commission may also recover such a penalty against persons who are not directly covered by an order if such persons have actual knowledge that acts or practices are unlawful under an existing order against a third party. The FTC may also recover a maximum $10,000 penalty for the violation of trade regulation rules.

Forty-nine states and the District of Columbia have laws based on the FTC Act's prohibition against deceptive and unfair acts and practices. Alabama is the exception.* Such statutes are commonly called *consumer protection statutes* or *little FTC acts.* All such statutes prohibit "deceptive" or "misleading" acts or practices. About one-half also prohibit "unfair" practices in their little FTC act. See, e.g., Mass. Ann. Laws ch. 93A §2.

---

* Survey of Consumer Fraud Law, chart at p.122, published by The National Institute of Law Enforcement and Criminal Justice (1978).

Although there is no private right of action under the FTC Act, nearly all of the little FTC acts allow such an action. See, e.g., Mo. Ann. Stat. §407.025. Since most states give great weight to FTC cease and desist orders and trade regulation rules, the use of a state act's private right of action along with a substantive finding of deception or unfairness by the FTC in such an action may in effect give the consumer counsel the private right of action that would otherwise be missing.

All statutes providing for individual action allow actual damages. About one-third of the jurisdictions allowing the private right of action also allow multiple damages. See, e.g., D.C. Code Ann. §28-3905(K); Ohio Rev. Code §1345 (treble damages).

Finally, it should be noted that the Federal Trade Commission has no jurisdiction over financial institutions, but those entities are now under the control of the Consumer Financial Protection Bureau, which was formed by the Dodd-Frank Act (2010). The CFPB took over the functions of many other federal agencies that had mandates to protect consumers in financial matters, and has been very active in issuing rules and regulations to carry out that function.

B. Non-Disclosure

Is it ever fraud to keep silent and not speak up? In the famous case of Peek v. Gurney, 6 H.L. 377 (1873), the House of Lords decided that there is never a duty to disclose no matter how morally censurable silence may be. Some courts still adhere to this. See Swinton v. Whitinsville Savings Bank, 311 Mass. 677, 42 N.E.2d 808 (1942) (no duty to mention that termites were being sold along with the house). Others disagree, Obde v. Schlemeyer, 56 Wash. 2d 449, 353 P.2d 672 (1960) (a termites case coming out the other way), following the suggestion of Professor Page Keeton that "silent fraud" should be actionable whenever "justice, equity, and fair dealing demand it"; Keeton, Fraud: Concealment and Non-Disclosure, 15 Tex. L. Rev. 1, 31 (1936). Keeton said that disclosure is most called for when silence will allow a dangerous condition to go undiscovered. See Annot., 22 A.L.R.3d 972.

RESTATEMENT (SECOND) OF CONTRACTS

§161. WHEN NON-DISCLOSURE IS EQUIVALENT TO AN ASSERTION

A person's non-disclosure of a fact known to him is equivalent to an assertion that the fact does not exist in the following cases only:

(a) where he knows that disclosure of the fact is necessary to prevent some previous assertion from being a misrepresentation or from being fraudulent or material.

(b) where he knows that the disclosure of the fact would correct a mistake of the other party as to a basic assumption on which that party is making the contract and if non-disclosure of the fact amounts to a failure to act in good faith and in accordance with reasonable standards of fair dealing.

(c) where he knows that disclosure of the fact would correct a mistake of the other party as to the contents or effect of a writing, evidencing or embodying an agreement in whole or in part.

(d) where the other person is entitled to know the fact because of a relation of trust and confidence between them.

STAMBOVSKY v. ACKLEY
New York Supreme Court, Appellate Division, 1991
169 App. Div. 2d 254, 572 N.Y.S.2d 672

RUBIN, Justice. Plaintiff, to his horror, discovered that the house he had recently contracted to purchase was widely reputed to be possessed by poltergeists, reportedly seen by defendant seller and members of her family on numerous occasions over the last nine years. Plaintiff promptly commenced this action seeking rescission of the contract of sale. Supreme Court reluctantly dismissed the complaint, holding that plaintiff has no remedy at law in this jurisdiction.

The unusual facts of this case, as disclosed by the record, clearly warrant a grant of equitable relief to the buyer who, as a resident of New York City, cannot be expected to have any familiarity with the folklore of the Village of Nyack. Not being a "local," plaintiff could not readily learn that the home he had contracted to purchase is haunted. Whether the source of the spectral apparitions seen by defendant seller are parapsychic or psychogenic, having reported their presence in both a national publication ("Readers' Digest") and the local press (in 1977 and 1982, respectively), defendant is estopped to deny their existence and, as a matter of law, the house is haunted. More to the point, however, no divination is required to conclude that it is defendant's promotional efforts in publicizing her close encounters with these spirits which fostered the home's reputation in the community. In 1989, the house was included in a five-home walking tour of Nyack and described in a November 27th newspaper article as "a riverfront Victorian (with ghost)." The impact of the reputation thus created goes to the very essence of the bargain between the parties, greatly impairing both the value of the property and its potential for resale. The extent of this impairment may be presumed for the purpose of reviewing the disposition of this motion to dismiss the cause of action for rescission (Harris v. City of New York, 147 A.D.2d 186, 188-189, 542 N.Y.S.2d 550) and represents merely an issue of fact for resolution at trial.

While I agree with the Supreme Court that the real estate broker, as agent for the seller, is under no duty to disclose to a potential buyer the phantasmal reputation of the premises and that, in his pursuit of a legal remedy for fraudulent misrepresentation against the seller, plaintiff hasn't a ghost of a chance, I am nevertheless moved by the spirit of equity to allow the buyer to seek rescission of the contract of sale and recovery of his downpayment. New York law fails to recognize any remedy for damages incurred as a result of the seller's mere silence, applying instead the strict rule of caveat emptor. Therefore, the theoretical basis for granting relief, even under the extraordinary facts of this case, is elusive if not ephemeral.

Buyer can seek rescission

"Pity me not but lend thy serious hearing to what I shall unfold" (William Shakespeare, Hamlet, Act I, Scene V [Ghost]).

From the perspective of a person in the position of plaintiff herein, a very practical problem arises with respect to the discovery of a paranormal phenomenon: "Who you gonna' call?" as the title song to the movie "Ghostbusters" asks. Applying the strict rule of caveat emptor to a contract involving a house possessed by poltergeists conjures up visions of a psychic or medium routinely accompanying the structural engineer and Terminix man on an inspection of every home subject to a contract of sale. It portends that the prudent attorney will establish an escrow account lest the subject of the transaction come back to haunt him and his client — or pray that his malpractice insurance coverage extends to supernatural disasters. In the interest of avoiding such untenable consequences, the notion that a haunting is a condition which can and should be ascertained upon reasonable inspection of the premises is a hobgoblin which should be exorcised from the body of legal precedent and laid quietly to rest.

It has been suggested by a leading authority that the ancient rule which holds that mere non-disclosure does not constitute actionable misrepresentation "finds proper application in cases where the fact undisclosed is patent, or the plaintiff has equal opportunities for obtaining information which he may be expected to utilize, or the defendant has no reason to think that he is acting under any misapprehension" (Prosser, Law of Torts §106, at 696 [4th ed. 1971]). However, with respect to transactions in real estate, New York adheres to the doctrine of caveat emptor and imposes no duty upon the vendor to disclose any information concerning the premises (London v. Courduff, 141 A.D.2d 803, 529 N.Y.S.2d 874) unless there is a confidential or fiduciary relationship between the parties (Moser v. Spizzirro, 31 A.D.2d 537, 295 N.Y.S.2d 188, affd., 25 N.Y.2d 941, 305 N.Y.S.2d 153, 252 N.E.2d 632; IBM Credit Fin. Corp. v. Mazda Motor Mfg. (USA) Corp., 152 A.D.2d 451, 542 N.Y.S.2d 649) or some conduct on the part of the seller which constitutes "active concealment" (see, 17 East 80th Realty Corp. v. 68th Associates, 173 A.D.2d 245, 569 N.Y.S.2d 647 [dummy ventilation system constructed by seller]; Haberman v. Greenspan, 82 Misc. 2d 263, 368 N.Y.S.2d 717 [foundation cracks covered by seller]). Normally, some affirmative misrepresentation [citations omitted] or partial disclosure [citations omitted] is required to impose upon the seller a duty to communicate undisclosed conditions affecting the premises [citations omitted].

Caveat emptor is not so all-encompassing a doctrine of common law as to render every act of non-disclosure immune from redress, whether legal or equitable. "In regard to the necessity of giving information which has not been asked, the rule differs somewhat at law and in equity, and while the law courts would permit no recovery of *damages* against a vendor, because of mere concealment of facts *under certain circumstances*, yet if the vendee refused to complete the contract because of the concealment of a material fact on the part of the other, equity would refuse to compel him so to do, because equity only compels the specific performance of a contract which is fair and open, and in regard to which all material matters known to each have been communicated to the other" (Rothmiller v. Stein, 143 N.Y. 581, 591-592, 38 N.E. 718 [emphasis added]). Even as a principle of law, long before exceptions were embodied in statute law (see, e.g., UCC 2-312, 2-313, 2-314, 2-315; 3-417[2][e]), the doctrine was held inapplicable to contagion among animals, adulteration of food, and insolvency of a maker of a promissory note and of a tenant substituted for another under a lease (see, Rothmiller v. Stein, supra, at 592-593, 38 N.E. 718 and cases cited therein). Common law is not moribund. *Ex facto jus oritur* (law arises out of facts). Where fairness and common sense dictate that an exception should be created, the evolution of the law should not be stifled by rigid application of a legal maxim.

The doctrine of caveat emptor requires that a buyer act prudently to assess the fitness and value of his purchase and operates to bar the purchaser who fails to exercise due care from seeking the equitable remedy of rescission (see, e.g., Rodas v. Manitaras, 159 A.D.2d 341, 552 N.Y.S.2d 618). For the purposes of the instant motion to dismiss the action pursuant to CPLR 3211 (a)(7), plaintiff is entitled to every favorable inference which may reasonably be drawn from the pleadings [citations omitted], specifically, in this instance, that he met his obligation to conduct an inspection of the premises and a search of available public records with respect to title. It should be apparent, however, that the most meticulous inspection and the search would not reveal the presence of poltergeists at the premises or unearth the property's ghoulish reputation in the community. Therefore, there is no sound policy reason to deny plaintiff relief for failing to discover a state of affairs which the most prudent purchaser would not be expected to even contemplate (see, Da Silva v. Musso, 53 N.Y.2d 543, 551, 444 N.Y.S.2d 50, 428 N.E.2d 382).

The case law in this jurisdiction dealing with the duty of a vendor of real property to disclose information to the buyer is distinguishable from the matter under review. The most salient distinction is that existing cases invariably deal with the physical condition of the premises (e.g., London v. Courduff, supra [use as a landfill]; Perin v. Mardine Realty Co., 5 A.D.2d 685, 168 N.Y.S.2d 647, affd., 6 N.Y.2d 920, 190 N.Y.S.2d 995, 161 N.E.2d 210 [sewer line crossing adjoining property without owner's consent]), defects in title (e.g., Sands v. Kissane, 282 App. Div. 140, 121 N.Y.S.2d 634 [remainderman]), liens against the property (e.g., Noved Realty Corp. v. A.A.P. Co., supra), expenses or income (e.g., Rodas v. Manitaras, supra [gross receipts]) and other factors affecting its operation. No case has been brought to this court's attention in which the property value was impaired as the result of the reputation created by information disseminated to the public by the seller (or, for that matter, as a result of possession by poltergeists).

Where a condition which has been created by the seller materially impairs the value of the contract and is peculiarly within the knowledge of the seller or unlikely to be discovered by a prudent purchaser exercising due care with respect to the subject transaction, nondisclosure constitutes a basis for rescission as a matter of equity. Any other outcome places upon the buyer not merely the obligation to exercise care in his purchase but rather to be omniscient with respect to any fact which may affect the bargain. No practical purpose is served by imposing such a burden upon a purchaser. To the contrary, it encourages predatory business practice and offends the principle that equity will suffer no wrong to be without a remedy.

Defendant's contention that the contract of sale, particularly the merger or "as is" clause, bars recovery of the buyer's deposit is unavailing. Even an express disclaimer will not be given effect where the facts are peculiarly within the knowledge of the party invoking it. [Citations omitted.] Moreover, a fair reading of the merger clause reveals that it expressly disclaims only representations made with respect to the physical condition of the premises and merely makes general reference to representations concerning "any other matter or things affecting or relating to the aforesaid premises." As broad as this language may be, a reasonable interpretation is that its effect is limited to tangible or physical matters and does not extend to paranormal phenomena. Finally, if the language of the contract is to be construed as broadly as defendant urges to encompass the presence of poltergeists in the house, it cannot be said that she has delivered the premises "vacant" in accordance with her obligation under the provisions of the contract rider. . . .

In the case at bar, defendant seller deliberately fostered the public belief that her home was possessed. Having undertaken to inform the public at large, to whom she has no legal relationship, about the supernatural occurrences on her property, she may be said to owe no less a duty to her contract vendee. It has been remarked that the occasional modern cases which permit a seller to take unfair advantage of a buyer's ignorance so long as he is not actively misled are "singularly unappetizing" (Prosser, Law of Torts §106, at 696 [4th ed. 1971]). Where, as here, the seller not only takes unfair advantage of the buyer's ignorance but has created and perpetuated a condition about which he is unlikely to even inquire, enforcement of the contract (in whole or in part) is offensive to the court's sense of equity. Application of the remedy of rescission, within the bounds of the narrow exception to the doctrine of caveat emptor set forth herein, is entirely appropriate to relieve the unwitting purchaser from the consequences of a most unnatural bargain. . . .

All concur except MILONAS, J.P. and SMITH, J., who dissent in an opinion by SMITH, J.

SMITH, Justice (dissenting). I would affirm the dismissal of the complaint by the motion court. . . . "It is settled law in New York that the seller of real property is under no duty to speak when the parties deal at arm's length. The mere silence of the seller, without some act or conduct which deceived the purchaser, does not amount to a concealment that is actionable as a fraud. [Citations omitted.] The buyer has the duty to satisfy himself as to the quality of his bargain pursuant to the doctrine of caveat emptor, which in New York State still applies to real estate transactions." London v. Courduff, 141 A. D.2d 803, 804, 529 N.Y.S.2d 874, app. dismd., 73 N.Y.2d 809, 537 N.Y.S.2d 494, 534 N.E.2d 332 (1988).

The parties herein were represented by counsel and dealt at arm's length. This is evidenced by the contract of sale which, inter alia, contained various riders and a specific provision that all prior understandings and agreements between the parties were merged into the contract, that the contract completely expressed their full agreement and that neither had relied upon any statement by anyone else not set forth in the contract. There is no allegation that defendants, by some specific act, other than the failure to speak, deceived the plaintiff. Nevertheless, a cause of action may be sufficiently stated where there is a confidential or fiduciary relationship creating a duty to disclose and there was a failure to disclose a material fact, calculated to induce a false belief. [Citation omitted.] However, plaintiff herein has not alleged and there is no basis for concluding that a confidential or fiduciary relationship existed between these parties to an arm's length transaction such as to give rise to a duty to disclose. In addition, there is no allegation that defendants thwarted plaintiff's efforts to fulfill his responsibilities fixed by the doctrine of caveat emptor. See London v. Courduff, supra, 141 A.D.2d at 804, 529 N.Y.S.2d 874.

Finally, if the doctrine of caveat emptor is to be discarded, it should be for a reason more substantive than a poltergeist. The existence of a poltergeist is no more binding upon the defendants than it is upon this court.

Based upon the foregoing, the motion court properly dismissed the complaint.

IV. DURESS

TOTEM MARINE TUG & BARGE v. ALYESKA PIPELINE SERVICE CO.
Supreme Court of Alaska, 1978 584 P.2d 15

BURKE, J. This appeal arises from the superior court's granting of summary judgment in favor of defendants-appellees Alyeska Pipeline Services, et al., in a contract action brought by plaintiffs-appellants Totem Marine Tug & Barge, Inc., Pacific, Inc., and Richard Stair.

The following summary of events is derived from the materials submitted in the summary judgment proceedings below.

Totem is a closely held Alaska corporation which began operations in March of 1975. Richard Stair, at all times relevant to this case, was vice-president of Totem. In June of 1975, Totem entered into a contract with Alyeska under which Totem was to transport pipeline construction materials from Houston, Texas, to a designated port in southern Alaska, with the possibility of one or two cargo stops along the way. In order to carry out this contract, which was Totem's first, Totem chartered a barge (the "Marine Flasher") and an ocean-going tug (the "Kirt Chouest"). These charters and other initial operations costs were made possible by loans to Totem from Richard Stair individually and Pacific, Inc., a corporation of which Stair was principal stockholder and officer, as well as by guarantees by Stair and Pacific.

By the terms of the contract, Totem was to have completed performance by approximately August 15, 1975. From the start, however, there were numerous problems which impeded Totem's performance of the contract. For example, according to Totem, Alyeska represented that approximately 1,800 to 2,100 tons of regular uncoated pipe were to be loaded in Houston, and that perhaps another 6,000 or 7,000 tons of materials would be put on the barge at later stops along the west coast. Upon the arrival of the tug and barge in Houston, however, Totem found that about 6,700 to 7,200 tons of coated pipe, steel beams and valves, haphazardly and improperly piled, were in the yard to be loaded. This situation called for remodeling of the barge and extra cranes and stevedores, and resulted in the loading taking thirty days rather than the three days which Totem had anticipated it would take to load 2,000 tons. The lengthy loading period was also caused in part by Alyeska's delay in assuring Totem that it would pay for the additional expenses, bad weather and other administrative problems.

The difficulties continued after the tug and barge left Houston. It soon became apparent that the vessels were travelling more slowly than anticipated because of the extra load. In response to Alyeska's complaints and with its verbal consent, on August 13, 1975, Totem chartered a second tug, the "N. Joseph Guidry." When the "Guidry" reached the Panama Canal, however, Alyeska had not yet furnished the written amendment to the parties' contract. Afraid that Alyeska would not agree to cover the cost of the second tug, Stair notified the "Guidry" not to go through the Canal. After some discussions in which Alyeska complained of the delays and accused Totem of lying about the horsepower of the first tug, Alyeska executed the amendment on August 21, 1975.

By this time the "Guidry" had lost its preferred passage through the Canal and had to wait two or three additional days before it could go through. Upon finally meeting, the three vessels encountered the tail of a hurricane which lasted for about eight or nine days and which substantially impeded their progress.

The three vessels finally arrived in the vicinity of San Pedro, California, where Totem planned to change crews and refuel. On Alyeska's orders, however, the vessels instead pulled into port at Long Beach, California. At this point, Alyeska's agents commenced off-loading the barge, without Totem's consent, without the necessary load survey, and without a marine survey, the absence of which voided Totem's insurance. After much wrangling and some concessions by Alyeska, the freight was off-loaded. Thereafter, on or about September 14, 1975, Alyeska terminated the contract. Although there was talk by an Alyeska official of reinstating the contract, the termination was affirmed a few days later at a meeting at which Alyeska officials refused to give a reason for the termination.

Following termination of the contract, Totem submitted termination invoices to Alyeska and began pressing the latter for payment. The invoices came to something between $260,000 and $300,000. An official from Alyeska told Totem that they would look over the invoices but that they were not sure when payment would be made — perhaps in a day or perhaps in six to eight months. Totem was in urgent need of cash as the invoices represented the debts which the company had incurred on 10-30 day payment schedules. Totem's creditors were demanding payment and according to Stair, without immediate cash, Totem would go bankrupt. Totem then turned over the collection to its attorney, Roy Bell, directing him to advise Alyeska of Totem's financial straits. Thereafter, Bell met with Alyeska officials in Seattle, and after some negotiations, Totem received a settlement offer from Alyeska for $97,500. On November 6, 1975, Totem, through its president Stair, signed an agreement releasing Alyeska from all claims by Totem in exchange for $97,500.

On March 26, 1976, Totem, Richard Stair, and Pacific filed a complaint against Alyeska, which was subsequently amended. In the amended complaint, the plaintiffs sought to rescind the settlement and release on the ground of economic duress and to recover the balance allegedly due on the original contract. In addition, they alleged that Alyeska had wrongfully terminated the contract and sought miscellaneous other compensatory and punitive damages.

Before filing an answer, Alyeska moved for summary judgment against the plaintiffs on the ground that Totem had executed a binding release of all claims against Alyeska and that as a matter of law, Totem could not prevail on its claim of economic duress. . . .

II

As was noted above, a court's initial task in deciding motions for summary judgment is to determine whether there exist genuine issues of material fact. In order to decide whether such issues exist in this case, we must examine the doctrine allowing avoidance of a release on grounds of economic duress.

This court has not yet decided a case involving a claim of economic duress or what is also called business compulsion. At early common law, a contract could be avoided on the ground of duress only if a party could show that the agreement was entered into for fear of loss of life or limb, mayhem or imprisonment. 13 Williston on Contracts, §1601 at 649 (3d ed. Jaeger 1970). The threat had to be such as to overcome the will of a person of ordinary firmness and courage. Id., §1602 at 656. Subsequently, however, the concept has been broadened to include myriad forms of economic coercion which force a person to involuntarily enter into a particular transaction. The test has come to be whether the will of the person induced by the threat was overcome rather than that of a reasonably firm person. Id., §1602 at 657.

At the outset it is helpful to acknowledge the various policy considerations which are involved in cases involving economic duress. Typically, those claiming such coercion are attempting to avoid the consequences of a modification of an original contract or of a settlement and release agreement. On the one hand, courts are reluctant to set aside agreements because of the notion of freedom of contract and because of the desirability of having private dispute resolutions be final. On the other hand, there is an increasing recognition of the law's role in correcting inequitable or unequal exchanges between parties of disproportionate bargaining power and a greater willingness to not enforce agreements which were entered into under coercive circumstances.

There are various statements of what constitutes economic duress, but as noted by one commentator, "The history of generalization in this field offers no great encouragement for those who seek to summarize results in any single formula." Dawson, Economic Duress—An Essay in Perspective, 45 Mich. L. Rev. 253, 289 (1947). Section 492(b) of the Restatement of Contracts defines duress as:

> any wrongful threat of one person by words or other conduct that induces another to enter into a transaction under the influence of such fear as precludes him from exercising free will and judgment, if the threat was intended or should reasonably have been expected to operate as an inducement.

Professor Williston states the basic elements of economic duress in the following manner:

1. The party alleging economic duress must show that he has been the victim of a wrongful or unlawful act or threat, and
2. Such act or threat must be one which deprives the victim of his unfettered will.

13 Williston on Contracts, §1617 at 704 (footnotes omitted).

Many courts state the test somewhat differently, eliminating use of the vague term "free will," but retaining the same basic idea. Under this standard, duress exists where: (1) one party involuntarily accepted the terms of another, (2) circumstances permitted no other alternative, and (3) such circumstances were the result of coercive acts of the other party. [Citations omitted.] The third element is further explained as follows:

> In order to substantiate the allegation of economic duress or business compulsion, the plaintiff must go beyond the mere showing of reluctance to accept and of financial embarrassment. There must be a showing of acts on the part of the defendant which produced these two factors. The assertion of duress must be proven by evidence that the duress resulted from defendant's wrongful and oppressive conduct and not by the plaintiff's necessities.

W. R. Grimshaw Co. [v. Nevil C. Withrow Co., 248 F.2d 896, 904 (8th Cir. 1957)].

As the above indicates, one essential element of economic duress is that the plaintiff show that the other party by wrongful acts or threats, intentionally caused him to involuntarily enter into a particular transaction. Courts have not attempted to define exactly what constitutes a wrongful or coercive act, as wrongfulness depends on the particular facts in each case. This requirement may be satisfied where the alleged wrongdoer's conduct is criminal or tortious but an act or threat may also be considered wrongful if it is wrongful in the moral sense. Restatement of Contracts, §492, comment (g); [citations omitted].

In many cases, a threat to breach a contract or to withhold payment of an admitted debt has constituted a wrongful act. [Citations omitted.] Implicit in such cases is the additional requirement that the threat to breach the contract or withhold payment be done in bad faith. [Citations omitted.]

Economic duress does not exist, however, merely because a person has been the victim of a wrongful act; in addition, the victim must have no choice but to agree to the other party's terms or face serious financial hardship. Thus, in order to avoid a contract, a party must also show that he had no reasonable alternative to agreeing to the other party's terms, or, as it is often stated, that he had no adequate remedy if the threat were to be carried out. [Citations omitted.] What constitutes a reasonable alternative is a question of fact, depending on the circumstances of each case. An available legal remedy, such as an action for breach of contract, may provide such an alternative. [Citations omitted.] Where one party wrongfully threatens to withhold goods, services or money from another unless certain demands are met, the availability on the market of similar goods and services or of other sources of funds may also provide an alternative to succumbing to the coercing party's demands. [Citations omitted.] Generally, it has been said that "[t]he adequacy of the remedy is to be tested by a practical standard which takes into consideration the exigencies of the situation in which the alleged victim finds himself." Ross Systems [v. Linden Dari-Delite, Inc., 35 N.J. 329, 173 A.2d 258, 261 (1961)].

An available alternative or remedy may not be adequate where the delay involved in pursuing that remedy would cause immediate and irreparable loss to one's economic or business interest. For example, in *Austin Instrument*, supra, and Gallagher Switchboard Corp. v. Heckler Electric Co., 36 Misc. 2d 225, 232 N.Y.S.2d 590 (N.Y. Sup. Ct. 1962), duress was found in the following circumstances: A subcontractor threatened to refuse further delivery under a contract unless the contractor agreed to modify the existing contract between the parties. The contractor was unable to obtain the necessary materials elsewhere without delay, and if it did not have the materials promptly, it would have been in default on its main contract with the government. In each case such default would have had grave economic consequences for the contractor and hence it agreed to the modifications. In both, the courts found that the alternatives to agreeing to the modification were inadequate (i.e., suing for breach of contract or obtaining the materials elsewhere) and that modifications therefore were signed under duress and voidable.

[handwritten margin note: when an alternative is Not Adequate]

Professor Dalzell, in Duress by Economic Pressure II, 20 N. Carolina L. Rev. 340, 370 (1942), notes the following with regard to the adequacy of legal remedies where one party refuses to pay a contract claim:

> Nowadays, a wait of even a few weeks in collecting on a contract claim is sometimes serious or fatal for an enterprise at a crisis in its history. The business of a creditor in financial straits is at the mercy of an unscrupulous debtor, who need only suggest that if the creditor does not care to settle on the debtor's own hard terms, he can sue. This situation, in which promptness in payment is vastly more important than even approximate justice in the settlement terms, is too common in modern business relations to be ignored by society and the courts.

This view finds support in Capps v. Georgia Pacific Corporation, 253 Or. 248, 453 P.2d 935 (1969). There, the plaintiff was owed $157,000 as a commission for finding a lessee for defendant's property but in exchange for $5,000, the plaintiff signed a release of his claim against the defendant. The plaintiff sued for the balance of the commission, alleging that the release had been executed under duress. His complaint, however, was dismissed. On appeal, the court held that the plaintiff had stated a claim where he alleged that he had accepted the grossly inadequate sum because he was in danger of immediately losing his home by mortgage foreclosure and other property by foreclosure and repossession if he did not obtain immediate funds from the defendant. One basis for its holding was found in the following quote by a leading commentator in the area of economic duress:

The most that can be claimed [regarding the law of economic duress] is that change has been broadly toward acceptance of a general conclusion — that in the absence of specific countervailing factors of policy or administrative feasibility, restitution is required of any excessive gain that results, in a bargain transaction, from impaired bargaining power, whether the impairment consists of economic necessity, mental or physical disability, or a wide disparity in knowledge or experience.

Dawson, Economic Duress — An Essay in Perspective, 45 Mich. L. Rev. 253, 289 (1947).

III

Turning to the instant case, we believe that Totem's allegations, if proved, would support a finding that it executed a release of its contract claims against Alyeska under economic duress. Totem has alleged that Alyeska deliberately withheld payment of an acknowledged debt, knowing that Totem had no choice but to accept an inadequate sum in settlement of that debt; that Totem was faced with impending bankruptcy; that Totem was unable to meet its pressing debts other than by accepting the immediate cash payment offered by Alyeska; and that through necessity, Totem thus involuntarily accepted an inadequate settlement offer from Alyeska and executed a release of all claims under the contract. If the release was in fact executed under these circumstances,[5] we think that under the legal principles discussed above that this would constitute the type of wrongful conduct and lack of alternatives that would render the release voidable by Totem on the ground of economic duress. We would add that although Totem need not necessarily prove its allegation that Alyeska's termination of the contract was wrongful in order to sustain a claim of economic duress, the events leading to the termination would be probative as to whether Alyeska exerted any wrongful pressure on Totem and whether Alyeska wrongfully withheld payment from Totem.[6]

One purpose of summary judgment, however, is to pierce the allegations in the pleadings in an effort to determine whether genuine issues of fact exist. As the moving party, Alyeska had the burden of showing that there were no such genuine issues and that it was entitled to judgment as a matter of law. E.g., Brock v. Rogers and Babler, Inc., 536 P.2d 778, 782 (Alaska 1975). Alyeska showed that Totem had executed the release, that Totem

[handwritten margin note: If Proved to be True, It Would Constitute econ Duress]

---

5. By way of clarification, we would note that Totem would not have to prove that Alyeska admitted to owing the precise sum Totem claimed it was owed upon termination of the contract but only that Alyeska acknowledged that it owed Totem approximately that amount which Totem sought.

6. We make no comment as to whether Alyeska's termination of the contract was wrongful nor as to the truth of Totem's other allegations.

had been represented by counsel at the negotiating session leading to the settlement and release and that appellant Stair, who actually signed the release on behalf of Totem, was fully aware of the consequences of such a release. Such evidence, by itself, would have entitled Alyeska to summary judgment in its favor. As a matter of law, there is no doubt that a valid release of all claims arising under a contract will bar any subsequent claims based on that contract.

To avoid summary judgment once the moving party meets its burden, the non-moving party must produce competent evidence showing that there are issues of material fact to be tried. Id. The respondent must set forth specific facts showing that it could produce admissible evidence reasonably tending to dispute the movants' evidence or establish an affirmative defense. Id. The court then must draw all reasonable inferences in favor of the non-moving party and against the movant. E.g., Clabaugh v. Bottcher, 545 P.2d 172, 175 n.5 (Alaska 1976).

In entering summary judgment against Totem, the court below reasoned as follows:

> The plaintiffs, specifically Mr. Stair, assert the release and settlement should be held for naught because of duress and coercion exerted upon him and his corporation by the defendants' action.
>
> Mr. Stair fails to show that the release and settlement negotiated by his attorneys was involuntary on his part. Mr. Stair did not personally participate in the negotiations which resulted in the release and settlement. No affidavit or other suggestion of evidence has been submitted to demonstrate that upon trial the plaintiffs could sustain their burden of proof required to set aside the release and settlement.

As thus stated, the superior court's decision clearly misstated the standard applicable on motions for summary judgment. A party opposing summary judgment need not establish that he will ultimately prevail at trial. Gablick v. Wolfe, 469 P.2d 391, 395 (Alaska 1970). Although we may affirm a trial court's grant of summary judgment, if alternative grounds exist for upholding its judgment, Moore v. State, 553 P.2d 8, 21 (Alaska 1976), we do not believe that summary judgment was properly granted in this case.

[*margin note: Don't Need to show to Jou will at trial To survive a Summary Judgement*]

Our examination of the materials presented by Totem in opposition to Alyeska's motion for summary judgment leads us to conclude that Totem has made a sufficient factual showing as to each of the elements of economic duress to withstand that motion. There is no doubt that Alyeska disputes many of the factual allegations made by Totem and drawing all inferences in favor of Totem, we believe that genuine issues of material fact exist in this case such that trial is necessary. Admittedly, Totem's showing was somewhat weak in that, for example, it did not produce the testimony of Roy Bell, the attorney who represented Totem in the negotiations leading to the settlement and release. At trial, it will probably be necessary for Totem to produce

[*margin note: Issue of Fact still exist*]

this evidence if it is to prevail on its claim of duress. However, a party opposing a motion for summary judgment need not produce all of the evidence it
may have at its disposal, but need only show that issues of material fact exist.
10 C. Wright and A. Miller, Federal Practice and Procedure: Civil, §2727 at
546 (1973). Therefore, we hold that the superior court erred in granting
summary judgment for appellees and remand the case to the superior court
for trial in accordance with the legal principles set forth above.

Holding

Reversed

Reversed and remanded.

QUESTION

What exactly were the "wrongful act(s)" committed by Alyeska? For a
more extended discussion of the "wrongful act" element, see Continental
Bank of Pa. v. Barclay Riding Acad., Inc., 93 N.J. 153, 459 A.2d 1163 (1983).

EVERBANK v. MARINI
Supreme Court of Vermont, 2015
134 A.3d 189

EATON, J.

¶ 1. This appeal stems from a decision of the Addison Superior Court,
Civil Division, granting summary judgment in favor of defendant Caroline
Marini on plaintiff EverBank's complaint for foreclosure on a mortgage that
Caroline signed in 2009 together with her co-defendant and then-husband
Gary Marini. In ruling on cross-motions for summary judgment, following a
hearing, the trial court concluded that Caroline was entitled to judgment as a
matter of law on EverBank's foreclosure complaint because the undisputed
material facts established that Caroline signed the mortgage under the
threat of physical violence from Gary and thus the mortgage was void as
to her. . . . We reverse the decision granting summary judgment in favor
of Caroline on the issue of whether the mortgage is void, and direct the
trial court to enter judgment for EverBank on that issue. We remand for
trial the issues of whether the mortgage is voidable and, if so, whether it is
enforceable because it was ratified by Caroline. . . .

¶ 2. The record developed before the civil division reveals the following
facts. In June 2005, Caroline and Gary Marini purchased a family home in
the Town of Middlebury. Several years later, in early 2009, Gary began contemplating borrowing money against the Middlebury home. Caroline,
however, believed that borrowing more money against their home was
"financially unhealthy" for their family, and opposed the idea.

¶ 3. Several months later, in early-March 2009, Caroline became aware
that Gary had been communicating with Quicken Loans Inc. about the

possibility of additional loans. Caroline contacted the person at Quicken with whom Gary had been communicating and informed him that their "debt to income ratio was impossible and that another loan was not in [her] best interest." The Marinis did not secure a loan with Quicken.

¶ 4. Around the same time, Caroline and Gary spoke with an attorney about the possibility of debt restructuring. Gary, however, was "adamantly opposed" to the idea of bankruptcy, and following the meeting with the attorney, "was highly emotional and upset," and "expressed thoughts of suicide repeatedly over the following days and weeks." At some point thereafter, Gary told Caroline that he would mortgage the family home "whether [she] liked it or not," and regardless of whether she agreed.

¶ 5. Shortly thereafter, in mid-March 2009, Gary again sought to apply for an additional loan, this time through LendingTree Loans. When Caroline found out that Gary was once again attempting to secure a loan against the family home, she contacted LendingTree and informed a loan officer there that she did not want the loan, that she and Gary were in marital counseling, and that the mortgage was "a very bad thing for [them]." The LendingTree loan officer advised Caroline not to sign the mortgage documents, and stated that she would stop the process if the mortgage was not in Caroline's best interests. Notwithstanding these initial conversations, the loan officer subsequently informed Caroline that the loan application had already entered underwriting and that she was unable to stop it at that point.

¶ 6. Around April 3, 2009, Gary informed Caroline that a notary would come to the house that weekend to witness her signature on the mortgage documents. Caroline told Gary that she would not sign. On April 5, 2009, the LendingTree notary called the Marini household to confirm the appointment. Caroline answered the call and told the notary that she disagreed with the loan and that she would not sign. The LendingTree notary did not come to the Marini house.

¶ 7. In the evening of April 5, 2009, LendingTree sent Gary an email, informing him that it had "just received confirmation from [its] notary service that [Caroline] has cancelled this transaction. Please advise. Under VT state laws, she would have needed to sign documents as well and she is refusing to at this point." Upon receipt of the email, Gary became "extremely angry." Gary brought Caroline and two of their children, ages eight and nineteen, into the kitchen and made them sit at the kitchen table while he berated Caroline, repeatedly stating that she was not a competent adult, that the children were no longer to consider her an adult, and that he was going to divorce her. Gary then removed a pair of large scissors from the knife drawer and waved them back and forth while repeating that Caroline was incompetent. Caroline was frightened for her and her children's physical safety, and told Gary that she would sign the mortgage documents if he would leave the children alone.

¶ 8. The following evening, a LendingTree notary came to the Marini home to witness Caroline's signature on the mortgage documentation. When the notary asked Caroline if her signature was her free act and deed, she replied, "it is what it is." At some point on that same day, Gary also executed a note payable to the order of "Home Loan Center, Inc., dba LendingTree Loans, a California Corporation" in the principal amount of $311,200.00. The mortgage granted Mortgage Electronic Registration System, Inc. (MERS), as nominee for LendingTree, a security interest in the Marini's Middlebury home and was recorded with the Middlebury town clerk's office on April 15, 2009. Although Caroline signed the mortgage paperwork, she did not sign the note; however, the mortgage names both Caroline and Gary as "borrowers" with LendingTree as the "lender," and MERS acting as the nominee for LendingTree. A portion of these loan proceeds were used to refinance the existing debt on the Marinis' Middlebury home and discharge the underlying mortgage, approximately $40,000 went to paying off some of Gary's Bank of America credit card debt, and another portion stayed with Gary in cash.

¶ 9. Almost immediately after the Marinis signed the loan and mortgage paperwork with LendingTree in April 2009, LendingTree assigned the rights to both instruments to Bank of America, N.A., successor by merger to Countrywide Home Loans, Inc. Around the end of November 2009, Caroline became aware of the assignment, and contacted Bank of America in an attempt to explain that she had "disagreed with the loan" and to "register [her] position that the loan was not what [she] wanted and what they had done was wrong." The representative from Bank of America with whom she spoke informed her that only Gary was listed on the loan documents and therefore the representative could not talk to Caroline about it.

¶ 10. Thereafter, around April or May 2011, the Marinis stopped making monthly payments on the loan and defaulted. In anticipation of the impending foreclosure, MERS assigned the mortgage to Bank of America, which initiated the foreclosure action in the Addison Superior Court, Civil Division on December 3, 2012. On December 31, 2012, Caroline filed a verified answer; Gary did not answer until May 13, 2013. In her verified answer, Caroline asserted the affirmative defense of duress, contending that the mortgage was void as to her because she had "signed the Mortgage Deed under duress, namely, implicit threat by [Gary] of physical harm with a sharp object in the presence of her children." Additionally, Caroline argued that the mortgage was voidable as to her, alleging duress arising from her "desire to protect her children from further exposure to parental disagreement, to protect herself from further humiliation, and continuing verbal pressure to burden the house with further debt."

¶ 11. On May 21, 2013, more than five months after Caroline answered, Bank of America moved for summary judgment against Caroline, and judgment for foreclosure by sale. Bank of America's motion for summary judgment did not address Caroline's counterclaim or affirmative defense of duress, nor did it indicate there were any factual disputes regarding Caroline's filings. In early July 2013, Caroline opposed Bank of America's motion and cross-moved for summary judgment in her favor, arguing that she was entitled to judgment as a matter of law because the undisputed material facts showed that she signed the mortgage under the threat of violence and thus it was void as to her. . . . On November 13, 2013, Bank of America moved to substitute EverBank as a party, as both the mortgage and the note had been assigned to EverBank on July 15, 2013.

¶ 12. On December 6, 2013, the trial court held a hearing on the pending cross-motions for summary judgment, at which counsel for Bank of America, Caroline with her counsel, and Gary appeared. . . . When the trial court inquired with Gary whether he agreed with Caroline's recitation of the facts, he responded:

> Yes. Quite frankly, I was very surprised that the notary accepted it based on the statement of saying "it is what it is." There was clearly no desire to sign that mortgage. And, in all honesty, that was probably the basis of our subsequent divorce over this issue. You know, clearly, she was not a willing signer to this mortgage.

Upon the trial court inquiring as to whether Gary "forced her to sign" the mortgage documents, the following exchange occurred:

> [Gary]: I — yeah, I'm not a violent person, but I can't speak for how she perceived — I was very angry, you know, on what was going on at the time.
> [Judge]: So you forced her to sign it?
> [Gary]: I guess I did from that standpoint because I was very angry. I didn't physical[ly] put her hand on the paper, but I was very angry.

. . . . The trial court concluded that the undisputed facts showed that Caroline had been subjected to duress such that the mortgage was void and was therefore entitled to judgment as a matter of law. . . .

¶ 17. Resolution of this [appeal] requires us first to examine the defense of duress to the formation of a contract. . . .

¶ 18. Generally speaking, improper pressure during the bargaining process, i.e., duress, operates to undermine a party's manifestation of assent and thus undermines one of the foundational cores of any agreement. See Restatement (Second) of Contracts ch. 7, topic 2, intro. note; 28 Williston on Contracts §71:8 (4th ed. 2015) ("Duress, like . . . other invalidating causes, may completely prevent the mutual assent necessary for the formation of a contract . . . , or, as is more frequently the case, may be merely a ground for allowing the avoidance of a bargain by its victim, whose expression of mutual assent was improperly obtained."). The specific question for our resolution on appeal is when that improper pressure is of such a quality that it makes an agreement "void," which is to say there effectively never was an agreement at all, and when it makes an agreement merely "voidable," which allows a victim of duress to subsequently repudiate and thus avoid the consequences of the agreement. The distinction between a "void" contract and a "voidable" contract is not simply a theoretical exercise; indeed, it has important potential consequences because, "[f]or example, a victim of duress may be held to have ratified the contract if it is voidable, but not if it is 'void'" and "a good faith purchaser may acquire good title to property if he takes it from one who obtained voidable title by duress but not if he takes it from one who obtained 'void title' by duress." Restatement (Second) of Contracts §174 cmt. b.

¶ 19. The parties agree, in essence, to this basic formulation — that duress can take two forms and that the impact on the validity of the underlying agreement varies depending on which applies. The parties also agree that duress by "physical compulsion" renders an agreement "void." The parties disagree, however, as to precisely what constitutes "physical compulsion." EverBank contends that only where one person physically compels another to give apparent consent, such as by manually forcing the victim to sign a document, is there no true expression of assent such that the purported agreement is void. Anything short of that, EverBank argues, does not prevent the victim from forming actual intent to be bound to the agreement, albeit an intent induced by improper means, although the circumstances of the agreement may create an inequity such that the agreement is later voidable by the victim. To this end, EverBank appears to concede that the civil division's alternative conclusion was correct that, even if the mortgage was not void, it was voidable by Caroline.

¶ 20. Caroline argues that EverBank's formulation of "physical compulsion" is underinclusive. She asserts that in addition to "actual physical compulsion," i.e., manually forcing the victim to sign, the threat of application of immediate physical force sufficient to place a person in the position of the signer in actual, reasonable, and imminent fear of death, serious personal injury, or actual imprisonment, is sufficient to render an agreement void from the start. See United States ex rel. Trane Co. v. Bond, 322 Md. 170, 586 A.2d 734, 740 (1991) (finding in addition to physical force, duress sufficient to render contract void consists of "the threat of application of immediate physical force sufficient to place a person in the position of the signer in actual, reasonable, and imminent fear of death, serious personal injury, or actual imprisonment."). To that end, Caroline suggests that the lethal force inherent in items such as guns, knives, scissors, baseball bats, fireplace pokers, or poison darts are all "sufficient to render the frightened victim 'a mere mechanical instrument'" and thus render a contract void for lack of mutual assent.

¶ 22. . . . The Restatement (Second) of Contracts, chapter 7, topic 2, addresses the concept of "duress and undue influence" and discusses at length the two forms of duress noted above — duress by physical compulsion, which renders an agreement void, see id. §174, and duress by improper threat, which results in an agreement that is voidable by the victim, see id. §§175, 176. The introductory note explains the basic distinction between the two as follows:

> In one, a person physically compels conduct that appears to be a manifestation of assent by a party who has no intention of engaging in that conduct. The result of this type of duress is that the conduct is not effective to create a contract. In the other, a person makes an improper threat that induces a party who has no reasonable alternative to manifesting his assent. The result of this type of duress is that the contract that is created is voidable by the victim. This latter type of duress is in practice the more common and more important.

Id. ch. 7, topic 2, intro. note.

¶ 23. As to duress by physical compulsion, the Restatement provides the general formulation: "If conduct that appears to be a manifestation of assent by a party who does not intend to engage in that conduct is physically compelled by duress, the conduct is not effective as a manifestation of assent." Id. §174. In other words, this section

> involves an application of [the principle that a party's conduct is not effective as a manifestation of the party's assent if the party does not intend to engage in it] to those relatively rare situations in which actual physical force has been used to compel a party to appear to assent to a contract.

Id. cmt. a (emphasis added). "The essence of this type of duress is that a party is compelled by physical force to do an act" that the party has no intention of doing; the party is therefore "a mere mechanical instrument" with the result being that "there is no contract at all, or a 'void contract' as distinguished from a voidable one." Id. The following illustration is provided:

> 1. A presents to B, who is physically weaker than A, a written contract prepared for B's signature and demands that B sign it. B refuses. A grasps B's hand and compels B by physical force to write his name. B's signature is not effective as a manifestation of his assent, and there is no contract.

Id. cmt. a, illus. 1.

¶ 24. As to duress by improper threat, the Restatement provides a two-prong test: "[i]f a party's manifestation of assent is induced by an improper threat by the other party that leaves the victim no reasonable alternative, the contract is voidable by the victim." Id. §175(1). Thus, there must be both an inducement by an "improper threat" and the victim must have no "reasonable alternative" but to succumb. A threat is improper if "what is threatened is a crime or a tort." Id. §176(1)(a); id. cmt. b ("A threat is improper if the threatened act is a crime or a tort, as in the traditional examples of threats of physical violence and of wrongful seizure or retention of goods. Where physical violence is threatened, it need not be to the recipient of the threat, nor even to a person related to him, if the threat in fact induces the recipient to manifest his assent."). Such a threat "may be expressed in words or it may be inferred from words or other conduct. Past events often import a threat." Id. §175 cmt. a. Improper threats do not constitute duress, however, "if the victim has a reasonable alternative to succumbing and fails to take advantage of it." Id. cmt. b. This standard does not require that "the threat must arouse such fear as precludes a party from exercising free will and judgment or that it must be such as would induce assent on the part of a brave man or a man of ordinary firmness"; rather, "[t]he rule stated in this Section omits any such requirement because of its vagueness and impracticability" and "[i]t is enough if the threat actually induces assent on the part of one who has no reasonable alternative." Id. "The standard is a practical one under which account must be taken of the exigencies in which the victim finds himself." Id. The Restatement provides the following relevant illustrations:

> 1. A is a good faith purchaser for value of a valuable painting stolen from B. When B demands the return of the painting, A threatens to poison B unless he releases all rights to the painting for $1,000. B, having no reasonable alternative, is induced by A's threat to sign the release, and A pays him $1,000. The threatened act is both a crime and a tort, and the release is voidable by B.
> 2. A threatens B that he will kill C, an employee of B, unless B makes a contract to sell A a tract of land that B owns. B, having no reasonable alternative, is induced by A's threat to make the contract. The threatened act is both a crime and a tort, and the contract is voidable by B.

Id. §176 cmt. b, illus. 1, 2.

¶ 25. In sum, under the Restatement, the fundamental distinction between the two varieties of improper conduct hinges on whether an actual manifestation of assent to enter a binding agreement existed at the time the victim signed or entered the agreement. Both varieties recognize that the manifestation of assent is flawed, but in the "voidable" context, the assent itself is compelled by circumstances that remove any reasonable alternative; in the "void" situation, there is but a shell of a manifestation of assent to enter an agreement as the victim was the conduit through which the hand of the wrongdoer acted. We generally agree with these distinctions and this approach. . . . Thus, in general, where one party is but a conduit through which an individual physically compels a victim to appear to manifest assent, one of the fundamental pillars of contract formation is fatally flawed and the agreement is void. On the other hand, where a party's manifestation of assent is unwillingly made but is induced by improper means without the victim having a reasonable means of avoidance, the agreement is subsequently voidable by the victim.

¶ 26. But this does not end our inquiry as it does not address whether the meaning of "physical compulsion" encompasses the sort of conduct Caroline argues that it should. As is clear from the above, the Restatement draws a seemingly clear line between a person manually manipulating a victim to appear to endorse an agreement and a person cajoling a victim through tortious or criminal behavior to actually endorse the same. What the Restatement does not explicitly address is the sort of immediately present lethal tortious or criminal behavior that Caroline argues effectively creates the same result as a situation involving the manual manipulation of a victim's hand. That is, according to Caroline, there is no meaningful distinction between a person with a gun to her head or a knife to her throat and a person of weaker physical ability who has her hand physically manipulated by a stronger person. To the extent that the Restatement does address this sort of potentially lethal conduct, it appears to consider it within the realm of conduct that would render an agreement voidable, but not void. See Restatement (Second) of Contracts §176 cmt. b, illus. 2.

¶ 27. . . . Other commentators have noted that situations involving the immediate application of lethal force, such as the proverbial gun to the head, have no meaningful distinction from a situation where a stronger individual grabs a victim's hand and physically compels the victim to appear to manifest assent. As is explained in Williston on Contracts, in discussing the sort of improper behavior that would render a contract void under the Restatement (Second) of Contracts:

> A similar outcome should occur where the physical force or compulsion is somewhat more remote, though no less compelling, as where the victim is forced to sign a document reflecting a bargain at gunpoint; here, too, although the act appears to be that of the victim, it is no more voluntary or intentional than where the coercing party actually manipulates the victim's arm.

28 Williston on Contracts, supra, §71:1. We agree with this reasoning. Thus, we conclude that in addition to "actual physical compulsion" as discussed in the Restatement, i.e., grabbing the hand of the victim and forcing the victim to appear to manifest assent, a contract may also be held void where "a threat of imminent physical violence is exerted upon the victim of such magnitude as to cause a reasonable person, in the circumstances, to fear loss of life, or serious physical injury . . . for refusal to sign the document." Trane, 586 A.2d at 740.

¶ 28. We therefore conclude that under Vermont law improper conduct sufficient to render a contract void, as opposed to voidable, consists of the actual application of physical force that is sufficient to, and does, cause a victim to appear to assent to the execution of a document, as well as the threat of immediate application of physical force sufficient to place a person in the position of the signer in actual, reasonable, and imminent fear of death or serious personal injury. In the absence of the application of physical force, it is the immediacy of the threat of the application of the significant physical force which leaves the signer with no reasonable choice except to sign the document. We recognize, of course, that there is an overlap between what the Restatement deems to be conduct rendering an agreement voidable and conduct that we hold today renders a contract void. "Necessarily, the determination of duress is dependent upon the circumstances of each individual case," id., and we have no doubt that our courts are capable of distinguishing between the varieties of improper conduct.

¶ 29. In this case, the undisputed facts before the trial court on the parties' cross-motions for summary judgment reveal that, leading up to Caroline's signing of the mortgage, Gary and Caroline's financial situation had been tenuous, and it was taking a tremendous toll on them individually and as a couple. Gary had made repeated attempts at securing a loan, mostly arranged without Caroline's involvement or knowledge, and Caroline, upon discovery, had routinely thwarted his attempts by, for example, contacting would-be lenders directly to get them to stop the loans and by telling the notary from LendingTree not to come. Gary had also threatened to mortgage the family home "whether [Caroline] liked it or not," and regardless of whether she agreed. Finally, on the evening prior to Caroline signing the mortgage paperwork, and after Caroline had again intervened to stop Gary's attempt at securing a loan, Gary had brought Caroline and their two children into the kitchen and made them sit at the kitchen table while he berated Caroline, repeatedly stating that she was not a competent adult, that the children were no longer to consider her an adult, and that he was going to divorce her. He then removed a pair of large scissors from the knife drawer and waved them back and forth while repeating that Caroline was incompetent. This scared Caroline and, in an attempt to protect her children, she told Gary that she would sign the mortgage documents if he would leave the children alone, which she did the following day in front of a notary public.

¶ 30. Even under this expanded definition of "physical compulsion," the mortgage is not void as to Caroline as a matter of law. Nothing in the record indicates, nor does Caroline argue, that Gary overpowered Caroline and manually manipulated her hand to appear to assent. Nor does the record reveal any evidence of a threat of imminent physical violence upon Caroline such that she reasonably feared loss of life or serious physical injury at the time she signed the document, which was the day following the incident with the scissors. Although the facts present a tense situation the night prior to Caroline signing, Gary's conduct in waving the scissors and threatening to divorce Caroline if she would not sign, while obviously threatening and dangerous to some degree at the time of the conduct, was removed in time and context from Caroline's signing of the mortgage paperwork itself the next day in front of an independent person. Accordingly, the civil division erred in concluding that the undisputed material facts compelled the conclusion that the mortgage was void as a matter of law as to Caroline. We therefore reverse the trial court's decision that the mortgage was void.

¶ 31. Although EverBank appears to accept that the record establishes that Gary's conduct around the time Caroline signed the mortgage renders the mortgage voidable, and thus argues that the civil division erred in its ratification analysis, our review of the record leads us to a different conclusion. For summary judgment purposes, the record is insufficient to compel a conclusion as a matter of law that the mortgage was voidable by Caroline for improper threat. As noted above, to constitute improper conduct such that an agreement can be held voidable, there must be both an inducement by an "improper threat" and the victim must have no "reasonable alternative" but to succumb. In this case, even though Gary's scissor waving the night prior to Caroline signing the mortgage constitutes an improper threat as contemplated by the Restatement, see Restatement (Second) of Contracts §176 (defining "when a threat is improper"), the record is devoid of any evidence that Caroline was without a reasonable alternative but to succumb. In this case, the improper threat occurred the night before Caroline actually signed her name to the mortgage document, and there is no indication in the record at all that the threat was so persistent that it continued through that time nor is there any indication at all that Caroline was without ability to exfiltrate herself from Gary's control. Construing the record in favor of EverBank as we must, . . . we cannot conclude that the undisputed facts establish as a matter of law that Caroline was subjected to an improper threat for which she had no reasonable alternative but to succumb. We therefore remand the matter of whether the mortgage is voidable to the trial court. . . .

NOTE AND QUESTION

Everbank highlights the distinction between contracts that are *void* (meaning that they never actually came into existence) and merely *voidable* (meaning that they exist until the victim takes steps to disaffirm them). This dichotomy matters because a victim cannot be bound by a void contract, but can lose her power to back out of a voidable contract. Indeed, under Restatement (Second) of Contracts §380, "[t]he power of a party to avoid a contract is lost if, after the circumstances that made the contract voidable have ceased to exist, he manifests to the other party his intention to affirm it or acts with respect to anything that he has received in a manner inconsistent with disaffirmance." Even if the trial court on remand finds the loan voidable, can you see why EverBank might be able to argue that Carolyn ratified the agreement? Did she accept the loan proceeds? Did she make any monthly payments?

Problem 120

Herbert was charged with kidnapping. After being advised by his attorney and the prosecutor that there was a possibility of a death penalty, Herbert pleaded guilty and received a sentence of 50 years. Herbert decided to challenge his plea as being voidable because of duress. Is it? Would your answer change if after he pleads guilty the statute prescribing the death penalty for kidnapping is declared unconstitutional? See Brady v. United States, 397 U.S. 742 (1970). Is a plea enforceable if the defendant pleads guilty so that his or her spouse will not be prosecuted? Compare Kent v. United States, 272 F.2d 795 (1st Cir. 1959) ("[i]f a defendant elects to sacrifice himself for such motives, that is his choice") with Crow v. United States, 397 F.2d 284 (10th Cir. 1968) (threat to a third person may show sufficient duress to rescind plea bargain); see also Cicchini, Broken Government Promises: A Contract-Based Approach to Enforcing Plea Bargain Agreements, 38 N.M. L. Rev. 159 (2008).

V. UNDUE INFLUENCE

Courts sometimes state that "where great weakness of mind concurs with gross inadequacy of consideration, or circumstances of suspicion, the transaction will be presumed to have been brought about by undue influence." Ayers v. Shaffer, 286 Va. 212, 748 S.E.2d 83 (2013). The next famous case elaborates on that idea.

ODORIZZI v. BLOOMFIELD SCHOOL DISTRICT
California District Court of Appeal, 1964
246 Cal. App. 2d 123, 54 Cal. Rptr. 533

FLEMING, J. Appeal from a judgment dismissing plaintiff's amended complaint on demurrer.

Plaintiff Donald Odorizzi was employed during 1964 as an elementary school teacher by defendant Bloomfield School District and was under contract with the District to continue to teach school the following year as a permanent employee. On June 10 he was arrested on criminal charges of homosexual activity, and on June 11 he signed and delivered to his superiors his written resignation as a teacher, a resignation which the District accepted on June 13. In July the criminal charges against Odorizzi were dismissed under Penal Code, section 995, and in September he sought to resume his employment with the District. On the District's refusal to reinstate him he filed suit for declaratory and other relief.

Odorizzi's amended complaint asserts his resignation was invalid because obtained through duress, fraud, mistake, and undue influence and given at a time when he lacked capacity to make a valid contract. Specifically, Odorizzi declares he was under such severe mental and emotional strain at the time he signed his resignation, having just completed the process of arrest, questioning by the police, booking, and release on bail, and having gone for forty hours without sleep, that he was incapable of rational thought or action. While he was in this condition and unable to think clearly, the superintendent of the District and the principal of his school came to his apartment. They said they were trying to help him and had his best interests at heart, that he should take their advice and immediately resign his position with the District, that there was no time to consult an attorney, that if he did not resign immediately the District would suspend and dismiss him from his position and publicize the proceedings, his "aforedescribed arrest" and cause him "to suffer extreme embarrassment and humiliation"; but that if he resigned at once the incident would not be publicized and would not jeopardize his chances of securing employment as a teacher elsewhere. Odorizzi pleads that because of his faith and confidence in their representations they were able to substitute their will and judgment in place of his own and thus obtain his signature to his purported resignation. A demurrer to his amended complaint was sustained without leave to amend. . . . In our view the facts in the amended complaint are insufficient to state a cause of action for duress, menace, fraud, or mistake, but they do set out sufficient elements to justify rescission of a consent because of undue influence. We summarize our conclusions on each of these points.

1. No duress or menace has been pleaded. Duress consists in unlawful confinement of another's person, or relatives, or property, which causes him to consent to a transaction through fear. (Civ. Code, §1569.) Duress is often used interchangeably with menace (Leeper v. Beltrami, 53 Cal. 2d 195, 203, 1 Cal. Rptr. 12, 347 P.2d 12, 77 A.L.R.2d 803), but in California menace is technically a threat of duress or a threat of injury to the person, property, or character of another. (Civ. Code, §1570; Restatement, Contracts, §§492, 493.) We agree with respondent's contention that neither duress nor menace was involved in this case, because the action or threat in duress or menace must be unlawful, and a threat to take legal action is not unlawful unless the party making the threat knows the falsity of his claim. (Leeper v. Beltrami, 53 Cal. 2d 195, 204, 1 Cal. Rptr. 12, 347 P.2d 12, 77 A.L.R.2d 803.) The amended complaint shows in substance that the school representatives announced their intention to initiate suspension and dismissal proceedings under Education Code, sections 13403, 13408 et seq. at a time when the filing of such proceedings was not only their legal right but their positive duty as school officials. (Ed. Code, §13409; Board of Education, etc. v. Weiland, 179 Cal. App. 2d 808, 4 Cal. Rptr. 286.) Although the filing of such

proceedings might be extremely damaging to plaintiff's reputation, the injury would remain incidental so long as the school officials acted in good faith in the performance of their duties. (Schumm by Whymer v. Berg, 37 Cal. 2d 174, 185-186, 231 P.2d 39, 21 A.L.R.2d 1051.) Neither duress nor menace was present as a ground for rescission.

No Fraud

2. Nor do we find a cause of action for fraud, either actual or constructive. (Civ. Code, §§1571 to 1574.) Actual fraud involves conscious misrepresentation, or concealment, or nondisclosure of a material fact which induces the innocent party to enter the contract. (Civ. Code, §1572; Pearson v. Norton, 230 Cal. App. 2d 1, 7, 40 Cal. Rptr. 634; Restatement, Contracts, §471.) A complaint for fraud must plead misrepresentation, knowledge of falsity, intent to induce reliance, justifiable reliance, and resulting damage. (Sixta v. Ochsner, 187 Cal. App. 2d 485, 489, 9 Cal. Rptr. 617; Zinn v. Ex-Cell-O Corp., 148 Cal. App. 2d 56, 68, 306 P.2d 1017.) While the amended complaint charged misrepresentation, it failed to assert the elements of knowledge of falsity, intent to induce reliance, and justifiable reliance. A cause of action for actual fraud was therefore not stated. (Norkin v. United States Fire Ins. Co., 237 Cal. App. 2d 435, 47 Cal. Rptr. 15.)

No Constructive Fraud

Constructive fraud arises on a breach of duty by one in a confidential or fiduciary relationship to another which induces justifiable reliance by the latter to his prejudice. (Civ. Code, §1573.) Plaintiff has attempted to bring himself within this category, for the amended complaint asserts the existence of a confidential relationship between the school superintendent and principal as agents of the defendant, and the plaintiff. Such a confidential relationship may exist whenever a person with justification places trust and confidence in the integrity and fidelity of another. [Citations omitted.] Plaintiff, however, sets forth no facts to support his conclusion of a confidential relationship between the representatives of the school district and himself, other than that the parties bore the relationship of employer and employee to each other. Under prevailing judicial opinion no presumption of a confidential relationship arises from the bare fact that parties to a contract are employer and employee; rather, additional ties must be brought out in order to create the presumption of a confidential relationship between the two. (Anno., 100 A.L.R. 875.) The absence of a confidential relationship between employer and employee is especially apparent where, as here, the parties were negotiating to bring about a termination of their relationship. In such a situation each party is expected to look after his own interests, and a lack of confidentiality is implicit in the subject matter of their dealings. We think the allegations of constructive fraud were inadequate.

No Mistake

3. As to mistake, the amended complaint fails to disclose any facts which would suggest that consent had been obtained through a mistake of fact or of law. The material facts of the transaction were known to both parties. Neither party was laboring under any misapprehension of law of which the other took advantage. The discussion between plaintiff and the school district representatives   principally   attempted   to   evaluate   the   probable

consequences of plaintiff's predicament and to predict the future course of events. The fact that their speculations did not forecast the exact pattern which events subsequently took does not provide the basis for a claim that they were acting under some sort of mistake. The doctrine of mistake customarily involves such errors as the nature of the transaction, the identity of the parties, the identity of the things to which the contract relates, or the occurrence of collateral happenings. (Restatement, Contracts, §502, comment e.) Errors of this nature were not present in the case at bench.

4. However, the pleading does set out a claim that plaintiff's consent to the transaction had been obtained through the use of undue influence. . . . Undue influence, in the sense we are concerned with here, is a shorthand legal phrase used to describe persuasion which tends to be coercive in nature, persuasion which overcomes the will without convincing the judgment. (Estate of Ricks, 160 Cal. 467, 480-482, 117 P. 539.) The hallmark of such persuasion is high pressure, a pressure which works on mental, moral, or emotional weakness to such an extent that it approaches the boundaries of coercion. In this sense, undue influence has been called overpersuasion. (Kelly v. McCarthy, 6 Cal. 2d 347, 364, 57 P.2d 118.) Misrepresentations of law or fact are not essential to the charge, for a person's will may be overborne without misrepresentation. By statutory definition undue influence includes "taking an unfair advantage of another's weakness of mind; or . . . taking a grossly oppressive and unfair advantage of another's necessities or distress." (Civ. Code, §1575.) While most reported cases on undue influence involve persons who bear a confidential relationship to one another, a confidential or authoritative relationship between the parties need not be present when the undue influence involves unfair advantage taken of another's weakness or distress. [Citations omitted.] We paraphrase the summary of undue influence given the jury by Sir James P. Wilde in Hall v. Hall, L.R. 1, P&D 481, 482 (1868): To make a good contract a man must be a free agent. Pressure of whatever sort which overpowers the will without convincing the judgment is a species of restraint under which no valid contract can be made. Importunity or threats, if carried to the degree in which the free play of a man's will is overborne, constitute undue influence, although no force is used or threatened. A party may be led but not driven, and his acts must be the offspring of his own volition and not the record of someone else's.

In essence undue influence involves the use of excessive pressure to persuade one vulnerable to such pressure, pressure applied by a dominant subject to a servient object. In combination, the elements of undue susceptibility in the servient person and excessive pressure by the dominating person make the latter's influence undue, for it results in the apparent will of the servient person being in fact the will of the dominant person.

Undue susceptibility may consist of total weakness of mind which leaves a person entirely without understanding (Civ. Code, §38); or, a lesser weakness which destroys the capacity of a person to make a contract even though he is not totally incapacitated (Civ. Code, §39; Peterson v. Ellebrecht, 205

First
Element

lesser Weakness

Second Element

unfair Advantage

Cal. App. 2d 718, 721-722, 23 Cal. Rptr. 349); or, the first element in our equation, a still lesser weakness which provides sufficient grounds to rescind a contract for undue influence. [Citations omitted.] Such lesser weakness need not be long-lasting nor wholly incapacitating, but may be merely a lack of full vigor due to age [citations omitted], physical condition (Weger v. Rocha, 138 Cal. App. 109, 114-115, 32 P.2d 417), emotional anguish (Moore v. Moore, 56 Cal. 89, 93; 81 Cal. 195, 197-198, 22 P. 589, 874), or a combination of such factors. The reported cases have usually involved elderly, sick, senile persons alleged to have executed wills or deeds under pressure. (Malone v. Malone, 155 Cal. App. 2d 161, 317 P.2d 65 (constant importuning of a senile husband); Stewart v. Marvin, 139 Cal. App. 2d 769, 294 P.2d 114 (persistent nagging of elderly spouse).) In some of its aspects this lesser weakness could perhaps be called weakness of spirit. But whatever name we give it, this first element of undue influence resolves itself into a lessened capacity of the object to make a free contract.

In the present case plaintiff has pleaded that such weakness at the time he signed his resignation prevented him from freely and competently applying his judgment to the problem before him. Plaintiff declares he was under severe mental and emotional strain at the time because he had just completed the process of arrest, questioning, booking, and release on bail and had been without sleep for forty hours. It is possible that exhaustion and emotional turmoil may wholly incapacitate a person from exercising his judgment. As an abstract question of pleading, plaintiff has pleaded that possibility and sufficient allegations to state a case for rescission.

Undue influence in its second aspect involves an application of excessive strength by a dominant subject against a servient object. Judicial consideration of this second element in undue influence has been relatively rare, for there are few cases denying persons who persuade but do not misrepresent the benefit of their bargain. Yet logically, the same legal consequences should apply to the results of excessive strength as to the results of undue weakness. Whether from weakness on one side, or strength on the other, or a combination of the two, undue influence occurs whenever there results "that kind of influence or supremacy of one mind over another by which that other is prevented from acting according to his own wish or judgment, and whereby the will of the person is overborne and he is induced to do or forbear to do an act which he would not do, or would do, if left to act freely." (Webb v. Saunders, 79 Cal. App. 2d 863, 871, 181 P.2d 43, 47.) Undue influence involves a type of mismatch which our statute calls unfair advantage. (Civ. Code, §1575.) Whether a person of subnormal capacities has been subjected to ordinary force or a person of normal capacities subjected to extraordinary force, the match is equally out of balance. If will has been overcome against judgment, consent may be rescinded.

The difficulty, of course, lies in determining when the forces of persuasion have overflowed their normal banks and become oppressive flood waters. There are second thoughts to every bargain, and hindsight is still better than foresight. Undue influence cannot be used as a pretext to avoid bad bargains or escape from bargains which refuse to come up to expectations. A woman who buys a dress on impulse, which on critical inspection by her best friend turns out to be less fashionable than she had thought, is not legally entitled to set aside the sale on the ground that the saleswoman used all her wiles to close the sale. A man who buys a tract of desert land in the expectation that it is in the immediate path of the city's growth and will become another Palm Springs, an expectation cultivated in glowing terms by the seller, cannot rescind his bargain when things turn out differently. If we are temporarily persuaded against our better judgment to do something about which we later have second thoughts, we must abide the consequences of the risks inherent in managing our own affairs. (Estate of Anderson, 185 Cal. 700, 706-707, 198 P. 407.) However, overpersuasion is generally accompanied by certain characteristics which tend to create a pattern. The pattern usually involves several of the following elements: (1) discussion of the transaction at an unusual or inappropriate time, (2) consummation of the transaction in an unusual place, (3) insistent demand that the business be finished at once, (4) extreme emphasis on untoward consequences of delay, (5) the use of multiple persuaders by the dominant side against a single servient party, (6) absence of third-party advisers to the servient party, (7) statements that there is no time to consult financial advisers or attorneys. If a number of these elements are simultaneously present, the persuasion may be characterized as excessive. The cases are illustrative: Moore v. Moore, 56 Cal. 89, 93, and 81 Cal. 195, 22 P. 589, 874. The pregnant wife of a man who had been shot to death on October 30 and buried on November 1 was approached by four members of her husband's family on November 2 or 3 and persuaded to deed her entire interest in her husband's estate to his children by a prior marriage. In finding the use of undue influence on Mrs. Moore, the court commented:

[handwritten margin note: Characteristics to show overpersuasion]

> It was the second day after her late husband's funeral. It was at a time when she would naturally feel averse to transacting any business, and she might reasonably presume that her late husband's brothers would not apply to her at such a time to transact any important business, unless it was of a nature that would admit of no delay. And as it would admit of delay, the only reason which we can discover for their unseemly haste is, that they thought that she would be more likely to comply with their wishes then than at some future time, after she had recovered from the shock which she had then so recently experienced. If for that reason they selected that time for the accomplishment of their purpose, it seems to us that they not only took, but that they designed to take, an unfair advantage of her weakness of mind. If they did not, they probably can explain why they selected that inappropriate time for the transaction of business which might have been delayed for weeks without injury to anyone. In the absence of any explanation, it appears to us that the time was selected with reference to just that condition of mind which she alleges that she was then in.

Taking an unfair advantage of another's weakness of mind is undue influence, and the law will not permit the retention of an advantage thus obtained. (Civ. Code, §1575.)

Weger v. Rocha, 138 Cal. App. 109, 32 P.2d 417. Plaintiff, while confined in a cast in a hospital, gave a release of claims for personal injuries for a relatively small sum to an agent who spent two hours persuading her to sign. At the time of signing plaintiff was in a highly nervous and hysterical condition and suffering much pain, and she signed the release in order to terminate the interview. The court held that the release had been secured by the use of undue influence. Fyan v. McNutt, 266 Mich. 406, 254 N.W. 146 (1934). At issue was the validity of an agreement by Mrs. McNutt to pay Fyan, a real estate broker, a five-percent commission on all moneys received from the condemnation of Mrs. McNutt's land. Earlier, Fyan had secured an option from Mrs. McNutt to purchase her land for his own account and offer it for sale as part of a larger parcel to Wayne County for an airport site. On July 25 Fyan learned from the newspapers that the county would probably start condemnation proceedings rather than obtain an airport site by purchase. Fyan, with four others, arrived at Mrs. McNutt's house at 1 A.M. on July 26 with the commission agreement he wanted her to sign. Mrs. McNutt protested being awakened at that hour and was reluctant to sign, but Fyan told her he had to have the paper in Detroit by morning, that the whole airport proposition would fall through if she did not sign then and there, that there wasn't time to wait until morning to get outside advice. In holding the agreement invalid the Michigan Supreme Court said:

> The late hour of the night at which her signature was secured over her protest and plea that she be given until the next day to consider her action, the urge of the moment, the cooperation of the others present in their desire to obtain a good price for their farm lands, the plaintiff's anxiety over the seeming weakness of his original option, all combined to produce a situation in which, to say the least, it is doubtful that the defendant had an opportunity to exercise her own free will. . . . A valid contract can be entered into only when there is a meeting of the minds of the parties under circumstances conducive to a free and voluntary execution of the agreement contemplated. It must be conceived in good faith and come into existence under circumstances that do not deprive the parties of the exercise of their own free will.

The difference between legitimate persuasion and excessive pressure, like the difference between seduction and rape, rests to a considerable extent in the manner in which the parties go about their business. For example, if a day or two after Odorizzi's release on bail the superintendent of the school district had called him into his office during business hours and directed his attention to those provisions of the Education Code compelling his leave of absence and authorizing his suspension on the filing of written charges, had told him that the District contemplated filing written charges against him, had pointed out the alternative of resignation available to him, had informed him he was free to consult counsel or any adviser he wished and to consider the matter overnight and return with his decision the next day, it is extremely unlikely that any complaint about the use of excessive pressure could ever have been made against the school district.

But, according to the allegations of the complaint, this is not the way it happened, and if it had happened that way, plaintiff would never have resigned. Rather, the representatives of the school board undertook to achieve their objective by overpersuasion and imposition to secure plaintiff's signature but not his consent to his resignation through a high-pressure carrot-and-stick technique — under which they assured plaintiff they were trying to assist him, he should rely on their advice, there wasn't time to consult an attorney, if he didn't resign at once the school district would suspend and dismiss him from his position and publicize the proceedings, but if he did resign the incident wouldn't jeopardize his chances of securing a teaching post elsewhere.

Plaintiff has thus pleaded both subjective and objective elements entering the undue influence equation and stated sufficient facts to put in issue the question whether his free will had been overborne by defendant's agents at a time when he was unable to function in a normal manner. It was sufficient to pose "... the ultimate question ... whether a free and competent judgment was merely influenced, or whether a mind was so dominated as to prevent the exercise of an independent judgment." (Williston on Contracts, §1625 [rev. ed.]; Restatement, Contracts, §497, comment c.) The question cannot be resolved by an analysis of pleading but requires a finding of fact.

We express no opinion on the merits of plaintiff's case, or the propriety of his continuing to teach school (Ed. Code, §13403), or the timeliness of his rescission (Civ. Code, §1691). We do hold that his pleading, liberally construed, states a cause of action for rescission of a transaction to which his apparent consent had been obtained through the use of undue influence. *Holding*

The judgment is reversed. *Reversed*

Problem 121

As he was backing out of his driveway on the way to his law office, Sam Ambulance ran over his next-door neighbor, Ruth Garden. Horrified, he called for help and went with her to the hospital. To his relief the doctor told him that it looked like she had nothing more than a broken arm and minor cuts. That evening, after she had had her supper in her hospital bed, Sam came by with flowers. He also brought with him a release from liability that he asked her to sign. The release provided that he would pay all of her current hospital bills plus $1,000, in return for which she agreed to forgo suing him for "all injuries, known or unknown, arising from this unfortunate incident." She said that she would like to talk to a lawyer, to which he replied that *he* was a lawyer, and it was the usual release. She sighed and confessed that she was feeling all right and did want to settle this now. Sam gave her a pen and she signed. The next day she went home and a week later collapsed in her garden while working. She proved to have severe brain damage, and two operations were necessary. When Sam refused to pay these new hospital bills, she brought suit. What arguments will the parties make? How should this come out?

- undue Influence
- Excessive pressure
- mutual mistake
- Fraud

VI. ILLEGALITY

The word *illegal* in contract law means more than simply criminal, although it certainly includes criminal contracts (contracts to commit murder, for example). But illegal in a contractual setting means that the contract or clause involved is void as a matter of *public policy,* whether or not technically criminal. Thus agreements to commit a tort, prenuptial contracts wherein one fiancé promises not to seek support from the other, or contractual clauses that are so harsh as to take unfair advantage of the weaker party, may all be declared illegal in a contracts suit. This argument, all too often forgotten by attorneys, may be a powerful theory.

A. The Effect of Illegality

BENNETT v. HAYES
California Court of Appeal, 1975
53 Cal. App. 3d 700, 125 Cal. Rptr. 825

Upon certification by the superior court, we ordered transfer of the appeal in this case, pursuant to section 911 of the Code of Civil Procedure, in order to settle an important question of law, to wit, whether an automobile repair dealer's failure to give his customer a written estimate prior to repair of the customer's automobile, as required by section 9884.9 subdivision (a), of the Business and Professions Code, bars any recovery for work performed. With certain additions and modifications, we have adopted the excellent opinion of the appellate department of the superior court, as follows:

Issue

> Plaintiff appeals from a judgment for defendant on an action for breach of a written contract and for recovery of an agreed price, entered February 28, 1975 in the Municipal Court. . . .

On August 24, 1973, defendant-respondent brought his 1964 Jaguar sedan to The European Stable, plaintiff-appellant's foreign car repair shop in Menlo Park, California. In the course of an oral discussion, respondent agreed to pay appellant $70.00 for the repair of one front brake, $100.00 for a radio and $17.00 for lubrication. Although specific sums were mentioned, appellant was unsure of the exact price of all the parts involved. Appellant failed to give respondent a written estimate for this work.

[handwritten margin note: *Exact price was never determined*]

On September 28, 1973, after appellant had telephoned respondent to say that he had completed the repairs, respondent traveled from his home in San Luis Obispo to Menlo Park to pick up the car. When he arrived, appellant told him the car was inoperable because the rear brakes were in need of repair. When asked to restore the car to its original state, appellant indicated this could not be done without additional cost. Having no other viable alternative, respondent then verbally authorized appellant to repair and replace the rear brakes for $200.00 and returned to his home in San Luis Obispo.

Respondent did not receive or sign a detailed written description of the work to be performed on his car until it was later delivered to him in San Luis Obispo, where he was billed for $500.00.

The issue is whether under Business and Professions Code §9884.9 [handwritten margin note: *issue*] appellant's failure to give respondent a written estimate prior to repairing respondent's car bars any recovery for the work performed.

Business and Professions Code §9884.9(a) at the time of the instant transaction provided in part as follows:

> The automotive repair dealer shall give to the customer a written estimated price for labor and parts necessary for a specific job and shall not charge for work done or parts supplied in excess of the estimated price without the oral or written consent of the customer which shall be obtained at some time after it is determined that the estimated price is insufficient and before the work not estimated is done or the parts not estimated are supplied. Nothing in this section shall be construed as requiring an automotive repair dealer to give a written estimated price if the dealer does not agree to perform the requested repair.

It is clear from §9884.9 in August, 1973 and as since amended that if work is done in excess of the written estimate without the consent of the customer, the repairman may not charge for the additional work.[1]

---

1. Section 9884.9, subdivision (a), of the Business and Professions Code, presently reads as follows:

> The automotive repair dealer shall give to the customer a written estimated price for labor and parts necessary for a specific job. No work shall be done and no charges shall accrue before authorization to proceed is obtained from the customer. No charge shall be made for work done or parts supplied in excess of the estimated price without the oral or written consent of the customer which shall be obtained at some time after it is determined that the estimated price is insufficient and before the work not estimated is done or the parts not estimated are supplied. Nothing in this section shall be construed as requiring an automotive repair dealer to give a written estimated price if the dealer does not agree to perform the requested repair.

The Automotive Repair Act became law in 1971 and as yet there are no appellate decisions interpreting the applicable provisions. The Attorney General has stated that "the purposes of the Act are to foster fair dealing (and) to eliminate misunderstandings." 55 Opinions of the Attorney General 278 (1972).

Appellant argues that the Automotive Repair Act sufficiently protects consumers by vesting in the Director of the Bureau of Automotive Repair the discretion to suspend or revoke the licenses of non-complying repairmen. The trial court concluded that allowing appellant to recover despite his failure to provide a written estimate would circumvent the purposes of the Act.

City Lincoln-Mercury Co. v. Lindsey, 52 C[al.] 2d 267[, 339 P.2d 851] (1959), involved a similar consumer protection statute. The underlying facts are as follows: The defendant purchased a new Lincoln on a conditional sales contract from the plaintiff's company. At the time the defendant signed the sales order, the time price differential and the contract balance were not filled in as required by Subdivision (a) of Section 2982 of the Civil Code. After making two installment payments, the defendant returned the automobile to the seller who in turn resold it and brought an action against the defendant for the deficiency. The defendant answered contending that the contract was illegal and unenforceable.

The court held that,

> The provisions of section 2982(a) . . . is for the protection of the purchaser; a violation of the subdivision in this respect makes the contract unenforceable by the seller.

In the case at bar appellant gave respondent no written estimate and no precise oral estimate of the costs or extent of the repairs to be performed. . . . This violation of B&P Code §9884.9 rendered the contract unenforceable by this appellant-dealer.

While recognizing the factor of unjust enrichment, the primary purpose of the rule of unenforceability is the discouragement of practices forbidden by law. Because appellant could have easily complied with B&P Code §9884.9, no reason exists for declining to apply this rule in this case.

Appellant argues he is entitled to quantum meruit equitable relief. However, he failed to advance this theory in his pleadings and offered no evidence at trial as to the reasonable value of his services. This precludes such relief on appeal.

Even if appellant had presented this issue properly on appeal, he would be denied relief. Tiedje v. Aluminum Taper Milling Co., 46 C[al.] 2d 450[, 296 P.2d 554] (1955), states the general rule that "the guilty party to an illegal contract cannot bring an action to enforce the contract or to recover on principles of quasi contract the benefits he has conferred under it." See also Fong v. Miller, 105 C[al.] A[pp.] 2d 411[, 233 P.2d 606] (1951).

Appellant auto repair dealer has violated B&P Code §9884.9 enacted for the protection of respondent, his customer.

This violation renders the repair contract unenforceable at law. Equitable relief is granted in such cases only under narrowly drawn exceptions to the general rule designed to discourage such violations by refusing relief. Appellant does not fall within these exceptions. *[handwritten: Contract is unenforceable]*

The judgment of the municipal court is affirmed. *[handwritten: Affirmed]*

QUESTION AND NOTE

1. Guilty parties to an illegal contract (those *in pari delicto*—of "equal fault") are literally "outlaws"—outside the protection of the law. The law leaves such guilty parties where it finds them, and, as the preceding case holds, will not even grant them quasi-contractual relief.

In Superior Vending, Inc. v. Dick's Bar of Hudson, Inc., 2010 WL 4386663 (W.D. Wis. 2010), the parties to a contract to sell and maintain poker machines in violation of Wisconsin law were denied any relief by the court, which left the parties "just as it found them." The opening paragraph of the decision says:

> Victor Hugo writes that in 15th Century Paris, rogues who lived on the wrong side of the law judged each other by their own strict rules in the Court of Miracles. That may have been a better venue for this lawsuit than federal court, because plaintiff seeks to enforce a contract that countenances illegal payouts from video poker machines. Superior Vending, Inc. believes that it has been double-crossed by Dick's Bar and Grill; this appears to be true but it is irrelevant, at least in this court: as Dick's Bar unabashedly proclaims, its contract with Superior is unenforceable because it is essentially an agreement to split unlawfully obtained money. . . .

The court had little sympathy for arguments such as one made by the plaintiff that voiding the contract would encourage parties to similar poker machine contracts all over Wisconsin to simply walk away from them. To this the court replied, "Those who enter a contract for illegal activity do so at their own risk and likely have extralegal means for enforcing those agreements."

Innocent parties caught up in an illegal contract, or those whose fault is much less than the other, can sometimes get relief either on the contract (by severing the illegal portion) or at least the amount of unjust enrichment that would otherwise obtain if the contract is voided. See Maudlin v. Pacific Decision Sciences Corp., 137 Cal. App. 4th 1001, 40 Cal. Rptr. 3d 724 (2006). Given these rules, if the defendant in Bennett v. Hayes had paid the $500, could *he* get it back? *[handwritten: Innocent Parties]*

Courts can sever the illegal portion of the contract and enforce the legal parts

2. *Severability.* If contracted services are already performed and some of the services are legal, a court may determine the relative value of the lawful services and enforce it, while severing the illegal portion; see Marathon Entertainment, Inc. v. Blasi, 42 Cal. 4th 974, 70 Cal. Rptr. 3d 727, 174 P.3d 741 (2008).

CARNES v. SHELDON
Michigan Court of Appeals, 1981
109 Mich. App. 204, 311 N.W.2d 747

RILEY, J. Plaintiff, Bonnie Lee Carnes, appeals as of right from a judgment rendered by a Wayne County Circuit Court judge denying her request for an equitable division of property held by defendant, Charles D. Sheldon, and denying her request for the custody of defendant's minor child, Mary Ellen Sheldon.

Prior to 1967, defendant was married to Constance Sheldon (now Constance Ward). Of this marriage four children were born, one of whom is Mary Ellen, the subject of the present custody dispute. Constance left defendant in 1967 and did not take the children with her. Shortly thereafter, defendant became acquainted with plaintiff, who was also separated from her husband, and who was the mother of three children. In May, 1967, plaintiff and two of her children moved into defendant's house with defendant and his children. The move was prompted by plaintiff's need for a place to live and defendant's need for someone to care for his children. In 1968, defendant obtained a divorce from his wife and was granted custody of all four children.

Plaintiff was unemployed at the time she moved in with defendant and remained so until September of 1970, when she worked part-time as a school bus driver. In 1972, her status was that of a full-time driver. For the most part, plaintiff continued at this job from 1972 through 1979, either part- or full-time, although she did collect unemployment compensation for the 1974-1975 school year.

At about the time plaintiff began working in 1970, the defendant bought a new home into which plaintiff, defendant, and the children moved. According to plaintiff, defendant had been anxious about the bills which would accompany the purchase of a new home and that she obtained her job in order to help pay the bills so as to quell defendant's anxieties. Plaintiff testified that her wages, which she received bi-weekly, were used to pay utilities and to purchase food. She then would give the balance to defendant, who, in turn, would tender back to plaintiff an amount sufficient to cover the next week's bills. Plaintiff testified that she does not know what defendant did with the money left over.

Plaintiff testified that from the beginning, and at various times during her relationship with defendant, she was told by defendant that they would get married as soon as her divorce from Mr. Carnes was final. Plaintiff's divorce, funded by defendant, was obtained some time in 1977. Plaintiff testified that defendant changed his story after her divorce, saying that she was "using" him and that he did not trust her. Defendant's refusal to marry her ultimately led to the demise of the relationship.

At first, plaintiff testified that she and defendant never held discussions pertaining to a division of property between them. Later she testified that, while there had been discussions on this subject, there was never any agreement that any of the property they accumulated would be divided between herself and defendant. She testified that "[h]e's always felt everything was his and nothing was mine. . . ." In addition, plaintiff testified that at the children's school she was known as Bonnie Sheldon and that the school principal referred to her as Sheldon. Defense counsel, however, produced a letter from the school principal addressed to Mrs. Bonnie Carnes. Plaintiff's driver's license and social security card were in the name of Carnes, and the parties' tax returns were filed separately. Plaintiff's bank accounts were in her name only. Plaintiff made no payments on the house, which was in defendant's name only. Defendant had a credit card, but plaintiff did not have access to it. Although defendant sometimes purchased items for plaintiff using the card, he told her that she would have to reimburse him for the cost of purchasing such items.

Defendant testified that there was no agreement to share his property with plaintiff and that he never promised to place title to any of his property in her name. According to defendant, throughout their relationship he always told plaintiff that he "couldn't see getting married because I couldn't see a woman changing her mind and taking half of what you own just because she decides she don't want you anymore. . . ." Defendant testified that plaintiff offered to go to a lawyer to sign an agreement stating that she would receive no property in the event of a divorce. Plaintiff admitted that she made this offer.

On April 24, 1979, plaintiff filed the instant suit, seeking an equitable division of the property accumulated during the years she and defendant lived together and seeking custody of Mary Ellen Sheldon.

The trial judge granted custody of the child to its natural mother, Constance Ward. With respect to her claim for an equitable distribution of property, the court held that plaintiff had failed to sustain her burden of proving that an express agreement existed between the parties regarding the ownership of personal and real property accumulated during their years of unmarried cohabitation. The court noted that plaintiff's claim of an express agreement was based in part on asserted promises by the defendant to marry (and thus share property accumulated from joint efforts) in the future. The trial court found that defendant did not make such a promise and on this point found defendant's testimony credible. Further, the court denied

Denied Implied Contract Theory

recovery on plaintiff's implied contract theory holding that implied contracts in this setting have been neither recognized by case law nor authorized by the Legislature. . . .

By statutory enactment in Michigan, common-law marriages are valid only if contracted before January 1, 1957. M.C.L. §551.2; M.S.A. §25.2, People v. Stanford, 68 Mich. App. 168, 242 N.W.2d 56 (1976). Since that time, Michigan has refused to recognize such marriages with the result that the property rights afforded a legally married couple have not been extended to those engaged in meretricious relationships. Michigan has also abolished the civil cause of action for breach of contract to marry. M.C.L. §551.301; M.S.A. §25.191.

This state will not enforce contracts made in consideration of meretricious relationships. In Tyranski v. Piggins, 44 Mich. App. 570, 205 N.W.2d 595 (1973); however, this Court recognized that the existence of a meretricious relationship does not render all agreements between the parties illegal. In *Tyranski* supra, 573-574, 205 N.W.2d 595, the Court said:

Rule

> But where there is an express agreement to accumulate or transfer property following a relationship of some permanence and an additional consideration in the form of either money or of services, the courts tend to find an independent consideration.

To the extent the rule announced in *Tyranski* concerns an express oral agreement entered into during the course of a meretricious relationship, it is inapplicable to plaintiff's implied contract claim.

With respect to implied contracts, only one case in Michigan has recognized a cause of action based upon a contract implied in fact in the context of a meretricious relationship. In Roznowski v. Bozyk, 73 Mich. App. 405, 251 N.W.2d 606 (1977), the defendant owned and managed a resort which had a tavern on its premises. The plaintiff previously had worked as a cocktail waitress in other local establishments but in 1968 moved into defendant's home, whereupon the parties began living together as husband and wife. She aided the defendant in operating his resort, including painting and cleaning the cabins and working in the bar. In addition, plaintiff performed most of the domestic chores in the home. In return, the defendant paid all of their expenses, including upkeep of their home, the plaintiff's insurance premiums, car payments, clothing, food, and medical bills.

In 1974, the relationship deteriorated, the parties split up, and plaintiff commenced suit claiming wages under an alleged express contract of employment entered into at the time she moved in with the defendant. She also sought recovery for the value of the services received by the defendant on a theory of implied contract. The trial court found that the plaintiff had not proved an express contract and further found that an employer-employee relationship did not exist. The court did find that the defendant was benefited by the plaintiff's services in connection with his tavern business and that she was entitled to recover for this. The trial court, significantly, excluded the plaintiff's claim for services rendered in the home, finding that these were gratuitous. See, generally, Anno: Recovery for Services Rendered by Persons Living in Apparent Relation of Husband and Wife without Express Agreement for Compensation, 94 A.L.R.3d 552.

On appeal, the defendant argued that, absent proof of an express agreement, the services rendered by plaintiff must be presumed to have been gratuitous. This Court disagreed, stating that the presumption of gratuity may be rebutted where it is established that when the services were rendered the plaintiff expected to receive and the defendant expected to pay wages therefor. The Court held that in order to recover the plaintiff must establish a contract implied in fact, which requires proof of the expectations of the parties.

> Without proof of the expectations of the parties, the presumption of gratuity will overcome the usual contract implied by law to pay for what is accepted. Weessies v. Van Dyke's Estate, 159 Mich. 180, 183, 123 N.W. 608 (1909). Cf. King v. First Michigan Bank & Trust Co. of Zeeland, 11 Mich. App. 144, 160 N.W.2d 721 (1968). The issue is a question of fact, to be resolved by consideration of all of the circumstances, including the type of services rendered, duration of services, closeness of relation of the parties, and the expressed expectations of the parties. *Roznowski* supra, 409, 251 N.W.2d 606.

The Court held that there was more than sufficient evidence to present a question of fact as to the parties' expectations and, therefore, granted the plaintiff a new trial. As noted, the trial court had excluded the plaintiff's claim for services rendered in the home as gratuitous, and this Court did not alter that exclusion.

Roznowski establishes a theory of recovery pursuant to a contract implied in fact under circumstances similar to those in the instant case. *Roznowski* is distinguishable from the instant case for several reasons, however. There the plaintiff sued for wages or for the value of services rendered, whereas, in the instant case, plaintiff does not ask for wages and has not alleged that she expected them. In addition, the *Roznowski* Court did not extend the principles of contracts implied in fact to household services. The plaintiff was allowed to recover only for services of a commercial nature. In the instant case, plaintiff's services to defendant were only of a household nature.

The courts of this state have been willing to grant equitable relief, in certain circumstances, to putative spouses. In cases involving putative spouses, one or both of the parties mistakenly believe in good faith that they are legally married, only to discover at a subsequent date that they are not. In Walker v. Walker, 330 Mich. 332, 335, 47 N.W.2d 633 (1951), the Court announced the principle that in the putative spouse situation a concealment of material facts by one spouse may constitute actionable fraud and permit the defrauded spouse to recover a portion of the property accumulated during the period of cohabitation.

P Alleges Fraud

Court rejects

In the instant case, despite the fact that plaintiff concedes that both parties knew that they were not married legally to each other, she argues that there was fraud present here because defendant promised to marry her but refused to do so. We reject this contention for several reasons. First, the trial court's finding that defendant did not promise to marry plaintiff is supported by the evidence. Second, plaintiff's unilateral expectation of marriage cannot be attributed to the defendant as a fraudulent act on his part. Third, the parties were not putative spouses. Finally, plaintiff is essentially asking for relief based on a breach of promise to marry, an action which has been specifically abolished by legislative fiat.

Further, plaintiff asks us to fashion remedies implied in law, similar to those suggested by the California Supreme Court in the now famous case of Marvin v. Marvin, 18 Cal. 3d 660, 134 Cal. Rptr. 815, 557 P.2d 106 (1976), where the Court suggested that the judiciary should begin formulating remedies appropriate to nonmarital relationships based on the presumption that cohabitants intend "'to deal fairly with each other.'" Id., 683, 134 Cal. Rptr. 815, 557 P.2d 106. The Court held that, in the absence of an express agreement, the courts should inquire into the conduct of the parties to determine whether the conduct demonstrates an implied contract, an agreement of partnership or joint venture, or some other tacit understanding of the parties. The Court further held that remedies such as quantum meruit, constructive trusts, or resulting trusts may be employed in the context of unmarried cohabitants.

Want Against Public Policy

The trial court, in the case at bar, held that Michigan does not allow such recovery and further held that it would be against the public policy of this state to do so. We agree with the trial judge.

In a New York decision, McCullon v. McCullon, 96 Misc. 2d 962, 410 N.Y.S.2d 226, 231 (1978), the Court, in discussing Marvin stated as follows:

"Marvin"

> As Justice Tobriner stated in his decision, the Marvin discussion was not intended to equate unmarried cohabitation with married couples or create common law marriage. What Marvin did was give the nonmarital partners, "the same rights to enforce contracts and to assert her equitable interest in property acquired through her effort *as does any other unmarried person.*" (Emphasis in original.)

In a recent Illinois decision, Hewitt v. Hewitt, 77 Ill. 2d 49, 57-58, 31 Ill. Dec. 827, 394 N.E.2d 1204 (1979), the Illinois Supreme Court, in a well-written and comprehensive opinion, stated the problem somewhat differently:

> The issue of unmarried cohabitants' mutual property rights, however, as we earlier noted, cannot appropriately be characterized solely in terms of contract law, nor is it limited to considerations of equity or fairness as between the parties to such relationships. There are major public policy questions

involved in determining whether, under what circumstances, and to what extent it is desirable to accord some type of legal status to claims arising from such relationships. Of substantially greater importance than the rights of the immediate parties is the impact of such recognition upon our society and the institution of marriage. Will the fact that legal rights closely resembling those arising from conventional marriages can be acquired by those who deliberately choose to enter into what have heretofore been commonly referred to as "illicit" or "meretricious" relationships encourage formation of such relationships and weaken marriage as the foundation of our family-based society? In the event of death shall the survivor have the status of a surviving spouse for purposes of inheritance, wrongful death actions, workmen's compensation, etc.? And still more importantly: what of the children born of such relationships? What are their support and inheritance rights and by what standards are custody questions resolved? What of the sociological and psychological effects upon them of that type of environment? Does not the recognition of legally enforceable property and custody rights emanating from nonmarital cohabitation in practical effect equate with the legalization of common law marriage?

We are of the opinion that public policy questions of such magnitude are best left to the legislative process, which is better equipped to resolve the questions which inevitably will arise as unmarried cohabitation becomes an established feature of our society. While the judicial branch is not without power to fashion remedies in this area, see, e.g., *Tyranski* supra, *Roznowski* supra, and *Walker*, supra, we are unwilling to extend equitable principles to the extent plaintiff would have us do so, since recovery based on principles of contracts implied in law essentially would resurrect the old common-law marriage doctrine which was specifically abolished by the Legislature. Although, as previously noted, the *Marvin* Court denied that the effect of its decision would be to resurrect the principle of common-law marriages, commentators have been less certain. Quoting from *Hewitt*, supra, 65-66, 31 Ill. Dec. 827, 394 N.E.2d 1204:

> "[T]he effect of these cases is to reinstitute common-law marriage in California after it has been abolished by the legislature." (Clark, The New Marriage, Willamette L.J. 441, 449 (1976)). "[*Hewitt*] is, if not a direct resurrection of common-law marriage contract principles, at least a large step in that direction." Reiland, Hewitt v. Hewitt: Middle America, *Marvin* and Common-Law Marriage, 60 Chi. B. Rec. 84, 88-90 (1978).

In conclusion, we concur with the trial judge's ruling that judicial restraint requires that the Legislature, rather than the judiciary, is the appropriate forum for addressing the question raised by plaintiff. We believe a contrary ruling would contravene the public policy of this state "disfavoring the grant of mutually enforceable property rights to knowingly unmarried cohabitants." Id., 66, 31 Ill. Dec. 827, 394 N.E.2d 1204. . . .

Remanded. We retain jurisdiction.

NOTES AND QUESTIONS

1. Is this case right? It has been the experience of your authors that a class vote on this question can produce a discussion that has to be put out with a fire hose. For a case allowing a "palimony" suit along the same lines, see Estate of Roccamonte, 174 N.J. 381, 808 A.2d 838 (2002).

2. In more recent years many jurisdictions have been forced to deal with the fact that many couples are living together and never plan to marry, and this has led to some adjustments in the law. Wilco v. Trautz, 427 Mass. 326, 693 N.E.2d 141 (1998);

We have not previously passed on the validity of written agreements between two unmarried cohabitants that attempt to define the rights of the parties as to services rendered and property acquired during their relationship. Our early decisions precluded the enforcement of an agreement between unmarried parties if the agreement was made in consideration that the parties should cohabit. See, e.g., Zytka v. Dmochowski, 302 Mass. 63, 63-64, 18 N.E.2d 332 (1938) (if money is given by one party to the other "entirely or partially in consideration that the parties should cohabit, then the parties have no standing to invoke the aid of a court of equity to compel the repayment of the money and they have no rights which are cognizable in equity"). See also Otis v. Freeman, 199 Mass. 160, 85 N.E. 168 (1908). More recently, we have held valid oral promises between unmarried cohabitants so long as "illicit sexual relations were [not] an inherent aspect of the agreement or a 'serious and not merely an incidental part of the performance of the agreement.'" Margolies v. Hopkins, 401 Mass. 88, 92, 514 N.E.2d 1079 (1987), quoting Green v. Richmond, 369 Mass. 47, 51, 337 N.E.2d 691 (1975).

Social mores regarding cohabitation between unmarried parties have changed dramatically in recent years and living arrangements that were once criticized are now relatively common and accepted. "As an alternative to marriage, more couples are choosing to cohabit. These relationships may be of extended duration, sometimes lasting as long as many marriages. In many respects, these cohabitation relationships may be quite similar to conventional marriages; they may involve commingling of funds, joint purchases of property, and even the birth of children." (Footnotes omitted.) Perry, Dissolution Planning in Family Law: A Critique of Current Analyses and a Look Toward the Future, 24 Fam. L.Q. 77, 78 (1990) (hereinafter Perry). With the prevalence of nonmarital relationships today, a considerable number of persons live together without benefit of the rules of law that govern property, financial, and other matters in a marital relationship. Thus, we do well to recognize the benefits to be gained by encouraging unmarried cohabitants to enter into written agreements respecting these matters, as the consequences for each partner may be considerable on termination of the relationship or, in particular, in the event of the death of one of the partners. "In recent years, increased attention has focused on the advisability of unmarried couples entering into cohabitation contracts in which they . . . detail the financial consequences of dissolution." Perry, *supra*. This may be especially important in a jurisdiction like Massachusetts where we do not recognize common law marriage, do not extend to unmarried couples the rights possessed by married couples who divorce, and reject equitable remedies that might have the effect of dividing property between unmarried parties.

Courts in other jurisdictions have concluded, as we did in Margolies v. Hopkins, *supra,* that an express agreement between adult unmarried persons living together is unenforceable only to the extent that it explicitly and inseparably is founded on sexual relations. [Citations omitted.] Furthermore, such agreements are not invalid merely because the parties may have contemplated the creation or continuation of a nonmarital relationship when they entered into the agreement. Marvin v. Marvin, *supra* at 670, 134 Cal. Rptr. 815, 557 P.2d 106. As the New York Court of Appeals stated in Morone v. Morone, *supra* at 486, 429 N.Y.S.2d 592, 413 N.E.2d 1154, "[t]he theory of these cases is that while cohabitation without marriage does not give rise to the property and financial rights which normally attend the marital relation, neither does cohabitation disable the parties from making an agreement within the normal rules of contract law."

3. Not all jurisdictions agree. The court in Schwegmann v. Schwegmann, 441 So. 2d 316 (La. Ct. App. 1983), held the same way as the *Carnes* court did concerning breach of an implied contract between a cohabitating couple. The plaintiff in *Schwegmann* asked for quasi-contractual relief for domestic services and business services. The court denied recovery for domestic services, finding that they were so completely intertwined with her illegal cohabitation as to be utterly indistinguishable therefrom.

With respect to the business services, the court stated:

> Plaintiff testified she performed business services for Mr. Schwegmann and his corporations by (1) helping him write editorials for Schwegmann's newspaper advertisements; (2) rendering investment advice; (3) assisting and rendering advice as to Mr. Schwegmann's political career; and (4) keeping him informed of things she saw in the stores which could have an adverse effect on the business. Under our law, the plaintiff may be entitled to compensation for the rendition of the services if the services were in fact rendered and do meet the prerequisites of the equitable principles formulated by the jurisprudence for recovery. In the *Bonaventure* case, supra, the Third Circuit clearly stated the equitable principle upon which recovery can be had:
>
> > Our jurisprudence appears settled to the effect that predicated upon equitable principles, the claims of a paramour and concubine will be   *Rule*

recognized and enforced with respect to joint or mutual commercial ventures, provided such enterprises arose independently of the illicit relationship. Heatwole v. Stansbury, 212 La. 685, 33 So. 2d 196; Sparrow v. Sparrow, 231 La. 966, 93 So. 2d 232; Foshee v. Simkin, La. App., 174 So. 2d 915.

Rationale

The rationale of the rule pronounced in the *Heatwole, Sparrow* and *Foshee* cases, supra (and the numerous authorities therein cited) is that where the concubinage is merely incidental to the business arrangement, the equitable rights of both parties will be recognized and enforced provided they be established by strict and conclusive proof. Stated otherwise, the rule is that if the commercial enterprise is independent of the illegal cohabitation, each party may assert his rights in the common endeavor.

Since the issue arose on a motion for summary judgment the trial judge concluded and we agree the plaintiff must be given every benefit of the doubt. Conceivably given the opportunity to do so, she could establish real and substantial business services performed for the defendants, including Mr. Schwegmann, that have not been previously compensated and which were separate and distinct from the concubinage relationship. Accordingly, we agree with the trial judge's ruling excepting her claim of compensation for business services from the summary dismissal of her claims.

4. The American Law Institute has weighed in on this issue, publishing "The Principles of the Law of Family Dissolution — Analysis and Recommendations" (2002), which urges the courts to treat longtime cohabitating couples who break up in the same manner as married couples, and to give them similar rights to a division of assets. The Principles contain a number of model rules on point, and apply whether the parties are same- or opposite-sex couples.

B. Licenses

RESTATEMENT (SECOND) OF CONTRACTS

§181. Effect of Failure to Comply with Licensing or Similar Requirement

If a party is prohibited from doing an act because of his failure to comply with a licensing, registration or similar requirement, a promise in consideration of his doing that act or of his promise to do it is unenforceable on grounds of public policy if

(a) the requirement has a regulatory purpose, and
(b) the interest in the enforcement of the promise is clearly outweighed by the public policy behind the requirement.

Problem 122

Sam Ambulance failed the bar exam three times. Undaunted, he hung out his shingle anyway and started extensive advertising for clients. He drafted a very good will for Mary Wealth, and she agreed to pay him $400 for doing so. Before he could collect, however, she learned the truth and refused to pay, though she kept the will. What can Sam do about her debt to him? If Sam had gotten a license but failed one year to send in his attorney registration form along with the required fee, would this misstep void contracts made with his clients before he corrected the problem? See Benjamin v. Koeppel, 85 N.Y.2d 549, 650 N.E.2d 829 (1995).

Problem 123

The state required all merchants who intended to extend consumer credit to obtain a license to do so from the State Attorney General's Office. The purpose of the licensing requirement was to finance a Consumer Protection Agency. Garfield Department Store never applied for a license but sold much merchandise under its own credit card plan. Must its customers pay their bills?

C. Contracts in Restraint of Trade

Agreements that limit competition, fix prices, create a monopoly, and so on are heavily regulated by both state and federal antitrust laws. The law here is complicated and beyond the scope of this course. But common law challenges to certain contractual covenants not to compete do involve the doctrine of illegality. Two primary situations create the argument that such clauses are unnecessary restraints on trade and hence illegal:

1. *Sales of a business.* If the seller of an existing business sells the buyer the "goodwill" of the business (its value over and above its tangible assets; i.e., its reputation with its customers), the seller frequently also expressly contracts not to set up a competing business in the immediate locale for a set period of time.
2. *Employment contracts.* When beginning a new job, the employee often must sign a contract containing a covenant not to compete with the employer on termination of the employment.

If the seller or employee violates these promises and goes into a competing business, the buyer or employer may sue, asking for damages for the harm caused and an injunction to prevent further competition during the life of the original contract. Because courts hate to deprive a person of the right to earn a living, courts are very suspicious of such restraints on trade. The courts tend not to enforce these agreements unless (1) the seller or employee has *unique* talents, knowledge, or abilities (no court is going to restrain a janitor from sweeping floors for someone else), (2) the area the injunction will cover is reasonable (the *spatial limitation*), and (3) the time period of restraint is also reasonable (the *temporal limitation*). See Fields Foundation v. Christensen, 103 Wis. 2d 465, 309 N.W.2d 125 (1981). Since injunctions are equitable remedies, the old maxim that "equity casts a wide net" means that before granting such relief the court will take into account the needs of the entire community; thus if the injunction against, say, a doctor who leaves one medical practice to start another would leave the surrounding area without adequate medical help, the court will withhold its hand and limit the parties to damages only.

Elements

In some states, covenants not to compete that are entered into by employees are void by command of statute. See, e.g., Ala. Code §8-1-1-1, Cal. Bus. & Prof. Code §§16600-16602.

Problem 124

Fancy Auto Repairs, Inc. hired young Lee Matheson when he was only 18 and sent him to a special school to learn foreign auto repairs. When he made top honors at the school, Fancy Auto hired him for a five-year period, making him sign a covenant not to compete in a 100-mile radius of its home city for three years after leaving employment. During the next year he worked in the foreign auto department under the tutelage of a master technician, all the while earning a respectable wage. At the end of the year he was pronounced ready to head the foreign auto repair department, and the master technician moved on to a different division of the company in another state. Matheson almost immediately quit his job and signed on with a cross-town rival of Fancy Auto, running the foreign auto repair department. Fancy Auto, pointing out all the money that it had spent in training Matheson, asked a court for an injunction forbidding him from violating the covenant not to compete. Should the court grant this? Would it make a difference if he had worked for Fancy Auto for ten years and then jumped to the new job? See Reddy v. Community Health Foundation of Man, 171 W. Va. 368, 298 S.E.2d 906 (1982).

WHITE v. FLETCHER/MAYO/ASSOCIATES

Supreme Court of Georgia, 1983
251 Ga. 203, 303 S.E.2d 746

BELL, J. This is a suit by a former employee of an advertising company for a declaration that certain noncompetition covenants he agreed to are unenforceable because they are against public policy.

In 1973 appellant Eldredge White graduated from college and was hired by Fletcher/Mayo/Associates, Inc., (FMA) a marketing, advertising, and sales promotion company based in St. Joseph, Missouri. He was transferred to Atlanta in November of 1977 as a corporate vice-president and manager of the Atlanta office, and was named a senior vice-president in May, 1981.

FMA began merger negotiations with appellee Doyle Dane Bernbach International, Inc., a New York advertising firm, culminating in a March, 1982 merger which was accomplished by Doyle Dane forming a subsidiary Delaware corporation, the other appellee in this case, which acquired FMA and took its name. Doyle Dane paid $3.1 million for FMA, which had a book value of $1.7 million; the difference between book value and the total price was money paid for the goodwill of FMA. White had no control over the decision to seek a merger and took no part in the merger negotiations. Prior to the merger FMA had encouraged its employees to invest in the company through stock purchases. At the date of merger White, through stock bonuses and his own purchases, owned 7114 shares of FMA common stock, which represented 4.62 percent of the total FMA stock and were worth a book value of about $85,000. Sixty-nine of FMA's employees held stock, and among them White ranked fifth in size of holdings. Two shareholders, Fletcher and Mayo, together held 43.38 percent of the stock. They were FMA's principal officers and the only officers or shareholders who sat on FMA's Board of Directors. FMA shareholders voted March 16, 1982 on the issue of merger with Doyle Dane. Those voting in favor of merger received Doyle Dane common stock in exchange for their FMA stock at a rate of 1.2991 Doyle Dane shares for each FMA share. Those who dissented received no Doyle Dane stock and instead received the fair market value of their shares. White voted in favor of merger and received, according to the standard exchange rate for all stockholders, Doyle Dane stock worth about $145,000, thus realizing a paper profit of about $60,000 on the corporate acquisition.

Prior to the merger White had no written employment contract with FMA. Doyle Dane conditioned its purchase of FMA on White signing agreements containing restrictive covenants in favor of FMA and Doyle Dane. Only three other employees of FMA—Fletcher, Mayo, and the chief financial officer—signed such agreements; no others, including the fourth largest shareholder and two other senior vice-presidents, made such agreements. White testified that at the time FMA told him he should sign the agreements because they were necessary to guarantee his job and secure broader career opportunities for him. There was trial testimony for appellees that FMA's biggest client was serviced out of the Atlanta office, that White supervised service of this and other accounts, and that he was asked to sign the covenants because, in light of his client contacts, he was considered a key employee.

Soon after the merger White was fired. He filed suit to determine whether he had to honor the covenants he'd agreed to. The learned trial judge, after careful consideration of the evidence and past decisions of this court, found the covenants overbroad but also found that they'd been entered into ancillary to the sale of FMA, and that the court therefore had the authority to blue pencil[1] the covenants into a more limited form. The judge extensively edited them, declared them enforceable as rewritten, and enjoined White from breaching them. White appeals. Appellees argue that White was a seller, but stipulate that if we decide that the covenants should be treated as ancillary to White's employment, then they are entirely unenforceable. We hold for White, and reverse.

"A covenant not to compete ancillary to an employment contract is enforceable only where it is strictly limited in time and territorial effect and is otherwise reasonable considering the business interest of the employer sought to be protected and the effect on the employee." Howard Schultz & Assoc. v. Broniec, 239 Ga. 181(1), 183, 236 S.E.2d 265 (1977). If such a covenant as read in its entirety is unenforceable, then under the doctrine announced in Rita Personnel Services, Inc. v. Kot, 229 Ga. 314, 191 S.E.2d 79 (1972), it cannot be judicially rewritten so as to sever the objectionable portion, because to do so would violate public policy. In the *Rita Personnel Services* case Kot entered into a franchise agreement with Rita, and covenanted not to compete with Rita for two years after termination of the franchise agreement in three named counties "or in any territorial area in which a franchise has been granted by Rita." The franchise was ended, and Rita sought to have the court obliterate the quoted phrase, which was clearly unreasonable, and enforce the remainder. The trial court refused the requested judicial surgery, and this court affirmed, concluding that although there were good reasons for severance, they were offset by the potential in terrorem effect on employees who don't challenge their contractual obligations. *Rita Personnel Services*, id. at 317, 191 S.E.2d 79, citing Blake, 73 Harv. L. Rev. 625, 682-683 (1960).[2]

---

1. This term is broadly applied in Georgia to include judicial editing of covenants which were not written in such a way that they are divisible by simply excising certain parts or words from them. [Citations omitted.]

2. Because Blake succinctly states the argument against severance in employment contracts, he is worth repeating here:

> Courts and writers have engaged in hot debate over whether severance should ever be applied to an employee restraint. The argument against doing so is persuasive. For every covenant that finds its way to court, there are thousands which exercise an in terrorem effect on employees who respect their contractual obligations and on

Accord, *Howard Schultz & Assoc.*, supra, 239 Ga. at 186, 236 S.E.2d 265.

On the other hand, if a covenant not to compete has been made by a seller ancillary to the sale of a business, the seller "may be enjoined from competing to the extent that it is found essential, by clear and convincing evidence, to protect the purchaser, despite the overbreadth of the covenant." Redmond v. Royal Ford, Inc., 244 Ga. 711, 713, 261 S.E.2d 585 (1979), citing Jenkins v. Jenkins Irrigation, Inc., 244 Ga. 95, 259 S.E.2d 47 (1979). In the *Jenkins* case Jenkins owned 50 percent of the stock of Jenkins Irrigation; he sold his interest and covenanted not to compete in that business for five years in the State of Georgia. The territorial restriction of the covenant was too broad, and hence unreasonable, but we held that Jenkins could be enjoined from competing in a more limited geographical area in which the buyer could show by clear and convincing evidence that protection from competition by Jenkins was essential for the buyer's protection. In reaching this conclusion we found that *Rita Personnel Services*, supra, was distinguishable:

[handwritten margin note: Need clear and convincing evidence]

> When a person sells a business and covenants not to compete in a certain territory, the buyer pays and the seller receives a part of the total purchase price as consideration for that covenant. The buyer frequently would not buy the business if the seller were free to begin competing immediately. By restricting the territory to an area less than that specified in the covenant, the court requires the seller to do that which the buyer and seller bargained for, yet in a smaller area than that agreed to by the seller. The reasons for rejecting severability in employee covenants, Rita Personnel Services v. Kot, supra, are not applicable to covenants not to compete made in conjunction with the sale of a business. Many courts in this country apply the "blue pencil" to covenants not to compete. 14 Williston on Contracts (3rd) 285, §1647B (1972). Without disapproving Rita Personnel Services v. Kot, supra, we join those courts as to covenants not to compete made in conjunction with the sale of a business.

---

competitors who fear legal complications if they employ a covenantor, or who are anxious to maintain gentlemanly relations with their competitors. Thus, the mobility of untold numbers of employees is restricted by the intimidation of restrictions whose severity no court would sanction. If severance is generally applied, employers can fashion truly ominous covenants with confidence that they will be pared down and enforced when the facts of a particular case are not unreasonable. This smacks of having one's employee's cake, and eating it too.

Blake, [Employee Agreements Not to Compete, 73 Harv. L. Rev. 625, 682-683].

Blake went on to note that not all employment contracts are adhesion contracts and that requiring employers to exactly tailor covenants to each employee would generally place upon them an impossible administrative burden. He suggested that if the employer acted in good faith in accord with a policy and practice to design restraints which are fair and only protect his legitimate interests, then the courts should engage in partial severance on the employer's behalf. Id. at 683-684. This court has not followed this approach, but it is noteworthy that even under Blake's test FMA and Doyle Dane apparently could not meet the burden of showing either that the terms of White's covenants were actually negotiated with him or that Doyle Dane's "policy and practice with regard to such restraints generally has been devised with reasonable regard to avoiding undue burdens on employees." Id. at 684.

Jenkins, supra 244 Ga. at 100, 259 S.E.2d 47.

In short, we do not blue pencil in employment contract cases, but do in sale of business cases. For this reason, if we are confronted with a case challenging the enforceability of a noncompetition covenant, our threshold task is to classify the agreement containing the covenant. In cases such as *Rita* and *Jenkins* the classification is obvious. Indeed, there are four cases, including *Rita*, which are cited in *Jenkins* as dealing with types of covenants which "have been treated by this court like employee covenants ancillary to employment contracts," *Jenkins*, supra at 97-98, 259 S.E.2d 47; an examination of these cases shows the typology in each was either assumed or cursory. See Rakestraw v. Lanier, 104 Ga. 188, 30 S.E. 735 (1898) (professional partnership agreement); *Rita*, supra (franchise agreement); Barrett-Walls, Inc. v. T.V. Venture, Inc., 242 Ga. 816, 251 S.E.2d 558 (1979) (distributorship agreement); *Howard Schultz*, supra (contract for services by independent contractor).

That the classification is less obvious where the covenant is in an agreement which is contended to be ancillary to both employment and the sale of an interest in a business became evident in the case of Redmond v. Royal Ford, supra. See 32 Mercer L. Rev. 25, 27-29 (1980). Redmond had been hired by Royal Ford as a salesman; later he was promoted to executive, in connection with which he signed a contract containing covenants not to compete, bought a 10 percent stock interest in Royal Ford, and gave the company an option upon termination of his employment to repurchase the stock at 20 percent over book value. He later left the company, and Royal Ford repurchased his stock, then sought to enforce the covenants. The restraints were overbroad, and the issue on appeal was whether they could be blue penciled. We first found the contract was clearly ancillary to his employment, but that there was still a question whether the stock option forced the agreement into the sale of business category. In a per curiam decision in which two justices concurred, two concurred specially, and three dissented, the majority opinion applied the *Jenkins* analysis and held that the case under consideration was distinguishable because, in contrast to cases such as *Jenkins*, supra, and Hood v. Legg, 160 Ga. 620, 128 S.E. 891 (1925), in which the promissors had sold the goodwill of their businesses and had been compensated for it, Redmond was a *buyer* who had made his covenants not to compete in conjunction with the acquisition of an interest in Royal Ford. [Citations omitted.]

The factual situation facing us now is more complex than *Redmond*'s, since although the covenants in question were clearly ancillary to White's employment and contemporaneous with his acquisition of an interest in Doyle Dane, they were also contemporaneous with White's profitable relinquishment of his interest in the pre-merger FMA. However, the profit White made on his exchange of stock was strictly proportional to that which was received by all other shareholders, ninety-four percent of whom were not asked to make such covenants. Compare Alexander & Alexander, Inc., v.

Wohlman, 19 Wash. App. 670, 578 P.2d 530, 537-538 (Wash. App. 1978) (stock of acquiring company was distributed to employees in proportion to amount of income each generated, not in proportion to percentage of shares owned in acquired company). Thus, it is problematical whether his profit constituted consideration for his covenants not to compete, or whether the sole consideration flowing to White in return for those covenants was his continued employment.

Even assuming the validity of appellees' contentions that White, Esau-like, improvidently gave up his major economic asset (for White, his right to use his specialized job skills) for a $60,000 mess of pottage, see generally Blake, supra at 648, there remains a question whether White, because of his employee status, had the same unfettered bargaining capacity as the seller of a business. It is clear that despite his ownership of a relatively small interest in FMA and his potential veto power over the merger, White had no control over overall management of FMA, and in fact had so little bargaining clout within FMA that he was unable to prevent his own termination. He was nothing more than an employee, albeit an important one, and as an employee White could reasonably have assumed that if he did not do as FMA and Doyle Dane wished he would be stigmatized as not being a team player, thereby jeopardizing his career prospects with FMA.

Pretermitting the question whether FMA and Doyle Dane in fact took advantage of their dominant bargaining power to extract White's promises, we find that redrafting the covenants would create a serious danger of sapping the vitality of the *Rita Personnel Services* doctrine. Such redrafting would encourage a purchaser of an existing business to genteelly coerce an employee of the acquired business to agree to an employment contract which contains noncompetition covenants and which appears to be the result of a true bargain but is actually a contract of adhesion. See note 1, supra; Restatement (2d) of Contracts §164, Comment b (1981) (Courts will not redraft overbroad agreements extracted by taking advantage of dominant bargaining power.). For this reason we hold today that where a trial judge is asked to determine the enforceability of a noncompetition covenant which the buyer of a business contends was given ancillary to the covenantor's relinquishment of his interest in the business to the buyer, and not given solely in return for the covenantor's continued employment, the judge must determine the covenantor's status. If it appears that his bargaining capacity was not significantly greater than that of a mere employee, then the covenant should be treated like a covenant ancillary to an employment contract, and "[a]s such, it should be enforced as written or not at all." *Redmond*, supra 244 Ga. at 715, 261 S.E.2d 585. Because we find that White was an employee, we conclude that the trial court erred in blue penciling White's covenants and in granting the injunction to enforce them in their judicially edited form.

Judgment reversed.

QUESTIONS

1. The court draws a distinction in its willingness to "blue pencil" between covenants restraining the seller of a business and a former employee. What is the policy justification for such a distinction?

2. Some courts are more willing than others to blue pencil. In Deborah Hope Doelker, Inc. v. Kestly, 87 A.D.2d 763, 449 N.Y.S.2d 52 (1982), for example, the court supplied a spatial limitation that was totally missing from the employee's covenant not to compete; in Fullerton Lumber Co. v. Torborg, 270 Wis. 133, 70 N.W.2d 585 (1955), the court found a ten-year period too long and sent the case back to the trial court with instructions to set a more reasonable period. As a matter of policy, is blue penciling a good idea? Consider the following case.

The courts are less likely to enforce covenants not to compete entered into by those in the learned professions. It is the American Bar Association's position that restrictive covenants for lawyers are unethical, and in some states — New York, for example — the Code of Professional Responsibility provides that a lawyer cannot enter into any agreement with prior associates or employers restricting his or her ability to practice law after resignation or discharge (except as such a restriction applies to retirement). Since 1980 the American Medical Association has taken the position that physicians' non-compete agreements impact negatively on health care and are not in the public interest, though it does not forbid them entirely. See AMA Code of Medical Ethics §E-9.02 and the discussion in Murfreesboro Medical Clinic, P.A. v. Udom, 166 S.W.3d 674 (Tenn. 2005).

VII. INCAPACITY

A. Minors

Those below the "age of majority" (18 in most jurisdictions) are responsible for their torts and crimes but are allowed to disaffirm the contracts they make. Why? The answer is not difficult if the child is only 7, but what if the "infant" is 17 and looks and acts all of 25? Why shouldn't the courts inquire into the sophistication of the particular individual and stop drawing arbitrary distinctions based on chronological age?

The infant (sometimes called a *minor*) may not disaffirm a contract for *necessaries* (food, clothing, shelter, etc.). In all jurisdictions special statutes deprive infants of the power to disaffirm certain contracts: bail bonds, military service, bank accounts, for example. Why would these exceptions be made?

VALENCIA v. WHITE

Court of Appeals of Arizona, 1982
134 Ariz. 139, 654 P.2d 287

BIRDSALL, J. The appellee, Valencia, commenced this action in the trial court seeking an injunction to prohibit the sale of his truck-tractor, upon which the appellant, White, claimed an artisan's lien (A.R.S. §33-1021 et seq.), and for return of the tractor. He alleged fraud in Count Two of his complaint, and the return of a trailer and damages for loss of use of his tractor resulting from the alleged fraud in Count Three. The trial court dismissed Counts Two and Three at the conclusion of the appellee's evidence, and no cross-appeal has been taken.

P's complaint

The appellants (hereinafter referred to as appellant) filed a counter-claim alleging that the appellee owed $13,783 on open account for repairs to his tractor, trailer and other trucking business vehicles. Counts Two and Three of the counterclaim sought alternative quantum meruit relief and a lien on the tractor.

Counter-claim

In his reply to the counterclaim, in addition to denying the open account liability, the appellee asserted that he lacked the capacity to contract because of his minority. Actually, the original complaint filed November 10, 1977, was filed by the appellee's mother as his guardian ad litem and the appellee was substituted as plaintiff sometime after he became 18 on November 20, 1977. [The trial court held that the plaintiff was entitled to $7,100, which was the amount the appellee had paid the appellant under the contract to purchase the truck-tractor.]

Appellee Asserted lack of capacity

We reverse and remand.

The questions presented on appeal are (1) whether a minor who owns and successfully operates a business may disaffirm contracts for necessary expenses of that business and (2) if he may so disaffirm, what are the rights between the parties?

Issues

The appellee also contends that the evidence shows that the services performed by the appellant were provided on the credit of the appellee's father. Although we do not agree that the evidence supports such a finding, assuming arguendo that it did, that fact would not be relevant. The appellee relies on the rule that a minor is not liable for necessaries if they have been furnished on the credit of another person. Burnand v. Irigoyen, 30 Cal. 2d 861, 186 P.2d 417 (1947). Since we agree with the finding of the trial court that the garage bill was not a necessity, it matters not that the appellant relied on the father's good credit.

Turning now to the issues raised by the appellant, we commence with a factual background. The appellee was a sophomore in high school, 17 years old, when his father established him in the trucking business in 1976 by giving him two truck-tractor semi-trailer rigs. The appellee hired drivers, secured jobs hauling produce and managed the business at a profit, as

Facts

much as $26,000 in 1978. The appellee was single and lived at home with his parents, although his father left the home in December, 1976. He was furnished his food, clothing, and housing during his minority by his parents (his father continued to support the family although not living in the home).

The appellant owned and operated a garage in Nogales for the repair of motor vehicles, including large trucks and trailers. He serviced and repaired the appellee's equipment from 1976 to July, 1977, when their disagreements commenced. In December, 1976, the appellee brought in one of his trucks with a major engine problem and the appellant agreed to replace its GMC engine with a Cummins to be built by the appellant. The charge for this engine, approximately $10,700, was the major item on the open account. The engine was installed and the truck was delivered to the appellee in May, 1977. He experienced troubles with this truck shortly thereafter and returned it to the appellant. The evidence was in conflict as to whether the new engine, other mechanical defects, or misuse, caused this breakdown. The trial court found that the minor's acts caused the damage to the engine. Since there is evidence to support this finding of fact it is binding on appeal. K&K Mfg., Inc. v. Union Bank, 129 Ariz. 7, 628 P.2d 44 (App. 1981). Periodic payments by the appellee on the account totaled $7,100, resulting in a balance of about $12,900 owing to the appellant except for the disaffirmance of the contract.

After the commencement of the action the truck and trailer were returned to the appellee, but the appellant retained the damaged engine, which had been disassembled for repair, and the radiator and transmission, which had been removed from the truck in order to determine what was wrong with the engine.

The appellant first argues that the garage bill was a necessity and the appellee cannot disaffirm. We disagree.

The trial court found that the services performed for the appellee by the appellant were not necessities of the minor. Whether contracts of a minor are for necessities is ultimately a question of fact if there is some reasonable basis upon which the goods or services furnished could be considered necessaries. 42 Am. Jur. 2d Infants §68; Haynie v. Dicus, 210 Ark. 1092, 199 S.W.2d 954 (1947). Where the contract is for a purpose benefiting the minor's employment or business there is a question to be decided upon the particular facts and circumstances of each case. [Citations omitted.] Although the judgment does not expressly state whether this finding was intended to be one of fact or law, we will consider it to be a finding of fact, and the record supports the finding. Since the appellee was provided board, room, clothing, medical needs and education, it was not necessary that he engage in business. We cannot fault this reasoning. The appellant argues that Worman Motor Co. v. Hill, 54 Ariz. 227, 94 P.2d 865, 124 A.L.R. 1363 (1939), contains language supporting his position:

The evidence does not show for what purpose the plaintiff used the automobile. It does not even show what his employment was. In the oral argument, as we recall, his business was stated to be that of picking cotton. But, even so, the evidence fails to show the car was necessary for him to go to and from his work, or for what purpose it was being used. For all we know, it may have been used only as a pleasure car. 54 Ariz. at 236-237, 94 P.2d 865.

These observations of the supreme court follow a quotation from Braham & Co. v. Zittel, 232 App. Div. 406, 250 N.Y.S. 44 (1931), which recognizes the rule we have already stated, i.e., whether an item is a necessity for a minor must be determined on the facts of each case, and then states there was no evidence in that case to support the minor's need. The Arizona Supreme Court merely found the same lack of record in *Worman*.

Rule restated

The appellant next contends the filing of the complaint ratified the contract. Again we disagree. In the complaint the appellee alleged his minority and alleged that the lien claimed on the tractor "is null and void" because he was a minor and incapable of contracting. In his reply to the counterclaim, he again alleged lack of capacity to contract because of minority. Although the complaint arose out of the contract, the appellee did not seek to enforce the contract or gain any benefits from it.

Second Argument

The appellant argues further that claims for attorney fees in each count of the complaint, pursuant to A.R.S. §12-341.01, constitute a ratification. Since the complaint arises out of the contract these claims may properly be made. Amphitheater Public Schools v. Eastman, 117 Ariz. 559, 574 P.2d 47 (1977). Even if the contract is disaffirmed, this is an action arising out of a contract. There has been no ratification.

Third Argument

The appellant's last contention concerns the trial court's attempt to restore the parties to a "status quo" after disaffirmance. He argues that requiring him to return monies paid on the account and refusing to allow him any remuneration for the services performed was error. We agree.

Fourth Argument

The trial court correctly recognized that the New Hampshire case of Porter v. Wilson, 106 N.H. 270, 209 A.2d 730, 13 A.L.R.3d 1247 (1965), adopts a minority view that a minor who disaffirms a contract may be held liable for benefits received even though they are not necessaries and even though the benefits cannot be returned in kind. The court in *Porter* held that the minor must pay for legal services furnished him in a guardianship matter, and his liability was the reasonable value of such services that were of benefit to him and not the amount he had agreed to pay or that had been charged. The matter was remanded to the trial court to determine that amount, which we understand could still be the same amount charged if the trial court found that was the reasonable value of those services.

Minority view

The New Hampshire court itself recognized that this "benefit rule" represents a minority view but found that it was a doctrine which has received approval of those who have given the matter serious consideration, citing 2 Williston on Contracts §238, p. 43 (3d ed. Jaeger 1959):

"Benefit Rule"

In some states the ordinary rule prevailing in regard to necessaries has been extended so far as to hold an infant bound by his contracts, where he fails to restore what he has received under them to the extent of the benefit actually derived by him from what he has received from the other party to the transaction. This seems to offer a flexible rule which will prevent imposition upon the infant and also tend to prevent the infant from imposing to any serious degree upon others.

Rule #

[W]e [are] persuaded that the rule which requires a minor to account for the benefit he has received is much the better rule. The Court of Appeals of Ohio has observed that:

> At a time when we see young persons between 18 and 21 years of age demanding and assuming more responsibilities in their daily lives; when we see such persons emancipated, married, and raising families; when we see such persons charged with the responsibility for committing crimes; when we see such persons being sued in tort claims for acts of negligence; when we see such persons subject to military service; when we see such persons engaged in business and acting in almost all other respects as an adult, it seems timely to re-examine the case law pertaining to contractual rights and responsibilities of infants to see if the law as pronounced and applied by the courts should be redefined. Haydocy Pontiac, Inc. v. Lee, 19 Ohio App. 2d 217, 250 N.E.2d 898, 900 (1969).

Other state courts have adopted the Minnesota rule in varying degrees. [Citations omitted.] Under the trial court's judgment in the instant case the appellant is not only precluded from recovering for parts and labor furnished the appellee in his going, successful business, he is required to repay monies paid to him on account of those services. In return he is only permitted to retain a disassembled engine that was damaged by the appellee's acts. No evidence suggests that the appellant took advantage of the appellee because of his age, lack of experience or judgment. Likewise no evidence suggests that the contract was disadvantageous to the appellee. . . .

In order to properly apply the rule in this case the trial court should have determined what benefits, if any, the minor actually received from the entire transaction. The only evidence presented in this regard is that the reasonable value of the parts and labor, including the Cummins engine, was $19,998.76. The parts and labor furnished the minor by the appellant were of benefit to him in that amount. The repair of the minor's business vehicles enabled him to successfully operate his trucking business. In addition to showing the profits from that business the evidence shows he purchased a pickup truck and a dragster from those profits. Obviously the parts and labor cannot be returned in kind to the appellant. Likewise the Cummins engine, having been damaged by acts attributable to the minor, cannot be returned in anywhere near the same condition as when it was acquired from the appellant. [Citations omitted.]

We find that to restore both parties to a status quo, the disassembled engine and the other parts in the possession of the appellant should be returned to the appellee; that the appellee received benefits having a value to him of $19,998.76; that the $7,100 paid by the appellee should be credited against the value of the benefits, leaving a balance of $12,898.71 which the appellee must pay to the appellant.   *Holding*

We reverse and remand with directions to enter judgment in favor of the appellants and against the appellee, in that amount and to order the return of the engine and other parts to the appellee.

NOTE

To disaffirm, the infant simply indicates (even in an informal way) that he or she no longer wants to be bound by the contract. If the infant reaches majority, the period of disaffirmance continues for a reasonable period of time and even thereafter unless the other side relies on the infant's apparent *ratification.* Compare Cassella v. Tiberio, 150 Ohio St. 27, 80 N.E.2d 426   *Ratification* (1948) (delay of 11 years excused), with Bobby Floars Toyota, Inc. v. Smith, 48 N.C. App. 580, 269 S.E.2d 320 (1980) (accepting benefits and making payments for ten months after reaching age of majority was ratification). In In re Apple In-App Purchase Litigation, 855 F. Supp. 2d 1030 (N.D. Cal. 2012), the court allowed parents, as guardians of their children, to disaffirm "game currencies" purchased by the children when playing games on apps created by Apple. However, in C.M.D. v. Facebook, Inc., 2014 WL 1266291 (N.D. Cal. 2014), the court would not allow minors using Facebook to disaffirm portions of their Facebook contracts while continuing to use Facebook and reaping the benefits of that social medium. In Lopez v. Kmart Corporation, 2015 WL 2062606 (N.D. Cal. 2015), a high school student who worked at Kmart turned 18, sued the company over a labor dispute, and promptly disaffirmed the agreement he had with Kmart requiring him to arbitrate all such grievances.

Problem 125

Mordred, though only 16 years old, looked to be in his late twenties. He went down to Tennyson Motors and signed a contract to purchase a new, expensive car, which he drove off the lot, around the block, and into a very immobile tree. He staggered back to Tennyson Motors and told Arthur King, the manager, that he was an infant and wanted his $500 down payment back. King, on learning the location and condition of the vehicle, refused, pointing to a clause in the contract stating, "I hereby affirm that I am over 18 years of age." Answer these questions: What is the effect of Mordred's written

Margin notes (handwritten):
- Some states will estopp the defense of lack of capacity
- Some states Disaffirm the contract but held him liable for tort of fraud

contractual statement that he was of age? What if he had told an oral lie as to this? See Kiefer v. Fred Howe Motors, Inc., 39 Wis. 2d 20, 158 N.W.2d 288 (1968) (minor could still disaffirm if fraud involved, but liable in tort for damages; court discusses alternative approaches taken by other jurisdictions in refusing to allow disaffirmance). If the minor's parent signs the contract, can the minor still disaffirm? See Berg v. Traylor, 148 Cal. App. 4th 809, 56 Cal. Rptr. 3d 140 (2007). Would it matter that Mordred was an emancipated minor, married, with a child of his own? If the contract had been for emergency medical services, could the infant still disaffirm? See Yale Diagnostic Radiology v. Estate of Harun Fountain, 267 Conn. 351, 838 A.2d 179 (2004) (contracts for necessities of life not disaffirmable).

Margin note (handwritten): - If parent signed for minor, then parent liable

By statute in some jurisdictions and by common law rule in others, infants must return consideration they received from the other side if it is possible to do so.

The infant's power of disaffirmance is not shared by the other party to the contract (unless he or she is also an infant). Thus infancy is an exception to the general rule of mutuality of obligation, which in bilateral contracts requires that both parties be bound or neither is. If the infant's obligation is backed by that of a surety, the surety is not permitted to raise the incapacity defense of the principal; see UCC §3-305(d) (promissory notes) and §34(1)(b) of the Restatement (Third) of the Law of Suretyship and Guaranty.

The protection the law gives to minors is extraordinary. The message behind these rules is quite clear: *Don't contract with our children!* If one must deal with children, get the approval of their guardians (or at least get the infant's promise guaranteed by a surety, who may not take advantage of the infant's incapacity).

B. Mental Infirmity

RESTATEMENT (SECOND) OF CONTRACTS

§15. MENTAL ILLNESS OR DEFECT

(1) A person incurs only voidable contractual duties by entering into a transaction if by reason of mental illness or defect

(a) he is unable to understand in a reasonable manner the nature and consequences of the transaction, or

(b) he is unable to act in a reasonable manner in relation to the transaction and the other party has reason to know of his condition.

(2) Where the contract is made on fair terms and the other party is without knowledge of the mental illness or defect, the power of avoidance under Subsection (1) terminates to the extent that the contract has been so performed in whole or in part or the circumstances have so changed that avoidance would be unjust. In such a case a court may grant relief as justice requires.

Problem 126

Rex Lear, age 58, depended on his daughters for day-to-day living, although he owned substantial assets that they held for him. For many years he had been mentally ill, coming in and out of periods of mental health. Even at his worst Rex appeared competent, although his conduct was often bizarre. One day he went into the Kent Dance Studio and inquired about dance lessons. He was neatly dressed and most courteous (in fact he kissed the hand of each woman he met, customers and clerks alike). He announced that he wanted to become the world's greatest dancer and compete in the Olympics (there is no such event, as Kent employees well knew). Every plan Kent mentioned, Lear agreed to immediately, while loudly laughing and dancing around with the employees. By the time he left the studio, he had signed contracts to learn ballroom dancing, hip hop, Latin forms, old world dances, dance instruction techniques, and New Wave, all totaling $28,000 (payable over the next five years). When he failed to show for any lessons or pay a cent, Kent Dance Studios inquired. He said that he had no memory of the day and had always hated dancing. When he refused to pay, Kent sued. Who prevails here? See Shoals Ford, Inc. v. Clardy, 588 So. 2d 879 (Ala. 1991) ($18,000 in punitive damages assessed against dealer who sold car to man over his mother's pleas that he was mentally incompetent). Would it matter if Rex had purchased a car and had had the use of it for one month? See 718 Associates v. Banks, 21 A.3d 977 (D.C. 2011).

Problem 127

Because of his bizarre conduct, Rex Lear was finally declared incompetent by a court proceeding, and a guardian was appointed to run his affairs. Five years went by, during which Lear received treatment, and to everyone's amazement he got steadily better. Eventually the doctors pronounced him cured, his guardian congratulated him, and Lear resumed control of his financial life. He never went through the legal steps necessary to have a court confirm his recovery. Two years later a business deal proved unprofitable for him, so he renounced the contract he had signed, claiming incompetency and pointing out that his guardian had not signed the contract. Can he do this?

Problem 128

When Edgar Poe awoke one morning with a tremendous hangover, he was startled to realize that the last thing he remembered was going into the Raven Tavern and having a few drinks with the boys. When he lurched into the living room he was amazed to find sitting by the front door a very large painting of a nude woman. The painting, titled *Annabel Lee*, had hung over the Raven's bar for decades. Later that afternoon, when his head quit hurting so much, he phoned the tavern and learned from Amontillado, the owner, that he had written an $8,000 check for the painting in a moment of high spirits the night before. He told Amontillado that he had no intention of keeping *Annabel Lee* (he was certain his wife, Lenore, would disapprove). Although Amontillado protested, Edgar hung up, phoned the bank, and stopped payment on the check. Amontillado sued. Must Edgar pay?

Handwritten margin notes:
- *Intoxication is a Voluntary Incapacity*
- *Need to show Not Voluntary*
  - *Alcoholic*
  - *Drug Addict*

VIII. UNCONSCIONABILITY

One of the most dramatic developments in late twentieth and early twenty-first century contract law has been the rise of non-negotiated form contracts. Indeed, it is virtually impossible to order goods, accept a job, open a bank or credit card account, or sign up for phone, cable, or Internet service without being forced to accept a slate of fine print terms. These so-called adhesion contracts earned their nickname because the nondrafting party has two choices: walking away from the transaction or "adhering" to the standardized terms.

As we discussed in Chapter 1, courts sometimes find that consumers and employees do not manifest assent to adhesion contracts. For example, as we mentioned, a computer user who simply visits a website does not agree to its terms of service unless he or she either was aware of the terms or should have been aware of them.

More often, courts police adhesion contracts by striking down *specific* harsh provisions under the defense of unconscionability. Very roughly, an unconscionable provision is one that is too unfair to be enforced. Once one has accepted this premise, the question becomes primarily one of drawing the line between a mere hard bargain and one-sided boilerplate that amounts to "carrying a good joke too far." Campbell Soup v. Wentz, 172 F.2d 80, 83 (3d Cir. 1948). Contracts containing harsh, unnegotiated terms that are simply presented to the other side on a "take it or leave it" basis are called *adhesion* contracts, because one party must adhere to the will of the other. They are said to resemble a law more than a contract. See Kessler, Contracts of Adhesion: Some Thoughts About Freedom of Contract, 43 Colum. L. Rev. 629 (1943). The idea that a contract

Handwritten margin note: Adhesion Contracts

may be *unconscionable* and therefore unenforceable in whole or in part is an old concept, with us at least as early as the mid-1700s. Similar devices were available in Roman law. The chief source for modern thought on the topic is §2-302 of the Uniform Commercial Code:

> 1. If the court as a matter of law finds the contract or any clause of the contract to have been unconscionable at the time it was made the court may refuse to enforce the contract, or it may enforce the remainder of the contract without the unconscionable clause, or it may so limit the application of any unconscionable clause as to avoid any unconscionable result.
>
> 2. When it is claimed or appears to the court that the contract or any clause thereof may be unconscionable the parties shall be afforded a reasonable opportunity to present evidence as to its commercial setting, purpose and effect to aid the court in making the determination.

QUESTIONS

1. Is the conscionability of the contract a question for judge or jury? Reread the first clause of subsection (1) carefully to answer this question. For what arguable policy reason would the Code drafters have made the choice they did on this issue?

2. Is the hearing mentioned in subsection (2) mandatory before a finding of unconscionability is made? See State v. AVCO Financial Services, 50 N.Y.2d 383, 429 N.Y.S.2d 181, 406 N.E.2d 1075 (1980).

3. If the contract was not unconscionable when signed but circumstances have made it so, does UCC §2-302 offer relief?

4. How do we define *unconscionability*? Is it, like Justice Potter Stewart's famous definition of *obscenity*, something we all "know when we see it"? Official Comment 1 to §2-302 explains that the "principle is one of the prevention of oppression and unfair surprise." Does that help? Compare that definition with the one advanced by Judge J. Skelly Wright in the famous case that follows.

WILLIAMS v. WALKER-THOMAS FURNITURE CO.
United States Court of Appeals, District of Columbia Circuit, 1965
350 F.2d 445

Wright, Circuit Judge. Appellee, Walker-Thomas Furniture Company, operates a retail furniture store in the District of Columbia. During the period from 1957 to 1962 each appellant in these cases purchased a number of household items from Walker-Thomas, for which payment was to be made in installments. The terms of each purchase were contained in a printed form contract which set forth the value of the purchased item and purported to lease the item to appellant for a stipulated monthly rent payment. The contract then provided, in substance, that title would remain in Walker-Thomas until the total of all the monthly payments made equaled the stated value of the item, at which time appellants could take title. In the event of a default in the payment of any monthly installment, Walker-Thomas could repossess the item.

The contract further provided that "the amount of each periodical installment payment to be made by [purchaser] to the Company under this present lease shall be inclusive of and not in addition to the amount of each installment payment to be made by [purchaser] under such prior leases, bills or accounts; *and all payments now and hereafter made by [purchaser] shall be credited pro rata on all outstanding leases, bills and accounts* due the Company by [purchaser] at the time each such payment is made." (Emphasis added.) The effect of this rather obscure provision was to keep a balance due on every item purchased until the balance due on all items, whenever purchased, was liquidated. As a result, the debt incurred at the time of purchase of each item was secured by the right to repossess all the items previously purchased by the same purchaser, and each new item purchased automatically became subject to a security interest arising out of the previous dealings.

On May 12, 1962, appellant Thorne purchased an item described as a Daveno, three tables, and two lamps, having total stated value of $391.10. Shortly thereafter, he defaulted on his monthly payments and appellee sought to replevy all the items purchased since the first transaction in 1958. Similarly, on April 17, 1962, appellant Williams bought a stereo set of stated value of $514.95.[1] She too defaulted shortly thereafter, and appellee sought to replevy all the items purchased since December 1957. The Court of General Sessions granted judgment for appellee. The District of Columbia Court of Appeals affirmed, and we granted appellants' motion for leave to appeal to this court.

Appellants' principal contention, rejected by both the trial and the appellate courts below, is that these contracts, or at least some of them, are unconscionable and, hence, not enforceable. In its opinion in Williams v. Walker-Thomas Furniture Company, 198 A.2d 914, 916 (1964), the District of Columbia Court of Appeals explained its rejection of this contention as follows:

> Appellant's second argument presents a more serious question. The record reveals that prior to the last purchase appellant had reduced the balance in her account to $164. The last purchase, a stereo set, raised the balance due to $678. Significantly, at the time of this and the preceding

---

1. At the time of this purchase her account showed a balance of $164 still owing from her prior purchases. The total of the purchases made over the years in question came to $1,800. The total payments amounted to $1,400.

purchases, appellee was aware of appellant's financial position. The reverse side of the stereo contract listed the name of appellant's social worker and her $218 monthly stipend from the government. Nevertheless, with full knowledge that appellant had to feed, clothe and support both herself and seven children on this amount, appellee sold her a $514 stereo set.

We cannot condemn too strongly appellee's conduct. It raises serious questions of sharp practice and irresponsible business dealings. A review of the legislation in the District of Columbia affecting retail sales and the pertinent decisions of the highest court in this jurisdiction disclose, however, no ground upon which this court can declare the contracts in question contrary to public policy. We note that were the Maryland Retail Installment Sales Act, Art. 83 §§128-153, or its equivalent, in force in the District of Columbia, we could grant appellant appropriate relief. We think Congress should consider corrective legislation to protect the public from such exploitive contracts as were utilized in the case at bar.

We do not agree that the court lacked the power to refuse enforcement to contracts found to be unconscionable. In other jurisdictions, it has been held as a matter of common law that unconscionable contracts are not enforceable. While no decision of this court so holding has been found, the notion that an unconscionable bargain should not be given full enforcement is by no means novel. In Scott v. United States, 79 U.S. (12 Wall.) 443, 445 (1870), the Supreme Court stated:

> If a contract be unreasonable and unconscionable, but not void for fraud, a court of law will give to the party who sues for its breach damages, not according to its letter, but only such as he is equitably entitled to.

Since we have never adopted or rejected such a rule, the question here presented is actually one of first impression.

Congress has recently enacted the Uniform Commercial Code, which specifically provides that the court may refuse to enforce a contract which it finds to be unconscionable at the time it was made. 28 D.C. Code §2-302 (Supp. IV 1965). The enactment of this section, which occurred subsequent to the contracts here in suit, does not mean that the common law of the District of Columbia was otherwise at the time of enactment, nor does it preclude the court from adopting a similar rule in the exercise of its powers to develop the common law for the District of Columbia. In fact, in view of the absence of prior authority on the point, we consider the congressional adoption of §2-302 persuasive authority for following the rationale of the cases from which the section is explicitly derived. Accordingly, we hold that where the element of unconscionability is present at the time a contract is made, the contract should not be enforced.

Unconscionability has generally been recognized to include an absence of meaningful choice on the part of one of the parties together with contract terms which are unreasonably favorable to the other party. Whether a meaningful choice is present in a particular case can only be determined by consideration of all the circumstances surrounding the transaction. In many cases the meaningfulness of the choice is negated by a gross inequality of bargaining power. The manner in which the contract was entered is also relevant to this consideration. Did each party to the contract, considering his obvious education or lack of it, have a reasonable opportunity to understand the terms of the contract, or were the important terms hidden in a maze of fine print and minimized by deceptive sales practices? Ordinarily, one who signs an agreement without full knowledge of its terms might be held to assume the risk that he has entered a one-sided bargain. But when a party of little bargaining power, and hence little real choice, signs a commercially unreasonable contract with little or no knowledge of its terms, it is hardly likely that his consent, or even an objective manifestation of his consent, was ever given to all the terms. In such a case the usual rule that the terms of the agreement are not to be questioned should be abandoned and the court should consider whether the terms of the contract are so unfair that enforcement should be withheld.

In determining reasonableness or fairness, the primary concern must be with the terms of the contract considered in light of the circumstances existing when the contract was made. The test is not simple, nor can it be mechanically applied. The terms are to be considered "in the light of the general commercial background and the commercial needs of the particular trade or case."[11] Corbin suggests the test as being whether the terms are "so extreme as to appear unconscionable according to the mores and business practices of the time and place." 1 Corbin [§128].[12] We think this formulation correctly states the test to be applied in those cases where no meaningful choice was exercised upon entering the contract.

Because the trial court and the appellate court did not feel that enforcement could be refused, no findings were made on the possible unconscionability of the contracts in these cases. Since the record is not sufficient for our deciding the issue as a matter of law, the cases must be remanded to the trial court for further proceedings.

So ordered.

DANAHER, Circuit Judge (dissenting). The District of Columbia Court of Appeals obviously was as unhappy about the situation here presented as any of us can possibly be. Its opinion in the *Williams* case, quoted in the majority text, concludes: "We think Congress should consider corrective legislation to protect the public from such exploitive contracts as were utilized in the

11. Comment, Uniform Commercial Code §2-30[2].
12. See Henningsen v. Bloomfield Motors, Inc.[, 32 N.J. 358, 161 A.2d 69 (1960)]; Mandel v. Liebman, 303 N.Y. 88, 100 N.E.2d 149 (1951). The traditional test as stated in Greer v. Tweed, 13 Abb. Pr., N.S. [427] at 429 [N.Y. 1872], is "such as no man in his senses and not under the delusion would make on the one hand, and as no honest or fair man would accept, on the other."

case at bar." My view is thus summed up by an able court which made no finding that there had actually been sharp practice. Rather the appellant seems to have known precisely where she stood.

There are many aspects of public policy here involved. What is a luxury to some may seem an outright necessity to others. Is public oversight to be required of the expenditures of relief funds? A washing machine, e.g., in the hands of a relief client might become a fruitful source of income. Many relief clients may well need credit, and certain business establishments will take long chances on the sale of items, expecting their pricing policies will afford a degree of protection commensurate with the risk. Perhaps a remedy when necessary will be found within the provisions of the "Loan Shark" law, D.C. Code §§26-601 et seq. (1961).

I mention such matters only to emphasize the desirability of a cautious approach to any such problem, particularly since the law for so long has allowed parties such great latitude in making their own contracts. I dare say there must annually be thousands upon thousands of installment credit transactions in this jurisdiction, and one can only speculate as to the effect the decision in these cases will have.

I join the District of Columbia Court of Appeals in its disposition of the issues.

NOTE AND QUESTION

Unconscionability is a wild card doctrine in our law. Dealing as it does with basic fairness, the concept has been attacked as meaningless, untamable, dangerous. The seminal law review article advocating this view was the late Professor Arthur Leff's Unconscionability and the Code: The Emperor's New Clause, 115 U. Pa. L. Rev. 485 (1967), in which the author proposed a two-part test for unconscionability that has proved very popular with the courts. Leff stated that before a court could deem a contract or any part thereof unconscionable, the court must find both *procedural* and *substantive* unconscionability. Procedural unconscionability, according to Leff, meant unfairness in the bargaining process (typically because one party, having the superior position, dictates the terms and refuses to bargain at all). Substantive unconscionability, on the other hand, refers to harsh terms in the resulting contract. How does this compare with the definition of unconscionability given by Judge J. Skelly Wright in the last case?

NOTE ON DOOR-TO-DOOR SALES

Buyers trapped in their homes and subjected to hours of sales pitch all too frequently sign up for foolish ventures. Recognizing that those who are purchasing items in their own homes do not have the bargaining position of someone who is in the seller's store (and thus free to walk away), the Federal Trade Commission has promulgated a regulation permitting such buyers to void the contract without reason if a notice of rescission is mailed to the seller before expiration of midnight of the third business day following the date of sale. Further, the three-day period does not even begin to run until the seller has furnished the buyer with a form explaining this right to cancel. The rule does not apply to the sale of insurance or real estate or to transactions in which buyer is the one who initiates the contact. See Federal Trade Commission Regulations for Door-to-Door Sales, 16 C.F.R. §429.

Problem 129

Star General Construction Company contacted Wong Air Conditioning Contractors and offered to give Wong the air conditioning subcontract on a construction project recently awarded to Star General if Wong could supply the air conditioning units at $8,000 each. Wong replied that it would lose money at that rate, but Star General said that $8,000 was the best it could do. Wong is a tiny new business and needs to build its reputation. If it agrees to do the project at the quoted rate, can it later use UCC §2-302 to reform the contract and receive a greater price? Does §2-302 protect *merchants* in sales contracts?

WEAVER v. AMERICAN OIL CO.
Supreme Court of Indiana, 1971
257 Ind. 458, 276 N.E.2d 144

ARTERBURN, C.J. In this case the appellee oil company presented to the appellant-defendant leasee [sic], a filling station operator, a printed form contract as a lease to be signed, by the defendant, which contained, in addition to the normal leasing provisions, a "hold harmless" clause which provided in substance that the leasee operator would hold harmless and also indemnify the oil company for any negligence of the oil company occurring on the leased premises. The litigation arises as a result of the oil company's own employee spraying gasoline over Weaver and his assistant and causing them to be burned and injured on the leased premises. This action was initiated by American Oil and Hoffer (Appellees) for a declaratory judgment to determine the liability of appellant Weaver, under the clause in the lease. The trial court entered judgment holding Weaver liable under the lease.

Clause three (3) of the lease reads as follows:

Lessor, its agents and employees shall not be liable for any loss, damage, injuries, or other casualty of whatsoever kind or by whomsoever caused to the person or property of anyone (including Lessee) on or off the premises, arising out of or resulting from Lessee's use, possession or operation thereof, or from defects in the premises whether apparent or hidden, or from the installation existence, use, maintenance, condition, repair, alteration, removal or replacement of any equipment thereon, whether due in whole or in part to negligent acts or omissions of Lessor, its agents or employees; and Lessee for himself, his heirs, executors, administrators, successors and assigns, hereby agrees to indemnify and hold Lessor, its agents and employees, harmless from and against all claims, demands, liabilities, suits or actions (including all reasonable expenses and attorneys' fees incurred by or imposed on the Lessor in connection therewith) for such loss, damage, injury or other casualty. Lessee also agrees to pay all reasonable expenses and attorneys' fees incurred by Lessor in the event that Lessee shall default under the provisions of this paragraph.

It will be noted that this lease clause not only exculpated the leasor oil company from its liability for its negligence, but also compelled Weaver to indemnify them for any damages or loss incurred as a result of its negligence. The appellate court held the exculpatory clause invalid, 261 N.E.2d 99, but the indemnifying clause valid, 262 N.E.2d 663. In our opinion, both these provisions must be read together since one may be used to effectuate the result obtained through the other. We find no ground for any distinction and we therefore grant the petition to transfer the appeal to this court.

This is a contract, which was submitted (already in printed form) to a party with lesser bargaining power. As in this case, it may contain unconscionable or unknown provisions which are in fine print. Such is the case now before this court.

The facts reveal that Weaver had left high school after one and a half years and spent his time, prior to leasing the service station, working at various skilled and unskilled labor oriented jobs. He was not one who should be expected to know the law or understand the meaning of technical terms. The ceremonious activity of signing the lease consisted of nothing more than the agent of American Oil placing the lease in front of Mr. Weaver and saying "sign," which Mr. Weaver did. There is nothing in the record to indicate that Weaver read the lease; that the agent asked Weaver to read it; or that the agent, in any manner, attempted to call Weaver's attention to the "hold harmless" clause in the lease. Each year following, the procedure was the same. A salesman, from American Oil, would bring the lease to Weaver, at the station, and Weaver would sign it. The evidence showed that Weaver had never read the lease prior to signing and that the clauses in the lease were never explained to him in a manner from which he could grasp their legal significance. The leases were prepared by the attorneys of American Oil Company, for the American Oil Company, and the agents of the American Oil Company never attempted to explain the conditions of the lease nor did they advise Weaver that he should consult legal counsel, before signing the lease. The superior bargaining power of American Oil is patently obvious and the significance of Weaver's signature upon the legal document amounted to nothing more than a mere formality to Weaver for the substantial protection of American Oil.

Had this case involved the sale of goods it would have been termed an "unconscionable contract" under sec. 2-302 of the Uniform Commercial Code as found in Burns' Ind. Stat. sec. 19-2-302, IC 1971, 26-1-2-302. The statute reads as follows:

> 19-2-302. *Unconscionable contract or clause.* — If the court as a matter of law finds the contract or any clause of the contract to have been unconscionable at the time it was made the court may refuse to enforce the contract, or it may enforce the remainder of the contract without the unconscionable clause, or it may so limit the application of any unconscionable clause as to avoid any unconscionable result.
>
>   (2) When it is claimed or appears to the court that the contract or any clause thereof may be unconscionable the parties shall be afforded a reasonable opportunity to present evidence as to its commercial setting, purpose and effect to aid the court in making the determination. (Acts 1963, ch. 317, sec. 2-302 p. 539.)

According to the Comment to Official Text, the basic test of unconscionability is whether, in light of the general commercial background and the commercial needs of the particular trade or case, the clauses involved are so one-sided as to be unconscionable under the circumstances existing at the time of the making of the contract. Subsection two makes it clear that it is proper for the court to hear evidence upon these questions.

> An "unconscionable contract" has been defined to be such as no sensible man not under delusion, duress or in distress would make, and such as no honest and fair man would accept. There exists here an "inequality so strong, gross and manifest that it is impossible to state it to a man of common sense without producing an exclamation at the inequality of it." "Where the inadequacy of the price is so great that the mind revolts at it the court will lay hold on the slightest circumstances of oppression or advantage to rescind the contract." It is not the policy of the law to restrict business dealings or to relieve a party of his own mistakes of judgment, but where one party has taken advantage of another's necessities and distress to obtain an unfair advantage over him, and the latter, owing to his condition, has encumbered himself with a heavy liability or an onerous obligation for the sake of a small or inadequate present gain, there will be relief granted. Stiefler v. McCullough (1933), 97 Ind. App. 123, 174 N.E. 823.

The facts of this case reveal that in exchange for a contract which, if the clause in question is enforceable, may cost Mr. Weaver potentially thousands of dollars in damages for negligence of which he was not the cause, Weaver must operate the service station seven days a week for long hours, at a total yearly income of $5,000-$6,000. The evidence also reveals that *the clause was in fine print* and *contained no title heading* which would have identified it as an indemnity clause. It seems a deplorable abuse of justice to hold a man of poor education, to a contract prepared by the attorneys of American Oil, for the benefit of American Oil which was presented to Weaver on a "take it or leave it basis." Justice Frankfurter of the United States Supreme Court spoke on the question of inequality of bargaining power in his dissenting opinion in United States v. Bethlehem Steel Corp. (1942), 315 U.S. 289, 326.

> [I]t is said that familiar principles would be outraged if Bethlehem were denied recovery on these contracts. But is there any principle which is more familiar or more firmly embedded in the history of Anglo-American law than the basic doctrine that the courts will not permit themselves to be used as instruments of inequity and injustice? Does any principle in our law have more universal application than the doctrine that courts will not enforce transactions in which the relative positions of the parties are such that one has unconscionably taken advantage of the necessities of the other?
>
> These principles are not foreign to the law of contracts. Fraud and physical duress are not the only grounds upon which courts refuse to enforce contracts. The law is not so primitive that it sanctions every injustice except brute force and downright fraud. More specifically, the courts generally refuse to lend themselves to the enforcement of a "bargain" in which one party has unjustly taken advantage of the economic necessities of the other.

The traditional contract is the result of free bargaining of parties who are brought together by the play of the market, and who meet each other on a footing of approximate economic equality. In such a society there is no danger that freedom of contract will be a threat to the social order as a whole. But in present-day commercial life the standardized mass contract has appeared. It is used primarily by enterprises with strong bargaining power and position. The weaker party, in need of the goods or services, is frequently not in a position to shop around for better terms, either because the author of the standard contract has a monopoly (natural or artificial) or because all competitors use the same clauses.

Judge Frankfurter's dissent was written nearly twenty years ago. It represents a direction and philosophy which the law, at that time was taking and is now compelled to accept in our modern society over the old principle known as the *parole* [sic] *evidence rule.* The parole evidence rule states that an agreement or contract, signed by the parties, is *conclusively presumed* to represent an integration or meeting of the minds of the parties. This is an archaic rule from the old common law. The objectivity of the rule has as its only merit its simplicity of application which is far outweighed by its failure in many cases to represent the actual agreement, particularly where a printed form prepared by one party contains hidden clauses unknown to the other party is submitted and signed. The law should seek the truth or the subjective understanding of the parties in this more enlightened age. The burden should be on the party submitting such "a package" in printed form to show that the other party had knowledge of any unusual or unconscionable terms contained therein. The principle should be the same as that applicable to implied warranties, namely that a package of goods sold to a purchaser is fit for the purposes intended and contains no harmful materials other than that represented. Caveat lessee is no more the current law than caveat emptor. Only in this way can justice be served and the true meaning of freedom of contract preserved. The analogy is rational. We have previously pointed out a similar situation in the Uniform Commercial Code, which prohibits unconscionable contract clauses in sales agreements.

Caveat lessee

When a party can show that the contract, which is sought to be enforced, was in fact an unconscionable one, due to a prodigious amount of bargaining power on behalf of the stronger party, which is used to the stronger party's advantage and is unknown to the lesser party, causing a great hardship and risk on the lesser party, the contract provision, or the contract as a whole, if the provision is not separable, should not be enforceable on the grounds that the provision is contrary to public policy. The party seeking to enforce such a contract has the burden of showing that the provisions were explained to the other party and *came to his knowledge* and there was in fact *a real and voluntary meeting of the minds and not merely an objective meeting.*

Burden is on the party seeking to enforce contract

Unjust contract provisions have been found unenforceable, in the past, on the grounds of being contrary to public policy, where a party has a greater superior bargaining position. In Pennsylvania Railroad Co. v. Kent (1964), 136 Ind. App. 551, 198 N.E.2d 615, Judge Hunter, speaking for the court said that although the proposition that "parties may enter into such contractual arrangement as they may desire may be conceded in the general sense; when, however, such special agreement may result in affecting the public interest and thereby contravene public policy, the abrogation of the rules governing common carriers must be zealously guarded against." We do not mean to say or infer that parties may not make contracts exculpating one of his negligence and providing for indemnification, but it must be done *knowingly* and *willingly* as in insurance contracts made for that very purpose.

It is the duty of the courts to administer justice and that role is not performed, in this case, by enforcing a written instrument, not really an agreement of the parties as shown by the evidence here, although signed by the parties. The parole evidence rule must yield to the equities of the case. The appeal is transferred to this court and the judgment of the trial court is reversed with direction to enter judgment for the appellant.

Reversed

GIVAN, DEBRULER and HUNTER, JJ., concur.

PRENTICE, J., dissents, with opinion.

Dissent

PRENTICE, J. (dissenting). . . . The identical clause which Defendant here seeks to avoid was held not to be against public policy in the case of Loper v. Standard Oil Co. (1965), 138 Ind. App. 84, 211 N.E.2d 797. Defendant directs our attention, however, to Henningsen et al. v. Bloomfield Motors, Inc., et al. (1960), 32 N.J. 358, 161 A.2d 69, 75 A.L.R.2d 1, cited in Am. Jur. 2d

Contract §188, where, according to Defendant, it is said: "It has been held that clauses limiting liability are given rigid scrutiny by the courts, and will not be enforced unless the limitation is fairly and honestly negotiated and understandingly entered into." The Appellate Court has accepted this statement at face value although there appears to be no Indiana authority in support of such rule. It has been given limited application in other jurisdictions and, as limited, appears to be reasonable and workable. But the defendant appears to mislead us by failing to complete the quotation, which is completed as follows: ". . . this is especially true where the contract involves services of a public or semipublic nature, but has also been applied in some controversies involving private contracts, particularly where, as in the case of a public or semipublic contract *the private contract is the only means one of the parties has of filling an important need.*" (Emphasis added.) The *Henningsen* case involved an action by a consumer against the vendor of an automobile, wherein the court declined to enforce the provision of the sales contract that provided that the express warranty was in lieu of all others expressed or implied. The case has no application to the issues raised on this appeal. Neither do the facts as found by the trial court, together with additional facts mentioned, suggest a disparity of bargaining positions warranting the application of exceptions to reasonable and well established rules or offend against my concept of fair business negotiations. A general disparity of economic or intellectual positions, while factors to be considered along with others in such cases, do not, in and of themselves, give one who is dominant in such attributes an unconscionable advantage in the particular transaction. Whether or not the contract was "understandingly entered into" by Defendant, we, of course, cannot say; but we see nothing to indicate that he was deprived of the opportunity to understand it by any acts or omissions of American. It would be a strange, and in my opinion impossible, rule if one party to a contract were to be held the guardian of the other and accountable to him for both the advantages he hoped to gain thereunder and the risks or losses that he may have failed to consider. Under such a rule, the less one knew of the provisions of the written contract which he executed, the better would be his position in the event of later dissatisfaction.

[margin note: Nothing deprived him the opportunity to read the clause]

Chief Justice Arterburn, speaking for a majority of this Court, has concluded that the defendant was in an inferior position with respect to the lease and treats the lease as we might treat an *adhesion* contract. I find justification for neither. An adhesion contract is one that has been drafted unilaterally by the dominant party and then presented on a "take it or leave it" basis to the weaker party, who has no real opportunity to bargain about its terms. (Restatement 2d, Conflict of Law §332 a, Comment e) (17 C.J.S. Contracts §10, p. 581.) Here we have a printed form contract prepared by American. There was great disparity between the economic positions of American and Defendant; and Defendant was a man of limited educational and business background. However, there is nothing from which we can find or infer that the printed lease provisions were not subject to negotiation or that, with

[margin note: Not an Adhesion contract]

Chose Not to read but elected to Accept

The small print is Not The reasn he dront read It

respect to this particular lease, Defendant was not in a bargaining position equal to that of American. The fact that Defendant did not avail himself of the opportunity to read the agreement but elected to accept it as presented does not warrant the inference that his only options were to "take it or leave it." That the "hold harmless" clause was or might have been in small print, as suggested by the majority, can hardly have significance in light of the claim and finding that the defendant did not read any portion of the document.

The majority places great reliance upon the dissenting opinion of Justice Frankfurter in United States v. Bethlehem Steel Corp. (1942), 315 U.S. 289, 326. I agree that it is a well reasoned opinion and that the philosophy there expressed has had a great impact upon the parole evidence rule and rightfully so. However, I find no similarity between the actual situations under consideration. In the *Bethlehem Steel* case, the national security of the United States hung in the balance while the terms of the contract in question were negotiated. Although the negotiators for the government had a theoretical choice between accepting the proposed contract or taking over the operation of Bethlehem, the latter subjected the nation to such grave peril as to amount to no choice at all. Bethlehem's actions clearly amounted to the taking of an unconscionable advantage of the circumstances, and there was ample authority for relieving the government of the harsh terms thusly coerced. The court there had merely to apply the fundamental principles of law that the courts will not enforce a bargain where one party has unconscionably taken advantage of the necessities and distress of the other. In the case at bar, the defendant was under no compulsion to act. There is nothing to indicate that he was motivated by any purpose other than to improve his own economic position, that the lease arrangement was to be more beneficial to American than to him, that he was financially, intellectually or emotionally incompetent or disadvantaged, that his necessities or potential distress were in any way involved or that his bargaining position with respect to this particular transaction, was not substantially equal to that of American.

The case of the Pennsylvania Railroad Co. v. Kent (1964), 136 Ind. App. 551, 198 N.E.2d 615, has no application, as it was determined upon an issue of public interest and the rules governing common carriers. Also, it is clear that the Uniform Commercial Code sections on sales cited by the majority can have no application; and Chief Justice Arterburn was careful to point out that it was referred to only to illustrate the acceptance of legal philosophies permitting and fostering fair dealings and substantive justice rather than blind and often unjust adherence to hard and fast rules. But we have neither the duty nor the right to abandon established principles whenever, in our judgment, it is necessary to avert a hardship. And should the Legislature see fit to vest us with either or both, I question that we have the requisite wisdom. It is for this reason, I believe, that our mandate is not simply to administer justice but to do so *under the law.* I hold no special interest in preserving the policy of enforcing indemnity and exculpatory contracts. It may well be that they should be greatly curtailed. But the majority opinion does not so hold.

Defendant's dilemma does not spring from an unconscionable advantage taken of him either by deceit of American or by virtue of a superior bargaining position. It clearly stems from either an unwillingness or indifference upon his part to utilize the resources available to him or from a willingness to assume the risks in exchange for the rewards that he hoped to gain. Presumably he has had the benefits contracted for, and the majority decision is a grant of retrospective unilateral contractual immunity to the careless and speculative and places a premium upon ignorance. I fear that it will stand as an invitation to any litigant, who finding himself burdened by his own contract, will say that he did not understand its provisions and ask us for relief that we have neither the duty, right nor wisdom to grant.

willingness to assume the risk

I would accept transfer of this cause, set aside the decision of the Appellate Court, as modified, and affirm the decision of the trial court.

QUESTIONS

1. What is the difference between an exculpatory clause and an indemnity clause? Which was which here? Why not simply declare all exculpatory clauses void as against public policy?

2. Was there both procedural and substantive unconscionability here?

3. Can any language in the case be cited for the proposition that Indiana has abandoned the parol evidence rule entirely? See Grande v. General Motors Corp., 444 F.2d 1022 (7th Cir. 1971).

4. If you were advising American Oil Company, how should it proceed in the future to make sure these clauses would be enforceable?

━━━━━━━━━━━━

The chief reporter of the UCC, and its guiding spirit, was Professor Karl Llewellyn of Columbia Law School. Llewellyn was one of the great legal minds of his day and the author of many famous discussions of commercial problems. When he tackled the problem of unconscionability, he came up with his celebrated "true answer" to the issue of enforcing harsh clauses in contracts:

> The answer, I suggest, is this: Instead of thinking about "assent" to boilerplate clauses, we can recognize that so far as concerns the specific, there is no assent at all. What has in fact been assented to, specifically, are the few dickered terms, and the broad type of the transaction, and but one thing more. That one thing more is a blanket assent (not a specific assent) to any not unreasonable or indecent terms the seller may have on his form, which do not alter or eviscerate the reasonable meaning of the dickered terms. The fine print which has not been read has no business to cut under the reasonable meaning of those dickered terms which constitute the dominant and only real expression of agreement.

Llewellyn, *The Common Law Tradition: Deciding Appeals* 370 (1960).

Problem 130

When she went to check her coat at La Casa Restaurant, Portia Moot failed to notice a sign on the coatroom wall that stated "Not Responsible for Lost Items" in rather large letters. When she went to retrieve the coat after her meal, it was missing. Did the sign exculpate the restaurant from liability? Would it help the defense if the claim check she had been given also repeated this language? What if the cause of the loss was because an employee of the restaurant had stolen the customer's coat? See American Litho, Inc. v. Imation Corp., 2010 WL 681298 (D. Minn. 2010) (exculpatory clause will not protect "gross or willful negligence").

NOTE ON UNCONSCIONABILITY IN THE LEASING OF GOODS

Article 2A of the UCC on the lease of goods contains an unconscionability section modeled on §2-302, but going a bit further. Like its predecessor, §2A-108 does not define unconscionability but does have the following rules:

§2A-108. Unconscionability

(1) If the court as a matter of law finds a lease contract or any clause of a lease contract to have been unconscionable at the time it was made the court may refuse to enforce the lease contract, or it may enforce the remainder of the lease contract without the unconscionable clause, or it may so limit the application of any unconscionable clause as to avoid any unconscionable result.

(2) With respect to a consumer lease, if the court as a matter of law finds that a lease contract or any clause of a lease contract has been induced by unconscionable conduct or that unconscionable conduct has occurred in the collection of a claim arising from a lease contract, the court may grant appropriate relief.

(3) Before making a finding of unconscionability under subsection (1) or (2), the court, on its own motion or that of a party, shall afford the parties a reasonable opportunity to present evidence as to the setting, purpose, and effect of the lease contract or clause thereof, or of the conduct.

(4) In an action in which the lessee claims unconscionability with respect to a consumer lease:
  (a) If the court finds unconscionability under subsection (1) or (2), the court shall award reasonable attorney's fees to the lessee.
  (b) If the court does not find unconscionability and the lessee claiming unconscionability has brought or maintained an action he [or she] knew to be groundless, the court shall award reasonable attorney's fees to the party against whom the claim is made.

> (c) In determining attorney's fees, the amount of the recovery on behalf of the claimant under subsections (1) and (2) is not controlling.

It is possible that this expanded set of rules will influence the courts in nonlease situations when it is applied by analogy (for example, to forbid unconscionable behavior in the collection process).

STIRLEN v. SUPERCUTS
California Court of Appeals, 1997
60 Cal. Rtpr. 2d 138

KLINE, Presiding Justice.

The San Francisco Superior Court refused to enforce a compulsory arbitration clause of an employment contract on the grounds it was . . . unconscionable. We find this determination correct.

I

Defendants Supercuts, Inc., and David E. Lipson, its president and chief executive officer (hereinafter collectively referred to as "Supercuts"), appeal from an order denying their motion to compel arbitration of a dispute relating to the termination from employment of plaintiff William N. Stirlen.

Supercuts, a Delaware corporation that conducts a national hair care franchise business, employed Stirlen as its vice president and chief financial officer from January 1993 until March 1994, when he was terminated.

Stirlen commenced this wrongful discharge case in December 1994. . . . Supercuts moved to compel arbitration under the compulsory arbitration provision of an employment contract between the parties. The court denied the motion, as we have said, on the grounds the provision, considered in its entirety, was unconscionable and therefore unenforceable.

II

The complaint alleges that on numerous occasions in late 1993 and early 1994 Stirlen informed Lipson and other corporate officers of various operating problems he felt contributed to the general decline in Supercuts' retail profits and of "accounting irregularities" he feared might be in violation of state and federal statutes and regulations. Stirlen also expressed concern that the decline in profits "was being hidden in the books and from public shareholders." At a meeting in November 1993, Stirlen provided senior managers quarterly statements indicating that, before accounting "adjustments," Supercuts' earnings level moved only laterally or actually declined during the previous seven quarters. Though Lipson assertedly expressed anger at the production of these statements, Stirlen reiterated his concerns in a memo to Lipson in January of 1994. After Stirlen brought these concerns to the company's auditor, Lipson allegedly reprimanded him, accused him of being a "troublemaker" and told him that if he did not reverse his position on the issues taken to the auditor he would no longer be considered a "member of the team."

At the end of February 1994, Lipson called Stirlen to his office and suspended him from his job. He was terminated the following month. . . .

III

[Under both the Federal Arbitration Act, 9 U.S.C. §1-16 ("FAA") and California Code of Civil Procedure §1281], "the court shall order the petitioner and respondent to arbitrate [a] controversy if it determines that an agreement to arbitrate the controversy exists. . . ." In a petition to compel arbitration under this statute, "the moving party, in essence, requests specific performance of a contractual agreement to arbitrate the controversy. . . ." [However, under both §2 of the FAA and Cal. Code Civ. Proc. §1281, courts can refuse to enforce arbitration clauses] "upon such grounds as exist for the revocation of any contract."

IV

Paragraph 11 of the employment contract is entitled "Submission to Jurisdiction; Arbitration" and comprises what we refer to in this opinion as the "arbitration clause." This provision consists of four subparagraphs.

Subparagraph (a), which pertains to claims that need not be submitted to arbitration, provides as follows: "Any action initiated by the Company seeking specific performance or injunctive or other equitable relief in connection with any breach or violation of Paragraphs 7, 8, 9, or 10 of this Agreement may be maintained in any federal or state court having jurisdiction over Marin County, California. . . ."

Subparagraph (b) of Paragraph 11 states that, "[e]xcept as provided in Paragraph 11.a. hereinabove, in the event there is any dispute arising out of Executive's employment with the Company, the termination of that employment, or arising out of this Agreement, whether such dispute gives rise or may give rise to a cause of action in contract or tort or based on any other theory or statute, including but not limited to the California Fair Employment & Housing Act, Title VII of the Civil Rights Act of 1964, the Age Discrimination in Employment Act, the Americans with Disabilities Act, or any other act or statute, Executive and the Company agree that exclusive recourse shall be to submit any such dispute to final and binding arbitration . . . upon a request submitted in writing in accordance with the notice provisions of this Agreement to the other party to this Agreement within one (1) year of the date the dispute arose, or, in the case of a dispute arising out of the termination of Executive's employment, within one (1) year of the date Executive's employment was terminated. The failure to timely request arbitration hereunder shall constitute a complete waiver of all rights to raise any claims in any forum, arising out of any dispute described herein. The one (1) year limitations period within which to request arbitration shall not be subject to tolling, equitable or otherwise."

Subparagraph (c) of Paragraph 11 restricts the remedies available in arbitration. The parties agree that "in arbitration, the exclusive remedy for alleged violation of this Agreement or the terms conditions, or covenants of employment, and for any harm alleged in connection with any dispute subject to arbitration hereunder (including, without limitation, causes of action arising in tort), shall be a money award not to exceed the amount of actual damages for breach of contract, less any proper offset for mitigation of such damages, and the parties shall not be entitled to any other remedy at law or in equity, including but not limited to other money damages, exemplary damages, specific performance, and/or injunctive relief."

The final subparagraph of Paragraph 11, subparagraph (d), prescribes the method for choosing an arbitrator and provides that the arbitrator's decision "will be final and binding on the parties," the arbitrator's fees will be shared by the parties, the arbitration shall be held in Marin County, and "the arbitrator shall not have the power to alter, amend, or modify any of the provisions of this agreement." . . .

V

The trial court succinctly explained its conclusion that the arbitration clause was "so one-sided as to be unconscionable" as follows: "Defendants can use the court system for certain claims, but the plaintiff must use arbitration for all his, with very limited damages. The plaintiff gives up significant rights, and defendant is protected from liability for all fraud, willful injury or violation of law."

In 1979, . . . the Legislature enacted Civil Code section 1670.5, and thereby adopted the doctrine of unconscionability enunciated in Section 2–302 of the Uniform Commercial Code (U.C.C.), except that section 1670.5 applies to all contracts, not just those for the sale of goods. . . .

Under the U.C.C. provision, [u]nconscionability has generally been recognized to include an absence of meaningful choice on the part of one of the parties together with contract terms which are unreasonably favorable to the other party. Phrased another way, unconscionability has both a "procedural" and a "substantive" element.

procedural

The procedural element focuses on two factors: oppression and surprise. Oppression arises from an inequality of bargaining power which results in no real negotiation and an absence of meaningful choice. Surprise involves the extent to which the supposedly agreed-upon terms of the bargain are hidden in the prolix printed form drafted by the party seeking to enforce the disputed terms.

Substantively

Substantive unconscionability is less easily explained. Cases have talked in terms of "overly harsh" or "one-sided" results. [H]owever, unconscionability turns not only on a "one-sided" result, but also on an absence of justification for it, which is only to say that . . . a contract is largely an allocation of risks between the parties, and therefore that a contractual term is substantively suspect if it reallocates the risks of the bargain in an objectively or unreasonable or unexpected manner. . . .

One commentator sums up the matter as follows: "'[p]rocedural unconscionability' has to do with matters relating to freedom of assent. 'Substantive unconscionability' involves the imposition of harsh or oppressive terms on one who has assented freely to them." Hawkland UCC Series §302:02 (Art. 2), p. 246.) The prevailing view is that these two elements must both be present in order for a court to exercise its discretion to refuse to enforce a contract or clause under the doctrine of unconscionability.

Issue

In the present case, the threshold question is whether the subject arbitration clause is part of a contract of adhesion, thereby establishing the necessary element of procedural unconscionability. . . .

Definition of Adhesion Contract

The standard definition of a "contract of adhesion" is a standardized contract, which, imposed and drafted by the party of superior bargaining strength, relegates to the subscribing party only the opportunity to adhere to the contract or reject it.

D's Contention No Superior Bargaining Power

Supercuts maintains that the contract here is not adhesive because it did not have superior bargaining strength. It emphasizes that Stirlen was not a person desperately seeking employment but a successful and sophisticated corporate executive Supercuts sought out and "hired away" from a highly paid position with a major corporation "by offering him an annual salary of $150,000, and then agreeing to remunerative 'extras' not included in the standard executive employment agreement," such as generous stock options, a bonus plan, a supplemental retirement plan, and a $10,000 "signing bonus." We are unpersuaded. . . .

Terms of K offered to him after he Accepted employment

Stirlen appears to have had no realistic ability to modify the terms of the employment contract. Undisputed evidence shows that the terms of the contract, which were cast in generic and gender neutral language, were presented to him after he accepted employment and were described as standard provisions that were not negotiable. The only negotiating between the parties regarding the conditions of Stirlen's employment related to the stock options, bonus and retirement plans, and other "extras," but these matters were the subject of a separate letter agreement Stirlen executed on January 25, 1993, more than a month before he signed the employment contract. Moreover, the letter agreement adverted to the "standard employment contract" Stirlen would be required to sign, noting that the terms of the letter agreement did not supplant but were "[i]n addition to the standard provisions of the contract . . ." Stirlen's assertions that the employment contract was presented to him on a "take it or leave it basis" and that every other corporate officer was required to and had signed an identical agreement, were not disputed. We agree with the trial court's determination that the agreement to arbitrate was part of a contract of adhesion.

Having determined that the procedural element of unconscionability is present in this case, we turn to the matter of substantive unconscionability. . . .

Finally coming to grips with the issue at the heart of this case, Supercuts alternatively claims the arbitration clause is not one-sided, and therefore unconscionable, because the apparent disparities are actually reasonable and fair. . . .

While it may often be advantageous for employees to submit employment disputes to arbitration, it may also be disadvantageous. For example, arbitral discovery is ordinarily much more limited than judicial discovery, which may seriously compromise an employee's ability to prove discrimination or unfair treatment. [Citations omitted.] Procedural protections available in arbitration are inferior in other ways to those employees may obtain in a judicial forum. As the Ninth Circuit noted in Prudential Ins. Co. of America v. Lai (9th Cir. 1994) 42 F.3d 1299, in California "the privacy rights of victims of sexual harassment are protected by statutes limiting discovery and admissibility of plaintiff's sexual history in a judicial proceeding." (Id., at p. 1305, fn. 4.) No such statutory protection is provided an employee compelled to arbitrate a claim of sexual harassment against an employer under an agreement of the sort presented here, in which the parties do not agree that the civil discovery statutes shall apply.

Further, except in extraordinary circumstances, parties who submit a dispute to private arbitration also give up their right to review of an adverse decision. Thus, unlike Supercuts, which can obtain judicial review of an adverse judicial determination of its claims, its employees must accept adverse rulings on their employment claims even if an error of fact or law appears on the face of the arbitrator's ruling and causes substantial injustice.

One of the most significant discrepancies, of course, is the unilateral restriction on employee remedies and the nature of the rights employees are deprived of in this manner. While Supercuts is deprived of no common law or statutory remedies that may be available to it under Paragraphs 7, 8, 9 and 10 of the employment contract, remedies available to employees in employment disputes are severely curtailed. Not only are employees denied punitive damages for tort claims, they are also denied relief for statutory claims. . . . The only remedy left to employees—actual damages for breach of contract—may bear no relation whatsoever to the extent of the wrong and the magnitude of the injuries suffered at the hands of the employer. This would amount to denial of the underlying cause of action, which would be preserved in name only.

In short, the arbitration clause provides the employer more rights and greater remedies than would otherwise be available and concomitantly deprives employees of significant rights and remedies they would normally enjoy. Considering the terms of the arbitration clause in the light of the commercial context in which it operates and the legitimate needs of the parties at the time it was entered into, we have little difficulty concluding that its terms are "'so extreme as to appear unconscionable according to the mores and business practices of the time and place.' . . ." (Williams v. Walker–Thomas Furniture Co. (D.C. Cir. 1965) 350 F.2d 445, 449-450.)

NOTES AND QUESTIONS

1. Disputes over whether a party can be forced into arbitration take place in the shadow of the Federal Arbitration Act ("FAA"). At common law, judges, who were suspicious of arbitration, invented special rules called the "ouster" and "revocability" doctrines to make it impossible for a party to obtain specific performance of an agreement to arbitrate a future dispute. Congress passed the FAA in 1925 to abolish this hostility to arbitration. The FAA does so through its centerpiece, §2, which states that a "written provision in any . . . contract evidencing a transaction involving commerce to settle by arbitration a controversy thereafter arising . . . shall be valid, irrevocable, and enforceable, save upon such grounds as exist at law or in equity for the revocation of any contract." 9 U.S.C. §2. Section 2 therefore mandates that judges apply conventional contract doctrines such as fraud, duress, and unconscionability—not unique anti-arbitration rules like the ouster and revocability doctrines—to invalidate arbitration clauses.

2. In the 1990s and 2000s, some drafters began trying to use arbitration clauses in consumer, franchise, and employment contracts to tilt the scales of justice in their favor. Unconscionability became the weapon of choice for judges to combat this trend. They found arbitration clauses to be unconscionable for (among other things) (1) mandating confidentiality, see Sprague v. Household Int'l, 473 F. Supp. 2d 966, 974 (W.D. Mo. 2005), (2) barring the award of particular remedies, see Simpson v. MSA of Myrtle Beach, Inc., 644 S.E.2d 663, 671 (S.C. 2007), (3) selecting distant locations for the hearing, see Nagrampa v. MailCoups, Inc., 469 F.3d 1257, 1285 (9th Cir. 2006), (4) limiting discovery, see Ferguson v. Country-wide Credit Indus., Inc., 298 F.3d 778, 786 (9th Cir. 2002), and (5) imposing hefty costs on the plaintiff, see Gutierrez v. Autowest, Inc., 7 Cal. Rptr. 3d 267, 277 (Ct. App. 2003).

3. The most controversial intersection of arbitration and unconscionability involved "class arbitration waivers." These provisions require plaintiffs not only to arbitrate, but to do so on an *individual* basis (rather than as part of

a class action). In Discover Bank v. Superior Court, 113 P.3d 1100, 1104-1108 (Cal. 2005), the California Supreme Court held that a class arbitration waiver was unconscionable where a credit card company had allegedly cheated its customers out of about $30 each. The court reasoned that because no single plaintiff will spend the time and money necessary to pursue such a small claim, the class arbitration waiver functioned as a "get out of jail free card" for corporate liability. Id. at 1108. Several other courts applied this "*Discover Bank* rule" to strike down class arbitration waivers when a "plaintiff's only reasonable, cost-effective means of obtaining a complete remedy [was] as either the representative or a member of a class." Kinkel v. Cingular Wireless LLC, 857 N.E.2d 250, 275 (Ill. 2006). However, corporate lawyers had an ace up their sleeve. To address the objection that class arbitration waivers deterred small-dollar complaints, some companies began to offer rewards for plaintiffs to arbitrate those claims on an individual basis. For example, AT & T promised to pay a bounty of between $5,000 and $10,000 and double attorney's fees to any consumer who won an award in arbitration that exceeded the company's last written settlement offer. Our next case reveals that AT & T's gambit paid off.

AT & T MOBILITY v. CONCEPCION
United States Supreme Court, 2011
563 U.S. 333

Justice SCALIA delivered the opinion of the Court.

Section 2 of the Federal Arbitration Act (FAA) makes agreements to arbitrate "valid, irrevocable, and enforceable, save upon such grounds as exist at law or in equity for the revocation of any contract." 9 U.S.C. §2. We consider whether the FAA prohibits States from conditioning the enforceability of certain arbitration agreements on the availability of class-wide arbitration procedures.

I

In February 2002, Vincent and Liza Concepcion entered into an agreement for the sale and servicing of cellular telephones with AT & T Mobility LCC (AT & T). The contract provided for arbitration of all disputes between the parties but required that claims be brought in the parties' "individual capacity, and not as a plaintiff or class member in any purported class or representative proceeding." . . . The agreement authorized AT & T to make unilateral amendments, which it did to the arbitration provision on several occasions. The version at issue in this case reflects revisions made in December 2006, which the parties agree are controlling.

The revised agreement provides that customers may initiate dispute proceedings by completing a one-page Notice of Dispute form available on AT & T's Web site. AT & T may then offer to settle the claim; if it does not, or if the dispute is not resolved within 30 days, the customer may invoke arbitration by filing a separate Demand for Arbitration, also available on AT & T's website. In the event the parties proceed to arbitration, the agreement specifies that AT & T must pay all costs for non-frivolous claims; that arbitration must take place in the county in which the customer is billed; that, for claims of $10,000 or less, the customer may choose whether the arbitration proceeds in person, by telephone, or based only on submissions; that either party may bring a claim in small claims court in lieu of arbitration; and that the arbitrator may award any form of individual relief, including injunctions and presumably punitive damages. The agreement, moreover, denies AT & T any ability to seek reimbursement of its attorney's fees, and, in the event that a customer receives an arbitration award greater than AT & T's last written settlement offer, requires AT & T to pay a $7,500 minimum recovery and twice the amount of the claimant's attorney's fees.

The Concepcions purchased AT & T service, which was advertised as including the provision of free phones; they were not charged for the phones, but they were charged $30.22 in sales tax based on the phones' retail value. In March 2006, the Concepcions filed a complaint against AT & T in the United States District Court for the Southern District of California. The complaint was later consolidated with a putative class action alleging, among other things, that AT & T had engaged in false advertising and fraud by charging sales tax on phones it advertised as free.

In March 2008, AT & T moved to compel arbitration under the terms of its contract with the Concepcions. The Concepcions opposed the motion, contending that the arbitration agreement was unconscionable and unlawfully exculpatory under California law because it disallowed class-wide procedures. The district court denied AT & T's motion. It described AT & T's arbitration agreement favorably, noting, for example, that the informal dispute-resolution process was "quick, easy to use" and likely to "promp[t] full or . . . even excess payment to the customer *without* the need to arbitrate or litigate"; that the $7,500 premium functioned as "a substantial inducement for the consumer to pursue the claim in arbitration" if a dispute was not resolved informally; and that consumers who were members of a class would likely be worse off. Laster v. T-Mobile USA, Inc., 2008 WL 5216255, *11-*12 (S.D. Cal., Aug. 11, 2008). Nevertheless, relying on the California Supreme Court's decision in Discover Bank v. Superior Court, 36 Cal. 4th 148, 30 Cal. Rptr. 3d 76, 113 P.3d 1100 (2005), the court found that the arbitration provision was unconscionable because AT & T had not shown that bilateral arbitration adequately substituted for the deterrent effects of class actions. *Laster*, 2008 WL 5216255, *14.

The Ninth Circuit affirmed, also finding the provision unconscionable under California law as announced in *Discover Bank*. Laster v. AT & T Mobility

LLC, 584 F.3d 849, 855 (2009). It also held that the *Discover Bank* rule was not preempted by the FAA because that rule was simply "a refinement of the unconscionability analysis applicable to contracts generally in California." 584 F.3d, at 857. In response to AT & T's argument that the Concepcions' interpretation of California law discriminated against arbitration, the Ninth Circuit rejected the contention that "class proceedings will reduce the efficiency and expeditiousness of arbitration" and noted that "*Discover Bank* placed arbitration agreements with class action waivers on the *exact same footing* as contracts that bar class action litigation outside the context of arbitration." *Id.*, at 858 (quoting Shroyer v. New Cingular Wireless Services, Inc., 498 F.3d 976, 990 (C.A.9 2007)).

We granted certiorari, 560 U.S. _____, 130 S. Ct. 3322, 176 L. Ed. 2d 1218 (2010).

II

The FAA was enacted in 1925 in response to widespread judicial hostility to arbitration agreements. See Hall Street Associates, L.L.C. v. Mattel, Inc., 552 U.S. 576, 581, 128 S. Ct. 1396, 170 L. Ed. 2d 254 (2008). Section 2, the "primary substantive provision of the Act," Moses H. Cone Memorial Hospital v. Mercury Constr. Corp., 460 U.S. 1, 24, 103 S. Ct. 927, 74 L. Ed. 2d 765 (1983), provides, in relevant part, as follows:

"A written provision in any maritime transaction or a contract evidencing a transaction involving commerce to settle by arbitration a controversy thereafter arising out of such contract or transaction . . . shall be valid, irrevocable, and enforceable, save upon such grounds as exist at law or in equity for the revocation of any contract." 9 U.S.C. §2.

We have described this provision as reflecting both a "liberal federal policy favoring arbitration," *Moses H. Cone, supra,* at 24, 103 S. Ct. 927, and the "fundamental principle that arbitration is a matter of contract," Rent-A-Center, West, Inc. v. Jackson, 561 U.S. _____, _____, 130 S. Ct. 2772, 2776, 177 L. Ed. 2d 403 (2010). In line with these principles, courts must place arbitration agreements on an equal footing with other contracts [citations omitted].

The final phrase of §2, however, permits arbitration agreements to be declared unenforceable "upon such grounds as exist at law or in equity for the revocation of any contract." This saving clause permits agreements to arbitrate to be invalidated by "generally applicable contract defenses, such as fraud, duress, or unconscionability," but not by defenses that apply only to arbitration or that derive their meaning from the fact that an agreement to arbitrate is at issue. Doctor's Associates, Inc. v. Casarotto, 517 U.S. 681, 687, 116 S. Ct. 1652, 134 L. Ed. 2d 902 (1996); see also Perry v. Thomas, 482 U.S. 483, 492-493, n.9, 107 S. Ct. 2520, 96 L. Ed. 2d 426 (1987). The question in this case is whether §2 preempts California's rule classifying most collective-arbitration waivers in consumer contracts as unconscionable. We refer to this rule as the *Discover Bank* rule.

CA Law

Under California law, courts may refuse to enforce any contract found "to have been unconscionable at the time it was made," or may "limit the application of any unconscionable clause." Cal. Civ. Code Ann. §1670.5(a) (West 1985). A finding of unconscionability requires "a 'procedural' and a 'substantive' element, the former focusing on 'oppression' or 'surprise' due to unequal bargaining power, the latter on 'overly harsh' or 'one-sided' results" [citations omitted].

Conscionability

Discover Bank Holding

In *Discover Bank,* the California Supreme Court applied this framework to class-action waivers in arbitration agreements and held as follows:

"[W]hen the waiver is found in a consumer contract of adhesion in a setting in which disputes between the contracting parties predictably involve small amounts of damages, and when it is alleged that the party with the superior bargaining power has carried out a scheme to deliberately cheat large numbers of consumers out of individually small sums of money, then ... the waiver becomes in practice the exemption of the party 'from responsibility for [its] own fraud, or willful injury to the person or property of another.' Under these circumstances, such waivers are unconscionable under California law and should not be enforced." *Id.,* at 162, 30 Cal. Rptr. 3d 76, 113 P.3d, at 1110 (quoting Cal. Civ. Code Ann. §1668). . . .

III

A

P contention

The Concepcions argue that the *Discover Bank* rule, given its origins in California's unconscionability doctrine and California's policy against exculpation, is a ground that "exist[s] at law or in equity for the revocation of any contract" under FAA §2. Moreover, they argue that even if we construe the *Discover Bank* rule as a prohibition on collective-action waivers rather than simply an application of unconscionability, the rule would still be applicable to all dispute-resolution contracts, since California prohibits waivers of class litigation as well. See America Online, Inc. v. Superior Ct., 90 Cal. App. 4th 1, 17-18, 108 Cal. Rptr. 2d 699, 711-713 (2001).

When state law prohibits outright the arbitration of a particular type of claim, the analysis is straightforward: The conflicting rule is displaced by the FAA. Preston v. Ferrer, 552 U.S. 346, 353, 128 S. Ct. 978, 169 L. Ed. 2d 917 (2008). But the inquiry becomes more complex when a doctrine normally thought to be generally applicable, such as duress or, as relevant here, unconscionability, is alleged to have been applied in a fashion that disfavors arbitration. In Perry v. Thomas, 482 U.S. 483, 107 S. Ct. 2520, 96 L. Ed. 2d 426 (1987), for example, we noted that the FAA's preemptive effect might extend even to grounds traditionally thought to exist "at law or in equity for the revocation of any contract." *Id.,* at 492, n.9, 107 S. Ct. 2520 (emphasis deleted). We said that a court may not "rely on the uniqueness of an agreement to arbitrate as a basis for a state-law holding that enforcement would be unconscionable, for this would enable the court to effect what . . . the state legislature cannot." *Id.,* at 493, n.9, 107 S. Ct. 2520.

An obvious illustration of this point would be a case finding unconscionable or unenforceable as against public policy consumer arbitration agreements that fail to provide for judicially monitored discovery. The rationalizations for such a holding are neither difficult to imagine nor different in kind from those articulated in *Discover Bank.* A court might reason that no consumer would knowingly waive his right to full discovery, as this would enable companies to hide their wrongdoing. Or the court might simply say that such agreements are exculpatory—restricting discovery would be of greater benefit to the company than the consumer, since the former is more likely to be sued than to sue. See *Discover Bank, supra,* at 161, 30 Cal. Rptr. 3d 76, 113 P.3d, at 1109 (arguing that class waivers are similarly one-sided). And, the reasoning would continue, because such a rule applies the general principle of unconscionability or public-policy disapproval of exculpatory agreements, it is applicable to "any" contract and thus preserved by §2 of the FAA. In practice, of course, the rule would have a disproportionate impact on arbitration agreements; but it would presumably apply to contracts purporting to restrict discovery in litigation as well.

Other examples are easy to imagine. The same argument might apply to a rule classifying as unconscionable arbitration agreements that fail to abide by the Federal Rules of Evidence, or that disallow an ultimate disposition by a jury (perhaps termed "a panel of twelve lay arbitrators" to help avoid preemption). Such examples are not fanciful, since the judicial hostility towards arbitration that prompted the FAA had manifested itself in "a great variety" of "devices and formulas" declaring arbitration against public policy. Robert Lawrence Co. v. Devonshire Fabrics, Inc., 271 F.2d 402, 406 (C.A.2 1959). And although these statistics are not definitive, it is worth noting that California's courts have been more likely to hold contracts to arbitrate unconscionable than other contracts. Broome, An Unconscionable Applicable of the Unconscionability Doctrine: How the California Courts are Circumventing the Federal Arbitration Act, 3 Hastings Bus. L.J. 39, 54, 66 (2006); Randall, Judicial Attitudes Toward Arbitration and the Resurgence of Unconscionability, 52 Buffalo L. Rev. 185, 186-187 (2004).

The Concepcions suggest that all this is just a parade of horribles and no genuine worry. "Rules aimed at destroying arbitration" or "demanding procedures incompatible with arbitration," they concede, "would be preempted by the FAA because they cannot sensibly be reconciled with [s]ection 2." Brief for Respondents 32. The "grounds" available under §2's saving clause, they admit, "should not be construed to include a [s]tate's mere preference for procedures that are incompatible with arbitration and 'would wholly eviscerate arbitration agreements.'" *Id.,* at 33 (quoting Carter v. SSC Odin

Operating Co., LLC, 237 Ill. 2d 30, 50, 340 Ill. Dec. 196, 927 N.E.2d 1207, 1220 (2010)).

We largely agree. Although §2's saving clause preserves generally applicable contract defenses, nothing in it suggests an intent to preserve state-law rules that stand as an obstacle to the accomplishment of the FAA's objectives. [Citations omitted.] As we have said, a federal statute's saving clause "cannot in reason be construed as [allowing] a common law right, the continued existence of which would be absolutely inconsistent with the provisions of the act. In other words, the act cannot be held to destroy itself." American Telephone & Telegraph Co. v. Central Office Telephone, Inc., 524 U.S. 214, 227-228, 118 S. Ct. 1956, 141 L. Ed. 2d 222 (1998) (quoting Texas & Pacific R. Co. v. Abilene Cotton Oil Co., 204 U.S. 426, 446, 27 S. Ct. 350, 51 L. Ed. 553 (1907)).

We differ with the Concepcions only in the application of this analysis to the matter before us. We do not agree that rules requiring judicially monitored discovery or adherence to the Federal Rules of Evidence are "a far cry from this case." Brief for Respondents 32. The overarching purpose of the FAA, evident in the text of §§2, 3, and 4, is to ensure the enforcement of arbitration agreements according to their terms so as to facilitate streamlined proceedings. Requiring the availability of class-wide arbitration interferes with fundamental attributes of arbitration and thus creates a scheme inconsistent with the FAA.

Purpose of The FAA [margin note]

B

The "principal purpose" of the FAA is to "ensur[e] that private arbitration agreements are enforced according to their terms." *Volt,* 489 U.S., at 478, 109 S. Ct. 1248; see also Stolt-Nielsen S.A. v. AnimalFeeds Int'l Corp., 559 U.S. _____, _____, 130 S. Ct. 1758, 1763, 176 L. Ed. 2d 605 (2010). This purpose is readily apparent from the FAA's text. Section 2 makes arbitration agreements "valid, irrevocable, and enforceable" as written (subject, of course, to the saving clause); §3 requires courts to stay litigation of arbitral claims pending arbitration of those claims "in accordance with the terms of the agreement"; and §4 requires courts to compel arbitration "in accordance with the terms of the agreement" upon the motion of either party to the agreement (assuming that the "making of the arbitration agreement or the failure . . . to perform the same" is not at issue). In light of these provisions, we have held that parties may agree to limit the issues subject to arbitration, Mitsubishi Motors Corp. v. Soler Chrysler-Plymouth, Inc., 473 U.S. 614, 628, 105 S. Ct. 3346, 87 L. Ed. 2d 444 (1985), to arbitrate according to specific rules, *Volt, supra,* at 479, 109 S. Ct. 1248, and to limit *with whom* a party will arbitrate its disputes, *Stolt-Nielsen, supra,* at _____, 130 S. Ct. at 1773.

§2 [margin note]

The point of affording parties discretion in designing arbitration processes is to allow for efficient, streamlined procedures tailored to the type of dispute. It can be specified, for example, that the decisionmaker be a specialist in the relevant field, or that proceedings be kept confidential to protect trade secrets. And the informality of arbitral proceedings is itself desirable, reducing the cost and increasing the speed of dispute resolution. 14 Penn Plaza LLC v. Pyett, 556 U.S. _____, _____, 129 S. Ct. 1456, 1460, 173 L. Ed. 2d 398 (2009); *Mitsubishi Motors Corp., supra,* at 628, 105 S. Ct. 3346. . . .

Contrary to the dissent's view, our cases place it beyond dispute that the FAA was designed to promote arbitration. They have repeatedly described the Act as "embod[ying] [a] national policy favoring arbitration," *Buckeye Check Cashing,* 546 U.S., at 443, 126 S. Ct. 1204, and "a liberal federal policy favoring arbitration agreements, notwithstanding any state substantive or procedural policies to the contrary," *Moses H. Cone,* 460 U.S., at 24, 103 S. Ct. 927; see also *Hall Street Assocs.,* 552 U.S., at 581, 128 S. Ct. 1396. Thus, in Preston v. Ferrer, holding preempted a state-law rule requiring exhaustion of administrative remedies before arbitration, we said: "A prime objective of an agreement to arbitrate is to achieve 'streamlined proceedings and expeditious results,'" which objective would be "frustrated" by requiring a dispute to be heard by an agency first. 552 U.S., at 357-358, 128 S. Ct. 978. That rule, we said, would "at the least, hinder speedy resolution of the controversy." *Id.,* at 358, 128 S. Ct. 978.

California's *Discover Bank* rule similarly interferes with arbitration. Although the rule does not *require* class-wide arbitration, it allows any party to a consumer contract to demand it *ex post.* The rule is limited to adhesion contracts, *Discover Bank,* 36 Cal. 4th, at 162-163, 30 Cal. Rptr. 3d 76, 113 P.3d, at 1110, but the times in which consumer contracts were anything other than adhesive are long past. [Citations omitted.] The rule also requires that damages be predictably small, and that the consumer allege a scheme to cheat consumers. *Discover Bank, supra,* at 162-163, 30 Cal. Rptr. 3d 76, 113 P.3d, at 1110. The former requirement, however, is toothless and malleable (the Ninth Circuit has held that damages of $4,000 are sufficiently small, see Oestreicher v. Alienware Corp., 322 Fed. Appx. 489, 492 (2009) (unpublished)), and the latter has no limiting effect, as all that is required is an allegation. Consumers remain free to bring and resolve their disputes on a bilateral basis under *Discover Bank,* and some may well do so; but there is little incentive for lawyers to arbitrate on behalf of individuals when they may do so for a class and reap far higher fees in the process. And faced with inevitable class arbitration, companies would have less incentive to continue resolving potentially duplicative claims on an individual basis.

Although we have had little occasion to examine class-wide arbitration, our decision in *Stolt-Nielsen* is instructive. In that case we held that an arbitration panel exceeded its power under §10(a)(4) of the FAA by imposing class procedures based on policy judgments rather than the arbitration agreement itself or some background principle of contract law that would affect its interpretation. 559 U.S., at _____, 130 S. Ct. at 1773-1776. We then held that the agreement at issue, which was silent on the question of class procedures, could not be interpreted to allow them because the "changes brought about by the shift from bilateral arbitration to class-action arbitration" are "fundamental." *Id.*, at _____, 130 S. Ct. at 1776. This is obvious as a structural matter: Class-wide arbitration includes absent parties, necessitating additional and different procedures and involving higher stakes. Confidentiality becomes more difficult. And while it is theoretically possible to select an arbitrator with some expertise relevant to the class-certification question, arbitrators are not generally knowledgeable in the often-dominant procedural aspects of certification, such as the protection of absent parties. The conclusion follows that class arbitration, to the extent it is manufactured by *Discover Bank* rather than consensual, is inconsistent with the FAA.

First, the switch from bilateral to class arbitration sacrifices the principal advantage of arbitration — its informality — and makes the process slower, more costly, and more likely to generate procedural morass than final judgment. "In bilateral arbitration, parties forgo the procedural rigor and appellate review of the courts in order to realize the benefits of private dispute resolution: lower costs, greater efficiency and speed, and the ability to choose expert adjudicators to resolve specialized disputes." 559 U.S., at _____, 130 S. Ct. at 1775. But before an arbitrator may decide the merits of a claim in class-wide procedures, he must first decide, for example, whether the class itself may be certified, whether the named parties are sufficiently representative and typical, and how discovery for the class should be conducted. A cursory comparison of bilateral and class arbitration illustrates the difference. According to the American Arbitration Association (AAA), the average consumer arbitration between January and August 2007 resulted in a disposition on the merits in six months, four months if the arbitration was conducted by documents only. AAA, Analysis of the AAA's Consumer Arbitration Caseload, online at www.adr.org/si.asp?id=5027 (all Internet materials as visited Apr. 25, 2011, and available in Clerk of Court's case file). As of September 2009, the AAA had opened 283 class arbitrations. Of those, 121 remained active, and 162 had been settled, withdrawn, or dismissed. Not a single one, however, had resulted in a final award on the merits. Brief for AAA as *Amicus Curiae* in *Stolt-Nielsen*, O.T. 2009, No. 08-1198, pp. 22-24. For those cases that were no longer active, the median time from filing to settlement, withdrawal, or dismissal — not judgment on the merits — was 583 days, and the mean was 630 days. Id., at 24.

The dissent claims that class arbitration should be compared to class litigation, not bilateral arbitration. *Post*, at 6-7. Whether arbitrating a class is more desirable than litigating one, however, is not relevant. A State cannot defend a rule requiring arbitration-by-jury by saying that parties will still prefer it to trial-by-jury.

Second, class arbitration *requires* procedural formality. The AAA's rules governing class arbitrations mimic the Federal Rules of Civil Procedure for class litigation. Compare AAA, Supplementary Rules for Class Arbitrations (effective Oct. 8, 2003), online at http://www.adr.org/sp.asp?id = 21936, with Fed. Rule Civ. Proc. 23. And while parties can alter those procedures by contract, an alternative is not obvious. If procedures are too informal, absent class members would not be bound by the arbitration. For a class-action money judgment to bind absentees in litigation, class representatives must at all times adequately represent absent class members, and absent members must be afforded notice, an opportunity to be heard, and a right to opt out of the class. Phillips Petroleum Co. v. Shutts, 472 U.S. 797, 811-812, 105 S. Ct. 2965, 86 L. Ed. 2d 628 (1985). At least this amount of process would presumably be required for absent parties to be bound by the results of arbitration.

We find it unlikely that in passing the FAA Congress meant to leave the disposition of these procedural requirements to an arbitrator. Indeed, class arbitration was not even envisioned by Congress when it passed the FAA in 1925; as the California Supreme Court admitted in *Discover Bank,* class arbitration is a "relatively recent development." 36 Cal. 4th, at 163, 30 Cal. Rptr. 3d 76, 113 P.3d, at 1110. And it is at the very least odd to think that an arbitrator would be entrusted with ensuring that third parties' due process rights are satisfied.

Third, class arbitration greatly increases risks to defendants. Informal procedures do of course have a cost: The absence of multilayered review makes it more likely that errors will go uncorrected. Defendants are willing to accept the costs of these errors in arbitration, since their impact is limited to the size of individual disputes, and presumably outweighed by savings from avoiding the courts. But when damages allegedly owed to tens of thousands of potential claimants are aggregated and decided at once, the risk of an error will often become unacceptable. Faced with even a small chance of a devastating loss, defendants will be pressured into settling questionable claims. Other courts have noted the risk of "in terrorem" settlements that class actions entail, see, *e.g.,* Kohen v. Pacific Inv. Management Co. LLC, 571 F.3d 672, 677-678 (C.A.7 2009), and class arbitration would be no different.

Arbitration is poorly suited to the higher stakes of class litigation. In litigation, a defendant may appeal a certification decision on an interlocutory basis and, if unsuccessful, may appeal from a final judgment as well. Questions of law are reviewed *de novo* and questions of fact for clear error. In contrast, 9 U.S.C. §10 allows a court to vacate an arbitral award *only* where the award "was procured by corruption, fraud, or undue means"; "there was evident partiality or corruption in the arbitrators"; "the arbitrators were guilty of misconduct in refusing to postpone the hearing . . . or in refusing to hear evidence pertinent and material to the controversy[,] or of any other misbehavior by which the rights of any party have been prejudiced"; or if the "arbitrators exceeded their powers, or so imperfectly executed them that a mutual, final, and definite award . . . was not made." The AAA rules do authorize judicial review of certification decisions, but this review is unlikely to have much effect given these limitations; review under §10 focuses on misconduct rather than mistake. And parties may not contractually expand the grounds or nature of judicial review. *Hall Street Assocs.*, 552 U.S., at 578, 128 S. Ct. 1396. We find it hard to believe that defendants would bet the company with no effective means of review, and even harder to believe that Congress would have intended to allow state courts to force such a decision. . . .

The dissent claims that class proceedings are necessary to prosecute small-dollar claims that might otherwise slip through the legal system. See *post*, at 9. But States cannot require a procedure that is inconsistent with the FAA, even if it is desirable for unrelated reasons. Moreover, the claim here was most unlikely to go unresolved. As noted earlier, the arbitration agreement provides that AT & T will pay claimants a minimum of $7,500 and twice their attorney's fees if they obtain an arbitration award greater than AT & T's last settlement offer. The District Court found this scheme sufficient to provide incentive for the individual prosecution of meritorious claims that are not immediately settled, and the Ninth Circuit admitted that aggrieved customers who filed claims would be "essentially guarantee[d]" to be made whole, 584 F.3d, at 856, n.9. Indeed, the District Court concluded that the Concepcions were *better off* under their arbitration agreement with AT & T than they would have been as participants in a class action, which "could take months, if not years, and which may merely yield an opportunity to submit a claim for recovery of a small percentage of a few dollars." *Laster,* 2008 WL 5216255, at *12.

. . .

Because it "stands as an obstacle to the accomplishment and execution of the full purposes and objectives of Congress," Hines v. Davidowitz, 312 U.S. 52, 67, 61 S. Ct. 399, 85 L. Ed. 581 (1941), California's *Discover Bank* rule is preempted by the FAA. The judgment of the Ninth Circuit is reversed, and the case is remanded for further proceedings consistent with this opinion.

It is so ordered.

[Justice Thomas's concurring opinion is omitted.]

Justice BREYER, with whom Justice GINSBURG, Justice SOTOMAYOR, and Justice KAGAN join, dissenting.

The Federal Arbitration Act says that an arbitration agreement "shall be valid, irrevocable, and enforceable, *save upon such grounds as exist at law or in equity for the revocation of any contract.*" 9 U.S.C. §2 (emphasis added). California law sets forth certain circumstances in which "class action waivers" in *any* contract are unenforceable. In my view, this rule of state law is consistent with the federal Act's language and primary objective. It does not "stan[d] as an obstacle" to the Act's "accomplishment and execution." Hines v. Davidowitz, 312 U.S. 52, 67, 61 S. Ct. 399, 85 L. Ed. 581 (1941).

And the Court is wrong to hold that the federal Act pre-empts the rule of state law.

I

The California law in question consists of an authoritative state-court interpretation of two provisions of the California Civil Code. The first provision makes unlawful all contracts "which have for their object, directly or indirectly, to exempt anyone from responsibility for his own . . . violation of law." Cal. Civ. Code Ann. §1668 (West 1985). The second provision authorizes courts to "limit the application of any unconscionable clause" in a contract so "as to avoid any unconscionable result." §1670.5(a).

The specific rule of state law in question consists of the California Supreme Court's application of these principles to hold that "some" (but not "all") "class action waivers" in consumer contracts are exculpatory and unconscionable under California "law." Discover Bank v. Superior Ct., 36 Cal. 4th 148, 160, 162, 30 Cal. Rptr. 3d 76, 113 P.3d 1100, 1108, 1110 (2005). In particular, in *Discover Bank* the California Supreme Court stated that, when a class-action waiver is found in a consumer contract of adhesion in a setting in which disputes between the contracting parties predictably involve small amounts of damages, and when it is alleged that the party with the superior bargaining power has carried out a scheme to deliberately cheat large numbers of consumers out of individually small sums of money, then . . . the waiver becomes in practice the exemption of the party "from responsibility for [its] own fraud, or willful injury to the person or property of another." *Id.,* at 162-163, 30 Cal. Rptr. 3d 76, 113 P.3d, at 1110.

In such a circumstance, the "waivers are unconscionable under California law and should not be enforced." *Id.,* at 163, 30 Cal. Rptr. 3d 76, 113 P.3d, at 1110.

The *Discover Bank* rule does not create a "blanket policy in California against class action waivers in the consumer context." Provencher v. Dell, Inc., 409 F. Supp. 2d 1196, 1201 (C.D. Cal. 2006). Instead, it represents the "application of a more general [unconscionability] principle." Gentry v. Superior Ct., 42 Cal. 4th 443, 457, 64 Cal. Rptr. 3d 773, 165 P.3d 556, 564 (2007). Courts applying California law have enforced class-action waivers where they satisfy general unconscionability standards. [Citations omitted.] And even when they fail, the parties remain free to devise other dispute mechanisms, including informal mechanisms that, in context, will not prove unconscionable. See Volt Information Sciences, Inc. v. Board of Trustees of Leland Stanford Junior Univ., 489 U.S. 468, 479, 109 S. Ct. 1248, 103 L. Ed. 2d 488 (1989).

II

A

The *Discover Bank* rule is consistent with the federal Act's language. It "applies equally to class action litigation waivers in contracts without arbitration agreements as it does to class arbitration waivers in contracts with such agreements." 36 Cal. 4th, at 165-166, 30 Cal. Rptr. 3d 76, 113 P.3d, at 1112. Linguistically speaking, it falls directly within the scope of the Act's exception permitting courts to refuse to enforce arbitration agreements on grounds that exist "for the revocation of *any* contract." 9 U.S.C. §2 (emphasis added). The majority agrees. *Ante,* at 9. . . .

III

The majority's contrary view (that *Discover Bank* stands as an "obstacle" to the accomplishment of the federal law's objective, *ante,* at 9-18) rests primarily upon its claims that the *Discover Bank* rule increases the complexity of arbitration procedures, thereby discouraging parties from entering into arbitration agreements, and to that extent discriminating in practice against arbitration. These claims are not well founded. . . .

Where does the majority get its contrary idea — that individual, rather than class, arbitration is a "fundamental attribut[e]" of arbitration? *Ante,* at 9. The majority does not explain. And it is unlikely to be able to trace its present view to the history of the arbitration statute itself. . . .

Because California applies the same legal principles to address the unconscionability of class arbitration waivers as it does to address the unconscionability of any other contractual provision, the merits of class proceedings should not factor into our decision. If California had applied its law of duress to void an arbitration agreement, would it matter if the procedures in the coerced agreement were efficient?

Regardless, the majority highlights the disadvantages of class arbitrations, as it sees them. See *ante,* at 15-16 (referring to the "greatly increase [d] risks to defendants"; the "chance of a devastating loss" pressuring defendants "into settling questionable claims"). But class proceedings have countervailing advantages. In general agreements that forbid the consolidation of claims can lead small-dollar claimants to abandon their claims rather than to litigate. I suspect that it is true even here, for as the Court of Appeals recognized, AT & T can avoid the $7,500 payout (the payout that supposedly makes the Concepcions' arbitration worthwhile) simply by paying the claim's face value, such that "the maximum gain to a customer for the hassle of arbitrating a $30.22 dispute is still just $30.22." Laster v. AT & T Mobility LLC, 584 F.3d 849, 855, 856 (C.A.9 2009).

What rational lawyer would have signed on to represent the Concepcions in litigation for the possibility of fees stemming from a $30.22 claim? See, e.g., Carnegie v. Household Int'l, Inc., 376 F.3d 656, 661 (C.A.7 2004)

("The *realistic* alternative to a class action is not 17 million individual suits, but zero individual suits, as only a lunatic or a fanatic sues for $30"). In California's perfectly rational view, nonclass arbitration over such sums will also sometimes have the effect of depriving claimants of their claims (say, for example, where claiming the $30.22 were to involve filling out many forms that require technical legal knowledge or waiting at great length while a call is placed on hold). *Discover Bank* sets forth circumstances in which the California courts believe that the terms of consumer contracts can be manipulated to insulate an agreement's author from liability for its own frauds by "deliberately cheat[ing] large numbers of consumers out of individually small sums of money." 36 Cal. 4th, at 162-163, 30 Cal. Rptr. 3d 76, 113 P.3d, at 1110. Why is this kind of decision — weighing the pros and cons of all class proceedings alike — not California's to make? . . .

IV

By using the words "save upon such grounds as exist at law or in equity for the revocation of any contract," Congress retained for the States an important role incident to agreements to arbitrate. 9 U.S.C. §2. Through those words Congress reiterated a basic federal idea that has long informed the nature of this Nation's laws. We have often expressed this idea in opinions that set forth presumptions. See, e.g., Medtronic, Inc. v. Lohr, 518 U.S. 470, 485, 116 S. Ct. 2240, 135 L. Ed. 2d 700 (1996) ("[B]ecause the States are independent sovereigns in our federal system, we have long presumed that Congress does not cavalierly pre-empt state-law causes of action"). But federalism is as much a question of deeds as words. It often takes the form of a concrete decision by this Court that respects the legitimacy of a State's action in an individual case. Here, recognition of that federalist ideal, embodied in specific language in this particular statute, should lead us to uphold California's law, not to strike it down. We do not honor federalist principles in their breach.

With respect, I dissent.

NOTES AND QUESTIONS

1. *Concepcion* has been accused of destroying the consumer and employment class action. See, e.g., Jessica Silver-Greenberg and Robert Gebeloff, Arbitration Everywhere, Stacking the Deck of Justice, N.Y. Times (Oct. 31, 2015), https://nyti.ms/2m8xZdj. Why might the opinion have such a dramatic impact? Would this be a good or a bad outcome?

2. Although the law is still evolving, the consensus appears to be that *Concepcion* prohibits judges from finding class arbitration waivers to be unconscionable, but does *not* generally prohibit courts from deeming *other*

unfair portions of arbitration clauses to be unconscionable. See, e.g., Chavarria v. Ralphs Grocery Co., 733 F.3d 916, 919 (9th Cir. 2013).

3. In July 2017, the Consumer Financial Protection Bureau (CFPB) issued a rule banning class arbitration waivers in the financial services sector. See Arbitration Agreements, 82 Fed. Reg. 33,210 (July 19, 2017). However, several months later, the Senate voted 51 to 50 (with Vice President Pence breaking the tie) to repeal the rule. See Act of Nov. 1, 2017, Pub. L. No. 115-74, 131 Stat. 1243, 1243; Jessica Silver-Greenberg, Consumer Bureau Loses Fight to Allow More Class-Action Suits, N.Y. Times (Oct. 24, 2017), https://perma.cc/Z5FP-NG4M. Thus, drafters remain free to use fine print as a shield against aggregate liability.

4. Recently, there has been rising interest in empirical studies of arbitration results. Although arbitration is private, several states have statutes that require arbitration providers (such as the American Arbitration Association and JAMS) to publish data about the outcomes of their consumer and employment arbitrations. Using these statistics, researchers have discovered that "repeat players" (companies that arbitrate multiple times) are more likely to prevail on the merits than "one-shotters" (companies that arbitrate just once). See, e.g., Alexander J.S. Colvin, An Empirical Study of Employment Arbitration: Case Outcomes and Processes, 8 J. Emp. Leg. Stud. 1 (2011); Alexander J.S. Colvin and Mark D. Gough, Individual Employment Rights Arbitration in the United States: Actors and Outcomes, 68 ILR Rev. 1019 (2015); David Horton and Andrea Cann Chandrasekher, Arbitration Nation: Data from Four Providers, 107 Calif. L. Rev. (forthcoming 2019); David Horton and Andrea Cann Chandrasekher, After the Revolution: An Empirical Study of Consumer Arbitration, 104 Geo. L.J. 57 (2015); David Horton and Andrea Cann Chandrasekher, Employment Arbitration After the Revolution, 65 DePaul L. Rev. 457 (2016).

A NOTE ON BOILERPLATE TERMS AND UNCONSCIONABILITY

As discussed in Chapter 1, when consumers purchase goods and services online they are frequently required to agree to boilerplate terms either by simply purchasing the product or specifically clicking an "I Agree" icon ("browsewrap" versus "clickwrap"). Similarly products can arrive with boilerplate terms included in the package with an instruction to return the product if the buyer does not agree to the terms, and some courts will allow these late-arriving additions to become part of the contract. In either situation the percentage of people actually reading the terms is tiny, and those who do often fail to understand or appreciate the significance of the matters covered. Such harsh "I Win, You Lose" boilerplate clauses routinely do the following:

1.   Arbitration is required for all disputes; even though the seller gets to choose the arbitrator, the consumers frequently have to bear the costs of the arbitration if they lose, and there is no appeal from an adverse decision made by the seller's arbitrator.

2.   Class actions are forbidden in both lawsuits filed in court or in arbitration. This means that small matters are not worth pursuing even though the retailer makes a lot of money by the volume of shady charges imposed, while the consumer has no realistic remedy at all.

3.   The seller exculpates itself from liability for consequential damages even if caused by negligent behavior in creating the product. Frequently warranties of quality are also disclaimed or severely limited, with the end result that product failure results in no remedy for the consumer.

4.   A forum selection clause requires all legal actions to be brought in a jurisdiction favorable to the seller either because the laws there discriminate against consumers or because filing a lawsuit in that jurisdiction is often too difficult or expensive for the injured party. In a famous case on point, Carnival Cruise Lines, Inc. v. Shute, 499 U.S. 585 (1991), the United States Supreme Court upheld a forum selection clause that required cruise line passengers who purchased a ticket in the state of Washington to sue in Florida, where the cruise line was headquartered, even though the ship on which they were injured sailed from California and the boilerplate language came with the ticket after they had already paid for it.

In a major book entitled Boilerplate: The Fine Print, Vanishing Rights, and the Rule of Law (2012), Professor Margaret Jane Radin discusses boilerplate from many angles. She begins by comparing two worlds: "World A," where parties actually negotiate the terms of their contract, and "World B," where one party dictates all the terms and refuses to negotiate at all. In World B she states that the so-called contracts are in reality "contracts *not* to contract." Rather, the contracts are dictated by the superior party and filled with what she calls "boilerplate rights deletion schemes." Professor Radin has a raft of solutions: legislative action to forbid such clauses, private rating systems of contracts according to how odious they are, etc., but when it comes to judicial treatment of offending boilerplate she urges the courts to look beyond existing doctrines like unconscionability and treat the use of harmful boilerplate as an intentional tort resulting in both punitive damages and attorney fees.

IX. IMPOSSIBILITY

Everything is deemed possible except that which is impossible
in the nature of things.
— California Civil Code §1597

If an event occurs *before* the contract is formed that causes trouble with its performance, the law of mistake is generally used to solve the difficulty. If the problem arises *after* contract formation, the rules that follow are more appropriate (though courts are not always careful to observe this distinction).

When life goes wrong and the contract cannot be performed, who bears what risk? Where do the losses fall? Again our leading case comes from Great Britain.

TAYLOR v. CALDWELL
Queen's Bench, 1863
3 B.&S. 826, 122 Eng. Rep. 309

BLACKBURN, J. In this case the plaintiffs and defendants had, on the 27th May, 1861, entered into a contract by which the defendants agreed to let the plaintiffs have the use of The Surrey Gardens and Music Hall on four days then to come, viz., the 17th June, 15th July, 5th August and 19th August, for the purpose of giving a series of four grand concerts, and day and night fêtes at the Gardens and Hall on those days respectively; and the plaintiffs agreed to take the Gardens and Hall on those days, and pay £100 for each day.

The parties inaccurately call this a "letting," and the money to be paid a "rent"; but the whole agreement is such as to shew that the defendants were to retain the possession of the Hall and Gardens so that there was to be no demise of them, and that the contract was merely to give the plaintiffs the use of them on those days. Nothing however, in our opinion, depends on this. The agreement then proceeds to set out various stipulations between the parties as to what each was to supply for these concerts and entertainments, and as to the manner in which they should be carried on. The effect of the whole is to shew that the existence of the Music Hall in the Surrey Gardens in a state fit for a concert was essential for the fulfilment of the contract, — such entertainments as the parties contemplated in their agreement could not be given without it.

After the making of the agreement, and before the first day on which a concert was to be given, the Hall was destroyed by fire. This destruction, we must take it on the evidence, was without the fault of either party, and was so complete that in consequence the concerts could not be given as intended.

And the question we have to decide is whether, under these circumstances, *Issue*
the loss which the plaintiffs have sustained is to fall upon the defendants.
The parties when framing their agreement evidently had not present to their
minds the possibility of such a disaster, and have made no express stipulation
with reference to it, so that the answer to the question must depend upon the
general rules of law applicable to such a contract.

There seems no doubt that where there is a positive contract to do a
thing, not in itself unlawful, the contractor must perform it or pay damages
for not doing it, although in consequence of unforeseen accidents, the
performance of his contract has become unexpectedly burthensome or
even impossible. The law is so laid down in 1 Roll. Abr. 450, Condition
(G), and in the note (2) to Walton v. Waterhouse (2 Wms. Saund. 421 a.
6th ed.), and is recognised as the general rule by all the Judges in the much
discussed case of Hall v. Wright (E.B.&E. 746). But this rule is only applicable
when the contract is positive and absolute, and not subject to any condition
either express or implied: and there are authorities which, as we think,
establish the principle that where, from the nature of the contract, it
appears that the parties must from the beginning have known that it
could not be fulfilled unless when the time for the fulfilment of the contract arrived some particular specified thing continued to exist, so that,
when entering into the contract, they must have contemplated such
continuing existence as the foundation of what was to be done; there,
in the absence of any express or implied warranty that the thing shall
exist, the contract is not to be construed as a positive contract, but as
subject to an implied condition that the parties shall be excused in
case, before breach, performance becomes impossible from the perishing
of the thing without default of the contractor.

There seems little doubt that this implication tends to further the great
object of making the legal construction such as to fulfil the intention of those
who entered into the contract. For in the course of affairs men in making
such contracts in general would, if it were brought to their minds, say that
there should be such a condition. . . .

There is a class of contracts in which a person binds himself to do
something which requires to be performed by him in person; and such
promises, e.g. promises to marry, or promises to serve for a certain time,
are never in practice qualified by an express exception of the death of the
party; and therefore in such cases the contract is in terms broken if the
promisor dies before fulfilment. Yet it was very early determined that, if
the performance is personal, the executors are not liable; Hyde v. The
Dean of Windsor (Cro. Eliz. 552, 553). See 2 Wms. Exors. 1560, 5th ed.,
where a very apt illustration is given. "Thus," says the learned author, "if
an author undertakes to compose a work, and dies before completing it, his
executors are discharged from this contract: for the undertaking is merely
personal in its nature, and, by the intervention of the contractor's death, has
become impossible to be performed." For this he cites a dictum of Lord

Lyndhurst in Marshall v. Broadhurst (1 Tyr. 348, 349), and a case mentioned by Patteson J. in Wentworth v. Cock (10 A.&E. 42, 45-46). In Hall v. Wright (E.B.&E. 746, 749), Crompton J., in his judgment, puts another case. "Where a contract depends upon personal skill, and the act of God renders it impossible, as, for instance, in the case of a painter employed to paint a picture who is struck blind, it may be that the performance might be excused." It seems that in those cases the only ground on which the parties or their executors, can be excused from the consequences of the breach of the contract is, that from the nature of the contract there is an implied condition of the continued existence of the life of the contractor, and, perhaps in the case of the painter of his eyesight.

It may, we think, be safely asserted to be now English law, that in all contracts of loan of chattels or bailments if the performance of the promise of the borrower or bailee to return the things lent or bailed, becomes impossible because it has perished, this impossibility (if not arising from the fault of the borrower or bailee from some risk which he has taken upon himself) excuses the borrower or bailee from the performance of his promise to redeliver the chattel.

The great case of Coggs v. Bernard (1 Smith's L.C. 171, 5th ed.; 2 L. Raym. 909) is now the leading case on the law of bailments, and Lord Holt, in that case, referred so much to the Civil law that it might perhaps be thought that this principle was there derived direct from the civilians, and was not generally applicable in English law except in the case of bailments; but the case of Williams v. Lloyd (W. Jones, 179), above cited, shews that the same law had been already adopted by the English law as early as The Book of Assizes. The principle seems to us to be that, in contracts in which the performance depends on the continued existence of a given person or thing, a condition is implied that the impossibility of performance arising from the perishing of the person or thing shall excuse the performance.

In none of these cases is the promise in words other than positive, nor is there any express stipulation that the destruction of the person or thing shall excuse the performance; but that excuse is by law implied, because from the nature of the contract it is apparent that the parties contracted on the basis of the continued existence of the particular person or chattel. In the present case, looking at the whole contract, we find that the parties contracted on the basis of the continued existence of the Music Hall at the time when the concerts were to be given; that being essential to their performance.

We think, therefore, that the Music Hall having ceased to exist, without fault of either party, both parties are excused, the plaintiffs from taking the gardens and paying the money, the defendants from performing their promise to give the use of the Hall and Gardens and other things. Consequently the rule must be absolute to enter the verdict for the defendants.

Rule absolute.

QUESTIONS

1. How does the court know that the burning of the music hall is an excusing event? How do you know it?

2. Would the court reach the same result if the defendant had burned down the music hall deliberately? Negligently?

3. Return to the facts of Problem 66 in Chapter 3. Would the plane crash that occurred be an event that excused the delivery company of liability to Bill Gilbert?

Problem 131

(a) Behemoth Construction Company agreed to build an office building for the city of Jordan. When the office building was 95 percent completed, it was destroyed by fire due to an act of God. There was no clause in the contract providing what was to happen in such an event (such a clause is called a *force majeure* clause, or, in Latin, a *vis major* clause). Must Behemoth Construction start over, or is the law of impossibility an excuse? See United States Fidelity & Guarantee Co. v. Parsons, 147 Miss. 335, 112 So. 469 (1927); Stees v. Leonard, 20 Minn. 494 (1874).

(b) Job Paint Contractors agreed to paint the City Council meeting room for the city of Jordan, with the city promising to pay $20,000 on completion. When Job was three-fourths done, the building holding the meeting room was destroyed in an earthquake. May Job Paint Contractors recover anything? See Albre Marble & Tile Co. v. John Bowen Co., 338 Mass. 394, 155 N.E.2d 437 (1959).

NISSHO-IWAI CO. v. OCCIDENTAL CRUDE SALES
United States Court of Appeals, Fifth Circuit, 1984
729 F.2d 1530

GOLDBERG, Circuit Judge. This diversity action involves a contract dispute between the Nissho-Iwai Company, Ltd. ("Nissho") and Occidental Crude Sales, Inc. ("Occidental"). Occidental appeals from a jury verdict awarding Nissho contract damages and fraud damages arising from Occidental's failure to perform a crude oil agreement. We hold that there was no reversible error in the finding that Occidental was liable for breach of contract. We reverse the damage award, however, and remand for a new trial limited to determining contract damages. Finally, we reverse the fraud verdict.

FACTS

Nissho is a Japanese corporation that distributes oil to Japanese buyers. Occidental is an American corporation that explores for and produces oil. In 1965, Occidental obtained a number of "oil concessions" from the High Petroleum Council and the Council of Ministers of Libya. The concessions permitted Occidental to drill for oil in two separate blocks of property ("Concession 102" and "Concession 103"). The producing wells were managed by the Libyan Government, and Occidental was responsible for pipelines that transported oil from the wells to an export terminal in Zueitina. Each concession agreement provided for a royalty payment of 12.5 percent and a tax payment of 50 percent to the Government on each barrel of oil.

On September 1, 1969, a Revolutionary Government under Colonel Moammar Khadafy deposed the King of Libya and assumed control. In January 1970, Colonel Khadafy formed a committee to negotiate higher prices with Libyan oil producers; but the companies were unwilling to comply. Khadafy imposed a series of production restrictions; and in August 1973, he nationalized 51 percent of Occidental's concessions.

THE CONTRACT

Occidental had been under contract since 1971 to provide Nissho with "Zueitina Medium" crude oil produced from Concession 102. Zueitina Medium is a low sulphur oil that is particularly useful to electric utility companies required to meet air pollution standards. After receiving the oil, Nissho would resell it to various Japanese power companies.

In 1973, Occidental, aware of the past difficulties with the Libyan Government, renegotiated its contract with Nissho. On October 4, 1973, Occidental and Nissho signed the new agreement, known as Contract 1038. Nissho agreed to purchase and Occidental agreed to supply 750,000 barrels of oil a month through December 31, 1978. The contract contains a "force majeure" clause excusing nonperformance caused by

> executive or administrative orders or acts [of the Libyan Government], . . . or by breakdown or injury to . . . producing . . . or delivering facilities, . . . or by any other event, whether or not similar to the causes specified above . . . , which shall not reasonably be within the control of the party against whom the claim would otherwise be made (i.e. Occidental in this case).

The contract also provides that it is to be governed by the laws of California.

[handwritten margin notes: "Parties renegotiated and signed a New Contract"; ""force Majeure" clause"]

EVENTS LEADING UP TO BREACH OF CONTRACT 1038

UNDERLIFTINGS BY NISSHO

The parties performed their respective duties for several months. Troubles developed, however, in 1974. First, during several months in 1974 and 1975, Nissho failed to "lift" its required allotment of oil. The reasons for these "underliftings" are disputed. There is evidence that Occidental supplied reduced quantities during January and March, 1974, because of the Arab-Israeli War. There is also evidence that some of the underliftings in late 1974 were caused by the Nereus Shipping Company ("Nereus") which "nominated" ships to receive oil at such close intervals that Occidental could not fill them. (Nereus was required to supply tankers pursuant to a contract of affreightment with Nissho.) The parties, however, continued to work under the contract. As one officer of Occidental testified, the company elected not to take legal action against Nissho, preferring to reach a commercial solution. Trial Transcript at 1101.

ACTIONS OF THE LIBYAN GOVERNMENT

During this period, actions of the Libyan Government affected Occidental's production. On February 7, 1974, the Government and Occidental entered into an Exploration and Production Sharing Agreement under which the Government received 81 percent of oil production. In the following months, the Government ordered increases or decreases in production from various wells. Occidental objected to some of the charges and negotiated remedial production quotas.

The parties reached an impasse in the summer of 1975, however. On July 31, the Government announced that Occidental's production exceeded the limits set in Petroleum Regulation Number 8 and that the wells in Concession 103 would be closed temporarily for testing. Then, on August 28, 1975, the Government issued a cutback order to become effective September 1, 1975. Occidental objected to the cutback, arguing that it violated the concession agreements and that Occidental would have "a right to look to the Government for reimbursement of all direct and consequential damages." Plaintiff's Exhibit 11. In a separate letter, Occidental objected to the Government's failure to pay for certain oil exploration (as required by the Exploration and Production Sharing Agreement).

When the Government failed to restore production within seven days, Occidental sought arbitration of the claims. In addition, on September 30, Occidental withheld $117 million that it owed the Government: including $40 million for oil purchased from the Government, and $77 million in back taxes and royalties.

The Government notified Occidental that if the payments were not made, the Government would prevent Occidental from exporting oil after

October 1, 1975. Occidental refused to pay and the government placed an embargo on exports. Thus, Occidental was unable to perform its contract with Nissho that month.

The embargo on exports lasted until Occidental and the Government settled their disputes on December 3, 1975. Pursuant to the settlement agreement, the embargo order was lifted, the pending arbitrations were withdrawn, and the production of Occidental was restored to 300,000 barrels per day.

PIPELINE BREAKDOWNS

Breakdowns in the oil pipeline leading from Concession 102 to Zueitina also affected Occidental's ability to perform the contract with Nissho. Leaks appeared in early 1975; and Occidental shut down the pipeline for repairs from June 20 to July 10. The leaks persisted, however; and in October, Occidental began major repairs: the pipeline was pressure tested, holes were dug, and a section of the pipeline was removed.

After the oil embargo ended in December, 1975, Occidental attempted to reconnect the pipeline and repair any remaining leaks. Yet, when the pipeline was reattached, Occidental discovered sand in the line. To correct that problem, Occidental again had to remove a section of the line. Consequently, the pipeline was shut down from October, 1975, through May 10, 1976, and no oil was produced from Concession 102 during that period.

BREACH BY OCCIDENTAL

In sum, Occidental failed to supply Nissho with any oil during the last four months of 1975 and the first four months of 1976. The oil embargo prevented performance between October and December, 1975. Then, pipeline problems stopped the flow of oil until May, 1976. The reason for the breach in September, 1975, is unclear. However, Occidental wrote Nissho on more than one occasion in August and early September, stating that the September cargo would not be available because of production restrictions. That representation was untrue. . . .

Occidental raises a number of challenges to the judgment in this case. It argues that Judge O'Conor erred in the first trial by recalling the jury to reconsider its verdict; thus, the original verdict should stand and Occidental is entitled to a directed judgment. We do not even reach this claim, however. Regardless of whether it was proper to recall the jury, Judge O'Conor had broad discretion to declare a mistrial and order a new trial when he detected confusion in the jury verdict.

Occidental also raises a number of issues concerning the second trial. It argues, first, that the judge erred in charging the jury about the Force Majeure clause. Occidental claims that the trial court should not have instructed the jury to consider whether an excusing event under the clause was within the reasonable control of Occidental. We hold that the instruction was proper. Moreover, we hold that Judge O'Conor properly refused a qualifying charge that Occidental had requested. . . .

CHALLENGES TO THE SECOND TRIAL

FORCE MAJEURE

Occidental raises several supposed errors in the second trial as grounds for reversing that judgment. Occidental objects to the giving of one jury instruction and the failure to give another with regard to force majeure. At trial, Occidental attempted to defend its nonperformance on the ground that acts of the Libyan Government (in particular, the embargo) and pipeline breakdowns prevented Occidental from supplying oil. Both excuses come within specific provisions of the "Force Majeure" clause in Contract 1038, which provides in pertinent part:

[handwritten margin note: Defense for Non-Performance]

[handwritten margin note: force majeure]

> Neither party shall be liable for . . . loss, damage, claims or demands of any nature whatsoever due to delays or defaults in performance . . . caused by impairment in any manner of [Occidental's] crude oil supply, [by] *executive or administrative orders or acts* . . . of any . . . government, [by] *breakdown or injury to . . . producing . . . or delivering facilities,* [by] *imposition of restrictions* . . . by any . . . government, . . . or by *any other event,* whether or not similar to the causes specified above . . . , *which shall not be reasonably within the control of the party* against whom the claim would otherwise be made.

Plaintiff's Exhibit 88, at 4, §XV (emphasis added).

> Judge O'Conor instructed the jury that [i]n order to find that Occidental's nonperformance was excused under the force majeure clause you must find from a preponderance of the evidence (1) that the excusing event or events relied upon by Occidental actually prevented Occidental's performance, *and* (2) that the excusing event or events were not reasonably within the control of Occidental or its supplier.

[handwritten margin note: Rule — Jury Instructions]

Record at 210. Occidental objects to the second element of the charge, which required the jury to consider whether pipeline difficulties and the Libyan oil embargo were within the reasonable control of Occidental. According to Occidental, the contract clause distinguishes between specifically enumerated events and the general category of "any other event"; only the latter must be beyond the reasonable control of the Seller. Occidental points out that in California, a limiting exception applies only to the last phrase preceding it, unless the context indicates otherwise. See, e.g., In re Estate of Colyear, 17 Cal. App. 3d 173, 94 Cal. Rptr. 696, 702 (1971); Grant v. Hipsher, 257 Cal. App. 2d 375, 383, 64 Cal. Rptr. 892 (1967).

[handwritten margin note: Occ. objects to 2nd element]

CA law

⚡

In this case, however, the California law of force majeure requires us to apply a reasonable control limitation to each specified event, regardless of what generalized contract interpretation rules would suggest. Thus, Judge O'Conor did not err in giving such an instruction. "Force majeure" has traditionally meant an event which is beyond the control of the contractor. See Squillante and Congalton, Force Majeure, 80 Comm. L.J. 4, 5 (1979).

No error

Rule ⚡

The common law defense of impossibility due to Act of God requires the defendant to prove that an excusing event is beyond his control, id. at 5; and contractual force majeure provisions typically incorporate this requirement, see Eastern Air Lines v. McDonnell Douglas, 532 F.2d 957, 991 (5th Cir. 1976).

"Reasonable Control" ①

Two Part Test

The term "reasonable control" has come to include two related notions. First, a party may not affirmatively cause the event that prevents his performance. The rationale behind this requirement is obvious. If a contractor were able to escape his responsibilities merely by causing an excusing event to occur, he would have no effective "obligation to perform." The second aspect of reasonable control is more subtle. Some courts will not allow a party to rely on an excusing event if he could have taken reasonable steps to prevent it. See Oosten v. Hay Haulers Dairy Employees & Helpers Union, 45 Cal. 2d 784, 291 P.2d 17, 20-21 (1955); 6 Corbin on Contracts, §1342, at 328; Anderson, supra. The rationale behind this requirement is that the force majeure did not actually prevent performance if a party could reasonably have prevented the event from occurring. The party has prevented performance and, again, breached his good faith obligation to perform by failing to exercise reasonable diligence. . . .

CA standard

The California Supreme Court has read into contractual force majeure provisions both aspects of "reasonable control" — good faith in not causing the excusing event and diligence in taking reasonable steps to ensure performance. In Oosten, supra, the parties had entered into a contract for the sale of milk. Clause 12 of the contract provided:

> In case of strike, lockout, or other labor trouble . . . which shall render it impossible for [either party to perform], no liability for non-compliance with this agreement caused thereby . . . shall exist or arise.

291 P.2d at 19. The clause did not explicitly refer to "reasonable control." Yet, the Court invoked the concept in describing the obligations of a party relying on a force majeure clause:

> In the instant case we construe clause 12, with respect to impossibility of performance, the same as it is construed generally in contract law with regard to whether performance has been made impossible. The only things the clause adds are that certain things — labor disputes, strikes — may excuse

performance, when without it they might not, but the question remains whether those things have been made impossible. As has been said: "We cannot always be sure what 'causes are beyond the control' of the contractor. Many fires can be prevented by the use of foresight and sufficient expenditure. Most strikes can be avoided by a judicious yielding or by an abject surrender to demands. No contractor is excused under such an express provision unless he shows affirmatively that his failure to perform was proximately caused by a contingency within its terms; that, in spite of skill, diligence and good faith on his part, performance became impossible or unreasonably expensive."

Id. at 20-21. See also Butler v. Nepple, 54 Cal. 2d 589, 6 Cal. Rptr. 767, 772-773, 354 P.2d 239, 244-245 (1960) (affirming *Oosten* rule that party must take reasonable steps to ensure performance).

To be sure, the facts in *Oosten* are distinguishable from our case. Nevertheless, the words of the California Court provide the most definitive statement of California law concerning the relationship between contractual force majeure clauses and the reasonable control limitation. The Court, in effect, requires proof that a party relying on a force majeure clause did not exercise reasonable control over the excusing event. California law supports Judge O'Conor's decision to apply the control limitation to each of the specified events in the force majeure clause of Contract 1038. Finally, we note that the Northern District of Illinois reached the same result in construing a force majeure clause under Michigan law. See Chemetron v. McLouth Steel, 381 F. Supp. 245, 256 (N.D. Ill. 1974), aff'd, 522 F.2d 469 (7th Cir. 1975). The clause at issue in that case provided:

> The failure of either Seller or Buyer to perform any of its obligations hereunder, if caused by an . . . explosion . . . or by any other circumstances beyond the reasonable control of the party so failing, shall not subject such party to any liability to the other party.

Id. The seller McLouth attempted to excuse its nonperformance because of explosions in its compressor. The District Court rejected the defense, in part because "there was not an adequate showing that the explosions were beyond McLouth's control." Id. The court was clearly applying the "reasonable control" requirement to the specified event (explosions).

In sum, we conclude that Judge O'Conor was correct in requiring Occidental to prove that pipeline breakdowns or the acts of the Libyan Government were beyond its reasonable control. . . .

As we have seen, however, California law requires Occidental to take extra steps to prevent the embargo unless "extreme and unreasonable difficulty, expense, injury, or loss[es] are involved." Butler v. Nepple, supra, 354 P.2d at 245; *Oosten* supra, 291 P.2d at 20. Whether a third party violates a contract in demanding extra money from Occidental is certainly a factor in determining whether that expense is unreasonable. It is not dispositive, however. For example, if the Libyan Government had demanded that Occidental pay five extra dollars, the expense (though unlawful) would not be unreasonable in terms of Occidental's good faith obligation to perform its contract with Nissho. Therefore, Occidental's requested instruction was not accurate.

Nor was the trial court required to decide the issue of reasonable control as a matter of law. The issue is a classic jury question. Though we may disagree with the jury's result, we cannot reverse if there is substantial evidence to support the judgment. See Boeing Co. v. Shipman, 411 F.2d 365, 374 (5th Cir. 1969). If reasonable men could find that Occidental was able to prevent the embargo without incurring unreasonable expense, then we must affirm. See id. A review of the record in this case reveals that there was sufficient evidence to support such a verdict.

It is clear Occidental was aware of the threatened embargo and could have prevented it by paying $117 million. This sum in itself was not unreasonable, since the entire figure represented back taxes, royalties, and oil costs that Occidental already owed the Libyan Government. Of course, even if Occidental had paid this sum and averted the embargo, it would still have faced production restrictions. A reasonable jury could have found, though, that Occidental would be able to recoup through arbitration or settlement any losses that might result from the restrictions. The company had already commenced arbitration proceedings against the Libyan Government; and, in December, it was able to reach a settlement. To be sure, the withheld payments and the resulting embargo were factors producing that settlement. That is not to say, however, that a settlement would not have been reached in the absence of an embargo. In the past, Occidental had been able to convince the Government to back down from production restrictions. A reasonable jury might have found that Occidental would again have been able to negotiate a reasonable settlement, particularly given the threat of the arbitration proceedings.

Similarly, there was sufficient evidence to support the view that Occidental had reasonable control over pipeline breakdowns. During 1975 and 1976, Occidental conducted numerous repairs on the pipeline leading from Concession 102 to Zueitina. In October, 1975, Occidental began repairs and disconnected a section of the line. The line remained severed until after the embargo ended in December. There was testimony that Occidental left the line disconnected because it did not want to spend money for repairs until after it had settled its dispute with Libya. Trial Transcript at 581. When the line was reconnected, Occidental discovered that it was clogged with sand. A reasonable jury could have found that the blockage of the line or the failure to discover the blockage earlier was caused by Occidental's delay in repairing and reconnecting the line. The evidence supported a finding that the pipeline breakdown was within Occidental's reasonable control.

In sum, there was no reversible error in either the force majeure charge given by Judge O'Conor or the jury's result. . . .

No error

======

Problem 132

In 2025, when the United States began regular flights to and from the moon, strange cracking problems began to plague the barges the spaceships towed behind them. The government advertised for bids for a contractor/ inventor who would guarantee the government a solution to the problem. The government explained in its advertisement that it was unsure whether current technology was advanced enough to solve the problem at all. Edison Tomorrow Company submitted the only bid and was awarded the job. After two years of steady effort, Edison Tomorrow threw in the towel and demonstrated to the satisfaction of everyone that the project was impossible; there was no way that the cracking could be prevented at this date. Edison Tomorrow then submitted its bill for its expenses, and the government refused to pay, pointing to the guarantee Edison Tomorrow had signed when awarded the contract. Edison Tomorrow took refuge in the law of impossibility. How should this come out? *-- NO*

No,
— Knew risks,
but assumed
anyway

=======================

UNIFORM COMMERCIAL CODE

§2-615. EXCUSE BY FAILURE OF PRESUPPOSED CONDITIONS

Except so far as a seller may have assumed a greater obligation . . .

(a) Delay in delivery or non-delivery in whole or in part by a seller who complies with paragraphs (b) and (c) is not a breach of his duty under a contract for sale if performance as agreed has been made impracticable by the occurrence of a contingency the non-occurrence of which was a basic assumption on which the contract was made or by compliance in good faith with any applicable foreign or domestic governmental regulation or order whether or not it later proves to be invalid.

(b) Where the causes mentioned in paragraph (a) affect only a part of the seller's capacity to perform, he must allocate production and deliveries among his customers but may at his option include regular customers not then under contract as well as his own requirements for further manufacture. He may so allocate in any manner which is fair and reasonable.

(c) The seller must notify the buyer seasonably that there will be delay or non-delivery and, when allocation is required under paragraph (b), of the estimated quota thus made available for the buyer. . . .

Comment 4. Increased cost alone does not excuse performance unless the rise in cost is due to some unforeseen contingency which alters the essential nature of the performance. Neither is a rise or a collapse in the market in itself a justification, for that is exactly the type of business risk which business contracts made at fixed prices are intended to cover. But a severe shortage of raw materials or of supplies due to a contingency such as war, embargo, local crop failure, unforeseen shutdown of major sources of supply or the like, which either causes a marked increase in cost or altogether prevents the seller from securing supplies necessary to his performance is within the contemplation of this section.

What constitutes Non-Performance

Problem 133

Hiram Walker contracted to sell T. C. Sherwood a cow called Rose of Aberlone. Prior to the date of delivery, Rose died. Is Walker in breach of contract? See UCC §2-613. What if Rose is very sick on the delivery date? What if Hiram Walker died before the delivery date?

No fault   *UCC*

Problem 134

Mona's Kitchen contracted with the U.S. Navy to supply it with 100,000 chicken pot pies every year for ten years at an agreed upon price. Mona's had always purchased its chickens from the Chicken Ranch of Best, Texas, with whom it had done business for 80 years. The Chicken Ranch suddenly closed its doors, a totally unexpected event, and Mona's Kitchens was unable to find substitute chickens at a price that made the contract with the Navy profitable. Is this an excusing event? See Ecology Services, Inc. v. Granturk Equipment, Inc., 443 F. Supp. 2d 756 (D. Md. 2006).

Not Impossible
- See Comment 5 (2-615)

Problem 135

Farmer McGregor contracted to sell 10,000 potatoes to the Potter Grocery Store. Both parties knew McGregor expected to grow the potatoes on his own farm, though the contract said nothing about the expected source of the potatoes. A tornado swept through McGregor's farm and destroyed the potato crop. Is this an excusing event under UCC §2-615? See its Official Comment 9. What if the problem was caused by rabbits? See Clark v. Wallace County Coop. Equity Exch., 26 Kan. App. 2d 463, 986 P.2d 391 (1999).

Depends if they understood if potatoes were to come from exclusively from the farm

- Could claim mutual misunderstanding
- Not for rabbits
* → Can control this*

SUNFLOWER ELECTRIC COOPERATIVE, INC.
v. TOMLINSON OIL CO.
Kansas Court of Appeals, 1981
7 Kan. App. 2d 131, 638 P.2d 963

HERD, J. This is a breach of contract action in which the trial court relieved appellee of liability for breach under the doctrine of impossibility of performance. Sunflower Electric appeals.

Appellant, Sunflower Electric Cooperative, Inc., a member of the R.E.A. family, is a public utility in the business of generating electricity for wholesale to eight member cooperatives. Its main generating facility is located in Finney County. Appellee, Tomlinson Oil Company, Inc., is a corporation involved in oil and gas production. It owned a number of oil and gas leases in an area known as the Stranger Creek gas field in Leavenworth County.

On November 29, 1973, the parties executed an agreement for the sale and purchase of natural gas which is the subject of this action. Under the agreement, Tomlinson promised to sell and Sunflower to buy 3 MMCF (million cubic feet) of gas per day from the reserves in the Stranger Creek field. Tomlinson also promised to develop its reserves so as to guarantee delivery of 7 MMCF per day. The price was fifty-five cents per MCF (thousand cubic feet) for the first year after initial delivery, increasing one cent per MCF each year for three years. After the fourth year the price would be renegotiated or submitted to arbitration. Under an exchange agreement with Kansas-Nebraska Natural Gas Co., Inc., the gas would be delivered to a Cities Service storage facility in Leavenworth County. Kansas-Nebraska would then deliver an equivalent amount of gas to a point four miles south of Sunflower's generating facility in Finney County. Tomlinson had to build a 13.2 mile pipeline to the Cities Service storage facility and Sunflower a 4.5 mile pipeline to the Kansas-Nebraska exchange delivery point. For purposes of appeal, the following provisions of the agreement are particularly relevant:

Section I. *Gas to be Purchased and Sold Hereunder.* The gas to be sold by Seller and purchased by Buyer under the terms of this agreement shall be produced from Seller's gas reserves now existing and that will exist during the term of this agreement under Seller's Leasehold Area. . . .

Section III. *Dedication of Acreage.* Seller shall dedicate to Buyer a gas supply from the reserves under the Seller's Leasehold Area up to 7 MMCF per day for a period of fifteen (15) years. . . .

Section IV. *Deliverability and Development.* Seller shall deliver not less than 3 MMCF of gas per day at the commencement of delivery of gas as herein provided for, and shall proceed to systematically and expeditiously develop its leases in Seller's Leasehold Area in such a manner as to guarantee the maximum deliverability herein contracted for at the earliest possible time and to continue the maximum deliverability for the full term of this agreement.

Section XII. *Specific Performance.* Buyer and Seller each expressly recognize that the purchase of gas and the availability of gas to the Buyer is the essence of this Agreement, that gas is a valuable and depleting natural resource, and that the private interests of Buyer as well as the interests of the consuming public of electricity served by Buyer would be irreparably damaged in the event that Seller failed to make the deliveries of gas herein agreed upon. . . . The Seller and Buyer stipulate that the payment of money damages would not be adequate to satisfy the claims of Buyer or Seller for the breach of this agreement, and that by reason thereof this agreement shall be enforceable by specific performance, and that either party may seek specific performance thereof against the other.

Both parties constructed their respective pipelines which were completed by November 1974. Tomlinson breached the contract the first day and was never able to deliver the minimum amount of gas called for by the contract thereafter. In 1975 Tomlinson delivered only 88,479 MCF compared with 985,500 MCF it would have had to deliver to meet the minimum. In July 1976, Tomlinson stopped all production in the Stranger Creek field and hence deliveries under the contract. Sunflower had to look elsewhere for its natural gas supply. Sunflower then filed this action.

The trial court's findings of fact may be summarized as follows. The Stranger Creek field is located five to six miles northeast of an older field known as the McLouth field, now used as a storage area. The McLouth field, developed in the 1930's, at one time had 90 producing gas wells. Its history was extensively analyzed in a 1941 publication of the Kansas Geological Survey known as Bulletin 53. One of the early developers of the Stranger Creek field was Bill Iverson. Iverson was the consulting geologist on approximately fifteen wells in this field. From 1968 to 1970 Iverson and his partners, encouraged by Bulletin 53 and similarities to the older McLouth field, bought leases of 1200 acres in the Stranger Creek field. They then sold this acreage to J. A. Allisen in mid-1970. Allisen acquired additional leases and bought leased wells upon which pipe was set. In the fall of 1971, Allisen sold a one-half interest to Tomlinson and later another one-fourth interest. Ultimately Allisen and Tomlinson acquired 80 leases covering 9874.62 acres in the Stranger Creek field.

Prior to entering into the contract with Sunflower in November of 1973, Tomlinson had purchased 6 wells and drilled 6 wells. Of these twelve wells, only five (Pauley #1, Collins #1, Feverly #2, Kellison and Jones #1) were potential producers, with the remainder being dry holes or abandoned as not commercial. Multipoint back pressure tests, most of which were performed in October, 1972, by Cities Service revealed gas flows for these five wells as follows: Pauley #1 (675 MCF), Collins #1 (1200 MCF), Feverly #2 (846 MCF), Kellison (3680 MCF), and Jones #1 (589 MCF). A multipoint back pressure test measures the relationship of short-term gas flow to the back pressure of a pipeline but is not a measure of the well's long-term capacity or the gas reserves. The presence of heavy oil in all these wells was noted early.

long-term supply not known

In November, 1974, the five wells were connected to the pipeline Tomlinson had constructed to the Cities Service storage facility and gas was produced and sold under the contract starting December, 1974. Tomlinson experienced problems with heavy oil immediately but was unconcerned because three wells, Pauley, Feverly and Collins, had been shut in for some time. The Pauley well never produced as the weight of fluid was heavier than the gas. The other four wells went on the line at a good flow of gas but went into a rapid decline. On February 4, 1975, E. B. Kreiter, production manager for Tomlinson, prepared a progress report in which he noted that the wells were "declining at an abnormally high rate which would indicate a small reservoir or one of limited permeability." On April 29, Tomlinson checked fluid levels on these wells and calculated bottom hole pressure. All wells had a decline in pressure and were full of fluid. In May of 1975, Tomlinson drilled Jones #2 and Edmonds #1, neither of which were commercial wells. In June of 1975, Feverly #2 was temporarily abandoned. The remaining wells produced some small amount of gas through July of 1976, when all production stopped.

problems with 3 wells

↓ All production stopped

As production declined, Tomlinson found heavy oil fouling up all of its separators, tubing and meters. Kerosene and steam would not clean this equipment. The oil changed to a solid-like asphalt. A sample of the heavy oil from the Pauley #1 well was found to have a viscosity of 100,000 centipoise at 100°F with a pour point of 90°F. Normal crude oil has a viscosity of 10 to 100 centipoise. Because of the heavy oil problem, Tomlinson decided not to spend any additional time or money in developing or producing in the Stranger Creek field. . . .

From this conflicting testimony the trial court found:

Testimony

> [T]hat the gas in the Stranger Creek field is exhausted and that heavy oil is a problem only because of the depletion of gas. The Tomlinson estimates of reserves when the contract was signed were over optimistic. However, the Tomlinson development program and operation after the contract was signed was reasonable and prudent and further efforts by anyone at this time would not result in production of any significant amount of gas from the Stranger Creek gas field.

In its conclusions of law, the trial court first held that the agreement was subject to the Uniform Commercial Code and that Sunflower's measure of damages under K.S.A. 84-2-712(2) was the difference between the cost of "cover," i.e., fuel purchased in substitution for that due from Tomlinson, and the contract price. The court found that Sunflower's calculation of $2,614,011.13 based on the cost of replacement fuel for the four years of the agreement for which the price of gas was set was proper as damages

Damages under UCC

Amount is Not challenged

Liability is ## challenged

under this formula. This amount is not challenged on appeal. Based on its finding that the gas in Stranger Creek was exhausted, the court denied specific performance.

The court then considered Tomlinson's liability for damages. The agreement contained an "uncontrollable forces" clause which the court held inapplicable. Again, this ruling is not challenged on appeal. The court did hold, however, that Tomlinson should be relieved under the doctrine of impossibility of performance. In so finding the court stated in part:

[T]his is a contract where a particular gas field was being developed and a supply of gas from the leases and acreage dedicated in that field is a basic assumption of the contract and the only source contemplated. Failure of the Stranger Creek gas field to produce sufficient quantities of gas to fulfill the contract for any reason other than the fault of the defendant is an excuse for non-performance under Restatement of Contracts, supra, §283 or §286, unless the defendant assumed this risk.

. . . Nothing in the contract guarantees, warrants or promises that a sufficient reserve exists and will exist to fulfill the contract and the Court cannot conclude that one party rather than the other assumed the risk of a particular reserve.

The defendant has contended throughout that this is a case of supervening impossibility due to the unexpected problem with heavy oil. There is little question but what oil with a viscosity 10,000 times that of normal crude oil would and did produce unique and probably unsolvable problems with production. However, the weight of the evidence seems to now suggest that the Stranger Creek gas field is not similar to the McLouth field and the gas reserves in this field were quite small when the contract was signed. If this is correct, then we are dealing with original impossibility. This still makes no difference from a legal standpoint, so long as defendant Tomlinson was not at fault in failing to foresee this contingency. When the contract was signed, Tomlinson had five apparently good gas wells with multipoint back pressure tests indicating tremendous quantities of gas. Most of the geologists found similarities to the highly successful McLouth field nearby. Gas reserves are difficult to estimate prior to actual production and the plaintiff's witnesses thought the data insufficient to even try. Whether better data prior to execution of the contract would have given a better picture of the reserves is speculative. In order to accurately project reserves, it is necessary to have production, which requires a pipeline and a market, hence the contract. The Court finds that defendant Tomlinson was not at fault in failing to foresee the rapid depletion of the Stranger Creek field. The parties contracted on the basic assumption that the Stranger Creek leases contained substantial gas reserves. The defendant Tomlinson proceeded as a prudent and diligent developer in building the pipeline and then expanding its exploration. They are to be excused by reason of objective impossibility of performance, whether original or supervening. Restatement of Contracts, supra, §§281, 283, 286(1).

The court also denied charges to Sunflower for the $262,209.55 it had spent on the pipeline constructed under the agreement in Finney County. From these rulings, Sunflower appeals. . . .

Accordingly, this court must determine whether the trial court's findings of fact are supported by the evidence and whether those findings support the legal conclusion that Tomlinson should be excused from its obligation under the contract because of the doctrine of impossibility of performance. The latter determination is one of law. Restatement (Second) of Contracts, ch. 11, Introductory Note, pp. 309-310 (1981). Moreover, insofar as determination of this case requires interpretation of the agreement itself, the standard of review is that regardless of the construction of a written instrument made by the trial court, on appeal the instrument may be construed and its legal effect determined by the appellate court. State Bank of Parsons v. First National Bank in Wichita, 210 Kan. 647, Syl. ¶1, 504 P.2d 156 (1972).

The law has long since recognized that impossibility, or as stated by the more modern authorities, impracticability of performance *may* relieve a promisor of liability for breach of contract. Such impracticability may arise after the contract, in which case it is referred to as "supervening" or may exist at the time of the contract, in which case it is referred to as "original" or "existing." The trial court found this to be a case of existing impracticability in that the weight of the evidence suggested that Stranger Creek never contained sufficient reserves to meet the contract requirement. The general rule as to existing impracticability is stated in Restatement (Second) of Contracts §266 (1981):

> Where, at the time a contract is made, a party's performance under it is impracticable without his fault because of a fact of which he has no reason to know and the non-existence of which is a basic assumption on which the contract is made, no duty to render that performance arises, unless the language or circumstances indicate the contrary.

This statement of the general rule encompasses the exceptions to relief: (1) the impracticability must not have been caused by the promisor (fault), (2) the promisor must have had no reason to know of the impracticability (foreseeability); and (3) the language or circumstances may indicate that the promisor not be relieved because of the impracticability (assumption of the risk).

The Restatement rule adopts in large part the rationale of section 2-615 of the Uniform Commercial Code. The Code clearly applies here. The sale of gas contemplated by the agreement was the "sale" of "goods." K.S.A. 84-2-105 to 106. See Amoco Pipeline Co. v. Admiral Crude Oil Corp., 490 F.2d 114 (10th Cir. 1974). K.S.A. 84-2-615 provides in pertinent part:

Except so far as a seller may have assumed a greater obligation. . . . (a) Delay in delivery or nondelivery in whole or in part by a seller . . . is not a breach of his duty under a contract for sale if performance as agreed has been made impracticable by the occurrence of a contingency the nonoccurrence of which was a basic assumption on which the contract was made. Official comments 5 and 8 indicate that fault and foreseeability, as well as assumption of the risk are exceptions to relief under this provision.

A distinction is also drawn between impracticability which is "subjective" and "objective." This has been described as the difference, respectively, between "I cannot do it" and "the thing cannot be done." See State Highway Construction Contract Cases, 161 Kan. 7, 67, 166 P.2d 728 (1946). Only objective impracticability may serve to relieve a party of his or her contractual obligation.

There appears to be no real dispute that the existence of sufficient reserves in Stranger Creek to meet the contract requirements was a "basic assumption" of the agreement. Since under the trial court's findings sufficient reserves do not exist, the general rule provides that Tomlinson should be relieved from liability, unless one of the exceptions applies. Sunflower's six points on appeal are overlapping and repetitious but may be reduced to the following: (1) the impracticability of performance was subjective, (2) Tomlinson was at fault in developing Stranger Creek, (3) lack of sufficient reserves was foreseeable by Tomlinson, (4) Tomlinson assumed the risk of impracticability, and (5) it would be inequitable to grant relief under the circumstances of this case.

We first consider the argument that this is a case of subjective impossibility. As the trial court found, most of the Kansas cases which have considered the doctrine of impossibility of performance have been found to involve subjective impossibility and thus relief has been denied. The general rule is stated in White Lakes Shopping Center, Inc. v. Jefferson Standard Life Ins. Co., 208 Kan. 121, Syl. ¶2, 490 P.2d 609 (1971):

When one agrees to perform an act *possible in itself* he will be liable for a breach thereof although contingencies not foreseen by him arise which make it difficult, or even beyond his power, to perform and which might have been foreseen and provided against in the contract. (Emphasis added.)

In *White Lakes* the alleged impossibility was that more financing was needed for a construction project than had previously been agreed to in a loan commitment. Impossibility, if it was such, was held to be subjective. . . .

Sunflower's argument that the agreement for the sale of gas is a thing possible "in itself" ignores the agreement which was expressly limited to sale of gas produced from Stranger Creek. The trial court's findings of fact that Stranger Creek is exhausted and further efforts by anyone would not result in production is supported by the evidence. The trial court's finding also disposes of Sunflower's argument that "the use of pumping units and bottom hole heaters could have been utilized to improve production. . . ." Thus, the sale of gas from Stranger Creek is impossible for anyone to perform, making this a case of objective impossibility.

Second, Sunflower argues that the fault exception applies to Tomlinson because it failed to expeditiously develop Stranger Creek. This argument appears to be based on the fact only five wells were connected to the pipeline constructed to deliver gas under the agreement, and after it became apparent these wells would not produce sufficient gas to meet the contract requirements, only two additional wells were drilled, neither of which produced. This argument must fail for two reasons. First, the trial court found "defendant Tomlinson proceeded as a prudent and diligent developer in building the pipeline and then expanding its exploration." This finding is supported by the evidence. Secondly, failure to drill additional wells cannot be deemed "fault" in light of the trial court's finding that the reserves are exhausted. Failure to develop Stranger Creek, whether expeditiously or not, did not contribute to the impracticability involved in this case, i.e., the lack of reserves.

Because of the manner in which we dispose of this case we will discuss Sunflower's third and fourth arguments together. Those arguments are: the lack of reserves was foreseeable by Tomlinson and Tomlinson assumed the risk that the reserves would be insufficient. As both the Restatement and the Code indicate, the language *or circumstances* of a contract may indicate that a party has assumed an obligation to perform despite impracticability. Such an assumption of the risk may be implied and foreseeability may be a factor in such a determination. . . .

Was the lack of reserves in Stranger Creek "sufficiently foreshadowed" at the time of contracting to be considered a risk assumed by Tomlinson? The trial court found Tomlinson was not "at fault" in failing to foresee the lack of reserves in Stranger Creek. This was based on the fact that when the contract was signed, Tomlinson had five wells with multipoint back pressure tests indicating sufficient gas to meet the contract requirements and the fact that most of the geologists found similarities to the successful McLouth field. The court also found, however, that multipoint back pressure tests do not provide a measure of reserves. The court specifically found that "[g]as reserves are difficult to estimate prior to actual production and the plaintiff's witnesses thought the data insufficient to even try." We think the court applied too strict a standard of foreseeability. It may well be true under prudent business standards, Tomlinson *assumed* it has reserves in Stranger Creek. However, the evidence is overwhelming and the trial court's own findings are to the effect that such reserves are inherently unknown. Tomlinson, in its brief, supports this conclusion when it states that "[a]ll the experts agreed one does not know what is below the ground and that the responsible estimates can be way off." Green and Yates gave Tomlinson a negative report on reserves. The favorable reserve reports were by

Tomlinson's employees. They based their opinion on Bulletin 53 pertaining to the McLouth field and a pressure test which admittedly did not pertain to reserves. We conclude Tomlinson should have foreseen Stranger Creek might not contain sufficient reserves. . . .

Court said it was foreseeable

Tomlinson would have us abandon the rule that if the event was foreseeable the parties must make provision for it in the contract or be bound. It points out that Williston finds this rule "descended in the law from a time when it was more nearly true than it now is, because impossibility was more rarely an excuse." 18 Williston on Contracts §1953 (3d ed. 1978), p. 118. That treatise proposes the following test which Tomlinson would have us apply here:

> If the event causing the impossibility in question could not only have been anticipated but its occurrence could have been guarded against by the promisor (not the effect of it by a provision in the contract but the occurrence itself by preventing its happening), it is reasonable to assume that the promisor took the risk of the continued possibility of performance. p. 119.

Even were we to adopt this test of foreseeability, however, the present case falls within the next sentence of §1953, which provides:

> A similar argument is appropriate where the promisor, although having no power to prevent the contingency, had superior knowledge of the possibility of its happening.

Here, Tomlinson, as a company in the business of oil and gas production, and as the owner of the Stranger Creek leases, and as the party making the estimates as to reserves, must be held to have had superior knowledge as to the possibility that the reserves might prove insufficient.

Having concluded that the lack of reserves was foreseeable to Tomlinson, we also conclude that Tomlinson assumed the risk that such would prove to be the case. The trial court correctly found that the agreement contains no express assumption of such an obligation by Tomlinson, but as indicated above, this may be implied by the circumstances of a particular case. Besides the factor that the lack of reserves was foreseeable to Tomlinson, we note that the agreement provided that "the purchase of gas and the availability of gas to Buyer is the essence of this agreement" and that Tomlinson was to develop the field so as to "guarantee" the maximum deliverability under the agreement. We find these provisions, particularly the former, significant. Sunflower agreed to build a 4.5 mile pipeline and loan Tomlinson the cost of its gathering system, a total outlay of in excess of a half million dollars, based on Tomlinson's assurances of adequate reserves.

Most cases with analogous facts are simply applications of the general rule that relief will be allowed absent one of the exceptions. The general rule is particularly applicable where the existence of a specific thing is necessary for the performance of the contract and that specific thing is destroyed or fails to come into existence. See Restatement (Second) of Contracts §263 (1981). Thus, one who contracts to sell and deliver a crop of fruit, vegetables, grain, or hay then growing on a specific tract of land, or to be grown on such a tract within a specified growing season, is discharged from duty by the destruction of that crop without fault. Mercantile Co. v. Canning Co., 111 Kan. 68, 206 P. 337 (1922). This rule has been applied to an oil sales contract when the well which was the subject of the contract ceased to produce. North American Oil Co. v. Globe Pipe Line Co., 6 F.2d 564 (8th Cir. 1925). See also Housing Auth. v. E. Tenn. Etc. Co., 183 Va. 64, 31 S.E.2d 273 (1944), where it was held that a contract to supply natural gas which the parties contemplated would come from a particular field was excused when the field ceased to produce. It is of note that this was a jury case and that the instructions provided that the supplier must not have assumed the risk of failure of the field. The jury verdict for the supplier was affirmed.

Even when a specific thing is necessary for performance, however, the circumstances may demonstrate that a party has assumed the risk. 6 Corbin on Contracts §1339 (1962), states: "In any such case, however, the expressions of the parties, interpreted reasonably, may show that one party has assumed the whole risk, has warranted the possibility of performance or made himself an insurer. One who contracts to supply pasturage on specific land for a number of cattle may be found to have warranted that grass will grow and water run [citing Berg v. Erickson, 234 F. 817 (8th Cir. 1916)]. One who promises to supply water for irrigation must look out for droughts and find the water at the favorable time and place; [citing Northern Irr. Co. v. Watkins, 183 S.W. 431 (Tex. Civ. App. 1916)]; it is the risk of drought, usual and unusual, that the promisee expects to eliminate. The water company may, of course, protect itself by a clause respecting drought and other causes beyond its control." p. 398.

A reasonable interpretation of the contract in this case shows that it was the risk of obtaining a supply of natural gas, which the contract recognized as a "depleting natural resource" which Sunflower sought to eliminate. The fact that the agreement was specifically tied to the Stranger Creek field is significant in determining whether Tomlinson should be relieved. We gave effect to this limitation regarding Sunflower's argument of subjective impossibility. In light of the other circumstances, however, we conclude that the fact the agreement was so limited does not in itself compel relief for Tomlinson.

This is not a case where a crop failed through some natural disaster or even where an oil or gas field which had been producing so as to meet contract requirements failed. In this case a contract was entered into to supply a specified quantity of gas before it was determined that that quantity existed and without any provision being made in the contract for such a contingency. . . .

That Tomlinson assumed the risk reserves might be insufficient is, we think, demonstrated by (1) the language of the contract making purchase and availability of gas to Sunflower the essence of the agreement, (2) Tomlinson's foreseeability that the reserves might not be sufficient, and (3) Tomlinson's expertise and superior knowledge as to the possibility of inadequate reserves. This compels a finding that Tomlinson not be relieved of liability for its breach. To hold otherwise would mean an oil or gas producer could enter into a long term supply contract, borrow money on it, gamble on the extent of its supply, know the purchaser is relying and expending sums thereon, then escape with impunity when the supply proves inadequate. If the producer wishes to be relieved of liability where its reserves are unknown, appropriate language can be inserted in the contract. In this case, it was not. . . .

Reversed

The judgment is reversed and remanded with directions to enter judgment for plaintiff in the amount of $2,806,298.13 and costs.

QUESTIONS

1. How do we distinguish this case from the destruction of the potato crop in Problem 135?

2. How do we distinguish this case from the death of the cow in Problem 133?

KRELL v. HENRY
Court of Appeal, King's Bench, 1903
2 K.B. 740

Agreed to rent rooms for coronation

Event was cancelled, king got sick

The plaintiff, Paul Krell, sued the defendant, C. S. Henry, for 50£, being the balance of a sum of 75£, for which the defendant had agreed to hire a flat at 56A, Pall Mall on the days of June 26 and 27, for the purpose of viewing the processions to be held in connection with the coronation of His Majesty. The defendant denied his liability, and counterclaimed for the return of the sum of 25£, which had been paid as a deposit, on the ground that, the processions not having taken place owing to the serious illness of the King, there had been a total failure of consideration for the contract entered into by him.

The facts, which were not disputed, were as follows. The plaintiff on leaving the country in March, 1902, left instructions with his solicitor to let his suite of chambers at 56A, Pall Mall on such terms and for such period (not exceeding six months) as he thought proper. On June 17, 1902, the defendant noticed an announcement in the windows of the plaintiff's flat to the effect that windows to view the coronation processions were to be let. The defendant interviewed the housekeeper on the subject, when it was pointed out to him what a good view of the processions could be obtained from the premises, and he eventually agreed with the housekeeper to take the suite for the two days in question for a sum of 75£.

On June 20, the defendant wrote the following letter to the plaintiff's solicitor: —

> I am in receipt of yours of the 18th instant, inclosing form of agreement for the suite of chambers on the third floor at 56A, Pall Mall, which I have agreed to take for the two days, the 26th and 27th instant, for the sum of 75£. For reasons given you I cannot enter into the agreement, but as arranged over the telephone I inclose herewith cheque for 25£ as deposit, and will thank you to confirm to me that I shall have the entire use of these rooms during the days (not the nights) of the 26th and 27th instant. You may rely that every care will be taken of the premises and their contents. On the 24th inst. I will pay the balance, viz., 50£, to complete the 75£ agreed upon.

On the same day the defendant received the following reply from the plaintiff's solicitor: —

> I am in receipt of your letter of to-day's date inclosing cheque for 25£ deposit on your agreeing to take Mr. Krell's chambers on the third floor at 56A, Pall Mall for the two days, the 26th and 27th June, and I confirm the agreement that you are to have the entire use of these rooms during the days (but not the nights), the balance, 50£, to be paid to me on Tuesday next the 24th instant.

The processions not having taken place on the days originally appointed, namely, June 26 and 27, the defendant declined to pay the balance of 50£ alleged to be due from him under the contract in writing of June 20 constituted by the above two letters. Hence the present action. Darling J., on August 11, 1902, held, upon the authority of Taylor v. Caldwell and The Moorcock, that there was an implied condition in the contract that the procession should take place, and gave judgment for the defendant on the claim and counter-claim.

The plaintiff appealed.

WILLIAMS, L.J. [After discussing Taylor v. Caldwell and Roman civil law, the court continued:] I do not think that the principle of the civil law as introduced into the English law is limited to cases in which the event causing the impossibility of performance is the destruction or non-existence of some thing which is the subject-matter of the contract or of some condition or state of things expressly specified as a condition of it. I think that you first have to ascertain, not necessarily from the terms of the contract, but, if required, from necessary inferences, drawn from surrounding circumstances recognised by both contracting parties, what is the substance of the contract, and then to ask the question whether that substantial contract needs for its foundation the assumption of the existence of a particular state of things. If it does, this will limit the operation of the general words, and in such case, if the contract becomes impossible of performance by reason of the nonexistence of the state of things assumed by both contracting parties as the foundation of the contract, there will be no breach of the contract thus limited. Now what are the facts of the present case? The contract is contained in two letters of June 20 which passed between the defendant and the plaintiff's agent, Mr. Cecil Bisgood. These letters do not mention the coronation, but speak merely of the taking of Mr. Krell's chambers, or, rather, the use of them, in the daytime of June 26 and 27, for the sum of 75£, 25£ then paid, balance 50£ to be paid on the 24th. But the affidavits, which by agreement between the parties are to be taken as stating the facts of the case, shew that the plaintiff exhibited on his premises, third floor, 56A, Pall Mall, an announcement to the effect that windows to view the Royal coronation procession were to be let, and that the defendant was induced by that announcement to apply to the housekeeper on the premises, who said that the owner was willing to let the suite of rooms for the purpose of seeing the Royal procession for both days, but not nights, of June 26 and 27. In my judgment the use of the rooms was let and taken for the purpose of seeing the Royal procession. It was not a demise of the rooms, or even an agreement to let and take the rooms. It is a licence to use rooms for a particular purpose and none other. And in my judgment the taking place of those processions on the days proclaimed along the proclaimed route, which passed 56A, Pall Mall, was regarded by both contracting parties as the foundation of the contract; and I think that it cannot reasonably be supposed to have been in the contemplation of the contracting parties, when the contract was made, that the coronation would not be held on the proclaimed days, or the processions not take place on those days along the proclaimed route; and I think that the words imposing on the defendant the obligation to accept and pay for the use of the rooms for the named days, although general and unconditional, were not used with reference to the possibility of the particular contingency which afterwards occurred. It was suggested in the course of the argument that if the occurrence, on the proclaimed days, of the coronation and the procession in this case were the foundation of the contract, and if the general words are thereby limited or qualified, so that in the event of the non-occurrence of the coronation and procession along the proclaimed route they would discharge both parties from further performance of the contract, it would follow that if a cabman was engaged to take some one to Epsom on Derby Day at a suitable enhanced price for such a journey, say 10£, both parties to the contract would be discharged in the contingency of the race at Epsom for some reason becoming impossible; but I do not think this follows, for I do not think that in the cab case the happening of the race would be the foundation of the contract. No doubt the purpose of the engager would be to go to see the Derby, and the price would be proportionately high; but the cab had no special qualifications for the purpose which led to the selection of the cab for this particular occasion. Any other cab would have done as well. Moreover, I think that, under the cab contract, the hirer, even if the race went off, could have said, "Drive me to Epsom; I will pay you the agreed sum; you have nothing to do with the purpose for which I hired the cab," and that if the cabman refused he would have been guilty of a breach of contract, there being nothing to qualify his promise to drive the hirer to Epsom on a particular day. Whereas in the case of the coronation, there is not merely the purpose of the hirer to see the coronation procession, but it is the coronation procession and the relative position of the rooms which is the basis of the contract as much for the lessor as the hirer; and I think that if the King, before the coronation day and after the contract, had died, the hirer could not have insisted on having the rooms on the days named. It could not in the cab case be reasonably said that seeing the Derby race was the foundation of the contract, as it was of the licence in this case. Whereas in the present case, where the rooms were offered and taken, by reason of their peculiar suitability from the position of the rooms for a view of the coronation procession, surely the view of the coronation procession was the foundation of the contract, which is a very different thing from the purpose of the man who engaged the cab — namely, to see the race — being held to be the foundation of the contract. Each case must be judged by its own circumstances. In each case one must ask oneself, first, what, having regard to all the circumstances, was the foundation of the contract? Secondly, was the performance of the contract prevented? Thirdly, was the event which prevented the performance of the contract of such a character that it cannot reasonably be said to have been in the contemplation of the parties at the date of the contract? If all these questions are answered in the affirmative (as I think they should be in this case), I think both parties are discharged from further performance of the contract. I think that the coronation procession was the foundation of this contract, and that the non-happening of it prevented the performance of the contract; and, secondly, I think that the non-happening of the procession, to use the words of Sir James Hannen in Baily v. De Crespigny, was an event "of such a character that it cannot reasonably be supposed to have been in the contemplation of the contracting parties when the contract was made, and that they are not to be held bound by general words which, though large enough to include, were not used with reference to the possibility of the particular contingency which afterwards happened." The test seems to be whether the event which causes the impossibility was or might have been anticipated and guarded against. It seems difficult to say, in a case where both parties anticipate the happening of an event, which anticipation is the foundation of the contract, that either party must be taken to have anticipated, and ought to have guarded against, the event which prevented the performance of the contract. . . .

I myself am clearly of opinion that in this case, where we have to ask ourselves whether the object of the contract was frustrated by the non-happening of the coronation and its procession on the days proclaimed, parol evidence is admissible to shew that the subject of the contract was rooms to view the coronation procession, and was so to the knowledge of both parties. When once this is established, I see no difficulty whatever in the case. It is not essential to the application of the principle of Taylor v. Caldwell that the direct subject of the contract should perish or fail to be in existence at the date of performance of the contract. It is sufficient if a state of things or condition expressed in the contract and essential to its performance perishes or fails to be in existence at that time. In the present case the condition which fails and prevents the achievement of that which was, in the contemplation of both parties, the foundation of the contract, is not expressly mentioned either as a condition of the contract or the purpose of it; but I think for the reasons which I have given that the principle of Taylor v. Caldwell ought to be applied. This disposes of the plaintiff's claim for 50£ unpaid balance of the price agreed to be paid for the use of the rooms. The defendant at one time set up a cross-claim for the return of the 25£ he paid at the date of the contract. As that claim is now withdrawn it is unnecessary to say anything about it. . . .

Appeal dismissed.

QUESTIONS

1. How does this case differ from the burning of the music hall in Taylor v. Caldwell?

2. Do you agree with the learned judge's resolution of his hypothetical concerning the Derby Day cab?

3. If the defendant had not dropped his cross-claim for the return of the deposit, how would the issue have been decided?

Problem 136

Henry Higgins asked Eliza Doolittle to go with him to the Embassy Ball and for that purpose ordered a special gown to be made for her by Shaw of London, a famous designer. Shaw created the dress for her after several fittings, but before it could be delivered Eliza suddenly died. Must Higgins pay for the dress? What if the Embassy Ball were cancelled? See In re Estate of Sheppard, 328 Wis. 2d 533, 789 N.W.2d 616 (Wis. App. 2010) (estate was sued for failure of deceased to pay for flying lessons not yet received because of his death during the contract period).

Problem 137

In 1970, Monopoly Oil Company entered into a ten-year contract with Icarus Airlines by which it contracted to furnish the airline with all the gasoline it would need for that period at a set price per barrel. The next year the oil-producing countries created for the first time a cartel to fix oil prices and suddenly the price of oil skyrocketed. Monopoly Oil Company, unable to get oil at the cheap old price, tells you, its attorney, that it will go bankrupt if it is forced to honor its contract with Icarus. Advise your client. Does UCC §2-615 provide an avenue of escape? Read it and its Official Comment 4 carefully.

[handwritten margin note: UCC 2-615]

[handwritten: — Assume risk of extreme price risk]

[handwritten: — Not Impossible]

———

Some mention should be made of the famous (and controversial) case of Aluminum Co. of America v. Essex Group, 499 F. Supp. 53 (W.D. Pa. 1980), in which the court completely rewrote the contract to give each party the profits originally expected. The *Alcoa* fact pattern, however, is unique. In that case the parties had employed eminent economist Alan Greenspan (later chair of the Federal Reserve System) to devise a pricing index for the sale of aluminum. When the index chosen proved to be dramatically out of line with the expectations of the parties (because of the unexpected actions of OPEC in the early 1970s the pricing formula awarded one party huge gains while costing the other a loss of $75 million), the court reformed the contract to bring it back into line with the original understanding. The case was settled rather than appealed, leaving on the books a citation permitting a court enormous freedom to rewrite contracts where the need to do so is strong.

The economic downturn of 2008 resulted in many breaches when funds to make payments, provide services or goods, to buy or sell services or real estate, and so on dried up. Often defendants tried to utilize impossibility or frustration of purpose doctrines as a legal excuse to meet their performance obligations. The courts' response was that financial conditions vary from time to time and are thus foreseeable, hence not an excusable event. See, e.g., Flathead Michigan I, LLC v. Pennisula Development, LLC, 2011 WL 940048 (E.D. Mich. 2011).

CHAPTER 6 ASSESSMENT

Multiple Choice Questions

1. To help with a charity golf tournament, the Klick-Lewis car dealership donated a new Chevrolet Beretta GT and placed it on the ninth tee with a sign saying "HOLE-IN-ONE wins this car courtesy of Klick-Lewis, Inc." No one made a hole-in-one during the tournament. Two days later, before Klick-Lewis got around to removing the car or taking down the sign, Amos

Cobaugh was playing in another tournament on the same course and made a hole-in-one on the ninth hole. Is he entitled to the car?

a. Yes, he is. He has fulfilled all of the terms of the offer by making the hole-in-one, which was his acceptance of this unilateral contract. He was unaware of the fact that the dealership no longer meant to be making this offer, and its delay in taking down the sign is its own problem. There isn't even a mistake here, since the dealership meant to make the offer and was negligent in revoking it. He furnished consideration by playing in the tournament, which had this exciting possibility as part of it, and thereby helping the charity and contributing to the good publicity the dealership got from participating in the event.

b. No, he doesn't get the car. Even if there was still an offer in the air, he was mistaken in believing it was still available. In any event he gave the dealership no consideration. How did his hole-in-one benefit it in any way?

c. He loses. The contract is founded on a mistake: The dealership did not mean to make the offer in the second tournament, and even though this is a unilateral mistake it is unfair to hold it to its offer, making it come up with a new car when he is not out anything other than the disappointment of not getting a windfall. It's hard to feel sorry for him since he still gets bragging rights for having made a hole-in-one.

d. He loses. Making a hole-in-one is not a matter of skill, but luck. Even professional golfers can play all their lives and not make such a shot. Thus this is a gambling contract and void for illegality, and the guilty parties to such a contract, those *in pari delicto*, which include both the golfer and dealership, cannot enforce the contract.

2. When Clayton Crandall graduated with top honors with a degree in computer science from Stanford University he went to work for Air Outfitters, which performed custom redesigns for airplanes and fleets of airplanes. It was an at-will contract, so that either party could terminate Clayton's employment at any time, but Clayton did sign an employment agreement with his employer that included a clause stating that if he left the company he could not accept employment in the same airplane redesign field anywhere in the world for five years. After three years of working for Air Outfitters, Clayton, who had become well known due to write-ups both in print and online about what a genius he was, left Air Outfitters for a very lucrative position and a ten-year contract with Air Outfitter's major rival. Air Outfitters sued both Clayton and his new employer, asking for an injunction to prevent him from taking the new job, and a decree of specific performance that he must return to work at Air Outfitters. What result?

a. The court should issue the requested writs. This is a reasonable covenant not to compete. Air Outfitters has been instrumental in his training and it would be unfair to allow him to benefit from that training and then take it to a major competitor. The covenant not to compete is reasonable both in time (five years is not all that long) and, given how the world has shrunk when it comes to commerce, even geographic reach.

b. The contract he had with Air Outfitters in illusory to begin with since it is unilateral: He is paid only so long as he works, but once he leaves the contract ceases to have any legal effect and shouldn't bar his future efforts to find a better job. Restraints on trade are not favored in our law, and this one is ludicrous given the flimsy nature of the at-will agreement.

c. The contract is perfectly valid. Covenants not to compete are frequently made even for at-will employments. Here Air Outfitters will train him and it would be unfair for him to take his unique abilities, which were amplified during the early years he worked there, and bolt the company, going to work for the company's chief rival. The clause is not overly broad: Five years is a reasonable period, especially considering he can take jobs in his field as long as they are not with an airplane outfitting enterprise, and the scope of the restriction (worldwide) is not large considering there are not a great many such companies and what few exist are located in different parts of the globe. Both writs should be granted.

d. Same answer as C except for the last sentence. The injunction to keep him from going to work for the new company should be granted, but a writ of specific performance that makes him return to Air Outfitters would smack of slavery and require the court to supervise his work, under penalty of contempt of court should he not work up to his full potential. Such a writ would also violate the "at will" terms of the original agreement.

3. Alice Smith lived in the slums in a large city and suffered from irreversible brain damage due to lead poisoning she got from the housing project she grew up in. When she was 16 her whole family sued the project and recovered a judgment that would pay each member of the family a monthly check of nearly $1,000, with yearly increases. Those payments were guaranteed for 35 years. The checks began arriving shortly thereafter. Alice managed to squeak through high school even though the confusion in her head was so bad she could barely read, but the day she turned 18 a kindly woman, dressed nicely in a business suit, took her to lunch and made her an offer of an immediate payment of $63,000 if she would sell the rights to the future checks to the company the woman represented. Alice, much in need of money, signed the contract and took the check. Two years later when Alice's mother asked her why her

monthly checks weren't coming in, Alice explained what had happened and said she used the money to attend beauty school until she dropped out. The mother, very upset, contacts you, a lawyer at Legal Aid. Alice had been scheduled to receive 420 monthly checks adding up to nearly $574,000 (a present value of roughly $338,000). In a *Washington Post* article from 2015 you read that while most settlements are paid in their entirety, so-called "structured settlements" are stretched out over years "to protect vulnerable recipients from immediately spending the money. Since 1975, insurance companies have committed an estimated $350 billion to structured settlements. This has given rise to a secondary market in which dozens of firms compete to purchase the rights to those payments for a fraction of their face value." The article can be found at http://readersupportednews.org/news-section2/318-66/32051-how-companies-make-millions-off-lead-poisoned-poor-blacks. Will a lawsuit to void Alice's contract succeed?

a. Probably. While Alice was of legal age to make a contract, the company that bought the right to the structured settlement checks knew that lead poisoning had damaged her mental capacity to understand what she was doing. The law should stretch to protect those who cannot protect themselves and not those who profit from the inability of some people to understand the complexities of financial decisions. Alice did not have sufficient mental capacity to enter into this contract so it's voidable at her option.

b. Not likely. Alice needed that $63,000 now, when she signed the check, and the promise of many future small checks couldn't help her at a time when the larger amount would enable her to better herself by getting vocational training. Whether that training worked out or not, Alice made that decision. Yes, she has some mental difficulties, but she graduated from high school and can read and write, and she will testify that it seemed like the right thing to do when she signed the contract. We all make decisions in life that we later regret, but we don't get a "do-over" that cancels contracts we knowingly made.

c. Alice should prevail under a theory of unconscionability and/or fraud. As for unconscionability, there is procedural unconscionability in taking advantage of someone who doesn't have sufficient intelligence to make the obviously right choice, and substantive unconscionability in stealing a big amount of money for a comparatively small amount. Fraud requires a misrepresentation and here Alice was told this would be a good deal for her when it was not. Perhaps undue influence would also work: Alice was pressured into signing a contract at a moment when she was very vulnerable and unable to appreciate the smart thing to do. Our law should stretch to protect people who are scammed in this ugly fashion.

4. Skyline Sweaters became well known for the beautiful sweaters that it created with wonderfully intricate designs made with dyed angora hair. Its announced 2021 fall collection was much anticipated, and Tres Bien, a fashion designer in Paris, contracted in late 2020 to buy half of the announced quantity of such sweaters (yet to be manufactured) from Skyline at a set price. Everyone knew that 96 percent of the world's market for angora hair was produced in China, where it came from rabbits, though a small amount was available from sources outside of that country. Shortly after the sales contract was signed a civil war in China shut down all commercial production of goods and no angora hair was allowed to leave the country. Skyline sadly told Tres Bien that it would be unable to fulfill the sales contract, claiming impossibility. The buyer responded that this would be a breach of their contract because (a) Skyline took the risk of a shutdown in supply, and (b) there was enough angora hair available outside of China to fill the order. A lawsuit followed. You are the attorney for Skyline. Your client tells you that non-Chinese angora hair costs double what the Chinese sell it for, and it would ruin the company to have to buy non-Chinese angora hair. Is this an excusing event? See Uniform Commercial Code §2-615 (Failure of Presupposed Condition), and especially its Official Comments 4 and 5.

    a. Yes, the availability of angora hair at the Chinese price was the very basis on which the contract was formulated, and when this source of supply shut down the seller's obligation goes with it; see Official Comment 5, which excuses performance where "a particular source of supply is shown by the circumstances to have been contemplated or assumed by the parties at the time of contracting."

    b. No. Official Comment 4 clearly states that "increased cost alone does not excuse performance unless the rise in cost is due to some unforeseen contingency which alters the essential nature of the performance." Skyline can still buy the hair from other sources and if that makes it a party to a losing contract, that's the very sort of risk contracts at a fixed price create for sellers. Seller should have protected itself by buying insurance against such a supply failure, or putting in a clause escalating the price if the hair had to be bought from a different source.

    c. Yes. That same Comment goes on to say that "a severe shortage of raw materials or of supplies due to a contingency such as war, embargo, local crop failure, unforeseen shutdown of major sources of supply or the like, which either causes a marked increase in cost or altogether prevents the seller from securing supplies necessary to his performance, is within the contemplation of this section." That is exactly what happened here: a war causing a marked increase in cost.

    d. No. The seller bore this risk unless it put a clause in the contract excusing performance in the event of the shutdown of the supply of angora hair coming from China. If you put all your eggs in one basket, you should guard against the loss of the basket in obvious ways, one of which is drafting a "Failure of Supplier" clause in your sales documents.

Answers

1. A is the best answer, and the arguments he makes here were persuasive to the court in the actual case, though there was a dissenter who bought the illegality argument in D and would have voided the whole contract on that ground. See Cobaugh v. Klick-Lewis, Inc., 385 Pa. Super. 587, 561 A.2d 1248 (1989).

2. D has the best argument. No writ of specific performance would ever be issued to force someone to work for another, but the injunction seems fair for the reasons given. Air Outfitters will have the burden of convincing the court that the covenant not to compete is fair and doesn't unduly restrict commerce, and it's hard to see why this one wouldn't meet that standard.

3. Who knows? Close cases like this almost always depend on what judge you get: the liberal who will grant relief to those tricked out of their money or the conservative who will uphold the need to make valid contracts with the poor as well as the rich. Structured settlement sales like these are an ugly business, and some states have regulated them or forbidden them entirely. It is your job as an attorney to make the sorts of arguments that were presented above as skillfully as you can, and in cases of this kind preparation should include lots of statistics and real-life examples both pro and con.

4. Any of these arguments might carry the day in court. Factors that may influence the decision would include (a) how foreseeable was the Chinese civil war, (b) did Tres Bien have notice that the hair would come from China, and/or (c) is it common in this industry to draft clauses explaining what happens when a shortage of supplies occurs?

7

CONDITIONS AND PROMISES: PERFORMANCE AND BREACH

Contracts contain promises stating what the parties must do in order to perform. In addition, contracts also have clauses placing limitations on these promises (for example, "seller must perform only if the price of oil is below $65 per barrel"). These clauses are "conditions" and create their own difficulties, as we shall see. Further, the parties may have specified which promise must be performed first or perhaps left that question to implication, in which case the court must decide the order of performance. Finally, judges must consider whether substantial but imperfect performance satisfies the promise, and to what extent certain clauses in the contract can be ignored or have been waived by the parties. There is much of importance to the attorney in these matters, and we will work our way through it all in this chapter.

[margin annotations: conditions; order of performance; Post-performance]

I. BASIC CONCEPTS

In this chapter, we are not concerned with whether the parties have a contract; we assume a contract is formed. This chapter explores when, if ever, the performances that each party promised are due — the law of promises and conditions. A *promise* (sometimes called a *covenant*) is simply a contractual undertaking, breach of which leads to liability for damages or equitable relief. A *condition* is a fact, the occurrence or nonoccurrence of which determines when and if a party must perform.

[margin annotation: conditions]

The parties may have agreed that their performances are (a) due on a specified date or (b) due upon the occurrence or nonoccurrence of some event other than the passage of time (for example, if the price for gold is more than $700 per ounce, or the government repeals a certain law, or a buyer is able to obtain a mortgage at a specific interest rate). If the parties have expressed an intent that performance is dependent upon the occurrence or nonoccurrence of an event not certain to occur, the performance

[margin annotation: Expressed Condition]

obligation is said to be subject to an *express condition*. What happens if the event that must occur does not arise? At first thought, the answer to this query seems simple: The party whose obligation is dependent upon the event no longer has any obligation. But is this fair if the other contracting party has already performed and stands to lose a great amount solely because of the nonoccurrence of the event? What if the nonoccurrence of the event appears to have been a minor issue to the parties at the time of the agreement?

The parties may have exchanged a number of promises and said nothing about the order of performances. The court may still infer the parties' intent concerning the order of performances from their conduct, the surrounding circumstances, and the sense of the contract—a condition *implied in fact.* Conversely, where the parties' intent is unclear, a court may use a *constructive condition*—a condition *implied in law*—to fill in the blanks concerning the timing of performances. For example, if X has promised to build a bridge for Y, the court may find that the completion of the bridge is a constructive condition of Y's promise to pay X.

[handwritten margin note: Implied In Fact]

[handwritten margin note: Implied in Law]

Problem 138

[handwritten margin note: Condition]

Your insurance policy provides that you must give notice of an insured-against event within ten days of its occurrence or the company is not liable. Suppose that you fail to do so. Must the insurance company pay your claim? If not, why not? Can the insurance company sue you for failure to give the contracted-for notice? If not, why not?

Problem 139

[handwritten margin note: Covenant]

[handwritten margin note: $50/20,000]

[handwritten margin note: → This is key]

Nebuchadnezzar hired the Hanging Gardens Construction Company to build a terrace for $20,000, agreeing to pay for it in stages upon the completion of various parts of the building, less a percentage retained until the end of the project. One month, by accident, Nebuchadnezzar's check was $50 short of the correct amount. Hanging Gardens' president calls you, its attorney. Can it sue Nebuchadnezzar if the money is not immediately paid? For this reason alone could it refuse to perform further on the construction job? Why or why not?

Problem 140

[handwritten margin note: hybrid]

Deciding that she needed a new, distinctive briefcase, Portia Moot, well-known appellate lawyer, hired a leather craftsman who promised to make her one for court appearances. She agreed to pay him $400 on completion. On the date the briefcase was to be delivered, she went to his shop. He had moved to Arizona. She had the same briefcase made elsewhere for $600. May she sue him for the damages his breach has caused her? Must she pay him first? Why or why not?

II. EXPRESS CONDITIONS AND IMPLIED-IN-FACT CONDITIONS

A. *The Policy Concerns*

HOWARD v. FEDERAL CROP INSURANCE CORP.
United States Court of Appeals, Fourth Circuit, 1976
540 F.2d 695

WIDENER, Circuit Judge. Plaintiff-appellants sued to recover for losses to their 1973 tobacco crop due to alleged rain damage. The crops were insured by defendant-appellee, Federal Crop Insurance Corporation (FCIC). Suits were brought in a state court in North Carolina and removed to the United States District Court. The three suits are not distinguishable factually so far as we are concerned here and involve identical questions of law. They were combined for disposition in the district court and for appeal. The district court granted summary judgment for the defendant and dismissed all three actions. We remand for further proceedings. Since we find for the plaintiffs as to the construction of the policy, we express no opinion on the procedural questions.

Federal Crop Insurance Corporation, an agency of the United States, in 1973, issued three policies to the Howards, insuring their tobacco crops, to be grown on six farms, against weather damage and other hazards.

The Howards (plaintiffs) established production of tobacco on their acreage, and have alleged that their 1973 crop was extensively damaged by heavy rains, resulting in a gross loss to the three plaintiffs in excess of $35,000. The plaintiffs harvested and sold the depleted crop and timely filed notice and proof of loss with FCIC, but, prior to inspection by the adjuster for FCIC, the Howards had either plowed or disked under the tobacco fields in question to prepare the same for sowing a cover crop of rye to preserve the soil. When the FCIC adjuster later inspected the fields, he found the stalks had been largely obscured or obliterated by plowing or disking and denied the claims, apparently on the ground that the plaintiffs had violated a portion of the policy which provides that the stalks on any acreage with respect to which a loss is claimed shall not be destroyed until the corporation makes an inspection.

The holding of the district court is best capsuled in its own words:

> The inquiry here is whether compliance by the insureds with this provision of the policy was a condition precedent to the recovery. The court concludes that it was and that the failure of the insureds to comply worked a forfeiture of benefits for the alleged loss.[1]

There is no question but that apparently after notice of loss was given to defendant, but before inspection by the adjuster, plaintiffs plowed under the tobacco stalks and sowed some of the land with a cover crop, rye. The question is whether, under paragraph 5(f) of the tobacco endorsement to the policy of insurance, the act of plowing under the tobacco stalks forfeits the coverage of the policy. Paragraph 5 of the tobacco endorsement is entitled *Claims.* Pertinent to this case are subparagraphs 5(b) and 5(f), which are as follows:

> 5(b) *It shall be a condition precedent* to the payment of any loss that the insured establish the production of the insured crop on a unit and that such loss has been directly caused by one or more of the hazards insured against during the insurance period for the crop year for which the loss is claimed, and furnish any other information regarding the manner and extent of loss as may be required by the Corporation. (Emphasis added.)
>
> 5(f) The tobacco stalks on any acreage of tobacco of types 11a, 11b, 12, 13, or 14 with respect to which a loss is claimed *shall not be destroyed until the Corporation makes an inspection.* (Emphasis added.)

The arguments of both parties are predicated upon the same two assumptions. First, if subparagraph 5(f) creates a condition precedent, its violation caused a forfeiture of plaintiffs' coverage. Second, if subparagraph 5(f) creates an obligation (variously called a promise or covenant) upon plaintiffs not to plow under the tobacco stalks, defendant may recover from plaintiffs (either in an original action, or, in this case, by a counterclaim, or as a matter of defense) for whatever damage is sustained because of the elimination of the stalks. However, a violation of subparagraph 5(f) would not, under the second premise, standing alone, cause a forfeiture of the policy.

---

1. The district court also relied upon language in subparagraph 5(b), infra, which required as a condition precedent to payment that the insured, in addition to establishing his production and loss from an insured case, "furnish any other information regarding the manner and extent of loss as may be required by the Corporation." The court construed the preservation of the stalks as such "information." We see no language in the policy or connection in the record to indicate this is the case.

Generally accepted law provides us with guidelines here. There is a general legal policy opposed to forfeitures. United States v. One Ford Coach, 307 U.S. 219, 226 (1939); Baca v. Commissioner of Internal Revenue, 326 F.2d 189, 191 (5th Cir. 1963). Insurance policies are generally construed most strongly against the insurer. Henderson v. Hartford Accident & Indemnity Co., 268 N.C. 129, 150 S.E.2d 17, 19 (1966). When it is doubtful whether words create a promise or a condition precedent, they will be construed as creating a promise. Harris and Harris Const. Co. v. Crain and Denbo, Inc., 256 N.C. 110, 123 S.E.2d 590, 595 (1962). The provisions of a contract will not be construed as conditions precedent in the absence of language plainly requiring such construction. *Harris* 123 S.E.2d at 596. And *Harris,* at 123 S.E.2d 590, 595, cites Jones v. Palace Realty Co., 226 N.C. 303, 37 S.E.2d 906 (1946), and Restatement of the Law, Contracts, §261.

Plaintiffs rely most strongly upon the fact that the term "condition precedent" is concluded in subparagraph 5(b) but not in subparagraph 5 (f). It is true that whether a contract provision is construed as a condition or an obligation does not depend entirely upon whether the word "condition" is expressly used. Appleman, Insurance Law and Practice (1972), vol. 6A, §4144. However, the persuasive force of plaintiffs' argument in this case is found in the use of the term "condition precedent" in subparagraph 5(b) but not in subparagraph 5(f). Thus, it is argued that the ancient maxim to be applied is that the expression of one thing is the exclusion of another.

The defendant places principal reliance upon the decision of this court in Fidelity-Phenix Fire Insurance Company v. Pilot Freight Carriers, 193 F.2d 812, 31 A.L.R.2d 839 (4th Cir. 1952). Suit there was predicated upon a loss resulting from theft out of a truck covered by defendant's policy protecting plaintiff from such a loss. The insurance company defended upon the grounds that the plaintiff had left the truck unattended without the alarm system being on. The policy contained six paragraphs limiting coverage. Two of those imposed what was called a "condition precedent." They largely related to the installation of specified safety equipment. Several others, including paragraph 5, pertinent in that case, started with the phrase, "It is further warranted." In paragraph 5, the insured warranted that the alarm system would be on whenever the vehicle was left unattended. Paragraph 6 starts with the language: "The assured agrees, by acceptance of this policy, that the foregoing conditions precedent relate to matters material to the acceptance of the risk by the insurer." Plaintiff recovered in the district court, but judgment on its behalf was reversed because of a breach of warranty of paragraph 5, the truck had been left unattended with the alarm off. In that case, plaintiff relied upon the fact that the words "condition precedent" were used in some of the paragraphs but the word "warranted" was used in the paragraph in issue. In rejecting that contention, this court said that "warranty" and "condition precedent" are often used interchangeably to create a condition of the insured's promise, and "[m]anifestly the terms 'condition precedent' and 'warranty' were intended to have the same meaning and effect." 193 F.2d at 816.

Fidelity-Phenix thus does not support defendant's contention here. Although there is some resemblance between the two cases, analysis shows that the issues are actually entirely different. Unlike the case at bar, each paragraph in *Fidelity-Phenix* contained either the term "condition precedent" or the term "warranted." We held that, in that situation, the two terms had the same effect in that they both involved forfeiture. That is well established law. See Appleman, Insurance Law and Practice (1972), vol. 6A, §4144. In the case at bar, the term "warranty" or "warranted" is in no way involved, either in terms or by way of like language, as it was in *Fidelity-Phenix*. The issue upon which this case turns, then, was not involved in *Fidelity-Phenix*.

The Restatement of the Law of Contracts states:

§261.   Interpretation of Doubtful Words as Promise or Condition

Where it is doubtful whether words create a promise or an express condition, they are interpreted as creating a promise; but the same words may sometimes mean that one party promises a performance and that the other party's promise is conditional on that performance.

Two illustrations (one involving a promise, the other a condition) are used in the Restatement:

2. A, an insurance company, issues to B a policy of insurance containing promises by A that are in terms conditional on the happening of certain events. The policy contains this clause: "provided, in case differences shall arise touching any loss, *the matter shall be submitted to impartial arbitrators*, whose award shall be binding on the parties." This is a promise to arbitrate and does not make an award a condition precedent of the insurer's duty to pay.

3. A, an insurance company, issues to B an insurance policy in usual form containing this clause: "In the event of disagreement as to the amount of loss it shall be ascertained by two appraisers and an umpire. The loss shall *not be payable until 60 days after the award of the appraisers when such an appraisal is required*." This provision is not merely a promise to arbitrate differences but makes an award a condition of the insurer's duty to pay in case of disagreement. (Emphasis added.)

We believe that subparagraph 5(f) in the policy here under consideration fits illustration 2 rather than illustration 3. Illustration 2 specifies something to be done, whereas subparagraph 5(f) specifies something not to be done. Unlike illustration 3, subparagraph 5(f) does not state any conditions under which the insurance shall "not be payable," or use any words of like import. We hold that the district court erroneously held, on the motion for summary judgment, that subparagraph 5(f) established a condition precedent to plaintiffs' recovery which forfeited the coverage.

From our holding that defendant's motion for summary judgment was improperly allowed, it does not follow the plaintiffs' motion for summary judgment should have been granted, for if subparagraph 5(f) be not construed as a condition precedent, there are other questions of fact to be determined. At this point, we merely hold that the district court erred in holding, on the motion for summary judgment, that subparagraph 5(f) constituted a condition precedent with resulting forfeiture.

The explanation defendant makes for including subparagraph 5(f) in the tobacco endorsement is that it is necessary that the stalks remain standing in order for the Corporation to evaluate the extent of loss and to determine whether loss resulted from some cause not covered by the policy. However, was subparagraph 5(f) inserted because without it the Corporation's opportunities for proof would be more difficult, or because they would be impossible? Plaintiffs point out that the Tobacco Endorsement, with subparagraph 5(f), was adopted in 1970, and crop insurance goes back long before that date. Nothing is shown as to the Corporation's prior 1970 practice of evaluating losses. Such a showing might have a bearing upon establishing defendant's intention in including 5(f). Plaintiffs state, and defendant does not deny, that another division of the Department of Agriculture, or the North Carolina Department, urged that tobacco stalks be cut as soon as possible after harvesting as a means of pest control. Such an explanation might refute the idea that plaintiffs plowed under the stalks for any fraudulent purpose. Could these conflicting directives affect the reasonableness of plaintiffs' interpretation of defendant's prohibition upon plowing under the stalks prior to adjustment?

We express no opinion on these questions because they were not before the district court and are mentioned to us largely by way of argument rather than from the record. No question of ambiguity was raised in the court below or here and no question of the applicability of paragraph 5(c) to this case was alluded to other than in the defendant's pleadings, so we also do not reach those questions. Nothing we say here should preclude FCIC from asserting as a defense that the plowing or disking under of the stalks caused damage to FCIC if, for example, the amount of the loss was thereby made more difficult or impossible to ascertain whether the plowing or disking under was done with bad purpose or innocently. To repeat, our narrow holding is that merely plowing or disking under the stalks does not of itself operate to forfeit coverage under the policy.

The case is remanded for further proceedings not inconsistent with this opinion.

NOTES AND QUESTIONS

1. How do we know if a clause in a contract is a condition, a promise, or both? Is it a question of fact? Of law?

2. What is the effect of the court finding an express condition? A promise? What is the effect of language that creates both a promise and a condition?

3. The court makes much of the fact that in one part of the contract the drafter said clearly that a condition precedent was intended, but failed to use similar language in the part at issue in the case. The Latin phrase for this idea is *expressio unius est exclusio alterius* ("the expression of one thing is the exclusion of another"). Prudent drafting of the contract's language is the answer to the dilemma. Be careful, future lawyers, not to state that something is a condition precedent in one part of the agreement and leave off this language in another segment where such a condition is nonetheless intended. And by all means if your client truly wants a condition precedent, make certain to draft language making that unmistakably clear. For another example of a court finding a promise and not a condition primarily because express condition precedent language was not used, see Solar Applications Engineering, Inc. v. T.A. Operating Corp., 327 S.W.3d 104 (Tex. 2010).

4. Because conditions lead to forfeitures, and it is a common law maxim that "the law abhors a forfeiture," courts tend to struggle against the destruction of liability that conditions create. The relevant Latin phrase here is *ut res magis valeat quam pereat* ("let it be saved rather than destroyed"), a concept that has utility throughout contracts law.

JONES ASSOCIATES v. EASTSIDE PROPERTIES
Court of Appeals of Washington, 1985
41 Wash. App. 462, 704 P.2d 681

SWANSON, Judge. Jones Associates, Inc. (Jones Associates) appeals the superior court judgment (1) dismissing its action against Eastside Properties, Inc., et al., (Eastside) for money due under a professional services contract of $15,030 plus interest and (2) awarding Eastside Properties $7,500 for costs, expenses, and attorney fees. We reverse and remand for trial.

In early 1977 Jones Associates, an engineering, consulting, and surveying firm, and Eastside Properties, a real estate development corporation, entered into a professional services agreement. The contract signed by the parties was a preprinted form commonly used by Jones Associates which was modified by an Eastside representative.

Under the contract for a $17,480 fixed fee, including short plat application fees, Jones Associates was to provide a feasibility study, master plan, nine record surveys, and nine short plats for Eastside's 180-acre land parcel. In May, 1978 Jones Associates submitted Eastside's short plat application to the King County Building and Land Development Division, which in July, 1978, gave its preliminary approval with numerous conditions attached. Eastside unsuccessfully appealed the conditions imposed.

To enable Eastside to comply with the imposed conditions, the parties entered into a June 19, 1979 amendment to the original contract, which amendment expressly incorporated all of the original contract's terms.

For a $12,550 fixed fee, under the change order Jones Associates was to provide an updated feasibility study, a roadway plan and profile, a design for a water system if not provided by the water district, storm drainage plans submitted for approval, and revised short plats filed for recordation.

Jones Associates claims that it performed all required services under the original contract and the change order. According to Eastside Properties, however, the following two conditions precedent to payment were not met: the original and the updated feasibility studies were not proven to be satisfactory to Eastside, and King County final plat approval was not obtained.

Eastside paid $15,000 to Jones Associates in April, 1980. In March, 1981 Jones Associates brought a money due action against Eastside. At the time of trial Eastside's short plat application still had not been approved, and the extension period to obtain final county approval had expired.

At the end of the plaintiff's evidence the trial court granted Eastside's motion to dismiss the complaint and awarded Eastside $7,500 attorney fees pursuant to the parties' contract. The court's oral decision stated that the dismissal was based upon its interpretation of the unambiguous contract language that obtaining county approval was a condition precedent to contractual payment, which condition had not been met. Jones Associates' reconsideration motion was denied, and this appeal followed.

The issue is whether the trial court erred in dismissing Jones Associates' action against Eastside Properties. Eastside Properties claims that the following contract provision creates a condition precedent to payment: "Engineer shall be responsible for obtaining King County approval for all platting as set forth above." Jones Associates, however, contends that the provision is not a condition precedent but rather merely states that it was to perform all necessary engineering, consulting, and surveying services related to Eastside's short plat application. We conclude that the provision is a promise rather than a condition precedent; thus dismissing the action was error. . . .

A condition precedent is an event occurring after the making of a valid contract which must occur before a right to immediate performance arises. [Citations omitted.] In contrast to the breach of a promise, which subjects the promisor to liability for damages but does not necessarily discharge the other party's duty of performance, the nonoccurrence of a condition prevents the promisee from acquiring a right or deprives him of one but subjects him to no liability. Ross v. Harding, 64 Wash. 2d 231, 236, 391 P.2d 526 (1964); 5 S. Williston, Contracts §665, at 132 (3d ed. 1961).

Whether a provision in a contract is a condition, the nonfulfillment of which excuses performance, depends upon the intent of the parties, to be ascertained from a fair and reasonable construction of the language used in the light of all the surrounding circumstances. 5 Williston, Contracts (3d ed.) §663, p.127.

Ross, supra at 236, 391 P.2d 526; accord, *Koller*, supra, 73 Wash. 2d at 860, 441 P.2d 126. Where it is doubtful whether words create a promise or an express condition, they are interpreted as creating a promise. *Ross*, supra.

[handwritten marginalia: Words That State a Condition Precedent]

> An intent to create a condition is often revealed by such phrases and words as "provided that," "on condition," "when," "so that," "while," "as soon as," and "after."

Vogt v. Hovander, 27 Wash. App. 168, 178, 616 P.2d 660 (1979). Here no such words were used, and it is unclear whether the parties intended obtaining King County approval to be a condition precedent to payment under the contract.

Where the parties' contractual language is ambiguous, the principal goal of construction is to search out the parties' intent. Jacoby v. Grays Harbor Chair & Mfg. Co., 77 Wash. 2d 911, 918, 468 P.2d 666 (1970).

> Determination of the intent of the contracting parties is to be accomplished by viewing the contract as a whole, the subject matter and objective of the contract, all the circumstances surrounding the making of the contract, the subsequent acts and conduct of the parties to the contract, and the reasonableness of respective interpretations advocated by the parties.

[Citations omitted.] Here an examination of the entire contract, circumstances surrounding the contract's formation, the parties' subsequent conduct, and the reasonableness of the parties' respective interpretations indicates that the parties intended Jones Associates' assumption of responsibility for obtaining King County approval to be a duty under the contract but not a condition precedent to payment.

First, the relevant provision's language in the second typewritten paragraph under "Scope of Services" does not expressly indicate that if King County approval was not obtained, Eastside would not be responsible for any costs whatsoever, as does the preceding typewritten paragraph[4] containing an express condition precedent regarding a satisfactory economic feasibility study. Since the two typewritten paragraphs were inserted into the contract by Eastside, the first typewritten paragraph provides evidence of Eastside's ability clearly and unambiguously to express a condition precedent to payment. Moreover, ambiguous contract language is strictly

---

4. The first typewritten paragraph states:

[handwritten marginalia: Condition]

> Engineer shall promptly complete feasibility study and if said study establishes to Client's satisfaction that the development project is economic, the Engineer shall be required to fulfill the entire scope of services as set forth in this agreement. In the event said feasibility study is not satisfactory to Client, this entire agreement shall be considered terminated and Client shall not be responsible for any costs or charges whatsoever.

construed against the drafter. *Jacoby,* supra; Taylor-Edwards Warehouse v. Burlington Northern, 715 F.2d 1330, 1334 (9th Cir. 1983).

Further, other portions of the original contract support Jones Associates' contention that it contemplated its contractual duty to be to perform necessary services related to the short plat application rather than that obtaining King County final plat approval was to be a condition precedent to payment. The "Description of Final Product" lists, besides a development feasibility report and master plan, nine record surveys and nine short plats "in King County format," not "approved by King County." Similarly, the contract states under "Completion of Assignment" that the short plats were to be ready for submission by a certain date, not that they were to have King County approval by a certain date. In addition, while the change order is in accord with Jones Associates' assuming responsibility for obtaining King County final plat approval, the language implies a duty rather than an express condition precedent: One of Jones Associates' services to be performed under the change order was to revise and "file for recordation," not obtain county approval of, the short plats.

Moreover, the respondent's conduct subsequent to the making of the contract supports the interpretation that the parties did not intend the relevant provision to be a condition precedent. First, rather than refusing to pay the fixed fee because of the nonoccurrence of a condition precedent, Eastside did tender in April, 1980, $15,000 of the $30,030 that was due under the original contract and its amendment. In addition, Eastside did, though not without argument, enter into a contractual amendment for $12,550 for Jones Associates to perform additional services so that it could comply with King County's imposed conditions rather than insisting that the condition precedent of obtaining King County approval contemplated that the original contract encompassed any necessary additional services to secure such approval.

> Further, it is well-established that forfeitures are not favored in law and are never enforced in equity unless the right thereto is so clear as to permit of no denial.

Kaufman Bros. Constr. v. Olney, 29 Wash. App. 296, 300, 628 P.2d 838 (1981) (quoting Dill v. Zielke, 26 Wash. 2d 246, 252, 173 P.2d 977 (1946)).[5] The Restatement (Second) of Contracts §227(1) (1981) states:

> In resolving doubts as to whether an event is made a condition of an obligor's duty, . . . an interpretation is preferred that will reduce the obligee's risk of forfeiture, unless the event is within the obligee's control or the circumstances indicate that he has assumed the risks.

5. The Restatement (Second) of Contracts §227 comment b (1981) defines "forfeiture" as the resulting denial of compensation where the nonoccurrence of a condition of an obligor's duty causes the obligee to lose his right to the agreed exchange after he has relied substantially on the expectation of that exchange, as by preparation or performance.

The Restatement §227 comment b continues:

> If the event is within [the obligee's] control, he will often assume this risk [of forfeiture]. If it is not within his control, it is sufficiently unusual for him to assume the risk that, in case of doubt, an interpretation is preferred under which the event is not a condition.

Assuming the risk

Here since obtaining King County final plat approval was not within Jones Associates' control, it was sufficiently unusual for it to assume the risk of forfeiture so that where doubt exists, as in this case, the preferred interpretation is that the event was not a condition. No circumstances have been shown to indicate that it assumed the risk of forfeiture; rather, Harry P. Jones, Jones Associates' president, testified to the contrary. Moreover, conditions precedent are not favored by the courts. Thomas v. French, 30 Wash. App. 811, 819, 638 P.2d 613 (1981). An examination of the entire contract, the circumstances of its formation, the parties' conduct and the reasonableness of their interpretations supports the conclusion that obtaining King County final plat approval was intended to be Jones Associates' duty under the contract but not a condition precedent to payment. . . .

Court looked at formation of contract, parties conduct

However, since it is undisputed that King County approval was not secured, Jones Associates may be liable for breach of its promise to obtain King County final plat approval.

> One who makes a promise which cannot be performed without the consent or cooperation of a third person is not excused from liability because of inability to secure the required consent or cooperation, unless the terms or nature of the contract indicate that he does not assume this risk.

Fischler v. Nicklin, 51 Wash. 2d 518, 523, 319 P.2d 1098 (1958). By signing the original contract, which included the typewritten paragraph regarding responsibility for obtaining King County approval, and its amendment, which incorporated the original contract's terms, Jones Associates assumed the risk that King County might not approve Eastside's short plat application so that if such approval was not obtained, it would be liable for breach of the parties' contract.

Jones Associates contends that it cannot be liable for not obtaining King County final plat approval because such approval was dependent upon certain factors, some of which were in the respondent's discretion or ability to perform. There being no findings of fact, the record is not clear as to why final county plat approval was not obtained. However, all contracts embody an implied condition that the parties will not interfere with each other's performance, but will cooperate in good faith. [Citations omitted.] Proof of a party's interference with the performance of the other party's obligation under the contract will work to discharge the other party's duty. [Citations omitted.] Upon remand both parties will have the opportunity to show any

Implied Condition Not to Interfere with Performance

conduct of the other party that prevented it from obtaining the full benefit of performance.

The judgment is reversed and the cause is remanded for trial and the determination of damages, if any, to be offset against any money due Jones Associates under the contract as well as an attorney fee award to the prevailing party pursuant to the parties' contract.

Reversed [handwritten]

QUESTION

What will the parties argue on retrial?

BRIGHT v. GANAS
Court of Appeals of Maryland, 1937
171 Md. 493, 189 A. 427

SLOAN, J. The plaintiff, Paul Ganas, sued the defendant, Robert S. Bright, executor of James G. Darden, deceased, on an alleged testamentary contract for the sum of $20,000. The judgment being for the plaintiff for $8,990, the defendant appeals. . . .

Paul Ganas, the plaintiff, a native of Greece, at the age of thirteen, came to this country about twenty-seven years ago, whither he had been preceded by his father, then engaged in the restaurant business at Roanoke, Va. He worked at various places, principally as a waiter, finally going to Washington, where he became acquainted with Col. James G. Darden, a picturesque and mysterious character, who lived luxuriously and seemed to be supplied with plenty of money, though we are not informed as to the nature or size of his estate. Col. Darden settled in Cambridge in 1929, where he bought a house, and in May of that year engaged Ganas as a servant or man of all work, more or less personal in its nature, and there Ganas continued until Darden's death in November, 1933 at about the age of sixty-eight. . . . [T]here is nothing contained in the record which proves or tends to prove anything except a specific agreement for the payment of $20,000 out of Col. James G. Darden's estate, at his death, to Paul Ganas, if he served the colonel faithfully and continuously to that time.

[handwritten margin note: Condition was to serve P faithfully until his death]

Col. Darden was ill for several months continuously to the day of his death. So far as he knew, during that time, the plaintiff was serving him faithfully, and assisted in nursing him. On or about the last day of August, 1933, Mrs. Darden had left her husband's room late at night (the plaintiff was downstairs at the time), and had gone to her room, where she there found on her bed an envelope containing a letter addressed to her by the plaintiff. It would serve no worthy purpose to quote it or to even summarize its contents, except to say that this plaintiff had designs on his employer's

[handwritten margin note: P wrote a letter]

wife, which he was intent on revealing to her. She testified that the next morning she took the letter to her mother, who lived in Cambridge, asked her to read it, and asked her advice. She told Dr. Wolfe, her husband's physician (since deceased), about it, and he advised her against telling her husband. She said, "I wanted to that night, but I knew he could not stand it." Asked on cross-examination, "You spoke of locking your door after the burial. There was never any effort on Paul's part to follow this up was there?" She answered, "He did not have a chance. I had someone near me all the time." About two hours after Col. Darden's funeral she showed Mr. Bright, the executor, the letter and told him the plaintiff must get out of the house. He being told by Mr. Bright that he must leave, he rebelled, and the next day he was told by his attorney he had to go, and then did.

The plaintiff must have had some conception of the gravity and consequences of his offense, for on the envelope containing the letter he wrote: "If I lose my job by this note — at least I would gain my peace of mind — ." When asked at the trial what led him to write the letter he gave a long, incoherent, unresponsive answer, which showed no reason or excuse for writing it, and that it was inspired by moral depravity or a disordered, disorderly mind, with no conception of the proprieties, especially when his employer, who seemed to be fond of him, and whose confidence was thus betrayed, was so ill that his physician forbade any communication with him on the subject. This record discloses no excuse or justification for the plaintiff's behavior. He is the one who offended against all the rules of propriety and decency, and he ought to pay the penalty instead of reaping a reward. There was nothing in the wife's conduct inviting such an outburst from the plaintiff. If this act of the plaintiff was such as to justify his immediate and summary discharge, if his employer had known of the incident, then, in our opinion, it is as available to the executor as a defense, as it would have been to the decedent in his lifetime. . . . [T]his from Labatt's Master and Servant (2d ed.) §299, p.930: "Every servant impliedly stipulates that both his words and his behavior in regard to his master and his master's family shall be respected and free from insolence. A breach of this stipulation is unquestionably a valid reason for dismissing the servant, especially when it is accompanied by other conduct which would of itself justify a rescission of the contract." As we have indicated, this is one entire contract, and the plaintiff was entitled to the full consideration of his contract or none of it. Schneider v. Hagerstown Brewing Co., 136 Md. 151, 154, 110 A. 218; 39 C.J. 145, 149. On the theory of an entire contract, if the act of unfaithfulness and disloyalty here charged against the plaintiff was sufficient to warrant his immediate discharge by his employer, had it been known to him, then his right to compensation has been forfeited (20 A.&E. Ency. Law (2d ed.) 20), for it cannot be assumed that the employer would not have done the thing that common decency and loyalty to his wife would have required him to do. The question for us then is, whether it is one of law for the court or of fact for the jury, the legal sufficiency of the evidence to support a verdict for the plaintiff having been submitted by the fourth prayer of the defendant for a directed verdict which was refused and exception taken. If held to be for the jury, then the defendant's sixth and ninth prayers, which instructed the jury to find for the defendant if they found the plaintiff to have been unfaithful to his employer, should have been granted.

The rule with respect to the province of the court and jury as stated in 26 C.J. 1016, and quoted in Dorrance v. Hoopes, supra, is: "What constitutes good and sufficient cause for the discharge of a servant is a question of law, and where the facts are undisputed, it is for the court to say whether the discharge was justified. But where the facts are disputed, it is for the jury to say upon all the evidence whether there were sufficient grounds to warrant the discharge," and in that case, 122 Md. 344, at page 352, 90 A. 92, 95, Ann. Cas. 1916A, 1012, this court said: "There are cases . . . so flagrant and so manifestly contrary to the implied conditions arising from . . . master and servant which should exist between them that they can be decided by the court as matters of law." 39 C.J. 212.

In this case the violation of the agreement by the plaintiff was so flagrant, unjustified, and inexcusable as to justify his discharge, and, if by it he earned his discharge, then he cannot recover. It was not contradicted, denied, nor even explained, so that, in accordance with the rule herein stated, in our opinion the plaintiff was not entitled to recover, and the defendant's fourth prayer should have been granted. 13 C.J. 790, §1011. . . .

Judgment reversed without a new trial with costs to the appellant.

NOTES AND QUESTIONS

1. The court refuses to reprint the plaintiff's letter, but (as reported in L. Fuller and R. Braucher, *Basic Contract Law* 659 (1964)), it appeared in the court record in this fashion:

> My dear Margaret:
> We seem to talk to each other in a secret language. You often communicate to me that you desire my friendship; you treat me not like a servant. This is what torments me! God knows, at times I would like to kiss you and all most eat you — for love is physical — otherwise what is beauty for?
> Yes a man needs a woman to draw power into his being. And what is a woman that no one loves? Or a woman that does not love anyone? A mere piece of physical mechanism and that is all.
> You too, often seem to me to be frigid, incapable of loving; and I don't believe you ever loved me. I, on the other hand have loved you deeply from my heart — and have suffered mental and physical agony. Yes such is love!
> I would have gone to hell for you once, for I thought you loved me. But now I know better — and that's why I try hard to forget you.
> Now you ought to try to forget me — for one thing you do not have to depend on me for your lively-hood.

I always wanted to see you taken care of financially — your income in the future will be 3 times larger than mine — Besides I am not ready for marriage. I want to study and be something first — But sometimes I feel that without love I am simply a lost atom in the universe — and cannot accomplish much.

I often feel that you just want to dominate me — to put me under your heels — that's all.

Yes you are a puzzle to me — If I only knew your secret goal!

Without love,

Paul

2. Do you agree with the court's characterization of this letter? With the court's result? In answering this, consider that written on the envelope containing the letter were the following words: "If I lose my job with this note — at least I would gain my peace of mind — ."

3. What pedagogical point is being made by the inclusion of this case at this point in the chapter?

B. Conditions Precedent vs. Conditions Subsequent

When we classify conditions as *express, implied-in-fact,* or *constructive,* the classification has to do with how the condition arose (by explicit agreement of the parties, as implied by their conduct, or implied in law).

In *Howard* the court was trying to determine whether the contested clause was a condition *precedent* (pronounced pre-SEE-dent, *not* PRESS-ident). When we speak of *conditions precedent* and *conditions subsequent,* the classification has to do with the time when the conditioning event is to happen in relation to the promisor's duty to perform. A condition is precedent if an event must occur *before* the performance is due. A condition is subsequent if the performance obligation is due but will cease to exist upon the occurrence of the specified event.

GRAY v. GARDNER

Supreme Judicial Court of Massachusetts, 1821

17 Mass. 188

ASSUMPSIT on a written promise to pay the plaintiff 5,198 dollars, 87 cents, with the following condition annexed, viz., "on the condition that if a greater quantity of sperm oil should arrive in whaling vessels at *Nantucket* and *New Bedford,* on or between the first day of April and the first day of October of the present year, both inclusive, than arrived at said places, in whaling vessels, on or within the same term of time the last year, then this obligation to be void." Dated April 14, 1819.

The consideration of the promise was a quantity of oil, sold by the plaintiff to the defendants. On the same day another note unconditional had been given by the defendants, for the value of the oil, estimated at sixty cents per gallon; and the note in suit was given to secure the residue of the price, estimated at eighty-five cents, to depend on the contingency mentioned in the said condition.

At the trial before the chief justice, the case depended upon the question whether a certain vessel, called the *Lady Adams*, with a cargo of oil, arrived at *Nantucket* on the first day of October, 1819, about which fact the evidence was contradictory. The judge ruled that the burden of proving the arrival within the time was on the defendants; and further that, although the vessel might have, within the time, gotten within the space which might be called *Nantucket Roads*, yet it was necessary that she should have come to anchor, or have been moored, somewhere within that space before the hour of twelve following the first day of October, in order to have *arrived*, within the meaning of the contract.

The opinion of the chief justice on both these points was objected to by the defendants, and the questions were saved. If it was wrong on either point, a new trial was to be had; otherwise judgment was to be rendered on the verdict, which was found for the plaintiff.

Whitman, for the defendants. As the evidence at the trial was contradictory, the question on whom the burden of proof rested, became important. We hold that it was on the plaintiff. This was a condition precedent. Until it should happen, the promise did not take effect. On the occurrence of a certain contingent event, the promise was to be binding, and not otherwise. To entitle himself to enforce the promise, the plaintiff must show that the contingent event has actually occurred.

On the other point saved at the trial, the defendants insist that it was not required by the terms of this contract that the vessel should be moored. It is not denied that such would be the construction of a policy of insurance containing the same expression. But every contract is to be taken according to the intention of the parties to it, if such intention be legal, and capable of execution. The contemplation of parties to a policy of insurance is, that the vessel shall be safe before she shall be said to have arrived. So it is in some other maritime contracts. But in that now in question, nothing was in the minds of the parties, but that the fact of the arrival of so much oil should be known within the time limited. The subject matter in one case is safety, in the other it is information only. In this case the vessel would be said to have arrived, in common understanding, and according to the meaning of the parties.

PARKER, C.J. The very words of the contract show that there was a promise to pay, which was to be defeated by the happening of an event, viz., the arrival of a certain quantity of oil, at the specified places, in a given time. It is like a bond with a condition; if the obligor would avoid the bond, he must show performance of the condition. The defendants, in this case, promise to pay a certain sum of money, on condition that the promise shall be void on the happening of an event. It is plain that the burden of proof is upon them; and if they fail to show that the event has happened, the promise remains good.

The other point is equally clear for the plaintiff. Oil is to arrive at a given place before twelve o'clock at night. A vessel with oil heaves in sight, but she does not come to anchor before the hour is gone. In no sense can the oil be said to have arrived. The vessel is coming until she drops anchor, or is moored. She may sink, or take fire, and never arrive, however near she may be to her port. It is so in contracts of insurance; and the same reason applies to a case of this sort. Both parties put themselves upon a nice point in this contract; it was a kind of wager as to the quantity of oil which should arrive at the ports mentioned, before a certain period. They must be held strictly to their contract, there being no equity to interfere with the terms of it.

Judgment on the verdict.

The boat didn't Arrive yet

NOTES AND QUESTIONS

1. Why would the parties have made such a contract?

2. Why did it matter whether the condition here was precedent or subsequent?

3. Reread the first Problem in this chapter and compare it with the following clause from an insurance policy. If we assume that the relevant language creates express conditions, which one illustrates a condition precedent and which a condition subsequent?

> If the company does not pay the insured's claim, whether valid or not, within one year of the occurrence of the insured-against event, the company shall have no further liability unless the insured shall file suit within the one-year period.

4. The Restatement (Second) of Contracts has dropped the precedent/subsequent distinction, and only conditions precedent are called "conditions" under the new lexicon. Conditions subsequent have been downgraded to simply "events that terminate a duty." See Restatement (Second) of Contracts §230. This is because of the difficulty in distinguishing between the two and the relative unimportance of the issue in most contract cases. That is not to say that the practical significance in distinguishing between the two has completely disappeared as is demonstrated by the following Federal Rules of Civil Procedure:

Rule 9.   Pleading Special Matters . . .

(c) *Conditions Precedent.* In pleading the performance or occurrence of conditions precedent, it is sufficient to aver generally that all conditions precedent have been performed or have occurred. A denial of performance or occurrence shall be made specifically and with particularity.

Rule 8. General Rules of Pleading . . .

(c) *Affirmative Defenses.* In pleading to a preceding pleading, a party shall set forth affirmatively accord and satisfaction, arbitration and award, assumption of risk, contributory negligence, discharge in bankruptcy, duress, estoppel, failure of consideration, fraud, illegality, injury by fellow servant, laches, license, payment, release, res judicata, statute of frauds, statute of limitations, waiver, and any other matter constituting an avoidance or affirmative defense. When a party has mistakenly designated a defense as a counterclaim or a counterclaim as a defense, the court on terms, if justice so requires, shall treat the pleading as if there had been a proper designation.

5. A court always has the power to alter the usual burdens of pleading and proof in situations where one party has superior ability to present the relevant evidence, or where, for one reason or another, justice requires a different allocation. For example, it is easier to prove a positive ("John Doe was in Houston on February 25th") than a negative ("John Doe was *not* in Houston on February 25th"), so the court may decide to place the burden of proof on the person with best access to the evidence of the positive happening. In Buick Motor Co. v. Thompson, 138 Ga. 282, 75 S.E. 354 (1912), the contract was to supply cars "conditions permitting," and the court placed the burden of proving the issue on the defendant, even though traditional analysis would probably deem this a condition precedent to the plaintiff's case.

6. The historical setting of this famous case and a discussion of the law it created are found in Nyquist, A Contract Tale from the Crypt, 30 Hous. L. Rev. 1205 (1993).

III. SOME TYPES OF EXPRESS CONDITIONS, INCLUDING CONDITIONS OF SATISFACTION

CHODOS v. WEST PUBLISHING CO.
United States Court of Appeals, Ninth Circuit, 2002
292 F.3d 992

REINHARDT, Circuit Judge.

This case presents the question whether a publisher retains the right to reject an author's manuscript written pursuant to a standard industry agreement, even though the manuscript is of the quality contemplated by both

Issue

parties. In this case, attorney Rafael Chodos entered into a standard Author Agreement with the Bancroft-Whitney Publishing Company under which he agreed to write a treatise on the intriguing subject of the law of fiduciary duty. The agreement is widely used in the publishing industry for traditional literary works as well as for specialized volumes. Bancroft-Whitney thought that the treatise would be successful commercially and that it would result in substantial profits for both the author and the publisher. After Chodos had spent a number of years fulfilling his part of the bargain and had submitted a completed manuscript, Bancroft-Whitney's successor, the West Publishing Company, came to a contrary conclusion. It declined to publish the treatise, citing solely sales and marketing reasons. Like a good lawyer, Chodos responded by suing for damages, first for breach of contract, and then, after amending his complaint to drop that claim, in quantum meruit. The district court held that under the terms of the contract West's decision not to publish was within its discretion, and granted summary judgment in West's favor. Chodos appeals, and we reverse.

I. Background

Rafael Chodos is a California attorney whose specialty is the law of fiduciary duty. His practice consists primarily of matters involving fiduciary issues such as partnership disputes, corporate dissolutions, and joint ventures. Prior to being admitted to the bar in 1977, Chodos worked as a software engineer. Beginning in approximately 1989, Chodos began developing the idea of writing a treatise on the law of fiduciary duty that included a traditional print component as well as an electronic component that incorporated search engines, linking capabilities, and electronic indexing. Chodos sought to draw on both his legal and technological expertise, and was motivated in part by the fact that there was, and continues to be, no systematic scholarly treatment of the law of fiduciary duty.

In early 1995, Chodos sent a detailed proposal, which included a tentative table of contents, to the Bancroft-Whitney Corporation. Bancroft was at the time a leading publisher of legal texts. William Farber, an Associate Publisher, promptly responded to Chodos's proposal, and informed him that the Bancroft editorial staff was enthusiastic about both the subject matter and the technological features of the proposed project. In July, 1995, Bancroft and Chodos entered into an Author Agreement, which both parties agree is a standard form contract used to govern the composition of a literary work for hire.

The Author Agreement provided for no payments to Chodos prior to publication, and a 15% share of the gross revenues from sales of the work. Farber informed Chodos that a typical successful title published by Bancroft grossed $1 million over a five-year period, although Chodos's work, of course, might be more or less successful than the average. Chodos sought publication of the work not only for the direct financial rewards, but also for the enhanced professional reputation he might receive from the publication of a treatise, which in turn might result in additional referrals to his practice and increased fees for him.

From July, 1995 through June, 1998, Chodos's principal professional activity was the writing of the treatise. He significantly limited the time spent on his law practice, and devoted several hours each morning as well as most weekends to the book project. Chodos estimates that he spent at least 3600 hours over the course of three years on writing the treatise and developing the accompanying electronic materials. He did so with the guidance of Bancroft staff. For example, in late 1995 or early 1996, Farber instructed Chodos that because Bancroft viewed the book as a practice aid and not as an academic work, he should delete an introductory chapter that was primarily historical and disperse the historical material throughout the text, in footnote form. As Chodos completed each of the chapters, he submitted them to Bancroft on a CD-ROM; the seventh and final chapter was sent to the publisher in February, 1998. When finished, the book consisted of 1247 pages.

In mid-1996, Bancroft-Whitney was purchased by the West Publishing Group, and the two entities merged at the end of the year. The Bancroft editors, now employed by West, continued to work with Chodos in preparing the work for publication, although West did establish a management position that ultimately had a direct bearing on Chodos's career as a treatise-writer, that of Director of Product Development and Management for the Western Market Center. Between February and June, 1998, after the entire treatise had been submitted, Chodos reviewed the manuscript to ensure that the formatting was consistent and that no substantive gaps existed. In the summer of 1998 the West editors provided him with detailed notes and suggestions, to which he diligently responded. In November, 1998, West again sent Chodos a lengthy letter including substantive editorial suggestions related to the organization of the book. In early December, 1998, West sent Chodos yet another letter, this time apologizing for delays in publication, and assuring him that publication would take place in the first quarter of 1999. Burt Levy, who replaced Farber as Chodos's editor, informed Chodos that copy editors were preparing the manuscript for release in the early part of that year.

After receiving no communication from Levy in January, 1999, Chodos contacted West to check on the status of his treatise. On February 4, 1999, Chodos received a response from Nell Petri, a member of the marketing department. Petri informed Chodos that West had decided not to publish the book because it did not "fit within [West's] current product mix" and because of concerns about its "market potential." West admits, however, that the manuscript was of "high quality" and that its decision was not due to any literary shortcomings in Chodos's work.

The decision not to publish the treatise on fiduciary duty was made by Carole Gamble, who joined West as Director of Product Development and Management for the Western Market Center at about the same time that Chodos completed the manuscript. In late 1998, West developed new internal criteria to guide publication decisions. Applying these criteria, Gamble decided not to go forward with the publication of the treatise. She did not in fact read what Chodos had written, but instead reviewed a detailed outline of the treatise and the original proposal for it. Gamble did not prepare a business analysis prior to making her decision. After Chodos informed West that in his view the publisher had breached its contract, West did prepare an economic projection that concluded that the publication of Chodos's work would be an unprofitable venture. Thus, this legal action was born.

Proceedings Below

Chodos filed an action against West for breach of contract in Los Angeles Superior Court in March, 1999, shortly after the publisher's decision not to publish his work, and West removed the case to federal court on the basis of diversity jurisdiction. Chodos immediately moved for summary judgment, which was denied. Shortly thereafter, he amended his complaint to seek restitution on a quantum meruit basis and dropped the breach of contract claim. West moved to dismiss the amended complaint for failure to state a claim, and the motion was denied. At the conclusion of discovery, West moved for summary judgment, and Chodos sought to amend the complaint again, in order to add a claim for fraud. The district court granted West's motion and entered judgment in its favor; it simultaneously denied Chodos leave to amend his complaint.

II. Discussion

Chodos makes two alternative arguments: first, that the standard Author Agreement is an illusory contract, and second, that if a valid contract does exist, West breached it. Under either theory of liability, Chodos contends that he is entitled to recover in quantum meruit.

A.   The Author Agreement Is Not Illusory

In support of his first argument, Chodos correctly notes that in order for a contract to be enforceable under California law, it must impose binding obligations on each party. Bleecher v. Conte 29 Cal. 3d 345, 350, 213 Cal. Rptr. 852, 698 P.2d 1154 (1981). The California Supreme Court has held that "if one of the promises leaves a party free to perform or to withdraw from the agreement at his own unrestricted pleasure, the promise is deemed illusory and it provides no consideration." Mattei v. Hopper, 51 Cal. 2d 119, 122, 330 P.2d 625 (1958). Chodos contends that because the contract required him to produce a work of publishable quality, but allowed West, in its discretion, to decide unilaterally whether or not to publish his work, the contract violates the doctrine of mutuality of obligation and is therefore illusory.

California law, like the law in most states, provides that a covenant of good faith and fair dealing is an implied term in every contract. [Citations omitted.] Thus, a court will not find a contract to be illusory if the implied covenant of good faith and fair dealing can be read to impose an obligation on each party. See, e.g., Third Story Music v. Waits, 41 Cal. App. 4th 798, 805-06, 48 Cal. Rptr. 2d 747 (1995) ("[T]he implied covenant of good faith is also applied to contradict an express contractual grant of discretion when necessary to protect an agreement which otherwise would be rendered illusory and unenforceable."). The covenant of good faith "finds particular application in situations where one party is invested with a discretionary power affecting the rights of another." Carma, 2 Cal. 4th at 372, 6 Cal. Rptr. 2d 467, 826 P.2d 710.

It is correct that the agreement at issue imposes numerous obligations on the author but gives the publisher "the right in its discretion to terminate" the publishing relationship after receiving the manuscript and determining that it is unacceptable. However, we conclude that the contract is not illusory because West's duty to exercise its discretion is limited by its duty of good faith and fair dealing. [Citations omitted.] More specifically, because the standard Author Agreement obligates the publisher to make a judgment as to the quality or literary merit of the author's work—to determine whether the work is "acceptable" or "unacceptable"—it must make that judgment in good faith, and cannot reject a manuscript for other, unrelated reasons. See Third Story Music, 41 Cal. App. 4th at 804, 48 Cal. Rptr. 2d 747. Thus, Chodos's first argument fails.

B. WEST BREACHED THE AGREEMENT

Chodos's alternative argument—that a contract exists and it was breached—is more persuasive. West contends that the Author Agreement allowed it to decline to publish the manuscript after Chodos completed writing it for *any* good-faith reason, regardless of whether the reason was related to the quality or literary merit of Chodos's manuscript. However, West's right to terminate the agreement is a limited one defined in two related provisions of the agreement. The first, the "acceptance clause," establishes that West may decline to publish Chodos's manuscript if it finds the work to be "unacceptable" in form and content. The acceptance clause, paragraph eight of the agreement, provides that:

After timely receipt of the Work or any portion of the Work prepared by Author, Publisher shall review it as to both form and content, and notify Author whether it is acceptable or unacceptable in form and content under the terms of this Agreement. In the event that Publisher determines that the Work or any portion of the Work is unacceptable, Publisher shall notify Author of Publisher's determination and Publisher may exercise its rights under paragraph 4.

[handwritten: Second Provision]

[handwritten: "Failure to Perform"]

The second relevant provision (referred to in the acceptance clause as West's "rights under paragraph 4") allows West to terminate the publishing agreement if the author does not cure a failure in performance after being given an opportunity to do so. This provision, numbered paragraph four of the contract and entitled "Author's Failure to Perform," states:

> [I]f Publisher determines that the Work or any portion of it is not acceptable to publisher as provided in paragraph 8 [the acceptance clause] . . . [a]fter thirty (30) days following written notice to author if Author has not cured such failure in performance Publisher has the right in its discretion to terminate this Agreement.

The district court agreed with West that in determining whether a manuscript is satisfactory in form and content under the acceptance clause of the standard Author Agreement, the publisher may in good faith consider solely the likelihood of a book's commercial success and other similar economic factors. We unequivocally reject the view that the relevant provisions of the Author Agreement may be so construed in the absence of additional language or conditions.

[handwritten: No conditional language to the economic success of the Book]

The expansive reading of the acceptance clause suggested by West is inconsistent with the language of the two contract clauses. Under the agreement, the publisher may deem a manuscript unacceptable only if it is deficient in "form and content." Thus, had Chodos submitted a badly written, poorly researched, disorganized or substantially incomplete work to West, the publisher would have been well within its rights to find that submission unacceptable under the acceptance clause — as it would were it to reject any work that it believed in good faith lacked literary merit. A publisher bargains for a product of a certain quality and is entitled to reject a work that in its good faith judgment falls short of the bargained-for standard. Nothing in the contract, however, suggests that the ordinary meaning of the words "form and content" was not intended, and nowhere in the contract does it state that the publisher may terminate the agreement if it changes its management structure or its marketing strategy, or if it revises its business or economic forecasts, all matters unrelated to "form and content." To the contrary, the fact that the contract required West to afford Chodos an opportunity to cure any deficient performance supports our straightforward reading of the acceptance clause as a provision that relates solely to the quality or literary merit of a submitted work.[4] As noted above, if West determined that Chodos's submission was unacceptable, he was to be given a period of time to cure his failure in performance. The inclusion of this provision indicates that a deficiency in "form and content" is one that the author has some power to cure. Chodos has no power to "cure" West's view that the marketplace for books on fiduciary duty had changed; nor could he "cure" a change in West's overall marketing strategy and product mix; nor, indeed, could he be expected to do much about a general downturn in economic conditions. The text and structure of the contract thus demonstrate that West's stated reasons for terminating the agreement were not among those contemplated by the parties.

The uncontroverted evidence in this case is that Chodos worked diligently in cooperation with West — indeed, with West's encouragement — to produce a work that met the highest professional standard, and that he was successful in that venture. His performance was induced by an agreement that permitted rejection of the completed manuscript only for deficiencies in "form and content." Chodos thus labored to complete a work of high quality with the expectation that, if he did so, it would be published. He devoted thousands of hours of labor to the venture, and passed up substantial professional opportunities, only for West to decide that due to the vagaries of its internal reorganizations and changes in its business strategies or in the national economy or the market for legal treatises, his work, albeit admittedly of high quality, was for naught. It would be inequitable, if not unconscionable, for an author to be forced to bear this considerable burden solely because of his publisher's change in management, its poor planning, or its inadequate financial analyses at the time it entered into the contract, or even because of an unexpected change in the market-place. Moreover, to allow a publisher to escape its contractual obligations for these reasons would be directly contrary to both the language and the spirit of the standard Author Agreement.

West urges us to affirm the district court's ruling because, in its view, it is well-accepted that, regardless of the contract's failure to mention economic circumstances or market demands, publishers have broad discretion under the acceptance clause of the standard Author Agreement to reject manuscripts for any good faith commercial reason. For this proposition, the district court cited two cases from the Second Circuit involving that same clause. Although at least one of the cases contains dicta that would support the district court's decision, both are distinguishable factually and legally. Moreover, to the extent that either case suggests that a publisher bound by

---

4. In the case of technical, scientific or legal work, the term "quality" may be more descriptive of the permissible subject of the publisher's exercise of its discretion, while in the case of a less specialized publication, such as a novel, a book of poetry of essays, or a biography or other historical work, the term "literary merit" may be more fitting.

the standard Author Agreement may terminate the contract for *any* reason so long as it acts in good faith, we respectfully reject that view.

In *Doubleday & Co. v. Curtis*, 763 F.2d 495, 496 (2d Cir. 1985), a publisher rejected a manuscript by the well-known actor but neophyte author, Tony Curtis, on the basis of its poor literary quality. There, as here, the publishing agreement allowed the publisher to reject a submission if it was not satisfactory as to "form and content." Id. However, in *Doubleday*, in direct contrast to the circumstances here, it was agreed that the manuscript was *unsatisfactory* in form and content. Id. at 500. In *Doubleday*, Curtis's claim was that the publisher had a good-faith obligation under the contract to re-write his admittedly unsatisfactory manuscript and to transform it into one of publishable quality. Id. The Second Circuit held that a publisher's good faith obligation does not stretch that far; thus, the Second Circuit's essential holding in *Doubleday* has no bearing on the present case.

It is true that the Second Circuit appears to have stated its holding in *Doubleday* more broadly than the case before the court warranted. The court said:

> [W]e hold that a publisher may, in its discretion, terminate a standard publishing contract, provided that the termination is made in good faith, and that the failure of an author to submit a satisfactory manuscript was not caused by the publisher's bad faith.

Id. at 501. Still, read in context, the holding does not make it clear whether the court meant that a publisher may reject a manuscript for reasons wholly unrelated to its literary worth or that it may do so only if it determines in good faith that the submitted work is unsatisfactory on its literary merits. If the former is the Second Circuit's view of the law, we respectfully disagree.

The district court also relied on *Random House, Inc. v. Gold*, 464 F. Supp. 1306 (S.D.N.Y. 1979). That case is more apposite than *Doubleday* in that the district court there held that a publisher may consider economic circumstances when evaluating a manuscript's "form and content" under the standard publishing agreement. Id. at 1308-09. Although we disagree with that holding for the reasons set forth above, and are certainly not bound by it, we note that even in *Random House* the court did not go so far as to state that economic considerations may be the *sole* reason for a publisher to decline to publish a manuscript that is in every other respect acceptable. In *Random House,* as in *Doubleday*, the submitted manuscript was not of publishable quality. In contrast to Chodos's work, the editor at Random House considered the manuscript at issue to be "shallow and badly designed." Id. at 1308.

In sum, we reject the district court's determination that West acted within the discretion afforded it by the Author Agreement when it decided not to publish Chodos's manuscript. Because West concedes that the manuscript was of high quality and that it declined to publish it solely for

Holding

commercial reasons rather than because of any defect in its form and content, we hold as a matter of law that West breached its agreement with Chodos.

[margin: Damages]

The district court ruled that if West breached the contract, Chodos could proceed in quantum meruit, but only if the damages were not determinable under the contract. It also stated that a question of material fact existed as to whether contract damages were determinable. It then granted West summary judgment on the quantum meruit claim because it held that there was no breach of contract. As we have already determined above, the district court erred in finding that no breach occurred. Accordingly, we must consider the remaining issues relevant to Chodos's quantum meruit claim.

[margin: QM]

Under California law, a party who has been injured by a breach of contract may generally elect what remedy to seek. In a leading case on election of remedies, the California Supreme Court stated:

> It is well settled in this state that one who has been injured by a breach of contract has an election to pursue any of three remedies, to wit: He may treat the contract as rescinded and may recover upon a quantum meruit so far as he has performed; or he may keep the contract alive, for the benefit of both parties, being at all times ready and able to perform; or, third, he may treat the repudiation as putting an end to the contract for all purposes of performance, and sue for the profits he would have realized if he had not been prevented from performing.

Alder v. Drudis, 30 Cal. 2d 372, 381-82, 182 P.2d 195 (1947) (internal quotation marks omitted).

In employment contracts and contracts for personal services, like the one before us, the first option, an action in quantum meruit, is generally limited to cases in which the breach occurs after partial performance and the party seeking a recovery does not thereafter complete performance. "Where [a party's] performance is not prevented, the injured party may elect instead to affirm the contract and complete performance. If such is his election, his exclusive remedy is an action for damages." B.C. Richter Contracting Co. v. Continental Casualty Co., 230 Cal. App. 2d 491, 500, 41 Cal. Rptr. 98 (1964) (citing House v. Piercy, 181 Cal. 247, 251, 183 P. 807 (1919)). Thus, if a plaintiff has fully performed a contract, damages for breach is often the only available remedy. Oliver v. Campbell, 43 Cal. 2d 298, 306, 273 P.2d 15 (1954).

[margin: QM usually for Partial Performance]
[margin: If Full Performance, then usually the only remedy is Breach]

The California Supreme Court has, however, recognized an exception to the general rule. In *Oliver,* the court stated:

[margin: Exception]

> The remedy of restitution in money is not available to one who has fully performed his part of a contract, if the only part of the agreed exchange for such performance that has not been rendered by the defendant is a sum of money constituting a liquidated debt; *but full performance does not*

[margin: Rule]

> *make restitution unavailable if any part of the consideration due from the defendant in return is something other than a liquidated debt.*

Id. at 306, 273 P.2d 15 (adopting Restatement of Contracts §350) (emphasis added).

Assuming that Chodos fully performed his end of the bargain by delivering a completed manuscript to West, then whether Chodos can recover on a quantum meruit claim turns on whether the 15% of the gross revenues provided for in the agreement constitutes a "liquidated debt." According to Black's Law Dictionary, "[a] debt is liquidated when it is certain what is due and how much is due. That which has been made certain as to amount due by agreement of parties or by operation of law." Black's Law Dictionary 931 (6th ed. 1990). The term "liquidated debt" is similar to the term "liquidated damages," which the California courts have defined as "an amount of compensation to be paid in the event of a breach of contract, the sum of which is fixed and certain by agreement. . . ." Kelly v. McDonald, 98 Cal. App. 121, 125, 276 P. 404 (1929) (citation omitted), overruled in part on other grounds, McCarthy v. Tally, 46 Cal. 2d 577, 297 P.2d 981 (1956).

Chodos's entitlement to 15% of the revenues from his book on fiduciary duty is not a liquidated debt under California law, as it was not a certain or readily ascertainable figure. The mere existence of a fixed percentage royalty in a contract does not render that royalty a "liquidated debt," if the revenues to which that percentage figure is to be applied cannot be calculated with reasonable certainty. Here, it is impossible to determine even now what those revenues would have been had West not frustrated the completion of the contract. Had West honored its contractual obligations and published the treatise, the revenues would have depended on any number of circumstances, including how West chose to market the book, and how it was received by readers and critics.[10] Accordingly, under *Oliver,* Chodos is entitled to sue for restitution for the time and effort he reasonably invested in writing the manuscript. See also O'Hare v. Peacock Dairies, 26 Cal. App. 2d 345, 79 P.2d 433, 442-43 (1938) (holding future profits to be unascertainable where plaintiffs are owed a future revenue stream from a dairy that had ceased operation). We express no opinion as to how restitution should be calculated in this case, nor do we intimate any suggestion as to the appropriate amount of such recovery. . . .

---

10. It might also be reasonably argued that West's publishing of Chodos's treatise was an additional element of consideration to which Chodos was entitled, since substantial benefits other than the royalties he would have received might have accrued to him as a result of publication, including enhanced reputation and additional client referrals. Because restitution is available if "*any* part of the consideration due from the defendant in return is something other than a liquidated debt," *Oliver,* 43 Cal. 2d at 306, 273 P.2d 1 (emphasis added), restitution might be available under this theory regardless of whether the potential royalties are considered a "liquidated debt."

III. Conclusion

Because West breached its contract with Chodos by rejecting his manuscript for a reason not permitted by the contract between the parties and because Chodos is entitled to recover for the breach in quantum meruit, we REVERSE the district court's grant of summary judgment in West's favor, and REMAND the case to the district court with instructions to enter summary judgment as to liability in Chodos's favor, and for further proceedings consistent with this opinion. . . .

Reversed

NOTE

Like West in *Chodos*, parties sometimes grant themselves the power to terminate the contract if they are not satisfied with the other party's performance. This might be seen as an illusory promise, but courts avoid that by limiting the discretion of the party with the right to be dissatisfied. In general, they do so by imposing an *objective* standard in which the party with discretion can invoke the satisfaction clause if a *reasonable person* would have been dissatisfied. This is particularly true if the subject matter of the contract involves commercial quality, operative fitness, or mechanical utility (issues that are easy to assess objectively). Alternatively, when a contract revolves around fancy, taste, or aesthetics, the test is *subjective*: whether the party with discretion actually was dissatisfied. See Restatement (Second) §228.

Problem 141

(a) Oscar Wilde went to James Whistler and asked to have his portrait painted, agreeing to pay Whistler £40 if he was satisfied with the painting. Whistler produced what all agree to be a masterpiece, but Wilde pooh-poohed it, proclaiming it "crude and mean." Whistler sued. Must Wilde pay? Is this an illusory contract? Who has the burden of proof here?

(b) When Scarlett decided to sell her ancestral home, Tara, she engaged the services of Mitchell Realty, agreeing to pay a 10 percent commission if the company could produce a "satisfactory" buyer. Mitchell Realty scouted around and found a millionaire named John Doe, who agreed to pay cash. Investigation showed him to be a shy, quiet recluse. She turned him down as unsatisfactory, and Mitchell sued her for its fee. How should this come out? Would it influence your answer if the seller were a corporation?

(c) Four Star Construction Company built a $4 million building for Octopus National Bank, with payments to be made as the project progressed. Fifteen percent of each progress payment was to be withheld in a retainage

[margin notes: — Condition Subsequent → Performance is owed, unless Architect is satisfied]

account to be paid at the end of the project after Four Star had obtained a certificate of approval from the architect hired by the bank to supervise the project. The building was built according to specifications, and Four Star was so proud of its work that it called in industry magazines to write up the job. Nonetheless, the architect inspected the project and pronounced the work unsatisfactory, refusing to elaborate beyond saying that the "workmanship is ugly." Four Star sued. Is it entitled to the retainage? Does it matter what the motivation of the architect is?

[margin note: — Could sue for QM for work completed]

GULF CONSTRUCTION CO. v. SELF
Court of Appeals of Texas, 1984
676 S.W.2d 624

UTTER, J. This is an appeal of two separate lawsuits which were tried jointly by agreement of all parties before the Honorable Rachel Littlejohn sitting as judge of the 156th and 36th District Courts of San Patricio County. Each case involved a suit by a subcontractor against a general contractor and its bonding company to recover payment for labor and materials furnished by the subcontractors to the general contractor. The parties waived a jury trial, and the case was tried to the court. Separate judgments were rendered against appellants in favor of each appellee-subcontractor. From such separate judgments, appellants appeal. We affirm the judgments of the trial court.

Appellant Gulf Construction Company, Inc., as general contractor, entered into two contracts with Good Hope Chemical Corporation, as owner, for the construction of various buildings to be located at Good Hope Chemical's plant site near Ingleside in San Patricio County. A performance and payment bond was executed by appellant Mid Continent Casualty as surety for Gulf Construction.

Appellant Gulf Construction then entered into three separate subcontracts with each of the appellees, Shaw Plumbing Company and Calvin Self, individually and d/b/a Industrial Electric Company. During the construction of the project, the owner, Good Hope Chemical, encountered financial problems and directed that all work at the plant site cease. After they were ordered to stop their work, the subcontractors each demanded that Gulf Construction pay the balance owed for the work performed. After they each made their demands, the subcontractors filed mechanic's and materialman's liens after giving the appropriate notice. Also, the subcontractors perfected their claims on the performance and payment bond furnished by appellant Gulf Construction and executed by appellant Mid Continent Casualty Company as surety. When the general contractor, Gulf Construction, refused and failed to pay the balance owed to each of the subcontractors, the subcontractors, Shaw Plumbing and Self, filed suit. Appellants defended against the subcontractors' claims on the basis of the ninth paragraph of the subcontracts which reads as follows:

> Ninth. When the owner or his representative advances or pays the general contractor, the general contractor shall be liable for and obligated to pay the sub-contractor up to the amount or percentage recognized and approved for payment by the owner's representative less the retainage required under the terms of the prime contract. Under no circumstances shall the general contractor be obligated or required to advance or make payments to the sub-contractor until the funds have been advanced or paid by the owner or his representative to the general contractor.

It was the position of appellants that, since the owner, Good Hope Chemical, had filed for bankruptcy and was unable to pay appellant, appellant Gulf Construction was under no obligation, pursuant to the ninth paragraph of the subcontracts, to pay the balance owed to each of the subcontractors.

Resolution of the issues presented in appellant's first through sixth points of error on appeal depends on the construction of the language of the ninth paragraph of the subcontracts in question as either (1) a condition precedent to Gulf Construction's obligation to pay the balance owed to each subcontractor or (2) merely a covenant dealing with the "terms of payment" or "manner of payment." A condition precedent may be either a condition to the formation of a contract or to an obligation to perform an existing agreement. Conditions may, therefore, relate either to the formation of contracts or liability under them. Hohenberg Brothers Company v. George E. Gibbons & Co., 537 S.W.2d 1 (Tex. 1976). Conditions precedent to an obligation to perform are those acts or events which occur subsequently to the making of the contract that must occur before there is a right to immediate performance and before there is a breach of contractual duty. Ibid. While no particular words are necessary for the existence of a condition, such terms as "if," "provided that," "on condition that," or some other phrase that conditions performance usually connote an intent for a condition rather than a promise. In the absence of such a limiting clause, whether a certain contractual provision is a condition, rather than a promise, must be gathered from the contract as a whole and from the intent of the parties. Ibid. The Texas Supreme Court in Citizens National Bank in Abilene v. Texas and Pacific Railway Company, 136 Tex. 333, 150 S.W.2d 1003 (1941), stated:

> It is the duty of the Court, in determining the meaning and intent of a contract, to look to the entire instrument; that is, the contract must be examined from its four corners. Stated in another way, the contract must be considered and construed as an entire instrument, and all of its provisions must be considered and construed together. It is not usually proper to consider a single

paragraph, clause, or provision by itself, to ascertain its meaning. To the contrary, each and every part of the contract must be construed and considered with every other part, so that the effect or meaning on any other part may be determined.

Rule

However, where the intent of the parties is doubtful or where a condition would impose an absurd or impossible result, then the agreement should be interpreted as creating a covenant rather than a condition. Also, it is a rule of construction that a forfeiture, by finding a condition precedent, is to be avoided when possible under another reasonable reading of the contract. Schwarz-Jordan, Inc. of Houston v. Delisle Construction Company, 569 S.W.2d 878 (Tex. 1978). "Because of their harshness and operation, conditions are not favorites of the law." Sirtex Oil Industries, Inc. v. Erigan, 403 S.W.2d 784 (Tex. 1966). The rule, as announced in Henshaw v. Texas National Resources Foundation, 216 S.W.2d 566 (Tex. 1949), is that:

Law Abhors a Forfeiture

Since forfeitures are not favored, courts are inclined to construe the provisions in a contract as covenants rather than as conditions. If the terms of the contract are fairly susceptible of an interpretation which will prevent a forfeiture, they will be so construed.

Generally, a writing is construed most strictly against its author and in such a manner as to reach a reasonable result consistent with the apparent intention of the parties. Republic National Bank of Dallas v. Northwest National Bank of Fort Worth, 578 S.W.2d 109 (Tex. 1978). The first sentence of the ninth paragraph of the subcontract in question, by itself, does not set forth a condition precedent to appellant's obligation to make payment but only utilizes language similar to that in contractual provisions construed in Thos. J. Dyer Company v. Bishop International Engineering, Inc., 303 F.2d 655 (6th Cir. 1962); Prickett v. Lendell Builders, Inc., 572 S.W.2d 57 (Tex. Civ. App. — Eastland 1978, no writ); Wisznia v. Wilcox, 438 S.W.2d 874 (Tex. Civ. App. — Corpus Christi 1909, writ ref'd n.r.e.); and Mignot v. Parkhill, 237 Or. 450, 391 P.2d 755 (1964), wherein the courts held that such language set forth only a covenant regarding "terms of payment" or "manner of payment" and not a condition precedent. However, the additional question presented is: Does the second sentence of the ninth paragraph which provides that "Under no circumstances shall the general contractor be obligated or required to advance or make payments to the sub-contractor until the funds have been advanced or paid by the owner or his representative to the general contractor," when read in context within the entire contract, create a condition precedent or does it modify or explain the preceding sentence as to "terms of payment" or "manner of payment?" In Thos. J. Dyer Company v. Bishop International Engineering Company, supra, the United States Sixth Court of Appeals was called upon to construe a provision in a subcontract which provided that no payment was due the subcontractor

Issue

until five days after the owner of the construction project made payment to the general contractor. The general contractor had not been paid by the owner and contended that, since it had not been paid, the condition precedent to his obligation to make payment had not yet been met; and, hence, it should not be subject to any liability. In rejecting the general contractor's claim, the United States Sixth Court of Appeals stated:

> It is, of course, basic in the construction business for the general contractor on a construction project of any magnitude to expect to be paid in full by the owner for the labor and material he puts into the project. He would not remain long in business unless such was his intention and such intention was accomplished. That is a fundamental concept of doing business with another. The solvency of the owner is a credit risk necessarily incurred by the general contractor, but various legal and contractual provisions, such as mechanics liens, and installment payments, are used to reduce these to a minimum. These evidence the intention of the parties that the contractor be paid even though the owner may ultimately become insolvent. This expectation and intention of being paid is even more pronounced in the case of a subcontractor whose contract is with the general contractor, not with the owner. In addition to his mechanic's lien, he is primarily interested in the solvency of the general contractor with whom he has contracted. Normally and legally, the insolvency of the owner will not defeat the claim of the subcontractor against the general contractor. Accordingly, in order to transfer this normal credit risk incurred by the general contractor from the general contractor to the subcontractor, the contract between the general contractor and the subcontractor should contain an express condition clearly showing that to be the intention of the parties.

The Court of Appeals for the Sixth Circuit held that, in accordance with "the normal construction of the relationship of the parties," said provision did not shift the normal credit risk from the general contractor to the subcontractor and that the provision was a reasonable provision designed to postpone payment for a reasonable period of time after the work was completed, during which time the general contractor would be afforded the opportunity of procuring from the owner the funds necessary to pay the subcontractor. Furthermore, the United States Court of Appeals held that to construe the provision as requiring the subcontractor to wait to be paid for an indefinite time until the general contractor has been paid by the owner, which may never occur, is to give it an unreasonable construction which the parties did not intend at the time the subcontract was entered into.

In Mignot v. Parkhill, the Oregon Supreme Court construed the following subcontract provision which is similar to the second sentence of the ninth paragraph in question:

> It is fully understood by and between the parties hereto that the contractor [defendant] shall not be obligated to pay subcontractor [plaintiff] for any

of the work until such time as contractor has himself received the money from Bate Lumber Company.

As in the instant case, the above-quoted provision in *Mignot* was followed by an unconditional agreement to pay a certain amount to the subcontractor as consideration for the subcontractor's performance under the contract. The Oregon Supreme Court construed the contractual provision in the following manner:

> We take the contract at its four corners. The defendant's engagement to pay the stipulated consideration is expressed in unconditional terms and the provision in question, in our opinion, does no more than affect the time of payment. In unambiguous language, the defendant agreed to pay designated sums, not upon receiving the money from Bate Lumber Co., but upon completion of various portions of the work on specified days, subject only to approval by the forest service representative. The contract does not state that the defendant shall not be obligated if the money is not received from Bate Lumber Company nor that payment shall be made to plaintiff "out of" funds received by defendant from Bate Lumber Company (as in so many cases holding the provision a condition precedent) but that defendant shall not be obligated "*until such time as*" the money is received by him. The clause is in the nature of a modification of the time provisions which immediately precede it and is followed by an unconditional agreement of the defendant to pay plaintiff $123,700 in consideration of latter's prompt and faithful performance of the work.

As in *Mignot*, we hold that the contract in question does not state that Gulf Construction shall not be obligated *if* the money is not received from the owner, Good Hope Chemical, nor that the payment shall be made to the subcontractors "out of" funds received by Gulf Construction but that Gulf Construction shall not be obligated or required to make payments *until* the money has been received by the owner. The second sentence of the ninth paragraph is in the nature of a modification of the time provision which immediately precedes it in the first sentence of the ninth paragraph.

Furthermore, we note that the following of the trial court's findings of law filed in support of its judgment are consistent with a reasonable interpretation of the above-quoted language of *Thos. J. Dyer Company*, as applied to the instant case:

> (1) The court finds as a matter of law that the risk of non-payment by an owner on a construction contract rests on the contractor who contracts with such owner rather than on a subcontractor who has no privity of contract with the owner.
> (2) The court finds as a matter of law that the risk of non-payment by the owner on a construction contract is not shifted from the contractor to the subcontractor unless there is a clear, unequivocal and expressed agreement between the parties to do so.

(3) The court finds as a matter of law that there was <u>no intent</u> on the part of the parties to the subcontract of the risk of non-payment by the owner (Good Hope Chemical Corp.) should be shifted from the contractor (Gulf Construction Company, Inc.) to the subcontractors (Calvin Self, Individually and d/b/a Industrial Electric Company, and Shaw Plumbing Company).

(4) The court finds as a matter of law that the ninth paragraph of the subcontracts between the parties <u>does not clearly</u>, unequivocally and expressly shift the risk of non-payment by the owner from the contractor (Gulf Construction Company) to the subcontractors (Calvin Self, Individually and d/b/a Industrial Electric Company and Shaw Plumbing Company).

We hold that the ninth paragraph of the subcontracts merely provides a covenant dealing with "terms of payment" or "manner of payment" rather than a condition precedent. Appellants' first through sixth points of error are overruled. . . .

[handwritten margin note: clause is a covenant]

The judgment of the trial court in favor of appellee Shaw is modified to reflect the correct total judgment against Gulf Construction Company in the amount of $40,726.84, and, as modified, both judgments against Gulf Construction Company, Inc., and Mid-Continent Casualty Company are affirmed.

NOTES AND QUESTIONS

1. What facts relevant to conditions might lead you to a different conclusion?

2. What happened to the "time" portion of the agreement? Since payment was not to be made until the time the general contractor was to be paid, and this never happened, how did the duty of payment arise?

3. It has been held in California that even an express condition precedent in the form of a "pay if paid" clause is unenforceable as a matter of public policy because it serves to deny the subcontractor its rights to a mechanic's lien under the California Constitution. Wm. R. Clarke Co. v. Safeco Insur., 64 Cal. Rptr. 2d 578, 938 P.2d 372 (1997). Other courts take a decidedly different approach by upholding language clearly stating that it is a condition precedent to the subcontractor's payment that the contractor is paid by the owner; Transtar Electric, Inc. v. A.E.M. Servs. Corp., 140 Ohio St. 3d 193, 16 N.E.3d 645 (2014).

Problem 142

Every time his rich Aunt Augusta came to town, she gave Algernon a gift of $1,000. Her next visit was scheduled for the first of April, but Algernon ran short of funds before that date. He went to his friend John Worthing and asked to borrow $200, signing a promissory note in which he agreed to repay the money "when Aunt Augusta next arrives in town." Unfortunately, Aunt Augusta died suddenly, leaving all of her fortune to her daughter Gwendoline. Must Algernon pay when John Worthing presents the promissory note? See Mularz v. Greater Park City Co., 623 F.2d 139 (10th Cir. 1980).

Problem 143

Scarlett contracted to sell her ancestral home, Tara, to Rhett Butler "provided he is able to obtain satisfactory financing by June 4, 2021." June 4 was the date set for the closing. Does this agreement oblige him to try to obtain financing? That is, has he made a *promise* to do so? See Stackhouse v. Gaver, 801 N.W.2d 260 (Neb. App. 2011). If he does not try at all, could she procure it for him? Would he have to take it?

IV. PERFORMANCE AND CONSTRUCTIVE CONDITIONS

A. Need for Constructive Conditions of Exchange

KINGSTON v. PRESTON
Court of King's Bench, 1773
2 Doug. 689, 99 Eng. Rep. 437

Non-Performance

It was an action of debt, for non-performance of covenants contained in certain articles of agreement between the plaintiff and the defendant. The declaration stated; — That, by articles made the 24th of March, 1770, the plaintiff, for the considerations therein-after mentioned, covenanted, with the defendant, to serve him for one year and a quarter next ensuing, as a covenant-servant, in his trade of a silk-mercer, at £200 a year, and in consideration of the premises, the defendant covenanted, that at the end of the year and a quarter, he would give up his business of a mercer to the plaintiff, and a nephew of the defendant, or some other person to be nominated by the defendant, and give up to them his stock in trade, at a fair valuation; and that, between the young traders, deeds of partnership should be executed for 14 years, and from and immediately after the execution of the said deeds, the defendant would permit the said young traders to carry on the said business in the defendant's house. — Then the declaration stated a covenant by the plaintiff, that he would accept the business and stock in trade, at a fair valuation, with the defendant's nephew, or such other person, etc., and execute such deeds of partnership, and, further, that the plaintiff should, and would, at, and before, the sealing and delivery of the deeds, cause and procure good and sufficient security to be given to the defendant, to be approved of by the defendant, for the payment of £250 monthly, to the defendant, in lieu of a moiety of the monthly produce of the stock in trade, until the value of the stock should be reduced to £4,000. — Then the plaintiff averred, that he had performed, and been ready to perform, his covenants, and assigned for breach on the part of the defendant, that he had refused to surrender and give up his business, at the end of the said year and a quarter. — The defendant pleaded, 1. That the plaintiff did not offer sufficient security; and, 2. That he did not give sufficient security for the payment of the £250, etc. — And the plaintiff demurred generally to both pleas. — On the part of the plaintiff, the case was argued by Mr. Buller, who contended, that the covenants were mutual and independent, and, there-fore, a plea of the breach of one of the covenants to be performed by the plaintiff was no bar to an action for a breach by the defendant of one of which he had bound himself to perform, but that the defendant might have his remedy for the breach by the plaintiff, in a separate action. On the other side, Mr. Grose insisted, that the covenants were dependent in their nature, and, therefore, performance must be alleged: the security to be given for the money, was manifestly the chief object of the transaction, and it would be highly unreasonable to construe the agreement, so as to oblige the defendant to give up a beneficial business, and valuable stock in trade, and trust to the plaintiff's personal security, (who might, and, indeed, was admitted to be worth nothing,) for the performance of his part. — In deli-vering the judgment of the Court, Lord Mansfield expressed himself to the following effect: There are three kinds of covenants: 1. Such as are called mutual and independant, where either party may recover damages from the other, for the injury he may have received by a breach of the covenants in his favour, and where it is no excuse for the defendant, to allege a breach of the covenants on the part of the plaintiff. 2. There are covenants which are conditions and dependant, in which the performance of one depends on the prior performance of another, and, therefore, till this prior condition is performed, the other party is not liable to an action on his covenant. 3. There is also a third sort of covenants, which are mutual conditions to be per-formed at the same time; and, in these, if one party was ready, and offered, to perform his part, and the other neglected, or refused, to perform his, he who was ready, and offered, has fulfilled his engagement, and may maintain an action for the default of the other; though it is not certain that either is obliged to do the first act. — His Lordship then proceeded to say, that the dependance, or independance, of covenants, was to be collected from the evident sense and meaning of the parties, and, that, however transposed they might be in the deed, their precedency must depend on the order of time in which the intent of the transaction requires their performance. That, in the case before the Court, it would be the greatest injustice if the plaintiff should prevail: the essence of the agreement was, that the defendant should not trust to the personal security of the plaintiff, but, before he delivered up his stock and business, should have good security for the payment of the money. The giving such security, therefore, must necessarily be a condition precedent. — Judgment was accordingly given for the defendant, because the part to be performed by the plaintiff was clearly a condition precedent.

[handwritten margin note: Essence of the Agreement]

[handwritten margin note: Holding → condition precedent]

SHAW v. MOBIL OIL CORP.
Oregon Supreme Court, 1975
272 Or. 109, 535 P.2d 756

DENECKE, J. The question is, what is the obligation of the plaintiff, a service station lessee and operator, to pay rent to the defendant, Mobil Oil Corporation, the lessor and gasoline supplier of plaintiff?

In 1972 the parties entered into a service station lease and a retail dealer contract. The contract required the dealer to purchase not less than 200,000 gallons of gasoline per year and Mobil to sell to the dealer the amount of gasoline ordered by the dealer, but not more than 500,000 gallons per year.

The lease required the dealer to pay as rent, 1.4 cents per gallon of gasoline delivered, but "no less than the minimum amount . . . specified in said schedule for a calendar month." The schedule specified a minimum rental of $470 per month. The lease further provided: "If at the end of a month, the gallonage payments are less than the minimum rental, Tenant shall pay the deficiency promptly. . . ."

In order for the rent per gallon to equal the minimum rental per month, Mobil was required to deliver 33,572 gallons per month. In July 1973 the dealer ordered 34,000 gallons, but Mobil delivered only 25,678 gallons. The reason for Mobil's delivery of less than the gallonage ordered was that it was complying with a request by the Federal Energy office that it allocate its existing gasoline supply among its dealers. Mobil demanded that the plaintiff dealer pay the minimum rental for July as specified in the lease. Plaintiff brought this declaratory judgment proceeding to have determined its obligation to pay the minimum rental under the circumstances stated. The trial court decided the dealer had to pay the minimum rental.

[handwritten margin note: mobile delivered less because of a federal request]

[handwritten margin note: D still demanded same rent from P]

The retail dealer contract provided: "[T]he amounts so sold and purchased within such limits [minimum of 200,000 and maximum of 500,000 gallons per year] to be those ordered by Buyer [lessee]." Mobil's District Sales Manager and the trial court both interpreted this clause to mean what it appears to state; that is, that Mobil had a duty to deliver to the dealer as much as the dealer ordered. This duty is at least partially subject to an excuse clause which will be discussed later.

The trial court found that the service station lease and the retail dealer contract "were executed contemporaneously, constituted an integrated contract and are to be construed together." We agree.

The dealer contended in the trial court and contends here that his promise to pay the minimum rental is a dependent promise; that is, it is conditioned upon Mobil's performing its obligation to deliver the quantities of gasoline ordered by the dealer.

[handwritten margin note: P claimed it's a dependent Promise]

The law in Oregon on dependent promises, which is similar to the law in other jurisdictions, is stated in First Nat. Bank v. Morgan, 132 Or. 515, 528-529, 284 P. 582, 286 P. 558 (1930):

> Whether covenants are dependent or independent is a question of the intention of the parties as deduced from the terms of the contract. If the parties intend that performance by each of them is in no way conditioned upon performance by the other, the covenants are independent, but if they intend performance by one to be conditioned upon performance by the other, the covenants are mutually dependent: 5 Page on Contracts, §§2941-2951, et seq.; Williston on Contracts, §824; Burkhart v. Hart, 36 Or. 586, 60 P. 205.
>
> *[handwritten margin note: whether it's dependent or independent is a matter of intent; "Mutually Dependent"]*
>
> . . . While there is no fixed definite rule of law by which the intention in all cases can be determined, yet we must remember, as stated by Professor Williston, that, since concurrent conditions protect both parties, courts endeavor so far as is not inconsistent with the expressed intention to construe performances as concurrent conditions. 2 Williston on Contracts, §835. See also 5 Page on Contracts, §2948. The necessity of construing these covenants as concurrent in order to avoid gross injustice in the instant case is apparent for without a delivery of the stock the whole consideration for which the note was given must of necessity fail. Accord, R.C.A. Photophone v. Sinnott, 146 Or. 456, 459, 30 P.2d 761 (1934).

Corbin prefers to label the promise "conditional," rather than "dependent." 3A Corbin, Contracts, 46, §637 (1960).

In Associated Oil Co. v. Myers, 217 Cal. 297, 18 P.2d 668, 670 (1933), the defendants leased their property to the plaintiff, Associated Oil Co. The lease provided for a rent of 4 cents per gallon of gasoline sold to defendants for resale with a minimum rental of $10 per month. The parties simultaneously entered into a licensing agreement whereby defendants agreed to sell the oil company's products exclusively. The oil company brought this suit to enjoin the defendants from selling other brands of petroleum products from the station. The court held the promises of the parties were dependent and one party's obligation to perform was conditional upon the other party's performance.

In Rosenthal Paper Co. v. National Folding Box & Paper Co., 226 N.Y. 313, 123 N.E. 766 (1919), the court held a promise to pay a minimum royalty was conditioned upon the performance of another promise by the other contracting party. Seligstein held a patent on a type of box and assigned the exclusive right to manufacture this type of box to the defendant. The agreement provided the manufacturer would pay Seligstein a royalty of $1 per thousand boxes manufactured. The royalty agreement further provided, "'. . . it is expressly understood that the payment by the said . . . [manufacturer] to said Seligstein for the right to manufacture and sell boxes under said letters patent shall not be less than the sum of five hundred dollars ($500.00) for each and every year during the life of this contract.'" 123 N.E. at 767.

The manufacturer paid Seligstein $1 per thousand boxes manufactured; however, this was not sufficient to equal the minimum rental. Seligstein's assignee brought this action for the difference between the amount paid per thousand boxes sold and the minimum rental. The manufacturer contended it had no obligation to pay the minimum rental because that obligation was conditioned upon Seligstein performing other promises which Seligstein failed to perform.

The court stated the issue:

> We take up first the question whether or not the agreement of the defendant to pay the minimum royalty and the agreements of Seligstein to protect the letters patent from substantial infringement, and to refrain from selling, within the designated territory, any box manufactured under the patent, or any rights for any clothing, millinery, or suit box to any one for the territory were dependent or independent of each other. 123 N.E. at 767-768.

The court held the promises were "dependent." It reasoned that the parties must have intended that the manufacturer undertook an obligation to pay a minimum royalty for the exclusive right to manufacture in reliance on Seligstein's promise to maintain the exclusiveness of manufacturer's right by not licensing any one else to manufacture and by not selling such boxes.

In the present case we believe it equally apparent that the dealer undertook his obligation to pay a minimum rental in reliance on Mobil's fulfillment of its obligation to deliver the quantity of gasoline ordered by the dealer.

We conclude that the dealer's promise to pay the minimum rental was conditioned or dependent upon Mobil's delivery of the amount of gasoline ordered by the dealer.

The primary contention of Mobil and seemingly the chief reason for the trial court's decision was that under a provision of the contract Mobil was excused from delivering the quantity of gasoline ordered by the dealer because of a request to Mobil by the Federal Energy office to allocate its gasoline supply among its dealers.

Assuming that the contract does excuse Mobil from performance under these circumstances, nevertheless, the dealer is not obligated to pay the minimum rental.

The clause Mobil relies upon states:

> Seller shall not be liable for loss, damage or demurrage due to any delay or failure in performance (a) because of compliance with any order, request or control of any governmental authority or person purporting to act therefor.

Interpreting this clause most favorably to Mobil, its meaning can be no more than that Mobil cannot be held responsible for breach of contract if it does not perform its promises because of a government request.

[handwritten margin note: D cannot be held liable for breach of contract]

A party has no obligation to perform a promise that is conditioned upon the other party's performance when the other party failed to perform even though the other party's failure to perform is excused and is not a breach of contract.

[handwritten margin note: Rule]

An example of this situation is when the other party fails to perform its promise upon which the promisor's performance is conditioned because of the impossibility of performance. Eggen v. Wetterborg, 193 Or. 145, 237 P.2d 970 (1951), is such a case. Plaintiffs leased the premises from the defendants for use as a gasoline station and tavern. The buildings were destroyed by fire. This court held that the lessees' obligations, including their obligation to pay rent, and the lessors' obligations were dependent upon the existence of the buildings. The court stated:

> When parties enter into a contract on the assumption that some particular thing necessary to its performance will continue to exist and be available for the purpose, and neither party agrees to be responsible for its continued existence and availability, the contract must be regarded as subject to the implied condition that, if before the time for performance, and without the default of either party, the particular thing ceases to exist or be available for the purpose, the contract shall be dissolved and the parties excused from performing it. 193 Or. at 152-153, 237 P.2d at 974.

Corbin states the rule:

> [I]f one of these promises becomes impossible of performance, the party who made it may be excused from legal duty. His failure to perform is not a breach of contract. But the fact that the law excuses him from performance does not justify him in demanding performance by the other party. 6 Corbin, Contracts 510-511, §1363 (1962).

Williston is to the same effect. 6 Williston, Contracts 131, 139, §838 (3d ed. 1962).

The dealer is not obligated to pay the minimum rental although Mobil might be excused from delivering the quantity of gasoline ordered by the dealer.

Reversed.   *[handwritten: Reversed]*

B. Ordering Performances Through Constructive Conditions

RESTATEMENT (SECOND) OF CONTRACTS

§234. ORDER OF PERFORMANCES

(1) Where all or part of the performances to be exchanged under an exchange of promises can be rendered simultaneously, they are to that extent due simultaneously, unless the language or the circumstances indicate to the contrary.

Problem 144

Travis decided to sell a houseboat to his good friend Meyer for the sum of $35,000. They agreed that Meyer would pay by check and that the sale would be made at noon on the first day of August on board the boat. On that date neither showed up at the appointed time. Meyer was at a conference, and Travis was at home reading an adventure story. When Meyer returned from the conference, he sued Travis for breach of contract. As judge, would you let his suit succeed without more? On these facts would Travis succeed in a similar suit against Meyer? See UCC §2-309, Official Comment 5, and consider the UCC sections that follow.

Uniform Commercial Code §2-507(1)

(1) Tender of delivery is a condition to the buyer's duty to accept the goods and, unless otherwise agreed, to his duty to pay for them. Tender entitles the seller to acceptance of the goods and to payment according to the contract.

Uniform Commercial Code §2-511(1)

(1) Unless otherwise agreed tender of payment is a condition to the seller's duty to tender and complete any delivery.

Problem 145

Travis agreed to sell a houseboat to his good friend Meyer, to be delivered on the first of August. It was to be paid for by a check for $1,000 on the first of each month thereafter, starting in September until a total of $35,000 had been paid. Travis failed to deliver the boat on the date agreed, and

Meyer sued on August 10. Must he tender payment in order to prevail in his suit? How does he avoid the language of UCC §2-511(1)?

To call conditions *concurrent* means that they must occur at the same time. Where it is not clear whose performance is to come first (as in Problem 143), tender is the concurrent condition imposed on each party. Until one party tenders, neither is in breach and cannot be sued. The UCC sections just quoted reflect this idea.

Uniform Commercial Code §2-307

Delivery in Single Lot or several Lots

Unless otherwise agreed all goods called for by a contract for sale must be tendered in a single delivery and payment is due only on such tender but where the circumstances give either party the right to make or demand delivery in lots the price if it can be apportioned may be demanded for each lot.

Problem 146

When Mausolus was building a crematorium, he ordered 12,000 fancy bricks from Caria Brick Works, agreeing to pay $6,000 for them. Caria promised to deliver the bricks by the first of June. On the fifth of May, Caria delivered 6,000 of the bricks, informing Mausolus that the rest would be delivered shortly and presenting an invoice for $3,000. Mausolus refused to pay until all the bricks were delivered. Caria announced that unless Mausolus paid the bill, no further bricks would be delivered. Who is right?

UCC 2-307

Problem 147

CL
Services Contract

Bill Gilbert agreed to write the lyrics for a musical show to be produced the following year. After writing one-half of the lyrics, Bill approached the producer and demanded that the producer pay him one-half of the promised price. The producer refused, and Bill quit writing and said he would write no more. The producer hired another lyricist, and Bill sued. What result? Consider the following section of the Restatement (Second) of Contracts and the comment. How would you draft the contract for Bill to reach the result he desires?

Cant have Concurrent exchange of Performance takes a long time

§234. Order of Performance ... *CL*

(2) Except to the extent stated in Subsection (1) [quoted before Problem 144] where the performance of only one party under such an exchange requires a period of time, his performance is due at an earlier time than that of the other party, unless the language or the circumstances indicate the contrary. . . .

- If Service takes long time, service is required before payment

- Exception: Paying before going to the movies

Comment

Where the performance of one party requires a period of time and the performance of the other party does not, their performance cannot be simultaneous. Since one of the parties must perform first, he must forego the security that a requirement of simultaneous performance affords against disappointment of his expectation of an exchange of performances, and he must bear the burden of financing the other party before the latter has performed. . . . Of course the parties can by express provision mitigate the harshness of a rule that requires that one completely perform before the other perform at all. They often do this, for example, in construction contracts by stating a formula under which payment is to be made at stated intervals as work progresses. But it is not feasible for courts to devise such formulas for the wide variety of such cases that come before them in which the parties have made no provision. Centuries ago, the principle became settled that where work is to be done by one party and payment is to be made by the other, the performance of the work must precede payment, in the absence of a showing of a contrary intention. It is sometimes supposed that this principle grew out of employment contracts, and reflects a conviction that employers as a class are more likely to be responsible than are workmen paid in advance. Whether or not the explanation is correct, most parties today contract with reference to the principle, and unless they have evidenced a contrary intention it is at least as fair as the opposite rule would be.

C. Substantial Performance of Constructive Conditions

JACOB & YOUNGS, INC. v. KENT
Court of Appeals of New York, 1921
230 N.Y. 239, 129 N.E. 889

CARDOZO, J. The plaintiff built a country residence for the defendant at a cost of upwards of $77,000, and now sues to recover a balance of $3,483.46, remaining unpaid. The work of construction ceased in June, 1914, and the defendant then began to occupy the dwelling. There was no complaint of defective performance until March, 1915. One of the specifications for the plumbing work provides that —

> All wrought-iron pipe must be well galvanized, lap welded pipe of the grade known as "standard pipe" of Reading manufacture.

The defendant learned in March, 1915, that some of the pipe, instead of being made in Reading, was the product of other factories. The plaintiff was accordingly directed by the architect to do the work anew. The plumbing was then encased within the walls except in a few places where it had to be exposed. Obedience to the order meant more than the substitution of

P used wrong Pipe

other pipe. It meant the demolition at great expense of substantial parts of
the completed structure. The plaintiff left the work untouched, and asked
for a certificate that the final payment was due. Refusal of the certificate was
followed by this suit.

The evidence sustains a finding that the omission of the prescribed
brand of pipe was neither fraudulent nor willful. It was the result of the
oversight and inattention of the plaintiff's subcontractor. Reading pipe is
distinguished from Cohoes pipe and other brands only by the name of the
manufacturer stamped upon it at intervals of between six and seven feet.
Even the defendant's architect, though he inspected the pipe upon arrival,
failed to notice the discrepancy. The plaintiff tried to show that the brands
installed, though made by other manufacturers, were the same in quality, in
appearance, in market value, and in cost as the brand stated in the contract—that they were, indeed, the same thing, though manufactured in
another place. The evidence was excluded, and a verdict directed for the
defendant. The Appellate Division reversed, and granted a new trial.

We think the evidence, if admitted, would have supplied some basis for
the inference that the defect was insignificant in its relation to the project.
The courts never say that one who makes a contract fills the measure of his
duty by less than full performance. They do say, however, that an omission,
both trivial and innocent, will sometimes be atoned for by allowance of the
resulting damage, and will not always be the breach of a condition to be
followed by a forfeiture. Spence v. Ham, 163 N.Y. 220, 57 N.E. 412, 51
L.R.A. 238; Woodward v. Fuller, 80 N.Y. 312; Glacius v. Black, 67 N.Y. 563,
566; Bowen v. Kimbell, 203 Mass. 364, 370, 89 N.E. 542, 133 Am. St. Rep. 302.
The distinction is akin to that between dependent and independent promises, or between promises and conditions. Anson on Contracts (Corbin's
ed.) §367; 2 Williston on Contracts, §842. Some promises are so plainly
independent that they can never by fair construction be conditions of one
another. Rosenthal Paper Co. v. Nat. Folding Box & Paper Co., 226 N.Y. 313,
123 N.E. 766; Bogardus v. N.Y. Life Ins. Co., 101 N.Y. 328, 4 N.E. 522. Others
are so plainly dependent that they must always be conditions. Others,
though dependent and thus conditions when there is departure in point
of substance, will be viewed as independent and collateral when the departure is insignificant. 2 Williston on Contracts, §§841, 842; Eastern Forge
Co. v. Corbin, 182 Mass. 590, 592, 66 N.E. 419; Robinson v. Mollett, L.R.,
7 Eng. & Ir. App. 802, 814; Miller v. Benjamin, 142 N.Y. 613, 37 N.E. 631.
Considerations partly of justice and partly of presumable intention are to tell
us whether this or that promise shall be placed in one class or in another.
The simple and the uniform will call for different remedies from the multi-
farious and the intricate. The margin of departure within the range of normal expectation upon a sale of common chattels will vary from the margin to
be expected upon a contract for the construction of a mansion or a
"skyscraper." There will be harshness sometimes and oppression in the
implication of a condition when the thing upon which labor has been

expended is incapable of surrender because united to the land, and equity and reason in the implication of a like condition when the subject-matter, if defective, is in shape to be returned. From the conclusion that promises may not be treated as dependent to the extent of their uttermost minutiae without a sacrifice of justice, the progress is a short one to the conclusion that they may not be so treated without a perversion of intention. Intention not otherwise revealed may be presumed to hold in contemplation the reasonable and probable. If something else is in view, it must not be left to implication. There will be no assumption of a purpose to visit venial faults with oppressive retribution.

Those who think more of symmetry and logic in the development of legal rules than of practical adaptation to the attainment of a just result will be troubled by a classification where the lines of division are so wavering and blurred. Something, doubtless, may be said on the score of consistency and certainty in favor of a stricter standard. The courts have balanced such considerations against those of equity and fairness, and found the latter to be the weightier. The decisions in this state commit us to the liberal view, which is making its way, nowadays, in jurisdictions slow to welcome it. Dakin & Co. v. Lee, 1916, 1 K.B. 566, 579. Where the line is to be drawn between the important and the trivial cannot be settled by a formula. "In the nature of the case precise boundaries are impossible." 2 Williston on Contracts, §841. The same omission may take on one aspect or another according to its setting. Substitution of equivalents may not have the same significance in fields of art on the one side and in those of mere utility on the other. Nowhere will change be tolerated, however, if it is so dominant or pervasive as in any real or substantial measure to frustrate the purpose of the contract. Crouch v. Gutmann, 134 N.Y. 45, 51, 31 N.E. 271, 30 Am. St. Rep. 608. There is no general license to install whatever, in the builder's judgment, may be regarded as "just as good." Easthampton L.&C. Co., Ltd. v. Worthington, 186 N.Y. 407, 412, 79 N.E. 323. The question is one of degree, to be answered, if there is doubt, by the triers of the facts (Crouch v. Gutmann; Woodward v. Fuller, supra), and, if the inferences are certain, by the judges of the law (Easthampton L.&C. Co., Ltd. v. Worthington, supra). We must weigh the purpose to be served, the desire to be gratified, the excuse for deviation from the letter, the cruelty of enforced adherence. Then only can we tell whether literal fulfillment is to be implied by law as a condition. This is not to say that the parties are not free by apt and certain words to effectuate a purpose that performance of every term shall be a condition of recovery. That question is not here. This is merely to say that the law will be slow to impute the purpose, in the silence of the parties, where the significance of the default is grievously out of proportion to the oppression of the forfeiture. The willful transgressor must accept the penalty of his transgression. Schultze v. Goodstein, 180 N.Y. 248, 251, 73 N.E. 21; Desmond-Dunne Co. v. Friedman-Doscher Co., 162 N.Y. 486, 490, 56 N.E. 995. For him there is no occasion to mitigate the rigor of implied conditions. The transgressor whose default is unintentional and trivial may hope for mercy if he will offer atonement for his wrong. Spence v. Ham, supra.

In the circumstances of this case, we think the measure of the allowance is not the cost of replacement, which would be great, but the difference in value, which would be either nominal or nothing. Some of the exposed sections might perhaps have been replaced at moderate expense. The defendant did not limit his demand to them, but treated the plumbing as a unit to be corrected from cellar to roof. In point of fact, the plaintiff never reached the stage at which evidence of the extent of the allowance became necessary. The trial court had excluded evidence that the defect was unsubstantial, and in view of that ruling there was no occasion for the plaintiff to go farther with an offer of proof. We think, however, that the offer, if it had been made, would not of necessity have been defective because directed to difference in value. It is true that in most cases the cost of replacement is the measure. Spence v. Ham, supra. The owner is entitled to the money which will permit him to complete, unless the cost of completion is grossly and unfairly out of proportion to the good to be attained. When that is true, the measure is the difference in value. Specifications call, let us say, for a foundation built of granite quarried in Vermont. On the completion of the building, the owner learns that through the blunder of a subcontractor part of the foundation has been built of granite of the same quality quarried in New Hampshire. The measure of allowance is not the cost of reconstruction. "There may be omissions of that which could not afterwards be supplied exactly called for by the contract without taking down the building to its foundations, and at the same time the omission may not affect the value of the building for use or otherwise, except so slightly as to be hardly appreciable." Handy v. Bliss, 204 Mass. 513, 519, 90 N.E. 864, 134 Am. St. Rep. 673. ... The rule that gives a remedy in cases of substantial performance with compensation for defects of trivial or inappreciable importance has been developed by the courts as an instrument of justice. The measure of the allowance must be shaped to the same end.

The order should be affirmed, and judgment absolute directed in favor of the plaintiff upon the stipulation, with costs in all courts.

McLaughlin, J. I dissent. The plaintiff did not perform its contract. Its failure to do so was either intentional or due to gross neglect which, under the uncontradicted facts, amounted to the same thing, nor did it make any proof of the cost of compliance, where compliance was possible.

Under its contract it obligated itself to use in the plumbing only pipe (between 2,000 and 2,500 feet) made by the Reading Manufacturing Company. The first pipe delivered was about 1,000 feet and the plaintiff's superintendent then called the attention of the foreman of the subcontractor, who was doing the plumbing, to the fact that the specifications annexed to the contract required all pipe used in the plumbing to be of the Reading Manufacturing Company. They then examined it for the purpose of ascertaining whether this delivery was of that manufacture and found it was. Thereafter, as pipe was required in the progress of the work, the foreman of the subcontractor would leave word at its shop that he wanted a specified number of feet of pipe, without in any way indicating of what manufacture. Pipe would thereafter be delivered and installed in the building, without any examination whatever. Indeed, no examination, so far as appears, was made by the plaintiff, the subcontractor, defendant's architect, or any one else, of any of the pipe except the first delivery, until after the building had been completed. Plaintiff's architect then refused to give the certificate of completion, upon which the final payment depended, because all of the pipe used in the plumbing was not of the kind called for by the contract. After such refusal, the subcontractor removed the covering or insulation from about 900 feet of pipe which was exposed in the basement, cellar, and attic, and all but 70 feet was found to have been manufactured, not by the Reading Company, but by other manufacturers, some by the Cohoes Rolling Mill Company, some by the National Steel Works, some by the South Chester Tubing Company, and some which bore no manufacturer's mark at all. The balance of the pipe had been so installed in the building that an inspection of it could not be had without demolishing, in part at least, the building itself.

I am of the opinion the trial court was right in directing a verdict for the defendant. The plaintiff agreed that all the pipe used should be of the Reading Manufacturing Company. Only about two-fifths of it, so far as appears, was of that kind. If more were used, then the burden of proving that fact was upon the plaintiff, which it could easily have done, since it knew where the pipe was obtained. The question of substantial performance of a contract of the character of the one under consideration depends in no small degree upon the good faith of the contractor. If the plaintiff had intended to, and had, complied with the terms of the contract except as to minor omissions, due to inadvertence, then he might be allowed to recover the contract price, less the amount necessary to fully compensate the defendant for damages caused by such omissions. Woodward v. Fuller, 80 N.Y. 312; Nolan v. Whitney, 88 N.Y. 648. But that is not this case. It installed between 2,000 and 2,500 feet of pipe, of which only 1,000 feet at most complied with the contract. No explanation was given why pipe called for by the contract was not used, nor that any effort made to show what it would cost to remove the pipe of other manufacturers and install that of the Reading Manufacturing Company. The defendant had a right to contract for what he wanted. He had a right before making payment to get what the contract called for. It is no answer to this suggestion to say that the pipe put in was just as good as that made by the Reading Manufacturing Company, or that the difference in value between such pipe and the pipe made by the Reading Manufacturing Company would be either "nominal or nothing." Defendant contracted for pipe made by the Reading Manufacturing Company. What his reason was for requiring this kind of pipe is of no importance. He wanted that and was entitled to it. It may have been a mere whim on his part, but even so, he had a right to this kind of pipe, regardless of whether some other kind, according to the opinion of the contractor or experts, would have been "just as good, better, or done just as well." He agreed to pay only upon condition that the pipe installed were made by that company and he ought not to be compelled to pay unless that condition be performed. [Citations omitted.] The rule, therefore, of substantial performance, with damages for unsubstantial omissions, has no application. [Citations omitted.]

What was said by this court in Smith v. Brady, supra, is quite applicable here:

> I suppose it will be conceded that every one has a right to build his house, his cottage or his store after such a model and in such style as shall best accord with his notions of utility or be most agreeable to his fancy. The specifications of the contract become the law between the parties until voluntarily changed. If the owner prefers a plain and simple Doric column, and has so provided in the agreement, the contractor has no right to put in its place the more costly and elegant Corinthian. If the owner, having regard to strength and durability, has contracted for walls of specified materials to be laid in a particular manner, or for a given number of joists and beams, the builder has no right to substitute his own judgment or that of others. Having departed from the agreement, if performance has not been waived by the other party, the law will not allow him to allege that he has made as good a building as the one he engaged to erect. He can demand payment only upon and according to the terms of his contract, and if the conditions on which payment is due have not been performed, then the right to demand it does not exist. To hold a different doctrine would be simply to make another contract, and would be giving to parties an encouragement to violate their engagements, which the just policy of the law does not permit. (17 N.Y. 186, 72 Am. Dec. 442).

I am of the opinion the trial court did not err in ruling on the admission of evidence or in directing a verdict for the defendant.

For the foregoing reasons I think the judgment of the Appellate Division should be reversed and the judgment of the Trial Term affirmed....

Order affirmed, etc.

NOTES AND QUESTIONS

1. Is Cardozo holding that the Reading pipe clause was a mere promise and not a condition?

2. Traditionally, it is said that conditions "fail" and promises are "breached." This distinction is not religiously observed; note that Cardozo speaks of "breach of condition."

3. Corbin believes that it is wrong to state that substantial performance "satisfies the condition"; in his view substantial performance *is* the condition. Corbin §701.

4. The doctrine of substantial performance does not apply to *express* conditions; there must be strict compliance with express conditions. Oppenheimer v. Oppenheim, Appel, Dixon & Co., 86 N.Y.2d 685, 636 N.Y. S.2d 734, 660 N.E.2d 415 (1995). Considering that the following clause was in the contract (as reported in J. Dawson and W. Harvey, *Cases on Contracts and Contract Remedies* 744 (2d ed. 1969)), did Cardozo adhere to this doctrine?

> Any work furnished by the Contractor, the material or workmanship of which is defective or which is not fully in accordance with the drawings and specifications, in every respect, will be rejected and is to be immediately torn down, removed and remade or replaced in accordance with the drawings and specifications, whenever discovered.

5. If the owner of the house had some particular reason for desiring Reading pipe above all others, how should the clause be worded to make certain that no other pipe would do as well?

Problem 148

When ordering supplies for the construction of the Dickens Orphanage, Mr. Bumble, president of the Bumble Construction Company, saw that the specifications called for the installation of Reading pipe throughout the building. He told his clerk, Oliver, to order Cohoes pipe instead because it was cheaper and more or less the same thing as Reading pipe. When the directors of the orphanage learned of the substitution, they refused to make the final progress payment. Bumble sued. Who should prevail? See VRT, Inc. v. Dutton-Lainson Co., 530 N.W.2d 619 (Neb. 1995).

D. Material and Total Breach

The doctrine of substantial performance was developed in the context of a builder's breach of a construction contract to deal with the potentially harsh effects of constructive conditions. Even the breaching builder can still recover under the contract if the builder's performance is substantial, with any remaining defects in performance recompensed as a mere breach of promise, with a set-off for any damages caused. If substantial performance has not occurred, the builder is stripped of the ability to sue on the contract and is limited to a remedy in quasi-contract, with damages measured by the excess of benefit conferred over and above harm caused, the contract price being the upper limit. See the discussion of quasi-contract in Chapter 3.

Outside of this context, courts apply a similar approach that revolves around whether one party has *materially* and *totally* breached the contract. Any breach of contract entitles the nonbreaching party to sue for damages. However, an *immaterial* breach of contract has precisely the same effect as substantial performance. Although the breaching party is liable for damages, the nonbreaching party must continue to perform its own duties. Conversely, a *material* breach entitles the nonbreaching party not just to sue for damages, but to temporarily stop its own performance and wait to see whether the breaching party can *cure* the defect. If the breaching party cures, the nonbreaching party must treat the contract as intact and continue to perform. However, if a material breach is not cured (or cannot be cured), it becomes *material and total*, which means that the nonbreaching party can both recover damages and treat the contract as broken, withholding any remaining performance.

According to the Restatement (Second) of Contracts, court decide (1) whether a breach is material and (2) if so, whether it is material and total, by examining several factors:

§241.   Circumstances Significant in Determining Whether a Failure Is Material

In determining whether a failure to render or to offer performance is material, the following circumstances are significant:

a. the extent to which the injured party will be deprived of the benefit which he reasonably expected;
b. the extent to which the injured party can be adequately compensated for the part of that benefit of which he will be deprived;
c. the extent to which the party failing to perform or to offer to perform will suffer forfeiture;
d. the likelihood that the party failing to perform or to offer to perform will cure his failure, taking account of all the circumstances including any reasonable assurances;
e. the extent to which the behavior of the party failing to perform or to offer to perform comports with standards of good faith and fair dealing.

§242.   Circumstances Significant in Determining When Remaining Duties are Discharged

In determining the time after which a party's uncured material failure to render or to offer performance discharges the other party's remaining duties to render performance . . . , the following circumstances are significant:

a. those stated in §241;
b. the extent to which it reasonably appears to the injured party that delay may prevent or hinder him in making reasonable substitute arrangements;
c. the extent to which the agreement provides for performance without delay, but a material failure to perform or to offer to perform on a stated day does

not of itself discharge the other party's remaining duties unless the circumstances, including the language of the agreement, indicate that performance or an offer to perform by that day is important.

━━━━━━━━━━

Article 25 of the United Nations Convention on Contracts for the International Sale of Goods is roughly similar. It borrows from civil law the concept of "fundamental breach." Fundamental breach is similar to material breach in the Restatement.

Article 25

A breach of contract committed by one of the parties is fundamental if it results in such detriment to the other party as substantially to deprive him of what he is entitled to expect under the contract, unless the party in breach did not foresee, and a reasonable person of the same kind in the same circumstances would not have foreseen, such a result.

On a finding of fundamental breach, the aggrieved party is given a broader range of remedies (including contract termination) than for non-fundamental breaches. See, e.g., Articles 49, 51(2), 64, 72, 73.

━━━━━━━━━━

WALKER & CO. v. HARRISON
Michigan Supreme Court, 1957
81 N.W.2d 352

This is a suit on a written contract. The defendants are in the dry-cleaning business. Walker & Company, plaintiff, sells, rents, and services advertising signs and billboards. These parties entered into an agreement pertaining to a sign. The agreement is in writing and is termed a "rental agreement." It specifies in part that:

"The lessor agrees to construct and install, at its own cost, one 18'9" high x 8'8" wide pylon type d.f. neon sign with electric clock and flashing lamps . . . . The lessor agrees to and does hereby lease or rent unto the said lessee the said SIGN for the term, use and rental and under the conditions, hereinafter set out, and the lessee agrees to pay said rental . . . .
"(a) The term of this lease shall be 36 months . . . .
"(b) The rental to be paid by lessee shall be $148.50 per month for each and every calendar month during the term of this lease; . . . .
"(d) Maintenance. Lessor at its expense agrees to maintain and service the sign together with such equipment as supplied and installed by the lessor to operate in conjunction with said sign under the terms of this lease; this

service is to include cleaning and repainting of sign in original color scheme as often as deemed necessary by lessor to keep sign in first class advertising condition and make all necessary repairs to sign and equipment installed by lessor. . . ."

At the "expiration of this agreement," it was also provided, "title to this sign reverts to lessee." This clause is in addition to the printed form of agreement and was apparently added as a result of defendants' concern over title, they having expressed a desire "to buy for cash" and the salesman, at one time, having "quoted a cash price."

The sign was completed and installed in the latter part of July, 1953. The first billing of the monthly payment of $148.50 was made August 1, 1953, with payment thereof by defendants on September 3, 1953. This first payment was also the last. Shortly after the sign was installed, someone hit it with a tomato. Rust, also, was visible on the chrome, complained defendants, and in its corners were "little spider cobwebs." In addition, there were "some children's sayings written down in here." Defendant Herbert Harrison called Walker for the maintenance he believed himself entitled to under subparagraph (d) above. It was not forthcoming. He called again and again. "I was getting, you might say, sorer and sorer. . . . Occasionally, when I started calling up, I would walk around where the tomato was and get mad again. Then I would call up on the phone again." Finally, on October 8, 1953, plaintiff not having responded to his repeated calls, he telegraphed Walker that:

> "You Have Continually Voided Our Rental Contract By Not Maintaining Signs As Agreed As We No Longer Have A Contract With You Do Not Expect Any Further Remuneration."

Walker's reply was in the form of a letter. After first pointing out that "your telegram does not make any specific allegations as to what the failure of maintenance comprises," and stating that "We certainly would appreciate your furnishing us with such information," the letter makes reference to a prior collateral controversy between the parties, "wondering if this refusal on our part prompted your attempt to void our rental contract."

No additional payments were made and Walker sued in assumpsit for the entire balance due under the contract, $5,197.50 . . . . Defendants filed answer and claim of recoupment, asserting that plaintiff's failure to perform certain maintenance services constituted a prior material breach of the agreement, thus justifying their repudiation of the contract and grounding their claim for damages. The case was tried to the court without a jury and resulted in a judgment for the plaintiff. The case is before us on a general appeal.

Defendants urge upon us again and again, in various forms, the proposition that Walker's failure to service the sign, in response to repeated requests, constituted a material breach of the contract and justified repudiation by them. Their legal proposition is undoubtedly correct. Repudiation is one of the weapons available to an injured party in event the other contractor has committed a material breach. But the injured party's determination that there has been a material breach, justifying his own repudiation, is fraught with peril, for should such determination, as viewed by a later court in the calm of its contemplation, be unwarranted, the repudiator himself will have been guilty of material breach and himself have become the aggressor, not an innocent victim.

Case-by-case Analysis

What is our criterion for determining whether or not a breach of contract is so fatal to the undertaking of the parties that it is to be classed as "material"? There is no single touchstone. Many factors are involved . . . .

We will not set forth in detail the testimony offered concerning the need for servicing. Granting that Walker's delay (about a week after defendant Herbert Harrison sent his telegram of repudiation Walker sent out a crew

Holding

and took care of things) in rendering the service requested was irritating, we are constrained to agree with the trial court that it was not of such materiality as to justify repudiation of the contract, and we are particularly mindful of the lack of preponderant evidence contrary to his determination. The trial court, on this phase of the case, held as follows:

> Now Mr. Harrison phoned in, so he testified, a number of times. He isn't sure of the dates but he sets the first call at about the 7th of August and he complained then of the tomato and of some rust and some cobwebs. The tomato, according to the testimony, was up on the clock; that would be outside of his reach, without a stepladder or something. The cobwebs are within easy reach of Mr. Harrison and so would the rust be. I think that Mr. Bueche's argument that these were not materially a breach would clearly be true as to the cobwebs and I really can't believe in the face of all the testimony that there was a great deal of rust seven days after the installation of this sign. And that really brings it down to the tomato. And, of course, when a tomato has been splashed all over your clock, you don't like it. But he says he kept calling their attention to it, although the rain probably washed some of the tomato off. But the stain remained, and they didn't come. I really can't find that that was such a material breach of the contract as to justify rescission. I really don't think so.

Tomato is really the Issue

✗

Nor, we conclude, do we. There was no valid ground for defendants' repudiation and their failure thereafter to comply with the terms of the contract was itself a material breach, entitling Walker, upon this record, to judgment . . . .

Affirmed

NOTES AND QUESTIONS

1. A deteriorating contractual relationship places the parties in a tricky situation. If Party A believes that Party B has materially breached, Restatement (Second) §241 entitles Party A to suspend her own performance and

see if Party B can cure. But if Party A asserts her rights too forcefully, then Party A may be the first party to materially breach — and perhaps, as in *Walker*, materially and totally breach. If you were Harrison's lawyer, what would you have advised him to do when Walker did not reply to Harrison's phone calls in September?

2. The court holds that Harrison's October 8 telegram was an anticipatory repudiation of the contract. As we will discuss in Chapter 8, an anticipatory repudiation is a clear expression of intent to do something that *will* be a material and total breach. Can you see why the telegram met this standard? Because it did, it meant that Harrison materially and totally breached, denying him the right to withhold future payments and subjecting him to damages.

CARTER v. SHERBURNE CORP.
Vermont Supreme Court, 1974
132 Vt. 88, 315 A.2d 870

SHANGRAW, C.J. This is an appeal by the defendant from a judgment of the Rutland County Court. The subject matter of the litigation is work done and materials furnished by the plaintiff in connection with a development of the defendant's near Sherburne Mountain. The plaintiff claimed that he was not fully paid for labor and materials furnished under written contracts, and that he was entitled to further amounts on a quantum meruit basis for labor and materials furnished without express agreement as to price. The defendant claimed defective performance and payment for everything due, and asserted a counterclaim for expense necessitated by plaintiff's alleged failure to fulfill contractual commitments. The Court found that plaintiff was in substantial compliance under his contracts, that the defendant had no right to terminate the contracts, and that the defendant's counterclaim was without foundation. The Court also found that the plaintiff performed other work for the defendant without compensation under a promise for additional work which was not fulfilled by the defendant. Plaintiff was awarded various sums for unpaid invoices, payment for other work done for the defendant, and interest. The defendant corporation has appealed.

The facts as found by the Court are, in substance, as follows:

There were four written contracts between the parties covering (a) the furnishing and placing of gravel on one road, (b) the drilling and blasting of rock on various residential roads, (c) road construction, and (d) the cutting and grubbing of a gondola lift-line. The contracts called for weekly progress payments based upon work completed with a provision for retaining 10 percent until ten days after final acceptance. The billings from the plaintiff to the defendant amounted to $52,571.25, of which $41,368.05 was paid by the defendant. The difference between the $52,571.25 billed, and $41,368.05 paid, comprised $4,596.45 retained by the defendant under its holdback provision, and adjustments claimed by the defendant of $6,606.75. The Court found that adjustments in the amount of $4,747.25 was improperly taken by the defendant and that amount was decreed to the plaintiff. In addition the Court found that the plaintiff was entitled to all the retainage held by the defendant.

As to the defendant's contention that the plaintiff's performance was unsatisfactory and, in particular, that the plaintiff failed to abide by the completion schedules in the contracts, the Court found that on the whole, the plaintiff rendered substantial performance under the contracts without major complaints from the defendant up to the time it terminated the contracts. The Court found further, that time was not of the essence of the contracts, that many of the delays were due to the directions of the defendant in constantly shifting the plaintiff's activities from one contract to another, and that other delays were financial in origin, in that plaintiff had difficulty meeting his outstanding obligations because of payments withheld by the defendant without justification.

The Court also found that the defendant's representatives promised the plaintiff extensive additional work contracts, that in return for this promise the plaintiff agreed to do certain work without compensation, that the plaintiff did in fact do some of this work, and that the additional work promised by the defendant was not awarded to the plaintiff. The Court held that the plaintiff was justified in his reliance on defendant's promise, and that he could recover his expenses and the value of his services from the defendant on a quantum meruit basis.

Defendant claims the Court erred in its ruling that the plaintiff was in substantial compliance under his contracts and in its finding that the plaintiff was entitled to recover certain sums under the gondola lift-line contract. In addition, defendant claims that the Court was in error in allowing the plaintiff recovery on a quantum meruit basis as parole evidence was improperly admitted, and the recovery granted was not in accordance with the terms of the contract....

The defendant's primary contention is that the Court's ruling that the plaintiff was in substantial compliance under his contracts is error. The contention is that this ruling was based on the erroneous conclusion that time was not of the essence of the contracts, and that as time was of the essence and plaintiff failed to perform within the time specified, plaintiff was not in substantial compliance and defendant is entitled to the amounts withheld as retainage.

Where time is of the essence, performance on time is a constructive condition of the other party's duty, usually the duty to pay for the performance rendered. Jones v. United States, 96 U.S. 24 (1877). Time may be made of the essence of a contract by a stipulation to that effect, Cheney v. Libby, 134 U.S. 68 (1890), or by any language that expressly provides that the contract will be void if performance is not within a specified time. Sowles v. Hall, 62 Vt. 247, 20 A. 810 (1890). Where the parties have not expressly declared their intention, the determination as to whether time is of the essence depends on the intention of the parties, the circumstances surrounding the transaction, and the subject matter of the contract. Kennedy v. Rutter, 110 Vt. 332, 6 A.2d 17 (1939).

[margin: If NOT expressly stated...]

As a general rule, time is not of the essence in a building or construction contract in the absence of an express provision making it such. 13 Am. Jur. 2d Building and Construction Contracts §47.

*[margin: * General Rule]*

Construction contracts are subject to many delays for innumerable reasons, the blame for which may be difficult to assess. The structure . . . becomes part of the land and adds to the wealth of its owner. Delays are generally foreseen as probable; and the risks thereof are discounted. . . . The complexities of the work, the difficulties commonly encountered, the custom of men in such cases, all these lead to the result that performance at the agreed time by the contractor is not of the essence. 3A A. Corbin, Contracts §720, at 377 (1960).

We conclude, then, that time was not of the essence of any of the contracts considered here. None of the four contracts included express language making time of the essence, and we can find nothing in the circumstances surrounding these contracts that would lift them out of the operation of the general rule. Two of the contracts called for completion dates and forfeitures for non-completion on schedule, but the inclusion of dates in construction contracts does not make time of the essence. De Sombre v. Bickel, 18 Wis. 2d 390, 118 N.W.2d 868 (1963). Moreover, the inclusion of penalty or forfeiture provisions for non-completion on schedule is strong evidence that time is not of the essence and that performance on time is not a condition of the other party's duty to accept and pay for the performance rendered. 3A A. Corbin, Contracts §720 (1960).

*[margin: * Court concluded time was NOT of the essence / Analysis]*

*[margin: * Penalty or forfeiture clauses or strong evidence that time isn't of the essence]*

Ordinarily, in contracts where time is not of the essence, a failure to complete the work within the specified time will not terminate the contract, but it will subject the contractor to damages for the delay. See 13 Am. Jur. 2d Building and Construction Contracts §47. However, in this case, most of the delays were due to the actions of the defendant corporation in constantly shifting the plaintiff's activities from one contract to another, cf. 17A C.J.S. Contracts §502(4), and in improperly withholding the plaintiff's payments. Cf. Orange, Alexandria and Manassas R. R. Co. v. Placide, 35 Md. 315 (1871). Delay in the performance of a contract will, as a rule be excused where it is caused by the act or default of the opposite party, Schneider v. Saul, 224 Md. 454, 168 A.2d 375 (1961); District of Columbia v. Camden Iron Works, 181 U.S. 453 (1901); 17 Am. Jur. 2d Contracts §389; 13 Am. Jur. 2d Building and Construction Contracts §48, or by the act or default of persons for whose conduct the opposite party is responsible. See Annot. 152 A.L.R. 1390 (1944). Where this is the case, the contractor will not be held liable, under a provision for liquidated damages or otherwise, for his

[margin: When delay is excused]

non-compliance with the terms of the contract, . . . and his non-compliance will not be considered a breach. See District of Columbia v. Camden Iron Works, supra. An obligation of good faith and fair dealing is an implied term in every contract, H. P. Hood and Sons v. Heins, 124 Vt. 331, 205 A.2d 561 (1964); Shaw v. E. I. DuPont De Nemours & Co., 126 Vt. 206, 226 A.2d 903 (1967), and a party may not obstruct, hinder, or delay a contractor's work and then seek damages for the delay thus occasioned.

Defendant also disputes the Court's conclusions with respect to the gondola lift-line contract. Defendant informed the plaintiff in April, 1968, that no more progress payments would be made on the gondola contract. At that time, plaintiff had completed a substantial portion of the contracted work, but had not yet invoiced it. After defendant's notice, plaintiff continued to work on the lift-line, but was forced to stop for financial reasons. Defendant claims that the plaintiff is not entitled to recover for work done or invoiced after the notice concerning termination of payments.

Defendant's April notice concerned only the progress payments due the plaintiff. It was not a notice of contract termination. In the absence of a total disavowal of the contract, failure of payment does not require an immediate cessation of performance. Williams v. Carter, 129 Vt. 619, 285 A.2d 735 (1971). The contracts between the plaintiff and the defendant were not terminated until June of 1968. The termination was without legal justification, and the plaintiff is entitled to recover the contract price for all work done before the termination date. . . .

With respect to the recovery granted the plaintiff, failure to perform the agreed exchange gives rise to several remedies, one of which is recovery on a quantum meruit basis. An action in quantum meruit is distinct from one for damages. Its purpose is to require the wrongdoer to restore what he has received from the plaintiff's performance of the contract, Gilman v. Hall, 11 Vt. 510 (1839), and the measure of recovery is the reasonable value of the performance rendered, uncontrolled by the contract price or by any other terms of the express contract. Derby v. Johnson, 21 Vt. 17 (1848); 5 A. Corbin, Contracts §§1112, 1113 (1964). The Court's finding and conclusions are therefore correct.

Judgment affirmed.

NOTES AND QUESTIONS

1. As *Carter* demonstrates, if a construction contract calls for completion by a certain date but does not specifically state that "time is of the essence," most courts deem the clause a promise only, thus avoiding the forfeiture of monies due that would otherwise occur. However, the omission of a "time is of the essence" clause does not mean that courts will always ignore unambiguous deadlines that when missed result in termination of contractual rights; see the strong language to this effect in

In re Nextmedia Group, Inc., 440 B.R. 76 (Bankr. D. Del. 2010). Nevertheless, in a majority of the cases deciding that time was not of the essence, the absence of such a clause proved to be very persuasive that a condition precedent was not intended; see, e.g., Nippon Life Ins. Co. of Am. v. One Source Mgmt., 2011 WL 1782089 (Ohio App. 2011). Likewise, in other contexts, courts generally refuse to construe performance deadlines as conditions. See, e.g., Coldwell v. Moore, 85 N.E.3d 262, 270 (Ohio Ct. App. 2017) (refusing to adopt an "iron-clad rule that, where an agreement to purchase real estate includes a closing date, the purchase agreement becomes unenforceable if the deal is not closed on the specified closing date").

2. Alternatively, when a contract expressly says that "time is of the essence," courts tend to treat untimely performance as nonsatisfaction of a condition. See, e.g., In re 1111 Myrtle Ave. Grp. LLC, 575 B.R. 567, 579 (Bankr. S.D.N.Y. 2017) ("If time is of the essence, failure to close on the designated law day by either party is a default of the agreement."); Querencia Properties, S. de R.L. de C.V. v. New Querencia Capital Partners, L.L.C., 224 S.W.3d 348, 352 (Tex. App. 2006); but cf. Restatement (Second) §242 cmt. D (explaining that "stock phrases as 'time is of the essence'" do not necessarily make timely performance a condition, but can tip the scales toward a breach being material and total).

[handwritten margin note: If expressly stated, Then its a Condition]

Problem 149

Scarlett entered into a valid option contract to sell her ancestral home, Tara, to Rhett if he brought the entire payment in cash to Tara between the hours of noon and 1:00 P.M. tomorrow. The next day he arrived with the proper amount at 1:23 P.M. and tendered the money. By this time she had changed her mind and refused to go through with the deal. If he sued in equity, asking for specific performance after paying the money into court, would you, as judge, grant him relief? Was "time of the essence" here? Would your answer change if the parties had already formed a valid contract that called for payment by 1:00 P.M. the next day, and Rhett was simply late in paying?

Problem 150

Fibber McGee and his wife Molly had lived in their apartment for ten years. Every two years they went down to the landlord's office and signed a new lease, the lease ending every two years on May 31. One year they were amazed when the landlord refused their offer of renewal on June 1, noting that their option had expired at midnight of the day before and saying that he planned to raze the building and turn it into a parking lot. They come to your office for help. Do they have a case? Should there be a different rule for the exercise of an option to renew a lease than to purchase real property?

Problem 151

When Howard Mortus signed up for a $1 million life insurance policy from the Norisk Insurance Company he was able to make only a small down payment. For the bulk of the initial premium, he gave the insurance company a promissory note payable on July 1, 2020, six months from the date the insurance became effective. He became ill early in 2020 and failed to make the payment in July as he had promised. He died on September 25 of that year. The company had not contacted him in any way between the first of July and his death. Must Norisk pay his estate the $1 million, or is his failure to make the July payment an excusing event?

RESTATEMENT (SECOND) OF CONTRACTS

§240. PART PERFORMANCES AS AGREED EQUIVALENTS

If the performances to be exchanged under an exchange of promises can be apportioned into corresponding pairs of part performances so that the parts of each pair are properly regarded as agreed equivalents, a party's performance of his part of such a pair has the same effect on the other's duties to render performance of the agreed equivalent as it would have if only that pair of performances had been promised.

Problem 152

Tracthouses, Inc., contracted with NewTown of New Jersey to build ten identical houses for $50,000 each on lots owned by NewTown.

(a) Tracthouses built the first three houses, but NewTown, financially embarrassed, was unable to make the payments. Advise Tracthouses what to do. Should it stop building and sue? Should it keep building and sue? If it does sue, should it sue for breach on the first three houses only or for all ten? See Pakas v. Hollingshead, 184 N.Y. 211, 77 N.E. 40 (1906).

(b) Tracthouses built nine of the houses perfectly, but had huge labor problems and could not complete the tenth, which it left in a half-finished condition. NewTown had agreed to pay when all ten houses were finished.

Must it pay anything now that Tracthouses has defaulted? If Tracthouses is in material breach is it entitled to sue for anything?

Uniform Commercial Code §2-612

"Installment Contracts"

(1) An "installment contract" is one which requires or authorizes the delivery of goods in separate lots to be separately accepted, even though the contract contains a clause "each delivery is a separate contract" or its equivalent.

(2) The buyer may reject any installment which is non-conforming if the non-conformity substantially impairs the value of that installment and cannot be cured or if the non-conformity is a defect in the required documents; but if the non-conformity does not fall within subsection (3) and the seller gives adequate assurance of its cure the buyer must accept that installment.

(3) Whenever non-conformity or default with respect to one or more installments substantially impairs the value of the whole contract there is a breach of the whole. But the aggrieved party reinstates the contract if he accepts a non-conforming installment without seasonably notifying of cancellation or if he brings an action with respect only to past installments or demands performance as to future installments.

Problem 153

The Lincoln Railway Company ordered 12 shipments of split rails from the Douglas Timber Corporation, contracting for the delivery of one shipment per month of 500 rails each. The shipments were to be delivered by the end of the first week of each month for a one-year period. The first shipment arrived on time, but contained only 497 rails. May Lincoln Railway refuse to accept? Cancel the contract? The next month Douglas Timber shipped 500 rails, but they arrived on the ninth day of the month. May Lincoln Railway reject? If Lincoln Railway refused to pay for the second shipment until Douglas Timber provided evidence of its ability to make future shipments in the proper quantity and on time, and Douglas Timber refused to make further shipments until Lincoln Railway paid for the second, who is in breach here? What should have been done, and by whom? See UCC §1-207 (§1-308 in the revised version of Article 1). The leading classic case on delivery problems in installment contracts is Norrington v. Wright, 115 U.S. 188 (1885).

- Installment Contract
↳ Cant drop
↳ Doesnt Substantially Impair, and Can be cured

The nuanced substantial performance and material/total breach rules have never (at least in theory) applied to single-delivery contracts between merchants. Learned Hand once stated that "[t]here is no room in commercial contracts for the doctrine of substantial performance."

✶ Does NOT apply to Single Delivery Contracts

Mitsubishi Goshi Kaisha v. J. Aron & Co., 16 F.2d 185, 186 (2d Cir. 1926). Instead, traditional law (which is now codified in §2-601 of the Uniform Commercial Code) requires that seller make a "perfect tender" of the goods, and if this doesn't happen, the buyer is given the option to accept the defective tender or reject it. Read UCC §§2-601, 2-602, 2-606, and 2-607.

PRINTING CENTER OF TEXAS, INC.
v. SUPERMIND PUBLISHING CO.
Texas Court of Appeals, 1984
669 S.W.2d 779

CANNON, J. Appellee sued appellant for refund of a deposit made under a written contract to print 5,000 books entitled "Supermind Supermemory." Appellee alleged that it rightfully rejected the books upon delivery under Tex. Bus. & Com. Code Ann. §2.601 (Tex. UCC) (Vernon 1968) and that it has a right to cancel the contract and recover the part of the purchase price paid under Tex. Bus. & Com. Code Ann. §2.711 (Tex. UCC) (Vernon 1968). The trial court awarded appellee refund of its $2,900 deposit . . . .

We note that appellee may have tried this suit on the wrong legal theory and if so, the judgment of trial court is not supported by the jury findings. The parties tried this suit on the assumption that the provisions of the Texas Uniform Commercial Code governed their contract for the printing of books. Chapter 2 of the Business and Commerce Code is limited to transactions involving the sale of goods. Tex. Bus. & Com. Code Ann. §2.102 (Vernon 1968). A contract to print books involves the sale of both goods and services. The printer sells goods which consist of paper and ink and services consisting of binding, typesetting, proofing, etc. "In such hybrid transactions, the question becomes whether the dominant factor or essence of the transaction is the sale of materials or of services." G-W-L, Inc. v. Robichaux, 643 S.W.2d 392, 394 (Tex. 1982).

It appears to us that the services are the essence or the dominant factor of a printing contract; therefore, Chapter 2 of the Business and Commerce Code would not apply. Special issue number one inquired of the jury whether the books delivered to appellee failed in any respect to conform to the contract. The affirmative answer to this issue does not give the purchaser a right to reject and to recover a refund of the purchase price under the common law of contracts as it would under Chapter 2 of the Code.

Appellant has not assigned a point of error as to whether the trial court's judgment is supported by the verdict of the jury. Therefore any error concerning this point is waived. [Citations omitted.] We indulge in the doubtful assumption that Chapter 2 of the Business and Commerce Code governs the contract between parties to enable us to adequately consider appellant's points of error. . . .

Appellant contends in its second point of error that jury finding that the books failed to conform to the contract is so against the great weight and preponderance of the evidence as to be manifestly unjust. In re King's Estate, 150 Tex. 662, 244 S.W.2d 660 (1952). This finding is related to whether appellee had a right to reject the books under Tex. Bus. & Com. Code Ann. §2.601 (Vernon 1968) which states in part: ". . . if the goods or tender of delivery fail in any respect to conform to the contract, the buyer may (1) reject the whole. . . ." This provision has been called the perfect tender rule because it supposedly allows a buyer to reject whenever the goods are less than perfect. This statement is not quite accurate; under §2-601 the tender must be perfect only in the sense that the proffered goods must conform to the contract in every respect. Conformity does not mean substantial performance; it means complete performance. The longstanding doctrine of sales law that "there is no room in commercial contracts for the doctrine of substantial performance" is carried forward into §2.601 of the Code . . . .

In analyzing whether tendered goods are conforming, the contract of the parties must first be determined. "Conform" is defined in Tex. Bus. & Com. Code Ann. §2.106(b) (Vernon 1968), as "in accordance with the obligations under the contract." . . . A buyer has a right to reject goods under §2.601 if the goods fail to conform to either the express or implied terms of the contract.

Once the contract of the parties has been determined, the evidence must be reviewed to see if the right goods were tendered at the right time and place. If the evidence does establish nonconformity in some respect, the buyer is entitled to reject if he rejects in good faith. Bus. & Com. Code Ann. §1.203 provides that, "Every contract or duty within this Act imposes an obligation of good faith in its performance or enforcement." Since the rejection of goods is a matter of performance, the buyer is obligated to act in good faith when he rejects the goods. Where the buyer is a merchant, his standard of good faith rejection requires honesty in fact and observance of reasonable commercial standards of fair dealing in the trade. Tex. Bus. & Com. Code Ann. §2.103(2). If the seller alleges that the buyer rejected in bad faith, the seller has the burden of proof on this issue. Evidence of circumstances which indicate that the buyer's motivation in rejecting the goods was to escape the bargain, rather than to avoid acceptance of a tender which in some respect impairs the value of the bargain to him, would support a finding of rejection in bad faith. Neumiller Farms Inc. v. Cornett, 368 So. 2d 272 (Ala. 1979). Thus, evidence of rejection of the goods on account of a minor defect in a falling market would in some instances be sufficient to support a finding that the buyer acted in bad faith when he rejected the goods.

The written contract between the parties which is expressed in a bid proposal dated July 31, 1981 covers only essential terms such as quantity, trim size, and type of paper and cover. The type of paper specified in the contract was thirty pound white newsprint. Appellee's witness testified that he was shown a sample of the newsprint to be used and that the tendered books

Evidence of ∆ Non-Conforming

were not the same color as the sample. The witness stated the pages of the books were gray while the sample was white. This testimony is evidence of nonconformity because any sample which is made part of the basis of the bargain creates an express warranty that the whole of the goods shall conform to the sample. Tex. Bus. & Com. Code Ann. §2.313(a)(3) (Tex. UCC) (Vernon 1968).

Court looked ∆ at usage of trade

Other nonconformities which appellee alleges and offers proof of are off center cover art, crooked pages, wrinkled pages and inadequate perforation on a pull out page. The contract does not expressly address any of these matters. Although evidence of trade usage may have indicated that these conditions are contrary to the standards of commercial practice within the publishing industry, appellant failed to offer evidence of trade usage to supplement the contract. However, appellant knew that appellee wanted the books printed for sale to the public. In these circumstances, it is implied in the contract that the books be commercially acceptable and appealing to the public. Section 2.314 Tex. Bus. & Com. Code Ann. (Tex. UCC) (Vernon 1968) states that a warranty that the goods shall be merchantable is implied in a contract for their sale and that for goods to be merchantable, they must pass without objection in the trade and be fit for the ordinary purposes for which such goods are used. A jury could reasonably conclude that books with crooked and wrinkled pages, off center cover art, and inadequate perforation are not fit for sale to the public. We find sufficient evidence to support the jury's finding that the books did not conform to the contract.

"Implied" Condition

Books were Non-conforming

Appellant didn't meet Burden of proof

Appellant contends that if nonconformities exist, they are minor and that appellee rejected the books in bad faith. Appellant has failed to carry its burden to prove that appellee rejected the books in bad faith. First, we do not agree with appellant's contention that the alleged nonconformities should be classified as minor. Second, there is no evidence which indicates that appellee's primary motivation in rejection of the books was to escape a bad bargain. We also note that appellant has waived its defense of rejection in bad faith by its failure to request an issue on this defense, because it has not conclusively established it under the evidence. Tex. R. Civ. P. 279.

. . .

Affirmed

The judgment of the trial court is affirmed.

CAPITOL DODGE SALES v. NORTHERN CONCRETE PIPE, INC.

Michigan Court of Appeals, 1983
131 Mich. App. 149, 346 N.W.2d 535

PETERSON, J. Defendant appeals by leave granted from a district court judgment, affirmed on appeal to the circuit court, awarding plaintiff damages for breach of contract for sale of a new 1979 Dodge pickup truck.

Defendant claims that the trial court erred in finding that it had accepted the truck and in concluding that it had thereafter wrongfully attempted a revocation of the sale. We agree, finding that the evidence shows no acceptance within the meaning of the Uniform Commercial Code, MCL 440.2606; MSA 19.2606, and that defendant had an absolute right to reject the truck, MCL 440.2601; MSA 19.2601.

The evidence shows that on November 8 or 9, 1978, an officer of defendant, William Washabaugh, called at plaintiff's place of business to discuss the possible purchase of a pickup truck with a snowplow attachment. The truck in question was of the type desired and plaintiff's salesman, John Fuller, took Mr. Washabaugh for a test drive in the vehicle. Washabaugh liked the truck. However, before the test drive was completed, the engine overheated. There was a conflict in the testimony of Fuller and Washabaugh which was not addressed by the opinion of the trial judge: Washabaugh testified that the temperature gauge was "all the way over" and that there was steam coming from under the hood; Fuller testified that the truck was just running warm, that there was no overheating, and that he saw no steam coming from the engine compartment.

Whichever version is correct, the significant fact is that the topic of engine overheating was specifically addressed by Fuller and Washabaugh. Washabaugh expressed concern about the matter, and indicated past experience with other vehicles suffering engine damage from overheating. Fuller said that overheating resulted from incorrect positioning of the snow-plow blade in front of the radiator. Washabaugh was willing to buy the truck if Fuller's statement was correct. Fuller assured him that that was in fact the case, documents of purchase were executed, and Washabaugh gave Fuller a check for the full payment of the purchase price. They agreed that employees of defendant would pick up the truck the following day and that they would be instructed on the proper positioning of the plow blade.

On the following day, Stanley Reid and Leon LaFave came to plaintiff's place of business to pick up the truck for defendant. Fuller personally showed them how to properly position the blade, and it was so positioned in Fuller's presence before Reid and LaFave left for defendant's place of business near Potterville. When they arrived there, the engine was overheating and steaming. A mechanic employed by defendant could find no apparent defects from a visual inspection, so a telephone call was made to plaintiff's office. An employee in plaintiff's service department advised rechecking the blade position, refilling the radiator, and taking the truck out for another drive. This was done. Reid and LaFave drove to Potterville, about two miles from defendant's place of business, and back. The engine again overheated, the temperature gauge rose to the maximum, and there was an eruption of water and steam.

LaFave again called plaintiff's office and was told to bring the truck into plaintiff's service department. He did so, and when he arrived the engine was again overheating and steaming. He was told that the problem might be with a thermostat but that the truck would be ready and could be picked up the following afternoon.

On the next afternoon (the third day, be it November 10 or 11), LaFave went to Lansing and picked up the truck. He was told that a radiator cap had been replaced. By the time he got back to defendant's place of business, the engine was again overheating. On Washabaugh's orders, LaFave immediately notified plaintiff by telephone that defendant was not taking the truck, that payment was being stopped on the check, and that plaintiff should come get the truck. Plaintiff sent a wrecker and crew that evening and towed the truck back to its lot.

D Immediately Notified P that he was returning the truck

In the following days, plaintiff did nothing to the truck by way of inspection or repair. It was left sitting on plaintiff's lot. On November 15 or 16, the purchase and registration documents were taken by plaintiff to a branch office of the Secretary of State. On November 15 or 16, plaintiff received notice from its bank that defendant had stopped payment on the check.

P Didn't seasonably cure the defect

Title to the truck was issued in defendant's name by the Secretary of State on December 1, 1978. Both parties retained counsel, and defendant made an effort to tender title to plaintiff so the truck could be resold. Plaintiff rejected the tender, taking the position that the transaction was complete and that it could not resell the truck because defendant held title, and commenced this suit.

... [T]he opinion of the trial judge contains no findings of fact, discussion, or conclusion as to an acceptance of the truck by defendant within the meaning of the Uniform Commercial Code, although the conclusion that acceptance had occurred can be implied from the opinion's statement of the issues as being: (1) whether the defendant had sustained the burden of proving the truck defective so as to justify a revocation after acceptance; (2) if the truck was defective, whether plaintiff was given an opportunity to seasonably cure the defect; and (3) whether plaintiff had a duty to resell the truck.

We find the trial judge's decision on such issues inapposite, holding that on these facts the implied finding that there had been an acceptance of the truck by defendant is erroneous.

The Uniform Commercial Code, §2-606 (MCL 440.2606; MSA 19.2606), provides:

UCC §2-606

(1) Acceptance of goods occurs when the buyer

(a) after a reasonable opportunity to inspect the goods signifies to the seller that the goods are conforming or that he will take or retain them in spite of their nonconformity; or

(b) fails to make an effective rejection (subsection (1) of section 2602), but such acceptance does not occur until the buyer has had a reasonable opportunity to inspect them; or

(c) does any act inconsistent with the seller's ownership; but if such an act is wrongful as against the seller it is an acceptance only if ratified by him.

(2) Acceptance of a part of any commercial unit is acceptance of that entire unit.

This language, in defining what constitutes an acceptance, clearly contemplates an act of the buyer beyond taking delivery or possession of the goods. Possession during the time necessary for the "reasonable opportunity" to inspect is contemplated prior to acceptance. Similarly, §2-602 of the code allows a rejection of goods for nonconformance "within a reasonable time *after their delivery.*" Thus, while transfer of possession or title may be acts bearing on the question of acceptance, they are not in themselves determinative thereof. White & Summers, Handbook of the Law under the Uniform Commercial Code (2d ed.), §8-2, p. 296. . . .

Zabriskie [Zabriskie Chevrolet v. Smith, 228 A.2d 848 (D.C. 1967)] is pertinent for two reasons. In the first place, when dealing with acceptance under the UCC, it speaks to the relationship between the manufacturer and seller of complex machines or devices on the one hand and the dependent buyer on the other hand. The buyer may be expert in the use of the machine or device but he generally has no expertise as to the mechanical, electronic, chemical, and engineering components that combine to produce the intended performance. *Zabriskie* recognized this buyer dependency on the seller's expertise in holding that something more than a mere visual inspection is appropriate before the buyer can be held to have accepted the machine. We agree. A "reasonable time to inspect" under the UCC must allow an opportunity to put the product to its intended use, or for testing to verify its capability to perform as intended.

Zabriskie is also important for its holding that the adoption of the Uniform Commercial Code, §2-601, which provides that the buyer may reject goods which "fail in any respect to conform to the contract," creates a "perfect tender" rule replacing pre-code cases defining performance of a sales contract in terms of substantial compliance. We agree with that construction of the code. . . .

In the instant case, there was no acceptance. Nothing that defendant did can be construed under §2-606(1)(a), as signifying, after a reasonable opportunity to inspect, that the truck conformed or that defendant would retain the truck in spite of its nonconformity. Defendant had the absolute right to reject the truck for nonconformity within a reasonable time, and to seasonably notify the plaintiff thereof. MCL 440.2602; MSA 19.2602. It did so.

Reversed and remanded for entry of judgment in favor of defendant. Costs to defendant.

NOTES AND QUESTIONS

1. What exactly is the difference between the substantial performance limitation and the good faith limitation on rejection that the court finds in *Printing Center?*

2. Do you feel the court in *Capitol Dodge* would have necessarily arrived at a different decision under the facts of *Printing Center*?

If the buyer of goods has clearly made an "acceptance" of them as that term is defined in §2-606, the buyer may no longer reject the goods under §2-602. But if the buyer subsequently discovers a major defect with the goods, may the buyer avoid the contract? The common law would give relief under the idea of rescission, but the Uniform Commercial Code avoids using that term and instead calls the avoidance mechanism "revocation of acceptance." Read §2-608.

COLONIAL DODGE, INC. v. MILLER
Michigan Supreme Court, 1984
420 Mich. 452, 362 N.W.2d 704

KAVANAGH, J. This case requires the court to decide whether the failure to include a spare tire with a new automobile can constitute a substantial impairment in the value of that automobile entitling the buyer to revoke his acceptance of the vehicle under MCL 440.2608; MSA 19.2608.

We hold it may and reverse.

On April 19, 1976, defendant Clarence Miller ordered a 1976 Dodge Royal Monaco station wagon from plaintiff Colonial Dodge which included a heavy-duty trailer package with extra wide tires.

On May 28, 1976, defendant picked up the wagon, drove it a short distance where he met his wife, and exchanged it for her car. Defendant drove that car to work while his wife returned home with the new station wagon. Shortly after arriving home, Mrs. Miller noticed that their new wagon did not have a spare tire. The following morning defendant notified plaintiff that he insisted on having the tire he ordered immediately, but when told there was no spare tire then available, he informed the salesman for plaintiff that he would stop payment on the two checks that were tendered as the purchase price, and that the vehicle could be picked up from in front of his home. Defendant parked the car in front of his home where it remained until the temporary ten-day registration sticker had expired, whereupon the car was towed by the St. Clair police to a St. Clair dealership. Plaintiff had applied for license plates, registration, and title in defendant's name. Defendant refused the license plates when they were delivered to him.

According to plaintiff's witness, the spare tire was not included in the delivery of the vehicle due to a nation-wide shortage caused by a labor strike. Some months later, defendant was notified his tire was available.

Plaintiff sued defendant for the purchase price of the car. On January 13, 1981, the trial court entered a judgment for plaintiff finding that defendant wrongfully revoked acceptance of the vehicle. The Court of Appeals decided that defendant never accepted the vehicle under MCL 440.2606; MSA 19.2606 of the Uniform Commercial Code and reversed. 116 Mich. App. 78, 85; 322 N.W.2d 549 (1982). On rehearing, the Court of Appeals, noting the trial court found the parties had agreed that there was a valid acceptance, affirmed the trial court's holding there was not a substantial impairment in the value sufficient to authorize defendant to revoke acceptance of the automobile.

[handwritten: Appeals Court Reverse]

[handwritten: Then Affirmed]

Defendant argues that he never accepted the vehicle under MCL 440.2606; MSA 19.2606, claiming mere possession of the vehicle is not sufficient according to the UCC. Plaintiff contends defendant did accept the vehicle by executing an application for Michigan title and driving the vehicle away from the dealership. The trial court stated "[t]he parties agree that defendant Miller made a valid acceptance of the station wagon under §2.606 of the Uniform Commercial Code. . . ." We are not persuaded that, had the matter been contested in the trial court, a finding of acceptance would be warranted on this record. However, since defendant did not submit the question to the trial judge, but in effect stipulated to acceptance, we will treat the matter as though there was acceptance.

[handwritten: D's Contention]

[handwritten: D Never Agreed whether he Accepted or Not, Just that he revoked]

We are satisfied defendant made a proper revocation under MCL 440.2608(1)(b); MSA 19.2608(1)(b). This section reads:

> (1) The buyer may revoke his acceptance of a lot or commercial unit whose non-conformity substantially impairs its value to him if he has accepted it
>
>> (a) on the reasonable assumption that its non-conformity would be cured and it has not been seasonably cured; or
>>
>> (b) without discovery of such non-conformity if his acceptance was reasonably induced either by the difficulty of discovery before acceptance or by the seller's assurances.
>
> (2) Revocation of acceptance must occur within a reasonable time after the buyer discovers or should have discovered the ground for it and before any substantial change in condition of the goods which is not caused by their own defects. It is not effective until the buyer notifies the seller of it.
>
> (3) A buyer who so revokes has the same rights and duties with regard to the goods involved as if he had rejected them.

Plaintiff argues the missing spare tire did not constitute a substantial impairment in the value of the automobile, within the meaning of MCL 440.2608(1); MSA 19.2608(1). Plaintiff claims a missing spare tire is a trivial defect, and a proper construction of this section of the UCC would not permit defendant to revoke under these circumstances. It maintains that since the spare tire is easy to replace and the cost of curing the nonconformity very small compared to the total contract price, there is no substantial impairment in value.

[handwritten: P's Contention - Not Substantial Impairs Value]

However, MCL 440.2608(1); MSA 19.2608(1) says "[t]he buyer may revoke his acceptance of a lot or commercial unit whose nonconformity

[Margin note: " To him "]

substantially impairs its value *to him.* . . ." (Emphasis added.) Number two of the Official Comment to MCL 440.2608; MSA 19.2608 attempts to clarify this area. It says that

> [r]evocation of acceptance is possible only where the nonconformity substantially impairs the value of the goods to the buyer. For this purpose the test is not what the seller had reason to know at the time of contracting; the question is whether the nonconformity is such as will in fact cause a substantial impairment of value to the buyer though the seller had no advance knowledge as to the buyer's particular circumstances.

[Margin note: facts to show value of the tire to the defendant]

We cannot accept plaintiff's interpretation of MCL 440.2608(1); MSA 19.2608(1). In order to give effect to the statute, a buyer must show the nonconformity has a special devaluing effect on him and that the buyer's assessment of it is factually correct. In this case, the defendant's concern with safety is evidenced by the fact that he ordered the special package which included special tires. The defendant's occupation demanded that he travel extensively, sometimes in excess of 150 miles per day on Detroit freeways, and often in the early morning hours. Mr. Miller testified that he was afraid of a tire going flat on a Detroit freeway at 3 A.M. Without a spare, he testified, he would be helpless until morning business hours. The dangers attendant upon a stranded motorist are common knowledge, and Mr. Miller's fears are not unreasonable.

[Margin note: Holding]

We hold that under the circumstances the failure to include the spare tire as ordered constituted a substantial impairment in value to Mr. Miller, and that he could properly revoke his acceptance under the UCC.

[Margin note: §2-608(1)(b)]
[Margin note: Non-conformity was hard to Discover]

That defendant did not discover this nonconformity before he accepted the vehicle does not preclude his revocation. There was testimony that the space for the spare tire was under a fastened panel, concealed from view. This out-of-sight location satisfies the requirement of MCL 440.2608(1)(b); MSA 19.2608(1)(b) that the nonconformity be difficult to discover.

[Margin note: D Notified Seller in reasonable time]

MCL 440.2608(2); MSA 19.2608(2) requires that the seller be notified of the revocation of acceptance and that it occur within a reasonable time of the discovery of the nonconformity. Defendant notified plaintiff of his revocation the morning after the car was delivered to him. Notice was given within a reasonable time.

Plaintiff argues that defendant failed to effectively revoke acceptance because he neglected to sign over title to the car to plaintiff.

Defendant, however, had no duty to sign over title absent a request from plaintiff that he do so. Under MCL 440.2608(3); MSA 19.2608(3), "[a] buyer who so revokes has the same rights and duties with regard to the goods involved as if he had rejected them." And a buyer who has rejected goods in his possession "is under a duty . . . to hold them with reasonable care at the seller's disposition for a time sufficient to permit the seller to remove them; but the buyer has no further obligations with regard to the goods. . . ."

MCL 440.2602(1)(b) and (c); MSA 19.2602(1)(b) and (c). Defendant's notice to plaintiff and holding of the car pending seller's disposition was sufficient under the statute, at least in the absence of evidence that defendant refused a request by the plaintiff to sign over title.

Plaintiff contends defendant abandoned the vehicle, denying it any opportunity to cure the nonconforming tender as prescribed in MCL 440.2508; MSA 19.2508. We find that defendant's behavior did not prevent plaintiff from curing the nonconformity. Defendant held the vehicle and gave notice to the plaintiff in a proper fashion; he had no further duties. *Reversed*

Reversed.

RYAN, J. (dissenting). I dissent.

While I agree that MCL 440.2608(1)(b); MSA 19.2608(1)(b) establishes what is essentially a subjective test to measure the buyer's authority to revoke an acceptance of nonconforming goods, the requisite impairment of the value of the goods to the buyer must be *substantial*. It is not sufficient that the nonconformance be worrisome, aggravating, or even potentially dangerous. It must be a nonconformity which diminishes the value of the goods to the buyer to a substantial degree. The mere possibility that the new car in this case would have a flat tire in the early hours of the morning in an unsafe area of the City of Detroit, leaving its driver with no spare tire, although real, is unlikely. In all events, it is not a possibility which can reasonably be said to elevate the absence of a spare tire, a temporary deficiency easily remedied, to the level of a "substantial impairment" of the value of the new automobile for its ordinary use as a motor vehicle.

Consequently, I would reverse the judgment of the Court of Appeals and affirm the finding of the trial court on this issue.

BOYLE, J. (dissenting). I disagree with the conclusion reached by the majority for the reasons stated by Judge Cynar in his dissent in the Court of Appeals. 116 Mich. App. 78, 87; 322 N.W.2d 549 (1982) (Cynar, P.J., dissenting). I agree with Judge Cynar's analysis of the law of substantial impairment and its application to the facts in this case. As he succinctly summarized:

> A buyer may properly revoke acceptance where the nonconformity substantially impairs its value. The existence of such nonconformity depends on the facts and circumstances of each case. Jorgensen v. Pressnall, 274 Or. 285; 545 P.2d 1382 (1976). The determination of substantial impairment has been made from the buyer's subjective view, considering particular needs and circumstances. See Summers & White, Handbook of the Law Under the Uniform Commercial Code (2d ed.), §8-3, p. 308; Committee Comment 2 to MCL 440.2608; MSA 19.2608. An objective approach was utilized in Fargo Machine & Tool Co. v. Kearney & Trecker Corp., 428 F. Supp. 364 (E.D. Mich., 1977), and an objective and subjective test was employed in Jorgensen, supra.

The purpose of the requirement of substantial impairment of value is to preclude revocation for trivial defects or defects which may be easily corrected. Rozmus v. Thompson's Lincoln-Mercury Co., 209 Pa. Super. 120; 224 A.2d 782 (1966).

The trial judge's determination that the temporarily missing spare tire did not constitute a substantial impairment in value under either the subjective or objective test was not clearly erroneous. Id., pp. 88-89.

Therefore, I do not agree that defendant Miller properly rejected the vehicle, and I would affirm the trial court's finding on that issue.

NOTES AND QUESTIONS

1. Increasingly, courts have used a subjective and objective test in making a determination of "substantial impairment." First, the subjective test: Did the buyer have a specific need that, in the buyer's mind, was not met by the product? The objective test is whether a reasonable person in the shoes of the buyer would find the product failed to meet the need. Such objective evidence can go to the effect the failure had on the buyer's safety as in the current case or other factors such as the timing of breakdowns and the number of such breakdowns. Midwest Mobile Diagnostic Imaging, L.L.C. v. Dynamics Corp. of Am., 965 F. Supp. 1003 (W.D. Mich. 1997).

2. Was the court correct in usurping the jury's findings regarding the substantial impairment issue?

3. Note that one of the effects of an acceptance is that the burden of proof shifts from the seller to the buyer per UCC §2-607(4). This means that prior to acceptance, the seller has the burden of establishing a perfect tender under §2-601 (or a substantial one under §2-612 for installment sales), but after the buyer accepts the goods, the buyer must prove a substantial impairment and the other elements necessary to revoke acceptance under §2-608.

4. The right of rejection is subject to the right to cure under §2-508. Did the buyers in the last two cases give the seller the right to cure? How?

5. The right of the breaching party to cure is not unlimited. "[T]he buyer . . . is not bound to permit the seller to tinker with the article indefinitely in the hope that it may ultimately be made to comply with the warranty." Orange Motors of Coral Gables, Inc. v. Dade County Dairies, Inc., 258 So. 2d 319, 321 (Fla. Dist. Ct. App. 1972).

6. Use by the buyer of goods after attempted revocation or rejection may show a waiver of the right to reject or revoke. However, use by the buyer may be allowed if reasonable and relatively short term. For example, if the buyer is using the product for a time after revocation in a good faith attempt to mitigate damages, the defendant has given no contra instructions to the buyer, and the defendant is not harmed, such use may be allowed. Wilk Paving, Inc. v. Southworth-Milton, Inc., 162 Vt. 552, 649 A.2d 778 (1994).

Further, buyer's use for a limited time when the buyer has no real option may not prohibit rejection or revocation. Consider that the party who has revoked acceptance of a mobile home may have no other place to live while the right of revocation is litigated. See, e.g., Performance Motors, Inc. v. Allen, 280 N.C. 385, 186 S.E.2d 161 (1972). Also consider Johnson v. General Motors Corp., Chevrolet Motor Div., 233 Kan. 1044, 668 P.2d 139 (1983) (continuing use of defective truck after revocation was permissible buyer would have had to purchase another vehicle while paying for the defective one). Contra Gasque v. Mooers Motor Car Co., 227 Va. 154, 313 S.E.2d 384 (1984) (dicta that any use of an automobile after revocation is improper).

V. EXCUSE

A. Prevention and Cooperation

SULLIVAN v. BULLOCK
Court of Appeals of Idaho, 1993
124 Idaho 738, 864 P.2d 184

WALTERS, Chief Judge.

The issue at trial in this action was whether it was the homeowner or the contractor who breached a written contract to remodel several rooms in a home. The jury returned a special verdict finding that although the contractor had not substantially performed under the contract, he had been prevented from doing so by the homeowner. The jury awarded $2,956.40 in damages to the contractor, essentially the balance of the contract price. The homeowner filed a motion for judgment n.o.v. or for a new trial, which was denied. The homeowner appeals the judgment and denial of her motion. She contends that the jury's verdict is contrary to the law and the evidence presented. She also claims that the trial court erroneously rejected one of her proposed jury instructions, excluded evidence, and awarded costs and attorney fees to the contractor.

We affirm the denial of the motions in so far as the decision below holds that the homeowner prevented the contractor's complete performance. However, we reverse and remand the decision to the extent it approved an erroneous measure of damages in favor of the contractor. We also vacate the award of attorney fees and remand for further consideration by the district court.

I. Facts

The evidence presented at trial established that in April 1991, Cora Sullivan hired Dallas Bullock, doing business as New Home Development, to remodel her kitchen, hallway, utility room, bathroom and sewing room, for a total price of $6,780. The written contract set out the major aspects of the project but lacked detail. No design sketches were agreed to by the parties. Less than detailed communications between Mrs. Sullivan and Mr. Bullock resulted in misunderstandings regarding exactly what the final product would look like. Eventually the contract was breached in several respects. The work was not begun or completed by the dates set out in the contract. Mrs. Sullivan, however, assented to the delays. Evidence was presented that the work performed by Mr. Bullock and the subcontractors he hired was sometimes below the industry standard for the area, not as Mrs. Sullivan had requested, and was not performed to her satisfaction. In other words, according to Mrs. Sullivan and other witnesses, the improvements were not "constructed and completed in a good and workmanlike manner" as expressly required by the contract. However, evidence was presented that during the time the work was being performed, Mrs. Sullivan did not clearly convey to Mr. Bullock her dissatisfaction and he continued with the perception that the project was progressing with approval. During the project, Mr. Bullock incurred costs not provided for in the contract, primarily for electrical work to bring the kitchen up to code and for plumbing. There was no evidence that Mrs. Sullivan approved the extra costs for the electrical work.

For a period while construction was progressing, Mrs. Sullivan did not live at the home. Eventually, however, she moved in while the remodeling continued. At one time, Mrs. Sullivan told Mr. Bullock that she would not be at home on a certain day and, feeling protective of her personal belongings, she did not want the workmen there while she was gone. Unfortunately, and unbeknownst to Mr. Bullock, one of the workmen entered the home through a window to complete some work while Mrs. Sullivan was gone. This so upset Mrs. Sullivan that she angrily confronted Mr. Bullock and told him that neither he nor his workmen were to ever set foot in her house again. Further requests by Mr. Bullock and others to enter the home and continue the project were refused by Mrs. Sullivan. On July 1, 1991, Mr. Bullock submitted a "final" bill to Mrs. Sullivan for $2,956.40, purportedly for work completed, but also representing the contract balance for the completed project.

II. Procedural History

In October 1991, Mrs. Sullivan filed a complaint in the district court, asserting that Mr. Bullock's workmanship was grossly defective and that he had been unresponsive to requests to improve his product. The complaint sought damages in the amount of $19,703 to completely redo the work Mr. Bullock had started and return of the $5,932 she had already paid him. Mr. Bullock answered Mrs. Sullivan's complaint and filed a counter-claim. He alleged that his work was satisfactory, that any unsatisfactory work could be fixed, but that Mrs. Sullivan had prohibited him from finishing the project or fixing defects. He stated that Mrs. Sullivan had paid $5,906 and he requested $2,956.40 in damages for the work he had performed. He also asserted a claim against Mrs. Sullivan, seeking damages for slander.

The trial addressed the breach of contract claim. The counterclaim alleging slander was voluntarily dismissed. The jury returned a special verdict finding that Mr. Bullock had not substantially performed under the contract, but that he had been prevented or substantially hindered from performing by Mrs. Sullivan. The jury awarded him $2,956.40, and the court awarded him costs and attorney fees as provided by the contract. Mrs. Sullivan moved for judgment n.o.v. or new trial. Her motion was denied. She appeals the judgment and the denial of her motion.

III. ANALYSIS . . .

1A. PREVENTION

First, we examine the jury's finding that Mrs. Sullivan prevented or hindered Mr. Bullock's performance. Implied in every contract is a condition to cooperate. In any case where the plaintiff's performance requires the cooperation of the defendant, as in a contract to serve or to make something from the defendant's materials or on his land, the defendant, by necessary implication, promises to give this cooperation and if he fails to do so, he is immediately liable although his only express promise is to pay money at a future day. Indeed, there is generally in a contract subject to either an express or an implied condition an implied promise not to prevent or hinder performance of the condition. Such prevention, if the condition could otherwise have been performed, is, therefore, an immediate breach of contract, and if of sufficiently serious character, damages for the loss of the entire contract may be recovered. In construction contracts, the duty to cooperate encompasses allowing access to the premises to enable the contractor to perform the work. 17A C.J.S. Contracts §468.

The duty to cooperate is recognized in Idaho. In McOmber v. Nuckols, 82 Idaho 280, 353 P.2d 398 (1960), our Supreme Court held that the plaintiff who had refused to allow the defendant to perform the rental service for which he had been contracted, or who had imposed conditions which made performance by the defendant impracticable, could not recover damages. A similar result was found in Molyneux v. Twin Falls Canal Co., 54 Idaho 619, 35 P.2d 651 (1934), wherein the Court held that a party to a contract to construct a drainage tunnel could recover damages if he had been prevented by the other party from completing the project. In other words, nonperformance under the contract was excused if the other party prevented the performance.

Conduct of Π Preventing Party

To excuse a party's nonperformance, however, the conduct of the party preventing performance must be "wrongful" and "in excess of their legal rights." 17A C.J.S. Contracts §468. Other authorities have stated that the conduct of the party preventing performance must be outside what was permitted in the contract and "unjustified," or outside the reasonable contemplation of the parties when the contract was executed. Our Supreme Court has echoed this standard in *Molyneux* by stating:

> If, at the time appellant [the canal company] ordered respondent [Molyneux] to stop work, it intended to drill the tunnel any additional length and then or later should proceed with the tunnel without having previously *in good faith and pursuant to the contract* determined to terminate the tunnel, it was obligated to let respondent do the work, and if it did not permit respondent to do such work appellant would, in such case, have breached its contract with respondent.

Molyneux, 54 Idaho at 629, 35 P.2d at 655 (emphasis added).

Jury Instructions were proper

Here, the trial court's instructions to the jury properly reflected this statement of the law. Jury instruction twenty-one set out the elements required to be proved by Mrs. Sullivan for her to prevail on her complaint. It also set out the elements required of Mr. Bullock in his counterclaim. The issue of prevention was described in instruction twenty-two, which follows the theory stated in *Molyneux* that the act of prevention must have been unreasonable, in other words, outside the contemplation of the parties as expressed in the contract.

The jury returned a verdict stating that Mr. Bullock had not substantially performed but that Mrs. Sullivan had unreasonably prevented his performance. There was substantial evidence from which the jury could conclude that Mr. Bullock's failure was to be excused by Mrs. Sullivan's act of denying access to her home. True, an employee did enter Mrs. Sullivan's home when he was not supposed to. However, when Mrs. Sullivan denied any further access to the home she acted in a manner that was outside the contemplation of the contract or the parties when they executed the contract. Viewing the record in the light most favorable to Mrs. Sullivan, we hold that a reasonable view of the evidence supports the verdict. . . .

Affirmed

QUESTION

Well, what do you think? Do you believe Mrs. Sullivan should have allowed admittance to her home?

Problem 154

Sangazure General Construction Company signed a contract with Point-dextre Plumbing and Fixtures to use the latter for the plumbing work on the new building for Wells & Associates. The contract provided that Sangazure could dismiss the subcontractor if Pointdextre Plumbing at any point became insolvent. The construction lasted for a two-year period. During the second year, Sangazure General Construction Company itself had financial problems, leading it to be late on a number of occasions with the progress payments it was required to make to Pointdextre Plumbing. This in turn upset the delicate financial status of Pointdextre so that it became insolvent—under any definition of the term—whereupon Sangazure exercised the insolvency clause and dismissed Pointdextre, planning to do the plumbing itself. Pointdextre sued, and Sangazure pointed to the insolvency clause as its defense. Is that clause effective in this circumstance?

Problem 155

When Bob Cratchit interviewed for a job with the firm of Scrooge and Marley, Mr. Marley told him that he would be permanently employed there at a salary to be negotiated from time to time. They agreed on a starting salary, and Cratchit took the position. He worked tirelessly for three years, pleasing both of the partners. Then Mr. Marley died and Scrooge became harder and harder to please. On a Tuesday, he fired Cratchit, saying that he couldn't stand to see his face one more day. Advise Cratchit, who is in your law office asking whether a lawsuit against Scrooge has any chance of succeeding. See Foley v. Interactive Data Corp., 47 Cal. 3d 654, 254 Cal. Rptr. 211, 765 P.2d 373 (1988); Metcalf v. Intermountain Gas Co., 116 Idaho 622, 778 P.2d 744 (1989).

NOTE ON GOOD FAITH

Concepts of good faith, cooperation, and prevention are closely related. When one party actively attempts to torpedo the contractual relationship, the court may find a material breach of an implied promise (covenant): (a) not to prevent the other party from performing; (b) to cooperate in ensuring performance is achieved; or (c) to act in good faith. Just as the material breach of an express promise can result in the discharge of performance, the material breach of such an implied promise can provide a viable defense for nonperformance by the nonbreaching party. The boundaries of the duty of good faith, etc., are generally defined by the parties' intent and reasonable expectations in entering into the contract. See, e.g., Cross & Cross Properties, Ltd. v. Everett Allied Co., 886 F.2d 497 (2d Cir. 1989). Generally, there can be no breach of the implied covenant of good faith if a party is only doing what it is entitled to do under the contract provisions. PDQ Lube Center, Inc. v. Huber, 949 P.2d 792 (Utah Ct. App. 1997). In essence, the typical good faith claim is another breach of contract claim typically used as an excuse for nonperformance because the other party seeking relief exercised bad faith in its duty to meet the defendant's reasonable expectations of performance. Occasionally, courts find that the breach of the implied covenant of good faith gives rise to remedies for the breach of the good faith obligation itself. For example, courts in a number of states have allowed an insured to recover for breach of the implied covenant of good faith by an insurer. See, e.g., Karas v. Liberty Ins. Corp., 2014 WL 3579524 (D. Conn. 2014). California courts have permitted such an action in a variety of other contracts, including an agreement to make mutual wills (Brown v. Superior Court, 34 Cal. 2d 559, 212 P.2d 878 (1949)); to sell real property (Osborne v. Cal-Am Financial Corp., 80 Cal. App. 3d 259, 145 Cal. Rptr. 584 (1978)); employee incentive contracts (Foley v. U.S. Paving Co., 262 Cal. App. 2d 499, 68 Cal. Rptr. 780 (1968)); leases (Cordonier v. Central Shopping Plaza Associates, 82 Cal. App. 3d 991, 147 Cal. Rptr. 558 (1978)); and contracts to provide leasing services (Masonite Corp. v. Pacific Gas & Electric Co., 65 Cal. App. 3d 1, 135 Cal. Rptr. 170 (1976)). In some states, the breach of an implied covenant of good faith may also constitute a tortious act giving rise to damages. McEvoy by Finn v. Group Health Co-op. of Eau Claire, 213 Wis. 2d 507, 570 N.W.2d 397 (1997). California has also led the league in this type of action. For a discussion of the history of the development of this tort and its limitations, see the discussion in both the majority and dissent in Seaman's Direct Buying Service v. Standard Oil, 36 Cal. 3d 752, 206 Cal. Rptr. 354, 686 P.2d 1158 (Cal. 1984). See also Viles v. Security National Ins. Co., 788 S.W.2d 566 (Tex. 1990), an insurance case, adopting the view that a tort will lie only in those cases in which a special relationship exists between the parties. Quinn Cos. v. Herring-Marathon Group, Inc., 299 Ark. 431, 773 S.W.2d 94 (1989) (limiting the tort to contractual relationships involving insurance claims). However, the general rule is that the duty of good faith does not give rise to an independent cause of action but only to a right to defend against a party's own failure to perform; that is, because of the breach of the implied condition of good faith the party argues that its own performance obligation was excused. See the Official Comment to §1-203 [§1-304 in the revised version of Article 1].

One issue that won't go away is whether a bank can be liable for suddenly cutting off an agreed line of credit. Such "lender liability" lawsuits sound in contract, and sometimes involve allegations that the bank has failed to act in good faith (which is required by both the common law and §1-203 — §1-304 in the revised version of Article 1 — of the Uniform Commercial Code). In the leading case of K.M.C. Co. v. Irving Trust Co.,

757 F.2d 752 (6th Cir. 1985), the bank cancelled a line of credit without notice and the court held that this breach of the implied obligation of good faith exposed the bank to $7,000,000 in damages! See also Reid v. Key Bank of Southern Maine, 821 F.2d 9 (1st Cir. 1987) (similar facts, $100,000 in damages); In re JPMorgan Chase Bank Home Equity Line of Credit Litigation, 2011 WL 2600573 (N.D. Ill. 2011) (such conduct also violated the federal Truth in Lending Act). Although banks and other lenders often win these lawsuits (for example, if the obligation is one payable on demand rather than at a certain date, faith restrictions do not apply), cases like those cited should make them leery of precipitous actions when dealing with their customers. Alarmed by this expanding liability, many states have passed statutes prohibiting any action on an oral commitment to lend. And courts in this situation have shown an increasing reluctance to find any basis of independent relief based on breach of good faith obligations.

B. Forfeiture as an Excuse

BURGER KING CORP. v. FAMILY DINING, INC.
United States District Court, Eastern District of Pennsylvania, 1977
426 F. Supp. 485, aff'd, 566 F.2d 1168 (3d Cir. 1977)

HANNUM, District Judge. Presently before the Court is defendant's motion for an involuntary dismissal in accordance with Rule 41(b), Federal Rules of Civil Procedure, advanced at the close of plaintiff's case. The trial is before the Court sitting without a jury.

In bringing the suit plaintiff seeks a determination under the Declaratory Judgment Act, Title 28, United States Code §2201, that a contract between the parties, by its own terms, is no longer of any force and effect. A request for declaratory relief is appropriate in a case such as this where the primary question is whether such a termination has occurred. See: Wright and Miller, Federal Practice and Procedure: Civil §2765, n. 35.

Jurisdiction of the parties is based on diversity of citizenship in accordance with Title 28, United States Code §1332(a).

FACTS ESTABLISHED IN PLAINTIFF'S CASE

Plaintiff Burger King Corporation (hereinafter "Burger King") is a Florida corporation engaged in franchising the well-known Burger King Restaurants. In 1954, James W. McLamore, founder of Burger King Restaurants, Inc. (the corporate predecessor of Burger King) built the first Burger King Restaurant in Miami, Florida. In 1961 the franchise system was still of relatively modest size having only about 60 or 70 restaurants in operation outside of Florida. By 1963, however, Burger King began to experience significant growth and was building and operating, principally through franchisees, 24 restaurants per year. It was also at this time that Burger King's relationship with defendant Family Dining, Inc. (hereinafter "Family Dining") was created.

Family Dining is a Pennsylvania corporation which at the present time operates ten Burger King Restaurants (hereinafter "Restaurant") in Bucks and Montgomery Counties in Pennsylvania. Family Dining was founded and is currently operated by Carl Ferris who had been a close personal friend of McLamore's for a number of years prior to 1963. In fact they had attended Cornell University together in the late 1940's. It would seem that this friendship eventually led to the business relationship between Burger King and Family Dining which was conceived in the "Burger King Territorial Agreement" (hereinafter "Territorial Agreement") entered on May 10, 1963.

In accordance with the Territorial Agreement Burger King agreed that Family Dining would be its sole licensee, and thus have an "exclusive territory," in Bucks and Montgomery Counties provided Family Dining operated each Restaurant pursuant to Burger King license agreements[1] and maintained a specified rate of development. Articles I and II of the Territorial Agreement are pertinent to this dispute. They provide as follows:

I

For a period of one year, beginning on the date hereof, Company will not operate or license others for the operation of any Burger King restaurant within the following described territory hereinafter referred to as "exclusive territory," to-wit: The counties of Bucks and Montgomery, all in the State of Pennsylvania as long as Licensee operates each Burger King restaurant pursuant to Burger King restaurant licenses with Company and faithfully performs each of the covenants contained.

This agreement shall remain in effect and Licensee shall retain the exclusive territory for a period of ninety (90) years from the date hereof, provided that at the end of one, two, three, four, five, six, seven, eight, nine and ten years from the date hereof, and continuously thereafter during the next eighty years, Licensee has the following requisite number of Burger King restaurants in operation or under active construction, pursuant to Licenses with Company:

- One (1) restaurant at the end of one year;
- Two (2) restaurants at the end of two years;
- Three (3) restaurants at the end of three years;
- Four (4) restaurants at the end of four years;
- Five (5) restaurants at the end of five years;
- Six (6) restaurants at the end of six years;
- Seven (7) restaurants at the end of seven years;
- Eight (8) restaurants at the end of eight years;

1. Each Restaurant is opened pursuant to a separate Burger King license agreement.

- Nine (9) restaurants at the end of nine years;
- Ten (10) restaurants at the end of ten years;

and continually maintains not less than ten (10) restaurants during the next eighty (80) years.

Licensee and company may mutually agree to the execution of a restaurant license to a person other than the Licensee, herein, if such restaurant license is executed same will count as a requisite number as set forth in paragraph above.

II

If at the end of either one, two, three, four, five, six, seven, eight, nine or ten years from the date hereof, or anytime thereafter during the next eighty (80) years, there are less than the respective requisite number of Burger King operations or under active construction in the "exclusive territory" pursuant to licenses by Company, this agreement shall terminate and be of no further force and effect. Therefore, Company may operate or license others for the operation of Burger King Restaurants anywhere within the exclusive territory, so long as such restaurants are not within the "Protected Area," as set forth in any Burger King Restaurant License to which the Licensee herein is a party.

[margin handwritten: Express Condition]

The prospect of exclusivity for ninety years was clearly intended to be an inducement to Family Dining to develop the territory as prescribed and it appears that it had exactly this effect as Family Dining was to become one of Burger King's most successful franchisees. While Burger King considered Carl Ferris to be somewhat of a problem at various times and one who was overly meticulous with detail, it was nevertheless through his efforts which included obtaining the necessary financing and assuming significant risks, largely without assistance from Burger King, that enabled both parties to benefit from the arrangement.

[margin handwritten: Exclusivity in the region was bargained for consideration]

On August 16, 1963, Family Dining opened the First Restaurant at 588 West DeKalb Pike in King of Prussia, Pennsylvania. The second Restaurant was opened on July 2, 1965, at 409 West Ridge Pike, Conshohocken, Pennsylvania, and the third Restaurant was opened October 19, 1966, at 2561 West Main Street, Norristown, Pennsylvania.

However, by April, 1968, Family Dining had not opened or begun active construction on a fourth Restaurant which, in accordance with the development rate, should have been accomplished by May 10, 1967, and it was apparent that a fifth Restaurant would not be opened by May 10, 1968, the date scheduled. On May 1, 1968, the parties entered into a Modification of the Territorial Agreement (hereinafter "Modification") whereby Burger King agreed to waive Family Dining's failure to comply with the development rate. There is nothing contained in the record which indicates that Burger King received anything of value in exchange for entering this agreement. However, McLamore testified that if the fourth and fifth Restaurants would be built nearly in compliance with the development rate for the fifth year he would overlook the year or so default in the fourth Restaurant. This attitude seems to be consistent with his overall view toward the development rate with

[margin handwritten: Behind development schedule]

[margin handwritten: Modified contract]

respect to which, he testified, was "designed to insure the company of an orderly process of growth which would also enable the company to produce a profit on the sale of its franchises and through the collection of royalties that the restaurants would themselves produce." The fourth Restaurant was opened on July 1, 1968, at 1721 North DeKalb Pike, Norristown, Pennsylvania, and the fifth Restaurant was opened on October 17, 1968, at 1035 Bustleton Pike in Feasterville, Pennsylvania.

More delays

On April 18, 1969, Ferris forwarded a letter to McLamore pertaining to certain delays in site approval and relating McLamore's earlier statement that there would be no problem in waiving the development schedule for the sixth Restaurant. The letter expressed Ferris' concern regarding compliance with the development rate. By letter dated April 26, 1969, from Howard Walker of Burger King, Ferris was granted a month extension in the development rate. With respect to this extension McLamore testified that "it never crossed my mind to call a default of this agreement on a technicality." On October 1, 1969, the sixth Restaurant was opened at 1515 East High Street in Pottstown, Pennsylvania. The seventh Restaurant was opened on February 2, 1970, ahead of schedule, at 560 North Main Street in Doylestown, Pennsylvania.

Granted extension

Promoted

At this point in time Burger King was no longer a modest sized franchise system. It had become a wholly owned subsidiary of the Pillsbury Company and had, in fact, evolved into a complex corporate entity. McLamore was elevated to Chairman of the Board of Burger King and, while he remained the chief executive officer for a time, Arthur A. Rosewall was installed as Burger King's President. Ferris was no longer able to expect the close, one to one relationship with McLamore that had previously obtained in his dealings with the company. It seems clear that as a result Family Dining began to experience difficulties in its day to day operations with Burger King.

One of the problem areas which arose concerned site selection. In a typical situation when a franchisee would seek approval for a building site an application would be submitted to the National Development Committee comprised of various Burger King officials. Based on Ferris' prior showing regarding site selection it could be expected that he would have little difficulty in obtaining their approval. In McLamore's view, Ferris was an exceptionally fine franchisee whose ability to choose real estate locations was exceptional. However, in August, 1970, a Frankford Avenue location selected by Ferris was rejected by the National Development Committee. The reasons offered in support of the decision to reject are not entirely clear and it seems that for the most part it was an exercise of discretion. The only plausible reason, given Ferris' expertise, was that the site was 2.7 miles from another Burger King franchise operated by Pete Miller outside Family Dining's exclusive territory. Yet Burger King chose not to exercise its discretion in similar circumstances when it permitted another franchisee to build a Restaurant in Devon, Pennsylvania, approximately 3 miles away from an existing Family Dining Restaurant.

In his August 25, 1970, memo to the Carl Ferris file McLamore observed that Burger King "had sloppy real estate work involved in servicing him and that [Burger King was] guilty of many follow up delinquencies." This was during a time, as Burger King management was well aware, where it was one thing to select a location and quite another to actually develop it. That is, local governing bodies were taking a much stricter view toward allowing this type of development. It was also during this time, as McLamore's memo points out, Burger King realized that the Bucks-Montgomery territory was capable of sustaining substantially more Restaurants than originally thought.

Amidst these circumstances, the eighth Restaurant was opened ahead of schedule on October 7, 1970, at 601 South Broad Street in Lansdale, Pennsylvania. And in December, 1971, Burger King approved Family Dining's proposed sites for two additional Restaurants in Ambler, Pennsylvania and Levittown, Pennsylvania.

In early 1972, Arthur Rosewall became the chief executive officer of Burger King. At this time it also became apparent that the ninth Restaurant would not be opened or under construction by May 10, 1972. On April 27, 1972, in a telephone conversation with McLamore, Ferris once again expressed his concern to Burger King regarding compliance with the development rate. Burger King's position at that time is evidenced by McLamore's Memo to the Carl Ferris file dated April 28, 1972, wherein he provides that "Ferris' territorial arrangement with the company is such that he must have his ninth store (he has eight open now) under construction next month. I indicated to him that, due to the fact that he was in the process of developing four sites at this time, the company would consider he had met, substantially, the requirements of exclusivity." McLamore testified that at that time he had in mind a further delay of 3 to 6 months.

In April, 1973, Burger King approved Family Dining's proposed site for a Restaurant in Warminster, Pennsylvania. However, as of May 10, 1973, neither the ninth or the tenth Restaurant had been opened or under active construction.

A letter dated May 23, 1973, from Helen D. Donaldson, Franchise Documents Administrator for Burger King, was sent to Ferris. The letter provides as follows:

> Dear Mr. Ferris:
> During a periodic review of all territorial agreements we note that as of this date your development schedule requiring ten restaurants to be open or under construction by May 10, 1973, has not been met. Our records reflect eight stores open in Bucks and/or Montgomery County, and one site approved but not manned.
> Under the terms of your territorial agreement failure to have the required number of stores in operation or under active construction constitutes a default of your agreement.

[handwritten margin note: Letter stating breach of compliance with development schedule]

If there are extenuating circumstances about which this office is not aware, we would appreciate your earliest advice.

It is doubtful that the Donaldson letter was intended to communicate to Ferris that the Territorial Agreement was terminated. The testimony of both Rosewall and Leslie W. Paszat, an executive of Burger King, who worked closely with Rosewall on the Family Dining matter indicates that even Burger King had not settled its position at this time. Ferris' letter dated July 27, 1973, to Rosewall, and Rosewall's reply dated August 3, 1973 also fail to demonstrate any understanding that the Territorial Agreement was terminated.

It seems that throughout this period Burger King treated the matter as something of a "hot potato" subjecting Ferris to contact with several different Burger King officials. Much of Ferris' contact with Rosewall was interrupted by Rosewall's month long vacation and a meat shortage crisis to which he had to devote a substantial amount of his time. Ultimately Paszat was given responsibility for Family Dining and it appears that he provided Ferris with the first clear indication that Burger King considered the Territorial Agreement terminated in his letter of November 6, 1973. Burger King's corporate structure had become so complex that the question of who, when or where the decision was made could not be answered. The abrupt manner in which Burger King's position was communicated to Family Dining, under the circumstances, was not straightforward.

First clear indication it was terminated

From November, 1973, until some point early in 1975, the parties attempted to negotiate their differences with no success. The reason for the lack of success is understandable given that Burger King from the outset considered exclusivity a non-negotiable item. It was during this period on September 7, 1974, that Family Dining began actual construction of the ninth Restaurant in Warminster, Pennsylvania.

Several months before the instant litigation was begun Family Dining informed Burger King that it intended to open a ninth Restaurant on or about May 15, 1975, on Street Road, Warminster, Pennsylvania. In February, 1975, Burger King notified Family Dining that a franchise agreement (license) had to be entered for the additional Restaurant without which Family Dining would be infringing Burger King's trademarks. A similar notice was given in April, 1975, in which Burger King indicated it would retain counsel to protect its rights. Nevertheless Family Dining proceeded with its plans to open the Warminster Restaurant.

In May, 1975, Burger King filed a complaint, which was the inception of this lawsuit, seeking to enjoin the use of Burger King trademarks by Family Dining at the Warminster Restaurant. The Court granted a Temporary Restraining Order until a hearing on the complaint could be held. On May 13, 1975, the parties reached an agreement on terms under which the Burger King trademarks could be used at the Warminster Restaurant. Pursuant to the agreement Burger King filed an amended complaint seeking the instant declaratory relief. Subsequently and also pursuant to this agreement Family Dining opened its tenth Restaurant in Willow Grove, Pennsylvania, the construction of which began on March 28, 1975.

DISCUSSION

Family Dining raises several arguments in support of its motion pursuant to Rule 41(b). One of its principal arguments is that the termination provision should be found inoperative because otherwise it would result in a forfeiture to Family Dining. For reasons which have become evident during the presentation of Burger King's case the Court finds Family Dining's position compelling both on legal and equitable grounds and is thus persuaded that the Territorial Agreement should not be declared terminated. Under Rule 41(b) when a plaintiff in an action tried by the Court without a jury has completed the presentation of his evidence, the defendant, without waiving his right to offer evidence in the event the motion is not granted, may move for a dismissal on the ground that upon the facts and the law plaintiff has shown no right to relief. Inasmuch as termination is the only relief sought by Burger King, it follows that dismissal of the action is appropriate.

In bringing this suit Burger King maintains that the Territorial Agreement is a divisible contract wherein Family Dining promised to open or have under active construction one new Restaurant in each of the first ten years of the contract in exchange for which Burger King promised to grant one additional year of exclusivity for each new Restaurant. This, to be followed by an additional eighty years of exclusivity provided the first ten Restaurants were built on time. In support Burger King relies on the opening language of Article I of the Territorial Agreement which provides that "[f]or a period of one year, beginning on the date hereof, Company will not operate or license. . . ." It is thus argued that since Family Dining clearly failed to perform its promises the Court must, in accordance with the express language of Article II, declare the contract terminated. Burger King further argues that because Family Dining did not earn exclusivity beyond the ninth year, upon termination, it could not be found that Family Dining would forfeit anything in which it has an interest.

Contrary to the analysis offered by Burger King, the Court considers the development rate a condition subsequent, not a promise, which operates to divest Family Dining of exclusivity. Where words in a contract raise no duty in and of themselves but rather modify or limit the promisees' right to enforce the promise such words are considered to be a condition. Whether words constitute a condition or a promise is a matter of the intention of the parties to be ascertained from a reasonable construction of the language used, considered in light of the surrounding circumstances. Feinberg v. Automobile Banking Corporation, 353 F. Supp. 508, 512 (E.D. Pa. 1973); Williston, Contracts, §§665, 666. It seems clear that the true purpose of the

Territorial Agreement was to create a longterm promise of exclusivity to act as an inducement to Family Dining to develop Bucks and Montgomery Counties within a certain time frame. A careful reading of the agreement indicates that it raises no duties, as such, in Family Dining. Both Article I and Article II contain language which refers to ninety years of exclusivity subject to limitation. For instance, Article I provides in part that "[t]his Agreement shall remain in effect and licensee shall retain the exclusive territory for a period of ninety (90) years from the date hereof, provided that at the end of one, two. . . ." Failure to comply with the development rate operates to defeat liability on Burger King's promise of exclusivity. Liability, or at least Family Dining's right to enforce the promise, arose upon entering the contract. The fact that Burger King seeks affirmative relief premised on the development rate and the fact that it calls for a specified performance by Family Dining tend to obscure its true nature. Nevertheless, in the Court's view it is a condition subsequent. 8 P.L.E. Contracts §264 (1971).

Furthermore, the fact that performance is to occur in installments does not necessarily mean that the contract is divisible. Once again, this is a question of the intention of the parties ascertained, if possible, from a reasonable interpretation of the language used. Continental Supermarket Food Service, Inc. v. Soboski, 210 Pa. Super. 304, 232 A.2d 216, 217 (1967). In view of the fact that there was a single promise of exclusivity to have a ninety year duration, assuming the condition subsequent did not occur by a failure to comply with the development rate, the Court believes, consistent with the views previously expressed herein, that the contract was intended to be entire rather than severable.

The question arises whether Burger King has precluded itself from asserting Family Dining's untimeliness on the basis that Burger King did not demand literal adherence to the development rate throughout most of the first ten years of the contract. Nothing is commoner in contracts than for a promisor to protect himself by making his promise conditional. Ordinarily a party would be entitled to have such an agreement strictly enforced, however, before doing so the Court must consider not only the written contract but also the acts and conduct of the parties in carrying out the agreement. As Judge Kraft, in effect, provided in Dempsey v. Stauffer, 182 F. Supp. 806, 810 (E.D. Pa. 1960), after one party by conduct indicates that literal performance will not be required, he cannot without notice and a reasonable time begin demanding literal performance.

In the early going Burger King did not demand that Family Dining perform in exact compliance with the development schedule. It failed to introduce any evidence indicating that a change in attitude had been communicated to Family Dining. At the time of the Donaldson letter Family Dining's non-compliance with the development rate was no worse than it was with respect to the fourth and fifth Restaurants. The letter itself was sent by a documents administrator rather than a Burger King official and it seems to imply that the Territorial Agreement would not be terminated. Assuming that at some point between May and November, or even at the time of the Donaldson letter, Ferris realized literal performance would be required, the circumstances of this type of development are such that Burger King was unreasonable in declaring a termination such a short time after, if not concurrent with, notice that literal performance would be required.

[margin note: was Not given reasonable time]

Considerable time was consumed in negotiations between November, 1973, until shortly before suit although it appears that these efforts were an exercise in futility given Burger King's view on exclusivity. Moreover, it could be expected that Burger King would have sued to enjoin any further progress by Family Dining, during this lengthy period, just as it did when Family Dining attempted to get the ninth Restaurant under way. The upshot being that the hiatus in development from November, 1973, until active construction began on the ninth and tenth Restaurants is not fully chargeable to Family Dining.

Based on the foregoing the Court concludes that Burger King is not entitled to have the condition protecting its promise strictly enforced.

[margin note: No strict enforcement]

Moreover and more important, even though a suit for declaratory relief can be characterized as neither legal nor equitable, United States Fidelity & Guaranty Co. v. Koch, 102 F.2d 288, 290 (3d Cir. 1939), giving strict effect to the termination provision involves divesting Family Dining of exclusivity, which, in the Court's view, would amount to a forfeiture. As a result the Court will not ignore considerations of fairness and believes that equitable principles, as well, ought to govern the outcome of this suit. Barraclough v. Atlantic Refining, 230 Pa. Super. 276, 326 A.2d 477 (1974).

[margin note: would result in forfeiture]

The Restatement, Contracts, §302 provides:

> A condition may be excused without other reason if its requirement
> (a) will involve extreme forfeiture or penalty, and
> (b) its existence or occurrence forms no essential part of the exchange for the promisor's performance.

[margin note: Rule]

Taking the latter consideration first, it seems clear that throughout the early duration of the contract Burger King was more concerned with a general development of the territory than it was with exact compliance with the terms of the development rate. Burger King offered no evidence that it ever considered literal performance to be critical. In fact, the evidence indicates quite the contrary. Even though McLamore testified that he never contemplated a delay of the duration which occurred with the ninth and tenth Restaurants, he felt a total delay of approximately 19 months with respect to the fourth and fifth Restaurants was nearly in compliance. On the basis of his prior conduct and his testimony considered in its entirety his comments on this point command little weight.

Clearly Burger King's attitude with respect to the development rate changed. Interestingly enough it was sometime after Burger King realized Bucks and Montgomery Counties could support substantially more than ten

Restaurants as had been originally thought. It was also at a time after Rose-wall replaced McLamore as chief executive officer.

Burger King maintains that Ferris' conduct indicates that he knew strict compliance with the development rate was required. This is based on the several occasions where Ferris expressed concern over non-compliance. However, during the presentation of Burger King's evidence it was established that Ferris was an individual who was overly meticulous with details which caused him to be, in many respects, ignored by Burger King officials. Given this aspect of his personality and Burger King's attitude toward him very little significance can be attached to Ferris' expressions of concern. In short, the evidence fails to establish that either Burger King or Family Dining considered the development rate critical. If it eventually did become critical it was not until very late in the first ten years and in such a way that, in conscience, it cannot be used to the detriment of Family Dining.

As previously indicated, the Court believes that if the right of exclusivity were to be extinguished by termination it would constitute a forfeiture. In arguing that by termination Family Dining will lose nothing that it earned, Burger King overlooks the risks assumed and the efforts expended by Family Dining, largely without assistance from Burger King, in making the venture successful in the exclusive territory. While it is true that Family Dining realized a return on its investment, certainly part of this return was the prospect of continued exclusivity. Moreover, this is not a situation where Burger King did not receive any benefit from the relationship.

In making the promise of exclusivity Burger King intended to induce Family Dining to develop its Restaurants in the exclusive territory. There is no evidence that the failure to fulfill the time feature of this inducement was the result of any intentional or negligent conduct on the part of Family Dining. And at the present time there are ten Restaurants in operation which was all the inducement was intended to elicit. Assuming all ten were built on time Burger King would have been able to expect some definable level of revenue, a percentage of which it lost due to the delay. Burger King did not, however, attempt to establish the amount of this loss at trial.

In any event if Family Dining were forced to forfeit the right of exclusivity it would lose something of incalculable value based on its investment of time and money developing the area, the significant risks assumed and the fact that there remains some 76 years of exclusivity under the Territorial Agreement. Such a loss would be without any commensurate breach on its part since the injury caused to Burger King by the delay is relatively modest and within definable limits. Thus, a termination of the Territorial Agreement would result in an extreme forfeiture to Family Dining.

In accordance with the foregoing the Court finds that under the law and based upon the facts adduced in Burger King's case, it is not entitled to a declaration that the Territorial Agreement is terminated. Therefore, Family Dining's Rule 41(b) motion for an involuntary dismissal is granted.

QUESTION

If Burger King had come to you, its attorney, when the corporate decision was made that the exclusive franchise arrangement with Family Dining was unwisely granted, what would you have advised your client to do about it?

NOTE ON THE DIFFERENT USES OF THE FORFEITURE CONCEPT

In the first part of this chapter, we saw that the concept of forfeiture is sometimes used to justify an interpretation of contract clauses as language of promise rather than of condition. If a court feels that the consequence of interpreting language as an express condition is an unfair loss of a bargained-for benefit for one party, the court will be more apt to find the parties intended only a promise.

Despite the possibility of forfeiture, the court may feel compelled to find the existence of a condition because the intent of the parties is clear. Or the court may feel it necessary to find a constructive condition so that there is some order to the performances of the parties. However, if the consequence of the failure of the conditioning event is a potential "disproportionate forfeiture," the court may find that the condition is excused. The Restatement (Second) accepts this approach:

§229.   Excuse of a Condition to Avoid Forfeiture

To the extent that the non-occurrence of a condition would cause disproportionate forfeiture, a court may excuse the non-occurrence of that condition unless its occurrence was a material part of the agreed exchange.

As you might expect, the line between these two uses of the forfeiture concept blurs in the real world as courts try to give effect to the parties' agreement and traditional contract doctrine while reaching a just result.

INMAN v. CLYDE HALL DRILLING CO.
Supreme Court of Alaska, 1962
369 P.2d 498

DIMOND, J. This case involves a claim for damages arising out of an employment contract. The main issue is whether a provision in the contract, making written notice of a claim a condition precedent to recovery, is contrary to public policy.

Inman worked for the Clyde Hall Drilling Company as a derrickman under a written contract of employment signed by both parties on November

16, 1959. His employment terminated on March 24, 1960. On April 5, 1960, he commenced this action against the Company claiming that the latter fired him without justification, that this amounted to a breach of contract, and that he was entitled to certain damages for the breach. In its answer the Company denied that it had breached the contract, and asserted that Inman had been paid in full the wages that were owing him and was entitled to no damages. Later the Company moved for summary judgment on the ground that Inman's failure to give written notice of his claim, as required by the contract, was a bar to his action based on the contract.[2]

The motion was granted, and judgment was entered in favor of the Company. This appeal followed.

A fulfillment of the thirty-day notice requirement is expressly made a "condition precedent to any recovery." Inman argues that this provision is void as against public policy. In considering this first question we start with the basic tenet that competent parties are free to make contracts and that they should be bound by their agreements. In the absence of a constitutional provision or statute which makes certain contracts illegal or unenforceable, we believe it is the function of the judiciary to allow men to manage their own affairs in their own way. As a matter of judicial policy the court should maintain and enforce contracts, rather than enable parties to escape from the obligations they have chosen to incur.

We recognize that "freedom of contract" is a qualified and not an absolute right, and cannot be applied on a strict, doctrinal basis. An established principle is that a court will not permit itself to be used as an instrument of inequity and injustice. As Justice Frankfurter stated in his dissenting opinion in United States v. Bethlehem Steel Corp., "The fundamental principle of law that the courts will not enforce a bargain where one party has unconscionably taken advantage of the necessities and distress of the other has found expression in an almost infinite variety of cases." In determining whether certain contractual provisions should be enforced, the court must look realistically at the relative bargaining positions of the parties in the framework of contemporary business practices and commercial life. If we find those positions are such that one party has unscrupulously taken

---

2. The portion of the contract with which we are concerned reads:

You agree that you will, within thirty (30) days after any claim (other than a claim for compensation insurance) that arises out of or in connection with the employment provided for herein, give written notice to the Company for such claim, setting forth in detail the facts relating thereto and the basis for such claim; and that you will not institute any suit or action against the Company in any court or tribunal in any jurisdiction based on any such claim prior to six (6) months after the filing of the written notice of claim hereinabove provided for, or later than one (1) year after such filing. Any action or suit on any such claim shall not include any item or matter not specifically mentioned in the proof of claim above provided. It is agreed that in any such action or suit, proof by you of your compliance with the provisions of this paragraph shall be a condition precedent to any recovery.

advantage of the economic necessities of the other, then in the interest of justice — as a matter of public policy — we would refuse to enforce the transaction. But the grounds for judicial interference must be clear. Whether the court should refuse to recognize and uphold that which the parties have agreed upon is a question of fact upon which evidence is required.

The facts in this case do not persuade us that the contractual provision in question is unfair or unreasonable. Its purpose is not disclosed. The requirement that written notice be given within thirty days after a claim arises may have been designed to preclude stale claims, and the further requirement that no action be commenced within six months thereafter may have been intended to afford the Company timely opportunity to rectify the basis for a just claim. But whatever the objective was, we cannot find in the contract anything to suggest it was designed from an unfair motive to bilk employees out of wages or other compensation justly due them.

There was nothing to suggest that Inman did not have the knowledge, capacity or opportunity to read the agreement and understand it; that the terms of the contract were imposed upon him without any real freedom of choice on his part; that there was any substantial inequality in bargaining positions between Inman and the Company. Not only did he attach a copy of the contract to his complaint, which negatives any thought that he really wasn't aware of its provisions, but he also admitted in a deposition that at the time he signed the contract he had read it, had discussed it with a Company representative, and was familiar with its terms. And he showed specific knowledge of the thirty-day notice requirement when, in response to a question as to whether written notice had been given prior to filing suit, he testified:

> A. Well now, I filed — I started my claim within 30 days, didn't I, from the time I hit here. I thought that would be a notice that I started suing them when I first came to town.
> Q. You thought that the filing of the suit would be the notice?
> A. That is right.

Under these circumstances we do not find that such a limitation on Inman's right of action is offensive to justice. We would not be justified in refusing to enforce the contract and thus permit one of the parties to escape his obligations. It is conceivable, of course, that a thirty-day notice of claim requirement could be used to the disadvantage of a workman by an unscrupulous employer. If this danger is great, the legislature may act to make such a provision unenforceable.[11] But we may not speculate on what in the future may be a matter of public policy in this state. It is our function to act only

11. In Oklahoma the constitution (art. XXIII, §9) provides: "Any provision of any contract or agreement, express or implied, stipulating for notice or demand other than such as may be provided by law, as a condition precedent to establish any claim, demand, or liability, shall be null and void." See Brakebill v. Chicago, R.I.&P. Ry., 37 Okl. 140, 131 P. 540 (1913).

where an existent public policy is clearly revealed from the facts and we find that it has been violated. That is not the case here.

Inman's claim arose on March 24, 1960. His complaint was served on the Company on April 14. He argues that since the complaint set forth in detail the basis of his claim and was served within thirty days, he had substantially complied with the contractual requirement.

Service of the complaint probably gave the Company actual knowledge of the claim. But that does not serve as an excuse for not giving the kind of written notice called for by the contract. Inman agreed that no suit would be instituted "prior to six (6) months *after the filing of the written notice of claim.*" (Emphasis ours.) If this means what it says (and we have no reason to believe it does not), it is clear that the commencement of an action and service of the complaint was not an effective substitute for the kind of notice called for by the agreement. To hold otherwise would be to simply ignore an explicit provision of the contract and say that it had no meaning. We are not justified in doing that.

The contract provides that compliance with its requirement as to giving written notice of a claim prior to bringing suit "shall be a condition precedent to any recovery." Inman argues that this is not a true condition precedent—merely being labelled as such by the Company—and that non-compliance with the requirement was an affirmative defense which the Company was required to set forth in its answer under Civ. R. 8(c). He contends that because the answer was silent on this point, the defense was waived under Civ. R. 12(h).

The failure to give advance notice of a claim where notice is required would ordinarily be a defense to be set forth in the answer. But here the parties agreed that such notice should be a condition precedent to any recovery. This meant that the Company was not required to plead lack of notice as an affirmative defense, but instead, that Inman was required to plead performance of the condition or that performance had been waived or excused. The Company may not be charged under Civ. R. 12(h) with having waived a defense which it was not obliged to present in its answer.

Relying upon the doctrine of anticipatory breach of contract, Inman argues that when the Company discharged him it repudiated the employment agreement, and he was then excused from any further performance, including performance of the condition precedent of giving written notice of his claim.

What the Company allegedly did was not an anticipatory breach of contract in the strict sense of the term. Such a breach would have been committed only if the Company had repudiated its contractual duty before the time fixed for its performance had arrived. That was not the case here. Both parties had commenced performance on November 16, 1959, and they continued to perform until March 24, 1960. We believe Inman's real claim is that there was a breach of an existing duty accompanied by words or acts disclosing the Company's intention to refuse performance in the future, and that this conferred upon him the privilege to deal with the contract as if broken altogether.

But even assuming that there had been a breach which excused Inman from further performance of his contractual obligation to work for the Company for the full term of the contract, it does not follow that he was also excused from performing the condition precedent to commencement of this action for damages. He did not allege, nor does the record indicate, that his failure to give notice was caused by the Company's fault. There is no showing nor any inference that the Company, by words or conduct, induced Inman not to give the required notice, or led him to believe that giving notice would be a futile gesture. In fact, he admitted in his deposition that his reason for not complying with the condition was because he thought the filing of the suit would constitute the required notice.

Inman's last point is that the trial court erred in entering a final judgment. He argues that the failure to give written notice was merely a matter in abatement of his action until the condition could be performed, and that the most the court ought to have done was to dismiss the action without prejudice.

This argument is unsound. At the time judgment was entered Inman could no longer perform the condition precedent to recovery by giving written notice of his claim within thirty days after the claim arose, because this time limitation had expired. In these circumstances his right to seek redress from the court was barred and not merely abated. Final judgment in the Company's favor was proper.

The judgment is affirmed.

NOTE

This has been a much-discussed case. Robert Childress in Conditions in the Law of Contracts, 45 N.Y.U. L. Rev. 33, 34-35 (1970), took a dim view of *Inman* and the use of condition theory to avoid nonperformance.

> [T]he law of contracts has been forced by pressure for just decisions to develop numerous doctrines to nullify what is said to be the law of conditions. Waiver, estoppel, substantial performance and abhorrence of forfeitures are among the doctrines which have allowed the law of conditions to survive by making it inoperative. Since most cases end well, it would be a simple matter to conclude that all is well with the law of contract conditions. But the failure to articulate the real ground of decision misleads the profession and thereby promotes uncertainty and litigation. Some might still argue that the traditional law of conditions is a stabilizing influence in the law of contracts. A look at the present function of the doctrine will show why this is not so. Its sole function today is to allow a disputant to make a fact or event operative beyond the scope of its demonstrated materiality in the circumstances. As in *Inman*, courts still occasionally claim to allow an irrelevancy to be decisive in litigation. This tempts people to try to escape contract duties by asserting irrelevancies. They rarely succeed, but the attempts make the traditional law of conditions quite the opposite of a stabilizing influence. . . .

Because of its function, the law of conditions claims to bar analysis based upon good faith contract performance. In fact, it only drives such analysis underground where it is conducted under the mysterious shrouds of waiver, estoppel and the other various repealers of the law of conditions. The operation of these repealers is not mysterious and obscure by accident. Obscurity is necessary to the survival of rules about the law of conditions. It continues to be said to exist, but it is allowed to be decisive only in cases whose decisions would go unchanged if there were no law of conditions.

C. Waiver and Estoppel

PHH MORTGAGE CORP. v. RAMSEY
Ohio Court of Appeals, 2014
17 N.E.3d 629

BROWN, J.

[¶1] PHH Mortgage Corporation (individually "PHH") fka Cendant Mortgage Corporation dba Coldwell Banker Mortgage (individually "Coldwell Banker"), plaintiff-appellant, appeals judgments of the Franklin County Court of Common Pleas, in which the court granted judgment in favor of Andrew Ramsey ("appellee") and Precision Real Estate Group, LLC ("Precision"), defendants-appellees (referred to singularly as "appellee").

[¶2] In 2003, appellee purchased real estate for use as a rental property. He executed a promissory note payable to Coldwell Banker and used the funds to finance the real estate purchase. The note was secured by a mortgage in favor of Coldwell Banker. After the closing, appellee deeded the property to Precision. PHH subsequently became the holder of the note and mortgage.

[¶3] Appellee made timely monthly payments until August 2009, at which time he attempted to pay his monthly mortgage through a "pay now" link on PHH's website, referred to as "Speedpay," as he had been doing for six years. However, when he attempted to do so on August 3, 2009, he received an error message informing him that his payment could not be processed. He tried again on August 6 and 10 but received the same error message. On August 13, 2009, appellee tried to pay online again via Speedpay, and this attempt appeared successful, but he did not receive a confirmation number. Appellee telephoned the Coldwell Banker help line and was told this his payment would be "pushed" through the system, and he was given a confirmation number for his August 2009 payment.

[¶4] On August 16, 2009, PHH sent a notice to appellee informing him that his payment was late. Appellee again telephoned the help line and was told that the website was having problems but his payment would be processed.

[¶5] On September 3, 2009, appellee went to PHH's website to make his September payment, and he realized that his August 2009 payment had still not been credited. He attempted to make an online payment via Speedpay and received an error message.

[¶6] Appellee telephoned Coldwell Banker and explained the circumstances. The representative told him that his payment would be processed, but the late payment would be reported to credit bureaus, and there was no one else who could help him. Appellee insisted on speaking to another customer service representative who had the authority to help him, but the help line representative refused and hung up the phone.

[¶7] On September 8, 2009, PHH issued appellee a notice of intent to foreclose.

Foreclosure Notice

[¶8] On September 9, 2009, appellee traveled to Coldwell Banker's physical office to make payments but he was told by representatives that the office did not accept payments. Appellee contacted the real estate agent who sold him the house and the agent gave him the name of a Coldwell Banker representative. Appellee spoke to the representative but the representative never contacted him again as to a solution.

[¶9] On September 10, 2009, appellee mailed a payment for August and September 2009 to Coldwell Banker, with an explanation of the circumstances, but the payment was never processed or returned to him.

[¶10] On October 5, 2009, appellee mailed to Coldwell Banker a payment for October and November 2009, along with an explanation of the circumstances, but the payment was never processed or returned. Appellee made no attempt at payments after December 2009.

[¶11] During the time PHH was attempting to foreclose on the property, appellee had a renter leasing the property. On numerous occasions, PHH's representatives attempted to "winterize" the home and change the door locks, ultimately resulting in appellee's inability to continue renting the premises to a tenant.

Had renter lease on property

[¶12] On November 10, 2009, PHH filed a complaint in foreclosure against appellee, as well as several others. PHH later added Precision as a defendant. On April 27, 2011, PHH filed a motion for summary judgment, which the trial court granted. Appellee appealed, and we reversed the trial court's decision in PHH Mtge. Corp. v. Ramsey, 10th Dist. No. 11AP-559, 2012-Ohio-672, 2012 WL 566777 ("*Ramsey I*"), finding there existed genuine issues of material fact regarding whether appellee defaulted in his payment of the note.

SJ was granted for PHH reversed

[¶13] On remand, the matter was heard before a magistrate pursuant to a bench trial. On July 17, 2013, the magistrate filed a decision, in which the magistrate denied PHH foreclosure and awarded appellee judgment for $1,550. PHH filed objections to the magistrate's decision. On October 2, 2013, the trial court overruled the objections. On January 17, 2014, the trial court issued a nunc pro tunc judgment related to the October 2, 2013 judgment. PHH appeals the judgments of the trial court, asserting the following assignments of error:

    I. The trial court erred by denying PHH Mortgage a judgment on its note against Mr. Ramsey.

    II. The trial court erred by not granting foreclosure of the mortgage.

    III. The trial court erred by not addressing the reformation of mortgage in its decision. . . .

    [¶16] In its decision in the present case, the trial court adopted the magistrate's decision and overruled PHH's objections. The magistrate found that appellee did not default on the terms of the note and mortgage. The magistrate determined that, despite PHH's claim that appellee did not have the contractual right to make his payments electronically; PHH waived the terms of the contract by accepting electronic payments from appellee for six years without objection. The magistrate concluded that the August 2009 payment was properly made. The magistrate observed that the contract contemplated, via the provision for late fees, that payment would occasionally be technically late but still within the proper performance obligations of appellee, and PHH waived strict performance of the term relating to the contractual due date by accepting appellee's payments after the deadline on many occasions. The magistrate also found the anti-waiver provisions in the note and mortgage were inoperative under the present facts. With regard to the anti-waiver provision in the note, the magistrate found the provision was only operative if there was a default, and there was no default here. With regard to the anti-waiver provision in the mortgage agreement, the magistrate found that the provision was only operative when the lender accepted partial or insufficient payment, which was not the situation in the present action.

    [¶17] PHH argues herein that appellee tendered neither the August 1, 2009 payment nor sufficient payments thereafter and, thus, was in default. PHH asserts that appellee could not rely upon his attempts to pay via Speedpay because that system was controlled by Western Union and not PHH and, as such, did not constitute payments "tendered" to PHH. PHH contends that appellee needed to show not simply that he sent a payment through Speedpay, but that PHH had knowledge and receipt of the payment, which it did not. Therefore, PHH argues, appellee was in breach of the agreement when he failed to tender his August 1, 2009 payment, and when he later tried to tender his August, September, October, and November payments without the late charges and other expenses required under the agreement; he was in continued breach of the agreement.

    [¶18] After a review of the record and testimony in this case, we agree with the magistrate's findings. Under Section 1 of the note, appellee promised to "pay" the lender the mortgage amount, plus interest, in the form of "cash, check or money order." Under Section 3 of the note, appellee agreed to "pay" the lender by making a payment on the first day of each month. Also under Section 3, appellee agreed to make payment at an address specified in the note, "or at a different place if required by the Note Holder." Section 6 of the note provided, in pertinent part, that if PHH did not "receive" the full amount of the monthly payment by the end of 15 calendar days after the date it was due, appellee would pay a late charge to PHH. Section 6 further provided that if appellee did not "pay" the full amount of each monthly payment on the date it was due, appellee would be in default.

[¶19] This court explained the rule of waiver as it applies to contracts in EAC Properties, L.L.C. v. Brightwell, 10th Dist. No. 10AP-853, 2011-Ohio-2373, 2011 WL 1944101, ¶21-23:

"Rule of waiver" *(handwritten margin note)*

> As applied to contracts, waiver is a voluntary relinquishment of a known right. State ex rel. Wallace v. State Med. Bd. of Ohio, 89 Ohio St. 3d 431, 435, 732 N.E.2d 960, 2000-Ohio-213. "Waiver assumes one has an opportunity to choose between either relinquishing or enforcing of the right." Chubb v. Ohio Bur. of Workers' Comp.[,] 81 Ohio St. 3d 275, 279, 690 N.E.2d 1267, 1998-Ohio-628. A party who has a duty to perform and who changes its position as a result of the waiver may enforce the waiver. *Id.* at 279 . . . . The party asserting waiver must prove the waiving party's clear, unequivocal, decisive act. Automated Solutions Corp. v. Paragon Data Sys., Inc., 167 Ohio App. 3d 685, 856 N.E.2d 1008, 2006-Ohio-3492, ¶28.
>
> *express or implied (handwritten margin note)*
>
> "[W]aiver of a contract provision may be express or implied." Lewis & Michael Moving & Storage, Inc. v. Stofcheck Ambulance Serv., Inc., 10th Dist. No. 05AP[-]662, 2006-Ohio-3810 [2006 WL 2056636], ¶29 . . . . "'[W]aiver by *Rule (handwritten margin note)* estoppel' exists when the acts and conduct of a party are inconsistent with an intent to claim a right, and have been such as to mislead the other party to his prejudice and thereby estop the party having the right from insisting upon it." (Emphasis omitted.) *Id.* . . . . "Waiver by estoppel allows a party's inconsistent conduct, rather than a party's intent, to establish a waiver of rights." *Id.* . . . .
>
> Whether a party's inconsistent conduct amounts to waiver involves a fac- *Question of fact (handwritten margin note)* tual determination within the province of the trier of fact. *Id.* at ¶30 . . . . Review of a trial court's factual determinations involves some degree of deference, and we will not disturb a trial court's findings of fact where the record contains competent, credible evidence to support such findings. Wiltberger v. Davis (1996), 110 Ohio App. 3d 46, 52, 673 N.E.2d 628.

[¶20] In the present case, PHH argues that appellee neither "tendered" nor made a "payment" of the mortgage, relying upon various passages from Jenkins v. Mapes, 53 Ohio St. 110, 41 N.E. 137 (1895). PHH contends there was no payment here, citing *Jenkins,* because "[p]ayment is consummated by an acceptance of the thing tendered, and is incomplete until then." *Id.* at 115, 41 N.E. 137. PHH also asserts, citing *Jenkins,* that there was no tender here because, "there can be no tender of a thing unless the person to whom the tender is made has, by himself or agent, knowledge of it." *Id.* at 117, 41 N.E. 137. Relying upon these provisions in *Jenkins,* PHH claims that appellee could not simply show he sent a payment through Speedpay, but he needed to show that PHH had knowledge of the payment. PHH concludes that it did not have knowledge of a payment or accept or receive the payment because Speedpay is owned and controlled by Western Union.

[¶21] At trial, PHH presented the testimony of one witness, Ron Casperite, complex liaison for PHH, who testified that Speedpay is maintained by Western Union. However, he admitted he was not familiar how a PHH customer accesses the Speedpay website to make a mortgage payment.

[¶22] Appellee testified at the hearing that he had always paid his mortgage online. He described the payment process, as it related to the website of PHH's predecessor, Coldwell Banker:

> You log into their [Coldwell Banker's] website and you — there's a pay now button, and you basically click on that, you put in the money that you're going to pay, plus additional principal, and it redirected you to another site seamlessly and just processed your payment, and at the end it gave you a confirmation number.

(Tr. 26.)

[¶23] Appellee then answered questions about the circumstances surrounding his attempted payment of the mortgage on August 3, 2009:

> Q.   All right. Andrew, you just testified you're current through July of 2009. What happened starting with your payment toward the mortgage and note in August 2009?
> A.   I tried to make the payment online like I normally would and the website was erroring out and wouldn't let you submit your payment. So I waited — it's actually — it happened before in the past, and normally it would just, you know, if you try the next day or so, or three days it would work. So that's exactly what I did.

(Tr. 27.)

[¶24] Appellee said he "waited a few days like I normally did, because, like I said, this was a routine occurrence, it just happens, so I waited three days and I tried again, and I received the same message." (Tr. 28.) He received this second error message on August 6, 2009. Appellee testified that he again tried to pay his mortgage through the website of PHH's predecessor, Coldwell Banker, on August 10, 2009, but he received another error message.

[¶25] Appellee testified that he then called the help line for Coldwell Banker to discuss the issue:

> Q.   And what was discussed?
> A.   Well, basically, I, you know, hey, I can't make the payments, you know, can I make this payment or whatever? And they told me that the payments would go through, you know, that there was, you know, a system problem that they were having.

Q. Okay. And were you told to do anything else or not to worry about it at that time, or what?

A. Yeah. Well, I was told to try to go — try to make another payment.

Q. Okay. And did you?

A. Yeah, I did actually try to make another payment, yeah.

(Tr. 30-31.)

[¶26] Appellee further testified that, on August 16, 2009, he received a notification from Coldwell Banker that the August 2009 payment was late. In response to the late notification, he again called the help line for Coldwell Banker. A customer service representative told him that his payment would be processed and gave him a confirmation number. As of that time, appellee believed he had made his August 2009 mortgage payment.

p believed he made Aug payment

[¶27] Appellee testified that, on September 3, 2009, he went on the Coldwell Banker website to make his September 2009 payment but received another error message. At that time, he realized that his August 2009 payment had never been credited. Appellee called the help line for Coldwell Banker to ask about the uncredited August 2009 payment and his credit score being affected, but the customer service representative told him there was nothing she could do about it and hung up the phone.

[¶28] Appellee testified that he then went to a physical location for Coldwell Banker, but employees there told him that they do not process payments or deal with these types of issues at that location.

went to physical location

[¶29] Appellee then testified that, on September 10, 2009, he mailed a check to Coldwell Banker for nearly four times the mortgage amounts for August and September 2009, along with a letter explaining the situation. These payments were not processed and not returned.

Mailed payment

[¶30] Appellee testified that, on October 5, 2009, he sent another letter and check for nearly four times the amount of mortgage payments due for October and November 2009 to the Coldwell Banker address listed for mailing mortgage payments, but the check was never cashed or returned. Appellee testified that, at all relevant times, he had sufficient funds in his bank account to cover his mortgage payments, his attempted online payments, and the checks he wrote.

[¶31] Appellee also related a story during his testimony about how he contacted his former realtor, who had originally worked for Coldwell Banker and who had helped him with a similar issue a few months after the mortgage commenced. His former realtor again connected him with the same contact person at Coldwell Banker who had resolved his prior problem, but the person, "Sherrie," never called him back after she said she would look into the matter.

[¶32] Initially, the testimony of PHH's sole witness, Casperite, was brief and minimally helpful to the pertinent matters. The main issue revolved around appellee's attempted use of Speedpay online, a subject about which Casperite admitted he knew little. What Casperite did know about

Speedpay was that it was owned by Western Union, which PHH attempts to use as support for its argument that appellee never actually "tendered" or made "payment" to PHH itself. However, this argument misses the point.

[¶33] PHH fails to directly address the basis relied upon by the trial court to find that no default occurred here; that is, that PHH waived any claim that appellee did not have the contractual right to make his payments electronically by accepting electronic payments from appellee for six years without objection, and PHH waived strict performance of the due date term by accepting appellee's payments after the due date on many prior occasions. Initially, a promissory note is a contract, and rules of contract interpretation apply to the interpretation of promissory notes. [Citations omitted.] It is well-established that every contract has an implied covenant of good faith and fair dealing that requires not only honesty but also reasonableness in the enforcement of the contract. Littlejohn v. Parrish, 163 Ohio App. 3d 456, 2005-Ohio-4850, 839 N.E.2d 49, ¶21 (1st Dist.). "'Good faith performance or enforcement of a contract emphasizes faithfulness to an agreed common purpose and consistency with the justified expectations of the other party.'" Id. at ¶26, quoting Restatement of the Law 2d, Contracts, Section 205, Comment a (1981). Bad faith may consist of inaction, or may be the "'abuse of a power to specify terms, [or] interference with or failure to cooperate in the other party's performance.'" Id., quoting Restatement of the Law 2d, Contracts, Section 205, Comment d (1981). "'Good faith' is a compact reference to an implied undertaking not to take opportunistic advantage in a way that could have not been contemplated at the time of drafting, and which therefore was not resolved explicitly by the parties." Ed Schory & Sons, Inc. v. Soc. Natl. Bank, 75 Ohio St. 3d 433, 443-44, 662 N.E.2d 1074 (1996), quoting Kham & Nate's Shoes No. 2, Inc. v. First Bank of Whiting, 908 F.2d 1351, 1357 (7th Cir. 1990). Relatedly, "[w]here the obligations arising under a contract have attached, and subsequent thereto one party without the consent of the other does some act or makes some new arrangement which prevents the carrying out of the contract according to its terms, he cannot avail himself of this conduct to avoid his liability to the other party." Suter v. Farmers' Fertilizer Co., 100 Ohio St. 403, 126 N.E. 304 (1919), paragraph four of the syllabus.

[¶34] In the present case, PHH was not reasonable in its enforcement of the promissory note. Despite PHH's attempt to portray the Speedpay website as an unrelated entity for which it could bear no responsibility, PHH, through its predecessor, explicitly agreed to permit its mortgage customers to pay their mortgages using the service. By permitting and, in fact, encouraging, its customers to pay their mortgages online by providing a Speedpay link on the predecessor's own website, PHH gave its customers a justified expectation that the Speedpay system would work properly. Here, it obviously did not work as intended and expected, and PHH, through its predecessor, explicitly assured appellee that his payment would be credited through the Speedpay system. PHH's actions here demonstrate a genuine failure to cooperate with appellee to make sure his mortgage payment would be properly credited. It is difficult to imagine anything more that appellee could have done, given the circumstances and past dealings between the parties as to how payments were handled and credited.

[¶35] Furthermore, although it is beyond dispute that the actual promissory note did not contain an explicit provision for payments via the internet, it did indicate that the borrower could make a payment "at a different place if required by the Note Holder." Likewise, although it could be disputed whether an online payment via Speedpay technically met the requirement of Section 1 of the note that payment be made in "cash, check or money order," for PHH to rely upon this provision, while at the same time encouraging borrowers to pay their mortgages through a link on their own website, violates the covenant of good faith by taking "opportunistic advantage in a way that could have not been contemplated at the time of drafting." *Ed Schory & Sons, Inc.*, at 444, 662 N.E.2d 1074. By unilaterally offering Speedpay as a service to appellee, PHH offered appellee a new arrangement to make payments that prevented appellee from explicitly carrying out the terms of the contract in this instance, and PHH cannot now claim that appellee should have never relied on Speedpay.

[¶36] On these bases, we agree with the trial court that PHH waived any argument that appellee did not have the contractual right to make his payments electronically because it accepted electronic payments from appellee for six years without objection. Even if the contract did not explicitly permit electronic payments, PHH accepted Speedpay as a form of payment from appellee from the commencement of the loan and never disputed that this was a valid form of payment.

[¶37] Furthermore, we agree that PHH waived strict performance of the due date term because it accepted appellee's payments after the due date on many prior occasions. Appellee testified that he had before received the same error when attempting an online payment through Speedpay, but would, in the past, always be able to make the payment when he tried a day or two later. There was no evidence that PHH ever objected to his payments on these terms or considered appellee in default or sought foreclosure. Appellee justifiably relied upon PHH's past actions to believe his past payments were not in default or grounds for foreclosure. As the trial court explained, given PHH's past inactions and the late-fee provision in the contract, appellee demonstrated that PHH contemplated that late payments would still properly fulfill appellee's obligations under the contract.

[¶38] As for the anti-waiver provisions contained in the mortgage and note, PHH does not contest the trial court's conclusions on this issue in its appellate brief. Notwithstanding, we agree with the trial court that the anti-waiver provisions in the note and mortgage were not operative here because appellee was not in default, and PHH never accepted partial or insufficient payment, which were the respective requisites for the application of the anti-waiver provisions in the note and mortgage. For all of the foregoing reasons, we find the trial court did not err when it denied PHH judgment on its note against appellee. Therefore, PHH's first assignment of error is overruled. . . .

Judgments affirmed.

Affirmed

NOTES

1. Speaking to the issue in the last case, Professor Grant Gilmore, one of the drafters of the Uniform Commercial Code once said, "[C]ourts pay little attention to clauses which appear to say that meaningful acts are meaningless and that the secured party can blow hot or cold as he chooses." G. Gilmore, *Security Interests in Personal Property* §44.1, at 1214 (1965). Thus anti-waiver clauses themselves can be waived and can be reinstated only on notice to that effect; accord, Moe v. John Deere Co., 516 N.W.2d 332 (S.D. 1994).

2. Courts rarely distinguish between estoppel and waiver. In fact either doctrine is arguably applicable under the facts of the instant case: Debtor was attempting to demonstrate its rights under the contract (to retain the collateral) still existed because of the creditor's actions in ignoring missed payment and not treating the obligation in default. Debtor was arguing that creditor should not be able to proceed because it would be unfair to allow the creditor to proceed without notice because debtor relied upon creditor's ignoring the late payments: estoppel. Such action may also show waiver: the intentional relinquishment of a known right. However, when a party attempts to establish contractual rights counter to those in the express agreement that provide the basis for affirmative relief, courts will typically refuse the use of estoppel doctrine. See, e.g., Bennett v. Farmers Ins. Co., 150 Or. App. 63, 945 P.2d 595 (1997). On the related issue of the implied covenant of good faith see the note on good faith earlier in this chapter.

3. *Installment payment obligations.* Under traditional contract doctrine, if a debtor fails to pay an installment payment, the creditor is entitled to sue only for the missed installment even though the missed payment might represent a repudiation of the entire obligation. This presents a dilemma for the creditor who must wait as each installment becomes past due before suing. Instead, the creditor can include in the agreement an *acceleration clause*—a clause allowing the creditor to treat the entire obligation as due, once a payment has been missed.

Problem 156

Mr. and Mrs. America bought a $28,000 automobile from Swank Motors, promising to make installment payments on the first of each month. The contract provided that "time is of the essence," and the failure to make payments as agreed was a ground for declaring a default and repossessing. Nonetheless, they were frequently late on the payments, some months as much as ten days late. After seven months of late payments, Swank had had enough, and without warning it repossessed the car. The Americas sued for conversion and breach of contract. Who should win the lawsuit? See UCC §2-208.

(a) Would it affect your answer if each month Swank had vigorously protested the late payment, and threatened repossession if it happened again?

(b) Would it affect your answer if the contract contained a clause saying that the "acceptance of late payments shall not be construed as a waiver of the right to declare a default because payments are not made as agreed; in spite of the acceptance of such late payments, time remains of the essence"?

(c) Swank Motors calls you, its attorney, with this question. It knows that its acceptance of the late payments has probably resulted in a waiver of the ability to repossess, but it has grown weary of the sloppy payment practices of the Americas. Is it possible to reinstate the "time is of the essence" clause? What procedure would you advise? See UCC §2-209(5).

Problem 157

Wong Construction Company signed a contract to build an auditorium for the City of Thebes, Utah. The agreement had a clause that required all changes to the duties of the contractor to be in writing. Nonetheless, as construction proceeded the city official in charge of the project constantly demanded additions, and when Wong's manager asked for these changes to be put in writing, she was told "Don't worry about it." When the time came for payment, the city was unwilling to pay for modifications unsupported by written change orders. Will this argument succeed?

In addressing this common fact pattern, Justice Michael Musmano of the Pennsylvania Supreme Court in Wagner v. Graziano Const. Co., 390 Pa. 445, 136 A.2d 82 (1957), famously said:

> The most ironclad written contract can always be cut into by the acetylene torch of parol modification supported by adequate proof. . . .
>
> Even where the contract specifically states that no non-written modification will be recognized, the parties may yet alter their agreement by parol negotiation. The hand that pens a writing may not gag the mouths of the assenting parties. The pen may be more precise in permanently recording what is to be done, but it may not still the tongues which bespeak an improvement in or modification of what has been written.

D. Election

Waived ~> Waived express Compliance

Waived Compliance by company had an "election" to waive the Notice requirement

Problem 158

Mr. and Mrs. America took out insurance policies with NoRisk Insurance Company on each of their lives. The policies provided that notice of death had to be given in writing within ten days of occurrence or the insurance company had no liability. Mr. America suffered a heart attack while jogging and died. The next afternoon, Mrs. America phoned the NoRisk office and informed the company of his death. The person who took the call expressed sympathy. Two weeks later a claims adjuster from the company called on Mrs. America and had her fill out the appropriate forms. He discussed with Mrs. America the possibility of settling the claim for one-half its face value "because of some concern about the insurance application." Two days after that she received a letter from the company stating that its review of the file revealed that she had never given a written notice of her husband's death as required by the policy, so it was denying liability. Distraught, Mrs. America phones you, her attorney. What is your theory? Can she prove reliance here? Does it matter?

E. Impossibility

As with the contract as a whole, impossibility of performance can excuse the performance of conditions in the contract. If this occurs, the courts must adjust the resulting contractual liabilities. If a condition's occurrence becomes impossible, is the contract at an end? In resolving this issue, courts look to the same risk allocation factors we explored in the section on impossibility.

Impossibility ~> Affirmative defense to damages by Act of God

Problem 159

Opera singer Beverly Pipes was engaged to sing the role of Michelle in a new opera entitled *Obama*. The opera went into rehearsal in May, with a scheduled opening date of September 1. During the first week of August, Ms. Pipes fell ill with pneumonia and missed all subsequent rehearsals. The producer of the opera engaged another soprano to take over the role, and the show opened as scheduled. It was a tremendous sensation. At the end of the first week of performances, Beverly Pipes showed up at the opera house, ready to sing. She said that she felt fine and that her voice was never better.

She knew the role and wanted it back. The producer refused and a lawsuit followed. Is Ms. Pipes in breach for failing to rehearse? Is the manager in breach for failing to give her the part back? This Problem is based on the well-known case of Poussard v. Spiers & Pond, 1 Q.B.D. 410 (1876).

Problem 160

Luciano Uvula, world-renowned tenor, was engaged by the Chicago Opera Association to sing a series of roles in famous operas, all of which were already in his extensive repertoire. He agreed to come to Chicago on May 1 and begin rehearsals with the company, but he came down with a cold and didn't show up in Chicago until May 15, at which time he announced he was ready to rehearse. The opera season was scheduled to start July 1 and extend through April of the next year. The management refused to let Uvula rehearse, saying that missing the beginning of rehearsals was too serious. He sued. How should this come out? The case is Bettini v. Gye, 1 Q.B.D. 183 (1876).

F. A Short Drafting Exercise

Problem 161

The City of Fargo, North Dakota, was delighted to receive the award of the Winter Olympics for the year 2030. You are the city attorney, and the city officials have asked you to draft a contract with Sports Facilities, Inc., a construction firm that the city has hired to build a bobsled run. The bobsled run *must* be completed by October 1, 2029, in time for the pre-Olympics trials, or the city will be ruined. The city officials tell you that they do not want to have to pay a cent if the bobsled run is not completed by that date. Which of the following clauses would you use?

(a) "Sports Facilities, Inc., hereby promises to complete the bobsled run by October 1, 2029."

(b) "Unless the bobsled run is completed by October 1, 2029, the City shall not be liable for any amount."

(c) "Sports Facilities, Inc., hereby promises to complete the bobsled run by October 1, 2029, and unless it does so the City shall not be liable for any amount."

Draft your own clause or clauses to make sure the city gets what it wants and be prepared to read it aloud in class.

CHAPTER 7 ASSESSMENT

Multiple Choice Questions

1. When the longtime host of Laugh Central, a popular quasi-news late night show, retired after many years, the network hired a new host, Alex Pretoria, to take over starting on December 1, seven months away. The network also asked renowned artist Venus Flowers to design and paint the new set, agreeing to pay her $50,000 provided she could finish it at least one week before the opening. She promptly went to work creating her design, and ran the preliminary sketches by the network's agents, who were thrilled with them. The designs all incorporated images of Alex Pretoria in various comic situations. On the first day of November Pretoria suddenly died in a car accident, and Laugh Central decided to delay indefinitely any new opening. When Flowers submitted her bill for $50,000, the network declined to pay her anything, on the theory that Pretoria's death was an event that excused it from liability to her. She promptly filed a lawsuit. How should it come out?

    a. The network should win. The contract has become impossible to perform because the continued existence of Pretoria was a constructive condition precedent to the promise of the network to pay Flowers. The fact that she made her designs all about Pretoria shows that she too understood that his continued existence was a condition to the payment of any money to her.

    b. Flowers should win. The continued existence of Pretoria was a risk the network took as part of running a television show. Anytime a major player dies, which, alas, can happen, the network has to work around that. Since the risk was on the network, the contract with Flowers was in no way intended by either party to depend on something that industry custom places on the producer of a television show.

    c. Flowers should only prevail for the amount she is out of pocket. If she is paid the full amount, she would reap a windfall because she saved some expenses by not having to complete her designs and paint them on the set. All she should recover is what she has spent to date.

    d. Flowers should get the full contract price minus whatever expenses she did save by not having to complete the contract. Since the risk was on the network, Flowers should be made whole, which includes the profits she would have made on the deal, so all that should be subtracted are expenses actually saved.

2. On November 1, when Kaitlyn was down on her luck and about to be evicted from her apartment for lack of money to pay the rent, her sister Madison came by that evening and gave her a large check for the amount past due. "This is only a loan," Kaitlyn insisted when she accepted the check. "Well," Madison replied, "if you say so." "Yes," Kaitlyn said, and

she added, "I promise to pay you back the moment we meet at the family Christmas party." Smiling, the sisters shook hands. Before that party, however, two things happened: Kaitlyn won the lottery and Madison suddenly fell ill and died. When Madison's son and only heir told Kaitlyn to make the payment to him, she responded that Madison's death relieved her of the obligation to repay what was only a gift to begin with. Is that right?

a. Yes. The so-called contract between the two women was just a gift disguised as a contract and created no liability to pay. Family members frequently do this sort of thing with no intent to create legal liability. Even if good morals would require Kaitlyn to pay, the law does not.

b. No. The women shook hands and that shows they were serious about this not being a gift, but instead being a binding contract. Particularly where it is no hardship for Kaitlyn to repay the debt is the law likely to make her do so.

c. No. Even if there was a contract there was an unfulfilled condition precedent to the promise to pay: meeting in person at the family Christmas party. Since that condition did not occur, Kaitlyn's promise to pay likewise fails.

d. No. There was contractual intent to repay the debt and the so-called condition was really only a term of the contract as to when payment would be made. It meant that the payment would be tendered at the time of the party, and was not meant to condition the liability to pay at all. This was merely an agreement as to time, not a condition, and certainly the parties would not have thought that the death of either of them had anything to do with liability under the contract. Kaitlyn can still pay Madison's heir at the party, and a court will decree that's what is required.

3. Sky Trails Lodge was a ski resort and hired ski instructors for the winter season each year, agreeing to give them room and board during the four months that the lodge was open to the public, and to pay them an additional $9,000 at the end of the four-month period, in return for which the ski instructors would teach guests how to ski and protect them while on the mountain. Albert North was such an instructor, and was in fact the best of the three instructors Sky Trails hired that season. Two-thirds of the way through the season his appendix ruptured and he was taken to the hospital for surgery. This meant that he missed the rest of the season. When he asked for two-thirds of his salary Sky Trails replied that he had to finish the season before he would have been eligible for any amount. He sued. How does this come out?

a. He should win. The employer got two-thirds of his performance and should pay a similar amount, here $6,000. Yes, there was a condition precedent to his ability to get the whole amount (lasting the whole season), but that became impossible to perform through no fault of Albert, so it is excused.

b. He loses. There was a clear condition precedent to the payment of the $9,000, and he didn't fulfill that condition. He always took the risk that various factors would prevent him from lasting the season, but he was willing to take that risk for the security of the room and board and the ability to put this employment on his resume. He certainly hasn't "substantially" performed; one-third of his performance is a large chunk of what was still due.

c. Albert may lose on the contract due to his failure to perform the condition precedent to payment, but he at least may sue in quasi-contract for the value of services conferred on Sky Trails prior to the unfortunate termination of his employment when he fell ill. The parties have valued that at $6,000, so that's the amount he should recover in quantum meruit.

d. Same answer as C but Albert should in no way be limited in quasi-contract by the amount of the contract. Instead, if he can prove that his performance before his illness was worth more than $6,000 he should recover that.

4. When Octopus National Bank loaned Amelia and Jacob Smith $170,000 to buy their dream home it made them sign a promissory note that requires monthly payments to be made on the first of every month. There was a clause providing that "time is of the essence" and that if the payment was late even one day the note would mature and the entire debt immediately become due. There was also a clause stating: "The acceptance of a late payment shall not be a waiver of the necessity of making future payments on time, even if this is done often, and the lender reserves the right, without notice, to accelerate the entire debt if any one payment is missed even after forgiving late ones on prior occasions." The Smiths made their payments on time for the first year of the 30-year mortgage period, but in year two they twice made payments one day late. In year three they made payments late six of the twelve months, but never more than three days late, and ONB always accepted the payments without saying anything. In year four the Smiths made similar late payments on eight of the months, again without any protest from ONB. In the fifth year the stock market crashed and a recession occurred. The first month of the fifth year the Smiths were one day late when making the mortgage payment, at which point ONB informed them that the debt was being accelerated and the entire balance was due immediately. The Smiths are in your law office asking for advice. They certainly don't have the money to pay off the entire debt. Can you save their home?

a. Yes. This agreement that late payments having no real damage can suddenly cause such a terrible penalty is unconscionable. It is procedurally unconscionable because consumers like the Smiths have no bargaining power over boilerplate terms like these, so this is an adhesion contract. It is substantively unconscionable because it's outrageous to make such a small mistake lead to the loss of their home in foreclosure. An unconscionable condition that pretends "time is of the essence" when it is not can be stricken from the contract, or, at least not available to the bank unless it gives adequate notice that it will be reinstated.

b. No. Contracts mean what they say. Here there is a well-drafted clause that explains the payment rules very clearly and warns the borrowers that there can be large consequences from missing the condition that payments be made on time. Yes, the bank was nice to them in the past, but the contract allowed that without it being a waiver because the contract warned them that no waiver was occurring. When the financial situation changed so drastically the Smiths should have been aware that the bank was likely to insist on strict compliance with payment terms. At that point making the payment late allowed the bank to do just what it did: call the loan.

c. Yes. Contract law stretches to protect justified reliance, and here the Smiths had come to rely on the ability to make payments a few days late without having the dire consequence of enforcing a condition that was a technicality to begin with. All the bank really cared about was getting paid, and payments a few days late are no big deal. What is really going on here is that the bank is looking for an excuse to call the mortgage and improve its own financial position at the expense of its innocent customers. A court is likely to say that both the "time is of the essence" clause and the "anti-waiver" clause were waived by a years-long course of performance in which payments were routinely made late with no complaint by the bank. If the bank wanted to reinstate the payment clause, it should have given them a new warning to that effect.

Answers

1. D is the best answer. For the reasons mentioned in B, a court is highly likely to place the risk of Pretoria's death on the network, and thus his demise is not a condition precedent to the network's promise to honor Flowers's contract. However, to the extent she does save some expenses by not having to complete the contract, those amounts should be deducted from the $50,000, thus giving her sufficient money to protect both her current expenses and the profit she was to make from the contract's completion.

2. B and D are the best answers. Sometimes clauses are awkwardly phrased as a condition when they are merely descriptive of a term, such as the time

when something will occur. As we saw in the last chapter, if some occurrence renders a term of the contract incapable of performance, the courts will ask what would the parties have thought should happen if they had thought about this possibility occurring. Though phrased as a condition, the "meeting at the party" was meant only as the time of payment, and that time can still occur though the meeting itself cannot. But neither Kaitlyn nor Madison would have likely believed that Madison's death would have excused the promise to repay the loan.

3. C is the best answer. The condition precedent was not met, but quasi-contract should help him out here. The parties have valued his performance at roughly $6,000 for two-thirds of it occurring, and the courts are not likely to second guess that. The rule of United States v. Algernon Blair (Chapter 3) allowing a party to sue for more than the contract amount is only available where the defendant is the breaching party, and that is not the case here. Sky Trails is not in breach. Albert is likely to get $6,000 in quantum meruit.

4. C is the best answer. Most (but not all) courts will say that both "time is of the essence" and "anti-waiver" clauses can be waived in just this sort of fact pattern. The Smiths have justifiably come to expect they have the right to make payments a day or so late without the bank caring. In effect, the course of performing this contract has led to a modification of it to allow slightly late payments. If the bank wanted to reinstate the waived clause, it should give the Smiths a clear "no more nice guy" notice so they will be warned that they could lose their home if they make future payments even one day late.

CHAPTER
8
ANTICIPATORY REPUDIATION

If one of the parties to an existing contract announces that it is not going to perform or does something to make its own performance impossible, that's an "anticipatory repudiation" in the language of the law of contracts. Such a repudiation raises a number of issues: must the other side accept the repudiation, can an immediate lawsuit be brought, may the repudiation be retracted if there has been no reliance on it, etc. This chapter will explore these and other issues.

Problem 162

For a trip to the moon from the space station in 2030, NASA requested bids on a gravity-free scooter capable of making the trip. It awarded the contract in early 2022 to Venture's Vehicles, a company specializing in experimental craft. The contract price was $32 billion payable on delivery in 2030. In mid-2026, Venture's Vehicles sent NASA a letter sadly informing the agency that it was unable to fulfill its contract by the date scheduled. NASA was able to purchase a substitute vehicle elsewhere for $56 billion. Can it recover from Venture's Vehicles now (in 2026), or must it wait until 2030, the scheduled date of delivery?

HOCHSTER v. DE LA TOUR
Queen's Bench, 1853
2 El. & Bl. 678, 118 Eng. Rep. 922

Lord CAMPBELL, C.J. now delivered the judgment of the Court. On this motion in arrest of judgment, the question arises, Whether, if there be an agreement between A. and B., whereby B. engages to employ A. on and from a future day for a given period of time, to travel with him into a foreign country as a courier, and to start with him in that capacity on that day,

A. being to receive a monthly salary during the continuance of such service, B. may, before the day, refuse to perform the agreement and break and renounce it, so as to entitle A. before the day to commence an action against B. to recover damages for breach of the agreement; A. having been ready and willing to perform it, till it was broken and renounced by B. The defendant's counsel very powerfully contended that, if the plaintiff was not contented to dissolve the contract, and to abandon all remedy upon it, he was bound to remain ready and willing to perform it till the day when the actual employment as courier in the service of the defendant was to begin; and that there could be no breach of the agreement, before that day, to give a right of action. But it cannot be laid down as a universal rule that, where by agreement an act is to be done on a future day, no action can be brought for a breach of the agreement till the day for doing the act has arrived. If a man promises to marry a woman on a future day, and before that day marries another woman, he is instantly liable to an action for breach of promise of marriage; Short v. Stone (8 Q.B. 358). If a man contracts to execute a lease on and from a future day for a certain term, and, before that day, executes a lease to another for the same term, he may be immediately sued for breaking the contract; Ford v. Tiley (6 B.&C. 325). So, if a man contracts to sell and deliver specific goods on a future day, and before the day he sells and delivers them to another, he is immediately liable to an action at the suit of the person with whom he first contracted to sell and deliver them; Bowdell v. Parsons (10 East, 359). One reason alleged in support of such an action is, that the defendant has, before the day, rendered it impossible for him to perform the contract at the day: but this does not necessarily follow; for, prior to the day fixed for doing the act, the first wife may have died, a surrender of the lease executed might be obtained, and the defendant might have repurchased the goods so as to be in a situation to sell and deliver them to the plaintiff. Another reason may be, that, where there is a contract to do an act on a future day, there is a relation constituted between the parties in the meantime by the contract, and that they impliedly promise that in the meantime neither will do any thing to the prejudice of the other inconsistent with that relation. As an example, a man and woman engaged to marry are affianced to one another during the period between the time of the engagement and the celebration of the marriage. In this very case, of traveller and courier, from the day of the hiring till the day when the employment was to begin, they were engaged to each other; and it seems to be a breach of an implied contract if either of them renounces the engagement. This reasoning seems in accordance with the unanimous decision of the Exchequer Chamber in Elderton v. Emmens, which we have followed in subsequent cases in this Court. The declaration in the present case, in alleging a breach, states a great deal more than a passing intention on the part of the defendant which he may repent of, and could only be proved by evidence that he had utterly renounced the contract, or done some act which rendered it impossible for him to perform it. If the plaintiff has no remedy for breach of the contract unless he treats the contract as in force, and acts upon it down to the 1st June 1852, it follows that, till then, he must enter into no employment which will interfere with his promise "to start with the defendant on such travels on the day and year," and that he must then be properly equipped in all respects as a courier for a three months' tour on the continent of Europe. But it is surely much more rational, and more for the benefit of both parties, that, after the renunciation of the agreement by the defendant, the plaintiff should be at liberty to consider himself absolved from any future performance of it, retaining his right to sue for any damage he has suffered from the breach of it. Thus, instead of remaining idle and laying out money in preparations which must be useless, he is at liberty to seek service under another employer, which would go in mitigation of the damages to which he would otherwise be entitled for a breach of the contract. It seems strange that the defendant, after renouncing the contract, and absolutely declaring that he will never act under it, should be permitted to object that faith is given to his assertion, and that an opportunity is not left to him of changing his mind. If the plaintiff is barred of any remedy by entering into an engagement inconsistent with starting as a courier with the defendant on the 1st June, he is prejudiced by putting faith in the defendant's assertion: and it would be more consonant with principle, if the defendant were precluded from saying that he had not broken the contract when he declared that he entirely renounced it. Suppose that the defendant, at the time of his renunciation, had embarked on a voyage for Australia, so as to render it physically impossible for him to employ the plaintiff as a courier on the continent of Europe in the months of June, July and August 1852: according to decided cases, the action might have been brought before the 1st June; but the renunciation may have been founded on other facts, to be given in evidence, which would equally have rendered the defendant's performance of the contract impossible. The man who wrongfully renounces a contract into which he has deliberately entered cannot justly complain if he is immediately sued for a compensation in damages by the man whom he has injured: and it seems reasonable to allow an option to the injured party, either to sue immediately, or to wait till the time when the act was to be done, still holding it as prospectively binding for the exercise of this option, which may be advantageous to the innocent party, and cannot be prejudicial to the wrongdoer. An argument against the action before the 1st of June is urged from the difficulty of calculating the damages: but this argument is equally strong against an action before the 1st of September, when the three months would expire. . . .

Upon the whole, we think that the declaration in this case is sufficient. It gives us great satisfaction to reflect that, the question being on the record, our opinion may be reviewed in a Court of Error. In the meantime we must give judgment for the plaintiff.

Judgment for plaintiff.

NOTES AND QUESTIONS

1. Does it follow, as Lord Campbell says, that the desirability of allowing the aggrieved party to mitigate also necessarily means that suit may be brought before the date set for performance? See Corbin §960.

2. Is allowing the early suit good policy? What factors militate in either direction? See Corbin §961. For an economic analysis, see Jackson, Anticipatory Repudiation and the Temporal Element of Contract Law: An Economic Inquiry into Contract Damages in Cases of Prospective Nonperformance, 31 Stan. L. Rev. 69 (1978).

3. In general, there are two kinds of anticipatory repudiations: *express* and *implied.* An *express* anticipatory repudiation occurs when a party unequivocally declares its intent to do something that would materially and totally breach the contract. An *implied* repudiation occurs when a party does something that makes it unable (or apparently unable) to perform. See Restatement (Second) §250. Finally, repudiations can be retracted until the nonrepudiating party either (1) notifies the other party that it has repudiated or (2) changes position in reliance on the repudiation. See, e.g., UCC §2-611. Our next case features all of these issues.

TAYLOR v. JOHNSTON
California Supreme Court, 1975
539 P.2d 425

SULLIVAN, Justice.

. . . Plaintiff was engaged in the business of owning, breeding, raising and racing thoroughbred horses in Los Angeles County. Defendants were engaged in a similar business, and operated a horse farm in Ontario, California, where they furnished stallion stud services. In January 1965 plaintiff sought to breed his two thoroughbred mares, Sunday Slippers and Sandy Fork to defendants' stallion Fleet Nasrullah. To that end, on January 19 plaintiff and defendants entered into two separate written contracts—one pertaining to Sunday Slippers and the other to Sandy Fork. Except for the mare involved the contracts were identical.

The contract provided that Fleet Nasrullah was to perform breeding services upon the respective mares in the year 1966 for a fee of $3,500, payable on or before September 1, 1966. . . .

On October 4, 1965, defendants sold Fleet Nasrullah to Dr. A. G. Pessin and Leslie Combs II for $1,000,000 cash and shipped the stallion to Kentucky. Subsequently Combs and Pessin syndicated the sire by selling various individuals 36 or 38 shares, each share entitling the holder to breed one mare each season to Fleet Nasrullah. . . .

On the same day defendants wrote to plaintiff advising the latter of the sale and that he was "released" from his "reservations" for Fleet Nasrullah. Unable to reach defendants by telephone, plaintiff had his attorney write to them on October 8, 1965, insisting on performance of the contracts. . . . On October 27, defendants advised plaintiff by letter that arrangements had been made to breed the two mares to Fleet Nasrullah in Kentucky. . . .

In January 1966 plaintiff shipped Sunday Slippers and Sandy Fork to [Kentucky]. At that time, however, both mares were in foal and could not be bred. . . .

On April 17, 1966, Sunday Slippers foaled and Frazier immediately notified Dr. Pessin. The latter assured Frazier that he would make the necessary arrangements to breed the mare to Fleet Nasrullah. On April 26, the ninth day after the foaling, Frazier, upon further inquiry, was told by Dr. Pessin to contact Mrs. Judy who had charge of booking the breedings and had handled these matters with Frazier in the past. Mrs. Judy, however, informed Frazier that the stallion was booked for that day but would be available on any day not booked by a shareholder. She indicated that she was acting under instructions but suggested that he keep in touch with her while the mare was in heat.

Sunday Slippers came into heat again on May 13, 1966. Frazier telephoned Mrs. Judy and attempted to book the breeding for May 16. She informed him that Fleet Nasrullah had been reserved by one of the shareholders for that day, but that Frazier should keep in touch with her in the event the reservation was cancelled. On May 14 and May 15 Frazier tried again but without success; on the latter date, Sunday Slippers went out of heat.

On June 4, the mare went into heat again. Frazier again tried to book a reservation with Fleet Nasrullah but was told that all dates during the heat period had been already booked. He made no further efforts but on June 7, on plaintiff's instructions, bred Sunday Slippers to a Kentucky Derby winner named Chateaugay for a stud fee of $10,000.

Sandy Fork, plaintiff's other mare awaiting the stud services of Fleet Nasrullah, foaled on June 5, 1966. Frazier telephoned Mrs. Judy the next day and received a booking to breed the mare on June 14, the ninth day after foaling. On June 10, 1966, however, she cancelled the reservation because of the prior claim of a shareholder. Frazier made no further attempts and on June 14 bred Sandy Fork to Chateaugay. . . .

The court found the facts to be substantially as stated above and further found and concluded that by selling Fleet Nasrullah defendants had "put it out of their power to perform properly their contracts," that the conduct of defendants and their agents Dr. Pessin and Mrs. Judy up to and including June 13, 1966, constituted a breach and plaintiff "was then justified in treating it as a breach and repudiation of their contractual obligations to him," and that defendants unjustifiably breached the contracts but plaintiff did not. The court awarded plaintiff damages for defendants' breach in the sum of $103,122.50.

Defendants' main attack on the judgment is two-pronged. They contend: First, that they did not at any time repudiate the contracts; and second, that they did not otherwise breach the contracts because performance was made impossible by plaintiff's own actions. . . .

Nevertheless both aspects of defendants' argument require us at the outset to examine the specifications for performance contained in the contracts. We note that the reservation for 'one services' for Fleet Nasrullah was 'for the year 1966.' As the evidence showed, a breeding is biologically possible throughout the calendar year, since mares regularly come into heat every 21 days, unless they are pregnant. The contracts therefore appear to contemplate breeding with Fleet Nasrullah at any time during the calendar year 1966. The trial court made no finding as to the time of performance called for by the contracts. There was testimony to the effect that by custom in the thoroughbred racing business the breeding is consummated in a "breeding season" which normally extends from January until early July, although some breeding continues through August. It is possible that the parties intended that the mares be bred to Fleet Nasrullah during the 1966 breeding season rather than the calendar year 1966.

However, in our view, it is immaterial whether the contract phrase "for the year 1966" is taken to mean the above breeding season or the full calendar year since in either event the contract period had not expired by June 7 and June 14, 1966, the dates on which Sunday Slippers and Sandy Fork respectively were bred to Chateaugay and by which time, according to the findings defendants had repudiated the contracts. There can be no actual breach of a contract until the time specified therein for performance has arrived. Although there may be a breach by anticipatory repudiation; by its very name an essential element of a true anticipatory breach of a contract is that the repudiation by the promisor occur before his performance is due under the contract. In the instant case, because under either of the above interpretations the time for performance had not yet arrived, defendants' breach as found by the trial court was of necessity an anticipatory breach and must be analyzed in accordance with the principles governing such type of breach. To these principles we now direct our attention.

Anticipatory breach occurs when one of the parties to a bilateral contract repudiates the contract. The repudiation may be express or implied. An express repudiation is a clear, positive, unequivocal refusal to perform; an implied repudiation results from conduct where the promisor puts it out of his power to perform so as to make substantial performance of his promise impossible.

When a promisor repudiates a contract, the injured party faces an election of remedies: he can treat the repudiation as an anticipatory breach and immediately seek damages for breach of contract, thereby terminating the contractual relation between the parties, or he can treat the repudiation as an empty threat, wait until the time for performance arrives and exercise his remedies for actual breach if a breach does in fact occur at such time. However, if the injured party disregards the repudiation and treats the contract as still in force, and the repudiation is retracted prior to the time of performance, then the repudiation is nullified and the injured party is left with his remedies, if any, invocable at the time of performance.

[D]efendants clearly repudiated the contracts when, after selling Fleet Nasrullah and shipping him to Kentucky, they informed plaintiff "(y)ou are, therefore, released from your reservations made to the stallion." However, the trial court additionally found that "(p)laintiff did not wish to be 'released' from his 'reservations' . . . insist(ed) on performance of the stud service agreements . . . (and) threaten(ed) litigation if the contracts were not honored by defendants. . . ." Accordingly defendants arranged for performance of the contracts by making Fleet Nasrullah available for stud service to plaintiff in Kentucky through their agents Dr. Pessin and Mrs. Judy. Plaintiff elected to treat the contracts as in force and shipped the mares to Kentucky to effect the desired performance. The foregoing facts lead us to conclude that the subsequent arrangements by defendants to make Fleet Nasrullah available to service plaintiff's mares in Kentucky constituted a retraction of the repudiation. Since at this time plaintiff had not elected to treat the repudiation as an anticipatory breach and in fact had shipped the mares to Kentucky in reliance on defendants' arrangements, this retraction nullified the repudiation. Thus, plaintiff was then left with his remedies that might arise at the time of performance.

The trial court found that after the mares had arrived in Kentucky, had delivered the foals they were then carrying and were ready for servicing by Fleet Nasrullah, plaintiff was justified in concluding from the conduct of defendants, their agent Dr. Pessin, and their subagent Mrs. Judy, that "defendants were just giving him the runaround and had no intention of performing their contract in the manner required by its terms" and in treating such conduct "as a breach and repudiation of their contractual obligation to him." Since, as we have explained, defendants retracted their original repudiation, this subsequent conduct amounts to a finding of a second repudiation.

There is no evidence in the record that defendants or their agents Dr. Pessin and Mrs. Judy ever stated that Sunday Slippers and Sandy Fork would not be serviced by Fleet Nasrullah during the 1966 breeding season or that they ever refused to perform. Frazier, plaintiff's agent who made arrangements for the breeding of the mares admitted that they had never made such a statement to him. Accordingly, there was no express repudiation or unequivocal refusal to perform.

The trial court's finding of repudiation, expressly based on the "conduct of the defendants" and their agents suggests that the court found an implied repudiation. However, there is no implied repudiation, i.e., by conduct equivalent to an unequivocal refusal to perform, unless the promisor puts it out of his power to perform. Once the mares arrived in Kentucky, defendants had the power to perform the contracts; Fleet Nasrullah could breed with the mares. No subsequent conduct occurred to render this performance impossible. Although plaintiff was subordinated to the shareholders with respect to the priority of reserving a breeding time with Fleet Nasrullah, there is no evidence in the record that this subordination of reservation rights rendered performance impossible. Rather it acted to postpone the time of performance, which still remained within the limits prescribed by the contracts. It rendered performance more difficult to achieve; it may even have cast doubt upon the eventual accomplishment of performance; it did not render performance impossible.

Because there was no repudiation, express or implied, there was no anticipatory breach. . . .

To recapitulate, Sandy Fork was in foal in January 1966, the commencement of the 1966 breeding season, and remained so until June 5, 1966. Throughout this period Fleet Nasrullah could not perform his services as contracted due solely to the conduct of plaintiff in breeding Sandy Fork in 1965. Biologically the first opportunity to breed Sandy Fork was on June 14, 1966, nine days after foaling. Frazier telephoned Mrs. Judy on June 6, 1966, and received a booking with Fleet Nasrullah for June 14, 1966. On June 13 Mrs. Judy telephoned Frazier and informed him she would have to cancel Sandy Fork's reservation for the following day because one of the shareholders insisted on using that day. Mrs. Judy gave no indication whatsoever that she could not or would not breed Sandy Fork on any of the following days in that heat period or subsequent heat periods. Frazier made no further attempts to breed Sandy Fork with Fleet Nasrullah. Thus, plaintiff, who delayed the possibility of performance for five months, asserts that the delay of performance occasioned by defendants' cancellation of a reservation on the first day during the six-month period that plaintiff made performance possible amounts to an unequivocal refusal to perform, even though there was adequate opportunity for Fleet Nasrullah to perform within the period for performance specified in the contract and even though defendants never stated any intention not to perform. We conclude that as a matter of law this conduct did not amount to an unequivocal refusal to perform and therefore did not constitute an anticipatory breach of the contract covering Sandy Fork.

Sunday Slippers foaled on April 17, 1966, first came into heat on April 26 and then successively on May 13 and June 4, 1966. Mrs. Judy informed Frazier that she would breed Sunday Slippers on any day that one of the shareholders did not want to use the stallion. Frazier unsuccessfully sought to breed the mare of April 26, May 14, May 15 and June 4, 1966, Fleet Nasrullah being reserved on those dates. Mrs. Judy continued to assure Frazier that the breeding would occur. Sunday Slippers was due to come into heat again twice during the breeding season: June 25 and July 16, 1966. At most this conduct amounts to delay of performance and a warning that performance might altogether be precluded if a shareholder were to desire Fleet Nasrullah's services on all the remaining days within the period specified for performance in which Sunday Slippers was in heat. We conclude that as a matter of law this conduct did not amount to an unequivocal refusal to perform and therefore did not constitute an anticipatory breach of the contract covering Sunday Slippers.

In sum, we hold that there is no evidence in the record supportive of the trial court's finding and conclusion that defendants repudiated and therefore committed an anticipatory breach of the contracts.

NOTES AND QUESTIONS

1. The defendant's October 4, 1965 letter "releasing" the plaintiffs from the contract was an express anticipatory repudiation. Why, then, did the court ultimately hold that the *plaintiffs* materially and totally breached the contract?

2. In addition to express and implied repudiations, parties can repudiate by *failing to provide adequate assurances* that they will perform. The material that follows examines this issue.

UNIFORM COMMERCIAL CODE

§2-609. Right to Adequate Assurance of Performance

(1) A contract for sale imposes an obligation on each party that the other's expectation of receiving due performance will not be impaired. When reasonable grounds for insecurity arise with respect to the performance of either party the other may in writing demand adequate assurance of due performance and until he receives such assurance may if commercially reasonable suspend any performance for which he has not already received the agreed return.

(2) Between merchants the reasonableness of grounds for insecurity and the adequacy of any assurance offered shall be determined according to commercial standards.

(3) Acceptance of any improper delivery or payment does not prejudice the aggrieved party's right to demand adequate assurance of future performance.

(4) After receipt of a justified demand failure to provide within a reasonable time not exceeding thirty days such assurance of due performance as is adequate under the circumstances of the particular case is a repudiation of the contract.

RESTATEMENT (SECOND) OF CONTRACTS

§251. When a Failure to Give Assurance May Be Treated as a Repudiation

(1) Where reasonable grounds arise to believe that the obligor will commit a breach by non-performance that would of itself give the obligee a claim for damages for total breach . . . the obligee may demand adequate assurance of due performance and may, if reasonable, suspend any performance for which he has not already received the agreed exchange until he receives such assurance.

(2) The obligee may treat as a repudiation the obligor's failure to provide within a reasonable time such assurance of due performance as is adequate in the circumstances of the particular case.

Problem 163

Assume that in the same basic fact pattern as in the last Problem, NASA had phoned Venture's Vehicles in 2026 and inquired how production was going. John Venture, president of the company, replied, "Well, I'm really not sure if we are going to be able to do the job. We've encountered some glitches on this one." May NASA immediately take steps to mitigate? What should NASA do? See UCC §2-609 and its Official Comment. If NASA sent a §2-609 notice, which of the following responses by Venture's Vehicles would be satisfactory in your opinion?

(a) "We're sorry if we worried you. Production is now on schedule and we will deliver as agreed."

(b) "We have solved our internal difficulties and will produce the scooters as agreed. Please send your personnel to our offices and we'll make our plans and schedules available to them for inspection."

(c) "Our local bank is willing to issue you a letter of credit for the damages payable in the event we default."

Restatement (Second) of Contracts §251 is similar to UCC §2-609. However, under the Restatement provision the demand for assurance need not be in writing and there is no 30-day limit on the time to provide adequate assurances of due performance. For a comparison of UCC §2-609 and Restatement §251 and an interesting study of their application in actual lawsuits, see White, Eight Cases and Section 251, 67 Cornell L. Rev. 841 (1982); for a comprehensive discussion of §2-609, see Garvin, Adequate Assurance of Performance: Of Risk, Duress, and Cognition, 69 U. Colo. L. Rev. 71 (1998).

HOPE'S ARCHITECTURAL PRODUCTS v.
LUNDY'S CONSTRUCTION
United States District Court, District of Kansas, 1991
781 F. Supp. 711

LUNGSTRUM, District Judge. This case presents a familiar situation in the field of construction contracts. Two parties, who disagreed over the meaning of their contract, held their positions to the brink, with litigation and loss the predictable result of the dispute. What is rarely predictable, however (and what leads to a compromise resolution of many construction disputes when cool heads hold sway), is which party will ultimately prevail. The stakes become winner-take-all.

Plaintiff Hope's Architectural Products (Hope's) is a New York corporation that manufactures and installs custom window fixtures. Defendant Lundy's Construction (Lundy's) is a Kansas corporation that contracted to buy windows from Hope's for a school remodeling project. Defendant Bank IV Olathe (Bank IV) is a national banking organization with its principal place of business in Kansas. Bank IV acted as surety for a statutory bond obtained by Lundy's for the remodeling project.

Hope's contends that Lundy's breached the contract to buy windows, entitling Hope's to damages in the amount of the contract price of $55,000. Hope's also contends that Bank IV wrongfully refused to pay Hope's on the bond when Lundy's breached the contract. Hope's has sued for breach of contract, and in the alternative, for recovery under the theory of quantum meruit. A trial to the court was held December 4 and 5, 1991. Two issues emerged as pivotal to the resolution of this case: (1) when was delivery of the windows due, and (2) if delivery was late, could Hope's lawfully suspend performance and demand certain assurances (including ultimately, a demand for prepayment in full), that Lundy's would not back charge for the late delivery under the authority of K.S.A. §84-2-609? Because the court finds that a determination of these issues leads to the conclusion that Hope's was the party in breach of this contract, the plaintiff's request for relief is denied.

I. FACTS

The following findings of fact are entered pursuant to Fed. R. Civ. P. 52. On June 13, 1988, defendant Lundy's entered into a contract with the Shawnee Mission School District as general contractor for the construction of an addition to the Rushton Elementary School. Lundy's provided a public works bond in connection with the Rushton project as required by K.S.A. §60-1111 (1983). The purpose of the bond was to insure that Lundy's paid any outstanding indebtedness it incurred in the construction of the project. The statutory bond was secured through defendant Bank IV.

Plaintiff Hope's is a manufacturer of custom-built windows. The initial contact between Hope's and Lundy's occurred through Mr. Richard Odor, a regional agent for Hope's in Kansas City. On June 29, 1988, Hope's contracted with Lundy's to manufacture ninety-three windows for the Rushton project. The contract price, including the cost of labor and materials for the windows, was $55,000.

Although the contract included a term pertaining to the time for delivering the windows, there is some controversy over the meaning of this provision. Even under the most favorable interpretation to Hope's, however, delivery was due twelve to fourteen weeks after Hope's received approved shop drawings from Lundy's on July 18. Thus, delivery was due no later than October 24, 1988.

During the late summer and fall of 1988, several discussions took place between Hope's and Lundy's concerning when the windows would be delivered to the job site. Production of the windows was delayed by events that, according to the testimony of Mr. Odor, were not the fault of Lundy's. On September 27, 1988, Mark Hannah, vice president of Lundy's wrote to Hope's requesting that installation of the windows begin October 19, and be completed by October 26. On October 14 Hannah again wrote to Hope's, threatening to withhold "liquidated damages" from the contract price if Hope's did not comply with these deadlines. Although there was no provision in the contract for liquidated damages, Hope's did not make any response to the October 14 letter.

The windows were shipped from Hope's New York plant to Kansas City on October 28. Delivery to the Rushton site was anticipated on November 4. On November 1, Hannah called Hope's office in New York to inquire about the windows. He spoke to Kathy Anderson, Hope's customer service manager. The substance of this conversation is disputed. Hope's claims that Hannah threatened a back charge of $11,000 (20% of the contract price) for late delivery of the windows. Hannah testified, however, that although the possibility of a back charge was discussed, no specific dollar amount was mentioned. Hannah specifically denies that he threatened to withhold $11,000 from the contract.

After her conversation with Hannah, Anderson immediately informed Chris Arvantinos, vice president of Hope's, of the threatened back charge. Arvantinos called Hannah to discuss the back charge, but he does not recall hearing Hannah mention the $11,000 figure. Arvantinos requested that Hannah provide assurances that Lundy's would not back charge Hope's, but Hannah was unwilling to provide such assurances.

In a letter written on November 2, Arvantinos informed Hannah that Hope's was suspending delivery of the windows until Lundy's provided assurances that there would be no back charge. Hannah received this letter on the morning of November 3, shortly before Mr. Odor visited Hannah at Lundy's.

Odor, who had spoken with Arvantinos about the back charge, issued a new
demand that Lundy's had to meet before Hope's would deliver the windows.
He gave Hannah an invoice for the full amount of the contract price,
demanding prepayment before the windows would be delivered.

[handwritten margin: request 2]
[handwritten margin: full k price]

Odor set out three ways that Lundy's could meet this demand: (1)
payment of the contract price in full by cashier's check; (2) placement of
the full contract price in an escrow account until the windows were installed;
or (3) delivery of the full contract amount to the architect to hold until the
windows were installed. All three options required Lundy's to come up with
$55,000 before the windows would be delivered. Hannah believed that the
demand presented by Odor superseded the letter from Arvantinos he
received earlier that morning.

Hannah informed Odor that there was no way for Lundy's to get an
advance from the school district at that time to comply with Hope's request.
The meeting ended, Lundy's did not prepay, and Hope's did not deliver the
windows. On November 7, 1988, Lundy's terminated the contract with
Hope's. Thereafter, Lundy's obtained an alternate supplier of the windows.

[handwritten margin: Hope never delivered the windows]

On February 15, 1989, Hope's notified defendant Bank IV of Lundy's
failure to pay the contract price and demanded payment from Bank IV on
the public works bond. Bank IV refused to pay Hope's claim. This action was
filed by Hope's on March 20, 1989. Jurisdiction of the matter rests with this
court pursuant to 28 U.S.C. §1332. . . .

II. Discussion . . .

A. PLAINTIFF'S CONTRACT CLAIM AGAINST DEFENDANT LUNDY'S

This case turns on the resolution of two central and interrelated issues:
(1) when was delivery due under the contract, and (2) could Hope's lawfully
demand the assurances it demanded from Lundy's under K.S.A. §84-2-609.[2]

[handwritten margin: Two Issues]

If the demands for assurances were proper, then Hope's would have
been justified in suspending its performance and withholding delivery and
Lundy's failure to provide assurances and subsequent termination of the
contract amounted to a total breach. If, however, the demands for

[handwritten margin: Proper v. Not Proper Request]

---

2. Section 2-609 provides:

§84-2-609. Right to adequate assurance of performance.
(1) . . . When reasonable grounds for insecurity arise with respect to the performance
of either party the other may in writing demand adequate assurance of due performance and until he receives such assurance may if commercially reasonable suspend
any performance for which he has not already received the agreed return.
(2) Between merchants the reasonableness of grounds for insecurity and the adequacy
of any assurance offered shall be determined according to commercial standards.

K.S.A. §84-2-609 (1983).

assurances were not proper under §84-2-609 then Hope's breached the contract by wrongfully withholding delivery of the windows and Lundy's was entitled to cancel the contract. The delivery date issue is addressed first because the matter of whether or not Hope's was already in breach for late delivery goes directly to the propriety of its demand for assurances.

1. Delivery Date

Even under Hope's interpretation of the delivery term, delivery of the windows was not timely.[3] At trial, Chris Arvantinos, Hope's vice president, testified that Hope's committed to deliver the windows twelve to fourteen weeks after July 18, 1988, the day Hope's received approved shop drawings. This would make delivery due between October 10 and October 24. In fact, the windows did not arrive in Kansas City until November 4, fifteen and one-half weeks after July 18. Hope's claims that this delay was "immaterial" and did not excuse Lundy's from its duties under the contract. Hope's is unable to cite any controlling authority to support this argument, however. Moreover, this argument misses the point. Even if an "immaterial" delay did not excuse future performance by Lundy's, no performance was due from Lundy's until the windows were delivered to the job site, which never occurred.

Hope's also argues, almost in passing, that the delay was caused by problems that were outside of its control, thus excusing Hope's from responsibility for the late delivery. Under a clause in the contract, Hope's disclaimed responsibility "for delayed shipments and deliveries occasioned by strikes, fires, accidents, delays of common carriers or other causes beyond our control. . . ." During the course of production, Hope's experienced problems with its "bonderizing" and prime paint system, which resulted in a delay in production of approximately two weeks. Hope's produced no evidence at trial, however, to show that this was a matter which was beyond its control. Moreover, it is interesting to note that Hope's did not contemporaneously seek from Lundy's any extension of the delivery date under this provision or notify Lundy's that it might result in a delay beyond October 24. It appears that reference to this clause is more of an afterthought born of litigation than a bona fide excuse for modifying the delivery date.

Hope's also contends that a three to four day delay resulted when Lundy's asked for a change in the design of the windows to include "weep holes" after production had already begun. However, Hope's representative, Odor, testified that nothing Lundy's did delayed Hope's manufacturing.

---

3. "Delivery" is defined by Black's Law Dictionary as "[t]he act by which the res or substance thereof is placed within the actual or constructive possession or control of another. . . . What constitutes delivery depends largely on the intent of the parties." Black's Law Dictionary 385 (5th ed. 1979). In this case, the parties bargained for more than mere shipment of the windows. Arvantinos testified that Hope's committed to delivering the windows to the job site between October 10 and October 24. Thus, delivery was to occur under the parties' agreement when the windows arrived in Kansas City and were available for installation at the Rushton job site.

Moreover, even accounting for this delay, Hope's was a week late delivering the windows.

2.   Section 2-609 Demand for Assurances

The framework for judging demands for assurances under 84-2-609 was set forth in LNS Investment Co., Inc. v. Phillips 66 Co., 731 F. Supp. 1484, 1487 (D. Kan. 1990):

> To suspend its performance pursuant to [84-2-609], defendant must (1) have had reasonable grounds for insecurity regarding plaintiff's performance under the contract, (2) have demanded in writing adequate assurance of plaintiff's future performance and (3) have not received from plaintiff such assurance.

[handwritten margin note: UCC]

White and Summers note that what constitutes a "reasonable ground" for insecurity and an "adequate assurance" are fact questions. J. White & R. Summers, Uniform Commercial Code §6-2, at 236 (3d ed. 1988). Reasonableness and adequacy are determined according to commercial standards when, as is the case here, the parties are merchants. K.S.A. §84-2-609(2) (1983).

Although nothing in the record indicates that Hope's expressly claimed any rights under §84-2-609 during the course of this transaction, Hope's asserted at trial that the October 14 letter from Lundy's demanding delivery by October 16 and threatening liquidated damages gave Hope's reasonable grounds for insecurity. Delivery was not due until October 24 under Hope's version of the parties' agreement, and Lundy's had no right to demand performance early, let alone broach the withholding of liquidated damages. This letter might have justified a demand for assurances under §84-2-609. However, Hope's made no such demand after receiving the letter. Instead of invoking its rights under §84-2-609, Hope's chose not to respond at all to Lundy's threat of liquidated damages. This event merely came and went without any legal consequence.

[handwritten margin note: unreasonable request]

Hope's in effect invoked its rights under §84-2-609 in response to Lundy's threat of a back charge during the November 1 phone conversations. Two separate demands for assurances were made in response to this threat. Initially, Chris Arvantinos demanded assurances that Lundy's would not back charge Hope's for the delayed shipment in a telephone conversation with Mark Hannah later in the day on November 1. Arvantinos memorialized this demand in a letter composed on that day and mailed on the second of November. In their telephone conversation, Hannah refused to provide assurances that Lundy's would not back charge Hope's.

[handwritten margin note: Two separate Demands were made (1)]

Hope's made a second demand for assurances on November 3, when Richard Odor presented Hope's invoice to Hannah demanding payment in full. Thus, Hope's demanded assurances that it would not be back charged

[handwritten margin note: (2)]

on November 1, and when that demand was refused, Hope's made a second demand on November 3. The court finds that Hope's was not entitled to invoke §84-2-609 on either occasion.

p. already Breached

When Hope's made its first demand for assurances on November 1, it was already in breach of the parties' agreement. Delivery of the windows was due by October 24, but the windows did not arrive in Kansas City until November 4. A party already in breach is not entitled to invoke §2-609 by demanding assurances. United States v. Great Plains Gasification Associates, 819 F.2d 831, 835 (8th Cir. 1987); cf. Sumner v. Fel-Air, Inc., 680 P.2d 1109 (Alaska 1984) (Section 2-609 does not apply after a breach has already

Policy

occurred). To hold otherwise would allow a party to avoid liability for breaching its contract by invoking §2-609 to extract from the nonbreaching party an assurance that no damages will be sought for the breach. A nonbreaching party in need of prompt performance could be coerced into giving up its right to damages for the breach by giving in to the demands in order to receive the needed performance. This court refuses to endorse such a result.

The assurances which Hope's demanded, moreover, were excessive. "What constitutes 'adequate assurance' is to be determined by factual conditions; the seller must exercise good faith and observe commercial standards; his satisfaction must be based upon reason and must not be arbitrary or capricious." Richmond Leasing Co. v. Capital Bank, N.A., 762 F.2d 1303, 1310 (5th Cir. 1985). "If the assurances he demands are more than 'adequate' and the other party refuses to accede to the excessive demands, the court may find that the demanding party was in breach or a repudiator." J. White & R. Summers, supra, §6-2, at 236.

①

Lundy's argues that Hope's demand for assurances in the November 2 letter from Arvantinos was overly broad and unreasonable. The letter informed Lundy's that Hope's would not deliver the windows to the job site until it received assurances that it would not "be backcharged or otherwise held responsible for liquidated damages, delay charges *or any extra costs on account of time of delivery of the windows*" (emphasis added). When this demand was made, the windows had not yet arrived in Kansas City. Therefore, the parties did not know at this time whether the proper quantity of windows had been shipped, whether the windows were the correct size, or whether they otherwise met Lundy's specifications. If there were any nonconformities in the shipment, there could have been another delay in the time of delivery while Hope's corrected the problem. Yet, Hope's demanded a blanket assurance that it would not be held responsible for *any extra costs* incurred because of "time of delivery of the windows." This demand was overly broad on its face and unreasonable under §84-2-609.

unreasonable

②

The assurances Hope's demanded on November 3 were also excessive. In his meeting with Mark Hannah, Richard Odor insisted that Lundy's pre-pay the contract price, deliver a cashier's check to the architect, or place the full contract price in an escrow account before the windows would be delivered. Yet, Lundy's never gave any indication that it was unable or unwilling to pay the amount it owed to Hope's when the windows were delivered and the bond stood as security for Lundy's obligation. Such a demand was unreasonable and amounted to a breach by Hope's. [Citations omitted.] The payment terms under the contract were "Progress payments by the 10th of each month covering 90% of the total value of materials delivered and installation performed during the previous month with final payment upon completion of our [Hope's] work." By demanding prepayment, Hope's essentially attempted to rewrite this term of the contract. [Citations omitted.]

unreasonable

Payment Terms of contract

Although Hope's contends that a threatened back charge of $11,000 for a one week delay in shipment justified its demand for prepayment, the court is not persuaded that Lundy's made any specific demand for $11,000. The testimony on this issue was controverted, but only Kathy Anderson, Hope's customer service manager, testified, in a perfunctory manner, that an $11,000 back charge was threatened. Mark Hannah specifically denied making such a demand. Neither Chris Arvantinos nor Richard Odor testified to recalling receiving such a demand. There was also testimony at trial from one witness for Hope's that the threatened back-charge was in the amount of $5,000. The court is not persuaded that Lundy's went beyond making unspecified threats of a back charge for possible damages it would incur because of Hope's delay.

By threatening to withhold damages from the contract price, Lundy's was merely exercising its rights under K.S.A. §84-2-717,[4] which entitles a buyer to deduct from the amount owing on the contract any damages from the seller's breach. [Citations omitted.] Giving notice of its intention to avail itself of a legal right did not indicate that Lundy's was unwilling or unable to perform under the contract. Indeed, the very nature of the right invoked by Lundy's manifests an intention that it would continue performing and pay the contract price due, less damages caused by Hope's delay. Thus, the demand for prepayment was unreasonably excessive when there was no indication that Lundy's would not pay Hope's when performance was due.

★

Both Hope's delay in delivering the windows and Hope's excessive demands entitled Lundy's to treat Hope's as in breach and to cancel the contract, which it did on November 7, 1988. K.S.A. §84-2-711 (1983) ("Where the seller fails to make delivery or repudiates . . . the buyer may cancel. . . ."). Thus, Hope's is not entitled to recover under its claim for breach of contract.

Holding

4. "§84-2-717. *Deduction of damages from the price.* The buyer on notifying the seller of his intentions to do so may deduct all or any part of the damages resulting from any breach of the contract from any part of the price still due under the same contract." K.S.A. §84-2-717 (1983).

B. PLAINTIFF'S QUANTUM MERUIT CLAIM

Hope's also claims that it is entitled to compensation from Lundy's under the theory of quantum meruit. "Quantum meruit," which literally means "as much as he deserves," is a phrase used often in older cases to describe an equitable doctrine premised on the theories of unjust enrichment and restitution. Black's Law Dictionary 1119 (5th ed. 1979). Recovery was allowed under this theory when a benefit had been received by a party and it would be inequitable to allow the party to retain it. E. Farnsworth, Contracts §2.20, at 103 n.4 (2d ed. 1990). Instead of labeling it quantum meruit, courts today speak in terms of restitution. See Pioneer Operations Co. v. Brandeberry, 14 Kan. App. 2d 289, 789 P.2d 1182 (1990).

To recover in restitution, a breaching plaintiff must have conferred a benefit on the nonbreaching party. See Walker v. Ireton, 221 Kan. 314, 559 P.2d 340 (1977) (right to restitution limited to expenditures or services that benefited other party); Restatement (Second) of Contracts §374 (1979). The burden is on the breaching party to prove the extent of the benefit conferred, and doubts will be resolved against him. Restatement (Second) of Contracts §374 comment b (1977).

In this case, Hope's conferred no benefit on Lundy's. The windows manufactured by Hope's were never used in the Rushton project, and the court is not persuaded that the installation advice provided by Christiansen Steel Erection for Hope's improved the project. Hope's admits that the only labor it claims to have provided at the Rushton job site was consultation work performed by Christiansen Steel Erection, a company Hope's subcontracted with to install the windows. Mike and John Christiansen visited the job site on several occasions to advise Lundy's on how to prepare the window openings for installation. The advice they provided, however, related to the installation of windows that were never used on the project. When Lundy's canceled its contract with Hope's, it obtained an alternate supplier of a different type of windows. These windows did not require the same careful preparation of the window openings as the Hope's windows. Lundy's job foreman testified that the Christiansen's advice became moot when the alternate supplier was obtained. "[A] party's expenditures in preparation for performance that do not confer a benefit on the other party do not give rise to a restitution interest." Restatement (Second) of Contracts §370 comment a (1977). Thus, because no benefit was conferred upon Lundy's, Hope's has no valid claim to restitution.

III. CONCLUSION

After careful consideration of the facts and law, this Court holds that Hope's breached the contract in question. Therefore, defendant Lundy's was entitled to cancel its performance and defendant Bank IV was not obligated to pay Hope's under the statutory bond.

It is therefore ordered that plaintiff's claims for relief are hereby denied, and judgment is entered in favor of defendants.

It is so ordered.

RESTATEMENT (SECOND) OF CONTRACTS

§252. Effect of Insolvency

(1) Where the obligor's insolvency gives the obligee reasonable grounds to believe that the obligor will commit a breach under the rule stated in §251, the obligee may suspend any performance for which he has not already received the agreed exchange until he receives assurance in the form of performance itself, an offer of performance, or adequate security.

(2) A person is insolvent who either has ceased to pay his debts in the ordinary course of business or cannot pay his debts as they become due or is insolvent within the meaning of the federal bankruptcy law.*

Problem 164

Assume NASA had agreed to make progress payments of $1 million monthly to Venture's Vehicles starting in January 2022. After NASA had made payments through October of that year, it learned that Venture's Vehicles was insolvent and had defaulted on a similar job it had with the European Space Agency. May NASA treat this as a repudiation? May it cut off the progress payments?

Problem 165

To heat the music hall for the evening's performance each evening, the manager had to turn up the furnace by four o'clock in the afternoon. One February day the advertised event was a rock concert by the Body Bags, a popular group touring New England. They were still in a city 80 miles away on the date of the performance, and traffic had been made impossible by a New England blizzard that stranded everyone. Certain that they would not show up, and figuring that in any event no audience would, the manager

---

*The Bankruptcy Code uses a purely bookkeeping test for insolvency: more liabilities than assets; see Bankruptcy Code §101(32). The Restatement test tacks on to this the so-called equity definition of *insolvency*: failure to pay debts as they occur, which is much easier to prove than the test in the Bankruptcy Code.

decided to cancel that evening's performance; he did not heat the music hall. It was understood by all parties that the performers, if they were ready, willing, and able to perform, were to be paid even though weather conditions caused the performance to be cancelled. Half an hour before showtime, the musicians did arrive; they had rented snowmobiles to get through. When they learned that there would be no show and no payment, they sued. The manager defended by pointing to their prospective inability to perform and the doctrine of impossibility. How would this come out in a court in which you were the judge? See Hathaway v. Sabin, 63 Vt. 527, 22 A. 633 (1891).

Problem 166

After his horse Bucephalus won the Kentucky Derby, Alexander agreed to sell him to Phillip on September 1 for $15 million. On July 10, Phillip learned that Alexander had sold Bucephalus to Darius for $20 million. Phillip sued immediately, but Alexander contended that no breach could possibly occur until September 1. Who is right here? See Official Comment 2 to UCC §2-610.

Problem 167

Travis contracted to sell a houseboat to his friend Meyer for $35,000. They agreed to meet on the boat on August 1 and swap the boat for a check for that amount. On July 15 Meyer phoned Travis and told him that the deal was off. Travis refused to accept the cancellation and brought suit on August 10 for breach of contract. If Meyer can show that Travis never formally tendered the houseboat, is this a defense? If Travis had promised to paint the houseboat prior to delivery, is it a defense that he never did so after Meyer's call? If you were a judge, what would you require Travis to allege and prove here?

GREGUHN v. MUTUAL OF OMAHA INSURANCE CO.
Supreme Court of Utah, 1969 23
Utah 2d 214, 461 P.2d 285

Tuckett, J. The plaintiff filed a separate action against each of the defendants to recover benefits due under health and accident policies issued by the defendants. The two cases were consolidated for trial. From an adverse verdict and judgment of the court below the defendants have appealed to this court.

On May 12, 1962, the defendant United Benefit Life Insurance Company issued a policy to the plaintiff, and on May 8, 1964, the defendant Mutual of Omaha Insurance Company issued a policy to the plaintiff. Both policies insured the plaintiff against loss arising from sickness or accident. At the time the policies were issued and for more than 20 years prior thereto the plaintiff had worked as a brick mason. During his adult life, except for a short period of time in the army and during another six-month interval when the plaintiff worked at a brewery, he had followed the trade of a brick mason. The record shows that the plaintiff's schooling had ended at the fifth grade.

The pertinent provisions of the policies we are here concerned with are: The Mutual of Omaha policy defines injuries as follows: "Injuries mean accidental bodily injuries received while this policy is in force and resulting in a loss independently of sickness and other causes." In the same policy the phrase "total loss of time" means "that period of time during which you are unable to engage in any other gainful work or service for which you are reasonably fitted by education, training or experience." In the policy issued by United Benefit Life Insurance Company the insuring clause of the policy states that the policyholder is insured "against loss of life, limb, or sight resulting directly and independently of all other causes from accidental bodily injuries received while this policy is in force," and the term "loss of time" means "that period of time for which the insured is able to perform none of his occupational duties." On September 21, 1964, while the plaintiff was working as a brick mason, a plank which was a part of the scaffold on which he was working fell from beneath him. The plaintiff caught himself with one hand on the wall and the other hand on the scaffold which prevented him from falling to the ground below. The plaintiff remained hanging until a fellow employee assisted him in regaining a position on the scaffold. Approximately an hour after this incident the plaintiff began to suffer pain in his back.

The next day the plaintiff continued to suffer pain in his lower back which radiated down his left leg. The plaintiff consulted Dr. Robert H. Lamb, an orthopedic surgeon. Dr. Lamb examined the plaintiff and took X-rays of the plaintiff's back and as a result he concluded that the plaintiff had a pre-existing condition of the back known as spondylolisthesis. This defect might be either congenital or acquired. Dr. Lamb was also of the opinion that the plaintiff had received an injury causing pressure on the new nerve roots at the lower lumbar level accounting for the plaintiff's numbness and pain.

The plaintiff was treated by a course of physical therapy in the hospital which treatment did not relieve his symptoms, and subsequently two surgical procedures were performed in an effort to effect a cure of the plaintiff's back problems.

The defendants made payments to the plaintiff pursuant to the terms of the policies until on or about June 1965 when the defendants notified the plaintiff that the plaintiff's ailment would be considered a loss due to illness without confinement, and that a payment of $300 would represent the final payment of benefits under the policies. Upon failure of the defendants to further perform, these actions resulted.

Trial was had in the court below on the issues as to whether or not the plaintiff was totally and permanently disabled within the terms and conditions of the policies, and whether or not the accidental fall of the plaintiff activated and precipitated a latent condition of the plaintiff's back to a disability condition. During the course of the trial the plaintiff testified that he had experienced no back problems prior to the accident of September 21, 1964, and that he had continuously worked as a brick mason for approximately 30 years except for two short periods. The plaintiff's attending physician, Dr. Lamb, testified that he was of the opinion that the plaintiff would be unable in the future to continue on with the trade of brick masonry. The defendants also called medical experts who testified as to the plaintiff's condition. The testimony of these physicians conflicted in some respects with the testimony of Dr. Lamb, but it was generally agreed that the plaintiff would be unable to follow his trade as a brick mason. There was some testimony to the effect that the plaintiff might be physically capable of engaging in some other line of work such as brick masonry contracting.

The jury returned a general verdict finding the issues in favor of the plaintiff. After the verdict was returned, the court calculated the amount due under the terms of the policies together with interest to the time of trial. In addition thereto the court found that the defendants had repudiated their contracts of insurance and concluded that the plaintiff was entitled to a lump sum judgment for future benefits which would accrue under the terms of the policies. The court received evidence as to the life expectancy of the plaintiff and based thereon calculated and made a finding as to future benefits.

The defendants are here contending that the evidence failed to show that the plaintiff was totally disabled and that his disability did not result from the accident alone exclusive of all other causes. While it is true that plaintiff suffered from a condition of the back, there is no dispute in the evidence that the plaintiff had carried on his trade as a brick mason over a long period of time without being aware that he had a defect known as spondylolisthesis and without that condition interfering with his work. It must be concluded that the defendants when they issued their policies of health and accident insurance took the plaintiff in the condition they then found him. There is evidence of record from which the jury could conclude that the plaintiff's disability resulted proximately from the accident and that the nondisabling and dormant condition of the plaintiff's back was precipitated into a disabling condition by the accident in question. While the defendants excepted to the court's instructions to the jury and also excepted to the refusal of the court to give certain of the defendants' requested instructions, from our review of the instructions we are of the opinion that the issues were fairly and adequately submitted to the jury and we find no grounds for reversal of the verdict.

This brings us to what we consider the most critical problem in the case. Did the court err in granting an award for future disability under the doctrine of anticipatory breach? This problem is one of first impression in this jurisdiction. While the defendants cite the case of Colovos v. Home Life Insurance Co. of New York as being an expression by this court as to what the rule is, an examination of the case reveals that the doctrine of anticipatory breach was not before the court. The decisions of a number of the states permit an insured to recover a money judgment for the present value of future payments based upon the insured's life expectancy. However, the great majority of decisions permit recovery under a disability policy only of installments accrued and unpaid. The doctrine of anticipatory breach has not ordinarily been extended to unilateral contracts. As stated in the Restatement of Contracts: In unilateral contracts for the payment in installments after default of one or more, no repudiation can amount to an anticipatory breach of the rest of the installments not yet due. We are of the opinion that it was error for the trial court to enter judgment for future benefits to become due under the policies.

The verdict and the decision of the trial court amounts to a determination that the plaintiff is entitled to the monthly payments as specified in the insurance policies so long as he is totally and permanently disabled. Defendants are not relieved of the obligation of making the payments unless the plaintiff should recover or die. Should the defendants fail in the future to make payment in accordance with the terms of the policies without just cause or excuse and the plaintiff is compelled to file another action for delinquent installments, the court at that time should be able to fashion such relief as will compel performance.

This matter is remanded to the trial court with directions to modify its judgment so as to eliminate that part of the judgment pertaining to future benefits under the policies. Plaintiff (respondent) is entitled to costs.

CROCKETT, C.J., and CALLISTER and HENROID, JJ., concur.

ELLETT, Justice (dissenting). I dissent.

The plaintiff claimed that he was totally and permanently disabled under the terms of the policies written by the defendants. After making some periodic payments, the defendants denied any liability to make further payments on the grounds that if the plaintiff had any disability, it was not related to causes covered in the policies.

By rendering its verdict in favor of the plaintiff, the jury found that plaintiff was permanently and totally disabled under the terms of the policies. There was evidence to support the verdict and, therefore, the issue of the permanency and totality of the disability under the policies has been concluded, and the prevailing opinion accepts these facts.

While the majority of cases listed in the digests have held that recovery in actions involving health and accident policies is limited to accrued and past-due installments, there is respectable and, in my opinion, better reasoned authority to the contrary.

In those actions which have been brought to interpret, apply, or enforce the terms of a policy and where no repudiation of further liability is involved, then the recovery is properly limited to accrued and past-due installments. However, where there is a repudiation of all contractual obligations, I think it is the better policy to allow full recovery in one action, as was done in the case now before us.

Some of the cases which limit recovery to past-due installments do so because of a provision in the policy requiring the insured to furnish proof of continued disability as a condition of liability to pay. This should not be necessary where there has been a determination in court that the disability is *total* and *permanent.*

It does not appeal to me as being just or fair to permit an insurer which has breached its contractual obligation to pay, to insist that the insured must *abide* by the terms of the contract insofar as those terms favor the insurer. One who abrogates his contract is in no position to compel the other party to be bound by the terms of the contract.

Some of the cases which limit recovery to past-due installments do so upon the ground that to permit a recovery beyond the installments as set out in the contract would be in abrogation of the express provisions of the contract.

Such a holding confuses a suit for specific performance with an action in damages for breach of contract.

At common law an action of Debt would lie for money due under a contract, but only one cause could be brought on the contract. Where a contract was to be performed in installments, an action could not be maintained until all installments were due. The action of Assumpsit changed the law so that recovery could be had as soon as there had been a nonperformance of any installment obligation. However, the idea that only one action would lie for breach of a contract still persisted, and so a plaintiff had to recover all damages in one action, including installments not yet due. He got judgment for the total amount promised when there was a breach of the one installment of the contract.

Later on in the process of development of the law, installment contracts came to be regarded as divisible into separate parts, and thus an action of Indebitatus Assumpsit (he promised to pay) would lie upon each installment as it became due. See Corbin on Contracts, §949. . . .

There can be no quarrel with the rule that where the contract has become wholly unilateral, as where nothing further is to be done by the plaintiff, the mere failure to pay one or more installments when due would not, in and of itself, be considered a repudiation of the contract as to future payments, since the breach does not go to the essence of the contract. However, where there is a failure to pay one installment, coupled with an announcement by the insurer that no future payments will be made, then damages for the partly anticipatory breach should be allowed. See Corbin on Contracts, Sec. 966.

Since the plaintiff in this case was determined to be totally and permanently disabled, the defendants cannot relitigate those matters. By assuming the defendants would pay according to the contract, the prevailing opinion ignores the fact that the plaintiff sued for damages, not specific performance, and would compel him to abide by terms of the contract when neither party requests such a ruling. The decision grants to the defendants an opportunity to refuse gain to pay the installments to plaintiff and says that in such an event the trial court "should be able to fashion such relief as will compel performance." I am unable to know just what relief the decision has in mind. Under the pleadings as framed in this case, the relief to which plaintiff was entitled has already been given him.

[handwritten margin note: sue for specific performance, Not merely damages]

If it appears, as in this case, that a party to a contract makes an outright refusal to comply with the terms thereof and so notifies the other party, then I can see no legal reason why that other party may not accept the anticipatory breach of the contract and sue for his damages. What reason is there in law or good conscience to give a locus penitentiae to the party whose wrongful conduct precipitates a lawsuit? Why should an appellate court set the stage for further litigation when the matters have already been fully determined?

[handwritten margin note: There should Anticipatory Breach in Installment contracts]

By informing the plaintiff herein that no further payments would be made upon the policies, the defendants were guilty of an executory breach of the contracts which entitled the plaintiff to sue for his damages and to put an end to further litigation.

[handwritten margin note: would prevent future litigation]

I would affirm the judgment of the trial court and in so doing would ignore the dictum in the case of Colovos v. Home Life Ins. Co. of New York, 83 Utah 401, 412, 28 P.2d 607 (1934).

QUESTIONS

1. Do you agree with the majority or the dissent here?

2. What policy reasons support the majority's position? Which would point the other way?

3. The most common type case in which this issue arises occurs where a party owes installment payments on a loan or a credit purchase. The debtor misses a payment and indicates he refuses to pay any future obligations. The easiest resolution of this matter is for the creditor to put an acceleration clause in the contract. "If you miss a payment, we can accelerate the entire debt and sue now for the entire remaining obligation." This will work. Issues still arise when such acceleration clauses apply to incidents beyond missed payments as triggering events. For example, the creditor may have a provision in the contract that says all payments become due "at will" or if the creditor "deems itself insecure." Interpretation as to just when such an

[margin note: Must be m. good faith]

event occurs has created much litigation. Interestingly, the Uniform Commercial Code blesses such insecurity clauses, while adding that they can only be exercised in good faith; UCC §1-309.

4. Could the court have solved the problem in the instant case by a decree of specific performance with respect to future installments as they come due? See Corbin §969; John Hancock Mutual Life Insurance Co. v. Cohen, 254 F.2d 417 (9th Cir. 1958).

CORBIN ON CONTRACTS §965

What the plaintiff asks for and what he is given is a judgment for money damages. It is merely an accidental circumstance that where the contractual duty is a duty to pay money, the performance that is expressly promised is identical in character with the performance that is required by a judgment for money damages. Obviously, a judgment for money damages is not a judgment for the specific performance of a promise to deliver goods, to convey land, or to render service. In the case of an express contract for the payment of money, however, a judgment for money damages may appear to one who looks at the matter only superficially to be a judgment for specific performance. This it certainly is not if the judgment is not for the full sum promised, but is merely for its present value after making proper discount for advance collection. Furthermore, in an action for damages for breach of a promise to make a money payment, the plaintiff can get judgment for much more than the amount promised him if he can prove with reasonable certainty the amount of additional losses that the defendant had reason to foresee. Therefore, a plaintiff should not be deprived of his remedy in damages for an anticipatory repudiation merely because the promised performance is similar in character to the performance that is required by the judicial remedy that is commonly given for all kinds of breaches of contract.

Problem 168

Return to the facts of the first Problem in this chapter wherein NASA contracted with Venture's Vehicles for the space scooter to be delivered on July 1, 2030, and on April 5, 2026, the company informed NASA by letter that it was repudiating the contract. NASA's purchasing director was dumbfounded by this news but immediately began casting about for a substitute, which NASA found on September 10, 2026, signing a contract on that date to pay the new company $48 billion for delivery of the scooter as agreed. Assume that the price for such scooters specified in the contract was

$32 billion and that the market price for the scooters would be $45 billion on April 5, 2026, and $55 million on July 1, 2030.

(a) You are the chief attorney for NASA and your phone rings with these questions. *Must* NASA sue now? Take mitigatory action now? Or may it treat the repudiation as a *brutum fulmen* (Latin for "empty noise") and await performance in 2030 as agreed? At what moment will its damages be measured? See UCC §§2-610, 2-713, and 2-723. Do these sections conflict? What does "learned of the breach" mean in §2-713? See Cosden Oil & Chem. Co. v. Karl O. Helm Aktiengesellschaft, 736 F.2d 1064 (5th Cir. 1984).

(b) If NASA does nothing, may Venture's Vehicles change its mind, retract the repudiation, and reinstate the contract? See UCC §2-611. If NASA had contracted with another company for the space scooter on learning of the repudiation, would Venture's Vehicles have been able to do this?

CHAPTER 8 ASSESSMENT

Multiple Choice Questions

1. Star Management was a company that represented entertainers by financing and setting up events at which the entertainer could perform. It contracted with rock star Cindy Taylor to do this for a December performance of her songs at a production created by a convention center in Las Vegas, agreeing to send her $30,000 in travel expenses and make all the arrangements for a successful event, in return for a percentage of the money she would be paid for the performance by the Las Vegas event producer. One month before the event, Star Management sent her $15,000, and she replied with an email asking where the rest of the money was. Star Management replied that it would be forthcoming soon. Taylor emailed back, "This deal is off—you were supposed to send it all at once." Star Management emailed back, "Are you sure?" Two hours later Taylor emailed, "Are you going to send the rest of the money?" Hearing nothing for the rest of the day, Taylor sent an email shortly before midnight stating, "Deal back on, but assuming you will send the rest of the money soon." The next morning Star Management cancelled the Las Vegas event, and then each party sued the other for breach of contract. It was not clear from the contract whether Star Management had to pay the $30,000 as a lump sum or not. How should this come out?

   a. Taylor should win. Star Management was in breach when it didn't send the full amount, she demanded it clear this up, and instead it cancelled the contract while negotiations were going on. She did not make an anticipatory repudiation of the deal with her first reply because it indicated she was claiming breach of contract by Star

Management. Even if this was a repudiation, subsequent emails between the parties revived the deal, and Taylor made it clear she was going to perform as long as Star Management also did so, but then it unilaterally called off the event, which was a breach of contract. The law favors a compromise and Star Management behaved badly after one had been reached.

b. Star Management should win. She clearly repudiated the contract by saying "This deal is off." That anticipatory repudiation entitled Star Management to believe her and call off the Las Vegas performance. The intervening emails never worked out a new agreement, and that was Taylor's fault for being so definite in her original cancellation.

c. There never was a contract since the parties had not agreed on what both thought was a key term: the amount of travel expenses Star Management was required to pay up front.

2. When Mary Jones filed for divorce from her husband Ronald Jones the parties negotiated a settlement agreement by which he would send her $4,000 each month for the next seven years. He did so for two years, but then fell in love with another woman and stopped making the payments, saying he was done with supporting her when she could well afford to support herself. Mary sued him and asked for damages in the amount of the money due during the remainder of the contract, discounted to present value. Should the court award her this amount?

a. Yes. His repudiation of the settlement agreement is a breach and gives rise to full damages. He must pay all that she has lost under the contract, which is the remaining amount, though it is only fair to reduce it by the present value of that amount (meaning an amount of money that if invested would, by earning interest, add up to the total sum over a seven-year period). Otherwise she'd have to bring a lawsuit every month, wasting time and money for everyone, including the trial court.

b. No. If the contract has been fully performed on one side, as here, and all that remains is the future payment of money, the court will not make all the payments due early, even with a discount to present value. Doing so would be a sort of super specific performance, giving her a lump sum that the contract would never have awarded her. She can only sue for the amounts he promised to pay as they come due.

Answers

1. A is the best answer. The law does favor a compromise, and even though Taylor did make an anticipatory repudiation the nonbreaching party did not accept it, but instead made an inquiry as to whether the deal was still on. While there were serious negotiations on this issue still in process, Taylor sent a message clearly retracting the repudiation and reinstating

the contract. Yes, there was still a dispute about timing of the remaining travel expenses payment, but that could have been worked out. This meant that Star Management was in breach when it precipitously cancelled the event. The actual case on which this question is based is Vision Entertainment Worldwide, LLC v. Mary Jane Productions, Inc., 2014 WL 5369776 (S.D.N.Y. 2014).

2. It depends on the jurisdiction. In the Utah case reprinted above the court reached answer B, but Corbin pooh-poohs the "specific performance" rationale, saying all that is going on is allowing the injured party her damages now (with a proper discount for interest so that she doesn't receive more money than performance would have given her). The policy justification for the Corbin view is that otherwise she is faced with a hopeless series of lawsuits to rectify a big injury that occurs at the moment Ronald repudiates all future payments.

CHAPTER
9
THIRD-PARTY BENEFICIARIES

I. TYPES OF THIRD-PARTY BENEFICIARIES

Although we think of a contract as involving the two parties who negotiated it, agreements often affect many others. For example, if parties to a divorce settlement make promises to each other about financing the education of their children, those children, while not parties to the contract, may have a legitimate claim to enforce the provisions that were made for their benefit. It is no surprise then that our law will allow some strangers to the contract to sue to enforce it, while drawing lines to bar that same right to others even if those others will benefit from the contract's enforcement (like the education institutions in which the children enroll). In this chapter we will explore which "third-party beneficiaries" to a contract are eligible for this valuable enforcement right, and which outside parties are not.

Problem 169

Judge Hardy promised his son Andy that he would buy him the used car that Andy had been admiring down at MGM Motors if Andy would agree to go to law school instead of pursuing a career in the theater. Andy did go to law school, which, of course, he loved so much he gave up any further thoughts of an alternative career. Judge Hardy failed to buy the promised car, but Andy was so happy in his studies that he didn't care. MGM Motors cared, however, and it brought suit against Judge Hardy for failing to buy the car from the dealership. MGM claimed to be the third-party beneficiary of the promise Judge Hardy made to Andy. Should this suit succeed? Try to articulate your reasons for deciding either way.

Problem 170

Judge Hardy paid MGM Motors $20,000 upon MGM's promise to deliver a new car to Andy Hardy on his fifteenth birthday. Judge Hardy never made it to Andy's birthday, and MGM never delivered the car to Andy. Andy has sued. Should he recover from MGM? Would your answer differ if Judge Hardy had owed Andy $20,000 as opposed to it being a gift?

A.   *The Historical Development of Beneficiary Rights*

The preceding Problems address the issue of when, if ever, a third person, X, not a party to a contract between A and B, should be able to enforce B's promise to A. The traditional English approach was not to allow X to enforce B's promise under contract law (although some English courts used the fiction of an equitable trust to get to the same place). The following decision, Lawrence v. Fox, is the classic case demonstrating a more liberal American approach. Following *Lawrence* are two other famous New York cases representing attempts to extend the potential class of third parties who can enforce a contract to which they are not a party.

LAWRENCE v. FOX
Court of Appeals of New York, 1859
20 N.Y. 268

Appeal from the Superior Court of the city of Buffalo. On the trial before Mr. Justice Masten, it appeared by the evidence of a bystander, that one Holly, in November, 1857, at the request of the defendant, loaned and advanced to him $300, stating at the time that he owed that sum to the plaintiff for money borrowed of him, and had agreed to pay it to him the then next day; that the defendant in consideration thereof, at the time of receiving the money, promised to pay it to the plaintiff the then next day. Upon this state of facts the defendant moved for a nonsuit, upon three several grounds, viz.: That there was no proof tending to show that Holly was indebted to the plaintiff; that the agreement by the defendant with Holly to pay the plaintiff was void for want of consideration, and that there was no privity between the plaintiff and defendant. The court overruled the motion, and the counsel for the defendant excepted. The cause was then submitted to the jury, and they found a verdict for the plaintiff for the amount of the loan and interest, $344.66, upon which judgment was entered; from which the defendant appealed to the Superior Court, at general term, where the judgment was affirmed, and the defendant appealed to this court. The cause was submitted on printed arguments.

GRAY, J. The first objection raised on the trial amounts to this: That the evidence of the person present, who heard the declarations of Holly giving directions as to the payment of the money he was then advancing to the defendant, was mere hearsay and therefore not competent. Had the plaintiff sued Holly for this sum of money no objection to the competency of this evidence would have been thought of; and if the defendant had performed his promise by paying the sum loaned to him to the plaintiff, and Holly had afterwards sued him for its recovery, and this evidence had been offered by the defendant, it would doubtless have been received without an objection from any source. All the defendant had the right to demand in this case was evidence which, as between Holly and the plaintiff, was competent to establish the relation between them of debtor and creditor. For that purpose the evidence was clearly competent; it covered the whole ground and warranted the verdict of the jury. But it is claimed that notwithstanding this promise was established by competent evidence, it was void for the want of consideration. It is now more than a quarter of a century since it was settled by the Supreme Court of this State — in an able and pains-taking opinion by the late Chief Justice Savage, in which the authorities were fully examined and carefully analysed — that a promise in all material respects like the one under consideration was valid; and the judgment of that court was unanimously affirmed by the Court for the Correction of Errors. (Farley v. Cleaveland, 4 Cow., 432; same case in error, 9 id., 639.) In that case one Moon owed Farley and sold to Cleaveland a quantity of hay, in consideration of which Cleaveland promised to pay Moon's debt to Farley; and the decision in favor of Farley's right to recover was placed upon the ground that the hay received by Cleaveland from Moon was a valid consideration for Cleaveland's promise to pay Farley, and that the subsisting liability of Moon to pay Farley was no objection to the recovery. The fact that the money advanced by Holly to the defendant was a loan to him for a day, and that it thereby became the property of the defendant, seemed to impress the defendant's counsel with the idea that because the defendant's promise was not a trust fund placed by the plaintiff in the defendant's hands, out of which he was to realize money as from the sale of a chattel or the collection of a debt, the promise although made for the benefit of the plaintiff could not enure to his benefit. The hay which Cleaveland delivered to Moon was not to be paid to Farley, but the debt incurred by Cleaveland for the purchase of the hay, like the debt incurred by the defendant for money borrowed, was what was to be paid. That case has been often referred to by the courts of this State, and has never been doubted as sound authority for the principle upheld by it. (Barker v. Buklin, 2 Denio, 45; Hudson Canal Company v. The Westchester Bank, 4 id., 97.) It puts to rest the objection that the defendant's promise was void for want of consideration. The report of that case shows that the promise was not only made to Moon but to the plaintiff Farley. In this case the promise was made to Holly and not expressly to the plaintiff; and this difference between the two cases presents the question, raised by the defendant's objection, as to the want of privity between the plaintiff and defendant. As early as 1806 it was announced by the Supreme Court of this State, upon what was then regarded as the settled law of England, "That where one person makes a promise to another for the benefit of a third person, that third person may maintain an action upon it." Schermerhorn v. Vanderheyden (1 John. R., 140), has often been reasserted by our courts and never departed from. . . . But it is urged that because the defendant was not in any sense a trustee of the property of Holly for the benefit of the plaintiff, the law will not imply a promise. I agree that many of the cases where a promise was implied were cases of trusts, created for the benefit of the promiser. The case of Felton v. Dickinson (10 Mass., 189, 190), and others that might be cited, are of that class; but concede them all to have been cases of trusts, and it proves nothing against the application of the rule to this case. The duty of the trustee to pay the *cestuis que trust*, according to the terms of the trust, implies his promise to the latter to do so. In this case the defendant, upon ample consideration received from Holly, promised Holly to pay his debt to the plaintiff; the consideration received and the promise to Holly made it as plainly his duty to pay the plaintiff as if the money had been remitted to him for that purpose, and as well implied a promise to do so as if he had been made a trustee of property to be converted into cash with which to pay. The fact that a breach of the duty imposed in the one case may be visited, and justly, with more serious consequences than in the other, by no means disproves the payment to be a duty in both. The principle illustrated by the example so frequently quoted (which concisely states the case in hand) "that a promise made to one for the benefit of another, he for whose benefit it is made may bring an action for its breach," has been applied to trust cases, not because it was exclusively applicable to those cases, but because it was a principle of law, and as such applicable to those cases. It was also insisted that Holly could have discharged the defendant from his promise, though it was intended by both parties for the benefit of the plaintiff, and therefore the plaintiff was not entitled to maintain this suit for the recovery of a demand over which he had no control. It is enough that the plaintiff did not release the defendant from his promise, and whether he could or not is a question not now necessarily involved; but if it was, I think it would be found difficult to maintain the right of Holly to discharge a judgment recovered by the plaintiff upon confession or otherwise, for the breach of the defendant's promise; and if he could not, how could he discharge the suit before judgment, or the promise before suit, made as it was for the plaintiff's benefit and in accordance with legal presumption accepted by him (Berley v. Taylor, 5 Hill, 577-584, et seq.), until his dissent was shown. The cases cited, and especially that of Farley v. Cleaveland, establish the validity of a parol promise; it stands then upon the footing of a written one. Suppose the defendant had given his note in which, for value received of Holly, he had promised to pay the plaintiff and the plaintiff had accepted the promise, retaining Holly's liability. Very clearly Holly could not have discharged that promise, be the right to release the defendant as it may. No one can doubt that he owes the sum of money demanded of him, or that in accordance with his promise it was his duty to have paid it to the plaintiff; nor can it be doubted that whatever may be the diversity of opinion elsewhere, the adjudications in this State, from a very early period, approved by experience, have established the defendant's liability; if, therefore, it could be shown that a more strict and technically accurate application of the rules applied, would lead to a different result (which I by no means concede), the effort should not be made in the face of manifest justice.

The judgment should be affirmed.

JOHNSON, C.J., DENIO, SELDEN, ALLEN and STRONG, JJ., concurred. JOHNSON, C.J., and DENIO, J., were of opinion that the promise was to be regarded as made to the plaintiff through the medium of his agent, whose action he could ratify when it came to his knowledge, though taken without his being privy thereto.

COMSTOCK, J. (Dissenting.) The plaintiff had nothing to do with the promise on which he brought this action. It was not made to him, nor did the consideration proceed from him. If he can maintain the suit, it is because an anomaly has found its way into the law on this subject. In general, there must be privity of contract. The party who sues upon a promise must be the promisee, or he must have some legal interest in the undertaking. In this case, it is plain that Holly, who loaned the money to the defendant, and to whom the promise in question was made, could at any time have claimed that it should be performed to himself personally. He had lent the money to the defendant, and at the same time directed the latter to pay the sum to the plaintiff. This direction he could countermand, and if he had done so, manifestly the defendant's promise to pay according to the direction would have ceased to exist. The plaintiff would receive a benefit by a complete execution of the arrangement, but the arrangement itself was between other parties, and was under their exclusive control. If the defendant had paid the money to Holly, his debt would have been discharged thereby. So Holly might have released the demand or assigned it to another person, or the parties might have annulled the promise now in question, and designated some other creditor of Holly as the party to whom the money should be paid. It has never been claimed, that in a case thus situated, the right of a third person to sue upon the promise rested on any sound principle of law. We are to inquire whether the rule has been so established by positive authority.

The cases which have sometimes been supposed to have a bearing on this question, are quite numerous. In some of them, the dicta of judges, delivered upon very slight consideration, have been referred to as the decisions of the courts. Thus, in Schermerhorn v. Vanderheyden (1 John., 140), the court is reported as saying, "We are of opinion, that where one person makes a promise to another, for the benefit of a third person, that third person may maintain an action on such promise." This remark was made on the authority of Dalton v. Poole (Vent., 318, 332), decided in England nearly two hundred years ago. It was, however, but a mere remark, as the case was determined against the plaintiff on another ground. Yet this decision has often been referred to as authority for similar observations in later cases. . . .

The cases in which some trust was involved are also frequently referred to as authority for the doctrine now in question, but they do not sustain it. If A delivers money or property to B, which the latter accepts upon a trust for the benefit of C, the latter can enforce the trust by an appropriate action for that purpose. (Berly v. Taylor, 5 Hill, 577.) If the trust be of money, I think the beneficiary may assent to it and bring the action for money had and received to his use. If it be of something else than money, the trustee must account for it according to the terms of the trust, and upon principles of equity. There is some authority even for saying that an express promise founded on the possession of a trust fund may be enforced by an action at law in the name of the beneficiary, although it was made to the creator of the trust. Thus, in Comyn's Digest (Action on the case upon Assumpsit, B. 15), it is laid down that if a man promise a pig of lead to A, and his executor give lead to make a pig to B, who assumes to deliver it to A, an assumpsit lies by A against him. The case of The Delaware and Hudson Canal Company v. The Westchester County Bank (4 Denio, 97) involved a trust because the defendants had received from a third party a bill of exchange under an agreement that they would endeavor to collect it, and would pay over the proceeds when collected to the plaintiffs. A fund received under such an agreement does not belong to the person who receives it. He must account for it specifically; and perhaps there is no gross violation of principle in permitting the equitable owner of it to sue upon an express promise to pay it over. Having a specific interest in the thing, the undertaking to account for it may be regarded as in some sense made with him through the author of the trust. But further than this we cannot go without violating plain rules of law. In the case before us there was nothing in the nature of a trust or agency. . . .

GROVER, J., also dissented. Judgment affirmed.

SEAVER v. RANSOM

Court of Appeals of New York, 1918
224 N.Y. 233, 120 N.E. 639

POUND, J. Judge Beman and his wife were advanced in years. Mrs. Beman was about to die. She had a small estate, consisting of a house and lot in Malone and little else. Judge Beman drew his wife's will according to her instructions. It gave $1,000 to plaintiff, $500 to one sister, plaintiff's mother, and $100 each to another sister and her son, the use of the house to her husband for life, and remainder to the American Society for the Prevention of Cruelty to Animals. She named her husband as residuary legatee and executor. Plaintiff was her niece, 34 years old in ill health sometimes a member of the Beman household. When the will was read to Mrs. Beman, she said that it was not as she wanted it. She wanted to leave the house to plaintiff. She had no other objection to the will, but her strength was waning, and, although the judge offered to write another will for her, she said she was afraid she would not hold out long enough to enable her to sign it. So the judge said, if she would sign the will, he would leave plaintiff enough in his will to make up the difference. He avouched the promise by his uplifted hand with all solemnity and his wife then executed the will. When he came to die, it was found that his will made no provision for the plaintiff.

This action was brought, and plaintiff recovered judgment in the trial court, on the theory that Beman had obtained property from his wife and induced her to execute the will in the form prepared by him by his promise to give plaintiff $6,000, the value of the house, and that thereby equity impressed his property with a trust in favor of plaintiff. Where a legatee promises the testator that he will use property given him by the will for a particular purpose, a trust arises. [Citations omitted.] Beman received nothing under his wife's will but the use of the house in Malone for life. Equity compels the application of property thus obtained to the purpose of the testator, but equity cannot so impress a trust, except on property obtained by the promise. Beman was bound by his promise, but no property was bound by it; no trust in plaintiff's favor can be spelled out.

An action on the contract for damages, or to make the executors trustees for performance, stands on different ground. Farmers' Loan & Trust Co. v. Mortimer, 219 N.Y. 290, 294, 295, 114 N.E. 389. The Appellate Division properly passed to the consideration of the question whether the judgment could stand upon the promise made to the wife, upon a valid consideration, for the sole benefit of plaintiff. The judgment of the trial court was affirmed by a return to the general doctrine laid down in the great case of Lawrence v. Fox, 20 N.Y. 268, which has since been limited as herein indicated.

Contracts for the benefit of third persons have been the prolific source of judicial and academic discussion. [Citations omitted.] The general rule, both in law and equity (Phalen v. United States Trust Co., 186 N.Y. 178, 186, 78 N.E. 943, 7 L.R.A. [N.S.] 734, 9 Ann. Cas. 595), was that privity between a plaintiff and a defendant is necessary to the maintenance of an action on the contract. The consideration must be furnished by the party to whom the promise was made. The contract cannot be enforced against the third party, and therefore it cannot be enforced by him. On the other hand, the right of the beneficiary to sue on a contract made expressly for his benefit has been fully recognized in many American jurisdictions, either by judicial decision or by legislation, and is said to be "the prevailing rule in this country." Hendrick v. Lindsay, 93 U.S. 143; Lehow v. Simonton, 3 Colo. 346. It has been said that "the establishment of this doctrine has been gradual, and is a victory of practical utility over theory, of equity over technical subtlety." Brantly on Contracts (2d ed.) p. 253. The reasons for this view are that it is just and practical to permit the person for whose benefit the contract is made to enforce it against one whose duty it is to pay. Other jurisdictions still adhere to the present English rule (7 Halsbury's Laws of England, 342, 343; Jenks' Digest of English Civil Law, §229) that a contract cannot be enforced by or against a person who is not a party (Exchange Bank v. Rice, 107 Mass. 37, 9 Am. Rep. 1). But see, also, Forbes v. Thorpe, 209 Mass. 570, 95 N.E. 955; Gardner v. Denison, 217 Mass. 492, 105 N.E. 359.

In New York the right of the beneficiary to sue on contracts made for his benefit is not clearly or simply defined. It is at present confined, first, to cases where there is a pecuniary obligation running from the promisee to the beneficiary, "a legal right founded upon some obligation of the promisee in the third party to adopt and claim the promise as made for his benefit." Farley v. Cleveland, 4 Cow. 432, 15 Am. Dec. 387; Lawrence v. Fox, supra; [citations omitted]. Secondly, to cases where the contract is made for the benefit of the wife, affianced wife, or child of a party to the contract [citations omitted]. The close relationship cases go back to the early King's Bench case (1677), long since repudiated in England, of Dutton v. Poole, 2 Lev. 211 (s. c., 1 Ventris, 318, 332). See Schemerhorn v. Vanderheyden, 1 Johns. 139, 3 Am. Dec. 304. The natural and moral duty of the husband or parent to provide for the future of wife or child sustains the action on the contract made for their benefit. "This is the farthest the cases in this state have gone," says Cullen, J., in the marriage settlement case of Borland v. Welch, 162 N.Y. 104, 110, 56 N.E. 556.

The right of the third party is also upheld in, thirdly, the public contract cases, where the municipality seeks to protect its inhabitants by covenants for their benefit; and, fourthly, the cases where, at the request of a party to the contract, the promise runs directly to the beneficiary although he does not furnish the consideration [citations omitted]. It may be safely said that a general rule sustaining recovery at the suit of the third party would include but few classes of cases not included in these groups, either categorically or in principle.

The desire of the childless aunt to make provision for a beloved and favorite niece differs imperceptibly in law or in equity from the moral duty of the parent to make testamentary provision for a child. The contract was made for the plaintiff's benefit. She alone is substantially damaged by its breach. The representatives of the wife's estate have no interest in enforcing it specifically. It is said in Buchanan v. Tilden that the common law imposes moral and legal obligations upon the husband and the parent not measured by the necessaries of life. It was, however, the love and affection or the moral sense of the husband and the parent that imposed such obligations in the cases cited, rather than any common-law duty of husband and parent to wife and child. If plaintiff had been a child of Mrs. Beman, legal obligation would have required no testamentary provision for her, yet the child could have enforced a covenant in her favor identical with the covenant of Judge Beman in this case. De Cicco v. Schweizer, supra. The constraining power of conscience is not regulated by the degree of relationship alone. The dependent or faithful niece may have a stronger claim than the affluent or unworthy son. No sensible theory of moral obligation denies arbitrarily to the former what would be conceded to the latter. We might consistently either refuse or allow the claim of both, but I cannot reconcile a decision in favor of the wife in Buchanan v. Tilden, based on the moral obligations arising out of near relationship, with a decision against the niece here on the ground that the relationship is too remote for equity's ken. No controlling authority depends upon so absolute a rule. . . . Kellogg, P.J., writing for the court below well said:

> The doctrine of Lawrence v. Fox is progressive, not retrograde. The course of the late decisions is to enlarge, not to limit, the effect of that case.

The court in that leading case attempted to adopt the general doctrine that any third person, for whose direct benefit a contract was intended, could sue on it. The headnote thus states the rule. Finch, J., in Gifford v. Corrigan, 117 N.Y. 257, 262, 22 N.E. 756, 15 Am. St. Rep. 508, says that the case rests upon that broad proposition; Edward T. Bartlett, J., in Pond v. New Rochelle Water Co., 183 N.Y. 330, 337, 76 N.E. 211, 213, calls it "the general principle"; but Vrooman v. Turner, supra, confined its application to the facts on which it was decided. "In every case in which an action has been sustained," says Allen, J., "there has been a debt or duty owing by the promisee to the party claiming to sue upon the promise." 69 N.Y. 285, 25 Am. Rep. 195. As late as Townsend v. Rackham, 143 N.Y. 516, 523, 38 N.E. 731, 733, we find Peckham, J., saying that, "to maintain the action by the third person, there must be this liability to him on the part of the promisee." . . .

But, on principle, a sound conclusion may be reached. If Mrs. Beman had left her husband the house on condition that he pay the plaintiff $6,000, and he had accepted the devise, he would have become personally liable to pay the legacy, and plaintiff could have recovered in an action at law against him, whatever the value of the house. [Citations omitted.] That would be because the testatrix had in substance bequeathed the promise to plaintiff, and not because close relationship or moral obligation sustained the contract. The distinction between an implied promise to a testator for the benefit of a third party to pay a legacy and an unqualified promise on a valuable consideration to make provision for the third party by will is discernible, but not obvious. The tendency of American authority is to sustain the gift in all such cases and to permit the donee beneficiary to recover on the contract. [Citation omitted.] The equities are with the plaintiff, and they may be enforced in this action, whether it be regarded as an action for damages or an action for specific performance to convert the defendants into trustees for plaintiff's benefit under the agreement. . . .

Judgment affirmed.

QUESTIONS

1. What factual variation in this case keeps the doctrine of Lawrence v. Fox from being directly on point? That is, given *Lawrence*, why was it necessary to litigate *Seaver* at all?

2. If the aunt here was making a *gift* to her niece, and gift promises are not enforceable until delivery, how can the niece sue to enforce the gift promise? If it is the policy of the law not to enforce unperformed gift promises, isn't that policy violated here?

3. What harm would come from denying donee beneficiaries the power to sue the promisor? The worst thing they are out is a gift.

NOTE ON TERMINOLOGY

In third-party beneficiary problems there are always at least three parties: the promisor, the promisee, and the third-party beneficiary. It is particularly crucial to your success in this area that you are able to put the right label on the characters presented by the facts (and you should practice doing it with the materials that follow). How do you sort them out? After all, in a bilateral contract *both* of the original contracting parties will be promisors.

To find the promisor, ask yourself which one of the original contracting parties made a promise to the other that benefits a third party. The answer will reveal the promisor for purposes of third-party beneficiary analysis. The promisor is almost always the defendant.

The promisee will be the original contracting party to whom the promise is made. As we shall see, it is the promisee's relationship to the third-party beneficiary that determines many of the legal results.

The third-party beneficiary will be a stranger to the original contract who is benefitted thereby. This stranger will almost always be the plaintiff.

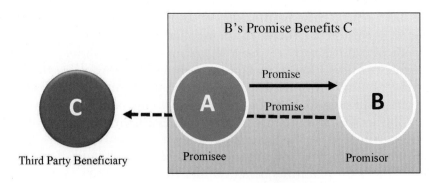

Third Party Beneficiary

H. R. MOCH CO. v. RENSSELAER WATER CO.
Court of Appeals of New York, 1928
247 N.Y. 160, 159 N.E. 896

Appeal from Supreme Court, Appellate Division, Third Department. Action by the H. R. Moch Company, Inc., against the Rensselaer Water Company. From a judgment of the Appellate Division (219 App. Div. 673, 220 N.Y.S. 557), reversing an order of the Special Term, and granting defendant's motion for judgment dismissing the complaint for failure to state facts sufficient to constitute a cause of action, plaintiff appeals. Affirmed. . . .

CARDOZO, C.J. The defendant, a waterworks company under the laws of this state, made a contract with the city of Rensselaer for the supply of water during a term of years. Water was to be furnished to the city for sewer flushing and street sprinkling; for service to schools and public buildings; and for service at fire hydrants, the latter service at the rate of $42.50 a year for each hydrant. Water was to be furnished to private takers within the city at their homes and factories and other industries at reasonable rates, not exceeding a stated schedule. While this contract was in force, a building caught fire. The flames, spreading to the plaintiff's warehouse nearby, destroyed it and its contents. The defendant, according to the complaint, was promptly notified of the fire, "but omitted and neglected after such notice, to supply or furnish sufficient or adequate quantity of water, with adequate pressure to stay, suppress, or extinguish the fire before it reached the warehouse of the plaintiff, although the pressure and supply which the defendant was equipped to supply and furnish, and had agreed by said contract to supply and furnish, was adequate and sufficient to prevent the spread of the fire to and the destruction of the plaintiff's warehouse and its contents." By reason of the failure of the defendant to "fulfill the provisions of the contract between it and the city of Rensselaer," the plaintiff is said to have suffered damage, for which judgment is demanded. A motion, in the nature of a demurrer, to dismiss the complaint, was denied at Special Term. The Appellate Division reversed by a divided court.

Liability in the plaintiff's argument is placed on one or other of three grounds. The complaint, we are told, is to be viewed as stating: (1) A cause of action for breach of contract within Lawrence v. Fox, 20 N.Y. 268; (2) a cause of action for a common-law tort, within MacPherson v. Buick Motor Co., 217 N.Y. 382, 111 N.E. 1050, L.R.A. 1916F, 696, Ann. Cas. 1916C, 440; or (3) a cause of action for the breach of a statutory duty. These several grounds of liability will be considered in succession.

(1) We think the action is not maintainable as one for breach of contract.

No legal duty rests upon a city to supply its inhabitants with protection against fire. [Citation omitted.] That being so, a member of the public may not maintain an action under Lawrence v. Fox against one contracting with the city to furnish water at the hydrants, unless an intention appears that the promisor is to be answerable to individual members of the public as well as to the city for any loss ensuing from the failure to fulfill the promise. No such intention is discernible here. On the contrary, the contract is significantly divided into two branches: One a promise to the city for the benefit of the city in its corporate capacity, in which branch is included the service at the hydrants; and the other a promise to the city for the benefit of private takers, in which branch is included the service at their homes and factories. In a broad sense it is true that every city contract, not improvident or wasteful, is for the benefit of the public. More than this, however, must be shown to give a right of action to a member of the public not formally a party. The benefit, as it is sometimes said, must be one that is not merely incidental and secondary. [Citation omitted.] It must be primary and immediate in such a sense and to such a degree as to bespeak the assumption of a duty to make reparation directly to the individual members of the public if the benefit is lost. The field of obligation would be expanded beyond reasonable limits if less than this were to be demanded as a condition of liability. A promisor undertakes to supply fuel for heating a public building. He is not liable for breach of contract to a visitor who finds the building without fuel, and thus contracts a cold. The list of illustrations can be indefinitely extended. The carrier of the mails under contract with the government is not answerable to the merchant who has lost the benefit of a bargain through negligent delay. The householder is without a remedy against manufacturers of hose and engines, though prompt performance of their contracts would have stayed the ravages of fire. "The law does not spread its protection so far." Robins Dry Dock & Repair Co. v. Flint, 48 S. Ct. 134.

So with the case at hand. By the vast preponderance of authority, a contract between a city and a water company to furnish water at the city hydrants has in view a benefit to the public that is incidental rather than immediate, an assumption of duty to the city and not to its inhabitants. Such is the ruling of the Supreme Court of the United States. German Alliance Ins. Co. v. Homewater Supply Co., 226 U.S. 220. Such has been the ruling in this state . . . , though the question is still open in this court. Such with few exceptions has been the ruling in other jurisdictions. Williston, Contracts, §373, and cases there cited; Dillon, Municipal Corporations (5th ed.) §1340. The diligence of counsel has brought together decisions to that effect from 26 states. Only a few states have held otherwise. Page, Contracts, §2401. An intention to assume an obligation of indefinite extension to every member of the public is seen to be the more improbable when we recall the crushing burden that the obligation would impose. Cf. Hone v. Presque Isle Water Co., 104 Me. 217, at p. 232, 71 A. 769. The consequences invited would bear no reasonable proportion to those attached by law to defaults not greatly different. A wrongdoer who by negligence sets fire to a building is liable in damages to the owner where the fire has its origin, but not to other owners who are injured when it spreads. The rule in our state is settled to that effect, whether wisely or unwisely. If the plaintiff is to prevail, one who negligently omits to supply sufficient pressure to extinguish a fire started by another assumes an obligation to pay the ensuing damage, though the whole city is laid low. A promisor will not be deemed to have had in mind the assumption of a risk so overwhelming for any trivial reward.

The cases that have applied the rule of Lawrence v. Fox to contracts made by a city for the benefit of the public are not at war with this conclusion. Through them all there runs as a unifying principle the presence of an intention to compensate the individual members of the public in the event of a default. For example, in Pond v. New Rochelle Water Co., 183 N.Y. 330, 76 N.E. 211, the contract with the city fixed a schedule of rates to be supplied, not to public buildings, but to private takers at their home. In Matter of International R. Co. v. Rann, 224 N.Y. 83, 85, 120 N.E. 153, the contract was by street railroads to carry passengers for a stated fare. In Smyth v. City of New York, 203 N.Y. 106, 96 N.E. 409, and Rigney v. New York Cent. & H.R.R. Co., 217 N.Y. 31, 111 N.E. 226, covenants were made by contractors upon public works, not merely to indemnify the city, but to assume its liabilities. These and like cases come within the third group stated in the comprehensive opinion in Seaver v. Ransom, 224 N.Y. 233, 238, 120 N.E. 639. The municipality was contracting in behalf of its inhabitants by covenants intended to be enforced by any of them severally as occasion should arise.

(2) We think the action is not maintainable as one for a common-law tort. . . .

(3) We think the action is not maintainable as one for the breach of a statutory duty. . . .

The judgment should be affirmed, with costs. . . .

Judgment affirmed, etc.

NOTE ON MUNICIPAL CONTRACTS

Consider the case of Koch v. Consolidated Edison Co. of New York, 62 N.Y.2d 548, 479 N.Y.S.2d 163, 468 N.E.2d 1 (1984), which concerned a defendant who had been found liable for a citywide blackout in the city of New York. Part of the defendant's appeal concerned the lower court's failure to dismiss the city's claim based on Con Edison's contracts with the Power Authority of the State of New York (PASNY). The Power Authority had purchased two generating plants from Con Edison, and Con Edison had agreed to continue to provide transmission and delivery of the electricity produced in the two plants to all existing recipients, including the city of New York. A service agreement was entered into in which was recited Con Edison's willingness, by use of its existing facilities, to assist PASNY in serving the needs of the Astoria-Indian Point customers. Con Edison was obligated to provide the same quality of service to PASNY's customers as it did to its own customers, under Con Edison's regular tariff schedules. In a simultaneously executed "Contract for the Sale of Power and Energy," Con Edison agreed to provide sufficient energy to meet the requirements of PASNY's affected customers.

The appellate court upheld the trial court; the city was a third-party beneficiary. In its decision on this point, the appellate court felt compelled to distinguish *Moch* and another famous case, Kornblut v. Chevron Oil Co. (cited in the following quotation). In the latter case, the court refused third-party beneficiary status to the estate of a person who died in his auto alongside the New York Thruway while waiting for the assistance of the defendant's repair truck. The defendant had contracted with an agency of the state to provide "rapid and efficient roadside automotive service." The following is an excerpt from the court's distinction in *Koch*.

> To be distinguished are our holdings in Moch Co. v. Rensselaer Water Co., 247 N.Y. 160, 159 N.E. 896 [contract between water company and city to supply water for fire hydrants did not create a duty to member of the public] and Kornblut v. Chevron Oil Co., 62 A.D.2d 831, 407 N.Y.S.2d 498, affd. on opn. below, 48 N.Y.2d 853, 424 N.Y.S.2d 429, 400 N.E.2d 368 [contract with Thruway Authority to provide repair services did not create duty to members of the public]. In neither of those cases did the operative contract provide that the service was to be rendered other than for the contracting party, city or authority. Moreover, in *Moch* we noted the distinction between the agreement of the water company, there in issue, to furnish water at the hydrants and the agreement of the water company to provide direct service to members of the public at their homes and factories (247 N.Y., at pp. 164, 166, 159 N.E. 896). In the present instance, the purpose of the enabling legislation was expressly stated to be "To preserve reliability of electric service in the metropolitan area of the city of New York" (Public Authorities Law, §1001-a, subd. 1), and the service agreement contained the express obligation to "operate and maintain all the facilities necessary to deliver power to Astoria-Indian Point Customers [which included plaintiffs] in accordance with good utility operating practice." Indeed, the essence of the responsibility of a public utility is to provide services to the consuming public.

QUESTIONS

Is the court's rationale persuasive? What policy considerations are at play? Are the consequences of loss of power to a city caused by a utility's failure to adequately provide the power any more foreseeable than the consequences of a loss of water to an entity that depends on the water in part for fire protection? Finally, why is it important that the court found that a city has no duty to protect its citizens from fires?

B. *The Need for the Restatement (Second) Changes*

The concepts developed in the three preceding New York Court of Appeals cases were incorporated wholesale into the original Restatement of Contracts (1932):

§133. Definition of Donee Beneficiary, Creditor Beneficiary Incidental Beneficiary

(1) Where performance of a promise in a contract will benefit a person other than the promisee, that person is, except as stated in Subsection (3):

(a) a donee beneficiary if it appears from the terms of the promise in view of the accompanying circumstances that the purpose of the promisee in obtaining the promise of all or part of the performance thereof is to make a gift to the beneficiary or to confer upon him a right against the promisor to some performance neither due nor supposed to be asserted to be due from the promisee to the beneficiary;

(b) a creditor beneficiary if no purpose to make a gift appears from the terms of the promise in view of the accompanying circumstances and performance of the promise will satisfy an actual or supposed or asserted duty of the promisee to the beneficiary, or a right of the beneficiary against the promisee which has been barred by the Statute of Limitations or by a discharge in bankruptcy, or which is unenforceable because of the Statute of Frauds;

(c) an incidental beneficiary if neither the facts stated in Clause (a) nor those stated in Clause (b) exist.

(2) Such a promise as is described in Subsection (1a) is a gift promise. Such a promise as is described in Subsection (1b) is a promise to discharge the promisee's duty.

(3) Where it appears from the terms of the promise in view of the accompanying circumstances that the purpose of the promisee is to benefit a beneficiary under a trust and the promise is to render performance to the trustee, the trustee, and not the beneficiary under the trust, is a beneficiary within the meaning of this Section.

As time went on the three categories of third-party beneficiaries established by the New York Court of Appeals and given the imprimatur of the first Restatement of Contracts (creditor, donee, and incidental) proved embarrassing because they did not quite describe all the possible beneficiaries who ought to be allowed to sue. The next Problem illustrates a typical situation, but to understand it you need to know something about mechanic's liens.

A *lien* is a property interest given to creditors in the debtor's property to protect a credit extension. Some liens are voluntarily incurred by the debtor (a mortgage, for example), but many liens arise either by operation of common law or by statute to protect certain worthy creditors (for example, those who perform work on personal property, such as garage mechanics, are given an *artisan's lien* on the property in their possession for the value of their services remaining unpaid).

Mechanic's liens are statutory liens given to those who perform work on or supply materials to a construction project. The lien is for unpaid wages or goods delivered and it attaches to the realty under construction. If the lienors remain unsatisfied and have followed certain formalities (filing a notice of intention to claim the mechanic's lien, for example), the realty can be sold under judicial supervision and the proceeds of the sale are used to pay off the lienors. This is true even if the owner of the realty has already made payment in full to the general contractor, who failed to pass the money on to those actually doing the labor or supplying the materials. The idea here is to keep the owner very interested in making sure that the project's laborers and suppliers get paid.

Problem 171

When John Adams decided to build his dream house, he hired the Hoban Construction Company to do the work. Worried about the possibility of mechanic's liens, Adams made Hoban Construction get a surety who would post a bond promising to pay all those who performed work on the project or who delivered materials to the job site. The Jefferson Surety Company, at Hoban's request, issued such a bond making the payment promise to Adams. During the construction Adams made periodic progress payments to Hoban Construction, withholding 15 percent as retainage to be paid on completion of the job. When Adams' architect certified that Hoban had completed the construction properly, and Hoban issued a certificate stating that it had paid off all of the laborers and suppliers, Adams released the retainage to Hoban. Two months later the Washington Brick Company realized that it had never been paid for the bricks it had delivered to the Adams project. The time for the filing of intention to claim a mechanic's lien had passed, and Hoban Construction, the only entity with which it had had a contract, was bankrupt. Washington Brick knew about the surety bond promising to pay off the suppliers, and so made a claim for payment from the surety. When the request was refused, Washington Brick brought suit against Jefferson Surety, claiming to be a third-party beneficiary of the promise made in the bond. Answer these questions:

(a) Who is the promisor here? The promisee?

(b) What kind of third-party beneficiary is Washington Brick: creditor, donee, or incidental? You may assume that Adams had no contract with Washington Brick, which contracted only with Hoban Construction.

(c) Is the last question easier to answer if the owner of the realty who demanded the bond was the United States government rather than a private individual like Adams? (You should know that no one can get a mechanic's lien on public property — on the post office, for example.)

(d) In deciding whether the parties intended some third person to be a beneficiary with a right to sue, is the intention of the promisor or the promisee most important? See Owner-Operator Independent Drivers Ass'n, Inc. v. Concord EFS, Inc., 59 S.W.3d 63 (Tenn. 2001).

NOTE ON THE MILLER ACT

Under the Miller Act, 40 U.S.C. §270, the general contractor must furnish a *payment* bond, guaranteeing payment to those who work on the project or provide materials for the construction. Although property of the United States is not subject to any mechanic's lien, subcontractors and suppliers who meet specific time and procedural requirements under the act can sue the surety directly if payment is not made; 40 U.S.C. §270(b). Suit can, therefore, be brought directly under the act rather than under the common law concerning third-party beneficiaries.

The Miller Act also requires general contractors to provide a *performance* bond to the United States. The performance bond insures that the performance will be completed in the time required. Performance bonds are also often used in private construction contracts. Although there is some split of authority, it is generally accepted that third-party suppliers and subcontractors are not third-party beneficiaries of performance contracts. See, e.g., Frommeyer v. L.&R. Construction Co., 139 F. Supp. 579 (D.N.J. 1956).

Situations like that presented in the last Problem led to an overhaul of third-party beneficiary terminology when the Restatement (Second) of Contracts was created:

§302. Intended and Incidental Beneficiaries

(1) Unless otherwise agreed between promisor and promisee, a beneficiary of a promise is an intended beneficiary if recognition of a right to performance in the beneficiary is appropriate to effectuate the intention of the parties and either

(a) the performance of the promise will satisfy an obligation of the promisee to pay money to the beneficiary; or
(b) the circumstances indicate that the promisee intends to give the beneficiary the benefit of the promised performance.

(2) An incidental beneficiary is a beneficiary who is not an intended beneficiary.

Comment d to this section states that "if the beneficiary would be reasonable in relying on the promise as manifesting an intention to confer a right on him, he is an intended beneficiary."

II. EXPANDING USE OF THIRD-PARTY BENEFICIARY CONCEPTS

In more than one case, plaintiff's attorney has felt compelled to raise the third-party beneficiary claim in circumstances that might be characterized as "facts requiring a grasping of at least one straw." Sometimes the beneficiary argument is used to supplement a tort claim in a case in which there is at least some question concerning the validity of the tort. Consider the next two cases.

BLAIR v. ANDERSON
Supreme Court of Delaware, 1974
325 A.2d 94

DUFFY, J. This appeal submits for decision a sovereign immunity defense by the State of Delaware to a claim arising out of incarceration in a Delaware Correctional institution.

I

Plaintiff, formerly a Federal prisoner, alleges that while incarcerated in the New Castle County Correctional Institution he was attacked by a fellow prisoner and that defendants, including the State, were negligent in permitting such assault. The Superior Court granted the State's motion to dismiss the action on the ground that it is barred by the doctrine of sovereign immunity whether the claim be regarded as based on contract or in tort. 314 A.2d 919 (1973). Our analysis of the legal issues in the case persuades us that the Court's conclusion was correct as to tort but not as to the contract claim.

II

By statute, 11 Del. C. §6505(a)(13), the Department of Correction is authorized:

> To agree with the proper authorities of the United States for payment to the General Fund of the State of such sums as shall be fixed by the Department for the maintenance and support of offenders committed to the Department by authority of the United States.

Under that statute the Department, on December 8, 1968, entered into a contract with the United States Department of Justice (Bureau of

Prisons);[1] the service to be performed by the State is described therein as "[s]afekeeping, care and subsistence of persons held under authority of any United States statute . . ." and among the rules and regulations governing custody and treatment of such persons is this:

1. Responsibility for Prisoners' Custody

It is the responsibility of the sheriff, jailer, or other official responsible for the administration of the institution to keep the prisoners in safe custody and to maintain proper discipline and control.

The State argues that it may not be sued by plaintiff because the doctrine of sovereign immunity permits such suit only after waiver by a legislative act and the General Assembly has not passed such an act.

III

The Delaware Constitution provides that "[s]uits may be brought against the State, according to such regulations as shall be made by law," Art. 1, §9, Del. C. Ann., and the judicial history of the provision makes it plain that the defense of sovereign immunity may be "waived by legislative act and only by legislative act." George & Lynch, Inc. v. State, Del. Supr., 197 A.2d 734 (1964); Shellhorn & Hill, Inc. v. State, Del. Supr., 187 A.2d 71 (1962). It is clear, however, that waiver need not be made in express statutory language. Specifically, when the General Assembly authorizes a contract to be made it implicitly and necessarily waives immunity to suit for breach by the State of that contract. George & Lynch, Inc. v. State, supra. While the justice of that proposition stands on its own merit, we do note also that there is a tendency (recognized by the Court below) to narrow the doctrine of sovereign immunity. Cf. Wilmington Housing Authority v. Williamson, Del. Supr., 228 A.2d 782 (1967); Holden v. Bundek, Del. Super., 317 A.2d 29 (1972).

IV

First, as to plaintiff's claim in tort, a suit by a Federal prisoner for injury caused by a fellow prisoner is apparently within the scope of the Federal Tort Claims Act, 28 U.S.C. §§1346(b), 2671-2680; United States v. Muniz, 374 U.S. 150 (1963). But we find no basis, in statutory waiver or otherwise, for departing from the well established Delaware law as to immunity. Therefore,

---

1. The Bureau of Prisons is required to provide, inter alia, for the "[s]afekeeping, care, and subsistence" of a prisoner and for his "protection." 18 U.S.C. §4042.

so much of the decision below as accords that defense to the State against a tort claim by plaintiff will be affirmed. Shellhorn & Hill, Inc. v. State, supra.

V

Considering now plaintiff's second theory, it is clear that to the extent of the contract with the United States the State has waived sovereign immunity in a suit for its own breach of that contract. Beyond doubt that is true as to any claim by the United States (which is the other contracting party), but we are concerned here, not with a suit by the Federal Government, but by a claimant who was committed to the State facility by authority of the United States (pursuant to the contract).

Upon examining the agreement the Superior Court concluded that plaintiff was a donee or incidental beneficiary thereof without standing to sue. In our view, he is a creditor beneficiary.

It is established Delaware law that a third party beneficiary of a contract may sue on it. Astle v. Wenke, Del. Supr., 297 A.2d 45 (1972). Generally, the rights of third-party beneficiaries are those specified in the contract; but if performance of the promise will satisfy a legal obligation which a promisee owes a beneficiary, the latter is a creditor beneficiary with standing to sue. Restatement of Contracts §133(1)(b). Compare Astle v. Wenke, supra.

Here, the United States obviously owed a duty of care and subsistence to a person it caused to be committed and it owed him a statutory duty of "safekeeping" and "protection." 18 U.S.C. §4042. By the contract Delaware agreed to perform that duty. And the terms of the agreement show that the duty amounts to more than the "room and board" minimum which the State argued; the duty included "safekeeping" and care as well.

While there may be semantic concerns about calling a prisoner a "creditor" or "beneficiary" (or both) of a Federal-State incarceration contract, the point is that plaintiff was the very subject of the agreement between governments. He was the person (for present purposes) whom the State contracted to safekeep, to care for and to provide with subsistence. Under these circumstances he has not only a direct interest in the contract but a right to enforce it as against the State if it fails to provide the requisite minimums.

In sum, we hold that the State, by entering into the contract with the United States, waived any defense available to it based upon the principle of sovereign immunity and that plaintiff is in law a creditor beneficiary of the agreement. It should be emphasized that we make no judgment as to any alleged breach of contract by the State nor as to any measure of damages to be applied. We decide only that the State may not avail itself to a defense of sovereign immunity to defeat plaintiff's contract claim. . . .

In conclusion we note that under the present state of the law a basic unfairness may result which the judiciary cannot correct. We hold here that plaintiff may sue the State and such a right may be denied by virtue of the sovereign immunity doctrine to State prisoners held in the same institution. But a different result would mean that plaintiff would be without a remedy which is available under the Federal Tort Claims Act, 28 U.S.C. §1346(b), etc., to other prisoners in a Federal prison. We can only suggest that the General Assembly and responsible officers in the Executive Branch consider the problem.

Reversed as to the contract claim.

BAIN v. GILLISPIE
Court of Appeals of Iowa, 1984
357 N.W.2d 47

SNELL, J. James C. Bain serves as a referee for college basketball games. During a game which took place on March 6, 1982, Bain called a foul on a University of Iowa player which permitted free throws to a Purdue University player. That player scored the point that gave Purdue a last-minute victory. Some fans of the University of Iowa team blamed Bain for their team's loss, asserting that the foul call was clearly in error.

John and Karen Gillispie operate a novelty store in Iowa City, specializing in University of Iowa sports memorabilia. The store is known as Hawkeye John's Trading Post. Gillispie's business is a private enterprise for profit having no association with the University of Iowa or its sports program.

A few days after the controversial game, the Gillispies began marketing T-shirts bearing a reference to Bain. It showed a man with a rope around his neck and was captioned "Jim Bain Fan Club." On learning of it, Bain sued the Gillispies for injunctive relief, actual and punitive damages. Gillispies counterclaimed, alleging that Bain's conduct in officiating the game was below the standard of competence required of a professional referee. As such, it constituted malpractice which entitles Gillispies to $175,000 plus exemplary damages. They claim these sums because Iowa's loss of the game to Purdue eliminated Iowa from the championship of the Big Ten Basketball Conference. This in turn destroyed a potential market for Gillispies' memorabilia touting Iowa as a Big Ten champion. Their claim for actual damages is for loss of earnings and business advantage, emotional distress and anxiety, loss of good will, and expectancy of profits. Exemplary damages are asked because Bain's calls as a referee were baneful, outrageous, and done with a heedless disregard for the rights of the Gillispies.

The trial court found the Gillispies had no rights and sustained a motion for summary judgment dismissing Gillispies' counterclaim. They appeal, contending the trial court erred in finding no genuine issue of material fact. The triable issues claimed are: 1) that Gillispies' damages were a reasonably foreseeable consequence of Bain's acts as a referee, or

2) that Gillispies are beneficiaries of an employment contract between Bain and the Big Ten Athletic Conference. . . .

"The question of whether a duty arises out of a parties' relationship is always a matter of law for the courts." Soike v. Evan Mathews and Co., 302 N.W.2d 841, 843 (Iowa 1981). Applying these maxims to Gillispies' tort claim, we find the trial court properly granted the summary judgment against the claim. It is beyond credulity that Bain, while refereeing a game, must make his calls at all times perceiving that a wrong call will injure Gillispies' business or one similarly situated and subject him to liability. The range of apprehension, while imaginable, does not extend to Gillispies' business interests. Referees are in the business of applying rules for the carrying out of athletic contests, not in the work of creating a marketplace for others. In this instance, the trial court properly ruled that Bain owed no duty. Gillispies have cited no authority, nor have we found any, which recognizes an independent tort for "referee malpractice." Absent corruption or bad faith, which is not alleged, we hold no such tort exists. [Citations omitted.] As the trial court properly reasoned:

> This is a case where the undisputed facts are of such a nature that a rational fact finder could only reach one conclusion—no foreseeability, no duty, no liability. Heaven knows what uncharted morass a court would find itself in if it were to hold that an athletic official subjects himself to liability every time he might make a questionable call. The possibilities are mind boggling. If there is a liability to a merchandiser like the Gillispies, why not to the thousands upon thousands of Iowa fans who bleed Hawkeye black and gold every time the whistle blows? It is bad enough when Iowa loses without transforming a loss into a litigation field day for "Monday Morning Quarterbacks." There is no tortious doctrine of athletic official's malpractice that would give credence to Gillispie's counterclaim.

The trial court also found that there was no issue of material fact on the Gillispies' claim that they were beneficiaries under Bain's contract with the Big 10. Gillispies argue that until the contract is produced, there exists a question of whether they are beneficiaries. There is some question of whether there is a contract between Bain and the Big 10. In his response to interrogatories, Bain stated that he had no written contract with the Big 10, but that there was a letter which defined "working relationship." Although this letter was never produced and ordinarily we would not decide an issue without the benefit of examining the letter's contents, we nevertheless find the issue presently capable of determination. By deposition Gillispies answered that there was no contract between them and Bain, the Big 10 Athletic Conference, the University of Iowa, the players, coaches, or with anybody regarding this issue. Thus, even if the letter were considered a contract, Gillispies would be considered third-party beneficiaries. Because Gillispies would not be privy to the contract, they must be direct beneficiaries to maintain a cause of action, and not merely incidental beneficiaries. . . .

Gillispies make no claim that they are creditor beneficiaries of Bain, the Big 10 Athletic Conference, or the University of Iowa. "The real test is said to be whether the contracting parties intended that a third person should receive a benefit which might be enforced in the courts." Bailey v. Iowa Beef Processors, Inc., 213 N.W.2d 642, 645 (Iowa 1973), cert. denied 419 U.S. 830 (1974). It is clear that the purpose of any promise which Bain might have made was not to confer a gift on Gillispies. Likewise, the Big 10 did not owe any duty to the Gillispies such that they would have been creditor beneficiaries. If a contract did exist between Bain and the Big 10, Gillispies can be considered nothing more than incidental beneficiaries and as such are unable to maintain a cause of action. Olney v. Hutt, 251 Iowa 1379, 1386, 105 N.W.2d 515, 518 (1960).

Consequently, there was no genuine issue for trial which could result in Gillispies obtaining a judgment under a contract theory of recovery. The ruling of the trial court sustaining the summary judgment motion and dismissing the counterclaim is affirmed.

Affirmed.

Problem 172

The boxing match between Bill Holt and Bobby Startup was the fight of the decade, but it ended badly when Bill was repeatedly floored in the ninth round and finally knocked out seconds before the bell. He never recovered consciousness. Everyone at the fight was outraged that the referee, ex-champion Killer Knight, allowed the fight to continue after the first two knockdowns in the beginning of the ninth round. Hearing the criticism later, Knight said, "You got to let them fight because the crowd likes blood." Knight was publicly condemned by the Referees' Association for failing to stop the fight long before the fatal blow. Bill Holt's estate filed suit against Killer Knight, contending that it was a third-party beneficiary of his contract with the boxing association that hired him to referee the fight. Will this theory succeed? See Wolfgang v. Mid-America Motorsports, Inc., 111 F.3d 1515 (10th Cir. 1997).

Problem 173

What arguments might be made either way on the following possible third-party beneficiary claims?

(a) An injured tort victim sues the insurance agency that issued a policy to the tortfeasor. Compare Delmar News v. Jacobs Oil Co., 584 A.2d 531 (Del. Super. 1990), with Flattery v. Gregory, 397 Mass. 143, 489 N.E.2d 1257 (1986).

(b) Corporate shareholders sue to prevent the breach of a merger agreement between their corporation and another. See Bush v. Brunswick Corp., 783 S.W.2d 724 (Tex. App. 1989).

(c) A school bus driver, injured when the brakes failed, sues the entity that sold the bus to the school district. See DuPont v. Yellow Cab Co. of Birmingham, 565 So. 2d 190 (Ala. 1990). See Uniform Commercial Code §2-318 (which gives the states three possible alternatives to adopt here).

(d) A bookstore employee who was raped when the security system's alarm failed sues the seller of the system. See Hill v. Sonitrol of Southwestern Ohio, 36 Ohio St. 3d 36, 521 N.E.2d 780 (1988); compare Rhodes v. United Jewish Charities of Detroit, 184 Mich. App. 740, 459 N.W.2d 44 (1990).

(e) After the mother died, the father stopped making payments under the divorce property settlement and is sued by his daughter for missed payments and the cost of going to college (also provided for in the settlement). See Morelli v. Morelli, 102 Nev. 326, 720 P.2d 704 (1986).

(f) An attorney commits malpractice in the drafting of a will, and the legatee who is cut out by this blunder sues. Is an attorney liable to anyone other than the client who wanted the will? See McIntosh County Bank v. Dorsey & Whitney, LLP, 745 N.W.2d 538 (Minn. 2008).

III. RIGHTS OF THE PARTIES

A. The Promisor's Defenses

The third-party beneficiary's rights are *derivative* from those of the promisee, so that the third-party beneficiary gets no better rights against the promisor than the promisee had. This means that the promisor is able to raise almost all defenses arising from the original contract regardless of whether sued by the promisee or the third-party beneficiary. The following Restatement provision reaches this result in a convoluted fashion.

RESTATEMENT (SECOND) OF CONTRACTS

§309. Defenses Against the Beneficiary

(1) A promise creates no duty to a beneficiary unless a contract is formed between the promisor and the promisee; and if a contract is voidable or unenforceable at the time of its formation the right of any beneficiary is subject to the infirmity.

(2) If a contract ceases to be binding in whole or in part because of impracticability, public policy, nonoccurrence of a condition, or present or prospective failure of performance, the right of any beneficiary is to that extent discharged or modified.

(3) Except as stated in subsections (1) and (2) and in section 311 or as provided by the contract, the right of any beneficiary against the promisor is not subject to the promisor's claims or defenses against the promisee or the promisee's claims or defenses against the beneficiary.

(4) A beneficiary's right against the promisor is subject to any claim or defense arising from his own conduct or agreement.

———————————

Subsection (3) is tricky. At first glance it appears to say that the third-party beneficiary is not subject to the promisor's defenses against the promisee, but that is incorrect. Note the words "or as provided in the contract." This means that the third-party beneficiary takes subject to claims and defenses that the promisor could have raised *with respect to the contract with the promisee.* For example, if the promisee obtained the agreement with the promisor by putting a gun to the promisor's head, the promisor can assert duress as a defense against both the promisee and the third-party beneficiary. (The rest of subsection (3) simply clarifies that the *other* claims or defenses—those that do *not* stem from the third-party beneficiary contract—do not diminish the third-party beneficiary's ability to recover from the promisor. For example, if the promisee once borrowed money from the promisor and failed to pay it back, this extraneous debt does not offset the third-party beneficiary's damages.) In sum, the third-party beneficiary's rights are derivative, and thus can be extinguished by a flaw in the agreement between the promisor and promisee.

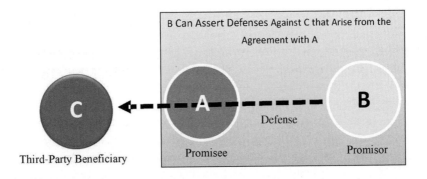

EMIRAT AG v. HIGH POINT PRINTING LLC
United States District Court for the Eastern District of Wisconsin, 2017
248 F. Supp. 3d 911

DECISION AND ORDER DENYING EMIRAT'S MOTION FOR PARTIAL SUMMARY JUDGMENT (DOC. 71) AND GRANTING WS PACKAGING'S MOTION FOR SUMMARY JUDGMENT (DOC. 68)

C. N. CLEVERT, Jr., U. S. District Judge

In this diversity action, Emirat AG sues WS Packaging Group, Inc. and High Point Printing LLC over the allegedly defective printing of combination game and telephone-use scratch-off cards. Emirat and WS Packaging have filed cross-motions for summary judgment . . . .

FACTS

Emirat AG is a foreign corporation registered in Germany, with its principal place of business in Munich, Germany. Emirat's business is risk management and related promotional aspects, which include commercial promotions and sweepstakes.

Defendant High Point Printing LLC was an Ohio limited liability company with its principal place of business in Aurora, Ohio. . . . However, High Point has not appeared in this action and has filed a Certificate of Dissolution with the Ohio Secretary of State on April 19, 2013. Prior to its dissolution, High Point was a commercial printer and print broker. Doug Szygenda was an owner and its principal agent.

Defendant WS Packaging Group, Inc., is a Wisconsin corporation with its principal place of business in Green Bay, Wisconsin. It manufactures printing and packaging products, including labels, tags, coupons, decals and game and sweepstakes printed products.

In the summer of 2007, a Dubai-based company introduced Emirat to Sabafon, a telephone services company based in Yemen, which led to a contract between Emirat and Sabafon for the printing of 25 million scratch-off phone cards. The scratch-off phone cards were intended to be purchased by consumers so they could get a prepaid activation code (a "PIN") for their telephones. The PIN on each card was to be covered by an opaque scratch-off coating.

The scratch-off phone cards would also include a promotional scratch-and-win game, which consisted of twenty-four boxes with a range of prizes also covered by scratch-off coating. According to the rules of the promotional game, if a player scratched six boxes that revealed the same prize, the player would win that prize. If the six boxes scratched off showed more than one prize or more than six boxes were scratched off, the player would get nothing. Every card had six boxes containing the same prize, and the remaining boxes had various other prizes; thus, each card was a potential winner.

On June 7, 2007, Emirat issued a quote to Sabafon for "25,000,000 high level EMIRAT Security Cards." The name "high level EMIRAT Security Cards" was a marketing term used by Emirat in the quote. The quote provided no further description of the level of security necessary for the cards, however it did indicate that "[t]he scratch cards have to be printed through EMIRAT." It is undisputed that Sabafon accepted the quote.

On each card, the chances that a player would pick the correct six boxes to scratch were small. The contract between Emirat and Sabafon detailed what percentage of cards would have the possibility of winning each level of prizes. Additionally, there were to be ten "guaranteed" grand prize winners on which all twenty-four boxes had the same prize of a car — thus a guaranteed win.

Emirat is not a printing company, and prior to its contract with Sabafon it had been involved with only one project involving the printing of scratch-off cards. Under the contract between the two companies, Emirat agreed to arrange for the printing of the 25 million scratch-off cards as requested. Initially, Sabafon agreed to pay Emirat an amount that included the cost of printing the cards and the cost of the prizes. Emirat assumed all responsibility for the prizes and agreed to obtain insurance for the prizes . . . .

On May 6, 2008, Emirat obtained a quote from High Point regarding the printing of the 25 million scratch-off cards (also called "scratch-and-reveal cards" or "scratch-n-reveal cards" or "game cards" in the evidence and this opinion) with overwrap. On May 9, 2008, Emirat accepted the quote, entering a contract with High Point. (Doc. 61 Ex. 2.) . . .

On May 23, 2008, High Point and WS Packaging entered a Letter of Indemnification agreement, stating among other things, that WS Packaging "assumes responsibility only for the accuracy of the printing" and states that WS Packaging does not "guarantee that a game construction cannot be tampered with, counterfeited or foiled." By its terms, the May 23, 2008 Letter of Indemnification covered game orders submitted by High Point to WS Packaging from May 2008 to June 2009. (Doc. 63, ¶ 3; Doc. 61 Ex. 4 at 1.) (The letter's contents are further discussed below.) . . .

Thereafter, High Point subcontracted with WS Packaging to print the cards. WS Packaging provided a quotation to High Point on September 16, 2008, for printing 25 million scratch-n-reveal cards. (Doc. 61 Ex. 7.) High Point then submitted a purchase order on September 23, 2008, to WS Packaging for 25 million "Scratch–N–Reveal" cards to be delivered to Yemen . . . .

At deposition, WS Packaging's Paula Hagen defined "candling" as "[s]how-through of game data." (Doc. 59 Ex. 10 at 28.) She agreed that a card is considered candled if someone "is able to read a significant portion of either the game data or the phone charge code." (Doc. id. at 79.) . . .

Pursuant to its contract with High Point, WS Packaging printed an initial run of 12.5 million cards and delivered them to Yemen in October 2008 . . . . A few weeks after the initial run of 12.5 million cards was shipped, Emirat contacted Szygenda at High Point to report that Sabafon had complained that "the pin numbers are readable with a light behind the card (candling) [sic]." Szygenda relayed that complaint to WS Packaging. WS Packaging requested that High Point return the 12.5 million scratch-off cards printed during the initial run of cards in 2008 and issued a return authorization, indicating that "[g]ame data is visible under the scratch off area on some cards when a high intensity light is flashed through the back of the card." WS Packaging's Hagen sent an email to WS Packaging's quality-management and customer-relations teams on November 12, 2008, discussing, among other things, the new equipment to be used for testing candling of scratch-off cards.

Although WS Packaging agreed to reprint the cards at no charge, Emirat communicated to High Point a number of changes to the cards' configuration. (Doc. 63, ¶ 8; Doc. 81 ¶ 8.) On February 11, 2009, WS Packaging issued a new quote to High Point for the reprinting of the cards; the quote reflected the requested changes. (Doc. 63, ¶ 8; Doc. 81 ¶ 8.)

On April 30, 2009, WS Packaging and High Point entered a second Letter of Indemnification containing nearly identical terms to the May 2008 Letter of Indemnification. By its terms, the April 30, 2009 Letter of Indemnification covered game orders submitted from April 2009 to May 2010. (Doc. 63, ¶ 3; Doc. 61 Ex. 5 at 1.) On May 21, 2009, WS Packaging's Kevin Fitzgerald emailed "game notes" to colleagues, stating that "GAME CARD MUST NOT CANDLE WHEN USING STRONGEST LIGHT BEAM WE HAVE IN HOUSE!!!" (Doc. 59 Ex. 19.)

On May 27, 2009, High Point issued a new purchase order to WS Packaging for 25 million scratch-n-reveal cards for a total remaining cost of over $700,000 . . . .

High Point ceased operations sometime in late 2009. (Doc. 59 Ex. 3 at 15.)

Representatives of Emirat were present at WS Packaging's plant in Neenah on October 23, 2009, to inspect the next shipment of cards and arrange for their shipment to Dubai . . . .

The October 23rd shipment of cards reached Dubai in November. Bargholz and Spannagel of Emirat were present in Dubai, along with representatives of Sabafon. Spannagel has testified that she and Barholz observed a representative of Sabafon use a flashlight to candle a game card and successfully scratch off six matching symbols out of twenty-four. (Doc. 57k, ¶ 32; Doc. 75, ¶ 32.) Bargholz and Spannagel have testified that, upon examination of some of the cards with an ordinary household flashlight, they were able to see phone-card PINs. When Spannagel and Bargholz tested the game cards in Dubai, they bent the cards, cracking the scratch layer, though the cracks could not be seen by the naked eye. (Doc. 79 Ex. F at 102.)

[Because High Point had gone out of business, Emirat filed a complaint alleging, among other things, that WS Packaging had breached its contract with High Point and that Emirat was a third-party beneficiary of that contract.]

DISCUSSION

... It is undisputed that WS Packaging contracted with High Point through the Letters of Indemnification signed in April 2008 and May 2009 and purchase orders received on September 23, 2008, and May 27, 2009. Emirat acknowledges that it is not a party to the WS Packaging/High Point contract and that it is not in privity with WS Packaging .... But its alternate argument is that it is a third-party beneficiary of the WS Packaging/High Point contract.

A person not a party to an agreement may recover under that agreement as a third-party beneficiary if the agreement was intentionally entered primarily and directly for the benefit of that person. [Citations omitted.] The contracting parties must intend to grant the third party an enforceable right. Corrugated Paper Prods., Inc. v. Longview Fibre Co., 868 F.2d 908, 911 (7th Cir. 1989) (discussing New Jersey and other general contract law). An indirect benefit incidental to the primary purpose of the contract is insufficient to confer third-party beneficiary status. [Citations omitted.] The Seventh Circuit has noted that in various jurisdictions

> courts have also been reluctant to recognize third-party rights based solely on the fact that the contracting parties were aware of the third person's relationship to the transaction. For example, courts have generally held that a third party is not a beneficiary of a sales agreement merely because both contracting parties knew that the product would be resold to the third party, or to a class of which the third party was a member. Even where the subsequent purchaser is mentioned by name in the contract, such a third party is "no more than a known remote buyer" in the absence of further evidence of an intent to benefit the third party.

Corrugated Paper Prods., Inc., 868 F.2d at 911.

WS Packaging contends that evidence that the agreement was intentionally entered directly and primarily for the benefit of another must be found within the agreement itself, and the agreements between WS Packaging and High Point did not by its terms confer any benefits on Emirat. This court disagrees that the written terms of a contract must confer the third-party benefit. In Hoida, the Supreme Court of Wisconsin said that to assert third-party status a plaintiff could attach a copy of a written contract so demonstrating or assert facts sufficient to show a primary and direct benefit. 2006 WI 69, ¶ 19, 291 Wis. 2d 283, 717 N.W.2d 17. In *Becker*, the Wisconsin Court of Appeals found a plaintiff to be a third-party beneficiary of an oral contract. The court found that "the evidence of the oral contract between the town and Crispell-Snyder is not specific enough for us to examine the parties' intent through specific express language. However, we can use the totality of the circumstances to evaluate whether the contract" conferred a benefit on the Beckers, limited the benefit to a well-defined group, and required the contractor to assume liability to third parties. 2009 WI App 24, ¶ 14, 316 Wis. 2d 359, 763 N.W.2d 192 (citing two Supreme Court of Wisconsin cases in which the court determined the parties' intent based on the facts and circumstances surrounding an oral contract). . . .

Whether Emirat was and is a third-party beneficiary of the May 2009 purchase order is an interesting question, as Emirat's representatives were a part of the order process throughout the High Point/WS Packaging relationship relating to this case, the purchase order mentions Emirat as responsible for shipping, and Emirat thereafter controlled the testing of the game cards. Notwithstanding the lack of any express writing confirming or denying Emirat's position as a third-party beneficiary, the parties' actions indicate that toward the end of the relationship regarding these scratch-off game cards Emirat was involved almost as much as High Point in the ordering process. . . .

On the other hand, Emirat might not be considered an intended beneficiary under the Restatement (Second) of Contracts §302 (1981), as WS Packaging's performance of the production contract would neither satisfy an obligation of High Point to pay money to Emirat nor serve as a gift to Emirat. See id. cmts. And two of the Restatement's illustrations suggest that if the promisee acts as an intermediary, the third party is at most an incidental beneficiary. See id. illustrations 3, 19 ("A contracts to erect a building for C. B then contracts with A to supply lumber needed for the building. C is an incidental beneficiary of B's promise, and B is an incidental beneficiary of C's promise to pay A for the building."). The author of Corbin on Contracts suggests that Emirat would not be considered a third-party beneficiary: "While a few cases recognize an owner as a third party beneficiary under a contract between the general contractor and subcontractor, the case law generally supports the view espoused in this treatise that the owner is typically not an intended beneficiary of such contracts." 9 John E. Murray, Jr., Corbin on Contracts §45.3 (rev. ed. 2007). . . .

But this court need not decide whether Emirat is a third-party beneficiary, because, even if so considered, its rights extend no further than the terms of the contract itself. The third-party "beneficiary's rights are defined and limited by the contract that created those rights." 9 Murray, supra, §46.5; accord III Farnsworth, supra, §10.9 ("Since an intended beneficiary's (C's) right is based on the contract between the promisor (A) and the promisee (B), it is measured by the terms of that contract and is generally subject to any defenses and claims of the promisor against the promisee arising out of that contract."). A promisor may assert against a third-party beneficiary any defense that it could assert against the promisee. See Restatement (Second) of Contracts §309 cmt. c. (1981) (stating that the beneficiary's right, like that of an assignee, "is subject to limitations inherent in the contract, and to supervening defenses arising by virtue of its terms").

And here the terms of the contract indicate that Emirat failed to sue within the contractual statute of limitations. The WS Packaging and High Point contract consists of the terms contained in the Letters of Indemnification, the quotes from WS Packaging to High Point, and the High Point purchase orders. . . . And importantly, the Letters include the following provision, in all-caps bold: "ANY ACTION BROUGHT BY BUYER MUST BE COMMENCED WITHIN ONE (1) YEAR AFTER THE DELIVERY OF THE PRODUCTS OR THE COMPLETION OF SERVICES NOTWITHSTANDING ANY STATUTORY PERIOD OF LIMITATION TO THE CONTRARY." (Doc. 61 Ex. 4, ¶ 18, Ex. 5, ¶ 18.)

The first shipment of replacement game cards was in Emirat's possession in the summer of 2009 . . . and the second shipment . . . was received by Emirat in Yemen in November 2009. Therefore, any claim about the condition or defective quality of those two shipments of cards had to be brought no later than one year after receipt — November 2010. Emirat filed this case on August 2, 2012, which was too late according to the Letters of Indemnification. . . .

Emirat argues that the statute of limitations has not run, because the limitations provision provides for a time period of one year after delivery of the products or completion of services, and WS Packaging has not completed its services inasmuch as third and fourth shipments remain outstanding. The limitations provision does not specify delivery of the products or the completion of services, whichever comes earlier or whichever comes later. So the court must interpret the language as written. As such, it finds that claims about the deliveries that were already made had to be brought within one year of each delivery. Thus, Emirat's lawsuit was still filed too late respecting the cards that were actually delivered. . . .

NOTES AND QUESTIONS

1. Can you label the parties under Emirat's legal theory? Who is the promisee, the promisor, and the potential third-party beneficiary?

2. Suppose there was evidence that High Point had misrepresented its ability to print cards that did not "candle" to WS Packaging during the parties' preliminary negotiations in the spring of 2008. How might that have affected Emirat's lawsuit?

Problem 174

When Cable TV Company signed Wanda Wonderful to star in a new television series it was producing, the contract between them required her to procure and maintain a $4 million life and health insurance policy payable to the company in the event she couldn't work for health reasons. Wanda took out such a policy with the NoRisk Insurance Company. She made the required monthly payments for the first six months but then missed two in a row. The company sent her numerous letters reminding her of the required amounts, but she ignored them. Tragically, she mysteriously drove her car off a canyon road. By coincidence, she and the grace period on the policy expired together. When Cable TV Company sent in a notice of claim, NoRisk Insurance responded that the policy had lapsed. Cable TV sued, arguing that once its rights were established, those rights existed wholly apart from the contract, unaffected by subsequent problems between the original contracting parties. How should this come out?

Problem 175

Nicely Johnson borrowed $500 from Sky Matheson but won it back in a floating craps game the next night. One of the losers was Nathan Detroit, who owed Nicely $350 of Nicely's winnings, and he promised Nicely to pay that amount to Sky Matheson the next day. When he did not do so, Sky sued Nathan. He argued that any defense of illegality pertained to the original gambling debt and did not taint the promise Nathan made to pay the money to him. How should this come out?

B. Vesting of the Beneficiary's Rights

Under the first Restatement, the original contracting parties remained free to change the contract to the detriment of the third-party beneficiary until the moment when the beneficiary's rights *vested*. Vesting was automatic for donee third-party beneficiaries but required reliance by creditor third-party beneficiaries before their rights vested. Once the creditor/donee distinction disappeared in the Restatement (Second), the vesting rules had to change also.

RESTATEMENT (SECOND) OF CONTRACTS

§311. Variation of a Duty to a Beneficiary

(1) Discharge or modification of a duty to an intended beneficiary by conduct of the promisee or by a subsequent agreement between promisor and promisee is ineffective if a term of the promise creating the duty so provides.

(2) In the absence of such a term, the promisor and promisee retain power to discharge or modify the duty by subsequent agreement.

(3) Such a power terminates when the beneficiary, before he receives notification of the discharge or modification, materially changes his position in justifiable reliance on the promise or brings suit on it or manifests assent to it at the request of the promisor or promisee. . . .

BOARD OF EDUCATION OF COMMUNITY SCHOOL DISTRICT NO. 220 v. VILLAGE OF HOFFMAN ESTATES
Appellate Court of Illinois, 1984
126 Ill. App. 3d 625, 81 Ill. Dec. 942, 467 N.E.2d 1064

SULLIVAN, J. Defendant Village of Hoffman Estates (Village) appeals from the granting of summary judgment for plaintiff Board of Education of Community School District No. 220 (District) in an action seeking a declaration of District 220's rights as a beneficiary under the terms of certain annexation agreements. The sole question before us is whether District 220 acquired any rights under the agreements which could not be altered by subsequent amendment mutually agreed to by the contracting parties.

The facts of the case are largely undisputed. In 1975, two groups of developers (Owners), desiring to have certain tracts of land annexed to the Village, entered into annexation agreements with the Village. Each agreement provided in relevant part that the Owners would pay to the Village "the sum of $135 per residential unit as developed." The funds paid were to be held in escrow "for the benefit of education," and the agreements further provided that during the 5-year period following execution of the agreements, the parties thereto would use their best efforts to cause the area annexed to be included within the boundaries of School District 15. If, at any time during the prescribed period, their efforts were successful, the funds were to be paid to School District 15. If, however, their efforts were unsuccessful, then at the end of the 5-year period the escrowed funds were to be paid to District 220.

The Owners and the Village were not successful in their attempts to have the area in question included within the boundaries of District 15, and shortly before the expiration of the 5-year period, they amended their agreements, extending the period to nine years and providing that they would use their best efforts to cause the area to be included within the boundaries of "School Districts 15 or 54." Again, if their efforts were unsuccessful, then at the end of the 9-year period the funds were to be paid to District 220. At all pertinent times, the land which is the subject of the annexation agreements has been within the boundaries of District 220, and it has provided free education for the children residing in that area, as it is required to do under the Illinois School Code. (Ill. Rev. Stat. 1981, ch. 122, par. 10-

20.12.) The funds required by the agreements have been paid and are currently being held in escrow.

After the 5-year period prescribed by the original annexation agreements expired, District 220 brought the instant action seeking a declaration that it was presently entitled to receive the escrowed funds on the ground that it was a donee beneficiary of the contracts between the Owners and the Village, and that the contracting parties had no power to alter the terms of their agreements without its consent. The trial court granted summary judgment for District 220, ruling that, as a matter of law, execution of the agreements created a vested right, subject to divestment, in District 220, and that the purported amendments were therefore ineffective. Since the 5-year period had elapsed, and the "divesting condition subsequent," i.e., inclusion of the land within the boundaries of School District 15, had not occurred, the trial court ordered that the escrowed funds be paid to District 220. This appeal followed.

OPINION

The issue presents us with the question of when the rights of a third-party beneficiary under a contract become "vested"; that is, at what point is the third-party's right to demand performance irrevocable and unamendable. The parties herein are in agreement that District 220's status is that of a donee beneficiary, since the promise made for its benefit was a gift rather than a means of repaying some debt owed it by the Village. This point being conceded, the sole issue is whether the Owners and the Village retained any right to amend that portion of their agreements which conferred a benefit upon District 220.

It is established that third-party beneficiaries have enforceable rights under contracts made for their benefit. (See, e.g., Carson Pirie Scott & Co. v. Parrett (1931), 346 Ill. 252, 178 N.E. 498 (creditor beneficiary); Riepe v. Schmidt (1916), 199 Ill. App. 129 (donee beneficiary).) However, we are aware of only one case directly concerned with the question of subsequent revocation or amendment. In Bay v. Williams (1884), 112 Ill. 91, 1 N.E. 340, Bay purchased land from Newman and Sissons, promising as partial consideration therefor to pay certain notes owed by them to Williams. Subsequently, Sissons agreed to release Bay from that promise. When Williams sought to recover from Bay, he asserted the release as a defense, and the supreme court, in a divided opinion, held that the promise to pay "invests the person for whose use it is made with an immediate interest and right, as though the promise had been made to him. This being true, the person who procures the promise has no legal right to release or discharge the person who made the promise, from his liability to the beneficiary." (112 Ill. 91, 97, 1 N.E. 340, 342-343.) Subsequent cases, relying on Bay, have stated that the rights of a creditor beneficiary become vested immediately upon execution of the contract [citations omitted], although none of those cases involved an attempted rescission or modification of an original agreement. It appears that the same rule is applied to contracts made for the benefit of a donee beneficiary (see, e.g., Joslyn v. Joslyn (1944), 386 Ill. 387, 54 N.E.2d 475), but it seems to be based more on an analogy to the law of trusts or gifts than to the law of contracts. We are aware that this rule is contrary to that expressed in the Restatement (Second) of Contracts, which states that, in the absence of language in the contract making the rights of a third-party beneficiary irrevocable, "the promisor and promisee retain power to discharge or modify the duty by subsequent agreement" until such time as the beneficiary, without notice of the discharge or modification, "materially changes his position in justifiable reliance on the promise or brings suit on it or manifests assent to it at the request of the promisor or the promisee." (Restatement (Second) of Contracts §311 (1979).) Furthermore, it appears that the majority of jurisdictions have now adopted the rule as set forth in the Restatement (see 17 Am. Jur. 2d Contracts §317 (1964); 17A C.J.S. Contracts §373 (1963), and cases cited therein), perhaps on the theory that the parties to a contract should remain free to amend or rescind their agreement so long as there is no detriment to a third party who has provided no consideration for the benefit received.

In the instant case, the Village does not contend that we should alter the rule established 100 years ago in Bay v. Williams, a rule which apparently has not been considered in the light of modern trends in the law of contracts, and we therefore need not express our views thereon. Instead, the Village asserts that the above rule is inapplicable where, as here, there are two possible beneficiaries of the promise, and the ultimate beneficiary could not be determined until certain specified events occurred. Under those circumstances, it maintains, no rights could have vested in District 220, since it was not assured of being a beneficiary of the promise, and the parties should therefore be free to alter their agreement. It is District 220's position that the right became vested as soon as the Owners and the Village executed the agreements, although the right was subject to divestment. Therefore, it posits, no amendment was possible. Unfortunately, although both sides cite several cases which purportedly support their arguments, none of the cases involve a situation even remotely analogous to the facts before us. All of the cases cited involved a single, identifiable beneficiary, whereas here, there are quite obviously two possible beneficiaries.

In considering this issue, we begin with the premise, accepted by most commentators, that a third-party beneficiary contract may exist even if the beneficiary is not named, not identifiable, or not yet in existence, so long as the beneficiary is identifiable or in existence when the time for performance arrives. These same commentators note, however, that such beneficiaries have no vested rights until they are identified, and that contracts made for their benefit may therefore be rescinded or modified by the parties thereto until such time as the beneficiaries are identified. [Citations omitted.] We have indicated that such agreements are valid in Illinois, as where a contract provides that final payment will be withheld until a general contractor provides proof that all materialmen and subcontracts have been paid. [Citations omitted.] Clearly, under such contracts, the third-party beneficiaries are not identifiable until they provide materials or service, and it could never be seriously contended that they had any vested rights prior to that time which would preclude the contracting parties from modifying the agreement.

Our courts have never considered the question of modification or rescission under similar facts, although the few cases from other jurisdictions which have addressed the issue indicate that until the third-party beneficiary is identified, no vested rights arise. In Stanfield v. W. C. McBride, Inc. (1939), 149 Kan. 567, 88 P.2d 1002, Stanfield was awarded judgment for injuries he suffered when struck by an automobile owned by Miller-Morgan Motor Co. (Miller-Morgan) and driven with its consent by an employee of W. C. McBride, Inc. (McBride). McBride paid the judgment, then sought to recover from Miller-Morgan's insurer, claiming that its employee was covered under the omnibus clause of Miller-Morgan's automobile policy. The evidence disclosed that the omnibus clause had been stricken from the policy eight days before the accident occurred, and the court ruled that while McBride's employee was a potential third-party beneficiary under the contract of insurance, he had no vested rights thereunder until such time as he became identified as an actual beneficiary, and the parties to the contract were free to modify or rescind their agreement prior to that time. Accord, Winchester v. Sipp (1960), 252 Iowa 156, 106 N.W.2d 55.

Similar reasoning is evident in Associated Teachers of Huntington, Inc. v. Board of Education, Union Free School, District No. 3, Town of Huntington (1973), 33 N.Y.2d 229, 306 N.E.2d 791, 351 N.Y.S.2d 670. There, a contract between the association and the school board provided that sabbatical leaves would be granted to as many as 3 percent of the staff per school term. Twenty-one teachers submitted applications, and it was understood that not all could be granted leave. Prior to considering the applications, the school board stated that, due to financial considerations, no leaves would be granted, and the association brought an action to enforce the agreement. The court noted that the individual teachers had no vested rights, since none was assured of being granted leave and the third-party beneficiaries under the contract had not yet been identified. However, the court went on to hold that the association, as promisee, had a right to enforce the contract.

While the cases cited are not directly on point, we believe that they are analogous. Here, although two entities are named in the contract, it could not be ascertained until certain events occurred which would be the third-party beneficiary. Thus, while it is true that the field of potential beneficiaries is much smaller than in the above-cited cases, ultimately — by the terms of the contract — there could be only one beneficiary of the funds held in escrow "for the benefit of education," and that beneficiary could not be identified until the time for performance arose; i.e., until the land was included within the boundaries of School District 15 or 5 years elapsed, whichever event occurred first. It does not appear to us that District 220 was any more certain to be the beneficiary than was District 15 or that it had any greater claim to the funds than did District 15. District 220 points out that during that 5-year period, it was providing education for the children residing in the area, and apparently asserts that we may conclude from that fact that the phrase "for the benefit of education" meant "for the benefit of District 220." We disagree. District 220, in providing education for the children, was doing what it is required to do under the School Code, a duty which it might have had for only a short time should the school boundaries have changed. It appears to us from the language of the contract that the parties thereto intended to confer a benefit on whichever school district would be serving the area over the long term, and they apparently hoped that that district would be District 15 rather than District 220.

Based on the clear language of the contract, it is our view that District 220 was merely a potential beneficiary of the promise to pay certain specified sums for the benefit of education, and the undisputed facts establish that the actual beneficiary of the promise had not yet been identified at the time the Village and the Owners modified their agreement. Since neither school district was identified as the beneficiary, neither had a vested right under the contract, and we hold that under those circumstances the parties were free to modify their agreement.

For the foregoing reasons, the order of the trial court is reversed, and the cause remanded for further proceedings not inconsistent with the views expressed herein.

Reversed and remanded.

Problem 176

Fox borrowed $300 from Holly and promised to repay it the following week to Lawrence, one of Holly's creditors to whom Holly owed the same amount. The next day Holly phoned Fox and said, "Forget repaying Lawrence the money. I've changed my mind and want you to repay the money directly to me next week. I'll settle my debt with Lawrence later." Fox didn't care, so he said it was fine with him. Lawrence learned of this modification agreement and, fearing that Holly would never get around to honoring the debt, Lawrence brought an action in equity to enjoin Fox from paying the debt to Holly. You are the judge. Do you issue the injunction? Would your decision be influenced by any of the following facts?

(a) The modification agreement was entered into before Lawrence ever became aware of the first promise by Fox.

(b) Instead of (a), Lawrence did learn of the original Fox promise but never acted on it in any way.

(c) On learning of the original Fox promise, Lawrence dropped his plans to sue Holly and garnish his wages.

(d) Do your answers depend in any way on the state of Holly's finances?

Problem 177

(This Problem appeared on the Indiana bar exam in July 1971.) In June 1968, John Good, having decided to retire and wishing to help his alma mater, ABC College, entered into a written lease agreement for the facilities of his small factory with his employee, Henry Work. The lease provided that for a period of ten years from the date of the lease, Henry Work, as lessee, would pay as rental the sum of $1,200 each month to ABC College.

John Good sent a copy of said lease agreement to ABC College and received the usual form letter acknowledging gifts.

Henry Work made the $1,200 monthly payments to ABC College until July 1970, when he advised John Good that the factory equipment was old and it would be impossible for him to continue in business unless he could purchase new equipment of the value of $15,000, and that he could not purchase the same unless the rent were reduced to $900 per month. John Good agreed to reduce the monthly rental to $900, and Henry Work purchased the new equipment.

ABC College learned of the reduction in rent when it received Henry Work's check for $900, which it refused to accept, and is now demanding $1,200 per month. John Good and Henry Work have come to you for advice as to their rights and liabilities. Advise them.

IV. MORTGAGES AND THIRD-PARTY BENEFICIARIES

A *mortgage* is a consensual lien on real property given by the mortgagor (the fee simple owner) to the mortgagee (the financing entity). Technically, the mortgage is a deed transferring the legal interest in the realty to the lender. Modern courts, however, have no trouble in concluding that this is merely a method of collateralizing a loan, and that the "real" owner is the mortgagor. Courts of equity have long recognized a right to redeem the property, even if the debt was recently defaulted, by paying off the mortgage and recovering the property. This right, called the *equity of redemption*, is what is meant by the "equity" homeowners are said to "build" in their property as they make mortgage payments.

Problem 178

Because the property was heavily mortgaged to the Gable State Bank and Scarlett was having trouble making the mortgage payments, she decided to sell her equity in her ancestral home, Tara, to Vivien, her next-door neighbor. Vivien was unable to finance her own mortgage, so Scarlett agreed to let Vivien *assume* (promise to pay) her mortgage commitment to the bank. Vivien then paid Scarlett $10,000 for her equity in Tara. Vivien made the required payments for two years and then stopped. The Gable State Bank brought a foreclosure proceeding and sold the property. The sale did not bring enough to pay the debt; there was a deficiency of $8,000. Answer these questions:

(a) Does Scarlett still owe the debt to Gable State Bank? Why or why not?

(b) If Gable State Bank wants to sue Vivien and phones you, its attorney, what is its cause of action against her, as she made no promise directly to the bank, and no one at the bank had ever met her?

An *assumption of the mortgage* means that the buyer of the property undertakes a personal liability to make the payments. Sometimes the buyer is not willing to shoulder this burden, but still wants to buy the property. In such a case, the buyer may contract only to purchase the property *subject to* the mortgage. What does this mean?

Obviously, there is no way that the mortgagor and the buyer of the equity can free the land from the mortgage lien simply by their agreement, so the buyer will always take the land subject to the mortgage. But if this is the only understanding between the parties, the buyer of the equity makes no binding promise to pay off the mortgage (though the buyer will *try* to do so in order to acquire the land free of the mortgage lien). If the buyer is unable to make the necessary payments, the bank will foreclose and take the property, but any deficiency is owed only by the original mortgagor (and anyone else who has *assumed* the mortgage debt). In actuality, a *subject to* purchaser is entering into a *unilateral* contract, hoping to make all the payments but avoiding any promissory liability guaranteeing their continuance.

Problem 179

When Scarlett agreed to sell her equity in Tara to Vivien, Vivien was only willing to take the property subject to the mortgage in favor of Gable State Bank. As a result, Scarlett charged her $14,000 for her equity. After two years of possession and steady payments made on time, Vivien wearied of

Tara and moved to Atlanta. She made no further payments. Answer these questions:

(a) Does Scarlett still owe the mortgage amounts to Gable State Bank? If she is forced to pay the bank, may she sue Vivien on any theory?

(b) If Gable State Bank brings suit against Vivien will it prevail? (Do you understand why Scarlett made Vivien pay $4,000 more in this contract than in the one in the last Problem?)

(c) Why would *Vivien* have been interested in a *subject to* purchase? What possible advantage does she get out of this arrangement?

In the situation in which the buyer of the equity of redemption assumes the mortgage, the assumption promise creates a Lawrence v. Fox pattern, with the bank in the position of the creditor third-party beneficiary. Obviously, the promisee here (the seller of the equity) wants the promise of payment in order to gain security from future liability. If the equity has been transferred many times and the current owner is only holding subject to the mortgage but the buyer assumes the mortgage, are similar third-party beneficiary rights created? Strangely enough, this problem arises often enough to be annoying.

Problem 180

Scarlett sold her equity in Tara to Vivien, who took subject to the mortgage but did not assume it. Three years later Vivien sold the equity in Tara to Clark, who assumed the mortgage debt owed to Gable State Bank. When Clark missed payments, Gable State repossessed the property and sold it at a foreclosure sale. The proceeds from this sale brought enough to pay all but $8,000 of the mortgage amount, so Gable State Bank brought suit against Clark, claiming to be a third-party beneficiary of his promise to Vivien to assume the mortgage. Clark argued that because Vivien did not owe any personal liability to Gable State Bank (and because no one ever makes gifts to banks), Gable State was at best an *incidental* beneficiary of his promise. How should this come out?

Why in the world would Vivien have made Clark undertake personal liability on a debt she herself did not owe? The leading case is Schneider v. Ferrigno, 110 Conn. 86, 147 A. 303 (1929). See also Kilmer v. Smith, 77 N.Y. 226 (1879) (reformation for mistake may be appropriate where there is a mistake as to the existence of a duty; see comment b to Restatement (Second) of Contracts §312).

CHAPTER 9 ASSESSMENT

Multiple Choice Questions

1. Holly loaned Fox $5,000, but at the time they made their agreement Holly happened to also owe that same amount to a man named Lawrence, so he made Fox promise to pay the $5,000 to Lawrence, which Fox agreed to. Before the due date of the loan Holly got drunk at a party at Fox's house and in a quarrel he punched Fox in the mouth, breaking his expensive dentures. When the loan matured Lawrence, who had been told all about the loan, came to collect and Fox told him he wasn't paying anything until it was clear how much it was going to cost him to have his dentures repaired. Lawrence calls you, his attorney. Can Fox do this to him?

   a. Yes. The rights of a third-party beneficiary are derivative and therefore Lawrence takes the contract with all the defenses that Fox could have raised against Holly, which includes the cost of the injury to his dentures. Lawrence will have to collect whatever Fox fails to pay from Holly, who stills owes him the debt.

   b. Same answer except that Holly doesn't owe anything to Lawrence anymore. Once he learned of the contract between Fox and Holly to pay the money to Lawrence, the original debt Holly owed was gone and replaced by the debt that Fox now owed to Lawrence.

   c. No, Fox can't subtract defenses against Holly that did not arise from the same contract that was assigned to Lawrence. A third-party beneficiary only takes subject to defenses that arise from the contract that created the third-party rights, and here Fox's defense arises from a separate incident that had nothing to do with the contract to pay the debt to Lawrence. Fox will have to pay Lawrence and bring a separate tort action against Holly.

2. Newton Money promised to give $1 million to Football University if it would give an honorary degree in Fine Arts to his daughter, Ripley Money, the well-known author of romance novels (involving heroines with large bodices falling in love with adventurers like pirates). After some haggling, a contract was signed to this effect. Ripley was thrilled and announced that this would happen on Facebook, on her website, and by having both new stationery and business cards printed that mentioned the new degree (she had never even gone to college before making millions as a writer). There was so much negative publicity around the deal between Newton and Football University, that, by agreement, they decided that the honorary degree would go to Newton himself, honoring his very respectable autobiography. Ripley promptly sued, claiming to be a third-party beneficiary of their contract. How does this come out?

   a. She loses. Ripley was an incidental beneficiary of the contract and has no right to sue. Her father owes her no debt, and his mistaken belief in her prowess as a writer is a delusion creating no obligation to go through with his temporary fantasy that she was worthy of this honor. The parties to a contract may always change it to the detriment of a third-party beneficiary who hasn't given separate consideration to seal the deal.

   b. She loses. The parties to a contract creating third-party beneficiary rights may always change it to the detriment of a third-party beneficiary unless the rights of the third-party beneficiary have vested, which occurs when the third-party beneficiary materially changes her position in justifiable reliance on the contract. Here nothing of import has happened to Ripley that causes her any harm if the contract is changed, and, indeed, cancelling the contract is probably in her best interest to avoid any further negative publicity focusing on how bad a writer she really is.

   c. She wins. The rule of law is stated in B, but she has justifiably relied on the original contract to give her the honorary degree by her wide publicity of this award and by going through the time and expense of changing her stationery and business cards. Once that happened her rights had vested and it was too late to alter the agreement without her consent.

3. After the financial collapse of 2008, Big National Bank (BNB) had much trouble getting payments from those to whom it had loaned money to purchase homes, and in generating new mortgages in a depressed market. It had always inserted a provision in the old mortgage agreements that forbade the mortgagors (the home buyers) from selling their mortgage contracts and having them assumed by others, but now it decided to drop this prohibition in order to keep those mortgages from going into default. Thus it sent a notice to mortgagors telling them it would consent to mortgage assumptions by responsible buyers of the mortgagors' equity in the properties. Ricardo Rivera received such a notice and immediately posted a notice on Facebook that he was interested in selling the equity in his home to someone who would take over the mortgage payments he owed to BNB. Fatima Feliz contacted him and said she was interested, and in subsequent negotiations they worked out the details and signed a contract entitled "Mortgage Assumption Agreement." In the contract Feliz "agreed that the property was covered by a mortgage for $100,000 owed to BNB, with monthly payments of $600 for 23 more years before the property would be free of the mortgage, if and when she made all the required payments." The contract said she admitted she was "subject to the mortgage." The two parties sent the contract to BNB, which approved it, and Feliz began making the mortgage payments two weeks later when she moved in. One year later Feliz lost her job and had no steady source of income, so she abandoned the house and stopped sending in the required monthly amounts. BNB promptly sued both Feliz and Rivera for the amounts due, and began foreclosure proceedings. How does this come out?

    a. They both lose and the bank wins. Unless the bank agreed at the time of the mortgage assumption to a novation, so that Rivera was excused from his promise to pay the mortgage debt and Feliz was substituted in his place, Rivera still owes the money when she stops paying. When she assumed his debt, her promise to Rivera to make the payments created creditor third-party beneficiary rights in BNB, and the bank can sue her in that posture.

    b. The bank loses. The bank must have understood that its approval of Feliz taking over the mortgage excused Rivera from liability now that she was on board. However, at no point in the new agreement did she actually "assume" the mortgage debt. The phrases demonstrate instead that she was taking the property "subject to" the mortgage. In that case she had made no *promise* to pay the monthly amounts (and thus there is no promise creating third-party beneficiary rights in the bank), but only a commitment to Rivera that she would try to make the monthly amounts and if she made them all she would have paid off the bank and then would take the property free of the mortgage lien of the bank. All the bank can do is foreclose on the property, and if that doesn't bring enough in the foreclosure sale to pay the outstanding loan, the bank must eat the loss.

    c. The bank wins. A novation is never presumed and takes clear evidence of an intent to substitute one party for another. No bank would excuse Rivera, the original mortgagor, from, in effect, being a guarantor of Feliz's promise to pay off the mortgage debt unless it had to, and there is no reason to do it here. Thus when she stops making the payments, he's liable for them. As for her, the contract she signed is called a "Mortgage Assumption Agreement" and the parties clearly meant just that: an *assumption* of Rivera's promise to the bank to pay the mortgage, which creates creditor third-party beneficiary rights in the bank to enforce the promise against her. Thus the bank gets three bites of the apple: Both Rivera and Feliz are personally liable for the payments, and the property still has a lien on it, allowing the bank to foreclose and sell the property through the foreclosure process.

Answers

    1. C is the best answer. A third-party beneficiary takes free of claims and defenses that arise from different transactions, like the damages from the brawl at the party. A third-party beneficiary does take subject to claims and defenses arising from the same transaction that created the rights of the third-party beneficiary. See Restatement (Second) of Contracts §309, quoted before the last case in this chapter.

2. C is the best answer, assuming the court finds her actions to be justifiable reliance and of sufficient substance that it is a definite loss to her if the award does not go through. Minds might differ on that, but recalling the award will be a definite blow to her reputation and the possible future sales of her books, whatever their literary worth.

3. Any of these things are possible, but C seems the most likely. We really need more facts including what Rivera and Feliz agreed to about her making payments: Was this a *promise* to do so? In that case, the bank is a third-party beneficiary. Rivera will want this to be the case, too, since it gives the bank another party to whom it can look for payments, and that's probably what he intended when he sold his equity in the property to Feliz.

10
ASSIGNMENT AND DELEGATION

In a bilateral executory contract each party is owed a performance obligation — a contract *right* — and each owes or will owe a performance obligation — a contract *duty*. These rights and duties are transferable to others, sometimes even before performance of the contract begins. In this chapter we will explore such *assignments of rights* and *delegations of duties*, and, after defining both, consider under what circumstances the courts will allow parties to sell their contracts to strangers. The financial world deals mightily in such transactions, so lawyers must master the rules if they want to be players in that arena.

I. INTRODUCTION

We begin with the proper terminology. Contract *rights* are *assigned*, and contract *duties* are *delegated*. These are words of art and must not be used interchangeably. In an assignment of rights, the person making the assignment (who will be one of the original contracting parties) is called the *assignor*. The person to whom the assignment of rights is made (who will be a stranger to the original contract) is called the *assignee*. The original contracting party whose obligation is assigned is the *obligor*.

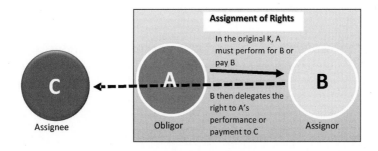

In a delegation of duties, the same parties are known as the *delegator*, the *delegatee*, and the *obligee*.

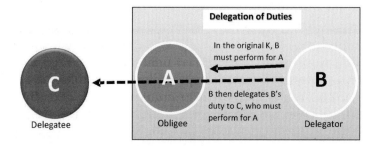

Unfortunately, courts sometimes also speak of parties *assigning the contract* (as opposed to merely assigning their rights under the contract). An assignment of the contract is *both* an assignment of a party's rights *and* a delegation of that party's duties. Because policymakers, judges, scholars, and litigants tend to use the term "assignment" without specifying whether they mean an assignment of rights or an assignment of the contract, it is important to read closely and pay careful attention to what they mean when they use that word.

Problem 181

Joseph Armstrong went down to Wonder Spa and signed a contract agreeing to pay the spa $1,000 in return for the use of its facilities for a two-year period. A week later the Nightflyer Finance Company sent him a payment booklet, stating that the contract he had signed with the spa had been purchased by Nightflyer. Label the type of transaction and the three parties involved using the terminology just discussed.

Problem 182

After Armstrong had worked out at the spa for six months, it changed ownership. The new owners agreed with the old owners to honor all existing contracts with the spa's customers. Label the type of the transaction and the parties to it.

NOTE ON NOVATION

A concept that it closely related to assignments and delegations is the *novation*. A novation occurs when one party exits the relationship and is replaced by a new party, which inherits the original party's rights and duties. Restatement (Second) of Contracts §280. Because novations are based on the agreement of all the parties, they do not need to comply with the traditional rules that limit assignments and delegations (which we discuss below). However, consent to a novation is never presumed; to the contrary, "all parties to the original contract must clearly and definitely intend the second agreement to be a novation and intend to completely disregard the original contract obligation." PNC Bank, N.A. v. Price, 64 N.E.3d 402, 412 (Oh. 2016).

Problem 183

Fox borrowed $300 from Holly and promised to repay Lawrence, a creditor to whom by chance Holly owed the same amount. Holly then told Lawrence about the new loan; Lawrence just grunted. When the debt from Fox came due, Lawrence contacted Fox and asked him when he could expect payment. Fox replied that he was financially embarrassed just at present. Lawrence then called Holly and told him all this. Holly replied that because Fox had promised to pay this debt, Holly felt that he no longer owed it, and Lawrence should look only to Fox for repayment. Is this consistent with the law? See First American Commerce Co. v. Washington Mutual Savings Bank, 743 P.2d 1193 (Utah 1987).

Problem 184

As part of their divorce agreement, George promised Martha that he would make her car payments until the vehicle was paid for completely. He was true to his promise for six months, but then he suddenly left the state and could not be found. The finance company to whom the automobile dealership sold the paper is hounding Martha for payment. She calls you, her divorce attorney. She doesn't owe this debt anymore, does she?

Problem 185

Professor Chalk of the Gilberts Law School was scheduled to make a speech in Detroit in late February. His fee for the speech was to be $1,000. He came down with a cold in early February and became worried about the advisability of going to Detroit just as he was recovering. He phoned his friend Professor Podium and asked him if he would make the speech in his stead. Podium agreed, so Chalk phoned the president of the group to whom he was to give the speech and asked if the substitution was acceptable. Because Podium was an even better speaker than Chalk, the president also agreed. When Podium failed to show up on the day scheduled, the organization sued Chalk for its wasted expenses. Is he liable?

II. VALIDITY OF THE ASSIGNMENT OR DELEGATION

Assignments of rights are generally valid. As soon as the obligor has notice of the assignment, the obligor must honor it and perform for the assignee, rather than the assignor. However, courts may refuse to enforce a purported assignment for several reasons, including when it places an undue burden on the obligor. An unenforceable assignment simply leaves the contracting parties in the status quo: Each must perform as originally agreed.

Delegations are permissible except when barred by the contract or public policy, or when the obligee's interests will be substantially harmed by having the delegatee — rather than the delegator — performing. A failed delegation is very different than a failed assignment of rights: It is an anticipatory breach of contract. Finally, even when a delegator has effectively transferred its obligations to the delegatee, the delegator can still face liability if the delegatee breaches the contract.

RESTATEMENT (SECOND) OF CONTRACTS

§317. ASSIGNMENT OF A RIGHT

. . . A contractual right can be assigned unless

(a) the substitution of a right of the assignee for the right of the assignor would materially change the duty of the obligor, or materially increase the burden or risk imposed on him by his contract, or materially impair his chance of obtaining return performance, or materially reduce its value to him, or

(b) the assignment is forbidden by statute or is otherwise inoperative on grounds of public policy, or

(c) assignment is validly precluded by contract.

RESTATEMENT (SECOND) OF CONTRACTS

§318. DELEGATION OF PERFORMANCE OF DUTY

(1) An obligor can properly delegate the performance of his duty to another unless the delegation is contrary to public policy or the terms of his promise.

(2) Unless otherwise agreed, a promise requires performance by a particular person only to the extent that the obligee has a substantial interest in having that person perform or control the acts promised.

(3) Unless the obligee agrees otherwise, neither delegation of performance nor a contract to assume the duty made with the obligor by the person delegated discharges any duty or liability of the delegating obligor.

UNIFORM COMMERCIAL CODE

§2-210. DELEGATION OF PERFORMANCE; ASSIGNMENT OF RIGHTS

(1) A party may perform his duty through a delegate unless otherwise agreed or unless the other party has a substantial interest in having his original promisor perform or control the acts required by the contract. No delegation of performance relieves the party delegating of any duty to perform or any liability for breach.

(2) Unless . . . otherwise agreed, all rights of either seller or buyer can be assigned except where the assignment would materially change the duty of the other party, or increase materially the burden or risk imposed on him by his contract, or impair materially his chance of obtaining return performance. A right to damages for breach of the whole contract or a right arising out of the assignor's due performance of his entire obligation can be assigned despite agreement otherwise . . .

(3) Unless the circumstances indicate the contrary a prohibition of assignment of "the contract" is to be construed as barring only the delegation to the assignee of the assignor's performance.

(4) An assignment of "the contract" or of "all my rights under the contract" or an assignment in similar general terms is an assignment of rights and unless the language or the circumstances (as in an assignment for security) indicate the contrary, it is a delegation of performance of the duties of the assignor and its acceptance by the assignee constitutes a promise by him to perform those duties. This promise is enforceable by either the assignor or the other party to the original contract.

(5) The other party may treat any assignment which delegates performance as creating reasonable grounds for insecurity and may without

prejudice to his rights against the assignor demand assurances from the assignee (Section 2-609).

A. *Performance Obligations*

MACKE CO. v. PIZZA OF GAITHERSBURG, INC.
Court of Appeals of Maryland, 1970
259 Md. 479, 270 A.2d 645

SINGLEY, J. The appellees and defendants below, Pizza of Gaithersburg, Inc.; Pizzeria, Inc.; The Pizza Pie Corp., Inc. and Pizza Oven, Inc., four corporations under the common ownership of Sidney Ansell, Thomas S. Sherwood and Eugene Early and the same individuals as partners or proprietors (the Pizza Shops) operated at six locations in Montgomery and Prince George's Counties. The appellees had arranged to have installed in each of their locations cold drink vending machines owned by Virginia Coffee Service, Inc., and on 30 December 1966, this arrangement was formalized at five of the locations, by contracts for terms of one year, automatically renewable for a like term in the absence of 30 days' written notice. A similar contract for the sixth location, operated by Pizza of Gaithersburg, Inc., was entered into on 25 July 1967.

On 30 December 1967, Virginia's assets were purchased by The Macke Company (Macke) and the six contracts were assigned to Macke by Virginia. In January, 1968, the Pizza Shops attempted to terminate the five contracts having the December anniversary date, and in February, the contract which had the July anniversary date.

Macke brought suit in the Circuit Court for Montgomery County against each of the Pizza Shops for damages for breach of contract. From judgments for the defendants, Macke has appealed.

The lower court based the result which it reached on two grounds: first, that the Pizza Shops, when they contracted with Virginia, relied on its skill, judgment and reputation, which made impossible a delegation of Virginia's duties to Macke; and second, that the damages claimed could not be shown with reasonable certainty. These conclusions are challenged by Macke.

In the absence of a contrary provision — and there was none here — rights and duties under an executory bilateral contract may be assigned and delegated, subject to the exception that duties under a contract to provide personal services may never be delegated, nor rights be assigned under a contract where delectus personae was an ingredient of the bargain. [Citations omitted.] Crane Ice Cream Co. v. Terminal Freezing & Heating Co., 147 Md. 588, 128 A. 280 (1925) held that the right of an individual to purchase ice under a contract which by its terms reflected a knowledge of the individual's needs and reliance on his credit and responsibility could not be assigned to the corporation which purchased his business. In Eastern Advertising Co. v. McGaw & Co., 89 Md. 72, 42 A. 923 (1899), our predecessors held that an advertising agency could not delegate its duties under a contract which had been entered into by an advertiser who had relied on the agency's skill, judgment and taste.

The six machines were placed on the appellees' premises under a printed "Agreement-Contract" which identified the "customer," gave its place of business, described the vending machine, and then provided:

Terms

1. The Company will install on the Customer's premises the above listed equipment and will maintain the equipment in good operating order and stocked with merchandise.

2. The location of this equipment will be such as to permit accessibility to persons desiring use of same. This equipment shall remain the property of the Company and shall not be moved from the location at which installed, except by the Company.

3. For equipment requiring electricity and water, the Customer is responsible for electrical receptacle and water outlet within ten (10) feet of the equipment location. The Customer is also responsible to supply the Electrical Power and Water needed.

4. The Customer will exercise every effort to protect this equipment from abuse or damage.

5. The Company will be responsible for all licenses and taxes on the equipment and sale of products.

6. This Agreement-Contract is for a term of one (1) year from the date indicated herein and will be automatically renewed for a like period, unless thirty (30) day written notice is given by either party to terminate service.

7. Commission on monthly sales will be paid by the Company to the customer at the following rate: . . .

The rate provided in each of the agreements was "30% of Gross Receipts to $300.00 monthly[,] 35% over [$]300.00," except for the agreement with Pizza of Gaithersburg, Inc., which called for "40% of Gross Receipts." We cannot regard the agreements as contracts for personal services. They were either a license or concession granted Virginia by the appellees, or a lease of a portion of the appellees' premises, with Virginia agreeing to pay a percentage of gross sales as a license or concession fee or as rent, . . . and were assignable by Virginia unless they imposed on Virginia duties of a personal or unique character which could not be delegated . . . .

The appellees earnestly argue that they had dealt with Macke before and had chosen Virginia because they preferred the way it conducted its business. Specifically, they say that service was more personalized, since the president of Virginia kept the machines in working order, that commissions were paid in cash, and that Virginia permitted them to keep keys to the machines so that minor adjustments could be made when needed. Even if we assume all this to be true, the agreements with Virginia were silent as to the details of the working arrangements and contained only a provision requiring Virginia to "install . . . the above listed equipment and . . . maintain the equipment in good operating order and stocked with merchandise." We think the Supreme Court of California put the problem of personal service in proper focus a century ago when it upheld the assignment of a contract to grade a San Francisco street:

> All painters do not paint portraits like Sir Joshua Reynolds, nor land-scapes like Claude Lorraine, nor do all writers write dramas like Shakespeare or fiction like Dickens. Rare genius and extraordinary skill are not transfer-able, and contracts for their employment are therefore personal, and cannot be assigned. But rare genius and extraordinary skill are not indispensable to the workmanlike digging down of a sand hill or the filling up of a depression to a given level, or the construction of brick sewers with manholes and covers, and contracts for such work are not personal, and may be assigned . . . .

Moreover, the difference between the service the Pizza Shops happened to be getting from Virginia and what they expected to get from Macke did not mount up to such a material change in the performance of obligations under the agreements as would justify the appellees' refusal to recognize the assignment . . . .

In support of the proposition that the agreements were for personal services, and not assignable, the Pizza Shops rely on three Supreme Court cases, Burck v. Taylor, 152 U.S. 634 (1894); Delaware County Commr. v. Diebold Safe & Lock Co., 133 U.S. 473 (1890); and Arkansas Valley Smelting Co. v. Belden Mining Co., 127 U.S. 379 (1888), all of which were cited with approval by our predecessors in Tarr v. Veasey, 125 Md. 199, 207, 93 A. 428 (1915). We find none of these cases persuasive. *Burck* held that the contrac-tor for the state capitol in Texas, who was prohibited by the terms of his contract from assigning it without the state's consent, could not make a valid assignment of his right to receive three-fourths of the proceeds. In *Delaware County*, Diebold Safe and Lock, which was a subcontractor in the construc-tion of a county jail, was barred from recovering from the county commis-sioners for its work on the theory that there had been a partial assignment of the construction contract by the prime contractor, which had never been assented to by the commissioners. This result must be limited to the facts: i.e., to the subcontractor's right to recover under the assignment, and not to the contractor's right to delegate. See Taylor v. Palmer and Devlin v. Mayor, Aldermen and Commonalty of the City of New York, both supra. *Arkansas Valley*, which held invalid an attempt to assign a contract for the purchase of ore, is clearly distinguishable, because of a contract provision which stipu-lated that payment for the ore was to be made after delivery, based on an assay to be made by the individual purchaser named in the contract. The court concluded that this was a confidence imposed in the individual purchaser's credit and responsibility and that his rights under the contract could not be transferred to another. Tarr v. Veasey involved a situation where duties were delegated to one person and rights assigned to another and our predecessors held the rights not to be assignable, because of the parties' intention that duties and rights were interdependent.

We find more apposite two cases which were not cited by the parties. In The British Waggon Co. & The Parkgate Waggon Co. v. Lea & Co., 5 Q.B.D. 149 (1880), Parkgate Waggon Company, a lessor of railway cars, who had agreed to keep the cars "in good and substantial repair and working order," made an assignment of the contract to British Waggon Company. When British Waggon Company sued for rent, the lessee contended that the assignment had terminated the lease. The court held that the lessee remained bound under the lease, because there was no provision making performance of the lessor's duty to keep in repair a duty personal to it or its employees.

Except for the fact that the result has been roundly criticized, see Corbin, supra, at 448-449, the Pizza Shops might have found some solace in the facts found in Boston Ice Co. v. Potter, 123 Mass. 28 (1877). There, Potter, who had dealt with the Boston Ice Company, and found its service unsatisfactory, transferred his business to Citizens' Ice Company. Later, Citizens' sold out to Boston, unbeknown to Potter, and Potter was served by Boston for a full year. When Boston attempted to collect its ice bill, the Massachusetts court sustained Potter's demurrer on the ground that there was no privity of contract, since Potter had a right to choose with whom he would deal and could not have another supplier thrust upon him. Modern authorities do not support this result, and hold that, absent provision to the contrary, a duty may be delegated, as distinguished from a right which can be assigned, and that the promisee cannot rescind, if the quality of the performance remains materially the same.

Restatement, Contracts §160(3) (1932) reads, in part:

> Performance or offer of performance by a person delegated has the same legal effect as performance or offer of performance by the person named in the contract, unless,
> (a) performance by the person delegated varies or would vary materially from performance by the person named in the contract as the one to perform, and there has been no . . . assent to the delegation. . . .

In cases involving the sale of goods, the Restatement rule respecting delegation of duties has been amplified by Uniform Commercial Code §2-210(5), Maryland Code (1957, 1964 Repl. Vol.) Art. 95B §2-210(5), which permits a promisee to demand assurances from the party to whom duties have been delegated. [Citations omitted.]

As we see it, the delegation of duty by Virginia to Macke was entirely permissible under the terms of the agreements. In so holding, we do not put ourselves at odds with Eastern Advertising Co. v. McGaw, supra, 89 Md. 72, 42 A. 923, for in that case, the agreement with the agency contained a provision that "the advertising cards were to be 'subject to the approval of Eastern Advertising Company as to style and contents,'" at 82, 42 A. at 923, which the court found to import that reliance was being placed on the agency's skill, judgment and taste, at 88, 42 A. 923. . . .

Judgment reversed as to liability; judgment entered for appellant for costs, on appeal and below; case remanded for a new trial on the question of damages.

QUESTION

Assume Macke had refused to provide the drink machines and the defendant had sued Virginia Coffee Service for breach. Would the delegation by Virginia be a defense to breach? Would there be a different result under UCC §2-210(1) (which is printed above)?

Problem 186

Jay Eastriver promised to sell to Gerald Czeck all of the mufflers that Gerald needed to operate the Czech Muffler Shop for the years 2021 through 2024. Gerald decided to sell the shop to a corporation called Texas Auto and assigned to it his right to purchase the mufflers from Jay. Jay now refuses to sell any mufflers to Texas Auto, complaining that the contract was not assignable. Who wins? Does Jay have any intermediate recourse if he is unsure of how Texas Auto will perform? Read UCC §§2-210, 2-306, and 2-609. Can §2-306 be used as an argument for Jay? For Texas Auto? See Official Comment 4. Does it matter if Texas Auto requires more or fewer mufflers than Gerald would have?

B. Payment Obligations

HERZOG v. IRACE
Supreme Judicial Court of Maine, 1991
594 A.2d 1106

BRODY, Justice. Anthony Irace and Donald Lowry appeal from an order entered by the Superior Court (Cumberland County, Cole, J.) affirming a

District Court (Portland, Goranites, J.) judgment in favor of Dr. John P. Herzog in an action for breach of an assignment to Dr. Herzog of personal injury settlement proceeds[1] collected by Irace and Lowry, both attorneys, on behalf of their client, Gary G. Jones. On appeal, Irace and Lowry contend that the District Court erred in finding that the assignment was valid and enforceable against them. They also argue that enforcement of the assignment interferes with their ethical obligations toward their client. Finding no error, we affirm.

The facts of this case are not disputed. Gary Jones was injured in a motorcycle accident and retained Irace and Lowry to represent him in a personal injury action. Soon thereafter, Jones dislocated his shoulder, twice, in incidents unrelated to the motorcycle accident. Dr. Herzog examined Jones's shoulder and concluded that he needed surgery. At the time, however, Jones was unable to pay for the surgery and in consideration for the performance of the surgery by the doctor, he signed a letter dated June 14, 1988, written on Dr. Herzog's letterhead stating:

> I, Gary Jones, request that payment be made directly from settlement of a claim currently pending for an unrelated incident, to John Herzog, D.O., for treatment of a shoulder injury which occurred at a different time.

Dr. Herzog notified Irace and Lowry that Jones had signed an "assignment of benefits" from the motorcycle personal injury action to cover the cost of surgery on his shoulder and was informed by an employee of Irace and Lowry that the assignment was sufficient to allow the firm to pay Dr. Herzog's bills at the conclusion of the case. Dr. Herzog performed the surgery and continued to treat Jones for approximately one year.

In May, 1989, Jones received a $20,000 settlement in the motorcycle personal injury action. He instructed Irace and Lowry not to disburse any funds to Dr. Herzog, indicating that he would make the payments himself. Irace and Lowry informed Dr. Herzog that Jones had revoked his permission to have the bill paid by them directly and indicated that they would follow Jones's directions. Irace and Lowry issued a check to Jones for $10,027 and disbursed the remaining funds to Jones's other creditors. Jones did send a check to Dr. Herzog but the check was returned by the bank for insufficient funds and Dr. Herzog was never paid.

Dr. Herzog filed a complaint in District Court against Irace and Lowry seeking to enforce the June 14, 1988 "assignment of benefits." The matter was tried before the court on the basis of a joint stipulation of facts. The court entered a judgment in favor of Dr. Herzog finding that the June 14, 1988 letter constituted a valid assignment of the settlement proceeds enforceable against Irace and Lowry. Following an unsuccessful appeal to the Superior

---

1. This case involves the assignment of proceeds from a personal injury action, not an assignment of the cause of action itself.

Court, Irace and Lowry appealed to this court. Because the Superior Court acted as an intermediate appellate court, we review the District Court's decision directly. See Brown v. Corriveau, 576 A.2d 200, 201 (Me. 1990). . . .

VALIDITY OF ASSIGNMENT

An assignment is an act or manifestation by the owner of a right (the assignor) indicating his intent to transfer that right to another person (the assignee). See Shiro v. Drew, 174 F. Supp. 495, 497 (D. Me. 1959). For an assignment to be valid and enforceable against the assignor's creditor (the obligor), the assignor must make clear his intent to relinquish the right to the assignee and must not retain any control over the right assigned or any power of revocation. Id. The assignment takes effect through the actions of the assignor and assignee and the obligor need not accept the assignment to render it valid. Palmer v. Palmer, 112 Me. 149, 153, 91 A. 281, 282 (1914). Once the obligor has notice of the assignment, the fund is "from that time forward impressed with a trust; it is . . . impounded in the [obligor's] hands, and must be held by him not for the original creditor, the assignor, but for the substituted creditor, the assignee." Id. at 152, 91 A. 281. After receiving notice of the assignment, the obligor cannot lawfully pay the amount assigned either to the assignor or to his other creditors and if the obligor does make such a payment, he does so at his peril because the assignee may enforce his rights against the obligor directly. Id. at 153, 91 A. 281.

Ordinary rights, including future rights, are freely assignable unless the assignment would materially change the duty of the obligor, materially increase the burden or risk imposed upon the obligor by his contract, impair the obligor's chance of obtaining return performance, or materially reduce the value of the return performance to the obligor, and unless the law restricts the assignability of the specific right involved. See Restatement (Second) Contracts §317(2)(a) (1982). In Maine, the transfer of a future right to *proceeds* from pending litigation has been recognized as a valid and enforceable equitable assignment. McLellan v. Walker, 26 Me. 114, 117-18 (1896). An equitable assignment need not transfer the entire future right but rather may be a partial assignment of that right. *Palmer,* 112 Me. at 152, 91 A. 281. We reaffirm these well established principles.

Relying primarily upon the Federal District Court's decision in *Shiro,* 174 F. Supp. 495, a bankruptcy case involving the trustee's power to avoid a preferential transfer by assignment, Irace and Lowry contend that Jones's June 14, 1988 letter is invalid and unenforceable as an assignment because it fails to manifest Jones's intent to permanently relinquish all control over the assigned funds and does nothing more than request payment from a specific fund. We disagree. The June 14, 1988 letter gives no indication that Jones attempted to retain any control over the funds he assigned to Dr. Herzog. Taken in context, the use of the word "request" did not give the court reason to question Jones's intent to complete the assignment and, although no specific amount was stated, the parties do not dispute that the services provided by Dr. Herzog and the amounts that he charged for those services were reasonable and necessary to the treatment of the shoulder injury referred to in the June 14 letter. Irace and Lowry had adequate funds to satisfy all of Jones's creditors, including Dr. Herzog, with funds left over for disbursement to Jones himself. Thus, this case simply does not present a situation analogous to *Shiro* because Dr. Herzog was given preference over Jones's other creditors by operation of the assignment. Given that Irace and Lowry do not dispute that they had ample notice of the assignment, the court's finding on the validity of the assignment is fully supported by the evidence and will not be disturbed on appeal.

ETHICAL OBLIGATIONS

Next, Irace and Lowry contend that the assignment, if enforceable against them, would interfere with their ethical obligation to honor their client's instruction in disbursing funds. Again, we disagree.

Under the Maine Bar Rules, an attorney generally may not place a lien on a client's file for a third party. M. Bar R. 3.7(c). The Bar Rules further require that an attorney "promptly pay or deliver to the client, as requested by the client, the funds, securities, or other properties in the possession of the lawyer which the client is entitled to receive." M. Bar R. 3.6(f)(2)(iv). The rules say nothing, however, about a client's power to assign his right to proceeds from a pending lawsuit to third parties. Because the client has the power to assign his right to funds held by his attorney, McLellan v. Walker, 26 Me. at 117-18, it follows that a valid assignment must be honored by the attorney in disbursing the funds on the client's behalf. The assignment does not create a conflict under Rule 3.6(f)(2)(iv) because the client is not entitled to receive funds once he has assigned them to a third party. Nor does the assignment violate Rule 3.7(c), because the client, not the attorney, is responsible for placing the incumbrance upon the funds. Irace and Lowry were under no ethical obligation, and the record gives no indication that they were under a contractual obligation, to honor their client's instruction to disregard a valid assignment. The District Court correctly concluded that the assignment is valid and enforceable against Irace and Lowry.

The entry is judgment affirmed.

All concurring.

NOTE AND QUESTION

Under the common law, purported assignments of pending tort claims violated public policy and were not enforceable. See, e.g., Comegys v. Vasse,

26 U.S. (1 Pet.) 193, 213 (1828) ("personal torts . . . are not capable of assignment"); Rice v. Stone, 83 Mass. (1 Allen) 566, 572 (1861) ("an assignment of a claim for a personal injury is void"). However, some states have carved out an exception for assignments of the *proceeds* of a pending lawsuit (rather than an assignment of the actual lawsuit itself). See, e.g., Richard v. Nat'l Transp. Co., 285 N.Y.S. 870, 875 (N.Y. Mun. Ct. 1936). Why might the law make this distinction? How would you characterize the assignment in *Herzog*?

Problem 187

Joseph Armstrong went down to Wonder Spa and signed a contract agreeing to pay the spa $1,000 in return for the use of its facilities for a two-year period. A week later the Nightflyer Finance Company sent him a notice that the contract he had signed with Wonder had been assigned to Nightflyer. Joseph read the notice but promptly forgot it and continued to pay Wonder, who pocketed the money. Wonder is bankrupt, and Nightflyer now insists that Joseph pay Nightflyer. Joseph told them they were crazy if they thought he was going to pay twice. Nightflyer has sued Joseph, and he has retained you. Does he owe the money or doesn't he? See UCC §9-406(a). Could he validly claim that his payment obligation was too personal to be assigned?

III. THE FORMALITIES OF AN ASSIGNMENT

A. *Gifts*

RESTATEMENT (SECOND) OF CONTRACTS

§332. REVOCABILITY OF GRATUITOUS ASSIGNMENTS

(1) Unless a contrary intention is manifested, a gratuitous assignment is irrevocable if

(a) the assignment is in a writing either signed or under seal that is delivered by the assignor; or

(b) the assignment is accompanied by delivery of a writing of a type customarily accepted as a symbol or as evidence of the right assigned.

(2) Except as stated in this Section, a gratuitous assignment is revocable and the right of the assignee is terminated by the assignor's death or

incapacity, by a subsequent assignment by the assignor, or by notification from the assignor received by the assignee or by the obligor.

(3) A gratuitous assignment ceases to be revocable to the extent that before the assignee's right is terminated he obtains

    (a) a payment or satisfaction of the obligation, or

    (b) judgment against the obligor, or

    (c) a new contract of the obligor by novation.

(4) A gratuitous assignment is irrevocable to the extent necessary to avoid injustice where the assignor should reasonably expect the assignment to induce action or forbearance by the assignee or a sub-assignee and the assignment does induce such action or forbearance.

(5) An assignment is gratuitous unless it is given or taken

    (a) in exchange for a performance or return promise that would be consideration for a promise; or

    (b) as security for or in total or partial satisfaction of a preexisting debt or other obligation.

Problem 188

The publication of her sensational memoirs made Lynn Brown a rich woman. One day she met her good friend Polly Travis on the street and, hearing Polly's tale of financial woe, said to her, "I'll tell you what. I have a savings account with Octopus National Bank that has a healthy amount in it. I have no need of the money, and I hereby give it to you." Polly thanked her with enthusiasm. Polly's friend Mary Bush was present throughout the conversation and is willing to testify to it. That evening Polly was shocked to hear that Lynn had been killed in a car accident. She was also shocked to learn that Octopus National Bank and Lynn's executor refused to give her the amount in the savings account. Will the law give it to her?

B. Assignments for Consideration

RESTATEMENT (SECOND) OF CONTRACTS

§324. Mode of Assignment in General

It is essential to an assignment of a right that the obligee manifest an intention to transfer the right to another person without further action or manifestation of intention by the obligee. The manifestation may be made to the other or to a third person on his behalf and, except as provided by statute or by contract, may be made either orally or by writing.

An assignment of an interest in real property requires a writing under the statute of frauds. If the assignment is a transfer of an interest in accounts receivable and is not exempt under UCC §9-109(d), Article 9 of the Code requires a written agreement signed by the assignor; see UCC §9-203. The same section mandates some sort of an authenticated record for any agreement using personal property or fixtures as collateral for a debt. Article 9 does not apply to the creation of interests in realty, wages, insurance, or certain other collateral described in §9-109(d). These matters are regulated either by the common law or by special statutory provisions.

NOTE ON WAGE ASSIGNMENTS

At one time creditors who loaned money to individuals often asked for security in the form of a "wage assignment." The obligor would agree to give the creditor a right in the obligor's wages for the repayment of the obligation. Such an assignment might begin to operate immediately, with the employer paying a portion of the debtor's wages directly to the creditor, or be designed to operate only when the debtor was in default.

Nearly every state has some limitation on the assignment of wages. (Why, do you suppose?) A few states, such as Alabama, Code Ann. §8-5-21, prohibit wage assignments entirely in most kinds of transactions. More commonly, states limit wage assignments only in certain loans made by "small loan companies" (specially licensed lenders who are allowed higher interest rates for loans with a principal not exceeding specified amounts. These are known as "finance companies" in many states.) Such small loan legislation generally is restricted to procedural and signature requirements. A common limitation, for example, requires the employer and the borrower's spouse to sign an agreement for a wage assignment.

A few states with comprehensive consumer credit codes limit wage assignments in all consumer credit transactions. Such limitations typically make all wage assignments voidable at will by the consumer. See Wis. Stat. §422.404.

IV. LIMITATIONS ON THE ASSIGNMENT

A right of a contracting party to performance under an executory contract was historically known as a *chose in action* (meaning the right to sue someone in contract or tort). Common law once prohibited the assignment of a chose in action because it was considered too personal in nature, but a major exception developed. A contracting party could give another party a *power of attorney*, which would enable the person holding the power to enforce the contract. There were procedural and substantive problems that restricted the use of this ruse, including a requirement that any action at law had to be brought and prosecuted in the name of the assignor. However, the rival courts of equity were quick to recognize a suit by an assignee in the assignee's own name. Not to be outdone in the race for more customers, common law courts loosened up some of the substantive restrictions placed on the power of attorney: for example, allowing the assignment to survive the death of the assignor. However, the common law courts still refused to allow a suit in the name of the assignee. Most states have adopted statutes of civil procedure that now permit, and in fact require, an action to be brought in the name of the assignee. See generally, Murray on Contracts §135 (4th ed. 2001). There are other statutes outside of the UCC that also encourage assignment. In resolving the following Problems, ask yourself what the cited UCC sections indicate about the drafters' feelings concerning the freedom of assignment.

Problem 189

Assume in a sale of goods transaction that the parties' contract contained the following provision:

> The parties promise not to assign this contract. Any purported assignment will be void from the beginning. The parties recognize the significance of this limitation and agree it controls over any trade usage or any other limitation allowing contract rights to be assigned.

Shortly after the contract was entered into, seller assigned its right to payment from buyer to Equity Farm Coop. Must the buyer pay Equity when seller delivers the bananas? See UCC §§2-210(2) (which can be found in the text above) and 9-401(b).

Problem 190

If the contract Joseph Armstrong originally signed with Wonder Spa had contained a clause stating that "The Spa promises that it will not assign this contract to a finance company," could he refuse to pay Nightflyer Finance Company when it proves to him that the contract was nonetheless assigned to it? See UCC §9-406(a) and its Official Comment 4. Would it make a difference if the clause had stated, "Any assignment of this contract to a finance company is void"?

DICK BROADCASTING COMPANY, INC. OF TENNESSEE v. OAK RIDGE FM, INC.

Supreme Court of Tennessee, 2013
395 S.W.3d 653

SHARON G. LEE, J.

The legal issues in this appeal revolve around the assignment of three agreements. The first is a Right-of-First-Refusal Agreement that allowed for an assignment with the consent of the non-assigning party. The agreement was silent as to the anticipated standard of conduct of the non-assigning party in withholding consent. The other two agreements—a Time Brokerage Agreement and a Consulting Agreement—were assignable without consent. The primary issue we address is whether the implied covenant of good faith and fair dealing applies to the non-assigning party's conduct in refusing to consent to an assignment when the agreement does not specify a standard of conduct. Oak Ridge FM, Inc. ("Oak Ridge FM") contractually agreed for Dick Broadcasting Company ("DBC") to have a right of first refusal to purchase Oak Ridge FM's WOKI-FM radio station assets. The agreement was assignable by DBC only with the written consent of Oak Ridge FM. When DBC requested Oak Ridge FM to consent to the assignment of the Right-of-First-Refusal agreement to a prospective buyer, Oak Ridge FM refused to consent. Oak Ridge FM also refused to consent to the assignment of the Consulting Agreement and Time Brokerage Agreement, neither of which contained a consent provision. DBC sued Oak Ridge FM and the other defendants, alleging breach of contract and violation of the implied covenant of good faith and fair dealing. The trial court granted the defendants a summary judgment. DBC appealed, and the Court of Appeals vacated the summary judgment. We hold that where the parties have contracted to allow assignment of an agreement with the consent of the non-assigning party, and the agreement is silent regarding the anticipated standard of conduct in withholding consent, an implied covenant of good faith and fair dealing applies and requires the non-assigning party to act with good faith and in a commercially reasonable manner in deciding whether to consent to the assignment. Because there are genuine issues of material fact in dispute, we affirm the judgment of the Court of Appeals and remand to the trial court.

I

DBC and its related companies were the Federal Communications Commission ("FCC") licensees for various radio stations, including WIVK, WIVK-FM, and WIOL in Knoxville, Tennessee, and WXVO-FM in Oliver Springs, Tennessee. Oak Ridge FM was the FCC licensee for radio station WOKI-FM in Knoxville. On June 23, 1997, three separate, but related, contracts (collectively "the WOKI-FM Agreements") were executed relating to WOKI-FM. The first agreement was a Time Brokerage Agreement between DBC and Oak Ridge FM wherein Oak Ridge FM sold substantially all of WOKI-FM's broadcast time to DBC. DBC was required to program the purchased broadcast time to include entertainment, music, news, commercials, and other matters for a period of seven years. The Time Brokerage Agreement was binding on the parties and their "successors and assigns" and contained no limitation on the right of either party to assign the agreement.

The second agreement was a Consulting Agreement between DBC and ComCon Consultants ("ComCon"), a partnership composed of John W. Pirkle and his son Jonathan W. Pirkle, employees at Oak Ridge FM. Under the Consulting Agreement, the Pirkles were paid to serve as consultants to DBC for seven years. The Consulting Agreement was binding on the parties and their "successors and assigns" and contained no limitation on the right of either party to assign the agreement.

The third agreement was a Right-of-First-Refusal Agreement between Oak Ridge FM and DBC that gave DBC the right of first refusal to purchase at a discounted price substantially all of Oak Ridge FM's assets used in the operation of WOKI. The critical part of the Right-of-First-Refusal Agreement for the purpose of this appeal is the assignment provision, which provides:

> This First Refusal Agreement shall be binding upon and inure to the benefit of the parties hereto and their respective successors and assigns, including, without limitation, any assignee of the FCC licenses for [WOKI-FM]. *No party may assign its rights, interests or obligations hereunder without the prior written consent of the other party,* and any purported assignment without such consent shall be null and void and of no legal force or effect; provided, however, that DBC shall be permitted to assign its rights and obligations under this First Refusal Agreement (1) to an entity controlled by James Allen Dick Jr., or by any one or more of the Dick family shareholders of DBC, or (2) to another entity provided that DBC shall be prevented from performing this First Refusal Agreement and provided that DBC shall guarantee the obligations of such other entity as DBC's assignee hereunder.

(Underlining in original; italics added).

On April 30, 2000, DBC entered into a written Asset Purchase Agreement with Citadel Broadcasting Company ("Citadel") selling most of its radio station assets, including its agreements with Oak Ridge FM, for a purchase price of $300,000,000.

On July 18, 2000, DBC sent a letter to Mr. Pirkle as president and principal shareholder of Oak Ridge FM advising him "of the pending acquisition" by Citadel of substantially all of DBC's assets, including the WOKI-FM Agreements, and asking him to consent to the assignment of the Right-of-First-Refusal Agreement. At nearly the same time, Mr. Pirkle, as president of Oak Ridge FM, sent a letter to DBC stating that he had learned of DBC's proposed deal with Citadel and that none of the agreements—the Time

Brokerage Agreement, the Consulting Agreement and the Right-of-First-Refusal Agreement — could be assigned without ComCon's and Oak Ridge FM's permission. Mr. Pirkle refused to consent unless they could agree on "an arrangement which satisfies our concerns allowing for the full or partial replacement of DBC with Citadel." In an affidavit filed in support of the motion for summary judgment, Mr. Pirkle acknowledged that on the advice of counsel he refused to agree to the assignment without additional consideration. His goal was to negotiate a "separate and more profitable agreement with Citadel."

To close the Citadel sale, DBC maintained that it had to obtain the assignment of all three agreements, and therefore DBC continued unsuccessfully to request Mr. Pirkle's consent. DBC offered to guarantee Citadel's obligations under the WOKI-FM Agreements, but Mr. Pirkle continued to withhold consent. Eventually DBC finalized the deal with Citadel without the assignment of the agreements and with a $10,000,000 reduction in the sales price.

On March 27, 2001, DBC sued Oak Ridge FM, ComCon, and Mr. Pirkle ("Defendants"), seeking a declaratory judgment that the Time Brokerage Agreement and the Consulting Agreement were assignable by DBC to Citadel without the consent of the Defendants and that Mr. Pirkle, on behalf of Oak Ridge FM, breached the agreements by wrongfully and unreasonably withholding consent to the assignments in order to extract money from the sale to Citadel. DBC further alleged that the implied covenant of good faith and fair dealing applied to the Right-of-First-Refusal Agreement and that the Defendants breached the agreement by failing to act reasonably and in good faith. The Defendants answered, admitting that Mr. Pirkle refused to consent to the assignment of the agreements but denying any breach of contract on their part.

Both sides filed a motion for summary judgment. Following a hearing on the parties' competing summary judgment motions, the trial court held that the implied covenant of good faith and fair dealing was not applicable to the Right-of-First-Refusal Agreement and that the Defendants did not breach the agreement. As to the Consulting Agreement, the trial court held that DBC's interests in this agreement were freely assignable without the Defendants' consent and that there was a genuine issue of fact regarding whether Mr. Pirkle's actions in insisting the agreement was not assignable without his consent, and in withholding that consent, were reasonable under the circumstances. The trial court nevertheless granted a summary judgment to the Defendants, stating that it was "unwilling to find that a party may be held liable for a breach of contract for holding out a good faith but mistaken interpretation of a contract provision," and dismissed the action.

DBC appealed. The Court of Appeals vacated the award of summary judgment, holding that the implied covenant of good faith and fair dealing applies to the assignment clause in the Right-of-First-Refusal Agreement and that genuine issues of material fact made the summary judgment improper.

Dick Broad. Co. of Tenn. v. Oak Ridge FM, Inc., No. E2010-01685-COA-R3-CV, 2011 WL 4954199, at *11 (Tenn. Ct. App. Oct. 19, 2011). DBC and the Defendants each filed an application for permission to appeal.

We granted both applications primarily to address the following issue: where the parties have contracted to allow assignment of an agreement with the consent of the non-assigning party, and the agreement is silent regarding the anticipated standard of conduct in withholding consent, does the implied covenant of good faith and fair dealing apply to require the non-assigning party to act with good faith and in a commercially reasonable manner in refusing to give its consent for the assignment of the agreement? We hold that the implied covenant of good faith and fair dealing applies to a silent consent clause of an assignment contract provision. When the agreement does not specify the standard of conduct for withholding consent, a party's decision to refuse consent must be made in good faith and in a commercially reasonable manner. We further hold that the trial court erred in considering Mr. Pirkle's testimony that he thought he had a contractual right to block DBC's assignment of the Consulting Agreement by withholding consent based on a discussion with his attorney.

II

Our task in this case involves the interpretation of a contract. We review issues of contractual interpretation de novo. Perkins v. Metro. Gov't of Nashville & Davidson Cnty., 380 S.W.3d 73, 80 (Tenn. 2012) (citing Allmand v. Pavletic, 292 S.W.3d 618, 624-25 (Tenn. 2009)). We are guided by well-settled principles and general rules of construction. "A cardinal rule of contractual interpretation is to ascertain and give effect to the intent of the parties." *Allmand,* 292 S.W.3d at 630 (citing Allstate Ins. Co. v. Watson, 195 S.W.3d 609, 611 (Tenn. 2006)). We initially determine the parties' intent by examining the plain and ordinary meaning of the written words that are "contained within the four corners of the contract." 84 Lumber Co. v. Smith, 356 S.W.3d 380, 383 (Tenn. 2011) (citing Kiser v. Wolfe, 353 S.W.3d 741, 747 (Tenn. 2011)). The literal meaning of the contract language controls if the language is clear and unambiguous. *Allmand,* 292 S.W.3d at 630. However, if the terms are ambiguous in that they are "susceptible to more than one reasonable interpretation," *Watson,* 195 S.W.3d at 611, we must apply other established rules of construction to aid in determining the contracting parties' intent. Planters Gin Co. v. Fed. Compress & Warehouse Co., 78 S.W.3d 885, 890 (Tenn. 2002). The meaning of the contract becomes a question of fact only if an ambiguity remains after we have applied the appropriate rules of construction. *Id.* (quoting Smith v. Seaboard Coast Line R.R., 639 F.2d 1235, 1239 (5th Cir. Unit B Mar. 1981) (per curiam))).

The clause in the Right-of-First-Refusal Agreement that is the subject of this controversy states: "[n]o party may assign its rights, interests or

obligations hereunder without the prior written consent of the other party."
This is known as a "silent consent" clause because, although it requires
consent of the non-assigning party, it is silent regarding the standard of
conduct required of a party desiring to refuse consent to a requested assignment. DBC argues that the implied covenant of good faith and fair dealing
should apply to the silent consent clause to require the non-assigning party
to act in good faith and in a commercially reasonable manner in denying
consent. The Defendants argue that the silent consent clause should be
interpreted to grant the non-assigning party unfettered discretion to deny
consent for any or no reason.

Whether the implied covenant of good faith and fair dealing applies to a
silent consent clause in an assignment provision of a right of first refusal
agreement is an issue of first impression in Tennessee. We hold that the
implied covenant of good faith and fair dealing is applicable. Our decision is
supported by the established common law of Tennessee and a majority of
other jurisdictions.

It is well-established that "[i]n Tennessee, the common law imposes a
duty of good faith in the performance of contracts." Wallace v. Nat'l Bank of
Commerce, 938 S.W.2d 684, 686 (Tenn. 1996). In *Wallace,* this Court
observed that "[i]t is true that there is implied *in every contract* a duty of
good faith and fair dealing in its performance and enforcement, and a
person is presumed to know the law." *Id.* (emphasis added) (quoting TSC
Indus., Inc. v. Tomlin, 743 S.W.2d 169, 173 (Tenn. Ct. App. 1987) (citing
Restatement (Second) of Contracts §205 (1979))). As early as 1922, this
Court imposed an implied condition of reasonableness in a contract requiring the sellers of land to find "satisfactory" the price of land sold at auction
in order for the auctioneers to be paid a commission. Robeson & Weaver v.
Ramsey, 147 Tenn. 25, 245 S.W. 413, 413 (1922). The contractual provision
at issue in *Robeson & Weaver* provided:

> It is agreed . . . that if the said property does not sell for a price that is
> satisfactory to the [sellers] that they are to pay to the [auctioneers] all actual
> and legitimate expenses incurred in putting on said sale, . . . but if the sale of
> said property is confirmed at the price it brought then the [sellers are] to pay
> the [auctioneers] 5%, five per cent., of the amount the property is sold for.

Id. at 413-14. The land sold at auction for a price "several thousand dollars
more" than it was worth, but two of the three sellers did not agree to confirm
the sale because they were not satisfied with the price. *Id.* at 414. The sellers
argued that under the express terms of the contract, they had an absolute
unfettered right to find the auction price "unsatisfactory" and refuse to
confirm the sale. This Court disagreed, holding that where the sales price
substantially exceeded the market price, then the price should be considered
satisfactory and the sellers would be "capricious" if dissatisfied with it. *Id.* at
415. The *Robeson & Weaver* Court concluded that because the farm brought

more than its value and an amount that should have satisfied a reasonable person, the auctioneers were entitled to their commission. *Id.* Thus, where the contract was silent as to the standard of conduct anticipated by the parties in the performance of the agreement, i.e., the sellers providing consent to the sale price as "satisfactory," the Court rejected a standard allowing the sellers to act capriciously and required them to act in a commercially reasonable manner. *Id.*; *see also* German v. Ford, 300 S.W.3d 692, 705 n.9 (Tenn. Ct. App. 2009) ("'When a contract is contingent on one party's satisfaction, that party must exercise his or her judgment in good faith and as a reasonable person, when a definite objective test of satisfaction is available; not arbitrarily without bona fide reason for his or her dissatisfaction.'" (quoting 13 Richard A. Lord, *Williston on Contracts* §38:24 (4th ed. 2000))).

These decisions are in accord with section 205 of the Restatement (Second) of Contracts (1979), which provides that "*[e]very contract* imposes upon each party a duty of good faith and fair dealing in its performance and its enforcement." (Emphasis added) . . . .

In some cases, the courts have expressed this principle as allowing the qualifying word "reasonable" and its equivalent "reasonably" to be read into every contract. [Citing cases.]

Courts in numerous other jurisdictions have similarly held that a clause requiring consent to the assignment of an agreement, if silent regarding the circumstances under which consent may be withheld, is interpreted in accordance with the implied covenant of good faith and fair dealing to require the exercise of reasonableness and good faith in deciding whether to consent to the assignment. [Citing cases.]

The Defendants argue that the position adopted by the courts in other jurisdictions cited and discussed above represents an unpersuasive "minority rule" and that a majority of the courts considering the silent consent clause issue have applied the traditional common law view that parties asked to consent to assignment may refuse arbitrarily or unreasonably refuse. *See generally* James C. McLoughlin, Annotation, *When Lessor May Withhold Consent Under Unqualified Provision in Lease Prohibiting Assignment or Subletting of Leased Premises Without Lessor's Consent,* 21 A.L.R.4th 188 (1983). Our research indicates that the former "majority rule" approach has steadily eroded over time and is now a minority position among the courts that have considered the issue. In 1977, the Alabama Supreme Court noted that although "[t]he general rule throughout the country has been that, when a lease contains an approval clause, the landlord may arbitrarily and capriciously reject proposed subtenants," the rule "has been under steady attack in several states in the past twenty years." *Homa-Goff Interiors,* 350 So. 2d at 1037; [citations omitted]. Alex M. Johnson, Jr., *Correctly Interpreting Long-Term Leases Pursuant to Modern Contract Law: Toward a Theory of Relational Leases,* 74 Va. L. Rev. 751, 753 (1988) (noting "the rapidly expanding list of state courts that have rejected the property rules on alienability of leaseholds and, by applying contract principles, have limited the lessor's right to restrict alienation arbitrarily").

Currently, some fourteen jurisdictions — Delaware, Georgia, Indiana, Kentucky, Massachusetts, Michigan, Minnesota, New Hampshire, New Jersey, New York, North Carolina, South Carolina, Vermont, and Washington [citations given in footnotes] — continue to adhere to the older common law view that a landlord may arbitrarily or unreasonably refuse to consent under a silent consent clause in a lease's anti-assignment provision. Seventeen jurisdictions have adopted the "modern" position discussed above, imposing an implied duty of good faith and fair dealing in interpreting a silent consent clause.

The Defendants argue that the trial court was correct in finding that the Right-of-First-Refusal Agreement was unambiguous and complete and holding that to interpret the contract in accordance with the implied covenant of good faith and fair dealing "would be in effect to add a new provision to the contract which the parties were free to add themselves." We disagree. It is true that "the common law duty of good faith does not extend beyond the agreed upon terms of the contract and the reasonable contractual expectations of the parties." *Wallace*, 938 S.W.2d at 687. Moreover, "'[t]he implied obligation of good faith and fair dealing does not . . . create new contractual rights or obligations, nor can it be used to circumvent or alter the specific terms of the parties' agreement.'" *Lamar Adver. Co.*, 313 S.W.3d at 791 (quoting *Barnes & Robinson Co.*, 195 S.W.3d at 643). However, while the implied covenant of good faith and fair dealing "does not create new contractual rights or obligations, it protects the parties' reasonable expectations as well as their right to receive the benefits of their agreement." *Long*, 221 S.W.3d at 9.

In this case, neither party is asking the Court to create a new contractual right or obligation, alter the terms of the Right-of-First-Refusal Agreement, or insert a new material and un-bargained for condition. *See Kendall*, 220 Cal. Rptr. 818, 709 P.2d at 847 ("It is not a rewriting of a contract, as respondent suggests, to recognize the obligations imposed by the duty of good faith and fair dealing, which duty is implied by law in every contract."). Both parties are asking the Court to infer a standard of conduct anticipated by the parties in carrying out the rights and liabilities provided for in the contract. The contractual language at issue provides that the Right-of-First-Refusal Agreement "shall be binding upon and inure to the benefit of the parties hereto and their respective successors and assigns, including, without limitation, any assignee of the FCC licenses for [WOKI-FM]. No party may assign its rights, interests or obligations hereunder without the prior written consent of the other party[.]" The parties anticipated the possibility of and made allowance for the assignment of the agreement. They also agreed that a party's attempt to exercise its right to assign the agreement triggers a duty on the part of the non-assigning party to consider and decide whether to consent. What standard of conduct did the parties anticipate the non-assigning party must exercise in granting or denying consent? DBC is asking the Court to infer the standard "consent shall not be unreasonably withheld." The Defendants are asking the Court to infer the standard "consent may be withheld in the decider's sole discretion, for any or no reason, however arbitrary or unreasonable." The parties could have inserted either provision into the Agreement, and either provision would generally have been enforceable as reflecting the bargained-for intent of the parties. *See Wallace*, 938 S.W.2d at 686 (observing that contracting parties "'may by agreement . . . determine the standards by which the performance of obligations are to be measured.'" (quoting Bank of Crockett v. Cullipher, 752 S. W.2d 84, 91 (Tenn. Ct. App. 1988))). But the contract in this case was silent on this point, leaving the resolution of the ensuing conflict to the courts. . . .

We conclude that where a contractual provision requiring consent to assign an agreement is silent regarding the standard of conduct governing a party's decision whether to consent, such decision must be made in good faith and in a commercially reasonable manner. *See Wallace*, 938 S.W.2d at 686 ("'In construing contracts, courts look to the language of the instrument and to the intention of the parties, and impose a construction which is fair and reasonable.'" (quoting *TSC Indus.*, 743 S.W.2d at 173)). The parties are free to contract for a standard of decision-making that is subject to a party's sole, absolute, unfettered discretion, allowing for the denial of consent for any reason, however arbitrary, or for no reason. Such an agreement will be enforceable absent any other public policy ground precluding it. *Wallace*, 938 S.W.2d at 686 (observing that parties may agree to "the standards by which the performance of obligations are to be measured" (quoting *Cullipher*, 752 S.W.2d at 91)). To avoid the imposition of the implied covenant of good faith and fair dealing, the parties must explicitly state their intention to do so. *See* 17A C.J.S. *Contracts* §437 (2011) ("*Absent an express disavowal by the parties,* every contract . . . generally contains an implied covenant or duty of good faith and fair dealing in its performance and enforcement." (emphasis added) (footnotes omitted)).

Our holding effectuates several desirable results: (1) it is consistent with established precedent in Tennessee case law and a majority of other jurisdictions as cited and discussed herein; (2) it establishes predictability, consistency, and bright-line clarity to contracting parties in the drafting and interpretation of agreements; (3) it guarantees full disclosure and clarity of understanding "on the front end" in reaching a deal if one or both parties want to retain complete and unfettered decision-making authority to provide or deny consent; and (4) it preserves and upholds the parties' right to freedom of contract . . . .

The Defendants argue that there could have been no breach of the Right-of-First-Refusal Agreement because there was never an offer to buy WOKI-FM's assets, and thus any right of first refusal remained "nascent" and untriggered by a potential sale. We do not agree. The Defendants cite no authority for this proposition other than a general description of the nature of a right of first refusal and how it generally works. The right of first refusal to buy the assets of WOKI-FM at a discounted rate of one million dollars less than an offer from another potential buyer is a valuable asset, and we have already determined that the parties anticipated and agreed this right would be assignable with the other party's consent. DBC's request for consent to assign the Right-of-First-Refusal Agreement triggered a duty on the part of Oak Ridge FM through Mr. Pirkle to consider and decide whether to consent and to exercise his discretion in good faith and in a commercially reasonable manner. DBC has alleged that Mr. Pirkle's failure to do so cost DBC more than ten million dollars, reflected in the reduction of the sales price in the agreement with Citadel and other expenses. It will be a matter for the fact-finder at trial to determine whether Mr. Pirkle withheld consent to the assignment unreasonably or in bad faith. . . .

III

In conclusion, we hold that where the parties have contracted to allow assignment of an agreement only with consent and the agreement is silent regarding the anticipated standard of conduct in withholding consent, the implied covenant of good faith and fair dealing requires a party to act with good faith and in a commercially reasonable manner in refusing consent to assign the agreement. The judgment of the Court of Appeals is affirmed. The trial court's summary judgment in favor of the Defendants is vacated, and the case is remanded to the Chancery Court for Knox County for such further action as may be necessary, consistent with this opinion. Costs on appeal are assessed to the Appellants, John W. Pirkle, Oak Ridge FM, Inc., and ComCon Consultants, and their respective sureties, for which execution may issue if necessary.

WILLIAM C. KOCH, JR., J., concurring.
I concur with the Court's decision to apply the implied duty of good faith and fair dealing to the three contracts involved in this case. I also concur with the Court's decision that neither party is entitled to a summary judgment because the current record reflects genuine disputes regarding the facts material to their claims and defenses. However, because there is no consensus regarding the scope of the implied duty of good faith and fair dealing in the context of arm's length commercial transactions, I write separately to address this important point.

The courts should tread cautiously when asked to recognize and enforce implied obligations that are not reflected in a written contract. The freedom to contract is "a vital aspect of personal liberty" that ensures the right of competent persons to enter into contracts or to decline to do so, as long as the contract is not illegal or against public policy. . . .

The courts should be cautious about imposing a set of morals on the commercial marketplace. *See* Brunswick Hills Racquet Club, Inc. v. Route 18 Shopping Ctr. Assocs., 864 A.2d at 399. Care must be taken to avoid overly broad applications of the implied duty of good faith and fair dealing that could "frustrate the policy interest in freedom of contract and undermine the parties' legitimate efforts to contractually determine their obligations." Sandra K. Miller, *Legal Realism, the LLC, and a Balanced Approach to the Implied Covenant of Good Faith and Fair Dealing*, 45 Wake Forest L. Rev. 729, 740 (2010). As the Honorable Michael D. Kirby, a former Justice of the High Court of Australia, has noted:

> The wellsprings of the conduct of commercial people are self-evidently impor-
> tant for the efficient operation of the economy. Their actions typically depend
> on self-interest and profit-making not conscience or fairness. In particular
> circumstances protection from unconscionable conduct will be entirely appro-
> priate. But courts should, in my view, be wary lest they distort the relationships
> of substantial, well-advised corporations in commercial transactions by sub-
> jecting them to the overly tender consciences of judges.

Austotel Pty Ltd. v. Franklins Selfserve Pty Ltd., (1989) 16 NSWLR 582, 585-86(CA).

Bad faith has been defined in various ways. This Court has construed "bad faith" as "actions in knowing or reckless disregard of . . . contractual rights." Glazer v. First Am. Nat'l Bank, 930 S.W.2d 546, 549-50 (Tenn. 1996). . . .

Thus, in this context, "bad faith" is not simply bad judgment or negligence. Borzillo v. Borzillo, 259 N.J. Super. 286, 612 A.2d 958, 961 (Ch. Div. 1992). It involves a dishonest purpose. Landry v. Spitz, 925 A.2d at 342. In general, "[b]ad faith . . . implies both actual or constructive fraud, or a design to mislead or deceive another, or a neglect or refusal to fulfill some duty or some contractual obligation, not prompted by an honest mistake as to one's rights or duties, but by some interested or sinister motive." Keller v. Beckenstein, 117 Conn. App. 550, 979 A.2d 1055, 1063-64 (2009). The Supreme Court of Montana has likewise held that the implied duty of good faith and fair dealing is breached "[w]hen one party uses discretion conferred by the contract to act [dishonestly] or to act outside of accepted commercial practices to deprive the other party of the benefit of the contract." Marshall v. State, 253 Mont. 23, 830 P.2d 1250, 1251 (1992).

Based on the evidence already obtained in discovery, there is little question that Dick Broadcasting Co., John W. Pirkle, and their related companies are knowledgeable and experienced actors in the commercial radio business. They were well represented when they negotiated and executed their contracts in 1997, and they were also well represented two years later when Dick Broadcasting negotiated and executed the agreement to sell its radio assets to Citadel Broadcasting Co.

The record also reflects that these parties were dealing at arm's length and that they were pursuing their own interests in their dealings with each other. Dick Broadcasting was seeking to maximize its financial advantage by negotiating sale of its radio assets to Citadel Broadcasting without advising or involving Mr. Pirkle. By the same token, Mr. Pirkle was pursuing his own self-interest when he contacted Citadel Communications directly after discovering that Dick Broadcasting had agreed to sell its radio assets to Citadel Communications.

Pursuing one's self-interest in a commercial transaction is not a breach of the implied duty of good faith and fair dealing. In order for a commercial actor's conduct to amount to such a breach, there must be evidence that it falls outside of the boundaries of acceptable commercial practice or it was motivated by a dishonest purpose, fraudulent intent, or ill will. The current record does not show that the actions of either party in this case fell outside the boundaries of acceptable commercial practice or that their actions were motivated by a dishonest purpose, a fraudulent intent, or ill will. Without such evidence, the best course will be "to let experienced commercial parties fend for themselves and [ ] not seek to 'introduce intolerable uncertainty into a carefully structured contractual relationship.'" Brunswick Hills Racquet Club, Inc. v. Route 18 Shopping Ctr. Assocs., 864 A.2d at 399 (quoting Brick Plaza, Inc. v. Humble Oil & Ref. Co., 218 N.J. Super. 101, 526 A.2d 1139, 1141 (Ct. App. Div. 1987)).

V. DEFENSES OF THE OBLIGOR

A. In General

Generally, the rights of an assignee, like those of a third-party beneficiary, are derivative. The assignee gets no better rights against the obligor than the assignor had, so that the obligor can assert contractual defenses when pursued by the assignee. For example, in the picture below, if B procured A's assent to the contract through fraud or duress, A could invoke these doctrines to resist a breach of contract claim filed by C.

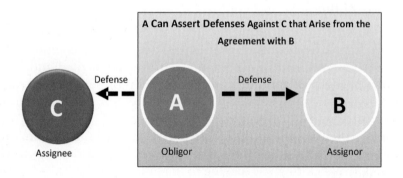

B. *Waiver of Defense Clauses*

There are two major exceptions to the basic idea that obligors can assert defenses against the assignee that stem from the contract with the assignor. The first comes from negotiable instruments law and the holder in due course doctrine (applicable to promissory notes and checks).

Problem 191

Joseph Armstrong signed a contract with Wonder Spa, and at the same time he signed a promissory note for $1,000, payable to the order of the spa. A week later he received a payment booklet from Nightflyer Finance Company, and he dutifully began making payments to it. Six months later the spa burned to the ground, so Armstrong stopped making payments. The finance company brought suit against him on the promissory note, claiming to be a "holder in due course" of the note, and thus free of his defense of failure of consideration. Must he pay? Under the complicated rules of Article 3 (see UCC §§3-302, 3-305(a) and (b)) a holder in due course (an innocent party acquiring the instrument) takes free of most defenses (called "personal" defenses), but not very serious ones (called "real" defenses). Mere failure of consideration, as here, is a personal defense.

Problem 192

Instead of the above, the original contract Armstrong signed with the spa provided that "Any problems the customer has with the spa will be settled by negotiations with the spa's management alone, and will in no way be asserted against any finance company to whom this obligation may be assigned." Is such a clause (called a *waiver of defenses against assignee* clause) valid to insulate the finance company from the same defense, i.e., the destruction of the spa by fire? Read UCC §9-403.

In the first part of the last century, the common law typically favored the finance company in these types of situations, using negotiable instruments law, the contractual waiver of defenses clause, or both to strip the consumer of defenses. The policy here was to promote the free marketability of the note or contract. Where such paper is signed by someone in business, this policy makes sense, but consumers, not having the bargaining ability or knowledge to avoid these tangles, are thought to deserve greater protection.

Consequently, the Federal Trade Commission has promulgated a regulation having the force of law that requires sellers of goods or services on credit to put on the contract a legend preserving the ability of consumers to assert defenses against assignees. See Federal Trade Commission Holder-in-Due-Course Regulations, 16 C.F.R. §433.1-433.3 (the legend preserving these defenses is quoted in the following case). State statutes frequently give similar protection to consumers and sometimes others, such as farmers.

WALES v. ARIZONA RV CENTERS, LLC
United States District Court, Eastern District of Louisiana, 2015
2015 WL 137260

Ivan L. R. Lemelle, District Judge.

I. Nature of Motion and Relief Sought

Before the Court is Defendant's, Bank of America, N.A. ("BOA"), Motion to Dismiss the claims asserted in Plaintiffs', Lyle and Judy Wales, Original and Amended Complaints pursuant to Fed. R. Civ. P. 12(b)(6) for failure to state a claim upon which relief may be granted. (Rec. Docs. 16, 1, 5, 20). Plaintiffs oppose the instant motion. (Rec. Doc. 21). For the reasons that follow,

IT IS ORDERED THAT Defendants' Motion is DENIED.

II. Facts and Procedural History

This case arises out of the purchase by Plaintiffs of a recreational vehicle ("RV"), to wit a 2013 DUTCHMEN VOLTAGE, VIN 47CFVTV38DC662699 (the "VOLTAGE"). (Rec. Doc. 20 at 3). Plaintiffs purchased the VOLTAGE on September 29, 2012 from Defendant Arizona RV Centers, LLC, a foreign limited liability company with registered agent for service of process in Phoenix, Arizona, and doing business as "Camping World RV Sales" ("Camping World"). (Rec. Doc. 20 at 2-3). The sales price of the VOLTAGE was $97,858.98, excluding finance charges. (Rec. Doc. 20 at 3). Plaintiffs made a net trade-in in the amount of $9,863.49 and purchased an extended service contract for $6,995.00. *Id.* In order to complete the purchase, Plaintiffs entered into a financing contract for the total transaction amount of $96,408.49. *Id.* The sales contract was thereafter assigned to Defendant BOA for management. *Id.*

Plaintiffs allege in their Second Amended Complaint ("SAC") that, within the first year of the purchase of the VOLTAGE, the RV began to manifest various defective conditions, the particular details of which are immaterial for present purposes. (Rec. Doc. 20 at 4). Plaintiffs further allege that they made repeated attempts to have the manufacturer, Defendant Keystone RV Company, a foreign corporation authorized to do and doing business in the State of Louisiana ("Keystone"), service and repair the defects present in the VOLTAGE. (Rec. Doc. 20 at 1, 5). According to Plaintiffs, many nonconforming and defective conditions were never repaired and the VOLTAGE continues to exhibit various defects to this day. (Rec. Doc. 20 at 5). As a result, Plaintiffs notified Defendants of their desire to rescind the sale, which request was declined, prompting initiation of the instant suit. In the SAC, Plaintiffs allege: (Count 1) Violations of Louisiana Redhibition Laws; (Count 2) Lender Liability on the part of Defendant BOA; (Count 3) Violation of the Magnusson-Moss Warranty Act, 15 U.S.C. §2301, et seq.; and (Count 4) Negligent Repair. (Rec. Doc. 20). Plaintiffs seek rescission of the sale, including collateral costs as of the time of sale, finance charges, insurance premiums, maintenance costs, repair costs, as well as applicable penalties and attorney's fees with legal interest from the date of judicial demand, which Plaintiffs allege exceed $100,000.00.

III. Contentions of Movant

BOA argues it is not a proper party to the instant suit in which Plaintiffs bring claims under Louisiana redhibition and negligence laws as well as the federal Magnuson-Moss Warranty Act, because BOA merely provided financing for the transaction at issue. Because these types of claims generally apply instead to sellers and manufacturers of the underlying products, BOA argues these types of claims are not properly asserted against it in its capacity as lender. The salient issue for purposes of the instant motion is whether a clause in the contract of sale, which must be included in this type of consumer contract under federal law, allows the buyer to bring a claim for affirmative relief against the lender in this type of transaction. The clause at issue, commonly referred to as the "FTC Holder Rule," reads:

> ANY HOLDER OF THIS CONSUMER CREDIT CONTRACT IS SUBJECT
> TO ALL CLAIMS AND DEFENSES WHICH THE DEBTOR COULD ASSERT
> AGAINST THE SELLER OF GOODS OR SERVICES OBTAINED WITH THE
> PROCEEDS HEREOF. RECOVERY HEREUNDER BY THE DEBTOR SHALL
> NOT EXCEEED AMOUNTS PAID BY THE DEBTOR HEREUNDER.

16 CFR §433.2 (1975). BOA argues this clause does not entitle the buyer to bring affirmative claims against the lender, but instead, merely entitles the buyer to assert the same defenses it would have against a seller against the lender under circumstances where the contract of sale has been assigned to the latter. In other words, the clause operates solely as a shield and not as a

sword. This, BOA reasons, is because the FTC Holder Rule was adopted primarily to foreclose the possibility of lenders invoking the "holder-in-due-course doctrine" to enforce the buyer's obligation to pay under a contract of sale even where the seller had breached its duty to perform as promised. In support of this position, BOA cites Federal Trade Commission ("FTC") guidelines explaining the impetus for adopting the rule as well as Louisiana precedent interpreting the rule. BOA further argues that the Louisiana Civil Code articles pertaining to redhibition do not contemplate assertion of that species of claim against non-sellers and non-manufacturers. Finally, BOA argues Plaintiffs have shown no entitlement to cancellation of the financing contract.

IV. Contentions of Opponents

Plaintiffs respond that the plain language of the FTC Holder Rule clearly reserves to buyers the right to assert "all *claims* and defenses" against lenders which they might enforce against sellers when the lender is the holder of the contract. Thus, Plaintiffs argue, they are entitled to affirmatively assert claims for relief against BOA that they might otherwise assert against the seller and manufacturer of the VOLTAGE. Further, Plaintiffs contend FTC guidelines make it clear that a consumer *can* maintain an affirmative action against a creditor who has received payments, but only where the seller's breach is so substantial that a court is persuaded that rescission and restitution are justified. Plaintiffs acknowledge a split of authority on the application of the Holder Rule in this respect.

Under one approach, courts hold buyers are entitled to affirmative recovery against the lender when there is a substantial breach by the seller warranting rescission or restitution. *See, e.g.,* Mount v. LaSalle Bank Lake View, 926 F. Supp. 759, 764 (N.D. Ill. 1996). Under the other approach, courts adhere to the plain language of the Holder Rule and allow any claims the buyer has against the seller to be asserted affirmatively against the lender. *See, e.g.,* Lozada v. Dale Baker Oldsmobile, Inc., 91 F. Supp. 2d 1087, 1095 (W.D. La. 2000). Because Plaintiff seeks rescission of the underlying contract, both approaches are presumably satisfied in the instant case. Finally, Plaintiffs argue BOA is a necessary party to the instant action under Fed. R. Civ. P. 19, to the extent that — if Plaintiffs prevail and obtain rescission and restitution of the sales contract — BOA must be joined in order to afford an opportunity for appropriate relief. . . .

VI. Discussion

As noted above, BOA challenges Plaintiffs' right to bring the claims asserted against it in its capacity as lender. As discussed fully below, the Court disagrees with BOA's legal conclusions in this respect.

To begin, the Court looks to the plain language of the clause, which reads: "this consumer credit contract is subject to all claims and defenses which the debtor could assert against the seller." *See* Hardt v. Reliance Standard Life Ins. Co., 560 U.S. 242, 251, 130 S. Ct. 2149, 176 L. Ed. 2d 998 (2010) ("We begin by analyzing the statutory language, assuming that the ordinary meaning of that language accurately expresses the legislative purpose.") (internal quotations omitted). This language unambiguously authorizes affirmative use. *See* Maberry v. Said, 911 F. Supp. 1393, 1402 (D. Kan. 1995) (reaching this same unavoidable conclusion applying a plain language analysis). Further, an examination of the history of the rule and guidelines pertaining thereto released by the FTC further support this interpretation. To be sure, the animating purpose of the promulgation of the rule may well have been to prevent invocation of the holder-in-due-course doctrine by lenders to foreclose the use of defenses by a buyer who had been aggrieved by some breach of the seller. This conclusion is supported by contemporaneous statements of the FTC:

> Our primary concern . . . has been the distribution or allocation of costs occasioned by seller misconduct in credit sale transactions. These costs arise from breaches of contract, breaches of warranty, misrepresentation, and even fraud. The current commercial system which enables sellers and creditors to divorce a consumer's obligation to pay for goods and services from the seller's obligation to perform as promised, allocates all of these costs to the consumer/buyer.

40 Fed. Reg. 53522 (Nov. 18, 1975). Beyond this point, however, Defendants' contentions as to the intent of the FTC are patently incorrect. The FTC proceeded to explain the Holder Rule as follows:

> It will require that all consumer credit contracts generated by consumer sales include a provision which allows the consumer to assert his sale-related claims and defenses against any holder of the credit obligation. From the consumer's standpoint, this means that a consumer can (1) defend a creditor suit for payment of an obligation by raising a valid claim against the seller as a setoff, and (2) *maintain an affirmative action against a creditor who has received payments for a return of monies paid on account.* The latter alternative will only be available where a seller's breach is so substantial that a court is persuaded that rescission and restitution are justified.

40 Fed. Reg. 53524 (Nov. 18, 1975) (emphasis added). Thus, the FTC clearly contemplated at the time of promulgation that the Rule would authorize affirmative claims against lenders by buyers, subject only to the requirement that any affirmative recovery be limited to the amount of monies paid in and only in the case of an underlying breach warranting rescission. This

conclusion is further supported by an advisory opinion released in 2012, following the development of the split of authority referenced above:

> The Commission affirms that the Rule is unambiguous, and its plain language should be applied. No additional limitations on a consumer's right to an affirmative recovery should be read into the Rule, especially since a consumer would not have notice of those limitations because they are not included in the credit contract. Had the Commission meant to limit recovery to claims subject to rescission or similar remedy, it would have said so in the text of the Rule and drafted the contractual provision accordingly. It remains the Commission's intent that the plain language of the Rule be applied, which many courts have done.

16 C.F.R. Part 433: Federal Trade Commission Trade Regulation Concerning the Preservation of Consumers' Claims and Defenses (The Holder Rule), Op. F.T.C. (May 3, 2012). While not binding authority, the above is certainly informative as to the FTC's intent concerning the Holder Rule. The history of the rule further reveals that the Commissioner considered and expressly rejected the position advanced by Defendants herein:

> Many industry representatives suggested that the rule be amended so that the consumer may assert his rights only as a matter of defense or setoff against a claim by the assignee or holder. Industry representatives argued that such a limitation would prevent the financier from becoming a guarantor and that any limitation in the extent of a third party's liability was desirable. The practical and policy considerations which militate against such a limitation on affirmative actions by consumers are far more persuasive.

40 Fed. Reg. 53256 (1975) (cited in *Maberry, supra,* 911 F. Supp. at 1402).

As the foregoing reveals, Defendant's contentions as to the ability of buyers to assert affirmative claims against lenders under the FTC Holder Rule are contradicted by the plain language and history of the Rule itself. Accordingly, Defendant's claims in this respect are without merit.

The Court is further unpersuaded with regard to Defendant's contentions that the language of the Louisiana Civil Code articles governing the implied warranty against redhibition limit application as between buyers, sellers, and manufacturers. While the Code articles might apply directly only as between such parties, the Holder Rule expressly makes applicable claims "the debtor could assert against the seller of goods." Thus, the articles' reference to buyers and sellers merely serves to emphasize that this type of claim falls under the express coverage of the Holder Rule. The FTC's statements above pertaining to breaches of warranty and "sale-related claims" underscore this point. Defendant's arguments to the contrary are without support in law and find no basis in inferential reasoning.

While the Court concludes that the Holder Rule limits affirmative recovery to circumstances where the seller's breach is so substantial as to warrant rescission, this is precisely the sort of claim brought by Plaintiffs in reliance on Louisiana's law of redhibition in the instant case. As such, there remains no issue as to Plaintiffs' ability to assert this form of claim against Defendants.

VII. Conclusion

The plain language and history of the FTC Holder Rule expressly permit affirmative claims by buyers against lenders in cases of a substantial breach warranting rescission of the sale. While it remains to be seen whether Plaintiffs will succeed in establishing such a breach, Defendant has failed to show that plaintiffs have not established "a plausible claim for relief" under the applicable Fed. R. Civ. P. 12(b)(6) standards. Accordingly,

IT IS ORDERED THAT Defendants' Motion to Dismiss is DENIED.

Business obligors do not escape as easily as consumers. Section 9-403 of the Code, which you should read, enforces waiver-of-defenses-against-assignee clauses where the obligor is not a consumer, except as to the very few defenses that are permitted against holders in due course (the so-called real defenses listed in §3-305(a)(1)). Before an assignee qualifies for the protection of §9-403, the assignee must take the assignment for value, in good faith, and without notice of problems with the obligation assigned; i.e., the assignee must meet the same qualifications imposed on someone trying to become a holder in due course of commercial paper (§3-302). A lawyer reviewing a contract for a client should alert the client to the consequences of waiving almost all defenses against later assignees of the paper, pointing out that even if the other side breaches the contract, the client will still have to pay the assignee.

When a business assigns its accounts receivable to a finance company, sometimes the parties agree that the finance company will collect the accounts as they mature. But because some account debtors become disturbed if they must deal with a strange creditor, and also for practical reasons of convenience, instead the assignor and assignee may agree to *nonnotification financing*, whereby the assignor collects the accounts and turns the money over to the assignee. While the common law courts had some doubts as to the validity of an assignment allowing the assignor such continued control over the accounts receivable, these procedures are now clearly authorized by the UCC. See §9-205.

C. Setoff and Recoupment

SEATTLE-FIRST NATIONAL BANK v. OREGON PACIFIC INDUSTRIES

Supreme Court of Oregon, 1972
262 Or. 578, 500 P.2d 1033

DENECKE, J. The plaintiff bank obtained a judgment against the defendant for the amount of an invoice assigned to the bank by Centralia Plywood. The trial court denied defendant's right to a setoff and defendant appeals.

The issue is the interpretation of the assignment section of the secured transactions chapter of the Uniform Commercial Code (ORS 79.3180).

On December 12, 1968, the defendant purchased plywood from Centralia. Centralia assigned the invoice evidencing the purchase to the bank on December 13, and the bank notified the defendant of the assignment. The defendant refused payment and the bank brought this action.

The defendant argues that it has a setoff against the bank's claim. Prior to the bank's assignment the defendant had placed two plywood orders, not included in the assigned invoice, with Centralia. Delivery was never made by Centralia and defendant contends it can set off the damages it suffered thereby against the bank's claim.

Centralia Plywood was insolvent when it assigned the invoice to the bank on December 12 and the bank knew of the insolvency at that time. Both Centralia and the bank are nonresidents. The defendant contends that because of these circumstances it is entitled to the setoff and cites our opinion in Pearson v. Richards, 106 Or. 78, 92, 211 P. 167 (1922), in support.

Assuming defendant's contention is correct in cases not involving the Code, we hold the principle contended for by defendant is not applicable when the Code applies. ORS 79.3180(1) provides:

> [T]he rights of an assignee are subject to:
> (a) All the terms of the contract between the account debtor and assignor and any defense or claim arising therefrom; and
> (b) Any other defense or claim of the account debtor against the assignor which accrues before the account debtor receives notification of the assignment.

The Code does not expressly provide that a claim can be set off if the assignor was insolvent at the time of the assignment and the assignee had knowledge of this fact or because the assignor and assignee are nonresidents.

One of the prime purposes of the Code was to create a statutory scheme incorporating within its provisions the complete regulation of certain types of commercial dealings. This purpose would be blunted if the rules created by some pre-code decisions and not expressly provided for in the statutory scheme were nevertheless grafted onto the Code by implication. In Evans Products v. Jorgensen, 245 Or. 362, 372, 421 P.2d 978 (1966), we held generally that we would not engage in this practice.

We recently observed in Investment Service Co. v. North Pacific Lbr. Co., Or., 492 P.2d 470-471 (1972), that the comment to this section of the Code states that this section "makes no substantial change in prior law." Upon further examination, we must acknowledge that while the Code retains the essence of the previous law of assignments, the Code has, by specific language, changed some of the details of the previous law of assignments.

The Code distinguishes "between what might be called the contract-related and the unrelated defenses and claims. Defenses and claims 'arising' from the contract can be asserted against the assignee whether they 'arise' before or after notification. . . . Under the Code, 'any other defense or claim' is available against the assignee only if it 'accrues before . . . notification.'" 2 Gilmore, Security Interests in Personal Property, 1090-1091, §41.4 (1965).

The setoff or claim the defendant seeks to assert is an unrelated setoff because it arises out of a breach of a contract not connected with the invoice assigned to the bank. For this reason the defendant can assert the setoff only if it accrued before the defendant was notified of Centralia's assignment to the bank.

The controversy thus narrows down to the issue of whether the setoff "accrued" to the defendant before it received notice of the assignment. We could be aided in defining "accrued" if we could determine why the accrual of the setoff was selected as the cutoff event. Accruing of the setoff, however, apparently, was selected arbitrarily. The choice of the event of the accrual was based upon previous decisions, some of which used the phrase "matured" rather than "accrued" claim. 4 Corbin, Contracts, 599, §897 (1951). 1 Restatement 211, Contracts §167(1), provided that the obligor could assert its setoff if the setoff was "based on facts arising . . . prior to knowledge of the assignment by the obligor." It was necessary to permit at least some setoffs to be asserted in order to protect the obligor from being unduly prejudiced by the assignment; but this right of setoff had to be limited in order to give some value and stability to the assignment so that it could be used as an effective security device. If an obligor could not assert any of the defenses or setoffs against an assignee which he could have asserted against his creditor, the assignor, the obligor would be extremely prejudiced by an assignment. On the other hand, if the obligation assigned could be obliterated or diminished by events happening after the assignment and notice of assignment to the obligor, the assignment would be precarious collateral.

The comments to the Oregon Code are of no assistance in interpreting "accrue." The comments to the Washington Code state: "The term 'accrues' appears to mean that the 'claim' shall exist as such, i.e., as a cause of action, before such knowledge." RCWA 62A.9-318, p. 439.

"Accrue," aside from its fiscal use, generally is used in the law to describe when a cause of action comes into being. Its chief use is to determine when the statute of limitations commences. We believe it is advisable to use "accrue" in the Code in its usual sense; that is, a claim or setoff accrues when a cause of action exists.

The parties stipulated that the "breaches of contract [the failure to deliver by Centralia] occurred on or about January 3, 1969." Therefore, the claim "accrued" at that time. Since the claim accrued after defendant had notification of the assignment, the setoff cannot be asserted successfully.

Defendant on appeal contends that by stipulating that the breaches of contract occurred on January 3 it did not intend to stipulate that the cause of action accrued at that time. The normal inference is that the cause of action accrues at the time the breach of contract occurs. In addition, the record indicates that the trial court and the parties so understood the import of the stipulation.

Affirmed.

QUESTION

The subtraction process that a debtor engages in when paying a creditor varies in terminology depending on the nature of the debt subtracted. If the debtor is relying on damages that arose from the *same* transaction, the subtraction process is called a *recoupment*. If the damages arose from a transaction *unrelated* to the assigned contract, the process is called a *setoff* (bankers, perversely, call it "offset").

Problem 193

Joseph Armstrong signed the usual contract with Wonder Spa. It contained the required FTC legend preserving his ability to assert defenses against assignees. The spa assigned his contract to Nightflyer Finance Company, which notified Armstrong that in the future he should make payment directly to it. Two weeks later one of the instructors at the spa negligently dropped a barbell on Armstrong's foot. May he subtract the doctor's bills from the payment to Nightflyer? What if the sole owner of the spa was driving around town in the spa's car and accidentally ran over Armstrong's dog? May Armstrong subtract the value of the dog from the payments due to Nightflyer? Does your answer to this last question change if the dog were already dead before Armstrong learned of the assignment of his contract to the finance company? To answer these questions, see UCC §9-404(a).

D. Modifications

════════

Problem 194

Prester John made maps for a living and sold them to National Auto Club. It was agreed that he would receive $5,000 for each map he produced under the contract. Needing money, Prester John went to Medieval National Bank and borrowed $30,000, assigning to the bank the payments due to him from National Auto Club. The quality of his maps was not as good as the parties had originally contemplated, and National Auto Club threatened to cancel and sue. Prester John agreed to accept $4,000 for each map, but Medieval National Bank protested this change. Is the bank bound by the modification in the contract? See UCC §9-405.

VI. WARRANTIES BY THE ASSIGNOR

The economic collapse of 2008 was largely caused by the outrageous creation of subprime mortgages for people who didn't need them or couldn't afford them. These mortgages, along with perfectly legitimate ones, were bundled together into trusts (a process called "securitization"), and then the trust sold bonds to investors, with the bonds supposedly being backed by the bundled mortgages.

When a mortgage is first created there are two primary documents signed at the closing. One is the *promissory note* by which the mortgagor (the home owner) promises to make payments to the mortgage (the payee on the note). The other is the *mortgage deed* itself, which creates a consensual lien on the real property, and which is then filed in the country real property records so that the property cannot be sold unless the mortgage is satisfied. During the feeding frenzy that fell apart in 2008 what happened to these two documents is most interesting. In theory they should have been kept together, or, more specifically, the current holder of the promissory note should always be the assignee of the mortgage. The common law rule is that "security follows the debt," with the security here meaning the mortgage following the promissory note (the "debt").* But in the mortgage mess the two were often separated.

Banks trying to foreclose on the mortgage were astounded to learn that Article 3 of the Uniform Commercial Code ("Negotiable Instruments") only permits foreclosure by someone in possession of the promissory note. Since in many cases the banks attempting to foreclose couldn't find the original promissory note, but at best a copy of that note, many courts simply denied foreclosure, pointing out that the home owner is only liable to the person in possession of the note and paying the wrong entity would expose the home owner to double liability. On top of this snafu the foreclosing banks frequently had trouble proving a clear chain of assignments of the mortgage itself from the originating bank through the various entities that had participated in the securitization trust, and without such proof the assignments did not convey title in the mortgage deed sufficient to make the suing bank the real party in interest in the foreclosure proceeding (a question of standing).

RESTATEMENT (SECOND) OF CONTRACTS

§333. WARRANTIES OF AN ASSIGNOR

(1) Unless a contrary intention is manifested, one who assigns or purports to assign a right by assignment under seal or for value warrants to the assignee

(a) that he will do nothing to defeat or impair the value of the assignment and has no knowledge of any fact which would do so;

(b) that the right, as assigned, actually exists and is subject to no limitations or defenses good against the assignor other than those stated or apparent at the time of the assignment;

(c) that any writing evidencing the right which is delivered to the assignee or exhibited to him to induce him to accept the assignment is genuine and what it purports to be.

(2) An assignment does not of itself operate as a warranty that the obligor is solvent or that he will perform his obligation.

(3) An assignor is bound by affirmations and promises to the assignee with reference to the right assigned in the same way and to the same extent that one who transfers goods is bound in like circumstances.

---

* "Security follows the debt" is codified in Article 9 of the Uniform Commercial Code. See UCC §9-203(g), which clearly states that possession of the promissory note automatically creates a security interest in the mortgage even without a formal assignment of same. For a more complete discussion of this issue and the UCC's requirement that possession of the promissory note is necessary for foreclosure of the mortgage, see Whaley's blog entry on point: douglaswhaley.blogspot.com/2010/11/update-mortgage-foreclosure-and-missing.html.

(4) An assignment of a right to a sub-assignee does not operate as an assignment of the assignee's rights under his assignor's warranties unless an intention is manifested to assign the rights under the warranties.

Problem 195

When Octopus National Bank bought the mortgage John and Mary Smith had signed on their home five years ago, the bank had major problems. It had purchased the mortgage by an assignment from Last National Bank, which had in turn purchased it from the trustee of a securitization trust. The original mortgagee was Pursuit National Bank, but it was no longer in business (closed down in a scandal over its creation of dubious mortgages). No one knew the current location of the promissory note the Smiths had signed at the closing, though Octopus National did have a copy of the note. After the foreclosure suit was thrown out by the court for these reasons, the bank's attorney was flummoxed when thinking about what to do next. Read Restatement (Second) §333 (which can be found in the text above) and advise the bank's attorney.

QUESTION

If in the previous Problem Octopus National Bank's attorney learns that Last National Bank has failed since selling the mortgage to ONB, what recourse does the bank have now? Does it have any rights against the securitization trust or are there privity issues with that? In answering this question see (4) of the above Restatement provision, and also consider what you learned in Chapter 9 of this book.

VII. DELEGATION OF DUTIES

LANGEL v. BETZ
Court of Appeals of New York, 1928
250 N.Y. 159, 164 N.E. 890

POUND, J. Plaintiff, on August 1, 1925, made a contract with Irving W. Hurwitz and Samuel Hollander for the sale of certain real property. This contract the vendees assigned to Benedict, who in turn assigned it to Isidor

Betz, the defendant herein. The assignment contains no delegation to the assignee of the performance of the assignor's duties. The date for performance of the contract was originally set for October 2, 1925. This was extended to October 15, 1925, at the request of the defendant, the last assignee of the vendees. The ground upon which the adjournment was asked for by defendant was that the title company had not completed its search and report on the title to the property. Upon the adjourned date the defendant refused to perform. The vendor plaintiff was ready, able, and willing to do so, and was present at the place specified with a deed, ready to tender it to the defendant, who did not appear.

The plaintiff as vendor brought this action against the defendant assignee for specific performance of the contract. Upon the foregoing undisputed facts he has had judgment therefor.

The question is: "Can the vendor obtain specific performance of a contract for the sale of real estate against the assignee of the vendee, where the assignee merely requests and obtains an extension of time within which to close title?"

Here we have no novation, no express assumption of the obligations of the assignor in the assignment, and no demand for performance by the assignee.

The mere assignment of a bilateral executory contract may not be interpreted as a promise by the assignee to the assignor to assume the performance of the assignor's duties, so as to have the effect of creating a new liability on the part of the assignee to the other party to the contract assigned. The assignee of the vendee is under no personal engagement to the vendor where there is no privity between them. [Citations omitted.] The assignee may, however, expressly or impliedly, bind himself to perform the assignor's duties. This he may do by contract with the assignor or with the other party to the contract. It has been held (Epstein v. Gluckin, 233 N.Y. 490, 135 N.E. 861) that, where the assignee of the vendee invokes the aid of a court of equity in an action for specific performance, he impliedly binds himself to perform on his part and subjects himself to the conditions of the judgment appropriate thereto. "He who seeks equity must do equity." The converse of the proposition, that the assignee of the vendee would be bound when the vendor began the action, did not follow from the decision in that case. On the contrary, the question was wholly one of remedy rather than right, and it was held that mutuality of remedy is important only so far as its presence is essential to the attainment of the ends of justice. This holding was necessary to sustain the decision. No change was made in the law of contracts nor in the rule for the interpretation of an assignment of a contract.

A judgment requiring the assignee of the vendee to perform at the suit of the vendor would operate as the imposition of a new liability on the assignee which would be an act of oppression and injustice, unless the assignee had, expressly or by implication, entered into a personal and binding contract with the assignor or with the vendor to assume the obligations of the assignor.

It has been urged that the probable intention of the assignee is ordinarily to assume duties as well as rights, and that the contract should be so interpreted in the absence of circumstances showing a contrary intention. The American Law Institute's Restatement of the Law of Contracts (section 164) proposes a change in the rule of interpretation of assigned contracts to give as full effect to the assumed probable intention of the parties as the law permits. The following statement is proposed:

> Section 164 Interpretation of Words Purporting to Assign a Bilateral Contract and Effect of Acceptance of the Assignment by the Assignee
>
> (1) Where a party to a bilateral contract which is at the time wholly or partially executory on both sides, purports to assign the whole contract, his action is interpreted, in the absence of circumstances showing a contrary intention, as an assignment of the assignor's rights under the contract and a delegation of the performance of the assignor's duties.
>
> (2) Acceptance by the assignee of such an assignment is interpreted, in the absence of circumstances showing a contrary intention, as both as assent to become an assignee of the assignor's rights and as a promise *to the assignor to assume the performance of the assignor's duties.*

This promise to the assignor would then be available to the other party to the contract. Lawrence v. Fox, 20 N.Y. 268; 1 Williston on Contracts, §412. The proposed change is a complete reversal of our present rule of interpretation as to the probable intention of the parties. It is, perhaps, more in harmony with modern ideas of contractual relations than is "the archaic view of a contract as creating a strictly personal obligation between the creditor and debtor" (Pollock on Contracts [9th ed.] 232), which prohibited the assignee from suing at law in his own name and which denied a remedy to third party beneficiaries. "The fountains out of which these resolutions issue" have been broken up if not destroyed (Seaver v. Ransom, 224 N.Y. 233, 237, 120 N.E. 639, 2 A.L.R. 1187), but the law remains that no promise of the assignee to assume the assignor's duties is to be inferred from the acceptance of an assignment of a bilateral contract, in the absence of circumstances surrounding the assignment itself which indicate a contrary intention.

With this requirement of the interpretation of the intention of the parties controlling we must turn from the assignment to the dealings between the plaintiff and the defendant to discover whether the defendant entered into relations with the plaintiff whereby he assumed the duty of performance. The assignment did not bring the parties together, and the request for a postponement differs materially from the commencement of an action in a court of equity, whereby the plaintiff submits himself to the jurisdiction of the court or from a contractual assumption of the obligations of the assignor. If the substance of the transaction between the vendor and the assignee of the vendee could be regarded as a request on the part of the latter for a postponement of the closing day and a promise on his part to assume the obligations of the vendee if the request were granted, a contractual relation arising from an expression of mutual assent, based on the exchange of a promise for an act, might be spelled out of it; but the transaction is at least as consistent with a request for time for deliberation as to the course of conduct to be pursued as with an implied promise to assume the assignor's duties if the request were granted. The relation of promisor and promisee was not thereby expressly established, and such relation is not a necessary inference from the nature of the transaction. When we depart from the field of intention and enter the field of contract, we find no contractual liability; no assumption of duties based on a consideration.

Plaintiff contends that the request for an adjournment should be construed (time not being the essence of the contract) as an assertion of a right to such adjournment, and therefore as a binding act of enforcement, whereby defendant accepted the obligations of the assignee. Here again we have an equivocal act. There was no demand for an adjournment as a matter of right. The request may have been made without any intent to assert a right. It cannot be said that by that act alone the assignee assumed the duty of performance.

Furthermore, no controlling authority may be found which holds that a mere demand for performance by the vendee's assignee creates a right in the complaining vendor to enforce the contract against him. H.&H. Corporation v. Broad Holding Corporation, 204 App. Div. 569, 198 N.Y.S. 763. See 8 Cornell L.Q., 374; 37 Harv. L. Rev., 162. That question may be reserved until an answer is necessary.

The judgment of the Appellate Division and that of the Special Term should be reversed and the complaint dismissed, with costs in all courts.

Judgments reversed, etc.

QUESTIONS

1. Read UCC §2-210(5). Section 328 of the Restatement (Second) of Contracts is similar to the UCC provision. It states:

(1) Unless the language or the circumstances indicate the contrary, as in an assignment for security, an assignment of "the contract" or of "all my rights under the contract" or an assignment in similar general terms is an assignment of the assignor's rights and a delegation of his unperformed duties under the contract.

(2) Unless the language or the circumstances indicate the contrary, the acceptance by an assignee of such an assignment operates as a promise to the

assignor to perform the assignor's unperformed duties, and the obligor of the assigned rights is an intended beneficiary of the promise.

    Caveat: The Institute expresses no opinion as to whether the rule stated in subsection (2) applies to an assignment by a purchaser of his rights under a contract for the sale of land.

What is the status of *Langel* under the Restatement section? See Kunzman v. Thorsen, 303 Or. 600, 740 P.2d 754 (1987).

    2. In the opinion at one point the court cites to Lawrence v. Fox, the famous third-party beneficiary case that began the last chapter. What is the relevance of that citation in this delegation of duty case?

Problem 196

    When ballet star Vera Toes suddenly got the chance to dance the part of Pat Nixon in the new ballet called *Watergate,* she was thrilled and quickly signed the contract with the Wilma Arts Dance Company. A week before rehearsals were to begin, the State Department asked Vera if she would be willing to tour South America as part of a cultural exchange program. She decided that helping her government was more important than the *Watergate* show, so she called her good friend Carla Pas de Deux and they agreed that Carla would assume her obligation to the dance company. Then Vera phoned Wilma Arts, president of the organization, and received her permission to substitute Carla in her stead. Vera went off to South America on the tour, but Carla never honored her agreement to appear in *Watergate.* When the dance company threatened suit, Carla replied that any contract she had was with Vera and not the Wilma Arts Dance Company. Is Vera liable here to the dance company? Is Carla? What are the legal theories involved?

ROUSE v. UNITED STATES
United States Court of Appeals, D.C. Circuit, 1954
215 F.2d 872

EDGERTON, Circuit Judge. Bessie Winston gave Associated Contractors, Inc., her promissory note for $1,008.37, payable in monthly installments of $28.01, for a heating plant in her house. The Federal Housing Administration guaranteed the note and the payee endorsed it for value to the lending bank, the Union Trust Company.

    Winston sold the house to Rouse. In the contract of sale Rouse agreed to assume debts secured by deeds of trust and also "to assume payment of $850 for heating plant payable $28 per Mo." Nothing was said about the note.

Winston defaulted on her note. The United States paid the bank, took an assignment of the note, demanded payment from Rouse, and sued him for $850 and interest.

Rouse alleged as defenses (1) that Winston fraudulently misrepresented the condition of the heating plant and (2) that Associated Contractors did not install it satisfactorily. The District Court struck these defenses and granted summary judgment for the plaintiff. The defendant Rouse appeals.

Since Rouse did not sign the note he is not liable on it. D.C. Code 1951, §28-119; N.I.L. Sec. 18. He is not liable to the United States at all unless his contract with Winston makes him so. The contract says the parties to it are not "bound by any terms, conditions, statements, warranties or representations, oral or written" not contained in it. But this means only that the written contract contains the entire agreement. It does not mean that fraud cannot be set up as a defense to a suit on the contract.[1] Rouse's promise to "assume payment of $850 for heating plant" made him liable to Associated Contractors, Inc., only if and so far as it made him liable to Winston; one who promises to make a payment to the promisee's creditor can assert against the creditor any defense that the promisor could assert against the promisee.[2] Accordingly Rouse, if he had been sued by the corporation, would have been entitled to show fraud on the part of Winston. He is equally entitled to do so in this suit by an assignee of the corporation's claim. It follows that the court erred in striking the first defense. We do not consider whether Winston's alleged fraud, if shown, would be a complete or only a partial defense to this suit, since that question has not arisen and may not arise.

We think the court was right in striking the second defense. "If the promisor's agreement is to be interpreted as a promise to discharge whatever liability the promisee is under, the promisor must certainly be allowed to show that the promisee was under no enforceable liability. . . . On the other hand, if the promise means that the promisor agrees to pay a sum of money to A, to whom the promisee says he is indebted, it is immaterial whether the promisee is actually indebted to that amount or at all. . . . Where the promise is to pay a specific debt . . . this interpretation will generally be the true one."[3] The judgment is reversed and the cause remanded with instructions to reinstate the first defense.

Reversed and remanded.

---

1. 3 Williston, Contracts §811A (rev. ed. 1936).
2. 2 id. §394.
3. 2 id. §399.

CHAPTER 10 ASSESSMENT

Multiple Choice Questions

1. When Alice Kramden decided to divorce her husband Ralph, she contacted Ed Norton, a well-known divorce lawyer, and they signed a contract by which Norton would represent her for a named fee. Norton, however, became overwhelmed by all the divorce work he had to do, so he called Nat Birnbaum, the best divorce lawyer in town, and asked him if he would take over some of Norton's cases, including the one with Alice Kramden. Birnbaum agreed, but when Alice protested that she wanted only Norton, he told her not to worry, that Birnbaum was the finest divorce lawyer in town. Assume this is true. Alice calls you, her attorney cousin, and asks if Norton can do this to her. What do you say?

    a. No. This is an assignment of rights without the consent of the obligee, and that is always forbidden.

    b. Yes. This is a delegation of duties, and that is allowed in most cases when the delegation doesn't hurt the obligee. Here the delegation actually helps her, so she can't complain.

    c. No. This is a breach of contract by Norton. A delegation of duties is not allowed where the delegator has special attributes that are important to the obligee, as here. She chose Norton because she trusted him, and she cannot be forced to hand over her divorce matter to a stranger she doesn't know, and this is true regardless of how good he is in the eyes of others.

2. In the same fact pattern, Norton does not delegate the duties to Birnbaum, but instead continues to represent Alice as agreed. However, he owes Birnbaum money, so he tells Alice that she should make all of the payments for his services to Birnbaum instead of to him. Alice is upset by this. She worries that if the payments are not going to Norton that he won't work as hard on her case. She calls you, her attorney cousin, again. Can she legally refuse to pay Birnbaum and keep paying Norton?

    a. No. This is not a delegation of duties. Norton is still performing the duties owed to Alice by handling the divorce. This is an assignment of a right to payment, which is almost always allowed in our law.

    b. Yes. For the reasons Alice told you she is legitimately worried that Norton won't handle her affairs as astutely as he would if he was getting the payments directly, so she can object to this assignment/delegation and continue to make the direct payments. If Norton then wants to pay the money to Birnbaum, so be it, but at least he will have touched her money before he parts with it.

3. Alice was happy to hear that Birnbaum was taking over her divorce. She'd wanted him all along because he was the best divorce lawyer in town, so she told Norton, "Hooray! I'd love to be represented by Mr. Birnbaum!"

However, Birnbaum missed the first court date that was set up in her divorce, which was the very next day, and she had to represent herself. When she tried to contact Birnbaum to see why he hadn't shown, he wouldn't return her phone calls. She's never met him, and they have signed no formal agreement. "Do I have a cause of action against him?" she asks you, her attorney cousin.

   a. No. She should have signed a detailed contract with him, just as she did with Norton, before assuming he would really want to be her lawyer. Even if he told Norton he would take on her case, a new contract has to be signed before he has any liability to her.

   b. Yes. When Norton delegated his duties under the contract with Alice and also assigned Birnbaum his right to payment from her, Birnbaum agreed to this arrangement. When Birnbaum told Norton he would take over the case, that promise to Norton created creditor third-party beneficiary rights in Alice. Birnbaum is the promisor, Norton is the promisee, and Alice is the third-party beneficiary. There is no reason this promise has to be in writing, so Birnbaum can be sued for breach of the promise by Alice.

Answers

1. C is the best answer. Where the person who wants to delegate duties has reasonably been chosen for personal characteristics, no delegation is possible without the consent of the obligee (the other party to the contract being delegated). Representation in a divorce is a very personal decision, and a stranger can't be foisted on her without her agreement.

2. A is the best answer. Commerce depends on the right to assign money, both due and to be due in the future, and the person who owes the money, here Alice, has no right to object to an assignment of her duty of payment to a stranger as long as she's sure that Norton wants her to make the direct payments. It may be very important to Norton to have the monies go directly to Birnbaum (who might otherwise cut off a credit arrangement he's given Norton). If it has to go through him and then to Birnbaum that slows things down in a situation where speed of payment may be crucial.

3. B is the answer. Anytime there is a delegation of duties the promise of the delegatee to assume the duties creates creditor third-party beneficiary rights in the obligee. This is the only routine instance where there is an overlap between the law of assignments and the law of third-party beneficiaries.

TABLE OF CASES

Principal cases are italicized.

INDEX